URBAN SUSTAINABILITY

MICHIGAN STATE UNIVERSITY PRESS | East Lansing

A GLOBAL PERSPECTIVE

URBAN SUSTAINABILITY

edited by IGOR VOJNOVIC

Michigan State University Press
East Lansing, Michigan 48823-5245

Printed and bound in the United States of America.

19 18 17 16 15 14 13 1 2 3 4 5 6 7 8 9 10

LIBRARY OF CONGRESS CATALOGING-IN-PUBLICATION DATA
Urban sustainability : a global perspective / edited by Igor Vojnovic.
p. cm.
Includes bibliographical references.
ISBN 978-1-61186-055-9 (lithocase : alk. paper) 1. Urban ecology (Sociology) 2. Sustainable urban development. 3. City planning—Environmental aspects. I. Vojnovic, Igor.
HT241.U7275 2012
338.9'27091732—dc23
2011050530

ISBN 978-1-61186-055-9 (cloth) / ISBN 978-1-60917-347-0 (ebook)

Book and cover design by Charlie Sharp, Sharp Des!gns, Lansing, Michigan
A picture of Prague (Czech Republic) from the Prague Clock Tower used courtesy of Igor Vojnovic.

green press INITIATIVE

Michigan State University Press is a member of the Green Press Initiative and is committed to developing and encouraging ecologically responsible publishing practices. For more information about the Green Press Initiative and the use of recycled paper in book publishing, please visit www.greenpressinitiative.org.

Visit Michigan State University Press at www.msupress.org.

Dedicated to my son,
Noah Georgis Vojnovic

CONTENTS

■ HARM DE BLIJ

FOREWORD

When historians of the distant future reflect on momentous transformations in the geographic fabric of the world, a milestone being passed in this early stage of the twenty-first century will surely draw their attention: for the first time in human history, the majority of planet Earth's human inhabitants reside in urban settings. Given the dimensions of the twentieth century's population explosion, coupled with the long-term ascendancy of the industrial revolution, it is noteworthy that this urbanizing threshold was not crossed earlier. Today the rush to the cities accelerates from China, where it constitutes the greatest short-term migration of its kind in human history, and India, also urbanizing, although at a still-slower pace, to other parts of the global periphery, including sub-Saharan Africa and Southeast Asia.

Optimistic demographic projections suggest that this sustained urbanization will be accompanied by spatially uneven but globally significant declines in the rate of natural increase, leading some analysts to predict that the world's population will stabilize at approximately 10 billion by the end of the present century. Such extrapolations are risky, but even if they turn out to be prescient, the implications are that the planet will have to accommodate some 3 billion additional inhabitants, that the overwhelming majority of this population will swell the numbers of the global periphery, and that most will dwell in burgeoning megacities.

This book addresses the key questions arising from these prospects in the contexts of the sustainability of the process (how economic and social stability can be preserved and ecological impacts constrained) and the pursuit of equity (securing long-term participatory fairness and social justice). These concepts are not new—sustainable development and issues of equity have been debated for decades in academic and other venues—but they are taking on greater urgency in an era of economic, cultural, and political globalization and associated neoliberal policies. Some early forecasts of urbanization's impacts, based on the European experience, included assumptions that were mistaken—for example, the notion that urban agglomeration would reduce population pressures in rural areas resulting in ecological benefits for urban hinterlands. In reality, the demands of urban dwellers, ranging from shelter to diets, are far greater per capita than those of rural residents, so that consumption of construction materials and meat products grows exponentially as urbanization proceeds. In rural areas, logging and pastures are but two of the visible impacts of the city on the ecology of the countryside.

These and other influences reflect the power of cities in this era of rapid urbanization. Although farm lobbies still exert significant influence in some national governments, decisions affecting rural ecologies tend to be made in urban settings, and few edicts made in the countryside have any effect on cities (although China's villagers currently are staging thousands of public protests annually to denounce the often ruthless exploitation of their land by powerful, city-based capitalists). And in this era of globalization, city-hinterland linkages are losing their relevance in the search for sustainability and equity: the demands of urban consumers in the United States or Japan now affect ecologies (terrestrial as well as marine) from Nigeria's Niger Delta to Antarctic waters off New Zealand. Even the cities of the poorer global periphery, whose per-capita consumer demands are less intense and more local, nevertheless generate environmental and biological impacts on large populations over wide areas, ranging from atmospheric pollution and sewage discharge to water contamination and associated health hazards.

Looming over the entire combination of issues addressed in this book are the gigantic dimensions of the problem, the huge numbers of the populations of the megacities in the global core today and in the periphery tomorrow. Tokyo may constitute the largest conurbation in the former, but São Paulo and Mexico City are not far behind, and the future is evident from Jabotabek (centered on Jakarta, Indonesia, approaching 30 million), Mumbai, India (22 million), and Lagos, Nigeria (16 million). Urban regions covering hundreds of square miles and accommodating 40 or 50 million people or more will require a reconsideration of the city as we have conceived of it, lending new urgency to the issues this book addresses.

Although the current wave of globalization is not the first manifestation of a phenomenon that has had religious, colonial, and other acquisitive and control-driven motivations in the past, its current neoliberal expression reflects the virtually unbridled economic opportunism of our times and sets the bar higher for those who espouse the objectives inherent in the title of this book. While the debate over globalization's merits continues, and supporters point to South Korea and Dubai as evidence of its promise, critics focus on data that reflect the growing inequities lurking behind the gleaming facades of the emblematic high-rise towers of globalization's urban nodes. Take the photograph in the chapter "Advancing towards Urban Sustainability" (fig. 1): many of the residents of the shantytown flanking Carter Road in Mumbai earn a pittance working for the wealthy owners of the condominium building rising above their slum—a global pattern at all levels of scale, but whose inherent inequities are exacerbated by globalization. Lack of regulatory restraint and minimal (if any) protection of the rights of workers—consider the fate of the mostly South Asian workers building the skyscrapers supposedly symbolizing Arab globalization—is creating Gini coefficients that should give pause to all involved. Growth without a trend toward equity constitutes a risk to the future stability of many of the countries with statistically fast-growing economies.

The global economic crisis that began in 2008 (but whose roots were older) proved the need for international fiscal coordination and multinational cooperation. When the crisis passes, the world is likely to return to the practices of the past until another emergency arises; it is the cycle of history. To achieve progress in this age of globalization—toward the more intractable goals of urban sustainability and greater social equity, requiring policy formulations designed to constrain the demands of those present in consideration for those yet to be born—will take more than municipal or county governments can accomplish. Such coordination needs nothing less than a permanent, global initiative involving national as well as local administrations, comparable to the United Nations Millennium Declaration and its Development Goals.

PREFACE

This book explores the multiple dimensions and complexity of urban sustainability within the context of globalization and the growing concentration of wealth and power within global urban centers, particularly within wealthy countries. In the twenty-first century, with the world population becoming urban and with the rapid emergence of megacities in poor countries, the importance of addressing environmental, economic, political, social, gender, ethnic and racial, and health concerns in cities has become more relevant than ever. The stresses experienced in cities have been rapidly evolving and increasing, and they will likely be the most significant pressures on world governments and governance over the coming decades. The need to address these urban stresses has also been accentuated by new levels of socioeconomic inequality that has paralleled the diffusion of neoliberalism.

The rise in the number of people living in poverty and the increasing inequality in the distribution of resources has been recognized globally. By the mid-2000s, while the richest 20 percent of the world's population accounted for some 75 percent of global income, the poorest 40 percent accounted for only 5 percent of world income.[1] It is not only that great inequality exists, but also that the inequality has been increasing. Over the past five decades, the growing disparity between the wealthy and the poor has been experienced almost ubiquitously "between" and "within" countries. For instance, while in 1970 the average income of a country in the top quarter of the world income distribution was twenty-three times the average income of a country in the bottom quarter, by 2010 the average income of a country in the top quarter of world income distribution had increased to twenty-nine times that of a country in the bottom quarter.[2] In fact, for thirteen countries in the bottom quarter of the world income distribution, the real average income of its population in 2010 was lower than in 1970.[3]

Despite the promises offered by deregulation and free trade advocates, the fact remains that the more that countries have pursued neoliberal policies, open trade, and globalization, the more that inequality has been evident worldwide. While some select countries and urban regions have benefited from globalization, this is not the case for many, as the above figures show. It should be recognized, however, that the increase in inequality is not just evident between countries, but also within countries. By 2007 over 80 percent of the world population lived in countries where income inequality was on an increase, and given the current global economic crisis, this figure has likely been on the rise.[4]

With regard to pressures on the natural environment, it should become immediately evident that inequality in the distribution of resources and wealth has direct implications on the nature of environmental harms. The impacts of an unequal resource distribution will parallel vastly differing levels of consumption between the wealthy and the poor, reflecting on the subgroup populations that are responsible for global resource demands and, consequently, negative anthropogenic environmental impacts. This has been recently recognized by the World Bank. Their calculations for 2005, for instance, reveal that while the wealthiest 20 percent of the world population accounted for some 76.6 percent of total private consumption, the poorest 20 percent accounted for just 1.5 percent.[5]

The implications on the world's poor from these developing patterns of resource distribution and consumption are significant, and perhaps most evident with health impacts among some of the most vulnerable populations, the world's young. In 2008, for instance, some 8.8 million children died before the age of five due to poverty. Stated alternatively, over 24,100 children died each day before their fifth birthday as a result of poverty, and this number would be significantly higher if ages five, six, and seven were also considered in these figures.[6]

This book is intended to explore the interplay and the coupling of environmental, physical, political, socioeconomic, racial and ethnic, gender, and health relationships that have emerged in cities as we have entered this new era of the urban world. The chapters reveal the scope, the multiplicity, and the intricacies of urban stresses within different global settings, ultimately revealing the necessary complexity of policy initiatives pursuing sustainability. This collection of essays has been gathered with an attempt to be inclusive of a wide range of voices—scientific and theoretical—in an exploration of urban sustainability.

There are many people that need to be thanked in making this volume possible. Ellen White worked diligently to ensure the production of necessary maps. I am grateful to the many authors who submitted such excellent chapters. These are urban researchers, colleagues, and friends whose works have shaped my own research and understanding of cities, issues of justice, and environmental stresses. There are a few particularly close and influential people in my life on a personal level that are part of this collection. They include Zenia Kotval, Daniel Sui, Joseph Messina, June Thomas, Joe Darden, Assefa Mehretu, Pierre Filion, Ricardo Gomez-Insausti, and a special recognition needs to go out to my PhD adviser Carl Amrhein, a person who has been very supportive throughout my career.

I would also like to thank the over eighty different reviewers from six continents that took extensive periods of time from their busy schedules to provide detailed and thoughtful critiques and recommendations to the chapters in this book. They all added important contributions to this collection and have helped improve its quality.

Over the years, I have had a number of very close friends and colleagues who are not part of this project, but who have engaged with me in great discussions and have helped me better understand cities, the natural environment, sustainability, and justice. They include Alan Arbogast and Randy Schaetzl at Michigan State University; Jonathan Phillips at University of Kentucky; David Cairns, Clarissa Kimber, Bob Bednarz, and Andrew Klein at Texas A&M University; Bob Knippen at Ab Initio in Boston; Daniel Griffith at University of Texas at Dallas; Anne Chin at University of Colorado at Denver; Michael Bradfield at Dalhousie University; Shoukry Roweis and Alan Waterhouse at University of Toronto; and, finally, two of my dear University of Toronto friends, with whom I have had the pleasure of enjoying the past ten Christmas dinners at their home—in addition to many other wonderful and intellectually stimulating engagements—discussing the most recent rounds of international climate agreements, Canadian and American history and geography, and the new world economic order: Claude Marchand and Richard Peltier.

A number of other colleagues at Michigan State University also need to be recognized in making this book possible. I am very grateful to Laura Reese for her ongoing support of this volume. There are many who read Laura's books and articles and know her as a profound and prolific author on cities. I have had the privilege over the past six years of getting to know her as a colleague and a friend. We have been very fortunate here at Michigan State University that she took the position as director of the Global Urban Studies Program (GUSP). Laura's support and funding from GUSP was critical in enabling this collection to be published.

I would also like to thank Paul Hunt and Michigan State University Research. The very generous publishing subvention from MSU Research enabled the printing of this book. This volume would not have been produced if it were not for the university's support. Julie L. Loehr, Kristine Blakeslee and Michigan State University Press need to be acknowledged for taking on this large collection and making it possible. Thank you to everyone at the Press.

I have also been very lucky to have a great family that has been very encouraging throughout my career. I would like to recognize my parents, Zoran and Branka Vojnovic, who have been very supportive of my work and particularly this project. They have such a great passion for planting vegetable gardens and fruit trees that feed the neighborhood more than themselves. The degree of joy that they get from watching neighborhood kids pick fruit from their trees is worthy of celebration. I am indebted to them for showing me how to appreciate the beauty of life and how to enjoy it. They were also important for instilling in me the importance of travel and adventures.

Another dear family member that has been very supportive of this project, and an important influence in the selection of my career, is my uncle Milan Vojnovic. As a professor of architecture at University of Sarajevo, he was the first to introduce me to academia and to the appreciation of the urban built environment. Visiting Milan and seeing his architectural drawings and going on his tours of Sarajevo—as well as towns and cities throughout Croatia when he took me on family vacations—are still moments that are deeply and fondly imprinted in my memory. Everyone should have an uncle like Milan.

I am also very lucky to have a sister- and brother-in-law whose company is always inspirational. Wanda Georgis and Steve Yap (along with Zak, Naz, and Jonah), live life being dedicated to and exploring how to improve the world around them. Their gusto in recycling everything from clothing to toys, and from electronics to furniture, is unparalleled. From providing health services to newly arrived immigrants, to ensuring the development and success of community gardens, to buying real estate in the expensive Toronto market with the purpose of renting it out to those in need—and at a financial loss to themselves—they live life encompassing the spirit of sustainability more than anyone else I know.

Finally, my warmest thanks go to my wife, Ghada Georgis, for her years of support, patience, and intellectual inspiration. She brought peace to my life and also great wisdom. Ghada was always there in engaging the world with me as an urbanist, even though this is far from her profession. I am so appreciative of all of our great adventures together that have spanned across the world's continents. From Jericho to Tokyo, and from Sydney to Pugwash, I have been very fortunate to have such a great companion in life.

NOTES

1. United Nations Development Program, *Fighting Climate Change: Human Solidarity in a Divided World* (New York: United Nations Development Program, 2007), 25.
2. United Nations Development Program, *The Real Wealth of Nations: Pathways to Human Development* (New York: United Nations Development Program, 2010), 42.
3. Ibid.
4. United Nations Development Program, *Fighting Climate Change*, 25.
5. World Bank, *World Development Indicators 2008* (Washington, DC: World Bank, 2008), 4.
6. UNICEF, *The State of World's Children* (New York: United Nations Children's Fund, 2009), 18–19.

REFERENCES

UNICEF. *The State of World's Children.* New York: United Nations Children's Fund, 2009.

United Nations Development Program. *Fighting Climate Change: Human Solidarity in a Divided World.* New York: United Nations Development Program, 2007.

United Nations Development Program. *The Real Wealth of Nations: Pathways to Human Development.* New York: United Nations Development Program, 2010.

World Bank. *World Development Indicators 2008.* Washington, DC: World Bank, 2008.

■ JEB BRUGMANN

OVERVIEW

The promise of the worn maxim "think global, act local" is that myriad, diverse local actions, particularly in the design, planning, and management of cities can produce positive, cumulative global outcomes. For nearly forty years we have been putting that maxim to the test. There have surely been some cumulative positive results. In the late 1970s, for instance, local and even household-based measures contributed significantly to a 15 percent reduction in per capita energy consumption in the United States.[1] Solid waste recycling programs in industrialized countries have significantly reduced waste volumes going into landfills. Water conservation programs, better water utility management, and new plumbing fixtures have reduced unit consumption of water in many areas of industrial, institutional, and household operations. But the good news of these and other demonstrated links between local action and global change are much tempered by other trends over which localities have found it harder to gain real leverage or control. By the late 1990s, for instance, the U.S. energy efficiency gains of the 1970–1980s were eliminated, largely by the introduction and aggressive promotion of sport utility vehicles. Decreases in the percentage of household waste going to landfills were overshadowed by increased overall waste volumes, in large part due to increased packaging in the early 1990s, and then by overall increases in consumption related to cheaper developing-country production. Improved efficiencies in water consumption are overshadowed by the worldwide trend toward lower density suburbanization on urban peripheries, which compromises groundwater sources and watersheds, reduces efficiencies of utility operations, and increases water demand for landscaping.

As these examples suggest, local action alone, in spite of an amazing number of initiatives, is not proving the maxim. Similar examples are well known with regard to urban poverty alleviation and urban services provision to low-income communities. This, I argue, reflects a critical shortcoming in strategy on the part of the "urban sustainability" project, one that will be resolved only through a new round of coordinated research, theory, and practice that focuses on a more complete ecological understanding of the nature of the city in a global context. The principle challenge we face in bringing about urban sustainability, as both a process and a condition, is the reality that cities exist, grow, and operate at many scales. Our "act local" efforts have focused largely on the neighborhood, district, urban municipality, and sometimes metropolitan region. But as William Rees and other ecological economists so aptly describe within the ecological frame, and as the world cities literature so aptly describes within the political-economic frame, this urban thing that we are trying to make sustainable functions also as a system of consumption, production, and ecological reengineering at continental and global scales.[2] In forty years, the expanding global urban system has transformed much of the matured planetary ecosystem, at its many scales, into the semi-ecology of a global City.

While there is much to be achieved, we have nonetheless come a long way in consolidating "urban sustainability" as a new domain of practice. It is worth taking stock of this new enterprise. Global affairs management has traditionally been a domain of national and international policy and of corporate and military strategy. These institutions often viewed the primary challenges of global affairs, as in the invasion of Iraq, the negotiation of a UN climate convention, or the establishment of a new international trade regime, as matters of global (modern) institutional alignment. With alignment, the collaborative ability of modern institutions to achieve shared institutional objectives by reengineering society and ecology, as in the Green Revolution or the more recent global liberalization project, could be assumed. Efforts to understand the changing human system at the ground level were a secondary concern, left to be explored by the specialist academician, managed by the local technician, and governed by the least influential of modern institutions, the municipality. But events over the last decades have steadily shaken this approach. Developing from specific city contexts, the 2003 SARS epidemic, the local social-cultural complexities confounding U.S. military strategy in Iraq, the rise of new transnational urban crime organizations like the MS-13, the development of disruptive business innovations like Indian outsourcing, and the subprime mortgage crisis have each demonstrated the shortcomings of modern strategy in a rapidly urbanizing world.

The chapters in this book reflect a new capacity to explore global conditions as defined by a worldwide geography of urban complexity. These studies of the granular aspects of recognized global problems suggest a new strategic frame of reference: that global challenges on an urbanizing planet need to be understood *in an urban context.* Contrary to the "world is flat" perspective, local particularities and events now amplify more quickly into global opportunities and crises. SARS in urban Guangdong Province, disaster in New Orleans, poverty and political marginalization in the slums of Nairobi, Gaza, or Caracas all produce disruptive global events because in a predominantly urbanized world the changing nature of the city is the changing nature of the world.

The book's first principle, that global sustainability is a matter of urban context, may seem self-evident today, but it represents a Copernican shift in thinking. Among the major modern institutions, only the corporation has developed practices for viewing strategic options through an urban lens and for pursuing institutional objectives within the context of cities. Ever more dependent on urban markets and infrastructure, the corporate sector is nonetheless daunted by the chaotic, seemingly ungovernable nature of such a rapidly evolving system. Corporate thinking about cities is therefore self-contained to known territories (e.g., central business districts) and metrics (e.g., local rents and cost structures), often still blinkered by the modernist framing of the city as something municipal or as a project location or intervention site.

Perhaps the most profound indication of insufficient theory and empirical research on the extra-local nature of the global city system is found in the 2007 Fourth Assessment Report of the Intergovernmental Panel on Climate Change (IPCC). Even when cities have been the first to officially commit to Kyoto targets (even before the Framework Convention on Climate Change process began),[3] the first to demonstrate that substantial reductions in carbon emissions could be achieved without economic disruption, and the first jurisdictions to achieve Kyoto targets, the IPCC still lacks an analysis of the urban dynamics and urban geography of greenhouse gas emissions. The physical science section of the Fourth Report makes no reference to cities. It refers to "settlements" among the other euphemistic "human systems" that are driving climate change, including "society," "technology," "trade," "sociocultural preferences," "production and consumption patterns," "health," and "literacy"—but it falls short of an analytical recognition that these things are and will remain largely unmanageable euphemisms unless they are understood and approached as they are organized and function in the world: as the integrated material, energetic systems that we call cities. The mitigation section of the Fourth Report briefly discusses urban transportation energy demand, the urban heat island effect, and methane recovery from solid waste landfills, but there is no overall concept of the city as an energy system that can be comprehensively designed. The IPCC and Kyoto process still quantify emissions and define responses in terms of economic sectors and end-uses, without a view as to the urban system that shapes and binds them all together. The city still remains peripheral to such sincere, sophisticated, and critically important endeavors, I believe, because we lack the analytical framework and tools to understand it as a steerable system—that is, as a domain of strategy.

Nonetheless, progress has been made in consolidating this domain. This book reflects three particular consolidations of thinking and practice since "urban sustainability" emerged as a scholarly, technical, and managerial project.

In the first instance, the book reflects the project's evolution beyond the often fractious separation of discourse about the city into two distinct geographical and socioeconomic camps, which posed themselves as separate, even oppositional urban reform projects in the 1970s to 1990s. In the 1992 UN Earth Summit process, for example, these projects were defined and debated in terms of a "Green Agenda" and (or *versus*) a "Brown Agenda." The green camp arose from the Western environmental movement and problematized the *chronic* challenge of the city as an un- or even anti-ecological resource processing, consumption, and waste production system that threatened planetary ecology. The Club of Rome's *Limits to Growth*, the urban materials and energy balance analyses undertaken under UNESCO's Man, Nature and Biosphere Programme, the Ecological Footprint analysis, the eco-efficiency movement of architects, industrial designers and engineers in Europe and Japan, and the works of ecological economists were representative of this *problematique*.

The brown camp arose from the social movements of the slum dwellers and urban poor, and it problematized the *acute* challenges of urban land tenure, legal exclusion, and other injustices reproducing housing, public health, and economic crisis for growing urban majorities. The discourses of the 1976 UN Habitat Conference, the research and publications of the International

Institute for Environment and Development, the advocacy of the Habitat International NGO coalition, and the works of critical geographers, sociologists, and legal scholars in different country contexts were representative of this *problematique*. Throughout the 1970s to 1990s these two camps promoted competing platforms at all the scales, from international forums to national capitals to local city councils. The Green Agenda focused on investments to contain urban pollution and land conversion. It promoted pollution control laws, sewerage treatment infrastructure, mass transit, energy efficiency, and reduced consumption, all of which delivered little apparent benefit to poor people working in hazardous conditions, lacking basic sanitation, taking residence in environmentally sensitive lands, and seeking an increase in basic consumption. The Brown Agenda focused on housing expansion, infrastructure, water, and energy services for the poor. Pollution control, to the extent that it was a concern, focused on removing wastes from living and work environments, not on what happened to wastes once removed. The two agendas, though not inherently oppositional, organized through, and became part of, the local class-based politics of cities and the broader geopolitical division between the OECD and G77+China blocks.

This book manifests a more colorblind reconceptualization of urban sustainability that has been emerging in the twenty-first century. It presents a more holistic view of the city as a socioeconomic and ecological phenomena to be developed in an integrated fashion within a local context, and not so much as the political territory of a social movement to be rallied to a cause. The viability of accommodation between the two old camps was demonstrated first by the "best practices" of cities themselves (e.g., in Curitiba, Porto Alegre, Rio de Janeiro, Chicago, San Francisco Bay Area, Vancouver, Jinja, and Bangalore), where green and brown reform measures were integrated into single local investment and reform programs. The broader possibility of convergence was reinforced by major international programs like Local Agenda 21 and Healthy Cities, and ultimately by UN Habitat.[4] Discursively, we have seen the emergence of "environmental justice" and "just sustainability" as an intellectual fulcrum balancing the acute and chronic, and the brown and green agendas on a singular intellectual and practice platform. After decades of contention, "urban sustainability" has finally been accepted as an exploration and practice of the whole city, not of specific reform programs for it.

Simultaneous with the bridging of these solitudes, there was a broadening of interdisciplinary collaboration regarding the city as a phenomenon. Urban sustainability has been consolidated as a truly multidisciplinary domain in which geographers, sociologists, engineers, planners, political economists, and ecologists receive funding to understand the city as a unit of systemic development and change. This is a major shift from the earlier period when disciplines problematized the city in separate texts and programs. One observes a principled effort on the part of scholars and practitioners alike to focus on points of convergence between historic ideological projects, or to simply study urbanization phenomena as they appear and not with reference to entrenched discourses for policy advocacy and program funding.

The third consolidation of urban sustainability as a domain of scholarship and practice has been a steady recognition of the city as a biotic and political-economic geography in its own right, not as a subsidiary jurisdiction to be managed by municipalities, reformed by social movement projects, and shaped by national and international programs or corporate interests. For instance, there has been a noted shift in economic development theory and practice from the city as a "location" seeking comparative cost advantages to the urban region as a unique source of competencies and historical legacies for new industry development, and to the urban regime as an entrepreneurial force on a global landscape.[5] Rigid normative readings of city development phenomena are being challenged. For instance, the nearly doctrinaire dismissal of the residential suburb has been somewhat suspended, providing space to investigate the suburb as an urban landscape that can be completed through further cycles of investment. "Urban ecologists" have shifted focus from studies of the adaptations of "natural" species living in urban environments to full-scale studies of the ecological dynamics of cities themselves and of urbanization as a form of ecological engineering.

Along with these consolidations of scholarship and practice, we have seen a broadening public and mass media discourse about the city. Urban affairs reportage can now be regularly found in the *Economist* and the *New Yorker* and in the news and business sections of daily newspapers around the world. Little more than a decade ago, our debates about urban indicators were a marginal, specialist concern; today there seems to be a whole industry producing comparative indicators and indices on the livability, affordability, cultural life, and cuisine of cities. Corporate consulting firms like Monitor Group and McKinsey have developed business lines for benchmarking and analyzing cities. Yet, in spite of this recognition of the city as a phenomena to be measured and reported, our practices vis-à-vis the city remain archaic. Science-based institutions and processes, like the IPCC and the World Health Organization (WHO) and its national centers for disease control, do comparatively little science and policy with reference to the city, whether at the local level or as a global urban system of materials, energy, and biological/viral exchange. Corporations and their consultants still relate to cities in a tactical way as facilities locations with different cost structures, and analyze them using the most simplistic benchmarking methods, but rarely do they study and invest in cities strategically as productive, creative communities and systems. And we, the urban sustainability scholars and practitioners, still focus most of our attention and work on the city as we have earlier understood it, as a local scale phenomenon, even as our discourse treats it as a phenomenon of global scale.

We have tried to extend our practices to other scales of urban reality. For instance, intercity networks that once functioned merely to "share best practices" and build a sense of community amongst jurisdictionally separated local practitioners have evolved into nascent mechanisms for bioregional governance with a sense of common jurisdiction. The Great Lakes Mayors network of the 1990s, for example, has evolved into the Great Lakes and St. Lawrence Cities Initiative with a coordinated policy agenda that embraces the common economic and environmental interests of a huge extended urban geography.[6] Similarly, there is an evolution of practice focused on monitoring and managing the cumulative impacts of a global city system. For instance, the ICLEI Cities for Climate Protection campaign, a program that assists more than 750 cities to quantify, monitor, and reduce their greenhouse gas emissions, is building capacity to better aggregate local inventories of urban greenhouse gas emissions into an urban system assessment that is reported to the Kyoto process. But we still lack the kind of researched, analytical frame and tools to support a substantial evolution of urban sustainability practice beyond the municipal scale—scientifically, technically, politically and institutionally—into a new practice for coordinated development of cities as an extra-local system.

I have earlier argued that a major shortcoming in the Local Agenda 21 (LA21) approach, which by UN/ICLEI accounts catalyzed development planning processes in more than 10,000 cities and towns in more than 115 countries, was its lack of a well-articulated global political project to match the globally conceived and far more sophisticated liberalization project of the time.[7] The lack of a "think local, act global" strategy and reform program allowed the 1990s liberalization project to articulate in such a way that its development and consumption influences in our cities—the just-in-time delivery of standardized suburban subdivisions and retail franchise centers, the SUVs, the rising resource consumption and waste, the continued shortage of affordable, formal sector housing, and growing gaps in urban services and health care—overwhelmed our LA21 and other "act local" efforts.

Liberalization also created a tectonic shift in urban "institutional ecology" that disrupted the development of urban sustainability as a practice. Early sustainability practice, like LA21, was conceived within a state-centric context (i.e., reforms anchored in public planning and investment, environmental regulation, and overseas development assistance). It sought a civic, "participatory" rejuvenation and reform of the local state, but it did so just as the state's footings were being shaken, stripping our work of known tactics and tools. Yet liberalization also revealed contours of the emerging city system, which had been obscured by state-centric and technocratic framings of the city.

The rapid embrace of market liberalization by cities everywhere—whether evidenced by "competitive cities" strategies (as a LA21 counterpoint), the emergence of a transnational urban development industry, or even the global articulation and growth of the informal economic sector—brought the entrepreneurial, mercantile, and communitarian character of cities to the fore. Informal labor and housing markets expanded and matured, redefining the real character of so-called slums. Particular ethnic or caste communities advanced their holds on traditional economic sectors. A parallel system of foreign direct investment (FDI)—totaling some $300 billion in annual remittances between the lower-income urban classes, city-to-city[8]—fueled more urban migration, new construction, and enterprise in the informal sector and in formal low-income districts. Slum-based businesses became semiformal and globalized, and hawkers developed scaled product-sourcing and distribution operations. Even as liberalization delivered McUrbanization, a commandeering of central cities by transnational corporate interests, and growing income inequality and spatial marginalization of the poor, it also revealed the limits of global capital's urban claims. Alongside the "rise of the creative class," the city's informal and illegal economic sectors vastly expanded their claims and territories to the City at every scale.

In 2004 I made a trip to Johannesburg with a Goldman Sachs banker to identify investment opportunities in township-based black enterprises. Upon arrival we discovered that Goldman Sachs' security protocols would not allow the banker to visit most township areas. Our limited itinerary for the week thereby symbolized the extent of traditional capital's containment in the city. More substantively, water service concessions held by Europe's private water titans were failing in South Africa's urban districts, in spite of the country's extremely conducive foreign direct investment policy environment. The South African government became an investor in Johannesburg's rough-and-tumble informal taxi sector, which carries a large percentage of the city's commuters, even as the city privatized urban services and the international airport. The scene was hardly monolithic.

As much as liberalization confounded urban sustainability practice, traditional capital faced unexpected barriers to entry in the city during the first decade of liberalization. This has clarified the strategic challenge confronting planners and technocrats, nongovernmental organizations, and corporations alike in steering the city's development. The raw economic advantages of cities—in particular their density and scale economies—prove to be a public good that can be leveraged by many different social groups according to their means and traditions. The result is a diversity of entrepreneurial and commercial strategies to secure global advantage in and through the city: formal, informal, and illegal. Whereas the strategies of the "poor" could once be marginalized and locally contained by force, as cities integrate into the City system, these strategies are consolidating into parallel and competing *forms of political-economy* within a splintered, not a monolithic, capitalist mode of production. The scaled territory of the City supports powerful communitarian, migrant-entrepreneurial, and criminal strategies, which define urban spatial geographies and financial and human flows as much as traditional corporate strategy.

Urban strategy and reform today demands the reform of different political-economic forms toward progressive ends, at multiple scales. One cannot simply intervene in a local system. Neither can national or global policy reforms prevent local realities from amplifying into globalized events. Multiscalar strategy is required. NGOs have led the way in developing practices for this new environment. Filling the regulatory and development assistance roles left by the state's retreat, functioning as a form of private governance, their coordinated global campaigns against leading brands have amplified the settlement of specific local cases into worldwide changes in business practices. Their co-regulatory regimes, like the Forest Stewardship Council or Fairtrade, have provided frameworks for the simultaneous reform of local practices in hundreds of locations. Their micro-credit and micro-insurance networks have provided an infrastructure for capitalization of uncounted local development interventions. Urban sustainability practice can learn much from their approaches.

Given the complexities of urban systems, however, the advancement of urban sustainability practice will also require deeper understanding of the nature of the City as a multiscalar ecological and political-economic system. We can accelerate this understanding by pushing the above-mentioned "consolidations" of urban sustainability scholarship to their fuller logical conclusion in our research undertakings; that is, by contextualizing the unit of analysis in our studies within the extended urban systems of which they are a part, and by suspending the twentieth century's normative projects for the city—the Livable City, the Good Governance City, and the Sustainable City—enough to allow fresh, interdisciplinary attempts to more fully characterize the urban system and its dynamics.

To start, I believe it is time to explore the possibilities of a new consolidation, between the urban sustainability project and the world cities project. Both fields of scholarship have much to gain. On the one hand, the world cities undertaking has very substantially explored the extra-local phenomena of the City system. It encompasses very advanced efforts to collect data and analyze material, financial, and human flows between cities, thereby supporting characterizations of extra-local urban formations. By matching this high-level or top-down view of the City with the current bottom-up view of the urban sustainability domain, we can create a fuller picture of the City. It would also force creative reconciliation between the neostructuralist orientation of the world cities project with urban sustainability's theorization of how local cultural, political, and institutional impacts produce (overdetermine) extra-local outcomes—in other words, how the local articulates upward into global patterns. This would be no easy task, but it would likely be ideologically cleansing.

On the other hand, the urban sustainability undertaking brings many frames and tools to the table that can fill out the world cities characterization of the City as a socioeconomic phenomenon driven by formal corporate investment.[9] In addition to the commodity, financial, and human flows of world cities analysis, the City also constitutes energy, noncommodity materials (e.g., siltation, dust), and nonhuman biological flows that substantially impact global conditions. Ecological economics offers a complementary theorization of the City, and of specific city networks or supply chains, as semi-ecological systems in a process of development, lacking the necessary feedback mechanisms required to analyze and regulate consumption, distribution, and entropy in the system. Altogether, such a collaboration could support a discourse about the City that gives it the necessary salience in forums like the IPCC; that is, as a system forming, operating and extending itself through essentially nonstate mechanisms, creating acute and chronic problems at each scale, which can be redesigned, reformed, and regulated to achieve desired global outcomes.

Such an approach, I believe, would help us engage with the city more as it is today, and to more precisely describe the origins of global changes, which have been left abstractly explained as disembedded processes under the catch-all heading of "globalization." By exploring the City as a multiscalar phenomenon, we can understand how crises or innovations get articulated into the City system through individual cities, as systems (as opposed to "sites") shaped by unique cultural traditions and economic histories. Accepted interpretations of technology, such as the Internet and mobile phones, as disembedding people from the city and place, can be reexplored as part of an extended urban infrastructure that has started to embed us in a new interurban body politic and self-organizing order (e.g., via the global social regulation of transnational corporate practices by civil society networks).

The studies presented in this book show that, for all its complications, the city is still a designable, governable, and manageable unit of change that influences and is influenced by its articulation into a larger urban system. Creating an understanding of the multiscalar workings of cities has been the implicit project of urban sustainability from its beginnings. This book is a start to a more complete theorizing of how this City is put together and works at all these scales to reengineer global ecology. The body of research presented here sheds extensive light on the potential and challenges for re-engineering the City through design, technology, governance, and management into a new kind of anthropomorphic biome (i.e., a stable ecosystem), which is ultimately required for any truly sustainable global development outcome.

NOTES

1. DeGolyer and MacNaughton, *Twentieth Century Petroleum Statistics* (Dallas, TX: DeGolyer and MacNaughton, 1997), 108.
2. William Rees, Understanding Urban Ecosystems: An Ecological Economics Perspective, in *Understanding Urban Ecosystems*, ed. Berkowitz et al (New York: Springer-Verlag, 2003); Manuel Castells, *The Rise of the Network Society* (Cambridge, MA: Blackwell,

1996); John Friedmann, The World City Hypothesis, *Development and Change* 4 (1986): 12–50; Fu-Chen Lo and Yue-Man Yeung, *Emerging World Cities in Pacific Asia* (Tokyo: United Nations University Press, 1996); Paul Knox and Peter Taylor, eds., *World Cities in a World System* (Cambridge: Cambridge University Press, 1995).

3. The Framework Convention on Climate Change was open for signature in 1992. In 1990 Toronto officially committed to a 20 percent reduction in its carbon dioxide (equivalent) emissions from 1988 levels.
4. Jeb Brugmann, Locating the Local Agenda: Preserving Public Interest in the Evolving Urban World, in *Scaling the Urban Environmental Challenge: From Local to Global and Back*, ed. Peter Marcotullio and Gordon McGranahan (London: Earthscan, 2007).
5. Michael Storper, *The Regional World: Territorial Development in a Global Economy* (New York: Guilford Press, 1997); Sharad Chari, *Fraternal Capital: Peasant-Workers, Self-Made Men, and Globalization in Provincial India* (Stanford: Stanford University Press, 2004); Susan Clarke and Gary Gaile, *The Work of Cities* (Minneapolis: University of Minnesota Press, 1998).
6. See http://www.glslcities.org/.
7. Brugmann, Locating the Local Agenda.
8. This is equivalent to 40 percent of worldwide official foreign direct investment (FDI) in 2006.
9. The focus of world cities scholarship on the socioeconomic impacts of the global financial and business services industry in particular has led, I believe, to a narrowly applied theory, represented in the preoccupation with classifying individual cities into economic typologies and hierarchical rankings on this narrow basis (Beaverstock et al., World-City Network). In practice, these classifications have been used more to promote the economic competition between cities on the basis of generic cost, labor market and amenity comparisons (for the benefit of these industries) rather than supporting reform of urban development and policy in favor of more holistic, progressive development of the city system. Although world cities research forces us to come to terms with problems of global data insufficiency on cities (Kentor et al, *The World-System's City System*), it can distract from the larger project of understanding the system itself, with its interdependent economic, ecological, social, and political dimensions.

REFERENCES

Beaverstock, Jonathan, Richard Smith, and Peter Taylor. World-City Network: A New Metageography? *Annals of the Association of American Geographers* 90:1 (2000): 123–34.

Brugmann, Jeb. Locating the Local Agenda: Preserving Public Interest in the Evolving Urban World. In *Scaling the Urban Environmental Challenge: From Local to Global and Back*, ed. Peter Marcotullio and Gordon McGranahan, 331–54. London: Earthscan, 2007.

Castells, Manuel. *The Rise of the Network Society.* Cambridge, MA: Blackwell, 1996.

Chari, Sharad. *Fraternal Capital: Peasant-Workers, Self-Made Men, and Globalization in Provincial India.* Stanford: Stanford University Press, 2004.

Clarke, Susan, and Gary Gaile. *The Work of Cities.* Minneapolis: University of Minnesota Press, 1998.

DeGolyer and MacNaughton. *Twentieth Century Petroleum Statistics, 1997.* Dallas, TX: DeGolyer and MacNaughton, 1997.

Friedmann, John. Where We Stand: A Decade of World City Research. In *World Cities in a World System*, ed. Paul Knox and Peter Taylor, 21–47. Cambridge: Cambridge University Press, 1995.

———. The World City Hypothesis. *Development and Change* 4 (1986): 12–50.

Kentor, Jeffrey, David Smith, and Michael Timberlake. *The World-System's City System: A Research Agenda.* 2004. http://www.irows.ucr.edu/conferences/globgis/papers/Smith.htm.

Knox, Paul, and Peter Taylor, eds. *World Cities in a World System.* Cambridge: Cambridge University Press, 1995.

Lo, Fu-Chen, and Yue-Man Yeung. *Emerging World Cities in Pacific Asia.* Tokyo: United Nations University Press, 1996.

Rees, William. Understanding Urban Ecosystems: An Ecological Economics Perspective. In *Understanding Urban Ecosystems*, ed. Alan Berkowitz, Charles Nilon, and Karen Hollweg, 115–36, New York: Springer-Verlag, 2003.

Storper, Michael. *The Regional World: Territorial Development in a Global Economy.* New York: Guilford Press, 1997.

Taylor, Peter. Hierarchical Tendencies amongst World Cities: A Global Research Proposal. *Cities* 14:6 (1997): 323–32.

■ IGOR VOJNOVIC

Advancing toward Urban Sustainability

THE PURSUIT OF EQUITY

The concept of *sustainability,* while gaining popularity in the late 1980s, appears for the first time within a human-environment context in the Club of Rome's *The Limits to Growth* (1972). The Club of Rome Executive Committee argued that the "world system is simply not ample enough nor generous enough to accommodate much longer such egocentric and conflictive behavior by its inhabitants." Their solution was to pursue "a society in a steady state of economic and ecological equilibrium," with the goal of establishing a "condition of ecological and economic stability that is sustainable far into the future."[1] In the midst of a world economy and energy crisis, the idea of a global system characterized by long-term social and ecological stability resonated strongly in the world community.

Another dimension of the sustainability debate, pursuing social equity, was introduced in 1974 at the World Council of Churches conference on Science and Technology for Human Development. At the conference, the concept of a "sustainable society" was first introduced and sustainability became closely aligned with the pursuit of equity and social justice.[2]

Some six year later, in 1980, *the term sustainable development* was first used in the International Union for Conservation of Nature and Natural Resources' (IUCN) report *World Conservation Strategy: Living Resource Conservation for Sustainable Development.* Similar to other academic and UN publications on sustainable development advanced in later years, the IUCN advocated "the management of human use of the biosphere so that it may yield the greatest sustainable benefit to present generations while maintaining its potential to meet the needs and aspirations of future generations."[3]

The concept of sustainable development received particular attention after the publication of *Our Common Future* (1987) by the World Commission on Environment and Development (WCED). The WCED claimed that industrialization had resulted in unprecedented changes to our planet, threatening our social and ecological stability. The WCED's response was the need to pursue sustainable development, "development that meets the needs of the present without compromising the ability of future generations to meet their own needs."[4] The WCED also stressed the equitable access to resources within and amongst nations—and particularly in addressing the essential needs of the world's poor—as a critical dimension of sustainability.[5]

In the current literature, sustainable development and sustainability continue to be largely variants of the IUCN and the WCED definitions, and rarely do the descriptions offer greater specificity. As pointed out by the WCED, what their report had proposed was a description of sustainable development in "general terms."[6] In fact, what researchers and analysts have provided is the "spirit" of the concept, which advocates human activities that can maintain the quality of natural resources and the environment over time while meeting the needs of multiple generations. The spirit of sustainability and its benefits to society have been recognized for centuries, but a mechanism for advancing toward sustainability, and the physical reality of this condition, continue to be elusive.

In exploring the complexity involved in the sustainability advocacy, this collection of works will focus on cities. The concentration on urban sustainability has been encouraged by a number of global trends that have placed cities at the forefront of world issues. More than half the world population currently lives in urban areas, and virtually all world population growth over the next three decades is expected to be in cities (see table 1).[7] In addition, into the twenty-first century the anticipated resource demands, the scale of direct and indirect environmental degradation resulting from urban inhabitants, and the social and health stresses expected in cities will likely be the most significant pressures on world governments and governance (see fig. 1). Finally, increasing economic globalization—evident with the deregulation of markets and the decentralization of economic activities—and the general diffusion of neoliberalism, while enhancing the condition of certain urban populations has also placed new and increasing stresses on many urban subgroups. To this extent, this collection of works is intended to illustrate the multiple dimensions of urban sustainability in different spatial, cultural, political, and socioeconomic contexts. While there is no consensus on a mechanism for achieving urban sustainability, this collection intends to illustrate that the pursuit of inter- and intragenerational equity will be the common global thread in promoting social and ecological stability over time.

Sustainability Initiatives

While the relevance of sustainability is clearly apparent, there is an absence of agreement on exactly how to achieve this condition. Current debates have thus concentrated on the proposed mechanisms necessary to achieve sustainability. These debates have ranged widely. On the one end, theorists such as Wolfgang Sachs and Ted Trainer have advocated the pursuit of sustainability by means of fundamental structural changes in socioeconomic and political organization.[8] On the other end, in what critics consider a public relations exercise with no fundamental impact on corporate behavior, commercial interests such as the Business Council for Sustainable Development and the chemical industry's Responsible Care offer the view that the global community needs to pursue sustainable economic development, combining ongoing economic growth and

Table 1. Urban population by region and percentage of world population that is urban by region, 1950–2020 (projected)

Urban population (millions)

	1950	1960	1970	1980	1990	2000	2020*
World	**733**	**993**	**1,330**	**1,737**	**2,273**	**2,857**	**4,215**
Africa	33	52	83	129	199	295	568
Asia	232	338	486	693	1,012	1,367	2,214
Europe	280	343	413	475	516	529	540
Latin America and Caribbean	70	108	163	234	314	393	542
North America	110	143	171	189	214	250	322
Oceania	8	10	14	16	19	23	30

Percentage urban

	1950	1960	1970	1980	1990	2000	2020*
World	**29.1**	**32.9**	**36.0**	**39.2**	**43.2**	**47.1**	**55.9**
Africa	14.9	18.6	23.2	27.5	31.9	37.1	47.8
Asia	16.6	19.8	22.7	26.3	31.9	37.1	48.5
Europe	51.2	56.7	62.9	68.6	71.5	72.7	76.6
Latin America and Caribbean	41.9	49.3	57.4	64.9	71.1	75.5	82.3
North America	63.9	69.9	73.8	73.9	75.4	79.1	84.8
Oceania	60.6	65.9	70.6	71.1	70.1	72.7	74.2

* Projected
Source: United Nations, *World Urbanization Prospects: The 2003 Revision* (New York: United Nations, 2004).

conservation.[9] In fact, by the early 1990s, a decade after the concept was first used by IUCN, over eighty definitions of the term "sustainable development" existed.[10]

Within this context, criticism has also been cast on the very idea of sustainable development. A contradiction is seen between the term "development," considered synonymous with high consumption and the protection of material privileges, and the term "sustainability," concerned with the maintenance of natural environmental quality and the robustness of ecological systems.

Despite the absence of a clear mechanism for advancing toward sustainability, and despite the lack of knowledge of whether it is even physically attainable, considerable global political effort has been devoted to pursuing sustainability. In 1992 the UN Conference on Environment and Development (UNCED) in Rio de Janeiro included 172 countries and revealed that much of the world considered sustainability desirable. Five notable documents emerged from UNCED—*Agenda 21, The Rio Declaration, The Framework Convention on Climate Change, The Convention on Biological Diversity,* and *The Forest Principles.* However, by the 1995 UN Climate Change Convention in Berlin it was evident that not much progress was being made in pursuit of UNCED initiatives. At the 1997 Kyoto Conference and the 1997 UN General Assembly Session in New York City similar frustrations were also expressed.

In 2002, ten years after the Rio Summit, the World Summit on Sustainable Development

PHOTO BY SHAILESH KARAMCHANDANI

Figure 1. A slum on Carter Road in Mumbai

(WSSD) was held in Johannesburg, South Africa. During the WSSD, the pursuit of the Rio principles was strongly reaffirmed. However, George W. Bush and his administration's boycott of the summit, and Washington's rejection of binding targets to cut pollution and reduce poverty, paralyzed the potential for any significant global initiatives. In addition, the WSSD revealed, once again, the ongoing contentions in the design of actual mechanisms for achieving sustainability.

The inability to initiate international agreements supporting sustainability was more recently evident with the Kyoto Protocol. The Kyoto Protocol was drawn up in 1997 and was an addendum to the 1992 United Nations Framework Convention on Climate Change adopted at UNCED in Rio. The 1997 Protocol set mandatory limits on carbon emissions, replacing the voluntary goals of the 1992 treaty. Despite coming into force in 2005, the Kyoto Protocol lacked the ratification by the United States and Australia, and did not require many newly industrializing countries, including China and India, to reduce emissions. The Kyoto Protocol illustrated that even when there is a clearly articulated objective, in this case stabilizing greenhouse gas concentrations in the atmosphere, it is difficult to establish unanimous support for international environmental agreements. It should also be acknowledged that in many countries that had signed the 2005 Protocol, emissions have continued to increase.

By December of 2007, however, there was a new hope that an international agreement on climate change would eventually include all the wealthy nations. After the November 27, 2007, Australian elections, the new Prime Minister Kevin Michael Rudd ratified the Kyoto Protocol as the first act of the new Australian government. In addition, shortly after, in December 2007, at the International Climate Change Conference in Bali, 187 countries, including the United States, agreed to negotiate a new accord on climate change by 2009. This new treaty would lead to a post-2012 international climate change accord, replacing the Kyoto Protocol's first period of emission reductions upon its expiration at the end of 2012.[11]

While the United States ultimately agreed to the adoption of the 2007 Bali roadmap, U.S. negotiators were once again viewed as obstructionists in the talks. It was recognized that President George W. Bush—with strong constituency support from mining, oil, and natural gas industries—maintained little interest in establishing mandatory climate measures.[12] In fact, due to U.S. pressures, the *Bali Action Plan* contained no binding commitments, which European representatives were aggressively pursuing. As the new rounds of negotiations were to proceed, the United States was viewed as the main obstacle to an international climate change agreement. The George W. Bush administration and other members of the Republican Party insisted that the United States would not agree to any binding emission limits.[13]

The 2008 U.S. presidential election gave new promise of a change in the U.S. climate policy agenda. In mid-December 2008, as then President-elect Barack Obama introduced his team on energy and climate, and his own environmental policy challenges, he argued that "this time it must be different. . . . This will be a leading priority of my presidency and a defining test of our time. We cannot accept complacency, nor accept any more broken promises."[14]

One year later, on December 18, 2009, at the UN Climate Change Conference in Copenhagen, President Obama announced his goal of reducing carbon emissions in the United States by 17 percent from 2005 levels by 2020. With the new president, there was clearly greater U.S. interest in the drafting of a legally binding international climate treaty evident at the Copenhagen Summit. As stated by Lisa Jackson, a U.S. Environmental Protection Agency Administrator and President Obama's cabinet member in charge of environmental protection, "We are seeking robust engagement with all of our partners around the world."[15]

The Copenhagen Accord was drafted at the 2009 Summit and received widespread, but not full, commitment from both wealthy and poor countries. The Copenhagen Accord, reinforced by the Cancun Agreements of December 2010, managed to keep the pursuit of an international climate agreement alive despite the many difficulties that remain ahead.

The Copenhagen Accord and the Cancun Agreements committed short- and long-term financial support from wealthy to poor countries for technology development and transfer, forest conservation, capacity building, and the impacts of global change. The agreements also reinforced the international interest in keeping global warming to below 2°C and committed countries to reviewing a 1.5°C goal by 2015, reinforcing the recognition that a 2°C goal is likely inadequate.

The case still remains, however, that the accord does not have a legally binding structure and that there is still no international treaty to succeed the Kyoto Protocol past 2012.[16] The voluntary national emission reduction proposals for the year 2020 are also considered insufficient to meet even the objective of keeping global warming to below 2°C.[17] In addition, the United States, China, and India are still not bound to mandatory reductions under the Kyoto Accord. Akira Yamada, Japan's deputy director general for Global Issues, likened these three top emitters as "spectators" at a soccer match that the rest of the world was playing.[18] Yamada maintained that this jeopardized any post-2012 treaty extension, and he called for the big three emitters to "come down to the field to play with us, to score against global warming."[19] Matters were further complicated in 2011 when Canada formally withdrew from the Kyoto Protocol.

Urban Sustainability Initiatives

As with sustainability in general, there is considerable ambiguity with the concept of urban sustainability. Defining urban sustainability as part of general sustainability has been considered critical in maintaining links between the local and the global.[20] The pursuit of urban sustainability, therefore, must ensure the pursuit of socioeconomic processes that enable the achievement of local and global sustainability.

Urban sustainability can be loosely defined as the outcome of a social, economic, and physical organization of urban populations in ways that accommodates the needs of current and future generations while preserving the quality of the natural environment and its ecological systems over time. As with the concept of sustainability, current descriptions of urban sustainability are considered too vague for any practical purpose, such as defining policy.

On the one hand, the benefit of not having a precise definition is that communities will conceptualize the sustainability condition differently, depending on their particular values, circumstances, and unique urban stresses. The design of local sustainable initiatives will be very different in Nairobi, Kenya, and London, England. In fact, sustainability initiatives will also differ between cities in a single country, depending on the local conditions. One just needs to think of the differences in the nature of urban stresses between Beijing and Shanghai, Brasilia and São Paulo, or San Francisco and Detroit.

However, the lack of a clear definition of sustainability has contributed to our inability to implement urban sustainability policies. In addition, our understanding of what makes urban sustainability is deficient. Little is known about the role of governments in advancing sustainability, the design and implementation of successful urban sustainability programs, and the structure of institutional and social relations necessary to support sustainable human activities.

As in the case of sustainability, the first attempts to design programs promoting local sustainability emerged from the Rio Summit. Developing from UNCED was the *Rio Declaration on Environment and Development*, which outlined twenty-seven principles to guide the global pursuit of sustainability. To advance these principles, *Agenda 21* was adopted as the action plan for implementing sustainability, and in chapter 28 of the *Agenda* municipal expectations were outlined.[21] By 2001 there were 6,416 cities and towns in 113 countries that had programs classified as Local Agenda 21, and this number had increased to over 10,000 cities and towns by 2007.[22] However, in an evaluation of Local Agenda 21 programs, Jeb Brugmann (who conceived and launched Local Agenda 21) states the following:

> What requires little assessment is the fact that few cities and towns stand today as models of sustainability. Many have made significant . . . progress in specific areas, such as reductions of air pollutants, waste diversion, improved governance, or increased sanitation services. However, these "best practices" are not a sufficient basis on which to claim success, particularly in the face of continued negative global trends.[23]

In Brugmann's review of Local Agenda 21 initiatives, he cites variables such as lack of understanding in the design and implementation of sustainability programs, insufficient municipal finances and institutional capacity, perverse subsidies, and traditional legislation that inhibits the adoption of new technologies and practices as being the most significant limitations to the development of effective urban sustainability initiatives. Thus, despite the apparent popular global support, little progress has been made in defining and implementing urban sustainability into practice.

In 1996 the UN Conference on Human Settlement (Habitat II) in Istanbul was made a focal point for the advancement of sustainable settlements. The main goal was to establish an international consensus for the pursuit of sustainable cities. The preparatory committee recommended the following objective as the guiding principle: "To increase the world awareness of the problems and potentials of human settlements—as important inputs to social progress and economic growth—and to commit the world's leaders to making our cities, towns, and villages healthy, safe, just, and sustainable."[24]

David Satterthwaite notes that while the documents that emerged from Habitat II can be viewed favorably in recognizing the need for global poverty reduction, they are "weakest where they need to be strongest—in agreeing on the kind of national and international frameworks that would ensure sustainable development goals are addressed in cities."[25] Similarly, Michael Cohen argues, "the biggest gap in the Istanbul discussions was the lack of progress in operationalizing the notion of environmentally sustainable development. . . . Further while the term 'sustainable development' was mentioned repeatedly, little progress was made in suggesting how it could be operationally applied to urban areas."[26]

Thus the central theme in the urban sustainability discourse, as with sustainability, continues to be the absence of a mechanism, or mechanisms, for advancing toward the sustainability condition. As many of the authors in this volume stress, despite the long-standing discourse on sustainability, and the ongoing implementation of extensive sustainability policies worldwide, the actual impact on environmental quality from these initiatives is limited, being overwhelmed by ongoing consumption practices and resource demands. This is particularly evident in the wealthy nations. The most critical issue within the sustainability discourse remains defining environmental policies that can convert the growing global interest in preserving the environment into actual improvements in environmental well-being.[27]

Broader global targets in the pursuit of sustainability—such as reductions in poverty, limiting greenhouse gas emissions, and reducing sulfur dioxide concentrations—will require innumerable *effective* local, regional, national, and international policies depending on the specific spatial contexts. In fact, the complexity of urban stresses within different spatial, cultural, political, and socioeconomic contexts, and the different conceptualizations of sustainability depending on particular local values and circumstances, will make the development of common global mechanisms in the pursuit of urban sustainability unlikely. This customized requirement in shaping sustainability policies contributes to the difficulty of developing effective policies that actually contribute significantly to improvements in environmental quality. This collection of works will show that a critical common thread in the global urban sustainability discourse, and ultimately in the design of urban sustainability policies, is the pursuit of equity, both inter- and intragenerational. The pursuit of equity, however, will vary considerably, depending on the particular regional and national conditions and the nature of local urban stresses.

The Spirit of Sustainability

The advocacy of encouraging economic activity that recognizes intergenerational concerns while considering the welfare of the community as a whole can be traced back more than two thousand years to Aristotle's work on ethics and politics. Aristotle defined two types of economic activity. The first, *oikonomia,* is the "management of a household, in so far as the art of household management must either find ready to hand, or itself provide, such things necessary to life, and useful for the community of the family or state."[28] Aristotle also believed that this type of household and community management is "the element of true riches; for the amount of property which is needed for a good life is not unlimited." Like sustainability, *oikonomia* takes a long-run perspective and considers the social welfare of the household, the community, and the state as a whole. It also recognizes limited resource accumulation and consumption as necessary in the interest of the community. Aristotle contrasted *oikonomia* with a second form of economic activity, *chrematistics,* which he argued "is commonly and rightly called an art of wealth-getting, and has in fact suggested the notion that riches and property have no limit."[29] This type of economic behavior is based on maximizing short-term value and returns through the manipulation of wealth and property. While *oikonomia* evolved into the modern term "economics," it is clear that behavior in the existing global economy is more closely aligned with *chrematistics*—maximizing short-term monetary exchange value.

Another example of the spirit of sustainability was evident with the North American Mohawk natives, who were successful in integrating elements of sustainability into tribal decision-making. In decisions that could affect future generations of the tribe, a member called the *representative of the seventh generation* had the power to veto decisions that would adversely affect the coming generations.[30]

Over the past century, the obligation of the current generation to ensure the survival of future generations was also debated in the industrializing West. In 1908 President Theodore Roosevelt created the National Conservation Commission and appointed Gifford Pinchot as its chair. The task of the commission was to perform a natural resource inventory of the United States. In the report, the commission outlined the importance of resource stocks and flows by arguing the following:

> It is high time to realize that our responsibility to the coming millions is like that of parents to their children, and that in wasting our resources we are wronging our descendents. . . . If we of this generation destroy the resources from which our children would otherwise derive their livelihood, we reduce the capacity of our land to support a population, and so either degrade the standard of living or deprive the coming generations of their right to life on this continent.[31]

The members of the commission went on to argue that:

> The duty of man to man, on which the integrity of nations must rest, is no higher than the duty of each generation to the next; and the obligation of the nation to each actual citizen is no more sacred than the obligation to the citizen to be, who, in turn, must bear the nation's duties and responsibilities.[32]

Not everyone did agree with the position of the commission. As Colorado senator Henry Teller argued in 1909, "I do not believe there is either a moral or any other claim upon me to postpone the use of what nature has given me, so that the next generation or generations may have an opportunity to get what I myself ought to get."[33] Nonetheless, despite the opposition in certain camps, a new appreciation for resource conservation and preservation did emerge in America in the early 1900s. Similar social and political movements during this period were evident throughout the West—including in Germany, France, the UK, Switzerland, Sweden, and Canada.[34]

In the United States, the responsibility of the current generation to ensure a resource base to meet the needs of future generations was also strengthened in the post–World War II period by the President's Materials Policy Commission (1951), also known as the Paley Commission. Similar to the National Conservation Commission, the Paley Commission's task was to examine the "adequacy of materials to meet the needs of the . . . world in the years ahead."[35] One of the commission's key recognitions was that the "current generation is responsible for passing on to the next as best it can the prospects of continued well-being."[36] In the discussion on the issue of "conserving for the future," the commission identified and advocated "this generation's responsibility to provide for the next."[37]

The Spirit of Sustainable Cities

As in the case of sustainability, the "spirit" of sustainable cities also has a long history. Utopian visions of settlements that maintain a balance between humans and their natural surroundings, such as that by Sir Thomas More (1516), began to receive particular attention during the nineteenth century. This interest was largely generated by the condition of the growing underclass and the disorder of early industrial cities. The extensive literature on the topic, the various experiments to establish utopian communities, and the political campaigns by urban reformers—including William Morris, Edward Bellamy, Peter Kropotkin, Jane Adams, William Dubois, and Robert Owen—provide examples of nineteenth-century advocacies that supported the building of cities that fostered environmental, socioeconomic, gender, and/or racial and ethnic harmony. These urban reformers encouraged a balanced coexistence between cities and their surrounding natural environment, promoted communities that advanced self-sufficiency and health, and advocated for socioeconomic, racial, ethnic, and gender equity.

Ebenezer Howard's *Garden Cities of Tomorrow* (1902), for instance, advocated a socioeconomic structure in which "town and country *must be married,* and out of this joyous union will spring a new hope, a new life, a new civilization."[38] The Garden City was proposed as a 32,000 person, largely self-sustained community. Each city was limited to 1,000 acres, with an industrial belt along the edge, surrounded by farms producing the local food supply, and all clustered within a pristine natural setting. Once the 32,000 person limit was met, a new Garden City would be built and linked by public transit. The size and density of the Garden City ensured that its residents could walk and bike to almost all destinations.

Similarly, Frank Lloyd Wright's Broadacre City advanced the merging of the urban and the rural, and the harmonious coexistence of citizens with nature. In the words of Wright, "to live in nature as the trees are native to the wood or grass is to the field." As maintained by Wright, "Broadacre would be so built in sympathy with nature that a deep feeling for the beauty of the terrain would be a fundamental qualification in the new city-builders." Similar to Howard, Wright's visions advocated a social structure based on high degrees of industrial and agrarian self-sufficiency. As noted by Wright, "normally each factory, farm or dwelling would be within a ten-mile radius of vast, variegated wayside fresh-food and manufacturers' markets so that each might serve the other units simply and effectively, all directly serving population living or working in its particular neighborhood."[39]

The advocacy by nineteenth- and early twentieth-century reformers, promoting socially, racially, ethnically, and economically just and healthy communities—while advancing substantial and important policies that improved the condition of early industrial cities—never did fully materialize. Class, racial, and gender inequities, along with inadequate public health, are still central issues in cities worldwide. Similarly, the pursuit of a harmonious coexistence between the city and the surrounding natural environment was never realized either. The ongoing interest in the development of communities that exist within their bioregional carrying capacity demonstrates this concern.[40]

In addition, while up to the mid-twentieth century, urban environmental concerns were largely local, focusing on smog (air pollution), local water supplies, sewage provision, and waste management, in the latter twentieth century, awareness of urban-environmental issues became increasingly transboundary and global. A new recognition was placed on the impacts of automobile and factory emissions on global warming; the use of chlorofluorocarbons (CFCs) in aerosols, refrigerators, and air conditioners and its effects on ozone depletion; and sulfur dioxide concentrations from coal and oil burning and its resulting transboundary impact of acid rain.

The discourse on the socioeconomic and the structural organization of cities, and its articulation in the context of *sustainable cities* proper, begins to appear in the 1980s, in part a reaction to a series of environmental local stresses with significant national and international consequences. Chernobyl, Love Canal, and Three Mile Island placed urban environmental issues at the forefront of urban debates. In addition, the emergence of megacities, particularly in low-income countries, placed a new interest on urban development processes and stresses in these large urban agglomerations. Reversing historical urban growth trends, an increasing proportion of the largest cities in the world began to emerge in poorer countries (see table 2). Within this context, increasing concern began to center on the management of fiscally distressed megacities and the condition of urban residents in poorer countries in general (see table 3).

Urban Sustainability and Resource Consumption

While urban areas make up approximately 2 percent of the Earth's land surface, urban inhabitants consume over 75 percent of the Earth's resources depleted in any year.[41] With most of the world resource stocks directed to urban areas—which are the aggregation of global economic wealth (see

Table 2. Twenty largest urban agglomerations, 1950–2015 (projected)

1950

RANK	URBAN AGGLOMERATION	POPULATION
1	New York	12,338,000
2	Tokyo	11,275,000
3	London	8,361,000
4	Paris	5,424,000
5	Moscow	5,356,000
6	Shanghai	5,333,000
7	Rhein-Ruhr North*	5,295,000
8	Buenos Aires	5,041,000
9	Chicago	4,999,000
10	Calcutta	4,446,000
11	Osaka	4,147,000
12	Los Angeles	4,046,000
13	Beijing	3,913,000
14	Milan	3,633,000
15	Berlin	3,337,000
16	Philadelphia	3,128,000
17	Mumbai	2,981,000
18	Rio de Janeiro	2,930,000
19	Saint Petersburg	2,903,000
20	Mexico City	2,883,000
Average size of top 20 urban agglomerations		**5,088,450**

1975

RANK	URBAN AGGLOMERATION	POPULATION
1	Tokyo	26,615,000
2	New York	15,880,000
3	Shanghai	11,443,000
4	Mexico City	10,690,000
5	Osaka	9,844,000
6	São Paulo	9,614,000
7	Buenos Aires	9,143,000
8	Los Angeles	8,926,000
9	Paris	8,630,000
10	Beijing	8,545,000
11	Calcutta	7,888,000
12	Moscow	7,623,000
13	Rio de Janeiro	7,557,000
14	London	7,546,000
15	Mumbai	7,347,000
16	Chicago	7,160,000
17	Seoul	6,808,000
18	Rhein-Ruhr North*	6,448,000
19	Cairo	6,437,000
20	Tianjin	6,160,000
Average size of top 20 urban agglomerations		**9,515,200**

2000

RANK	URBAN AGGLOMERATION	POPULATION
1	Tokyo	34,450,000
2	Mexico City	18,066,000
3	New York	17,846,000
4	Paris	17,099,000
5	Mumbai	16,086,000
6	Calcutta	13,058,000
7	Shanghai	12,887,000
8	Buenos Aires	12,583,000
9	Delhi	12,441,000
10	Los Angeles	11,814,000
11	Osaka	11,165,000
12	Jakarta	11,018,000
13	Beijing	10,839,000
14	Rio de Janeiro	10,803,000
15	Cairo	10,398,000
16	Dhaka	10,159,000
17	Moscow	10,103,000
18	Karachi	10,032,000
19	Metro Manila	9,950,000
20	Seoul	9,917,000
Average size of top 20 urban agglomerations		**13,535,700**

Projected 2015

RANK	URBAN AGGLOMERATION	POPULATION
1	Tokyo	36,214,000
2	Mumbai	22,645,000
3	Delhi	20,946,000
4	Mexico City	20,647,000
5	São Paulo	19,963,000
6	New York	19,717,000
7	Dhaka	17,907,000
8	Jakarta	17,498,000
9	Lagos	17,036,000
10	Calcutta	16,798,000
11	Karachi	16,155,000
12	Buenos Aires	14,563,000
13	Cairo	13,123,000
14	Los Angeles	12,904,000
15	Shanghai	12,666,000
16	Metro Manila	12,637,000
17	Rio de Janeiro	12,364,000
18	Osaka-Kobe	11,359,000
19	Istanbul	11,302,000
20	Beijing	11,060,000
Average size of top 20 urban agglomerations		**16,875,200**

*The urban agglomeration around Essen, Germany.
Source: United Nations, *World Urbanization Prospects: The 2003 Revision* (New York: United Nations, 2004).

Table 3. Income inequities and urban slums

COUNTRIES	INCOME RATIO (RICHEST 20% : POOREST 20%)	SLUM DWELLERS (% OF URBAN POPULATION)
Sierra Leone	57.6	96.0
Nicaragua	48.8	81.0
Guatemala	46.0	62.0
South Africa	45.9	33.0
Lesotho	43.4	57.0
Honduras	42.7	18.0
Nigeria	40.8	79.0
Cameroon	36.6	67.0
Kenya	36.1	71.0
Cambodia	33.8	72.0
India	33.5	55.0
Central African Republic	32.7	92.0
Bolivia	32.0	61.0
Morocco	30.9	33.0
Lao's People Democratic Republic	30.6	66.0
Ghana	30.1	70.0

Source: United Nations Human Settlement Programme (UN-Habitat), *The State of the World's Cities* (London: Earthscan, 2004).

Table 4. Selected city contributions to gross national product, 2003

COUNTRIES	POPULATION IN MILLIONS (2003)	POPULATION % OF NATIONAL TOTAL (A)	GNP % OF NATIONAL TOTAL (B)	RATIO (B/A)
São Paulo, Brazil	17.9	8.6	36.1	4.20
Buenos Aires, Argentina	13.0	35.0	53.0	1.51
Santiago de Chile, Chile	5.5	35.6	47.4	1.33
Lima, Peru	7.9	28.1	43.1	1.53
Guayaquil, Ecuador	2.3	13.1	30.1	2.30
Mexico City, Mexico	18.7	14.2	33.6	2.37
San Salvador, El Salvador	1.4	25.8	44.1	1.71
Casablanca, Morocco	3.6	12.1	25.1	2.07
Abidján, Cote d'Ivoire	3.3	18.1	33.1	1.83
Nairobi, Kenya	2.6	5.2	20.1	3.87
Karachi, Pakistan	11.1	6.1	16.1	2.64
Shanghai, China	12.8	1.2	12.5	10.42
Manila, Philippines	10.4	12.1	25.1	2.07
Bangkok, Thailand	6.5	10.9	37.4	3.43
Moscow, Russia	10.5	5.8	10.9	1.88

Source: United Nations Human Settlement Programme (UN-Habitat), *The State of the World's Cities* (London: Earthscan, 2004).

table 4)—cities are the source of much of the global environmental degradation. Cities themselves, however, do not have significant capacity in generating material resources, such as food and energy, and little ability to absorb or recycle waste or to clean air and water to any reusable extent. Urban inhabitants rely on large natural areas beyond urban boundaries for resource inputs and environmental services to meet the basic necessities and continued functioning of urban systems. In fact, since cities rely on natural areas and agricultural lands beyond their own boundaries, and even on regions outside national boundaries, Eugene Odum has gone as far as arguing that cities are "parasites on the biosphere."[42]

The reliance of urban areas on surrounding natural lands leads to the notion of a settlement's ecological footprint, the total area necessary to support a given population. While a city's ecological footprint will vary according to different per capita consumption levels, this urban support region is spatially much larger than that area contained within the physical urban footprint. For instance, the 1.8 million people of the Lower Fraser Valley—a roughly 1,544 square-mile urban-agricultural region within which Vancouver (Canada) is located—requires an area that is some nineteen times larger than its territory to support the material standards of its population.[43]

The notion of the ecological footprint also leads to the distinction in resource demands in different parts of the world based on wealth. In comparing global resource consumption, Wackernagel and Rees show that while as a world average the ecological footprint of the human population is 4.5 acres per person, there is considerable variation in resource consumption between countries (see table 5).[44] In terms of environmental impacts, if everyone consumed at North American standards, Wackernagel and Rees argue that three Earths would be required—assuming 32.3 billion acres of land, with 21.9 billion productive acres and 10.4 billion marginally productive or unproductive acres—to meet the aggregate material demand.[45]

The links between local and global sustainability should become evident upon considering urban resource requirements. Even with sustainability initiatives that are not classified specifically as urban, given the scale of resource demands in cities, and particularly among the wealthy, the most significant impacts of sustainability programs will be disproportionately experienced by affluent urban inhabitants.

Table 5. Comparing people's average consumption per person in the United States, Canada, India, and the world

CONSUMPTION PER PERSON IN 1991	USA	CANADA	INDIA	WORLD
CO_2 emission (tons/yr)	21.5	16.8	0.9	4.6
Purchasing power ($US)	22,130	19,320	1,150	3,800
Vehicles per 100 persons	57	46	0.2	10
Paper consumption (lb/yr)	699	545	4	97
Fossil energy use (GJ/yr)*	287	250	5	56
Fresh water withdrawal (ft^3/yr)	65,968	59,611	21,613	22,743
Ecological footprint (acres/person)	**12.6**	**10.6**	**1.0**	**4.5**

* GJ = 10^9 joules
Source: Mathis Wackernagel and William Rees, *Our Ecological Footprint: Reducing Human Impact on the Earth* (Philadelphia: New Society Publishers, 1996).

Table 6. Life expectancy, literacy, school enrollment and gross domestic product per capita for high-, medium-, and low-income countries, 2001–2002

REGION	LIFE EXPECTANCY AT BIRTH (YEARS)	ADULT LITERACY RATE (% AGES 15+)	COMBINED GROSS ENROLLMENT RATION FOR PRIMARY, SECONDARY, AND TERTIARY SCHOOLS (%)	GDP PER CAPITA (PPP $US)
Arab States	66.3	63.3	60	5,069
East Asia and the Pacific	69.8	90.3	65	4,768
Latin America and the Caribbean	70.5	88.6	81	7,223
South Asia	63.2	57.6	54	2,658
Sub-Saharan Africa	46.3	63.2	44	1,790
Central and Eastern Europe and Commonwealth of Independent States	69.5	~99.0	79	7,192
OECD	77.1	~99.0	87	24,904
High-income OECD	78.3	~99.0	93	29,000
High income	*78.3*	*~99.0*	*92*	*28,741*
Middle income	*70.0*	*80.4*	*71*	*5,908*
Low income	*49.1*	*54.3*	*51*	*2,149*
World	**66.9**	—	**64**	**7,804**

Source: United Nations Development Program, *Human Development Report 2004: Cultural Liberty in Today's Diverse World* (New York: United Nations Development Program, 2004).

The notion of the ecological footprint also recognizes an important distinction between high- and low-consumption countries. As the World Bank illustrated in the mid-1990s, while approximately 59 percent of the world's population falls within the low-income/low-consumption category (maintaining an average per capita GNP of $390), 15 percent of the world's population lives in the high-income/high-consumption category, with an average per capita GNP of $22,160.[46] A decade earlier, the WCED recognized a similar condition, noting that roughly one-quarter of the world's population, mostly from industrialized countries, consumed roughly three-quarters of the world's resources. Tables 6 and 7 illustrate more recent global distinctions among a number of socioeconomic indicators.

Into the twenty-first century, as recognized by the United Nations Development Program, not much has changed in terms of the existing global socioeconomic inequalities. By 2007, while the richest 20 percent of the world's population accounted for some 75 percent of the global income, the poorest 40 percent of the world's population accounted for only 5 percent of world income.[47] The nature of this income distribution has also translated into parallel characteristics in resource consumption. While the wealthiest 20 percent of the world population accounted for some 76.6 percent of total private consumption, the poorest 20 percent accounted for only 1.5 percent.[48]

The extreme condition of these global inequities has recently emerged with a public health concern that has become prominent in the West: the obesity epidemic. While key urban health concerns in low-income countries focus on access to potable water, sewerage, and disposing waste, a critical urban health concern in the West is obesity. In the United States, some 300,000 deaths annually are attributed to obesity-related causes, while some 830 million people worldwide suffer serious health risks, including death, from malnutrition (see table 8).[49]

It is not just between nations, but also within nations, that considerable inequalities exist. These inequalities vary substantially among countries, reflecting the distinction in emphasis that nations place on the elimination of inequality within their borders (table 9).

Urban Implications of National Disparities

The differences in levels of prosperity across nations are reflected in environmental circumstances and conditions within metropolitan regions. At the risk of oversimplification, there are three general patterns evident globally. First, in wealthy, industrial countries, cities have long reached economic maturity, as reflected in their slow, and in some cases, negative growth. These cities are characterized by high incomes, high consumption rates, and high per capita ecological footprints (fig. 2). It should be recognized that while these cities maintain the concentration of global wealth, a large and growing underclass still remains within these urban centers. Pollutant emissions within these cities, and especially biological pollution, are controlled by technological means (water and sewage treatment providing examples). Major issues within these cities are focused on

PHOTOGRAPH BY IGOR VOJNOVIC

Figure 2. Shinjuku in Tokyo.

Table 7. Gross yearly incomes and rents for selected cities, 2003 (U.S. dollars)

CITY	GROSS YEARLY INCOME			AVG. PER HOUR GROSS INCOME	NORMAL HOUSEHOLD RENT PER MONTH
	INDUSTRIAL WORKERS	PRIMARY SCHOOL TEACHERS	ENGINEERS		
Central and Eastern Europe					
Bratislava	5,600	4,100	9,100	2.50	350
Bucharest	3,500	1,800	12,800	1.80	150
Budapest	9,400	6,200	15,100	4.20	440
Istanbul	15,100	10,400	18,600	4.60	890
Kiev	5,300	600	3,700	1.30	310
Ljubljana	12,000	17,800	14,100	5.40	170
Moscow	3,800	1,800	3,400	2.90	590
Prague	6,800	5,700	10,200	3.10	310
Sofia	3,300	2,100	4,300	1.40	150
Tallinn	6,400	5,100	9,200	3.20	100
Vilnius	5,900	3,700	10,100	2.90	340
Riga	10,100	2,400	7,700	3.20	140
Warsaw	6,900	5,300	11,300	3.40	440
Western Europe					
Amsterdam	40,600	34,300	36,300	16.60	890
Athens	20,700	19,500	26,800	8.90	620
Barcelona	17,700	25,500	32,400	9.80	590
Basel	52,600	78,500	76,900	25.10	930
Berlin	32,600	45,000	50,600	16.40	630
Brussels	37,800	30,600	39,900	17.50	590
Copenhagen	47,700	42,500	63,500	25.50	940
Dublin	35,700	41,700	46,900	16.30	1,320
Frankfurt	34,300	41,900	54,800	18.00	920
Geneva	49,600	76,400	62,200	23.40	1,630
Helsinki	32,300	30,500	48,500	15.00	560
Lisbon	10,300	16,000	18,700	6.10	810
London	28,800	33,700	40,800	16.90	1,930
Lugano	51,400	59,500	69,900	21.70	950
Luxembourg	30,700	58,000	71,800	17.90	700
Madrid	16,800	27,600	41,300	9.10	740
Milan	16,100	20,600	33,200	11.40	1,660
Oslo	54,200	35,700	46,000	24.40	1,000
Paris	19,300	24,900	42,900	13.70	1,270
Rome	15,700	17,300	25,800	9.50	1,210
Stockholm	40,000	32,300	47,700	16.60	750
Vienna	29,100	28,900	40,600	14.30	1,020
Zurich	59,600	75,300	81,300	25.70	1,380

CITY	GROSS YEARLY INCOME: INDUSTRIAL WORKERS	GROSS YEARLY INCOME: PRIMARY SCHOOL TEACHERS	GROSS YEARLY INCOME: ENGINEERS	AVG. PER HOUR GROSS INCOME	NORMAL HOUSEHOLD RENT PER MONTH
Africa					
Lagos	2,700	1,700	3,200	1.30	100
Nairobi	2,900	1,900	1,900	1.10	320
Johannesburg	15,900	7,500	7,500	4.90	480
Middle East					
Dubai	13,300	22,800	42,500	6.80	1,350
Manama	22,500	13,300	51,000	5.90	800
Tel Aviv	13,300	13,400	43,300	8.40	790
Latin America					
Bogota	4,100	4,100	14,400	2.10	200
Buenos Aires	5,100	2,400	10,500	2.00	150
Caracas	10,700	3,500	14,900	2.30	290
Lima	6,800	4,100	16,800	2.60	300
Rio de Janeiro	6,900	2,400	14,600	2.10	230
Santiago de Chile	8,300	5,900	15,500	3.20	430
São Paulo	6,500	2,700	13,400	2.70	200
North America					
Chicago	43,800	47,200	57,100	21.20	1,430
Los Angeles	43,400	46,700	74,500	18.60	1,060
New York	47,000	54,200	75,000	21.70	1,790
Mexico City	3,600	8,300	9,000	2.30	770
Miami	40,900	34,000	54,000	16.00	700
Montreal	28,700	30,700	48,500	12.90	410
Toronto	29,800	26,500	66,200	13.50	850
Southeast Asia and Pacific Rim					
Bangkok	4,200	4,200	9,800	1.80	120
Hong Kong	17,300	47,100	39,200	8.00	1,750
Jakarta	3,300	2,300	6,700	1.70	1,110
Karachi	1,300	2,000	4,700	0.90	90
Kuala Lampur	11,100	10,200	15,900	3.70	460
Manila	4,200	4,000	5,500	1.40	650
Mumbai	1,900	1,400	6,000	0.80	200
Seoul	34,600	27,200	32,900	7.90	710
Shanghai	4,600	4,300	12,100	3.30	480
Singapore	1,700	23,000	26,700	6.90	790
Sydney	18,400	24,300	32,400	10.30	1,010
Taipei	22,200	22,300	25,800	8.30	1,410
Tokyo	50,000	45,800	71,500	17.60	1,010

Source: Union Bank of Switzerland, *Price and Earning around the Globe* (Zurich: UBS, 2003).

Table 8. Socioeconomic indicators in low-income countries, 2000

REGION	LIVING ON LESS THAN ONE DOLLAR (PPP $US) A DAY	TOTAL POPULATION UNDERNOURISHED	CHILDREN AGE 5 DYING	PEOPLE WITHOUT ACCESS TO IMPROVED WATER SOURCES	PEOPLE WITHOUT ACCESS TO ADEQUATE SANITATION
Sub-Saharan Africa	323,000,000	185,000,000	5,000,000	273,000,000	299,000,000
Arab States	8,000,000	34,000,000	1,000,000	42,000,000	51,000,000
East Asia and the Pacific	261,000,000	212,000,000	1,000,000	453,000,000	1,004,000,000
South Asia	432,000,000	312,000,000	4,000,000	225,000,000	944,000,000
Latin America and the Caribbean	56,000,000	53,000,000	0	72,000,000	121,000,000
Central and Eastern Europe and Commonwealth of Independent States	21,000,000	33,000,000	0	29,000,000	—
World	**1,100,000,000**	**831,000,000**	**11,000,000**	**1,197,000,000**	**2,742,000,000**

Source: United Nations Development Program, *Human Development Report 2004: Cultural Liberty in Today's Diverse World* (New York: United Nations Development Program, 2004).

maintaining their extensive and potentially decaying infrastructure, and in some cases reversing economic and demographic decline. Such urban stresses are evident in Manchester, Glasgow, and Liverpool (United Kingdom), Leipzig and Halle (Germany), and Detroit (United States).

Second, in industrializing countries many cities are experiencing accelerated population and income growth, paralleled by rapidly increasing levels of consumption (fig. 3). A major focus in

PHOTOGRAPH BY IGOR VOJNOVIC

Figure 3. Beijing, Drum Town area, contrasting with new developments in the background.

Table 9. Income or consumption inequality across selected countries

COUNTRIES	SURVEY YEAR	RICHEST 10% TO POOREST 10%	RICHEST 20% TO POOREST 20%	GINI INDEX*
UNDP high HDI index				
Norway	2000†	6.1	3.9	25.8
Australia	1994†	12.5	7.0	35.2
Canada	2000†	9.4	5.5	32.6
Sweden	2000†	6.2	4.0	25.0
Switzerland	2000†	9.0	5.5	33.7
Japan	1993†	4.5	3.4	24.9
Netherlands	1999†	9.2	5.1	30.9
France	1995†	9.1	5.6	32.7
Finland	2000†	5.6	3.8	26.9
United States	2000†	15.9	8.4	40.8
Spain	2000†	10.3	6.0	34.7
Denmark	1997†	8.1	4.3	24.7
United Kingdom	1999†	13.8	7.2	36.0
Italy	2000†	11.6	6.5	36.0
Hong Kong, China (SAR)	1996†	17.8	9.7	43.4
Germany	2000†	6.9	4.3	28.3
Israel	2001†	13.7	7.9	39.2
Singapore	1998†	17.7	4.7	42.5
Korea (Republic of)	1998†	7.8	4.7	31.6
Argentina	2004†	40.9	17.8	51.3
Mexico	2004‡	24.6	12.8	46.1
Russian Federation	2002‡	12.7	7.6	39.9
Brazil	2004†	51.3	21.8	57.0
UNDP medium HDI index				
Venezuela	2003†	48.3	16.0	48.2
Colombia	2003†	63.8	25.3	58.6
Ukraine	2003‡	5.9	4.1	28.1
Thailand	2002‡	12.6	7.7	42.0
China	2004†	21.6	12.2	46.9
Turkey	2003‡	16.8	9.3	43.6
Jordan	2002–03‡	11.3	6.9	38.8
Peru	2003†	30.4	15.2	52.0
Iran	1998‡	17.2	9.7	43.0
El Salvador	2002†	57.5	20.9	52.4
Algeria	1995‡	9.6	6.1	35.3
Vietnam	2004‡	6.9	4.9	34.4
Egypt	1999–00‡	8.0	5.1	34.4
South Africa	2000‡	33.1	17.9	57.8
Morocco	1998–99‡	11.7	7.2	39.5
India	2004–05‡	8.6	5.6	36.8
Pakistan	2002‡	6.5	4.3	30.6
Kenya	1997‡	13.6	8.2	42.5
Yemen	1998‡	8.6	5.6	33.4
UNDP low HDI index				
Senegal	2001‡	12.3	7.4	41.3
Nigeria	2003‡	17.8	9.7	43.7
Tanzania	2000–01‡	9.2	5.8	34.6
Guinea	2003‡	10.5	6.6	38.6
Rwanda	2000‡	18.6	9.9	46.8
Benin	2003‡	9.4	6.0	36.5
Malawi	2004–05‡	10.9	6.7	39.0
Zambia	2004‡	32.3	15.3	50.8
Côte d'Ivoire	2002‡	16.6	9.7	44.6
Burundi	1998‡	19.3	9.5	42.4
Ethiopia	1999–00‡	6.6	4.3	30.0
Mozambique	2002–03‡	18.8	9.9	47.3
Mali	2001‡	12.5	7.6	40.1
Niger	1995‡	46.0	20.7	50.5
Burkina Faso	2003‡	11.6	6.9	39.5
Sierra Leone	1989‡	87.2	57.6	62.9

*A value of 0 on the index represents absolute equality and a value of 100 represents absolute inequality.
† Income shares by percent of population, ranked by per capita income.
‡ Consumption (expenditure) shares by percent of population, ranked by per capita consumption (expenditures).
Source: United Nations Development Program. *Human Development Report 2005* (New York: United Nations, 2005).

PHOTOGRAPH BY ASSEFA MEHRETU AND TEGEGNE GEBRE-EGZIABHER

Figure 4. Addis Ababa's Merkato area, consisting of piecemeal housing construction for low-income families.

these cities is providing and expanding urban infrastructure networks. While cities in industrialized countries have experienced similar expansion pressures over the last 200 years, cities in industrializing countries have little to learn from these earlier experiences. The unprecedented scales of population growth, the accelerated pace of technological innovation, and the rapidly changing global markets have forced these urban agglomerations to create their own development paths. The new economic opportunities within these centers, however, are not being shared by all, generating increasing income inequities and socioeconomic polarization. The per capita and aggregate ecological footprint of these cities is also rapidly increasing. In addition, there is growing pressure to expand the use of technological instruments to control the increasing pollution. Examples of such cities include Seoul (South Korea), Mumbai and Delhi (India), Shanghai (China), Mexico City (Mexico), and São Paulo (Brazil).

The third urban grouping consists of cities in poor, nonindustrial countries (fig. 4). These cities are experiencing rapid population growth, with stagnant and, in some cases, declining economies. Due to extreme poverty, these urban centers are characterized by acute urban stresses. Basic infrastructure provision is absent and the majority of the population is living in severely poor conditions. The per capita ecological footprint of these urban inhabitants is low, but the environmental and biological impacts of these urban concentrations on the local population are grievous. Examples of such cities include Lagos (Nigeria), Kinshasa (Democratic Republic of Congo), and Addis Ababa (Ethiopia).

Benefits of Urban Agglomerations

Despite the high resource demands, there are extensive benefits to living in cities, particularly when compared to scattered settlements. Concentrating people at safe densities in urban areas—which can be heightened in cities with a rich provision of urban services and amenities—reduces land requirements for any given population. The impacts of low density dispersed developments on land consumption and the degradation of sensitive ecosystems, such as wetlands and agricultural lands, provides an example of the environmental harms that emerge when populations are dispersed. This first benefit of urban living is closely tied to its second advantage, service provision.

Concentrating populations in urban areas minimizes the cost of providing rich urban services and high service standards. The cost of providing infrastructure such as roads, public transit, water and sewage networks, health care, education, and household waste collection and disposal can all be reduced as population densities increase. While household waste disposal might emerge as an issue in large cities, it is the high densities that can accommodate effective recycling programs, and when applied with waste reduction initiatives safe disposal is manageable.

The largest world cities, and cities in poorer countries, also confront pressures with sewage disposal. If sewage from urban areas is not properly treated it can generate considerable harm to the environment, such as reductions in the biological productivity of aquatic ecosystems. Untreated sewage can also facilitate outbreaks of water-borne diseases, such as typhoid and cholera. There are many examples, however, of safely recycling treated sewage effluent, particularly when it can be directed to nonpotable uses including crop irrigation, urban agriculture, industrial cooling, and for watering lawns of commercial and industrial sites. It should be recognized that the reduced costs in service provision realized with more compact developments result from lower levels of material and energy use in service delivery, illustrating the integrative relationship between preservation, conservation, affordability, and increased economic performance.

Urban living in higher densities can also generate less resource-intensive transportation patterns. More compact developments increase the number of destinations that can be reached by walking and biking while also accommodating the effective provision of public transit. In turn, the use of the private automobile and the transport truck can be minimized, reducing fossil fuel use and associated pollution emissions. Inefficient urban decentralization is an issue of particular importance in wealthy countries—such as the United States, Australia, and Canada—which maintain some of the highest levels of per capita energy consumption and pollutant emissions.

Compact urban developments also minimize energy requirements for the heating and cooling of buildings, which are achieved through the benefits of shared walls and shading from proximate structures. In addition, higher densities (to reasonable extents) reduce capital energy requirements in buildings, realized with reductions of resource materials in building construction and in the provision of infrastructure (such as roads, sidewalks, and water and sewage networks).

Cities have also historically been the centers of culture, science, and innovation. Literature,

Figure 5. A view of the Acropolis in Athens from Ancient Agora, the hub of ancient Athens.

theater, music, arts, and architecture have flourished within urban areas. In fact, many cities themselves have developed into cultural artifacts (figs. 5 and 6). With the cultural economy emerging as an important economic sector of the twenty-first century, unique cultural centers have become heritage hubs and drivers of regional economies. Similar to preserving the natural heritage, preserving the cultural heritage becomes a central aspect of urban sustainability.

The high concentration of people in urban areas can also foster rich social economies—nonprofit-oriented economic activities supported by cooperatives, social firms, and self-help groups that focus on raising the purchasing power of lower-income residents. One example is provided with the worldwide proliferation of local exchange trading systems, which are community exchange networks that enable goods and services to be traded without currency. These systems stimulate local economies and create local wealth. Less formal social economies are evident with the extensive number of volunteers who provide educational services and other support systems for the youth, as well as services for the elderly, the disabled, and individuals with special needs.

Research has shown that urban populations, by embracing their unique environmental and cultural heritage—as well as the advantages of urban living—can facilitate a socioeconomic organization that reduces natural resource use while increasing the aggregate welfare of the community.[50] Globally this will likely require very different local initiatives, based on specific urban stresses, and local values and circumstances. However, as this collection will show, the common

PHOTOGRAPH BY IGOR VOJNOVIC

Figure 6. Via Dolorosa, Jerusalem.

thread in the global urban sustainability discourse, and ultimately in the design of urban sustainability policy, is the pursuit of equity—both inter- and intragenerational.

Advancing toward Sustainability: The Pursuit of Equity

In developing sustainable urban policies, a characteristic that must be evident in local initiatives is integration—links between the environmental, social, and economic dimensions of urban policy. The integration of environmental and socioeconomic variables can be achieved in the pursuit of two social conditions, inter- and intragenerational equity. Intergenerational equity is concerned with ensuring the survival of future generations by maintaining the quality of natural resources and their services over time. One generation can meet this obligation if they leave the next generation an inheritance of resource wealth no less than what they inherited. This is the first basic condition of sustainability.

Intragenerational equity, on the other hand, is based on promoting the equitable access to resources within existing generations. This would encompass addressing all the local problems that would ensure the elimination of poverty, hunger, and disease. Even if one generation passes to the next generation an inheritance of resource wealth equivalent to what they inherited, if millions starve in the existing generation in order to meet this requirement, it would be difficult to argue that sustainability has been achieved.

Intergenerational Equity

An analysis of the intergenerational equity requirements entails an overview of the composition of natural capital. There are three different types of environmental resources that make up natural capital. The first is the natural environment's ability to act as a waste sink. This is nature's capacity to convert waste into environmentally useful or neutral products—such as the ability of vegetation to absorb pollutants and release oxygen. A Douglas-fir, for example, is capable of absorbing 39.6 pounds (18 kilograms) of sulfur-dioxide from the atmosphere on an annual basis.[51] The second type of natural capital consists of renewable resources, which include regenerating resources such as fresh water, fish stocks, and forests. The third type consists of exhaustible resources, environmental stocks that are not replenishable (non- or slow-regenerating resources such as minerals and fossil fuels).

The requirements for advancement toward sustainability with the first two types of capital stocks are clearly evident. First, waste discharge needs to be maintained at, or below, the assimilative capacity of the natural environment, ensuring the ongoing capacity of the biosphere to recycle waste. Second, renewable resources cannot be used at rates greater than their regeneration rate. Meeting these two conditions would preserve the assimilative capacity of the natural environment over time while also ensuring a sustainable yield of renewable resources.

Addressing the sustainability requirements of exhaustible resources is more difficult because, as the name implies, once consumed it is difficult to reuse or recycle. As long as exhaustible resources continue to be consumed, their resource pool will decline, and no generation will have the ability to pass to the next generation an inheritance of resource wealth that is equal to what they inherited.

The consumption of exhaustible resources is the first difficulty confronted in the pursuit of sustainability. Two propositions have been advanced in addressing this dilemma. Neither of the two proposals would allow for the achievement of sustainability, but they would enable the global community to advance toward the sustainability condition, ensuring that ecological and social stability is prolonged.

The first proposition advocates that when possible the productive functions of reduced exhaustible resources should be replaced with substitutable renewable resources. The increased capacity for producing renewable resource yields are intended to maintain the environmentally productive functions of the reduced exhaustible resources. For instance, the ongoing consumption of fossil fuels can be offset by investments that enable the increased production of wind, solar, and tidal energy. While not guaranteeing future generations a constant stock of exhaustible resources, it does allow future generations access to the same productive functions of a particular exhaustible resource as its stock declines.

The second proposition advanced to address the difficulty in dealing with exhaustible resources is a market approach, based on optimal resource allocation. Resource economists have argued that the incorporation of correct pricing strategies—encouraging pricing according to scarcity or replacement value—would safeguard exhaustible resources. If the depletion of an exhaustible resource is occurring at rates considered to be dangerously high, the price of the resource will be bid up and its rate of depletion slowed or stopped.[52]

A number of difficulties exist with the market-based approach. Correct pricing strategies would involve the incorporation of costs of all natural resources (renewable resources, nonrenewable resources, and the environment's assimilative capacity) into the price of resource inputs. Due to market failures, however, most environmental resources are not priced, or are underpriced, a condition that promotes their continued degradation. In fact, there are many environmental processes that are essential to human survival, but they are not recognized as resources by markets, maintaining a price of zero and thereby encouraging their overuse.

Environmental resources, a significant portion being common goods with no clear ownership, rarely have associated prices. An example of overconsumption associated with the underpricing of a commonly held resource is evident with water in North America, where water charges seldom include the price of water itself. Municipalities pay for the treatment and pumping of the water to their households, but the very idea of charging for water is unfamiliar, largely since it is a common-held resource. The underpricing of water, however, leads to its overuse by both residential and commercial consumers, a classic example of the tragedy of the commons.

In addition, the natural environment provides extensive services, such as converting waste discharge into environmentally useful or neutral products, climate stabilization, and photosynthesis, that are not priced by markets. Natural lands, for instance, act as green infrastructure—maintaining water pollution control, groundwater recharge, storm water management, and increasing the capacity to support biodiversity—with no market being able to assess the value and the price of these environmental services. While these natural functions are essential for the survival of humankind, since markets do not exist for these environmental services they are provided for free, generating their overuse and degradation.

The absence of markets for common resources, in addition to encouraging their overuse, also ensures that markets cannot provide a signal anticipating the threat or destruction of a critical ecological function or the depletion of a resource stock. For instance, the increased concentration of greenhouse gases in the atmosphere and the ongoing depletion of the ozone layer occur with little apparent social and economic disruption, yet Bill Gates announces his transition out of heading Microsoft and the world economy panics, with extensive market fluctuations and adjustments.

Another critical aspect of resource markets is associated with the absence of a variable that reflects the willingness to pay for resources by future generations. Even with resources that have markets and prices, these resources remain underpriced because they do not reflect the preferences and the willingness to pay of relevant economic agents who have not been born. Simply, future generations are not represented in negotiations over resources. In the context of sustainability, resource pricing must incorporate a variable, a futures or a sustainability tax, that recognizes the value of existing resources to coming generations.

Intragenerational Equity

Given that sustainability is an environmental and socioeconomic condition that ensures that basic needs of the global human population are met over multiple generations while maintaining long-term ecological stability, sustainability necessitates meeting intragenerational equity requirements—an equitable access to resources among members of the current generations. This scenario encompasses providing existing generations with basic needs, adequate nutrition, shelter, potable water, sewage, waste disposal, and employment. Simply put, it is meaningless to encourage conservation to satisfy human needs indefinitely while people in the current generation starve. After all, what makes the needs of future generations any more important than the needs of the current one?

While all countries face the complex grouping of global environmental stresses, there are countries that confront an added dimension to their urban pressures. Dealing with basic survival needs of disadvantaged populations, stresses particularly apparent in poorer countries, makes wider global environmental interests secondary in many parts of the world. The priority for over a billion people is basic survival. The deficient state of human welfare in poorer countries is reflected in the fact that in 2002, as noted by the United Nations Development Programme (UNDP), a child died approximately every three seconds.[53]

The intragenerational equity requirement will also be necessary in governance, since the cooperation that will be required between governments at the local, national, and international levels will not allow for tensions over meeting basic survival needs of existing generations. This tension has been evident in the international discussions for decades—as evident at the Rio Summit—with divisions apparent between wealthy and poor nations over forgoing current consumption to satisfy the needs of future generations.

One of the most important considerations in addressing intragenerational equity will be based on assumptions made about the scarcity of resources. If it is assumed that resources, while scarce, are sufficient to meet the needs of current and future generations, then the existing stresses associated with poverty and malnutrition are a sociopolitical condition that can be addressed through redistribution. However, if it is assumed that resource stocks cannot meet the needs of current and future generations, then intergenerational trade-offs will have to be made—in the form of weakening the above equity requirements—in order to move toward a condition that is at least a step closer to sustainability.

Core Urban Objectives

The inter- and intragenerational equity principles can be operationalized with six specific objectives in the building and organization of cities. These will be discussed in different regional contexts throughout the book. They include: (1) cities that satisfy basic equity criteria, providing essential social, economic, and health resources for all income groups; (2) cities that minimize resource use, particularly reliance on nonrenewable resources; (3) sociopolitical organization that facilitates democratic participation and guarantees political and personal freedoms; (4) built environments that reflect the needs of all income groups, encourage community cohesion, and preserve the cultural heritage of population subgroups; (5) urban development patterns that encourage increased harmony with nature, preserving environmental quality and life systems over time; and (6) urban environments that eliminate and avoid the creation of health risks. It should be recognized that while there is considerable overlap among the objectives, they have been differentiated for greater clarity and specificity.

With the world population continuing to concentrate in cities, the pursuit of the core objectives can facilitate existing urbanization processes while minimizing socioeconomic and environmental stresses of rapid urban growth. In addition, the pursuit of the objectives can ensure that the full advantages of living in cities, as discussed earlier in the chapter, are realized. This would enable communities to increase the welfare of their residents while minimizing the demands placed on global ecological systems.

Given the complexity of pursuing urban sustainability, due to various local, regional, and national stresses, the political interest in establishing a common global mechanism will be unlikely. The specific initiatives promoting the core objectives will vary, based on local socioeconomic and environmental pressures, local values, as well as local, regional, and national political and administrative structures. However, the shared global condition, and overarching principle, will be the pursuit of equity. Besides being the primary focus, inter- and intragenerational equity will also be the integrative aspect to the environmental, social, gender, racial, and economic dimensions of urban sustainability. To this extent, this collection intends to illustrate the complexity of pursuing urban sustainability within different spatial, cultural, and socioeconomic contexts, and to also emphasize the critical role of equity as a necessary universal condition in advancing toward urban sustainability.

The Structure of the Book

This volume of works explores regional socioeconomic and natural environmental stresses, many that have become particularly acute in recent decades due to increasing deregulation, opening of markets to more direct global competition (with accompanying global production and consumption complexities), and the diffusion of neoliberalism. The newly evolving global urban system has in many cases facilitated new levels of environmental and socioeconomic pressures, with expanding resource consumption, growing social and economic polarization, and increasing marginalization of the disadvantaged. As the chapters in this collection show, the backlash to this newly evolving economic and political system has already resulted in major national crises (as in Argentina and Thailand), and the growing pressures in other regions illustrate the difficulty of the long-term stability of this new global economic order. However, case studies in this book also illustrate important local, regional, and national efforts at preserving social stability and minimizing adverse natural environmental impacts, despite wider global trends.

The collection will begin by exploring cities in Asia. "Urban Environmental Management in Shanghai: A Multiscale Perspective" and "The Urban Expansion and Sustainability Challenge of Cities in China's West: the Case of Urumqi" examine the development of two Chinese cities, Shanghai and Urumqi, and the natural environmental impacts of their rapid growth, as well as the recent public initiatives introduced to respond to these environmental pressures. While the chapter on Shanghai presents a multiscale perspective in the exploration of urban sustainability, the Urumqi chapter explores the urban environmental transition discourse in exploring the development of this city in China's west. These two chapters effectively illustrate the importance of multiscale analysis—which can capture broader national and global impacts—in assessing the environmental burdens of growing urban metabolisms. "Sustainable Manufacturing in Nagoya: Exploring the Dynamics of Japan's Competitive Advantage" shifts the focus to sustainability and manufacturing. Ronald Kalafsky explores the concentration of Toyota's production plants in the Nagoya region and examines Japan's efforts to preserve its industrial sector, the well-being of its working class, and social stability in the context of increasing deregulation and globalization.

Continuing in the context of Asia, "The Sufficiency Economy, Sustainable Development, and Agricultural Towns in Thailand: The Case of Nang Rong" and "Deconcentration in the Tel Aviv Metropolitan Area: Governance, Markets, and the Quest for Sustainability" explore urban development processes and their impact on land and resource consumption. The first of these examines recent national reforms promoting increased environmental and social responsibility in Thailand, and how they are being translated locally in an agricultural town, Nang Rong. The second explores the largest metropolitan center in Israel, Tel Aviv, and government policy initiatives—from local to national—directed at limiting urban decentralization. Imad Salamay, through a study of Beirut, explores the role of political representation, equal rights, consociational democracy, and sustainability in a deeply divided pluralist society. The chapter explores the necessity of political reforms in achieving basic representation and advancing toward sustainability in Beirut's rapidly changing urban environment. In closing the review of cities in Asia, "Segmentation and Enclavization in Urban Development: The Sustainable City in India" examines the notion of the "inclusive sustainable city" in the context of India. Darshini Mahadevia explores how urban India has been moving away from inclusivity in urban governance and development as it deregulates markets to facilitate increased foreign investment.

In "Urban Sustainability and Automobile Dependence in an Australian Context" the collection shifts from Asia to Australia as Peter Newman and Jeffrey Kenworthy explore efforts at reducing automobile dependence by promoting transit-, pedestrian-, and green-oriented development in five Australian cities. The chapter explores efforts in Sydney, Melbourne, Brisbane, Perth, and Adelaide to promote mass transit and walking to reduce the detrimental environmental impacts associated with automobile travel.

The next three chapters center on urban-environmental and socioeconomic stresses in African cities. This shift in the collection focuses on regions experiencing some of the most severe global urban stresses. Brij Maharaj and Sultan Khan examine efforts in Durban at promoting sustainability within the context of a deregulating and globalizing economy increasingly shaped by neoliberalism. "Residential Marginality, Erasure, and Intractability in Addis Ababa" examines the urban-environmental stresses in one of the poorest urban regions in the world: Addis Ababa, Ethiopia. Through a study of struggles over housing and land in Addis, the chapter illustrates that recent patterns evident in many market-based economies—characterized by the displacement of the urban poor from city cores—are also apparent in dictatorial, nonmarket-based regimes. "Water Provision for and by the Peri-urban Poor: Public-Community Partnerships or Citizens Coproduction?" focuses on water provision and sustainability in examining two different models in water provision to the peri-urban poor, with a comparison of Dar es Salaam, Tanzania, and Caracas, Venezuela.

Following this geographic transition to South America, the next two chapters examine the pursuit of urban sustainability in two cities in the southern hemisphere of the Americas, one in Argentina and one in Brazil. Ricardo Gomez-Insausti and Analia Conte review urban sustainability within the context of deregulation, globalization, and the recent socioeconomic and political instability in Buenos Aires. In the next chapter, Brian Godfrey investigates the history of *favelas* in Rio de Janeiro and the different attempts of eradicating the urban poor from the city, with the most recent being incorporated as part of the sustainability movement.

"Neoliberal Restructuring, Poverty, and Urban Sustainability in Kingston, Jamaica" shifts the collection to the Caribbean and explores the role of the diaspora in building social sustainability transnationally. Beverley Mullings explores the impacts of neoliberal restructuring in Jamaica and the efforts of the urban poor to deal with the resulting social stresses through the transnationalization of the Jamaican family.

In the next six chapters, the volume transitions to a focus on cities in the United States and Canada. Victoria Basolo explores the importance of housing to urban sustainability within the context of building typologies and urban development in Los Angeles. The next two chapters explore the role of ethnicity, race, racial inequity, and justice in either hindering or promoting urban sustainability. "The Colors That Shaped a City: The Role of Racial and Class Tensions in Inhibiting Urban Sustainability, the Detroit Context" explores the role of racism and white flight in Detroit in encouraging excessive resource consumption and natural environmental degradation, while "The Role of Ethnicity and Race in Supporting Sustainable Urban Environments" examines ethnic communities in Chicago in sustaining the well-being of the city.

Within the Canadian context, Pierre Filion reviews recent planning and development initiatives in Toronto, particularly the policy emphasis on smart growth strategies in promoting a more compact, transit-oriented, and sustainable urban form. In "Planning for Sustainable Development in Montreal: A Qualified Success" Raphaël Fischler and Jeanne Wolfe explore urban-environmental stresses in Montreal and the provincial and local initiatives that have been shaping the city's sustainability program. The final Canada chapter examines food supply and sustainability through the study of decentralization and equity implications of urban supermarket locations in Edmonton, Alberta.

The last geographic focus in the collection is Europe. The chapter by Stephan Anderberg and Eric Clark explores Copenhagen and Malmö as environmental forerunners of urban sustainability. The chapter analyzes the relation between eco-branding and environmental quality improvements in the Øresund region, and the role that each has had in supporting the region's image as a leader in environmental innovation.

Michael Pacione, in the next chapter, assesses the policy framework for urban sustainability initiatives in the United Kingdom. After a review of the evolution of public programs for promoting sustainable urban development, the chapter focuses on the Thames Gateway Region in London and one of the largest European brownfield developments. The chapter examines how local, regional, and national sustainability programs are translated into local development practices.

"Sustainable Development in Portugal: An Analysis of Lisbon and Porto," by Carlos Balsas, examines sustainable development initiatives in Portugal and explores the experience of promoting sustainability through reinvestment and redevelopment programs in its two largest cities, Lisbon and Porto. Finally, the collection closes with the exploration of urban sustainability projects in traditional harbor communities, where the preservation and integration of heritage resources into a rapidly changing global economy has become critical in ensuring social and economic stability. The focus of the chapter is on the Italian port cities of Naples and Genoa.

NOTES

I am very grateful to the reviewers of this chapter—Professors Zenia Kotval, Jeanne Wolfe, Pierre Filion, Raphaël Fischler, Joe Darden, and Ricardo Gomez-Insausti—who provided valuable comments and suggestions.

1. Donella Meadows, *The Limits to Growth* (New York: Universe Books, 1972), 24, 192, 196.
2. Paul Abrecht, *Faith, Science, and the Future* (Geneva: World Council of Churches, 1978), 3.
3. International Union for Conservation of Nature and Natural Resources (IUCN), *World Conservation Strategy: Living Resource Conservation for Sustainable Development* (Gland, Switzerland: International Union for Conservation of Nature and Natural Resources, United Nations Environmental Protection Programme, and World Wildlife Fund, 1980), 1.
4. World Commission on Environment and Development, *Our Common Future* (New York: Oxford University Press, 1987), 43.
5. Ibid., 46–49.
6. Ibid., 46.
7. United Nations, *World Urbanization Prospects: The 2003 Revision* (New York: United Nations, 2004).
8. Wolfgang Sachs, ed., *Global Ecology—A New Arena of Political Conflict* (New Jersey: Zed Books, 1993); Wolfgang Sachs, Fair Wealth: Eight Shifts towards a Light Economy, in *Sustainable Everyday: Scenarios of Urban Life,* ed. Ezio Menzini (Milan: Edizioni Ambiente, 2003), 41–44; Ted Trainer, *The Conserver Society: Alternatives for Sustainability* (London: Zed Books, 1995); Ted Trainer, Development, Charity, and Poverty: The Appropriate Development Perspective, *International Journal of Social Economics* 29 (2002): 54–72.
9. Ward Morehouse, *Accountability, Regulation, and Control of Multinational Corporations* (London: Permanent People's Tribunal on Environmental Hazards and Human Rights, 1994); Andrew Rowell, *Green Backlash: Global Subversion of the Environment Movement* (New York: Routledge, 1996).
10. Jorge Hardoy, Diana Mitlin, and David Satterthwaite, *Environmental Problems in Third World Cities* (London: Earthscan, 1992).
11. Rahmat Witoelar, *The Bali Roadmap: Address to Closing Plenary,* UN Climate Change Conference (Bali, Indonesia: UN Climate Change Conference, December 15, 2007); UN Climate Change Conference, *Bali Action Plan* (Bali, Indonesia: UN Climate Change Conference, 2007).
12. Tora Skodvin and Steinar Andresen, An Agenda for Change in U.S. Climate Policies? Presidential Ambitions and Congressional Powers, *International Environmental Agreements: Politics, Law, and Economics* 9 (2009): 263–80.
13. Peter Gelling and Andrew Revkin, Climate Talks Take on Added Urgency after Report, *New York Times,* December 3, 2007, A3.
14. John M. Broder and Andrew C. Revkin, Hard Task for New Team on Energy and Climate, *New York Times,* December 16, 2008, A24, http://www.nytimes.com/2008/12/16/us/politics/16energy.html.
15. Barack Obama, Remarks by the President at the Morning Plenary Session of the United Nations Climate Change Conference (Copenhagen, Denmark) (Washington, DC: White House, Office of the Press Secretary, December 18, 2009), http://www.whitehouse.gov/the-press-office/remarks-president-morning-plenary-session-united-nations-climate-change-conference; Juliet Eilperin, In Copenhagen, U.S. Pushes for Emissions Cuts from China, Developing Nations, *Washington Post,* December 10, 2009, http://www.washingtonpost.com/wp-dyn/content/story/2009/12/09/ST2009120904931.

html?sid=ST2009120904931.
16. Michel G. J. den Elzen, Andries F. Hof, Angelica Mendoza Beltran, Giacomo Grassi, Mark Roelfsema, Bas van Ruijven, Jasper van Vliet, and Detlef P. van Vuuren, The Copenhagen Accord: Abatement Costs and Carbon Prices Resulting from the Submissions, *Environmental Science and Policy* 14 (2011): 28–39.
17. Joeri Rogelj, Julia Nabel, Claudine Chen, William Hare, Kathleen Markmann, Malte Meinshausen, Michiel Schaeffer, Kirsten Macey, and Niklas Höhne, Copenhagen Accord Pledges Are Paltry, *Nature* 464 (2010): 1126–1128; Michel G. J. den Elzen, Andries F. Hof, Angelica Mendoza Beltran, Giacomo Grassi, Mark Roelfsema, Bas van Ruijven, Jasper van Vliet, and Detlef P. van Vuuren, The Copenhagen Accord: Abatement Costs and Carbon Prices Resulting from the Submissions, *Environmental Science and Policy* 14 (2011): 28–39.
18. Juliet Eilperin and William Booth, Cancun Agreements Put 193 Nations on Track to Deal with Climate Change, *Washington Post*, December 11, 2010, http://www.washingtonpost.com/wp-dyn/content/article/2010/12/11/AR2010121102308.html?wprss=rss_nation.
19. Ibid.
20. Igor Vojnovic, Inter-generational and Intra-generational Equity Requirements for Sustainable Development, *Environmental Conservation* 22:3 (1995): 223–28; Paul Selman, *Local Sustainability: Managing and Planning Ecologically Sound Places* (London: Paul Chapman, 1996); Graham Haughton, Environmental Justice and the Sustainable City, *Journal of Planning Education and Research* 18 (1999): 233–43.
21. UNCED, *Agenda 21* (New York: United Nations, 1992).
22. Jeb Brugmann, Locating the "Local Agenda": Preserving Public Interest in the Evolving Urban World, in *Scaling Urban Environmental Challenges: From Local to Global and Back*, ed. Peter Marcotullio and Gordon McGranahan (London: Earthscan, 2007), 331–54; Jeb Brugmann, Locating the Local Agenda: Preserving Public Interest in the Evolving Urban World, in *Scaling the Urban Environmental Challenge: From Local to Global and Back*, ed. Peter Marcotullio and Gordon McGranahan (London: Earthscan, 2007), 331–54.
23. Jeb Brugmann, Agenda 21 and the Role of Local Government, in *Earth Summit 2002*, ed. Felix Dodds (London: Earthscan, 2000), 40.
24. Pii Elina Berghall, *Habitat II and the Urban Economy* (Helsinki: UNU World Institute for Development Economics Research, 1995), 4.
25. David Satterthwaite, Sustainable Cities or Cities that Contribute to Sustainable Development? in *Sustainable Cities*, ed. David Satterthwaite (London: Earthscan, 2001), 101.
26. Michael Cohen, Habitat II: A Critical Assessment, *Environmental Impact Assessment Review* 16 (1996): 433.
27. In part, the lack of success in converting the global interest in environmental preservation into actual improvements in environmental well-being and advancement toward sustainability has been facilitated by, as noted by Jeb Brugmann in the overview to this volume, the absence of a clearly articulated and supported global initiative that parallels the neoliberal project. The wide-ranging political, corporate, and public coalitions that have so effectively diffused neoliberalism have simply not been evident with the sustainability movement and the pursuit of equity. The difficulty in drafting a global climate change agreement is reflective of this lack of broad-based support. Such a global initiative and commitment, with truly wide-ranging coalitions, will ultimately be necessary if the global community is to advance toward sustainability.
28. Aristotle, *Nicomachean Ethics, Book 1*, and *Politics, Book 1*, trans. W. D. Ross (New York: Gateway Editions, 1954), 51.
29. Aristotle, *Nicomachean Ethics, Book 1, and Politics, Book 1*, trans. W. D. Ross (New York: Gateway Editions, 1954), 51; Herman E. Daly and John B. Cobb, *For the Common Good: Redirecting the Economy toward Community, the Environment, and a Sustainable Future*, updated ed. (Boston: Beacon Press, 1994).
30. Royal Commission on the Future of the Toronto Waterfront, *Regeneration* (Toronto: Minister of Supply and Services Canada and Queen's Printer of Ontario, 1992).
31. Commission of Conservation, *Report of the National Conservation Commission (Volume I)* (Washington, DC: Government Printing Office, 1909), 2–3.
32. Ibid., 13.
33. Talbot Page, *Conservation and Economic Efficiency: An Approach to Materials Policy* (Baltimore: Johns Hopkins University Press, 1977), 1.
34. Karl Ditt, Nature Conservation in England and Germany 1900–1970; Forerunners of Environmental Protection? *Contemporary European History* 5:1 (1996): 1–28; Commission of Conservation of Canada, *First Annual Report* (Ottawa: Mortimer Co., 1910); Anna Bramwell, *Ecology in the 20th Century* (New Haven: Yale University Press, 1989), 23–63.

35. President's Materials Policy Commission, *Resources for Freedom* (Washington, DC: Resources for the Future, 1952), 1.
36. Ibid., 4.
37. Ibid., 23.
38. Ebenezer Howard, *Garden Cities of Tomorrow* (London: Faber & Faber, 1965), 48.
39. Frank Lloyd Wright, *When Democracy Builds* (Chicago: University of Chicago Press, 1945), 7, 63, 67.
40. Urban decentralization and the merging of the urban and rural that was advocated by nineteenth- and twentieth-century urban reformers generated their own socioeconomic and environmental stresses as excessive suburbanization proliferated across the urban landscape throughout much of the West.
41. Herbert Girardet, "Cities and the Culture of Sustainability," in *Earth Summit 2002: A New Deal*, ed. Felix Dodds (London: Earthscan, 2000), 204.
42. Eugene Odum, *Ecology: A Bridge between Science and Society* (Sunderland, MA.: Sinauer Associates, 1997), 290.
43. Mathis Wackernagel and William Rees, *Our Ecological Footprint: Reducing Human Impact on the Earth* (Philadelphia: New Society Publishers, 1996), 86.
44. Ibid., 85.
45. Ibid., 89.
46. World Bank, *World Development Report* (Washington, DC: World Bank, 1994), 162.
47. United Nations Development Program, *Fighting Climate Change: Human Solidarity in a Divided World* (New York: United Nations Development Program, 2007), 25.
48. World Bank, *World Development Indicators 2008* (Washington, DC: World Bank, 2008), 4.
49. Ali H. Mokdad, James Marks, Donna Stroup, Julie Gerberding, Actual Causes of Death in the United States, *Journal of the American Medical Association* 291 (2004): 1238–45; United Nations Development Program, *Human Development Report 2005* (New York: United Nations, 2005), 24.
50. Peter Newman and Jeffrey Kenworthy, *Sustainability and Cities: Overcoming Automobile Dependence* (Washington, DC: Island Press, 1999); Vojnovic, Inter-generational and Intra-generational Equity Requirements; Igor Vojnovic, The Environmental Costs of Modernism, *Cities* 16 (1999): 301–13; Igor Vojnovic, Shaping Metropolitan Toronto: A Study of Linear Infrastructure Subsidies, *Environment and Planning B: Planning and Design* 27 (2000): 197–230.
51. Graham Haughton and Colin Hunter, *Sustainable Cities* (London: Jessica Kingley, 1996), 118.
52. Some environmental economists have even argued that given the existence of nonrenewable resources, the best that can be achieved by any one generation is to pass to the next generation not the physical stocks that they inherited, but rather a constant economic value. See David Pearce, Anil Markandya, and Edward Barbier, *Blueprint for a Green Economy* (London: Earthscan, 1989).
53. United Nations Development Program, *Human Development Report 2005* (New York: United Nations Development Program, 2005), 27.

REFERENCES

Abrecht, Paul. *Faith, Science, and the Future.* Geneva: World Council of Churches, 1978.

Aristotle. *Nicomachean Ethics, Book 1, and Politics, Book 1.* Trans. W. D. Ross. New York: Gateway Editions, 1954.

Berghall, Pii Elina. *Habitat II and the Urban Economy.* Helsinki: UNU World Institute for Development Economics Research, 1995.

Borgstrom, Georg. *The Hungry Planet.* New York: Macmillan, 1967.

Bramwell, Anna. *Ecology in the 20th Century.* New Haven: Yale University Press, 1989.

Broder, John M., and Andrew C. Revkin. Hard Task for New Team on Energy and Climate. *New York Times*, December 16, 2008, A24. http://www.nytimes.com/2008/12/16/us/politics/16energy.html.

Brugmann, Jeb. Locating the "Local Agenda": Preserving Public Interest in the Evolving Urban World. In *Scaling the Urban Environmental Challenge: From Local to Global and Back*, ed. Peter Marcotullio and Gordon McGranahan, 331–54. London: Earthscan, 2007.

———. Agenda 21 and the Role of Local Government. In *Earth Summit 2002*, ed. Felix Dodds, 40–48. London: Earthscan, 2000.

Cohen, Michael. *Habitat II: A Critical Assessment.* Environmental Impact Assessment Review, 1996.

Commission of Conservation. *Report of the National Conservation Commission (Volume I).* Washington, DC: Government Printing Office, 1909.

Commission of Conservation of Canada. *First Annual Report.* Ottawa: Mortimer Co., 1910.

Daly, Herman E., and John B. Cobb. *For the Common Good:*

Redirecting the Economy toward Community, the Environment, and a Sustainable Future. Updated ed. Boston: Beacon Press, 1994.

den Elzen, Michel G. J., Andries F. Hof, Angelica Mendoza Beltran, Giacomo Grassi, Mark Roelfsema, Bas van Ruijven, Jasper van Vliet, and Detlef P. van Vuuren. The Copenhagen Accord: Abatement Costs and Carbon Prices Resulting from the Submissions. *Environmental Science and Policy* 14 (2011): 28–39.

Ditt, Karl. Nature Conservation in England and Germany 1900–1970; Forerunners of Environmental Protection? *Contemporary European History* 5:1 (1996): 1–28.

Ehrlich, Paul R., and Anne H. Ehrlich. *The Population Explosion.* New York: Simon & Schuster, 1990.

Eilperin, Juliet. In Copenhagen, U.S. Pushes for Emissions Cuts from China, Developing Nations. *Washington Post,* December 10, 2009. http://www.washingtonpost.com/wp-dyn/content/story/2009/12/09/ST2009120904931.html?sid=ST2009120904931.

Eilperin, Juliet, and William Booth. Cancun Agreements Put 193 Nations on Track to Deal with Climate Change. *Washington Post,* December 11, 2010. http://www.washingtonpost.com/wp-dyn/content/article/2010/12/11/AR2010121102308.html?wprss=rss_nation.

Gelling, Peter, and Andrew Revkin. Climate Talks Take on Added Urgency after Report. *New York Times,* December 3, 2007, A3.

Girardet, Herbert. Cities and the Culture of Sustainability. In *Earth Summit 2002: A New Deal,* ed. Felix Dodds, 202–11. London: Earthscan, 2000.

Hardoy, Jorge, Diana Mitlin, and David Satterthwaite. *Environmental Problems in Third World Cities.* London: Earthscan, 1992.

Haughton, Graham. Environmental Justice and the Sustainable City. *Journal of Planning Education and Research* 18 (1999): 233–43.

Haughton, Graham, and Colin Hunter. *Sustainable Cities.* London: Jessica Kingley, 1996.

Howard, Ebenezer. *Garden Cities of Tomorrow.* London: Faber & Faber, 1965.

International Union for Conservation of Nature and Natural Resources (IUCN). *World Conservation Strategy: Living Resource Conservation for Sustainable Development.* Gland, Switzerland: International Union for Conservation of Nature and Natural Resources, United Nations Environmental Protection Programme, and World Wildlife Fund, 1980.

Meadows, Donella. *The Limits to Growth.* New York: Universe Books, 1972.

Mokdad, Ali H., James Marks, Donna Stroup, and Julie Gerberding. Actual Causes of Death in the United States. *Journal of the American Medical Association* 291 (2004): 1238–45.

Morehouse, Ward. *Accountability, Regulation, and Control of Multinational Corporations.* London: Permanent People's Tribunal on Environmental Hazards and Human Rights, 1994.

Newman, Peter, and Jeffrey Kenworthy. *Sustainability and Cities: Overcoming Automobile Dependence.* Washington, DC: Island Press, 1999.

Obama, Barack. Remarks by the President at the Morning Plenary Session of the United Nations Climate Change Conference (Copenhagen, Denmark). Washington, DC: White House. December 18, 2009. Office of the Press Secretary. http://www.whitehouse.gov/the-press-office/remarks-president-morning-plenary-session-united-nations-climate-change-conference.

Odum, Eugene. *Ecology and Our Endangered Life Support Systems.* Sunderland, MA: Sinauer Associates, 1993.

———. *Ecology: A Bridge between Science and Society.* Sunderland, MA.: Sinauer Associates, 1997.

Page, Talbot. *Conservation and Economic Efficiency: An Approach to Materials Policy.* Baltimore: Johns Hopkins University Press, 1977.

Pearce, David, Anil Markandya, and Edward Barbier. *Blueprint for a Green Economy.* London: Earthscan, 1989.

President's Materials Policy Commission. *Resources for Freedom.* Washington, DC: Resources for the Future, 1952.

Rogelj, Joeri, Julia Nabel, Claudine Chen, William Hare, Kathleen Markmann, Malte Meinshausen, Michiel Schaeffer, Kirsten Macey, and Niklas Höhne. Copenhagen Accord Pledges Are Paltry. *Nature* 464 (2010): 1126–28.

Rowell, Andrew. *Green Backlash: Global Subversion of the Environment Movement.* New York: Routledge, 1996.

Royal Commission on the Future of the Toronto Waterfront. *Regeneration.* Toronto: Minister of Supply and Services Canada and Queen's Printer of Ontario, 1992.

Sachs, Wolfgang. Fair Wealth: Eight Shifts toward a Light Economy. In *Sustainable Everyday: Scenarios of Urban Life,* ed. Ezio Menzini, 41–44. Milan: Edizioni Ambiente, 2003.

———, ed. *Global Ecology—A New Arena of Political Conflict.* New Jersey: Zed Books, 1993.

Satterthwaite, David. Sustainable Cities or Cities that Contribute to Sustainable Development? In *Sustainable Cities,* ed. David Satterthwaite, 80–106. London: Earthscan, 2001.

Selman, Paul. *Local Sustainability: Managing and Planning*

Ecologically Sound Places. London: Paul Chapman, 1996.

Skodvin, Tora, and Steinar Andresen. An Agenda for Change in U.S. Climate Policies? Presidential Ambitions and Congressional Powers. *International Environmental Agreements: Politics, Law, and Economics* 9 (2009): 263–80.

Trainer, Ted. *The Conserver Society: Alternatives for Sustainability*. London: Zed Books, 1995.

———. Development, Charity, and Poverty: The Appropriate Development Perspective. *International Journal of Social Economics* 29 (2002): 54–72.

UN Climate Change Conference. *Bali Action Plan*. Bali, Indonesia: UN Climate Change Conference, 2007.

UNCED. *Agenda 21*. New York: United Nations, 1992.

United Nations. *World Urbanization Prospects: The 2003 Revision*. New York: United Nations, 2004.

United Nations Development Program. *Fighting Climate Change: Human Solidarity in a Divided World*. New York: United Nations Development Program, 2007.

———. *Human Development Report 2005*. New York: United Nations, 2005.

Vojnovic, Igor. The Environmental Costs of Modernism. *Cities* 16 (1999): 301–13.

———. Inter-generational and Intra-generational Equity Requirements for Sustainable Development. *Environmental Conservation* 22:3 (1995): 223–28.

———. Shaping Metropolitan Toronto: A Study of Linear Infrastructure Subsidies. *Environment and Planning B: Planning and Design* 27 (2000): 197–230.

Wackernagel, Mathis, and William Rees. *Our Ecological Footprint: Reducing Human Impact on the Earth*. Philadelphia: New Society Publishers, 1996.

Witoelar, Rahmat. The Bali Roadmap: Address to Closing Plenary, UN Climate Change Conference. Bali, Indonesia: UN Climate Change Conference, December 15, 2007.

World Bank. *World Development Indicators 2008*. Washington, DC: World Bank, 2008.

———. *World Development Report*. Washington, DC: World Bank, 1994.

World Commission on Environment and Development. *Our Common Future*. New York: Oxford University Press, 1987.

Wright, Frank Lloyd. *When Democracy Builds*. Chicago: University of Chicago Press, 1945.

■ WEI TU / DANIEL SUI / WEICHUN MA

Urban Environmental Management in Shanghai

A MULTISCALE PERSPECTIVE

Since the late 1970s, Shanghai—China's economic capital and the largest city—has transformed rapidly from a deteriorating industrial center of the Maoist era to one of the most dynamic, vigorous, and fastest-growing metropolitan areas of the Asia-Pacific Rim.[1] The unprecedented urban redevelopment process has greatly improved the economic, social, and environmental conditions of Shanghai. Moreover, after successfully hosting the 2010 World Expo and with a Disney theme park under construction, the economic growth of Shanghai in the near future seems assured (figs. 1, 2, and 3). As cities become larger and wealthier, the driving forces and the manifestations of environmental burdens are also changing rapidly and becoming increasingly complex.[2] In particular, many scholars have observed the shift of urban environmental burdens from local and regional levels to national and even global levels.[3] It is indeed more urgent than ever that urban environmental management strategies be adjusted according to the spatial and temporal evolution of environmental problems in order to achieve the goal of urban sustainable development.

Due to Shanghai's pivotal role in China, the city's environmental problems have received rather extensive interdisciplinary attention in the literature. Some are overviews of general environmental quality and management issues;[4] some examine specific environmental threats, such as water and air pollution;[5] some analyze issues related to the environmental policies and management instruments;[6] others simulate and predict future environmental conditions.[7] The existing studies are valuable in helping to understand the current situation and evolution of the environmental burdens and policies in Shanghai. The spatial scale of most of the existing studies, however, has been largely limited to the intraurban level. Few studies were conducted to examine Shanghai's environmental issues from a multiscale perspective. By focusing solely on environmental issues at the intraurban level, important environmental processes operating at other spatial

PHOTOGRAPH BY WEICHUN MA

Figure 1. New central business district skyline, Pudong.

scales may be overlooked and the links among problems across different geographical scales may be ignored. For example, by discharging industrial wastewater into Changjiang River, water quality of the inner-city river might be improved, but one of the negative consequences is the deteriorating water quality in the Changjiang River Estuary and East China Sea, which will be costly to clean in the long run.

Aiming at bridging this gap in the literature, this study attempts to conduct an assessment of Shanghai's urban environmental issues and policies at three spatial scales: intra-urban, interurban/regional, and global. As such, the rest of this chapter has been organized into five sections. After a brief introduction in section 1, section 2 briefly discusses the importance of a multiscale perspective in understanding urban environmental burdens and policies. Section 3 examines Shanghai's urban environmental management at three spatial scales since the late 1970s, followed by section 4, which discusses the opportunities and challenges of formulating a multiscale environmental policy. The last section contains conclusions.

PHOTOGRAPH BY LOUIS E. SCHMIER

Figure 2. Apartments under construction, Pudong.

PHOTOGRAPH BY WEICHUN MA

Figure 3. Traffic flows on Sichuan Road, Puxi.

The Role of Spatial Scales in an Integrated Urban Environmental Assessment

Spatial scale refers to the unit or level of analysis in space.[8] Both the importance and relationship between macro-, meso-, and microscale phenomenon and processes have been discussed extensively in geography and environmental studies literature.[9] According to these studies, a multiscale approach is essential to understanding urban environmental problems and to achieving the goal of sustainable development.

First, urban environmental burdens are continuous in space, and macro-scale environmental problems tend to converge in microscale localities. Environmental problems at microscale localities, in turn, contribute to macroscale environmental conditions.[10] For example, climate change, a typical global issue, can be sensed by many coastal cities worldwide as the threat of rising sea levels escalates. And greenhouse gas emissions in cities, usually a localized environmental problem, are often cited as one of the major leading causes behind global warming.

Second, the magnitude of urban environmental burdens at different spatial scales is interrelated, although not necessarily positively correlated. Reducing local environmental burdens may either decrease or increase impacts at the regional scale.[11] Reclaiming land from sea, for example, can temporally alleviate land shortage caused by population growth at the local level; at the regional level, however, the coastal ecological systems may be increasingly disturbed, resulting in negative impacts on residents inland.

Third, urban environmental burdens at different spatial scales are featured by different characteristics. Local burdens, usually more acute and immediate, tend to generate short-term threats to a limited population in a small area. At the same time, local problems may also be easier to fix. The regional/global burdens, on the other hand, may be less obvious and urgent, but more likely to last longer, pose long-term threats to current as well as future generations, potentially affect larger areas, and be more difficult to deal with.

Fourth, because pollution does not respect administrative boundaries, environmental burdens generated at one locality usually impact a much larger geographical region. For example, behind a well-developed, affluent city with clean water and fresh air, there may be hidden stories about its wastes being deposited somewhere outside the city boundary, while a large amount of energy and natural resources are being imported from remote areas or other countries.

Last, spatial scale is also a critical factor that may impact the results of environment assessment. While a measure of environmental change at regional or global levels is more favorable to pro-environment groups, a measure of intra-urban environmental burden is usually the primary concern of local governments. The cross-boundary and/or global environmental burdens caused by a city are more likely to be ignored if an environmental assessment is to be conducted by local environmental officials.

In short, due to the close link and frequent interactions among environmental issues across different spatial scales, examination of environmental issues at only one scale often leads to the neglect of problems at other scales and/or inadequate analysis of the connections of problems across different scales. An integrated assessment of urban environment burdens that link the micro-, meso-, and macroscales will not only yield deeper understanding of environmental challenges from a particular locality; it will also provide a more holistic perspective for formulating policy solutions for long-term sustainable urban development.

In the following discussion, the macro-, meso-, and micro-scales correspond to the intra-urban, interurban/regional, and global scale, respectively. At the intra-urban scale, the central concern is how the quality of urban environments impacts the lives of urban residents living within the city; at the interurban/regional level, the focus is on the environmental impacts of urban development on its hinterland, ecosystems, and neighboring regions; at the global level, the emphasis is on the relationship between urban metabolism,[12] distant resource depletion, and worldwide environmental processes such as global warming.

Moreover, there is also an interesting link between the multispatial-scale analyses of urban environmental burdens and the three-stage urban environmental evolution model.[13] While the multiscale analysis takes a spatial perspective to examine urban environmental problems, the evolution model tackles the urban environmental issues from a temporal perspective. In general, the three stages of the urban environmental evolution model can roughly correspond to the three levels of the multiscale analysis. In stage 1, poverty-related environmental concerns (e.g., sanitation and drinking water) can largely be analyzed at the intra-urban level; in stage 2, production-related pollution (e.g., wastewater from an iron and steel plant) needs to be examined at both intraurban and interurban/regional levels due to the potential spatial relocation of pollutants; in stage 3, the consumption and lifestyle-associated environmental burdens (e.g., air pollution caused by traffic jams in big cities) have to be inspected at the global level because the materials/energy input and output of a big city are usually related to resource depletion and worldwide environmental processes.

Shanghai's Environmental Problems and Policies

Shanghai sits on the southeast edge of the Changjiang river delta, one of the most economically developed and densely settled regions in China (fig. 4). Together with three other special municipalities in the country, Shanghai Municipal Government (SMG) enjoys an administrative authority equivalent to that of a province and reports directly to the central government in Beijing. There are currently nineteen urban districts and one rural county under SMG's jurisdiction, with a total area of 2,448 square miles and a population of 17.42 million, including more than 3 million unregistered permanent residents. Shanghai's per capita Gross Domestic Product (GDP) topped US$6,000 in 2006 after a continuous two-digit annual GDP growth for more than fifteen years.[14]

Pre-reform Shanghai

Shanghai was one of the earliest Chinese cities open to Western trade after the Treaty of Nanjing in 1842. By 1936 it had become the world's seventh largest city and China's premier industrial and trading center. Despite the severe damage caused by the Sino-Japanese war of 1937–1945 and the following civil war between the communists and the nationalists, Shanghai remained China's most important seaport, trade center, and light manufacturing base by the end of the 1940s.

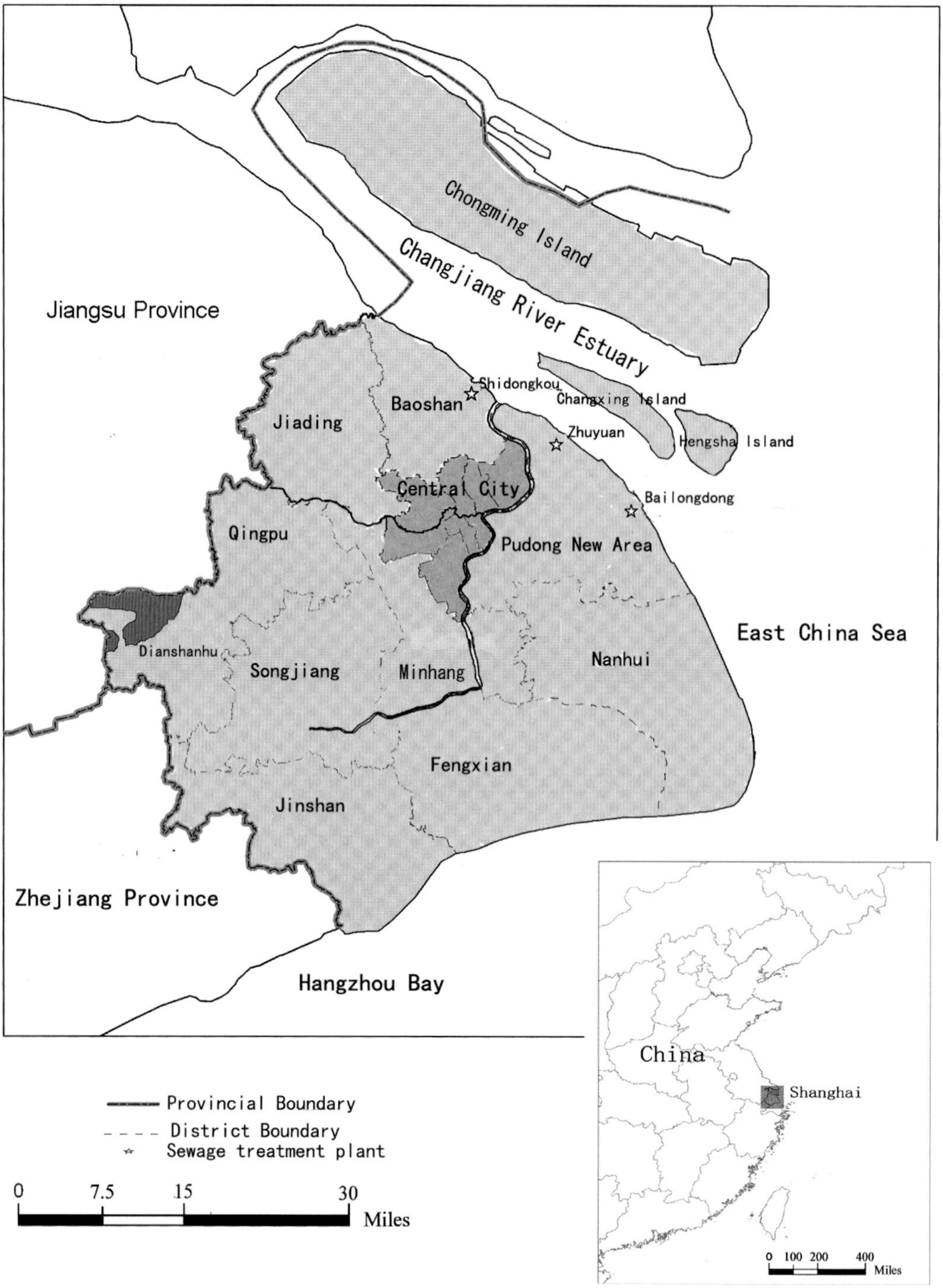

Figure 4. Shanghai and its location in China.

Shanghai's economy was radically transformed after Mao took over the country in 1949. Regarded by decision-makers as the more "productive" part of the economy, the heavy manufacturing sectors, such as petrochemicals and machineries, were encouraged to develop. In contrast, light industrial and tertiary sectors were substantially suppressed. Following the highly planned and command-driven economic system of the former Soviet Union, China's major cities became the main producers of industrial products for the country. Thus Shanghai was rapidly transformed into China's largest production city, contributing approximately 17 percent of the country's total annual revenue in the three decades after 1949.[15]

In efforts to promote industrialization, however, not only was the development of Shanghai's service sector greatly restrained; the service functions of the city—such as land use optimization, pollution mitigation, and improvement of urban infrastructure—were also ignored and delayed. As a result, the housing conditions, public transportation systems, municipal services, and urban infrastructure all deteriorated rapidly. In the 1930s the level of the urban development of Shanghai, at least inside the International Settlement and French Concession, had reached standards comparable to many European counterparts.[16] In contrast, the condition of urban infrastructure in Shanghai was even worse than that of many other economically less important Chinese cities by the mid-1980s.[17] In general, Shanghai's socialist-style urbanization process during Mao's era was characterized by a relatively slow growth rate, a heavily polluted urban environment, deteriorating urban infrastructure, and a mixture of residential, industrial, and commercial land use types under the work-units system.[18]

Postreform Shanghai

Since the late 1970s the unparalleled economic development and the rapid urbanization in Shanghai has occurred in the context of China's massive economic privatization and political decentralization. On the one hand, local governments such as Shanghai have gained much more power to determine the timing, pace, and spatial configuration of urban development. On the other hand, they were also required by the central government to take more responsibility for their own development. Because of the declining revenues from local state-owned enterprises (SOEs) and a reduced support from the central government, local governments had to seek new revenue sources to support their own development.[19] As a consequence, economic development zones were increasingly used as a development instrument to collect land rent, attract foreign direct investment (FDI), and stimulate urban redevelopment.[20] In May 1990 the central government announced a trans-century development plan to remake Shanghai into a world economic, financial, and trade center. Pudong District, on the east side of the Huangpu River, was designated as the focal point of this unprecedented national development plan, and four development zones (functional areas) were established to assume the different roles of urban development.[21]

The economic and urban development in Shanghai has been remarkable. Per capita GDP increased from US$500 in 1978 to more than US$6,000 in 2006, the highest among all Chinese cities (fig. 5).[22] The growing wealth in Shanghai has been clearly reflected in the changing consumption patterns. Compared to the level in 1980, the total consumption in 2006 increased more than eight times. Moreover, the consumption of basic necessities has been constantly declining,

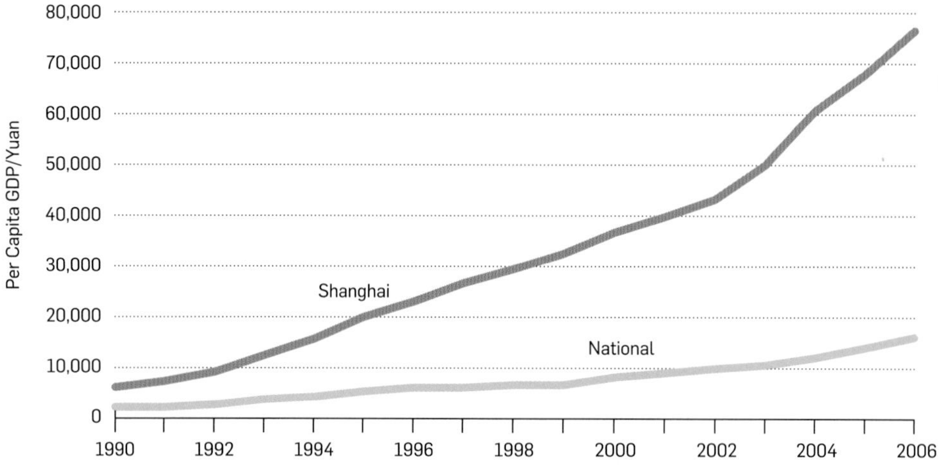

Figure 5. Per capita GDP of Shanghai and China, 1990–2006 (inflation unadjusted).

Source: SSB 2007.

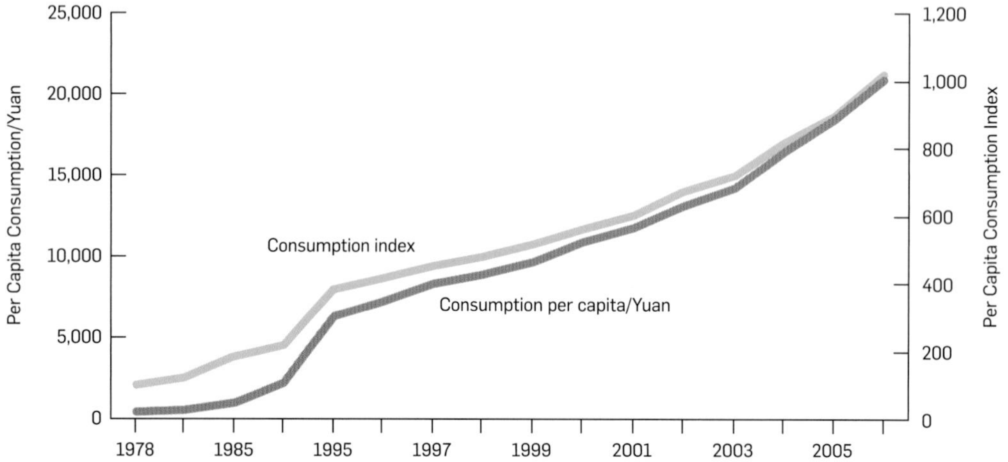

Figure 6. Per capita consumption and consumption index of Shanghai, 1978–2006.

Source: SSB 2007.

and spending on service, housing, transportation, and entertainment has been continuously increasing (figs. 6 and 7). In addition, housing markets have been maturing with the rapid formation of a land rent gradient since the late 1990s. The living conditions of the residents were greatly improved, although the housing prices have skyrocketed since 2003 (figs. 8 and 9).

In short, the transition from a highly planned to a market-oriented economy since the late 1970s has fundamentally transformed the structure and spatial pattern of urban land use in Shanghai. There has been a growth of specialized manufacturing zones, economic development areas, and science parks in the urban outskirts. There has also been a mushrooming of upscale

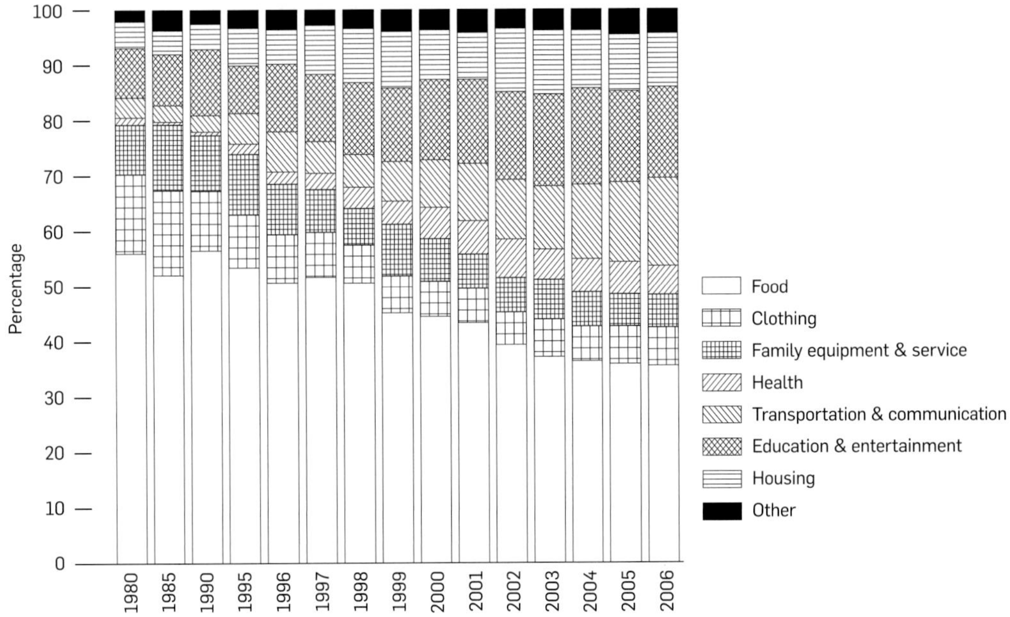

Figure 7. Consumption structure of Shanghai, 1980–2006.

Source: SSB 2007.

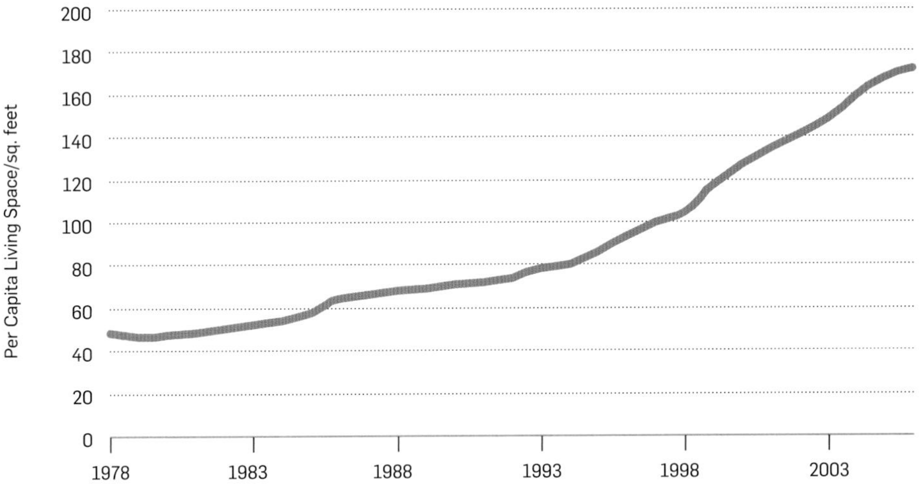

Figure 8. Per capita living space in Shanghai, 1978–2006.

Source: SSB 2007.

residential and commercial districts, as well as a maturing of the central business districts (CBDs). Urban land use has become much more functionally differentiated. Industrial pollution has been effectively controlled and the urban built environment has become much more diversified, environmentally friendly, and attractive. The unparalleled urban redevelopment process in postreform

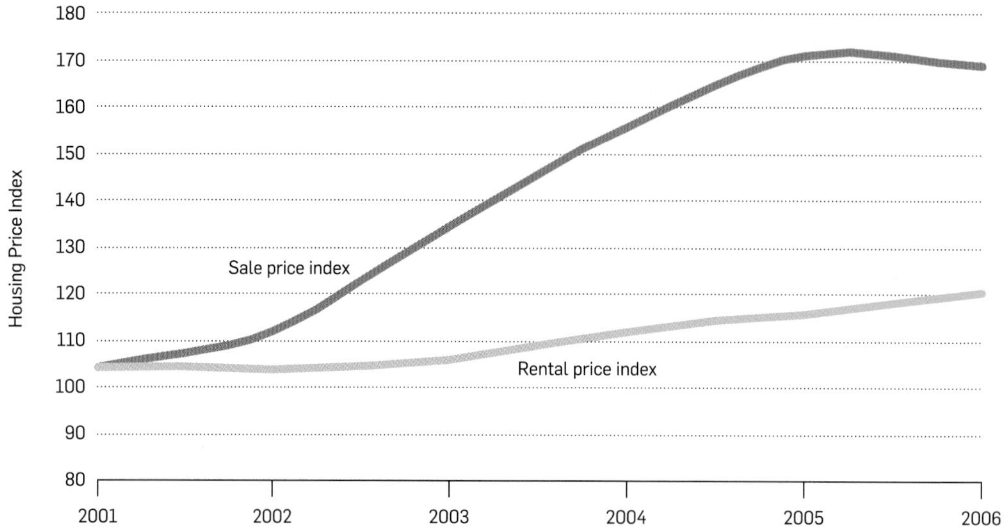

Figure 9. Housing price indices in Shanghai, 2001–2006.
Source: SSB 2007.

Shanghai can be characterized by large-scale investment on urban infrastructure projects, redevelopment of the old city, economic restructuring and relocation, and pollution abatement. The solid investment in environmental affairs has been crucial to ensure the significant improvement of Shanghai's environmental conditions at the intra-urban level (see table 1).

Urban Environmental Management in Shanghai since the Late 1970s

After three decades of neglect, urban environmental issues finally became one of the SMG's top priorities in the late 1970s. Between the late 1970s and the late 1980s systematic urban environmental management began in Shanghai. The Shanghai Environmental Protection Bureau (SEPB), now a prime agency under SMG in charge of environmental affairs, was founded in 1979. A series of city ordinances and regulations were enacted to tackle severe industrial pollution and other environmental nuisances that had been accumulating in the past decades. An environmental monitoring network was established to systematically collect data for checking environment quality and to enforce environmental standards. The industrial pollution was the main target of environmental management at this stage.

The 1990s witnessed the most dramatic urban redevelopment process in Shanghai's more than 1,000-year history. This decade featured large-scale construction of urban and environmental infrastructure, industrial pollution mitigation, and urban beautification. Both industrial and domestic wastes were systematically collected and treated, heavily polluted rivers were rehabilitated, and urban green space was created all over the city. More significantly, the role of Shanghai as the nation's production center was reexamined, and a service-oriented urban development goal was endorsed by the central government. Shanghai Land Use Master Plan (1997–2010), approved

Table 1. Investment in environmental protection and its share of total GDP in Shanghai, 1991–2006

	TOTAL ENVIRONMENTAL INVESTMENT (10^8 ¥)	SHARE IN TOTAL GDP (%)		TOTAL ENVIRONMENTAL INVESTMENT (10^8 ¥)	SHARE IN TOTAL GDP (%)
1991	7.60	0.90	1999	111.57	2.80
1992	15.20	1.40	2000	141.91	3.10
1993	32.13	2.10	2001	152.93	3.10
1994	39.09	2.00	2002	162.39	3.00
1995	46.49	1.90	2003	191.53	3.10
1996	68.83	2.40	2004	225.40	3.03
1997	82.35	2.50	2005	281.00	3.07
1998	102.13	2.80	2006	310.85	3.02

Source: Shanghai Statistical Bureau, *Shanghai Statistics Year Book, 1990–2007* (Shanghai: Shanghai Statistic Press, 2007).

by the Ministry of Land and Resources in 1997, was adopted by the SMG as a planning instrument to transform the residence-industry-business mixed land use pattern formed during Mao's era into a new land use model featured by various functional zones, high environmental standards, and attractive urban amenities for living, working, and investing.[23] In 1999 SMG formulated a local action plan under the national blueprint of Agenda 21, a resultant document from the 1992 Rio Summit (Implementing China's Agenda 21 Shanghai Leader Group, 1999). Although concrete action plans have yet to be made and implemented, this event indicates the official introduction of the concept of sustainable development in Shanghai's urban environmental management system.

More recently, SEPB released the "Shanghai Environmental Protection Three-Year Action Plan, 2005–2008" (SEPAP 05–08) under the direction of the National Tenth Five-Year (2006–2010) Plan for Environmental Protection.[24] SEPAP 05–08 set up four general goals of environmental management: continue to improve the basic environmental infrastructure (e.g., sewage treatment facilities, green space); continue to reduce domestic and industrial pollution (e.g., coal desulfurization); continue to improve environmental monitoring and management system (e.g., determine total allowed pollutant discharge based on environmental carrying capacity); and continue to improve environmental quality and quality of living (e.g., making Pudong District a national model for urban environment management).

An Assessment of Urban Environmental Burdens and Management

This section summarizes the urban environmental burdens at three spatial scales: intraurban, interurban/regional, and global. Major urban environmental impacts, such as water and air pollution, energy use, and land use, are examined individually under each spatial scale. From the perspective of the three-stage urban environmental evolution model, Shanghai largely passed stage 1 of the model by the end of the 1970s and can be positioned at stage 2 in the 1980s and most of the 1990s. More recently, Shanghai's position in the model has gradually shifted toward stage 3, although the environmental threats from stage 2 remain significant. It is understandable, then, that the most in-depth discussion below is given to the intra-urban level (stage 2) problems because the postreform urban environmental management in Shanghai has been focused on the environmental burdens at this particular level.

Intra-urban Scale

■ WATER QUALITY. Water pollution has been the most visible environmental problem in Shanghai because water surface covers about 11 percent of the city's total area. For centuries, the Huangpu River, widely regarded as the mother river by local residents, and its tributaries, served as the city's primary source of drinking water, transportation pathways, and sinks for domestic, industrial, and agricultural wastes. However, the worsening water quality of the Huangpu and many other rivers, especially the Suzhou Creek, Huangpu's largest tributary, has long been one of the most immediate health, environmental, and aesthetic concerns of Shanghai.

The major measures to improve the water quality of inner rivers include restructuring the economy, adopting a zoning system in land development (especially in the Pudong New Area), constructing sewage systems to collect and treat both industrial and domestic wastewater, tightening wastewater discharge regulations, and implementing environmental impact assessment (EIA) on major development activities.[25] These actions seemed to be quite effective. The total industrial wastewater discharge decreased 65 percent from 1990 to 2006, and the treatment rates of industrial wastewater reached 98.2 percent in 2000 (see table 2). Consequently, water quality in downstream Huangpu and Suzhou Creek has generally improved since 1995, indicated by the water quality monitoring results (see table 3). Currently, the inner river water quality is still not good enough to allow any recreational activities, such as swimming and fishing. However, Shanghai's rivers are much less odorous and unpleasant visually after more than two decades of ceaseless cleaning-up efforts.

The impacts of the overall surface water quality are more important in overall economic and aesthetic considerations. The quality of drinking water sources, on the other hand, is more directly related to human health. There are two major potable drinking water sources in Shanghai, upstream Huangpu River and the Changjiang River Estuary (from Xuliujing to the mouth of the Changjiang River). Although the Changjiang inlet is of relatively good quality in general,[26] the inlets on the Huangpu, which provide most of the drinking water for the city, are increasingly threatened by pollution from domestic, industrial, and agricultural sources (figs. 10, 11, and 12). According to a recent study, water in Minghang waterworks failed to meet Class IV of the Chinese Environmental Quality Standard for Surface Water (GB3808–2002).[27] In addition, the worsening water quality in upstream Huangpu River may indicate the declining water quality in Dianshan Lake and Tai Lake, the headwater of the Huangpu (table 3), which is closely related to nonpoint source pollution in the region.[28]

■ AIR QUALITY. Shanghai's air pollution comes from three main sources: the industrial and household coal combustion, gasoline consumption in transportation, and suspended particulates from

Table 2. Wastewater discharge and treatment in Shanghai, 1990–2006

	TOTAL (10^8 SHORT TON)	INDUSTRIAL (10^8 SHORT TON)	DOMESTIC (10^8 SHORT TON)	TREATMENT RATE (INDUSTRIAL %)
1990	18.13	12.08	6.05	N/A
1991	17.76	12.02	5.74	74.8
1992	18.40	12.43	5.97	77.0
1993	18.43	11.62	6.81	82.3
1994	18.48	10.71	7.77	82.2
1995	20.37	10.53	9.83	86.4
1996	20.73	10.35	10.38	93.7
1997	19.14	9.06	10.08	93.8
1998	18.88	8.16	10.71	95.3
1999	18.40	7.73	10.67	95.7
2000	17.57	6.58	11.00	98.2
2001	17.69	6.17	11.52	N/A
2002	17.43	5.89	11.54	N/A
2003	16.53	5.54	10.99	N/A
2004	17.54	5.12	12.43	N/A
2005	18.12	4.64	13.48	N/A
2006	20.29	4.38	15.91	N/A

Source: Shanghai Statistical Bureau, *Shanghai Statistics Year Book, 1990–2007* (Shanghai: Shanghai Statistic Press, 2007); SEPBb 2007.

construction sites. The common ambient pollutants used to monitor air pollution are SO_2, NO_x, CO, lead, and Total Suspended Particles (TSP). The main approaches to improve air quality include restructuring the economy, promoting clean energy (e.g., consume low-sulfur coal and replace coal with natural gas) and energy-saving technology, tightening emissions standards, developing public transportation, and limiting private vehicles.

After the central government determined to make Shanghai an international economic, financial, and trade center in the fourteenth session of the National Congress of the Communist Party in 1992, the share of the tertiary sectors in the economic pie increased significantly, from around 30 percent in 1990 to over 50 percent in 2006 (table 4). On the other hand, some highly polluting and low value-added industries (e.g., textiles) were gradually phased out. Thousands of manufacturing plants were either closed or relocated to specialized industrial development zones in urban outskirts, resulting in the concentration of the petrochemical industry in Jingshan district, electrical and mechanical units in Minghang district, and automobile (assembly and parts) industry in Jiading district. Between 1999 and 2005, the share of oil consumption in the total energy consumption increased 8.2 percent, compared to an 8.1 percent decrease of the use of coal (fig. 13). In addition, energy efficiency has also improved substantially. Between 1990 and 2005, Shanghai's total GDP increased more than eight times, while total energy consumption

Table 3. Water quality indices in three main water bodies in Shanghai, 1995–2005

	1995	1996	1997	1998	1999	2000	2001	2002	2003	2004	2005
Dianshan Lake											
Inlet	1.13	1.35	2.52	1.82	1.96	2.40	2.64	2.29	2.43	2.78	3.08
Outlet	1.13	0.94	1.42	1.57	1.43	1.55	1.66	1.77	1.91	2.32	2.14
Lake body	0.97	1.15	1.79	1.71	1.72	1.80	2.06	2.34	2.18	2.85	2.68
Lake side	0.99	1.10	1.51	1.63	1.49	1.80	1.91	1.98	2.12	2.56	2.31
Lake average	1.02	1.16	1.89	1.67	1.73	1.89	2.39	2.22	2.16	2.63	2.55
Huangpu River											
Dianfeng	0.86	0.95	0.99	0.97	1.03	1.15	1.17	1.41	1.37	1.67	1.46
Songpu Bridge	1.76	1.74	1.51	1.74	2.24	1.97	1.11	1.34	1.26	1.60	1.50
Lingjiang	1.24	1.28	1.31	1.38	0.97	0.96	0.69	0.81	0.82	1.00	0.89
Nanshi Waterworks	0.69	0.71	0.62	0.51	0.51	0.68	0.56	0.51	0.60	0.56	0.57
Yangpu Bridge	1.31	1.39	1.00	0.99	0.97	0.96	0.87	0.79	0.67	0.64	0.55
Wusong Kou	0.68	0.78	0.60	0.67	0.66	0.64	0.57	0.63	0.53	0.47	0.48
Suzhou Creek											
Zhao Tun	—	—	—	—	—	—	0.81	0.83	1.01	1.20	1.10
Bai He	0.92	1.03	1.91	1.87	1.93	0.88	1.42	1.48	1.03	1.30	1.12
Huang Du	1.03	1.06	0.87	0.93	0.95	0.56	0.73	1.16	0.71	0.87	0.77
Hua Cao	0.73	1.57	0.94	1.10	0.93	0.76	0.62	0.72	0.74	0.88	0.79
Beixingjing Bridge	2.52	1.94	2.89	1.92	1.50	1.54	1.20	0.97	0.82	0.94	0.96
Gubei Road Bridge	n/a	n/a	n/a	n/a	n/a	n/a	1.27	1.28	n/a	n/a	n/a
Wuning Road Bridge	2.33	2.03	1.91	2.73	1.61	1.13	1.01	0.95	0.84	0.95	0.87
Changhua Road Bridge	n/a	n/a	n/a	n/a	n/a	n/a	1.14	0.92	n/a	n/a	n/a
Zhejiang Road Bridge	2.05	1.89	1.54	1.67	1.46	1.19	0.77	0.79	0.83	0.84	0.75

Note: The water quality index (P_i) = $\frac{1}{n}\sum_{i=1}^{n}\frac{C_i}{S_i}$ (the smaller P_i, the better quality).
C_i = concentration of pollutant i
S_i = environmental standard for pollutant i
n = number of pollutants being included in the index
Source: SSB 2007; Shanghai Environmental Protection Bureau (SEPB). The Shanghai Environmental Protection Three-Year Action Plan (SEPAP), 2005–2008.

increased by only 150 percent (table 5). These measures effectively reduced the growth rate of the total industrial waste air emission (table 6), resulting in the decreasing concentration of major air pollutants such as SO_2 and TSP (fig. 14).

SMG also tried to control the increase in the number of automobiles to mitigate the air pollution from transportation. A city regulation became effective in 2001 making license plates for privately owned vehicles available only through public auction. The average bid for a plate exceeded US$6,500 in 2007. In addition, the mass transportation system has been extensively expanded since the early 1990s. The public transportation system (including subways, buses, and company commuting vehicles) now carries over 95 percent of total passengers. Compared

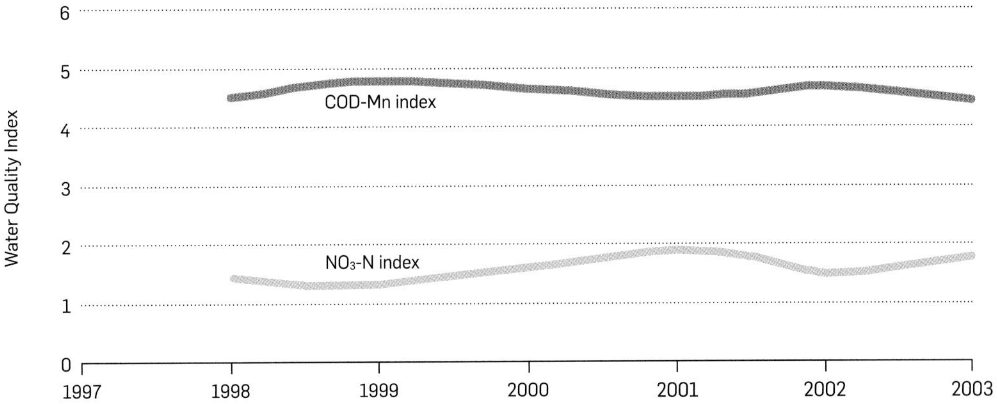

Figure 10. Water quality indices change at Songpu Bridge, Huangpu River, 1997–2002.

Source: SEPB 2007.

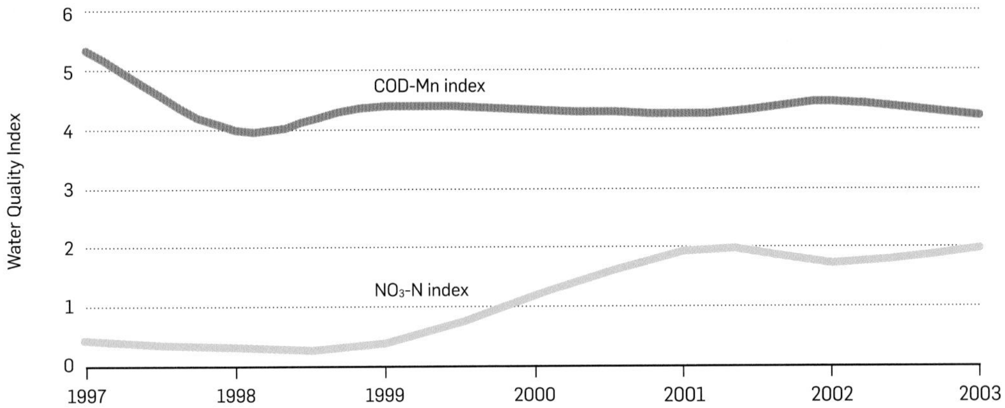

Figure 11. Water quality indices change at Minghang No. 2 Waterworks, Huangpu River, 1997–2002.

Source: SEPB 2007.

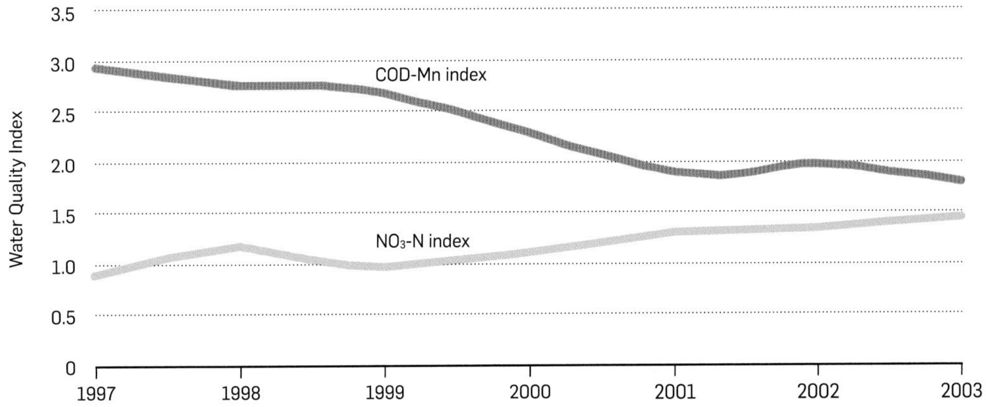

Figure 12. Water quality indices change at Chenghang Reservoir, Changjiang River, 1997–2002.

Source: SEPB 2007.

Table 4. Economic structural change in Shanghai, 1990–2006

	TOTAL GDP (10^8 ¥)	PRIMARY (%)	SECONDARY (%)	TERTIARY (%)
1990	781.66	4.4	64.7	30.9
1991	893.77	3.8	61.6	34.6
1992	1,114.32	3.1	60.8	36.1
1993	1,519.23	2.5	59.4	38.1
1994	1,990.86	2.4	57.7	39.9
1995	2,499.43	2.4	56.8	40.8
1996	2,957.55	2.3	54.0	43.7
1997	3,438.79	2.1	51.6	46.3
1998	3,801.09	1.9	49.3	48.8
1999	4,188.73	1.8	47.4	50.8
2000	4,771.17	1.6	46.3	52.1
2001	5,210.12	1.5	46.1	52.4
2002	5,741.03	1.4	45.7	52.9
2003	6,694.23	1.2	47.9	50.9
2004	8,072.83	1.0	48.2	50.8
2005	9,164.10	1.0	48.6	50.4
2006	10,366.37	0.9	48.5	50.6

Source: SSB 2007.

Table 5. The growth of energy consumption and GDP in Shanghai, 1990–2005

	ENERGY CONSUMPTION CONSUMPTION (10^8 SHORT TON COAL)	ENERGY TERMINAL CONSUMPTION (10^8 SHORT TON COAL)	ENERGY CONSUMPTION GROWTH RATE (%)	TOTAL GDP (10^8 ¥)	GDP GROWTH RATE (%)
1990	2,894.87	2,811.19		781.66	3.5
1991	3,144.76	3,050.73	8.52	893.77	7.1
1992	3,317.48	3,217.18	5.46	1,114.32	14.8
1993	3,580.39	3,432.84	6.70	1,519.23	15.1
1994	3,788.96	3,590.19	4.58	1,990.86	14.5
1995	4,051.35	3,855.92	7.40	2,499.43	14.3
1996	4,196.81	3,970.16	2.96	2,957.55	13.1
1997	4,317.11	4,087.48	2.96	3,438.79	12.8
1998	4,421.70	4,180.40	2.27	3,801.09	10.3
1999	4,644.03	4,444.82	6.33	4,188.73	10.4
2000	4,989.02	4,741.64	6.68	4,771.17	11.0
2001	5,347.63	5,034.57	6.18	5,210.12	10.5
2002	5,669.28	5,351.06	6.29	5,741.03	11.3
2003	6,165.50	5,800.95	8.41	6,694.23	12.3
2004	6,718.25	6,400.23	10.33	8,072.83	14.2
2005	7,320.43	6,996.15	9.31	9,164.10	11.1

Source: SSB 2007.

Table 6. Waste gas emissions in Shanghai, 1990–2006

	TOTAL (10^8 CU. YD.)	INDUSTRIAL (10^8 CU. YD.)		TOTAL (10^8 CU. YD.)	INDUSTRIAL (10^8 CU. YD.)		TOTAL (10^8 CU. YD.)	INDUSTRIAL (10^8 CU. YD.)
1990	4,624	N/A	1996	6,712	6,222	2002	10,335	9,731
1991	6,039	5,232	1997	6,865	6,219	2003	10,975	10,201
1992	6,684	5,779	1998	7,185	6,425	2004	12,381	11,554
1993	5,534	5,047	1999	7,168	6,470	2005	11,906	11,094
1994	5,986	5,472	2000	8,368	7,527	2006	13,138	12,331
1995	6,664	6,049	2001	9,967	9,109			

Source: SSB 2006.

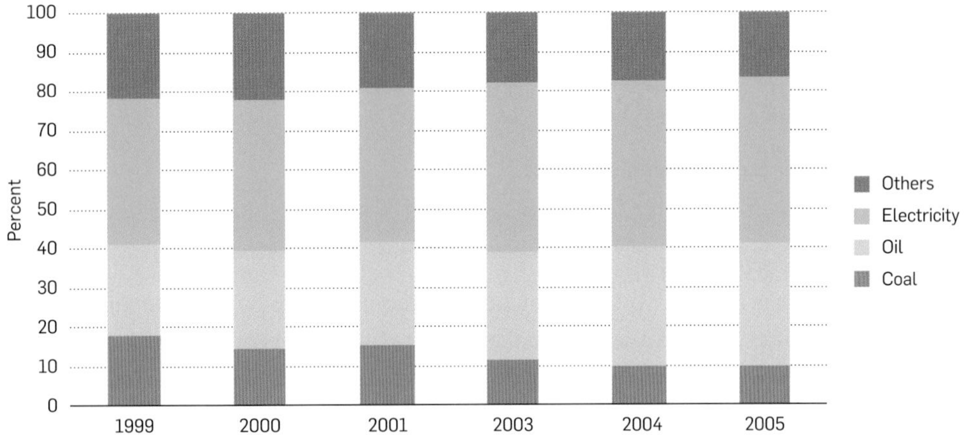

Figure 13. Structural changes in energy consumption in Shanghai, 1999–2005.

Source: SSB 2007.

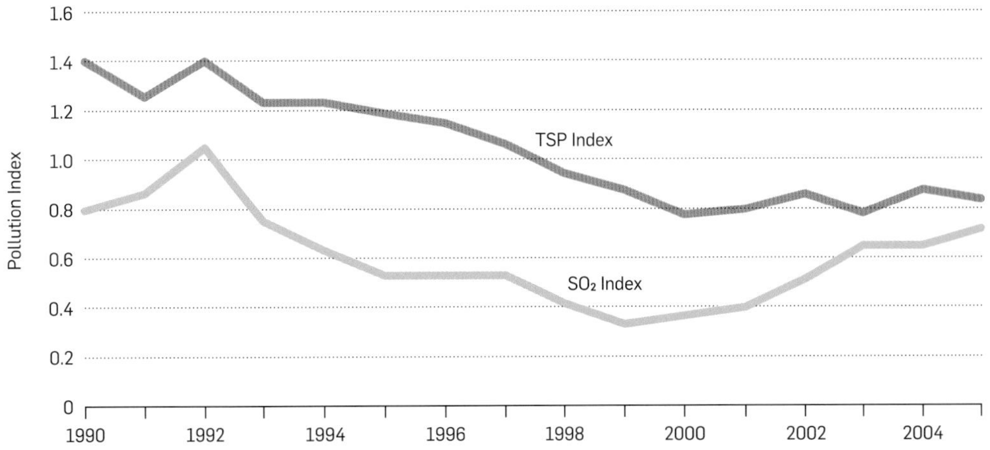

Figure 14. SO_2 and TSP pollution indices in Shanghai, 1990–2005.

Source: SSB 2007.

Table 7. Automobile-related air pollutant emissions in Shanghai, 1990–2003

	1990	1991	1992	1993	1994	1995	1996	2000	2003
Total vehicles (10,000)	21.2	22.9	26.6	32.1	37.4	37.86	41.68	100.32	171.04
CO (10^8 cu. yd.)	9.55	10.03	10.28	15.30	18.97	n/a	n/a	n/a	70.89
NOx (10^8 cu. yd.)	2.26	2.34	2.32	3.15	3.45	3.98	6.49	11.25	11.25

Sources: SAES 2006; SEMC 2006; SAES 2004.

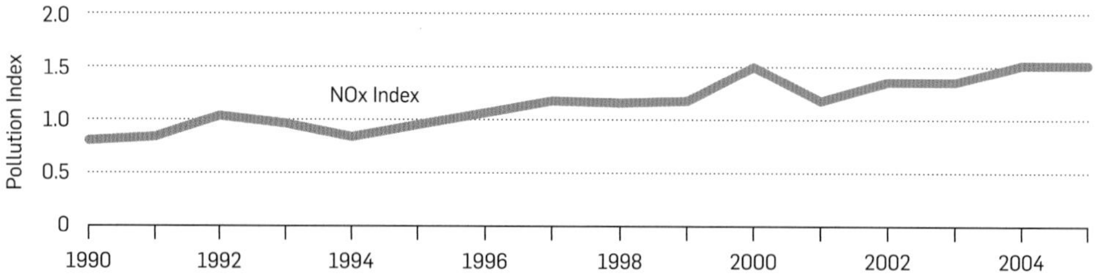

Figure 15. NOx pollution index in Shanghai, 1990–2005.

Source: SEPB 2007.

to Beijing, Shanghai has far fewer privately-owned automobiles, both by absolute and per capita measures, although Shanghai has a larger population and a higher level of per capita GDP.

Despite these efforts, however, the number of motorized vehicles in Shanghai increased eight times between 1990 and 2003. During the same period, motor vehicle-related NOx and NMHC emissions increased 373 percent and 393 percent, respectively. The NOx pollution index increased constantly from 0.8 in 1990 to about 1.4 in 2005 (fig. 15). It is also noteworthy that automobile ownership in Shanghai exceeded that of Seoul and Tokyo when they were at the same per capita GDP as Shanghai many years earlier. Thus the air pollution caused by the rapid motorization has become an increasingly important environmental burden in the city.[29]

■ LAND USE. Rapid urbanization is probably the most noticeable feature of Shanghai's land use change in the past three decades. The extent of the urbanized area, for example, increased from 255.86 mi^2 in 1987 to 870.51 mi^2 in 2004 (fig. 16). In addition, the rate of urbanization has accelerated, with average annual conversion rates of 6.83 mi^2, 1975–1981; 20.23 mi^2, 1990–1995; and 21.20 mi^2, 2000–2005.[30]

In addition, figures 17 and 18 indicate that land use structure has experienced significant transformation. The main trend of change has been characterized by increasing construction land, forest, and grass, and decreasing arable land, wild land, and water area. From 1987 to 2004, the average annual change of construction land, forest, grass, arable land, wild land, and water area was +30.22 mi^2, +0.45 mi^2, +1.82 mi^2, −24.80 mi^2, −0.51 mi^2, −1.88 mi^2, respectively. Moreover, the rates of change were also quite different among these land use types. For example, arable land has been decreasing at accelerating rates, with average annual changes of 13.35 mi^2 (1987–1990),

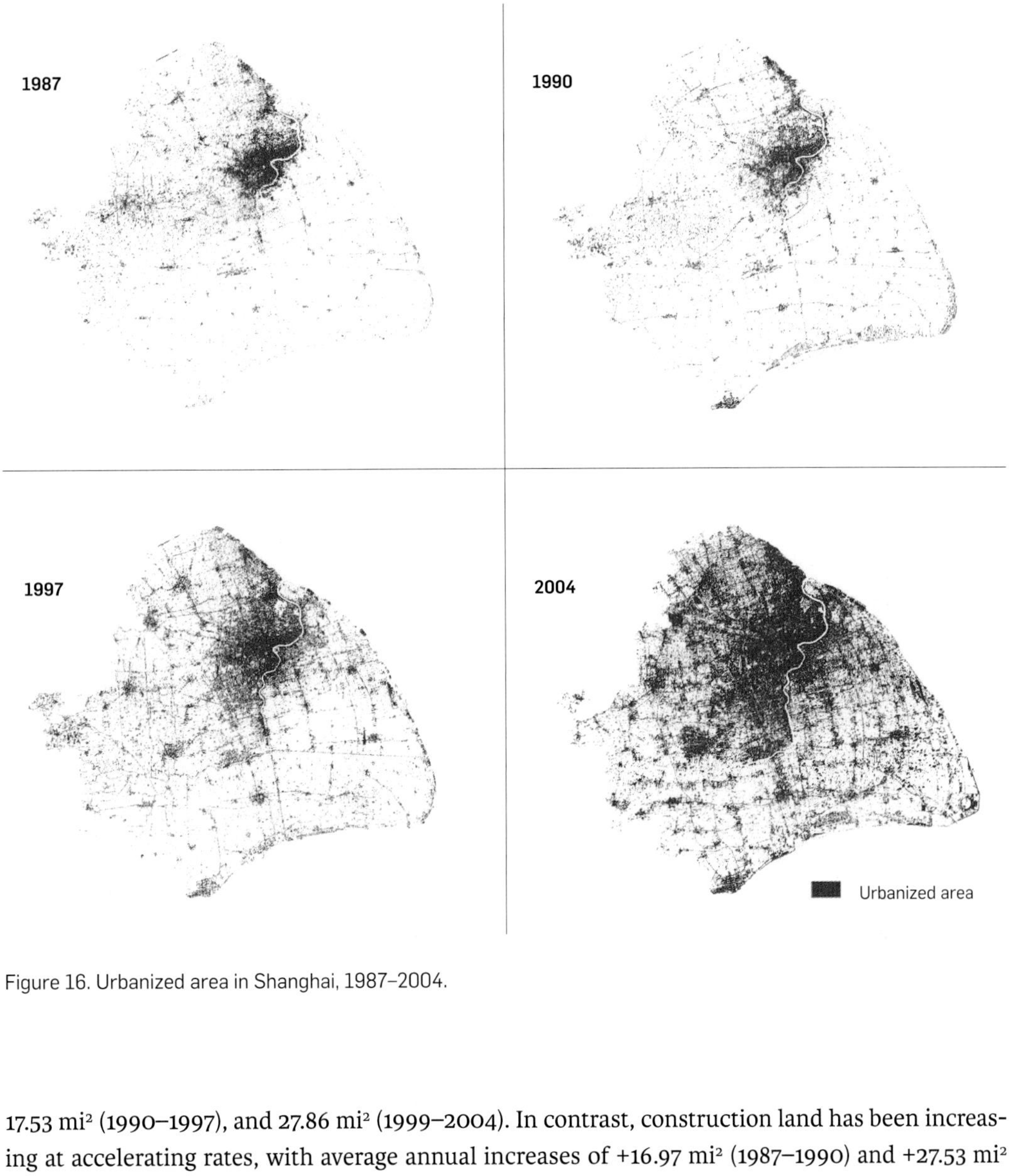

Figure 16. Urbanized area in Shanghai, 1987–2004.

17.53 mi^2 (1990–1997), and 27.86 mi^2 (1999–2004). In contrast, construction land has been increasing at accelerating rates, with average annual increases of +16.97 mi^2 (1987–1990) and +27.53 mi^2 (1999–2004). More data on land use changes can be found in table 8.

Moreover, the extensive urbanization process has also greatly transformed the spatial pattern of land use in Shanghai. The industrial-commercial-residential mixed land use pattern has been rapidly replaced by a new land use pattern featuring the specialization of land use with multinucleation, functional districts and multiple economic development zones. The grand urban redevelopment process, is considered "one of the great urban renewal stories of all time," and has resulted in greatly improved urban infrastructure, housing and living conditions, and urban amenities in general.[31] The negative environmental consequences of the massive urbanization have also been reported, including surface water pollution,[32] loss of ecological heterogeneity,[33] and increased level of energy/materials input and output.[34]

Table 8. Major land uses in Shanghai by area, 1987–2004

	ARABLE LAND (SQ. MI.)	FOREST (SQ. MI.)	GRASS (SQ. MI.)	WATER (SQ. MI.)	CONSTRUCTION LAND (SQ. MI.)	WILD LAND (SQ. MI.)
1987	1,602.2	13.4	4.2	73.1	101.5	16.7
1990	1,562.3	21.1	3.9	58.7	152.4	12.8
1997	1,439.5	25.3	24.3	49.1	350.5	11.8
1999	1,319.8	17.1	31.4	44.4	477.5	10.8
2004	1,180.5	21.1	35.1	41.2	615.1	8.0

Source: Shi 2007.

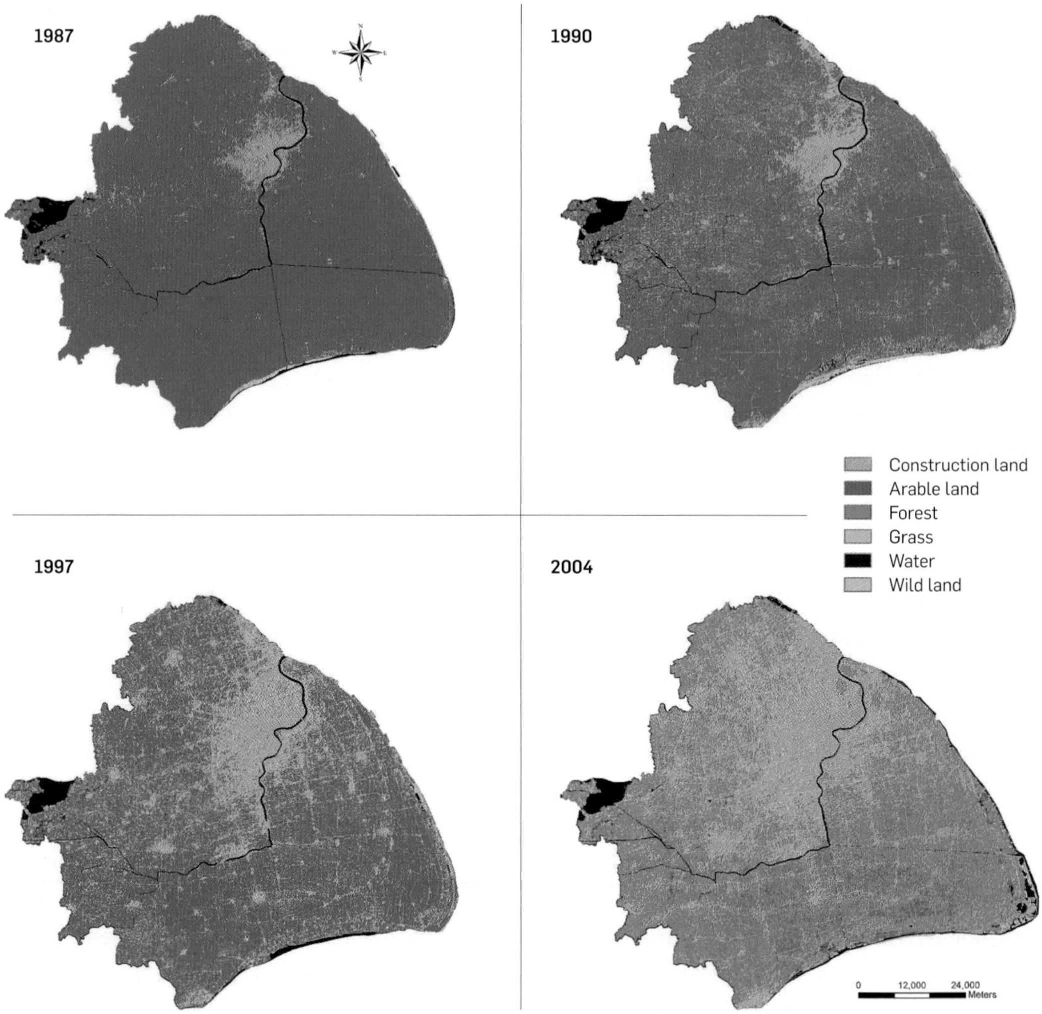

Figure 17. Land use change in Shanghai, 1987—2004.

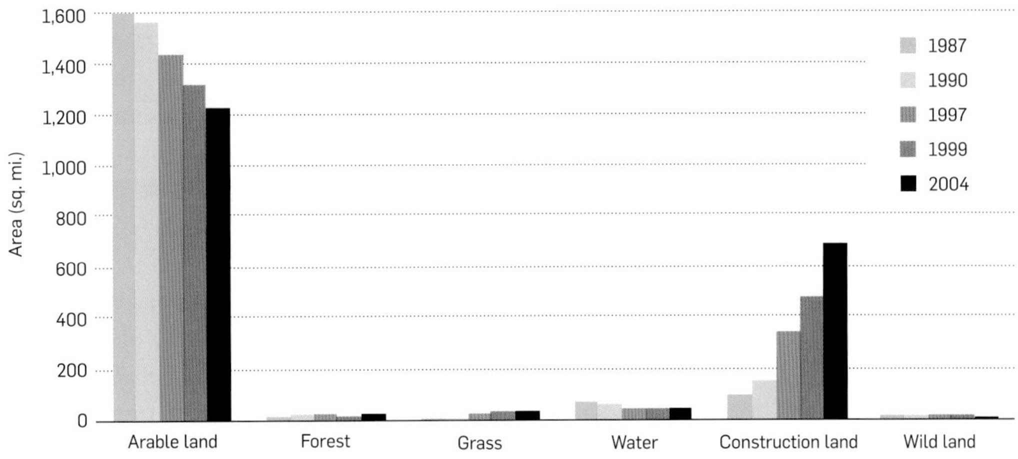

Figure 18. Land use change in Shanghai, 1987–2004 (by categories).

Source: Shi, C., S. M. Hutchinson, L. Yu, and S. Xu. "Towards a Sustainable Coast: An Integrated Coastal Zone Management Framework for Shanghai, People's Republic of China." *Ocean and Coastal Management* 44 (2001): 411–27.

Interurban/Regional Scale

Similar to all the other major cities in the world, Shanghai's urban and economic development has been dependent on its hinterland to obtain natural resources, to dispose of wastes, and to gain lands for expansion. The frequent and large-volume exchange of energy and material flows between Shanghai and its hinterland determines that the environmental burdens of the city would go beyond the city boundary to impact a much larger geographic area. At a regional level, these impacts are reflected most clearly in water and air pollution and the disturbance of ecosystems.[35]

■ WATER. Domestic and industrial wastewater, especially untreated or undertreated, is the major environmental threat to the marine environment of the Changjiang River Estuary and East China Sea. Shanghai generated more than 2.43 billion short tons of wastewater from both industrial and domestic sources in 2006. Part of the wastewater was collected by a centralized urban sewage system and after preliminary treatment discharged into the Changjiang River Estuary through deepwater outfalls. Currently, more than 3.14 million cu. yd. wastewater flows daily through Shidongkou, Zhuyuan, and Bailonggang outlets into the estuary (fig. 4).[36]

Many recent studies have associated the pollution of Changjiang River Estuary and East China Sea with wastewater discharge from Shanghai. Liu and his colleagues (2002), for example, found that the water body near Zhuyuan and Bailonggang outlets was in serious eutrophication status, with high concentrations of nitrogen, phosphorus, and COD. The same study also found that eutrophication in Changjiang River Estuary as a whole was much less severe but was increasing. Moreover, phase 3 of Shanghai Sewage Project (SSP3) will add 1.96 million cu. yd. more wastewater per day into the estuary after completion. The increased volume of wastewater may significantly worsen the water quality in not only the Changjiang River Estuary but also the Hangzhou Bay to the South if no further treatment measures other than preliminary treatment are provided. In addition, heavy metal concentrations (e.g., Fe, Zn, Ni, Mg, Co, and Mn) in the coastal and estuary sediments are actually much lower than expected. This may be explained by the strong diluting effects of the huge runoff and sediment flows from Changjiang and a relatively short period of industrialization in Shanghai and China.[37]

Nonpoint pollution from urban runoff, agricultural and aquacultural activities, animal husbandry farms, and small industries in rural areas, although much less studied, also contributes a considerable amount of pollutants to the urban hinterland. It is reported that about 145 short tons of pesticides in 2000 and an annual average of 18,530 short tons of nitrogen entered into the environment from the farmlands between 1996 to 2000.[38] Another study estimates that about 292,112 short tons of COD_{Cr}, 97,003 short tons of BOD_5, and 14,330 tons of NH_3 were contributed by nonpoint pollution sources in 2002.[39] The long-term regional environmental burden from nonpoint sources pollution has also been reported. For example, the concentrations of dichlorodiphenyltrichloroethane (DDTs) and hexachloro-cyclohexane (HCHs) are fairly high in the suspended matter of the Changjiang River Estuary and along the Zhejiang coastal area, although the applications of the two pollutants peaked between the 1960s and the 1980s.[40]

In addition, as the world's largest port, the Port of Shanghai handled a total of 592 million short tons of cargo in 2006. With the opening operation of the new Yangshan deep-water port in 2006,[41] the potential oil contamination associated with busy water transportation may become another important environmental concern to the regional water environment.

■ AIR POLLUTION. Similar to water pollution, air pollution is subject to the impact of cross-scale effects. The spatial effects of air pollution are in fact more challenging to identify and manage because the difficulty in defining individual "air sheds." Shanghai's air pollution certainly affects a much larger area than the city itself. According to one study, the mean concentration of NO, NO_x, SO_2, and CO in the six selected sites in the Changjiang River Delta region were all much higher than their background levels,[42] indicating the regional atmospheric environment has been contaminated by anthropogenic pollutants.[43] With a total of 1,233.1 billion cu. yd. industrial waste gas emissions in 2006, Shanghai is apparently one of the major air pollution sources in the region. One piece of evidence is the formation of a heat island in the Changjiang River Delta region relative to its adjacent regions and an urban heat sub-island in Shanghai in relation to the Changjiang River Delta region.[44] In addition, research has found a link between the SO_2 emission in Shanghai and the increasing acid rain events in the Changjiang River Delta.[45] Air pollution–related economic loss was also studied, and it was estimated that the yield of winter wheat in the Yangtze River Delta in 1999 and 2000 were reduced by about 20–30 percent due to the exposure to ambient ozone.[46]

■ URBANIZATION. About 62 percent of the land area of Shanghai was obtained from land reclamation, and close to 30.89 square miles of land were reclaimed in the past fifty years.[47] The urbanization induced regional environmental impacts that are mainly reflected in the damage of the vulnerable wildlife habitat and wetlands, reductions in biodiversity, and coastal erosion.[48] In the Sheshan area, the number of plant species has fallen from 535 in the 1980s to 254 by the end of the

1990s.[49] On Dajinshan Island, plant species declined rapidly from 254 in the 1980s to 145 in 2000.[50] The population of whistling swans wintering in the Chongming Island has been reduced from a few thousands in the 1980s to a few dozen at the beginning of the new millennium.[51] The severe shoreline retreat in the south coast adjacent to Hangzhou Bay has also been reported.[52] Moreover, the significant increase of urban green areas has come together with the increasing number of alien species and the loss of landscape heterogeneity.[53]

Global Scale

At the intra-urban and interurban levels, the analyses of urban environmental impacts emphasize the pressures caused by industrialization and urban development patterns in the city and its surrounding regions. At the global level, the focus is on the worldwide environmental consequences and resource depletion that are closely related to urban settlers' lifestyles and consumption. The analyses at a global level are especially important to more affluent urban settlements, considering their relatively high levels of energy/material use and waste production.[54] As Shanghai grows larger and becomes wealthier, the environmental impacts of the city at the global scale will become increasingly significant. For example, one study reports that per capita CO_2 emission (to provide goods and services for city residents) in Shanghai in 1997 was very close to Tokyo's level in 1995.[55] Thus it is necessary to examine Shanghai's environmental burdens at the global scale in addition to the analyses conducted at the other two spatial scales.

With a de facto population of more than 20 million and a rapidly increasing per capita consumption, Shanghai's ecological footprint (EF) and ecological deficiency (ED) have been increasing continuously since 1980. Compared to 1980 levels, Shanghai's EF and ED in 2003 increased 136 percent and 145 percent, respectively.[56] It is almost certain that Shanghai's total population and per capita consumption will continue to increase.[57] As a result, Shanghai's EF and ED will keep growing, and the only solution to balance the ED is to import carrying capacity from other regions in the world. In other words, the continuous economic and population growth and urban development in Shanghai will exert increasing environmental impacts globally. However, these global impacts have not been explicitly addressed in Shanghai's current environmental initiatives.

Summarizing Urban Environmental Burdens and Management Practices within the Context of Scale

Clearly, the environmental agenda of Shanghai in the past thirty years has been focused on the problems within the city's boundaries. Most of the efforts and resources were utilized to mitigate industrial pollution, upgrade environmental infrastructure, and restructure the urban economy. As a result, the environmental burdens at the intra-urban level have been effectively relieved. The ambient water and air quality has been generally improved, and the urban land use has been greatly transformed to a more environmentally friendly and economically efficient pattern.

The environmental problems at the regional level, however, were given a much lower priority and far less attention. The limited regional environmental measures tend to be piecemeal and passive. For example, the treatment facilities at the Zhuyuan and Bailonggang outlets were completed years after the sewage collecting system had started to collect and discharge wastewater into the Changjiang River Estuary, and these facilities provide only preliminary treatment to wastewater. The neglect of interurban/regional level problems has led to progressive displacement of environmental burdens from the central city to the suburbs, the larger urban hinterland, coastal ecosystems, and the entire Changjiang River Delta region.

Despite the rising EF and ED, Shanghai's environmental agenda seems to be least concerned with the global environmental processes and nonlocal resource depletion caused by a growing urban metabolism. However, Shanghai's local action plan for implementing China's Agenda 21 is an achievement that needs to be highlighted.[58] Although this document is more a political commitment to demonstrate the conformity of SMG to the central government's policy on environmental issues than a concrete environmental action plan, the concept of sustainable development and the local-regional-global nexus of environmental burdens were officially recognized by the policymakers and urban managers in Shanghai.

The environmental evolution in Shanghai over the past thirty years can be understood in the context of both the pro- and postreform political, economic, social, and institutional changes in China.[59] First, to take an end-of-pipe approach and follow a local-regional-global sequence to deal with environmental problems seems to be the only realistic choice for the city managers because of the severe and immediate pollution threats accumulated during Mao's era and the mounting environmental burdens created by the city's breathtaking economic growth.[60]

Second, the overlapping of sectoral (between various governmental agencies at different administrative levels) and regional (between administrative units) authorities and responsibilities on environmental affairs has also complicated environmental management beyond Shanghai's city boundary as the potential powers or interests wrestle among multiple governmental agencies and departments. For example, the Changjiang River Estuary is under the administration of Shanghai, Jiangsu Province, and Zhejiang Province based on a regional division; it is also under the supervision of specialized sectors, such as various levels of the State Oceanographic Administration and the State Environmental Protection Administration.

Third, the decentralization of power brought up by the political reform allows local governments to enjoy more administrative power but also to share much greater revenue responsibility.[61] The increased power and financial pressure of local governments greatly increased the competition among cities and regions. This process encouraged a pro-growth environment, gave local governments both incentives and means to formulate and implement inconsistent or selective environmental policies, and made the cooperation among Shanghai, Zhejiang, and Jiangsu more difficult in dealing with regional environmental problems.

Lastly, certain fundamental features of China's centralized authoritarian political and command economic system have remained almost intact in Shanghai's environmental governance. Under a hierarchical administrative system characterized by "bureaucratic and administrative centralism," the Chinese government dominates almost everything regarding environmental decisions and policymaking, including policy formulation, resource allocation, environmental assessment, and regulation enforcement.[62] This government-centered management style tends to focus on the intra-urban-level issues because local economic growth and improvement in environmental conditions are the only things that matter to the local officials.

Toward a Multiscale Urban Environmental Policy

Shanghai's environmental management during the past thirty years has been marked by a fairly successful pollution mitigation agenda in the urban sphere, a beginning but passive policy at the intra-urban/regional level, and a lack of any sustainable development policy at the global level. Considering Shanghai's political, economic, social, and institutional conditions, a new environmental agenda following a local-regional-global sequence seems to be the only viable choice for urban managers. However, a realistic approach does not mean that it is an optimal solution that will lead Shanghai to the path of sustainable development. If Shanghai is going to create another environmental miracle in the new millennium, the current environmental agenda has to be realigned and reprioritized based on the internal links and interactions of environmental burdens at three geographical scales. Shanghai is having great opportunities but also facing tough obstacles in the shift to a multiscale urban environmental policy.

Opportunities

Since the implementation of the open-door and reform policy in the late 1970s, China has been lurching between a continuous booming economy and a rapidly degrading environment.[63] While it ranked fourth globally in GDP—and had a growth rate of more than two times the world average in 2005[64]—its environmental sustainability index (ESI) was positioned as only 133 among 146 countries in the same year.[65] Facing pressure to confront serious pollution from both domestic and international communities, the central government has made it a national policy to balance economic prosperity, social equality, and environmental sustainability. This policy has been illustrated clearly in such national-level actions as the implementation of Agenda 21 in 1997 and the new Environmental Impact Assessment (EIA) Law that came into effect in 2003.[66] In addition, the State Council released another EIA-related document, "Plan-Level EIA Regulation," in late 2008. Overall, China has been taking a "learning by doing" approach with its social and economic reforms over the past three decades. It is almost certain that Shanghai will receive unreserved support from the central government to develop and experiment with a multi-scale environmental management model due to its prime geographic and economic status in the country.

Despite many problems, Shanghai's environmental management practice has laid a solid foundation to address intra-urban/regional and resulting global environmental burdens, and encouraging changes have been made by urban managers. For example, one of the two major goals of SEPAP05–08 was to reduce total resource consumption. Moreover, a nature reserve was scheduled to be established in the Chongming Island to protect the wetland and wildlife habitat according to SEPAP05–08.[67] In addition, Shanghai was also one of the first Chinese cities/regions to promote and experiment with the concept of the Circular Economy, a recycling-based economy that minimizes material and energy consumption by optimizing product design, restructuring life cycles of products, and recycling wastes from final products.[68] Pursuing the Circular Economy has not only been a key component in SEPAP05–08; it has also been highlighted in the Shanghai Eleventh Five-Year (2006–2010) Plan for Socioeconomic Development.

In addition, many existing studies on global issues suggest that the most effective way to get local governments to mitigate global issues is to encourage them to "think locally, act locally."[69] That is to say, there is the potential to link activities to address local issues with global problems. In fact, some localized strategies implemented by SMG recently have started to address some global environmental stresses such as green house gas (GHG) mitigation. The city policy to limit the quality of motorized vehicles by auctioning license plates for private vehicles and the national regulation of the production and use of plastic shopping bags are two good examples.[70] Although the intention of these local polices might not be to address global issues, they can provide positive environmental outcomes at the global level while controlling local pollution.

Obstacles

Unfortunately, considerable obstacles also exist that may prevent Shanghai from adapting to positive changes toward the implementation of a multi-scale urban environmental agenda. The first concerns the impacts of the postreform political economy on environmental governance. Because the current Chinese political system features a submissive political culture with a significant "rule of persons" (as opposed to "rule of law" in Western democracy) influence, the long-term environmental goals are often compromised in order to yield short-term political and economic gains. Moreover, nongovernment stakeholders play only marginal roles in environmental policymaking and management.

The next obstacle comes from the difficulty in sectoral and regional coordination concerning interurban/regional environmental issues, and this coordination may be further complicated by the regional protectionism exacerbated by the decentralization.

The third obstacle is funding. Shanghai has probably one of the best funded programs for environmental protection among all the provincial level governments in China. However, most of the environmental projects are very costly and do not provide short-term political and economic returns. In addition, policy incentives have not been established to internalize regional environmental costs. Thus the funding issue, especially funding environmental projects that do not directly benefit Shanghai, will hinder the implementation of projects at interurban/regional and higher levels. For example, one of the major reasons that concrete actions have not been followed after the release of the Local Agenda 21 plan in Shanghai may be due to the fact that the central government does not provide specific funding for any local agenda 21 plan.

Conclusions

With a main goal to rapidly alleviate severe industrial pollution, improve overall environmental quality, and upgrade urban amenities within the city boundary, Shanghai's urban environmental management in the past three decades has been focused primarily on the environmental problems at the intra-urban level. This end-of-pipe approach seems to be quite effective in mitigating domestic and industrial pollution that either accumulated during Mao's era or was generated in postreform era Shanghai. However, little has been done to deal with the environmental impacts at either the interurban/regional or global levels. More specifically, neither the spillover effect of Shanghai's environmental burdens nor the impact of Shanghai's production and consumption on global environmental processes and distant resource exploitation are carefully analyzed and considered in the environmental agendas.

It seems that SMG does not have a better option than following this local-regional-global sequence to formulate and implement environmental policies considering the political economy in postreform China. However, the much delayed or even ignored environmental policies in dealing with the environmental issues in the other two spatial scales has led to the geographic displacement of pollution and the mounting of EF and DF in the past three decades. Thus the major problem with urban environmental management in Shanghai is neither the lack of interest and attention of the central government nor the scarcity of capital and resources, but the lack of vision and expertise of the local government to establish and implement a multiscale urban environmental policy that can assess and address urban environmental impacts at a variety of geographic scales.

Entering a new millennium, China is lurching between a continuous economic growth and accelerating resource consumption and environmental degradation. Thus the successful transformation of Shanghai's current environmental policy, with a primary focus on intra-urban issues into a multiscale approach, will help Shanghai and hopefully other Chinese cities and regions to better gauge their development goals to achieve both socioeconomic and environmental sustainability. The support and cooperation from the central government, other local governments, and governmental agencies are essential to assist Shanghai in overcoming considerable political, institutional, and financial barriers to develop and carry out such policies. Standing at the forefront of China's reform and open policies, Shanghai's environmental policy will affect the future environment of Shanghai, the rest of China, and even the rest of the world.

NOTES

The authors would like to thank Xiaoxue Shi, Huijuan Han, and Wenjie Bao for their research assistance. We are also indebted to two manuscript reviewers and the book editor, Igor Vojnovic, for their constructive comments and suggestions on an earlier draft. Analyses and opinions in this article are entirely the responsibility of the authors.

1. J. M. Cai and V. F. S. Sit, Measuring World City Formation—The Case of Shanghai, *Annals of Regional Science* 37:3 (2003): 435–46; Institute of Chinese City Competition Capacity Studies (ICCCCS), Chinese City Competition Capacity Rank, 2003, *Information for Decision-makers* 2 (2004): 29 (in Chinese).
2. D. Satterthwaite, Sustainable Cities or Cities that Contribute to Sustainable Development, in *Sustainable Cities*, ed. D. Satterthwaite, 89–106 (London: Earthscan, 1999); X. Bai and H. Imura, A Comparative Study of Urban Environment in East Asia: Stage Model of Urban Environmental Evolution, *International Review for Environmental Strategies* 1:1 (2000): 135–58.
3. G. McGranahan, An Overview of Urban Environmental Burdens at Three Scales: Intra-urban, Urban-Regional, and Global, *International Review for Environmental Strategies* 5:2 (2005): 335–56; ed. P. J. Marcotullio and G. McGranahan, *Scaling Urban Environmental Challenges: From Local to Global and Back* (London: Earthscan Publications, 2007).
4. P. Abelson, Economic and Environmental Sustainability in Shanghai, in *Sustainable Cities in Developing Countries: Theory and Practice at the Millennium*, ed. C. Pugh, 185–202 (Earthscan: London, 2000); W. Tu and C. Shi, Urban Environmental Management in Shanghai: Achievements, Problems, and Prospects, *Environmental Management* 37:3 (2006): 307–21.
5. R. M. Ward and W. Liang, Shanghai Water Supply and Wastewater Disposal, *Geographical Review* 85 (1995): 141–56; G. Wu and C. Shi, Shanghai's Water

Environment, in *The Dragon's Head: Shanghai, China's Emerging Megacity*, ed. H. Foster, D. Lai, N. Zhou, 93–104 (Victoria, Canada: Western Geographical Press, 1998); W. Ren, Y. Zhong, J. Meligrana, B. Anderson, W. E. Watt, J. Chen, and H. L. Leung, Urbanization, Land Use, and Water Quality in Shanghai: 1947–1996, *Environment International* 29:1 (2003): 649–59; H. Kan, Chen B., C. Chen, Q. Fu, and M. Chen, An Evaluation of Public Health Impact of Ambient Air Pollution under Various Energy Scenarios in Shanghai, China, *Atmospheric Environment* 38:1 (2004): 95–102.

6. S. Hoyle, S. Power, and S. Hutchison, Environmental Impact Assessment in the People's Republic of China: A Case Study of the Shanghai Second Sewerage Project, *Environmentalist* 19 (1999): 251–57; L. X. Gu and W. R. Sheate, Institutional Challenges for EIA Implementation in China: A Case Study of Development versus Environmental Protection, *Environmental Management* 36 (2005): 125–42.
7. L. G. Ying and H. T. Kung, Forecasting up to Year 2000 on Shanghai's Environment Quality, *Environment Monitoring and Assessment* 63 (2000): 297–312; D. Gielenand C. Chen, The CO2 Emission Reduction Benefits of Chinese Energy Policies and Environmental Policies: A Case Study of Shanghai, Period 1995–2020, *Ecological Economics* 39 (2001): 257–70; W. Yuan and P. James, Evolution of the Shanghai City Region 1978–1998: An Analysis of Indicators, *Journal of Environmental Management* 64:3 (2002): 299–309; http://dx.doi.org/10.1016/j.compenvurbsys.2003.10.001 Z. Y. Yin, S. Walcott, B. Kaplan, J. Cao, W. Q. Lin, M. J. Chen, D. S. Liu, and Y. M. Ning, An Analysis of the Relationship between Spatial Patterns of Water Quality and Urban Development in Shanghai, China, *Computers, Environment and Urban Systems* 29:2 (2005): 197–221.
8. Other types of scale, such as temporal scale, are also critical in environmental studies, but they are beyond the scope of this paper. Scale refers to spatial scale in the rest of the paper unless otherwise explained.
9. Turner, B. L. II, R. E. Kasperson, W. B. Meyer, K. M. Dow, D. Golding, J. X. Kasperson, R. C. Mitchell, and S. J. Ratick, Two Types of Global Environmental Changes: Definitional and Special-Scale Issues in Their Human Dimensions, *Global Environmental Change* 1 (1990): 14–22; S. H. Schneider and T. L. Root, Ecological Implications of Climate Change Will Include Surprises, *Biodiversity and Conservation* 5 (1996): 1109–19; Rediscovering Geography Committee (RGC), Rediscovering Geography: New Relevance, in *Science and Society* (Washington, DC: National Academies Press, 1997); T. J. Wilbanks and R.W. Kates, Global Change in Local Places: How Scale Matters, *Climatic Change* 43:3 (1999): 601–28; Millennium Ecosystem Assessment (MEA), *Ecosystems and Human Well-Being: A Framework for Assessment* (Washington, DC: Island Press, 2003); R. B. McMaster and E. Sheppard, Introduction: Scale and Geographic Inquiry, in *Scale and Geographic Inquiry: Nature, Society, and Method*, ed. E. S. Sheppard and R. B. McMaster (Oxford: Blackwell, 2004), 1–22.
10. T. J. Wilbanks and R. W. Kates, Global Change in Local Places: How Scale Matters, *Climatic Change* 43:3 (1999): 601–28.
11. McGranahan, An Overview of Urban Environmental Burdens at Three Scales.
12. The concept of urban metabolism draws an analogy with the metabolic processes of organisms. In practice, the study of an urban metabolism requires quantification of the inputs, outputs, and storage of energy, water, nutrients, materials, and wastes in cities. E. H. Decker, S. Elliott, F. A. Smith, D. R. Blake, and F. S. Rowland, Energy and Material Flow through the Urban Ecosystem, *Annual Review of Energy and the Environment* 25 (2000): 685–740; C.A. Kennedy, J. Cuddihy, and J. Engel-Yan, The Changing Metabolism of Cities, *Journal of Industrial Ecology* 11:2 (2007): 43–59.
13. X. Baiand H. Imura, A Comparative Study of Urban Environment in East Asia: Stage Model of Urban Environmental Evolution, *International Review for Environmental Strategies* 1:1 (2000): 135–58; G. McGranahan and D. Satterthwaite, The Environmental Dimensions of Sustainable Development for Cities, *Geography* 87 (2002): 213–26.
14. Shanghai Statistical Bureau (SSB), *Shanghai Statistics Year Book, 1990–2007* (Shanghai: Shanghai Statistic Press, 2007).
15. Y. Yeung, Introduction, in *Shanghai: Transformation and Modernization under China's Open Door Policy*, ed. Y. Yeung and Y. W. Sung (Hong Kong: Hong Kong Chinese University Press, 1996), 2–23; F. Wu, Place Promotion in Shanghai, PRC, *Cities* 17:5 (2000): 349–61.
16. Yeung, Introduction, in *Shanghai*.; W. Wu, City Profile: Shanghai, *Cities* 16:3 (1999): 207–16; F. Wu, Place Promotion in Shanghai, PRC, *Cities* 17:5 (2000): 349–61.
17. Wu, Place Promotion in Shanghai.
18. I. Szelenyi, Cities under Socialism—And After, in *Cities after Socialism*, ed. G. Andrusz, M. Harloe, and I. Szelenyi (Oxford: Blackwell, 1996), 286–317; F.

Wu, The Transformation of Urban Space in Chinese Transitional Economy: With Special Reference to Shanghai, in *The New Chinese City: Globalization and Market Reform*, ed. John R. Logan (Oxford: Blackwell Publishers, 2002), 154–66.
19. S. S. Han, Shanghai between State and Market in Urban Transformation, *Urban Studies* 37:11 (2000): 2091–112.
20. F. F. Deng, Development Zones and Urban Land Reform in China, *Asian Geographer* 22:1–2 (2003): 5–25; F. Wu, Urban Restructuring in China's Emerging Market Economy: Towards a Framework for Analysis, *International Journal of Urban and Regional Research* 21:4 (1997): 640–63.
21. X. He, Development of Pudong and Optimization of Urban Area Structure in Shanghai, *Chinese Environment and Development* 4 (1993): 68–89; Z. Zhang and D. Zhang, Pudong Development and the Establishment of Shanghai's Position as the Center of Trade, *Journal of Asian Economics* 6:2 (1995): 279–89; S. Walcott and W. Xiao, High-tech Parks and Development Zones in Metropolitan Shanghai: From the Industrial to the Information Age, *Asian Geographer* 19 (2000):157–79.
22. Shanghai Statistical Bureau (SSB), *Shanghai Statistics 2005* (Shanghai: Shanghai Statistic Press, 2007).
23. F. Wu, Place Promotion in Shanghai, PRC, *Cities* 17:5 (2000): 349–61; Shanghai Municipal Housing, Land and Resource Administration Bureau, *Shanghai Land Use Master Plan (1996–2010)* (Shanghai: Municipal Housing, Land and Resource Administration Bureau, 1997).
24. Shanghai Environmental Protection Bureau (SEPB), *Shanghai Environmental Protection Three-Year Action Plan (SEPAP)*, 2005–2008, http://www.envir.gov.cn/info/2006/1/112278.htm.
25. P. Abelson, Economic and Environmental Sustainability in Shanghai, in *Sustainable Cities in Developing Countries: Theory and Practice at the Millennium*, ed. C. Pugh (London: Earthscan, 2000), 185–202.
26. G. Wu. and C. Shi, Shanghai's Water Environment, in *The Dragon's Head: Shanghai, China's Emerging Megacity*, ed. H. Foster, D. Lai, and N. Zhou, 93–104 (Victoria, Canada: Western Geographical Press, 1998).
27. According to GB3808–202, Class IV water is defined to be suitable for industrial or entertainment purpose only, but it is not suitable for direct contact with the human body. X. Bai, X. Zhang, Q. Sun, X. Wang, and B. Zhu, Effect of Water Source Pollution on the Water Quality of Shanghai Water Supply System, *Journal of Environmental Science and Earth*, Part A 1:7 (2006): 127–80.
28. A. E. Cha, In China, a Green Awakening, *Washington Post Foreign Service*, October 6, 2007, A01, http://www.washingtonpost.com/wp-dyn/content/article/2007/10/05/AR2007100502472_pf.html.
29. S. Dhakal, *Urban Energy Use and Greenhouse Gas Emissions in Asian Mega-cities: Policies for a Sustainable Future* (Japan, Kitakyush: Institute for Global Environmental Strategies, 2004), 123.
30. S. Zhao, L. Da, Z. Tang, H. Fang, K. Song, and J. Fang, Ecological Consequences of Rapid Urban Expansion: Shanghai, China, *Frontiers in Ecology and the Environment* 4:7 (2006): 341–46.
31. P. Yatsko, Work in Progress, *Far Eastern Economic Review* 7 (1997): 66–69; W. Wu, City Profile: Shanghai, *Cities* 16:3 (1999): 207–16; F. Wu, The Global and Local Dimension of Place-making: Remaking Shanghai as a World City, *Urban Studies* 37:8 (2000): 1359–77.
32. W. Ren, Y. Zhong, J. Meligrana, B. Anderson, W. E. Watt, J. Chen, and H. L. Leung, Urbanization, Land Use, and Water Quality in Shanghai: 1947–1996, *Environment International* 29:1 (2003): 649–59; http://dx.doi.org/10.1016/j.compenvurbsys.2003.10.001 Z. Y. Yin, S. Walcott, B. Kaplan, J. Cao, W. Q. Lin, M. J. Chen, D. S. Liu, and Y. M. Ning, An Analysis of the Relationship between Spatial Patterns of Water Quality and Urban Development in Shanghai, China, *Computers, Environment and Urban Systems* 29:2 (2005): 197–221.
33. L. Kong, J. Chen, N. Nakagoshi, and B. Zhao, The Impact of Urban Planning on Land Use and Land Cover in Pudong of Shanghai, China, *Journal of Environmental Sciences* 15:2 (2003): 205–14.
34. Gao Chengkang, Jiang Dahe, Wang Dan, and Yan Jonathan, Calculation of Ecological Footprint Based on Modified Method and Quantitative Analysis of Its Impact Factors: A Case Study of Shanghai, *Chinese Geographical Science* 16 (2006):4.
35. E. H. Decker, S. Elliott, F. A. Smith, D. R. Blake, and F. S. Rowland, Energy and Material Flow through the Urban Ecosystem, *Annual Review of Energy and the Environment* 25 (2000): 685–740.
36. C. Liu, H. E. Yun, J. H. Lee, and Z. Wang, Numerical Study on Environmental Impacts of the Third Shanghai Sewage Project, *International Journal of Sediment Research* 17:2 (2002): 165–73.
37. W. Zhang, L. Yu, S. M. Hutchinson, S. Xu, Z. Chen, and X. Gao, China's Yangtze Estuary: I. *Geomorphic Influence on Heavy Metal Accumulation in Intertidal Sediments Geomorphology* 41:2–3 (2001): 195–205;

Z. Chen, Y. Saito, Y. Kanai, T. Wei, L. Li, H. Yao, and Z. Wang, Low Concentration of Heavy Metals in the Yangtze Estuarine Sediments, China: A Diluting Setting Estuarine, *Coastal and Shelf Science* 60:1 (2004): 91–100.

38. G. F. Mao, Current Situation of Non-point Source Pollution of Chemical Fertilizer and Pesticide in Shanghai and Approach to Controlling Ways, *Acta Agriculturae Shanghai* 18:3 (2002): 56–60.
39. Z. X. Xu, S. F. Huang, and Z. C. Yan, Study on Non-point Source Pollution Load in Shanghai, *Shanghai Environmental Sciences* 22:z1 (2003): 112–16.
40. J. F. Chen, X. Xia, X. R. Ye, and H. Y. Jin, Marine Organic Pollution History in the Changjiang Estuary and Zhejiang Coastal Area—HCHs and DDTs Stratigraphical Records, *Marine Pollution Bulletin* 45:1–12 (2002): 391–96.
41. Asia Times, Shanghai Now the World's Largest Cargo Port, January 7, 2006, http://www.atimes.com/atimes/China_Business/HA07Cb02.html.
42. In the common practice of Environmental Impact Assessment (EIA), background level is defined as the concentration of a pollutant in an area before any significant anthropogenic impact has occurred.
43. H. X. Wang, X. Y. Tang, M. L. Wang, P. Yang, T. Wang, K. S. Shao, L. M. Zeng, H. F. Du, and L. M. Chen, Characteristics of Observed Trace Gases Pollutants in the Yangtze Delta, *Science in China* (Series D) 46 (2003): 397–404.
44. L. X. Chen, W. L. Li, W. Q. Zhu, X. J. Zhou, Z. J. Zhou, and H. L. Liu, Seasonal Trends of Climate Change in the Yangtze Delta and Its Adjacent Regions and Their Formation Mechanisms, *Meteorology and Atmospheric Physics* 92:1–2 (2006): 11–23.
45. V. N. Bashkin, *Environmental Chemistry: Asian Lessons* (Netherlands: Springer, 2003), 480.
46. H. X. Wang, C. S. Kiang, X. Tang, X. Zhou, and W. L. Chameides, Surface Ozone: A Likely Threat to Crops in Yangtze Delta of China, *Atmospheric Environment* 39:21 (2005): 3843–50.
47. J. Li, H. Xu, and H. Shen, A Research on the Exploitation of the Tidal Flats in Shanghai, International Geography Symposium: China and the World in the 21st Century, Hong Kong, 1998.
48. C. Shi, S. M. Hutchinson, L. Yu, and S. Xu, Towards a Sustainable Coast: An Integrated Coastal Zone Management Framework for Shanghai, People's Republic of China, *Ocean and Coastal Management* 44 (2001): 411–27.
49. B. S. Xu, S. H. Ou, and B. S. Yang, *Flora of Shanghai* (Shanghai: Shanghai Scientific and Technology and Document Press, 1999).
50. Y. C. Yang, L. J. Da, and X. K. Qin, A Study of the Flora on Dajinshan Island in Shanghai, *Chinese Journal of Wuhan Botanical Research* 20 (2002): 433–37.
51. X. Z. Yuan, H. Liu, J. J. Lu, The Ecological and Environmental Characteristics and Conservation of the Wetlands in the Changjiang Estuary, China, *Environmentalist* 22:4 (2002): 311–18.
52. X. Chen and Y. Zong, Coastal Erosion along the Changjiang Deltatic Shoreline, China: History and Prospective, *Estuarine, Coastal and Shelf Science* 46 (1998): 733–42.
53. L. Kong, J. Chen, N. Nakagoshi, and B. Zhao, The Impact of Urban Planning on Land Use and Land Cover in Pudong of Shanghai, China, *Journal of Environmental Sciences* 15:2 (2003): 205–14; L. J. Da, H. J. Fang, and X. X. Chen, *Woody Plant Species in Green Lands in Shanghai. Special Report on Investigation of Woody Plant Species in the Urban Area in Shanghai* (Shanghai: East China Normal University, 2005).
54. McGranahan, An Overview of Urban Environmental Burdens.
55. S. Dhakal, *Urban Energy Use and Greenhouse Gas Emissions in Asian Mega-cities: Policies for a Sustainable Future* (Japan, Kitakyush: Institute for Global Environmental Strategies, 2004), 123.
56. C. K. Gao, D. H. Jiang, D. Wang, and J. Yan, Calculation of Ecological Footprint Based on Modified Method and Quantitative Analysis of Its Impact Factors: A Case Study of Shanghai, *Chinese Geographical Science* 16:4 (2006): 306–13.
57. X. Peng, X. Guo, and H. X. Han, Future Prospects for Population Development in Shanghai: A Population Carrying Capacity Analysis, *Asian Population Studies* 1:3 (2005): 261–81.
58. W. Wang, Thoughts on Further Implementing China's Agenda 21, ACCA21 Newsletter, April 1999, http://www.acca21.org.cn/jx2e.html.
59. P. Gaubatz, China's Urban Transformation: Patterns and Processes of Morphological Change in Beijing, Shanghai and Guangzhou, *Urban Studies* 36:9 (1999): 1495–1521; W. Mao and P. Hills, Impacts of the Economic-Political Reform on Environmental Impact Assessment Implementation in China, *Impact Assessment and Project Appraisal* 20:2 (2002): 101–11.
60. An "end-of-pipe" approach uses technology to control pollutant releases or transfers from the manufacturing step of the product life cycle.
61. L. Gan, Implementation of Agenda 21 in China: Institutions and Obstacles, *Environmental Politics* 8:1 (1999): 318–26.
62. C. W. H. Lo, P. K. To, and K. C. Yip, The Regulatory Style of Environmental Governance in China:

The Case of EIA Regulation in Shanghai, *Public Administration and Development* 20:4 (2000): 305–18; E.N. Toteng, Urban Environmental Management in Botswana: Toward a Theoretical Explanation of Public Policy Failure, *Environmental Management* 28:1 (2001): 19–30.

63. J. Liu and J. Diamond, China's Environment in a Globalizing World, *Nature* 435 (2005): 1129–86.
64. The World Bank, China Data and Statistics, 2007, http://web.worldbank.org/WBSITE/EXTERNAL/COUNTRIES/EASTASIAPACIFICEXT/CHINAEXTN/0,,contentMDK:20601872~menuPK:318976~pagePK:141137~piPK:141127~theSitePK:318950,00.html.
65. Environmental Sustainability Index (ESI), 2005 Environmental Sustainability Index (ESI) Report, 2007, http://sedac.ciesin.columbia.edu/es/esi/.
66. L. Gan, Implementation of Agenda 21 in China: Institutions and Obstacles, *Environmental Politics* 8:1 (1999): 318–26; N. Stender, D. Wang, and J. Zhou, Impacting the Environment: China's New EIA Law, 2003, http://www.coudert.com/publications/articles/030115_14_eia_clp.pdf.
67. Shanghai Environmental Protection Bureau (SEPB), Shanghai Environmental Protection Three-Year Action Plan (SEPAP), 2005–2008, http://www.envir.gov.cn/info/2006/1/112278.htm.
68. N. Nakajima, A Vision of Industrial Ecology: State-of-the-Art Practices for a Circular and Service-Based Economy, *Bulletin of Science, Technology and Society* 20 (2000): 54–69; Y. Jiang, *Report on the Circular Economy in Shanghai, 2005* (Shanghai: Shanghai People's Publishing House, 2005).
69. M. Betsill, Mitigating Climate Change in US Cities: Opportunities and Obstacles, *Local Environment* 6:4: (2001): 393–406; S. Rayner and E. L. Malone, Zen and the Art of Climate Maintenance, *Nature* 390 (1997): 332–34; J. A. Kingdon, *Agendas, Alternatives and Public Policies,* 2nd ed. (New York: Harper-Collins, 1995).
70. The State Council of P.R. China, announcement on limiting the production, sale, and use of plastic shopping bags, http://www.gov.cn/zwgk/2008-01/08/content_852879.htm.

REFERENCES

Abelson, P. Economic and Environmental Sustainability in Shanghai. In *Sustainable Cities in Developing Countries: Theory and Practice at the Millennium,* ed. Cedric Pugh, 185–202. Earthscan: London, 2000.

Asia Times. Shanghai Now the World's Largest Cargo Port. Jan 7, 2006. http://www.atimes.com/atimes/China_Business/HA07Cb02.html.

Bai, Xiaohui, Xiaohong Zhang, Qun Sun, Xinze Wang, and Bin Zhu. Effect of Water Source Pollution on the Water Quality of Shanghai Water Supply System. *Journal of Environmental Science and Health Part A* 41:7 (2006): 1271–80.

Bai, Xuemei, and Hidefumi Imura. A Comparative Study of Urban Environment in East Asia: Stage Model of Urban Environmental Evolution. *International Review for Environmental Strategies* 1:1 (2000): 135–58.

Bashkin, Vladimir N. *Environmental Chemistry: Asian Lessons.* Netherlands: Springer, 2003.

Betsill, Michele M. Mitigating Climate Change in US Cities: Opportunities and Obstacles. *Local Environment* 6:4 (2001): 393–406.

Cai, Jianming, and Victor F. S. Sit. Measuring World City Formation—The Case of Shanghai. *Annals of Regional Science* 37:3 (2003): 435–46.

Cha, Ariana E. In China, a Green Awakening Washington Post Foreign Service. Saturday, October 6, 2007. http://www.washingtonpost.com/wp-dyn/content/article/2007/10/05/AR2007100502472_pf.html.

Chen, Jian-fang, Xiao-ming Xia, Xin-rong Ye, Hai-yan Jin. Marine Organic Pollution History in the Changjiang Estuary and Zhejiang Coastal Area—HCHs and DDTs Stratigraphical Records. *Marine Pollution Bulletin* 45:1–12 (2002): 391–96.

Chen, X., and Y. Zong. Coastal Erosion along the Changjiang Deltatic Shoreline, China: History and Prospective. *Estuarine, Coastal and Shelf Science* 46 (1998): 733–42.

Chen, L. X., W. L. Li, W. Q. Zhu, X. J. Zhou, Z. J. Zhou, and H. L. Liu. Seasonal Trends of Climate Change in the Yangtze Delta and Its Adjacent Regions and Their Formation Mechanisms. *Meteorology and Atmospheric Physics* 92:1–2 (2006): 11–23.

Chen, Z., Y. Saito, Y. Kanai, T. Wei, L. Li, H. Yao, and Z. Wang. Low Concentration of Heavy Metals in the Yangtze Estuarine Sediments, China: A Diluting Setting. *Estuarine, Coastal and Shelf Science* 60:1 (2004): 91–100.

Da, L. J., H. J. Fang, and X. X. Chen. *Woody Plant Species in Green Lands in Shanghai: Special Report on Investigation of Woody Plant Species in the Urban Area in Shanghai.* Shanghai: East China Normal University, 2005.

Decker, E. H., S. Elliott, F. A. Smith, D. R. Blake, and F. S.

Rowland. Energy and Material Flow through the Urban Ecosystem. *Annual Review of Energy and the Environment* 25 (2000): 685–740.

Deng, F. F. Development Zones and Urban Land Reform in China. *Asian Geographer* 22:1–2 (2003): 5–25.

Dhakal, S. *Urban Energy Use and Greenhouse Gas Emissions in Asian Mega-cities: Policies for a Sustainable Future.* Kitakyush, Japan: Institute for Global Environmental Strategies, 2004.

Environmental Sustainability Index (ESI). 2005 Environmental Sustainability Index (ESI) Report. http://sedac.ciesin.columbia.edu/es/esi/.

Gan, L. Implementation of Agenda 21 in China: Institutions and Obstacles. *Environmental Politics* 8:1 (1999): 318–26.

Gao, Chengkang, Jiang Dahe, Wang Dan, and Yan Jonathan. Calculation of Ecological Footprint Based on Modified Method and Quantitative Analysis of Its Impact Factors: A Case Study of Shanghai. *Chinese Geographical Science* 16:4 (2006): 306–13.

Gaubatz, P. China's Urban Transformation: Patterns and Processes of Morphological Change in Beijing, Shanghai and Guangzhou. *Urban Studies* 36:9 (1999): 1495–1521.

Gielen, D., and C. Chen. The CO2 Emission Reduction Benefits of Chinese Energy Policies and Environmental Policies: A Case Study of Shanghai, Period 1995–2020. *Ecological Economics* 39 (2001): 257–70.

Gu, L. X., and W. R. Sheate. Institutional Challenges for EIA Implementation in China: A Case Study of Development versus Environmental Protection. *Environmental Management* 36 (2005): 125–42.

Han, S. S. Shanghai between State and Market in Urban Transformation. *Urban Studies* 37:11 (2000): 2091–112.

He, X. Development of Pudong and Optimization of Urban Area Structure in Shanghai. *Chinese Environment and Development* 4 (1993): 68–89.

Hoyle, S., S. Power, and S. Hutchison. Environmental Impact Assessment in the People's Republic of China: A Case Study of the Shanghai Second Sewerage Project. *Environmentalist* 19 (1999): 251–57.

Institute of Chinese City Competition Capacity Studies (ICCCCS). Chinese City Competition Capacity Rank, 2003. *Information for Decision-makers* 2 (2004): 29 (in Chinese).

Jiang, Y. *Report on the Circular Economy in Shanghai, 2005.* Shanghai: People's Publishing House, 2005.

Kan, H., B. Chen, C. Chen, Q. Fu, and M. Chen. An Evaluation of Public Health Impact of Ambient Air Pollution under Various Energy Scenarios in Shanghai, China. *Atmospheric Environment* 38:1 (2004): 95–102.

Kennedy, C. A., J. Cuddihy, and J. Engel-Yan. The Changing Metabolism of Cities. *Journal of Industrial Ecology* 11:2 (2007): 43–59.

Kingdon, J. A. *Agendas, Alternatives and Public Policies.* 2d ed. New York: Harper-Collins, 1995.

Kong, L., J. Chen, N. Nakagoshi, B. Zhao. The Impact of Urban Planning on Land Use and Land Cover in Pudong of Shanghai, China. *Journal of Environmental Sciences* 15:2 (2003): 205–14.

Li, J., H. Xu, and H. Shen. A Research on the Exploitation of the Tidal Flats in Shanghai. International Geography Symposium: China and the World in the 21st Century, Hong Kong, 1998.

Liu, C., H. E. Yun, J. H. Lee, Z. Wang. Numerical Study on Environmental Impacts of the Third Shanghai Sewage Project. *International Journal of Sediment Research* 17:2 (2002): 165–73.

Liu, J., and J. Diamond. China's Environment in a Globalizing World. *Nature* 435 (2005): 1129–86.

Lo, C. W. H., P. K. To, and K. C. Yip. The Regulatory Style of Environmental Governance in China: The Case of EIA Regulation in Shanghai. *Public Administration and Development* 20:4 (2000): 305–18.

Mao, G. F. Current Situation of Non-point Source Pollution of Chemical Fertilizer and Pesticide in Shanghai and Approach to Controlling Ways. *Acta Agriculturae Shanghai* 18:3 (2002): 56–60.

Mao, W., and P. Hills. Impacts of the Economic-Political Reform on Environmental Impact Assessment Implementation in China. *Impact Assessment and Project Appraisal* 20:2 (2002): 101–11.

Marcotullio, P. J., and G. McGranahan, eds. *Scaling Urban Environmental Challenges: From Local to Global and Back.* London: Earthscan Publications, 2007.

McGranahan, G. An Overview of Urban Environmental Burdens at Three Scales: Intra-urban, Urban-Regional, and Global. *International Review Environmental Strategies* 5:2 (2005): 335–56.

McGranahan, G., and D. Satterthwaite. The Environmental Dimensions of Sustainable Development for Cities. *Geography* 87 (2002): 213–26.

McMaster, R. B., and E. Sheppard. Introduction: Scale and Geographic Inquiry. In *Scale and Geographic Inquiry: Nature, Society, and Method,* ed. E. S. Sheppard and R. B. McMaster, 1–22. Oxford, UK: Blackwell, 2004.

Millennium Ecosystem Assessment (MEA). *Ecosystems and Human Well-being: A Framework for Assessment.* Washington, DC: Island Press, 2003.

Nakajima, N. A Vision of Industrial Ecology: State-of-the-Art Practices for a Circular and Service-Based Economy. *Bulletin of Science, Technology and Society* 20 (2000): 54–69.

Peng, X., X. Guo, and H. X. Han. Future Prospects for

Population Development in Shanghai: A Population Carrying Capacity Analysis. *Asian Population Studies* 1:3 (2005): 261–81.

Rayner, S., and E. L. Malone. Zen and the Art of Climate Maintenance. *Nature* 390 (1997): 332–34.

Rediscovering Geography Committee (RGC).*Rediscovering Geography: New Relevance for Science and Society*. Washington, DC: National Academies Press, 1997.

Ren, W., Y. Zhong, J. Meligrana, B. Anderson, W. E. Watt, J. Chen, H. L. Leung. Urbanization, Land Use, and Water Quality in Shanghai: 1947–1996. *Environment International* 29:1 (2003): 649–59.

Satterthwaite, D. Sustainable Cities or Cities that Contribute to Sustainable Development. In *Sustainable Cities*, ed. D. Satterthwaite, 89–106. London: Earthscan, 1999.

Schneider, S. H., and T. L. Root. Ecological Implications of Climate Change Will Include Surprises. *Biodiversity and Conservation* 5 (1996): 1109–19.

Shanghai Environmental Protection Bureau (SEPB). The Shanghai Environmental Protection Three-Year Action Plan (SEPAP), 2005–2008. http://www.envir.gov.cn/info/2006/1/112278.htm.

Shanghai Municipal Housing, Land and Resource Administration Bureau. 1997. Shanghai Land Use Master Plan (1996–2010).

Shanghai Statistical Bureau (SSB). *Shanghai Statistics Year Book, 1990–2007*. Shanghai: Shanghai Statistic Press, 2007.

Shi, C., S. M. Hutchinson, L. Yu, and S. Xu. Towards a Sustainable Coast: An Integrated Coastal Zone Management Framework for Shanghai, People's Republic of China. *Ocean and Coastal Management* 44 (2001): 411–27.

State Council of P.R. China. 2007. Announcement on Limiting the Production, Sale, and Use of Plastic Shopping Bags. http://www.gov.cn/zwgk/2008–01/08/content_852879.htm.

Stender, N., D. Wang, and J. Zhou. 2003. Impacting the Environment: China's New EIA Law. http://www.coudert.com/publications/articles/030115_14_eia_clp.pdf.

Szelenyi, I. Cities under Socialism—and After. In *Cities after Socialism*, ed. Andrusz, Harloe and Szelenyi, 286–317. Oxford: Blackwell, 1996.

Toteng, E. N. Urban Environmental Management in Botswana: Toward a Theoretical Explanation of Public Policy Failure. *Environmental Management* 28:1 (2001): 19–30.

Tu, W., and C. Shi. Urban Environmental Management in Shanghai: Achievements, Problems, and Prospects. *Environmental Management* 37:3 (2006): 307–21.

Turner, B. L. II, R. E. Kasperson, W. B. Meyer, K. M. Dow, D. Golding, J. X. Kasperson, R. C. Mitchell, and S. J. Ratick. Two Types of Global Environmental Changes: Definitional and Special-Scale Issues in Their Human Dimensions. *Global Environmental Change* 1 (1990): 14–22.

Walcott, S., and W. Xiao. High-Tech Parks and Development Zones in Metropolitan Shanghai: From the Industrial to the Information Age. *Asian Geographer* 19 (2000): 157–79.

Wang, W. Thoughts on Further Implementing China's Agenda 21. ACCA21 Newsletter, April 1999. http://www.acca21.org.cn/jx2e.html.

Wang, H. X., X. Y. Tang, M. L. Wang, P. Yang, T. Wang, K. S. Shao, L. M. Zeng, H. F. Du, and L. M. Chen. Characteristics of Observed Trace Gases Pollutants in the Yangtze Delta. *Science in China (Series D)* 46 (2003): 397–404.

Wang, H. X., C. S. Kiang, X. Tang, X. Zhou, and W. L. Chameides. Surface Ozone: A Likely Threat to Crops in Yangtze Delta of China. *Atmospheric Environment* 39:21 (2005): 3843–50.

Ward, R. M., and W. Liang. Shanghai Water Supply and Wastewater Disposal. *Geographical Review* 85 (1995): 141–56.

Wilbanks, T. J., and R. W. Kates. Global Change in Local Places: How Scale Matters. *Climatic Change* 43:3 (1999): 601–28.

World Bank. 2007. China Data and Statistics. http://web.worldbank.org/WBSITE/EXTERNAL/COUNTRIES/EASTASIAPACIFICEXT/CHINAEXTN/0,,contentMDK:20601872~menuPK:318976~pagePK:141137~piPK:141127~theSitePK:318950,00.html.

Wu, F. The Global and Local Dimension of Place-making: Remaking Shanghai as a World City. *Urban Studies* 37:8 (2000): 1359–77.

———. Place Promotion in Shanghai, PRC. *Cities* 17:5 (2000): 349–61.

———. The Transformation of Urban Space in Chinese Transitional Economy: With Special Reference to Shanghai. In *The New Chinese City: Globalization and Market Reform*, ed. R. Logan John, 154–66. Oxford: Blackwell Publishers, 2002.

———. Urban Restructuring in China's Emerging Market Economy: Towards a Framework for Analysis. *International Journal of Urban and Regional Research* 21:4 (1997): 640–63.

Wu, G., and C. Shi. Shanghai's Water Environment. In *The Dragon's Head: Shanghai, China's Emerging Megacity*, ed. H. Foster, D. Lai, N. Zhou, 93–104. Victoria, Canada: Western Geographical Press, 1998.

Wu, W. City Profile: Shanghai. *Cities* 16:3 (1999): 207–16.

Xu, B. S., S. H. Ou, and B. S. Yang. *Flora of Shanghai*. Shanghai: Shanghai Scientific and Technology and Document Press, 1999.

Xu, Z. X., S. F. Huang, and Z. C. Yan. Study on Non-point Source Pollution Load in Shanghai. *Shanghai Environmental Sciences* 22:z1 (2003): 112–16.

Yang, Y. C., L. J. Da, and X. K. Qin. A Study of the Flora on Dajinshan Island in Shanghai. *Chinese Journal of Wuhan Botanical Research* 20 (2002): 433–37.

Yatsko, P. Work in Progress. *Far Eastern Economic Review* 7 (1997): 66–69.

Yeung, Y. Introduction. In *Shanghai: Transformation and Modernization under China's Open Door Policy*, ed. Y. Yeung and Y. W. Sung, 2–23. Hong Kong: Hong Kong Chinese University Press, 1996.

Yin, Z. Y., S. Walcott, B. Kaplan, J. Cao, W. Q. Lin, M. J. Chen, D. S. Liu, and Y. M. Ning. An Analysis of the Relationship between Spatial Patterns of Water Quality and Urban Development in Shanghai, China. *Computers, Environment and Urban Systems* 29:2 (2005): 197–221.

Ying, L. G., and H. T. Kung. Forecasting up to Year 2000 on Shanghai's Environment Quality. *Environment Monitoring and Assessment* 63 (2000): 297–312.

Yuan, X. Z., H. Liu, and J. J. Lu. The Ecological and Environmental Characteristics and Conservation of the Wetlands in the Changjiang Estuary, China. *Environmentalist* 22:4 (2002): 311–18.

Yuan, W., and P. James. Evolution of the Shanghai City Region 1978–1998: An Analysis of Indicators. *Journal of Environmental Management* 64:3 (2002): 299–309.

Zhang, W., L. Yu, S. M. Hutchinson, S. Xu, Z. Chen, and X. Gao. China's Yangtze Estuary: I. Geomorphic Influence on Heavy Metal Accumulation in Intertidal Sediments. *Geomorphology* 41:2–3 (2001): 195–205.

Zhang, Z., and D. Zhang. Pudong Development and the Establishment of Shanghai's Position as the Center of Trade. *Journal of Asian Economics* 6:2 (1995): 279–89.

Zhao, Z., L. Da, Z. Tang, H. Fang, K. Song, and J. Fang. Ecological Consequences of Rapid Urban Expansion: Shanghai, China. *Frontiers in Ecology and the Environment* 4:7 (2006): 341–46.

■ JIAGUO QI / PEILEI FAN / XI CHEN

The Urban Expansion and Sustainability Challenge of Cities in China's West

THE CASE OF URUMQI

Urban sprawl is a global-scale phenomenon that has raised serious environmental concerns.[1] Although the most rapid urban expansions tend to occur in coastal and well-developed regions across the globe, in recent decades we have witnessed large-scale urban development in traditionally resource-limited and environmentally vulnerable regions.

Urumqi, one of three large cities in China's west, has experienced rapid urban expansion in the past five decades. Its recent urban expansion is closely associated with institutional intervention, such as the West China Development Program (WCDP). The WCDP was advanced by the Chinese central government in 2000 as part of an economic development strategy to reduce regional disparities that hamper growth, social equity, and political stability. Although the motivation of the WCDP was economically sound, there have been concerns about sustainability and environmental consequences, as the ecological systems in regions like the Xinjiang Uyghur Autonomous Region (figs. 1 and 2) are extremely vulnerable to perturbations.

In this chapter, we use a case study of Urumqi, the capital of Xinjiang Uyghur Autonomous Region of China, to demonstrate urban expansion and its associated sustainability challenges, especially in regards to environmental changes. The name "Urumqi" means "the beautiful pasture land" in the ancient Mongolian language used by the Junggar tribe. The city of Urumqi (43.9°N, 87.48°E) is located in the central north of the Xinjiang Uyghur Autonomous Region and has a population of 2.08 million people from forty-nine ethnic groups. Multiethnic groups live in compact, mixed communities consisting of primarily Uyghur, Han, Hui, Kazak, Mongolian, Kirgiz, and Xibe ethnicities. The city was once an important town on the northern route of the Silk Road, essential to Sino-foreign economic and cultural exchanges.

Little is understood about the nature of Urumqi's urbanization, particularly its future sustainability at the current rate of growth. This is not surprising, as few studies have examined urban

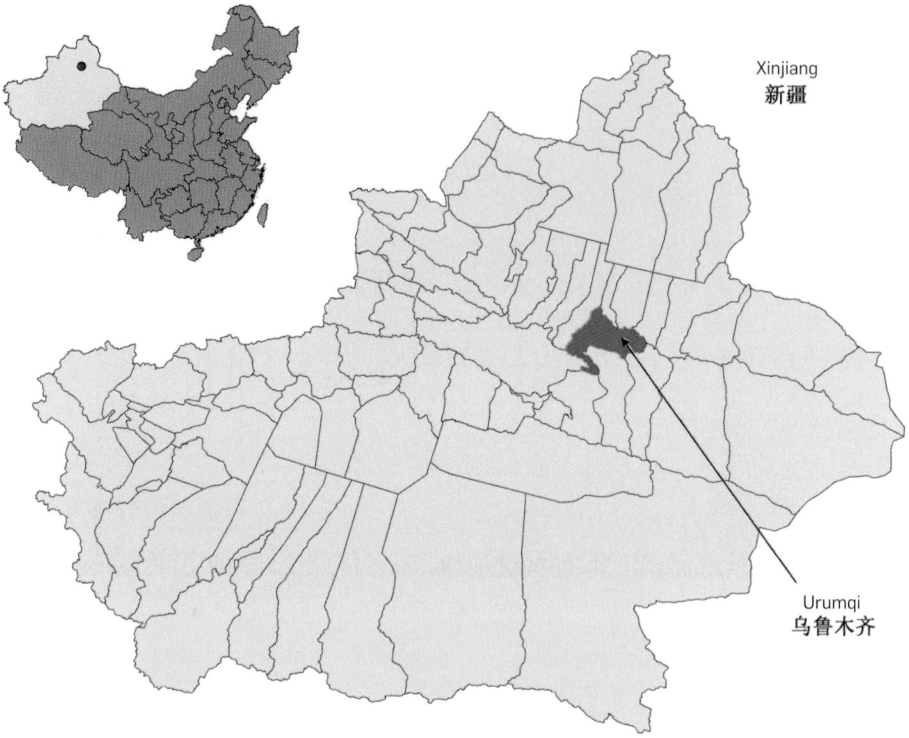

Figure 1. Geographic locations of the Xinjiang Autonomous Region and its capital city, Urumqi.
Source: Wikipedia, 2008.

sustainability issues of Chinese cities, and even fewer have investigated this remote city in China's west. As such, we raise the following specific research questions: What have been the spatial and temporal dynamics of urban expansion in Urumqi over the past four decades? What kind of urban sustainability challenges has rapid urban expansion in Urumqi caused? How have the various components of urban sustainability—that is, economic development, environmental challenges, and social stability—co-evolved over time? After reviewing Urumqi's urban development history and examining the urban environment, we explore Urumqi's current economic profile and associated environmental pressures. Particular focus in this discussion is placed on environmental characteristics (such as landscape morphology and resource availability) and institutional drivers (such as central government policies).

The rest of the chapter is organized as follows: we first introduce our theoretical framework for analysis, urban environmental transition theory. We then present the spatial-temporal development of the city, as observed from satellite imagery. Next, we analyze Urumqi's development in three general periods: the traditional period (before 1949), the Maoist period (1949–1978), and the postreform period (1978–present). We then assess the urban environmental situation of the city and compare it with the other provincial capitals. We discuss urban sustainability and the coevolution of urbanization, economic and social development, and environmental challenges using the urban environment transition theory before we summarize the findings and explore potential policy implications.

PHOTOGRAPH BY JIAGUO QI

Figure 2. The typical oasis system surrounded by desert.

The Urban Environment Transition Theory

We adopted the urban environment transition theory to interpret the interrelationship among economic development, the nature of urban growth, and environmental quality. The urban environment transition theory characterizes a city's economic development level with its environmental burden at local, regional, and global scales.[2] The urban environment transition theory argues the following:

1. Poor cities, or poor homes, neighborhoods, and workplaces principally located in the South tend to have localized environmental issues that lead to endemic health problems, such as diarrhea diseases due to inadequate household water supplies and acute respiratory infections caused by improper ventilation of cooking and heating fumes.
2. Middle-income cities, particularly those in the South and industrial cities of the formerly planned economies, have citywide or regional environmental problems, which are somewhat less acute threats to both human health and ecological sustainability. Typical examples include waterways polluted by untreated sewage and industrial wastewater and ambient air pollution due to concentration of smoke, sulfur dioxide, and particulates generated by industrial production.
3. Affluent cities generate global and intergenerational environmental burdens that are primary threats to sustainability. For instance, research indicates that affluent cities contributed the most to global carbon emissions; further, carbon dioxide emissions rise continuously with economic growth.[3]

In general, while poor cities institute few controls on pollution and create environmental problems that have a direct impact on their populations, affluent cities tend to implement strict protection measures for their own populations while disposing of environmental hazards elsewhere. The environmental impacts of poor cities are localized, while those of affluent groups, due to greater scales of consumption, reach far beyond their own communities. As a result, poor cities are burdened not only with localized problems, but also a greater share of environmental problems generated by resource demands of distant, wealthier populations.

This environmental disparity framework is particularly useful for examining cities in China, as they are at various stages of urban environmental transition. For instance, Urumqi can be considered a typical middle-income city that has environmental problems due to its rapid industrialization, especially the development of heavy industry driven extensively by external demand. Its sustainability is increasingly influenced by large mega cities in the coastal area, such as Beijing and Shanghai, that can be categorized as transitioning into the category of affluent cities due to the diminished role of the manufacturing sector in relation to the tertiary sector. High demands from these eastern coastal cities have led to a rapid exploration of natural resources in China's west, contributing to a wide range of environmental problems, including poor air quality and water shortages in the cities of the western region.

The increasingly complex production and consumption systems, particularly in a globalizing economy, effectively illustrate the shortcomings of simple local and/or regional analyses in exploring urban sustainability. For instance, the growing urban metabolism of cities like Shanghai, which is making considerable advancements in local environmental quality—as noted in "Urban Environmental Management in Shanghai"—masks its distant resource exploitation and the shifting of its environmental burdens to other geographic regions, including Urumqi.

In profiling local economic development and associated environment burdens in Urumqi, it is important to recognize the natural environmental characteristics (such as climate and resource availability) and the institutional drivers (such as central government policies) that have shaped development in the region. First, climatic and natural factors both facilitate and constrain development. For instance, partially due to natural conditions, Urumqi's air pollution is quite severe, especially during the winter months, when coal is used as the major source of heating. The mountains that surround the city prohibit air circulation out of the valley. In addition, dry air and eolian dust deposits from the surrounding deserts often generate "dirty" air when strong winds arrive in the spring and fall each year. Thus, these natural characteristics of Urumqi should not be neglected when assessing the city's environmental stresses.

We also argue that the institutional role in China is critical in shaping cities' trajectories, especially the central government policies and regulations on resource exploration and development. For instance, numerous bodies of research have indicated how the early open-door policy has dramatically changed the urbanization pace of cities in the coastal region.[4] Similarly, Urumqi's recent development has been significantly influenced by state policies, especially by the West China Development Program and the economic development zoning program (including the national level high-tech development zone), which we will detail later.

Spatiotemporal Change in Urumqi

To quantify the spatiotemporal urban expansion in Urumqi, we used remotely sensed images, acquired from space aircraft (image 1 of the remote sensing images of fig. 3), Landsat MSS (image 2 of the remote sensing images of fig. 3) and Landsat TM/ETM+ (images 3, 4, and 5 of the remote sensing images of fig. 3) satellites, to map urban and nonurban land uses, as our focus was to assess urban expansion. We adopted a simple visual interpretation classification technique in mapping urban lands because the images were visually distinct enough between urban and nonurban land uses. The classification accuracy, based on the results from our accuracy assessment by randomly selecting at least 200 points for each class with visual interpretation by our local collaborators, was

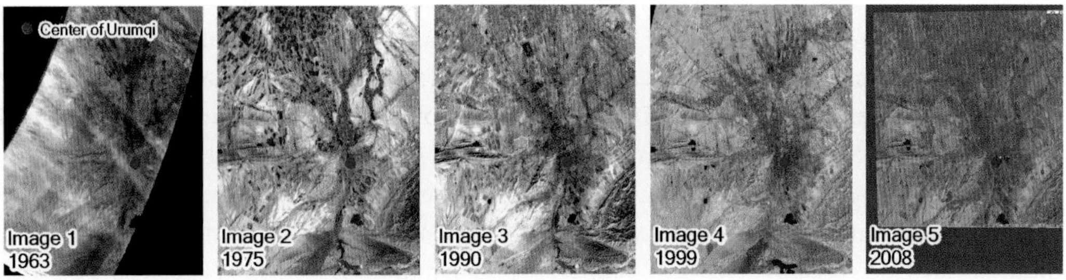

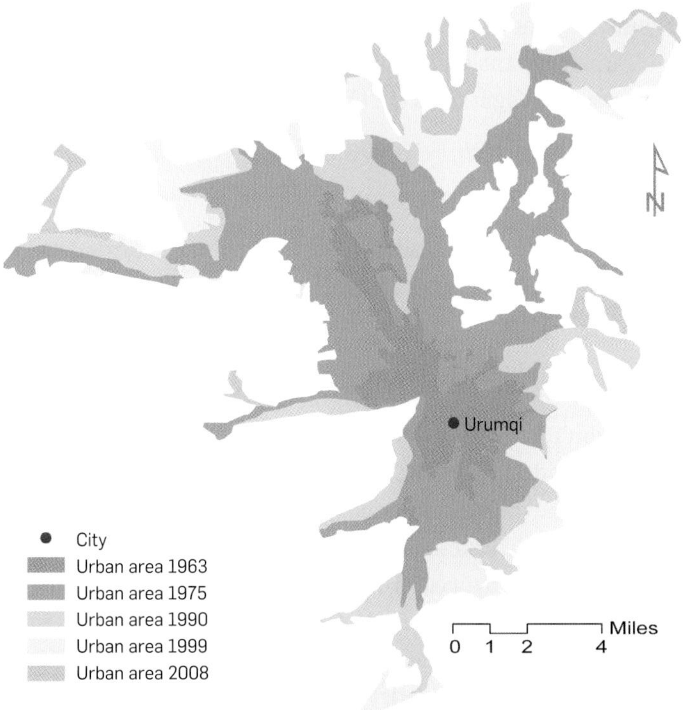

Figure 3. Remote sensing images (*top*) and urban expansion (*bottom*) of Urumqi, 1963–2008.

estimated to be at least 95 percent, in conjunction with information from existing historical maps. The accuracy may be deemed to be high, but keep in mind that in this analysis we only focused on two classes, urban and nonurban. Therefore, the visual interpretation is relatively straightforward and reliable.

As shown on the satellite images and the map (fig. 3), Urumqi's urban development is spatially asymmetric, expanding north and northeast from its original city center from the 1960s to 2008. The major spatial disparity is a result of geographic and geological constraints. The initial settlement was along the old riverbed (Hetian, in Chinese) that runs northwest to southeast. Early development was restricted to a small area around the city center. Later development drastically expanded the city to the northwest and southeast, converting some of the oasis ecosystems, which were cultivated during and shortly after the civil war that ended in 1949 (officially), into impervious urban lands. The urban expansion in the late 1990s was also partially due to the improvement of public transportation and increased use of private vehicles.

Similar to the spatial pattern of Urumqi's urban expansion, its temporal rate of expansion is also asymmetric, with a sharp increase in urban area from 1963 to 1975, followed by another relatively quick expansion from 1990 to 1999 (fig. 4). These two time periods corresponded, respectively, to the large migration from the inland in the 1960s and the later stage of China's economic reform, detailed in following sections. The overall rate of urban sprawl in Urumqi is alarming (fig. 4), on average about 2.32 square miles (1,485 acres) per year. Compared with 1990, the urban area increased 35 percent by 2008. This number may not seem high in comparison with other major cities in China, but given the scarcity of water (primarily provided by melting snow from the Tianshan Mountains) and agricultural resources in the region (which depend on oasis systems), such a rate of urban expansion is of major concern for long-term sustainability. This concern is even more warranted in light of recent changes in the region's climate.[5]

Urban Development of Urumqi

The observed urban expansion should be placed in the context of the city's development history, which can be divided into three general periods based on Gaubatz's work on Chinese cities.[6]

Before 1949: Traditional Urumqi

Due to its geographic location on the northern route of the Silk Road, Urumqi was an important trading center in Central Asia and a military base of China to ensure the safety of the trading route and China's borderline during the traditional period (before 1949, the establishment of the People's Republic of China). Migrants, mainly Han soldiers from the inland dispatched by various emperors in Chinese history, constantly mingled together with local Uyghur, Hui, and Kazak people, forming unique multicultural and multiethnic characteristics over the years.

Urumqi was first installed as a military post in the West Han Dynasty (about 2,000 years ago). Other dynasties, such as Tang (618 to 907) and Qing (1644 to 1912), continued to reinforce Urumqi's function of a military base for China. The city experienced large-scale development under Emperor Qian Long of the Qing Dynasty: city walls were erected and the city was expanded

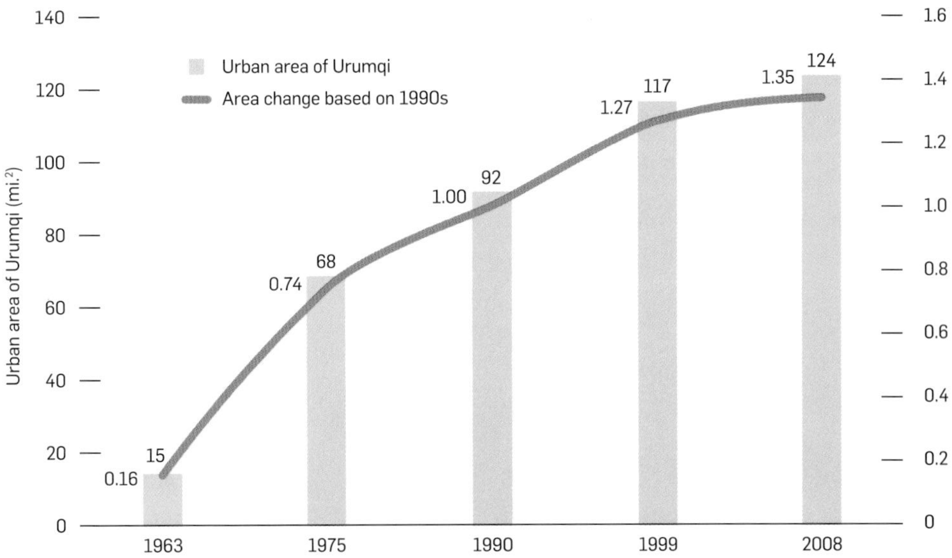

Figure 4. Rate of Urumqi's urban expansion as measured from satellite images. Note: The area is in square miles. The ratio was defined as the total area divided by that of 1990 (our reference year). The *x*-axis is non-equal temporal distance.

to accommodate the growing population. Inland migrants were encouraged to claim the land and cultivate agriculture products with lower taxation. Urumqi was named Dihua by Emperor Qian Long in 1763 and overtook Yili (or Ili) to become the military and political administrative center of the Xinjiang area. In 1884 the city officially became the capital of the new province Xinjiang.

The traditional city had a heavy focus on agriculture, trade, commerce, and handcrafts, with Uyghur people specializing in trading and handcrafts, whereas Han and Kazak people specialized in agriculture and animal husbandry, respectively. Like other traditional Chinese cities, Urumqi's residents formed communities according to their ethnicities, a tendency further facilitated by their occupations. For instance, the Erdaoqiao area was inhabited by the Uyghur people who were mostly merchants or craftsmen.

1949 to 1978: Maoist Urumqi

Urumqi was peacefully transitioned to the new Chinese government on September 25, 1949, after the Guomingdang (Chinese Nationalist Party) garrison commander in Xinjiang, Tao Zhiyue, defected to the Chinese Communist Party. Shortly thereafter, a city government under the new People's Republic of China (PRC) was officially established and the city was renamed Urumqi in 1954. Urumqi's development during the Maoist period (1949–1978) can be characterized by the ramp-up of the manufacturing sector and the Han migration from inland provinces.

During the Maoist period, the overall goal of urban planning in China was to create decentralized and self-sufficient urban centers by encouraging rapid industrialization. Less affected by the Second Sino-Japanese and civil wars than other inland and coastal cities in China, Urumqi quickly transformed itself from a consumption-oriented traditional city to a production-oriented

PHOTOGRAPH BY JIAGUO QI

Figure 5. The traditional trading spot of the Uyghur: Erdaoqiao.

industrial city. The city rapidly developed its relatively weak manufacturing sector. In 1952, the city started with an economic structure in which the primary, secondary, and tertiary sectors accounted for 6 percent, 31 percent, and 63 percent of total gross domestic product (GDP), respectively. The distribution changed to 3 percent, 49 percent, and 48 percent in 1978, indicating the rise of the manufacturing sector in the city's development.[7]

Like many cities in China, migration from other provinces to Urumqi was a major driving force for its industrialization during the Maoist period. Since the establishment of the PRC, a large number of migrants moved to Urumqi, including soldiers of the People's Liberation Army, manufacturing workers, and technicians. For instance, from 1958 to 1963, a total of 20,000 young people from the nine relatively developed provinces of Shanghai, Beijing, Jiangsu, Anhui, Henan, Hebei, Shandong, Hubei, and Sichuan migrated to Urumqi under the central government's directive to support the development of border provinces. After 1962, when the railway from Lanzhou in Gansu Province to Urumqi was completed, people from adjacent as well as faraway provinces, especially Gansu, Ningxia, Qinghai, Shanxi, and Henan, willingly came to Xinjiang for new job opportunities and also under the encouragement of the Chinese central government. Due to migration from inland and coastal regions, the population of Urumqi maintained a high annual growth rate of 7.8 percent during the Maoist era.

The urban structure during this period was mainly characterized by rapid industrialization, especially by the formation of *danwei* (working units), community units organized around a state-owned enterprise or government agency. The large, walled working units spread throughout the city and mixed with traditional communities. *Danwei,* as self-sufficient community units within the city, provided a working environment, housing facilities, food supplies, health care, and even education, moving the city toward a homogeneous but less integrated urban structure. The Han people, especially migrants, were meshed in these working units and newly developed industrial areas, a typical structure under the socialist system.

1978 to Present: Contemporary Urumqi

Contemporary Urumqi has undergone a rapid change since 1978 when Deng Xiaoping, the pioneer of China's Economic Reform, implemented the open-door policy. This period can be primarily characterized by exponential economic growth, especially in the 1990s, as illustrated by figure 6.

Although production increased in all three sectors, the manufacturing sector continued its dominance in Urumqi's economy. While in 1978 the city had 3 percent, 49 percent, and 48 percent of its total products from the primary, secondary, and tertiary sectors, in 2005 these figures changed to 1 percent, 54 percent, and 45 percent, reflecting a loss of 66 percent and 6 percent in the primary and tertiary sectors, respectively, but a 10 percent gain in the manufacturing sector. Since then the manufacturing sector has been further enhanced, as large energy companies continue to invest in Urumqi, especially in newly established economic development zones (a new

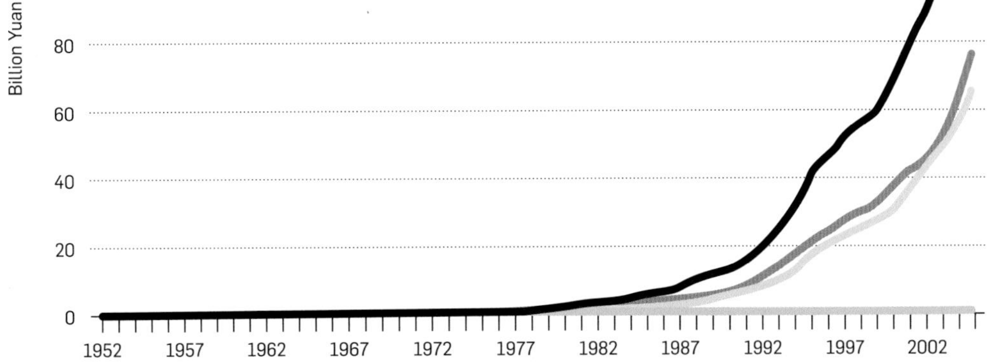

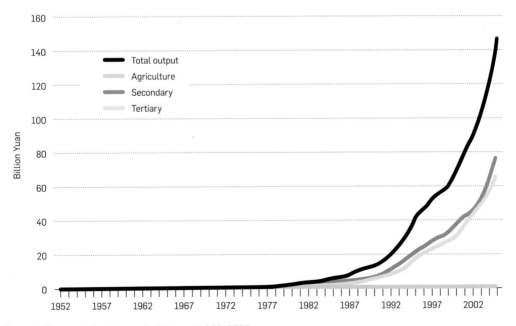

Figure 6. Economic development of Urumqi, 1952–2005.

Source: *Urumqi Statistical Yearbook*, 2006.

component of the traditional urban structure in China). Agriculture and animal husbandry have further declined in their relative importance. The rapid urban growth and decline in agriculture and livestock have created a mounting demand for food and water supplies. Given the limited quantity of arable lands surrounding Urumqi, the growing demand for resources has raised serious sustainability concerns and calls for the Chinese government to address urban sprawl, according to the official Xinhua News Agency.[8]

Urumqi has also developed a booming tertiary sector in recent years. As in other provincial capital cities in China, services such as finance, telecommunications, supply chain management, conference activities, and real estate development are flourishing. Due to its serendipitous location, Urumqi's international trade with Russia and other countries of the former Soviet Union has been thriving, reaching a total value of US$2.3 billion in import and export in 2006, leading major cities in China's west. Further, the unique natural aesthetics and multiethnic cultures enable the city to attract a wide range of tourists, making tourism an important source of revenues. The diverse ethnic lifestyles and colorful local customs of the city have attracted both domestic and international visitors and have made Urumqi one of the most popular tourist destinations in China. The development of the tourism industry has been facilitated by improvements to the transportation infrastructure, particularly the boom of the airline industry in the last decade. From 2001 to 2006, revenue generated from tourism doubled.

Since China's Economic Reform, Urumqi has not attracted a huge influx of migrant workers like other Chinese cities in the eastern region, although numbers of migrant workers were high in comparison with other cities in China's west. Its population grew at a steady rate of 2.4 percent annually from 1978 to 2006. Interestingly, the annual population growth rate from 2000 to 2006 (3.0 percent) was slightly higher than that of 1996 to 1999 (2.0 percent), implying that as the city's economy continues to develop, new employment opportunities are attracting more migrant workers. Urumqi's GDP per capita and average wage for staff and workers have followed the trend of its total GDP and industrial output—that is, GDP per capita grew much faster from 2000 to 2006 than from 1995 to 1999.

■ URUMQI IN COMPARISON WITH OTHER PROVINCIAL CAPITAL CITIES IN CHINA. Compared to thirty-three other major cities (provincial capitals and cities specially designated in the State Plan) in China, Urumqi is a rather small city, with only 2 million people. Nevertheless, economic indicators suggest that the level of Urumqi's economic development actually surpassed many other provincial capital cities, even some in the coastal region. For instance, Urumqi's GDP per capita of 32,417 yuan (US$4,066) ranked fifteenth, and the average annual salary of 23,677 yuan (US$2,970) ranked twelfth among the thirty-three cities compared. Its geographic advantage as a regional transportation hub was reflected by high volumes of passenger and freight traffic. Because of its unique location, Urumqi has become the thirteenth largest import and export hub. It should also be noted that the city has made a considerable investment in the treatment of environmental pollution, 585 yuan (US$73) per person, putting it at the ninth highest among the other major cities (table 1).

■ THE URUMQI METROPOLITAN ECONOMIC DEVELOPMENT AREA. Urumqi's economic development has expanded beyond its city boundaries and made a direct impact on surrounding areas. In 2003

Table 1. Urumqi's economic indicators in 2006 and its ranking among provincial capitals and cities specially designated by the central government

	TOTAL VALUE	VALUE (PER CAPITA)	RANKING (TOTAL VALUE)	RANKING (PER CAPITA)
Population (10,000)	202	—	31	—
GDP (10,000 ¥), per capita (¥)	6,543,019	32,417	30	15
Industrial value added (10,000 ¥), per capita (¥)	2,010,235	9,960	32	19
Passenger traffic (10,000 persons), per capita (persons)	3,945	20	31	15
Freight traffic (10,000 ton), per capita (ton)	14,182	70	16	1
Budgetary revenue of local government (10,000 ¥), per capita (¥)	570,356	2,826	29	12
Budgetary expenditure of local government (10,000 ¥), per capita (¥)	495,342	2,454	32	21
Investment in fixed assets (10,000 ¥), per capita (¥)	2,141,065	10,608	33	29
Average annual salary of staff and workers (¥)	23,677		12	
Value of import and export (US$10,000), per capita ($)	238,981	1,184	28	13
Investment in the treatment of environmental pollution (10,000 ¥), per capita (¥)	118,165	585	22	9

Source: Summarized and calculated by the authors based on *China Statistical Yearbook*, 2007. National Bureau of Statistics, *China Statistical Yearbook 2007* (Beijing: National Bureau of Statistics).

Urumqi and its six neighboring cities, Changji, Fukang, Miquan, Shihezi, Turpan, and Wujiaqu, established a regional economic organization called the Urumqi Metropolitan Economic Development Area (UMEDA) (table 2). Covering seven cities north of the Tianshan Mountains and an area of 14.8 million acres (23,173 square miles), UMEDA is the largest metropolitan economic development area in northwestern China. The formation of such an organization and cooperation signifies the new leading role of Urumqi in an era of integrated regional development. The purpose of this

Table 2. Urumqi metropolitan economic development area

CITY	MAIN ECONOMIC SECTORS
Urumqi	International commerce and trade center, tertiary industries
Changji	Electrical machinery, agriculture products processing, construction material
Miquan	Construction material, chemical industry, manufacturing
Fukang	Coal, petroleum gas, tourism
Shihezi	Livestock
Turpan	Tourism
Wujiaqu	High productivity agriculture, ecological tourism

Source: Urumqi City Government, *Urumqi Statistical Yearbook 2006* (Urumqi: Urumqi City Government, 2007).

organization is to promote codevelopment of the economy and attract more investment from other provinces and the central government. However, its role in the future urban development and sustainability of Urumqi remains uncertain.

Urban Environmental Quality

In sharp contrast with its rising economy in recent years, Urumqi's urban environmental quality has declined substantially, especially since the implementation of China's Economic Reform starting in 1978. Urumqi is rated as the worst of forty-six Chinese cities evaluated by the central

Table 3. Urban environment of Urumqi and the national average of thirty-one provincial capitals, 2006

	NATIONAL AVERAGE	STANDARD DEVIATION	URUMQI	URUMQI'S RANKING*
Air quality				
PM_{10} (oz./mi.^{3})	16.0	4.6	22.3	3
SO_2 (oz./mi.^{3})	7.6	3.2	16.6	1
NO_2 (oz./mi.^{3})	6.2	2.1	9.4	3
Days of air quality equal or above Grade II days†	307	38	246	29
Urban road traffic noise				
Average noise value (db)	68.5	1.3	70.4	2
Industrial waste and treatment				
Gas				
SO_2 emission (tons)	125,079	132,076	119,762	14
Soot emission (tons)	41,037	30,697	47,536	11
Dust emission (tons)	33,265	43,709	9,947	21
SO_2 removed as a percent of total waste generated	29	21	4	27
Soot removed as a percent of total waste generated	89	23	91	25
Dust removed as a percent of total waste generated	86	19	92	17
Water				
Total volume of waste water discharged (10,000 tons)	16,575	21,077	5,314	19
Industrial waste water meeting discharge standards (%)	90	12	79	28
Solid Waste				
Industrial solid waste generated (10,000 tons)	705	608	290	20
Ratio of Industrial solid waste utilized (%)	81	19	66	24

Source: Summarized and calculated by the authors based on data from the *China Statistical Yearbook, 2007*. National Bureau of Statistics, *China Statistical Yearbook 2007* (Beijing: National Bureau of Statistics).

*The ranking number indicates the pollution level of the city. The smaller the number the higher pollution level it indicates. For instance, a ranking of "1" of PM_{10} means that the city has the highest concentration of PM_{10} among all cities (i.e., the worst pollution in this category). The exceptions are rows of SO_2, soot, and dust removed as a percent of total waste generated, where the smaller the ranking indicates that the city has done a better job of removing the waste.

†In China, the government uses an air pollution index to indicate the air quality. The calculation of the air pollution index was based on the concentration of SO_2, NO_2, and PM_{10}. Currently, based on the value of the air pollution index, a city's air quality can be evaluated into one of the five grades. While Grades I and II refer to excellent and fine air quality, Grades III, IV, V represent a light, medium, and heavy degree of air pollution.

Table 4. Urumqi's urban air pollution, 2003–2006

	PARTICULATE MATTER (PM_{10}) (OZ./MI.^{3})	SULFUR DIOXIDE (SO_2) (OZ./MI.^{3})	NITROGEN DIOXIDE (NO_2) (OZ./MI.^{3})	DAYS OF AIR QUALITY EQUAL TO OR ABOVE GRADE II
National average				
2003	17.4	8.2	6.2	288
2004	16.5	8.1	6.0	294
2005	15.4	7.8	5.9	305
2006	16.0	7.6	6.2	307
Urumqi				
2003	18.7	14.3	8.1	282
2004	16.8	15.0	–	258
2005	16.8	17.1	8.2	256
2006	22.3	16.6	9.4	246

Source: Summarized by the authors based on data of *China Statistical Yearbook, 2007*. National Bureau of Statistics, *China Statistical Yearbook 2007* (Beijing: National Bureau of Statistics).

government, in terms of integrated environmental conditions, and one of the ten most polluted cities in the world according to the World Health Organization.[9] A comparison of recent urban air pollution in Urumqi with the national average shows that while provincial capitals on average improved air quality in all measures (PM_{10}, SO_2, NO_2, and days of air quality equal to or above Grade II), Urumqi showed a reverse trend of degrading air quality, and also ranked high in various pollution measurements. For instance, Urumqi was among the worst in SO_2 and third worst in PM_{10} and NO_2 in 1998. Further, in 2006 Urumqi had only 246 days when the air quality was equal to or above Grade II (air quality index exceeds 100), only better than two other heavily polluted cities: Lanzhou (205) and Beijing (241). In 2002 Urumqi reached a record of six continuous days of Grade V (air quality index > 300) air pollution.[10] (See tables 3 and 4.)

Municipal waste has also contributed significantly to the degradation of Urumqi's urban environment. Similar to many cities in the northwestern China, soot and dust are the primary sources of air pollution in Urumqi because coal is the major fuel used for heating and cooking. Situated in a valley of the Tianshan Mountains, Urumqi's air quality is very poor in the wintertime. For instance, between November 11 and 22, 2006, Urumqi had eight continuous days with severe air pollution, which was a major cause of concern for the health of locals.[11]

Furthermore, Urumqi's water resources are scarce and severely polluted. A temperate continental climate with little rainfall and a high evaporation all contribute to the scarcity of water resources in the city. Drinking water is primarily from snow melt from the Tianshan Mountains (through the Urumqi River), which also recharges the ground water. In total, available water per capital is only 129,180 gallons (489 m^3), a quarter of the national average and one-tenth of Xinjiang's average. Despite the water shortage, the city's water resources have been contaminated by uncontrolled waste disposal along waterways. The pollution is further aggravated by the contaminants from industrial wastes along the Urumqi River. Although they do not originate in the city, other forms of human activities, such as mushroom cultivation and overgrazing in surrounding grasslands, also contribute to water pollution.

Land Use Changes

Urumqi has a large land area of 2.8 million acres, mostly agricultural land (80 percent) and unused land (16.5 percent). The built-up, urban area only accounts for about 3.6 percent of the land. Pasture dominates the agricultural land by a large proportion, some 86 percent. Not surprisingly, most land in the built-up area is for residential, industrial, and mining uses (table 5).

In the past decade, as industries developed in the city, they facilitated Urumqi's urban sprawl. Residential, industrial, and mining land uses had the fastest expansion of about 2,400 acres each year from 1997 to 2004, as shown in table 6. Further, urban land converted from arable lands reached 1,951 acres, comprising a significant portion (26 percent) of the total acquired land for urban development (7,542 acres).

An examination of agricultural land composition and changes (table 7) reveals that arable lands and pastures had a notable loss over the past decades, while orchard lands more than doubled. This implies that more land was converted to orchards to pursue high value fruit production.

Assessing Urban Environment Transition Theory

Economic growth is the most conspicuous driving force for Urumqi's urban expansion, urban development, and the quality of the urban environment. According to urban environment transition theory, the environmental problems of a city are highly associated with its economic development level. For middle-income or industrial cities of formerly planned economies, major environmental problems usually are ambient air pollution and polluted waterways generated by industrial production and residential waste. The manufacturing sector currently is the major sector of Urumqi's economy, and the city is on its way toward an even higher level of industrialization. Recent investment in energy industries further aggravated this trend.

Data on air pollution, polluted waterways, and urban sprawl in terms of land conversion all seem to indicate that the industrial sector is the main cause for Urumqi's urban environmental degradation, supporting the urban environment transition theory. For instance, from 2003 to 2006, the concentration of three major air pollutants, particulate matter, sulfur dioxide, and nitrogen dioxide in Urumqi all increased significantly, a typical phenomenon for a middle-income/industrial city that intensifies its industrialization yet applies limited air pollution control. Interestingly, this is in sharp contrast to the national average, which showed a decline in the same indicators over the same time period. Further, data from the Urumqi's Land Resource Bureau show that industries and mining, along with residential lands, are the two largest uses of newly converted lands from 1997 to 2004. In addition, the industrial waste disposal from factories along the Urumqi River is a major cause of water pollution.

Urumqi has fallen behind other provincial capital cities in reducing the amount of industrial waste through waste treatment and strict emissions standards, making industrial waste the major pollutant in the city. Despite its investment in treating environmental pollutants, Urumqi's

Table 5. Land use in Urumqi, 2004

	VALUE (ACRES)	%
Agricultural land	**2,248,102**	**100.0**
Arable land	144,435	6.4
Orchard land	7,024	0.3
Forest land	135,578	6.0
Pasture	1,939,331	86.3
Other	21,734	1.0
Built-up area	**100,673**	**100.0**
Residential, industrial, and mining land	88,515	87.9
Transportation	7,820	7.8
Irrigation facilities	4,338	4.3
Unused land	**464,239**	**100.0**
Unused	399,159	90.8
Other	65,080	9.2
Total land	**2,813,014**	

Source: Urumqi Land Resource Bureau, 2008.

Table 6. Acquired land for different land uses, 1997–2004 (acres)

	LAND ACQUIRED		LAND ACQUIRED FROM ARABLE LAND	
CATEGORIES	VALUE	%	VALUE	%
Urban built up	954	13	191	10
Residential area in countryside	2,405	32	636	33
Industries and mining	2,407	32	522	27
Transportation	849	11	450	23
Irrigation facilities	148	2	8	0
Other	779	10	144	7
Total	**7,542**	**100**	**1,951**	**100**

Source: Urumqi Land Resource Bureau, 2008.

Table 7. Agricultural land composition and changes (acres)

	ARABLE LAND	ORCHARD LAND	FOREST LAND	PASTURE	TOTAL
1997	155,662	3,112	129,040	1,941,861	2,229,676
2004	144,435	7,024	135,578	1,939,331	2,248,102
Change	–11,227	3,912	6,537	–2,530	18,426
Change (%)	–7.2	125.7	5.1	–0.1	0.8

Source: Urumqi Land Resource Bureau, 2008.

industrial waste was not sufficiently controlled or effectively treated. Although Urumqi was on par with the national average in terms of emissions of SO_2, soot, and dust, its treatment efficiency (pollutants removed as a percentage of the total waste generated) fell behind most other provincial capital cities in China. Similarly, although in total quantity Urumqi discharged much less wastewater and generated much less solid waste than most other capital cities, it had much less stringent treatment standards. Only 78 percent of the industrial wastewater in Urumqi met discharge standards, whereas the national average was 90 percent. Likewise, only 66 percent of industrial solid waste was recycled in Urumqi, in comparison with the national average of 81 percent.

Large enterprises in the energy sector are the main producers of industrial waste in Urumqi.[12] Although we feel that the local government should impose stringent environmental regulations on these companies, revenues from these enterprises likely discourage the local government of Urumqi from enforcing environmental regulations, as it relies heavily on these key enterprises for local economic advancement.

Industrial pollution is not unique to Urumqi; many other Chinese cities have also experienced similar urban environmental degradation. It should be noted, however, that it is not just the local population in Urumqi that is responsible for these growing local and regional environmental burdens. As some large coastal provincial capitals move toward a more tertiary-sector-oriented economy, based on the so-called creative class,[13] manufacturing operations have become less important. They have been relocated from these city centers to suburban areas, or to other more remote cities like Urumqi, shifting pollution sources to increasingly distant locations. Further, the increasing use of automobiles and continued construction also contributed to the air pollution in major cities across China, thereby also increasing the global environmental burden. Urumqi may very well follow in the footsteps of these cities and experience a similar shift in environmental problems in the future.

In addition to economic growth, two other sets of variables are important driving forces shaping Urumqi's urban expansion, urban development, and the quality of the urban environment. The first are the natural environmental features of the region (such as physical landscape characteristics and natural resource availability) and the second are institutional structures (such as central government policies and shifts in global markets).

Considering the Natural Environment

Geomorphology is an important factor in both Urumqi's economic development and its severe environmental pollution, especially ambient air pollution. First, the rich natural resources in Urumqi, or Xinjiang at large, have led to the dominance of the energy sector in the region. The Xinjiang Autonomous Region, characterized by mountains (Tianshan Mountains) and dry basins (Turpan and Junggar basins), accounts for about one-sixth of China's total land area. However, it possesses over 30 percent of the oil and coal deposits in China and has become known as "the Sea of Hope" for the petroleum industry in China. Urumqi is bestowed with rich natural deposits of all kinds. A popular saying in Urumqi captures the richness of Xinjiang's natural resources: "Shan shan you bao, pen pen you you!" which means "Our mountains are filled with treasures and our basins are filled with oil."

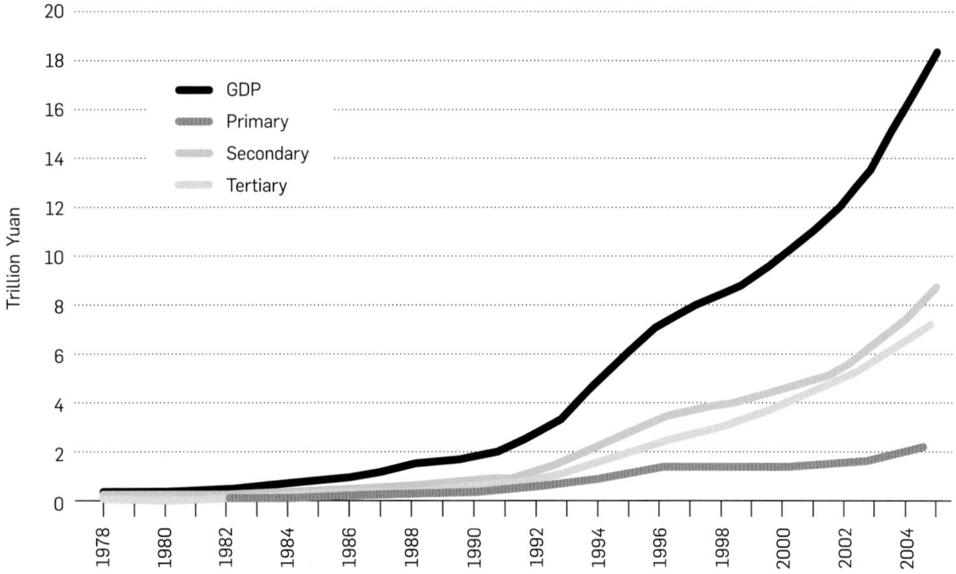

Figure 7. China's economic development, 1978–2005.

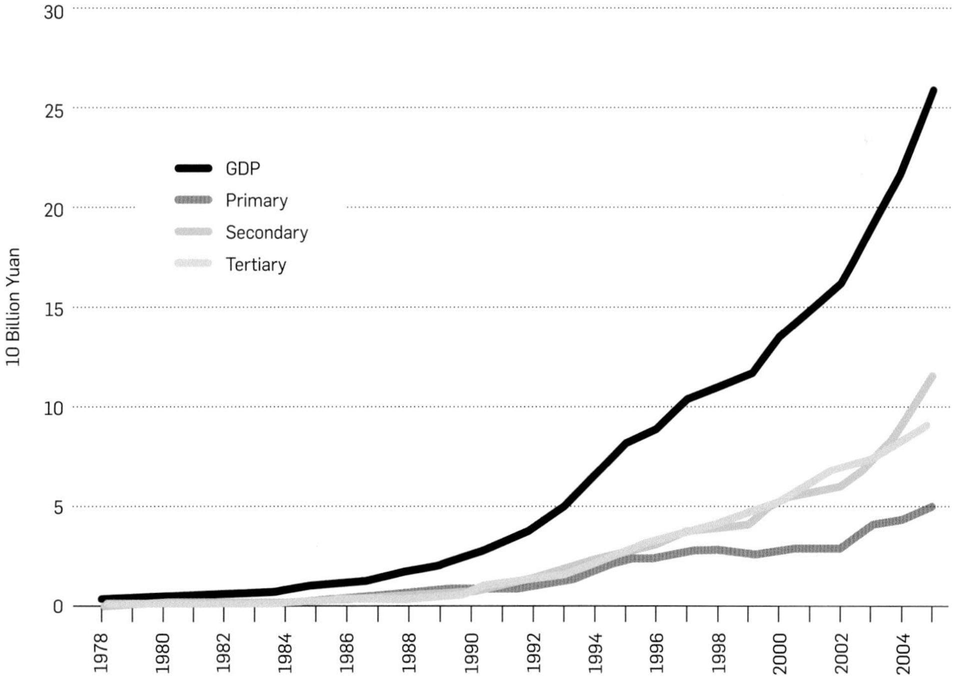

Figure 8. Xinjiang's economic development, 1978–2005.

Sources: *Xinjiang Statistical Yearbook*, 2007; *China Statistical Yearbook*, 2007.

Although Urumqi and Xinjiang have followed the general economic growth trend of China during the contemporary period (figs. 7 and 8), the economy of Urumqi, and to a larger extent Xinjiang, has specifically focused on natural resource related industries, especially petroleum and natural gas extraction, oil processing, coking, and nuclear fuel development. In 2006 the natural resource related industries contributed to 75 percent of Xinjiang's industrial revenue and employed 50 percent of Xinjiang's industrial employees, while the 2005 Chinese national average for these figures was only 14 percent and 13 percent, respectively. Urumqi's industrial structure drives Xinjiang's economy, as it is the largest city in the region and plays a leading role in regional economic development. For instance, Urumqi sits on top of a coalfield and is surrounded by more than 100 coal mines. In addition, the energy-related sectors account for three of the five main sectors in the Urumqi high-tech economic development zone, where the most recent industrial investment projects are located.

The economic future seems even brighter for Urumqi. PetroChina, the largest petroleum company in China, is preparing to acquire PetroKazakh, in order to transport 20 million tons of Kazakh oil annually through a pipeline to Eastern China via Urumqi. Apart from fossil fuels, Xinjiang is generously endowed with renewable energy resources such as wind and solar energy. It generates one-third of the wind energy in China. These natural resources lure investors to develop infrastructure and related facilities in the region, further driving rapid economic growth, urban sprawl, and environmental degradation in Urumqi.

With respect to landscape features, the location of Urumqi contributes to its severe ambient air pollution, especially during the winter months when coal-generated pollutants are trapped in the city's air by the surrounding mountains. The problems with poor air circulation are compounded in winter when Siberian cold fronts arrive from the north, effectively covering the valley with an invisible atmospheric lid. The northern winds also transport dust to the urban area of Urumqi, and this dust is trapped in the valley along with pollutants generated by domestic heating and cooking, coal-powered plants, and vehicle exhausts, causing heavy air pollution that is detrimental to human health.[14] Recent research on Urumqi's air quality further confirms the dramatic seasonal changes in air pollution in Urumqi. The average concentrations of PM_{10} in winter, spring, summer, and fall were 60,696, 28,849, 18,850, and 36,979 ounces per cubic mile (oz./mi.^{3}) in 2004; 58,903, 26,687, 17,218, and 26,349 oz./mi.^{3} in 2005; and 44,934, 21,026, 14,307, and 47,934 oz./mile^3 in 2006, respectively.[15]

Considering Institutional Structure

Due to the significant role of government in shaping the growth and form of China's cities, institutional drivers have been important in shaping Urumqi's development. At various stages, from its period as traditional city to contemporary Urumqi, government intervention dictated the city's development, particularly in terms of migration and economic profile. Urumqi is a migrant city by nature; migrants from the inland areas, soldiers dispatched by various emperors, and the youth sent by Mao Zedong in the 1950s and 1960s have been important drivers of Urumqi's urban growth. They provided the labor not only for the agricultural, industrial, and technology sectors, but also for urban construction, resulting in a rapid increase in both the urban population and the urban expansion.

■ URBAN LAND/PROPERTY MARKET IN CHINA. China's urban land and housing market in the postreform era has undergone three changes that significantly affected urban development in Urumqi.[16] First, China set up a new type of urban land tenure similar to Hong Kong's, in which government retains the ownership of land but sells land use rights (LUR) through a market mechanism.[17] Local governments are responsible for LUR transfer activities.[18] Second, China established a property market and created an urban land pricing system, the bench market price (BMP), at the city level.[19] However, a dual-track land use system exists in which both administrative land allocation and market LUR transfers are utilized simultaneously. Although BMPs of various land types and different land uses were frequently used by local governments to ensure minimum land prices, they are far from reflecting real market prices.[20] Third, closely related to privatization of property rights and the growth of the land market, China started to transition into a market-based urban housing system in 1993.[21]

The changing land/property market became an important driver for urban sprawl in China, expanding urban boundaries at an accelerating rate. Local government authorities became allied with local elites to form a growth machine during the economic decentralization process. Large scale private or quasi-private investments were particularly favored by local authorities due to the potential revenue that the land transaction could bring to the local government.[22] Urumqi certainly is not an exception; the economic development zone, which we will describe in more detail later, is one such example. Unlike other Chinese cities, however, in Urumqi both large national energy titans and emerging local elites pursuing the rising real estate markets are important players in the growth coalition with the local government.

■ WEST CHINA DEVELOPMENT PROGRAM. The WCDP implemented by the Chinese central government had a great impact on the development of Urumqi and Xinjiang as a whole. The region's economic development has been directed or restructured to satisfy projects aimed at taking advantage of the Xinjiang's rich natural resources to meet the energy needs of China's eastern region.

One of the central goals of the WCDP was to decrease the inequality of China's regional development. The first two decades of China's economic reform mainly benefited the eastern coastal area. As a result, the per capita income of the western region was less than 40 percent of the average level of the eastern region.[23] To promote economic development in the western region and bridge the widening gap among China's different regions, the State Council of China set up the WCDP led by the Premiers Zhu Rongji and Wen Jiabao in 2000. This economic development program covered six provinces (Gansu, Guizhou, Qinghai, Shannxi, Sichuan, and Yunnan), five autonomous regions (Guangxi, Inner Mongolia, Ningxia, Tibet, and Xinjiang), and one municipality (Chongqing) (fig. 9). Although it accounts for about 70 percent of China's total area, the western region had only 25 percent of the country's population and 16.6 percent of the GDP in 1999, as most of the land in this region is barren and uninhabitable.[24]

The main components of the WCDP include facilitating the development of infrastructure, enhancing ecological and environmental protection, restructuring industries, improving science and education, opening up the west, and deepening reforms. From 2000 to 2005, about seventy infrastructure megaprojects were funded with an investment of over 1 trillion yuan (US$120 billion). From this sum, 12.2 percent and 3.1 percent were invested in environmental protection and

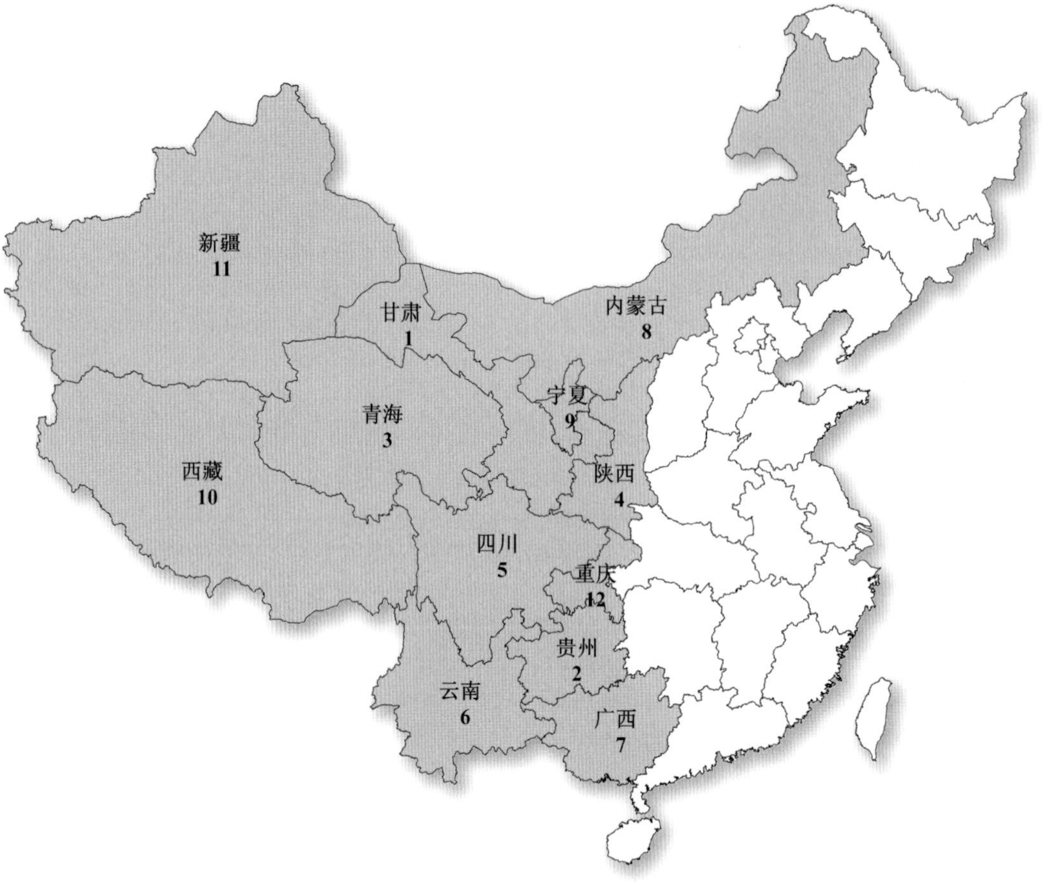

Figure 9. Area covered by the West China Development Program.

Source: State Council, West China Development Program, 2008, http://www.chinawest.gov.cn/.

Note: (1) Gansu; (2) Guizhou; (3) Qinghai; (4) Shannxi; (5) Sichuan; (6) Yunnan; (7) Guangxi; (8) Inner Mongolia; (9) Ningxia; (10) Tibet; (11) Xinjiang; (12) Chongqing.

improving living conditions in rural areas of the region, respectively.[25] In the first three years of the program, an additional 600 billion yuan (US$72 billion) in loans was provided by China's banks to the western region.[26] In 2006, six years after the initiation of the WCDP, the western region doubled its GDP and achieved an annual GDP growth rate of 10.6 percent.[27] As one of the most important participants of the WCDP, Xinjiang, and in particular Urumqi, took advantage of the program to achieve significant economic expansion, as illustrated in the previous section.

In addition to narrowing the economic gap among China's different regions, the WCDP had an implicit goal to satisfy the urgent energy needs of the rapidly expanding east by exploring the natural resources of the western region. Four large projects funded under this program reflect this goal by the Chinese central government: Xi Dian Dong Song (transporting electricity from the west to the east); Nan Shui Bei Diao (transporting water from the south to the north); Xi Qi Dong Shu (transporting natural gas from the west to the east); and Qing Zang Tie Lu (building a railway to the Tibetan Plateau).

Covering 16.7 percent of China's land area, Xinjiang has the largest land area among all provinces and autonomous regions in China.[28] Although Xinjiang leads other regions in natural resources, such as coal and natural gas, it has not been able to efficiently convert these resources into economic value due to the lack of transportation infrastructure inland. For instance, Xinjiang has estimated coal resources of 2.19 trillion tons, 40 percent of the national total. Although 40.8 million tons of coals were mined in 2004, only 2.5 million tons (5.9 percent) were transported out of Xinjiang via the Lan Xin Railway and National Highway 312.[29] The Xi Dian Dong Song program attempts to ease this problem by converting coal to electricity and then transporting it to the east through the power distribution grid.[30] Similarly, Xi Qi Dong Shu is a gigantic project that will build a total of 2,609 miles of pipelines to transport natural gas to the Lower Yangtze River Delta, the most developed region in the country,[31] from the west—especially Xinjiang, Qinghai, Sichuan, and Chongqing—which has rich natural gas resources. For instance, Xinjiang possesses natural gas resources of 2,399 cubic miles, with five of the basins in the western region that have rich natural gas resources, including Turpan Basin (estimated to have 22 percent of China's natural gas) and Junggar Basin. Urumqi, as the capital of the Xinjiang Autonomous Region, has been impacted dramatically by these projects through the inflow of investment and technology.

■ WEST CHINA DEVELOPMENT PROGRAM AND URUMQI IN THE 1990S AND 2000S. Benefiting from the WCDP, Urumqi's economic growth in the 1990s and 2000s has been mainly fueled by the secondary and the tertiary sectors, including trade and tourism. From 1995 to 2006, Urumqi achieved annual growth in gross regional product (GRP) of 11.9 percent, slightly ahead of the national average of 11.1 percent. However, if we divide the time span into two periods, the result implies that the WCDP made a dramatic impact on Urumqi's economic development. Before the WCDP implementation (1995–1999), the city's economic growth was very slow, as if there were no trickle down of the benefits from the national economic growth, even though Urumqi was one of the first few inland cities that pioneered the national policy of opening border cities in 1992. The GRP grew at 2.6 percent annually, much lower than the national average of 8.1 percent. However, when the WCDP started in 2000, the city's economy took off and its GRP jumped to 14.5 percent, well above the national average of 11.6 percent.

The WCDP also has an indirect impact on Urumqi's urban environment. It accelerated the industrialization of the city, especially through investment of the energy sector, leading to rapid urban sprawl to accommodate the industrial growth needs and the worsening air quality.

■ URUMQI'S HIGH-TECH DEVELOPMENT ZONE. Established in August 1992, Urumqi's High-Tech Development Zone (UHDZ) has been the growth engine for Urumqi's new economy. Its revenue and exports have grown at annual rates of 40 percent and 59 percent, respectively, much higher than Urumqi's GRP. While in 1995 it only contributed to 2 percent of Urumqi's GRP, in 2006 it generated 11.7 billion yuan (US$1.47 billion) in revenue and contributed to 18 percent of Urumqi's GRP (fig. 10).

UHDZ has several districts: Diamond City Central Business District (CBD), providing financial and business services; Torch Innovation Enterprises Zone, with a focus on research and development activities, such as high-tech start-ups for overseas returnees; North Manufacturing Zone and 500 Ku High-Tech Industrial Zone, which are concentrated on high-tech enterprises desired by UHDZ; and the Outer Zone Area that extends beyond the administrative boundary of UHDZ.

UHDZ is home to high-tech industries sought after by the local government, many of which are cleaner companies that generate much less pollution than traditional manufacturers. Thus the rapid development of UHDZ has positive environmental implications. The five main sectors in UHDZ are biomedical, electronic machinery, new energy, new materials, and petrochemicals, accounting for 95 percent of the total UHDZ gross outputs as of 2004. UHDZ also emphasizes developing industries and technologies using Xinjiang's unique agricultural products and renewable resources, such as tomatoes, safflowers,[32] wolfberries,[33] hops,[34] cotton, wind energy, and solar energy.

While important in generating revenues, industries based on Xinjiang's fossil fuel resources, such as coal and petroleum, may also jeopardize Urumqi's urban environment if appropriate environmental protection measures are not taken. Quite a few large energy enterprises—such as Shenhua Group, PetroChina Company, and the China Petroleum and Chemical Corporation (Sinopec)—have already opened branch offices in UHDZ to develop the energy industry and to implement Xi Dian Dong Song and Xi Qi Dong Shu programs. Although rapid development of related industries can quickly bring economic benefits to the city, relaxing environmental requirements for these enterprises will further deteriorate the city's quality of air and water. Moreover,

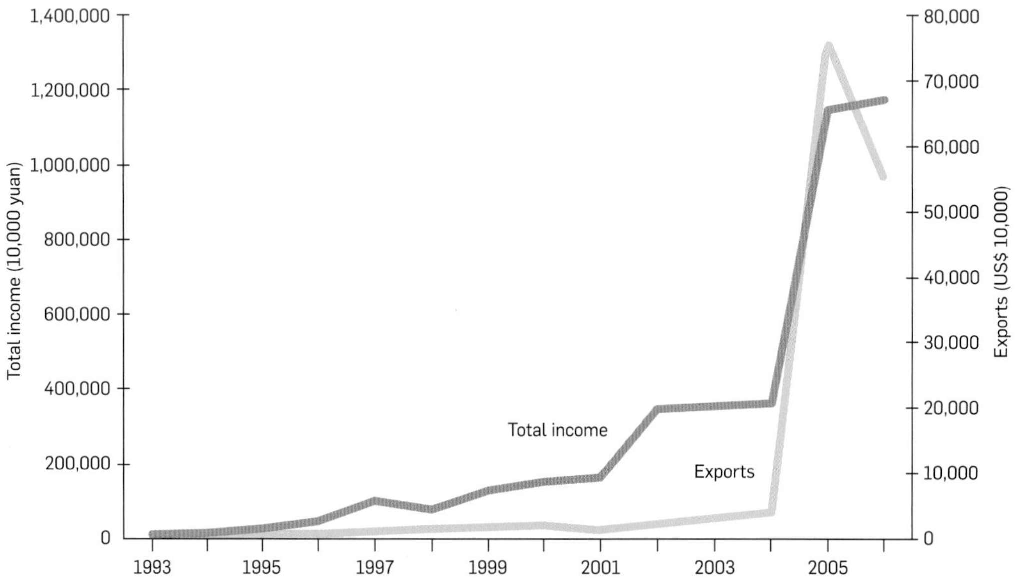

Figure 10. Urumqi high-tech development zone major economic indicator (1993–2006).

Source: *China Statistical Yearbook*, various years.

establishing a high-tech zone such as UHDZ implies that a significant portion of natural land would be converted to built-up areas. Currently, a large area of land that would otherwise be agricultural oases and grasslands is designated for the UHDZ (4,633 acres).

The rushed development of the UHDZ has generated unexpected consequences, including the rapid loss of cultivated land critical for food production, ownership disputes, and unplanned development against zoning regulations due to illegal land leases and transfers. An evaluation of UHDZ's land resources indicates that although UHDZ's land investment intensity is higher than other development zones in Xinjiang, its land utilization efficiency and land transfer rate are relatively low, only 36 percent and 39 percent, respectively.[35] Several issues related to UHDZ's development need to be addressed. First, the developed land has not been utilized sufficiently. Some existing manufacturing buildings and developed land remain unoccupied, and some land projects are kept as partially finished. Second, the UHDZ Management Committee, the main component in charge of acquisition of cultivated land, property rental, and transfer planning and registration, is not carrying out its duty effectively. There has been criticism that the political leaders of UHDZ should not be heavily involved in detailed operations of the committee and that they should not focus only on satisfying the requests of the investors. Third, the UHDZ lacks an investment and development strategy, leading to poor interrelationships among enterprises in the zone and a lack of clustering. The levels of land output and land profit are only 15 percent and 39 percent of the national average for development zones, respectively.[36] Fourth, due to the low demand resulting from competition with other development zones within and outside Xinjiang, the land value of UHDZ has been very low. For instance, the land price is only 33.3 percent of the average in the coastal area development zones.[37]

■ GLOBALIZATION. Developing Urumqi into an international trade hub in Central Asia and recovering Urumqi's reputation as the city connecting the East with the West is a vision shared by the Chinese central and local governments. Though Urumqi has a long history as a vibrant trade center in Central Asia, the implementation of such a vision has been associated closely with the evolution of China's open-door policy. After isolation from the rest of the world for many years, China opened its door to the West in 1978, first in the coastal areas in the 1980s and 1990s, then gradually in border provinces of China's west. The benefit of this policy shift can be easily observed: Urumqi's trade with Russia and other countries of the former Soviet Union is booming. The operation of the new railway, the so-called silk-road route from Beijing to Urumqi to Moscow, will further facilitate Urumqi's global connection. Continued implementation of the open-door policy in China's west may facilitate Urumqi's transition into an affluent city, as described by the urban environment transition theory, shifting its industry-oriented environmental burdens to consumption-oriented ones. For now, however, Urumqi continues to meet the heavy industry demand of increasingly service-oriented wealthy Chinese urban centers. In addition, with growing ties to Russia and other former Soviet countries, the increasingly complex production and consumption system that Urumqi is being integrated into is being translated into new and heightened scales of local environmental pressures.

The case of Urumqi is a reminder that with deregulation, the dispersal of global economic activity, and the decentralization of manufacturing, it has become difficult to determine the

PHOTOGRAPH BY JIAGUO QI

Figure 11. KFC and traditional business in Erdaoqiao.

populations responsible for the environmental burdens in specific geographic regions. The resource exploitation and environmental harms experienced in certain locations are shaped by resource demands from increasingly distant populations and urban centers. The claims of local and regional environmental improvements by some cities and regions thus might have little to do with overall advancements toward urban sustainability, and more with the effectiveness of these urban centers and their populations in shifting their resource extraction and environmental burdens to more distant locations.

Local and Regional Environment Management Initiatives

To cope with the deteriorating urban environment, governments of Xinjiang Uygur Autonomous Region and the Urumqi city implemented a series of environmental initiatives in recent years. The most well-known one is the Blue Sky Project initiated by Wang Lequan, the party secretary of Xinjiang in 1998, one year after Urumqi was rated as one of the top ten most polluted cities in the world by the World Health Organization. The project, officially introduced in April 1999, set an ambitious goal to resolve Urumqi's air pollution problems within five years and promised a clear sky in Urumqi.

The project has four main strategies. First, the city intends to improve its energy use efficiency by developing central heating systems and energy efficiency in buildings, and also by encouraging the use of clean energy sources based on geothermal heating, wind power, and electricity. Second, the city will decrease the overall pollution by implementing new energy-efficient manufacturing practices and serious measures to prevent and control industrial pollutions. Third, the city will improve environmental management by strengthening environmental monitoring, R&D capability, and environmental law enforcement. Fourth, the city will start to form a good urban ecology and control the development density of its central district.[38]

Prior to the 1998 initiatives, boilers using unprocessed coals for winter heating by different enterprises were the main source of ambient air pollution in Urumqi. The city therefore targeted boilers and invested extensively in developing central heating systems. Within only four years, from 1999 to 2002, the city demolished about 3,000 small boilers and 1,200 large boilers. Moreover, it invested 4 billion yuan (about US$500 million) to build forty-three utility stations to provide central heating in Urumqi, about 60 percent of city's heating needs.[39] From 2005 to 2008, the city has invested 100 million yuan (about US$12 million) annually in the demolition and improvement of boilers.

In 2008 Urumqi launched another four major initiatives to curtail ambient air pollution by 2012, the third five-year plan of the Blue Sky Project. In addition to enhancing central heating systems, three other measures involve eliminating old, high-emission buses, constructing wastewater treatment plants, and increasing the green coverage of the city from 25 percent to 35 percent

Figure 12. Wind power grid installed around Urumqi.

within the next five years.[40] These new initiatives are currently being implemented, and the results have yet to be seen.

In addition to these local initiatives, new policies and regulations over pollution have also been practiced with enhanced law enforcement. In January 2005 the first local law on environmental management, Urumqi Air Pollution Prevention and Management Regulation (hereafter referred to as "the regulation"), was passed by the People's Congress of the Xinjiang Uyghur Autonomous Region. It officially became effective as of December 30, 2008. With five chapters and thirty-four items, the new regulation provides basic guidelines to prevent and manage environment pollution, and it also imposes clear legal responsibility to the polluting enterprises. One interesting aspect of the regulation is the setup of the pollution warning system of the city. When the city is under a yellow (severe pollution) or red (very severe pollution) warning, Urumqi's environmental protection agency can take action, such as prohibiting the production and discharge of waste of the polluting enterprises and dispatching affected people to safe areas. Moreover, the regulation entails fines for violations of the law. For instance, when an enterprise discharges PM_{10}, SO_2, or other pollutants 50 percent more than the emissions standard, it will be subjected to a 50,000 yuan (about US$7,000) to 100,000 yuan (about US$15,000) fine.[41]

These new initiatives and policies have led to some positive changes in Urumqi's urban-environmental conditions. For instance, after continuous deterioration in air quality since 1998, in 2008 Urumqi's achieved its best air quality in ten years, with 261 days of good air quality. The monitoring system, with an investment of 34 million yuan (about US$4.22 million) and sixty-five real-time monitoring facilities, has also come into operation. The city now has a total of six automatic air quality monitoring stations to provide data for law enforcement.[42] In addition, since 2002 the city has also reforested 10,213 acres (62,000 mu) of bare land.[43]

However, the city has also been criticized in its inefficiency and double standard in dealing with urban-environmental issues. For instance, the city still has not dealt with some restaurants and retailers that use unprocessed coals for cooking or grilling. Furthermore, despite their heavy discharge of pollutants, some enterprises have been exempt from regulation due to their close connections with city government officials.[44] In our view, the growing coalition between local government and enterprises, and especially large national enterprises, has motivated the city to take a hands-off approach in dealing with large-revenue contributors, such as energy investors from the east, hindering the effectiveness of the new environmental policies. This suggests that urban environmental management has gone beyond the city boundary, affected implicitly by the energy demands of distant cities.

Urumqi's urbanization is strongly related to national policies on land use. Nationwide rapid urbanization since the economic reform has resulted in significant loss of arable land, particularly cropland at the urban fringe. Because the loss of this land threatens national food security, a series of new policies at both national and local levels have been implemented. For example, in 2004 the State Council issued "The Decision on Deepening Reforms and Strengthening Land Management" to restrict urban expansion and reduce the loss of arable land.[45] In the following year, 2005, Urumqi issued its own nine regulatory measures to implement the State Council's new policy, which specifies regulatory procedures required for urban development.[46] These measures were meant to ensure agricultural land for food production and security. Implementation of these regulatory measures has slowed down urban expansion, but it has not stopped illegal land conversion.

Conclusions

Installed as a Chinese military post about 2,000 years ago, Urumqi in its early history became an important trading center in Central Asia. During the Maoist period, 1949–1978, rapid industrialization and Han migration from the inland provinces propelled Urumqi's quick growth. In the post–economic reform period, manufacturing—and especially the large, recently established national energy companies in the UHDZ—have dominated Urumqi's economic and urban development.

In sharp contrast to the rising economy, Urumqi's urban environment has experienced severe deterioration, becoming one of the most polluted cities in China. In addition, significant arable land conversion to residential, industrial, and mining uses has directly affected local agricultural production and food supply. Urumqi's urban expansion has been occurring at the alarming rate of 1,484 acres per year from 1963 to 2008, as inferred from historical remotely sensed images.

The urban environment transition framework effectively captures the essence of environmental burdens of Urumqi as a typical industrial city. Within this context, institutional drivers, particularly those at the national and global scales, have been critical in shaping Urumqi's development and resulting natural environmental stresses. These include changes in the urban land/property market, the WCDP, the establishment of economic development zones, and globalization. The WCDP, implemented by the Chinese central government, has probably had the most significant impact on economic development, urban growth, and associated environmental burdens. Another significant variable in local economic development has been the mounting resource and industrial demands, particularly evident with energy, from distant Chinese cities whose urban metabolisms have been rapidly expanding.

Taking serious measures to manage and prevent environmental pollution, Urumqi implemented a number of new policies and programs. These pollution mitigating initiatives have achieved some positive results, though far from satisfactory. Enforcement of industrial waste treatment and strict emissions standards, along with a more diversified economic structure, is highly recommended as a means of further reducing local pollution. Furthermore, as Urumqi develops, and if it is successful in making the transition from an industry-oriented to a consumer-oriented economy, decision makers and city planners should anticipate a shift in environmental burdens.

In terms of current profile, however, the resource demands and the resource exploitation of distant cities from China's eastern coast, as well as policy changes at the national level, have affected the nature of Urumqi's economic development, urban growth, and its environmental burdens. Implementation of the WCDP program, mounting pressure for resources exploration driven by the nationwide rise in energy consumption, growing economic transactions with the former Soviet Union countries, and an increase in tourism are mostly exogenous factors, but they have a decisive impact on local economic development and resulting environment stresses. Within this context, the Urumqi case study suggests that the decentralization of manufacturing and economic globalization has made the assessment of urban sustainability in any one city difficult to evaluate.

Any assessments or strategies for advancement toward sustainability must ultimately be placed within national and global contexts.

NOTES

1. D. Clark, Global Patterns and Perspectives, in *Urban World/Global City*, ed. D. Clark (London: Routledge, 2003), 1–17. M. Moore, P. Gould, and B. S. Keary, Global Urbanization and Impact on Health, *International Journal of Hygiene and Environmental Health* 206 (2003): 269–78; O. Varis and L. Somlyody, Global Urbanization and Urban Water: Can Sustainability Be Afforded? *Water Science and Technology* 35:9 (1997): 21–32; W. R. Turner, T. Nakamura, and M. Dinetti. Global Urbanization and the Separation of Humans from Nature, *BioScience* 54:6 (2004): 585–90.
2. G. McGranahan, J. Songsore, and M. Kjellen, Sustainability, Poverty and Urban Environmental Transitions, in *Sustainability, the Environment and Urbanization*, ed. C. Pugh (London: Earthscan, 1996), 103–33; G. McGranahan, *The Citizens at Risk: From Urban Sanitation to Sustainable Cities* (London: Earthscan, 2001).
3. McGranahan, Songsore, and Kjellen, Sustainability, Poverty and Urban Environmental Transitions, 103–33.
4. C. C. Fan, Of Belts and Ladders-State Policy and Uneven Regional Development in Post-Mao China, *Annals of the Association of American Geographers* 85:3 (1995): 421–49; L. J. C. Ma, Urban Transformation in China, 1949–2000: A Review and Research Agenda, *Environment and Planning A* 34:9 (2002): 1545–69; G. C. S. Lin, Growth and Structural Change of Chinese Cities: A Contextual and Geographic Analysis, *Cities* 19:5 (2002): 299–316; S. F. Song and K. H. Zhang, Urbanisation and City Size Distribution in China, *Urban Studies* 39:12 (2002): 2317–27; John Friedmann, *China's Urban Transition* (Minneapolis: University of Minnesota Press, 2005).
5. E. Lioubimtseva, R. Cole, J. M. Adams, and G. Kapustin, Impacts of Climate and Land-Cover Changes Lands in Arid Lands of Central Asia, *Journal of Arid Environments* 62 (2005): 285–308; J. Schmidhuber and F. N. Tubiello, Global Food Security under Climate Change, *PNAS (Proceedings of National Academy of Sciences)* 104:50 (2007): 19703–8.
6. Piper Gaubatz, China's Urban Transformation, *Urban Studies* 36:9 (1999): 1495–1521.
7. Urumqi City Government, *Urumqi Statistical Yearbook 2006* (Urumqi: Urumqi City Government, 2007).
8. Xinhua News Agency, Chinese Leaders Caution against Urban Sprawl, August 23, 2006, http://en.chinagate.com.cn/english/48362.htm.
9. Juan Li, Guoshun Zhuang, Kan Huang, Yanfen Lin, Chang Xu, and Shulong Yu, Characteristics and Sources of Air-Borne Particulate in Urumqi, China: The Upstream Area of Asia Dust, *Atmospheric Environment* 42 (2008): 776–87.
10. Air quality of Grade V, fifth-degree pollution, is the worst degree of air pollution in China.
11. Tianshan Net, Start the Battle to Protect Urumqi's Urban Environment, January 11, 2007, http://www.tianshannet.com/news/content/2007–01/11/content_1591925_7.htm.
12. Urumqi County Science Net, Urumqi's Key Enterprises Became Major Sources of Pollution for the City, 2008, http://kj.wlmqx.gov.cn/Search/Content.aspx?Info_ID=f1d64115–5148–446b-84f4-e5097a2259ea.
13. Richard Florida, *The Rise of the Creative Class: And How It's Transforming Work, Leisure, Community and Everyday Life* (New York: Basic Books, 2002).
14. Li et al., Characteristics and Sources of Air-Borne Particulate in Urumqi, 776–87.
15. Ibid. The average concentrations of PM_{10} in winter, spring, summer, and fall were 412.8, 196.2, 128.2, and 251.5 μgm^{-3} in 2004; 400.6, 181.5, 117.1, and 179.2 μgm^{-3} in 2005; and 305.6, 143.0, 97.3, and 326 μgm^{-3} in 2006, respectively. 1 ug = $3.5274 * 10^{-8}$ oz, 1 m^3 = 2.3990×10^{-10} $mile^3$.
16. Sumei Zhang and Kenneth Pearlman, China's Land Use Reforms: A Review of Journal Literature, *Journal of Planning Literature* 19:1 (2004): 16–61.
17. Nelson Chan, Land-Use Rights in Mainland China: Problems and Recommendations for Improvement, *Journal of Real Estate Literature* 7:1 (1999): 53–63; Tung-Pi Chen, Emerging Real Estate Markets in Urban China, *International Tax and Business Lawyer* 8 (1990): 78–103; Ling Hin Li, Keith McKinnell, and Anthony Walker, Convergence of the Land Tenure Systems of China, Hong Kong and Taiwan, *Journal of Property Research* 17:4 (2000): 1–14; Wei Liu, Hong Kong's Impact on Shenzhen Real Property Law, *Hong Kong Law Journal* 27 (1997): 356–73.

18. Ping Xu, Acquiring Land Use Rights in China, *China Law* (March 1997): 94–96; Kenneth C. W. Keng, China's Land Disposition System, *Journal of Contemporary China* 5:13 (1996): 325–45; Xing Quan Zhang, Urban Land Reform in China, *Land Use Policy* 14:3 (1997): 187–99.
19. Ling Hin Li and Anthony Walker, Benchmark Pricing Behaviour of Land in China's Reforms, *Journal of Property Research* 13:3 (1996): 183–96; Fulong Wu, China's Recent Urban Development in the Process of Land and Housing Marketisation and Economic Globalisation, *Habitat International* 25 (2001): 273–89.
20. Jieming Zhu, Changing Land Policy and Its Impact on Local Growth: The Experience of the Shenzhen Special Economic Zone, China, in the 1980s, *Urban Studies* 31:10 (1994): 1611–23; Jieming Zhu, China's Urban Land Management Reforms in the Context of Gradualist Economic Transformation, *Asian Geographer* 17:1–2 (1999): 9–18.
21. Jean Jinghan Chen and David Wills, Urban Housing Reform in China—Policies and Performance, *Building Research and Information* 24:5 (1996): 311–17; Gill-Chin Lim and Man-Hyung Lee, Housing Consumption in Urban China, *Journal of Real Estate Finance and Economics* 6 (1993): 89–102; Zhongyi Tong and Allen R. Hays, The Transformation of the Urban Housing System in China, *Urban Affairs Review* 31:5 (1996): 625–58.
22. Yan Zhang and Ke Fang, Is History Repeating Itself: From Urban Renewal in the United States to Inner-City Redevelopment in China, *Journal of Planning Education and Research* 23:3 (2004): 286–98.
23. Ding Lu and William A. W. Neilson, Introduction: West China Development Issues and Challenges, in *China's West Region Development: Domestic Strategies and Global Implications*, ed. Ding Lu and William A. W. Neilson (Singapore: World Scientific, 2004), 1–14.
24. National Bureau of Statistics (NBS), *China Statistical Yearbook* (Beijing: National Bureau of Statistics, 2000).
25. Jie Han and Ruizhen Gu, Development and Reform Committee: The Initial Effect of West China Development: Doubling GDP in Six Years, Xinhua Net, September 6, 2006, http://news3.xinhuanet.com/fortune/2006–09/05/content_5051273.htm.
26. Ding Lu and William A. W. Neilson, Introduction: West China Development Issues and Challenges, in *China's West Region Development: Domestic Strategies and Global Implications*, ed. Ding Lu and William A. W. Neilson (Singapore: World Scientific, 2004), 1–14.
27. Han and Gu, Development and Reform Committee.
28. Dehua Li and Lixiao Yu, West China Development, Xinjiang Made a Solid Progress: An Interview with the Party Secretary of Xing Jiang Uygur Autonomous Region, Wang Lequan, China News Network, October 1, 2001, http://www.chinanews.com.cn/zhonghuawenzhai/2001–10–01/txt/18.htm.
29. Lan Xin Railway, from Lanzhou to Xinjiang, is the most important transportation route that connects Xinjiang with the rest of country.
30. Xinhua News Agency, China Plans to Build the North Path for Xi Dian Dong Song, June 6, 2006, http://www.ces.cn/html/2006–6/200666921321.shtml.
31. China Development Gateway, Xi Qi Dong Shu Project Q&A, China Development Gateway, February 27, 2007, http://cn.chinagate.com.cn/chinese/MATERIAL/281.htm.
32. Traditionally, the safflower (*hong hua* in Chinese) was grown for its seeds, as well as to color and flavor foods, make red and yellow dyes, and create medicines.
33. Wolfberry, also known as Chinese wolfberry, goji berry, barbary matrimony vine, bocksdorn, Duke of Argyll's tea tree, or matrimony vine (*gou qi* in Chinese), is a highly nutritious fruit and has been used in traditional Chinese medicine.
34. The flower cones of the *Humulus lupulus* (*pi jiou hua* in Chinese), known as hops, are used in the production of beer to impart bitterness, flavor, and preservative qualities.
35. "Land investment intensity" refers to the average investment on a unit of land—in this case, 10,000 yuan (US$1,254) per acre.
36. "Land output ratio" refers to the output per unit of land; "land profit ratio" refers to the profit—that is, output minus cost—per unit of land.
37. Qiaoshun Luo and Jun Hu, A Discussion on Land Use of Urumqi's High-Tech Economic Zone, http://www.lrn.cn/zjtg/academicpaper/200807/t20080704_249976.htm.
38. Dahao Wang, A Reflection of 10 Years Anniversary of the "Blue Sky Project" in Urumqi, September 23, 2008, http://www.guancha.com.cn/news_detail.php?id=2507&nowmenuid=4&cpath=&catid=0.
39. China Economic Network-Local Economies, Urumqi Invested 4 Billion Yuan to Implement "Blue Sky Project," February 26, 2003, http://www.ccchina.gov.cn/cn/NewsInfo.asp?NewsId=1553.
40. Urumqi Evening News, Four Measures to Manage Environment Pollution of Urumqi, January 18, 2008, http://news.h2o-china.com/information/china/676031200623369_1.shtml.
41. Urumqi On Line, "Urumqi Air Pollution Prevention

and Management Regulation" Will Be Implemented from the 30th of This Month, December 24, 2008, http://www.ucatv.com.cn/html/news/9/200812/24-38410.html.

42. Urumqi On Line, Urumqi Reached 261 Good Air Quality Days Last Year, January 7, 2009, http://www.wlmqwb.com/3688/200901/t20090107_400788.shtml.
43. "Mu" is a Chinese unit for area, 1 mu = 0.165 acre.
44. Wang, A Reflection of 10 Years Anniversary of the "Blue Sky Project."
45. China's State Council, The Decision on Deepening Reforms and Strengthening Land Management, 2004, http://www.gov.cn/ztzl/2006-06/30/content_323794.htm.
46. Urumqi Government. Nine Regulatory Measures of Deepening Reforms and Strengthening Land Management in Urumqi, 2005, http://renfang.urumqi.gov.cn/urumqi/webadmin1/ViewGW.asp?offset=285&ID=381.

REFERENCES

Chan, Nelson. Land-use Rights in Mainland China: Problems and Recommendations for Improvement. *Journal of Real Estate Literature* 7:1 (1999): 53–63.

Chen, Jean Jinghan, and David Wills. Urban Housing Reform in China—Policies and Performance. *Building Research and Information* 24:5 (1996): 311–17.

Chen, Tung-Pi. Emerging Real Estate Markets in Urban China. *International Tax and Business Lawyer* 8 (1990): 78–103.

China Development Gateway. Xi Qi Dong Shu project Q&A. China Development Gateway. February 27, 2007. http://cn.chinagate.com.cn/chinese/MATERIAL/281.htm.

China Economic Network-Local Economies. Urumqi Invested 4 Billion Yuan to Implement "Blue Sky Project." February 26, 2003. http://www.ccchina.gov.cn/cn/NewsInfo.asp?NewsId=1553.

China's State Council. 2004. The Decision on Deepening Reforms and Strengthening Land Management. http://www.gov.cn/ztzl/2006-06/30/content_323794.htm.

Clark, David. Global Patterns and Perspectives. In *Urban World/Global City*, ed. David Clark, 1–17. London: Routledge, 2003.

Fan, C. Cindy. Of Belts and Ladders—State Policy and Uneven Regional Development in Post-Mao China. *Annals of the Association of American Geographers* 85:3 (1995): 421–49.

Florida, Richard. *The Rise of the Creative Class: And How It's Transforming Work, Leisure, Community and Everyday Life*. New York: Basic Books, 2002.

Friedmann, John. *China's Urban Transition*. Minneapolis: University of Minnesota Press, 2005.

Gaubatz, Piper. China's Urban Transformation. *Urban Studies* 36:9 (1999): 1495–1521.

Han, Jie, and Ruizhen Gu. Development and Reform Committee: The Initial Effect of West China Development: Doubling GDP in Six Years. Xinhua Net. September 6, 2006. http://news3.xinhuanet.com/fortune/2006-09/05/content_5051273.htm.

Keng, Kenneth C. W. China's Land Disposition System. *Journal of Contemporary China* 5:13 (1996): 325–45.

Li, Dehua, and Lixiao Yu. West China Development, Xinjiang Made a Solid Progress, an Interview with the Party Secretary of Xing Jiang Uygur Autonomous Region, Wang Lequan. China News Network. October 1, 2001. http://www.chinanews.com.cn/zhonghuawenzhai/2001-10-01/txt/18.htm.

Li, Juan, Guoshun Zhuang, Kan Huang, Yanfen Lin, Chang Xu, and Shulong Yu. Characteristics and Sources of Air-borne Particulate in Urumqi, China: The Upstream Area of Asia Dust. *Atmospheric Environment* 42 (2008): 776–87.

Li, Ling Hin, Keith McKinnell, and Anthony Walker. Convergence of the Land Tenure Systems of China, Hong Kong and Taiwan. *Journal of Property Research* 17:4 (2000): 1–14.

Li, Ling Hin, and Anthony Walker. Benchmark Pricing Behaviour of Land in China's Reforms. *Journal of Property Research* 13:3 (1996): 183–96.

Lin, George C. S. The Growth and Structural Change of Chinese Cities: A Contextual and Geographic Analysis. *Cities* 19:5 (2002): 299–316.

Lim, Gill-Chin, and Man-Hyung Lee. Housing Consumption in Urban China. *Journal of Real Estate Finance and Economics* 6 (1993): 89–102.

Lioubimtseva, E., R. Cole, J. M. Adams, and G. Kapustin. Impacts of Climate and Land-Cover Changes Lands in Arid Lands of Central Asia. *Journal of Arid Environments* 62 (2005): 285–308.

Liu, Wei. Hong Kong's Impact on Shenzhen Real Property Law. *Hong Kong Law Journal* 27 (1997): 356–73.

Lu, Ding, and William A. W. Neilson. Introduction: West China Development Issues and Challenges. In *China's West Region Development: Domestic Strategies and Global Implications*, ed. Ding Lu and William A. W. Neilson, 1–14. Singapore: World Scientific, 2004.

Luo, Qiaoshun, and Jun Hu. A Discussion on Land Use of Urumqi's High-Tech Economic Zone. July 4, 2008. http://www.lrn.cn/zjtg/academicpaper/200807/t20080704_249976.htm.

Ma, Laurence J. C. Urban Transformation in China, 1949–2000: A Review and Research Agenda. *Environment and Planning A* 34:9 (2002): 1545–69.

McGranahan, Gordon. *The Citizens at Risk: From Urban Sanitation to Sustainable Cities*. London: Earthscan, 2001.

McGranahan, Gordon, Jacob Songsore, and Marianne Kjellen. Sustainability, Poverty and Urban Environmental Transitions. In *Sustainability, the Environment and Urbanization*, ed. Cedric Pugh, 103–33. London: Earthscan, 1996.

Moore, Melinda, Philip Gould, and Barbara S. Keary. Global Urbanization and Impact on Health. *International Journal of Hygiene and Environmental Health* 206 (2003): 269–78.

National Bureau of Statistics (NBS). *China Statistical Yearbook 2007* Beijing: National Bureau of Statistics, 2007.

———. *China Statistical Yearbook*. Beijing: National Bureau of Statistics, 2000.

Schmidhuber, Josef, and Francesco N. Tubiello. Global Food Security under Climate Change. *PNAS (Proceedings of National Academy of Sciences)* 104:50 (2007): 19703–8.

Song, Shunfeng, and Kevin Honglin Zhang. Urbanisation and City Size Distribution in China. *Urban Studies* 39:12 (2002): 2317–27.

Tianshan Net. Start the Battle to Protect Urumqi's Urban Environment. January 11, 2007. http://www.tianshannet.com/news/content/2007–01/11/content_1591925_7.htm.

Tong, Zhongyi, and Allen R. Hays. The Transformation of the Urban Housing System in China. *Urban Affairs Review* 31:5 (1996): 625–58.

Turner, Will R., Toshihiko Nakamura, and Marco Dinetti. Global Urbanization and the Separation of Humans from Nature. *BioScience* 54:6 (2004): 585–90.

Urumqi City Government. *Urumqi Statistical Yearbook 2006*. Urumqi: Urumqi City Government, 2007.

Urumqi County Science Net. 2008. Urumqi's Key Enterprises Became Major Sources of Pollution for the City. http://kj.wlmqx.gov.cn/Search/Content.aspx?Info_ID=f1d64115–5148–446b-84f4-e5097a2259ea.

Urumqi Evening News. Four Measures to Manage Environment Pollution of Urumqi. January 18, 2008. http://news.h2o-china.com/information/china/676031200623369_1.shtml.

Urumqi Government. 2005. Nine Regulatory Measures of Deepening Reforms and Strengthening Land Management in Urumqi. http://renfang.urumqi.gov.cn/urumqi/webadmin1/ViewGW.asp?offset=285&ID=381.

Urumqi On Line. "Urumqi Air Pollution Prevention and Management Regulation" Will Be Implemented from the 30th of This Month. December 24, 2008. http://www.ucatv.com.cn/html/news/9/200812/24–38410.html.

———. Urumqi Reached 261 Good Air Quality Days Last Year. January 7, 2009. http://www.wlmqwb.com/3688/200901/t20090107_400788.shtml.

Varis, Olli, and Laszlo Somlyody. Global Urbanization and Urban Water: Can Sustainability Be Afforded? *Water Science and Technology* 35:9 (1997): 21–32.

Wang, Dahao. A Reflection of 10 Years Anniversary of the "Blue Sky Project" in Urumqi. September 23, 2008. http://www.guancha.com.cn/news_detail.php?id=2507&nowmenuid=4&cpath=&catid=0.

Wu, Fulong. China's Recent Urban Development in the Process of Land and Housing Marketisation and Economic Globalisation. *Habitat International* 25 (2001): 273–89.

Xinhua News Agency. Chinese Leaders Caution against Urban Sprawl. August 23, 2006. http://en.chinagate.com.cn/english/48362.htm.

———. China Plans to Build the North Path for Xi Dian Dong Song. June 6, 2006. http://www.ces.cn/html/2006–6/200666921321.shtml.

Xu, Ping. Acquiring Land Use Rights in China. *China Law* March (1997): 94–96.

Zhang, Sumei, and Kenneth Pearlman. China's Land Use Reforms: A Review of Journal Literature. *Journal of Planning Literature* 19:1 (2004): 16–61.

Zhang, Xing Quan. Urban Land Reform in China. *Land Use Policy* 14:3 (1997): 187–99.

Zhang, Yan, and Ke Fang. Is History Repeating Itself? From Urban Renewal in the United States to Inner-City Redevelopment in China. *Journal of Planning Education and Research* 23:3 (2004): 286–98.

Zhu, Jieming. Changing Land Policy and Its Impact on Local Growth: The Experience of the Shenzhen Special Economic Zone, China, in the 1980s. *Urban Studies* 31:10 (1994): 1611–23.

———. China's Urban Land Management Reforms in the Context of Gradualist Economic Transformation. *Asian Geographer* 17:1–2 (1999): 9–18.

■ RONALD KALAFSKY

Sustainable Manufacturing in Nagoya

EXPLORING THE DYNAMICS OF JAPAN'S COMPETITIVE ADVANTAGE

As evidenced by the research presented throughout this book, metropolitan areas are viewed widely and justifiably as engines of economic development. Recent work also suggests that for well into the foreseeable future, cities will remain crucial to sustainable national and global economic growth.[1] There are many reasons for this relationship between urban growth and economic sustainability, but, in particular, it is because urbanized areas are centers of innovation and creativity, enduring as cores of economic dynamism. Findings from researchers as varied as Michael Porter, Edward Glaeser, Allen Scott, and Michael Storper have clearly demonstrated the importance of cities to economic sustainability.[2] The seminal research of these scholars has also shown that economically dynamic cities are intimately tied to wider domestic activity and global trade flows.

This chapter will examine the case of the extended Nagoya region and its main economic growth engine, the manufacturing sector. Nagoya, Japan's fourth largest city, has long been a focal point of the country's still-sizable secondary economic sector, particularly in such key industries as motor vehicles and machinery. Interestingly, this dynamic area is not immediately recognized by many observers located outside of Japan. Unlike most metropolitan areas in industrialized countries, the manufacturing sector continues to play a vital part in the economic growth across the Greater Nagoya region and, indeed, in much of Japan. This chapter, accordingly, will examine manufacturing activity in the extended Nagoya region, in terms of its impacts, competitive challenges, and, finally, its pivotal role in sustainable economic growth for this metropolitan area and Japan at large.

In addition to looking at overall manufacturing activities in Greater Nagoya, the machine tool sector will be used as a prime example of an advanced manufacturing industry that continues to be an indispensable element in the region's economic vitality and its continued development of human capital. The chapter concludes with a discussion of current and pending concerns about sustainable growth across the Nagoya metropolitan region and its globally dominant machine tool industry as both enter the second decade of the twenty-first century. Nagoya's success fits within the context of Japan's economic achievements over the past half-century. In many ways, Japan's economic growth has been exceptional among advanced market economies, in terms of rather low disparities in income distribution. The continued emphasis on advanced manufacturing in Japan is also emblematic of a type of economic growth that has been comparatively equitable and in some estimations has contributed to wide-ranging social stability by creating and sustaining a broad middle class.

Economic Development, Regulatory Environments, and Sustainability

Economic Development and Industrial Agglomeration

For decades there have been numerous discussions and analyses on the linkages between cities, regional economic development, and same-industry agglomerations of economic activity. Seminal works by Michael Porter, for example, have examined the factors that contribute to the growth and maintenance of a region's competitiveness.[3] The original framework envisioned by Porter can be illustrated as an interlinked group of elements that contribute to both industrial and regional growth, including firm strategies, factor conditions, related and supporting industries, and demand conditions.[4] Factor conditions include a skilled, educated workforce and physical infrastructure such as roads and seaports. Other elements, no less important, are the roles of government and chance in competitiveness and economic growth. In most urban economies there are significant linkages between government and the factor conditions mentioned here. These linkages are manifested in physical infrastructure and institutions such as educational systems.

Researchers extending as far back as Marshall and, more recently, Scott, Paul Krugman, and others have illustrated the benefits of similar industries or firms locating in close proximity to one another.[5] Positive externalities include shared skilled labor pools, innovation resulting from competition, and similar supplier bases. In essence, much of this research demonstrated that a number of interlinked factors are pivotal to maintaining viable economic growth. And, moreover, these conditions must be in place to enable firms and even entire industries to remain economically practicable in the long term.

There is also extensive work on the city itself as an economic unit. Glaeser, for example, demonstrated that while same-sector agglomerations are not preconditions for sustainable growth, other elements found in urbanized areas are indeed pivotal to viable economic health.[6] Such conditions include a skilled workforce and an adequate and appropriate infrastructure. Metropolitan areas provide fertile ground for innovation, especially in cutting-edge industries.[7] The destination of the products manufactured in a metropolitan area has an impact on the nature of economic growth. Research from Porter suggested that export-base industries are crucial to regional economic development.[8] Such industries provide salaries that are well above average. Products that are created for export markets (i.e., outside the local region) tend to be more research intensive and more innovative overall.

Institutions and Regulatory Environments

The study of economic activities of a region necessitates a brief discussion of the regulatory environment in which they take place. Government is an important element of a region's competitive advantage. The Japanese situation is certainly distinctive, given the mix of government intervention and market forces present during its rapid rebuilding process into what was the world's second largest economy, until 2011 when Japan's gross domestic product was surpassed by China. Institutional environments have been shown to influence the activities and performance of both firms and industries.[9] As Robert Boyer suggested, institutions indeed shape organizations such as companies, defining relations between different economic actors.[10] Japan is undoubtedly an example of the "Asian-based capitalism" described by Bruno Amable, with active government intervention during the initial stages of development.[11] During this developmental period, Japan blended market forces and government intervention, the mix being dependent on the particular industry and the global economic situation.[12] The Japanese model was emulated throughout many emerging economies across Asia, including Singapore, South Korea, and Taiwan, with the types and degrees of these public-private linkages varying among countries.

Many of the policy-led actions in Japan's economy were manifested through its Ministry of International Trade and Industry (MITI). This government organization took an active role in shaping Japan's industrial policy during the postwar period. Examples of policy-led guidance and intervention with the private sector included market research, industry targeting, and capital allocation.[13] Also critical were huge public investments in infrastructure to promote further development and efficiencies across the economy. Regulations also encouraged managed competition, in order to create efficient, internationally competitive firms. These governmental policies also extended to protecting firms against foreign competition through a variety of measures.

In addition to achieving an end-goal of rapid economic growth, a parallel goal for Japan's policymakers was to achieve this growth with stability and relatively little income inequality.[14] Such actions were pivotal in rebuilding Japan's industrial infrastructure. Many observers saw these goals and salutary policy consequences as contributing to Japan's meteoric economic growth and to the establishment of a large number of globally competitive firms.

Given Japan's long economic downturn during the 1990s and early 2000s, however, the policy environment and the relationships between government and industry have come under review. A 2000 analysis examined Japanese industry within the context of the post-bubble economic environment and found that some of the best performing industries over the long term were those that had the least government intervention and protection. Fortunately, in Nagoya's case many of the region's most successful manufacturing industries were subjected rather early to international market forces, and in recent decades they have received little government intervention. It is therefore not surprising that this region is home to some of Japan's strongest firms. There is little doubt, however, that these initial government policy actions helped to set Japan on a steep economic growth trajectory.

Sustainability, Equitable Growth, and the Case of Japan

An overarching issue found within discussions of economic growth in almost any region concerns sustainability. Japan provides an interesting case, due to long-standing ties between large companies and their workers, a large middle class, and, in OECD terms, relatively small income disparities. Advanced manufacturing in the urban environment does meet several of the needs outlined by Graham Haughton, and the introductory chapter of this book, concerning sustainable development in cities, including relative equity in wages.[15] On balance, a robust manufacturing sector has tended to provide far more sustainable entry-level positions than many other economic sectors.

The Japanese growth scenario aims at economic stability, which in many ways has an end goal of overall social solidity.[16] Related to this is the additional emphasis on modest income disparities, which cannot be emphasized enough. Certainly, the role of culture has played a large role in shaping these policies and growth trajectories as well. As described by Geert Hofstede, the acceptance of uncertainty (whether economic, political, or otherwise) in society varies widely among countries. In that respect, Japan prefers to minimize the impacts of societal upheavals that result from economic transitions that too often have downstream negative effects, such as unemployment, crime, and contentious domestic issues.[17]

The policy instruments used to achieve the Japanese economic situation were also mirrored in private corporations. Japanese firms may not be as lean as those found in the Anglo-Saxon model of corporate organization. Layoffs, historically, have been minimal. Companies retain core employees, and overall societal disruptions are diminished. When compared with many industrialized states, moreover, the public sector provides relatively fewer funds for education. Instead, the private sector takes responsibility for worker training. Of course, larger questions are raised about how long this can last, given trends in international markets.[18] Nonetheless, this corporate and societal structure appears to have contributed to the unique growth outcomes seen in Japan.

Nagoya and Its Economic Activities

The Nagoya metropolitan area is centrally located between the economic conurbations of Tokyo and Osaka, as seen in the inset of figure 1. For the purposes of this chapter, the Greater Nagoya region consists of the prefectures of Aichi (Nagoya's location), Gifu, and Mie.[19] This three-prefecture region has a total population of 11.2 million and a labor force of 7.5 million, a relatively high labor force percentage that works in the region's favor. According to the Greater Nagoya Initiative, this region, when taken alone, would constitute the eighteenth largest economy in the world.[20] At the outset, therefore, one finds a significant economic engine situated in Central Japan.

What constitutes economic activity across Greater Nagoya, and how does this differ from the rest of Japan? In this region, at least, manufacturing remains an essential component of the wider regional economy. Figure 1 also provides the manufacturing employment intensities for the three prefectures forming the Greater Nagoya Region. In each prefecture, the percentage of the workforce employed in manufacturing is well above the national average. For the region as a whole, roughly 21.3 percent of the workforce is involved in manufacturing versus 13.3 percent for all of Japan. These manufacturing percentages are also higher than many other metropolitan

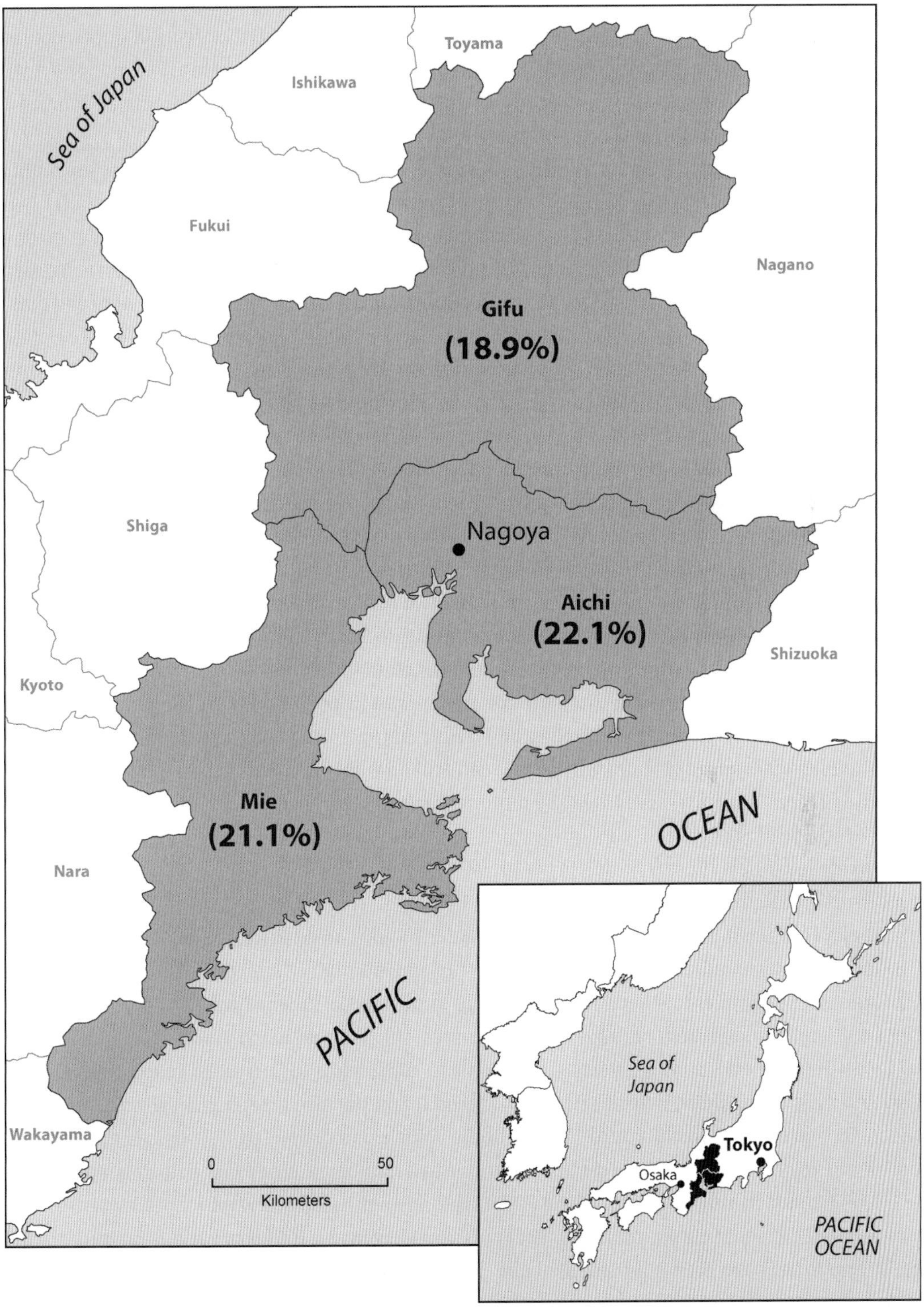

Figure 1. The Greater Nagoya Region and the percentage of the workforce employed in manufacturing.

Source: Ministry for Economy, Trade and Industry.

areas, including Tokyo. As one can see, the region has consistently maintained manufacturing employment intensities above the rest of Japan. Put another way, the location quotients for manufacturing-based employment for Aichi, Gifu, and Mie prefectures are 1.67, 1.42, and 1.59, respectively; all well above parity. So, at the outset, Greater Nagoya can confidently be labeled a manufacturing-intensive region.

While much of Japan's manufacturing sector suffered during the country's severe economic malaise of the 1990s and early 2000s, Aichi and surrounding prefectures were impacted far less during this time period.[21] In fact, advanced manufacturing activities began to concentrate during Japan's economic slowdown, with much of this recent agglomeration centering within the Nagoya region. The above numbers illustrate that the Greater Nagoya region is unique not only to Japan, but internationally as well.

What are the main manufacturing sectors within the Greater Nagoya region? First and foremost is the transportation equipment industry, employing over 322,000 workers in this region and an obvious driver of economic activity. Over 34 percent of Japan's transportation equipment employment is centered in the Nagoya region. The three-prefecture area also produces almost 15 percent more value-added per employee than the national average for this key industrial sector. Much of the region's advantage and prowess in transportation equipment is rooted in motor vehicle production; specifically, automobile manufacturing.

Why is motor vehicle production so important, both to the region and in general? This industry is regarded globally as *the* core manufacturing sector, in terms of its sheer employment numbers, its support of various upstream and downstream industries (i.e., forward and backward linkages), its technological spin-offs, and for the overall importance of transport to the world economy.[22] Given the products themselves and their manufacturing techniques, this industry is by far symbolic of advanced manufacturing that can still be viable in mature economies. It therefore benefits Greater Nagoya to have a healthy motor vehicle industry centered in this region.

Toyota, headquartered in Aichi prefecture, is an obvious leader in motor vehicle production. To provide just one indicator of this firm's growth, Toyota surpassed General Motors during a recent fiscal quarter in terms of worldwide automobile sales, so it stands to reason that this firm is a major player in the industrial powerhouse of Greater Nagoya. In addition to the obvious impact of Toyota itself, one should not neglect to include the large number of suppliers within the industry. The role of the supplier has become increasingly important as just-in-time (JIT) production systems are implemented, and, perhaps more important, the fact that many automakers now choose to focus on their core competencies. This focus, in turn, leads to increased responsibilities on various levels of suppliers, in terms not only of production but also research, design, and development. To this end, the world's third-largest motor vehicle parts supplier, Denso, is headquartered within the region, also in Aichi prefecture, along with a number of other Tier 1 and 2 suppliers.

The manufacturing engine that drives the region is not based solely on its production activities. Beyond the sheer output numbers, Toyota is also viewed as a leader of various manufacturing techniques that have been emulated globally. Toyota has obviously become a leader in high-end automobile production and research, incorporating technologies throughout their manufacturing and assembly processes. The JIT system is important, as are the high-precision technologies used in cars, such as the hybrids the firm is manufacturing. Toyota locates a majority of its design, management, and marketing in the Greater Nagoya region, and indeed many functions have recently moved to a new building in downtown Nagoya.

Another significant component of the transportation equipment sector that merits further mention is aerospace production. While Japan does not have a homegrown, large airframe assembler such as Airbus or Boeing, it does have a number of suppliers to these companies. Almost 50 percent of Japan's aircraft and related component production is centered in the Greater Nagoya region, which is home to firms such as Kawasaki Heavy Industries and Mitsubishi Heavy Industries. Incidentally, these two firms are among the top suppliers for Boeing's newest aircraft, the 787. The role of supplier has become increasingly important, as Boeing has made a concerted move toward becoming an assembler, rather than a manufacturer, of the majority of the aircraft's components.[23] Given the initial customer response to the 787, this industry has become another that could drive sustainable growth for the foreseeable future. Like the automobile industry and perhaps more so, this industry is also emblematic of advanced, sustainable manufacturing in the region.

The continued importance of manufacturing in Japan is an anomaly among other OECD countries. Across Japan, but particularly in the Nagoya region, there is an emphasis on *monozukuri*. This term is loosely translated from the Japanese as "the art of making things." This is an essential point to remember when examining the region and its core industries, as the term illustrates a focus on more than mere production numbers. In essence, manufacturing is viewed as a craft, and that artisan-like knowledge is passed from generation to generation of workers. This philosophy also dovetails with Japan's emphasis on the continual transition toward advanced manufacturing. In a series of visits to Japanese machine tool manufacturers during 2005 and 2006, firm representatives explained that while the emphasis within the region is on manufacturing, production numbers were not the sole focus of firms, but rather quality and innovation.[24] This underscores the importance of the workforce (and its development) in Japan's economic growth.

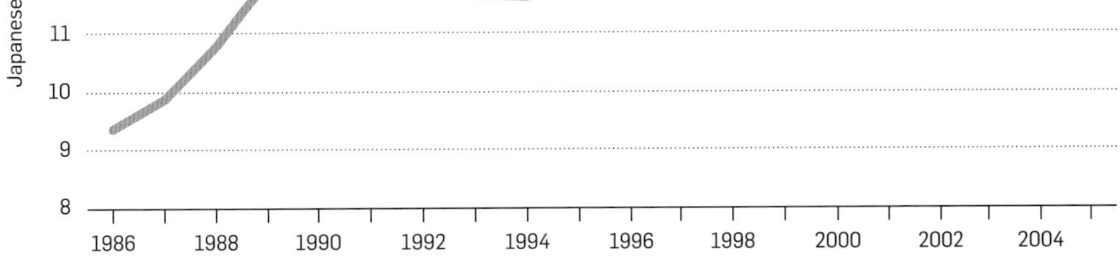

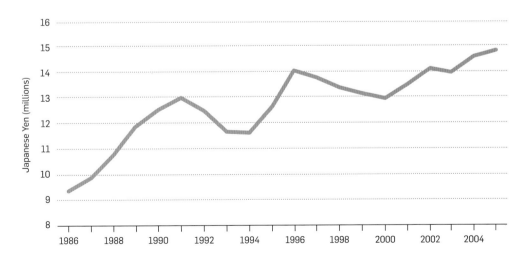

Figure 2. Value-added per manufacturing worker, Aichi Prefecture (in Japanese yen).

Source: Ministry for Economy, Trade and Industry.

On balance, there is evidence that Nagoya is moving toward higher-end manufacturing. Figure 2 indicates that value-added per worker in the Aichi Prefecture's (Nagoya's home) manufacturing sector has increased significantly since the mid-1980s. This provides an indication that workers are moving into higher-skilled activities and that producers are integrated, more capital-intensive, and becoming more efficient overall. Manufacturing employment, while declining, has not been in a steep decline as in most OECD economies. In Aichi, for example, total manufacturing sector employment has decreased by less than 1 percent since 2000.

If actual production activities are to remain in industrialized economies, the emphasis should be on advanced manufacturing—namely, more importance must be placed on research and development activities related to manufacturing. Related to the *monozukuri* concept, across much of Japan manufacturing is still considered to be a good profession. This sentiment is felt particularly in the Greater Nagoya region and, for that matter, in much of Central Japan. This view on the importance of manufacturing helps when firms are recruiting workers. To this day, manufacturers are still able to find some of the best engineers and plant-floor employees, unlike the dilemma seen in many mature economies. The *monozukuri* concept contributes to the high human capital levels of the Nagoya region and ties the economic and social structure tightly together. These advanced manufacturing industries, even at the production levels, pay a wage well above what is available in many other sectors. The motor vehicle and aircraft industries, while in many ways decidedly mature, can also be considered to have foreseeable growth prospects and could form the foundation of modern economies. These sectors also employ and train increasingly higher-skilled workers and form a relatively high value-added component of the economy.

The Machine Tool Industry and Economic Development

The following section provides a study of the machine tool industry and its role as an archetype of an industry that has enabled not only Greater Nagoya but also Japan to enjoy sustained economic growth while maintaining a fairly equitable income distribution. A machine tool is essentially a power-driven machine that shapes or forms metal.[25] In almost any industrialized nation, the machine tool sector is viewed as a core component of manufacturing, and in many ways it is still viewed by most observers as a gauge of a country's advancement in manufacturing technologies and overall health.[26] These viewpoints were certainly prevalent in Japan, where policymakers made the industry a foundation of the country's manufacturing sector reconstruction.[27]

The machine tool industry produces core manufacturing products that are often referred to as "mother machines" by observers both inside and outside of the industry. This sector is emblematic of the concentration on advanced manufacturing and also symbolic of the role that advanced manufacturing plays in the economic development across the Greater Nagoya region. In terms of the large aerospace and motor vehicle sectors discussed in this chapter, machine tool production directly impacts productivity and innovation in both industries. The linkages among these core industries are significant. For example, over 40 percent of the Japanese machine tool industry's output is destined for various customers involved in motor vehicle production.[28]

Over the past few decades, many observers have traced the Japanese machine tool industry's rapid rise into world dominance.[29] Without a doubt, policy-focused actions, including those by

MITI, helped the industry to rebuild after the war. These policy-led initiatives were basically focused on making this industry into a world leader and to support the reconstruction of the remainder of the manufacturing sector. Instead of initially raising import barriers to protect a sensitive industry, a different policy was used. Duties were actually lowered and/or waived for machine tools from leading production states such as France and the United States. The aim of this action was to assist with reverse engineering efforts.[30] In essence, Japan brought in the world's best tooling as a benchmark to what it should achieve at a minimum. Another example of policy-focused action stems from industry consolidation. Essentially, machine tool firms were encouraged to consolidate and to specialize in certain product lines. This created large firms that could weather market uncertainty and, at the same time, reduced undue competition among firms.

Relatively speaking, this industry is concentrated. Most firms are located in Aichi prefecture. The headquarters of Mori Seiki, for example, is actually located in downtown Nagoya, visible from the city's main rail station. Other leading firms, such as Okuma, Yamazaki Mazak, Toyoda, and Murata are headquartered in Aichi prefecture. Over twenty machine tool firms have production facilities in the Greater Nagoya region, with fourteen alone in Aichi. All told, approximately 40 percent of all Japanese machine tool production comes from this three-prefecture area. A location quotient for employment in industrial machinery production for the three prefectures is 1.67.[31] Like the overall manufacturing numbers, this figure is well above parity. The location quotient for this sector within Aichi prefecture itself (the core of Japanese machine tool production) is 1.78.

What advantage does locating in this region provide for machine tool manufacturers? Much of this locational advantage is supported by traditional research on industrial location and work from Porter. There is a tremendous amount of competition between firms (interfirm rivalry), which drives further innovations and improvements. Perhaps most important is a pool of available, high-skilled labor across the region. Given the skill levels required in modern, advanced manufacturing environments, this asset should continue to work toward Nagoya's advantage. Within the machine tool industry and, for that matter, most of Japan's core manufacturing industries, workers are an undeniably important factor in firm-level success. This is a point readily admitted by most machine tool manufacturers. The workers (at all levels) are an active part of the *kaizen,* or continuous improvement, process. This drives innovation, which in turn has led to the sustained importance of manufacturing in this region.

The next advantage concerns proximity to customers. Some of the industry's largest clients are in automobile production and the aerospace industry. Within Japan, both industries are clustered in the Greater Nagoya region. There is an integration of technologies and an exchange of ideas between machine tool manufacturers and their core customers.

Finally, the strategies of the machine tool firms themselves have contributed to the sector's continued dominance. Japan's machine tool producers have remained at the forefront of precision and flexibility. Determined not to go the way of other mature industries, such as textiles and shipbuilding, machine tool producers have developed equipment that can cut at ever-smaller tolerances and at higher speeds. Many of these advancements have been manifested in machining centers, which are multitasking machine tools that encompass the tasks of several pieces of equipment. These machines are highly flexible and programmable, so it stands to reason that they are in high demand in a rapidly evolving international manufacturing environment.[32] Several of the Greater Nagoya regions' largest producers are global leaders in this product line. This development has become important for the automobile industry, which expects ever-increasing quality, noise reduction, and performance. As mentioned, Toyota was viewed as the impetus for this, and interviews have revealed many firms who sold their products to Toyota or to one of their suppliers. These advantages have sustained the industry in recent decades—a notable achievement given the decline of many machine tool makers in other advanced economies, such as the United States and United Kingdom.

The machine tool industry in Japan has been increasingly export-based in nature, as selling outside of traditional market areas is important in maintaining the viability of this sector. Over 60 percent of all Japanese machine tool production is exported—a large percentage by any measure. Looking at the export activity of the industry from a different perspective, the amount of machine tool exports per employee has shown a marked increase since 1990, as seen in figure 3. From the sustainability and innovation perspectives, production for geographically distant markets keeps firms away from reliance on longtime, local customers, thereby avoiding path dependence and potential lack of innovation. The export dominance of the Japanese machine tool industry is important on a national scale as well. It has been suggested that exports kept the industry afloat during periods of dormant domestic demand.[33]

Export-focused industries provide higher-than-average salaries to a region, and increased value of exports per worker would provide a degree of support for Porter's work regarding the impact of extraregional shipments. Ideal industries for a region should increase their export output per capita over time. The emphases on continual innovation, advanced manufacturing, human capital, and export-driven success, which is often the result of the first three factors, appears to have allowed the Greater Nagoya region to remain economically robust well after the decline of urbanized areas such as Manchester or the Ruhr Valley industrial hearth, also located in advanced market economies. The Greater Nagoya Initiative still lists machine tools as one of its targeted sectors for growth, a noteworthy classification given its status as a mature industrial sector.[34]

Challenges for the Nagoya Region

The previous two sections provided short examinations of the manufacturing sector in Greater Nagoya and its role in the sustained economic growth of the region. Machine tool production, a core advanced industrial sector, was used as a specific case example of an industry that can sustain Nagoya's economy. While the current economic situation for manufacturing and machine tools looks robust and indeed appears it will remain that way into the near future, Greater Nagoya faces several competitive issues that may imperil the manufacturing sector and consequently impact sustainable growth for the region. Indeed, as numerous observers have noted, Japan is faced with many future challenges: political, demographic, and economic.[35] The issues, for the Nagoya region at least, essentially boil down to three problems: human capital shortages, the continued sustainability of the automobile industry, and global competition.

The main challenge could come from the skilled labor shortage. In order to remain competitive internationally and in order to retain domestic production sites, the industry's main source of competitive advantage is found in innovation. Skilled workers are at the center of this innovation.

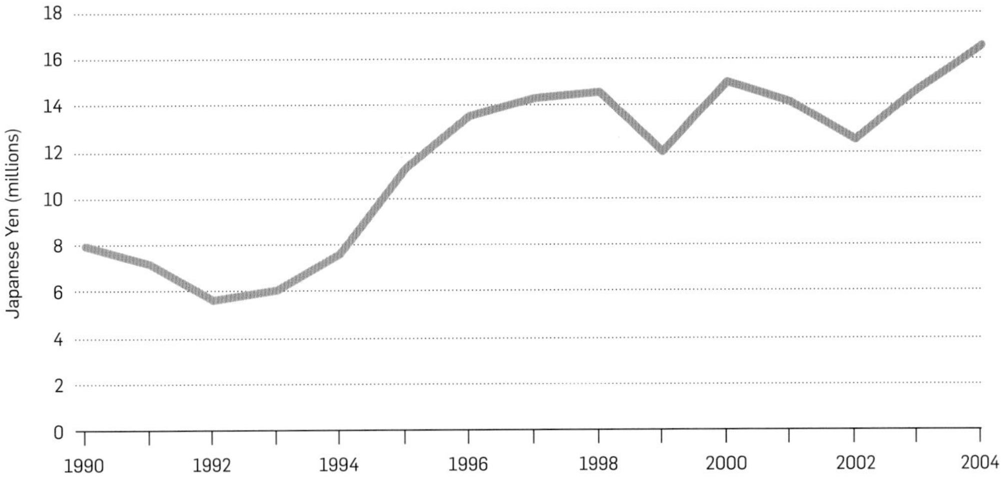

Figure 3. Machine tool exports per employee (in Japanese yen).

Source: Japan Machine Tool Builders Association, *Machine Tool Statistics Handbook* (Tokyo: JMTBA, 2006).

There is a problem, however, as current demographic trends indicate a continually shrinking and aging Japanese workforce. Indeed, across many of the manufacturing centers of Asia, finding skilled workers is one of the largest competitive issues facing firms.[36]

What are companies, the industry as a whole, and Nagoya to do? Already workers are being recruited from India and China for technical positions. Toyota, for example, is training these workers in Japanese language skills. Additionally, a number of production workers have been recruited into Greater Nagoya and its manufacturing sector from Brazil and Peru. While immigration to Japan is less than that of other high-income OECD countries, many manufacturers across this region have turned to immigration to address this shortage of skilled workers. The growth of the Greater Nagoya region and Japan's economic growth have been based on the social contract between large firms and their employees. In the machine tool industry, this seems to be the case. There is a worry, however, that global competition and capital flows will compel firms to break this contract.

There is also a growing impression that many young people do not want to enter the manufacturing field due to the perceived "Three Ks": *kitanai, kitsui,* and *kiken* (dirty, dangerous, and difficult).[37] Given that Japanese manufacturing firms (especially those in the machine tool industry) have been long known for highly skilled and very stable workforces, shifting demographic patterns and attitudes regarding manufacturing could negatively impact this industry. Already, the labor shortage is starting to hurt smaller manufacturers—maybe not machine tool producers per se, but labor shortages impact many of the myriad suppliers on which they rely.

While the economic situation described in this chapter appears to be relatively upbeat, many firm representatives across the region are guarded in their celebration over the recent boom. As one firm representative mentioned, "The economy is based on the success of one company, so what happens if it has problems?" Of course, the one company he alluded to is Toyota. Toyota's growth (even during the 1990s) contributed the sustained robustness of the Central Japan manufacturing sector and overall regional economy.[38] So, if something happens to Toyota, what happens to the fortunes for the rest of the Greater Nagoya region? Adding to this concern, many of the people interviewed readily recall the bubble economy of the 1980s, the subsequent burst of that bubble in 1990, and the resulting fifteen-year economic malaise. This memory causes many of the same people to temper their optimism about the continued viability of this economic growth. Certainly, firms are more concerned with stability than riding the next economic wave.

Increased global competition in the machine tool industries and other core Japanese manufacturing sectors cannot be ignored. The rapid ascent of China as a manufacturing power has cut into profit margins for many Nagoya manufacturers. In the machine tool industry, increased competition has come from South Korea and, to a lesser extent, from Taiwan. At the lower end of machine tool production, Chinese manufacturers have made some inroads as well. Japanese firms, to date, have been able to stay ahead of the curve by producing innovative, technologically advanced, and, in the case of machine tools, high-precision products. However, the changing geographies of global manufacturing and their accompanying challenges are readily acknowledged by Nagoya manufacturers.

Discussion

Why should manufacturing be viewed as an engine of economic growth and stability when this sector is, in many ways, so "old economy"? It is not manufacturing in general to which one should look for answers. Rather, it is advanced, high value-added manufacturing that can be a factor in sustainable economic growth into the future. As Porter, Hirotaka Takeuchi, and Mariko Sakakibara found in their study of industrywide and structural troubles in the Japanese economy, increased output, market share, and efficiencies are not enough to survive global competition.[39] Innovation is the key. The success of the motor vehicle, aerospace, and machine tool sectors epitomize the types of industries that can provide viable employment and sustained economic growth in the Greater Nagoya region and, for that matter, Japan. Beyond the usual financial metrics, manufacturing, in this particular case, can be viewed as a catalyst for stability and maintaining stability, both economically and socially.

A quick look at many measures of productivity would seem to indicate that Japanese firms and economic sectors do not rank as high as many of their OECD counterparts. Many observers have noted that, on balance, Japanese firms tend to have far more employees than their competitors located elsewhere. In some ways and in particularly in advanced manufacturing, this is important, as firms do not lose their skilled employees just because of an economic downturn. However, on a larger scale, some would suggest that this "overstaffing" is largely by design, as Japan policymakers and Japanese society at-large tend to view full employment as a sign of social stability.[40] In many advanced market economies, firms are much leaner and, accordingly, national unemployment rates are much higher. In many ways, the instability is shifted to society, whereas in Japan, companies work in concert with policymakers to ensure that this dislocation does not occur. The importance of harmony and the need to minimize risk and uncertainty in society is important in Japan and across much of Asia.[41]

The machine tool industry, heavily concentrated in Greater Nagoya, is used as an example of a core industry that has enabled Japanese manufacturing to remain competitive and, indeed, sustainable, even in light of increasing global pressures in the manufacturing sector. There is little doubt that Japan's manufacturing sector had initial help from MITI and other government agencies. Over time, however, these industries have become largely independent of public sector involvement. Growth and international success has stemmed from industrywide and firm-level initiatives, and regional advantages such as highly skilled workers. These are the exact kind of industries that maintain high human capital levels across Greater Nagoya.

The evidence presented in this chapter raises larger questions about the logic of jettisoning manufacturing as a viable component of advanced market economies. This chapter has attempted to illustrate how advanced manufacturing plays a pivotal role in Japan's economy. Beyond the obvious macroeconomic roles, the high skills and wages found within these industries have led to the development and maintenance of a large middle class. This raises a question: Does "creative destruction" of manufacturing sectors necessarily lead to the best outcomes or, for that matter, economic and social stability?

The Nagoya area appears to have the right conditions for sustained economic development. The leading core industries, such as machine tools and motor vehicle production, have moved into advanced manufacturing stages, beyond competition centered solely on low costs. Machine tool production is certainly representative of this trend, with its attention to precision, automation, and the focus on product niches such as machining centers.

Perhaps the most critical advantage of Greater Nagoya is that high-end human capital remains clustered in this region. In an advanced manufacturing environment, manufacturing skills will only be in higher demand. The Greater Nagoya region is a center of skilled machinists, designers, engineers, and numerous other skilled professions. Finally, the industries described in this chapter are leading exporters. While there is little doubt that there is still a healthy domestic market for many firms, their competitiveness on global markets spurs even further innovation. This relative stability will again depend on valuing the workers so crucial to firm-level and regionwide growth, which has long been a policy of many Japanese manufacturers.

In the Greater Nagoya region, manufacturing is doing quite well, and this economic sector remains at the core of its long-term growth plans. Manufacturing contributes to sustainable growth in the city and its environs. The challenge is, of course, to remain sustainable. Japan's demographic issues are adding to this challenge, with a shrinking working-age population, a problem exacerbated by a declining interest in manufacturing, though not at rates witnessed in other industrialized states. To retain manufacturing in Japan (and to avoid a wholesale move to overseas production), the answer is to remain innovative, which will require investments in the workforce—by firms and policymakers. Likewise, the immigration issue will also have to be continually revisited.

The dynamics of global capitalism and worldwide capital movements may put pressure on Japanese firms and the government to reevaluate the socioeconomic goals of the current systems and their costs. To this point, economic growth has resulted in relative stability and fewer income disparities than seen throughout much of the OECD. Will pressures to lower costs and to make manufacturing operations lean cause a move away from stability toward more inequality?

Additionally, will continued cost pressures that compel more Japanese manufacturers to move operations abroad also result in problems with this social contract?

Conclusion

This chapter has offered a look at the extended Nagoya region and the role of manufacturing in its continued positive economic trajectory. Nagoya is unique, in that there are not many examples of the manufacturing sector still serving as a driving force in metropolitan regions of advanced market economies. In most of the thriving economic clusters often described in the literature, manufacturing activities have been replaced largely by research and development activities and management (e.g., Silicon Valley) or, in cases where manufacturing is still prevalent, it is in protracted decline (e.g., Detroit and southern Michigan). Manufacturing overall remains important, even in advanced market economies, due to the types of jobs it can provide. Engineering and high-end research positions are, of course, important elements of manufacturing and regional growth. However, production-level positions are a large source of jobs that, on balance, pay higher than almost any other position for workers without advanced degrees. In this sense, Nagoya's manufacturing sector provides sustainable employment across all sectors, an urban-economic objective discussed in Igor Vojnovic's "Advancing toward Urban Sustainability." It contributes, moreover, to the earlier-discussed objectives regarding equity issues and stability.

Skilled employees are at the root of Japanese manufacturing competitiveness. So these companies must retain a base of highly skilled workers.[42] Beyond perceptions of overstaffing at private sector companies, the manufacturing sector in general fits into an Asian model of sustainable economic development and societal stability. Most would agree that advanced manufacturing jobs pay above-average wages and support a large middle class. In many ways, this reality underlies the importance of the manufacturing sector not only to Greater Nagoya but also to much of Japan. It also suggests that properly located advanced manufacturing still has a role to play in mature market economies.

NOTES

1. R. Florida, *The Flight of the Creative Class* (New York: HarperCollins, 2006).
2. M. E. Porter, *The Competitive Advantage of Nations* (New York: Free Press, 1990); E. L. Glaeser, The New Economics of Urban and Regional Growth, in *The Oxford Handbook of Economic Geography*, ed. G. L. Clark, M. P. Feldman, and M. S. Gertler (Oxford: Oxford University Press, 2000), 83–98; A. J. Scott and M. Storper, Regions, Globalization, Development, *Regional Studies* 37:6/7 (2003): 579–93.
3. M. E. Porter, *The Competitive Advantage of Nations* (New York: Free Press, 1990); M. E. Porter, The Adam Smith Address: Location, Clusters, and the "New" Microeconomics of Competition, *Business Economics* 33:1 (1998): 7–13; M. E. Porter, The Economic Performance of Regions, *Regional Studies* 37:6/7 (2003): 549–78.
4. M. E. Porter, *The Competitive Advantage of Nations.*
5. A. Marshall, *Principles of Economics* (London: Macmillan, 1890); Allen J. Scott, *New Industrial Spaces: Flexible Production Organization and Regional Development in North America* (London: Pion, 1988); P. Krugman, *Geography and Trade* (Cambridge, MA: MIT Press, 1991).
6. Glaeser, The New Economics of Urban and Regional Growth, 83–98.
7. M. J. Orlando and M. Verba, Do Only Big Cities Innovate? Technological Maturity and the Location

of Innovation, *Economic Review—Federal Reserve Bank of Kansas City* 90:2 (2005): 31–57.
8. Porter, The Economic Performance of Regions, 549–78.
9. P. A. Hall and D. Soskice, An Introduction to Varieties of Capitalism, in *Varieties of Capitalism: The Institutional Foundations of Comparative Advantage*, ed. P. A. Hall and D. Soskice (Oxford: Oxford University Press, 2001), 1–70; B. Amable, *The Diversity of Modern Capitalism* (Oxford: Oxford University Press, 2003).
10. R. Boyer, *The Regulation School: A Critical Introduction* (New York: Columbia University Press, 1990).
11. Amable, *The Diversity of Modern Capitalism.*
12. E. Sakakibara, *Beyond Capitalism: The Japanese Model of Market Economics* (Lanham, MD: University Press of America, 1993).
13. R. Komiya, M. Okuno, and K. Suzumura, *Industrial Policy of Japan* (Tokyo: Academic Press, 1988).
14. World Bank, *The East Asian Miracle: Economic Growth and Public Policy* (New York: Oxford University Press, 1993).
15. G. Haughton, Environmental Justice and the Sustainable City, in *The Earthscan Reader in Sustainable Cities*, ed. D. Satterthwaite (London: Earthscan, 1999), 62–79.
16. T. R. See Reid, *Confucius Lives Next Door: What Living in the East Teaches Us About Living in the West* (New York: Vintage Books, 2000).
17. Ibid.
18. K. Yamamura, Germany and Japan in a New Phase of Capitalism: Confronting the Past and the Future, in *The End of Diversity: Prospects for German and Japanese Capitalism*, ed. K. Yamamura and W. Streeck (Ithaca, NY: Cornell University Press, 2003), 115–46.
19. This three-prefecture definition of the Nagoya metropolitan region is also used by the Greater Nagoya Initiative (an interprefecture economic development group) and by other organizations.
20. Greater Nagoya Initiative, 2007, http://www.greaternagoya.org.
21. S. Banasick and R. Q. Hanham, Time Paths of Uneven Industrial Development in Japan, *Industrial Geographer* 3:2 (2006): 27–45.
22. P. Dicken, *Global Shift*, 5th ed. (New York: Guilford Press, 2007).
23. D. Pritchard and A. D. MacPherson, Industrial Subsidies and the Politics of World Trade: The Case of the Boeing 7E7, *The Industrial Geographer* 1 (2004): 57–73.
24. R. V. Kalafsky, Human Capital in Japanese Manufacturing: Evidence and Practices from a Key Capital Goods Sector, *Industrial Geographer* 4:1 (2006): 13–26.
25. In many countries, the machine tool industry encompasses both metal-cutting and metal-forming machinery. In Japan, it refers only to the former. The statistics in this chapter will therefore refer to metal-cutting machinery.
26. J. Graham, Firm and State Strategy in a Multipolar World: The Changing Geography of Machine Tool Production and Trade, in *Trading Industries, Trading Regions*, ed. H. Noponen, J. Graham, and A. Markusen (New York: Guilford Press, 1993), 140–74; J. F. Logan, Testimony of John F. Logan, Automation Group President—DT Industries, Chairman—AMT—The Association for Manufacturing Technology, before the Committee on Commerce, Science and Transportation, United States Senate, October 28, 1999.
27. R. Sarathy, The Interplay of Industrial Policy and International Strategy: Japan's Machine Tool Industry, *California Management Review* 31:3 (1989): 132–60.
28. Japan Machine Tool Builders Association, *Machine Tool Statistics Handbook* (Tokyo: JMTBA, 2006).
29. M. Dertouzos, R. Solow, R. Lester, and MIT Commission on Productivity, *Made in America: Regaining the Productive Edge* (Cambridge, MA: MIT Press, 1989); S. Kotha, and A. Nair, Strategy and Environment As Determinants of Performance: Evidence from the Japanese Machine Tool Industry, *Strategic Management Journal* 16:7 (1995): 497–518.
30. M. Tsuji and M. Ishikawa, Technology and Industrial Transformation: The Case of the Japanese Machine Tool Industry, *Oikonomika* 31 (1995): 155–69.
31. Prefecture-level data for specific machine tool industry employment were not available from METI or the Japan Machine Tool Builders Association.
32. M. Tsuji and M. Ishikawa, Technology and Industrial Transformation: The Case of the Japanese Machine Tool Industry, *Oikonomika* 31 (1995): 155–69.
33. Ibid.
34. http://www.greaternagoya.org.
35. M. E. Porter, H. Takeuchi, and M. Sakakibara, *Can Japan Compete?* (Cambridge, MA: Basic Books, 2000); K. Yamamura, Germany and Japan in a New Phase of Capitalism: Confronting the Past and the Future, *The End of Diversity: Prospects for German and Japanese Capitalism*, ed. K. Yamamura and W. Streeck (Ithaca, NY: Cornell University Press, 2003), 115–46.
36. Briefing: Asia's Skills Shortage—Capturing Talent, *Economist*, August 18, 2007, 59–61.

37. R. V. Kalafsky, Human Capital in Japanese Manufacturing: Evidence and Practices from a Key Capital Goods Sector, *Industrial Geographer* 4:1 (2006): 13–26.
38. Banasick and Hanham, Time Paths of Uneven Industrial Development in Japan, 27–45.
39. Porter, Takeuchi, and Sakakibara, *Can Japan Compete?*
40. Reid, *Confucius Lives Next Door.*
41. G. H. Hofstede and M. H. Bond, The Confucius Connection: From Cultural Roots to Economic Growth, *Organizational Dynamics* 16:4 (1988): 5–21; F. Trompenaars and C. Hampden-Turner, *Riding the Waves of Culture: Understanding Diversity in Global Business* (New York: McGraw-Hill, 1998).
42. R. V. Kalafsky, Human Capital in Japanese Manufacturing: Evidence and Practices from a Key Capital Goods Sector, *Industrial Geographer* 4:1 (2006): 13–26.

REFERENCES

Amable, Bruno. *The Diversity of Modern Capitalism.* Oxford: Oxford University Press, 2003.

Banasick, Shawn, and Robert Q. Hanham. Time Paths of Uneven Industrial Development in Japan. *Industrial Geographer* 3:2 (2006): 27–45.

Boyer, Robert. *The Regulation School: A Critical Introduction.* New York: Columbia University Press, 1990.

Dertouzos, Michael L., Robert M. Solow, Richard K. Lester, and MIT Commission on Productivity. *Made in America: Regaining the Productive Edge.* Cambridge, MA: MIT Press, 1989.

Dicken, Peter. *Global Shift.* 5th ed. New York: Guilford Press, 2007.

Economist. Briefing: Asia's Skills Shortage—Capturing Talent. *Economist*, August 18, 2007, 59–61.

Florida, Richard. *The Flight of the Creative Class.* New York: HarperCollins, 2006.

Glaeser, Edward L. The New Economics of Urban and Regional Growth. In *The Oxford Handbook of Economic Geography*, ed. Gordon L. Clark, Maryann P. Feldman, and Meric S. Gertler, 83–98. Oxford: Oxford University Press, 2000.

Graham, Julie. Firm and State Strategy in a Multipolar World: The Changing Geography of Machine Tool Production and Trade. In *Trading Industries, Trading Regions*, ed. Helzi Noponen, Julie Graham, and Ann R. Markusen, 140–74. New York: Guilford Press, 1993.

Greater Nagoya Initiative. 2007. http://www.greaternagoya.org.

Hall, Peter A., and David Soskice. An Introduction to Varieties of Capitalism. In *Varieties of Capitalism: The Institutional Foundations of Comparative Advantage*, ed. Peter A. Hall and David Soskice, 1–70. Oxford: Oxford University Press, 2001.

Haughton, Graham. Environmental Justice and the Sustainable City. In *The Earthscan Reader in Sustainable Cities*, ed. David Satterthwaite, 62–79. London: Earthscan Publications, 1999.

Hofstede, Geert, and Michael H. Bond. The Confucius Connection: From Cultural Roots to Economic Growth. *Organizational Dynamics* 16:4 (1988): 5–21.

Japan Machine Tool Builders Association. *Machine Tool Statistics Handbook.* Tokyo: Japan Machine Tool Builders Association, 2006.

Kalafsky, Ronald V. Human Capital in Japanese Manufacturing: Evidence and Practices from a Key Capital Goods Sector. *Industrial Geographer* 4:1 (2006): 13–26.

Komiya, Ryutaro, Masahiro Okuno, and Kotaro Suzumura. *Industrial Policy of Japan.* Tokyo: Academic Press, 1988.

Kotha, Suresh, and Anil Nair. Strategy and Environment as Determinants of Performance: Evidence from the Japanese Machine Tool Industry. *Strategic Management Journal* 16:7 (1995): 497–518.

Krugman, Paul. *Geography and Trade.* Cambridge, MA: MIT Press, 1991.

Logan, John F. Testimony of John F. Logan, Automation Group President—DT Industries, Chairman—AMT—The Association for Manufacturing Technology, before the Committee on Commerce, Science and Transportation, United States Senate, October 28, 1999.

Marshall, Alfred. *Principles of Economics.* London: Macmillan, 1890.

Orlando, Michael J., and Michael Verba. Do Only Big Cities Innovate? Technological Maturity and the Location of Innovation. *Economic Review—Federal Reserve Bank of Kansas City* 90:2 (2005): 31–57.

Porter, Michael E. The Adam Smith Address: Location, Clusters, and the "New" Microeconomics of Competition. *Business Economics* 33:1 (1998): 7–13.

———. *The Competitive Advantage of Nations.* New York: Free Press, 1990.

———. The Economic Performance of Regions. *Regional Studies* 37:6/7 (2003): 549–78.

Porter, Michael E., Hirotaka Takeuchi, and Mariko Sakakibara. *Can Japan Compete?* Cambridge, MA: Basic Books, 2000.

Pritchard, David, and Alan MacPherson. Industrial Subsidies and the Politics of World Trade: The Case of the Boeing 7E7. *Industrial Geographer* 1 (2004): 57–73.

Reid, T. R. *Confucius Lives Next Door: What Living in the East Teaches Us About Living in the West.* Vintage Books: New York, 2000.

Sakakibara, Eisuke. *Beyond Capitalism: The Japanese Model of Market Economics.* Lanham, MD: University Press of America, 1993.

Sarathy, Ravi. The Interplay of Industrial Policy and International Strategy: Japan's Machine Tool Industry. *California Management Review* 31:3 (1989): 132–60.

Scott, Allen J. *New Industrial Spaces: Flexible Production Organization and Regional Development in North America.* London: Pion, 1988.

Scott, Allen J., and Michael Storper. 2003. Regions, Globalization, Development. *Regional Studies* 37:6/7 (2003): 579–93.

Trompenaars, Fons, and Charles Hampden-Turner. *Riding the Waves of Culture: Understanding Diversity in Global Business.* New York: McGraw-Hill, 1998.

Tsuji, Masatsugu, and Mineo Ishikawa. Technology and Industrial Transformation: The Case of the Japanese Machine Tool Industry. *Oikonomika* 31 (1995): 155–69.

World Bank. *The East Asian Miracle: Economic Growth and Public Policy.* Oxford: Oxford University Press, 1993.

Yamamura, Kozo. Germany and Japan in a New Phase of Capitalism: Confronting the Past and the Future. In *The End of Diversity: Prospects for German and Japanese Capitalism*, ed. Kozo Yamamura and Wolfgang Streeck, 115–46. Ithaca, NY: Cornell University Press, 2003.

■ PARIWATE VARNAKOVIDA / JOSEPH MESSINA

The Sufficiency Economy, Sustainable Development, and Agricultural Towns in Thailand

THE CASE OF NANG RONG

During the late twentieth century, much of Southeast Asia adopted the pro-growth policies of the International Bank for Reconstruction and Development. The export-oriented growth model focused on development in the industrial and commercial sectors using resources from rural economies.[1] Following regional trends, Thailand from 1960 through the mid-2000s adopted the National Development Plan, which focused on rapid gross national product (GNP) growth through capital-intensive industrialization.[2] However, with the adoption of this development plan, uneven growth and significant equity imbalances resulted in highly disproportionate income distributions and extreme differences in basic living standards emerging between urban and rural areas.[3] Concurrently, land and other natural resources increasingly became maldistributed as early settlers acquired the last remaining available lands and, of course, preferentially selected the best lands with the best soil and water conditions, further exacerbating national inequities.

While Thailand was focusing on capital-intensive industrialization, in 1974 King Bhumibol Adulyadej introduced a new national development model: the philosophy of the sufficiency economy, which focused on investment in the rural agricultural sector, where traditionally the vast majority of the Thai population was and still is employed.[4] The sufficiency economy is explicitly sustainable based on the holistic concepts of moderation and contentment. The philosophy was introduced with the idea of production not just for profit maximization but also for advancement toward sustainability. Over the last four decades, these two competing development strategies—offering very different approaches to economic growth and resulting variably in social and environmental stresses—played important roles in shaping national, regional, and local policies in Thailand.

The World Commission on Environment and Development defined sustainable development as "development which meets the needs of the present without compromising the ability of the future generations to meet their own needs."[5] Sustainability and urban sustainability have long histories, as shown in Igor Vojnovic's "Advancing toward Urban Sustainability," but it has been argued that any movement toward sustainability requires that natural resource utilization include consideration of both intergenerational and intragenerational equities.[6] Intergenerational equity requires consuming resources at rates less than their regeneration rates and maintaining waste discharges at or below the carrying capacity of the natural environment. Intragenerational equity requires equitable access to resources among existing populations.[7] In the context of less developed regions, intragenerational equity must also satisfy the basic needs of the people in the existing generations. As argued by Cedric Pugh,[8] sustainable development is basically about maintaining environmental resources for the present generations while minimizing environmental degradation, thereby ensuring environmental and social well-being in the future.

In this chapter, we explore the history of Thailand, where the impacts of globalization and the adoption of an urban-based development policy have had considerable implications on basic issues of social equity and natural environmental stresses. The national pressures associated with increasing social disparities caused by some three decades of export-oriented growth development contributed, in part, to a military overthrow of the government in 2006. The coup set in motion the adoption of a new policy direction based on King Aduladej's sufficiency economy as Thailand attempts to pursue its own version of a more sustainable socioeconomic and environmental policy direction. Exploring the challenges in Thailand and the national conflicts of two very different contexts of development, this chapter uses the case of the Nang Rong district in Northeast Thailand to illustrate more explicitly how the different national policies have been translated into local initiatives and outcomes that have produced varying degrees of urban-environmental and urban-social stresses, as well as movements toward and away from the sustainability condition.

Urban Transitions and Development in Thailand and the Rise of the Sufficiency Economy

Located in central Southeast Asia, Thailand covers approximately 198,457 square miles. As of 2005 the total population was 62,418,054, with a population density of 315 persons per square mile.[9] The first Thai or Siamese state was founded in 1238 and was called the Sukhothai kingdom. The current (Ratthanakosin) era of Thai history began in 1782 following the establishment of Bangkok as capital of the Chakri dynasty under King Rama I the Great.[10]

King Rama V (1868–1910) promoted modern urban development in Bangkok by making it the center of a centralized administration. Critical infrastructure development began in the 1960s with the development of new roads and the extension of existing ones throughout the region to support the increasing population and the transportation of agricultural produce.[11]

With the implementation of the First to the Eighth National Development Plans (1957-2001), the primary interest was placed on economic growth through the promotion of export-oriented industries.[12] Plans were made for the establishment of industrial estates in cities, and growing disparities became evident between urban and rural areas. The growing pressures on small settlements throughout the country were also exacerbated by the rise of commercial agriculture, which began to replace small-scale, labor-intensive farming. The emerging economy not only promoted inequality in resource distribution and unbalanced and unstable growth throughout Thailand; it also placed severe pressures on natural ecological systems, particularly evident with increasing pollution and large-scale deforestation.[13]

In rural areas, the subsistence economy remains an important form of production. Peasants produce their own food, and in some cases their own clothing and other household utensils.[14] However, with globalization the expansion of the modern form of the free market economy has emerged and resulted in a more competitive and complex market for commercial agricultural production. The expansion of upland cash cropping occurred as a direct result of increased domestic and international demand for upland field crops.[15] Consumerism and extraregional demand further motivated households to clear forestlands and to extend cultivation of traditional field crops, as well as intensify paddy rice production.[16] Agricultural-based towns also faced added stresses due to a shift in policy focus, which began to increasingly concentrate new resource investments in large cities.

With growing social and environmental stresses, and growing political pressures for a new development direction, the government marketed the Ninth National Development Plan (2001-2006) as a starting point for implementing some of the king's sufficiency concepts. However, while some innovative programs from the Sufficiency Plan were introduced, it soon became clear that the government had no interest in implementing the full sufficiency strategy. Instead, a new tactic in its development plan was to directly inject investment into village development funds, resulting in more spending in the general economy. While production and investment were stimulated by the government spending, there was also growing evidence of increased corruption, authoritarianism, and the use of legal loopholes to support the government and this new national program. The growing political opposition facilitated a military coup in 2006, deposing the prime minister and setting a new national policy reliant much more fundamentally on the King's National Sufficiency Program. The introduction of the Tenth National Development Plan (2007–2011) implemented the king's concept of the sufficiency economy and was based on the "middle path" as a way of life.[17]

The Tenth National Development Plan dismantled the export-oriented economic approach of the last four decades. The goal for national development over the next ten to fifteen years will be based on the Green and Happiness Society according to the sufficiency economy philosophy and people-centered development.[18] The plan focuses on four objectives: developing the people to be knowledgeable and to have good moral standards; promoting equality and strengthening the society; reforming economic structure for sustainability and fairness; and developing good governance as a norm at all levels. Before Thailand's sufficiency plan is explored in more detail, the chapter will first review some of the socioeconomic and environmental stresses that gave rise to this program.

Globalization, Agricultural Production, and Growing Environmental Stresses under the Export-Oriented Growth Model

Driven by the National Development Plan during 1970s–1990s, Thailand's economy rapidly expanded, and the country was poised to join other Asian Tigers as a newly industrialized country (NIC). Thailand's export-oriented growth development policy produced gross domestic product

Table 1. Income share by quintile groups, 1975/1976–1992

QUINTILE	1975/1976	1981	1990	1992
Bottom	6.1	5.4	4.1	5.6
Second	9.7	9.1	7.4	8.7
Third	13.9	13.4	11.6	13.0
Fourth	21.0	20.6	19.7	20.0
Top	49.3	51.5	57.3	52.7

Source: Walden Bello, Shea Cunningham, and Li Kheng Poh, *A Siamese Tragedy: Development and Disintegration in Modern Thailand* (New York: Zed Books, 1998), 37.

(GDP) increases of 5.7 percent between 1970 and 1975, 7.8 percent between 1976 and 1980, and 9.9 percent between 1986 and 1990.[19] Urban centers and services expanded throughout the country. At the same time, Thailand evolved highly uneven patterns of development, particularly evident between high growth urban and disadvantaged rural areas. Environmental degradation was also rampant, with deforestation rates and pollution of all kinds increasing. However, the general economic strength of the country created an atmosphere of growth, prosperity, and security. Concerns over sustainability and equity were ignored by focusing only on the expansion of the economy.

With respect to socioeconomic pressures, the new prosperity was clearly not being distributed equally across the population. Thailand's growing reliance on the export-oriented growth model exacerbated inequities throughout the country. As table 1 shows, the majority of income was shared by the top quintile group, with the growing disparities in the rural areas evident since the 1970s throughout the 1980s and 1990s.

With globalization, the expansion of the market economy for agricultural products has resulted in a more open and competitive global market.[20] However, with the new global economy the growing demand for agricultural products has also placed natural ecological systems under increasing stress. Since the mid-1970s, deforestation and agricultural extensification in upland areas in Thailand were driven by the demand of European Economic Community (EEC) countries for calorie-rich livestock feed (see tables 2 and 3). In addition to increasing world market demand,

Table 2. Forest area in Thailand, 1950–2004

YEAR	SQUARE MILES	PERCENTAGE	YEAR	SQUARE MILES	PERCENTAGE
1950	132,819	67.00	1989	55,374	27.95
1961	105,649	53.33	1991	52,779	26.64
1973	85,602	43.21	1993	51,565	26.03
1976	76,609	38.67	1995	50,767	25.62
1978	67,654	34.15	1998	50,086	25.28
1982	60,464	30.52	2000	65,680	33.15
1985	58,250	29.40	2004	64,707	32.66
1988	55,525	28.03			

Source: The Royal Forest Department, 2006.

Table 3. Expansion of agricultural area (sq. mi.) in Thailand, 1986–1991

YEAR	FOREST	AGRICULTURAL AREA	HOUSING	RICE FIELD	CASH CROPS
1986	57,307	80,864	1,920	45,853	20,216
1987	56,398	81,052	1,940	44,584	20,669
1988	55,525	81,404	1,993	43,755	20,535
1989	55,374	81,441	2,029	43,361	20,471
1990	54,047	81,622	2,077	42,895	20,643
1991	52,779	82,210	2,134	42,782	20,702

Source: The Royal Forest Department, 1999.

upland cash cropping was facilitated by other factors, including improved infrastructure and the adoption of new technologies in farming.

Increasing globalization led to the emergence of large-scale commercial farmers who produced mainly for export markets. It also motivated small-scale farmers to change their agricultural patterns to be more competitive by switching to short-term-profit commercial upland cassava agriculture.[21] Most of the small-scale farmers own between fifteen to twenty rais of land (1 rai = 0.0006 square mile or 0.384 acre),[22] and while they make up approximately 50 percent of total farm population, they contribute only 25 percent of the total market value of agriculture production.[23] National statistics show that the number of small-scale farmers who held land less than six rais decreased 0.6 percent during 1993–1998 due to conversion to commercial agriculture. The number of large-scale farmers who own land between ten to thirty-nine rais, on the other hand, increased by 3.2 percent during the same period (see table 4).

Throughout this period, other coincidental exogenous factors—including the Asian Economic Crisis in 1997 and a severe drought—increasingly disrupted the socioecological system, accelerating environmental degradation and increasing rural poverty and inequality within Thailand.[24] The degree of inequality among subgroup populations and regional disparities remained high. The Gini coefficient (0.524 in 1990, 0.527 in 1994, 0.511 in 1998, and 0.511 in 2002) supports this assertion.

Table 4. Number of agricultural landholding by size of total area

TOTAL AREA HOLDING	NUMBER OF HOLDERS			PERCENTAGE OF HOLDINGS		
(ACRES)	1993	1998	2003	1993	1998	2003
Under 2.4	1,114,038	1,066,346	1,372,215	19.7	19.1	23.6
2.4–3.6	745,982	779,357	816,588	13.2	14.0	14.0
3.7–15.4	3,064,632	3,205,114	2,970,571	54.3	57.5	51.1
15.5–55.0	694,292	505,940	625,917	12.3	9.0	10.8
Over 55.0	28,564	21,438	29,338	0.5	0.4	0.5
Total	**5,647,508**	**5,578,195**	**5,814,629**	**100.0**	**100.0**	**100.0**

Source: National Statistical Office, 2004.

Table 5. Thailand's official poverty lines, 1988–2002*

REGION/AREAS	POVERTY LINES (BAHT PER CAPITA PER MONTH)								
	1988	1990	1992	1994	1996	1998	2000	2001	2002
Central	**476**	**526**	**599**	**622**	**714**	**876**	**882**	**925**	**930**
Rural/nonmunicipal	462	509	581	601	691	864	856	862	866
Urban/municipal	592	659	744	784	895	968	1,059	1,082	1,089
North	**459**	**498**	**563**	**581**	**702**	**791**	**777**	**828**	**830**
Rural/nonmunicipal	448	486	549	566	696	779	758	781	783
Urban/municipal	585	626	706	752	846	938	996	1,011	1,009
Northeast	**443**	**477**	**577**	**611**	**698**	**880**	**864**	**890**	**898**
Rural/nonmunicipal	435	469	570	599	687	869	850	856	864
Urban/municipal	597	641	734	773	883	1,064	1,057	1,059	1,068
South	**466**	**518**	**582**	**624**	**716**	**843**	**841**	**879**	**890**
Rural/nonmunicipal	441	492	553	593	684	804	797	806	819
Urban/municipal	620	682	763	829	951	1,108	1,100	1,123	1,129
Bangkok	**587**	**684**	**752**	**835**	**950**	**1,019**	**1,101**	**1,109**	**1,112**
Bangkok vicinity	**506**	**604**	**666**	**658**	**774**	**935**	**972**	**1,027**	**1,021**
Rural/nonmunicipal	474	537	596	614	710	894	884	896	886
Urban/municipal	568	681	749	838	931	1,015	1,107	1,113	1,110
Whole kingdom	**473**	**522**	**600**	**636**	**737**	**878**	**882**	**916**	**922**
Rural/nonmunicipal	445	485	566	592	690	840	825	835	841
Urban/municipal	590	672	746	816	930	1,020	1,086	1,086	1,090

*Monthly per capita income in baht at which one falls into poverty, shown by region. (100 baht equals US$3.23).
Source: The Office of National Economic and Social Development Board (NESDB), *Social Outlook* 2:1 (2005), 9.

Households with average per capita income below the poverty line, based on costs of basic needs, were considered as income poor. The poverty line was used as a tool to monitor and measure poverty incidence, and it revealed that the majority of impoverished households are found in rural/nonmunicipal areas. The increasing gap between urban and rural incomes revealed the severity of rural poverty and rural/urban inequality that emerged under the national export-oriented growth model program (see tables 5 and 6).

Under the export-oriented growth model, alternative forms of agriculture, particularly contract and high-tech farming, were introduced to rural areas. Local elite landowners hired the poor or landless to exploit the forests to acquire more land for cash crop agriculture. Small-scale farmers were pressured to enter wage labor arrangements to supplement falling, inflation adjusted incomes or to relinquish land—sometimes both. In some cases, farmers borrowed large amounts of money from creditors to pay for the higher input costs for fertilizers and pesticides. Many forfeited their land to creditors or sold it to repay the loans when incomes failed due to the wide fluctuations of the global rice or cassava markets, or due to the natural variation in climate.

In addition, the government promoted the export-oriented programs by providing low interest

Table 6. Poverty incidence in Thailand, 1988–2002

REGION/AREAS	POVERTY INCIDENCE (%)								
	1988	1990	1992	1994	1996	1998	2000	2001	2002
Central	**25.2**	**20.5**	**12.1**	**8.4**	**5.9**	**7.0**	**5.4**	**4.6**	**4.3**
Rural/nonmunicipal	28.8	22.9	14.7	9.7	6.9	8.1	6.4	4.5	4.8
Urban/municipal	10.6	8.6	2.1	5.2	1.6	2.3	2.0	5.0	3.0
North	**32.0**	**23.2**	**22.6**	**13.2**	**11.2**	**9.1**	**12.1**	**10.6**	**9.8**
Rural/nonmunicipal	34.3	25.5	25.9	15.0	13.1	10.2	13.9	11.0	10.9
Urban/municipal	14.3	11.3	5.2	3.8	3.6	3.3	3.4	9.0	6.0
Northeast	**48.4**	**43.1**	**39.9**	**28.6**	**19.4**	**24.0**	**28.1**	**24.5**	**17.7**
Rural/nonmunicipal	51.6	45.9	42.4	31.4	21.1	26.2	30.7	26.5	18.9
Urban/municipal	19.2	19.1	13.8	6.7	3.6	4.0	6.0	15.0	11.0
South	**32.5**	**27.6**	**19.7**	**17.3**	**11.5**	**14.6**	**11.0**	**13.5**	**8.7**
Rural/nonmunicipal	36.9	30.5	22.7	20.0	12.6	16.9	12.9	15.2	9.4
Urban/municipal	13.8	13.9	7.5	5.1	6.3	3.0	4.0	8.0	6.0
Bangkok	**3.8**	**3.3**	**1.9**	**0.6**	**0.3**	**1.0**	**0.0**	**1.0**	**1.0**
Bangkok vicinity	**8.7**	**3.0**	**1.7**	**1.6**	**1.0**	**0.5**	**0.7**	**1.0**	**2.0**
Rural/nonmunicipal	12.6	2.3	3.0	2.2	0.2	0.9	0.1	1.1	0.9
Urban/municipal	7.8	3.8	0.7	0.0	3.3	1.0	1.0	1.0	2.0
Whole kingdom	**32.6**	**27.2**	**23.2**	**16.3**	**11.4**	**13.0**	**14.2**	**13.0**	**9.8**
Rural/nonmunicipal	40.3	33.8	29.7	21.2	14.9	17.3	19.1	16.6	12.6
Urban/municipal	8.0	6.9	3.6	2.4	1.6	1.0	2.0	6.0	4.0

Source: The Office of National Economic and Social Development Board (NESDB), *Social Outlook* 2:1 (2005), 9.

loans intended to facilitate small-scale farmers to postpone the sale of their rice when world market prices were low.[25] However, middlemen and large-scale farmers received far greater benefits from the programs as opposed to the small-scale farmers, who often did not meet rice quality minimums to qualify. The quality problems resulted from the fact that many small-scale farmers simply did not have the mills or other technologies to keep their rice dry. This contributed to the lack of rice necessary to use as mortgage collateral during periods of severe drought.[26]

Overall, the growing competition that came along with globalization placed increasing pressures on local farmers, particularly small-scale farmers. In addition, new pressures were also evident as local farmers increasingly became dependent on uncontrollable external economic conditions. Conditions grew even more severe as Thai elites took advantage of the situation by acquiring lands from cash-strapped subsistence farmers. This led to more and more farmers changing from independent farmers to tenants or landless workers. These problems reinforced existing class inequities.

As farmers sold part, or all of their land, a new cycle of reinforced poverty emerged in Thailand. Their children were often forced to migrate and/or become landless laborers, who typically live under extreme conditions with very low living standards in urban slums. The export-driven model thus created issues of social and spatial unevenness in access to resources both within and between generations.

With regard to environmental stresses under the export-oriented growth program, several economic activities contributed to severe resource degradation, including logging, prawn farming, destructive methods of fishing, and wastewater from inland factories and households. The loss of the mangrove forests was an example of natural resource degradation influenced by the export-oriented growth model. Mangrove forests were cut down for prawn farming due to the high return investment and demand from world markets. In 1961 Thailand had mangroves of 1,420 square miles (2,299,375 rais). By 1992 more than half of the mangrove was destroyed, leaving 677 square miles (1,096,168 rais).[27] Forestry Department data in 1999 shows that mangrove forests were reduced to 647 square miles (1,047,387 rais), or 0.33 percent of the country by 1996.

In 1997 the period of economic growth came to an abrupt end. GDP had dropped to 0.0 percent in 1997 and –2.0 percent in 1998.[28] The Thai currency was devalued, and the government was essentially forced to change its policy of linking the value of its currency to the U.S. dollar.[29] Throughout the agricultural sector, defaults and indebtedness became widespread. All development within the country stalled, and new social, economic, and political pressures became evident.

The Roles of the King and Buddhism in Thailand

Before examining economic development and the concept of the sufficiency economy, two aspects of Thailand are worth exploring that have been fundamental in shaping Thailand's national policies. In Thailand the royal family, the Chakri dynasty, remains central to the country and Thai culture generally. The Chakri dynasty has ruled Thailand since the founding of the Ratthanakosin era in 1782. The current monarch, King Bhumibol, was crowned king of Thailand in 1950. In the Thai culture, the king is revered. He is considered to have "reigned with righteousness for the benefit and happiness of the Thai people," as manifest though his many social and economic development projects. Since the beginning of his reign, His Majesty has continually worked to enhance the livelihood of the poor. First, the king initiated royal projects on a small scale in the 1950s and 1960s using his personal funds. During the 1980s–1990s, the number of villages benefiting from royal initiative projects had expanded to about 4,000, or 7 percent of the villages in the kingdom.[30] Special attention was given to relatively remote areas inhabited by ethnic minorities and people who lacked access to resources. The aim was to create bonds that closely linked people from all sectors and to encourage unity, equity in accessibility to resources, preservation of the environment, and sustainable development. The king's royal speech given to the graduates of Kasetsart University on July 18, 1974, stated the following:

> Development of the nation must be carried out in stages, starting with the laying of the foundation by ensuring the majority of the people have their basic necessities through the use of economical means and equipment in accordance with theoretical principles. Once reasonable firm foundation has been laid and in effect, higher level of economic growth and development should be promoted.[31]

The king developed and promoted the philosophy of the sufficiency economy as an alternative to the export-oriented policies, and also as a related belief in the Buddhist way of life, which remains the dominant religion in Thailand among some 95 percent of the population.[32] Buddhism in Thailand is largely of the Theravada school, based on the religious movement founded in the sixth century B.C. by Siddhartha Gautama Sakyamuni, later known as the Buddha, who urged the world to relinquish the extremes of sensuality and self-mortification and follow the enlightened Middle Way. The Middle Way was the central and pervasive norm in the set of discourses that provided both the worldview and the philosophy that Buddhism applied to everyday life. Around the sixth century A.D., Theravada Buddhism reached present-day Thailand and was made the state religion of the Thai kingdom during the period of Sukhothai in the thirteenth century A.D. In Thailand, the king was, in principle, thought of as patron and protector of the religion (*sassana*) and the ordained Buddhist monks (*sangha*). In 1851 King Mongkut (Rama IV), who had been a monk for twenty-seven years, rose to power.[33] He institutionalized the sangha and the kingdom. The links between Buddhism and the state became increasingly integrated and hierarchical in nature.[34]

The King's Plan Toward the Sufficiency Economy

On the royal birthday in December 1998, the king in a national broadcast reemphasized the concept he had propounded since the 1970s: the sufficiency economy. The foundation of the king's concept was originally introduced to the graduates of Kasetsart University on December 4, 1974:

> No matter what others say—whether they will accuse Thailand of being old fashioned or obscurantist. So long as we have enough to live on and to live for—and this should be the wish and determination of all of us—without aiming for the apex of prosperity, we shall already be considered as the top in comparison with other countries in the present world.[35]

The sufficiency economy initiated by the king is different from the self-sufficiency concept. The sufficiency economy advocates taking the Middle Path in life—the path between two extremes, that of great luxury and great hardship—as the optimal route for personal conduct at all levels: individuals, families, and communities. It encourages self-reliance, honesty, and integrity while exercising knowledge with prudence.[36] Trade is allowed as long as individuals are able to live a reasonably comfortable life without excess or overindulgence in luxury. The foundations of King Bhumibol's theory included sustainability, moderation, and broad-based development. He promoted the virtues of leaving the chaos of modern urban life and capitalist economics and a return to what he perceived as more worthy and economically lasting agricultural enterprises, which he believed characterized the best of Thai heritage values. The concept focused on living a moderate, dependent life without greed or overexploitation of the environment and natural resources.[37]

The sufficiency economy model promotes the idea of limited production for the purpose of saving the environment and conserving scarce resources. It is an initiative with a strong sustainability scheme derived from the concept that replacement of natural capital is limited and that environmental quality should be maintained.

The sufficiency economy concept aims to preserve ecological sustainability, including soil and water quality, over time. Production is limited to the level adequate for family consumption. Equitable access of scarce and nonrenewable resources is emphasized. The use of natural resources is not encouraged for large-scale commercial activities but for household consumption. Activities such as rehabilitation of forests, soil, and water conservation systems are advocated, including the use of local knowledge and green technologies. The plan also actively promotes waste recycling and reuse.

The sufficiency economy also advanced the idea of production, not just for profit maximization but also for sustainable development for the individual, the household, and the larger community. In this model, food is not only an agricultural product or a hunter-gatherer subsistence activity. Excess beyond the needs of the household can be viewed as part of social responsibility and given to the broader society—for example, to monks, parents, relatives, and only then for sale. It was believed that these freely given community products were ways to redistribute resources. Under this scenario, people who received products would be expected under social norms to return the gifts when the opportunity arose.

For small-scale farmers, the sufficiency economy starts with a system that emphasizes the household farm. Farmers were encouraged to combine into groups or cooperatives. Goods and services could be exchanged to increase production efficiency and marketing,[38] while the cooperative members believed in the ethical values of honesty, openness, social responsibility, and caring for others. This way, the community will have a "self-immunity" to the changes created from endogenous and exogenous factors. People in the less developed areas with scarce resources could acquire the basic goods and services by exchanging available products or labor. Money, which was emphasized in the export-oriented growth model, is no longer promoted as the only instrument for exchange. The model stresses meeting the basic needs for all Thai people, with a particular focus placed on the disadvantaged.

It should be acknowledged that the king's plan still promotes industrial activity and trade, but the program's goals are to introduce a new set of values and conducts in dealing with globalization. For instance, it promotes investment in business only using funds not exceeding the company's assets. This philosophy encourages spending restraint and controlled expansion of activities and purposefully tries to limit the use of scarce resources. This should ensure that natural services and the quality of natural resources can be maintained over time. If fully adopted, the plan would promote natural resource quality and proper landscape composition, creating ecological stability. However, the plan recognizes that a balance needs to be found between Thailand's requirements to remain competitive in manufacturing, services, and other nonagricultural economic activities while promoting greater equity within and between generations.

The principles of the sufficiency economy include moderation, reasonableness, and self-immunity. Firms are encouraged to establish strong economic foundations by finding their niche, improving the quality of their products, and ensuring competitive costs in production. To this extent, material and energy efficiency are emphasized in the program. Firms are not encouraged to grow too fast by overborrowing or overexploiting resources.[39]

In addition, a new emphasis is placed on private corporations realizing their responsibilities to society and strengthening their connections within their communities. This is in recognition that the combination of private firms and broader Thai society can be extremely effective in mobilizing resources and playing an important role in helping the underprivileged help themselves over the long run.[40] Many Thai firms have already followed through with this new national mandate and have initiated corporate social responsibility programs and collaborations within their communities. For instance, the Thai Vegetable Oil Public Company Limited is currently operating in accordance with a new policy focusing on social responsibility achievements. The company donates money and products to schools for luncheon programs. It also established a student trainee program that aims to enlighten knowledge by self-learning. In addition, the company invested in a wastewater treatment system project to help improve environmental quality. Another example is provided by the Siam Cement Group, which established a sustainable development committee and a corporate policy that focuses on a three-pronged approach to greater community-corporate cohesion—promoting environmental preservation, community health and safety, and social responsibility.

The sufficiency economy is also being strengthened through government plans and legislation. The current constitution of Thailand is the supreme law of the kingdom, and it promulgated an interim constitution in October 2006, which stated that the government must encourage the sufficiency economy in order to ensure the economic, social, and sustainable development of the country. As noted earlier, the Ninth Thailand Economic and Social Development Plan (2002–2006) did integrate some of the sufficiency economy programs that emphasized sustainable development, quality of life issues, and environmental quality under globalization. The national plan focused on economics at the local level, but it also encouraged community level activities by, for instance, encouraging community savings for a village fund. The community was encouraged to expand their activities through reaching out to cooperative firms, banks, and other outside sources. The expansion across different levels of organizations or activities can be compared to developing a value chain in production. The expanded activities include raising funds, creating direct sales channels, and seeking funds for establishing community rice mills or cooperative stores.

The Tenth Thailand Economic and Social Development Plan (2007–2011) calls for a Green and Happiness Society.[41] The plan focuses on building strong communities to serve as building blocks for the nation and to develop a dependable community level economy to coexist harmoniously with nature and the surrounding environment. One significant goal was the preservation of forest areas for at least 33 percent of the country. Irrigated agriculture fields were also mandated to at least 31 million rais, or 19,151 square miles. The plan also explicitly promoted environmental quality and a healthy ecosystem as a necessity to support healthy living conditions.[42] The strategy to maintain natural resource quality from the tenth plan is illustrated in figure 1.

In the urban context, residents are encouraged to adopt the king's plan by giving away some of the excess goods to the community and to promote the redistribution of resources to rural areas. The Buddhist model expects the well-off to return some goods or resources to those who lack opportunities or the basic materials required for life. Residents are also encouraged to efficiently use resources. For instance, soils suitable for agriculture should not be exploited for urban expansion. Waste reduction is also promoted through recycling and reducing consumption. In addition, creditors and small businesses are encouraged to support cooperatives and small-scale farmers by purchasing their products. The plan lays the foundation for the establishment of a new culture,

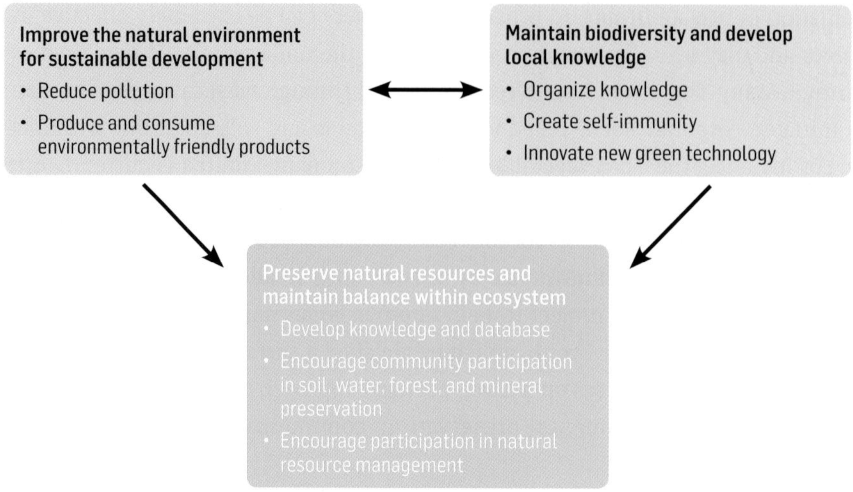

Figure 1. The environmental preservation context under the Tenth Thailand Economic and Social Development Plan (2007–2011).

where people in different places and in different generations can adapt the philosophy promoting social/corporate support systems into everyday life.

History of Settlement in Nang Rong

Nang Rong town is located within the Nang Rong subdistrict (Tambon) and Nang Rong district (Aumpur). The district was established within the Buriram province, located in northeast Thailand about 249 miles from Bangkok (fig. 2). Nang Rong district is one of twenty-one districts comprising Buriram Province. The district itself is further divided into fifteen subdistricts with one municipal center and several hundred villages.[43] Today, Nang Rong town is a tourism gateway providing access to the most significant ancient Khmer-sites in northeast Thailand. It is also a transportation hub to other provinces.

Nang Rong town lays on the Korat Plateau, which consists of Quaternary deposits.[44] The physical environment is characterized by relatively infertile soils, poor drainage, and a monsoonal but inconsistent climate and precipitation.[45] Nang Rong town has experienced some level of fluctuation in its population and increasing urbanization in the recent past due primarily to migration flows.[46] The legal town boundary, officially established in 1986, includes an area of eight square miles. Total population increased from 20,806 in 2001 to 21,153 in 2003. Population density increased from 2,600 to 2,644 persons per square mile. However, population in 2005 decreased to 20,923, with 10,026 males and 10,897 females. The density decreased from 2,644 to 2,615 persons per square mile in 2003–2005, almost entirely due to out-migration for wage labor in Bangkok. Conversely, the number of houses increased from 7,732 to 8,538.[47]

Nang Rong town provides important transportation and economic functions and services to the entire Northeastern region. The town is the regional central market, providing the

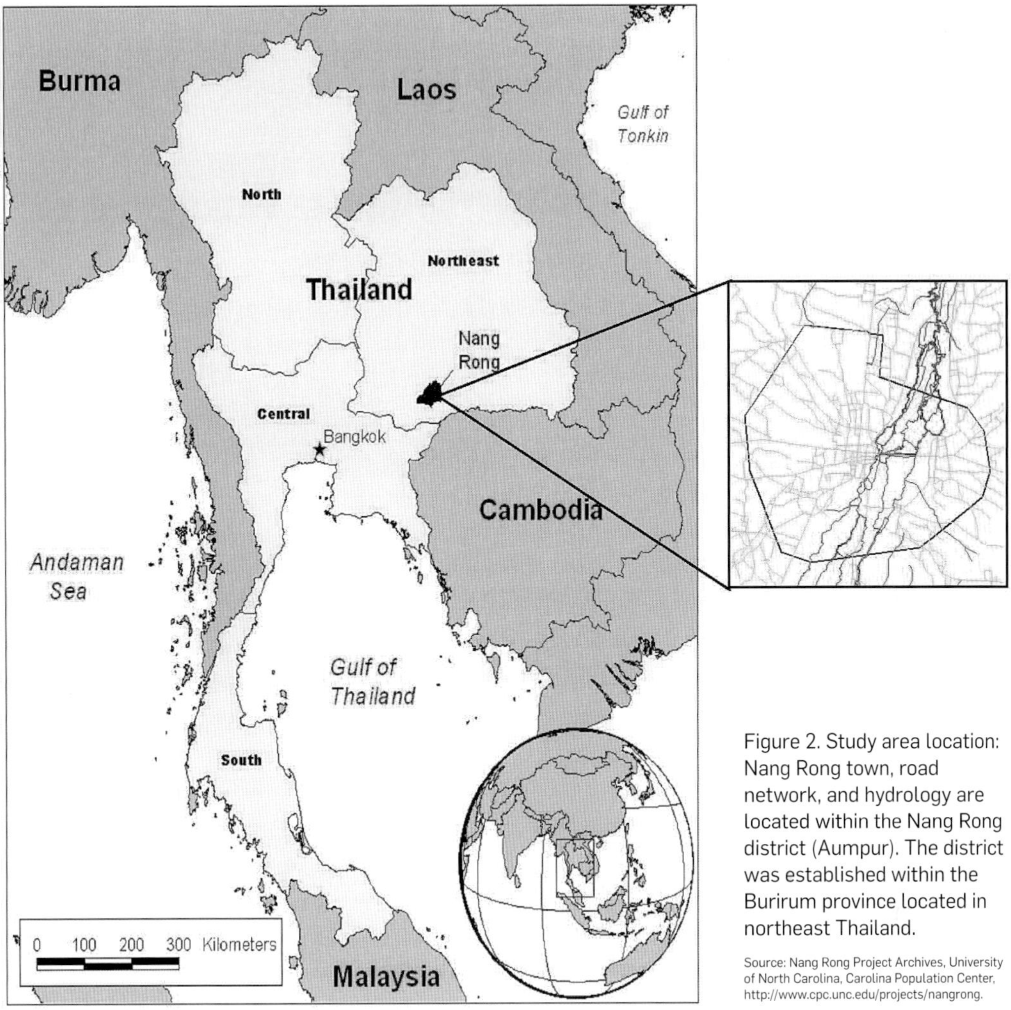

Figure 2. Study area location: Nang Rong town, road network, and hydrology are located within the Nang Rong district (Aumpur). The district was established within the Burirum province located in northeast Thailand.

Source: Nang Rong Project Archives, University of North Carolina, Carolina Population Center, http://www.cpc.unc.edu/projects/nangrong.

infrastructure for many economic and social activities, such as rice and cassava markets, general shopping, medical services, temples, and schools. Nang Rong is served by major highways connecting the city to Buriram and other urban centers. Over the past thirty years, the town has experienced rapid urbanization and demographic changes, often moving in uncorrelated and unsustainable trajectories. With frequent reverse migratory patterns, Nang Rong functions in the context of often declining population densities combined with increasing urbanization of adjacent natural and agricultural lands. The growing prevalence of these new settlement processes creates problems associated with increasing transformation of agricultural and natural lands for low-density residential urban uses. In the absence of an urban planning framework optimized for the Southeast Asian context, urban expansion takes place haphazardly and often develops over the best quality agricultural lands or lands not suitable for housing, such as on high risk floodplains. In the context of Southeast Asia, the demographic and physical infrastructural issues

PHOTOGRAPH BY PARIWATE VARNAKOVIDA

Figure 3. Rice fields in Nang Rong.

experienced in Nang Rong are typical. It is a small, rapidly changing town influenced directly by global processes (figs. 3 and 4).

The Role of the Natural Environment in Shaping Built Form

Significant social drivers aside, there are certain basic endogenous biophysical factors that have played an important role in shaping the built-environment morphology in the Nang Rong context. These factors include water resources, land availability, and soil quality. First, human settlement and general development of the area significantly depend on easy access to water and reliable supplies of water. Second, there are three issues impacting land availability: most previously forested lands have been settled, deforested, and converted to often marginal crop production; population growth has reduced the amount of land available to support new settlement and agricultural production; and with the passing of generations, farms have become subdivided into small pieces through kinship ties resulting in declining income potential and family capital. Third, soil quality determines to a great degree what types of land uses are viable in any area.

Water Resources

There are many natural water resources in northeast Thailand, including the three major rivers, the Mekong, the Chi, and the Mun, and innumerable smaller rivers and streams (*huay*). Nang Rong has four rivers (the word for river in the northeast is *lam*): Lam Plai Mat, Lam Nang Rong, Lam Pa Thia, and Lam Sai Yong. Some of these are technically intermittent. Despite the regular drought and/or floods, irrigation canals in Nang Rong are few. Agriculture in this area is almost entirely dependent upon rain fall.[48] In many areas, saline groundwater percolation combined with poor water retention characteristics have created widespread declining soil quality.[49]

Despite these challenges, the primary reason villagers have, over time, settled close to the natural water resources was not for agricultural water; rather, it was for general consumption by the villagers, their cattle, and for the provision of food such as fish, shellfish, and certain plants. If they could not settle along the edge of a river, the settlers would look for a place nearby, within one day's walk. Several permanent dams on streams for irrigation and water reservoirs were built. In the past, villagers did not use permanent dams and weirs during the rice-growing season; instead, they built temporary structures to control the flow of water through their fields. Villagers usually dug wells for drinking water and community consumption. Rainwater began to be regularly used for drinking only with the introduction of metal roofing about fifty years ago.[50]

One of the most critical water resource problems is directly the result of unmanaged wastes. Both human and industrial wastes are increasingly discharged directly into local streams and ponds, far exceeding the carrying capacity of the natural environment. Collectively, the phenomena explained are likely to reduce regional ecological stability and damage system resilience, violating basic tenets of sustainable development.

PHOTOGRAPH BY PARIWATE VARNAKOVIDA

Figure 4. Urbanization on the periphery of Nang Rong town, in former rice fields.

Soil Resources

Northeast Thailand geology is characterized by Cretaceous sandstone overlain with alluvial deposits that have eroded to form a succession of natural terraces. Most of Nang Rong is a combination of floodplains and upland areas of moderate slope.[51] Some areas are lateritic with weathered and leached soils generally deficient in nutrients and moisture. There is a layer of pebble and laterite extending to a 1.64 feet depth, which is generally not suitable for crops.[52] These laterized soils are very difficult to modify into good quality soils. Soil quality and water-holding capacity and drainage properties largely determine the areas suitable for paddy rice cultivation, the most important local crop.[53]

According to a report from the Office of Agricultural Economics,[54] in 1999 sugarcane in the Buriram Province covered 103 square miles (166,654 rais), an increase from 44 square miles (70,752 rais) in 1998 (a 111 percent increase in a single year). The area cultivated in cassava increased 58 percent in that same year, from 250 square miles (404,650 rais) to 394 square miles (637,400 rais). While cassava does grow well in the region, it also contributes to declining soil quality. Previously, kenaf was the dominant cultivar in these regions. With the emergence of commercial cassava agriculture, broad environmental impacts became evident—most significantly, soil exhaustion.[55]

In addition to the obvious impacts of deforestation, soil related impacts include localized erosion, increased runoff, increased flood events, increased soil salinity, and sedimentation problems.[56] The deforestation activities contributed to soil degradation and influenced the already challenged regional hydrological cycle. Despite the rural character of the region, the typically urban issue of impermeable surfaces has emerged. Some evidence of this is already occurring as infiltration rates and aboveground moisture retention in upland sites has decreased and consequently reduced ground water recharge.[57] This process reduces stream flow consistency while increasing the likelihood of flood events.

It is also likely that local surface temperatures may increase due to the temperature and evaporation effects of the deforestation and laterization processes. Some evidence of fluctuating amounts and spatial and temporal patterns of rainfall have been recorded in the northeast of Thailand, though this cannot be solely attributed to local changes.[58] The increasing severity of heavy rainfall events and their associated flooding have directly impacted Nang Rong. Recall that many recently developed areas are built on floodplains. Also, many of the newly built roads crossing Nang Rong are not usable during the rainy season. These problems limit travel efficiency for people inside and outside the areas.[59] Such impacts on ecological sustainability result in land unsuitable for agriculture and with limited reforestation potential.

Local Land Availability

For many centuries, the regional land cover was largely a mixed natural dry tropical forest and savanna. People moved into the region starting during the Khmer empire (879–1432 A.D.) searching for available natural resources. In the past fifty years, road building improved access to water and to available land, leading to rapid conversion to agriculture. This enhanced access is the primary driver for much of the regional land use and cover change.

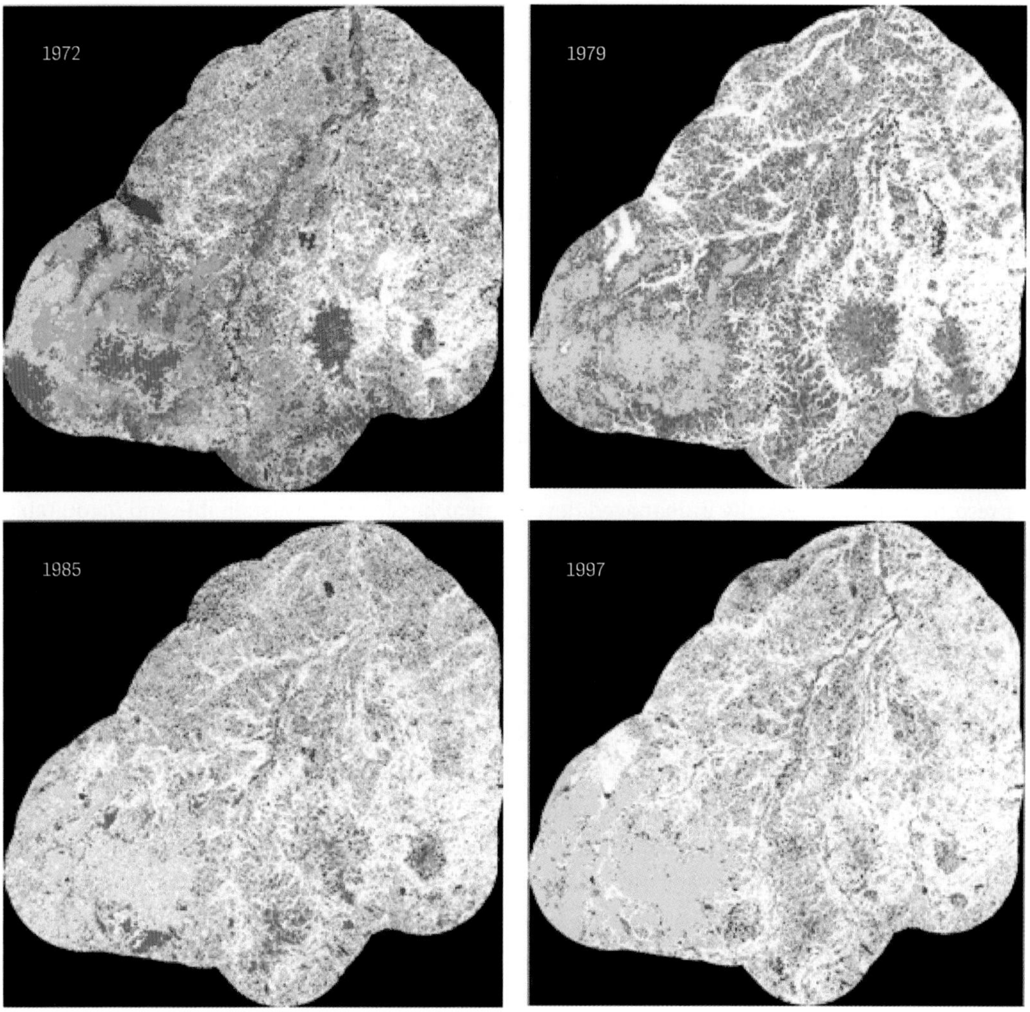

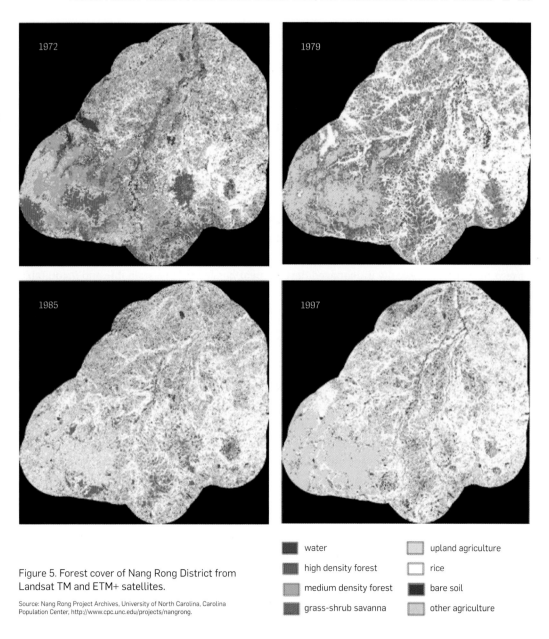

Figure 5. Forest cover of Nang Rong District from Landsat TM and ETM+ satellites.

Source: Nang Rong Project Archives, University of North Carolina, Carolina Population Center, http://www.cpc.unc.edu/projects/nangrong.

In-migration and family enlargement was influenced by commercial agriculture expansion, which was driven by international market demand for cassava.[60] Concurrently, villagers were encouraged to expand rice production beyond what was needed in the local economy and to also grow commercial crops for national and global markets. Even small-scale farmers ill-equipped to compete adopted commercial export-oriented farming. Chemical inputs, machinery, and hired labor were all used to increase crop yields.[61] Land was less available for distribution among siblings within households. Natural resources were overexploited, especially the forest areas in Nang Rong. Between 1954 and 2000, the percent of land in forest cover declined from 54.8 percent to 13.3 percent,[62] and now cover less than 10 percent of the landscape.[63] These changes have challenged ecological sustainability both locally and regionally.

Over the last several years, the rate of urban expansion has increased with major developments along lands adjacent to roads,[64] which have increased in Nang Rong town alone from approximately 5,000 to 9,000 land parcel units between 1994 and 2003.[65] Regionally, the number of villages also increased. The data sets for the Nang Rong Project archive at the University of North Carolina at Chapel Hill showed that Nang Rong District is an agricultural dominant society. In 1984 there were about 99 percent agricultural households, which slightly declined in 1994 to 90 percent and decreased dramatically in 2000 to 75 percent. The percentage of agricultural households that have been settled since 1984 declined from 99 percent to 50 percent in 2000.[66]

The combination of independent factors associated with social, geographical, and biophysical drivers has led to the widespread reduction in forest cover (fig. 5) and declining soil qualities. These factors have contributed to reduced quality of life driven by declining incomes and scarcity of resources. The historically unmanaged development has led to unsustainable and inequitable allocations of resources.

How Can the Sufficiency Economy Promote Sustainable Development in Nang Rong?

In Nang Rong, unsustainable commercial agriculture is an implicit factor in unsustainable urbanization. Nang Rong town and district have both been integrated into the national economy over the past few decades. National policies promoted local competition in the world market. These policies and plans directly influenced the conversion of forestlands to agricultural purposes. These parts of conversion were particularly evident between 1972 and 1997 (see tables 7, 8, 9, and 10). Rice paddy land (RP) increased by sixty-five square miles, while forest cover (FC) decreased by 144 square miles.

Satellite imagery from Landsat ETM+ shows that the Nang Rong town periphery expanded from 3.4 to 5.6 square miles, while the urban core increased from 0.61 to 1.95 square miles between 1990 and 2003 (see figs. 6 and 7). The average house size from the aerial photo interpretation was approximately 1,576 square feet in 1994, an increase from 1,407 square feet the previous decade. Only small patches of forest remain along the upland borders, and these have become increasingly spatially fragmented. The lowlands contain minimal patches of forest within extensive rice fields and settlements.[67] Widespread ecological fragility and increased economic risk have become important issues for land use and land cover suitability. Intrinsic land values declined in the more fragmented and depleted areas.

Land and Soil Resources: Effective Allocation of Land to Serve the Different Needs of Farm Households Using New Theory Farming

An example of the sufficiency economy was the "integrated farming practice according to the New Theory," which promoted step-by-step development, starting from satisfying basic needs at the household level.[68] There were six Royal Development Study Centers established throughout

Table 7. Land Use Land Cover cross-section areas (sq. mi.) by classification date

LULC CLASS	1972	1985	1997
Rice paddy land (RP)	272	298	337
Field crop land (FC)	14	82	66
Forest (uninhabited) (FOR)	183	117	118
Grass/scrub/savanna (GSS)	111	84	58
Terminal land use (TLU)	75	75	75

Table 8. Land Use Land Cover postclassification change in area (sq. mi.), 1972–1985

CHANGE FROM/TO	1985 RP	1985 FC	1985 FOR	1985 GSS	1985 TLU
1972 RP	209	28	10	24	0
1972 FC	1	8	4	2	0
1972 FOR	37	40	75	31	0
1972 GSS	51	6	28	26	0
1972 TLU	0	0	0	0	75

Source: William Welsh, Characterizing the Forest-Agricultural Land Flux within the Context of Soil Suitability Parameters in Nang Rong, Thailand, *Journal of The American Society for Photogrammetry and Remote Sensing*, Special Issue on Remote Sensing Data Fusion (June 2008): 765–773.
Note: RP = rice paddy land, FC = field crop land, FOR = forest, GSS = grass/scrub/savanna, TLU = terminal land use.

Table 9. Land Use Land Cover postclassification change in area (sq. mi.), 1985–1997

CHANGE FROM/TO	1997 RP	1997 FC	1997 FOR	1997 GSS	1997 TLU
1985 RP	236	3	40	19	0
1985 FC	31	37	8	6	0
1985 FOR	29	19	51	18	0
1985 GSS	42	7	20	15	0
1985 TLU	0	0	0	0	75

Source: William Welsh, Characterizing the Forest-Agricultural Land Flux within the Context of Soil Suitability Parameters in Nang Rong, Thailand, *Journal of The American Society for Photogrammetry and Remote Sensing*, Special Issue on Remote Sensing Data Fusion (June 2008): 765–773.
Note: RP = rice paddy land, FC = field crop land, FOR = forest, GSS = grass/scrub/savanna, TLU = terminal land use.

Table 10. Land Use Land Cover postclassification change in area (sq. mi.), 1972–1997

CHANGE FROM/TO	1997 RP	1997 FC	1997 FOR	1997 GSS	1997 TLU
1972 RP	223	1	35	14	0
1972 FC	1	11	1	1	0
1972 FOR	52	52	52	27	0
1972 GSS	61	3	30	17	0
1972 TLU	0	0	0	0	75

Source: William Welsh, Characterizing the Forest-Agricultural Land Flux within the Context of Soil Suitability Parameters in Nang Rong, Thailand, *Journal of The American Society for Photogrammetry and Remote Sensing*, Special Issue on Remote Sensing Data Fusion (June 2008): 765–773.
Note: RP = rice paddy land, FC = field crop land, FOR = forest, GSS = grass/scrub/savanna, TLU = terminal land use.

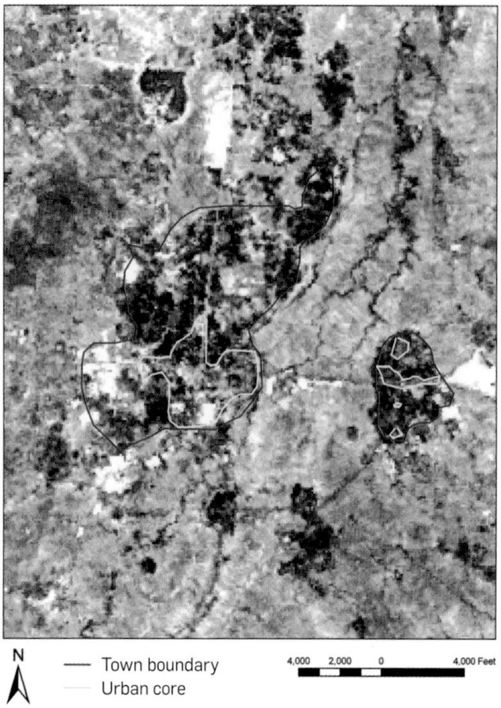

Figure 6. Urban cores and town periphery of Nang Rong town in January 1990 from Landsat TM.

Source: Nang Rong Project Archives, University of North Carolina, Carolina Population Center, http://www.cpc.unc.edu/projects/nangrong.

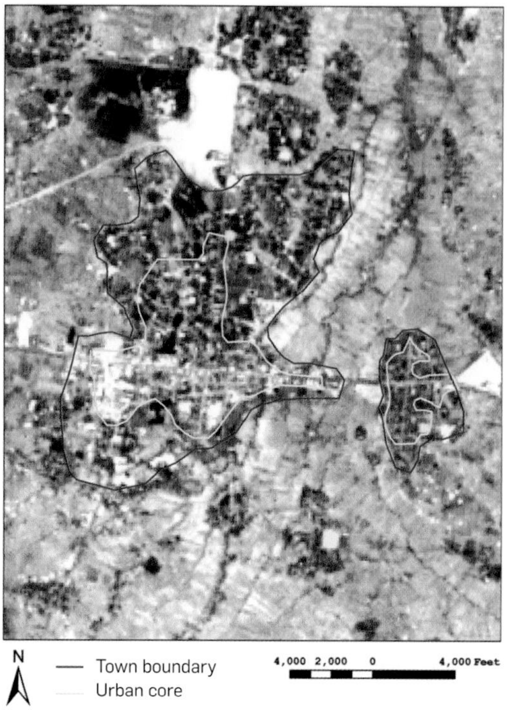

Figure 7. Urban cores and town periphery of Nang Rong town in January 2003 from Landsat ETM+ satellite.

Source: Nang Rong Project Archives, University of North Carolina, Carolina Population Center, http://www.cpc.unc.edu/projects/nangrong.

Thailand, each specializing in different unsustainable development problems. The Royal Development Study Centers were established to conduct studies and experiments on self-sufficiency and to promote appropriate development paths for each region. According to the Royal Development Projects Board:

> The purpose of the Royal Development Study Centers is to develop farmers' land by means of land development, water resources development, forest rehabilitation and application techniques in agriculture and animal husbandry. The center will serve as a central office to conduct development activities to improve the well-being of the people in the surrounding areas. Once the farmers upgraded their living standard, they might consider setting up a rice mill and rice bank in each village to get an opportunity to train themselves, to finally become self-supporting.[69]

The king's plan for New Theory farming for small-scale farmers was initiated in the 1980s. It focused on the application of integrated farming systems for poor farmers on small landholdings with scarce water resources, as in the Nang Rong region. Its main goal is to provide food security and to promote the principles of the sufficiency economy to the local poor population. Perhaps the most important goal of New Theory farming is to ensure the effective allocation of land to serve the diverse needs of small farm households, including paddy fields for rice, farm ponds for water and fish, cash crops and trees for income, and a defined residential area. In general practice, the area allocated to each kind of land use could be flexible, according to local resources, but a general land allocation is promoted under the plan. Rice is usually grown on 30 percent of the land, with another 30 percent excavated for a pond to be used during droughts or the annual dry season. Another 30 percent could be used for cash crops, vegetables, and fruits. The remaining 10 percent could be used for the household residential area.[70]

The New Theory farming land allocation model has been shown to be effective for household resource allocation and public uses. Of course, the most important objective is to produce sufficient goods for household consumption. Under the New Theory farming model, farmers will be less dependent on the whims of the market and less likely to incur debt.

Various agricultural development plans were studied at the closest center to Nang Rong, the Puparn Royal Development Center. The forests were replanted in an attempt to preserve the watershed. Soil and water conservation systems were studied, and topsoil erosion prevention was explored by growing vetiver grass.[71] Soil development enhancements included using organic fertilizer and green manure, creating compost, and constructing ponds. The sustainability goals in the northeast focused on small-scale farmers and encouraged the application of the test methods on their own lands to obtain enough rice yields for household consumption and to access water resources during dry periods.[72]

The evidence from field surveys and personal interviews by the authors suggest that farmers in Nang Rong who applied the integrated farming practice were able to obtain enough food for household consumption. Many families were able to rely on their integrated farming production to a certain extent without borrowing from creditors. The risks to the household were minimized. They did not have to rely solely on production for export and expose themselves to the fluctuations of the global cash crop markets. Farmers were encouraged to join the community cooperatives to form basic commercial enterprises focused on the production of local crafts. It was believed that these activities would help strengthen the social fabric of the community and reduce community risk from exogenous factors. It is also hoped that the new model can preserve small-scale farming, reduce out-migration to Bangkok and other large cities for wage labor, and minimize the conversion of agricultural lands to urban uses.

New Theory agriculture is an effective approach to preserve natural resources while maintaining agricultural production. Combined with the sufficiency economy plan, mixed land uses are encouraged. For example, fruit or other large trees are planted in and around the village core and individual households for household consumption and shade. Over time, the foliage from these trees and the plant biomass will cover the soil and prevent laterization and erosion, promoting the conservation of soils.[73] In addition, the system of the sufficiency economy promotes reduced deforestation and reduced extensification of urban and agricultural land uses. The approach provides a farming method and community economic model that may improve the quality of life for small-scale farmers. To date, this has resulted in reduced participation in commercial farming,[74] with concurrently more local farming groups formed. Furthermore, New Theory farming encourages reductions in insecticide and fertilizer use and a greater reliance on locally generated agricultural and animal wastes for replenishing soil nutrients. Farmers are also encouraged by the local government to cooperate with their neighbors so that they can lower raw material costs and increase their power to sell their surplus products to the market. Local governments have also received more funds for development projects influenced by the increased economic nationalism under the king's program.

After widespread adoption of these plans across the province, deforestation rates declined and access to water resources improved.[75] Highland runoff water is made usable by building check dams and fish-bone-shaped ditches, which also help preserve soil moisture during the dry season and support reforestation projects. River water and lowland sources are used in reservoirs for crop cultivation, animal husbandry, and fishery. In the reforestation area, indigenous tree species as well as trees for timber and fruit are replanted as village resources. While insufficient time has passed since the announcement of the king's plans, anecdotally there is now movement toward greater local equity.

Resources: King's Sufficiency Plan and Increased Funding for Water Provision

If communities implement the king's concept, farmers will be able to survive during periods of drought by bringing water from pond reserves to grow vegetables that require less water. Also, during floods, farmers can survive without relying as extensively on the government by using a variety of products (rice, fish, vegetables, and fruits), including those from their increased storage, as long as they are effectively preserved. After implementing principles of water supply from the sufficiency economy in the Nang Rong town plan, the local irrigation system was expanded to increase its support from 3,978 households in 2003 to 4,945 households in 2006. The local branch of the Royal Irrigation was able to produce approximately 107,145 cubic feet of clean water in 2003, which increased to 211,888 cubic foot in 2006.[76] There were only three wells built in Nang Rong town before 1982, while twenty-six wells were built between 1983 and 1999 (fig. 8).[77] According to the NRMO data, the out-migration of Nang Rong town population decreased from 4,326 to 2,601 from 2002 to 2006 (fig. 9). After the principles of the sufficiency economy were implemented in the 2003 municipal plan, people tended to stay in the region due to the improvement of accessibility to resources and a sense of equity in resource distribution. The town has been developing at a higher density and there has been less outward expansion into the agricultural areas.

The villages in the Nang Rong District received extensive funds for the sufficiency economy projects, including 141 million bahts, or US$4.5 million (US$1 = 31 bahts) for agriculture, 29 million bahts for household development projects, and 21 million bahts for local economic activities.[78] Two dams will also be built to supply water during the dry season in Nang Rong town. Rivers and streams will be dredged to help with water distribution and channel flow.[79] Budgets for the Nang Rong town irrigation system were increased from 2,598,300 for a three-year plan (2005–2007) to 3,968,835 bahts (2007–2009). Funding for environmental management and planning were also increased, with 4 million bahts budgeted for monitoring the quality of local resources, including water and soil quality, and 61 million bahts targeted to solving inequality issues within Nang Rong town.[80]

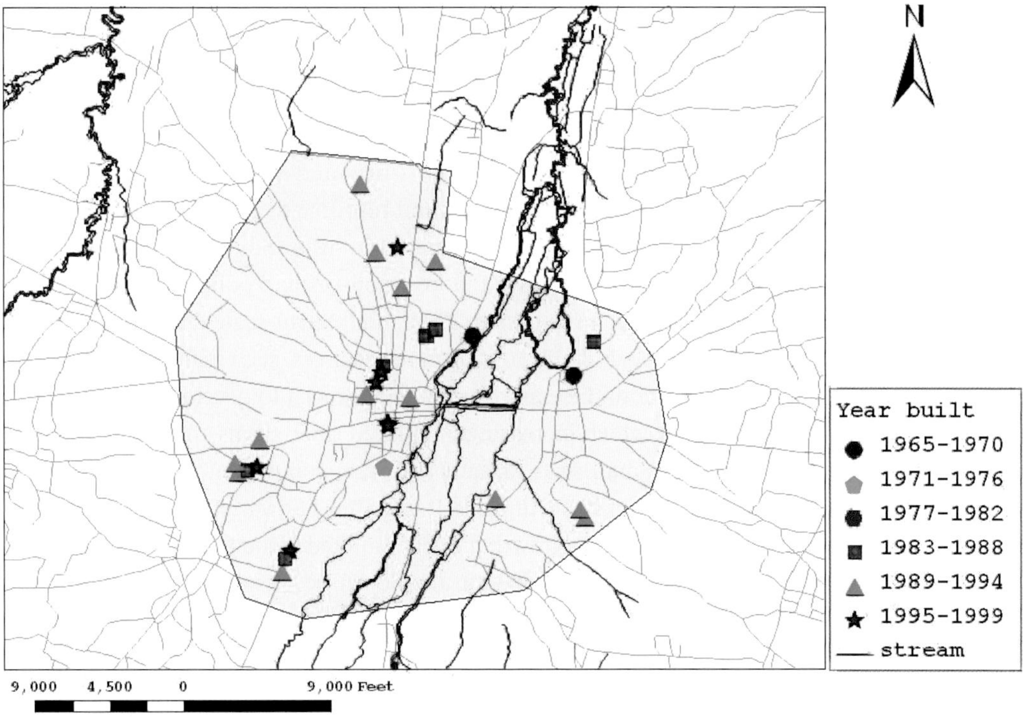

Figure 8. Well locations and year built in Nang Rong town.

Source: ONEP.

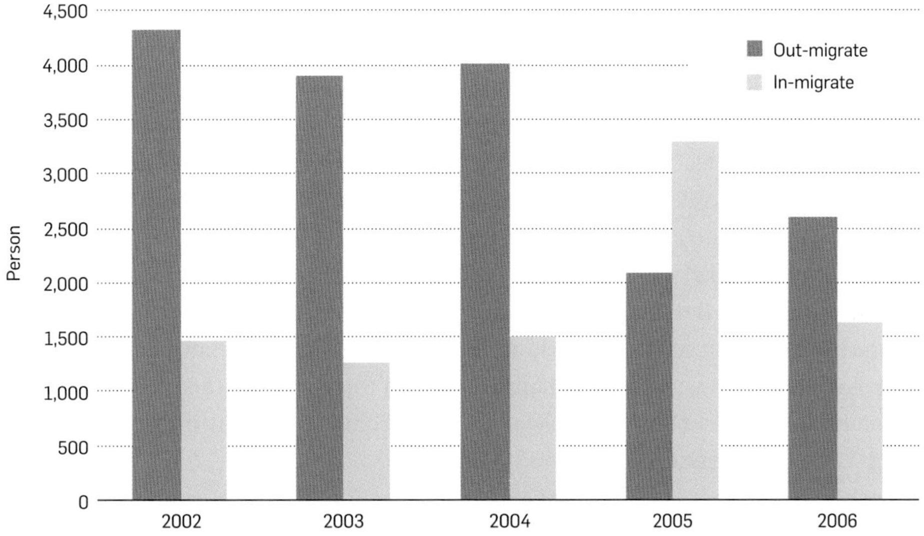

Figure 9. Out-migration and in-migration of Nang Rong town, 2002–2006.

Source: Nang Rong Municipal Office, *Three Years Development Plans 2004 to 2006* (Nang Rong, Thailand: Nang Rong Municipal Office, 2003); Nang Rong Municipal Office, *Three Years Development Plans 2007 to 2009* (Nang Rong, Thailand: Nang Rong Municipal Office, 2006).

How the Sufficiency Economy Can Be Applied toward Regional Sustainable Development

The export-oriented growth model was implemented via the Thailand national development plan from the early 1960s through the mid-2000s. The export-oriented growth model encouraged structural imbalances, environmental degradation, natural resource depletion, and inequalities in resource distribution. As has been amply demonstrated in other Southeast Asia contexts, urban populations under this model have received more resources and political attention than rural populations, and this has also been the case in Thailand.[81] Small-scale farmers suffered in particular, by becoming increasingly vulnerable to exogenous changes, such as fluctuation in crop prices in the world market. In addition, the export-oriented approach to development promoted large-scale commercial agriculture, which increasingly replaced small farms and labor-intensive activities, due to rising input costs. Small-scale farmers and rural populations were forced to sell their land and to move for employment opportunities. It was thus at a variety of different policy and outcome levels that the export-oriented growth model promoted inequalities.

The introduction of the Ninth National Economic and Social Development Plan set forth the shift from focusing on rapid development to more qualitative development. The main objective is "to improve the structure for national development in order to achieve a balance. This involves building fairness in society, and the ability to keep up with the changing world to render benefits for the mass majority of the country, thereby leading to sustainable development."[82] A new goal for developing the country was also defined in the Ninth Plan, shifting the focus from increasing wealth through expanding economic growth to forming a strong socioeconomic foundation and distributing the benefits of national development more equally across Thailand.[83]

The sufficiency economy model adapted in Thailand attempts to minimize population impacts and preserve water and soil quality, as well as preserve remaining forests. Waste discharges are converted into environmentally useful or ecologically neutral materials. Natural resources are used more properly, and excess production beyond the needs of the household can be redistributed. From the field work, it is evident that many farmers in Royal Development Center and Nang Rong adapted the king's concept by changing from monocrop agriculture to mixed-farming. They produced for their own needs and used surplus resources to produce for the appropriate market. They earned an increased income from selling surplus agricultural products leftover from household consumption, such as rice, seasonal fruits, and fish. The extra income was also a result of the dissemination of knowledge and new techniques by the Royal Development Center for making organic fertilizer from livestock waste. The local farmers established groups and exchanged resources and labor through cooperation within Nang Rong district. New crafts and products were made and sold through new marketing channels both in town and in other cities. The average annual income for people in Nang Rong town increased from 34,348 bahts in 2005 (US$1,108) to 41,729 bahts (US$1,346) in 2006.[84]

Sustainable development is scalable. Global sustainability requires regional sustainability, and regional sustainability requires local sustainability. The old adage, "think globally, act locally" certainly applies. The king's plan for the sufficiency economy starts at the family level, but this program also scales up to the community and the nation. The king's plans can be applied to other regions, especially in other Buddhist regions where the Middle Path principle is commonly understood. As His Majesty stated in a royal speech on December 4, 1998, "If one is moderate in one's desires, one will have less craving. If one has less craving, one will take less advantage of others. If all nations hold this concept of moderation, without being extreme or insatiable in one's desire, the world will be a happier place."

NOTES

1. Philip Hirsch and Larry Lohmann, Contemporary Politics of Environment in Thailand, *Asian Survey* 29:4 (1989): 439–51.
2. Chris Dixon, Thailand's Rapid Economic Growth: Causes, Sustainability and Lessons, in *Uneven Development in Thailand*, ed. Michael Parnwell (London: Ashgate, 1996).
3. Utis Kaothien, Regional and Urbanization Policy in Thailand: The Tertiary Sector as a Leading Sector in Regional Development, *Urban Studies* 28:6 (1991): 1027–43.
4. National Statistical Office (NSO), *Statistical Yearbook Thailand 2007* (Bangkok: Ministry of Information and Communication Technology, 2007).
5. World Commission on Environment and Development (WECD), *Our Common Future* (New York: Oxford University Press, 1987), 43.
6. Igor Vojnovic, Inter-generational and Intra-generational Equity Requirements for Sustainable Development, *Environmental Conservation* 22:3 (1995): 223–28.
7. Ibid.
8. Cedric Pugh, ed., *Sustainable Cities in Developing Countries: Theory and Practice at the Millennium* (London: Earthscan, 2001).
9. National Statistical Office (NSO), *Statistical Yearbook Thailand* (Bangkok: Ministry of Information and Communication Technology, 2006).
10. Robert Muscat, *The Fifth Tiger: A Study of Thai Development Policy* (Tokyo: United Nations University Press, 1994).
11. Dixon, Thailand's Rapid Economic Growth.
12. Michael Parnwell, *Uneven Development in Thailand* (London: Ashgate, 1996); Office of National Economic and Social Development Board (NESDB), National Sustainable Development Strategy for Thailand—A Guidance Manual, United Nations Environment Programme, Thailand Environment Institute, March 2008.
13. Guy Trebuil, Pioneer Agriculture, Green Revolution and Environmental Degradation in Thailand, in *Counting the Costs Economic Growth and Environmental Change in Thailand*, ed. Jonathan Rigg (Pasir Panjang, Singapore, Institute of Southeast Asian Studies, 1995).
14. Hans-Dieter Evers and Rudiger Korff, *Southeast Asian Urbanism: The Meaning and Power of Social Space* (Munich, Germany: LitVerlag, 2000).
15. Kriengsak Rojnkureesatien, Geographical Accessibility and Land-Use and Land-Cover Dynamics the Case of Nang Rong District, Northeast Thailand, PhD diss., Department of Geography, University of North Carolina–Chapel Hill, 2006.
16. Walden Bello, Shea Cunningham, and Li Kheng Poh, *A Siamese Tragedy: Development and Disintegration in Modern Thailand* (New York: Zed Books, 1998).
17. Thailand Board of Investment (BOI), Economic Planning: "A Green and Happy Society," *Thailand Investment Review* 16:8 (September 2006): 5.
18. Ibid.
19. National Statistical Office (NSO), *Statistical Yearbook Thailand* (Bangkok: Ministry of Information and Communication Technology, 1997).
20. Thanwa Jitsanguan, *Sustainable Agriculture Systems for Small-Scale Farmers in Thailand: Implications for the Environment*, FFTC book series no. 509 (Taipei: Food and Fertilizer Technology Center, 2001), http://www.agnet.org/library/eb/509/.
21. Kriengsak Rojnkureesatien, Geographical Accessibility and Land-Use and Land-Cover Dynamics the Case of Nang Rong District, Northeast Thailand, PhD diss., Department of Geography, University of North Carolina–Chapel Hill, 2006.
22. Aphiphan Pookpakdi, Sustainable Agriculture for Small Scale Farmers: A Farming System Perspective, in *Sustainable Agriculture for the Asian and Pacific Regions*, FFTC book series no. 44 (Taipei: Food and Fertilizer Technology Center, 1992).
23. Thanwa Jitsanguan, *Sustainable Agriculture Systems for Small-Scale Farmers in Thailand: Implications for the Environment,* FFTC book series no. 509, Taipei: Food and Fertilizer Technology Center, 2001, http://www.agnet.org/library/eb/509/.
24. William Welsh, Characterizing the

Forest-Agricultural Land Flux within the Context of Soil Suitability Parameters in Nang Rong, Thailand, *Journal of the American Society for Photogrammetry and Remote Sensing*, Special Issue on Remote Sensing Data Fusion (June 2008): 765–73.
25. Walden Bello, Shea Cunningham, and Li Kheng Poh, *A Siamese Tragedy: Development and Disintegration in Modern Thailand* (New York: Zed Books Ltd., 1998).
26. Michael Parnwell, *Uneven Development in Thailand*, (London: Ashgate, 1996).
27. Bello, Cunningham, and Kheng Poh, *A Siamese Tragedy*.
28. National Statistical Office (NSO), *Statistical Yearbook Thailand* (Bangkok: Ministry of Information and Communication Technology, 2004).
29. Thomas Crawford, Human-Environment Interactions and Regional Change in Northeast Thailand: Relationships between Socio-Economic, Environment, and Geographic Patterns, PhD diss., Department of Geography, University of North Carolina–Chapel Hill, 2000.
30. Muscat, *The Fifth Tiger*.
31. Office of the Royal Development Projects Board (RDPB), The Royal Development Centres and the Philosophy of Sufficiency Economy for the Ministerial Conference on Alternative Development: Sufficiency Economy, Thailand, 2004.
32. John Lawler, Diversity Issues in South-East Asia: The Case of Thailand, *International Journal of Manpower* 17:4/5 (1996): 152–67.
33. Muscat, *The Fifth Tiger*.
34. Susan Darlington, Rethinking Buddhism and Development: The Emergence of Environmentalist Monks in Thailand, *Journal of Buddhist Ethics* 7 (2000): 1–14.
35. RDPB, The Royal Development Centres and the Philosophy of Sufficiency Economy.
36. Ibid.
37. Ibid.
38. Jitsanguan, *Sustainable Agriculture Systems for Small-Scale Farmers in Thailand*.
39. Chirayu Isarangkun and Kobsak Pootrakool, Sustainable Economic Development through the Sufficiency Economy, The Crown Property of Bureau, 2004, http://www.sufficiencyeconomy.org.
40. Ibid.
41. BOI, Economic Planning: "A Green and Happy Society," 5.
42. NESDB, National Sustainable Development Strategy for Thailand—A Guidance Manual.
43. Nang Rong District Office (NRDO), *Nang Rong District Yearbook* (Burirum, Thailand: NRDO, 2006).
44. Charles Heckman, *Rice Field Ecology in Northeast Thailand* (The Hague: Junk, 1979).
45. Michael Parnwell, Rural Poverty, Development and the Environment: The Case of North-East Thailand, *Journal of Biogeography* 15 (1986): 199–208; Y. Kaida and V. Surarerks, Climate and Agricultural Land Use in Thailand, in *Climate and Agricultural Land Use in Monsoon Asia*, ed. Masatoshi Yoshino (Tokyo: University of Tokyo Press, 1984), 231–54; Ronald Rindfuss, Continuous and Discrete: Where They Have Met in Thailand, in *Linking People, Place, and Policy: A GIScience Approach*, ed. Stephen Walsh and Kelly Crews-Meyer (Boston: Kluwer Academic Publishers, 2002), 7–37.
46. Nang Rong Municipal Office (NRMO), *Three Years Development Plans 2004 to 2006* (Nang Rong, Thailand: Nang Rong Municipal Office, 2003); NRMO, *Three Years Development Plans 2007 to 2009*, Nang Rong, Thailand: Nang Rong Municipal Office, 2006.
47. Ibid.
48. Kriengsak Rojnkureesatien, Geographical Accessibility and Land-Use and Land-Cover Dynamics: The Case of Nang Rong District, Northeast Thailand, PhD diss., Department of Geography, University of North Carolina–Chapel Hill, 2006.
49. Seri Phongphit and Kevin Hewison, *Village Life: Culture and Transition in Thailand's Northeast* (Bangkok: White Lotus, 2001).
50. Ibid.
51. Khon Kaen University and Ford Cropping Systems Project, An Agroecosystem Analysis of Northeast Thailand, technical report, Faculty of Agriculture, Khon Kaen University, Thailand, 1982.
52. Rojnkureesatien, Geographical Accessibility and Land-Use and Land-Cover Dynamics.
53. Tom Evans, Integration of Community-Level Social and Environmental Data: Spatial Modeling of Community Boundaries in Northeast Thailand, PhD diss., Department of Geography, University of North Carolina at Chapel Hill, 1998.
54. Office of Agricultural Economics (OAE), *The Agricultural Statistics of Thailand* (Bangkok: Ministry of Agricultural and Cooperative, 2006).
55. Barbara Entwisle, Ronald Rindfuss, Stephen Walsh, and Philip Page, Population Growth and Its Spatial Distribution as Factors in the Deforestation of Nang Rong, Thailand, *Geoforum* 39 (2008): 879–97.
56. Somluckrat Grandstaff, Terry Grandstaff, Pagarat Rathakette, David Thomas, and Jureerat Thomas, Trees in Paddy Fields in Northeast Thailand, in *Traditional Agriculture in Southeast Asia: A Human*

Ecology Perspective, ed. Gerald G. Marten (Boulder: Westview Press, 1986), 273–92.

57. William Welsh, Agro-ecological Sustainability and Land Degradation Potential in Nang Rong, Thailand, PhD diss., University of North Carolina–Chapel Hill, 2001.
58. Jonathan Rigg, Homogeneity and Heterogeneity: An Analysis of the Nature of Variation in Northeastern Thailand, *Malaysian Journal of Tropical Geography* 22:1 (1991): 63–72.
59. Rojnkureesatien, Geographical Accessibility and Land-Use and Land-Cover Dynamics.
60. Entwisle et al., Population Growth and Its Spatial Distribution.
61. Bello, Cunningham, and Kheng Poh, *A Siamese Tragedy*.
62. Entwisle et al., Population Growth and Its Spatial Distribution.
63. NRDO, *Nang Rong District Yearbook*, 2006.
64. Rojnkureesatien, Geographical Accessibility and Land-Use and Land-Cover Dynamics.
65. NRMO, Three Years Development Plans 2004 to 2006.
66. Thanut Wongsaichue, Household Production Resources, Population Dynamics and Land Use / Land Cover Change in Rural Northeast Villages, Thailand, PhD diss., Mahidol University, Thailand, 2006.
67. Rojnkureesatien, Geographical Accessibility and Land-Use and Land-Cover Dynamics.
68. The Office of the National Research Council of Thailand (NRCT), The King's Sufficiency Economy and the Analyses of Meaning by Economists, National Research Council Committee on Economic Branch, 2003.
69. RDPB, The Royal Development Centres and the Philosophy of Sufficiency Economy.
70. Jitsanguan, *Sustainable Agriculture Systems for Small-Scale Farmers in Thailand.*
71. RDPB, The Royal Development Centres and the Philosophy of Sufficiency Economy.
72. Ibid.
73. Entwisle et al., Population Growth and Its Spatial Distribution.
74. OAE, The Agricultural Statistics of Thailand.
75. The Royal Forest Department, Forestry Statistics of Thailand, 2006, http://www.forest.go.th/stat/stat49/stat2549.htm
76. NRMO, *Three Years Development Plans 2007 to 2009.*
77. Office of Natural and Resources and Environmental Planning and Policy (NREPP), Ministry of Natural Resources and Environment, Thailand.
78. NRDO, *Nang Rong District Yearbook*, 2006.
79. NRMO, *Three Years Development Plans 2007 to 2009.*
80. Ibid.
81. Dixon, Thailand's Rapid Economic Growth.
82. *Chaipattana Foundation Journal*, December 2000, http://www.chaipat.or.th/chaipat/journal/dec00/eng/e_economy.html.
83. Ibid.
84. NRDO, *Nang Rong District Yearbook*, 2006.

REFERENCES

Bello, Walden, Shea Cunningham, and Li Kheng Poh. *A Siamese Tragedy: Development and Disintegration in Modern Thailand.* New York: Zed Books, 1998.

Chaipattana Foundation Journal. December 2000. http://www.chaipat.or.th/chaipat/journal/dec00/eng/e_economy.html.

Crawford, Thomas. Human-Environment Interactions and Regional Change in Northeast Thailand: Relationships between Socio-Economic, Environment, and Geographic Patterns. PhD diss., Department of Geography, University of North Carolina–Chapel Hill, 2000.

Darlington, Susan. Rethinking Buddhism and Development: The Emergence of Environmentalist Monks in Thailand. *Journal of Buddhist Ethics* 7 (2000): 1–14.

Dixon, Chris. Thailand's Rapid Economic Growth: Causes, Sustainability and Lessons. In *Uneven Development in Thailand*, ed. Michael Parnwell. London: Ashgate, (1996): 28–48.

Ekins, Paul, Sadrine Simon, Lisa Deutsch, Carl Folke, and Rudolf DeGroot. A Framework for the Practical Application of the Concepts of Critical and Strong Sustainability. *Ecological Economics* 44 (2003): 165–85.

Entwisle, Barbara, Ronald Rindfuss, Stephen Walsh, and Philip Page. Population Growth and Its Spatial Distribution as Factors in the Deforestation of Nang Rong, Thailand. *Geoforum* 39 (2008): 879–97.

Evans, Tom. Integration of Community-Level Social and Environmental Data: Spatial Modeling of Community Boundaries in Northeast Thailand. PhD diss., Department of Geography, University of North Carolina–Chapel Hill, 1998.

Evers, Hans-Dieter, and Rudiger Korff. *Southeast Asian Urbanism: The Meaning and Power of Social Space.* Munster, Germany: LitVerlag, 2000.

Grandstaff, Somluckrat, Terry Grandstaff, Pagarat Rathakette, David Thomas, and Jureerat Thomas. Trees in Paddy Fields in Northeast Thailand. In *Traditional Agriculture in Southeast Asia: A Human Ecology Perspective*, ed. Gerald G. Marten, 273–92. Boulder: Westview Press, 1986.

Heckman, Charles. *Rice Field Ecology in Northeast Thailand.* The Hague: Junk, 1979.

Hediger, Werner. Reconciling "Weak" and "Strong" Sustainability. *International Journal of Economics* 26:7/8/9 (1999): 1120–44.

Hirsch, Philip, and Larry Lohmann. Contemporary Politics of Environment in Thailand. *Asian Survey* 29:4 (1989): 439–51.

Isarangkun, Chirayu, and Kobsak Pootrakool. Sustainable Economic Development through the Sufficiency Economy. The Crown Property of Bureau. 2004. http://www.sufficiencyeconomy.org.

Jitsanguan, Thanwa. Sustainable Agriculture Systems for Small-Scale Farmers in Thailand: Implications for the Environment. FFTC book series no. 509. Food and Fertilizer Technology Center, Taipei, Taiwan. 2001. http://www.agnet.org/library/eb/509/.

Kaida, Y., and V. Surarerks. Climate and Agricultural Land Use in Thailand. In *Climate and Agricultural Land Use in Monsoon Asia*, ed. Masatoshi Yoshino, 231–54. Tokyo: University of Tokyo Press, 1984.

Kaothien, Utis. Regional and Urbanization Policy in Thailand: The Tertiary Sector as a Leading Sector in Regional Development. *Urban Studies* 28:6 (1991): 1027–43.

Khon Kaen University and Ford Cropping Systems Project. An Agroecosystem Analysis of Northeast Thailand. Technical report, Faculty of Agriculture, Khon Kaen University, Thailand, 1982.

Lawler, John. Diversity Issues in South-East Asia: The Case of Thailand. *International Journal of Manpower* 17:4/5 (1996): 152–67.

Muscat, Robert. *The Fifth Tiger: A Study of Thai Development Policy.* Tokyo, Japan: United Nations University Press, 1994.

Nang Rong District Office (NRDO). *Nang Rong District Yearbook.* Buriram, Thailand: NRDO, 2006. (In Thai.)

Nang Rong Municipal Office (NRMO). *Three Years Development Plans 2004 to 2006.* Nang Rong, Thailand: Nang Rong Municipal Office, 2003. (In Thai.)

———. *Three Years Development Plans 2007 to 2009.* Nang Rong, Thailand: Nang Rong Municipal Office, 2006. (In Thai.)

Nang Rong Project Archives. Carolina Population Center. University of North Carolina at Chapel Hill. http://www.cpc.unc.edu/projects/nangrong/.

National Statistical Office (NSO). *Statistical Yearbook Thailand.* Bangkok: Ministry of Information and Communication Technology, 1997.

———. *Statistical Yearbook Thailand.* Bangkok: Ministry of Information and Communication Technology, 2004.

———. *Statistical Yearbook Thailand.* Bangkok: Ministry of Information and Communication Technology, 2006.

———. *Statistical Yearbook Thailand 2007.* Bangkok: Ministry of Information and Communication Technology, 2007.

Office of Agricultural Economics (OAE). *The Agricultural Statistics of Thailand.* Bangkok: Ministry of Agricultural and Cooperative, 2006.

Office of National Economic and Social Development Board (NESDB). *Social Outlook* 2:1 (2005): 9. (In Thai.)

Office of the National Research Council of Thailand (NRCT). The King's Sufficiency Economy and the Analyses of Meaning by Economists. National Research Council Committee on Economic Branch, 2003.

———. National Sustainable Development Strategy for Thailand—A Guidance Manual. United Nations Environment Programme. Bangkok, Thailand Environment Institute, March 2008.

Office of Natural and Resources and Environmental Planning and Policy (NREPP). Bangkok: Ministry of Natural Resources and Environment, 2000.

Office of the Royal Development Projects Board (RDPB). The Royal Development Centres and the Philosophy of Sufficiency Economy for the Ministerial Conference on Alternative Development: Sufficiency Economy. Bangkok: RDPB, 2004.

Parnwell, Michael. Rural Poverty, Development and the Environment: The Case of North-East Thailand. *Journal of Biogeography* 15 (1986): 199–208.

———. *Uneven Development in Thailand.* London: Ashgate, 1996.

Phongphit, Seri, and Kevin Hewison. *Village Life: Culture and Transition in Thailand's Northeast.* Bangkok: White Lotus, 2001.

Pookpakdi, Aphiphan. Sustainable Agriculture for Small Scale Farmers: A Farming System Perspective. In *Sustainable Agriculture for the Asian and Pacific Regions.* Book series 44. Taipei: Food and Fertilizer Technology Center, 1992.

Pugh, Cedric, ed. *Sustainable Cities in Developing Countries: Theory and Practice at the Millennium.* London: Earthscan, 2001.

Rigg, Jonathan. Homogeneity and Heterogeneity: An Analysis of the Nature of Variation in Northeastern Thailand. *Malaysian Journal of Tropical Geography* 22:1 (1991): 63–72.

———. Rural-Urban Interactions, Agriculture and Wealth: A Southeast Asian Perspective. *Progress in Human*

Geography 22:4 (1996): 497–522.

Rindfuss, Ronald. Continuous and Discrete: Where They Have Met in Thailand. In *Linking People, Place, and Policy: A GIScience Approach,* ed. Stephen Walsh and Kelly Crews-Meyer, 7–37. Boston: Kluwer Academic Publishers, 2002.

Rojnkureesatien, Kriengsak. Geographical Accessibility and Land-Use and Land-Cover Dynamics the Case of Nang Rong District, Northeast Thailand. PhD diss., Department of Geography, University of North Carolina–Chapel Hill, 2006.

Royal Forest Department. Forestry Statistics of Thailand. 1999. http://www.forest.go.th/stat/stat42/stat2542.htm.

———. Forestry Statistics of Thailand. 2006. http://www.forest.go.th/stat/stat49/stat2549.htm.

Thailand Board of Investment (BOI). Economic Planning: "A Green and Happy Society." *Thailand Investment Review* 16:8 (September 2006): 5.

Trebuil, Guy. Pioneer Agriculture, Green Revolution and Environmental Degradation in Thailand. In *Counting the Costs Economic Growth and Environmental Change in Thailand*, ed. Jonathan Rigg, 67–89. Pasir Panjang, Singapore, Institute of Southeast Asian Studies, 1995.

Vojnovic, Igor. Inter-generational and Intra-generational Equity Requirements for Sustainable Development. *Environmental Conservation* 22:3 (1995): 223–28.

Welsh, William. Agro-ecological Sustainability and Land Degradation Potential in Nang Rong, Thailand. PhD diss., University of North Carolina–Chapel Hill, 2001.

———. Characterizing the Forest-Agricultural Land Flux within the Context of Soil Suitability Parameters in Nang Rong, Thailand. *Journal of the American Society for Photogrammetry and Remote Sensing.* Special Issue on Remote Sensing Data Fusion. (June 2008): 765–73.

Wongsaichue, Thanut. Household Production Resources, Population Dynamics and Land Use/Land Cover Change in Rural Northeast Villages, Thailand. PhD diss., Mahidol University, Thailand, 2006.

World Commission on Environment and Development (WECD). *Our Common Future.* New York: Oxford University Press, 1987.

■ ERAN RAZIN

Deconcentration in the Tel Aviv Metropolitan Area

GOVERNANCE, MARKETS, AND THE QUEST FOR SUSTAINABILITY

Israel is one of the densest countries in the world. It is a small developed country characterized by population growth rates that resemble those of some developing countries, due to a high natural increase of its Arab and ultrareligious Jewish population and to substantial in-migration. Population density according to official statistics reached about 803 persons per square mile (310.2 persons per square kilometer) in 2006, up from 279 persons per square mile (107.6 persons per square kilometer) in 1961 and 112 persons per square mile (43.1 persons per square kilometer) at the end of 1948.[1] Apart from tiny city states and island states, only a handful of countries are denser than Israel. Moreover, the Palestinian Territories, deeply intertwined with the Israeli settlement and environmental systems, are even denser than Israel. The southern half of Israel is a sparsely populated desert, thus densities in the populated parts of the country are even higher than what average figures indicate.

In 2006 over 80 percent of Israel's population of 6.85 million resided in Israel's four metropolitan areas: Tel Aviv, Haifa, Jerusalem, and Beer Sheva (fig. 1).[2] Given Israel's small size and the fact that the Tel Aviv metropolis is approaching the fringe areas of the Jerusalem and Haifa metropolitan areas, a two-tier metropolitan system seems to be emerging. Most of central Israel and much of its north gradually have evolved to be a continuous metropolitan region—although not characterized by a continuous built-up area—with Tel Aviv as a primary node, Jerusalem and Haifa as secondary nodes, and Beer Sheva as a peripheral node.

Environmental sustainability concerns associated with metropolitan expansion have frequently been obscured by the never-ending tensions of the Israeli-Arab conflict. The Society for the Protection of Nature—Israel's first environmental nongovernmental organization (NGO), established in 1953—initially engaged mainly in the protection of Israel's natural assets, such as flora, fauna, and water sources, and in the formation of nature reserves. This measure took place in

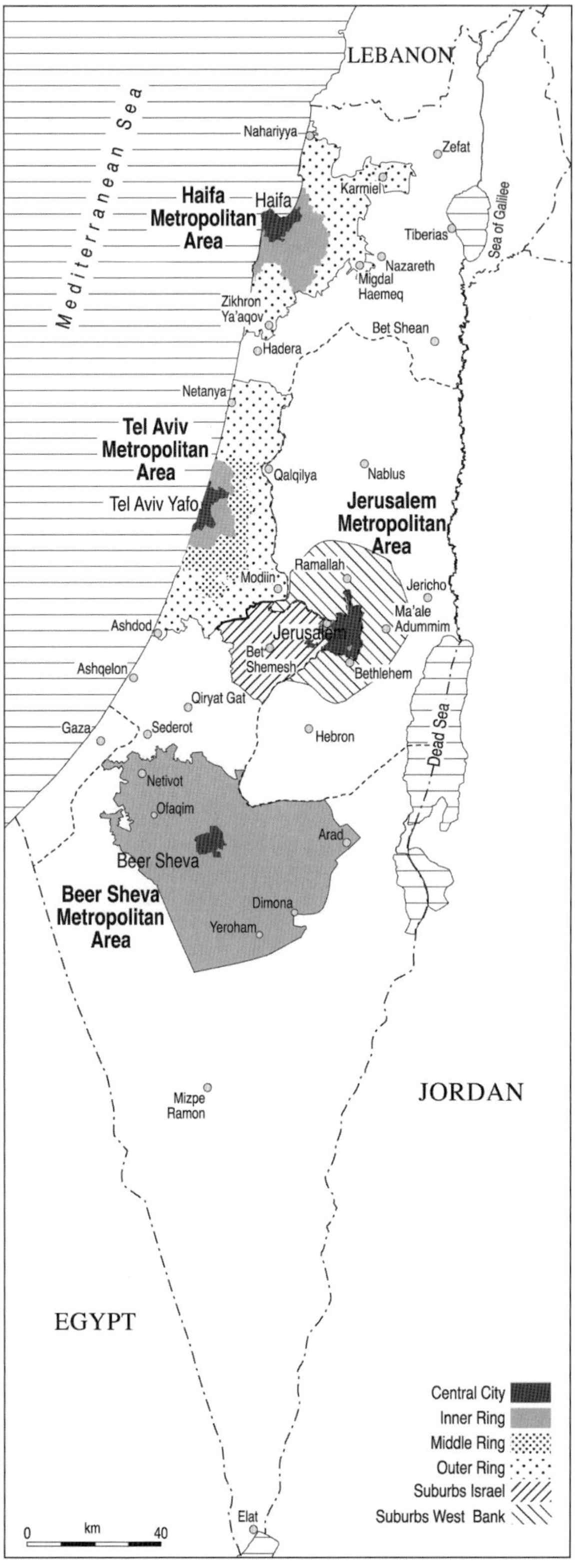

Figure 1. Israel's four metropolitan areas.

an era dominated by Zionist ideals of building a new Jewish state, settling a sparsely populated country, establishing new Jewish settlements, "making the desert bloom," and, in the words of poet Nathan Alterman: "we will dress you (the Land of Israel) in garb of concrete and cement."[3]

However, growing environmental awareness and accumulating pressures of population growth and urban development have produced an influential public agenda of sustainability, particularly since the 1990s. The Environmental Protection Service, established in 1973 within the Ministry of Interior, was the first central state action for the creation of a comprehensive environmental administration, active since its inception also in land use planning. In 1988 it became the independent Ministry of the Environment (Ministry of Environmental Protection since 2006). Environmental NGOs have also proliferated in the 1990s, becoming extensively engaged in land use planning procedures, utilizing judicial activism to oppose state supported development plans, and promoting long-term policy changes through legal action that led to precedent-setting court rulings. A significant milestone has been the establishment of Israel Union for Environmental Defense (Adam, Teva VaDin), specializing in legal environmental battles. Nearly one hundred NGOs have become affiliated with

Life and Environment—an organization active since 1974 that expanded in the late 1990s as an umbrella organization for NGOs that deal with public health, sustainable development, and public participation in planning. These NGOs have covered a broad range of national and local issues, including urban agendas such as promoting bicycle lanes, urban conservation, and principles of new urbanism. Local governments have also increasingly engaged in environmental agendas, some in the framework of joint municipal unions for the environment, established since the 1970s. Regional councils, practically controlling most open space in metropolitan fringe areas, have become engaged in the early 2000s in the preparation of master plans for sustainable development.[4] Conservation of open space through curbing suburban sprawl and promoting compact forms of urban development has become a foremost aspect in the environmental policy agenda, largely replacing the outdated focus on the preservation of agricultural land.

This chapter focuses on deconcentration processes in the Tel Aviv metropolitan area, providing evidence of the deconcentration of population and economic activities, and discussing the impact of governance and policy attributes on these processes. It sums up the emergence of a new planning doctrine that has attempted to counteract the liberalization of Israel's land policy in a context of a neoliberal transformation. The paper briefly presents two case studies in which public policy did arrest, at least to some extent, market processes of deconcentration. These demonstrate that public policy can challenge deconcentration and sprawl, despite prevailing perceptions that intensifying market-led trends cannot be reversed. The case studies indicate the emergence of a new mode of regulation in which environmental and social justice NGOs play a growing role in initiating and consolidating planning policies that promote environmental and social sustainability. However, such policies should be aware of constraints posed by the market, rather than unrealistically encourage development patterns that do not fit locational requirements of economic activities and residential preferences.

The Dominance of the Tel Aviv Metropolitan Area

The Tel Aviv metropolis, with over 3 million inhabitants, is Israel's dominant economic and cultural heart. Taking into account the gradual expansion of its boundaries, the share of the Tel Aviv metropolis has been fairly stable at around 44–45 percent of Israel's population. Major economic trends in the Tel Aviv metropolis included a decline in manufacturing and a rapid, nearly uninterrupted, increase in the share of financing and business services in metropolitan employment.

The dominance of the metropolis has probably become evident more than ever before since the 1990s, with the metropolis attracting young, professional, highly qualified labor, and seemingly draining other parts of the country from leading talent and creativity in business services, high-technology, entertainment, and culture. Whereas the share of the Tel Aviv metropolis in its present boundaries has declined steadily, from 47 percent of Israel's population in 1970 to around 40 percent in 2005 (excluding Ashdod), the share of the metropolis in Israel's employment has remained remarkably stable, at about 48 percent (table 1). This growing gap between the share of the metropolis in Israel's population and its share in employment indicates high rates of participation in the labor force, low unemployment, and increased commuting to the metropolis from beyond its boundaries.

Table 1. Population and employment in the Tel Aviv metropolitan area by rings, 1970–2005

	1970	1980	1990	1995	2000	2005
Number of inhabitants (% of the metro area)						
The city of Tel Aviv	27.0	18.7	16.0	14.8	13.6	13.3
Inner ring[a]	35.1	37.3	35.5	33.6	30.6	28.6
Middle and outer rings[b]	37.8	44.0	48.5	51.6	55.8	58.1
Total metro[c]	100	100	100	100	100	100
Total metro (thousands)[c]	1,420.1	1,795.1	2,126.5	2,358.3	2,611.5	2,839.8
Total metro (thousands), including Ashdod	—	—	—	—	2,785.7	3,040.4
Number of inhabitants (% of Israel—total)						
Total metro[c]	47.3	45.8	44.1	42.0	41.0	40.6
Total metro, including Ashdod	—	—	—	—	43.7	43.5
Number of employed persons—place of work (% of the metro area)						
The city of Tel Aviv	49.2	39.6	37.7	34.6	31.6	28.1
Inner ring[a]	18.8	21.0	24.5	24.9	22.9	22.3
Middle and outer rings[b]	32.0	39.4	37.9	40.5	45.5	49.6
Total metro[c]	100	100	100	100	100	100
Total metro (thousands)[c]	480.7	587.4	707.2	949.1	1065.4	1,200.0
Number of employed persons—place of work (% of Israel—total)						
Total metro[‡]	49.9	46.8	47.4	48.2	48.0	48.1

Source: Based on data of the Central Bureau of Statistics, Labor Force Surveys.
Note: The labor force survey data includes only the civilian labor force, not Palestinians residing in the Palestinian territories and working in Israel.
a. Rest of Tel Aviv District.
b. Central District. Figures of the outer ring exclude the city of Ashdod, located in the Southern District.
c. Excluding Ashdod.

Deconcentration of Population in the Tel Aviv Metropolis

Suburbanization in early post-independence years consisted primarily of state-sponsored public housing established at the far urban perimeter. Neighborhoods built in the 1950s were characterized by low densities, whereas those built in the 1960s and early 1970s were denser, largely consisting of low-standard large apartment blocks.[5] A marked transition occurred in the late 1970s and the 1980s, when a flow of middle class population into suburban and exurban space commenced, reflecting consumer preference for sprawling development of low-density and single-family housing.[6]

Mass immigration from the former Soviet Union has set in motion the evolution of a new outer ring of rapid metropolitan growth in the 1990s (fig. 2). A unique feature of this new outer ring has been the inclusion of rural regional councils, dominated by cooperative kibbutzim and moshavim that previously resisted urbanization.[7] The new outer ring includes new exurban settlements, epitomizing the new Israeli dream of a single-family house with a red roof and a backyard. Many, such as wealthy Karmei Yosef and lower middle class Bat Hefer, are located within the jurisdictional areas of regional councils (figs. 3 and 4). The kibbutzim and moshavim themselves

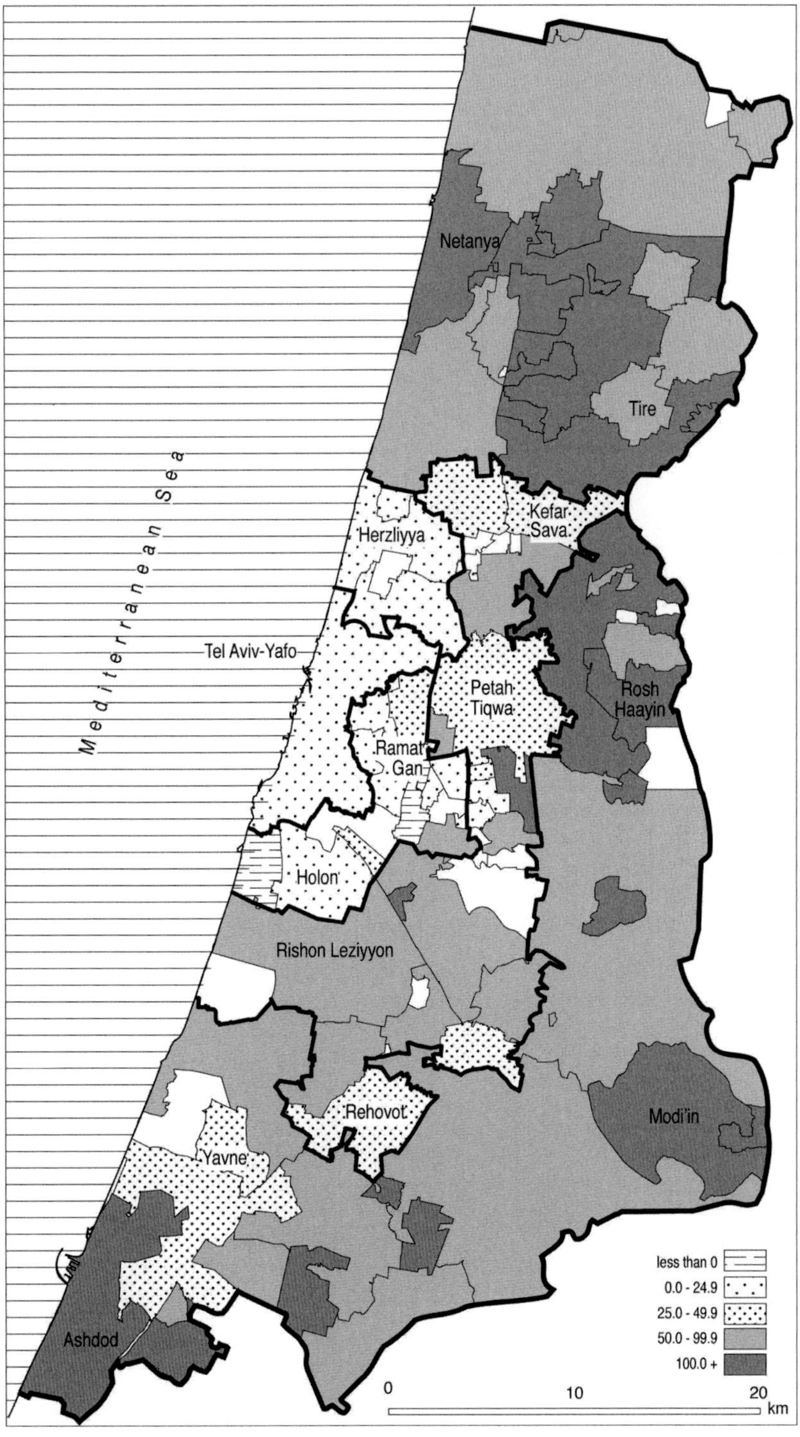

Figure 2. The Tel Aviv metropolitan area—percent population growth by local authority, 1989–2006.

PHOTOGRAPH BY ERAN RAZIN

Figure 3. High-density and low-density suburban residential development: Bat Hefer, an exurban settlement (Emeq Hefer Regional Council).

PHOTOGRAPH BY ERAN RAZIN

Figure 4. High-density and low-density suburban residential development: Karmei Yosef, an exurban settlement (Gezer Regional Council).

PHOTOGRAPH BY ERAN RAZIN

Figure 5. High-density and low-density suburban residential development: Modiin, a new suburban city.

Figure 6. High-density and low-density suburban residential development: Ashdod, a port town that became a suburb.

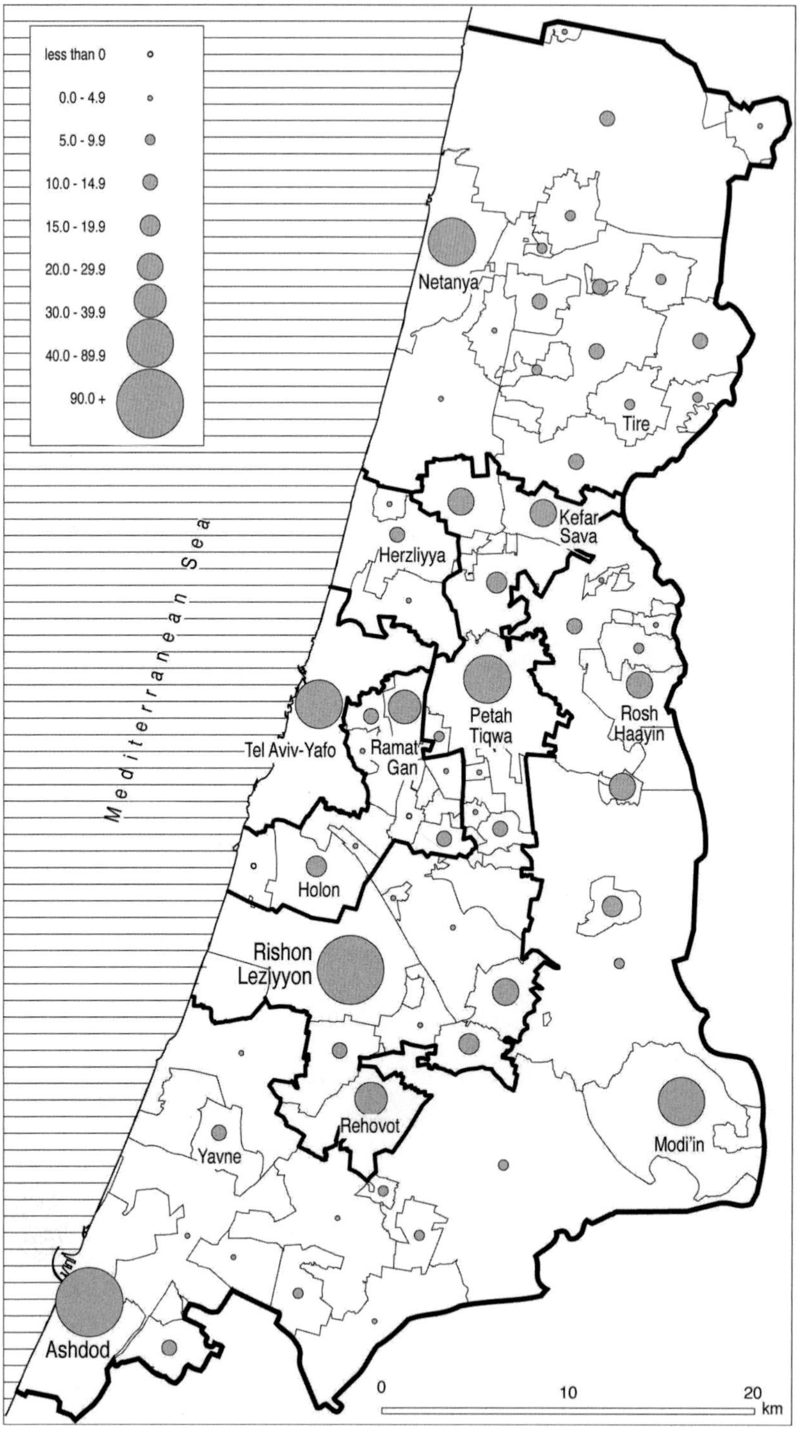

Figure 7. The Tel Aviv metropolitan area—population growth (number of persons) by local authority, 1989–2006.

are losing their unique cooperative structure, increasingly becoming rural suburbs and expanding through the development of new exurban neighborhoods. Many of the fastest growing local authorities since 1989 have been indeed regional councils, independent exurban local councils, and other small towns that attained an exurban character.

Metropolitan expansion, however, took place also in larger cities (figs. 5 and 6), either new cities such as Modiin and ultrareligious Elad, or cities previously functioning as nonmetropolitan regional centers. Ashdod, at the outer ring of the Tel Aviv metropolis, had the highest absolute population increase in the metropolis: 127,800 between 1989 and 2006. The outer ring cities of Modiin and Netanya also grew particularly fast, as did the central city of Tel Aviv and the middle ring city of Rishon Letzion (fig. 7).

The share of population residing in the city of Tel Aviv decreased continuously, reaching a low of 13.3 percent of total metropolitan population in 2005. The proportion of population residing in the inner ring has also declined steadily since 1980, whereas the share of the middle and outer rings grew, reaching about 60 percent in 2005. These changes mark a substantial transformation in Israel's urban system, not only because of their magnitude, but also because of their role in gradually merging the fringes of the Tel Aviv, Jerusalem, and Haifa metropolitan areas.

Deconcentration of Economic Activity

Job deconcentration in the Tel Aviv metropolis, particularly from the central city to the middle and outer rings, has been rapid, accelerating since the 1990s and becoming more rapid than the deconcentration of the population. The share of the city of Tel Aviv in metropolitan employment decreased from 50 percent to less than 30 percent, but rapid suburbanization of the population has kept the jobs/population ratio in Tel Aviv far higher than anywhere else. The share of employment in the inner ring also declined slightly, probably because the inner ring could not offer competitive land prices and lacked accessibility advantages of either the central city or the outer suburbs. Thus, most employment growth took place in the middle and outer suburbs.

Rapid deconcentration of retail, high-technology industries, warehousing and entertainment functions has followed earlier deconcentration of manufacturing. Deconcentration of office functions was more limited until the early 2000s but seems to be accelerating.[8] In fact, between 1995 and 2005, all major economic activities were rapidly deconcentrating, except for public services (including education and health). The deconcentration of retail, financial institutions, and business services from the city of Tel Aviv to the outer suburbs is a particularly significant phenomenon for the central city. Tel Aviv is losing its position as the retail hub of the metropolis, and its unique agglomeration economies in finance and business services could be eroding as well. Banking, insurance and financial institutions are the economic activity most concentrated in the city of Tel Aviv and in the Tel Aviv metropolis. However, whereas concentration of this sector in the Tel Aviv metropolis even increased, the dominance of the central city eroded. An even more marked process was evident in business services (table 2).

The emerging spatial pattern of employment in the Tel Aviv metropolis is polycentric, with some tendency toward scatteration. Despite substantial deconcentration, the city of Tel Aviv has retained its status as the dominant node of employment. The metropolitan central business

Table 2. Employed persons in the Tel Aviv metropolitan area by place of work and selected economic branches, 1995–2005

	MANUFACTURING			WHOLESALE, RETAIL TRADE, AUTOMOBILE REPAIRS			ACCOMMODATION SERVICES AND RESTAURANTS		
	1995	2000	2005	1995	2000	2005	1995	2000	2005
% of the metro area									
City of Tel Aviv	26.5	20.6	18.1	35.1	28.5	22.2	45.7	38.7	33.6
Inner ring	26.3	23.8	19.8	30.1	24.1	24.7	19.6	22.6	26.1
Middle and outer rings	47.2	55.6	62.1	34.8	47.4	53.2	34.7	38.7	40.3
Tel Aviv metro: total	100	100	100	100	100	100	100	100	100
% of Israel: total									
Tel Aviv metro: total	46.8	44.1	43.5	57.3	54.1	53.1	44.6	41.7	47.0

	TRANSPORT, STORAGE, AND COMMUNICATION			BANKING, INSURANCE, AND FINANCIAL INSTITUTIONS			BUSINESS SERVICES		
	1995	2000	2005	1995	2000	2005	1995	2000	2005
% of the metro area									
City of Tel Aviv	39.9	33.5	26.0	61.1	59.8	53.9	51.2	42.4	38.3
Inner ring	19.2	17.9	16.8	20.2	21.2	21.1	23.3	23.8	19.8
Middle and outer rings	40.9	48.6	57.3	18.7	19.0	25.0	25.5	33.8	41.9
Tel Aviv metro: total	100	100	100	100	100	100	100	100	100
% of Israel: total									
Tel Aviv metro: total	50.8	52.4	51.7	68.6	69.1	75.0	58.9	61.1	62.1

	PUBLIC ADMINISTRATION			EDUCATION		
	1995	2000	2005	1995	2000	2005
% of the metro area						
City of Tel Aviv	38.3	44.4	38.5	22.6	21.8	19.9
Inner ring	19.3	15.1	16.8	28.1	27.7	27.3
Middle and outer rings	42.4	40.5	44.7	49.2	50.5	52.8
Tel Aviv metro: total	100	100	100	100	100	100
% of Israel: total						
Tel Aviv metro: total	39.0	38.1	40.5	39.5	40.6	39.1

	HEALTH, WELFARE, AND SOCIAL SERVICES			COMMUNITY, SOCIAL, AND PERSONAL SERVICES		
	1995	2000	2005	1995	2000	2005
% of the metro area						
City of Tel Aviv	22.2	21.7	22.6	43.4	42.0	36.8
Inner ring	27.5	24.7	26.4	25.1	21.4	26.7
Middle and outer rings	50.3	53.6	51.0	31.6	36.6	36.6
Tel Aviv metro: total	100	100	100	100	100	100
% of Israel: total						
Tel Aviv metro: total	48.3	48.3	46.0	51.3	49.7	46.6

Source: Based on data of the Central Bureau of Statistics, Labor Force Surveys.

district spills over to adjacent Ramat Gan, but none of the suburban employment centers seem to be emerging as edge cities that rival Tel Aviv. Suburban locations such as Herzeliyya and Petah Tiqwa have managed to attract headquarters and high-end office activities, particularly in high-technology associated activities, but are far from rivaling Tel Aviv. Emerging patterns in retail have been rather scattered. Proximity to major highways, interchanges, and train stations has been a major consideration in the process of deconcentration. "Airport City"—a major logistics and office / high-tech hub close to the Ben Gurion International Airport, developed on state-owned agricultural land leased by moshav Bareket—is a prime example for such locational considerations.

The Governance Context

The governance context for metropolitan deconcentration refers to the roles of central government agencies (frequently acting as several stakeholders rather than pursuing a coherent public policy), local governments, NGOs and partnerships of these organizations with the private sector. Public policies to protect open space face pressures not only of local governments, land owners, and developers, but also of central government agencies.

Two major central government agencies involved in spatial development are the Planning Administration at the Ministry of Interior and Israel's Land Administration (ILA).[9] The Planning Administration operates the two upper tiers—national and district—of Israel's three-tier hierarchical statutory land use planning. The National Commission for Planning and Building at the Planning Administration is responsible for the preparation of statutory national outline plans (approved by the government), and for approval of statutory outline plans for Israel's six districts. The district planning committees form part of the six administrative districts of the Ministry of Interior. In addition to approving local plans, they are also responsible for the preparation of district outline plans. A majority of district committee members represent central state ministries, a minority represents local authorities, and one member is a professional planner.

ILA administers government-owned land and is practically engaged also with planning and development. ILA could be expected to promote policies devised by the Planning Administration, but in practice it has been more prodevelopment, being motivated also by the objective of revenue maximization. The Ministry of Housing is another central government stakeholder that tends to be more prodevelopment than the Planning Administration, its prime mission being to assure a certain volume of residential construction annually. The Ministry of Finance increasingly controls most spheres of public policy in Israel through its control of public spending and associated legislation. It is particularly influential in transportation development. The Ministries of Transportation, Environment, and Industry and Trade are also engaged in decisions that influence patterns of metropolitan development.

Local planning in Israel is largely in the hands of local authorities that serve as local planning committees, responsible for local planning, permits, and enforcement. Small local authorities are part of joint local planning committees that have less autonomy than independent local committees, because their chairperson is appointed by the Minister of Interior. Most planning decisions at the local level are subject to the approval of the district planning committee, which is in fact the major arena for substantial planning decisions at the local level. Local governments practically possess, however, more power than one could assume based on the formal division of powers. They can block quite effectively undesired plans and initiate plans. Approving "nonconforming use"—a temporary land use change—by the local authority is a tool to bypass national and district planning.[10] This measure provides a level of flexibility in otherwise rigid statutory land use plans. Granting these temporary permits is justified when the new use is required only for a limited time, or when the change is urgently needed while ordinary approval procedures could take years. This channel has been widely used to enable industrial and commercial land uses to enter old or even new agricultural structures, and particularly to enable retail in areas zoned for manufacturing, storage, or agriculture-related functions.

The influence of Israeli local authorities on deconcentration processes depends to a large extent on fiscal considerations. Attitudes and development policies of local authorities have been more in line with market processes than with central government policies.[11] Local authorities are substantially dependent on non–value-based property taxes,[12] and such taxes on businesses are usually their most profitable revenues.[13] Hence, the phenomenon frequently termed "fiscal zoning" or "the race for the ratables" prevails in Israel and encourages the dispersal of business land uses.

Another financial factor that encourages the rezoning of agricultural land is the substantial revenues from betterment levies on rezoned land. This levy consists of 50 percent of the increase in value of privately owned rezoned land; less in the case of publicly owned land. The betterment levy is paid to the local authority, thus providing an incentive to approve requests to rezone agricultural land. A fee paid to local authorities for the provision of "nonconforming use" permits also motivates local authorities to approve such "temporary" rezoning requests.

A profound change affecting metropolitan expansion since the late 1980s is the transformation of rural regional councils that control most open space in urban fringe areas. The regional councils were weak and rather passive in the past, when rural-cooperative organizations and the Jewish Agency engaged in service and development in the kibbutzim and moshavim. However, the crisis in agriculture and the collapse of most rural-cooperative organizations in the 1980s left the regional councils in a position of the sole public agents responsible for the provision of local public services in rural space. Facing growing fiscal needs, they joined the race for the ratables, displaying a more open attitude than in the past toward conversion of agricultural land.[14]

Contrastingly, Tel Aviv has pressed, with limited success, to reduce the amount of land allocated for economic land uses in metropolitan-edge areas. More intense were pressures of large suburban cities—Netanya, Kefar Sava, and Rehovot—to restrict the development of retail, industrial and office structures in adjacent regional councils. These suburban cities fear that their tax base would be eroded because of the movement of economic land uses from their jurisdictional areas to the surrounding regional councils that are able to offer lower rents, lower taxes and easier ability to open retail establishments on Saturdays.

Scarcity of land and growing fiscal disparities between local authorities have encouraged, since the 1990s, initiatives for tax base sharing and cooperation in the development of industrial and commercial land uses.[15] However, intermunicipal cooperation has faced substantial hurdles and has been mainly implemented in weak peripheral regions. Within metropolitan fringe areas, where the financial stakes and rewards are higher, cooperation is rare and hard to achieve.

Civic organizations have increasingly emerged as influential agents shaping Israel's public policy.[16] Preservation of open space has become a prime issue on the agenda of the green lobby, composed of NGOs such as the Society for the Protection of Nature and the Israel Union for Environmental Defense. These NGOs have lobbied to curb the deconcentration of land uses such as gas stations and commercial centers in rural areas and the extensive use of the nonconforming-use tool.[17] Action of civic organizations engaged in social justice and human rights agendas, such as the Democratic Mizrahi Coalition, has also influenced development patterns. Civic action consisted to a large extent of legal battles, taking advantage of growing activism of Israel's High Court of Justice. The High Court has become a major arena of societal conflicts, either aimed at challenging government decisions or dealing with issues that the legislature and government failed to resolve.[18]

National Policy Context

The Emergence of a New Planning Doctrine

National spatial planning in Israel was guided between the 1950s and 1980s by two major principles that formed the old planning doctrine:

1. Population dispersal from the Tel Aviv metropolitan area and the central coastal plain to peripheral regions, and an emphasis on planning peripheral regions.
2. Preservation of agricultural land.

Both principles favored curbing metropolitan expansion that comes at the expense of agricultural land and population dispersal to Israel's periphery. Population dispersal, largely justified by political and security considerations, was backed by statutory national outline plans prepared by the Planning Administration. Preservation of agricultural land was the task of the Commission for the Preservation of Agricultural Land—a most powerful tool established by the 1965 Planning and Building Law.[19] This commission effectively controlled the physical expansion of urban settlements in Israel, although the term "sprawl" by itself was not on the public agenda prior to the 1980s.

The foundations of the above doctrine eroded during the 1980s. Ideological change and the crises in agriculture and in the rural-cooperative sector made some of the assumptions of this doctrine obsolete, as did the rise of exurban settlements and of car-oriented shopping malls. Partial collapse of the old planning doctrine occurred under pressures of absorbing mass immigration in the 1990s.[20] Fearing acute housing shortages, the government opted in 1990 to approve the rezoning of substantial privately owned agricultural land, and it also set up emergency planning commissions that bypassed the local and district commissions. These emergency commissions practically stripped the Commission for the Preservation of Agricultural Land from its former power.

The emergency context and fears of the Planning Administration to lose control to the emergency planning commissions had a major role in inspiring a new round of planning efforts that led to the formulation of a new planning doctrine, from 1991 onward.[21] These consisted of new national plans—National Outline Plan (NOP) 31, Israel 2020 master plan, and NOP 35—as well as metropolitan development plans and six district plans. The main principles of the new doctrine are as follows:

1. For the first time since the establishment of Israel, a lower priority is given to the objective of population dispersal, in favor of successful immigrant absorption, economic growth, and environmental concerns.
2. Emphasis on planning at the metropolitan scale replaces earlier emphasis on peripheral regions.
3. A comprehensive multidisciplinary approach to land use planning is employed for the first time, referring to economic, social, and governance trends largely ignored previously by architects engaged in the preparation of physical plans. Environmental aspects are also internalized into the planning process.[22]
4. An emphasis on the extreme scarcity of land in Israel, and the dire consequences of "business as usual," trends on open space.[23]
5. The introduction of the (Dutch) concentrated dispersion concept—deconcentration into large and dense suburbs rather than to scattered sprawl.
6. Limiting search areas for future urban development to land bordering urban built-up areas, thus curbing leapfrog development in rural areas and encouraging compact development.
7. Developing a new planning vocabulary that defines several texture types, each with its own rules of development, from urban textures to rural conservation ones.

NOP 31—the first plan in this round of planning—was swiftly approved by the government in 1993, backed by a climate of an urgent need to absorb immigrants, and perhaps by stakeholders' unawareness of the far-reaching implications of an approved national plan on projects that contradict the plan. By the late 1990s stakeholders were fully aware of the significance of these plans. Thus, approval of NOP 35, prepared in 1998–1999, in which principles of the new planning doctrine were fully incorporated, was an uphill struggle. Stakeholders scrutinized every detail, challenging some aspects in the planning, political, and legal arenas. Major opposition to NOP 35 came from the rural regional councils, fearing that the plan would block profitable leapfrog development while legitimizing annexation of rural settlements to urban municipalities. The Ministry of Housing and ILA feared that the plan would tie their hands, particularly when it comes to the establishment of new settlements. NOP 35 was finally approved in autumn 2005, being one of the last decisions of the Sharon government.

The Tel Aviv metropolitan area was specifically handled in two district outline plans—the Tel Aviv and Central districts—and in a strategic metropolitan development plan. The three plans were prepared during the 1990s: the Central District plan (District Outline Plan 3/21) that includes the middle and outer rings of the Tel Aviv metropolis was approved in 2003, and the Tel Aviv District plan (DOP 5) that includes the metropolitan core and inner rings is in final approval stages (in 2008).[24] The three documents strongly favored policies of compact development, curbing sprawl, preserving open space, promoting public transportation oriented development, concentrating suburban business land uses in large nodes, developing metropolitan parks, and revitalizing and increasing densities of built-up areas in the metropolitan core. A particular innovation of the Central District plan concerned the definition of metropolitan recreation areas that are not necessarily prime open spaces but serve as a buffer for urban expansion. These plans have become influential even before their formal approval, guiding decisions of the Planning Administration in light of the new planning doctrine.

The Profound Shift in Land Policy—Semiprivatization of Publicly Owned Land

The shift in Israel's land policy was, at least for a time, even more far reaching than the shift in planning policy. Over 90 percent of Israel's land area is government owned, administered by ILA. Agricultural land of the ILA is leased to kibbutzim, moshavim, and private corporations. Until 1992, when such land was rezoned, its former lessees were usually entitled to receive compensation payment based only on the land's agricultural value; profits from rezoning were fully kept by the ILA. These conditions formed a formidable barrier for rezoning. Lessees of ILA agricultural land fiercely opposed attempts to rezone their land, unless compensated by similar land elsewhere.

The crisis in agriculture and in the kibbutzim and moshavim eroded the foundations of this land policy in the 1980s. The major change came in 1992, when decision 533 of ILA's council transformed radically the rules of the game, followed by the slightly modified decision 611 in 1993. According to these decisions, lessees of ILA agricultural land were entitled to compensation on land returned to the ILA, based on the value of the land after its rezoning. Moreover, they could request the ILA's permission to initiate by themselves nonagricultural development (residential, industrial, or commercial) on the leased land, being entitled to receive a reduced rate in the new lease contract and being exempt from a new tender on the land. Decision 611 gave the ILA the authority to grant an early approval (preruling) for lessees to initiate nonagricultural projects on the land, eliminating the risk of spending considerable funds on such initiatives only to learn later that the ILA opposes the step or prefers to rezone the land by itself. Such a pre-ruling by the ILA exerted considerable pressure on the planning commissions of the Planning Administration to approve plans that already enjoyed, in principle, the support of the ILA.

These decisions have changed dramatically the attitudes of kibbutzim and moshavim, which to a large extent ceased to be watchdogs of agricultural land and showed a growing interest in real estate profits. ILA decisions instigated a gold rush over rural land in the metropolitan fringes, largely directed by middleman entrepreneurs—developers and lawyers such as Shraga Biran.[25]

Since then, ILA's land policy has been a source for vociferous debate in the public, political, and legal arenas. The debates concerned the justification of sharing profits from rezoning public agricultural land with its former lessees, and the impact of this policy on encouraging sprawl. In 1994 the window of opportunity was partly closed—decision 611 was suspended and new decisions in 1994–1995 (666 and 727) revoked the entrepreneurial option, although retaining the principle of compensating lessees according to the value of the land after rezoning. These decisions continued to be a source for dispute. Three government-appointed commissions (in 1994, 1997, and 2000) recommended to retain the compensation principle, but to reduce the proportion of the profit given as compensation to the agricultural lessees. With the agricultural lobby unwilling to accept lower compensation, and some social justice lobbies challenging the whole principle, the government was unable to decide, and the conflict went to the courts.

A 2002 High Court of Justice ruling in an appeal of the Democratic Mizrahi Coalition—an NGO lobbying for social justice and the rights of the poorer segments of Israeli society—revoked ILA decisions. Based on principles of distributive justice, the court called for a much more minimal compensation for lessees on rezoning land owned by the public.[26] ILA responded with a new set of decisions, and these were again challenged in court. Policy debate in subsequent years mainly focused on privatization of the residential lots of kibbutzim and moshavim, whereas rezoning of state-owned agricultural land practically came to a halt.

Limiting compensation is indeed a powerful tool to control rezoning of agricultural land and curtailing urban expansion. It has a clear environmental benefit, but socially it is less clear who benefits from this step. Do the poor Mizrahi and Arabs really benefit from preventing kibbutzim and moshavim from making a profit from rezoning ILA agricultural land? Perhaps the court appeals mentioned represent an elitist approach backed by middle-class social activists. If housing prices rise and exurban space becomes out of reach for the less wealthy, then curbing unfair allocation of public resources to kibbutzim and moshavim may not necessarily favor the poor.

The Neoliberal Shift: Eroding the Welfare State

The recession in the Israeli economy between 1973 and 1990 encouraged local government entrepreneurialism, particularly the development of economic land uses that contribute to the local tax base. The economic boom of the 1990s consolidated entrepreneurial practices that evolved earlier, but the crisis of 2001–2003 fundamentally changed the power position of Israel's local government.[27] Public policy efforts to erode welfare state mechanisms, backed by a neoliberal vision, have led to increased fiscal disparities between local authorities that lack sufficient taxpaying businesses within their jurisdictional areas and those endowed with such facilities. The wider disparities than ever gave rise to calls for tax base sharing or even for nationalization of nonresidential property taxes.

Limited mechanisms of intermunicipal cooperation in the development and operation of industrial parks emerged through local initiatives in the 1990s. Whereas the prime motive for these agreements was initially to make land available for the development of economic land uses, with a secondary environmental agenda of concentrating development in large nodes, conditions of the early 2000s highlighted the potential role of such agreements in reducing disparities between adjacent local authorities. However, contrary to widespread perceptions, the main impact of proposed nationwide schemes for the redistribution of local tax revenues paid by nonresidential properties was not the transfer of revenues from wealthy rural regional councils to poor adjacent cities and towns, but rather from the central cities of Tel Aviv and Haifa to suburban locations and Arab local authorities in the periphery. Moreover, such proposals were viewed as a ploy of the Ministry of Finance to further erode the equalization grants.[28]

One can argue that the neoliberal shift creates a less comfortable environment for measures to control sprawl. The experience with Thatcher's government in Britain during the 1980s provides some support for this argument,[29] but it is difficult to conclude, in the Israeli context, whether economic ideologies and policies are clearly related to environmental ones. In fact, in the particular Israeli neoliberal regime, the concentration of power in the hand of central state economic and legal bureaucracies (the Ministries of Finance and of Law), could have created a more conducive environment for sustainable development policies than in a truly decentralized political system.[30]

Policy Evaluation Agenda

Three main policy evaluation issues associated with controlling sprawl can be defined in light of the transformations described here. The first concerns the move to strengthen land use statutory planning through the preparation of a new generation of national and district plans. Assessing the impact and limitations of plans and planning regulations imposed by upper levels of government is a major aspect of policy evaluation aimed at identifying best practices to control sprawl. Whereas most reporting in Israel has tended to emphasize means to bypass regulations, such as through pressures on political decision makers, tools such as nonconforming-use permits, or plain illegal construction, success stories are more rarely told. Cases where planning authorities above the local level were able to influence development can be studied in order to determine the conditions for effective action that influences patterns of deconcentration.

A second issue concerns the outcome of legal battles led by socially or environmentally conscious NGOs, particularly to halt the shift in Israel's land policy toward rezoning publicly owned agricultural land. The High Court ruling in the appeal of the Democratic Mizrahi Coalition demonstrated the effectiveness of NGO action in the legal arena. A long-term perspective should focus primarily on the ability of NGO action to reshape public policies in line with sustainability objectives, and to ensure effective implementation of such policies; and the ability and limits of judicial activism to reshape policy.

A final issue concerns the effectiveness of intermunicipal cooperation mechanisms as means to achieve sustainable land use development. Two such mechanisms in Israel include joint local planning committees and joint development and management of industrial parks and commercial centers that includes sharing tax revenues beyond those needed to serve the industrial park.

Evaluation of joint planning committees revealed that little planning coordination actually took place in these committees. At most, successful cooperation is considered to prevail when the local authorities agree on matters concerning the administrative functioning of the committee, and when they informally agree not to intervene in planning decisions in neighboring municipalities.[31] Experience gained so far with joint industrial parks reveals that this mode of cooperation has consolidated as an acknowledged option by local governments and the Planning Administration (incorporated in NOP 35). Emerging as a local initiative, the Ministry of Industry and Trade had a central role in encouraging, sometimes practically imposing, such initiatives in Israel's peripheral regions. Despite early skepticism, the new mechanism has survived, although the accumulating experience has also demonstrated weaknesses and risks of cooperation, particularly when municipalities do not honor signed agreements. In central metropolitan regions, market pressures, particularly the scarcity of land, could encourage cooperation, but intermunicipal cooperation faces greater obstacles as more is at stake and local authorities tend to be more powerful politically and economically.[32] Thus, the ability of cooperation mechanisms to modify land use development patterns, beyond a few local examples, is uncertain.

Case Studies—In Search of Best Practices

The two case studies discussed below largely focus on the first policy evaluation issue, in the context of prime real estate locations at the metropolitan fringe, where the potential for intermunicipal cooperation and coordination is minimal.

Yarkonim (Petah Tiqwa)

The Yarkonim concentration of big-box retail establishments, built illegally on agricultural land at a time when a procedure was undertaken to designate part of the land as a protected river park, is perhaps the most significant example in Israel for a planning and legal conflict that has resulted in partial closure of already functioning structures. It is located within the jurisdictional area of Petah Tiqwa—one of the largest suburban cities east of Tel Aviv (184,200 inhabitants in 2006). Yarkonim is a major interchange between a west-east highway that also serves as a beltway in the Tel Aviv metropolis and a north-south suburban highway. It is surrounded by privately owned agricultural land near the Yarkon River (fig. 8). Parts of this land were purchased in the early 1990s by businessmen well-connected in the Petah Tiqwa municipality (one of them an owner of a local football club). Whereas conversion of agricultural land has been a substantial barrier for development, the most appropriate location for big box retail near a major intersection, and the private (rather than public) ownership of the land, have been factors encouraging development.

Petah Tiqwa prepared a plan for a part of this area in the early 1990s, including commercial activities that were also supposed to finance conservation in the area allocated for the national river park. The District Committee did not approve the plan, since some of it overlapped with the river park plan in preparation. Petah Tiqwa opposed the river park plan, fearing also probable lawsuits of private land owners demanding compensation for lost development rights. Meanwhile, illegally built businesses opened on land planned to be incorporated into the river park: nurseries and outdoor event gardens. These closed down a few years later following negotiations with the National Parks Authority, but other illegal or semilegal structures were built near the interchange. In 1996 large retail establishments opened, based on permits for agricultural structures. Petah Tiqwa issued nonconforming-use permits for these establishments, but the District Committee revoked them because such permits on agricultural land require the approval of the Commission for the Preservation of Agricultural Land. Such an approval was not granted because of the location in the proposed national river park. Following a court ruling, these shops had to close down (figs. 9 and 10)—a rare occurrence in Israel.

Earlier, in 1991, Petah Tiqwa approved another plan for a large power center in an area adjacent to the Yarkonim interchange, to the north of a planned suburban train station. The District Committee was initially favorable toward the plan, but planning policies of the District Committee changed before completion of the planning approval procedures. In 1998 a power center opened for business on the land of the unapproved plan (figs. 9 and 10). The project received nonconforming

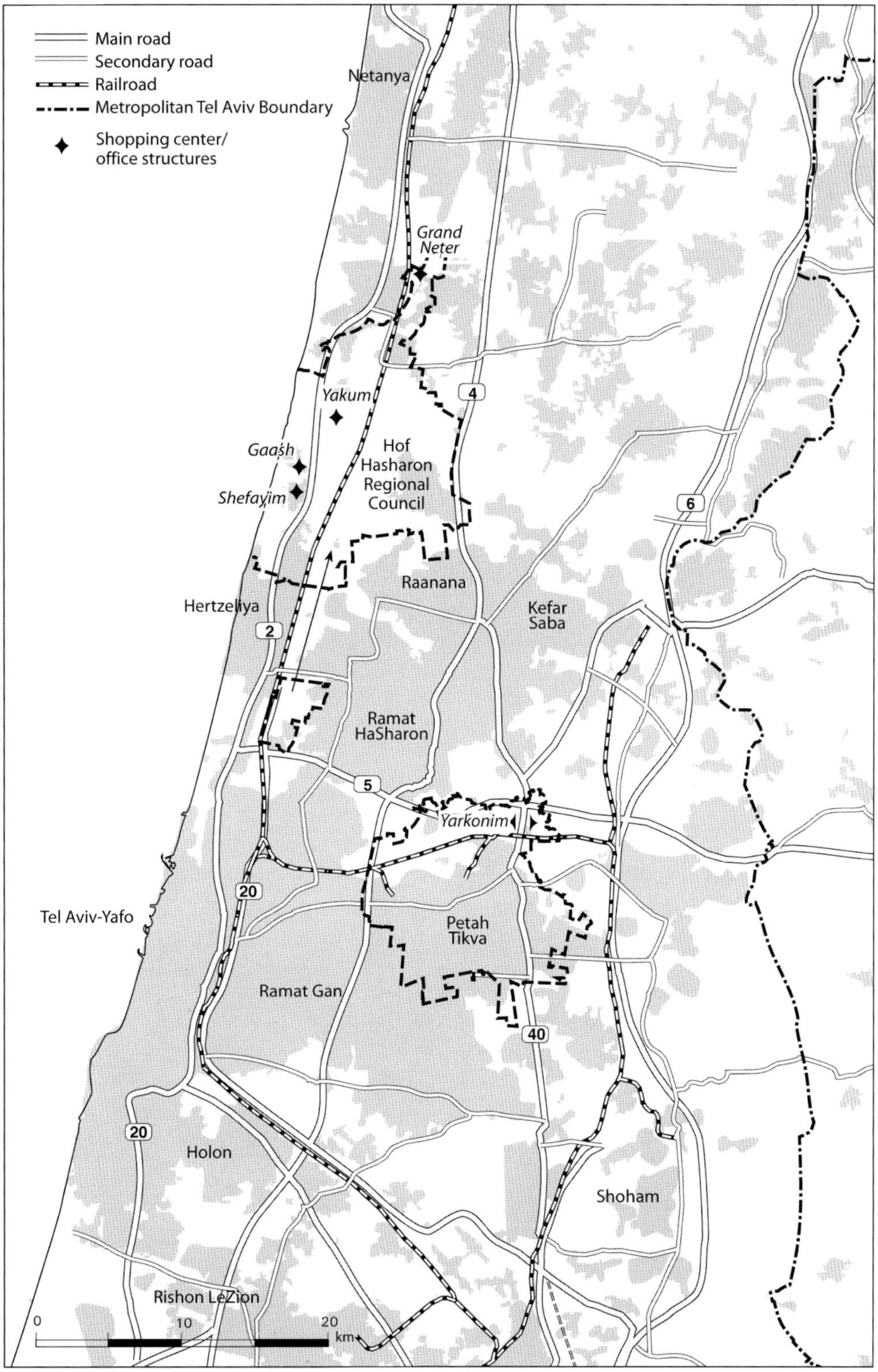

Figure 8. Location of the Yarkonim Junction and Hof HaSharon case studies.

PHOTOGRAPH BY ERAN RAZIN

Figure 9. Illegal commercial structures forced to close down at the Yarkonim Junction.

PHOTOGRAPH BY ERAN RAZIN

Figure 10. A functioning illegal power center adjacent to a train station at the Yarkonim Junction.

use permits from the city, but the Commission for the Preservation of Agricultural Land of the National Planning Administration refused to approve the permits. The case went to court, with the influential developers battling with the District Planning Committee. Another request for a nonconforming-use permit was refused in 2004. Legal battles continue (as of 2007), complicated by the fact that the new suburban train station practically depends on the infrastructure of this power center—parking lots, access road, sewerage, and electricity—for its functioning.

The Yarkonim case shows a clear conflict of interest between the Local Planning Committee (the city) and the District Planning Committee (the state). Such a conflict makes it more difficult to enforce closure and demolition of illegal structures, but it also reveals that planning controls do have some impact, even when confronting a powerful public-private coalition. This case shows that national planning can, in particular circumstances, overcome market forces represented by a powerful coalition of developers and the municipality. However, it also demonstrates that lengthy planning procedures and planning policies that change during the approval procedure are part of the problem, increasing uncertainty and risk for developers and motivating them to act without adhering to the legal procedures. If clear and realistic planning decisions concerning the river park were made on time, the uncertainty for developers and for the municipality would have been greatly reduced, and resources would not have been wasted on plans that clearly contradict the river park plan.

In a broader sense, the case demonstrates an early impact of the new planning doctrine. The Yarkonim development initiatives emerged during a period of a policy vacuum, or a window of opportunity created by the fall of the old planning doctrine in the early 1990s, but unlike perceptions of a one-way process toward privatization and market dominance, the new round of national and district planning has managed to gradually establish new rules of regulation. From the point of view of the developers, this process leads to complaints like "the bastards changed the rules and didn't tell me." However, even if some retail facilities are doomed to eventually close down, prolonged legal battles are clearly beneficial due to the high profits gained from each additional year of functioning. Nevertheless, the costs involved in prolonged battles deter other developers from following a similar path.

Hof HaSharon Regional Council

The Hof HaSharon regional council (9,800 inhabitants in thirteen settlements in 2006) is situated in a strategic location in the northern outer ring of the Tel Aviv metropolis, on the main Tel Aviv-Haifa highway. The regional council pioneered in approving an out-of-town power center, established in 1996 through the nonconforming-use permit channel (new structures supposedly for agriculture, warehousing, and manufacturing, but practically built for retail). It was also one of the first to practically permit opening large-scale retail businesses on Saturdays (the Jewish Sabbath). The Shefayim-Gaash power center (fig. 11) has become hugely popular and profitable. Part of it was formally approved subsequently for retail, but at a later stage the District Committee became stricter in its policy not to approve such functions in rural space, in line with the new district plan.

The regional council has been aggressive in the development of retail, industry, and offices in rural space, such as Euro Park in Yakum (fig. 12) and Grand Neter, all being typical leapfrog

PHOTOGRAPH BY ERAN RAZIN

Figure 11. Exurban commercial landscapes in Hof HaSharon: Shefayim power center.

PHOTOGRAPH BY ERAN RAZIN

Figure 12. Exurban commercial landscapes in Hof HaSharon: Euro Park.

developments surrounded by agricultural landscape, some illegal, but beneficial to the economy of the regional council and its kibbutzim and moshavim. It has sore relations with its urban neighbor to the north—the city of Netanya—due to the stiff competition over tax base. In the early 2000s, Hof HaSharon has also been the location of the first exurban gated community in Israel: the exclusive seaside village of Arsuf that separated itself from its surroundings by fence, gate, and security guards. Nearby, a second initiative has progressed to establish such exclusive enclosed community on land sold by kibbutz Gaash—Arsuf Cliffs.[33]

Hof HaSharon has become a prototype case—perhaps the most extreme case—of market-driven leapfrog sprawling development, beneficial to the regional council in fiscal terms. It demonstrates the outcome of the window of opportunity of the 1990s, in between the decline of the old planning doctrine and the consolidation of the new one. The kibbutzim of Hof HaSharon that fiercely opposed development pressures on agricultural land until 1990, in line with the old doctrine, have switched to a prodevelopment approach. The high visibility of this development has eventually made Hof HaSharon a case where environmental and social NGOs took action in order to halt further development and reverse at least partly illegal elements in the development that already took place. Attempts to check further leapfrog business development in Hof HaSharon consist mainly of court battles of adjacent municipalities and an opposition member of the council, with the aid of social justice and environmental NGOs. These oppose attempts to convert industrial structures and agricultural packaging houses into office space. Some such illegal structures have indeed remained vacant due to court orders. Action of Israel Union for Environmental Defense and a negative report of Israel's State Comptroller led the District Planning Committee to revoke the authority of the Local Planning Committee of Hof HaSharon to issue nonconforming-use permits on agricultural land or on existing agricultural facilities (storage, packaging, and agricultural industries) without the permission of the District Committee.[34] Whereas a detailed analysis of these conflicts is beyond the scope of this chapter, it should be noted that NGO action seemed more effective than central government control in initiating policy change: new planning policies, new regulatory tools, and enhanced enforcement. Such NGO action, backed by court rulings, has compelled government planning and enforcement agencies to become more active and effective at a later stage, and has enhanced the legitimacy of the new planning doctrine's tools—the national and district plans.

Conclusions

Sprawling patterns of metropolitan expansion present an acute policy issue in Israel, given the paucity of open space and the arguably dire consequences of market-led business-as-usual trends for a sustainable environmental future. Mass-immigration, coupled with political-ideological transformations, toppled down an old planning doctrine, giving way to rapid deconcentration, encouraged by policy notions supporting competition and privatization in a context of a neoliberal vision of economic growth. They have influenced considerably Israel's land policy, leading to its liberalization. However, the Israeli case demonstrates how the planning establishment, the third sector, and the courts have acted to offset erosion of planning controls that occurred in the first half of the 1990s, through the formation of a new planning doctrine that discourages environmentally unsustainable sprawling development. New statutory district and national outline plans have become prime tools to control sprawl, whereas alternative tools, such as inter-municipal cooperation, particularly in the development and management of industrial parks, have so far only marginally influenced patterns of deconcentration.

The approval of new district and national plans was at least partly achieved thanks to public and legal action of NGOs, producing a favorable public opinion and delegitimizing practices that bypass planning policy. Court rulings have also influenced the formulation of policy guidelines adopted by central government agencies. The legal channel for battling deviations from proclaimed public policies and from principles of sustainable development (mainly on grounds of either being illegal or contradicting principles of social justice) has become a frequent best practice to limit sprawl. It proved effective primarily when implemented in a context of a broader supportive coalition (green and social justice NGOs, the Planning Administration, environmental government agencies, and adjacent cities). This substantial impact of court rulings nevertheless inspires debates on the limits of judicial activism. To what extent do the courts have the legitimacy and professional capabilities to determine public policies that have numerous side-effects and unintended consequences? To what extent can the court judge the weight of conflicting considerations, such as distributive justice versus housing affordability, or rational land use planning versus flexibility crucial for economic development in a dynamic global economy?

In the early 2000s it has become extremely difficult to approve plans for commercial and business land uses on rural land at the metropolitan fringes and to rezone publicly owned agricultural land. The breach in the dam has been reduced considerably, even if it has not been completely sealed. Market forces remain powerful, but large-scale projects do aspire to function legally, thus planning controls, even when not completely effective, deter violations due to the cost and uncertainty involved in prolonged battles in planning committees and courts. This policy success, however, seems to have little effect on the accelerating trend of employment deconcentration, because most of this deconcentration is in cities and towns in suburban and exurban space. Moreover, the power of the new statutory plans has not yet been tested in the context of a prolonged hot real estate market.[35]

NOTES

Based on results of a research project sponsored by the European Commission's Fifth Framework, entitled Spatial Deconcentration of Economic Land Use and Quality of Life in European Metropolitan Areas (SELMA). The author thanks Eldad Berin, Gillad Rosen, and Dov Amrami for research assistance.

1. Based on Israel's formal boundaries: a territory of about 8,522 square miles (22,072 square kilometers) that includes annexed east Jerusalem and the Golan Heights, but not the rest of the West Bank and Gaza Strip.
2. Population within Israel's formal boundaries, not including West Bank settlements.
3. Nathan Alterman, *Shir boker lamoledet* (A morning song to the homeland), 1934.
4. N. Ben-Elia and E. Razin, Local Government and the Preservation of Open Space Policy. NB—Policy Analysis, Strategic Planning and Management, and The Open Land Institute, 2008 (Machon Deshe) (in Hebrew).
5. A. Gonen, *Between City and Suburb* (Aldershot, UK: Avebury, 1995).
6. A. Frenkel and M. Ashkenazi, The Integrated Sprawl Index: Measuring the Urban Landscape in Israel, *Annals of Regional Science* 42 (2008): 99–121.

7. Kibbutzim and moshavim are communal rural settlements that combined collective-socialist ideals with Zionist ones. These forms of settlement had a leading position in Israeli society and politics, primarily between the 1930s and 1970s.
8. E. Razin and A. Shachar, Deconcentration in the Context of Population Growth and Ideological Change: The Tel-Aviv and Beer-Sheva Metropolitan Areas, in *Employment Deconcentration in European Metropolitan Areas, Market Forces versus Planning Regulations*, ed. E. Razin, M. Dijst, and C. Vazquez (Dordrecht: Springer, 2007), 179–207.
9. R. Alterman, *Planning in the Face of Crisis, Land Use, Housing, and Mass Immigration in Israel* (London: Routledge, 2002).
10. I. Han, *Non-Conforming Use of Open Agricultural Areas* (Jerusalem: Jerusalem Institute for Israel Studies, 2004) (in Hebrew).
11. Z. Goldfisher, The Penetration of Non-Industrial Land Uses into Industrial Areas: Market Forces or Public Policy? M.A. thesis, Department of Geography, Hebrew University, 2003 (in Hebrew).
12. These are property taxes that are not based on the assessed value of the property, but on indirect measures, such as floor space, usage (residential or various types of businesses and other facilities), and location.
13. E. Razin, Needs and Impediments for Local Government Reform: Lessons from Israel, *Journal of Urban Affairs* 26 (2004): 623–40.
14. L. Applebaum and D. Newman, *Rural Trends in Israel and Their Implications on Local Government* (Jerusalem: Floersheimer Institute for Policy Studies, 1997) (in Hebrew).
15. E. Razin, Policies to Control Urban Sprawl: Planning Regulations or Changes in the "Rules of the Game," *Urban Studies* 35 (1998): 321–40.
16. G. Rosen and E. Razin, The Rise of Gated Communities in Israel: Reflections on Changing Urban Governance in a Neoliberal Era, *Urban Studies* 46 (2009): 1702–22; H. Yacobi, The NGOization of Space: Dilemmas of Social Change, Planning Policy, and the Israeli Public Sphere, *Environment and Planning D: Society and Space* 25 (2007): 745–58.
17. I. Han, *Planning Gas Stations and Commercial Centers in Rural Areas and Open Spaces* (Jerusalem: Jerusalem Institute for Israel Studies, 2002) (in Hebrew).
18. E. Razin and A. Hazan, Redrawing Israel's Local Government Map: Political Decisions, Court Rulings or Popular Determination, *Political Geography* 20 (2001): 513–33.
19. Alterman, *Planning in the Face of Crisis.*
20. E. Feitelson, Social Norms, Rationales and Policies: Reframing Farmland Protection in Israel, *Journal of Rural Studies* 15 (1999): 431–46; D. Newman and L. Applebaum, Defining the Rurban Settlement: Planning Models and Functional Realities in Israel, *Urban Geography* 10 (1989): 281–95.
21. A. Shachar, Reshaping the Map of Israel: A New National Planning Doctrine, *The Annals of the American Academy of Political and Social Science* 555 (1998): 209–18.
22. E. Feitelson, Muddling through Sustainability: The Transformation of Environmental Planning in Israel, *Progress in Planning* 49 (1998): 3–53.
23. A. Frenkel, The Potential Effect of National Growth-Management Policy on Urban Sprawl and the Depletion of Open Spaces and Farmland, *Land Use Policy* 21 (2004): 357–69.
24. Except for the city of Ashdod, which is located in the Southern District.
25. S. F. Biran, *Property Rights, Old and New, The Proposal for Social Privatization in Israel* (Tel Aviv: Hkibbutz Hameuchad, 2000) (in Hebrew).
26. D. Barak-Erez, Distributional Justice in Israel's Land: After the High Court Ruling on Agricultural Land, *HaMishpat* 18 (2004): 54–63 (in Hebrew).
27. E. Razin, Policies to Control Urban Sprawl; N. Ben-Elia, *The Fiscalization of Local Planning and Development* (Jerusalem: Floersheimer Institute for Policy Studies, 2000) (in Hebrew).
28. E. Razin and A. Hazan, *Redistributing Municipal Wealth in Israel, Reducing the Inequalities in the Revenues of Local Authorities* (Jerusalem: Floersheimer Institute for Policy Studies, 2006) (in Hebrew); E. Razin, G. Rosen, M. Dachoach-Halevi, and A. Hazan, Is the Role of the State in Local Governance Diminishing? in *Governing Metropolises.*
29. R. Schiller, *The Dynamics of Property Location, Value and the Factors which Drive the Location of Shops, Offices and Other Land Uses* (London: Spon, 2001).
30. *Eretz Acheret*, A State in Their Image: The Bureaucrats of the Treasury Are Reshaping Israelis, special issue, No. 43 (2008) (in Hebrew).
31. M. Dachoach-Halevi and E. Razin, Joint Planning Commissions: Municipal Cooperation, Planning Coordination, Cost Savings or a Tool of Control, *Planning, Journal of the Israel Association of Planners* 3:2 (2006): 18–35 (in Hebrew).
32. Razin, Rosen, Dachoach-Halevi, and Hazan, Is the Role of the State in Local Governance Diminishing?, in *Governing Metropolises.*
33. Rosen and Razin, The Rise of Gated Communities in Israel.

34. State Comptroller, Hof HaSharon Regional Council: The Local Planning Committee—Commercial and Business Centers, in *Reports on Auditing in Local Government* (Jerusalem: State Comptroller, 2005), 617–44 (in Hebrew).
35. The period 1997–2004 was characterized by a weak real estate market. An upward trend was evident between 2005 and 2007, apparently leveling in 2008.

REFERENCES

Eretz Acheret. A State in Their Image: The Bureaucrats of the Treasury Are Reshaping Israelis. Special issue. No. 43 (2008) (in Hebrew).

Alterman, Nathan. *Shir boker lamoledet* (A morning song to the homeland) 1934.

Alterman, R. *Planning in the Face of Crisis, Land Use, Housing, and Mass Immigration in Israel*. London: Routledge, 2002.

Applebaum, L., and D. Newman. *Rural Trends in Israel and Their Implications on Local Government*. Jerusalem: Floersheimer Institute for Policy Studies, 1997 (in Hebrew).

Barak-Erez, D. Distributional Justice in Israel's Land: After the High Court Ruling on Agricultural Land. *HaMishpat* 18 (2004): 54–63 (in Hebrew).

Ben-Elia, N. *The Fiscalization of Local Planning and Development*. Jerusalem: Floersheimer Institute for Policy Studies, 2000 (in Hebrew).

Ben-Elia, N., and E. Razin. 2008. Local Government and the Preservation of Open Space Policy. NB—Policy Analysis, Strategic Planning and Management, and The Open Land Institute (Machon Deshe) (in Hebrew).

Biran, S. F. *Property Rights, Old and New, The Proposal for Social Privatization in Israel*. Tel Aviv: Hkibbutz Hameuchad, 2000 (in Hebrew).

Dachoach-Halevi, M., and E. Razin. Joint Planning Commissions: Municipal Cooperation, Planning Coordination, Cost Savings or a Tool of Control. *Planning, Journal of the Israel Association of Planners* 3:2 (2006): 18–35 (in Hebrew).

Feitelson, E. Muddling through Sustainability: The Transformation of Environmental Planning in Israel. *Progress in Planning* 49 (1998): 3–53.

———. Social Norms, Rationales and Policies: Reframing Farmland Protection in Israel. *Journal of Rural Studies* 15 (1999): 431–46.

Frenkel, A. The Potential Effect of National Growth-Management Policy on Urban Sprawl and the Depletion of Open Spaces and Farmland. *Land Use Policy* 21 (2004): 357–69.

Frenkel, A., and M. Ashkenazi. The Integrated Sprawl Index: Measuring the Urban Landscape in Israel. *Annals of Regional Science* 42 (2008): 99–121.

Goldfisher, Z. 2003. The Penetration of Non-Industrial Land Uses into Industrial Areas: Market Forces or Public Policy? M.A. thesis, Department of Geography, Hebrew University (in Hebrew).

Gonen, A. *Between City and Suburb*. Aldershot: Avebury, 1995.

Han, I. *Planning Gas Stations and Commercial Centers in Rural Areas and Open Spaces*. Jerusalem: Jerusalem Institute for Israel Studies, 2002 (in Hebrew).

———. *Non-Conforming Use of Open Agricultural Areas*. Jerusalem: Jerusalem Institute for Israel Studies, 2004 (in Hebrew).

Newman, D., and L. Applebaum. Defining the Rurban Settlement: Planning Models and Functional Realities in Israel. *Urban Geography* 10 (1989): 281–95.

Razin, E. Needs and Impediments for Local Government Reform: Lessons from Israel. *Journal of Urban Affairs* 26 (2004): 623–40.

———. Policies to Control Urban Sprawl: Planning Regulations or Changes in the "Rules of the Game." *Urban Studies* 35 (1998): 321–40.

Razin, E., and A. Hazan. *Redistributing Municipal Wealth in Israel, Reducing the Inequalities in the Revenues of Local Authorities*. Jerusalem: Floersheimer Institute for Policy Studies, 2006 (in Hebrew).

———. Redrawing Israel's Local Government Map: Political Decisions, Court Rulings or Popular Determination. *Political Geography* 20 (2001): 513–33.

Razin, E., G. Rosen, M. Dachoach-Halevi, and A. Hazan. Is the Role of the State in Local Governance Diminishing? The Case of Israel's Metropolitan Areas. In *Governing Metropolises: Profiles of Issues and Experiments on Four Continents*, ed. J-P. Collin, and M. Robertson, 29–53. Quebec City: Presses de l'Université Laval, 2007.

Razin, E., and A. Shachar. Deconcentration in the Context of Population Growth and Ideological Change: The Tel-Aviv and Beer-Sheva Metropolitan Areas. In *Employment Deconcentration in European Metropolitan Areas, Market Forces versus Planning Regulations*, ed. E. Razin, M. Dijst, and C. Vazquez, 179–207. Dordrecht: Springer, 2007.

Rosen, G., and E. Razin. The Rise of Gated Communities in

Israel: Reflections on Changing Urban Governance in a Neoliberal Era. *Urban Studies* 46 (2009): 1702–22.

Schiller, R. *The Dynamics of Property Location, Value and the Factors which Drive the Location of Shops, Offices and Other Land Uses.* London: Spon, 2001.

Shachar, A. Reshaping the Map of Israel: A New National Planning Doctrine. *The Annals of the American Academy of Political and Social Science* 555 (1998): 209–18.

State Comptroller, Hof HaSharon Regional Council: The Local Planning Committee—Commercial and Business Centers. In *Reports on Auditing in Local Government,* 617–44. Jerusalem: State Comptroller, 2005 (in Hebrew).

Yacobi, H. The NGOization of Space: Dilemmas of Social Change, Planning Policy, and the Israeli Public Sphere. *Environment and Planning D: Society and Space* 25 (2007): 745–58.

IMAD SALAMEY

The Crisis of Consociational Democracy in Beirut

CONFLICT TRANSFORMATION AND SUSTAINABILITY THROUGH ELECTORAL REFORM

The pursuit of inter- and intragenerational equity across communities is essential for the achievement of social stability over time and, consequently, sustainability.[1] In cities whose communities are deeply divided, equity becomes crucially a political question where power-sharing arrangements among the various residing groups determine to a large extent the prospect of social stability and prospective sustainability. Pursuing appropriate urban resource and environmental management strategies becomes secondary to achieving political equity. As the case of the oil-rich city of Kirkuk in Iraq demonstrates, the agreement over appropriate political arrangement that provides an accommodating and equitable ethno-sectarian and sustainable coexistence remains a priori.

Most multiethnic, multiconfessional cities, particularly those in developing countries undergoing massive urbanization and demographic shifts, are confronting significant sociopolitical stress.[2] With urbanization claiming the majority of many developing countries' populations, the fate of nations becomes essentially tied to urban prosperity.[3] Governments' failing urban policies and inadequate state power-sharing arrangements may drive communities to develop primordial forms of informal urban networks, resorting to ethnic and sectarian mobilizations.[4] The result can deepen the division between urban communities while fueling ethno-sectarian competition over resources and political control, often radicalizing ethno-sectarian and separatist sentiments.[5] This has been manifested throughout many world multiethnic cities, whether in Sarajevo, Kirkuk, Belfast, Baghdad, Beirut, Jerusalem, Kabul, or Islam Abad. Deteriorating social and national cohesion is transcended at inter- and intragenerational levels, hindering the achievement of urban inter- and intragenerational equity or the establishment of accommodating ethno-sectarian arrangements that are essential for urban, and in turn, national sustainability.

Can urban democracy provide the appropriate power-sharing arrangement capable of satisfying the aspirations of the different groups and achieving social stability? The answer to this question varies widely along ideological perspectives. Proponents of democracy themselves vary along two prominent but opposed political structural propositions that have been advanced as appropriate arrangements for deeply divided communities in a plural society. The first is associated with the "integrationist" or "citizenship" nationalist, realist, and classic liberal theory models that advocate the submergence of divided communities into one within the nation-state while removing preferences to any particular religious, sectarian, ethnic, regional, or racial affiliation, thus achieving equal rights and sustainable relations. The second is associated with the multicultural and neoliberal theory that highlights diversity and stresses the importance of preserving ethnic, sectarian, religious, regional, gender, and racial particularities and necessitates differential political arrangements to citizen groups as a means of achieving sustainable community relations.[6] In essence, the division between both perspectives entails differences regarding the politicization or depoliticization of communities.

Modern experiences utilizing both paradigms have met with relative success. In deeply divided and pluralistic cities, historic grievances, geopolitical contexts, differential group sizes, countries' economic development, resources and services allocation, social mobility, demographic changes, linguistic and religious makeup, communities' spatial distribution, and state electoral systems have been among the many factors associated with the success of one political model over another. The debate goes on between proponents of the "citizenship" and "pluralism" perspectives as to the choice model for sustainable polity.

Arendt Lijphart, the founding father of "consociational democracy," summoned both paradigms as a situational choice. He suggested that whether a society is ethnically homogeneous or heterogeneous necessitates differential power-sharing arrangement strategies. For a homogeneous society, a majoritarian system is natural, while for an ethnically heterogeneous society more delegated power-sharing arrangements are required. For a diverse or heterogeneous society that is deeply divided, Lijphart suggested consociational democracy as a suitable model.[7] He defined consociationalism as "government by elite cartel designed to turn a democracy with a fragmented political culture into a stable democracy."[8] Thus, Lijphart initiated the foundation of ethno-democracy and strongly supported and devised a plural power-sharing model for a deeply divided society as a sustainable strategy.

Ideally, power distribution envisioned by Lijphart, as has been the case in Lebanon, necessitates agreements between the various ethnic groups and a continuous process of negotiation until consensus is reached. Yet, Lijphart's consociational democratic model for divided societies has undergone increasing challenges amid rising complexity in global ethnopolitics.

Serious problems awaiting Lijphart's consociationalism, however, is the fragility of any consensual agreement in response to rapidly changing demographic environments that often refuel contentions and conflict among communities over shrinking and contested space and resources. Evidently, severe ethno-sectarian conflicts have taken shape primarily in urban centers where intensive spatial and demographic changes have undermined inter-ethno-sectarian relations (such as in Baghdad, Kirkuk, Beirut, Belfast, Jerusalem, Los Angeles, and Paris). Therefore, consociationalism emerges as a need to readdress power-sharing formulation in such a way as to appropriately respond to the dynamism of a permanently changing and deeply divided urban environment.[9] As an alternative to the consociational approach for a deeply divided society, an adjunct approach may entail coercion that can easily emerge as unviable to peaceful transition and sustainability. Yet the question remains whether consociationalism or a synthetic power arrangement can be formulated in order to transform ethno-sectarian grievances within a political structural process, subsequently avoiding violent clashes and fostering sustainable coexistence.

Taking the urban experience of the city of Beirut, Lebanon, as a case study, this article examines confessional-consociationalism within the Lebanese power-sharing arrangement. The analysis of the confessional dynamic within Beirut provides important clues for the possibility of synthesizing both the consociational and the secular-national model in an integrative consociational proposition. The article explores the prospects for electoral urban reform that can absorb dynamic demographic changes and alleviate sectarian grievances within a systematic electoral framework.

The Dilemma of Urban Confessional-Consociationalism in Beirut

The political relationship between the various sectarian groups in Lebanon was originally formalized by a complex institutional political structure, known as "political confessionalism" (known in Arabic as *Al-Taefeyah As-Seyaseyah*). Confessionalism is a system of government that "proportionally" allocates political power among the various confessional/sectarian communities according to each community's percentage of the overall population. This sort of power-sharing arrangement has been referred to by political scientists as "consociational democracy" by virtue of its accommodating character.

Confessionalism was officially institutionalized in Lebanon by the Lebanese National Accord of 1943, which divided political and public offices "proportionally" amongst the various sectarian groups. This distribution was based on a national census conducted in 1932, which gave a slight demographic advantage to the Christian over the Muslim sects.[10]At that time, Beirut was predominantly inhabited by Christians and Sunni Muslim communities. Electoral and administrative districts were drawn in order to accommodate confessional distributions.

The Christian community in Lebanon, particularly the Maronites and the Roman Catholics, were among the first to experience confessionalism as a mobilizing force of capitalist modernization—political, economic, and cultural—beginning with the second half of the nineteenth century. This experience drove non-Christian communities to seek a similar mobilization to counterbalance the growth of Christian influence in modern Lebanon. With massive urbanization, cities such as Tripoli, Beirut, Zahleh, Sidon, and Tyre became the battleground for confessional mobilization. As a result, this type of urban modernization, which placed the confession as the core agent for change and for channeling group grievances, has come to characterize Lebanese national politics (see fig. 1).

A confessional-sectarian arrangement was established between the various urban groups demarcated by distinctive spatial, social, political, and economic foundations. Each confessional group has come to reside in particular neighborhoods or to build new ones around its respective religious institutions, community centers, schools, colleges, and other such community assets. Apartment buildings, shopping centers, streets, and highways were named after distinctive respective community and religious figures. Residents have been clustered in close proximity to

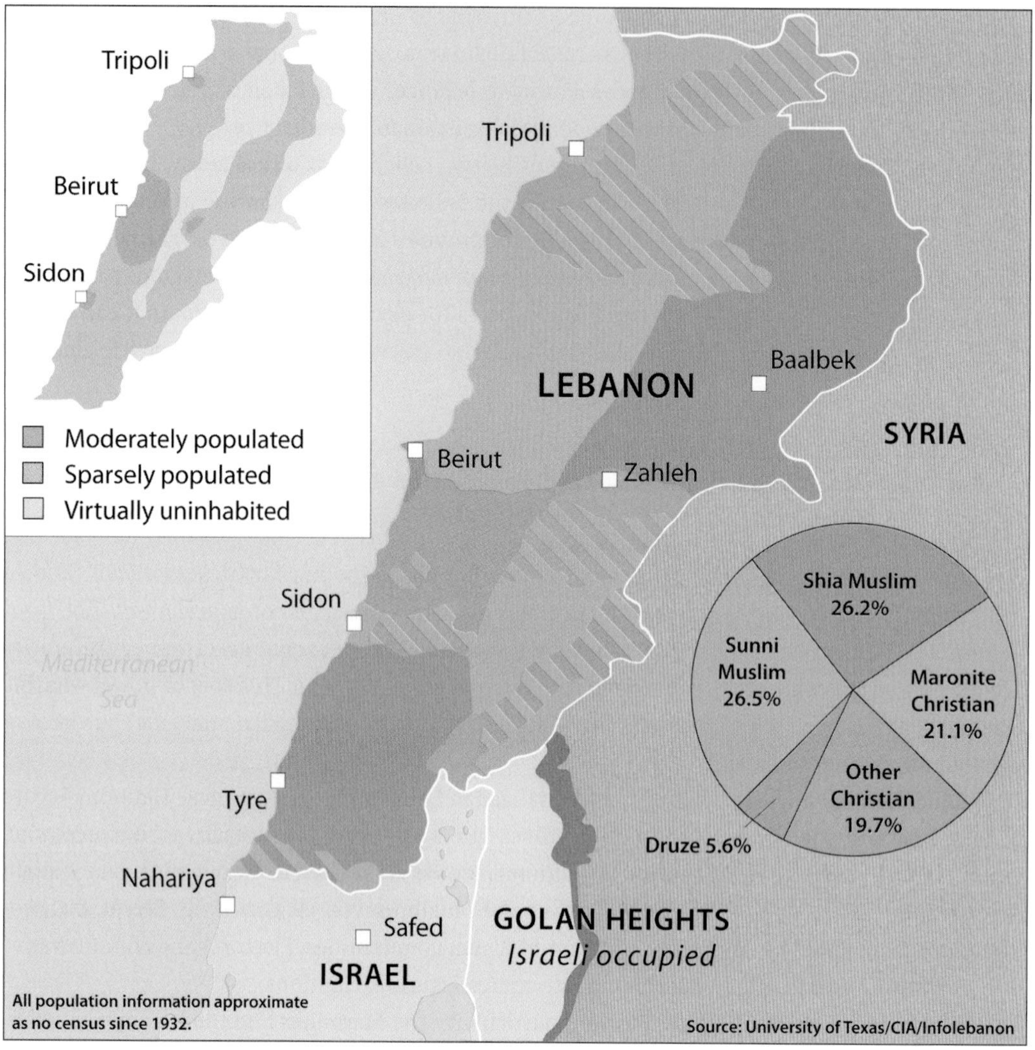

Figure 1. Approximate sectarian distribution in Lebanon, 1998.

their respective family members, clan, and fellow villagers. Community neighborhoods have become socially stratified along economic class lines. Personal status laws, particularly in marriage, inheritance, and divorce, have been confessionally based, undermining cross-confessional mixing. Lastly, public jobs, public services, public offices, and electoral seats and districts have been confessionally allocated in such a way as to further entrench confessionalism as a governing model among the different communities (see table 1).

The Sunni Muslim and Orthodox Christian communities became the predominant residential groups within the city of Beirut. The Beirut municipal city council was elected in 1998, the first since the last municipal election in Lebanon in 1963, with twenty-two seats evenly divided between Christians and Muslim sects and allocated as follows: Muslim: Sunni, nine; Shi'a, two;

Table 1. Confessional representation in Parliament, 2005

RELIGION	CONFESSION	REGISTERED VOTERS	%	ELECTED MPS	%
Christians	Maronites	667,556	22.19	34	26.56
	Greek Orthodox	236,402	7.86	14	10.94
	Greek Catholic	156,521	5.20	8	6.25
	Armenian Orthodox	90,675	3.01	5	3.91
	Armenian Catholic	20,217	0.67	1	0.78
	Protestant	17,409	0.58	1	0.78
Minorities*		47,018	1.56	1	0.78
Total Christians		1,235,798	41.08	64	50.00
Muslims	Sunni	795,233	26.44	27	21.09
	Shi'a	783,903	26.06	27	21.09
	Druze	169,293	5.63	8	6.25
	Alawite	23,696	0.79	2	1.56
	Ismaelite	0	0.00		
Total Muslims		1,772,125	58.92	64	50.00
Jewish		0	0.00	0	
Total		**3,007,923**	**100.00**	**128**	**100.00**

* Includes chaldean, Nestorian, Syriac, Jacobites, Latin, and Copt.
Source: Lebanese Ministry of Interior.

Druze, one; Roman Catholic, one; Maronite Catholic, two; Roman Orthodox, three; Armenian Orthodox, three; and Minorities, two. This sectarian distribution of municipal seats became an "informal norm" for acceptable sectarian allocation of seats in every election. At the same time, the Mayorship seat was reserved for a Sunni and the government-appointed city county executive for a Christian Orthodox. This distribution has been maintained over the years despite the disproportional growth of Sunni and Shi'a city population over the Christians (see table 2).

The southern suburbs of the city, particularly the Dahye and Ain Remeneh, that were by the

Table 2. Approximate sectarian distribution in Beirut and suburbs

NEIGHBORHOOD	MAJORITY SECT	SECONDARY SECT	MINOR SECT
West Beirut	Sunni	Shi'a	Orthodox
Ashrafieh	Orthodox	Maronite	Catholic
East Suburbs	Maronite	Orthodox	Catholic
South Beirut	Shi'a	Sunni	—
Dahye	Shi'a	Sunni	Druze
Baabda	Maronite	Shi'a	Druze
Ain Remeneh	Maronite	Shi'a	Sunni
Sea Port	Sunni	Shi'a	Others

Source: Approximation based on voter registration list, 2004.

Figure 2. Beirut, the city and the sea. Fishing at the Corniche.

early nineteenth century predominantly Christian (see fig. 4), by the early 1970s became inhabited by poor Shi'a and Sunni residents. Christian Maronites took residence in the eastern suburb of Beirut, alongside the Armenian Orthodox community who resided in the infamous poverty-stricken neighborhood of Bourj Hammoud.

The confessional power-sharing scheme succeeded in moderating interdenominational tension, allowing religious communities with varying histories and political aspirations to coexist within the city's boundaries. Periods of confessional coexistence preceded the 1975 civil war, with cross-confessional residents and commercial districts erecting in various areas such as Ras Beirut, Ashrafieh, Mazraa, and the downtown area.[11] Cross-confessional marriage was common. Secular popular political organizations, such as the Communist Party, the Syrian Social Nationalist Party, and the Baath Party, among others, recruited young members across confessional groups. Yet

PHOTOGRAPH BY DINA GEORGIS

Figure 3. A sample of Beirut's urban fabric. Rue Gouraud in the Gemmayze District.

the rapid modernization of the city from the 1950s to today exerted tremendous pressure on the confessional arrangement that refused to yield to the changing demography and emerging confessional urban groups, such as the relative growth of the city's Muslim population. The proportion of the Muslim population to the overall city population was further increased by the migration of Christians to the West.[12] The rigidity of this system (as advanced by Christians and other confessional elites who stand to lose by an adjustment in the confessional power distribution) has prevented any official population census since 1932 from assessing Beirut's modern demography.

By the end of the 1980s the city and its urban suburbs had attracted almost half of the country's population.[13] This population drift, with the confessional political structure in place, intensified confessional group competition and grievances over urban space, urban resources, and political access. The newly emerging urban Shi'a Muslims, for example, encountered

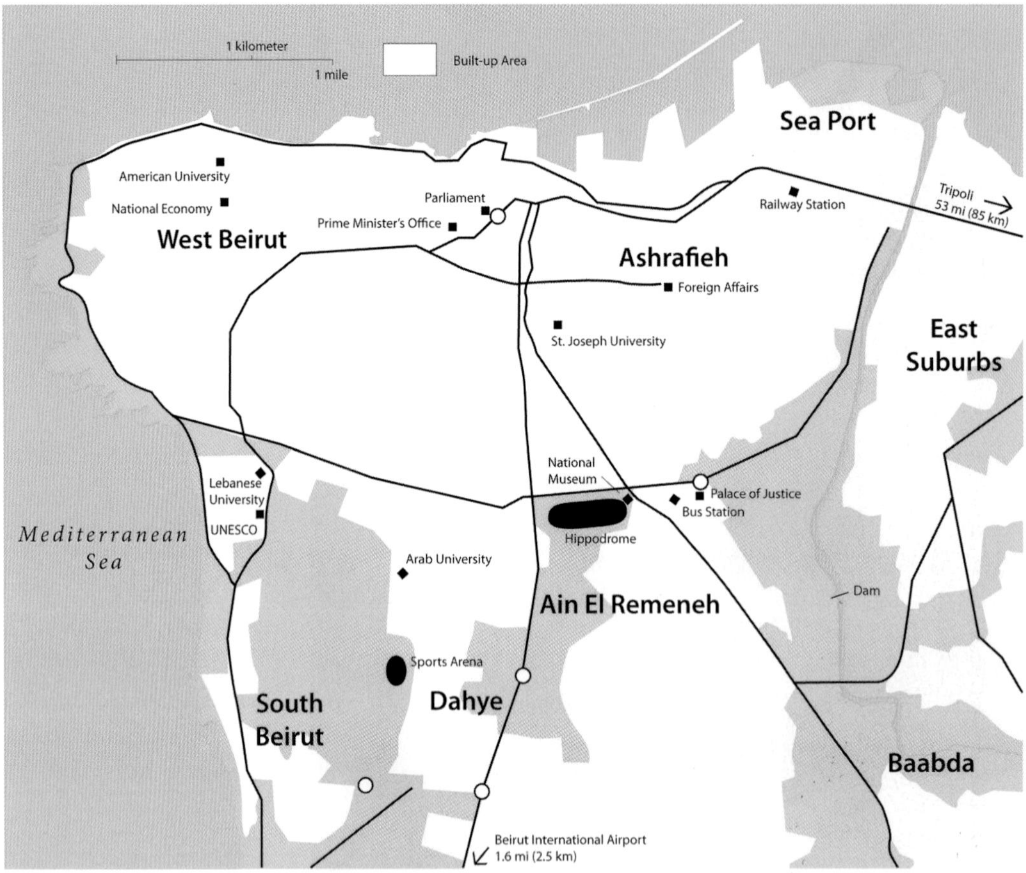

Figure 4. Map of Beirut and suburbs.

Source: City of Beirut.

systematic political and economic exclusion.[14] Throughout the city and its suburbs, neither municipal councils nor public offices were fairly accessible to Shi'a.[15] This forced the newly arrived Shi'a groups to develop, mainly in the southern suburb of Beirut, their economic, cultural, social, political, and welfare activities within the confines of their newly established confessional boundaries, often independent of the state and acting as a state against the state.[16] Defending confessional trenches and improving their power position relative to other confessional groups has drawn the support of their fellow sectarian groups and states in the region—namely, Iraq, Iran, and Syria—often undermining the very existence of the Lebanese confessional arrangement. Counterbalancing the growing threat of the Shi'a has set in motion a similar pattern of confessional patronage that has resulted in foreign countries intervening into Lebanese internal affairs and instigating internal confessional struggle (Saudi Arabia supporting the Sunnis, France, and the West supporting the Maronites).

At the end of this process the stage was set for a fragmented, uneven, and often conflictual urban transformation in contrast to a more integrative, "nationalized" form. For example, instead of assuming a nationally inclusive character, the city has emerged as divided along competing

PHOTOGRAPH BY R. M. KENNEDY

Figure 5. The imprints of conflict on the city. A building in Hamra District in West Beirut.

confessional enclaves, often sabotaging state-sponsored urban planning and development initiatives. This process has finally reached a confessional deadlock, adequately described by the Lebanese sociologist Waddah Sharrara as putting Beirut city "under arrest."[17]

As a consequence of the growing strains on the confessional division of the political pie, with growing external forces meddling in Lebanese affairs, national consensus broke down into two major civil wars, first in 1958 and then in 1975. Since 2004, the momentum for renewed conflict has begun to emerge once again as marked by a series of assassinations against confessional leaders and figures throughout Beirut. The escalation of sectarian conflict was culminated in May 2008 where anti-government opposition led by Shia Hezbollah waged an armed insurgency and occupied key parts of pro-government Sunni-dominated West Beirut. This only ended in the same month when the Qatari government along with the Arab League brokered the Doha Agreement that halted further escalation of violence.[18]

The Lebanese confessional power-sharing experience demonstrates the geopolitical challenges to consociationalism. Interconfessional struggles have increased regional and foreign interventions in Lebanon's affairs, territorially, politically, religiously, and economically, and have rendered power-sharing arrangements between the confessional groups fundamentally linked to regional and international power struggles.[19] Yet inward domestic factors have also emerged to significantly challenge the "ethnocized" state model.[20] These factors have been best manifested in the urbanization of Lebanon, whereby spatial and demographic fluidity have repeatedly undermined static traditional power-sharing arrangements.[21] During the past half century the country's urban population has grown from 33 percent in 1950 to 87 percent in 2000. The city of Beirut is now the home of half of the Lebanese population.[22] The tremendous urban growth, particularly that of Beirut over the last few decades, has made the city a focal point of confessional struggle. Urban trends have become the essence of national politics, with rigid confessional political arrangements turned into a catalyst for urban conflict rather than sustainable coexistence, fueling group grievances rather than consociation.

Thus, confessional population shifts, uneven regional economic development, foreign interventions, and growing unemployment rates were a prelude to the rural-to-urban migration that has challenged established spatial and political urban confessional boundaries. Acute social and radical sectarian mobilizations that disrupted the delicate balance soon followed.[23] The confessional state needed to act to absorb such currents, but it could not. The consociational balance of power structure prevented the political expression of the newly emerging social forces: political avenues were obstructed by the traditional arrangement.[24] Most crucially, the static consociational edifice was incapable of adapting to a changing demographic and spatial-sectarian environment. As a consequence, population influx to urban centers, driven by jobs, services and higher standards of living, transformed Lebanese confessionalism into a conflictual rather than accommodational political arrangement.

The Electoral Manifestation of Urban Confessionalism

The modern dynamism of confessional consociationalism in Beirut has repeatedly emerged as antithetical to a sustainable form of urbanization. This is evident in the confessional system tendency to strengthen sectarianism as a mobilizing political agent, and to make nonconfessional (secular) or cross-confessional affiliation a self-defeating aspiration. At the same time, it has provided the ground for a permanent unequal representation between the sects, nationally and locally, thus setting the different sectarian groups on an imminent clashing course (see table 3 that shows higher representative advantage of Beirut voters relative to those in the suburbs and elsewhere in the country). This phenomenon has manifested itself in the system's historical suppression and electoral accommodation of newly emerging urban residential groups, confessional, cross-confessional, and secular alike. The statistic confessional electoral institution has failed to absorb or adjust to the spatial and demographic communal reconfigurations, further amplifying the underlying causes of conflict.[25]

For instance, the system assigns voters to electoral districts of origin, not to residence, but, namely, to their villages and remote areas under sectarian control. Most voters who reside in mixed religious neighborhoods in Beirut or its suburbs have been driven to vote for sectarian candidates running in their respective villages and hometowns of origin.[26] This process has not only undermined geographic linkages between the candidates and their constituents; it has also tied

Table 3. Estimated (2001) distribution of Lebanese residential population per administrative voting districts versus parliamentarian representation, 2005

DISTRICT (MUHAFAZAH)	PERCENTAGE (ALL AGES)	NUMBER OF REPRESENTATIVES	PERCENTAGE OF REPRESENTATION
Beirut	8.7	19	14.8
Mount Lebanon: Beirut's suburbs	27.3	6	4.7
Rest of Mount Lebanon	16.2	29	22.7
North Lebanon	19.9	27	21.1
South Lebanon	9.7	12	9.4
Nabatieh	6.3	11	8.6
Bekaa	12.0	23	18.0

Source: Choghig Kasparian, *La Population Libanaise et ses Caracteristiques* (Beirut: University of Saint Joseph, 2003); and Imad Salamey and Rhys Payne, Parliamentary Consociationalism in Lebanon: Equal Citizenry vs. Quoted Confessionalism, *Journal of Legislative Studies* 14:4 (December 2008).

voters to sectarian politics and has further perpetuated traditional sectarian leadership. Emerging urban secular and cross-confessional communities have thus been denied political representation. Worse, this electoral mechanism has weakened residential ties to the living space, establishing exclusionary sectarianism and a fragmented sense of urban identity.

Unequal political representation and voting suppression have been manifested in permanent confessional gerrymandering. Since the 1992 election, parliamentary seats have been divided among six midsized administrative districts and subdivided into smaller electoral districts. In the 2000 and 2005 elections, the number of electoral districts expanded to fourteen. They differed in size and number of seats, varying between six seats in small districts, such as Beirut district 2, and seventeen seats in large districts, such as North Lebanon District 2. This distribution emerged as an outcome of various political and sectarian considerations and negotiations between the different groups. Candidates running for seats specifically designated for a minority confessional community in a confessionally mixed electoral district needed a majority of all votes to win election. Because each voter has the ability to vote for as many candidates on the list in a respective electoral district, confessional-majority voters determined the winning chances and, consequently, the selection of minority candidates. The consequence has been the suppression of minority votes in favor of majority sectarian composition. In Beirut, for example, majority Sunni voters have to a large extent determined the fate of Christian, Shi'a, and Druze parliamentary candidates (see table 4, showing overwhelming majority Sunni voters, which can ultimately determine the fate of all candidates in the three electoral districts of Beirut).

The system has also produced significant inequality in favor of Beiruti voters. Suburbanites, in contrast, were not only disfranchised but were also underrepresented in their place of origin relative to other Lebanese. In some districts of Beirut, approximately 3,500 sectarian votes were sufficient to be represented in a parliamentary seat, while in other districts over 20,000 votes per sect were required (see tables 5 and 6). In the 2005 election, candidates on an electoral list in Beirut were able to win a parliamentary seat with only 24,000 votes (District 3), while in South Lebanon 99,000 votes were needed to win. In North Lebanon, Suleiman Franjieh lost the

Table 4. Beirut political districting and voting distribution

	CHIITES	SUNNIS	DRUZE	MARONITES	GREEK ORTHODOX	GREEK CATHOLIC	ARMENIAN ORTHODOX	ARMENIAN CATHOLIC	SYRIAC	OTHER CHRISTIAN	TOTAL
First District											
Mazraa	4,607	55,313	182	1,043	3,617	767	299	160	395	690	6,773
Ashrafieh	3,181	4,984	283	7,252	14,762	6,002	7,418	2,763	3,720	3,199	53,564
Saifi	129	320	7	3,069	1,717	2,455	649	552	324	828	10,050
Total	7,917	60,617	472	11,314	20,096	9,224	8,398	3,475	4,429	4,717	130,687
MP	—	2	—	1	1	1	—	1	—	—	6
Second District											
Msaytbeh	8,736	31,755	1,784	1,771	5,558	1,495	783	272	4,479	1,511	58,144
Bachoura	19,669	15,436	92	1,485	764	911	1,340	390	781	1,286	42,154
Rmail	46	285	12	6,661	5,899	2,069	7,281	912	642	3,912	28,619
Total	28,451	47,479	1888	9,917	12,221	5,375	9,404	1,574	5,902	6,709	128,917
MP	1	2	—	—	1	—	1	—	—	1	6
Third District											
Ain Mreiseh	1,433	9,892	1,122	555	450	301	660	123	74	533	15,143
Ras Beirut	947	16,431	799	1,268	4,107	1,808	489	146	375	2,253	28,623
Mina El Hosn	790	2,066	43	1,798	1,184	809	849	168	170	5,949	13,826
Mdawar	528	3,728	23	2,613	1,589	1,170	26,232	3,050	491	3,097	42,512
Port	1,980	4,104	10	182	243	145	494	154	62	689	8,063
Zkak Blat	15,337	18,144	98	664	442	523	2,307	269	182	767	38,733
Total	21,015	54,365	2,095	7,080	8,006	4,756	31,031	3,910	1,354	13,288	146,900
MP	1	2	1	—	—	—	2	—	—	1	7

Source: Based on 2000 electoral lists, as published by Al-Anwar on December 22, 2000 (extracted from http://libanvote.com/).

Table 5. Mount Lebanon political districting and voting distribution

DISTRICT	MP/NO	NO	CHIITES	SUNNIS	DRUZE	MARONITES	GREEK ORTHODOX	GREEK CATHOLIC	ARMENIAN	ARMENIAN	OTHER CHRISTIAN	TOTAL
Chouf	—	voters	3,953	41,127	46,574	46,391	2,257	11,295	145	113	2,121	153,976
	8	MP	—	2	2	3	—	—	—	—	—	—
Aley/Baabda	—	voters	31,611	9,024	72,910	77,298	24,998	11,494	2,419	927	5,836	236.517
	11	MP	2	—	3	5	1	—	—	—	—	—
North Metn	—	voters	3,953	2,410	1,855	66,254	13,600	22,019	2,463	6,182	9,865	150,401
	8	MP	—	—	—	4	2	1	1	—	—	—
Jbeil/Keserwan	—	voters	12,592	2,135	9	114,122	5,273	4,495	2,450	889	3,493	145,478
	8	MP	1	—	—	7	—	—	—	—	—	—

Source: Based on 2000 electoral lists, as published by Al-Anwar on December 22, 2000 (extracted from http://libanvote.com/).

Table 6. South Lebanon political districting and voting distribution

	CHIITES	SUNNIS	DRUZE	MARONITES	GREEK ORTHODOX	GREEK CATHOLIC	ARMENIAN ORTHODOX	OTHER CHRISTIAN	TOTAL
First District									
Saida/Zahrani	56,749	37,739	80	10,788	825	11,922	288	557	118,948
Tyre	99,500	9,947	2	2,390	675	5,683	1,150	567	119,914
Bent Jbeil	78,218	793	2	9,025	111	2,482	47	195	90,873
Total	234,467	48,479	84	22,203	1,611	20,087	1,485	1,319	329,735
MP	9	2	—	—	—	1	—	—	12
Second District									
Marjeyoun	53,385	2,307	709	4,333	6,082	2,651	70	324	74,861
Hasbaya	589	15,805	10,805	1,841	4,029	912	35	77	34,093
Nabatieh	88,936	1,793	3	3,391	126	993	7	279	95,528
Jezzin	8,698	1,120	380	29,226	1,015	7,431	96	334	48,300
Total	156,608	21,025	11,895	38,791	11,252	11,987	208	104	252,782
MP	5	1	1	2	1	1	—	—	11

Source: Based on 2000 electoral lists, as published by Al-Anwar on December 22, 2000 (extracted from http://libanvote.com/).

parliamentary race despite receiving 82,670 votes, while in Beirut Ghinwa Jalloul won a seat with 23,731 votes.

The Beirut municipal city election reflects a similar pattern as that of the national parliamentary election. In the first place, the sectarian quotation of seats renders residential demographic change irrelevant to representation. As figure 6 shows, the proportion of the city's Sunni and Shi'a registered voters population is underrepresented in the municipal city council compared to that of the Christians. Yet, considering the city's overwhelming Sunni registered voter population, and considering that the municipal election is based on competing lists composed of individual candidates, Sunni-sponsored electoral lists are the only ones with winning chances. In both the 1998 and 2004 Beirut city municipal elections, electoral lists opposed to that endorsed by Sunni leader and former Prime Minister Rafic Hariri did not succeed in winning a single seat. Candidates of various sects were required to be supportive of the Sunni leadership if they were to be accepted on the Hariri endorsed electoral list.

Unequal representation and suppression of the minority vote have set in motion strong resentment of perceived privileged Beiruti voters and representatives, particularly by suburbanites; nonregistered city residents; and non-Sunni groups. At the same time, Beirut registered voters and traditional residential sects began to witness newly emerging migrant and displaced groups.[27] Sectarianism emerged as a crucial mobilizing agent in the struggle for urban reform or preservation.[28] From 2005 through 2008, political, religious, and sectarian parties mobilized respective supporters in this urban contest. With its strong suburban Shi'a base, Hezbollah led the campaign for "political inclusion," while the Sunni Future Movement and the Druze Progressive

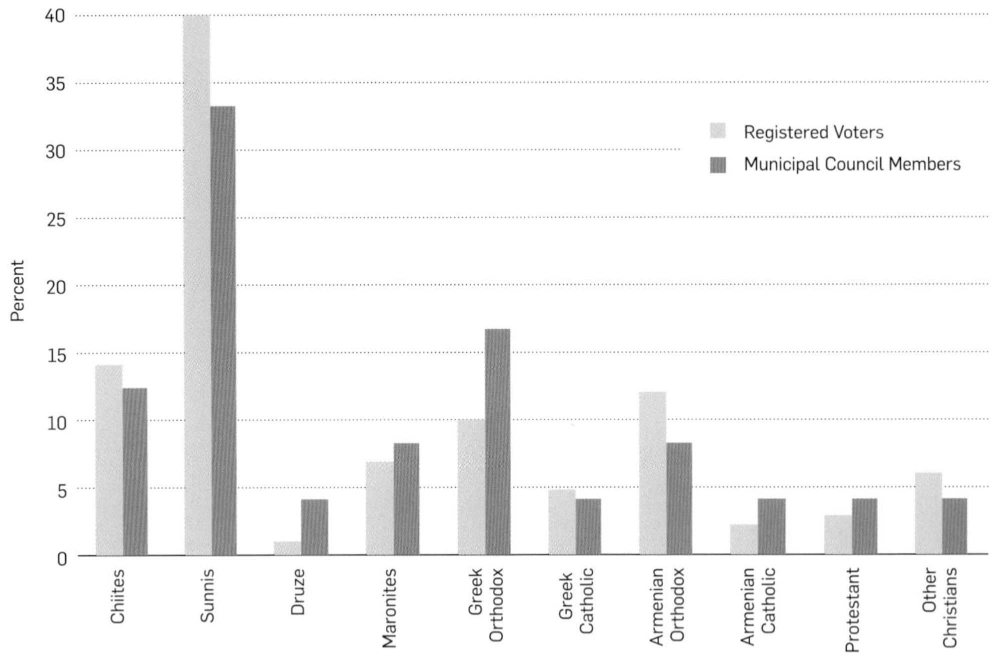

Figure 6. Percent of Beirut registered voters versus distribution of municipal council seats by sect, 2004.

Socialist Party called for the defense of the city. Finally, in May 2008 Hezbollah, in collaboration with the Shi'a Amal movement, militarily overran the Druze and the Sunni groups and took hold of West Beirut. Hezbollah and Amal ended their insurgency only after a Qatari and Arab League brokered agreement redistributed sectarian power to the disadvantages of both the Sunnis and the Druze.

Evidently, urban coexistence has emerged as the weakest link within the Lebanese consociational model and appears in urgent need of electoral reform. The existing confessional electoral structure has only deepened resentments amongst the various communities and has consequently led to sectarian tension, external intervention, and radicalization that have repeatedly undermined civil peace.[29]

Conflict Transformation through Electoral Reform

John Paul Lederach has adopted the view that conflict "is normal in human relationships, and conflict is a motor of change."[30] He considers conflict to be a normal and continuous dynamic within human relationships.[31] This specific conception of conflict is of crucial importance when proposing a sustainable resolution for a deeply divided city, since it implies no contradiction between conflict and sustainability. On the contrary, this view suggests that progressive change and sustainable urban relations at both inter- and intragenerational levels might be driven by a permanent conflict. Urban sustainability and conflict need not be exclusive propositions. What is needed is channeling or transforming conflict into a new form rather than illusively seeking its termination.

Lederach proposed synthesizing conflict and sustainability through "conflict transformation," defined as a way of "creating a constructive change process that reduces violence, increases justice in direct interaction and social structures, and responds to real-life problems in human relations."[32] Considering the deep-rooted confessionalism in Beirut, conflict transformation might be a suitable integrative-consociational proposition. Its implications may well foster the transformation of conflict into a situation that avoids extreme reactions while channeling differential communal grievances through a political structure that could culminate in group competition with the advantage of collective equity.

Over the past half century, confessional conflict in Beirut has been sustained by its resilient confessional system. Considering the deep-rooted confessionalism in Lebanese society and the various communal and plural orientations that have inspired the modern political institution and its contradictions, it would be difficult to imagine the withering away of confessionalism without a major social upheaval.[33] Yet transforming the conflictual dynamic of confessionalism, through gradualism and electoral reform, may present an opportunity for establishing the momentum toward urban sustainability in Beirut. Such a reform needs to include electoral formulations that would facilitate the transformation of political confessionalism from a confrontation geared toward a more constructive competitive paradigm.

Electoral law is among the key areas that can be reformulated in order to achieve critical structural conflict transformation. Engineering an electoral system that can accommodate the different community aspirations and promote cross-confessional alliances is the essence of integrative consociationalism. Such an electoral system would undermine the exclusionary tendencies within the urban process without undermining established community boundaries. In addition, it would facilitate cross-confessional integration in such a way as to establish a sense of common destiny without undermining political competition. Furthermore, the electoral system would have to abolish the domination of one confessional group over another without ruling out cross-confessional alliances and negotiation. Finally, and most critically, such a system would liberate the individual voter from confessional "predetermination" by providing citizenship rights through "self-determination" without necessarily excluding confessional representation.

Linking Residence with the Vote as a Means of Urban Inclusion

As stated earlier, most inhabitants of the city of Beirut and its suburbs are nonvoting residents and have been subjugated to systematic political exclusion from the city. The system has pitted residential against nonresidential confessional groups and has served as a catalyst for renewed conflict and violence in the city's recent history.[34] Therefore, the first urban "integrative" reform needed is one that links urban residency with political rights. An electoral integrative mechanism that moderates the wedge between various city inhabitants by linking urban residence with political representation is a fundamental requirement for urban sustainability. This can best be accomplished by making the urban voting districts, in both the city and its suburbs, inclusive of all permanent residents.[35] In the city of Beirut, this would require that confessionally dedicated seats be reallocated based on current confessional city and suburb residential populations. Such integrative electoral reform need not threaten "nativist" residents, because the accumulated number of representative seats, and consequently the services and political power gained for the city and its residing communities, would substantially increase.

Common Destiny through Integrative Electoral Districting

Unequal representation between the city and its suburbs in favor of the former has resulted in unequal development, thus instigating extreme sectarianism. As has been previously discussed, this reality has solidified confessional trenches between various urban communities and has undermined their common interests. The second condition for successful reform is nurturing a common destiny among all urban residents. This can be electorally achieved by unifying both the city and the suburbs within one political (electoral) entity through redistricting, where both become one voting district (Muhafazah of Metropolitan Beirut). Integrating both Beirut and its suburbs within one electoral district would undermine representational inequality in favor of common interest and purpose between the city and its suburbs. Competition within urban communities for electoral offices would continue to result in representatives seeking services and opportunities for their constituents, but the urban-suburban divide will be greatly diminished.

Community Representation through an Independent Confessional Vote

The current system fosters large-scale gerrymandering in favor of the current dominant confessional majority, subsequently suppressing or dominating minority votes, be they are secular or confessional. The earlier examination of the Lebanese majority district system has revealed that typical candidates for confessional seats within mixed districts seek a majority vote, which has necessitated winning the votes of the various confessional groups. Although a candidate seeking majority vote has seldom resulted in cross-confessional dialogue and alliance formation (which are associated with the moderation of extreme sectarianism), it has generally subjugated confessional minorities to the voting will of the majority. In Beirut, the Sunni registered voters have determined to a large extent the fate of Christian and Shi'a candidates, while in the suburbs of Beirut, Christians and Druze have determined the winning chances of Sunni and Shi'a hopefuls. The evidence suggests that this system has contributed to confessional resentment, further deepening the urban divide.

The third proposition for electoral reform is to establish means to prevent gerrymandering and achieve appropriate community representation. But because urban communities in Beirut and suburbs are substantially intermixed, it will be difficult to geographically redraw districts according to confessional distributions. Instead, electoral reforms should result in confessionally dedicated seats filled strictly by their respective confessional votes. Even though confessionally dedicated seats may contribute to confessional isolationalism, it will at the same time unleash long-held resentment against confessional domination and correct disproportionate confessional representation.

Self-Determination through the Dichotomy of Secular and Confessional Representation

The most rigid and controversial aspect of the present electoral system is its obligatory confessional nature, which refuses to provide electoral choices for secular, cross-confessional, or emerging electoral groups. By strictly dedicating electoral seats on a confessional basis, the electoral system disregards the proportional changes in confessional demography and disqualifies emerging nonconfessional sectarian groups. As a consequence, the system has set the stage for permanent disputes and conflicts among urban communities.

Arend Lijphart has suggested self-determination as a suitable proposition for both ethnic and nonethnic groups and individuals, which would guarantee all members of a plural society equal chances.[36] He has supported Theodore Hanf's recommendation for Lebanon—namely, to have a consociational arrangement based on the principle of self-determination that would make confessional group membership optional rather than obligatory. This proposition stands in sharp contrast to confessional predetermination.[37] Applying these recommendations within a confessionally diverse and divided city requires resolutions that stress political inclusion and common destiny without undermining a community's self-determination. The ultimate goal of this strategy is conflict transformation toward sustainable urbanism.[38]

Thus, the fourth and ultimate objective of transitional electoral reform is to seek the moderation of sectarianism through self-determination. What is needed in Beirut and its suburbs is a mixed electoral system that allocates electoral seats in proportion to confessional group sizes while opening the prospect for cross-confessional and secular representation. The latter reform area would be the most fundamental prerequisite in the transformation and advancement toward sustainability. This can be electorally achieved through the establishment of an inclusive Metropolitan Beirut voting district (Muhafazah Metropolitan Beirut) that allows for both confessional (seats dedicated to sectarian groups) and secular (seats elected on proportional basis) representations. The confessional seats would be allocated in proportion to the confessional constituencies throughout the Metropolitan Beirut District. For the confessional seats, each confessional group would elect its own representatives on a majoritarian cross-list basis. The nonconfessional seats will be determined on proportional list basis. This electoral scheme can also serve as an introduction to bicameral representation.[39]

Contrary to what the current system dictates, the proposed reform assures self-determination and makes confessional and secular identification voluntary rather than predetermined. Such a reform provides an internal corrective mechanism whenever demographic changes occur through its duality of proportional representation and a strict confessionally based vote. Consequently, it becomes viewed by the polity as being capable of adapting to permanent changes in urban demography. It could also be viewed as an avenue that transforms the present intersectarian competition into a more constructive sectarian-secular dichotomy.[40]

Confessionally allocated seats determined only by the voting members of the respective confessional community would assure the autonomy and self-determination of every group. On the other hand, secular proportional representation undermines sectarian differences, promotes cross-confessional and accommodating politics, and accounts for the dynamic and changing urban spatial-demography.

This proposed integrative consociational electoral model presents an opportunity for sustainable urban relations. In the long run, the sectarian-secular dichotomy would diffuse political sectarianism in favor of secularization by increasing the number of individuals participating in the secular voting process. The contention in urban relations would be transformed along a typical Western secular model. The resulting cultural diversity need not antagonize the city's political unity and common destiny. In the short and medium range, this integrative consociational electoral model would transform current confessional antagonisms by correcting representation and providing responsive accommodation to diverse confessional, cross-confessional, and secular urban groups.

Conclusion: Integrative Consociationalism as a Synthetic Urban Model for Sustainability

The dilemma of Beirut's urban relations remains typical of many deeply divided cities undergoing rapid urbanization amid the decline of small-state geopolitical independence. Demographic and spatial community momentum, along with the existing static political system, have set in motion a conflict dynamic that has repeatedly undermined group coexistence and sustainable relations. The fundamental challenge continues to be what type of power-sharing arrangement could accommodate the aspirations of the various groups, moderate external intervention, avoid internal splintering momentums, and achieve equitable and sustainable community relations.

Despite limits to electoral engineering in the formulation of a sustainable democracy in a divided society,[41] consociation remains a viable institutional choice. Alternatives to consociotionalism have led to the suppression of groups' rights for self-determination, inviting ongoing conflicts, dictatorship, and instability in such countries as Israel, Syria, Iraq, Turkey, Morocco, Sudan, Somalia, and Yemen. Fundamental to such a power-sharing arrangement is achievement of group accommodation and citizen self-determination. Such an arrangement, particularly in countries confronting rapid urbanization, must account for the social fluidity of the urban environment, demographically, spatially, and politically.

The examination of confessionalism in Beirut reveals grave consequences for the rigid power-sharing corporate consociational arrangement that refuses to accommodate a fast-changing urban environment. This arrangement awaits serious revisions before achieving sustainable urban relations. Such a task necessitates fundamental reconceptualization of our understanding of urban conflict in deeply divided cities, most importantly through rethinking conflict as a natural process that can be channeled in a positive direction. This implies that urban conflict and sustainability need not be contradictory propositions. On the contrary, synthesizing both through conflict transformation can provide an important contribution to the achievement of sustainable urban coexistence under duress.

In this chapter, integrative consociationalism has been advanced as a synthetic electoral urban model that would foster the preservation of sectarianism while accommodating the hybridization of permanently changing urban communities through proportional secular representation. As a result, sectarian-secular dichotomy would promote the transformation of urban conflict into more sustainable community relations. Such a transformation would further contribute to the removal of contentious sources of community conflict and thus undermine reasons for national fragmentation and external intervention.

NOTES

1. Julia Gardner, Decision Making for Sustainable Development: Selected Approaches to Environmental Assessment and Management, *Environmental Impact Assessment Review* 9 (1989): 342.
2. Dominique Tabutin, Bruno Schoumaker, Godfrey Rogers, Jonathan Mandelbaum, and Catriona Dutreuilh, The Demography of the Arab World and the Middle East from the 1950s to the 2000s: A Survey of Changes and a Statistical Assessment, *Population* 60:5/6 (2005): 505–91, 593–615.
3. Michael E. Bonine, Are Cities in the Middle East Sustainable? In *Population, Poverty, and Politics in Middle East Cities*, ed. Michael E. Bonine (Gainesville: University Press of Florida, 1997).
4. Samir Khalaf and Guilain Denoeux, Urban Networks and Political Conflict in Lebanon, in *Lebanon: A History of Conflict and Consensus*, ed. Nadim Shehadi and Dana Haffar Mills (London: Center for Lebanese Studies, 1988); Imad Salamey and Frederic Pearson, Hezbollah: A Proletarian Party with an Islamic Manifesto—A Sociopolitical Analysis of Islamist Populism in Lebanon and the Middle East, *Small Wars and Insurgencies* 18:3 (2007): 416–38.
5. Kirk Bowman and Jerrold Green, Urbanization and Political Instability in the Middle East, in *Population, Poverty, and Politics in Middle East Cities*, ed. Michael E. Bonine (Gainesville: University Press of Florida, 1997).
6. John McGarry and Brendan O'Leary, Iraq's Constitution of 2005: Liberal Consociation as Political Prescription, *International Journal of Constitutional Law* 5 (2007): 670–98.
7. Arend Lijphart, The Wave of Power-Sharing Democracy, in *The Architecture of Democracy: Constitutional Design, Conflict Management, and Democracy*, ed. Andrew Reynolds (Oxford: Oxford University Press, 2002), 37.
8. Arend Lijphart, Consociational Democracy, *World Politics* 21:2 (1969): 207–275.
9. Scott A. Bollens, *Urban Peace-Building in Divided Societies: Belfast and Johannesburg* (Boulder: Westview Press, 1999); Scott A. Bollens, City and Soul: Sarajevo, Johannesburg, Jerusalem, Nicosia, *City* 5:2 (2001): 169–87.
10. Non-Emigrant Residents of Lebanon (1932): Muslims = 386,469 (48.7%); Christians = 396,946 (50.03%); Jews =3,588 (0.5%); others = 6,393 (0.8%). Total = 793,396 (Source: Official Gazette, No. 2718, October 5, 1932).
11. Muslim constituted 40 percent of the 1975 population of "Christian" East Beirut; see Dona Stewart, Economic Recovery and Reconstruction in Postwar Beirut, *Geographic Review* 86:4 (1996): 487–504.
12. Youssef Duwayhe, Comprehensive Survey Study of Lebanese and Demographic Distribution (Arabic), *An-Nahar* (Beirut), November 13, 2006, 14; Joseph Jabbra and Nancy Jabbra, Consociational Democracy in Lebanon: A Flawed System of Governance, *Perspectives on Global Development and Technology* 17:2 (2001): 71–89; Julia Choukair, Finding a Path from Deadlock to Democracy, Carnegie Papers 64, 2006. Within the past 100 years various neighborhoods in the city of Beirut have experienced dramatic demographic changes in favor of the Muslims. The *Ain Al-Mreisah* neighborhood, for instance, had 54.64 percent Christian residents between 1907 and 1916, but by 2006 the Muslim residents constituted 80.78 percent. Similarly, the Port area experienced likewise trends, with the Muslims residents increasing from 38.64 percent to 84.27 percent for the same period. See Youssef Duwayhe, Comprehensive Survey Study of Lebanese and Demographic Distribution (in Arabic), *Annaha* (Beirut), November 13, 2006, 14.
13. Thomas Collelo, *Lebanon: A Country Study* (Washington, DC: Government Printing Office, 1987.
14. Salim Nasr and Dianne James, Roots of the Shi'i Movement, *MERIP Reports* 33 (1985): 10–16.
15. Hans Gebhardt et al., *History, Space and Social Conflict in Beirut: The Quarter of Zokak el-Blat* (Beirut: Orient Institute, 2005).
16. Waddah Sharrara, *Dawlat Hizballah, Lubnan Mujtama'a Islamiyya* (Hizballah's state, Lebanon—an Islamic society) (Beirut: DarAn-Naharli-Nashr, 1996).
17. Waddah Sharrara, *Al-Madenah Al-Mawkoufah* (Beirut: Dar Al-Matbouat Al-Sharkeyah, 1985) (in Arabic).
18. The Doha Agreement redistributed power to the disadvantage of the Sunnis through redistricting the

city of Beirut and reducing the Sunni voters from a majority to a minority status in two of the three electoral districts.

19. Michael Kerr, *Imposing Power Sharing: Conflict and Consensus in Northern Ireland and Lebanon* (Dublin: Irish Academic Press, 2005); Brenda M. Seaver, The Regional Sources of Power-Sharing Failure: The Case of Lebanon, *Political Science Quarterly* 115:2 (2000): 247–71; Oussama Safa, Lebanon Spring Forward, *Journal of Democracy* 17:1 (2006): 22–37.
20. Theodor Hanf, Coexistence in Wartime Lebanon: Decline of a State and Rise of a Nation, trans. John Richardson (London: Center for Lebanese Studies, in association with I.B. Tauris, 1993); Ghassan Salame, Lebanon: How "National" Is Independence? *Beirut Review* 6 (1993): 1–5; Imad Salamey and Frederic Pearson, Hezbollah: A Proletarian Party with an Islamic Manifesto—A Sociopolitical Analysis of Islamist Populism in Lebanon and the Middle East, *Small Wars and Insurgencies* 18:3 (2007): 416–38.
21. Samir Khalaf, *Cultural Resistance: Global and Local Encounters in the Middle East* (London: Saqi Books, 2001); Samir Khalaf, *Civil and Uncivil Violence in Lebanon: A History of the Internationalization of Communal Conflict* (New York: Columbia University Press, 2002); Imad Salamey and Frederic Pearson, Hezbollah: A Proletarian Party with an Islamic Manifesto—A Sociopolitical Analysis of Islamist Populism in Lebanon and the Middle East, *Small Wars and Insurgencies* 18:3 (2007): 416–38.
22. Dominique Tabutin, Bruno Schoumaker, Godfrey Rogers, Jonathan Mandelbaum, and Catriona Dutreuilh, The Demography of the Arab World and the Middle East from the 1950s to the 2000s: A Survey of Changes and a Statistical Assessment, *Population* 60:5/6 (2005): 572.
23. Joseph Jabbra and Nancy Jabbra, Consociational Democracy in Lebanon: A Flawed System of Governance, *Perspectives on Global Development and Technology* 17:2 (2001): 71–89.
24. Edward Shils, The Prospect for Lebanese Civility, in *Politics in Lebanon*, ed. Leonard Binder (New York: Wiley, 1960), 1–11.
25. Imad Salamey and Rhys Payne, Parliamentary Consociationalism in Lebanon: Equal Citizenry vs. Quoted Confessionalism, *Journal of Legislative Studies* 14:4 (2008): 451–73.
26. Fuad I. Khuri, *From Village to Suburb: Order and Change in Greater Beirut* (Chicago: University of Chicago Press, 1975), 192–93.
27. Imad Salamey and Paul Tabar, Opinion Study in Beirut and Suburbs Reveals the Demographic Dynamic of Political Division between Supporters of March 8th and 14th Alliance, *An-Nahar* (Beirut), January 30, 2007 (in Arabic).
28. Paul Tabar, Religious Ceremony in the Context of a Migrant Society, *Journal of Intercultural Studies* 23:3 (2002): 285–305.
29. Imad Salamey and Frederic Pearson, Hezbollah: A Proletarian Party with an Islamic Manifesto—A Sociopolitical Analysis of Islamist Populism in Lebanon and the Middle East, *Small Wars and Insurgencies* 18:3 (2007): 416–38.
30. John Paul Lederach, *The Little Book of Conflict Transformation* (Intercourse, PA: Good Books, 2003), 4.
31. Ibid., 15.
32. John Paul Lederach, Defining Conflict Transformation, *Peacework* 33:368 (2006): 26.
33. Julia Choukair, Finding a Path from Deadlock to Democracy, Carnegie Papers 64, 2006.
34. Hans Gebhardt et al, *History, Space and Social Conflict in Beirut: The Quarter of Zokak el-Blat* (Beirut: Orient Institute, 2005).
35. Nizar Sagheya and Rana Sagheya, *Propositions for Reforming the Electoral System in Lebanon* (Beirut: An-Nahar Publishing, 2004) (in Arabic).
36. Arend Lijphart, Self-Determination Versus Pre-Determination of Ethnic Minorities in Power-Sharing Systems, in *The Rights of Minority Cultures*, ed. Will Kymlika (Oxford: Oxford University Press, 2006), 285.
37. Theodor Hanf, The "Political Secularization" Issue in Lebanon, *Annual Review of the Social Science and Religion 5* (Amsterdam: Mouton, 1981), 249.
38. Alex Burkholder, Ethnic Conflict in Urban Environment, 3d prize winner in the Academic Category of the 1st Terry Writing Challenge (Canada: University of British Colombia, 2006); Samir Khalaf, *Cultural Resistance: Global and Local Encounters in the Middle East* (London: Saqi Books, 2001), 43–44.
39. The 1989 Taef Agreement, which sought to end the Lebanese Civil War, stipulated the eventual establishment of a bicameral Parliament, a confessionally based Upper House or a Senate along with a nonconfessionally based Lower House or a Chamber of Deputies. See the 1989 Taef Agreement: http://www.dailystar.com.lb/researcharticle.asp?article_id=54.
40. The sectarian-secular model necessitates wide ranging cross-sectarian alliance formations for winning elections.
41. Bassel Salloukh, The Limits of Electoral Engineering in Divided Societies: Elections in Postwar Lebanon, *Canadian Journal of Political Science* 39:2 (2006): 1–21.

REFERENCES

Anderson, Gordon. The Idea of a Nation-State Is an Obstacle to Peace. *International Journal on World Peace* 23:1 (2006): 75–85.

Bollens, Scott A. City and Soul: Sarajevo, Johannesburg, Jerusalem, Nicosia. *City* 5: 2 (2001): 169–87.

———. *Urban Peace-Building in Divided Societies: Belfast and Johannesburg*. Boulder: Westview Press, 1999.

Bonine, Michael E. Are Cities in the Middle East Sustainable? In *Population, Poverty, and Politics in Middle East Cities*, ed. Michael E. Bonine, 326–42. Gainesville: University Press of Florida, 1997.

Bowman, Kirk, and Jerrold Green. Urbanization and Political Instability in the Middle East. In *Population, Poverty, and Politics in Middle East Cities*, ed. Michael E. Bonine, 237–55. Gainesville: University Press of Florida, 1997.

Burkholder, Alex. Ethnic Conflict in Urban Environment. 3d prize winner in the Academic Category of the 1st Terry Writing Challenge. Vancouver: University of British Colombia, 2006.

Castles, Stephen, and Alastair Davidson. *Citizenship and Migration: Globalization and the Politics of Belonging*. Houndmills: Macmillan, 2000.

Choukair, Julia. Finding a Path from Deadlock to Democracy. Carnegie Papers 64. 2006.

Collelo, Thomas. *Lebanon: A Country Study*. Washington, DC: GPO for the Library of Congress, 1987.

Duwayhe, Youssef. Comprehensive Survey Study of Lebanese and Demographic Distribution (in Arabic). *An-Nahar* (Beirut), November 13, 2006, 14.

Gardner, Julia. Decision Making for Sustainable Development: Selected Approaches to Environmental Assessment and Management. *Environmental Impact Assessment Review* 9 (1989): 337–36.

Gulalp, Haldun. Citizenship vs. Nationality. In *Citizenship and Ethnic Conflict: Challenging the Nation State*, ed. Haldun Gulalp, 1–18. London: Routledge, 2006.

Gebhardt, Hans, et al. *History, Space and Social Conflict in Beirut: The Quarter of Zokak el-Blat*. Beirut: Orient Institute, 2005.

Hanf, Theodor. The "Political Secularization" Issue in Lebanon. *Annual Review of the Social Science and Religion 5*. Amsterdam: Mouton, 1981.

———. *Coexistence in Wartime Lebanon: Decline of a State and Rise of a Nation*, trans. John Richardson. London: Center for Lebanese Studies, in association with I.B. Tauris, 1993.

Jabbra, Joseph, and Nancy Jabbra. Consociational Democracy in Lebanon: A Flawed System of Governance. *Perspectives on Global Development and Technology* 17:2 (2001): 71–89.

Kasparian, Choghig. *La Population Libanaise et ses Caracteristiques*. Beirut: University of Saint Joseph, 2003.

Kerr, Michael. *Imposing Power Sharing: Conflict and Consensus in Northern Ireland and Lebanon*. Dublin: Irish Academic Press, 2005.

Khalaf, Samir. *Civil and Uncivil Violence in Lebanon: A History of the Internationalization of Communal Conflict*. New York: Columbia University Press, 2002.

———. *Cultural Resistance: Global and Local Encounters in the Middle East*. London: Saqi Books, 2001.

Khalaf, Samir, and Guilain Denoeux. Urban Networks and Political Conflict in Lebanon. In *Lebanon: A History of Conflict and Consensus*, ed. Nadim Shehadi and Dana Haffar Mills, 181–200. London: Center for Lebanese Studies, 1988.

Khuri, Fuad I. *From Village to Suburb: Order and Change in Greater Beirut*. Chicago: University of Chicago Press, 1975.

Lederach, John Paul. *The Little Book of Conflict Transformation*. Intercourse, PA: Good Books, 2003.

Lederach, John Paul. Defining Conflict Transformation. *Peacework* 33:368 (2006): 26–27.

Lijphart, Arend. Consociational Democracy. *World Politics* 21:2 (1969): 207–75.

———. Self-Determination versus Pre-Determination of Ethnic Minorities in Power-Sharing Systems. In *The Rights of Minority Cultures*, ed. Will Kymlika, 275–87. Oxford: Oxford University Press, 2006.

———. The Wave of Power-Sharing Democracy. In *The Architecture of Democracy: Constitutional Design, Conflict Management, and Democracy*, ed. Andrew Reynolds, 37–54. Oxford: Oxford University Press, 2002.

McGarry, John, and Brendan O'Leary. Iraq's Constitution of 2005: Liberal Consociation as Political Prescription. *International Journal of Constitutional Law* 5 (2007): 670–98.

Nasr, Salim, and Dianne James. Roots of the Shi'i Movement. *MERIP Reports* 33 (1985): 10–16.

Pasha, Mustapha Kamal. Predatory Globalization and Democracy in the Islamic World. *The ANNALS of the American Academy of Political and Social Science* 581 (2002): 121–31.

Safa, Oussama. Lebanon Spring Forward. *Journal of Democracy* 17:1 (2006): 22–37.

Sagheya, Nizar, and Rana Sagheya. *Propositions for Reforming the Electoral System in Lebanon*. Beirut: An-Nahar Publishing, 2004 (in Arabic).

Salame, Ghassan. Lebanon: How "National" Is

Independence? *Beirut Review* 6 (1993): 1–5.
Salamey, Imad, and Rhys Payne. Parliamentary Consociationalism in Lebanon: Equal Citizenry vs. Quoted Confessionalism. *Journal of Legislative Studies* 14:4 (December 2008): 451–73.
Salamey, Imad, and Frederic Pearson. Hezbollah: A Proletarian Party with an Islamic Manifesto—A Sociopolitical Analysis of Islamist Populism in Lebanon and the Middle East. *Small Wars and Insurgencies* 18:3 (2007): 416–38.
Salamey, Imad, and Paul Tabar. Opinion Study in Beirut and Suburbs Reveals the Demographic Dynamic of Political Division between Supporters of March 8th and 14th Alliance. *An-Nahar* (Beirut), January 30, 2007 (in Arabic).
Salloukh, Bassel. The Limits of Electoral Engineering in Divided Societies: Elections in Postwar Lebanon. *Canadian Journal of Political Science* 39:2 (2006): 1–21.
Seaver, Brenda M. The Regional Sources of Power-Sharing Failure: The Case of Lebanon. *Political Science Quarterly* 115:2 (2000): 247–71.
Sharrara, Waddah. *Al-Madenah Al-Mawkoufah*. Beirut: Dar Al-Matbouat Al-Sharkeyah, 1985 (in Arabic).
———. *Dawlat Hizballah, Lubnan Mujtama'a Islamiyya* (Hizballah's state, Lebanon—an Islamic society). Beirut: DarAn-Naharli-Nashr, 1996.
Shils, Edward. The Prospect for Lebanese Civility. In *Politics in Lebanon*, ed. Leonard Binder, 1–11. New York: Wiley, 1960.
Stewart, Dona. Economic Recovery and Reconstruction in Postwar Beirut. *Geographic Review* 86:4 (1996): 487–504.
Tabar, Paul. Islam in Tripoli: Identity in a Troubled City. Paper presented at the University of Notre Dame University Conference (in Arabic). Between the Rural and Urban: Space, Identity, and Urbanization in Northern Lebanon. Louaisi, Lebanon, 2002.
———. Religious Ceremony in the Context of a Migrant Society. *Journal of Intercultural Studies* 23:3 (2002): 285–305.
Tabutin, Dominique, Bruno Schoumaker, Godfrey Rogers, Jonathan Mandelbaum, and Catriona Dutreuilh. The Demography of the Arab World and the Middle East from the 1950s to the 2000s: A Survey of Changes and a Statistical Assessment. *Population* 60:5/6 (2005): 505–91, 593–615.

■ DARSHINI MAHADEVIA

Segmentation and Enclavization in Urban Development

THE SUSTAINABLE CITY IN INDIA

India is in the midst of an urban transformation, facilitated by deregulation, globalization, and investment-led economic growth. One outcome of this policy direction is a newly evolving exclusiveness emerging in India's cities. This is evident from local and state infrastructure and housing policies, which are extensively focused on upper income groups while being increasingly dismissive of the needs of the urban poor living in India's slums. With increasing deregulation and globalization there has been a new focus in urban India on policies promoting high end real estate developments, such as gated communities and hi-tech zones.

Not only is there almost no public interest in meeting the shelter and infrastructure needs of the urban poor, there also has been active state demolition and displacement of slums, with few getting rehabilitation.[1] In contrast, governments at all levels are extensively involved in facilitating the purchasing and consolidating of land parcels for upscale real estate projects. The inequities of this newly evolving development process have been the driver pushing India's cities away from inclusiveness and sustainability.

This chapter argues that the economic growth paradigm in India today is premised on a reality of excluding the needs of the urban poor through exclusive urban development while engaging in fragmented efforts to improve local environmental challenges. Ironically, the exclusionary urban development agenda includes ecological concerns. In other words, the processes of economic growth in India are being viewed in isolation from the concerns of equity and ecology. Thus, Indian cities are currently moving further away from the sustainability condition that existed prior to the introduction of new urban reforms and economic development strategies.

The next section of the chapter focuses on recent economic growth and urban development processes, followed by a discussion of the need to base the concept of urban sustainability on notions of equity and the conceptualization of sustainable cities as inclusive cities. The chapter then presents development concerns in India's cities, in particular concerns associated with various forms of deprivation. The fourth section reviews national efforts to boost economic growth through land-based development—specifically, the promotion of special economic zones (SEZs), enclaves, and gated communities on the urban periphery. The chapter then explores the case study of Aryaman, a gated community on the periphery of Ahmedabad City, which illustrates the inequities associated with exclusiveness in the context of Indian cities. The last section offers broad conclusions, expressing the author's concerns with sustainability in the context of the new economic growth efforts in urban India.

Economic Growth and Urban Development Processes in India

India's average annual economic growth between 2000 and 2005 was 6.7 percent in real terms, and it has increased to over 8 percent annually since 2004. High economic growth is expected to increase the rate and level of urbanization, which has historically been quite low. During the 1991–2001 decade, urbanization in India was at 2.65 percent per annum, and by 2001 just 27.5 percent of the population was living in urban areas.[2] While economic growth leads to urbanization, conversely it is argued that "no country in the industrial age has ever achieved significant economic growth without urbanization."[3] Cities are engines of economic growth, goes the popular policy saying as articulated by Jane Jacobs.[4]

Like China, India has adopted a development strategy of selective area-specific, investment-led growth.[5] China, the only other billion-plus country in the world today, has successfully implemented this policy over the past twenty-five years while maintaining about 10 percent growth. The government of India launched a new program named Jawaharlal Nehru Urban Renewal Mission (JNNURM) in December 2005, for improving infrastructure in sixty-three cities across the country over a seven-year period.[6] The national government has pledged 500 billion rupees (US$12.3 billion) as its contribution to the total expected investment of 1,250 billion rupees (US$30.8 billion) for these sixty-three cities.[7] It is the first time in India that urban development has received such major funding from the national government. Of the US$12.3 billion coming from the national government, US$4.55 billion has been targeted for constructing new housing for the urban poor. However, this sum would be able to cover only 10 percent of the required dwellings to house existing slum dwellers and the increase in the slum population expected by 2011.[8]

In 2004–2005, 53.6 percent of the national gross domestic product (GDP) was from the tertiary sector, whereas the primary and secondary sectors made up 22.4 percent and 24.0 percent, respectively.[9] Also, just 23.4 percent of the total workers are engaged in the tertiary sector and 17.6 percent in the secondary sector, leaving 59 percent depending on agriculture.[10] For continuing economic growth in India, the challenge will be to increase investment in the manufacturing sector and, like China, to push for infrastructure investment that not only increases economic efficiency but also creates employment in the secondary sector to offer options for those barely surviving in agriculture.

To achieve this goal, the national and the state governments have come up with several policy measures.[11] The first is the policy of promoting SEZs that would attract foreign direct investments (FDI) in the manufacturing sector through special tax incentives. This is a national government policy, but the SEZs have to be initiated by state governments and then seek permission from the national government to set them up to get tax benefits. The state government sees its role in this policy as that of land assembler—and, if need be, it also acquires land from the farmers—given the highly fragmented agricultural lands not suitable for putting up large development projects such as SEZs.[12]

Second, the government has also realized the importance of real estate development in not just attracting investments but also inducing growth and employment. This has led to the implementation of new township policies in different states in India, as well as a FDI policy for the townships at the national government level, to facilitate real estate development.

Third, the public realm actively moved on repealing the Urban Land Ceiling and Regulation Act (ULCRA) of 1976.[13] ULCRA restricted land assembly by a single real estate developer beyond the ceiling set under the legislation. The annulment of this legislation facilitates high valued, large enclave developments for residential and commercial purposes. The national government was first to repeal ULCRA, and then state governments responded. Some states responded on their own and some under the mandatory condition of the JNNURM,[14] which required the repeal of ULCRA if they were to receive national government contributions. The expectation is that the repeal of ULCRA will push up real estate growth and hence incomes and employment. This chapter illustrates that this has happened with gated communities, enclaves, and SEZs, which have been emerging around many large metropolitan centers.

At the center of these policies and programs introduced to infuse economic growth in India is the question of land—namely, the diversion of land, rural and urban, for economic growth. In this process, access to land for housing the urban poor is of little interest to the state.[15] While compulsions for economic growth remain in India, the concerns for equity are being overlooked. Sustainability challenges in India, however, need to be grounded in notions of equity.

The Discourse on Sustainable Cities in India

The urban policy discourse in India, while not having extensive initiatives defined as sustainability, is focused on improving urban infrastructure, urban efficiency, alleviating poverty and its manifestations (such as slums and squatter settlements), extending basic services networks, and extending participatory governance. Official public documents do not generally engage in discussions, or display concerns, about sustainable cities or sustainability of cities. However, development and poverty alleviation concerns are evident in both national and urban policy frameworks. Thus, while generally not engaging in the sustainability discourse, many public policy discussions and initiatives fall within what might be considered broadly as sustainability programs.

This is amply demonstrated by the preamble of the JNNURM, the flagship program of the national government:

> Cities and towns have a vital role in India's socio-economic transformation and change. Host to about 30 per cent of the country's population, they contribute 50–55 per cent of the GDP. At the same time, most cities and towns are severely stressed in terms of infrastructure and service availability, and their growth and development is constrained by indifferent implementation of the Constitution

> (seventy-fourth) Amendment Act, 1992, and continuation of statutes, systems and procedures that impede the operation of land and housing markets. . . . The JNNURM aims to encourage cities to initiate steps to bring about improvement in the existing service levels in a financially sustainable manner. . . . It is essential to create incentives and support urban reforms at state and city levels; develop appropriate enabling and regulatory frameworks; enhance the creditworthiness of municipalities; and integrate the poor with the service delivery system.[16]

One of the concerns of the JNNURM, as the paragraph above illustrates, is providing adequate shelter. In meeting this goal, the 2007 National Urban Housing and Habitat Policy (NUHHP) has been drawn up and accepted by the national government. While this policy is about ensuring *affordable shelter for all,* it also presents a rare case in public documentation where ecologically sustainable development is actually mentioned. The preamble of this policy states the following:

> Shelter is a basic human need next only to food and clothing. At the end of the 10th Five Year Plan, the housing shortage is estimated to be 24.7 million. However, urban areas in our country are also characterized by severe shortage of basic services like potable water, well laid out drainage system, sewerage network, sanitation facilities, electricity, roads and appropriate solid waste disposal. It is these shortages that constitute the rationale for policy focus on housing and basic services in urban areas. This policy intends to promote sustainable development of habitat in the country with a view to ensuring equitable supply of land, shelter and services at affordable prices to all sections of society. Given the magnitude of the housing shortage and budgetary constraints of both the Central and State Governments, it is amply clear that Public Sector efforts will not suffice in fulfilling the housing demand. In view of this scenario, the National Urban Housing and Habitat Policy, 2007 focuses the spotlight on multiple stake-holders namely, the Private Sector, the Cooperative Sector, the Industrial Sector for labor housing and the Services/Institutional Sector for employee housing. In this manner, the Policy will seek to promote various types of public-private partnerships for realizing the goal of Affordable Housing For All.[17]

In official policy documents, only the 2007 NUHHP has put the term "sustainable" in the main text and in other parts of the document, such as the preamble. The term "sustainable" within this policy is used in the ecological sense. In the section on "Balanced Regional Development," the policy mentions that the approach should be "ecologically sustainable."[18] However, how this is to be achieved is not stated.

In a subsequent subsection called "Development of Sustainable Habitats," the authors of the document state that the master plans, the regional plans, and the subregional plans would maintain an ecological balance and would have "a significant proportion of the total Master Plan area as 'green lungs of the city.'"[19] This is intended to be similar to the Master Plan of Delhi (2021) that provides 20 percent green areas. The subsection also states that "the bodies of water would be protected, with a special emphasis placed on floodplains of rivers passing through the cities. It also indicates that green belts would be developed around cities. Lastly, the sustainable habitat is to have 20–25 percent of the land area devoted to recreational uses (excluding bodies of water) for parks, playfields, and other open spaces (such as a specified park, an amusement park, a maidan,[20] a multipurpose open space, a botanical garden, [and] zoological parks."[21]

Overall, NUHHP summarizes the notions of sustainable cities. As the authors of NUHHP maintain:

> The ultimate goal of this Policy is to ensure sustainable development of all urban human settlements, duly serviced by basic civic amenities for ensuring better quality of life for all urban citizens. The Action Plan at the State/UT level in this regard must be prepared with the active involvement of all stakeholders. The NUHHP, 2007 also lays special emphasis on provision of social housing for the EWS/LIG categories so that they are fully integrated into the mainstream of ecologically well-balanced urban development.[22]

It should be acknowledged that whether and how this housing policy will be implemented depends on state governments. In the Indian federal system, national policies are implemented by the state governments only if its funding is provided by the national government. State governments are free to choose their investment priorities if they are to fund the projects themselves. During the writing of this chapter, none of the state governments of India had adopted the housing policy. It is at the state government level, therefore, that inclusion or exclusion of this initiative will occur.

It becomes evident that while two major national programs, JNNURM and NUHHP, have explicitly stated goals to improve basic services and housing for the urban poor in India, there is, in fact, no significant movement in achieving these goals. While NUHHP has no state adoption as of now, JNNURM, as noted earlier, does not have adequate funds for housing provision and infrastructure improvements to actually meet the needs of India's urban poor.

While national initiatives have been considered ineffective in addressing urban-environmental and social pressures, urban policy has actually exacerbated local stresses. Local policy has not only been used to actively dismiss the needs of the urban poor, but local master plans have become a tool for displacing slums from India's cities. The ecological considerations—for example, freeing the green belt from encroachments—in the Delhi Master Plan 2021 maintain strong exclusionary dimensions, particularly for the urban poor. The Delhi High Court also requested no tolerance of any violations of the master plan with regard to slums. As noted by Dupont and Ramanathan, the Delhi High Court[23] took an extremely legal view of slums on public lands as encroachments and asked that they be removed so that the public lands could be restored to the owning agency for public facilities, such as landfills.[24] It also dismissed the plea of resettlement, considering it as an act that would merely encourage dishonesty and violations, amounting to rewarding pickpockets, a brutal position that was subsequently stayed by the Supreme Court.[25] These litigation procedures are apparent not just in Delhi but also in other cities throughout India, including Mumbai. Thus master plans that can maintain an ecological sustainability agenda, as in the case of Delhi, are being used for the eviction of slums. There is therefore an increasing realization in urban India that ecological concerns are in conflict with equity concerns, particularly with the basic needs of India's urban poor.

At the local level, in addition to the master plans there are various fragmented urban environmental programs throughout the country. India now has the Eco City Programme, which aims to bring visible environmental improvements to six small and medium sized cities: Vrindavan, Tirupati, Puri, Ujjain, Kottayam and Thanjavur.[26] There are also a number of new environmental initiatives that have been developed, particularly in the area of solid waste management. Individual cities have taken initiatives to address the growing concerns of solid waste generated within their jurisdiction, partly in response to the Supreme Court ruling on mandatory collection and disposal of solid waste in cities with a population of more than 100,000. Research has shown that cities have a long way to go before meeting the Supreme Court Ruling, in spite of interesting new programs in some of India's urban centers.[27]

A number of cities—including Delhi, Ahmedabad, Pune, Hyderabad, and Bangalore—have also introduced Bus Rapid Transit (BRT), a low-cost mass public transit system. It is argued that a mass BRT system focuses on the concerns of the poor, since it keeps ticket prices low by virtue of its capital costs being far lower than those of an underground subway or an elevated Light Rail Transit (LRT) system.[28] The National Urban Transport Policy has also been promoting the design of roads for the BRT system, which accommodate bicyclists and pedestrians.

Two other initiatives are worth noting. JNNURM has infused investment in water and sanitation programs in sixty-three large cities, with 40 percent of the JNNURM funds committed to reach the poor. In addition, in large cities public buses and paratransit vehicles (three wheelers) have been converted to use compressed natural gas (CNG) in place of diesel to reduce particulate matter in the air.

Local environmental initiatives are clearly evident in cities throughout India. The BRT is notable since it meets both the environmental challenges as well as equity concerns. But, overall, urban development in India remains an excluding paradigm, with the inclusive agenda remaining on the margin, as illustrated with both the JNNURM and the NUHHP. Of particular concern is that the new ecological agendas are coming in direct conflict with issues of social equity, making the sustainable cities discourse in India more complex and contentious.

Given the nature of recent urban development processes in India, the definition of sustainable cities needs to ensure the adoption of an inclusive approach in urban planning, development, and governance.[29] Sustainable cities are those that keep the vision of the urban poor and marginal segments of society at the center of urban policy making.

The term "inclusive" can be used in two senses—inclusive of all people and inclusive of all dimensions of development— which suggests convergence of thinking and actions and convergence of different aspects of development. Only such a development process would address the prime concerns of the poor in a sustainable manner. When the poor are included in the development process, overall human development takes place in a sustainable manner. In addition, development and empowerment of the poor has to take place in a manner that protects the environment. If the urban environment deteriorates, it is the poor that are adversely affected first. Within this context, the role of the government, especially local government, is to see that the synergies are built between various development programs and various actors in the process of development (such as government and civil society, and micro- and macrolevel institutions).[30]

The concept of sustainable cities rests on four pillars: environmental sustainability, economic growth with redistribution, social justice (for women and all other excluded subpopulations),

Table 1. Number and incidence of absolute poor, India

YEAR	NUMBER (MILLIONS)	%
1983	70.94	40.79
1987–1988	75.17	38.20
1993–1994	76.34	32.36
2004–2005	80.80	25.70

Sources: India, Planning Commission, National Human Development Report, 2001 (New Delhi: Planning Commission, Government of India, 2002); Government of India, Press Information Bureau, Poverty Estimates from 2004–05, March (New Delhi: Government of India, 2007), http://planningcommission.nic.in/news/prmar07.pdf.

and political empowerment. These have to be simultaneously addressed in the development process, programs, and projects. The trade-off between any two of the mentioned pillars could lead to exclusions and social injustice. However, the urban development paradigm in this period of economic reforms in India, as it will become evident in this chapter, does not meet any of the stated requirements of sustainable cities. It is clear that the goal of "Inclusive Cities," or "Inclusive Growth," at least through national government policies, remain far from achievement.[31]

Urban Poverty and Deprivation

The official national definition of the urban poor in India is based on the caloric intake of food, but it does not include nutritional requirements. Individuals consuming less that 2,100 calories per day are considered to be living in poverty in urban areas. They are also called the *absolute poor.* By this measure, there are 80.8 million absolute urban poor in India (table 1), an increase from 70.9 million in 1983. However, the total urban population has increased at a much faster rate in the two decades from 1981 to 2001, at 2.9 percent per annum, than the increase in the number of urban poor, at 0.6 percent per annum between 1983 and 2004/2005.

In 2001 about 42.6 million or 15.0 percent of the total urban population in India lived in slums.[32] The proportion of the population living in slums and squatter settlements is much higher in the metropolitan areas than the average, with 24.1 percent, or 17.7 million, living in the million-plus metropolitan centers. In cities such as Mumbai, where land prices are high, 60 percent of the population lives in slums. Mahadevia has shown that except in the case of Mumbai, the availability of land for rehabilitation of the existing slum dwellers is attainable; land required to rehabilitate existing slum dwellers is less than 5 percent in other cities and 8.5 percent in Mumbai, at a floor space index (FSI) of 2.[33] However, there is little interest in allocating such small proportions of land to house the urban poor, despite the fact that considerable improvements in housing for the urban poor are possible (see figs. 1 and 2).

In fact, throughout India's cities, and in particular the large metropolitan centers, considerable resources have been devoted to the demolition and displacement of slums, with few getting rehabilitation.[34] For example, between November 2004 and March 2005, some 90,000 homes of slumdwellers in over forty-four localities were demolished.[35] In Delhi, from Yamun Pushta (banks) alone, 27,000 families have been evicted and about 100,000 families all over the city have been

PHOTOGRAPH BY DARSHINI MAHADEVIA

Figure 1. A slum in Mumbai.

PHOTOGRAPH BY DARSHINI MAHADEVIA

Figure 2. A redeveloped slum in Ahmedabad.

evicted from slums in the last eight years. According to an estimate, 42,000 families have faced demolitions in Kolkata since 2004. Furthermore, infrastructure development projects have led to large-scale slum displacements in Mumbai and other cities.[36]

It is not just housing supply that is lacking in cities throughout India. Critical stresses exist with what are considered basic urban services, as evident, for instance, with shortages of water supply and sanitation. It is estimated that 48.7 million urban households in India (73.7 percent) have access to tap water for domestic use.[37] This means that 17.7 million urban households do not have access to tap water and are dependent on their own sources. These sources include tubewells or shallow wells, handpumps to extract ground water, surface water sources (such as ponds, lakes, and rivers), and tankers. Just 29.5 million households (43.8 percent) have access to water sources meant for their exclusive use, indicating that more than half the urban households are sharing a water source, either at the level of the building (25.4 percent, or 17.1 million) or community (30.82 percent, or 20.8 million). Sharing water results in stress with regards to the quantity of water available and the increased potential for water conflicts. If the water has to be drawn from surface water sources, then women and girls end up spending a bulk of their time collecting water at the cost of their education and health. Also, 10.78 percent, or 7.26 million, urban households stated that water was not available throughout the year.

In 2007 an estimated 12.0 million urban households, that is one in every six urban households, did not have access to a latrine and therefore defecated in the open. Another 5.48 million used community latrines, and 13.1 million used shared latrines. One in every four households shared a latrine either with other households or with the community. Of the total urban households, 18.5 percent (or 12.5 million) did not have any access to drainage networks, and another 39.8 percent (or 26.8 million households) were connected to open drains. Only 41.7 percent of urban households, about 28.1 million, were connected to closed drains, either underground drains (29.2 percent) or covered drains on the surface. Two in every five households have latrines and bathrooms linked to open drains. In addition, with regard to waste management, only about 58 percent of the households have municipal garbage collection.[38]

The goal of providing housing and basic services to a large segment of India's urban population is still a distant reality. In select cities, JNNURM attempts to address some of these problems, but with inadequate funding. Meanwhile, cities have begun moving in their own directions, facilitated by public policies encouraging enclave developments, gated communities, and SEZs. These initiatives are changing the face of select segment(s) of cities, infusing capital investment, and encouraging selective growth.

Segmented City Forms

Friedmann and Wolff were the first to recognize the emergence of city segmentation in a globally linked city, what they called the World City. With the increasing inequality in cities, the rich began to live in isolated, enclosed, protected, and insulated neighborhoods, which Friedmann and Wolff call citadels. Such citadels first emerged amidst cities in the developed world, including La Défense in Paris and Battery Park in New York.[39] Citadels were also soon extended to cities in the developing economies.

In the developing world, the contrast between the very rich and the poor is starker than in developed countries. In the latter, while citadels for the rich emerge, poor tend to live in highly concentrated and segregated slums or ghettos. Relative segmentation of cities has been recently recognized in India. Marcuse and Kempen state that the new urban form in cities that have globalized include areas considered enclaves of the rich, the representatives of an extremely mobile upper class operating at the global level and living in exclusionary enclaves or citadels; gentrified areas of the professionals along with pockets of the poor; ethnic enclaves or minority enclaves (such as China towns, Latino towns, and African American communities in North American cities) or Muslim ghettos in Indian cities; and a new type of ghetto inhabited by the urban poor, fully and long-term excluded groups at the bottom of social stratification.[40]

In Mumbai, starting from the mid-1960s, every slum demolition in the city shifted the slum dwelling population out to the inaccessible parts of the eastern suburbs and exurbs.[41] Mumbai thus maintains a concentration of slums in its eastern suburbs. In the last decade, all the small housing units, each at 225 square feet (21 square meters) in size, which were constructed for rehabilitating slum dwellers evicted by the new developments, have been located in the eastern suburbs.[42]

Similar patterns of segmentation are also evident in Bangalore. North and west segments of Bangalore are industrial areas with housing for industrial workers. About 30 percent of the male workers in the city were employed in manufacturing in 1999–2000, and less than 5 percent of the male workers were employed in information technology (IT) and computer services.[43] Bangalore has an image as the Silicon Valley of India. But the new economy, as the IT related economic activities are called, is located in the eastern and the southern parts of Bangalore, near the airport. The high-end residential areas, housing those employed in the new economy, are also located in these parts of the city. Thus, the eastern and southern parts of Bangalore have emerged as exclusive enclaves, and the occupants of these parts of the city have very little or no contact with other Bangalore residents. In addition, parts of the northern industrial areas are being converted into IT enclaves with the support of the state government's industrial development agency, which is facilitating the transfer of lands to these new enclave developments.[44] The proposed international airport of Bangalore is also to be located in North Bangalore, with the necessary land already acquired from local farmers.

In Ahmedabad, the seventh largest metropolitan city and one of the richest urban governments in India, the western part of the city has been the focus of capital investment and globalized economic activities. The eastern part of the city, on the other hand, is industrial and has the concentration of the city's slum population.[45]

Ahmedabad City is divided by the Sabarmati River. Immediately to the east of the river is the old city core, which was once a walled city under the Mughal Sultanate.[46] At the end of the nineteenth century, cotton textile industries came up to the east of the walled city, and the emerging middle and upper classes began to move west, across the river. Bridges were built, and the western parts of the city emerged as mainly residential. The university and all the academic institutions are located in western Ahmedabad. Over the past century, the city's segmentation has continued following these patterns of development. It is the western periphery of the city that maintains all the commercial malls, expensive gated residential communities, and new proposed enclaves of high-end real estate development. It is here that the Ahmedabad Urban Development Authority (a planning and development authority for the peri-urban areas of the city) has concentrated its investment in infrastructure.[47] It is in the western periphery that one cannot find a single slum.

In contrast, the eastern parts of Ahmedabad, and its periphery, are characterized by high slum concentrations and severe infrastructure shortages.[48] These parts of Ahmedabad are inundated by every monsoon, and they regularly confront outbreaks of waterborne and vector-borne diseases.

Ahmedabad City has another axis of segmentation, the Muslim Ahmedabad and the non-Muslim Ahmedabad. The Muslim City of Ahmedabad is divided into four parts (two small and two large), whereas there is one Hindu City, or, more precisely, the non-Muslim city where the Hindu, the Jains, the Buddhists, the Christians, and the Sikhs live. About half the Muslim population of Ahmedabad City live in the two large Muslim concentrations, both on the periphery of the city. The first one is in an area named Juhapura, which is in the south and is where 33 percent of the Muslim population of the city live. The other large Muslim enclave is the Dani Limda ward, which is in the southeast part of the city, where 22 percent of the city's total Muslim population live. Both of these enclaves were, in fact, outside the limits of the Ahmedabad municipal government. But, with the expansion of Ahmedabad City in May 2006, they are now within the jurisdiction of this larger urban authority.[49]

The Muslims, displaced due to communal violence in 2002, have resettled in housing colonies in the southeast of Ahmedabad, in localities adjacent to Dani Limda ward and also in the Juhapura area.[50] The living conditions in the Muslim enclaves, particularly in Juhapura and the new developments outside Dani Limda ward, are considered squalid and inhuman. There is a new fear that the physical conditions within these communities, and the hopelessness among its population, encourage Muslim youth from these enclaves to be recruited for terror attacks.[51] More specifically, for the purposes of this chapter, these enclaves reveal that segmentation in Ahmedabad is evident along both socioeconomic and religious lines.

Special Economic Zones

A new form of city segmentation has emerged in the past decade and a half in many Indian cities, evident with the emergence of SEZs and gated communities or enclaves on the urban peripheries. The SEZs—emerging in China to support the dual economic system at the beginning of the nation's economic reforms initiated by Deng Xiaoping in 1978—are now looked at as a model that could promote economic growth while generating manufacturing sector employment in India. The SEZ policy, announced by the government of India, effective from April 1, 2000, is an aggressive policy to attract foreign investment in the manufacturing sector. The policy states that SEZs would provide an internationally competitive and hassle-free environment for production for the purpose of exports. These zones are designated duty-free enclaves and are deemed foreign territories for the purpose of trade operations, duties, and tariffs. A SEZ would typically be a manufacturing enclave, along with residences for a section of employees working in it.[52] The policy offers several fiscal and regulatory incentives to developers of the SEZs, as well as units within these zones. Many individual states in India have also come up with their own specific policies.

There is a long list of upcoming SEZs in the country, and the list is expanding, with new approvals regularly granted by the government of India. According to the Ministry of Commerce,[53] as of April 5, 2007, a total of 234 valid formal approvals for SEZs were granted, of which 63 SEZs were notified and 171 notifications of approved SEZs were pending.[54] Since then, 132 more SEZs have been approved, taking the total number of approved SEZs to 362, of which 136 have been notified.[55]

For instance, in the Mumbai Metropolitan Region (MMR), two large SEZs are to be developed by Reliance Industries. One of these, Navi Mumbai SEZ (NMSEZ), is located in Navi Mumbai (New Mumbai), a government planned and developed city outside of Mumbai intended to take some commercial development pressures from Mumbai city. The other SEZ, Maha Mumbai SEZ (MMSEZ), is located just outside the Navi Mumbai limits but within the MMR. The latter one was initially planned on 33,020 acres (13,363 hectares), but has been given permission to develop on only 12,700 acres (5,140 hectares). The size of the MMSEZ has been reduced because of the resistance to land acquisition by the local community. The NMSEZ contains within its boundaries the site of the proposed new international airport and the existing port of Mumbai, Jawaharlal Nehru Port (JNP), the largest port on the west coast of India. NMSEZ is spread over an area of 19.31 square miles (50 square kilometers), taking up about 14.5 percent of the area of Navi Mumbai. The NMSEZ would have independent townships within it, which would be developed by the private sector.[56]

The earlier SEZs have been set up on lands acquired by the government using land acquisition legislation. The state governments have acquired lands from farmers for the purpose of setting up SEZs, so that the industry gets access to large tracts of assembled and cheap land. As mentioned in the context of MMSEZ, and true for many other SEZ projects, farmers have resisted land acquisition, and sometimes the struggles end in violence, injuries, and deaths.[57] In some instances the government itself realized that the SEZ developers were engaging more in real estate development than manufacturing. Because of these occurrences, the national government, which is the authority sanctioning the SEZs, has devised a new set of rules, which include banning trading companies to be set up in the SEZs; requiring SEZs to be set up only on wastelands; and limiting SEZs to 12,355 acres (5,000 hectares).[58] The government is now also encouraging the private sector to purchase land directly from the farmers, as opposed to the government itself acquiring and assembling lands on their behalf.

Township Policies, New Towns, and Hi-Tech Zones

Since 2005 a number of state governments have made their own township policies after the government of India's decision to liberalize FDI norms in the construction sector. In the past, only nonresident Indians and people of Indian origin were allowed to invest in the housing and real estate sectors. Foreign investors other than nonresident Indians were allowed to invest only in the development of integrated townships and settlements either through a wholly-owned subsidiary or through a joint venture with a local partner. Through a notification in 2005, the Indian government has opened the real estate sector to 100 percent FDI in townships, built-up infrastructure, housing, and construction projects, which include housing, commercial premises, hotels, resorts, hospitals, educational institutions, recreational facilities, and city and regional level infrastructure projects.[59]

Each state has passed its own township policy. For example, Karnataka state's township policy has approved new towns in the 25 miles (40 kilometers) range of Bangalore. These would be well-planned and self-contained townships with civic amenities, commercial spaces, and residential land uses within the planned areas. The expected area of the five townships includes Bidadi, on 9,422 acres (3,813 hectares); Ramanagaram, on 3,991 acres (1,615 hectares); Sathanur, on 15,790 acres (6,390 hectares); Solur, on 12,185 acres (4,931 hectares); and Nandagudi, on 18,004 acres (7,286 hectares). The expected investment for these projects is around 300 billion rupees (US$7.38 billion). These are expected to house the IT and ITES (IT enabled services) companies. At least for Bidadi township, Karnataka Industrial Area Development Board (KIADB), a public agency, has acquired the lands from local farmers.[60] For the other townships it is not yet known whether lands would be privately acquired or whether public agency intervention will be sought.

Gujarat state has come up with an aggressive township policy for new towns between 25 acres (with minimum 200 million rupees, or US$4.92 million investment) and 200 acres (with 1,600 million rupees, or US$39.36 million investment).[61] The permitted uses in the new townships are residential, commercial, education, and health. It is expected that upper-income groups will find housing in the new townships.

One such township, named Shantigram, is to come up on 494 acres (200 hectares) of land just 5 miles (8 kilometers) outside of Ahmedabad. It will be developed by two local private business houses, one engaged in textile manufacturing and the other in a variety of businesses (including port development, airport development, and electricity production). Both the business houses also run their own real estate companies, which will construct this new township. This is to be an integrated township and will include apartments, individual bungalows, shopping malls, hospitals, two schools, two higher education institutions, offices, and entertainment complexes (including a civic center, a golf course, a cricket ground, and a recreation club with facilities, hotels, and restaurants). It will also include a 51 acres (20 hectare) IT/ITES SEZ. The total investment in the project is expected to be more than 45 billion rupees (US $1.11 billion).[62]

Another township, Venus Metropolis, is made up of 356 acres of land (144 hectares) just outside the new boundary of Ahmedabad. The project is to include an integrated development of bungalows, apartments, a hospital, schools, a college, and two hotels. It is to be designed by a foreign architecture firm, which has not yet been selected. In addition, two more townships, Sun Divine and DLF Township, are coming up in the vicinity of Shantigram and Venus Metropolis.[63]

In addition to new towns, many cities in India are developing hi-tech zones in their peripheries. One such IT enclave, Cyberabad, is 20.46 square miles (53 square kilometers), located outside the existing twin cities of Hyderabad-Secunderabad in the state of Andhra Pradesh. This new township has its own development authority and is not part of the Hyderabad-Secunderabad local government. The township includes the earlier setup of Hi-Tech City on 165 acres (67 hectares), an International School of Business, an Indian Institute of Information Technology, University of Hyderabad, a golf course, a sports complex, a lake, and a large number of IT companies.[64]

Similarly, outside Pune City, the eighth largest metropolitan center in India, which is rapidly emerging as India's IT city, two townships have been developed (one by the public sector and one by the private sector). The one developed by the private sector, Magarpatta City,[65] consists of 376 acres (152 hectares) and is located within the limits of the Pune municipal government. It has dedicated IT buildings, residential apartments, a school, a hospital, and various other leisure commercial spaces. In addition, about 30 percent of the space is being developed as green space.[66] The public sector development is called Rajiv Gandhi Infotech Park. Upon the completion of six phases of the park (as of now two are complete and land acquisition for the third has begun),[67] the total park area will be 5,948.4 acres (2,407.2 hectares).[68]

Gated Communities

Among the newly emerging exclusive developments in India are gated communities, the exclusive domains of urban elites in metropolitan India.[69] Typically enclaves where entry is restricted, these housing communities are surrounded by high walls capped with barbed wire fences. The gatekeepers belong to private security agencies. The communities set their own rules and meet the expenditures of security and property management. Throughout metropolitan centers in India, upper income groups are increasingly living in gated communities. Even in some of the older, upper-income housing developments, which were built traditionally and open to the larger city, walls and gates are being constructed for the purpose of security and exclusiveness.

It is not only that these communities have developed new forms of exclusiveness, but also that they have fundamentally altered traditional relationships that have facilitated access to basic amenities. For instance, given the extent of basic service deprivations, those without access to water traditionally depended on water facilities available in the housing of middle and upper income groups. Walls and gates end this dependency of the have-nots on the haves for access to basic facilities, such as water supply, facilitating even greater urban stresses among the absolute poor.

The Aryaman Housing Development

Ahmedabad is located in the state of Gujarat, in the western part of India that borders Pakistan. Gujarat is the second most industrialized and the fourth most urbanized state in India. In 2001, for instance, 37 percent of the state's population lived in urban areas, while India's urbanization level was only 27.5 percent. The state also maintains the fourth position in per capita income among the eighteen large states in India, a position it has held since the early 1990s. With this growing wealth, Gujarat is a state in which population segments are interested in high-end real estate. In addition, housing developments in the region are expected to attract the Gujarati community living in North America and the United Kingdom.[70]

In 2001 the population of the Ahmedabad Urban Agglomeration (AUA) was 4.52 million, making it the seventh largest metropolitan city in India. The population of the Ahmedabad Municipal Corporation (AMC) was 3.52 million in the same year, indicating that some 1 million people in the AUA were living in peri-urban areas. Given the outward population growth, in May 2006 the state government expanded the AMC boundary from 76.45 to 193.05 square miles (from 198 to 500 square kilometers),[71] thus amalgamating not only the peri-urban areas but also areas with potential urban use. The gated community Aryaman is located within the expanded limits of the AMC, but when this project was announced in 2006, the development was outside the AMC limits.

Figure 3 shows the location of new gated communities on the periphery of Ahmedabad City. To understand the significance of such developments, it is necessary to understand the planning system of the city. Urban planning is maintained through a system of town planning schemes. The development plan lays out broad zoning. The trunk infrastructure, including the road networks,

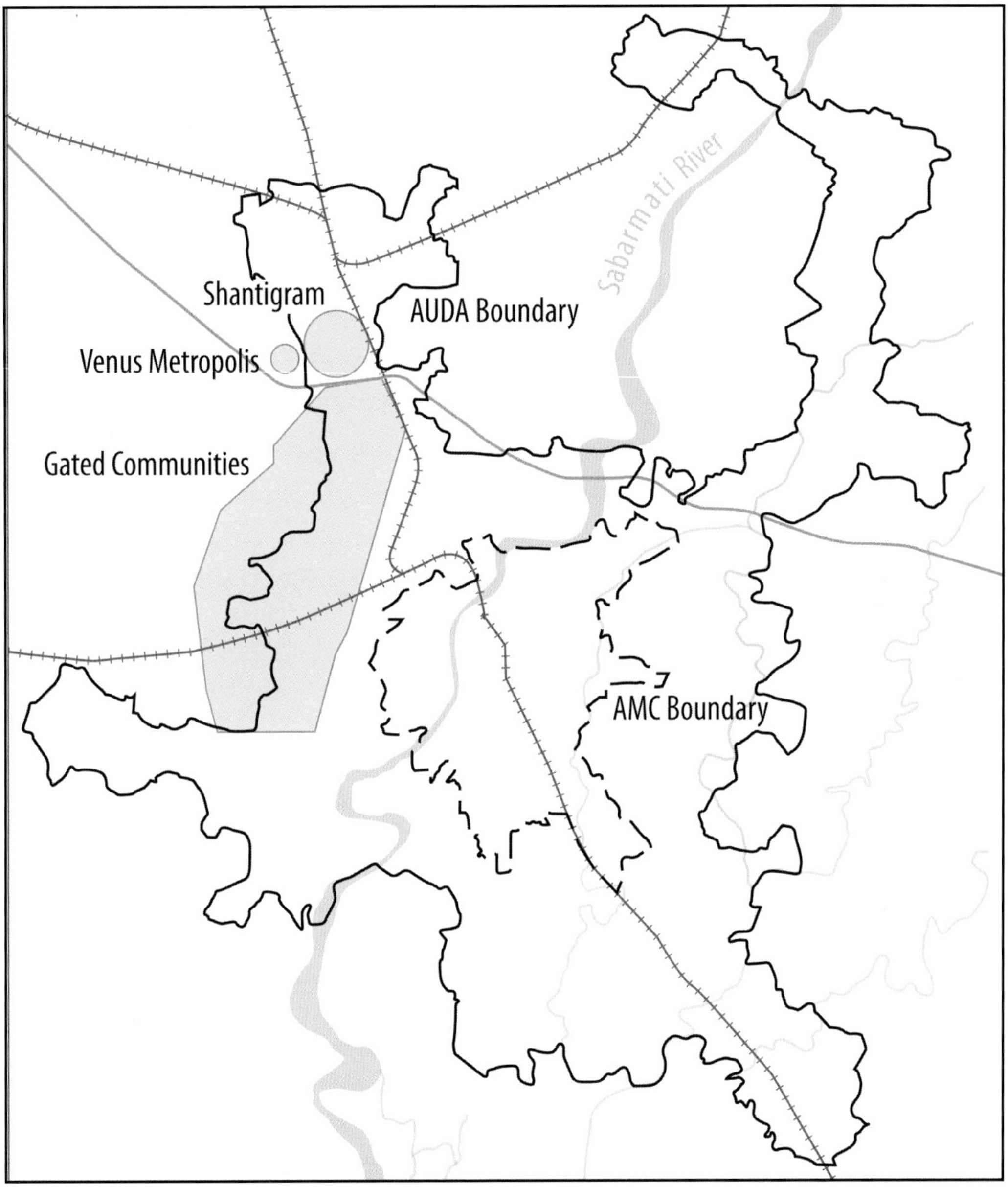

Figure 3. Map of Ahmedabad, with the location of a few enclaves.

are planned and laid out by the planning authority. The AMC carries out planning and development within its jurisdiction. For the peri-urban areas, a separate body, the Ahmedabad Urban Development Authority (AUDA), maintains authority. The AUDA demarcates the boundary within which it carries out its planning. Aryaman was located within the AUDA's planning limits when the project was announced in 2006.

According to development control regulations of AUDA's development plan, the areas within the AMC limits have a permissible FSI of at least 1.0 in residential zones for plots up to 10,764

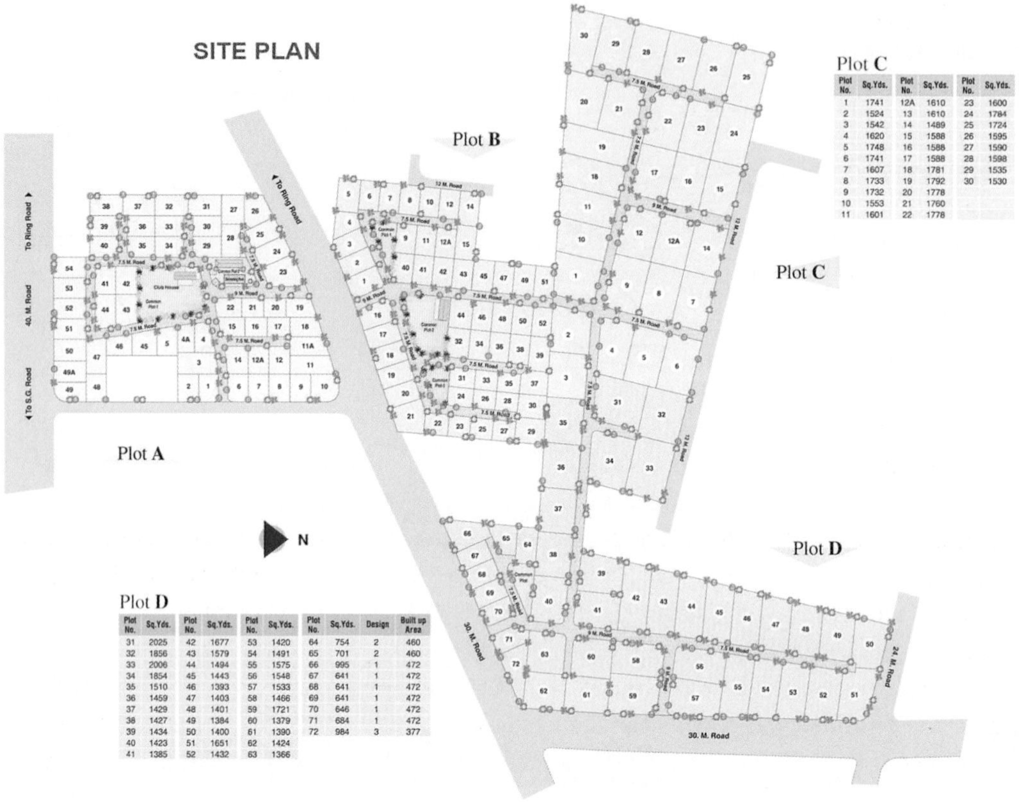

Plot C

Plot No.	Sq.Yds.	Plot No.	Sq.Yds.	Plot No.	Sq.Yds.
1	1741	12A	1610	23	1600
2	1524	13	1610	24	1784
3	1542	14	1489	25	1724
4	1620	15	1588	26	1595
5	1748	16	1588	27	1590
6	1741	17	1588	28	1598
7	1607	18	1781	29	1535
8	1733	19	1792	30	1530
9	1732	20	1778		
10	1553	21	1760		
11	1601	22	1778		

Plot D

Plot No.	Sq.Yds.	Plot No.	Sq.Yds.	Plot No.	Sq.Yds.	Plot No.	Sq.Yds.	Design	Built up Area
31	2025	42	1677	53	1420	64	754	2	460
32	1856	43	1579	54	1491	65	701	2	460
33	2006	44	1494	55	1575	66	995	1	472
34	1854	45	1443	56	1548	67	641	1	472
35	1510	46	1393	57	1533	68	641	1	472
36	1459	47	1403	58	1466	69	641	1	472
37	1429	48	1401	59	1721	70	646	1	472
38	1427	49	1384	60	1379	71	684	1	472
39	1434	50	1400	61	1390	72	984	3	377
40	1423	51	1651	62	1424				
41	1385	52	1432	63	1366				

Figure 4. Site map of Aryaman.

square feet (1,000 square meters) and more than 1.0 in commercial zones. In AUDA's development plan, two FSIs are permissible: 1.2 FSI (called residential type 2—R2 development) and 0.40 FSI (called R3 type development). Thus, Aryaman, being in AUDA and granted development permission by AUDA, has been planned with R2 and R3 types of development, ensuring that the peri-urban areas around Ahmedabad, coming under the planning jurisdiction of AUDA, develop as low density residential developments.

Aryaman is planned on twenty-five acres of land on a site located 4.4 miles (7 kilometers) to the west of the former boundary of the AMC.[72] It is a gated community that is still under construction, but it is planned to be occupied by the end of 2008. With the extensive road network planned by the AUDA on the western periphery of the city,[73] it does not take more than ten minutes to reach the site from the former boundary of the city. The scheme is planned for 154 individual villas, called bungalows in Ahmedabad, each having a private yard. Thus, each dwelling unit would be located on a separate land parcel, which measures between 4,500 square feet (418 square meters) to 16,200 square feet (1,505 square meters), and each bungalow maintains areas of 2,520–4,950 square feet (234–460 square meters), as per the permissible FSI on the plot. Figure 4 gives the site plan of the scheme.

An advertisement for the gated colony describes the new project:

> . . . beyond the horizon of densely urbanized city of Ahmedabad . . . Located at a crow-flying distance of 10 kilometers west from the commercial hub of S.G. Road. A unique residential community in the midst of green farm lands in the neighbourhood of this mega city. Self sustained, secured and yet serene. . . . . To make the entire community into one of the most coveted addresses of future Ahmedabad.

The community services in this development would include: 24 hours water supply of 2,000 litres per day for private garden and domestic requirement and adequate drainage connection; an artificial lake, a large swimming pool, a restaurant, a mini golf and cricket ground, all weather synthetic turf tennis court, a private and secured jogging track of more than 2.5 miles (4 kms), a community dump yard, a community nursery for plants and vegetation, and many other facilities.[74]

There are four sections in the development, marked as Plots A, B, C, and D in figure 4. Their irregular size is a result of piecemeal purchases of land from individual farmers, which are then consolidated for the development. It is for this reason that with large townships and SEZs, developers insist that the government should acquire lands from individual farmers. It can also be seen in figure 4 that some pockets of lands are not being developed. These land owners did not give up their lands to the developer, with some proceeding with their own construction and others holding out to get a better price for the land.

The project has fifty-six house plots in section A and twenty-six house plots in section B. Both these sections have land plots of less than 4,500 square feet (418 square meters), with dwelling units of no more than 3,150 square feet (293 square meters) (see table 2). Sections C and D are for larger plots, each measuring between 12,600–16,200 square feet (1,171–1,505 square meters), and are to be constructed as R3 development types. The units will measure about 4,500–4,950 square feet (418–460 square meters). There are thirty house plots in section C and forty-two house plots in section D.[75]

For houses in sections A and B, three house design types are suitable. Figures 5, 6, 7, and 10 are for houses in sections A and B. For houses in sections C and D, which are larger homes, eight house design types are offered by the developer. Figures 8 and 9 show structures in section C.[76] The individual structures have to keep the façade options suggested by the architect for the purpose of visual harmony.

Plot A has two entrances, both of which have gates with at least one guard. Plots B, C, and D can share three entrances, each one with a gate and at least one guard. All entry into the community is monitored at the gate, and visitors are admitted only by invitation of a homeowner, prohibiting informal sector vendors and service providers to gain entry into the project.

Table 2. Plot details, Aryaman

PLOT TYPE	NUMBER OF UNITS	DEVELOPMENT TYPE	FSI PERMITTED
A	56	R2	1.2
B	26	R2	1.2
C	30	R3	0.4
D	42	R3	0.4

PHOTOGRAPH BY DARSHINI MAHADEVIA

Figure 5. Entrance to a gated community, Aryaman, Ahmedabad.

PHOTOGRAPH BY DARSHINI MAHADEVIA

Figure 6. Internal roads in Aryaman.

PHOTOGRAPH BY DARSHINI MAHADEVIA

Figure 7. Villa in Aryaman.

PHOTOGRAPH BY DARSHINI MAHADEVIA

Figure 8. Common facility in Aryaman.

PHOTOGRAPH BY DARSHINI MAHADEVIA

Figure 9. Row of villas in Aryaman.

PHOTOGRAPH BY DARSHINI MAHADEVIA

Figure 10. Workers' housing outside a gated community, Aryaman.

With a low permissible FSI, the development has been planned so that 77 percent of its total land will remain open, with sprawling green lawns, ponds, community spaces, and roads. Among the common facilities, Aryaman has a clubhouse (advertised as "ultra modern"), a swimming pool, a health club, and 0.64 miles (1 kilometer) of private walking track. There is a party cottage to host gatherings for up to forty persons, a state-of the-art home theater, a large pantry, and an exclusive garden.

The gated community will be maintained by a private real estate management company. Each member of the community has given a deposit, an amount based on the size of the purchased lot. In addition, each member pays annual maintenance fees to the management company, who in turn manages the entire estate and takes care of all the maintenance and repairs within each house.

Aryaman has its own water supply through groundwater well access. Negotiations are under way to get water from the Narmada Project canal, some 6.25 miles (10 kilometers) away from the community. In a water scarce region, the community has promised twenty-four-hour water supply.[77] Trunk drainage lines have not been built outside the site of Aryaman, so the project will have common soak-pits for sewerage disposal. Each individual house will have their sewerage lines connected to an on-site network of sewerage, which for the time being will connect to a soak-pit. Once the trunk networks are built outside the project, the community's lines will be connected to the main trunk network.

In contrast, in the city a quarter of the population is living in slums, for which about 1.45–1.81 square miles (3.75–4.7 square kilometers) of land would be required for rehabilitation and the provision of housing, meaning that the 25 acres of Aryaman, which will house only 154 households, could house some 2–3 percent of Ahmedabad's urban poor. Thus, if the slum dwellers were to be housed on this piece of land, about 5,300 to 6,600 of Ahmedabad's poor could be housed on the site.

With regard to service provision, the norm for urban water supply in the state of Gujarat is about 39.6 gallons per capita per day (gpcd), or about 150 liters per capita per day (lpcd). Average water supply in Ahmedabad City is 37.8 gpcd (143 lpcd), slightly less than the state average.[78] However, only 36.4 percent of households in Ahmedabad have individual water connections.[79] In other metropolitan cities in Gujarat, the water supply situation is not any better. For example, Surat, the second largest city in the state, provides only 39.4 gpcd (149 lpcd) of water and only 37.1 percent of the population has individual water supply.

Furthermore, the water supply duration is also very low. Ahmedabad, on average, provides water for 2.5 hours per day and Surat for 3 hours per day. Hence, water has to be stored. Those who are able to store water are able to use more water, and those unable to do so have to make do with very low water use. In some Ahmedabad slums, average water use has been recorded at 1.3 gpcd (5 lpcd), and on an average, water use in slums is 2.1 gpcd (8 lpcd). Private gated communities in Ahmedabad, on the other hand, can have access to as much as 528 gallons (2,000 liters) of water per household per day, which amounts to 106–132 gpcd (400–500 lpcd) for a family of four or five.[80]

Conclusion

One outcome of India's globalization, urban transformation, and rapid growth—promoted by state policy—has involved land diversion for SEZs, townships, and gated communities, combined with the increasing exclusion and marginalization of slum communities. In addition, nationally, despite the NUHHP and the JNNURM, the unmet basic service and housing agenda remains large, and if the trajectory of the past decade continues, it will get even larger. The absolute poor living in India's slums are clearly not benefiting from the new emerging economy or the new development processes. Given the growing interest in the displacement of slums, and the greater levels of segmentation and enclavization, the absolute poor are increasingly being marginalized in India's society.

Furthermore, currently in India, while not explicitly framed within an urban sustainability agenda, urban-environmental stresses are being pursued through environmental management programs, albeit in a fragmented manner across the country. Urban development also continues to be viewed as an economic growth strategy, separate from environmental management initiatives. It is thus in multiple ways that cities in India are moving further away from the concept of the inclusive sustainable city.

Following wider national trends, growing exclusiveness is also evident in Ahmedabad, not only in the exclusionary policies that have increasingly dismissed the basic needs of the urban poor, but also in the emergence and diffusion of enclaves and gated communities throughout the metropolitan area. There have been some successful slum development schemes in Ahmedabad. One of them is an innovative partnership program called the Slum Networking Program (SNP), which has received international acclaim for its partnership between local government, the community, a nongovernmental organization, and the private sector in the initial projects. But, the pace of the SNP implementation has been so slow that it might take more than 100 years to reach out to the entire slum population.[81] Just twenty to twenty-five slums were upgraded by 2006, after which the Ahmedabad Municipal Corporation did not promote any new projects.[82]

In India, the action agenda for sustainable cities will remain, securing housing rights; provision and access to civic amenities; a clean, safe, and healthy living environment for all; adequate provision and access to public health facilities, basic education, safe and sufficient drinking water, and food security; freedom from violence and intimidation on the basis of social identity; sustainable livelihoods; and adequate and appropriate social security.[83] However, Indian cities are moving away from inclusive growth, the slogan of the incumbent national government, and inclusive sustainable development, which should be the conceptual framework for the development of India's cities.

NOTES

1. Darshini Mahadevia, Tall Claims and Sluggish Progress—Affordable Housing for All in UPA Regime, in *The People's Verdict—4th Civil Society Review of the National Common Minimum Programme*, ed. Wada Na Todo Abhiyan (New Delhi: Wada Na Todo Abhiyan, 2008), 7–11, http://www.wadanatodo.net/reports/download/250608/The%20People's%20Verdict_4th%20Civil%20

Society%20Review%20of%20the%20NCMP.pdf.

2. Darshini Mahadevia, *Globalisation, Urban Reforms and Metropolitan Response: India* (Delhi: Manak, 2003); K. C. Sivramakrishnan, Amitabh Kundu, and B. N. Singh, *Handbook of Urbanization in India: An Analysis of Trends and Processes* (New Delhi: Oxford University Press, 2005).
3. United Nations Population Fund, *State of World Population, 2007—Unleashing the Potential of Urban Growth* (New York: UNFPA, 2007), 1.
4. Jane Jacobs, *Cities and Wealth of Nations* (New York: Random House, 1984).
5. Anthony Gar-on Yeh and X. Xueqiang, Globalization and the Urban System in China, in *Emerging World Cities in Pacific Asia*, ed. Fu-chen Lo and Yue-man Yeung (New York: United Nations University Press, 1996, http://www.unu.edu/unupress/unupbooks/.
6. For details and critique of the program see Darshini Mahadevia, NURM and the Poor in Globalising Mega Cities, *Economic and Political Weekly* 41:31 (August 5, 2006): 3399–403.
7. Conversion rate as of September 10, 2007.
8. Darshini Mahadevia, House That for the *Aam Aadmi? Indian Express*, September 11, 2007, http://www.indianexpress.com/story/215596.html.
9. From Economic Survey, 2007–2008 of Government of India, http://indiabudget.nic.in/es2007–08/esmain.htm.
10. National Sample Survey Organisation, Employment and Unemployment Situation in India, 2004–05 (Part I), NSS 61st Round (July 2004–June 2005), Report No. 515 (61/10/1), Ministry of Statistics and Programme Implementation, Government of India, New Delhi, September 2006.
11. In the Indian federal structure, enshrined in the Indian constitution, there are certain responsibilities allocated to the central government, such as defense, communications, railways, etc., whereas land, water, and forest resources are under the jurisdiction of the state government. Hence, all land related policies are made by the state government. Urban development is also a state government subject.
12. In acquiring the land, there have been instances where the government has actually paid below market prices. There were also cases where farmers were able to negotiate prices that were more reflective of market value. The price paid to the farmers depends on a number of conditions, with the critical one being the ability of the farmers selling the land to organize and hold off on selling until they get better prices.
13. The ULCRA 1976 was introduced to socialize urban lands and make lands available to the local and state government for housing the urban poor.
14. Mahadevia, NURM and the Poor in Globalising Mega Cities.
15. Illustrated by Mahadevia (2009); Lalit Batra and Diya Mehra, Slum Demolitions and Production of Neo-liberal Space: Delhi, in *Inside the Transforming Urban Asia: Policies, Processes and Public Actions*, ed. Darshini Mahadevia (New Delhi: Concept, 2008), 391–414.
16. This is from the brochure of JNNURM, titled Towards Better Cities, Government of India: Ministry of Urban Employment and Poverty Alleviation and Ministry of Urban Development.
17. Ministry of Housing and Urban Poverty Alleviation, *National Urban Housing and Habitat Policy, 2007* (New Delhi: Government of India, 2007).
18. Ibid., 5.
19. Ibid., 7–8.
20. Open ground.
21. Ministry of Housing and Urban Poverty Alleviation, *National Urban Housing and Habitat Policy, 2007*, 8.
22. Ibid., 30.
23. Middle class citizens groups filed a litigation in the Delhi High Court stating that the Delhi Development Authority (DDA) had abdicated its responsibility of implementing the provisions of the master plan and allowed all forms of "illegal" developments—illegal in the sense that they violated the provisions of the master plan.
24. This decision can be construed as an environmental agenda for sustainable cities.
25. Veronique Dupont and Usha Ramanathan, The Courts and the Squatter Settlement in Delhi—Or the Intervention of the Judiciary in Urban Governance. Paper presented at the IDPAD seminar on New Forms of Urban Governance in Indian Mega-Cities, held at Jawaharlal Nehru University, New Delhi, January 10–11, 2005.
26. Ministry of Environment & Forests. *Annual Report. 2009-10* (New Delhi: Government of India). http://www.envfor.nic.in/report/report.html.
27. Darshini Mahadevia and Jeanne Wolfe, ed., *Solid Waste Management in Indian Cities: Status and Emerging Practices* (New Delhi: Concept, 2008).
28. Madhav G. Badami, Geetam Tiwari, and Dinesh Mohan, Access and Mobility for the Urban Poor in India, in *The Inclusive City—Infrastructure and Public Services for the Urban Poor in Asia*, ed. A. A. Laquian, V. Tewari, and L. M. Hanley (Washington, DC: Woodrow Wilson Center Press, 2007), 100–21.
29. Darshini Mahadevia, Sustainable Urban Development in India: An Inclusive Perspective, *Development in Practice*, 11:2/3 (2001): 242–59.

30. Ibid.
31. Ibid.; "Inclusive Growth" is the title and the theme of the Eleventh National Five Year Plan.
32. Office of the Registrar General and Census Commissioner, Slum Population, Series-1, Census of India, 2001 (New Delhi: Office of the Registrar General and Census Commissioner, India, 2005), 21; Mahadevia, Urban Land Market and Access of Poor.
33. FSI is the area of permissible built up area on a plot of land divided by the area of the plot of land. Built up on a plot of land can be two times the plot area. Thus, if the plot area is 1,000 square feet and FSI is 2, then a building with 2,000 square feet can be built on it (Mahadevia, Urban Land Market and Access of the Poor).
34. Mahadevia, Tall Claims and Sluggish Progress, 7–11.
35. Estimates on the number of homes demolished vary between 88,000 and 95,000 homes. Indian People's Tribunal on Environment and Human Rights—IPTEHR, Bulldozing Rights—A Report on the Forced Evictions and Housing Policies for the Poor in Mumbai (Mumbai: IPTEHR, 2005), 10.
36. Batra and Mehra, Slum Demolitions and Production of Neo-liberal Space, 391–414; personal communication, Indu Prakash Singh of Action Aid, India; Darshini Mahadevia and Harini Narayanan, Shanghaing Mumbai: Politics of Evictions and Resistance in Slum Settlements, in *Inside the Transforming Urban Asia: Processes, Policies and Public Actions*, ed. Darshini Mahadevia (New Delhi: Concept, 2008), 549–89.
37. This figure is calculated using the 2007 National Urban Housing and Habitat Policy (NUHHP) estimate of 67.4 million as total urban households in 2007. All the statistics in this paragraph and the next one are from National Sample Survey Organisation, Housing Condition in India—Housing Stock and Constructions, NSS 58th Round (July 2002–December 2002), Report No. 488 (58/1.2/1), Ministry of Statistics and Programme Implementation, Government of India, New Delhi, March, 2004.
38. Ibid.
39. John Friedmann and G. Wolff, World City Formation, *International Journal of Urban and Regional Research* 6 (1982): 306–44; Peter Marcuse and Ronald van Kempen, Introduction, in *Globalizing Cities—A New Spatial Order?* ed. Peter Marcuse and Ronald van Kempen (Oxford: Blackwell, 2000), 13.
40. Darshini Mahadevia, State Supported Segmentation of Mumbai: Policy Options in the Global Economy, *Review of Development and Change* 3:1 (1998); Mahadevia and Narayanan, Slumbay to Shanghai: Envisioning Renewal or Take Over? in *Inside the Transforming Urban Asia: Processes, Policies and Public Actions*, ed. Darshini Mahadevia (New Delhi: Concept, 2008), 94–131; Mahadevia and Narayanan, Shanghaing Mumbai, 549–89; Darshini Mahadevia and Harpreet Singh Brar, Changes and Continuities in Development Priorities, in *Inside the Transforming Urban Asia: Processes, Policies and Public Actions*, ed. Darshini Mahadevia (New Delhi: Concept, 2008), 132–67; Peter Marcuse and Ronald van Kempen, "Introduction," in *Globalizing Cities—A New Spatial Order?* ed. Peter Marcuse and Ronald van Kempen (Oxford: Blackwell, 2000), 4; for Ahmedabad, see Darshini Mahadevia, A City with Many Borders—Beyond Ghettoisation in Ahmedabad, in *Indian Cities in Transition*, ed. Annapurna Shaw (Hyderabad: Orient Longman, 2007), 315–40.
41. Mahadevia and Narayanan, Shanghaing Mumbai, 549–89.
42. Mahadevia and Narayanan, Slumbay to Shanghai, 94–131.
43. Darshini Mahadevia, Metropolitan Employment in India, in *Inside the Transforming Urban Asia: Policies, Processes and Public Actions*, ed. Darshini Mahadevia (New Delhi: Concept, 2008), 56–93.
44. "KIADB Gives Away Land for a Song," an article in the *Hindu*, August 19, 2007, states that seventy-eight acres of land valued at 4,000 million rupees was given away at just 392.7 million rupees for an IT park by the Karnataka Industrial Area Development Board (KIADB), a land acquisition and development agency of the state government of Karnataka state (http://www.hindu.com/2007/08/19/stories/2007081950400100.htm); Solomon Benjamin, Inclusive or Contested? Conceptualising a Globalised Bangalore, in *Inside the Transforming Urban Asia: Policies, Processes and Public Actions*, ed. Darshini Mahadevia (New Delhi: Concept, 2008), 170–93; Solomon Benjamin, R. Bhuvaneswari, P. Rajan, and Manjunath, "Fractured" Terrain, Spaces Left Over, or Contested?—A Closer Look at the IT-Dominated Territories in East and South Bangalore, in *Inside the Transforming Urban Asia: Policies, Processes and Public Actions*, ed. Darshini Mahadevia (New Delhi: Concept, 2008), 239–85.
45. Darshini Mahadevia, Interventions in Development: A Shift towards a Model of Exclusion, in *Poverty and Vulnerability in a Globalising Metropolis: Ahmedabad*, ed. Amitabh Kundu and Darshini Mahadevia (Delhi: Manak, 2002), 80–13; Darshini Mahadevia, Changing Economic Scenario: Informalisation and Increased Vulnerability, in *Poverty and Vulnerability in a Globalising*

Metropolis: Ahmedabad, ed. Amitabh Kundu and Darshini Mahadevia (Delhi: Manak, 2002), 30–79; Mahadevia and Singh Brar, Changes and Continuities in Development Priorities.

46. Mahadevia, Changing Economic Scenario, 30–79.
47. Mahadevia and Singh Brar, Changes and Continuities in Development Priorities, 132–167.
48. Mahadevia, Changing Economic Scenario, 30–79.
49. Mahadevia, A City with Many Borders, 315–40; Mahadevia, Changing Economic Scenario, 30–79.
50. Mahadevia, A City with Many Borders, 315–40.
51. The article calls them ghettos. This article appeared in *DNA* (Ahmedabad) on September 10, 2008, http://epaper.dnaindia.com/dnaahmedabad/epapermain.aspx?queryed=5&username=&useremailid=&pareneditioncode=5&eddate=9/10/2008 (accessed on September 10, 2008).
52. In Indian context, every new economic activity attracts an informal sector. Outside industrial townships, one finds growth of informal settlements. Hence, all those connected to an SEZ may not find a place to stay in the SEZ.
53. As per the *Fact Sheet on Special Economic Zones*, on the website of Ministry of External Affairs, developed by Federation of Industry and Commerce India (FICCI) and BISNET, 100 SEZs have been notified so far. (http://www.indiainbusiness.nic.in/industry-infrastructure/infrastructure/sez.htm).
54. Ibid.
55. BOA clears two SEZs of Infosys, In *Hindu*, August 9, 2007, http://www.hindu.com/2007/08/09/stories/2007080962182100.htm.
56. Navi Mumbai is a modern township spread over an area of around 350 square kilometers (http://www.navimumbaisez.com/overview.htm); Dionne Bunsha, Zone of Conflict, *Frontline* 23:12 (2006), www.hinduonnet.com/fline/fl2312/stories/20060630003711300.htm; http://www.hindu.com/2007/08/09/stories/2007080962182100.htm.
57. For details of the farmers' resistance in one article, see Rural Resistance, *Frontline* 23:20 (October 7–20, 2006), http://www.frontlineonnet.com/stories/20061020004700900.htm.
58. SEZ Doors Shut for Trading Units. In *The Economic Times*. July 3, 2006 http://economictimes.indiatimes.com/articleshow/1919918.cms; *Indian Express*, September 27, 2007, http://www.indianexpress.com/story/13458.html;
59. Sushma Ramachandran, 100 per cent FDI in Construction Industry through Automatic Route. In *Hindu*, February 25, 2005. http://www.hindu.com/2005/02/25/stories/2005022506990100.htm
60. Swathi Shivanand, BMDA Plans Townships. In *Hindu*, September 8, 2006. http://www.hindu.com/2006/09/08/stories/2006090813140300.htm.
61. Darshini Mahadevia, Mini SEZs through the Backdoor? *Times of India (Ahmedabad)*, December 18, 2006.
62. Ravi Teja, How Ahmedabad Is Changing, *Rediff*, January 6, 2007, http://www.rediff.com/money/2007/jan/06spec.htm.
63. From the website of the company. http://www.99acres.com/customised/newprojects/sunbuilders/.
64. C. Ramachandraiah and Sheela Prasad, The Makeover of Hyderabad—The "Model" IT City? in *High-Tech Urban Spaces—Asian and European Perspectives*, ed. C. Ramachandraiah, A. C. M. (Guus) van Westen and S. Prasad (New Delhi: Manohar, 2008), 293–318.
65. From the website of Magarpatta City. http://www.magarpattacity.com.
66. Mahadevia and Parashar, Dynamics of High Tech Urban Spaces, 341–66.
67. Land acquisition for the third phase has run into trouble with the farmers protesting on the streets, not allowing the government machinery to enter their villages, and firing by the police on the agitators, leading to government firing on the protestors and resulting in two injured protestors (P. Keskar, Mob of 7,000 Fight Police; 5 Officers, 4 Maan Residents Injured, *Indian Express*, March 10, 2006).
68. Mahadevia and Parashar, Dynamics of High Tech Urban Spaces, 341–66.
69. Some Internet articles are available on gated communities. See *The Gated Communities – Now Available in India*. http://urbanplanningblog.com/2007/07/19/gated-communities-now-available-in-india/; *Gated Communities the New Rage*, http://www.hindu.com/2005/01/05/stories/2005010516590300.htm.
70. Indira Hirway and Darshini Mahadevia, *The Gujarat Human Development Report, 2004* (Ahmedabad: Mahatma Gandhi Labour Institute, 2005). After Indian independences, states in India were reconstituted on a linguistic basis. Thus, Gujarat has a Gujarati-speaking population, which in essence has come to be identified as a community over time, in spite of caste and class differences. The term "Gujarati" refers to Gujarati-speaking Indian communities overseas.
71. Mahadevia and Singh Brar, Changes and Continuities in Development Priorities, 132–67.
72. 2.54 acres = 1 hectare. Thus, 1 acre = 0.4 hectares.
73. See Mahadevia and Singh Brar, Changes and

Continuities in Development Priorities, 132–67, for the development activities of AUDA since 2000.

74. From the advertisement brochure of Aryaman Scheme. Announcement of a gated community on agricultural lands outside and to the west of Ahmedabad City. http://www.saumyaconstructions.com/Aantarkshitij.htm.
75. Section C was added to the development after the housing scheme was announced.
76. These two sections of the development have not yet been constructed; hence no pictures are provided.
77. Indira Hirway and Darshini Mahadevia, *The Gujarat Human Development Report, 2004* (Ahmedabad: Mahatma Gandhi Labour Institute, 2005). Narmada is one of the largest and most controversial dam projects in India.
78. Ahmedabad Municipal Corporation and Ahmedabad Urban Development Authority, *City Development Plan Ahmedabad, 2006–2012* (Ahmedabad: AMC and AUDA, 2006).
79. Unless mentioned, data in this paragraph are from Urban Water Supply in Gujarat—Some Issues by Indira Hirway, an unpublished paper presented at the Gujarat Social Forum, held in Ahmedabad in January 2006.
80. From the website of the company. Saumya Constructions, Ahmedabad. http://www.saumyaconstructions.com/Aantarkshitij.htm.
81. For details of the SNP see Shrawan Kumar Acharya, Slum Networking in *Ahmedabad: An Alternate Approach, in Poverty and Vulnerability in a Globalising Metropolis: Ahmedabad*, ed. Amitabh Kundu and Darshini Mahadevia (Delhi: Manak, 2002), 349–372; Shyam Dutta, Partnerships for Urban Poverty Reduction: A Review Experience, in *Poverty and Vulnerability in a Globalising Metropolis: Ahmedabad*, ed. Amitabh Kundu and Darshini Mahadevia (Delhi: Manak, 2002), 237–67; Rajendra Joshi, Integrated Slum Development: Case of Pravinnagar-Guptanagar, in *Poverty and Vulnerability in a Globalising Metropolis: Ahmedabad*, ed. Amitabh Kundu and Darshini Mahadevia (Delhi: Manak, 2002), 268–308; Darshini Mahadevia, Urban Poor's Access to Land and Basic Services: Rhetoric, Reality and Dilemmas, *Nagarlok* 33:1 (2002): 66–85.
82. There are two reasons for the scaling back of the Slum Networking Program. First, under the JNNURM, the AMC has received funds to construct new low-cost housing for the urban poor. Second, the Ahmedabad Municipal Corporation's attention and efforts have been diverted to implementing projects funded under the JNNURM, such as the road widening projects and BRTS.
83. Mahadevia, Sustainable Urban Development in India, 242–59.

REFERENCES

Acharya, Shrawan Kumar. Slum Networking in Ahmedabad: An Alternate Approach. In *Poverty and Vulnerability in a Globalising Metropolis: Ahmedabad*, ed. Amitabh Kundu and Darshini Mahadevia, 349–72. Delhi: Manak, 2002.

Ahmedabad Municipal Corporation and Ahmedabad Urban Development Authority. *City Development Plan Ahmedabad, 2006–2012*. Ahmedabad: AMC and AUDA, 2006.

Badami, Madhav G., Geetam Tiwari, and Dinesh Mohan. Access and Mobility for the Urban Poor in India. In *The Inclusive City—Infrastructure and Public Services for the Urban Poor in Asia*, ed. A. A. Laquian, V. Tewari, and L. M. Hanley, 100–21. Washington, DC: Woodrow Wilson Center Press, 2007.

Batra, Lalit, and Diya Mehra. Slum Demolitions and Production of Neo-liberal Space: Delhi. In *Inside the Transforming Urban Asia: Policies, Processes and Public Actions*, ed. Darshini Mahadevia, 391–414. New Delhi: Concept, 2008.

Benjamin, Solomon, R. Bhuvaneswari, P. Rajan, and Manjunath. "Fractured" Terrain, Spaces Left Over, or Contested?—A Closer Look at the IT-Dominated Territories in East and South Bangalore. In *Inside the Transforming Urban Asia: Policies, Processes and Public Actions*, ed. Darshini Mahadevia, 239–85. New Delhi: Concept, 2008.

Benjamin, Solomon. 2008. Inclusive or Contested? Conceptualising a Globalised Bangalore. In *Inside the Transforming Urban Asia: Policies, Processes and Public Actions*, ed. Darshini Mahadevia, 170–93. New Delhi: Concept, 2008.

Bunsha, Dionne. Zone of Conflict. *Frontline* 23:12 (2006). http://singur-singur.blogspot.com/2007/01/zone-of-conflict.html

Dupont, Veronique, and Usha Ramanathan. The Courts and the Squatter Settlement in Delhi—Or the Intervention of the Judiciary in Urban Governance. Paper presented at the IDPAD seminar on New Forms of Urban Governance in Indian Mega-Cities, held at Jawaharlal Nehru University, New Delhi, January 10–11, 2005.

Dutta, Shyam. Partnerships for Urban Poverty Reduction: A Review Experience. In *Poverty and Vulnerability in a Globalising Metropolis: Ahmedabad*, ed. Amitabh Kundu and Darshini Mahadevia, 237–67. Delhi: Manak, 2002.

Friedmann, John, and G. Wolff. World City Formation. *International Journal of Urban and Regional Research* 6 (1982): 306–44.

Indian People's Tribunal on Environment and Human Rights—IPTEHR. *Bulldozing Rights—A report on the forced evictions and housing policies for the poor in Mumbai.* Mumbai: IPTEHR, 2005.

Hirway, Indira, and Darshini Mahadevia. *The Gujarat Human Development Report, 2004.* Ahmedabad: Mahatma Gandhi Labour Institute, 2005.

Jacobs, Jane. *Cities and Wealth of Nations.* New York: Random House, 1984.

Joshi, Rajendra. Integrated Slum Development: Case of Pravinnagar-Guptanagar. In *Poverty and Vulnerability in a Globalising Metropolis: Ahmedabad*, ed. Amitabh Kundu and Darshini Mahadevia, 268–308. Delhi: Manak, 2002.

Keskar, P. Mob of 7,000 Fight Police; 5 Officers, 4 Maan Residents Injured, *Indian Express,* March 10, 2006.

Mahadevia, Darshini. Changing Economic Scenario: Informalisation and Increased Vulnerability. In *Poverty and Vulnerability in a Globalising Metropolis: Ahmedabad*, ed. Amitabh Kundu and Darshini Mahadevia, 30–79. Delhi: Manak, 2002.

———. A City with Many Borders—Beyond Ghettoisation in Ahmedabad. In *Indian Cities in Transition*, ed. Annapurna Shaw, 315–340. Hyderabad: Orient Longman, 2007.

———. *Globalisation, Urban Reforms and Metropolitan Response: India.* Delhi: Manak, 2003.

———. House That for the Aam Aadmi? *Indian Express,* September 11, 2007.

———. Interventions in Development: A Shift towards a Model of Exclusion. In *Poverty and Vulnerability in a Globalising Metropolis: Ahmedabad*, ed. Amitabh Kundu and Darshini Mahadevia, 8–13. Delhi: Manak, 2002.

———. Metropolitan Employment in India. In *Inside the Transforming Urban Asia: Policies, Processes and Public Actions*, ed. Darshini Mahadevia, 56–93. New Delhi: Concept, 2008.

———. Mini SEZs through the Backdoor? *Times of India (Ahmedabad)*, December 18, 2006.

———. NURM and the Poor in Globalising Mega Cities. *Economic and Political Weekly* 41:31 (2006): 3399–403.

———. State Supported Segmentation of Mumbai: Policy Options in the Global Economy. *Review of Development and Change* 3:1 (1998): 12–41.

———. Sustainable Urban Development in India: An Inclusive Perspective. *Development in Practice* 11:2/3 (2001): 242–59.

———. Tall Claims and Sluggish Progress—Affordable Housing for All in UPA Regime. In *The People's Verdict—4th Civil Society Review of the National Common Minimum Programme*, ed. Wada Na Todo Abhiyan, 7–11. New Delhi: Wada Na Todo Abhiyan, 2008.

———. Urban Land Market and Access of the Poor. In *India: Urban Poverty Report 2009*, ed. India, Ministry of Housing and Urban Poverty Alleviation, 199–221. New Delhi: Oxford University Press, 2009.

———. Urban Poor's Access to Land and Basic Services: Rhetoric, Reality and Dilemmas. *Nagarlok* 33:1 (2002): 66–85.

Mahadevia, Darshini, and Appeeji Parashar. Dynamics of High Tech Urban Spaces: Case of Pune. In *High-Tech Urban Spaces—Asian and European perspectives*, ed. C. Ramachandraiah, A.C.M. (Guus) van Westen and Sheela Prasad, 341–66. New Delhi: Manohar, 2008.

Mahadevia, Darshini, and Harini Narayanan. Shanghaing Mumbai: Politics of Evictions and Resistance in Slum Settlements. In *Inside the Transforming Urban Asia: Processes, Policies and Public Actions*, ed. Darshini Mahadevia, 549–89. New Delhi: Concept, 2008.

———. Slumbay to Shanghai: Envisioning Renewal or Take Over? In *Inside the Transforming Urban Asia: Processes, Policies and Public Actions*, ed. Darshini Mahadevia, 94–131. New Delhi: Concept, 2008.

Mahadevia, Darshini, and Harpreet Singh Brar. Changes and Continuities in Development Priorities. In *Inside the Transforming Urban Asia: Processes, Policies and Public Actions*, ed. Darshini Mahadevia, 132–67. New Delhi: Concept, 2008.

Mahadevia, Darshini, and Jeanne Wolfe, eds. *Solid Waste Management in Indian Cities: Status and Emerging Practices.* New Delhi: Concept, 2008.

Marcuse, Peter, and Ronald van Kempen. Introduction. In *Globalizing Cities—A New Spatial Order?*, ed. Peter Marcuse and Ronald van Kempen, 1–21. Oxford: Blackwell, 2000.

Ministry of Housing and Urban Poverty Alleviation. National Urban Housing and Habitat Policy, 2007, Government of India.

Ministry of Statistics and Programme Implementation, Government of India, New Delhi. March 2004.

———. Employment and Unemployment Situation in India, 2004–05, (Part—I), NSS 61st Round (July 2004–June 2005), Report No. 515 (61/10/1). Ministry of Statistics and Programme Implementation, Government of India, New Delhi. September 2006.

National Sample Survey Organisation. Housing Condition in India—Housing Stock and Constructions, NSS 58th Round (July 2002–December 2002), Report No. 488 (58/1.2/1).

Office of the Registrar General and Census Commissioner. Slum Population, Series-1, Census of India, 2001. New Delhi: Office of the Registrar General and Census Commissioner, 2005.

Ramachandraiah, C., and Sheela Prasad. The Makeover of Hyderabad—The "Model" IT City? In *High-Tech Urban Spaces—Asian and European Perspectives*, ed. C. Ramachandraiah, A.C.M. (Guus) van Westen and S. Prasad. New Delhi: Manohar, 2008.

Ramachandran, Sushma. 100 per cent FDI in Construction Industry through Automatic Route. In *Hindu*, February 25, 2005. http://www.hindu.com/2005/02/25/stories/2005022506990100.htm

Shivanand, Swathi. BMDA Plans Townships. In *Hindu*, September 8, 2006. http://www.hindu.com/2006/09/08/stories/2006090813140300.htm

Sivramakrishnan, K. C., Amitabh Kundu, and B. N. Singh. *Handbook of Urbanization in India: An Analysis of Trends and Processes.* New Delhi: Oxford University Press, 2005.

Teja, Ravi. How Ahmedabad is Changing. *Rediff*, January 6, 2007. http://www.rediff.com/money/2007/jan/06spec.htm.

United Nations Population Fund. *State of World Population, 2007—Unleashing the Potential of Urban Growth.* New York: UNFPA, 2007.

Yeh, Anthony Gar-on and X. Xueqiang. 1996. Globalization and the Urban System in China. In *Emerging World Cities in Pacific Asia*, ed. Fu-chen Lo and Yue-man Yeung. New York: United Nations University Press.

■ PETER NEWMAN / JEFFREY KENWORTHY

Urban Sustainability and Automobile Dependence in an Australian Context

Urban sustainability is linked to automobile dependence through the triple set of bottom-line environmental, economic, and social issues, as outlined in table 1. These problems have been developing a synergy of stresses that is finally reaching a point where cities must change or begin to collapse. Whole suburbs of highly car-dependent cities are now being abandoned as the multiple problems of living where there is no option to reach work or services other than long-distance car trips is beginning to destroy the financial, social, and environmental values that once drove such land development. Jago Dodson and Neil Sipe in Australia have highlighted areas particularly vulnerable to mortgage stress created by rising fuel prices.[1]

The future is likely to make this process accelerate. Carbon will be taxed and traded to minimize its use as climate change governance becomes more and more politically driven on a global and local scale. Peak oil now threatens to make this even more dramatic as the price of fuel escalates from a growing inability to supply petroleum due to a diminishing resource base focused more and more in politically vulnerable areas.[2]

One response to these issues is a sense of fear and despair that adequate change is unlikely and that collapse of many car-dependent cities will follow. As David Lankshear and Neil Cameron said: "Peak oil has already become a magnet for post-apocalyptic survivalists who are convinced that western society is on the brink of collapse, and have stocked up tinned food and ammunition for that coming day."[3]

This chapter suggests that there is hope even in highly car-dependent cities as global and local politics center around climate change and peak oil. The solutions suggested here are summarized in the mantra of TOD, POD, and GOD—transit-oriented development, pedestrian-oriented development, and green-oriented development. These three policies, which are highly integrated, are outlined in concept and then applied to Australian cities.

Table 1. The sustainability problems of car dependence

Environmental	Economic	Social
• Oil vulnerability • Photochemical smog • Toxic air emissions • High greenhouse gas contributions • Urban sprawl • Greater storm-water problems from extra hard surface	• Traffic problems (noise, severance) • External costs from accidents, pollution, and health impacts • Congestion costs, despite road building • High infrastructure costs in new sprawling suburbs • Loss of productive rural land • Loss of urban land to bitumen • Obesity and other health impacts	• Loss of street life • Loss of community • Loss of public safety • Isolation in remote suburbs • Access problems for the car-less and those with disabilities • Road rage

Source: Peter Newman and Jeffrey Kenworthy, *Sustainability and Cities: Overcoming Automobile Dependence* (Washington, DC: Island Press, 1999).

Transit-Oriented Development.

Transit-oriented development (TOD) is now a core strategic focus in urban planning, which requires a commitment to centers and to transit as its core ingredients—together. Building centers linked to transit requires a strategic planning framework and a set of policy tools to help implement TODs. This chapter presents four strategic planning tools for implementing TODs. The model is applicable anywhere, but it is applied to Australian cities to demonstrate their application.

The four strategic planning tools for TODs are the following: a strategic policy framework that asserts where centers need to occur and at what kind of density and mix; a strategic policy framework that links centers with a rapid transit base, almost invariably electric rail; a statutory planning base that requires development to occur at the necessary density and design in each center, preferably facilitated by a specialized development agency; and a public-private funding mechanism that enables the transit to be built or refurbished through a linkage to the centers it will service.

A Strategic Policy Framework

Why do we need centers in a strategic plan?

■ CENTERS PROVIDE SERVICES AND AMENITY BASED ON ECONOMIES OF SCALE AND DENSITY. Most urban services and amenities cannot be provided unless a certain number of people are there to make them viable, which has been understood for centuries as the basis of the existence of cities as distinct from rural areas. However, in the era of the automobile, where transport to services and amenities could be assumed to be by car, the provision of centers of activity has been downplayed or decried. The UK Town and Country Planning Association's motto was "nothing gained by overcrowding"; this became the signal in many Anglo cities for the planning of car-dependent suburbs and the denial of the need for centers.[4]

Car dependence has reached its limits. Cities are now breaking down because of car dependence and the problems of climate change and peak oil are undermining the extremities of cities built this way. Governments and the market cannot provide the services and amenities of centers in any kind of viable system if houses and jobs are scattered and spaced without focus. In particular, they cannot provide a decent public transport system, and hence households are increasingly vulnerable to the price of driving, especially fuel prices. Thus centers are being reinvented in car-dependent cities in Australia and North America to help create the viability required across the city.[5]

The question that then follows is this: What kind of density and mix of activity can give rise to urban services and amenities in centers? Data from a series of studies have been collected to provide an answer to this question.[6] In figure 1 the kind of data found across cities everywhere illustrates how transport and density are linked (in this case the Sydney metropolitan area).

The curve is found to be universal and suggests a critical density at which car use increases dramatically. The data from global cities suggests that a minimum of 35 persons per hectare (14.2 persons per acre) of urban land is required *at a metropolitan scale* before transit, walking/biking, and short car trips combine to reduce the need for driving and significantly reduce energy use. The global cities data show that, on average, across the full sample of cities there are half as many jobs as there are people in cities. Thus the 35 persons per hectare (14.2 persons per acre) population density implies that to achieve the car use or energy use at that critical point on the graph, *whole cities* require a minimum of around 53 persons + jobs per hectare (21.5 persons + jobs per acre) of activity density, below which car use and transport energy use increase dramatically.

When we apply this idea *within cities*, as we have done in analyzing Australian cities, the picture is very similar, but with some caveats. First of all, within different areas of the same city, the ratio of jobs to population varies dramatically by local government area (LGA), and, of course, both

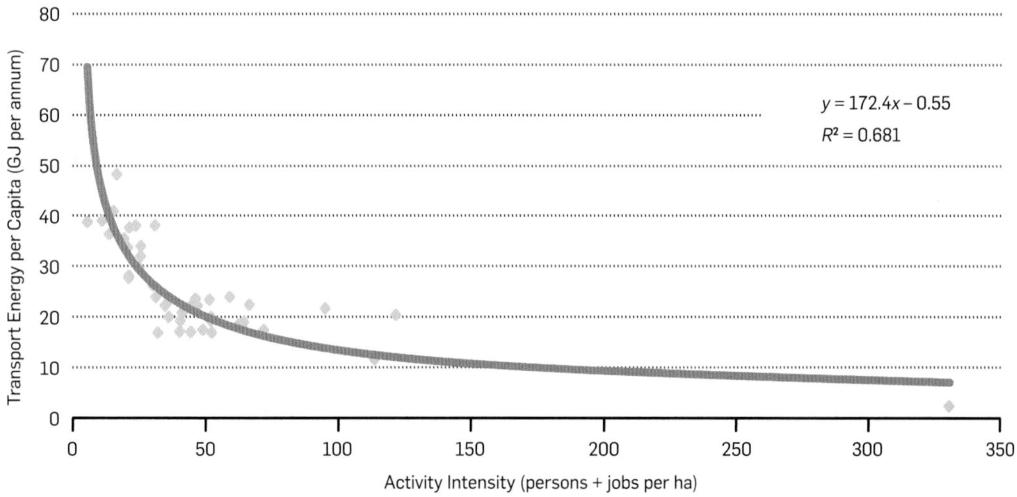

Figure 1. Total transport energy use versus activity intensity in Sydney, 2002.

are important in determining transport patterns. In the Sydney region, for example, the data by the 44 LGAs shows that the ratio of jobs to population varies from a low of 0.19 in the extreme outer areas to a high of 8.17 in the Sydney central city. Thus, if one wants to correlate car use or energy use with density, the true result is achieved only with activity densities, as in figure 1 (*r*-squared of 0.68). This graph shows that a minimum of 35 persons *and* jobs per hectare (14.2 persons *and* jobs per acre) are needed to minimize car use and energy use. The correlation of urban population density alone with transport energy use within Sydney results in a slightly weaker correlation (r-squared 0.55), and the line of best fit is a logarithmic curve, not a power function.

Overall, we can say that *within cities* a minimum activity density of 35 persons and jobs per hectare (14.2 persons and jobs per acre) is associated with a critical mass of urban services and amenities in a local center. If established within the limits of a 1 kilometer (0.62 mile) radius, a local center can be created with about 10,000 people and jobs. If within a 3 kilometer (1.86 mile) radius, then a town center can be created with around 100,000 population and jobs.

■ CENTERS ENABLE CAR DEPENDENCE TO BE REVERSED WITHOUT DESTROYING THE CHARACTER OF SUBURBS. The kind of TOD strategy outlined here suggests that if centers of an appropriate density and mix can be created, then not only are viable centers created, but the pressure on suburbs for unpopular infill is considerably reduced. Many suburbs will continue to be redeveloped, especially those where populations and services are declining. However, the wholesale rebuilding of suburbs can be avoided if centers are the focus of development. The kind of city envisaged by a TOD-oriented future can build on the character of many suburbs, yet still provide the services and amenities people are demanding, particularly a viable transit system. But central to this is the building of viable centers. People living in surrounding suburban areas are greatly benefited by the existence of dynamic, varied, and accessible centers within walking or cycling distance, or a short bus or car ride.

Linking Centers with a Rapid Transit Base

Why do we need rapid transit in a strategic plan?

■ RAPID TRANSIT ASSISTS CITIES IN THEIR WEALTH CREATION. Car dependence is expensive. The link between the wealth of a city and its car use is very weak; it is certainly not statistically significant (only 18 percent of the variation is explained).[7] The data for our main analyses relate to 1995 and at that time European cities tended to be the wealthiest in the world yet they have about one-third of the car use of U.S. cities; likewise wealthy Asian cities like Hong Kong, Tokyo, and Singapore, which are all strong economic engines, had ten times the per capita wealth of Bangkok, Jakarta, Kuala Lumpur, Manila, Surabaya, Seoul, and Beijing, but per capita car use was less. Many wealthy cities have put their wealth into good transit infrastructure. The result is not a city that is poorer because it wastes money on public transport, as suggested by many economists (particularly Treasury officials), but rather a place that becomes a desirable business location with greater livability and capacity to attract global capital and skilled, knowledge-based employment. Indeed, the data suggest that the more a city has committed itself to public transport infrastructure the less the city spends overall on passenger transport, both private and public, as a proportion of its gross domestic product; and the more a city has built itself around car dependence, the more of the city's wealth is wasted on just getting around.[8] Based on data from a few years ago before the Australian dollar exceeded the U.S. dollar in value, Australian car travel was estimated to cost around eighty-five cents in Australian dollars (then about 65 cents in U.S. dollars) per passenger kilometer (0.62 miles), compared to fifty to sixty cents in Australian dollars (then about thirty-eight to forty-six cents in U.S. dollars) per passenger kilometer (0.62 miles) in transit.[9]

There is an equity argument here too as the poor in Australian and American cities are increasingly moving out to car-dependent areas where they save money on housing but lose heavily on transport, with some families spending up to 40 percent of their income on transport.[10] Households in car-dependent cities in the United States are now spending more on transport than on their mortgages, which helps explain why oil price increases have helped to create the subprime mortgage meltdown in late 2007. Continuing nonviability of such car-dependent urban sprawl is already causing the abandonment of whole suburbs similar to the kind of inner-city abandonment found in U.S. cities in the 1960s.

On the other hand, TODs can offer cities economic advantages without this vulnerability. Much of the marketing benefit of TODs has been outlined by a Surface Transportation Policy Project (2005) study that showed that people living in TODs in the United States had the same age and income as those not living in TODs but had one less car per household (0.9 compared to 1.7 cars).[11] This scenario was found to lead to a 20 percent increase in available household wealth. As a tool for marketing TODs, it is not just of value to households, as local governments soon find that this extra available wealth is largely spent on local goods and services; buying a car would not do the same thing. Hence TODs are a means of helping create local economic development.

■ RAPID TRANSIT REDUCES THE EXTERNAL COSTS OF CAR DEPENDENCE. It has been well documented that car dependence is costly in terms of environmental, social, and economic externalities. For example, McGlynn and Andrews suggested an extra 20 cents per kilometer (.62 mile) in Australian dollars, or 15 cents in U.S. dollars in the early 1990s.[12] Government costs due to accidents, pollution, noise, and other external costs have been estimated and compared to the government revenue benefits of the road system in Australia, and there was an overall "road deficit" of AU$8 billion (about US$6.1 billion) in the late 1990s (using exchange rates at that time).[13] The biggest looming problem of car dependence is oil vulnerability, and here the historically derided "coalition of the willing" are still U.S. and Australian cities, which have by far the biggest vulnerability to the global oil production peak, which in all likelihood has already happened in late 2006.[14] Electric rail systems (with TOD built around stations) will withstand this crisis far better than urban areas with extensive car dependence. Electric rail continues to be the most efficient form of motorized transport, as it alone does not have to carry its own fuel. The data from our Global Cities Database are outlined in table 2.

■ RAPID TRANSIT SAVES TIME. People do not want to travel more than an hour a day on average—this proclivity has become known as the Marchetti Principle or Constant.[15] The switch to more sustainable modes of transport will not occur if it means people go beyond their travel time budget. Thus,

Table 2. Fuel efficiency and occupancy by mode in global cities, 1990

MODE	MJ PER PASSENGER KILOMETER (AVERAGE ALL CITIES)	MEASURED AVERAGE VEHICLE OCCUPANCY (AVERAGE ALL CITIES)
Car	2.91	1.52
Bus	1.56	13.83
Heavy rail (electric)	0.44	30.96
Heavy rail (diesel)	1.44	27.97
Light rail/tram	0.79	29.73

Note: Heavy and light rail occupancy is per wagon.

a city will only be truly moving toward a less car-dependent future if it can build a rapid transit system within every corridor that is faster than traffic and creates centers where walking, biking, or a short bus or car trip becomes the means of accessing urban services because they are local and hence quick to reach.

TOD can thus be used to save time for local and long distance travel. But TOD centers only attract the necessary development potential around them if they are linked by fast transit. Almost invariably, this transit is electric rail due to its speed (acceleration/deceleration, cruising speeds, and egress/ingress speeds, which are all significantly better than buses). Bus cities have transit speeds of around 20–25 kilometers per hour (12.4 to 15.5 miles per hour), while rail cities have transit speeds of 35–40 kilometers per hour (21.8 to 24.9 miles per hour), which are competitive with overall traffic speeds.[16] Commuter rail systems frequently offer speeds over 60 kilometers per hour (37 miles per hour). Rail gives transit an edge in speed, which is crucial to being competitive. In many emerging economy cities, and in some corridors where rail is not available, bus rapid transit is providing the extra speed required over traffic, though rarely as fast or with the capacity advantages of rail. The multiple advantages of "strong rail" cities over all other types of cities has been outlined quantitatively by Jeffrey Kenworthy.[17]

■ RAPID TRANSIT SAVES SPACE. The reason that many cities switch from buses to rail is that their city centers get jammed with slow buses. The Bangkok effect, or "bus bunching," is due to a capacity

Table 3. Modal capacities

MODE	CARRYING CAPACITY (PEOPLE PER HOUR)
Freeway lane	2,500
Bus lane	5,000–7,000
Light rail	10,000–20,000
Heavy rail line	50,000

Source: Vukan Vuchic, *Urban Transit: Planning, Operations and Economics* (New Jersey: John Wiley & Sons, 2005).

factor that is even more obvious with cars. Table 3 shows the relative capacities of modes, which has become a problem even in all the "famous" bus cities such as Curitiba, Ottawa, and Bogotá.

Thus the space requirements of car dependence are twenty times those of rail. The costs of such space are considerable and help to explain why most central cities cannot function without rail access. If the 200,000 per day of people who access central Sydney had to get there by car, it would mean an extra sixty-five freeway lanes and 782 hectares (1,932 acres) for car parks. Rail makes spatially constrained cities work.[18]

■ RAPID TRANSIT CREATES CITY SPACES SUITABLE FOR THE KNOWLEDGE/SERVICES ECONOMY. The key to the new economy based on transactions between knowledge/services professionals is the ability to meet and interact. Electronic communication can be used to follow up the creative interactions that occur face-to-face.[19] Cities therefore need centers that are dense, mixed, and walkable to create such interactions. This is the philosophy of the New Urbanists, and although their human-oriented urban designs are critical, so is the role of rail in creating spaces where bitumen (asphalt) is not the dominant land use.[20]

■ RAPID TRANSIT CREATES CERTAINTY FOR INVESTMENT. Transit, especially rail, is fixed and lasts a long time—certainly beyond the period most investors need to get their investment back. Bus routes change, and even bus lanes and busways are flexible and subject to political whims, though major rail and bus rapid transit systems cannot easily be moved. Transport planners have been heavily oriented to flexibility, but nothing can compete with the flexibility of cars if road space is sufficient—certainly no bus system can. However, once road space is constrained, the existence of fixed rail and bus rapid transit (BRT) systems becomes critical. If built, they provide the certainty investors need. Rail and BRT thus offer both a real transport solution and a real land investment opportunity. Robert Cervero has shown in over thirty studies in the United States that access to rail station land provided proven land value premiums.[21] An Australian developer has created a fund for doing TOD in Perth, as its rail projects offer potential for at least 15 percent higher return in the areas around stations due to the attraction of the new rail system, though their efforts have been greatly thwarted by a state and local planning system that does not translate its own policies and rhetoric into regulatory requirements.

A Statutory Planning Base

Why do we need a statutory planning process to require development in centers?

■ TODS CANNOT BE LEFT TO LOCAL POLITICS. Strategic planning is necessary but not sufficient. It needs to be translated into a statutory planning mechanism that requires density and mix in centers, which requires clear zoning and an urban design and planning system that can facilitate TODs. This planning is generally a partnership between local and state governments, as, invariably, if it is left just to local governments the regional perspectives are lost.

Local government is usually closely tied into local politics, and there are often groups opposed to redevelopment and density increases that undermine such TOD projects. Australian and

American cities are littered with examples of lost TODs. The rationale for the local reaction is often that density is socially dangerous, unhealthy, and brings too much traffic, though the evidence for this is not found in the literature or on the ground after such development.[22] If TOD implementation is going to be left to local councils to do by themselves, there will be much less achieved, as projects are generally watered down by local reactions.

One of the key benefits of TODs is that they enable affordable housing to be built as part of the project. Density can enable such affordability but generally needs to be required as part of the development through a statutory mechanism. Affordable housing strategies are needed to make the most social benefit out of TODs, though this is not usually what local communities would prioritize. Every city has different needs for affordable housing and different potential policies that can work. Vancouver has mostly required 15 percent affordable housing, and Boulder, Colorado, now requires 40 percent in each new development. Cali Gorowitz has summarized affordable housing techniques.[23]

Regional planning perspectives are necessary in the local political mix, but they do not often get a hearing in local media and decision-making. Australian and American planning will continue to emasculate TODs by local politics if that is all that is considered.

■ TODS REQUIRE REGIONAL PLANNING RESOURCES. Most TODs require repackaging of land parcels, redesign of roads, and reorientation toward the rail system. Proactive planning processes that create these land packages and offer detailed urban design are usually beyond local government resources. In the United States such planning is often done by private developers, and in Australia by land development agencies. Both need local government involvement, but the history of TOD development in Australia is such that without state government intervention—as in Perth, which declared Redevelopment Authority areas (discussed later)—little happens. The best TODs in recent times have come from the now defunct Federal Better Cities projects, which have been linked to state development agencies. Federal money essentially underwrote some of the perceived financial risk entailed in these groundbreaking TODs.

The role of government in facilitating TODs (such as Fortitude Valley in Brisbane, Pyrmont in Sydney, and Subiaco or East Perth in Perth) is not just in technical planning but also in public engagement and communication processes. Regional perspectives are needed to show why centers are required and viable regional transit systems cannot happen without such centers. Development corporations for TOD can bring the creative human resources for charettes, visioning workshops, and citizen juries to enable these issues to be considered.

In order to assist TODs there needs to be zoning that enables the specific benefits of TODs to be built into the planning system. A specific TOD zoning that enables these kind of mixed-use, dense centers with minimal parking (achieved through *maximum* rather than minimum parking requirements), and a proportion of affordable housing can assist considerably in their delivery.[24] Developers should be given special incentives if they build there, perhaps using density bonuses or time benefits in the approval process. Communities need to see there are benefits in such a zoning, perhaps with a Vancouver-like process where 5 percent of the cost of a development in a TOD goes to social infrastructure, such as community centers and public space landscaping, determined in partnership with the local community.

A Public-Private Funding Mechanism

Why do we need a financing mechanism for transit in TODs?

■ RAIL DEVELOPMENT HAS FLOUNDERED WHILE ROAD DEVELOPMENT HAS CREATIVELY FOUND FINANCING MECHANISMS. Transport funding in many Western democracies has had two radically different approaches in recent history. The first covers the period from the 1970s to the 1990s, the period of Centrist Road Planning. Federal funds in the United States and Australia were the major input into transport from the 1970s, but this was tightly controlled and channeled into roads. In this period in Australia about AU$42.8 billion (about US$32.5 billion using relevant historical exchange rates) went to roads, and approximately AU$5.4 billion to rail (about US$4.1 billion).[25] Rail managed to survive through state government, but it was rarely expanded. Only Perth did anything of significance in this period with new rail, and this was because of an intensely political process.[26] Brisbane's rail was electrified by a federal grant from the Whitlam ALP (Australian Labor Party) Government, the only significant venture by federal transport into rail. This era saw major roads built in all Australian cities feeding rapid urban sprawl and car dependence. The cost effectiveness of this effort was never challenged. Rail was never able to generate the political clout during this period to have tied funding (federal financial contributions) like roads, where no market process was ever considered necessary.

The second period of transport funding emerges in the 2000s and is characterized by increasing Market Road Planning. Tied road funding in Australian cities has stopped and has been given just to states for regional roads, though regional roads often seem to come into cities. Federal transport funds are still mostly for roads but can include freight rail in the AusLink program. States can fund roads or rail, but the politics of funding transport when health, education, and police are always higher on the agenda means that road funding has mostly had to go elsewhere. A market process was thus discovered by the states using toll roads, and after early models where government guarantees were needed, the system is now delivering major projects where the state government can not only get a road but also a substantial cash grant from the private consortium just for the right to build. Thus, in Sydney over AU$10 billion (at the time about US$7.6 billion) worth of toll roads has been built from the mid-1990s. Most other Australian cities are moving to tollways, only Perth has withstood this move. Similar processes have happened in the United States, where, increasingly, road funding is through toll roads. The difference in the United States is that federal funds can also be used to fund rail through partnership agreements.

Australia has very little history of market-based financing methods for rail such as the Portland tram in the United States. However, the election of the Rudd Labor Government in 2007 has seen the development of a new body called Infrastructure Australia designed to provide funds for Australian cities, particularly decent public transport. Its agenda is to link infrastructure provision to the sustainability agenda, which historically opens up a new era for Australian cities. One of the key mechanisms of Infrastructure Australia is the use of public-private partnerships (PPP) to facilitate rail projects and TODs.

Proposals for building fast, heavy rail using tollway financing have now been suggested—for example, Western Sydney Fast Rail and a new rail project in Melbourne. However, the majority of proposals are for building heavy and light rail using land development opportunities through PPPs.

Examples of both are found in other parts of the world. However, no mechanism has yet been facilitated by state governments in Australia though a new report on how it could be done in Perth has been produced.[27]

■ PUBLIC-PRIVATE PARTNERSHIPS FOR RAIL PROJECTS AUTOMATICALLY INTEGRATE CENTERS. Building a rail line entirely as a transport proposition by a state government can mean that it is optimized around rail operations (often focused on Park and Ride) without any consideration for the linking of centers or building of TODs. This has mostly been the history of rail development in Australia and the United States in recent years. However, if the private sector were to build a rail line in partnership with government, with land development financing, rail would automatically be integrated with land use, as that would be the major way of paying for it. Thus public-private funding arrangements for rail are an inherently more effective way of creating TODs than state funding alone.

Pedestrian-Oriented Development

TODs are the basic framework for rebuilding a car-dependent city. However, it is possible to make a mess of TODs unless they pay attention to detail on the street level. Transit is able to induce development around it at higher value than surrounding areas because it has so many people walking through the area. The land is valuable for many purposes, but only if pedestrians like walking through it. TODs must also be PODs.

In Copenhagen a new rail line has been paid for entirely through development profits around each station. Its patronage is now going well, as it serves a number of areas not previously on their suburban lines. However, in a stretch of the line in a new area (formerly military land) modernist, monumentalist architecture has been scattered around transit stops without any attempt at pedestrian linkages to the stations. No simple street grid was created, and it is now hard to reconstruct easy walkability between buildings and stations. The result has been much less usage of the train, much less usage of bikes or walking, and much more usage by cars, requiring substantial parking around the buildings. The TOD has been undermined by the lack of pedestrian qualities.

Pedestrian qualities are not just for aesthetic purposes (though this is not a small matter); they are also the basis of attracting new capital into cities. British planner Sir Peter Hall once said, "The new world will depend like the old world did on creativity and creativity happens when people come together face-to-face."[28] This is why the new capital associated with brain power jobs, is not attracted to car-dependent shopping centers. People need to meet in centers and they are doing so in traditional centers and increasingly in the new TODs. But TODs need to be PODs if they are going to really work at attracting the new jobs.

The development of strategies to increase the walkability of an urban center has been driven in recent years by the need to create attractive and livable urban areas that can attract the new economy jobs of services and tourism. Jan Gehl, a Danish urban designer, has now completed walkability strategies on each Australian city as well as many other major Anglo-Saxon cities, such as London, New York, and San Francisco. These strategies have emphasized how to enable people to come to the city without a car, how to keep them in the city without a car, and how to enable people to live, work, or study more easily in the city.[29]

The importance of walkability in city centers is now demonstrated, so it is time to apply the same principles to all TODs, wherever they are. Cities in the suburbs need to be walkable. For example, in Perth, Western Australia, in the 1990s the state government set up what is known as a Redevelopment Authority that covers a specific part of an inner suburb called Subiaco, centered on a suburban railway station and involving a lot of derelict light industrial and other inappropriate land uses. Redevelopment Authorities in Western Australia are aimed at taking full planning control of specific areas so that particular urban planning, transport, and urban design objectives can be achieved in a coherent manner. They are charged with the responsibility of breaking even financially. They purchase land, take care of all the urban services and infrastructure, amalgamate and resubdivide the land, and put it on the open market with strict guidelines to developers about how it must be developed. The guidelines are very prescriptive and very effective at achieving the urban planning visions set for the particular area.

During the 1990s, with money from the Australian federal government's Building Better Cities Programme, funds were obtained to sink the Subiaco railway line about 305 meters (1,001 feet) on both sides of Subiaco station so that the land on each side of the line could be joined together and new land above the rail line could be created. The Subiaco Redevelopment Authority then set about replanning the whole precinct around the station into a world-class TOD or walkable community. The plan consists of a range of medium to high density housing, with significant mixed land uses close to the station. The whole area is carefully planned, incorporating effective urban design principles to encourage walking and cycling, and since the development has reached a certain maturity, weekly patronage of the rail service through Subiaco station has skyrocketed. The public realm is superbly planned with generous sidewalks, tree-lined streets, a central lake and park/picnic area, and a demonstration sustainable house.

Perth has Redevelopment Authorities at Midland and Armadale stations, two terminus stations on other rail lines, as well as another Redevelopment Authority in East Perth, where a very large walkable community has been established within walking distance of another station. The same hallmarks of a quality public realm linked together with rich infrastructure provision for pedestrians and cyclists characterizes all these TOD developments around rail stations in Perth. The success of these walkable communities in the marketplace has led the private sector to replicate their successes at other stations on the new seventy-four-kilometer (forty-six-mile) southern suburbs rail line in Perth.

Green-Oriented Development

The agenda of the new sustainability economy is to design sustainable transportation, solar building, and green infrastructure together. TODs that have been well designed as PODs will also need to be GODs.

It will be important for green developers wanting to claim sustainability credibility to see that scattered developments, no matter how green in their buildings and renewable infrastructure, will be viewed as failures in a post-peak oil world. So far most of the new green buildings being accredited by the U.S. and Australian Green Building Council are in traditional centers. However, there are new TODs now being built that do not feature green buildings. TODs will need to ensure that they have full solar orientation, are renewably powered, have water sensitive design, use recycled and low-impact materials, and include innovations like Green Roofs and plug-in parking areas for plug-in hybrid electric vehicles (PHEV). Essentially, TODs will need to help cities become regenerative, not just curtail environmental damage.

An example of the kind of synergies likely to develop as new TOD-POD-GOD developments proceed comes from the Richard Meier–designed new cathedral in eastern Rome, which uses a titanium dioxide (TiO_2) compound called TXActive on its white sail-like roof, which is a self-cleaning material designed to prevent it from fouling and darkening due to dust and pollution. The material works much better than expected, as it catalyzes the oxidation of organic and NOx pollution from the atmosphere. As a result, trials have now shown how buildings and sidewalks using the material can clean the air up to 2.4 meters (8 feet) from the surface, thus reducing ambient air pollutants by 60 percent. A GOD with this material involved can be much more attractive to pedestrians.

One of the best examples of a TOD-POD-GOD is the redevelopment of Kogarah Town Square, an inner-city development in Sydney built on a large city council car park adjacent to the main train station and poorly performing businesses. The site is now a thriving mixed-use development consisting of 194 residences, 4,645 square meters (49,998 square feet) of office and retail space, and 3,252 square meters (35,004 square feet) of community space, including a public library and town square. The buildings are oriented for maximum use of solar shelves on each window (enabling shade in summer and deeper penetration of light into each room), photovoltaic collectors on the roof, and rainwater, which is collected in an underground tank and reused for toilets and garden irrigation. Recycled and low-impact materials were used in construction, and all residents, workers, and visitors have only a short walk to the train station, resulting in fewer parking requirements, enabling better and more productive use of the site. Compared to a conventional development, the Kogarah Town Square saves 42 percent of water and 385 metric tons (424 tons) of greenhouse gas per year not including the transport oil savings, which are hard to estimate but are likely to be even more substantial.

The 2000 Sydney Olympics and its Olympic Village in Newington are another example of sustainable transport married to sustainable buildings. The Olympic Village is one of the best examples of recycling a contaminated industrial site into several thousand houses, commercial space, hotels, and sports stadiums, all with green architecture. The houses have photovoltaic and solar water heating on their roofs and use recycled sewage to flush toilets and irrigate gardens. The sewage treatment works is part of the total complex and is so clean it recycles water back into lakes and all other water uses apart from drinking. The main Olympic stadium roof is a giant rainwater collector for recycling into gardens and toilets. All of these structures are built around a station that carried 50,000 people an hour during the Olympics, ensuring that (together with buses and ferries) the Sydney 2000 Olympics were car-free—a fitting way to begin the new century, but not one that has been copied much, yet.

Finally, the best example of sustainable transport and sustainable building being integrated is Vauban, in Freiburg, Germany. This project is a model for solar building. With around fifty commercial dwellings built to demonstrate their ability to deliver energy to the grid, the office block exports power from its photovoltaic system, and solar collectors are on all public buildings. Vauban also has some demonstration PLUS energy houses, which feed energy into the grid.

The project also features green infrastructure with full recycling of solid waste and sewage, and the development has a wood-based combined heat and power station. Thus it is a GOD but it is also a model for TOD and POD. Around half of the 5,000 inhabitants of Vauban have agreed to be car-free—that is, to live in the complex without a car. They have good light rail connections to the rest of the city (the LRT runs through the site on a grass track bed), and there are bicycle paths and facilities that lace the development. Those who have a car need to park in one of the two inexpensive solar garages, which store not only cars but also solar energy. The major linear green spaces are actually drainage swales that form part of the sustainable water management system. They feed water into compensation basins that are part of the landscaping features of the development and are used by children. The main result of this commitment to car-free TOD is that Vauban has much more space for playgrounds, vegetable gardens, and green space. Bitumen usually takes up around 30 percent of any car-dependent suburb, but in Vauban there is hardly any. Each of the neighborhood green spaces has been designed by the local residents, and many of them are wild and bushy despite being in the middle of a city. The most noticeable feature of the city is the way children use the car-free spaces. Without the fear of cars constantly confronting them, younger children play on the streets, older children run freely through the development, and parents supervise groups of babies in the playgrounds. Here is a clear contribution of the car-free space to help build social capital and community life—a model where, far from having to sacrifice for sustainability, families are gaining because the designs integrated sustainable transport and sustainable building dimensions. It is a glimpse of how a resilient and indeed regenerative city of the future could be.[30]

Applying the Principles to Australian Cities

The five main Australian cities covered in this chapter—Sydney (New South Wales), Perth (Western Australia), Melbourne (Victoria), Brisbane (Queensland), and Adelaide (South Australia)—are all state capitals.[31] Table 4 provides a basic profile of the cities using a set of carefully controlled comparative data for 2006. Even though the data are six years old, the same basic comparisons and perspectives hold true today.

The strategic planning approaches for these five cities have been evaluated and summarized in table 5 to show how they apply to the Australian urban context.

Table 4. A snapshot of Australian cities, 2006

CHARACTERISTIC	PERTH	ADELAIDE	MELBOURNE	SYDNEY	BRISBANE
Population	1,518,700	1,145,800	3,743,000	4,282,000	1,819,800
Urban density (persons per hectare)	11.3	11.9	15.6	19.5	9.7
Annual car use per person (pass kms.)	13,652	11,395	11,586	11,406	13,145
Total annual public transport use per person (pass kms.)	748	565	1,057	1,552	944
Parking in the central business district (spaces per 1,000 jobs)	501	486	268	206	216

Note: Latest Australian Bureau of Statistics Census figures for 2006.

Table 5. Application of a four-part TOD strategy to Australian cities

CITY	STRATEGIC POLICY FOR CENTERS	STRATEGIC POLICY FOR RAIL TRANSIT	STATUTORY PROCESS TO IMPLEMENT TOD	PUBLIC-PRIVATE FUNDING MECHANISM	INTEGRATED TOD, POD, AND GOD
Sydney	yes	weak in past decade; new rail project huge potential	yes, in new areas; centers being overhauled	possibly, but not yet	a few examples
Melbourne	yes, but struggling	weak; present rail mostly	yes, but not strong in implementation	no	best central business district, but little else
Brisbane	yes, but not well defined with clear goals for each center	yes; present rail mostly, but new rail lines and busways being built	no	no	very little
Perth	yes, but not well defined	yes	no	no	some examples
Adelaide	yes, but not well defined	weak on rail	no	no	very good central business district
Others: Canberra, Hobart, Newcastle	yes, but not well defined	no	no	no	no

Sydney

Sydney is the largest and oldest of the cities. It has by far the highest density inner-city area, the most extensive and well-used public transport system (especially rail), and also the least car use. It is Australia's largest city (Australia's "New York") and has the most complicated and hilly topography, making bicycling and walking less attractive than it might otherwise be given the densities and mixed land use over large areas of the city.

TODs can be found across Sydney—for example, in Chatswood, where the already very compact center is having three large residential towers built over the top of the new rail line from Epping using a PPP; St. Leonards, where CityRail sold capitalized air rights over the station for tens of millions of dollars in the 1980s; and Bondi Junction, Parramatta, and Edgecliff. And they have all been growing. Sydney has had a long history of locating major shopping centers around stations and hence has substantial TODs. The Kogarah Centre is quite possibly the best eco TOD in the world, together with Vauban.

The redevelopment or consolidation of Sydney has been quite dramatic in the central business district (CBD), North Sydney, and Parramatta. The new metropolitan strategy is based on extending this center-oriented development model, which is partly designed to take the pressure off suburbs, where redevelopment has been too rapid, and partly to make centers more viable in competing for new knowledge economy jobs and provision of services. It also seeks to facilitate six transit cities that can be linked by rapid transit and provide the basis of a less car-dependent

PHOTOGRAPH BY JEFFREY KENWORTHY

Figure 2. Sydney's central business district.

PHOTOGRAPH BY JEFFREY KENWORTHY

Figure 3. St. Leonard's station precinct on the Sydney rail system.

city.[32] Funding of strategic plans for each of these centers, with clear goals for population and jobs in each, has meant that Sydney's commitment to centers is very clear.

Rail vision is difficult in Sydney. Operational problems have not helped with the politics of rail, and thus the priority in the past decade shifted to roads and busways. The AU$10 billion (about US$7.6 billion at old exchange rates) worth of private tollways in the past ten years would not have been easy had rail not been so unmanageable. However, the most recent proposal for the Global Arc rail, which links the growth centers in the northwest and southwest through a new under-the-harbor tunnel, is a very large opportunity for TOD. It takes over from Perth's rail projects as being the most visionary rail proposal in the past fifty years in Australia. It is now generating TODs at all stations along its length, though no mechanism of value capture is being used to help build the rail system. If such a mechanism could be developed, it would enable the metropolitan strategy to have a market base for its plan to bring newcomers into redeveloped urban centers that are attractive and far less car-dependent. The politics of New South Wales is volatile, however, and nothing can be certain about this major project until it is built.

A statutory process to guide TODs is in place for the New Land Release areas through a development corporation with all the required powers to ensure density and design are sufficient to create a viable center. A range of different state-based processes have been created for designated development areas, such as TODs for the rest of the city, including some that are under the direction of the New South Wales government's Landcom.

Sydney has no rail public-private financing system in place, but it has much potential, demonstrating one possible mechanism through the development levy on new blocks in the Southwest Land Release area. It has also a proposal for a western fast rail that is entirely privately funded based on the tollway model. In addition, it has a light rail consortium prepared to look at ways of financing extensions to the small light rail transit system through a land development mechanism.

The new NW–SW Global Arc rail has the potential to provide the basis for this new funding mechanism, perhaps involving the federal government; it was suggested in the federal government's sustainable cities report that rail funding in cities should be on the federal agenda.[33] Regions of local governments having a vision for how TODs could work around this new fast rail system are likely to be in a strong position to take advantage of funding as it shifts away from car dependence to such locations.

Melbourne

Melbourne is an older city like Sydney with a very extensive, attractive, and quite dense inner area. It is linked together with the best inner-city rail and tram network of any Australian city, and it is possibly a global leader. This is the only tram system, apart from the Glenelg tram line in Adelaide, to have survived the period of tram removal in the 1950s and 1960s in Australia.

Melbourne is known for its attractive central area and extensive parklands and gardens. Its CBD has won awards for its walkability and livability. The region has a strategic policy for centers based on its Melbourne 2030 Strategy, requiring thirteen transit cities on its extensive heavy rail network. Melbourne, however, has a much less TOD-oriented past than Sydney, and many of its centers, especially large retail, are located off its rail network. Attempts to create more TODs in the

PHOTOGRAPH BY JEFFREY KENWORTHY

Figure 4. Trams in the Melbourne central business district showing intensive mixed modes of transportation.

PHOTOGRAPH BY JEFFREY KENWORTHY

Figure 5. The Southbank high-density mixed-use redevelopment on the Yarra River.

past around its rail system have met with virulent opposition.[34] One example was the rejection of the Camberwell Junction Transit City when a campaign run by film stars Geoffrey Rush and Barry Humphries managed to stop a five-story office block from being built on a car park site next to the station. Thus the success at implementing Melbourne 2030 so far has not been evident.

A rail vision for Melbourne is not yet clear despite several planning studies. They have an extensive rail network, especially its very large tram system, and it has been upgraded with fast rail out to its regional centers, including Ballarat and Bendigo. However, new rail lines are painfully slow and difficult to create. The proposed spur to Aurora is the first heavy rail extension, but this has been postponed, and the proposal for a Rowethorpe extension (through Monash University) has not been successful, despite linking a series of major knowledge economy centers with huge TOD potential. Light rail extensions have been completed successfully in Melbourne, which has extensive historical TODs of a linear nature along its large tram (streetcar) and LRT network. The tram system also has the potential for extensive future development using shop-top housing redevelopment. The need for a statutory process that requires TODs to be developed is obvious in Melbourne. The regional benefits are huge, but the local opposition is well organized and dramatically political. Creative public processes to resolve these tensions are necessary as well as the political nerve to implement them. This needs an institutional structure like a development corporation to assist local authorities. There is also no clear public-private financing mechanism for rail in Melbourne, despite some small attempts with light rail to the huge Docklands redevelopment and the city loop, both of which demonstrated clear TOD benefits.

Brisbane

Brisbane is a very fast growing city and is one of Australia's big focal points for the urban explosion along coastal areas, particularly in the nearby Gold Coast, which enjoys a subtropical climate. Brisbane is not like Sydney or Melbourne in having extensive areas of old inner-city row houses and terraces, but like Perth and Adelaide is more of a cottage city concerning important inner parts of the region. It does have an extensive and quite effective electric rail system, but it has over recent years been developing busways and has undergone significant new freeway/tollway construction.

Brisbane has a new strategic centers policy in its South East Queensland (SEQ) Regional Plan 2004. This plan sets aside 80 percent of the SEQ area as a "no go" for development in order to contain urban sprawl; instead, it concentrates development in a series of centers to support high frequency public transport. Higher density centers are not a feature of the SEQ region apart from the Brisbane CBD and the Gold Coast, hence there is some cynicism about whether such a strategy is feasible. However, the infrastructure to enable rail-oriented development has now been assigned, and thus new rail lines (complete with TODs) are being extended to the Sunshine Coast and Springfield, and with a Gold Coast Light Rail.

Rail patronage has continued to grow in the region despite the fact that most of the investment in recent years has been in expensive busways and most of the regional infrastructure plans are for tunnels and freeways. The new rail-orientation promises to assist the development of TODs in South East Queensland.

No statutory planning mechanism for TOD currently exists in Brisbane. The one-off

PHOTOGRAPH BY JEFFREY KENWORTHY

Figure 6. Intense inner-city residential development on the Brisbane River with City Cat ferry service.

PHOTOGRAPH BY JEFFREY KENWORTHY

Figure 7. Inner Brisbane infill redevelopment on the Brisbane River.

PHOTOGRAPH BY JEFFREY KENWORTHY

Figure 8. Brisbane's central business district showing intrusive freeways on the Brisbane River foreshore.

redevelopment project at Fortitude Valley, the most impressive example in Australia of a state-local partnership with very clear benefits to the public and private sectors, had a strong government institutional framework that came out of the 1980s Federal Government Better Cities program. A similar entity is required to make its TOD centers work.

No funding mechanism for rail involving public-private interests has happened, though the opportunity existed in the failed Brisbane Light Rail project. In addition, the much proposed Gold Coast Light Rail is now finally going ahead (scheduled opening mid-2014) and land development opportunities abound if a suitable public-private partnership can be developed to assist the process.

Perth

Perth, the youngest of the five cities, has the lowest inner-area density and the most car use. It has, however, done more since the late 1980s to develop its public transport system, in the form of new electric lines, than any other of the Australian cities. So far it has added 107 kilometers (66 miles) of new rail line since 1993; it has also extended its freeway system and has very high road availability and a relatively free-flowing traffic system compared to most cities.

Perth has a new strategic plan called "Directions 2031," which is designed to contain urban growth and focus on centers and corridors. It is less specific about a growth boundary than the other strategies in Australia, though a recent legal decision has shown that urban sprawl will not

PHOTOGRAPH BY JEFFREY KENWORTHY

Figure 9. Perth's central business district and inner suburbs looking west to the Indian Ocean.

PHOTOGRAPH BY JEFFREY KENWORTHY

Figure 10. Perth central railway station showing modern electric trains.

be allowed, as it is not sustainable. The plan is also less directive about how much of the future population or jobs should be directed into particular centers. However, it is clear that urban growth should be transit oriented, and a new TOD strategy is being developed through a cross-government TOD committee.

Perth has the most ambitious urban rail vision of all Australian cities, though it also had the least extensive urban rail system to build on. The completion in 2007 of the seventy-four kilometer (forty-six-mile) rail line to Mandurah, at a cost of AU$1.6 billion (about US$1.2 billion), has already been paid off due to the Western Australia (WA) mining boom. The system has around 171 kilometers (106 miles) of fast electric rail line with seventy-two stations, a huge turnaround for a city that had no electric rail line in 1990. Other potential lines have been suggested, and several light rail projects have been linked to new developments as possibilities.

Private sector proposals in partnership with local governments are now appearing all along the new rail system. There has been some statutory guidance on TOD for fifteen years in Perth, but that has been of absolutely no consequence in the planning of most station areas during the period in which the state government was making this substantial rail infrastructure investment. The only TODs in the past have occurred at Subiaco and East Perth due to state government intervention, with the Subiaco and East Perth Redevelopment Authorities and federal government involvement through Better Cities. Midland and Armadale subcenter redevelopments followed these earlier examples. No mechanism requiring local authorities to provide TODs existed until a recent state planning policy on urban growth and development made a very clear requirement for TODs.

The model of development that occurred in Subiaco and East Perth is possible for all TODs. The mooted Development Authority (combining the Redevelopment Authorities and LandCorp) could have responsibility for all TODs with clear powers to assist in their design and development. This partnership would appear to be necessary for widespread adoption of TODs, though a few examples of planned TODs along the new southern line are being developed by local authorities. Their implementation will need assistance. A TOD committee has been formed, with members from across government agencies, to try to remedy some of the lack of coordination and focus on TODs in Perth. This will help, but unless there is a clear statutory requirement guided by a state development agency, it is unlikely to succeed where previous attempts based purely on advice have failed.

No financing mechanism joining public and private interests exists for rail TODs in Perth, though proposals have occasionally appeared from the private sector.

A new development called North Port Quay is proposed to develop a model carbon-free city for 20,000 people adjacent to Fremantle, based on renewable power, a smart grid, and electric vehicles, as well as a TOD structure around a rail extension. This could become a world leader for TOD-POD-GOD development, though it is the subject of bitter community debate and is currently a victim of the global financial crisis.

Adelaide

Adelaide is the smallest of the five cities, having been through a protracted period of economic downturn and population stagnation. It is like Perth in its basic urban form, but unlike Perth, and indeed all other Australian cities, it has built virtually no urban freeway. Vast areas of the city are

PHOTOGRAPH BY JEFFREY KENWORTHY

Figure 11. Inner Adelaide showing new tram system.

built on a regular, highly planned grid of streets, which make it an easy city to navigate. The city is also mainly flat, making it potentially very attractive for pedestrians and cyclists. Adelaide retains a moribund diesel suburban rail service, though plans are prepared for its electrification. It has one of the world's few guided busway lines, the O-Bahn, serving one corridor of the city.

Adelaide has the most recent strategic plan, Planning Strategy for Metropolitan Adelaide (2005).[35] It too tries to contain growth and reduce car dependence through focusing on integrated land use around public transport. Centers are clearly delineated.

Adelaide's public transport is ready for revisioning. Its rail is slow, diesel-based, and old, so no TODs are attracted to it. The new light rail replacing the Glenelg tram, was extended to the City Station and beyond in 2007, with further extensions planned. It is the basis for the new rail vision announced in mid-2008, as well as electrification based around a TOD vision. Adelaide could become a national leader in Australia. Even though it was the last Australian city to begin a rail-oriented transition, its commitment to developing a public-private partnership to build the rail and its associated TODs can show every other city how to accomplish major urban development with a strong sustainability base.

No development control mechanism for TODs exists, and little experience of Development Commissions in TODs is apparent, though some are now being proposed by the SA Land Corp as the basis for the new approach. The next phase must now ensure that POD and GOD elements are included in these TODs.

Other Cities

Other cities in Australia have sometimes produced strategic plans (e.g., Canberra, Newcastle, Darwin, and Hobart) where centers are considered to be significant and public transport is focused. None are building rail, but since 2007 all are now planning light rail systems. None of the smaller cities have TOD plans of consequence. However, all now recognize that this is how they must seek to finance them. The Hunter and Illawarra regions of Newcastle in New South Wales are probably going to be the first to focus their development along their rail lines.

Conclusion

TODs have occurred occasionally in Australian urban development, though they have not been strategically or statutorily planned anywhere other than Sydney. The market is now exercising a bigger role in urban development, and the financial logic of TOD is coming to the fore. This is parallel with a strategic planning focus derived from the many aspects of sustainability pushing Australian cities toward centers and public transport. However, the four-part strategy necessary to guarantee the provision of transit-oriented development has not yet been fully put in place in any Australian city. Each city, therefore, should review its planning and transport strategies to ensure it has the following:

1. A strategic planning framework that asserts where centers need to occur, in what density and mix;
2. A strategic planning framework that links its centers with a rapid transit base, almost invariably with electric rail;
3. A statutory planning base that requires development to occur at the necessary density and design in each center, preferably with state government intervention;
4. A public-private funding mechanism that enables the electric rail to be built or refurbished through a linkage to the centers it will service; and
5. An integrative function that ensures TODs are also PODs and GODs.

The arrival of the new Infrastructure Australia governance process (2008) has the potential to accomplish all of these initiatives by linking its financing to sustainability objectives. Thus, states, local governments, and private sector interests, as well as local communities, must now face up to an agenda that requires focused subcenters and new transit to be linked and integrated with the broad agenda of overcoming automobile dependence.

NOTES

1. Jago Dodson and Neil Sipe, The Suburbs: Urban Location, Housing Debt and Oil Vulnerability in the Australian City, Urban Research Program, Research Paper 8 (Brisbane: Griffith University, 2006).
2. Peter Newman, Timothy Beatley, and Heather Boyer, *Resilient Cities: Responding to Peak Oil and Climate Change* (Washington, DC: Island Press, 2008).
3. David Lankshear and Neil Cameron, Peak Oil: A

Christian Response, *Zadok Perspectives* 88 (2005): 9–11.

4. Jane Jacobs, *Cities and the Wealth of Nations* (Harmondsworth, UK: Penguin, 1984); Louis Mumford, *The City in History* (Harmondsworth, UK: Penguin, 1961); Patrick Troy, *The Perils of Urban Consolidation* (Sydney: Federation Press, 1996); Allan King, Exporting Planning: The Colonial and Neocolonial Experience, *Urbanism Past and Present* 5 (1980): 12–22.
5. Peter Calthorpe, *The Next American Metropolis: Ecology and Urban Form* (New Jersey: Princeton Architectural Press, 1993); Peter Newman, Amy Thorpe, Shane Grieve, and Rachel Armstrong, Locational Advantage and Disadvantage in Public Housing, Rent Assistance and Housing Loan Assistance in Perth, Final Report, AHURI Project 80038 (Melbourne: AHURI, 2003).
6. Peter Newman and Jeffrey Kenworthy, Urban Design to Reduce Automobile Dependence, *Opolis* 2:1 (2006): 35–52.
7. Peter Newman and Jeffrey Kenworthy, *Sustainability and Cities: Overcoming Automobile Dependence* (Washington, DC: Island Press, 1999).
8. Ibid.
9. House of Representatives, *Sustainable Cities* (Canberra: Commonwealth of Australia, 2005). The currency exchange in this case, and throughout this chapter, was based on average rates for Australian and U.S. dollar exchanges for 2005 according to the Federal Reserve Bank of New York.
10. Surface Transportation Policy Project, *An Analysis of the Relationship between Highway Expansion and Congestion in Metropolitan Areas: Lessons from the 15 Year Texas Transportation Institute Study* (Washington, DC: STPP, 1998).
11. Surface Transportation Policy Project, *Driven to Spend: The Impact of Sprawl on Household Transportation Expenses* (Washington, DC: STPP, 2005).
12. Glen McGlynn and John Andrews, *The Economic Cost-Benefits of Urban Scenarios that Support ESD* (Melbourne: Australian Commission for the Future, 1991).
13. Phillip Laird, Peter Newman, Jeff Kenworthy, Mark Bachels, *Back on Track: Rethinking Australian and New Zealand Transport Policy* (Sydney: University of New South Wales Press, 2001).
14. Peter Newman, Beyond Peak Oil: Will Our Cities Collapse? *Journal of Urban Technology* 14:2 (2007): 15–30.
15. Ceasere Marchetti, Anthropological Invariants in Travel Behaviour, *Technical Forecasting and Social Change* 47:1 (1994): 75–78.
16. Jeffrey Kenworthy and Felix Laube, *An International Sourcebook of Automobile Dependence in Cities, 1960–1990* (Boulder: University Press of Colorado, 1999).
17. Jeffrey Kenworthy, An International Review of the Significance of Rail in Developing More Sustainable Urban Transport Systems in Higher Income Cities, *World Transport Policy and Practice* 14:2 (2008): 21–37.
18. Jeffrey Kenworthy, Response to the Industry Commission Inquiry on Urban Transport on Behalf of the Australian Railways Union, Perth, Murdoch University: Institute for Sustainability and Technology Policy (ISTP), January 1993.
19. Peter Hall, Reflections Past and Future in Planning Cities, *Australian Planner* 34:2 (1997): 83–89.
20. Calthorpe, *The Next American Metropolis.*
21. Robert Cervero, *Transit Oriented Development in America: Experiences, Challenges and Prospects* (Washington, DC: Transportation Research Board, National Research Council, 2003).
22. Peter Newman and Jeffrey Kenworthy, *Cities and Automobile Dependence: An International Sourcebook* (Aldershot: Gower, 1989).
23. Cali Gorowitz, Affordable Housing and TOD, Report for WA Government TOD Committee (Perth: Curtin University, Planning and Transport Research Centre, 2007).
24. Ibid.
25. Laird et al., *Back on Track.*
26. Peter Newman, Railways and Re-urbanisation in Perth, in *Case Studies in Planning Success*, ed. Jim Williams and Robert Stimson (New York: Elsevier, 2001).
27. J. McIntosh, P. Newman, T. Crane, and M. Mouritz, *Alternative Funding For Public Transport In Perth* (Perth: Committee for Perth and CUSP, 2011).
28. Hall, Reflections Past and Future in Planning Cities.
29. Jan Gehl and Lars Gemzoe, *Public Spaces, Public Life* (Copenhagen: Danish Architectural Press, 2004).
30. P. Newman, T. Beatley, and H. Boyer, *Resilient Cities: Responding to Peak Oil and Climate Change* (Washington, DC: Island Press, 2009).
31. Much of the information referring to specific developments and activities in Australian cities reflects the situation as it stood in October 2008 and is subject to rapid change and evolution. The principles, as set out in this chapter, and the basis of the evidence supporting those principles, are not, however, subject to change and are generally relevant and applicable to cities all over the world.
32. Newman and Kenworthy, Urban Design to Reduce

Automobile Dependence.

33. House of Representatives, *Sustainable Cities.*
34. Bob Birrell, Kevin O'Connor, Virginia Rapson, and Ernest Healy, *Melbourne 2030: Planning Rhetoric vs Urban Reality* (Melbourne: Monash University Press, 2005).
35. Minister for Urban Development and Planning, *Planning Strategy for Metropolitan Adelaide* (Adelaide: Planning SA, 2005).

REFERENCES

Birrell, Bob, Kevin O'Connor, Virginia Rapson, and Ernest Healy. *Melbourne 2030: Planning Rhetoric vs Urban Reality*. Melbourne: Monash University Press, 2005.

Calthorpe, Peter. *The Next American Metropolis: Ecology and Urban Form*. New Jersey: Princeton Architectural Press, 1993.

Cervero, Robert. *Transit Oriented Development in America: Experiences, Challenges and Prospects*. Washington, DC: Transportation Research Board, National Research Council, 2003.

Dodson, Jago, and Neil Sipe. *The Suburbs: Urban Location, Housing Debt and Oil Vulnerability in the Australian City*. Urban Research Program, Research Paper 8. Brisbane: Griffith University, 2006.

Gehl, Jan, and Lars Gemzoe. *Public Spaces, Public Life*. Copenhagen: Danish Architectural Press, 2004.

Gorowitz, Cali. *Affordable Housing and TOD*. Report for WA Government TOD Committee. Perth: Curtin University, Planning and Transport Research Centre (PATREC), 2007.

Hall, Peter. Reflections Past and Future in Planning Cities. *Australian Planner* 34:2 (1997): 83–89.

Hass-Klau, Carmen, Graham Crampton, Carsten Biereth, and Volker Deutsch. *Bus or Light Rail: Making the Right Choice—A Financial, Operational and Demand Comparison of Light Rail, Guided Buses, Busways and Bus Lanes*. Brighton: Environmental and Transport Planning, 2003.

House of Representatives. *Sustainable Cities*. Canberra: Commonwealth of Australia, 2005.

Jacobs, Jane. *Cities and the Wealth of Nations*. Harmondsworth, UK: Penguin, 1984.

Kenworthy, Jeffrey. An International Review of the Significance of Rail in Developing More Sustainable Urban Transport Systems in Higher Income Cities. *World Transport Policy and Practice* 14:2 (2008): 21–37.

———. Response to the Industry Commission Inquiry on Urban Transport on Behalf of the Australian Railways Union. Perth: Institute for Sustainability and Technology Policy (ISTP), 1993.

Kenworthy, Jeffrey, and Felix Laube. *An International Sourcebook of Automobile Dependence in Cities, 1960–1990*. Boulder: University Press of Colorado, 1999.

King, Allan. Exporting Planning: The Colonial and Neocolonial Experience. *Urbanism Past and Present* 5 (1980): 12–22.

Laird, Phillip, Peter Newman, Jeff Kenworthy, Mark Bachels. *Back on Track: Rethinking Australian and New Zealand Transport Policy*. Sydney: University of New South Wales Press, 2001.

Lankshear, David, and Neil Cameron. Peak Oil: A Christian Response. *Zadok Perspectives* 88 (2005): 9–11.

Marchetti, Ceasere. Anthropological Invariants in Travel Behaviour. *Technical Forecasting and Social Change* 47:1 (1994): 75–78.

McGlynn, Glen, and John Andrews. *The Economic Cost-Benefits of Urban Scenarios that Support ESD*. Melbourne: Australian Commission for the Future, 1991.

Minister for Urban Development and Planning. *Planning Strategy for Metropolitan Adelaide*. Adelaide: Planning SA, 2005.

Mumford, Louis. *The City in History*. Harmondsworth, UK: Penguin, 1961.

Newman, Peter. Beyond Peak Oil: Will Our Cities Collapse? *Journal of Urban Technology* 14:2 (2007): 15–30.

———. Railways and Re-Urbanisation in Perth. In *International Urban Planning Settings: Lessons of Success*, ed. Jim Williams and Robert Stimson, 295–10. New York: Elsevier, 2001.

Newman, Peter, Timothy Beatley, and Heather Boyer. *Resilient Cities: Responding to Peak Oil and Climate Change*. Washington, DC: Island Press, 2008.

Newman, Peter, and Jeffrey Kenworthy. *Cities and Automobile Dependence: An International Sourcebook*. Aldershot: Gower, 1989.

———. *Sustainability and Cities: Overcoming Automobile Dependence*. Washington, DC: Island Press, 1999.

———. Urban Design to Reduce Automobile Dependence. *Opolis* 2:1 (2006): 35–52.

Newman, Peter, Amy Thorpe, Shane Grieve, and Rachel Armstrong. *Locational Advantage and Disadvantage in Public Housing, Rent Assistance and Housing Loan Assistance in Perth*. Final Report, AHURI Project

80038. Melbourne: AHURI, 2003.

Surface Transportation Policy Project. *An Analysis of the Relationship between Highway Expansion and Congestion in Metropolitan Areas: Lessons from the 15 Year Texas Transportation Institute Study.* Washington, DC: STPP, 1998.

———. *Driven to Spend: The Impact of Sprawl on Household Transportation Expenses.* Washington, DC: STPP, 2005.

Troy, Patrick. *The Perils of Urban Consolidation.* Sydney: Federation Press, 1996.

■ BRIJ MAHARAJ / SULTAN KHAN

Urban Sustainability Rhetoric and Neoliberal Realities

DURBAN—A CITY IN TRANSITION

In their introduction to *The Sustainable Urban Development Reader,* Stephen Wheeler and Timothy Beatley contend that the "rising tide of inequity in many societies—in which some groups prosper while others suffer—is profoundly rooted in current patterns of urban development." The South African *State of the Cities Report 2006* also referred to the capacity of cities to "exclude, to marginalise, to reinforce patterns of inequality, and to create insiders and outsiders." This was especially evident with reference to unsustainable apartheid cities. The apartheid urban planning discourse was organized along the lines of racial separation and operationalized through spatial partition.[1]

In the postapartheid era the constitution of South Africa emphasized the need for the transformation of the apartheid city, especially ensuring democracy and the more effective delivery of services for all citizens, with a vision of equality, equity, and sustainability.[2] In keeping with international progressive trends, South Africa is a rights-based constitutional democracy. The South African constitution recognizes first-, second-, and third-generation rights—civic and political, social and economic, and environmental rights, respectively. More specifically, the Bill of Rights adopted in 1996 explicitly recognizes that everyone has the right to an environment that is not harmful to their health or well-being; everyone has the right to have access to healthcare services, including reproductive health care, sufficient food and water, and social security.[3]

It was envisaged that these rights would be primarily realized at the local or municipal level, and there was an explicit focus on sustainability. Section 152 (1) of the constitution elaborates that the functions of local government includes "sustainable provision of services to communities . . . and promoting a safe and healthy environment." More specifically, a local authority had to "structure and manage its administration and budgeting and planning processes to give priority to the basic needs of the community, and to promote the social and economic development of the community." There was also a general commitment to Local Agenda 21.[4]

However, this chapter argues that social, economic, and welfare indicators suggest that there are high levels of exclusion and polarization in South African cities, consequences of neoliberalism, which appear to be highly unsustainable and more divided than in the apartheid era. In the first section of the chapter macro policies and their urban impacts are critically assessed, including a brief overview of the Reconstruction and Development Program (RDP); the urban development strategy; the adoption of the growth, employment and redistribution (GEAR) strategy; an urban development framework; and developmental local government. The second section focuses on unsustainable urban realities and challenges in the city of Durban, providing a case study that reveals high levels of poverty and inequality, crises in housing and health, consequences of the commodification of the water supply, forced removals of the poor, exclusion of foreigners, and the rise of new social movements.

Reconstruction and Development Program

An attempt to introduce a new sustainable urban planning discourse in the postapartheid era started with the RDP, which emerged as the key strategy to address the social and economic inequalities of apartheid and to facilitate the transition to a nonracial democracy. The principles of the RDP were summarized by the African National Congress (ANC) as follows:

> An *integrated programme,* based on the *people,* that *provides peace and security for all* and *builds the nation, links reconstruction and development* and deepens *democracy.*[5]

The RDP was developed through a people-driven process and drawn up by the ANC in consultation with progressive labor and nongovernment organizations. The RDP emphasized the need to sustainably integrate reconstruction, development, and redistribution, and the "key to this link is an infrastructural programme that will provide access to modern and effective services like electricity, water, telecommunications, transport, health, education and training. . . . This programme will both meet basic needs and open up previously suppressed economic and human potential in urban and rural areas."[6]

The RDP played an important role from a policy perspective to ensure the "successful transition from separate development towards a more sustainable development future." However, many believed that the RDP was very ambitious and utopian, filled with good intentions, but with no indication as to how this would be realized. In spite of the basic needs focus, the majority were unlikely to benefit from economic growth initiated by the RDP. Rather, the white, Indian, and rapidly growing black middle classes would be the main beneficiaries.[7] Initial postapartheid urban reconstruction strategies were propelled by the RDP.

Urban Reconstruction and Egalitarianism

The Urban Development Strategy (UDS) of the Government of National Unity, released in October 1995, was influenced by the RDP in terms of being "people driven, integrated and sustainable, and implemented mainly through the reallocation of existing resources."[8] More specifically, the UDS identified five priority areas: integrating cities, investing in urban development, building safe environments, promoting economic development, and creating institutions for service delivery.

Integrating the Cities and Managing Urban Growth

The UDS aimed to integrate segregated cities by concentrating on rebuilding the townships, creating employment opportunities, providing housing and urban amenities, reducing commuting distances, and introducing sustainable urban management policies that were environmentally sensitive.[9]

Investing in Urban Development

Urban development investment focuses on upgrading existing houses and constructing new houses, restoring and extending infrastructure services, reducing environmental health hazards, encouraging investment, and providing job opportunities and social community facilities.[10]

Building Habitable and Safe Environments

The strategy focuses on human and social objectives in three areas:

1. *Social Development*—achieved through community-based development and the provision of health, educational, sport, and recreational services and opportunities;
2. *Social Security*—achieved by caring for the aged, neglected children, and broken families through social care and services;
3. *Safety and Security*—achieved by addressing socioeconomic conditions that perpetuate crime and violence and undermine development.[11]

Promoting Urban Economic Development

The new democratic government recognized cities as engines of economic growth, given that urban areas generated 80 percent of South Africa's gross domestic product (GDP). Urban development had to ensure the concomitant effect of generating greater economic activity, maximizing direct employment opportunities, and alleviating urban poverty.

Creating Institutions for Service Delivery

The primary task of delivering services was the responsibility of the local government, while the provincial government had to prioritize, monitor, and evaluate development. Central government had the responsibility to provide funding, which would be influenced by national reconstruction and development priorities. According to the UDS there was a need for new local government to improve administrative, planning, and implementation functions through the more efficient utilization of resources.[12] The UDS emphasizes a strong relationship between the private and public sector in the delivery of services.

Some have argued that the UDS was "mainly geared to rearranging cities for the benefit of multinational corporations and export-oriented producers." It was therefore not surprising that the UDS was largely welcomed by the private sector. However, the Centre for Development Enterprise (CDE), a private sector research and policy institute, was concerned that the emphasis on addressing basic needs and services in South African cities was lopsided. This was because of an insufficient focus on issues of local economic development that would generate the resources needed to provide services.[13]

Slide to Neoliberalism

Notwithstanding the laudable goals of the RDP and UDS, and demands from community and labor organizations to realize them, the government argued that the pressures of global economic restructuring forced a shift in the macroeconomic framework with the adoption of the neoliberal, macroeconomic GEAR strategy in June 1996, which the CDE summarized explicitly to be "consistent with the present strong international consensus on the efficiency of the market system." GEAR emphasized that economic development would be led by the private sector, there would be privatization of state-owned enterprises, government expenditure (especially social services) would be reduced, exchange control regulations would be relaxed, and there would be a more flexible labor market.[14]

Contrary to the government rhetoric, GEAR was viewed by many as a departure from the RDP. Local authorities would be forced to generate a larger proportion of their own revenues, and there was a strong emphasis on public-private partnerships. Within an urban setting, this would mean "privatisation and the promotion of the principle of cost recovery which will reflect in inadequate subsidies targeted at the poor." With regard to the provision of basic infrastructure and services, there was consensus in ANC government circles that "users should pay full cost-recovery, standards should be relatively low, and privatisation should be regularised."[15]

The influence of the World Bank is evident in the GEAR strategy, and some have described it as a "home-grown structural adjustment programme." The transition to neoliberal GEAR orthodoxy encountered an aberration with the basic needs-oriented RDP. GEAR's neoliberal orientation was criticized, as it would only address the needs of big business and foreign investors, the gap between the rich and poor would widen, and sociospatial inequalities distinctive of the apartheid era would be reproduced, perpetuating unsustainable practices. In fact, the virtual abandonment of the RDP would mean that the poor would "occupy the lowest rung on South Africa's new non-racial urban hierarchy."[16]

Two policy documents, the "Urban Development Framework" (UDF), released in 1997, and the "White Paper on Local Government," issued in March 1998, gave spatial impetus to the GEAR strategy.

Urban Development Framework

The aim of the UDF was to "outline the urban initiatives necessary to give substance to the imperatives outlined in the GEAR strategy." More efficient and sustainable urban centers were critical to reduce poverty and to forge a more equitable society. The UDF emphasized the importance of public-private partnerships in financing, managing, and delivering services. The UDF argued that based on international experience the "success or failure of national development initiatives will largely be shaped in cities and towns."[17]

The implementation of the UDF would depend on four key strategies: integrating the city, improving housing and infrastructure, promoting urban economic development, and creating institutions for service delivery. In its appraisal of contemporary urban realities, the UDF emphasized the urgency to control and regulate the city in terms of sustainability, economic efficiency, and participation. An important concern influencing the UDF was a need to examine the role and functions of cities against a background of increasing levels of globalization. Conventional wisdom suggests that cities must become more competitive, which was mainly expressed by their ability to attract more private capital and new economic activities. Although the UDF is not explicit about this, the GEAR strategy "would seem to indicate coherence to this convention."[18]

The CDE contended that "improving the management of cities and linking local urban management to economic development are vital for coping with the pressing problems of urban development and of expanding economic activity." However, local development policies have been characterized by a shift in emphasis away from the provision of social services and public goods toward accelerated growth in order to create jobs and increase the tax base of cities. Widespread concern has been raised about the gap between local economic development promises and outcomes. The assumption of the trickle down of benefits to the poor is questionable, and urban inequalities are often exacerbated.[19]

Integral to the success of GEAR and the UDF was good urban governance. Linked with the UDF framework was a radical restructuring of the role and function of local government in the late 1990s.

Developmental Local Government

In 1998 the "White Paper on Local Government" introduced the notion of developmental local government (DLG), which was committed to "working with citizens and groups within the community to find sustainable ways to meet their social, economic and material needs and improve the quality of their lives."[20] It reaffirms the ambitious vision that the public authorities had designed for the municipalities. The capacity to rapidly break with the past, address the backlogs in development, fight poverty, ensure sustainable growth, and provide a healthy and secure environment for all citizens will essentially depend on local government.

An important strategy to help municipalities become more developmental is integrated development planning (IDP), a strategic planning instrument established on the basis of consultation with local communities that must reflect a municipality's vision for its long-term development. It must include guidelines for land use management, a three-year financial plan, a plan for public transport, and essential elements for a municipal performance management system. Finally, it must also allow municipalities to coordinate activities among all development decision-making authorities, whether public or private, operating on their territory. However, a major weakness was that there were no institutional or financial mechanisms to translate these policies into practice.[21]

The CDE contended that the "White Paper on Local Government" was unable to deal with the tension between a need for strong local government to stimulate growth and development and the reality that there was a crisis in this sector. The document vacillated uncomfortably "between a development wish list and acknowledgement that gratification has to be deferred for sustained medium and long-term benefits." While the government identified inequality and poverty as the main economic challenges facing local authorities, the CDE argued that the key challenges were poverty, inequality, and economic growth. It argued that the priorities of cities should be determined through an economic lens. Increased economic growth would provide the resources to address basic needs, poverty, and inequality.[22]

Trade unions and community organizations were critical about whether DLG would achieve its goals. While the DLG focuses on supplying basic services, the emphasis should be on providing basic needs that are sustainable, which would only be possible if there were a funding system that would allow local authorities to meet these obligations. There was a failure to adequately consider the role that government intervention and funding would play in achieving the DLG objective of improving the quality of life of the poor.[23] Nonetheless, the trade unions represented by the Congress of South African Trade Unions (COSATU) failed to oppose the government's privatization strategies because of its political alliance with the ANC.

In 2001 the government decided that there was need to review and reformulate the UDF. In 2004 it announced its intention to develop an urban development framework for the second decade of democracy in South Africa, which would be based on the following principles:

- Increase the status of urban issues in public policy and programs
- Prevent institutional exclusion by fostering participatory, transparent, and democratic urban administration
- Maximize the impact of government action in urban areas by aligning policies, investment, and enforcement
- Introduce new instruments and incentives for urban reforms that meet social need, create economic opportunities, and protect the environment
- Improve intelligence or urban dynamics to inform policy, planning, and spending
- Develop human capacity for urban management and cooperative governance[24]

However, a coherent, national policy for cities is yet to emerge. In exploring how the national strategies are manifested locally, the next section focuses on unsustainable realities in Durban.

Unsustainable Urban Realities in Durban

A pervading concern of critical scholars is the impact of the postapartheid government's neoliberal strategies on the lives of the poor. A number of researchers have argued that postapartheid cities display high levels of poverty, inequality, and social exclusion, with limited opportunities for public participation—hallmarks of unsustainability and consequences of neoliberalism. By adopting Local Agenda 21, Durban was committed to sustainability, at least in theory. However, the city had to deal with the challenges relating to high levels of poverty and inequality; water commodification and disconnections; health and housing concerns; crime, grime, and inner-city decay; questionable tourism policies; an outbreak of xenophobic violence; and the rise of new social movements and mass action.[25]

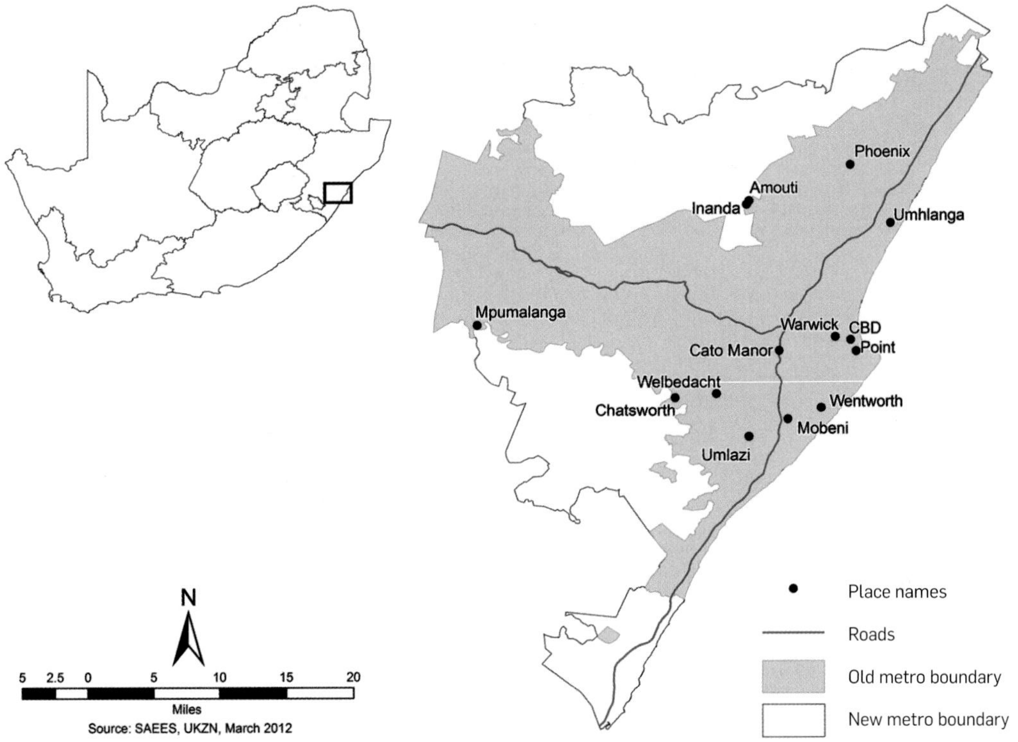

Figure 1. Map of Durban.

Durban—A Historical Perspective

Durban is situated on the east coast of South Africa in the province of KwaZulu-Natal (KZN) (fig. 1). It is bounded by the Indian Ocean on the east, and the warm Mozambique Current contributes to its pleasant climate. Durban has a subtropical climate, with temperatures ranging from 61°F to 77°F (16°C to 25°C) during winter, and 77°F to 90 °F (25°C and 32°C) during summer. Durban is one of the three most significant cities in South Africa, particularly because its spatial characteristics have always placed it in a favorable position, and the local economy has benefited tremendously from the development of the port.

The multicultural diversity of the city was linked to the presence of people of English, Zulu, and Indian origins. The English, who began settling in Durban in 1824, established a trading post in a region that belonged to the Zulu nation. The origin of South African Indians can be traced to the agricultural labor requirements of colonial Natal in the mid-nineteenth century, which some have viewed as a new form of slavery.

In 1996 the population of the Durban region was 2,751,193 people. According to the 2001 census, the population of Durban was 3,090,123 people, with a 12.32 percent increase in the population over five years and an annual growth rate of 2.3 percent. Recent surveys have suggested a decline in the rate of population growth, which was largely related to the impact of AIDS.[26] About half of the province's population live and work in the Durban Metro's industrial and commercial sectors.

OUTCOME	TRENDS	UNDESIRABLE EFFECTS
Inequalities	Many communities still do not have good access to metropolitan opportunities.	It is expensive and time consuming for poor people to move to places of employment and social facilities.
	Uneven distribution of employment opportunities exist.	Limited employment opportunities result in high levels of commuter traffic, particularly north–south movements.
	Public facilities and services are being scattered across community areas rather than grouped together at accessible points.	If community facilities are scattered in different locations then the thresholds (number of people needed) to promote local economic development activities and access to opportunities is decreased.
	While integration occurs to some extent in major commercial and high activity areas (the central business district), for the most part socio-economic barriers prevail.	There are high degrees of segregations between places of work and home and uneven access to social and economic activities within community areas. Private sector investment reinforces current imbalances.
Inefficiencies	Public transport system is being underutilized and land use patterns do not support efficiencies.	The underutilization costs are R418 million per year in transport subsidies. A poor transport service is being delivered to the public which impacts on the accessibility of opportunities for the poor.
	Centrally located urban areas continue to have generally low density development.	Two public transportation systems cannot operate efficient transport in a low density residential and business environment.
	The economic growth path of industry and commerce is decentralizing to outer areas and requires new platform infrastructure and logistics to be built.	The loss of employment opportunities associated with the changing character of the CBD has an opportunity cost. Expensive new bulk infrastructure is being built in greenfields when existing infrastructure in central areas is not being fully utilized.
	In situ low income housing is being formalized on the dense urban periphery.	The location of housing on the urban periphery means long and expensive journeys to work and social facilities. The cost of well located land falls outside the immediate affordability of the Provincial Housing Board subsidy scheme and the effect of the dispersed settlements places longer terms costs on the city.
Unsustainabilty	Some settlements on the urban periphery are being fully serviced for waterborne sanitation.	The money spent on providing expensive services to the urban periphery could be better and widely used if the units were more centrally located.
		Extended full services to certain urban periphery areas sets up expectations that all areas will be fully serviced with waterborne sanitation and the costs are high and uneconomic to sustain.
	Insufficient or no maintenance of existing Council physical infrastructure,	The people in outlying areas often have low per capita incomes, which often means that full services are unaffordable and this leads to non-payment which is financially unsustainable for the city and the poor.
		Council infrastructure is falling into disrepair and in the long term replacement costs will be substantial. Once disrepair reaches a critical point complete reconstruction is required at great cost.
	The municipality is losing market share of high spending tourists.	The municipality is losing an income opportunity. Luxury tourist accommodation establishments are under financial threat; the city is losing these establishments and this impacts on city's tourism image.
	Green space is being lost to other competing land uses.	Loss of free services with the green space, such as water supply, waste treatment, flood attenuation, food production, and nutrient cycling.
	Economic activity and human settlements are contributing toward air and water pollution.	Pollution impacts on human health and living conditions and limits future industrial development potential, with implications for export competitiveness, tourism potential, and health costs.
		Pressure on upper river catchment areas impacts on management issues related to air quality, flooding, water quality in the entire metro area.
	Current poor land management in human settlements, the clearing of vegetation, conversion of agricultural land and inadequate storm water provisions have high costs for remedial and mitigation actions, such as damages to roads after heavy rains.	Loss of soil fertility reduces opportunity for agriculture.
		Poor land management impacts on peri urban tourism potential and existing tourism resources.
		Blocking of storm water pipes causes repair and maintenance costs. Silting dams cause declining holding capacity and reduces the ability to limit flood damage.
		Loss of local food supply.

Like many South African cities, Durban does not function efficiently, "largely due to the legacy of apartheid." In this regard it is important to note that historically Durban was a pioneering "exponent of group race policy." The history of Durban in the twentieth century was largely about the contestation of economic and social space. The perceived economic threat from Indians (who were initially indentured laborers), consolidated a historical alliance between the white working class and the local state, and influenced the development of segregation policies that culminated in the Group Areas Act (1950). By the 1970s the sociospatial structuring of the apartheid city of Durban was complete. Economic imperatives influenced the development of gray areas in the early 1980s. Social movements with strong grassroots support demanded the transformation of the apartheid local state.[27]

Political contestation between the ANC and the Inkatha Freedom Party (IFP) resulted in the Durban region being wrecked by endemic violence since the 1980s. The high levels of crime and violence in the region have had a major impact on growth and development. The collapse of apartheid in the early 1990s and the imminent prospects of democracy brought about immense pressures for the deracialization of South African cities. In Durban the local state was forced to respond to a multitude of problems and demands as it attempted to come to terms with burgeoning numbers, a depressed economy, political demands for a nonracial city from civic organizations with strong grassroots, and land claims from those who had been dispossessed under apartheid. In 1994 Durban was the first South African city to adopt the Local Agenda 21 mandate.[28]

Local Agenda 21

Under the apartheid era unsustainability was the "hallmark of South African cities," where the planning imperative concerned space, economics, and racial segregation "rather than the need to create a healthy, viable and sustainable urban environment." In an attempt to address some of these concerns, the Durban Metro adopted Agenda 21, the "United Nations global action plan for socially, economically and environmentally sustainable development."[29]

The goal of the local Agenda 21 program in Durban is the "development of an environmental strategy and action plan for the Durban metropolitan area based on the principles of sustainable development and community participation."[30] In May 2002 the Durban municipality adopted the following definition of sustainability: "This means ensuring that our actions impact positively on the cash flow of Council, are affordable to the beneficiary communities, are supported by the communities, have no negative environmental impact or the negative impact can be mitigated, and that the institutional capacity exists to manage and maintain the developed areas."[31]

Since the adoption of Local Agenda 21, the state of Durban's environmental well-being continues to come under the spotlight of both environmentalists and policy makers. A major issue is the role of big manufacturing and multinational companies in abusing the environment in the apartheid and democratic eras. A good example is the Merebank-Wenthworth area in the south Durban industrial hub, which is home to the biggest oil refineries in the country, as well as numerous

◂ Figure 2 (opposite). Sustainability challenges in Durban.

wastewater treatment works, toxic waste landfill sites, and a multitude of chemical processing plants. The area has been dubbed by environmentalists as "Durban Poison," because it is known to seriously affect low-income communities' quality of health. In spite of serious opposition from local communities and environmental groups to pressure local and national governments to regulate the level of air, water, and soil pollution in the area, local communities have experienced very little relief from these hazards.

Notwithstanding the adoption of Local Agenda 21, in the second democratic decade many problems still persist. This is because the adoption of Local Agenda 21 in Durban operated largely at a rhetorical level, and there was a failure to operationalize it into reality, resulting in unemployment, inequality, and poverty (see fig. 2). A number of reasons have been identified for this failure:

- Lack of substantial political support
- A tendency to view sustainable development as a green issue that is implicitly antidevelopmental
- A lack of resources to build broad-based consensus
- Administrative power struggles
- Difficulty directing external resources to serve local rather than donor interests[32]

Further evidence of the failure of Local Agenda 21 was implicit in the Integrated Development Review in 2005/2006, which identified the following key development challenges in Durban: low economic growth and unemployment; poor access to basic household services; high levels of poverty; low levels of literacy and skills development; a sick and dying population affected by HIV/AIDS; exposure to an unacceptably high level of crime and risk; unsustainable development practices; and an ineffective, inefficient, inward-looking local government.[33] Chronic poverty and increasing inequalities were major problems in Durban.

Poverty and Inequality

Social, economic, and welfare indicators revealed that there were high levels of exclusion and polarization in South African cities, and Durban was no exception (fig. 3). There was a great deal of debate about poverty, especially about whether it was increasing, how it was measured, and the type of policies that would address the problem.[34] According to the United Nations Development Program, inequalities are widening:

> About 48.5 percent of the South African population (21.9 million people) currently falls below the national poverty line. Income distribution remains highly unequal and has deteriorated in recent years. This is reflected in the high Gini-coefficient, which rose from 0.596 in 1995 to 0.635 in 2001. The Human Development Index (HDI) for South Africa moved from 0.72 in 1990 to 0.73 in 1995 to 0.67 in 2003. Poverty and inequality continue to exhibit strong spatial and racial biases.[35]

According to the Durban municipality "poverty is about inadequate access to jobs, infrastructure and the full range of opportunities that a person might have. In short, it means societal inaccessibility, with a low income merely one aspect of this complex problem." In 1996 about

PHOTOGRAPH BY SULTAN KHAN

Figure 3. Informal settlements amidst middle income housing in Durban.

39 percent of the Durban population lived below the poverty line, this increased to 44.2 percent in 2004. According to the "strict definition of unemployment" 34.4 percent of the population in Durban was unemployed in 2006. This was significantly higher than the unemployment rate in Johannesburg (20 percent) and Cape Town (21 percent).[36]

In 1996 the Gini coefficient in Durban was 0.56, and this had increased to 0.61 in 2004. More startling in the city of Durban is that exclusively black areas such as Amaouti in Inanda compete internationally for the lowest ranking in the HDI, whereas Umhlanga, an overwhelmingly white area just next door to Amaouti, competes with California in terms of HDI.[37]

A quality of life study conducted by the city administration between 1998 and 2005 revealed that about 50 percent of households in Durban were unable to pay for health care, education, shelter, water, and electricity. The study estimated that the basic essentials for a family of four would cost US$240 (1,500 rand). In 2005, about 45 percent of the population earned less than US$240 (1,500 rand) per month. In this group 20 percent earned less than about US$185 (1,157 rand) per month and were referred to as being ultra poor. Poverty was highly gendered—58 percent of the women were poor compared to 29 percent of the men. Also, the probability of women falling into

PHOTOGRAPH BY SULTAN KHAN

Figure 4. Children growing up in Durban's poorly serviced informal settlements.

PHOTOGRAPH BY SULTAN KHAN

Figure 5. A shack defined as home by the poor in the city.

the ultra poor category was three times that of men. Further evidence of economic vulnerability was that 81.8 percent of residents in Durban were unable to save any money after meeting their monthly household costs.[38]

Such concerns have taken on an added urgency in South Africa given that the country is in the midst of a democratic transition, which has as its express goal the alleviation of the immiseration of the most poor and marginalized in the society. However, developmental and transformation strategies to address problems of poverty have been interpreted as being meaningless rhetoric with a minimal impact on the lives of the targeted communities.[39] Poverty impacts negatively on health and housing conditions.

Health and Housing

The majority of blacks are forced to live in informal settlements that lack basic amenities such as water and sanitation—living conditions that create a whole network of ill health (fig. 4). In Durban an estimated 257,000 households (one-third of the total population in the city) live in shacks in 540 recognized informal settlements (fig. 5).[40] Such settlements are also more susceptible to natural disasters such as floods and fires.[41]

Apart from the discriminatory legislation, structural violence, low wages, and unemployment that contribute to squatting, the inhabitants of the informal settlements have to contend with living in structures that offer only partial shelter against the elements, and have no, or inadequate, access to basic facilities such as water, sanitation, and refuse removal.[42] The majority of informal settlements in Durban did not have piped sewerage or indoor water, and the majority of the households dumped their refuse in piles outside their dwelling before burning it.

In Durban the demands of accelerated urbanization, particularly with regard to health care, is compounded by the legacy of apartheid planning, which has resulted in health service provision being fragmented along racial, administrative, financial, and spatial lines. While urbanization offers the promise of improved opportunities and a better lifestyle, the urban poor generally find themselves living in conditions detrimental to their health.

A devastating health issue is the scourge of HIV/AIDS. There was an HIV prevalence rate of 29–32 percent in urban areas in South Africa. However, in Durban the infection rate was 39 percent in 2004–2005, the highest in the country. AIDS-related deaths tend to perpetuate a vicious cycle of poverty, inequality, and social exclusion, and women and children are most vulnerable. More so in Durban than in the rest of the country, local government must integrate the consequences (such as cost and the impact on the structure of the skilled labor market) represented by the scourge of AIDS into the economic and social development policies. More resources will have to be allocated to addressing the consequences of HIV, including the "burden of sickness, hospitalisation, orphans, and social welfare."[43]

In Durban, and the rest of South Africa, health must be approached from a holistic perspective with an emphasis on sanitation, immunization, and nutrition that should be related to the provision of purified water, shelter, income generation opportunities, security, and a good, clean environment. Privatization of basic services like water has had a devastating impact on the lives of the poor.

Water Commodification, Cost Recovery, Disconnections

As an attempt to curb public opposition to privatization, the government emphasized the role of the private sector in the delivery of basic services such as water and electricity. The government presented privatization as being part of the restructuring process. The private sector, however, was driven by the profit motive and was unlikely to invest in poor areas where people could not afford to pay for services. Private companies are more profitable than those in the public sector because of their higher cost recovery rates. However, this profit is made at the expense of the poorest households not receiving any services.[44] Hence, sociospatial inequalities associated with the apartheid era were being reproduced through a market approach to provide basic services like water.[45]

In Durban water meters were installed in most low-income townships. However, the poor were unable to pay for water. Hence, in Durban commodification of water resulted in the metropolitan government disconnecting some 3,000 families per month at an annual cost of US$1,440,000 (9 million rand) flowing into the financial reserves of private contractors for the 2002–2003 financial year.[46] Subsequently, private sector ingenuity won the day through the introduction of prepaid meters (water and electricity) that consumers could disconnect themselves.

> Fiona Lumsden and Alex Loftus estimated that 800 to 1000 "disconnections" were taking place across the Durban municipality daily, amounting to roughly 4,000–5,000 per week. By June 2000, 23,786 households had been disconnected. Working on a conservative estimate of four persons per household, at least 100,000 people were without water. Some of these households have had their flow restored, but the problem of underconsumption of water due to water restrictors is clearly widespread in Durban. Consequently, "large sections of the townships in Durban are being pushed into the popular illegalities of clandestine water reconnections."[47]

Under the financial recovery system the prospect of poor people benefiting from a cost effective service was bleak. Subsidies from the general coffers of the state or from richer utility districts to poor ones were unlikely. It was more likely that people living in underdeveloped areas would pay significantly more for services than those in wealthy developed neighborhoods, as it costs more to bring services to an undeveloped area. Given the vast level of social and economic disparities and the racially fragmented spaces inherited from South Africa's past, the poorer areas bore the brunt of this neoliberal system of cost recovery.

This outcome was illustrated by Hameda Deedat and Eddie Cottle, who highlighted the relationship between cost recovery for water, disconnections, and their impact on the well-being of people. The outbreak of cholera in the northern part of KwaZulu-Natal province in August 2000 claimed the lives of 260 people and left 150,000 infected with the disease. It took South Africa's already ailing health authorities eighteen months to come to grips with this epidemic. The cholera epidemic was considered the worst in the history of the country. Deedat and Cottle concluded that the cause of this epidemic was the inability of the people to join the prepaid water scheme that led to the use of contaminated river water.[48]

The water business in South Africa has attracted such political controversy and exploitation by the private sector that even where services were provided, communities rejected them. The

PHOTOGRAPH BY SULTAN KHAN

Figure 6. Communal water stands provided by the city to informal settlement communities.

low-income Mpumalanga community in the western periphery of Durban rejected water services that were based on privatization principles. They were aware that after the pipes had been laid and the meters installed in the name of development, the bills would arrive. They did not have the money to pay these bills, and they consequently chased away contractors who had come to install water services. The cost recovery approach was unsustainable because of the high unemployment rate, as well as the high financial outlays to recoup repayments. Furthermore, in their mission to recoup costs, councilors and bureaucrats infringed the constitutional principles of equality and redress.[49]

Under pressure from community organizations and human rights lawyers, the Durban municipality argued that it provided six kiloliters of free water per household monthly in order to assist the poor (fig. 6). However, there was a caveat: "people with historic rental, electricity and water arrears are not entitled to the 6 kiloliter amount until they settle these arrears. Since the poor all have arrears that they cannot pay, they end up being excluded from the very policy that is meant to be for their benefit." Also, a large proportion of the poorest households did not have the required service infrastructure. Hence, "they do not receive the free basic service benefit." In 1996, 186,855 households did not have water on site in Durban, and this increased to 238,472 in 2001. Furthermore, many of the urban poor are excluded from the "pro-poor free benefit" because meters are used to determine consumption. The problem is that metered consumption "assumes a certain household size in determining the threshold quantum. This does not take into account the extensive reality of backyard dwellers and multi-family households. Residents in these situations often pay a premium given the high aggregate consumption through a single meter."[50]

A strategy that addresses historical inequalities and promotes social justice through decommodification of basic services needs critical exploration. An implicit assumption in the privatization debate is that the "market is more efficient than government at providing basic services." However, there are limits to what poor communities can achieve without active government intervention. Possible alternatives to cost recovery range from an immediate end to all forms of punitive action against those in arrears, and progressive block tariffs, to cross subsidization. Interestingly, white residents and the industrial sector benefited from such subsidies during the apartheid era. Added to pressures of inadequate water supply, a disturbing trend was an increase in forced removals of the poor, reminiscent of the apartheid era.[51]

Postapartheid Forced Removals

Housing issues, especially rents and affordability, have been central concerns in South Africa. In the 1980s and 1990s, the apartheid and postapartheid local states, respectively, attempted to dominate residents in public housing estates by imposing unbearable rent increases. In both instances, residents opposed these increases. Hence, public housing estates constituted a "terrain of resistance."[52]

Planned in terms of the Group Areas Act (1950), Chatsworth is a predominantly Indian dormitory township located in south Durban. Like most black townships in South Africa, it had a poorly developed infrastructure and very limited amenities and services, and residents faced enormous social and economic problems. In the 1960s there was a great deal of apprehension about moving to Chatsworth because rents for substandard dwellings increased by 78 percent and transport costs increased by 85 percent. It was difficult for stable communities to emerge, and similar to other relocated townships, such as the Cape Flats, social problems in the form of alcohol and drug addiction, gangs, and juvenile delinquency escalated.[53]

Sadly, these problems were aggravated in the postapartheid era. It has been argued that the "struggles in Chatsworth reveal much about the transition to democracy in South Africa." As the fledgling democracy's macroeconomic policy switched from the RDP to the GEAR Strategy, unemployment escalated (up to 40 percent) and the state began to abdicate its social and welfare responsibilities, a situation aggravated by rampant corruption and bureaucratic bungling. The plight of the poor across the country began to deteriorate, and Chatsworth was no exception. In 1999 a survey conducted in the Westcliffe and Bayview areas of Chatsworth revealed that "75 percent lived below the poverty line, 58 percent were unemployed and 42 percent dependent on welfare grants."[54]

As unemployment took its toll, flat-dwellers in Chatsworth found it increasingly difficult to pay their rents, as well as light and water tariffs. The response of the Durban Council was reminiscent of the apartheid era: "Their language of criminalising and stigmatising the poor, the arbitrary use of force, blaming the victim and continually increasing the cost of social services, is right out of the Hendrik Verwoerd manual." Those who were unable to pay their rents would be relocated to starter homes some distance from the city: "The community would be divided with the not-so-poor staying behind and the poor being forced out." The municipality attempted to defend its policy, arguing that it was different from the apartheid era: "Apartheid was about grouping races. This proposal is about grouping classes. Those in the same economic bracket will obviously stay together. It is racially blind. Normal business practice demands that if tenants can't pay rent, they must be evicted." A local resident leader responded as follows: "In the past we were moved because of race, now we are being forced out because we are poor. Is this not discrimination? Instead of compensation for the pain and suffering we suffered under apartheid, we are being exposed to humiliation, violence and evictions under the new government."[55]

However, all was not lost. The rise and growth of a postapartheid social movement, the Concerned Citizen's Group (CCG) in Chatsworth, headed by veteran antiapartheid activist and retired professor Fatima Meer, contributed toward the development of collective political consciousness across race barriers in Chatsworth. A major factor facilitating mobilization was material—the incapacity of the people to pay increasing rents in Chatsworth. Through organization, mobilization, and legal action, the CCG was able to prevent the evictions and relocations of the poor. While the Chatsworth experience has its own geographic and historical specificities, it does help to explain the dynamics underlying urban politics as poor marginalized communities challenge local and central government's neoliberal practices.

Crime, Grime, and Inner-City Decay

Inner-city problems have frequently been associated with changing economic, political, and social forces that operate at local, national, and international levels. Urban decline is sometimes causally linked to a changeover of power and racial composition of the city's population, and it is associated with a whole range of problems ranging from crime to delinquency. A major social consequence of this "phenomenon has been the concentration in the inner city of what is frequently termed an 'underclass' population. These are the poor and the disadvantaged who find it difficult to participate in the changing urban economy." Since the early 1990s there was considerable public debate about the decay of Durban's central business district (CBD) as reflected in newspaper articles, editorials, comments by estate agents, property managers, and the Durban Chamber of Commerce.[56]

There were concerns about falling property values and decline in standards in terms of maintenance and services in the CBD. This became apparent since the late 1980s when blacks began to move into predominantly white inner-city areas like Albert Park. However, to attribute this decline to the presence of blacks was unfair and racist. The slumlords were largely responsible for the lowering of standards because of their reluctance to invest in the maintenance and upkeep of premises largely occupied by blacks.[57]

As the demand for cheap accommodation in the city escalated, rents also increased. In order to meet rising rentals poorer tenants began to sublet their flats, contributing to overcrowding and increasing pressure on services. There were also unscrupulous landlords who charged excessively high rents and maximized their incomes by overcrowding their flats, but did not pay levies for service charges, leading to a decline in services and maintenance. Tenants were forced in live in "overcrowded and subhuman conditions."[58]

Changing economic and social conditions resulted in an escalation in survival activities like prostitution and informal trading. Basically, "capital disinvestment has created a space for those excluded from formal economic activity to gain a foothold in the urban system." These ventures were accompanied by many management problems, including a deluge of people to the city, as well as increasing numbers of street children (a consequence of the impact of AIDS).[59]

In Durban major private sector enterprises were relocating from the CBD to the suburbs, especially north of the city. Concerns about crime, grime, congestion, the escalation in street traders, and the failure to effectively implement by-laws were key factors influencing the decision to decentralize. These factors inevitably led to a decline in property values and redlining by financial institutions, which initiated a vicious downward spiral.

In Durban the local authority was acutely aware of the need to revitalize the CBD, which was perceived to be one of the most vibrant in South Africa. Activities in the CBD were being reoriented to cater for the needs of the large black consumer market. In addition, the CBD incubated emerging black enterprises. Globally, there has been rapid growth in the number of small businesses, and there are predictions that growth will be fastest in this sector of the economy, which will also provide the most opportunities for job creation. However, institutional approaches to urban renewal were poorly coordinated. Social justice has to be an important component of urban renewal strategies, especially for those who have been disadvantaged.[60]

Sustainable Tourism?

Durban has long earned its prime position as one of South Africa's most popular year-round tourist destinations due to its expansive beaches, warm ocean, sunny climates, and rich and diverse cultural heritage. Durban generates US$480 million (3 billion rand) annually from domestic tourism, the city's main source of tourism revenue. It supports an industry estimated to provide direct employment to over 65,000 people.[61]

Durban's tourism industry depended primarily on attracting white, middle-class visitors, and it was around this particular market that its main attractions and holiday accommodation were developed. Even the much vaunted uShaka Marine World was found to be too expensive, where the entrance fees cost about US$58 (360 rand) a day for an average family of four in 2004.[62]

The democratic transition of the 1990s provided many challenges, the most enduring of which was the need to cater to the emerging black tourist market. With shifts in both the international and domestic markets, an effort had to be made to reposition tourism in the city. New tourism attractions in Durban were needed that were appropriate for the African population, who constituted the core of Durban's domestic market. These attractions were likely to fundamentally alter the city's tourist landscape over the next decade.

Although tourism is labor-intensive in most counties, it is subjected to seasonal fluctuations. This fluctuation is particularly evident in Durban, where the number of nonpermanent employees is amongst the highest in the tourism sector. Large discrepancies also exist in income levels in tourism-related employment. White employees earn an average of three times more than black employees.[63]

In Durban, disparities existed in the distribution of labor market opportunities, especially in terms of race and gender within the tourism sector. The legacy of past discriminatory laws deliberately excluded black people from key jobs, training and development opportunities, and property ownership. With regard to employment in the tourism sector, black employees generally hold semi/unskilled positions, while white employees are employed at higher paid managerial and administrative levels.[64]

A serious threat to tourism is unemployment and the alienation of the majority of African people from the industry. Because of the legacy of apartheid, there is still a strong perception among African people in the city that tourism is a white preserve. Hence, a major challenge facing the promotion of tourism in Durban is the need to get local people to buy into the idea of pursuing tourism as a form of economic and urban regeneration activity.[65]

Durban—A Xenophobic City?

Undocumented migration and xenophobia have become a potentially explosive issue in South African cities, as the violence against foreigners in May 2008 revealed, and Durban was no exception. Illegal immigrants have been accused of taking away the jobs of locals, lowering wages, increasing crime, spreading diseases, and increasing the pressure on health, welfare, and other social services. However, groups that have been excluded from participating in the social, economic, and political life of the city—for example, women and migrants—are now more assertive and demand inclusion. From a constitutional and legislative perspective, the responsibility for addressing the needs of migrants falls on local government.[66]

The Durban response to the issue of foreign migrants has ranged from one of benign neglect to active hostility. Consequently, "foreign migrants are an irritant to be ignored and excluded from developmental plans of the local state and can therefore be marginalised." Almost all major policy documents of the eThekwini local authority make no reference to migrants. For example, the Draft IDP Review 2005/2006 recognizes the need to provide security for vulnerable groups, identified as the poor, women, and children. The Ombudsperson's Office is the only sector of the city's governance structure that makes some reference to issues facing foreign migrants. The Ombudsperson identified xenophobia as one of the "challenges ahead" that needs to be addressed. This recognition of migrants' problems is certainly laudable; however, the Ombudsperson went to great lengths to emphasize that in addressing migrants' problems South African citizens should not be disadvantaged. Migrants contribute actively to the economy of the city as workers, consumers, and entrepreneurs. Restricting the benefits of the city from migrants would be shortsighted, as they are unlikely to vanish, given the political and socioeconomic conditions that prevail on the African continent.[67]

Migrants and refugees in Durban received little support or assistance with regard to housing, employment, skills training, and education. In the absence of local government welfare support, migrants have depended on support from religious organizations, nongovernmental organizations, and informal networks. The experience of migrants in Durban and other parts of South Africa gives credence to the view that human rights operate at the rhetorical level and that there is an inability to translate them into tangible benefits.

Challenging Neoliberalism: New Social Movements and Mass Action

The immediate response of the poor is mass action. Local political dynamics in Durban have thrown up a number of distinctive organizations that stand outside party politics, representing the interests and views of the poor and the disadvantaged, which were largely marginalized through limited participatory opportunities. Such organizations have attempted to question the actions and views of officials and politicians, especially when their policies disadvantage the poor.

Ashwin Desai, Richard Ballard, Adam Habib, and Imraan Valodia offer remarkable insights into how the urban poor respond to landlessness, homelessness, evictions, privatization, water, and electricity disconnections. Organization and mobilization around these issues have provided the catalyst for new social movements to emerge, which is filling the vacuum in the absence of a political party that promotes the welfare of poor people beyond rhetoric. New social movements in Durban included the Concerned Citizens' Forum, the Social Movements Indaba, and branches of the Anti-Privatisation Forum (APF) and the Treatment Action Campaign (fig. 7).[68]

In his study of mobilization in Chatsworth, Desai argued that significant political transformation at the local level can be achieved via organization and mobilization of the working class in their living environments. Notable amongst these social movements is an increasing awareness amongst the poor that the source of their misery is related to the government's adoption of neoliberal macroeconomic policies.[69]

The APF, an umbrella organization that has gained prominence since 2000 in the fight against evictions, electricity and water disconnections, and job layouts as a result of restructuring represents the voices of impoverished communities against the state and other public actors. It is also networked with international social movements in the fight against neoliberal policies and their impact on social exclusion and polarization of the poor. The APF uses militant contestations with the state on its macroeconomic policies, and some of these are reminiscent of the communities' confrontation against the state's security apparatus in the apartheid era.[70]

The political stir created by these social movements was glorified to be the revival of the struggle against apartheid. Virtually every week thousands of demonstrators and unionized workers rallied in the streets in Durban and other cities to denounce both GEAR and the ANC. Grassroots organizations in the townships of Durban moved evicted families back into their homes, sometimes only minutes after authorities piled their household goods on the streets and bolted the doors.

There were also incidents in which private contractors had to use armed security personnel to disconnect services. The contradiction was soon to be seen. As soon as the contractors left, self-trained community technicians, males and females, reconnected services. Their fearlessness was fueled by desperation to survive the poverty cesspool in which many former apartheid township dwellers had been submerged. Such desperation has become a justification for conflict with the law. Since last year there have been several reports of violent conflicts with community leaders, police, security companies, and the state. Some of these confrontations were typical of those experienced in the apartheid regime.

Activist intellectual Ashwin Desai has poignantly captured the potential as well the challenges facing the new social movements:

PHOTOGRAPH BY SULTAN KHAN

Figure 7. A protest march in Durban.

These struggles, at first conducted in isolation from each other, have begun to jump the firebreaks of race and place. Will they continue to do so, and incinerate the fetters of old political allegiances and class compromise that have so immobilized us these last ten years? Or will the multitude be confined to the outer reaches of society doused by brigades of politicians, past masters of turning on and off the taps of struggle and expectation? Or will they stand side-by-side and in so doing light the way to a new society?[71]

Conclusion

At a macro policy level there was an awareness of the need to adopt sustainable approaches to urban development in South Africa, but there were problems in translating this intent at the microlevel. While postapartheid policy paid rhetorical lip service to sustainability discourses, in reality there was a "transparently neo-liberal strategy." It was therefore not surprising that "despite real attempts at moving sustainability into the centre of city strategy, there are relatively few areas where city actions have substantially been shaped by considerations of sustainability."[72]

While urbanization offers the promise of improved opportunities and a better lifestyle, the urban poor in Durban were excluded from such benefits and were denied basic services because of an inability to pay. New social movements emerged that maintained that unemployment, water and electricity disconnections, evictions, homelessness, and increasing poverty were a result of government's neoliberal macroeconomic policies.

Wheeler and Beatley have argued that "one of the most fundamental challenges to sustainable urban development is the need to redirect our economic engine into paths that are restorative rather than exploitative." South African cities face problems relating to sustainable urban growth—job creation, provision of basic services and infrastructure, and participatory planning. There have been suggestions that South Africa's democratic transition was largely technocratic—governed by bureaucratic laws and rules that have seriously limited democratic participation.[73]

In order to be sustainable, apartheid cities such as Durban must take the following into consideration: redistribution of resources, creating zones of opportunities for the historically disadvantaged, integrating the city so that urban resources are accessible to all citizens, and inviting people to participate in the planning process. Specific attention must focus on the environments within which the urban poor live, especially the impact of poor sanitation, crime, and the consequences of HIV/AIDS. Undocumented migrants are particularly vulnerable.

Addressing these problems will require a more direct intervention by the state than that currently envisaged by GEAR. Strong state intervention is both desirable and necessary in order to address the sociospatial inequalities of the apartheid era, as well as to create more sustainable cities.

NOTES

1. S. M. Wheeler and T. Beatley, eds., *The Sustainable Urban Development Reader* (London: Routledge, 2004), 2; South African Cities Network, *State of the Cities Report 2006*. Pretoria: South African Cities Network, 2006), 2.
2. Republic of South Africa, Constitution of the Republic of South Africa, Act 108 of 1996, 1996.
3. M. Olivier, Constitutional Perspectives on the Enforcement of Socio-Economic Rights: Recent South African Experiences, *VUWLR* 33 (2002): 117–51; Republic of South Africa, Constitution of the Republic of South Africa, Act 108 of 1996, section 153, 1996.
4. Republic of South Africa, Constitution of the Republic of South Africa, Act 108 of 1996, section 153, 1996; M. Sowman, Integrating Environmental Sustainability Issues into Local Government Planning and Decision-Making Processes, in *Democratising Local Government: The South African Experience*, ed. S. Parnell, E. Pieterse, M. Swilling, D. Wooldridge (Cape Town: University of Cape Town Press, 2002), 181–203.
5. African National Congress, *Reconstruction and Development Programme: A Policy Framework* (Johannesburg: Umanyo, 1994), 7.
6. B. Munslow and P. FitzGerald, Search for a Development Strategy: The RDP and Beyond, in *Managing Sustainable Development in South Africa*, ed. Patrick FitzGerald, Anne McLennan, Barry Munslow (Cape Town: Oxford University Press 1997), 47; African National Congress, *Reconstruction and Development Programme*, 6.
7. Munslow and FitzGerald, Search for a Development Strategy, 60; H. Marais, *South Africa: Limits to Change—The Political Economy of Transformation* (London: Zed Books, 1998); A. Adelzadeh and V. Padayachee, The RDP White Paper: Reconstruction and Development Vision? *Transformation* 25 (1994): 1–18.
8. *Government Gazette*, no. 16679, 1995, 15.

9. Ibid., 10.
10. Ibid.
11. Ibid., 11.
12. Ibid., 42.
13. Patrick Bond, Mzwanele Mayesiko, Darlene Miller, Mark Swilling, Response to Government's Draft Urban Development Strategy Document, *Urban Forum* 7 (1996): 101–20; Centre for Development Enterprise, Response to the Government's Draft Urban Development Strategy, *Urban Forum* 7 (1996): 90–100.
14. Response to the green paper on local government, Centre for Development Enterprise, November 1997; Department of Finance, *Growth, Employment and Redistribution—A Macro-Economic Strategy* (Pretoria: Government Printer, 1996).
15. S. Parnell and E. Pieterse, Developmental Local Government and Post-Apartheid Poverty Alleviation, *Africanus* 29 (1999): 61–84; P. Bond, *Unsustainable South Africa—Environment, Development and Social Protest* (Pietermaritzburg: University of Natal Press, 2002), 242.
16. O. Lehulere, The Political Significance of GEAR, *Debate* 3 (1997): 73; P. Bond, *Elite Transition: From Apartheid to Neoliberalism in South Africa* (London: Pluto Press, 2000); G. Saff, Claiming a Space in a Changing South Africa: The "Squatters" of Marconi Beam, Cape Town, *Annals of the American Association of Geographers* 86 (1996): 235–55.
17. Urban Development Framework, Pretoria: The Department of Housing, 1998, ii, 2.
18. Ibid., ix; A. Simone, "The Urban Development Framework," unpublished paper, 1998, 2, 7.
19. Centre for Development Enterprise, Response to the Government's Draft Urban Development Strategy, 31; D. Harvey, From Managerialism to Entrepreneurialism: The Transformation in Urban Governance in Late Capitalism, *Geografiska Annaler B* 71 (1989): 1–17; H. Leitner, Cities in Pursuit of Economic Growth—The Local State as Entrepreneur, *Political Geography Quarterly* 12 (1990): 146–70.
20. Republic of South Africa, *The White Paper on Local Government* (Pretoria: Department of Constitutional Development, 1998), 17.
21. *Government Gazette,* March 13, 1998, 39; Sowman, Integrating Environmental Sustainability Issues, 181–203.
22. A. Bernstein, Local Government's Second Chance Jeopardised, *Business Day,* March 6, 1998; A. Bernstein, Confused Response to Mounting Urban Crisis, *Business Day,* June 1, 1998.
23. South African Municipal Workers Union, Green paper on local government—An initial response from South Africa's Municipal Workers' Union. Unpublished paper, 1997.
24. South African Cities Network, *State of the Cities Report 2006,* 5–3.
25. Bond, *Unsustainable South Africa,* 242; A. Desai, *We Are the Poors: Community Struggles in Post-Apartheid South Africa* (New York: Monthly Review Press, 2002); Bond, *Elite Transition*; B. Maharaj and S. Narsiah, From Apartheid Apologism to Post-Apartheid Neo-Liberalism: Paradigm Shifts in South African Urban Geography, *South African Geography Journal* 84 (2002): 88–97.
26. South African Cities Network, *State of the Cities Report 2004.*
27. G. Williamson, Urban Planning Issues with Particular Reference to the Greater Durban Area, paper presented at Perspectives on Local Government Management and Development in Africa, University of Durban, Westville, 1994, 3; M. W. Swanson, Reflections on the Urban History of South Africa: Some Problems and Possibilities, with Special Reference to Durban, in *Focus on Cities,* ed. H. L. Watts (Durban: University of Natal, 1968), 142; P. Maylam and I. Edwards, eds., *The People's City: African Life in Twentieth Century Durban* (Pietermaritzburg: University of Natal Press, 1996); B. Maharaj, The Group Areas Act and Community Destruction in South Africa: The Struggle for Cato Manor in Durban *Urban Forum* 5:2 (1994): 1–25; B. Maharaj, Apartheid, Urban Segregation and the Local State: Durban and the Group Areas Act in South Africa, *Urban Geography* 18 (1997): 135–54; B. Maharaj, Urban Struggles and the Transformation of the Apartheid Local State: The Case of Community and Civic Organisations in Durban, *Political Geography* 15 (1996): 61–74.
28. M. Morris and D. Hindson, South Africa: Political Violence, Reform and Reconstruction, *Review of African Political Economy* 53 (1992): 43–59; D. Roberts and N. Diederichs, Durban's Local Agenda 21 Programme: Tackling Sustainable Development in a Post-Apartheid City, *Environment and Urbanisation* 14 (2002): 189–201.
29. D. Roberts, Durban's Local Agenda 21 Initiative—Preparing for a More Sustainable Future, *Urbanisation and Health Newsletter* 28 (1996): 63; D. Hindson and N. King, *Durban's Tomorrow Today: Sustainable Development in the Durban Metropolitan Area* (Durban: Indicator Press, 1996), 124.
30. Ibid., 12.
31. eThekwini Municipal Area Spatial Development Framework, Spatial Response to Long Term

Development Framework and Integrated Development Plan Draft, discussion document, May 2002, 4.

32. Roberts and Diederichs, Durban's Local Agenda 21 Programme, 18.
33. eThekwini Municipality Integrated Development Plan Review, 2005/2006.
34. M. Aliber, Chronic Poverty in South Africa: Incidence, Causes and Policies, *World Development* 31 (2003): 473–90; B. Roberts, "Empty Stomachs, Empty Pockets": Poverty and Inequality in Post-Apartheid South Africa, in *State of the Nation: South Africa 2004–2005*, ed. J. Daniel, R. Southall, and J. Lutchman (Pretoria: HSRC Press, 2005), 479–510.
35. United Nations Development Programme, *South African Human Development Report* (Cape Town: Oxford University Press, 2003), 5.
36. eThekwini Municipality Integrated Development Plan Review, 2005/2006, 18; eThekwini Economic Review, 2006/2007, 24–25.
37. eThekwini Economic Review, 2006/2007, 18, 25; R. Pattman and S. Khan, ed. *Undressing Durban* (Durban: Madiba Publishers, 2007), 17.
38. The currency exchange throughout the chapter was based on the U.S. Federal Reserve Bank of New York's average 2005 exchange rate of 0.16 South African Rand to the U.S. dollar. The Quality of Life of Durban's People, Trends: 1998–2005 (eThekwini Municipality), 28; eThekwini Municipality Integrated Development Plan Review, 2005/2006, 18; D. Casale and J. Thurlow, Poverty, Inequality and Human Development in the Durban Metropolitan Area, report prepared for the Economic Development Department, Durban Metropolitan Council, 1999, 7; South African Cities Network, *State of the Cities Report 2004*, 93.
39. D. Evaratt, The Politics of Poverty, in *The Real State of the Nation: South Africa after 1990. Development Update Special Edition*, ed. D. Evarett and V. Maphai 4 (2003): 75–100.
40. eThekwini Economic Review, 2006/2007, 57.
41. South African Cities Network, *State of the Cities Report 2004*.
42. D. Hindson and J. McCarthy, eds., *Here to Stay: Informal Settlements in KwaZulu-Natal* (Durban: Indicator Press, 1994).
43. South African Cities Network, *State of the Cities Report 2004*; eThekwini Economic Review, 2006/2007, 26; eThekwini Demographic Projections, Report for eThekwini Transport Authority, August 2004, 26.
44. J. E. Hardoy and D. Satterwaite, *Squatter Citizen—Life in the Urban Third World* (London: Earthscan, 1989), 160.
45. L. Smith and S. Hanson, Access to Water for the Poor in Cape Town: When Equity Meets Cost Recovery, *Urban Studies* (2003): 1517–48.
46. A. J. Loftus, A Political Ecology of Water Struggles in Durban, South Africa (PhD diss., University of Oxford, 2005).
47. F. Lumsden and A. Loftus, Inanda's Struggle for Water through Pipes and Tunnels: Exploring State-Civil Society Relations in a Post-Apartheid Informal Settlement, CCS Research Report No. 6, Durban, 2003, 11; A. Desai, *The Poors of Chatsworth* (Durban: Madiba Publishers, 2000), 79.
48. H. Deedat and E. Cottle, Cost Recovery, Prepaid Water Meters and the Cholera Outbreak in KZN, in *Cost Recovery and the Crisis of Service Delivery in South Africa*, ed. D. A. McDonald and J. Page (Pretoria: HSRC Publishers, 2002), 81–100.
49. Ibid.; Desai, *We Are the Poors*.
50. Desai, *We Are the Poors*, 76; South African Cities Network, *State of the Cities Report 2006*, 4–32; South African Cities Network, *State of the Cities Report 2004*, 79.
51. D. A. McDonald and J. Page, ed., *Cost Recovery and the Crisis of Service Delivery in South Africa* (Pretoria: HSRC Publishers, 2002); K. Bakker and D. Hemson, Privatising Water: BoTT and Hydropolitics in the New South Africa, *South African Geographical Journal* 82 (2000): 4; R. Stock, *Africa South of the Sahara—A Geographical Interpretation* (London: Guilford Press, 1995).
52. B. Maharaj, Urban Struggles and the Transformation of the Apartheid Local State: The Case of Community and Civic Organisations in Durban, *Political Geography* 15 (1996): 61–74.
53. Desai, *The Poors of Chatsworth*.
54. Ibid., 98; P. Dwyer, The Concerned Citizens' Forum—A Fight within a Fight, in *Voices of Protest—Social Movements in Post-Apartheid South Africa*, ed. R. Ballard, A. Habib, and I. Valodia (Pietermaritzburg: UKZN Press, 2006), 93.
55. Desai, *The Poors of Chatsworth*, 55, 56, 99.
56. R. A. Beauregard, *Voices of Decline: The Postwar Fate of US Cities* (Oxford: Blackwell, 1993); D. R. Diamond, Managing Urban Change: The Case of the British Inner City, in *Global Change Challenge: Geography in the 1990s*, ed. R. Bennett and R. Estell (London: Routledge, 1991), 219.
57. B. Maharaj and J. Mpungose, The Erosion of Residential Segregation in South Africa: The "Greying" of Albert Park in Durban, *Geoforum* 25 (1994): 19–32.
58. I. Mohammed, Report on the Rental Survey

and Profile of Buildings in Albert Park (Durban: Organisation of Civic Rights, 1999), 2.

59. L. Bremner, Re-inventing the Johannesburg Inner City, paper presented at a Research Seminar, Department of Architecture, University of Witswatersrand, 2000, 11.
60. R. Gittell and J. P. Thompson, Inner-City Business Development and Entrepreneurship: New Frontiers for Policy and Research, in *Urban Problems and Community Development*, ed. R. F. Ferguson and W. T. Dickens (Washington: Brookings Institute, 1999), 473–520; J. M. Thomas, Rebuilding Inner Cities: Basic Principles, in *The Inner City: Urban Poverty and Economic Development in the Next Century*, ed. T. D. Boston and C. L. Ross (New Brunswick: Transaction Publishers, 1997), 67–74.
61. G. Creemers and L. Wood, *The Economic Contribution of Tourism to the Province of KwaZulu-Natal* (Pietermaritzburg: KwaZulu-Natal Tourism Authority, 1997).
62. D. Gangaram, uShaka Prices Uproar—Growing Anger over Outrageous Entry Fees, *Daily News*, April 19, 2004.
63. A. M. Williams and G. Shaw, Tourism: Candyfloss Industry or Job Generator? *Town Planning Review* 59:1 (1988): 81–103; NALEDI, *Overview of the Current and Labour Market Conditions in South Africa* (Johannesburg: NALEDI, 2000).
64. B. Maharaj, V. Pillay, and R. Sucheran, Durban—A Tourism Mecca? Challenges of the Post-Apartheid Era, *Urban Forum* 16 (2006): 262–81.
65. Ibid.
66. M. Olivier, Constitutional Perspectives on the Enforcement of Socio-Economic Rights: Recent South African Experiences *VUWLR* 33 (2002): 117–51.
67. M. S. E. Vawda, Hidden Migration: Livelihoods, Identities and Citizenship—Malawians in the City of Durban (Ph.D. diss., University of KwaZulu-Natal, 2004); B. Maharaj, Durban—A Xenophobic City?, paper presented at the 16th ISA World Congress of Sociology, July 25–29, 2006.
68. Desai, *We Are the Poors*; R. Ballard, A. Habib, and I. Valodia, ed., *Voices of Protest—Social Movements in Post-Apartheid South Africa* (Pietermaritzburg: UKZN Press, 2006).
69. Desai, *The Poors of Chatsworth.*
70. S. Buhlungu, The Anti-Privatisation Forum: A Profile of a Post-apartheid Social Movement Research Report for Centre for Civil Society and School of Development Studies, University of KwaZulu-Natal, 2004.
71. Desai, *We Are the Poors*, 7.
72. Bond, *Unsustainable South Africa*, xvii; South African Cities Network, *State of the Cities Report 2006*, 4–18.
73. S. M. Wheeler and T. Beatley, ed., *The Sustainable Urban Development Reader* (London: Routledge, 2004), 2; J. Manor, Local Government in South Africa: Potential Disaster Despite Genuine Promise, SLSA Working Paper 8, 2001.

REFERENCES

Adelzadeh, A., and V. Padayachee. The RDP White Paper: Reconstruction and Development Vision? *Transformation* 25 (1994): 1–18.

African National Congress. *Reconstruction and Development Programme: A Policy Framework.* Johannesburg: Umanyo, 1994.

Aliber, M. Chronic Poverty in South Africa: Incidence, Causes and Policies. *World Development* 31 (2003): 473–490.

Bakker, K., and D. Hemson. Privatising Water: BoTT and Hydropolitics in the New South Africa. *South African Geographical Journal* 82 (2000): 3–12.

Ballard, R., A. Habib, and I. Valodia, ed. *Voices of Protest—Social Movements in Post-Apartheid South Africa.* Pietermaritzburg: UKZN Press, 2006.

Beauregard, R. A. *Voices of Decline: The Postwar Fate of US Cities.* Oxford, Blackwell, 1993.

Bernstein, A. Confused Response to Mounting Urban Crisis. *Business Day,* June 1, 1998.

———. A. Local Government's Second Chance Jeopardised. *Business Day,* March 6, 1998.

Bond, P. *Elite Transition: From Apartheid to Neoliberalism in South Africa.* London: Pluto Press, 2000.

———. *Unsustainable South Africa—Environment, Development and Social Protest.* Pietermaritzburg: University of Natal Press, 2002.

Bond, P., M. Mayekiso, and D. Miller. Response to Government's Draft Urban Development Strategy Document. *Urban Forum* 7 (1996): 101–20.

Bremner, L. Re-Inventing the Johannesburg Inner City. Paper presented at a Research Seminar, Department of Architecture, University of Witswatersrand, 2000.

Buhlungu, S. The Anti-Privatisation Forum: A Profile of a Post-Apartheid Social Movement. Research Report for Centre for Civil Society and School of Development Studies, University of KwaZulu-Natal, 2004.

Casale, B., and J. Thurlow. Poverty, Inequality and Human

Development in the Durban Metropolitan Area. Report prepared for the Economic Development Department, Durban Metropolitan Council, 1999.

Centre for Development Enterprise, Response to the Green Paper on Local Government. November 1997.

———. Response to the Government's Draft Urban Development Strategy. *Urban Forum*, 1996.

Creemers, G., and L. Wood. *The Economic Contribution of Tourism to the Province of KwaZulu-Natal.* Pietermaritzburg: KwaZulu-Natal Tourism Authority, 1997.

Deedat, H., and E. Cottle. Cost Recovery, Prepaid Water Meters and the Cholera Outbreak in KZN. In *Cost Recovery and the Crisis of Service Delivery in South Africa*, ed. D.A. McDonald and J. Page, 81–100. Pretoria: HSRC Publishers, 2002.

Department of Finance. *Growth, Employment and Redistribution—A Macro-Economic Strategy.* Pretoria: Government Printer, 1996.

Desai, A. *The Poors of Chatsworth.* Durban: Madiba Publishers, 2000.

———. *We Are the Poors: Community Struggles in Post-Apartheid South Africa.* New York: Monthly Review Press, 2002.

Diamond, D. R. Managing Urban Change: The Case of the British Inner City. In *Global Change Challenge: Geography in the 1990s*, ed. R. Bennett and R. Estell, 217–41. London: Routledge, 1991.

Dwyer, P. The Concerned Citizens' Forum—A Fight within a Fights. In *Voices of Protest—Social Movements in Post-Apartheid South Africa*, ed. R. Ballard, A. Habib, and I. Valodia, 89–110. Pietermaritzburg: UKZN Press, 2006.

eThekwini Municipality. Demographic Projections, Report for eThekwini Transport Authority. Durban: eThekwini Municipality, August 2004.

———. Economic Review, 2006/2007. Durban: eThekwini Municipality, 2006.

———. Integrated Development Plan Review, 2005/2006. Durban: eThekwini Municipality, 2006.

———. Municipal Area Spatial Development Framework, Spatial Response to Long Term Development Framework and Integrated Development Plan Draft. Durban: eThekwini Municipality, May 2002.

———. The Quality of Life of Durban's People, Trends: 1998–2005. Durban: eThekwini Municipality, 2005.

Everatt, D. The Politics of Poverty. *In The Real State of the Nation: South Africa after 1990*, ed. D. Everatt and V. Maphai. *Development Update Special Edition* 4 (2003): 75–100.

Gangaram, D. uShaka Prices Uproar—Growing Anger over Outrageous Entry Fees. *Daily News*, April 19, 2004.

Gittell, R., and J. P. Thompson. Inner-City Business Development and Entrepreneurship: New Frontiers for Policy and Research. In *Urban Problems and Community Development*, ed. R. F. Ferguson and W. T. Dickens, 473–520. Washington, DC: Brookings Institute, 1999.

Government Gazette. 39 (March 13, 1998); 16679 (1995).

Hardoy, J. E., and D. Satterwaite. *Squatter Citizen—Life in the Urban Third World.* London: Earthscan, 1989.

Harvey, D. From Managerialism to Entrepreneurialism: The Transformation in Urban Governance in Late Capitalism. *Geografiska Annaler B* 71 (1989): 1–17.

Hindson, D., and N. King. *Durban's Tomorrow Today: Sustainable Development in the Durban Metropolitan Area.* Durban: Indicator Press, 1996.

Hindson, D., and J. McCarthy, ed. *Here to Stay: Informal Settlements in KwaZulu-Natal.* Durban: Indicator Press, 1994.

Lehulere, O. The Political Significance of GEAR. *Debate* 3 (1997): 73.

Leitner, H. Cities in Pursuit of Economic Growth—The Local State as Entrepreneur. *Political Geography Quarterly* 12 (1990): 146–70.

Loftus, A. J. A Political Ecology of Water Struggles in Durban, South Africa. PhD diss., University of Oxford, 2005.

Lumsden, F., and A. Loftus. Inanda's Struggle for Water through Pipes and Tunnels: Exploring State-Civil Society Relations in a Post-Apartheid Informal Settlement. Durban: CCS Research Report No. 6, 2003.

Maharaj, B. Apartheid, Urban Segregation and the Local State: Durban and the Group Areas Act in South Africa. *Urban Geography* 18 (1997): 135–54.

———. The Group Areas Act and Community Destruction in South Africa: The Struggle for Cato Manor in Durban. *Urban Forum* 5:2 (1994): 1–25.

———. Urban Struggles and the Transformation of the Apartheid Local State: The Case of Community and Civic Organisations in Durban. *Political Geography* 15 (1996): 61–74.

Maharaj, B., and J. Mpungose. The Erosion of Residential Segregation in South Africa: The "Greying" of Albert Park in Durban. *Geoforum* 25 (1994): 19–32.

Maharaj, B., and S. Narsiah. From Apartheid Apologism to Post-Apartheid Neo-liberalism: Paradigm Shifts in South African Urban Geography. *South African Geography Journal* 84 (2002): 88–97.

Maharaj, B., V. Pillay, and R. Sucheran. Durban—A Tourism Mecca? Challenges of the Post-Apartheid Era. *Urban Forum* 16 (2006): 262–81.

Manor, J. Local Government in South Africa: Potential Disaster Despite Genuine Promise. SLSA Working Paper 8, 2001.

Marais, H. *South Africa: Limits to Change—The Political Economy of Transformation*. London: Zed Books, 1998.

Maylam, P., and I. Edwards, eds. *The People's City: African Life in Twentieth Century Durban*. Pietermaritzburg: University of Natal Press, 1996.

McDonald, D. A., and J. Page, eds. *Cost Recovery and the Crisis of Service Delivery in South Africa*. Pretoria: HSRC Publishers, 2002.

Mohammed, I. *Report on the Rental Survey and Profile of Buildings in Albert Park*. Durban: Organisation of Civic Rights, 1999.

Morris, M., and D. Hindson. South Africa: Political Violence, Reform and Reconstruction. *Review of African Political Economy* 53 (1992): 43–59.

Munslow, B., and P. FitzGerald. Search for a Development Strategy: The RDP and Beyond. In *Managing Sustainable Development in South Africa*, ed. P. FitzGerald, A. McLennan, B. Munslow, 41–61. Cape Town: Oxford University Press, 1997.

NALEDI. *Overview of the Current and Labour Market Conditions in South Africa*. Johannesburg: NALEDI, 2000.

Olivier, M. Constitutional Perspectives on the Enforcement of Socio-Economic Rights: Recent South African Experiences. *VUWLR* 33 (2002): 117–51.

Parnell, S., and E. Pieterse. Developmental Local Government and Post-Apartheid Poverty Alleviation. *Africanus* 29 (1999): 61–84.

Pattman, R., and S. Khan, ed. *Undressing Durban*. Durban: Madiba Publishers, 2007.

Republic of South Africa. The Constitution of the Republic of South Africa, Act 108 of 1996. 1996.

———. *The White Paper on Local Government*. Pretoria: Department of Constitutional Development, 1998.

Roberts, B. Empty Stomachs, Empty Pockets: Poverty and Inequality in Post-Apartheid South Africa. In *State of the Nation: South Africa 2004–2005*, ed. J. Daniel, R. Southall, and J. Lutchman, 479–510. Pretoria: HSRC Press, 2005.

Roberts, D. Durban's Local Agenda 21 Initiative—Preparing for a More Sustainable Future. *Urbanization and Health Newsletter* 28:63 (1996).

Roberts, D., and N. Diederichs. Durban's Local Agenda 21 Programme: Tackling Sustainable Development in a Post-Apartheid City. *Environment and Urbanization* 14 (2002): 189–201.

Saff, G. Claiming a Space in a Changing South Africa: The "Squatters" of Marconi Beam, Cape Town. *Annals of the American Association of Geographers* 86 (1996): 235–55.

Simone, A. The Urban Development Framework. Discussion paper, 1998.

Smith, L., and S. Hanson. Access to Water for the Poor in Cape Town: When Equity Meets Cost Recovery. *Urban Studies* 40:8 (2003): 1517–48.

South African Cities Network. *State of the Cities Report 2004*. Pretoria: South African Cities Network, 2004.

———. *State of the Cities Report 2006*. Pretoria: South African Cities Network, 2006.

Sowman, M. Integrating Environmental Sustainability Issues into Local Government Planning and Decision-Making Processes. In *Democratising Local Government: The South African Experience*, ed. S. Parnell, E. Pieterse, M. Swilling, and D. Wooldridge, 181–203. Cape Town: University of Cape Town Press, 2002.

Stock, R. *Africa South of the Sahara—A Geographical Interpretation*. London: Guilford Press, 1995.

Swanson, M. W. Reflections on the Urban History of South Africa: Some Problems and Possibilities, with Special Reference to Durban. In *Focus on Cities*, ed. H. L. Watts. Durban: University of Natal, 1968.

Thomas, J. M. Rebuilding Inner Cities: Basic Principles. In *The Inner City: Urban Poverty and Economic Development in the Next Century*, ed. T. D. Boston and C. L. Ross, 67–74. New Brunswick: Transaction Publishers, 1997.

UNDP. *South African Human Development Report*. Cape Town: Oxford University Press, 2003.

Urban Development Framework. Pretoria: Department of Housing, 1998.

Vawda, M. S. E. Hidden Migration: Livelihoods, Identities and Citizenship—Malawians in the City of Durban. Ph.D. diss., University of KwaZulu-Natal, 2004.

Wheeler, S. M., and T. Beatley, eds. *The Sustainable Urban Development Reader*. London: Routledge, 2004.

Williams, A. M., and G. Shaw. Tourism: Candyfloss Industry or Job Generator? *Town Planning Review* 59:1 (1988): 81–103.

Williamson, G. Urban Planning Issues with Particular Reference to the Greater Durban Area. Paper presented at Perspectives on Local Government Management and Development in Africa Conference, University of Durban-Westville, 1994.

■ ASSEFA MEHRETU / TEGEGNE GEBRE-EGZIABHER

Residential Marginality, Erasure, and Intractability in Addis Ababa

Addis Ababa is one of the most fascinating multicultural cities in Africa. The city's diversity is characterized not only by the physical environment of the built up area, but also by the social environment of the various peoples of Ethiopia who reside there and exhibit their various cultural and linguistic traits. The official language is Amharic, but people speak tens of their mother's dialects, and almost all who have had grade school education speak some English. News dailies are printed in Amharic, English, and a few of the major Ethiopian languages. The city is replete with contradictions. To a visitor who arrives at the Bole International Airport, the eastern part of the city, and proceeds to the city center, Addis resembles any modern metropolis, with double-lane tree-lined boulevards, multistory buildings, modern shops, cafés, and resplendent squares and roundabouts. If one proceeds from the center to the western outliers, one gets a completely different impression of the city: substandard housing, ramshackle shops, huge open markets, streets filled with people, and poor high-density residential neighborhoods. Some of the most advanced urban attributes and modern cultures characterize the eastern (Bole) sector of the city, while more authentic Ethiopian and traditional structures and ways of life abound in the poorer boroughs of Addis Ketema (fig. 1).

There are *tej bets* and *moseb bets* (traditional taverns that serve local brews and foods), contrasted by modern restaurants that would satisfy the most discriminating cosmopolitan palates. Addis has the largest African open market and is full of *suks* (tiny neighborhoods stalls) (fig. 2) and *goolits* (meaning squatting produce vendors with their goods spread on the ground) (fig. 3) serving the poor, as well as American-style malls for the affluent (fig. 4). Donkeys loaded with goods have as much claim to Addis Ababa's roads as Mercedes sedans (fig. 5). Slums and glossy high-rises are found side by side in the inner city (figs. 6 and 7). Most of the city's population lives in unhygienic slum conditions, but there are business, political, nongovernmental organization, and diplomatic

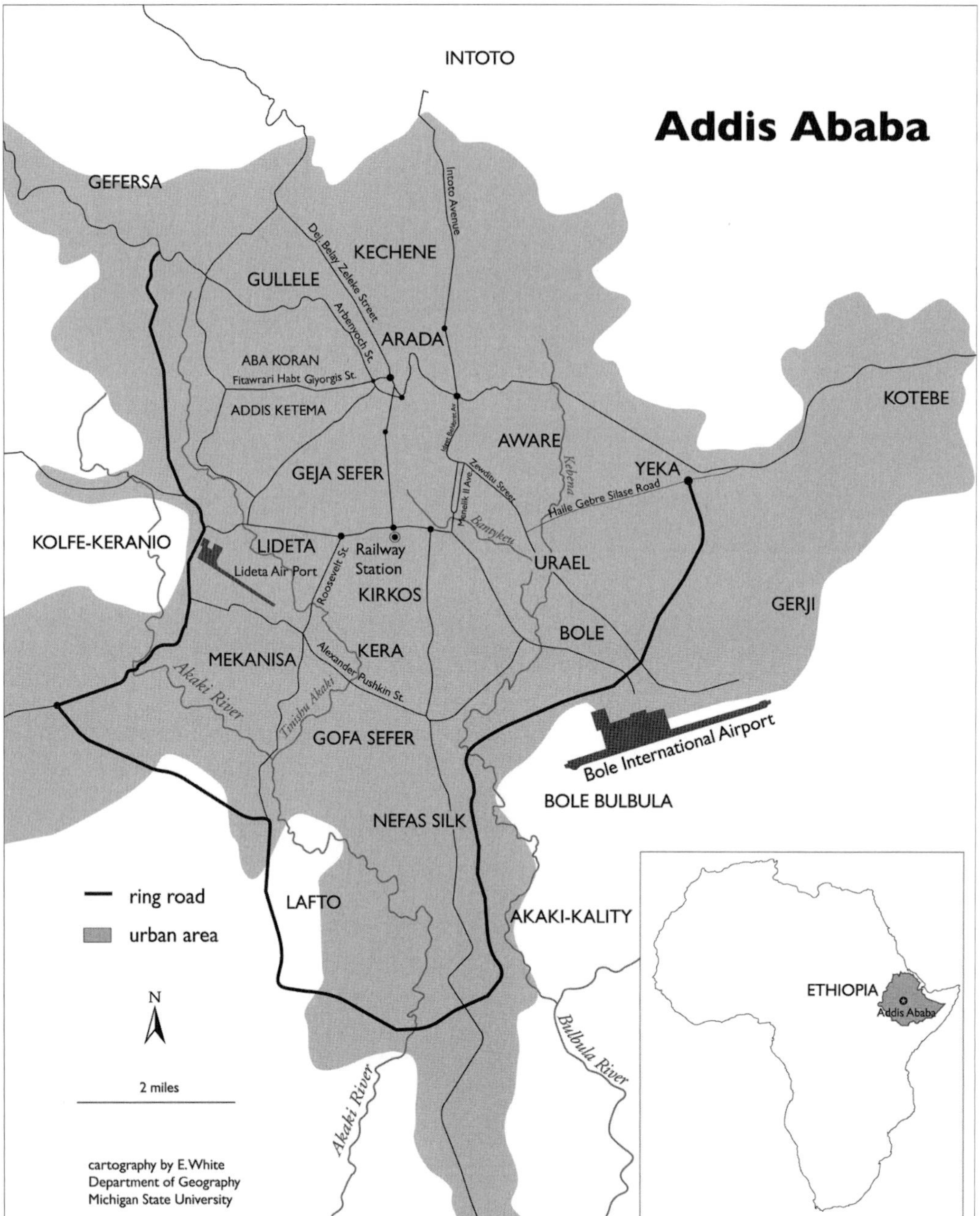

Figure 1. Addis Ababa street and location map.

elite that reside in multimillion dollar homes (fig. 8) in a city where the average annual household income is below $1,000 (table 1). Addis is a city of phenomenal contradictions. However, it continues to be a peaceful, relatively crime free, and effervescent city with courteous and friendly people.

The city has served as the hub of political power, industrial activity, and modernization since

Table 1. Distribution of households by income group, 1998

ANNUAL INCOME U.S. DOLLARS	NUMBER OF HOUSEHOLDS	INCOME PERCENT	INCOME CUMULATIVE PERCENT
Below 70	8,396	2.6	2.6
71–118	5,971	1.8	4.4
119–164	14,907	4.6	9.0
165–234	21,691	6.6	15.6
235–305	24,100	7.4	23.0
306–400	32,453	9.9	32.9
401–494	28,131	8.6	41.5
495–635	37,195	11.4	52.9
636–776	26,932	8.2	61.1
777–1058	38,655	11.8	72.9
1,059–1,482	32,314	10.0	82.9
1,483–1,905	15,742	4.8	87.7
1,906–2,352	11,194	3.4	91.1
2,353 and over	29,159	8.9	100.0
Total	**326,840**	**100.0**	**100.0**

Source: Central Statistical Authority, 2004.

PHOTOGRAPH BY ASSEFA MEHRETU AND TEGEGNE GEBRE-EGZIABHER

Figure 2. *Suks:* Small retail shops in poor neighborhoods.

PHOTOGRAPH BY ASSEFA MEHRETU AND TEGEGNE GEBRE-EGZIABHER

Figure 3. *Goolit:* A small outdoor produce retailer squatting in poor neighborhoods.

PHOTOGRAPH BY ASSEFA MEHRETU AND TEGEGNE GEBRE-EGZIABHER

Figure 4. Upscale shops and malls in Bole.

PHOTOGRAPH BY ASSEFA MEHRETU AND TEGEGNE GEBRE-EGZIABHER

Figure 5. Loaded donkeys in Arada streets of Addis.

PHOTOGRAPH BY ASSEFA MEHRETU AND TEGEGNE GEBRE-EGZIABHER

Figure 6. Substandard housing in the Arada area of Addis.

PHOTOGRAPH BY ASSEFA MEHRETU AND TEGEGNE GEBRE-EGZIABHER

Figure 7. Modern mid-rises in upscale neighborhoods of Addis.

PHOTOGRAPH BY ASSEFA MEHRETU AND TEGEGNE GEBRE-EGZIABHER

Figure 8. Upscale homes in Bole.

the Italian occupation in 1935. As one of the most indigenously authentic cities in Africa, Addis has few colonial relics that anchor its modern core. It grew from a collection of unplanned village settlements called *sefers* (meaning camps) with traditional architecture and building materials. The brief Italian occupation introduced some modern buildings, but it did not affect the traditional character of the city. From the end of the Italian occupation until 1974, the city's population grew rapidly, but there were hardly any urban plans to manage the city's land use and its growing population. There were hardly any zoning laws. Land and homes were privately owned and the market determined access to most land-based properties. Although most of the urban housing belonged to relatively few people, and the quality of the housing stock was generally poor, spatial mobility was free, and people made choices that improved their residential conditions by playing the open and free real estate market. The added advantage of a smaller population and slower urbanization in Addis at the time also made adequate housing provision more manageable.

Historical Background of Addis Ababa

Ethiopia is one of the largest countries in Sub-Saharan Africa (SSA) with a total population of over 73 million inhabitants in 2006, exceeded only by Nigeria. It is currently the sixteenth largest country in the world. However, Ethiopia has the lowest rate of urbanization of any SSA country except Burundi. With only 16 percent of its population urbanized, it is less than half of the rate of urbanization of SSA, which stood at 35.2 percent in 2005.[1] The principal reasons for Ethiopia's low rate of urbanization have been the slow pace of modernization and industrial development in the county's history. Ethiopia has always been primarily an agrarian society.

Although Ethiopia is one of the cradles of early civilization and urbanism, modern urban patterns have a relatively brief history, characterized by five principal periods. The first period began with the proclamation of Addis Ababa (new flower) by King of Kings (Atse) Menelik in 1892 and ended with the Italian occupation in 1935. The first period was characterized by many critical innovations by Atses Menelik and Haile Sellassie. Upon returning from the Battle of Adwa, his victorious campaign against colonial Italy in 1896, Atse Menelik, put an end to the then prevailing mode of roving national capitals and declared Addis Ababa as the first permanent capital of Ethiopia. The credit for making Addis the permanent capital of the kingdom is credited to his famous wife, Etege (Queen) Taitu, a first lady known for her beauty, charm, and intelligence and who was her husband's best counsel on a variety of issues of defense and statecraft.[2] She liked to bathe at the hot volcanic springs in the lower elevations of Addis, later known as Filwuha (hot water) or Finfine (spring) by the local residents, where she built a rest camp downhill from the original Menelik's encampment in the Entoto mountains north of the city. The introduction of eucalyptus trees from Australia by a Swiss adviser of Menelik to solve the fuel problem for cooking also contributed to the permanence of the capital. Furthermore, the location of the city at the geographical center of the country, with pleasant climate, thanks to its elevation of about 8,000 feet (2,438 meters) above sea level, despite its closeness to the equator (nine degrees north), and its strategic placement at the hub of the diverse and rich commodity hinterlands of Ethiopia, added to its attractiveness and later to its wealth.

Once the city was made the permanent capital, Atse Menelik made many more innovations by the first two decades of the twentieth century, such as introducing modern communication, transport (including the Franco-Ethiopian railway connecting Addis Ababa to the port city of Djibouti on the Red Sea), schools, hospitals, and banks, as well as allowing the foreign diplomatic community to build embassies in the city's eastern zone.[3] Upon his death in 1913 and following a brief rule by Menelik's daughter Etege Zewditu, Atse Haile Sellasie continued with and reinforced Menilik's innovations and added to the development of Addis Ababa and other urban centers in the country. During this earlier period, urban development was still dominated by military garrison settlements called *sefers* (encampments) often named after the head of the garrison, called *Ras* (meaning head), a trusted royal or commoner who was given land around the king's residence to distribute among his followers.

Atse Haile Sellassie, who was crowned King of Kings in 1930, began as a dedicated modernizer of Ethiopia. Upon his return from his European tours, Haile Sellassie decided to follow a more aggressive urban agenda, even though he encountered many challenges from the more conservative aristocrats.[4] His modernization plans included improvements to the functions of urban centers, making critical investments in public works, public services, schools, hospitals, places of worship, printing presses, newspapers, commercial institutions, and transport infrastructure, including an airline.[5]

The second phase of Ethiopia's urban development was during the five-year occupation by Fascist Italy from 1935 to 1940. Italy's defeat of Ethiopia's military and forcing of Atse Haile Sellassie into exile was a major success for Fascist Italy under Mussolini in its design to establish the Africa Orientale Italiana (AOI).[6] Although the Italian occupier endured constant challenge and attack by Ethiopian patriots, Italians tenaciously held on to cities like Addis with brutal means. While the occupation lasted only five years, the Italians introduced many changes in the Ethiopian urban system. First, they divided Ethiopia into six regions based on their understanding of the major ethnic groupings in Ethiopia, Somalia, and Eritrea (the latter two had been Italian colonies at the time), and centered each region with an administrative and commercial center. Second, they granted Addis Ababa status as an administrative center for AOI. Third, they offered cities like Addis Ababa an economic base (in secondary and tertiary activities) and introduced many modern initiatives in process and form with Italian-style architecture, piazzas, civil works, urban services, banks, and transport infrastructure. Fourth, the Italians also introduced the first major master plan, with zoning ordinances dividing the cities into various functions with central business districts, government sectors, parks, indigenous open markets, and differentiated and often segregated residential quarters. Fifth, they also initiated an impressive national network of roads that radiated from Addis Ababa and linked the city to all major centers of all the major regions of the AOI.[7] The Italians made a significant contribution to the physical and social modernization of the urbanization in Ethiopia.[8]

The third phase of urbanization followed the liberation of Ethiopia from Italian occupation in 1941. Upon his return from exile in England, Atse Haile Sellassie demonstrated nonvindictive statesmanship and magnanimity to Italian captive *soldatos* and invited them to stay in Ethiopia and engage themselves in whatever business they wished and still keep their Italian citizenship. That was a smart move on the part of the Atse to boost urban development. Many of the Italian former *soldatos* decided to stay in Ethiopian cities and began to engage themselves in modern services like shops, restaurants, engineering, electronics, communication, construction, automotives, and maintenance facilities, occupations that few Ethiopians did at the time. They also worked as drivers (*autistas*) of the mammoth long-distance Fiat trailer-rigs known as *trenta quatros* that began connecting Addis Ababa with the productive hinterlands and major market towns of Ethiopia. The Italian occupation and the contribution of Italian former *soldatos* who opted to live in Ethiopia helped Haile Sellassie's foreign image as a benevolent statesman. It worked to his advantage to push the modernization of the Ethiopian economy and the development of Addis Ababa, along with other strategic regional urban centers like Jimma in the south, Nekemte in the west, and Dire Dawa in the east, with a view to building an export economy based on Ethiopia's rich agricultural endowments. In order to support his development objectives, he began to build critical infrastructure, including a commercial school, a technical school, a university college, a modern civil service system, commercial banks, highway authorities, electric power authorities, a telecommunication ministry, water resource authorities, an international airline, and a tourist authority. He expanded educational and health-care establishments in major urban centers, and Addis Ababa received the bulk of such establishments, including high-quality colleges of arts and letters, education, engineering, science, building and architecture, and comprehensive universities that began to supply a highly trained work force. A major problem at the end of the third phase was the relative neglect of the countryside, where life continued to be hard and people, especially those with education, began to head for the major cities. This produced a tremendous pressure on cities like Addis Ababa, which did not have the jobs to absorb the new migrants. The countryside continued as it did for centuries, with little positive impact from the urban centers like Addis, whose growing inhabitants were polarized, with the majority becoming restive from lack of opportunities.

The fourth phase of Ethiopian urbanization began in 1974 with the overthrow of the pro-West monarchical order and the establishment of a Soviet Union–backed Marxist military junta called the Derg. The Derg ushered a very chaotic and traumatic era of one-party rule with little to no legitimacy on the part of Ethiopians. As is the case with such regimes, the Derg proclaimed a new urban government that relied on the nationalization of all land, rental property, and private industrial enterprises. It also empowered urban locality (*kebele*) associations to monitor *kebele* residents and public property, including nationalized vacant land and rental property. The shortsighted and often brutal ways in which the Derg tried to impose Soviet-style communism not only exacerbated the socioeconomic conditions in the cities but also destroyed the function of markets and transactions in urban and rental housing. The Derg period, which lasted until 1991, was disastrous for the country. Its amateurish rural land policies and the brutal suppression of its detractors led to the death of hundreds of thousands due to famine and summary killings in the "red terror" campaigns in the 1970s and 1980s.[9] In the case of Addis Ababa, the Derg had initiated some aggressive construction of low- and middle-income housing. However, although it was a significant innovation, it came at the expense of ill-advised total assault on the market-based development momentum that was in evidence prior to its taking power. Furthermore, its disruption of key urban institutions and their human capital by brutal means caused a massive loss of talent and competence as thousands of highly educated people became causalities of its summary killings or fled the country for their lives.

The fifth and final phase of Ethiopian urbanism began in 1990 when the Derg regime was replaced by another armed regime that had its roots as an ethnically inspired insurgency in northern

Ethiopia. The impact of this latest and current government on urbanism has so far been similar to that of the Derg's in many respects. First, in 1991, with little input from the population, it declared that urban land would remain under state ownership, and proceeded to remove land as an asset for private ownership capable of transfer, inheritance, exchange, and collateralization.[10] Second, with an apparent shift of focus from urban to rural development, it made pronouncements to decentralize and devolve power and development from the cities into the hinterland. Its positions on various economic, social, and political issues became overtly antiurban and populist in fervor. Conditions in Addis Ababa, for the majority of its residents, worsened with unemployment, low quality of life, and substandard housing.[11] Third, it instituted a system of federal administrative enclosures called *killils* that were to function as ethnolinguistic territories that, in effect, if not legal, began to be viewed as vesting special privileges to people who claimed ethnic origin in those territories. This has adversely affected the urban-rural nexus.[12] The government has recently realized the significance of urban development in national development and has issued plans that would moderate the spatial restrictedness implied in the *killil* arrangement.[13] What is not clear is what specifically it intends to do to reverse the crippling structures of state ownership of land assets and of the *kebele* and *killil* ordinances.

A Primate City in Distress

Rapid Population Growth

The postcolonial history of Addis Ababa is similar to other African primate cities.[14] But Addis has experienced more reverses in its recent developments than is the case with similar capitals like Nairobi, Dar es Salaam, Dakar, or Lagos. As all primate cities in Africa, Addis became an opportunity magnet from which few people with a modicum of skill could escape. Its size grew at a rate unmatched by the growth of basic industrial employment opportunities. Over the past thirty years, the population of Addis Ababa has tripled from nearly 1 million in 1975 to 3.2 million in 2006.[15] According to the 1994 census, 46.4 percent of the city's residents were immigrants. The current growth rate of Addis Ababa is estimated at 4.1 percent per year, which makes it one of the fastest growing cities in Africa.[16] According to UN projection, in 2015 Addis Ababa will become one of the five largest sub-Saharan African cities along with Lagos, Kinshsa, Lunada, and Abidjan, that will have an urban agglomeration of more than 5 million people.[17] Parallel with the fast population growth, the city has also experienced growth in the built up area. The current total built up area is estimated at 133,380 acres, up from 14,945 acres before 1975.[18]

Urban Poverty

With the real value of Ethiopia's income per capita remaining essentially unchanged (or declined) in thirty years, it currently stands at US$180 per annum.[19] The percent of the population living below the poverty line is nearly 45 percent, and Ethiopia's human development index (HDI) ranking is 170 of 177 countries, with an index value of only 0.371.[20] Ethiopia is one of the poorest countries in Africa, and Addis Ababa has been characterized as "one of the largest cities in the world to have ever occurred at such low income level" (see table 1). It is much lower than Mumbai's, which has the world's largest slum.[21] With this macroeconomic reality, the people heading for the city are poor and mostly unskilled. They add to the swelling ranks of the unemployed and underemployed making most of the city an impoverished mass of high-density substandard settlements.[22]

Together with high levels of unemployment, estimated at 33.6 percent in the early 2000s, the majority of residents in Addis Ababa have very low levels of income. The household income and expenditure survey made by the Central Statistical Authority revealed that 41.5 percent of the households in Addis earn income of less than $495 per year (or less than $1.40 per day). Almost two-thirds of the city's households earn less than $2.35 per day. Household sizes vary tremendously, but at an average of five persons per household, most of Addis residents live on less than fifty cents per capita per day.

Unstable Patterns in Recent Development

The city has had an unfortunate recent history that has made it subject to three different layers of land and housing policies in which each succeeding government tried to "improve" by wrecking both the good and the bad from the past. The pre-1974 governments introduced many innovations into Addis, as the city was a showpiece of Ethiopia's march toward modernization.[23] However, Addis remained an authentic African city in which the extension of the rural and traditional were more visible than the modern. Although there were a series of plans beginning in 1956 with Sir Abercombie's Master Plan, they were not fully implemented.[24] The city's growth, right up to the 1974 coup d'état by the Derg, was not adequately managed. However, there were a few positive dynamics prior to the mid-1970s that contributed to the city's charm, growth, and order. First, even though less than 10 percent of the population in Addis Ababa owned more than 90 percent of the urban land, access to housing of comparable quality for the poor was much easier and more affordable before 1974 than is the case today. Second, because of freedom of land markets, unencumbered by draconian government ordinances, residents had no restrictions to buy land and build their own homes in size, style, and building material of their choosing. Land was privately owned and served as valuable collateral to secure bank loans.[25] People were also free to move anywhere in the country and build land-based assets without the burden of navigating restrictive ordinances and crippling bureaucracies.

The period from 1974 to 1990 was the most traumatic for Addis Ababa and the one that has led to its phenomenal intractability. With a series of proclamations, the Derg regime gave the city's 1.5 million people at the time a radical array of ordinances, all of which contributed to the dispossession of private property, curtailed legal rights, and controlled movement.[26] With the nationalization of land and all rental dwellings, the government became the absentee proprietor and micromanager of slum dwellings as well as palaces. It declared Ethiopians noneligible to continue living in their own privately owned homes if their houses were defined by the regime to be "too large for Ethiopians." The owners of "large" homes were dispossessed and given smaller replacements. The larger houses were rented to foreigners or given to the government's functionaries. Initially, rents were lowered for all renters, but the nationalized properties were left neglected, exacerbating the depressive situation and making sections of the city where the government became the slumlord almost unlivable. Because of its Marxist ideological extremism, the Derg ignored the signs of urban dysfunction and the suffering of the poor.[27] Instead, it pushed the enforcement of its laws on an unwilling public by brutal means that finally led to its own downfall, leaving Addis Ababa and the country in a worse situation than when it took over.[28]

The current government that succeeded the Derg in 1991 had a decidedly different approach to urban issues, with its commitment to decentralized development with a focus on rural development. It also gave strong signals that it was undertaking market-oriented reforms to unleash the potentials frozen by the Derg's seventeen years of debilitating dictatorship.[29] But that hope faded very quickly. Since the new government conflated its political hegemony with national economic management, it repeated the Derg's mistakes of overregulating property rights and the national economy and gave rise to incompatible and unsustainable policies that adversely affected rural as well as urban development. First, it declared that government would continue to be the sole owner and distributor of land and that it would facilitate access to urban land by applying leasing or lottery arrangements for homes and businesses.[30] Second, as a government that emerged from an ethnic-based rural insurgency movement, it reflexively replaced the old multicultural and geographic provincial administrative regions with ethnolinguistic territories (*killils*) that implied local ethnic-based autonomy and reduced factor mobility and migration.[31] The traumatic social experiments by the Derg, followed by another layer of paternalistic hegemony by the current government on a whole set of social and property rights, meant an unsustainable regulatory burden that strained the coping ability of most residents of the city in trying to improve their lives.

Unsustainable Urban Ecology

Like many primate capitals in Africa, Addis Ababa's population had surpassed the capacity of the city's housing and infrastructure over thirty years ago, when it had only a fourth of the population that it has today. However, with free spatial mobility, private real estate markets, and almost nonexistent public housing, the inhabitants of the city had more spontaneous means of coping to improve their living conditions. The disruptive Derg ordinances on property rights that were aggravated by current land and housing policies, combined with the city's rapid population growth, have produced unsustainable social and ecological problems for Addis. The policies of both post-1974 governments neglected that "the goal of making cities more socially equitable, economically viable, politically participatory and ecologically sustainable" is at the heart of national development.[32] Community development has been severely curtailed by lack of security in ownership of land-based assets.[33] The current urban and rural policies on land have made Addis Ababa one of the most ecologically unsustainable cities in Africa. The city faces a disturbing combination of low incomes, high unemployment, substandard and insufficient housing, inadequate infrastructure, astronomical disparities in residential quality, and high rates of environmental pollution.

Solid waste is ranked as the highest and most prevalent environmental problem in the city.[34] In 2003 only 65 percent of the solid waste generated was collected. A quarter of the solid waste was disposed of illegally. Only 1 percent of the total liquid waste is collected (see table 2). The uncollected solid and liquid waste has made some urban sectors eyesores and health hazards, with all sorts of waste filling open ditches and open lots along the city's roads. The uncontrolled waste

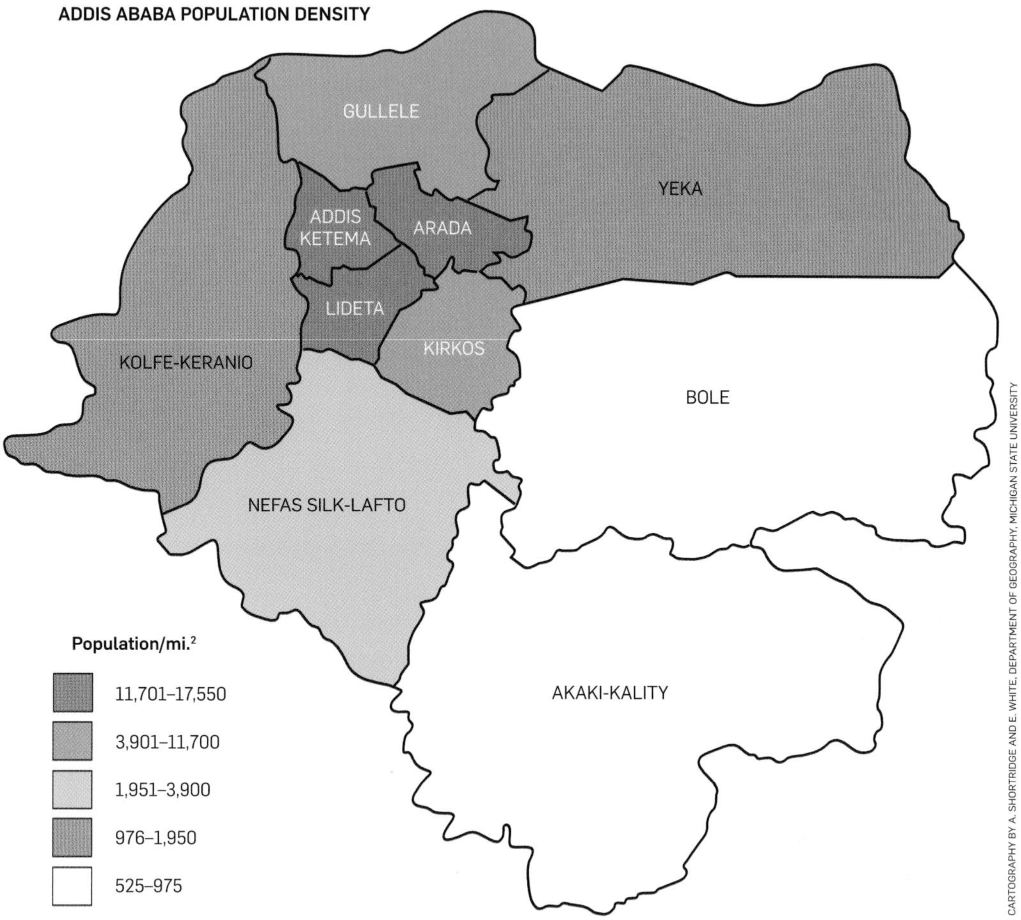

Figure 9. Map of Addis boroughs (*sefers*).

not only contributed to pollution of surface and ground water but also posed major health hazards by increasing morbidity and mortality, especially in poor high-density neighborhoods like Addis Ketema, Arada, and Lideta (fig. 9).[35]

The current sewer system in the city is designed to serve only 200,000 people, and it is often not in full capacity working condition.[36] At its best, the modern sewerage system serves only 0.3 percent of the housing units and only 2 percent of the city's population.[37] Much of the city depends on dry pit latrines and septic tanks. A 1996 survey estimated that only 8 percent of homes used flushed toilets, 82 percent used pit latrines, and the rest used fields/forests and other means to dispose of excreta. The problem of waste disposal in Addis is exacerbated by the lack of municipal sewage suction trucks to empty latrines, the high cost of private suction facilities, and the difficulty in accessing latrines with these trucks.[38]

Water pollution, particularly by industrial and institutional effluents, is a serious problem in the city. Inadequate waste disposal facilities have made the city's rivers and streams open sewers

Table 2. Waste generation and disposal in Addis Ababa

TYPE OF WASTE	MAGNITUDES
Annual solid waste generated	9,021,507 sq. ft.
Annual solid waste collection capacity	5,818,889 sq. ft.
Ratio of solid waste collected	65%
Ratio of solid waste illegally dumped	25%
Ratio of solid waste recycled/composted	10%
Sources of solid waste	
Households	76%
Industries/institutions	18%
Streets	6%
Daily liquid waste generated	211,360,000 gal.
Daily liquid waste collection capacity	2,113,600 gal.
Ratio of liquid waste collected	1%

Source: Bureau of Finance and Economic Development, 2007.

where toxic, hazardous effluents are dumped. Storm water disposal is another major problem in Addis. Drainage facilities consist of modern underground storm drainage pipes along the main roads and open ditches along streets of poorer neighborhoods. Both systems are abused and many of them are clogged with solid waste thrown into them from neighborhoods without alternative waste disposal systems.[39]

Air pollution has become a major problem in Addis. The sources range from burning wood or charcoals for household cooking to vehicular and industrial pollutants. Lack of strict zoning provisions has enabled some industrial, mining, and quarrying activities to be located within close proximity to residential neighborhoods contributing to both noise and toxic pollutions.

Addis lacks an environmental protection system commensurate with its size. The city has inadequate waste disposal facilities and uncontrolled air and water pollution. The magnitude of the environmental problem in Addis has severely stretched the capacity of the Addis Ababa Water and Sewerage Authority. A report on the city's waste disposal problems has indicated that "there is very low concern for environmental protection."[40] It was indicated in the report that the funds allocated for waste disposal and environmental protection were only 1 percent of the city's budget. Addis is heading toward an environmental crisis. It ranks poorly among cities of similar size and international significance with levels of pollution described as "beyond tolerable limit(s)."[41] (See table 3.)

Problems in Access to Residential Property

The urban land policy of the present government is essentially derived from the Derg's proclamation that nationalized all privately owned vacant urban land and rental property. Although both governments claimed that their program was to improve accessibility to housing, neither has achieved this goal. Current ownership patterns show that in Addis about 50 percent of the homes

Table 3. Indicators of water pollution for Addis Ababa

POLLUTION INDICATORS	UNITS	STANDARDS	ADDIS
Industrial point source			
Bio oxygen demand (BOD)	mg/lt	80	4,475
Chemical oxygen demand (COD)	mg/lt	250	14,702
Suspended solid (SS)	mg/lt	100	1,563
Treatment plant (PB)	mg/lt	0.5	4
Capital chromium (Cr)	mg/lt	2	6
Nonpoint source			
Bio oxygen demand (BOD) (clean water)	mg/lt	< 10	400
Chemical oxygen demand (COD) (clean water)	mg/lt	< 10	630
Suspended solid (SS)	mg/lt	—	575
E. coli (clean water)	mpn/100ml	1 to 2	30,000,00–100,000,000
Density of public parks	sq. ft./capita	65	7.1

Source: Bureau of Finance and Economic Development, 2007.

are privately owned as residences or rentals, and the government owns over 40 percent of the rental housing.[42] Even with such an unusual magnitude of government ownership of rentals, the ratio of housing units to households was given as 0.64, indicating a high degree of unmet demand.[43] Housing shortage has been on the rise. According to the Addis Ababa master plan,[44] the housing backlog in 2002 was 233,000 units. It is estimated that by 2010, 223,000 additional units will be needed. According to the Central Statistical Authority,[45] close to two-thirds of the dwelling units in Addis had only one or two rooms. As a result, overcrowding is a serious problem in the city. The majority of the houses are dilapidated and in substandard conditions. Homelessness is another major problem. It is indicated that there are 50,000–60,000 street children, of whom 15,000 are described as long-term street dwellers.[46]

The housing market has two principal sources, the old permit or rent system in private hands, and the new leasehold system by the government that, by law, owns all land in the country. However, there are also illicit transactions with hyperinflated prices for rent-system land. Access to land using any of these markets has been severely marginalizing to medium-income and low-income households. Land under the permit system is grandfathered in its tenure security and dispensation similar to what it was before the new law went into effect, except that the land can no longer "officially" be traded or collateralized. This has made the official exchange value of land nonexistent in the formal market for the tenant, restricting the official tradability only to the physical improvements on the land. However, the government reserves the sole right to appropriate, lease, or dispose in any way it wishes any urban land. This restriction, combined with the government's slow pace in putting more land into the market, has distorted the value of land-based assets leading to hyperinflationary, contraband land deals that the market cannot price in the open. According to some research findings, irrespective of what may be built on the land, in over 70 percent of permit land it is the undeclared price of the land that drives the value

Table 4. Average house price by type of houses

QUALITY OF HOUSE	NUMBER OF HOUSES	PERCENT	AVERAGE PRICE (US$)
Foundation only	37	33.6	25,673
Old houses	19	17.3	11,554
Houses in better condition	50	45.5	27,647
Houses in very good condition	4	3.6	34,618
Total (average)	**110**	**100.0**	**24,457**

Source: Wudineh Zenebe, Anti-corruption Commission to Investigate Real Estate Plot Grants, *Fortune* 8 (2006): 390.

of the property and not the market value of what is built on it.[47] In a survey of house values in the Nefas Silk, Bole, and Kolfe areas of the city, it has been shown that lands with only the foundation for houses sold for as much as lands with houses in good condition (see table 4).[48] Current prices for land under the permit system have made it almost impossible for low, middle, and even high-income inhabitants to afford a decent house in Addis. Predatory speculation of permit land by real estate agencies has made access to homes in the open market possible mostly for the very affluent and Diaspora communities.[49]

The leasehold system, which is used primarily for commercial allocation of land, has divided the city into five grades of land under each of the three city zones in Addis (table 5). The floor prices are supposed to be used as initial price for the bidding process. In fact, it is the last auction price that determines the market valuation of the land. The leasehold system puts out land for auction, and bidders compete for plots available for that year. The number of bidders per plot offered rose over time. The bidders plot ratio for 2000–2001 was 0.43. It jumped to 10 in 2001–2002 and to 14 in 2002–2003.[50] Most of the poor live in the inner-city neighborhoods, near the central business district, where the floor prices per unit area are at the highest. Households who have lands in the inner city but are too poor to develop them are subject to eviction with compensation only for the development on the land. The government has eminent domain to appropriate any land and then lease it to the highest bidder. The government's land law that states "the government may expropriate private property for public purposes subject to payment . . . of compensation commensurate to the value of the property" has often been used for dispossessing land from poor households and transferring the land to private developers.[51] The government, not the original landowner, appropriates the windfall benefits from high leasehold fees. Some have questioned the appropriateness of taking land from low-income households and transferring it to private developers under the guise of public purposes without compensating the poor households commensurate to the actual value of the land they lost.[52]

Leasehold land is also distributed by lottery. In this system, land is leased by the government to people who hold winning tickets on parcels that it makes available for access by lottery. The parcel sizes for provision of land in the lottery system vary, and they have been scaled down several times. They began at 1,883 square feet (175 square meters) and have been reduced to 1,130, 1,011, and 796 square feet (105, 94, and 74 square meters) over time. These are extremely small lots on which to build homes with yards and separate kitchens, which Ethiopians prefer. For any

Table 5. Benchmark/floor prices (in U.S. dollars per square foot) for leasehold land in Addis Ababa, 2002

GRADE	CENTRAL BUSINESS DISTRICT	ZONES OF TRANSITION	SUBURBAN AND URBAN FRINGES
1	14.18	10.78	2.99
2	12.91	7.86	2.52
3	11.13	6.80	1.83
4	9.13	5.74	1.61
5	7.52	4.67	—

Source: Addis Ababa City Government, 2002.

parcel size, there is a requirement to deposit a sizable amount of money to secure tenure, ranging from $1,941 for a 1,883 square feet lot to $1,294 for a 1,011 square feet lot. Low-income households, many of whom live on less than a dollar a day, cannot make such deposits. Only about 20 percent of the inhabitants in Addis can afford to put up such payments.[53] When poor city inhabitants get land by lottery without the ability to make the required payments, they are likely to "sell" their winnings to others who have the financial means to secure tenure for their own use or to speculate for subsequent transfer of the land with windfall profits in which, to abide by the law, the intrinsic value of the land is cleverly surrogated by an exaggerated value of developments made on the land.

The overall impact of the government's system for access to land is to marginalize low- and middle-income households and make their housing conditions unsustainable in a city that is rapidly growing and polarizing. Restrictions to upgrade *kebele* rentals have made close to 80 percent of the housing units in the inner cities inhospitable slums destined for eventual erasure.[54] This has resulted in further densification of severely crowded neighborhoods like Arada, Addis Ketema, Lideta and Kirkos (see table 6) and the proliferation of illegal squatting in the outskirts of the city that now comprises about 20 percent of the housing stock in Addis.[55]

Marginality, Erasure, and Intractability

When it comes to issues of urban land and urban housing, both the Derg and the current government had similar approaches—curtail and overregulate property rights.[56] Both regimes claimed that their measures were to help the poor have better access to land and housing. It appeared, however, that most of the regulatory mechanisms were either not suitable for or were improperly calibrated to the nature of the problems they were intended to solve.[57] This led to unsustainable urban conditions, and particularly as the city increased in size. The ill-conceived ideas of micromanaging urban affairs by draconian ordinances produced unintended adverse consequences of inequitable marginality and erasure of the very people the laws were intended to shelter, thereby culminating in urban systems' intractability.[58] By *overregulation* we mean the act of an administrative agency that places too many ineffective ordinances which are ill-suited to the problems at hand and with little institutional capacity or competence to monitor compliance and correct unintended consequences. By *marginality* we mean a position of disadvantage caused by a hegemonic

Table 6. Addis Ababa population density by boroughs, 2004

BOROUGH	POPULATION[1]	% OF TOTAL POPULATION	AREA[2]	% OF TOTAL AREA	DENSITY[3]
Arada	323.8	10.2	2,456.9	1.9	131.8
Addis Ketema	348.1	11.0	1,888.1	1.4	184.4
Lideta	321.7	10.0	3,027.0	2.3	106.3
Kirkos	364.3	11.5	3,749.5	2.8	97.2
Yeka	337.6	10.6	21,109.6	15.8	16.0
Bole	309.8	9.8	30,415.6	22.8	10.2
Akaki	188.8	6.0	31,609.6	23.7	6.0
Nifas Silk	348.7	11.0	14,928.7	11.2	23.4
Kolfe	283.8	9.0	16,162.2	12.1	17.6
Gulele	346.0	10.9	8,032.7	6.0	43.1
Total	3,172.5	100.0	133,379.8	100.0	23.8

1. In thousands. 2. In acres. 3. Persons per acre.
Source: UN-Habitat, *Situation Analysis of Informal Settlements in Addis Ababa* (Nairobi: United National Human Settlement Program, 2007).

administrative order that makes no provisions for relief from the inequitable consequences of its fiat.[59] *Erasure* is a systemic process that eventually leads to the loss by people of their property rights of tenure and exchange on land-based assets, followed by their removal without fair compensation or substitution.[60] *Intractability* is a condition of lack of good governance in a regulatory state in which policies produce externalities that negate planned or anticipated outcomes requiring subsequent concatenations of ineffective ordinances that lead to administrative paralysis.

The Derg's and the current government's land and housing policy is perhaps the most important reason for the current crisis in creating unsustainable housing conditions in Addis Ababa.[61] With the complicated history of the city, exacerbated by the Derg's misrule and its chaotic demise, what Addis needed was a bureaucracy-light option with a more equitable mixed-use redevelopment and mixed market model of urban housing and land administration that would offer more in situ improvement of "80 percent of the Addis Ababa's central areas (which) have been described as slums."[62] Instead, the present government advanced its new policies in its first year of rule in 1991 in its Economic Policy of the Transitional Period of Ethiopia, which was later followed by the 1993 Urban Lands Lease Holding Proclamation, both opting for bureaucracy-heavy methods that had little chance of being implemented and/or adequately monitored.[63] Its rigid, high-fee bearing and slow-moving land and housing policies—and the limited role it granted to the private sector in transacting land-based assets—made it almost impossible for individual urban residents, especially low- to middle-income households, to have land and/or build a home in Addis.[64]

Of the estimated housing stock of over 600,000 units in Addis, over a third are considered substandard and slum dwellings sustaining population densities as high as 324 people per acre.[65] Some estimates show that over three-fourths of the units have floor sizes smaller than 430 square feet, and about 20 percent of the substandard dwellings are smaller than 215 square feet.[66] There is also increasing discrepancy between the number of households in Addis and the housing available for them. In 1994 the unfulfilled demand for residential housing was estimated at about

10 percent; that has grown close to 25 percent in 2004.[67] This discrepancy is likely to grow as the population of the city rises in the face of continued dilapidation and abandonment of most of the houses in the inner city, including *kebele*-controlled high-density low-quality rentals (which have seen hardly any maintenance since the Derg's regime confiscated them from private owners). This will be exacerbated by the erasure of inner-city poor neighborhoods to give way for high-rent, low-density use.[68]

Such discrepancies between supply and demand for housing for the poor create two additional problems. One is increased densification of substandard housing in the inner city, which has grave consequences to residential hygiene and sustainability. The second is the rise in squatter settlements around Addis.[69] According to some estimates, there are now over 60,000 squatter units around Addis, which represents about 20 percent of the housing stock in the city.[70] These are illegal settlements and are often subject to demolition, but they continue to appear from nowhere, often built as "moonlight-houses" (so labeled because they are built at night in moonlight to avoid official detection).[71]

In the face of these overwhelming odds, the government's determination to continue centralizing the stewardship of urban land and urban housing will deepen the marginality of the poor, their gradual erasure from the city center, and the overall intractability of the urban system. Much of the city's land-based dynamics have therefore been left to the vagaries of informal dealings that have circumvented government directives.[72] In the end, the losers are the city poor, who do not have the means to cope with the complicated confluence of formal and informal methods for access to land and housing. Although the government takes a paternalistic stance to protect the interest of the poor, the outcome of its policies and projects to date did not serve that objective.[73] It is estimated that there is a need for 350,000 to 450,000 public housing units in Addis Ababa between now and 2017 at the rate of about 30,000 to 40,000 units per year. Just over 30,000 condominium units have been completed between 2003 and 2006.[74] The government's hope that the private sector would help in the construction of affordable housing on land provided by the government was misplaced. In an issue of *Fortune* magazine, Wudineh Zenebe indicated that real estate developers never built low-income housing on land that was made available. Instead, they transferred the land to third parties or built apartment units that were selling at prices that are out of reach for almost everyone in Addis except the very affluent.[75]

If condominiums continue to be the principal means of replacing *kebele* rentals, urban planners have to consider four fundamental problems with condominium units. First, *kebele* densities tend to be much higher (as high as 325 people per acre) than densities that the new low-rise or high-rise condos are designed for, which means inadequate coverage, especially for Addis boroughs like Arada, Addis Ketema, Lideta, and Kirkos. Second, condominium units erected by the government are expensive, costing close to $5,880 for a 550 square-feet, one-bedroom unit, which is unaffordable to the majority of *kebele* residents and inadequate to accommodate their sizable households.[76] Third, most condos are not located in the central city, where residents have enjoyed their social networks, low transit budgets, proximity to places of worship, and the social capital of neighborhood traditional self-help organizations (like *idir, mahber, and ekub*) that are essential to their livelihoods.[77] Although such residential disruptions also occur in urban renewal projects in more developed countries,[78] they are even more stressful in less developed communities where the social welfare resources for redress are almost nonexistent. Fourth, with an average size of more than five persons among poor households in Addis, even with tight controls on occupancy rates, it would lead to overuse and rapid depreciation of such projects, as has happened in such managed urban renewal schemes around the world.[79] There is a mismatch between the financial means of low-income households and the cost of access to condominiums. Despite the expressed aim of condominium projects to address the needs of the poor, studies have shown that a significant portion of these units are occupied by middle- and high-income households. Data from condominium sites located in several sectors of Addis (Aware, Gullele, Urael, Lideta, Mekanisa, and Bole-Gerji), showed that over 60 percent of the occupants are middle- and upper-income households. In the Bole-Gerji site, only 1.3 percent of condominium occupants are low-income households.[80]

A Tale of Two Cities: Boom and Bust in Addis

Addis Ababa is a metropolis of monumental contradictions between "poor" Addis of the unsightly slums in the city center of Arada, Addis Ketema, Lideta, and Kirkos and the "upscale" Addis of the gleamy high-rises and expensive homes in the Bole, Urael, and Kotebe neighborhoods.[81] Ironically, upscale Addis is currently booming, while poor Addis—which houses over 80 percent of the population, most of whom are very poor and unemployed—lives in marginalized and distressed neighborhoods under the strain of *kebele* strictures, with insecurity of tenure and inevitable erasure. As Rosemary Curran pointed out, "there is currently no strategy which allows low-income households to remain in their central city neighborhoods as major redevelopment (primarily commercial) takes place."[82] According to a recent study by UN's Habitat "the leasehold system . . . has remained insensitive to the housing plight of the urban poor" whose population "is living in run-down and slum settlements (considered) as one of the highest and poorest in the world."[83]

The principal challenge for the sustainability of Addis as a viable primate city is therefore the astronomical polarity between poor and upscale Addis, in which the former faces marginality and erasure to give way to the latter as the government's own action for urban renewal and its slow-moving machinery of redress for the poor is overtaken by contrarian events on the ground. The rapidly adjusting and relatively efficient informal market system has made it but intractable for the government's regulatory mechanism to work for the poor, thus deepening the plight of the people in poor Addis, whereas upscale Addis, perhaps by default, reaps windfall benefits. The land transfer from poor Addis to upscale Addis is facilitated by the government's commercial leasehold system as well as by a new breed of real estate agents that have become savvy in value surrogation for lawful transfer of land and housing to more affluent residents and businesses, including "members of the Ethiopian Diaspora."[84]

What is most astounding about Addis is how 80 percent of the central urban inhabitants live in slums of indescribable depravity in the midst of a building race of high-rises that outwardly tell a story of a boomtown. That in a sense manifests intractability, the failure by authorities to anticipate unintended outcomes of their policies that effectively marginalize and threaten erasure of poor inhabitants of the city center. Under the current government's policy, even middle-class earners are under severe stress to find decent housing. In the pre-1974 Addis Ababa, a middle-class family with income of $100 per month was able to afford a brick house on 5,400–10,800 square feet lots with multiple rooms and internal plumbing, with about 25 percent of its income (for rental or mortgage). Today, per capita incomes may have doubled for middle-income families, but "modern houses and apartments with toilets and hot and cold water—even when fairly modest—typically rent from $350 to $1,200" per month.[85] Most of Addis's inhabitants earn less than $85 per month, and over a third of the population lives below the poverty line.[86] Unless mid-income families are fortunate enough to live in grandfathered homes built before 1991, or homes constructed since then through the current government's narrow window of the lottery for access to public housing condominium units or land acquisition, it is almost impossible for an individual of low- or middle-income status to afford decent housing. The private sector, which is restricted to selling only improvements on the land and not the land itself, plays very little role in access to housing for most city inhabitants, as it posts prohibitive prices for homes of any quality because of the imputed shadow prices for land.[87]

Conclusion

There have always been poor residences in Addis, but conditions have deepened over the past thirty years. The period from 1974 to the present brought about a drastic change in the way the city has been administered. The two governments that ruled since then elected to micromanage the city's lands and housing stock with a promise of fairer access to urban housing for all, especially the poor. Ambitious regulatory mechanisms were put in place to manage such herculean tasks, but neither government was moved by the suffering and dislocation that its draconian directives created. These stresses in housing provision were amplified by continued urbanization and a growing Addis population. Low-income residents whom the laws were intended to help were left worse off in access to land and housing. Their mobility being severely restricted by the *kebele* (urban) and *killil* (federal) bureaucracies, their housing stock began to deteriorate toward uninhabitable slums due to overoccupancy, overcrowding, lack of maintenance, restrictions to making improvements by tenants, and lack of adequate sanitation and refuse collection facilities. On the contrary, the upper-income and affluent inhabitants of the city, who were better off to begin with, found ways to negotiate the governments' ordinances and experience living conditions that can match or excel any in Europe or the United States. The result is an astronomical disparity in quality of urban living that is unsustainable. Housing conditions for over 80 percent of the core city inhabitants have become intractable, with progressively marginalized people under the constant fear of erasure from their holdings. If current trends continue, the poor will be forced to evacuate the city or, more realistically, try to stay in more dense and dangerously unhygienic slum and squatter neighborhoods posing serious safety and health hazards to themselves and for the city as a whole.

The transformation of Addis Ababa into a viable and sustainable metropolis will need deregulated land-based ownership and transaction of assets, unrestricted spatial mobility of people, and a functionally integrated urban environment. The city has to serve the majority of its population that is poor and employed mostly in the informal sector with meager returns. A metropolis that marginalizes most of its inhabitants will be faced with serious instability. There are two principal systemic challenges that need to be tackled to address the current dilemma. Both have to do with moving Ethiopians toward an ownership and more mobile society by deregulating some of the draconian provisions on property rights and allowing markets to play a role in the allocation of scarce resources with appropriate public regulatory safeguards to protect vulnerable groups. In the case of Addis Ababa, all of its residents, rich and poor, should have as much stake in the dynamics of the city. The government has a legitimate role to facilitate access to low-income public housing as it has done with some success. However, it is unlikely to resolve the serious housing shortage with the current rate of supply faced with the astronomical magnitude in demand. Removing its rigid land policy and allowing land and housing to be transacted and collateralized in the open market will dislodge the current inflationary logjam in property markets. The records of the Derg and that of the current government with a paternalistic monopoly of stewardship of public land and housing assets have only led to a web of regulations whose negative outcomes have outweighed the benefits, especially for the poor. The overregulated environment on land and housing since the Derg may have vitiated property markets beyond repair in Ethiopia. However, robust public policies to sustain and strengthen the current role of the government to expand access to low-cost public housing combined with intelligent deregulation that would allow the right to own, inherit, and transact land-based assets, including land, would help resolve the growing intractability of Addis.

The second challenge has to do with functional integration of Addis with the countryside to facilitate residential and occupational mobility. Addis may soon have 4 million inhabitants—or may have reached or exceeded that number already.[88] In the current structure of *killils,* Addis enjoys the status of a federal capital in addition to being the quintessential primate city. It has a pull factor that is totally mismatched by the opportunities available in the city. This is a central problem in the sustainability of cities like Addis. Considering the current realities in job opportunities and access to quality housing, Addis is exceedingly overpopulated. In addition to improving conditions in the city, part of the solution resides in stemming the tide of immigrants into the city and liberalizing opportunities for Addis Ababans to "suburbanize" and move out into the greater metropolitan and exurban areas of the city for jobs, businesses, and/or residences. An important aspect of a master plan for Addis should incorporate the location and relocation of public as well as private job opportunities in the suburban satellite towns and exurban outliers, combined with affordable mass transit connecting the city center to nodes in suburbs and exurbs. On the public policy side, this will require the relaxation of strictures of both *kebele* and *killil* ordinances so that people can readily enjoy residential mobility and land ownership in and out of the city. Current urban developments in *killils* like Adama, Awasa, Bahr Dar, Dire Dawa, Jimma, Mekele, and Nekemte are encouraging signs. However, for a more dynamic future such emerging cities need to be functionally articulated to each other and to the national hub of Addis. *Killil* capitals and cities need to operate as open systems for free flow of innovations and factors of production with propensities to respond to regional, national, and international dynamics in trade, investment, development, and information exchange.

Finally, despite all the public reforms that have been put in place by the last two ruling regimes, the basic needs in housing and service provision of the Addis underclass are still unmet, and their conditions have deteriorated. In fact, with redevelopment initiatives and associated displacement of many in the inner city, the poor for the first time in history are actually being erased from Addis. The fact that the housing and infrastructure conditions of the middle-income groups have also deteriorated, since the introduction of state ownership over land and housing further exacerbates the urban housing crisis. The government regulatory mechanisms clearly do not have the technical or policy capacity to adequately or equitably improve the housing and infrastructure provision for the benefit of the urban poor. Freeing up the middle- and upper-income land and housing to increasing market forces, which have been shown globally to be effective in addressing the needs of the more privileged, would allow public initiatives, resources, energy, and effective action to be specifically concentrated in providing adequate land, housing, and infrastructure for the poor—which private markets have more difficulty in addressing. The public sector needs to show some degree of effectiveness in redressing disparities. Two decades of reforms in the name of meeting the needs of the urban poor have not prevented the most severe marginalization of the Addis underclass. On the contrary, if current trends continue to prevail, it appears that the poor face pervasive erasure from the Addis urban core.

NOTES

1. United Nations Population Division, *World Urbanization Prospects* (New York: UN Population Division, 2007).
2. Banru Zewde, *A History of Modern Ethiopia 1855–1991* (Oxford: James Currey, 2001), 114–20; Chris Prouty, *Empress Taytu and Menilek II: Ethiopia 1883–1910* (Trenton, NJ: Red Sea Press, 1986).
3. Bahru Zewde, *Pioneers of Change in Ethiopia* (Addis Ababa: Addis Ababa University Press, 2002); Paulos Gnogno, *Atse Menelik* (Addis Ababa: Bole Printing Press, 1991), 236–430 (in Amharic).
4. Zewde, *Pioneers of Change*, 79–98.
5. Richard Pankhurst, *The Ethiopians: A History* (Oxford, UK: Blackwell, 2001), 195–218.
6. Guida D'Italia, *Africa Orientale Italiana* (Milano: Consociazione Turistica Italiana, 1938).
7. Ibid., 474–94.
8. UN-Habitat, *Situation Analysis of Informal Settlements in Addis Ababa* (Nairobi: United National Human Settlement Program, 2007), 7.
9. Sigfried Pausewang, Kietil Tronvoll, and Lovise Aalen, A Process of Democratization or Control?, in *Ethiopia since the Derg: A Decade of Demographic Pretention and Performance*, ed. Siegfied Pausewang, Kjetil Tronvoll, and Lovise Aalen (London: Zed Books, 2002), 26–45.
10. Solomon Gebre, Urban Land Issues and Policies in Ethiopia, in *Land Tenure and Land Policy in Ethiopia after the Derg*, ed. Desalegn Rahmato (Addis Ababa: Institute of Development Research, 1994), 278–301; Tamrat Delelegne, Current Urban Land Policy Issues and Problems in Addis Ababa, in *Urban Development in Ethiopia and other Related Issues*, ed. Zewdie Serbarro and Zelleke Zewdie (Addis Ababa: Ministry of Works and Urban Development, 1998), 39–61; Solomon Haile and Reinfried Mansberger, Land Policy, Urban-Rural Interaction and Land Administration Differentiation in Ethiopia, paper at the Second FIG Regional Conference, Marakech, Morocco, 2003; World Bank, *Improving Access to Housing and Land in Addis Ababa: An Analytical Overview and Recommendations* (Washington, DC: World Bank, 2005).
11. UN-Habitat, *Situation Analysis*, 19.
12. Haile and Mansberger, Land Policy; Tegegne Gebre-Egziabher, Geographically Differentiated Strategy, Urbanization Agenda and Rural-Urban Linkages: An Assessment of Emerging Regional Development Strategies in Ethiopia, Addis Ababa University Regional and Local Development Studies Manuscript, 2007.
13. Ministry of Works and Urban Development, *Urban Development Policy* (Addis Ababa: Ministry of Works and Urban Development, 2006) (in Amharic).
14. Assefa Mehretu and Chris Mutambirwa, Cities of Sub-Saharan Africa, in *Cities of the World: Regional Development*, ed. Stanley D. Brunn, Jack F. Williams, and Donald Ziegler (New York: Rowman & Littlefield, 2003), 293–328.
15. Central Statistical Authority (CSA), *Statistical Abstract, Summary of Town Populations* (Addis Ababa: CSA, 2007); UN Population Division, *World Urbanization Prospects* (New York: UN Population Division, 2005).
16. Curran, Supplying Central City Housing.
17. B. Cohen, Urban Growth in Developing Countries: A

Review of Current Trends and a Caution Regarding Existing Forecasts, *World Development* 32 (2004): 1.

18. ORAAMP, Land Use and City Structure Studies of Addis Ababa and the Metropolitan Area, ORAAMP Executive Summary Report, 1999.
19. World Bank, *World Development Report* (Washington, DC: World Bank, 2008).
20. United Nations Development Program, *Human Development Report* (New York: UNDP, 2006).
21. Curran, Supplying Central City Housing, 15–16; Central Statistical Authority (CSA), Welfare Monitoring Survey, Statistical Bulletin 339-c (Addis Ababa: CSA).
22. UN-Habitat, *Situation Analysis*, 27.
23. Guida D'Italia, *Africa Orientale Italiana* (Milano: Consociazione Turistica Italiana, 1938); Zewde, *Pioneers of Change*, 35–98.
24. UN-Habitat, *Situation Analysis*, 7–10.
25. Gebre, Urban Land Issues, 278–301; Delelegne, Current Urban Land Policy Issues, 39–61.
26. UN-Habitat, *Situation Analysis*, 10–12.
27. Gebre, Urban Land Issues, 278–301.
28. UN-Habitat, *Situation Analysis*, 12.
29. Ibid., 12–14.
30. Gebre, Urban Land Issues, 278–301; Delelegne, Current Urban Land Policy Issues, 39–61; UN-Habitat, *Situation Analysis*, 12–13.
31. Haile and Mansberger, Land Policy.
32. Bureau of Finance and Economic Development, *Urban Development Indicators* (Addis Ababa: Addis Ababa City Administration, 2007).
33. Ibid.
34. Mesfin Tilaye, Identification and Prioritization of Environmental Problems: A Case Study among Citizens and Government Officials in Addis Ababa City (master's thesis, Wagengen Agricultural University, 1996); Camile De Stoop, Waste Collection and Disposal in Addis Ababa, in *Solid Waste Management in Addis Ababa: A Proceeding of a Workshop Held in Addis Ababa* (Addis Ababa: Solid Waste Management, 1998).
35. Bureau of Finance and Economic Development, *Urban Development Indicators* (Addis Ababa: Addis Ababa City Administration, 2007).
36. Sandra Dierig, *Urban Environmental Management in Addis Ababa: Problems, Policies, Perspectives and the Role of NGOs* (Hamburg: Institute of African Affairs, 1999).
37. Ibid.
38. Ibid.
39. Ibid.
40. Bureau of Finance and Economic Development, *Urban Development Indicators* (Addis Ababa: Addis Ababa City Administration, 2007).
41. Ibid.
42. Ibid.
43. Ibid.
44. Addis Ababa City Government, *Addis Ababa in Action: City Development Plan 2001–2010 Executive Summary* (Addis Ababa: City Government, 2002).
45. CSA, Welfare Monitoring Survey.
46. M. Crewes, What Is Up on the Streets of Addis? A Situational Analysis of Street Children and the NGOs Working with Them in Addis Ababa, Ethiopia, Preliminary Report, Retrak Ethiopia Project Development, Addis Ababa, 2006.
47. Wudineh Zenebe, Anti Corruption Commission to Investigate Real Estate Plot Grants, *Fortune* 8 (2006): 390.
48. Ibid.
49. Wondimu Abeje, A Right Approach for Adequate Housing: A Reflection in Light of the International Conventions and the Context of Urban Ethiopia, paper presented at the Conference on Urbanization and Urban Development in Ethiopia, RLDS, Addis Ababa University, 2005; UN-Habitat, *Situation Analysis*, 13.
50. Alebel Bayrau and Genanew Bekele, Investors' Willingness to Pay for Urban Land: The Case of Addis Ababa City, in *Proceedings of the Second International Conference on the Ethiopian Economy*, ed. Alemayehu Seyoum et al. (Addis Ababa: Ethiopian Economic Association, 2005).
51. Federal Democratic Republic of Ethiopia (FDRE), *The Constitution of the Federal Democratic Republic of Ethiopia* (Addis Ababa: FDRE, 1995).
52. Berrisford, *A New Legal Framework for Land Management*; Curran, Supplying Central City Housing, 35.
53. Curran, Supplying Central City Housing, 50.
54. Ibid., 9, 19; UN-Habitat, *Situation Analysis*, 27; World Bank, *Improving Access*.
55. Wudineh Zenebe, Anti Corruption Commission to Investigate Real Estate Plot Grants, *Fortune* 8 (2006): 390; UN-Habitat, *Situation Analysis*, 32.
56. UN-Habitat, *Situation Analysis*, 14.
57. Haile and Mansberger, Land Policy.
58. Curran, Supplying Central City Housing, 40.
59. Assefa Mehretu, Bruce Pigozzi, and Lawrence M. Sommers, Concepts in Social and Spatial Marginality, *Geografiska Annaler* 82 (2000): 89–101.
60. Berrisford, *A New Legal Framework for Land Management*; Rebecca R. Hart, Mapping, Erasing, Drifting, in *Julie Mehretu City Siting*, ed. Simon Allen, Rebecca R. Hart, and Kinsey Katchka (Detroit: Detroit Institute of Art, 2007), 55–59.

61. Curran, Supplying Central City Housing, 7–9; Delelegne, Current Urban Land Policy Issues, 39–61; UN-Habitat, *Situation Analysis*, 14.
62. Curran, Supplying Central City Housing, 8; UN-Habitat, *Situation Analysis*, 27.
63. Gebre, Urban Land Issues, 278–301; Delelegne, Current Urban Land Policy Issues, 39–61; Haile and Mansberger, Land Policy; World Bank, *World Development Report* (Washington, DC: World Bank, 2007); UN-Habitat, *Situation Analysis*.
64. Gebre, Urban Land Issues, 278–301; Curran, Supplying Central City Housing, 8; UN-Habitat, *Situation Analysis*, 7–8; Bihon, *Housing for the Poor*.
65. World Bank, *Improving Access*; Bihon, *Housing for the Poor*.
66. UN-Habitat, *Situation Analysis*, 29.
67. Bihon, *Housing for the Poor*.
68. World Bank, *Improving Access*.
69. UN-Habitat, *Situation Analysis*, 27.
70. Ibid., 27; Haile and Mansberger, Land Policy.
71. Delelegne, Current Urban Land Policy Issues, 39–61.
72. See also UN-Habitat, *Situation Analysis*, 31–33.
73. See also Curran, Supplying Central City Housing, 7; Delelegne, Current Urban Land Policy Issues, 39–61; UN-Habitat, *Situation Analysis*, 15; Bihon, *Housing for the Poor*.
74. Curran, Supplying Central City Housing, 7.
75. Wudineh Zenebe, Anti Corruption Commission to Investigate Real Estate Plot Grants, *Fortune* 8 (2006): 390.
76. World Bank, *Improving Access*, 5; Curran, Supplying Central City Housing, 7.
77. Curran, Supplying Central City Housing, 7.
78. Angelo Podagrosi and Igor Vojnovic, Tearing Down Freedmen's Town and African American Displacement in Houston: The Good, the Bad, and the Ugly, *Urban Geography* 29:4 (2008): 371–401.
79. Ibid.
80. Abadi Seyoum, Assessment on the Socio-Economic Composition of Condominium Housing Residents and Views towards the Quality of their Buildings in Addis Ababa (master's thesis, Regional and Local Development Studies, Addis Ababa University, 2007).
81. Delelegne, Current Urban Land Policy Issues, 39–61; UN-Habitat, *Situation Analysis*, 26–47.
82. Curran, Supplying Central City Housing, 9.
83. UN-Habitat, *Situation Analysis*, 15, 27.
84. See UN-Habitat, *Situation Analysis*, 13.
85. Curran, Supplying Central City Housing, 20.
86. Ibid., 7; World Bank, *World Development Report* (Washington, DC: World Bank, 2007).
87. Gebre, Urban Land Issues, 278–301.
88. Cohen, Urban Growth in Developing Countries, 1.

REFERENCES

Abeje, Wondimu. A Right Approach for Adequate Housing: A Reflection in Light of the International Conventions and the Context of Urban Ethiopia. Paper Presented at the Conference on Urbanization and Urban Development in Ethiopia. Addis Ababa: RLDS, Addis Ababa University, 2005.

Addis Ababa City Government. Addis Ababa in Action: City Development Plan 2001–2010 Executive Summary. Addis Ababa: City Government, 2002.

Bayrau, Alebel, and Genanew Bekele. Investors' Willingness to Pay for Urban Land: The Case of Addis Ababa City. In *Proceedings of the Second International Conference on the Ethiopian Economy*, ed. Alemayehu Seyoum, Assefa Admassie, Befekadu Degefe, Berhanu Nega, Mulat Demeke, Taddess Birru, and Wolday Amha, 533–52. Addis Ababa: Ethiopian Economic Association, 2005.

Berrisford, Stephen. *A New Legal Framework for Land Management in Addis Ababa: The Way Forward.* Addis Ababa: Institute of Housing Studies, 2002.

Bihon, Azeb. *Housing for the Poor in Addis Ababa.* Lund: Lund University Housing Development and Management, 2006.

Bureau of Finance and Economic Development. *Urban Development Indicators*. Addis Ababa: Addis Ababa City Administration, 2007.

Central Statistical Authority (CSA). Statistical Abstract, Summary of Town Populations. Addis Ababa: CSA, 2007.

———. Welfare Monitoring Survey. Statistical bulletin 339-C. Addis Ababa: CSA, 2004.

Cohen, B. Urban Growth in Developing Countries: A Review of Current Trends and a Caution Regarding Existing Forecasts. *World Development* 32:1 (2004): 23–59.

Crewes, M. What Is Up on the Streets of Addis? A Situational Analysis of Street Children and the NGOs Working with Them in Addis Ababa, Ethiopia. Preliminary Report. Retrak Ethiopia Project Development, Addis Ababa, 2006.

Curran, Rosemary T. Supplying Central City Housing for All Income Groups in Addis Ababa. Addis Ababa: Addis Ababa University Department of Urban and

Regional Planning Manuscript, 2007.

Delelegne, Tamrat. Current Urban Land Policy Issues and Problems in Addis Ababa. In *Urban Development in Ethiopia and Other Related Issues*, ed. Zewdie Serbarro and Zelleke Zewdie, 39–61. Addis Ababa: Ministry of Works and Urban Development, 1998.

Dierig, Sandra. *Urban Environmental Management in Addis Ababa: Problems, Policies, Perspectives and the Role of NGOs*. Hamburg: Institute of African Affairs, 1999.

D'Italia, Guida. *Africa Orientale Italiana*. Milano: Consociazione Turistica Italiana, 1938.

Federal Democratic Republic of Ethiopia (FDRE). The Constitution of the Federal Democratic Republic of Ethiopia. Addis Ababa: FDRE, 1995.

Gebre, Solomon. Urban Land Issues and Policies in Ethiopia. In *Land Tenure and Land Policy in Ethiopia after the Derg*, ed. Desalegn Rahmato, 278–301. Addis Ababa: Institute of Development Research, 1994.

Gebre-Egziabher, Tegegne. Geographically Differentiated Strategy, Urbanization Agenda and Rural-Urban Linkages: An Assessment of Emerging Regional Development Strategies in Ethiopia. Addis Ababa University Regional and Local Development Studies Manuscript, 2007.

Gnogno, Paulos. *Atse Menelik*. Addis Ababa: Bole Printing Press, 1991 (Amharic edition).

Haile, Solomon, and Reinfried Mansberger. Land Policy, Urban-Rural Interaction and Land Administration Differentiation in Ethiopia. Paper at the Second FIG Regional Conference, Marakech, Morocco, 2003.

Hart, Rebecca R. Mapping, Erasing, Drifting. In *Julie Mehretu City Siting*, ed. Simon Allen, Rebecca R. Hart, and Kinsey Katchka, 55–59. Detroit: Detroit Institute of Art, 2007.

Mehretu, Assefa, and Chris Mutambirwa. Cities of Sub-Saharan Africa. In *Cities of the World: Regional Development*, ed. Stanley D. Brunn, Jack F. Williams, and Donald Ziegler, 293–328. New York: Rowman & Littlefield, 2003.

Mehretu, Assefa, Bruce Pigozzi, and Lawrence M. Sommers. Concepts in Social and Spatial Marginality. *Geografiska Annaler B* 82 (2000): 89–101.

Ministry of Works and Urban Development. *Urban Development Policy*. Addis Ababa: Ministry of Works and Urban Development, 2006 (Amharic edition).

Office for the Revision of Addis Ababa Master Plan (ORAAMP). Land Use and City Structure Studies of Addis Ababa and the Metropolitan Area. Addis Ababa: ORAAMP Executive Summary Report, 1999.

Pankhurst, Richard. *The Ethiopians: A History*. Oxford, UK: Blackwell, 2001.

Pausewang, Sigfried, Kietil Tronvoll, and Lovise Aalen. A Process of Democratization or Control? In *Ethiopia since the Derg: A Decade of Demographic Pretention and Performance*, ed. Siegfied Pausewang, Kjetil Tronvoll, and Lovise Aalen, 26–45. London: Zed Books, 2002.

Podagrosi, Angelo, and Igor Vojnovic. Tearing down Freedmen's Town and African American Displacement in Houston: The Good, the Bad, and the Ugly. *Urban Geography* 29:4 (2008): 371–401.

Prouty, Chris. *Empress Taytu and Menilek II: Ethiopia 1883–1910*. Trenton, NJ: Red Sea Press, 1986.

Seyoum, Abadi. Assessment on the Socio-Economic Composition of Condominium Housing Residents and Views towards the Quality of Their Buildings in Addis Ababa. Master's Thesis, Regional and Local Development Studies, Addis Ababa University, 2007.

Stoop, Camile De. Waste Collection and Disposal in Addis Ababa. In *Solid Waste Management in Addis Ababa: A Proceeding of a Workshop Held in Addis Ababa*. Addis Ababa: Solid Waste Management, 1998.

Tilaye, Mesfin. Identification and Prioritization of Environmental Problems: A Case Study among Citizens and Government Officials in Addis Ababa City. Master's thesis, Wagengen Agricultural University, 1996.

United Nations Development Program (UNDP). *Human Development Report*. New York: UNDP, 2006.

UN-Habitat. *Situation Analysis of Informal Settlements in Addis Ababa*. Nairobi: United National Human Settlement Program, 2007.

United Nations Population Division. *World Urbanization Prospects*. New York: UN Population Division, 2005, 2007.

World Bank. *Improving Access to Housing and Land in Addis Ababa: An Analytical Overview and Recommendations*. Washington, DC: World Bank, 2005.

———. *World Development Report*. Washington, DC: World Bank, 2007, 2008.

Zenebe, Wudineh. Anti-corruption Commission to Investigate Real Estate Plot Grants. *Fortune* 8 (2006): 390.

Zewde, Banru. *A History of Modern Ethiopia, 1855–1991*. Oxford: James Currey, 2001.

———. *Pioneers of Change in Ethiopia*. Addis Ababa: Addis Ababa University Press, 2002.

■ ADRIANA ALLEN

Water Provision for and by the Peri-urban Poor

PUBLIC-COMMUNITY PARTNERSHIPS OR CITIZENS COPRODUCTION?

It is now widely recognized that the urban transition facing the developing world brings with it significant challenges in terms of meeting the water needs of the poor. In this context, it has become common place among international agencies and national governments alike to advocate governance arrangements for service provision that explicitly include the participation of civil society. However, underlying this apparent consensus there is a wide range of ideological positions. They range from pragmatic arguments for the participation of the so-called third sector to fill in the gaps left by the state and the private sector, to the more substantial redefinition of the role that citizens could and should play in the design and delivery of public policy.[1]

This chapter examines the institutional arrangements adopted in relation to emerging forms of citizen coproduction in water provision, looking in particular at the way in which these reinforce or bridge the gap between current government policies and practices by the peri-urban poor. The underlying assumption is that the reciprocal collaboration of government professionals and citizens engendered by a genuine process of coproduction has the capacity to positively transform those taking part. Such transformation implies that coproduction can lead to (1) a more sensitive approach from government professionals to the water needs, experience, and expectations of the beneficiaries—in particular of the water poor—and (2) the empowerment of the latter through their increased control of water management systems and the assertion of their right to water. Furthermore, the creation of an equal platform for interaction between government professionals and citizens plays an essential role not only in improving access to water by those typically excluded but also in making the system more accountable and environmentally sustainable.

While there are many well-documented projects aimed at linking public agencies and poor communities on a one-off basis, the focus here is on the emergence of institutionalized frameworks for service coproduction in the peri-urban interface (PUI) of metropolitan Dar es Salaam

(Tanzania) and Caracas (Venezuela).[2] The term "institutionalized frameworks" refers to the establishment of specific channels for government-citizen service coproduction that are explicitly backed up by the state at the policy level. Given the fact that neither the state or the formal private sector alone are likely to produce water services for the urban and peri-urban poor, a focus on institutionalized coproduction in comparison to one-off project partnerships is relevant because it allows the examination of the process and outcomes of experimenting with state-citizen interfaces aimed at addressing this challenge through sustainable mechanisms.

The importance of considering the coproduction of water services in peri-urban areas arises from the fact that these areas generally lie outside the coverage of formal networked water systems, which are in most cases restricted to a relatively small urban core. This is partly because many peri-urban settlements develop outside existing formal regulations, and this affects their formal right to basic services. In reality, peri-urban water supply is in the hands of a wide range of informal agents.[3]

Within the metropolitan context, the peri-urban interface is often the location of important environmental services and natural resources consumed in urban areas. The process of peri-urbanization is frequently accompanied by substantial pressures over natural resources (such as land and water) due to their increased marketability and greater volumes of pollution generated by higher concentrations of population and enterprises. Peri-urban areas are associated with both rural and urban physical and socioeconomic features, and their population consists of highly heterogeneous and rapidly changing socioeconomic groups. This diversity means that the needs and demands of peri-urban dwellers and water providers are also quite diverse and change rapidly over time. The identification of these needs is more complex than in urban or rural areas, due to the particular mix of newcomers and long-established dwellers, and also because farming, residential, and industrial land uses often coexist. Therefore, the peri-urban context is typically characterized by rapidly expanding unmet needs vis-à-vis a high level of experimentation in terms of the direct involvement of the poor in service provision through unorthodox organizational arrangements.[4]

In order to contextualize the ongoing debate on and experimentation with emerging forms of water provision, section 1 explores how the privatization of services widely spread in the 1990s has resulted in an "instrumentals state," in which the traditional functions of legislation, regulation, direct provision, and investment have been significantly transformed. However, as neither the public or the formal private sector are filling in the gap of meeting the water needs of the urban and peri-urban poor, this in turn has led to the exploration of various forms of citizen engagement in the delivery of basic services.

Section 2 examines the variety of practices through which the urban and peri-urban poor access water on the ground and the way in which the emergence of cooperative relations between grassroots actors and the state can be conceptualized as "citizen service coproduction." Building on this notion, section 3 examines two specific coproduction mechanisms: water users associations (WUAs) in Dar es Salaam and technical water fora (TWF) in Caracas. These two experiences represent different approaches to the involvement of citizens' groups in service delivery, in which the latter are also the principal beneficiaries. The final section examines the extent to which service coproduction in each case has been underlined by a process of citizens' empowerment or instrumentalization and reflects on the recent outcomes of these processes.

The Contested Governance of Water Provision

Central to the problematique outlined above is the question of who should do what. During the 1990s, the international debate became almost exclusively concerned with the question of whether these services were better run by the public or the private sector. On one side of this debate is the view that increased private sector participation (PSP) would resolve the failures of public water utilities, including their inability to reach the urban poor. On the other extreme, increased PSP is seen in fact as the problem, as it involves withdrawing from the policies and institutions required to achieve universal coverage and adequate water provision.

In this context, the international adherence to the definition of water as an economic good marks a paradigm shift in the governance of services delivery, bringing a market rationale to water management resources, arguing for the benefits of a clear separation between provider and regulator and the adoption of indicators that provide for "real" costs, water tariffs, and demand management. This line of argument foresees a reconciliation of financial and environmental concerns through the treatment of water as an economic good. The public-private controversy became then framed within the New Public Management (NPM) school of thought, assuming the failure of centralized government-led service delivery systems and the need for a more efficient division of labor usually under unbundled systems.[5] This perspective often refers in detail to the institutions (state, market, and civic society) of Western representative democracies and has been transplanted to the developing context through policy prescriptions, arguing that the market should be used as a model for political and administrative relationships.[6]

Jessica Budds and Gordon McGranahan argue that the above debate had very little to do with water per se but was rather subsumed in a highly ideological discussion about the effectiveness of the private sector in comparison to the public sector in almost any policy area.[7] In practice, during the last decade PSP in water provision dramatically increased in the most densely populated areas, where maintenance and investment costs are easier to recover. As contended by Karen Bakker, this has led to the geographical segregation of service providers around three different situations: larger cities where transnational corporations (TNCs) are currently the main providers; suburban and small urban areas, where nongovernmental organizations (NGOs) are seen as the main conduit for community service provision; and the rest, left to the state as direct provider.[8] This segregation is not incidental, and it corresponds with the potential profitability (market size and consumers' capacity to pay) of service provision in each area. A more disaggregated look reveals that the poor are not benefiting from increased PSP; rather, their exclusion from basic services has been exacerbated.[9]

In terms of governance, increased PSP has been associated with the notion of a reduced state. However, Matthias Finger claims that within this process, the state has not necessarily become weaker or obsolete but rather *instrumentalized* through the logic of partnership governance in a globalized economy, which advocates a small but strong state.[10] Such instrumentalization is evident in the transformation of the state's four traditional functions in the governance and management of basic services: legislation, regulation, operational provision of services, and investment. It is often assumed that the privatization of water services involves a substantial change in the last two functions: the state is not any longer in charge of direct provision and its investment function is reduced. But, as highlighted by Bakker, under increased PSP, the state still plays these four roles, although with a substantial twist.[11] First, it performs a central role in financing, although this is not just through direct investment but through contracting loans for the development and rehabilitation of service infrastructure from which TNCs are making a profit. Second, the state acts not only as a loans guarantor but also provides the legal stability and security required to ensure that contracts will be respected and bills paid. Third, the state also acts as a guarantor of regular revenues and a crucial risk bearer. In addition, it acts as a legitimate vehicle to enforce internationally agreed norms and standards that often exclude unorthodox practices and informal providers.

As the move toward privatization has run in parallel with calls for increased decentralization, changes in the state's functions also need to be examined in light of the increased role and responsibilities attributed to local governments either as direct providers, as regulators of the private sector, or in supporting alternative service providers to fill the gap. The instrumentalization resulting from increased PSP also extends to other actors. Financial institutions play a new function in this system and so do NGOs, who are often charged with the role of raising awareness, dwellers' contributions, and legitimization for PSP in informal settlements.

Access to Water Services by the Poor: Neither Public nor Private

When looking at the specific ways in which the urban and peri-urban poor gain access to water services, it is possible to identify a wide range of practices and arrangements (fig. 1). Some of these are formal, policy-driven mechanisms supported by institutional arrangements of the state. But in addition to these, there is a wide set of arrangements that operate on the basis of solidarity and reciprocity—such as when water is provided as a gift by some members of the community to others in need—as well as cases in which these practices operate on the basis of competition, as in the case of small independent water providers. These mechanisms can be characterized as being needs-driven and correspond to the wide spectrum of practices adopted by the poor, often with little or no support from the state, its policies, or its resources. While policy-driven mechanisms can be clearly identified from the perspective of production and provision, the arrangements identified on the right-hand side of the wheel are best examined and understood from the perspective of access and from the viewpoint of highly localized strategies.

The water supply wheel provides a schematic but comprehensive representation of both policy-driven and needs-driven strategies, showing the roles of the public, private, and civic society sectors and the extent to which these are based on cooperative or competitive principles. The three sectors are far from homogeneous, as the public sector might be present in the form of highly centralized state agencies or of decentralized bodies. Similarly, the private sector might involve TNCs, medium-sized licensed water providers, or informal vendors. The civic sector is not homogeneous either, as it might involve arrangements characterized by a certain degree of formalization, such as community schemes actively supported by the public sector or external NGOs, but also by more informal relations of cooperation established among members of the community.

Multiple hybrid combinations—some of which rely on some form of coproduction or systematic cooperation between government bodies and citizen groups—can be found in the urban context of developing countries. Many of these arrangements manage to do what the more

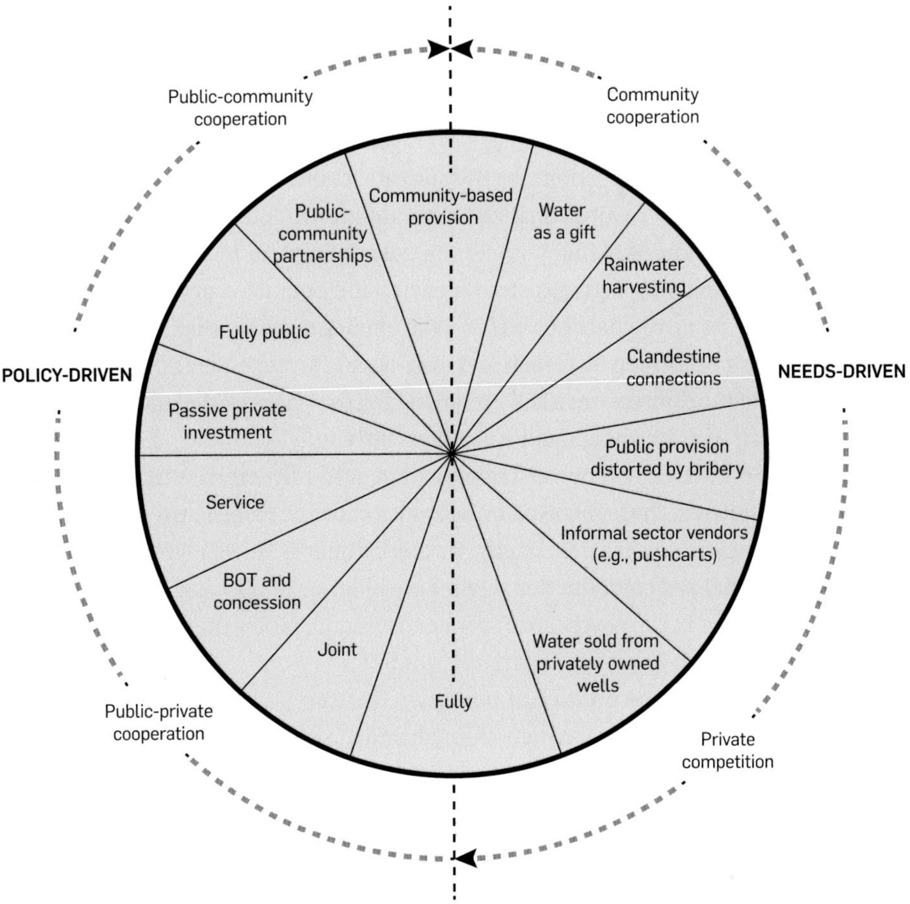

Figure 1. Water supply wheel.

Source: Adriana Allen, Julio D. Dávila, and Pascale Hofmann, *Governance of Water and Sanitation for the Peri-urban Poor: A Framework for Understanding and Action in Metropolitan Regions* (London: Development Planning Unit, 2006).

conventional formal public, public-private, and private arrangements in service delivery often fail to achieve: to reach the poor on a sustained basis.[12] Considering that coproduction in public services is increasingly a reality in the context of the developing world, it is surprising that, with a few exceptions, the bulk of the literature focuses on developed countries.

The term "coproduction" was initially coined in the 1970s by Elinor Ostrom and other academic sociologists and development economists looking at why neighborhood crime rates increased in Chicago when police stopped walking the streets and lost their connections with the local community.[13] Over time, the term was extended to tackle the question of why the mainstream model of service delivery—often run by large centralized, technocratic, and hierarchical structures—was failing to meet its objectives. In the 1980s a number of political scientists started to focus on citizen coproduction as a type of citizen activity intended to enhance the reach and quality of public services.[14] Thus, the literature on service coproduction evolved in tandem with a concern to bring a new perspective into the analysis and evaluation of public policy design and implementation.

Here I use the term "coproduction" to refer to the joint and direct involvement of citizens and public agencies to deliver a particular service, one in which "citizens can play an active role in producing public goods and services of consequence to them."[15] This is to be distinguished from the use of the term in reference to any interagent arrangement in service delivery characterized by the presence of two or more organizations, be they private, public, or civil society.

Furthermore, I focus on "institutionalized coproduction," defined by Anuradha Joshi and Mick Moore as "the provision of public services (broadly defined, to include regulation) through a regular long-term relationship between state agencies and organized groups of citizens, where both make substantial resource contributions."[16] This implies not only that cooperation between citizens and the state is backed up by formal and long-lasting arrangements but also that "power, authority and control of resources are likely to be divided (not necessarily equally), between the state and citizens in an interdependent and ambiguous fashion."[17]

Isabelle Lemaire characterizes coproduction as a give-and-take exercise that could either lead to a mere exchange between those involved or become a more transformative process.[18] As highlighted in the introduction, the central concern in this chapter is to examine the transformative capacity that institutionalized coproduction might have in terms of opening and/or expanding the political space for the poor in the governance of water provision, rather than on the actual material changes achieved in terms of improved water provision.

In their examination of the politics of poverty reduction policies, Neil Webster and Lars Engberg-Pedersen identify three dimensions through which political space manifests and can be expanded or constrained:

- The *institutional channels* through which policy formulation and implementation can be accessed, controlled, or contested by the poor;
- The *political discourses* through which poverty and poverty reduction are socially constructed, in terms of its causes, who is affected, why action should be taken to reduce it, who should take responsibility for this action, and so on;
- The *social and political practices of the poor* which can be used to influence decision making, agendas, policies and program implementation.[19]

The last section of this chapter returns to the above three dimensions, examining the extent to which citizen-government coproduction in Caracas and Dar es Salaam have deepened the political space for the peri-urban poor in the governance of water services.

Coproduction on the Ground

Within metropolitan areas and regions, demographic trends in the urbanization process are difficult to establish due to the frequent mismatch between jurisdictional boundaries and their spatial structure. Table 1 presents some estimates of population size and annual population growth rate of the two metropolitan contexts under consideration. What the table does not show is that in both cases the growth rate in the PUI is much higher than in the city as a whole.

According to the 2001 census, the Caracas Metropolitan Region (CMR) has a total population

Table 1. Overview of the two metropolitan areas/regions under study

	POPULATION 2000 (MILLIONS)	AREA (KM^2 / MI^2)	ANNUAL POPULATION GROWTH RATE	METROPOLITAN ADMINISTRATIVE STRUCTURE	WSS METROPOLITAN FORMAL SYSTEM
Dar es Salaam	2.5	1,350 / 521	7.2 %	Metropolitan Dar es Salaam: three semi-autonomous municipalities under the Greater Dar es Salaam Council	Public-private partnership with a community component
Caracas	4.2	6,207 / 2,397	3.3 %	Caracas Metropolitan Region: 17 municipalities belonging to 3 political-administrative entities (states)	Regional public agency to be devolved/transferred by 2007

Source: Based on Cariola and Lacabana (2004a) and Kombe and Lupala (2004a).

of 4.2 million, 65.5 percent of which live in Caracas City. Although a small metropolis in the Latin American context, the expansion of Caracas in the last decade has overflowed the boundaries of the metropolitan area, giving rise to the CMR (see fig. 2). The CMR embraces seventeen municipalities, five of which form the Caracas Metropolitan Area, while the other twelve are located in four large peripheral subregions. Among these, the Middle Tuy Valley (hereafter referred to as PUI

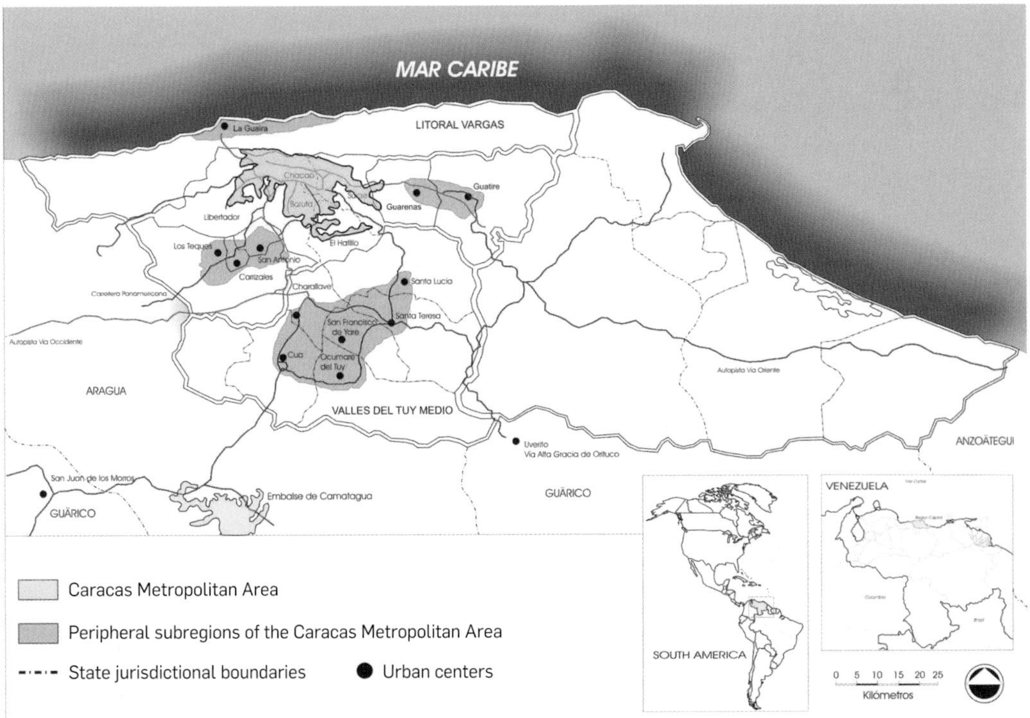

Figure 2. Metropolitan region of Caracas. Location of peri-urban areas analyzed in the Tuy Valley.

Tuy) is the fastest-growing subregion, recording a 50 percent increase of its population in the 1990–2001 period, which amounted to 534,752 inhabitants in 2001.[20] While the urbanized surface of the PUI Tuy almost doubled between 1992 and 2002 (from 5.6 percent to 10.7 percent of the total area), about 25 percent of the agricultural and forested surface were lost.[21]

The expansion of the CMR has been accompanied by a process of acute socioterritorial segregation, in which the Caracas Valley is occupied by the higher-income groups, the first peri-urban ring has become a residential alternative for vulnerable middle-income population groups, and the new emerging periphery (PUI Tuy) houses a downward-mobile population and a large part of the poor in the CMR.[22] According to the 2001 Household Survey, 70.1 percent of all households in the PUI Tuy were poor, while this category represented 52.6 percent of the households of the metropolitan area.[23]

The PUI Tuy plays a key role as a net water exporter region—about half of the water intake of the CMR water supply is located in this area—but at the same time its population suffers significant deficits. These include not only irregular and insufficient water supply but also serious sanitation problems. Parts of the population needs are met by municipal and private water trucks, the latter imposing high costs, especially on the poorer groups in the CMR periphery.[24]

Dar es Salaam is the primate city of Tanzania, accounting for 25 percent of the country's urban population. Population estimates for 2002 range from 2.5 to 3.5 million, with a daytime population of around 5 million.[25] Administratively, the metropolitan area comprises three autonomous

PHOTOGRAPHY BY J. DÁVILA

Figure 3. Informal peri-urban settlements in Charavalle. Tuy Valley, Metropolitan Region of Caracas.

PHOTOGRAPHY BY J. DÁVILA

Figure 4. New gated community in the Tuy Valley.

PHOTOGRAPHY BY J. DÁVILA

Figure 5. New housing in peri-urban Caracas, Paso Real 2000.

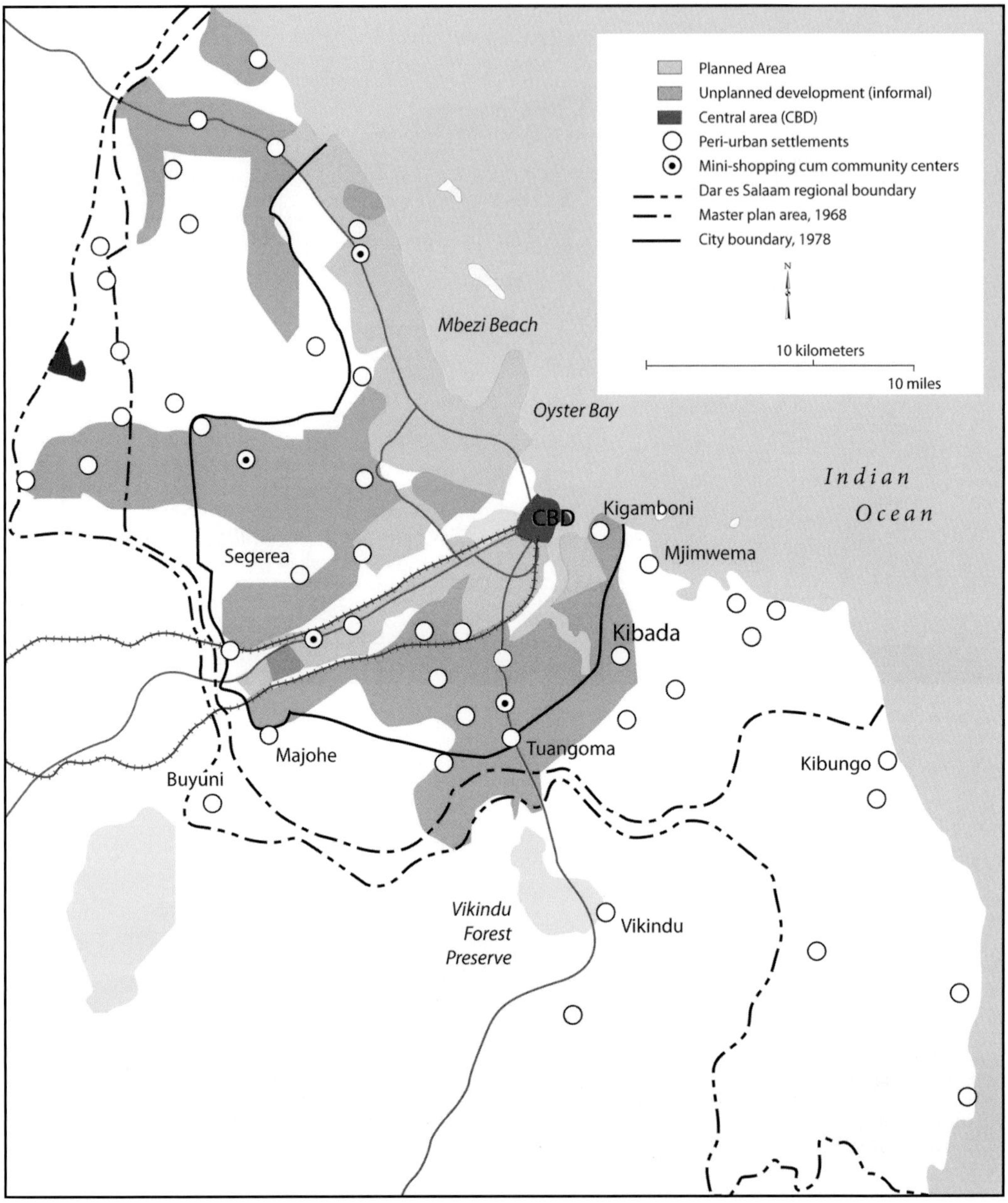

Figure 6. Metropolitan Dar es Salaam. Planned and unplanned land development and peri-urban settlements.

Source: Adapted from Wilbard Kombe, *Land Use Dynamics in Peri-urban Areas and Their Implications on the Urban Growth and Form: The Case of Dar es Salaam, Tanzania*, Habitat International 29 (2005): 113–35.

municipalities (Ilala, Kinondoni, and Temeke) that embrace seventy-three wards and fall under the Greater Dar es Salaam Council (see fig. 6). The population of Greater Dar es Salaam is increasing at an annual rate of 4.39 percent, which makes it the third fastest growing city in Africa.[26] Urban expansion primarily takes place along the coastline and the four arterial roads of Bagamoyo, Morogoro, Nyerere (Pugu), and Kilwa. Housing development between the arterial roads is mostly unplanned and lacks basic infrastructure. It is estimated that over 70 percent of the city population live in informal settlements, with more than 50 percent of the existing urban housing stock being informal.[27]

Urbanization in poverty characterizes the development of peri-urban Dar es Salaam, as poverty underpins changes in land use and land transactions, with poor migrants moving to the PUI both from inner-city areas and rural areas. This phenomenon is intimately linked to conflicting land tenure regimes and in particular to customary and quasi-customary land tenure systems in peri-urban areas. While these two systems facilitate access to unplanned and unsurveyed land for housing, some of the major adverse effects of informal urban growth include pollution and fecal contamination of groundwater sources as housing density increases.[28]

The PUI of Dar es Salaam comprises a diverse environment depicting a variety of socioeconomic activities. Agriculture is the main land use, with many households living in peri-urban areas subsidizing their demands for food from gardening activities. However, agriculture is gradually being displaced by housing, especially by those who cannot afford to rent a room or a house or buy land in the inner or intermediate city areas. There are also increasing number

PHOTOGRAPHY BY J. DÁVILA

Figure 7. Informal housing in peri-urban Caracas, Paso Real 2000.

PHOTOGRAPH BY A. ALLEN

Figure 8. A woman carrying water in a rapidly expanding peri-urban settlement (Tungi) within metropolitan Dar es Salaam.

of middle- and high-income households which have acquired large tracks of land in the PUI for gardening and animal husbandry purposes. Emerging livelihood opportunities in this area are associated with retailing and service areas, artisanship, farming, quarrying, renting rooms, land selling, and gardening.[29]

The Water Poor

Field interviews with peri-urban dwellers revealed that large segments of the populations in these settlements could be characterized as the water poor, due to their experience in terms of informal/illegal access to water, access to poor-quality water, and scanty access to water. Informal and/or illegal access to water is often linked to insecure tenure of land and housing rights. This is particularly crucial in the PUI, where customary and statutory systems coexist or overlap with each other and where the emerging structure of land use "is increasingly breaking away from normative urban land development norms, concepts and standards."[30]

Within the PUI Tuy, water supply and sanitation in the lower-income communities is highly heterogeneous. While some settlements lack these services entirely and only access water through public tank trucks, others tap illegally into any water main (whether it carries pure drinking water or untreated sewage), and a third group is fully connected to the networked water and sewer systems but suffer from irregular water supply. The insecurity associated with practices such as illegal connections was identified as a recurrent factor highlighted by most interviewees, as illustrated by a peri-urban resident:

> here is where the water problem is most visible, on Terrace 11. We have the connection to the pipe furthest away, on the main highway . . . we installed a small (illegal) tap, but it doesn't meet our needs. Water doesn't reach my house at least. . . . there are broken pipes and they aren't repaired.[31]

While in some areas the poor quality of water is a central concern, in other places the main problem affecting peri-urban communities is related to its irregular supply, this has significant gender implications. A woman in the PUI Tuy explains how this affects her life:

> When they give me water here every fourth day, I don't do any other chores, I just get water. . . . The next day I do all my chores, because water takes a lot of your time, fetching water, filling bottles, checking that there are no leaks.[32]

In peri-urban Dar es Salaam, contaminated shallow wells constitute one of the main sources for the poor. Other major sources include boreholes, rainwater, and water vendors. Many settlers in these areas cannot afford water supplied by vendors, which costs up to fifteen times the supply from wells, with water prices fluctuating depending on the availability of water and the distance walked from the water source to the customer. The deficiencies in water and sanitation suffered by the peri-urban poor bring about several diseases, including diarrhea, intestinal worms, cholera, and dysentery. In Tungi, one of the peri-urban localities studied in Dar es Salaam, the number of diarrhea cases almost tripled between 2001 and 2003 due to inadequate water supply.[33]

PHOTOGRAPHY BY J. DÁVILA

Figure 9. Hidrocapital free water supply in peri-urban Caracas.

The subward chairperson in Tungi recollects the fast changes affecting water and land use in the face of rapid peri-urbanization:

> Until the early 1990s most of the land was still under agricultural use. Most settlers would easily meet their water needs, from shallow wells. Then, we did not experience any water shortage for domestic and gardening. Water table was high; one did not require digging a deep well or drilling a borehole to get water. Now deep wells dry up, creating severe water shortages especially during extended dry season.[34]

In the face of expanding unmet water needs, many peri-urban dwellers found new livelihood opportunities. Mr. Rugenzi, a Sukuma and a former small-scale miner, recalls how he started his current business:

> I have not received any formal training in digging wells or drilling boreholes, but I acquired the skill while working in Gold mines in Geita. I came here to see my brother and realized he had no water. I used my skills and knowledge from the mines to dig a well, I got good water at around ten

Figure 10. Informal water vendor in peri-urban Dar es Salaam.

PHOTOGRAPH BY A. ALLEN

> meters depth. When the residents learnt about this they came one after another, requesting me to drill or dig wells for them. I started the business. I also fit pipes and pumps as well as do some maintenance of the wells when asked.[35]

Water vending, mostly by young men, is an important livelihood option and one of the main ways for households to access water in the study areas. Water vendors carry five to ten buckets of water, each with twenty-liter carrying capacity, and they collect water from different water sources, including boreholes, shallow wells, and public standpipes. There are also publicly run water sales outlets commonly known as water kiosks, where vendors collect water to sell to their customers. While the price of a twenty-liter bucket is twenty Tanzanian shillings (TShs) (equivalent to US$0.02) at the boreholes, shallow wells, public standpipes, and water kiosks, water vendors sell the same volume for between 100 and 500 TShs (US$0.1–0.5). A water vendor in Tungi explains how he came into the business:

> Before I started water vending business, I was running a vegetable stall and I ran short of capital. In 2002 I embarked on water vending business, because water was in high demand in Tungi.

> I bought a second hand bicycle for TShs 35,000 and 10 buckets each at TShs 2,000. Currently, I have 30 buckets; I carry 5 buckets per trip, and make five or six trips per day. Starting from September through to the beginning of rainy season in March, the business is very lucrative. Some customers who do not use salty water from wells buy as much as ten buckets per day. I earn between TShs 5,000 and 6,000 per day . . . I am paying fees for my children including TShs 80,000 for a boy studying at a Technical College in Arusha.[36]

Inadequate water supply in the PUI might bring livelihood opportunities for some, but it also restrains the survival and livelihood opportunities for many others and enhances competition for water and overextraction. In Dar es Salaam, many households living in peri-urban areas are subsidizing their demands for food from gardening activities. While peri-urban agriculture constitutes an important source of food for most households (65 percent of the city population),[37] it is also one of the main sources of unauthorized water connection in the city and of multiple disputes between the government and peri-urban dwellers. A group of residents from Sitakishari—another PU community studied in Greater Dar es Salaam—reflect on the impact of productive activities on the depletion of underground sources:

> A large number of residents here depend on urban agriculture, particularly gardening and livestock keeping that are mainly carried out in Msimbazi valley. Because of the competition in the utilization of land as well as water, the springs in this valley have been affected. Unlike in the past when water was available all the year round, water is now only available seasonally; hence people are forced to dig more wells to get water for irrigation. Besides, the springs that used to be public have been appropriated by one of the land owners.[38]

One of the main visible features in the PU in Dar es Salaam is that most of the entrepreneurial activities that depend on water are significantly undertaken by women. Subsequently, water shortages, unaffordable prices, or unsafe supplies hit women most. Lack of public regulatory frameworks that would check quality and improve access to water not only exacerbates hardships to which women are culturally bound, but also undermines the socioeconomic development of their households.

Institutional Background

The two case studies examined in this section fit within the notion of institutionalized service coproduction. In both cases, the emergence of cooperative arrangements between citizens and the state is laid out by a formal and long-term institutional framework.

Figure 12 provides a summary of the main problems affecting the water supply and sanitation (WSS) system in Greater Dar es Salaam and the Caracas Metropolitan Region before the reforms introduced in the early years of the twenty-first century. In both cases, the system was clearly in crisis, but the approaches adopted to restructure it were guided by very different interpretations of the roots of the problem.

Figure 11. Water as a gift. Women drawing water manually from a neighbor's well in peri-urban Dar es Dalaam.

In the case of Venezuela, the emergence of an institutionalized platform for service coproduction has to be examined in the light of the substantial changes introduced by the Chavez administration since 1998. In 1999 the country began a political, legal, economic, and social transition through the adoption of a new constitution and the beginning of the reorganization of the state, marking a shift from representative to participatory democracy. Since then, government's efforts to overcome poverty have focused on a strategy of social and productive integration through the active participation of the community and emphasis on increasing access to basic services with quality and equity.

Problems affecting the WSS system in the CMR prior to the reforms included one of the highest unaccounted for water rates in Latin America.[39] At the national level, about 55 percent of the population had water meters, but only 33 percent of them were in proper working order. In addition, more than 20 percent of water users were not registered on the cadastral system. Highly deficient measurement of water consumption was coupled by a low propensity to pay and meager legal support for penalizing fraud.[40] The fact that water billing revenue covered only 40 percent of the system's operating cost translated into a structural lack of capacity to expand and improve service and infrastructure on the basis of the system's own resources.[41] As a result, prior to the 2001 WSS reform, the revenue from water tariffs was insufficient to "cover the cost of operation and maintenance, let alone the financing of maintenance, replacement of assets or investments in new infrastructure."[42] The new system adopted a two-bracket tariff: one based on minimum adequate consumption and the other one penalizing wasteful consumption.[43] An indirect cross-cutting

Great Dar es Salaam	Caracas Metropolitan Region
• The distribution system did not cater for the whole (30% with access to tap water) • Piped network system was old and in a state of disrepair (60% of pumped water lost) • Low levels of water tariff collection (16%) and high level of "illegal" connections • Serious problems in terms of water quality and regularity • For the poor, access relying on multiple practices, significantly water vendors • Experimentation with public water kiosks, driven by NGOs	• PUI Tuy area participates in the metropolitan WSS system as a water "producer" • Encroachment of catchment areas through formal and informal settlements and high competition over water among peri-urban dwellers • Highs costs to treat water heavily polluted by effluents dumped into the Tuy River • Large numbers of "illegal" taps and informal distribution networks in informal settlements • Poor regularity: frequency of service, varying from every other day to every other twenty-seven days

Figure 12. The Water Supply and Sanitation (WSS) system prior to the reforms.

subsidy was introduced whereby some sectors (commercial, industrial, and high-income residential) would subsidize lower-income residential consumption.

Within the Chavez administration, the 2001 Organic Drinking Water and Sanitation Service Act (LOPSA) articulated a long-term regulatory framework to readdress an organizational crisis that affected the water system during the 1990s. More than 100 regulatory instruments for the water system had been created in that period, leading to clashes between municipal, regional, and national authorities. The act introduced a new institutional scheme separating policy, regulation, and management functions, transferring the service to the municipalities and activating the creation of TWF, designed as a direct channel between grassroots organizations and Hidrocapital, the public sector regional water supply company responsible for water provision in the CMR.

Historically, the absence of urban planning and the proliferation of informal settlements led the communities themselves to build precarious supply facilities through illegal connections to water taps from the main network. The 2001 act stipulated that thereafter the state and municipal governments and Hidrocapital must invest in the repair and refurbishment of this precarious and insufficient infrastructure. The plan included a process to transfer the operation of water supply services to the municipal level by 2007, through a concessionary regime in which municipalities, the private sector, and communities could participate individually or in association. In this context, the LOPSA anticipated that community participation in the service provision phase could take an organizational role through the TWF and involve direct operation of the service under concession. However, this has not yet been implemented, as the central government fears that the concessionary regime could open the door to multinational water companies. The LOPSA is currently in the process of being reformed to stop this possibility.[44] The discussion focuses on how to retain a strong role for the state to oversee the WSS system at the regional and national level while ensuring that the local operation of service provision is responsive to the needs of the poor.

In the case of Tanzania, for decades WSS provision has been the responsibility of the Dar es Salaam Water and Sanitation Authority (DAWASA), a public utility company. Historically, services were provided almost for free, with a minimum flat-rate charge that did not cover supply, operation, and maintenance costs, thus severely limiting the coverage and quality of services, estimated to meet only 45 percent of the total water demand. Thus, peri-urban dwellers were largely left to their own devices, accessing water through boreholes, shallow wells, rainwater harvesting, and water vendors.

Over the past decade, the role of DAWASA has been the subject of significant reforms, shifting from direct provider to enabler and regulator. In 2003, following the conditions imposed by the African Development Bank (ADB) to support the rehabilitation and operations of the city water facilities, DAWASA was transformed into a holding company, DAWASA Public Granting Authority (PGA), responsible for monitoring the performance of a private operator: City Water Services (CWS).

Initially CWS was granted a ten-year lease contract to deal with the billing, tariff collection, operation, and routine maintenance component of DAWASA's portfolio of responsibilities, while the rehabilitation and development of the whole system were to remain the responsibility of DAWASA. However, in 2005 the company was forced to withdraw when the government terminated the contract on grounds of failure to abide. A new public company (DAWASCO) was established to take over the role of CWS. According to the Tanzanian government, the WSS system in metropolitan Dar es Salaam, and particularly service provision in lower-income areas, deteriorated further during the operation of CWS.[45]

Prior to the reform, the WSS in Dar es Salaam had been in a state of disrepair for many years. A study conducted in 1995 estimated that the rehabilitation of the existing infrastructure and the network expansion to reach unconnected communities alone demanded over US$620 million.[46] A US$164 million loan was approved by various donors for the so-called Dar es Salaam Water Supply and Sanitation Project (DWSSP),[47] and the privatization of the billing and revenue collection system was implemented as part of the business plan to repay the loan. Key provisions in the DWSSP concerning informal settlements included "the resettlement of families illegally settled on the transmission lines and close to the stabilization ponds" and the disconnection of illegal users along the transmission lines.[48] In terms of expected impacts, the lending procurement acknowledged that small water vendors and larger tankers, as well as illegal users and illegal providers of service would be negatively affected by the project, whose main purpose was "to institute rational operation and discipline."[49]

Given that the private sector participation was intended to cover the management of the piped water supply in settlements occupied by high- and middle-income earners, the project provided for the creation of a Community Water Supply and Sanitation Programme (CWSSP)—operating under DAWASA with the assistance of specialized NGOs—"to provide a minimum service to low income communities who may not be immediately served by a piped water network."[50] The community component was allocated US$3.85 million, about 2.3 percent of the total cost of the project, and was conceived as a system of grants to be allocated by DAWASA to about

50 beneficiary communities for schemes "*based* on point sources or relying on a bulk supply from the network."[51]

The CWSSP aimed to scale-up some of community-managed water supply schemes supported by external NGOs that already operated in the lower income peri-urban areas of Greater Dar es Salaam. These were based on the organization of water users associations at the ward level, responsible for implementing and managing public water kiosks and standpipes, which provide water at a subsidized bulk tariff for resale to end users at affordable rates. With this purpose, DAWASA appointed Care International, PLAN International and WaterAid to support communities in the formulation of grant requests and their implementation.

Motivating Forces behind Citizen Coproduction

The drivers or organizational motivation for coproduction are varied, although often linked to the changing (and often declining) role of the state as a universal service provider. Joshi and Moore argue that a differentiation should be established between "governance drivers" and "logistical drivers."[52] Governance drivers arise in response to changes in the state's governance capacity, while logistical drivers emerge to address perceived problems in the effective delivery of services due to high transaction costs and/or highly complex environments. Although in reality, both governance and logistic drivers might be connected, the above distinction is useful to examine the impact that different organizational motivations might have on the emergence of services coproduction. A study by Tony Bovaird looks at six cases of coproduction in the developed and developing world, concluding that when linked to governance drivers, service users and communities are more likely to exert power over service planning, design, and management.[53] By contrast, he found that when coproduction arises from logistical drivers, the role of local communities is usually confined to service delivery.

In the two case studies analyzed, citizen coproduction emerged in the context of significant changes, associated with the withdrawal of the state as direct provider in the case of Dar es Salaam, and with the democratization and decentralization of roles and responsibilities in the case of Caracas. In the case of Tanzania, citizen coproduction became institutionalized out of need, as a way to fill in the gap left by the intended privatization of water provision. By contrast, in Venezuela it emerged out of a political project aimed at enforcing the water rights of the poor within their wider rights as citizens.

Confirming the thesis advanced by Bovaird, a significant difference can also be found in the application of service coproduction in the two case studies analyzed. While the Venezuelan approach establishes an institutional platform for citizens to participate in all the stages of service provision (from needs identification and design through delivery to assessment), in the case of Tanzania, community inputs were confined to self-provision by the poor, otherwise excluded from the process of needs assessment, water policy design, formulation, and monitoring of the system.

The rationale for the allocation of financial resources within each institutional platform reinforces the notion of a transformative versus instrumental logic in the adoption of service coproduction platforms in each case. In Caracas no ceiling capped the public financial resources allocated to poor communities. On the contrary, public investment prioritizes those in need.

Although the reform placed emphasis on improving the financial sustainability of the WSS system, the 2001 act provided for a social rate for households unable to pay the entire cost of their water supply service, as well as cross-cutting subsidies.

By contrast, in Dar es Salaam, the community program (CWSSP) was allocated a marginal percentage of the total infrastructure rehabilitation project costs to meet the needs of unplanned settlements. As argued by ActionAid: "donor resources, and the Tanzanian government's current and future tax revenues, will be used to fund a project in which 98% of the money will be spent on the richest 20% of the population."[54] A report by WaterAid also challenged many of the privatization assumptions and promises highlighting that in Temeke municipality—Dar es Salaam's major unplanned and unserviced area—"at least 120,000 out of a projected 200,000 households remain completely unconnected to the failing water system."[55] This report also highlights that the community water kiosks approach has improved access to water in some communities but still receives mixed reactions in unserved communities, "with residents preferring the flexibility of the present system, and vendors wary of losing trade."[56]

Who Drives Coproduction?

In theory the most distinctive aspect of coproduction refers to the interaction and interdependence of state agencies and citizens in the decision-making system. In this sense, citizen coproduction is often assumed as being based on a bilateral relationship between government/professionals and users/communities. However, in reality it often involves a wider set of relationships that usually evolve into fluid networks and complex adaptive systems.

Figure 13 provides a schematic representation of the two institutional arrangements under analysis.

In the case of Caracas, coproduction is at the heart of the WSS decision-making system through the TWF. This provides a universal mechanism for organized communities to interact with the state and the regional water company. The participation of the public sector is of key importance in view of Hidrocapital's preeminence in all phases of the water cycle. The new water regime does not allow private sector participation in the stages of water extraction and production, since water is defined as a public good and these activities are reserved to the public national company responsible for operating the major water production systems. In this context, the WSS is regulated through Hidrocapital and the National Superintendence of Water Service by the National Water Office, which in turn reports to the Ministry of the Environment and Natural Resources. Hidrocapital, for its part, undertook an organizational change to incorporate community participation into its operating procedures through the creation of the Community Management Office. The office has been instrumental in expediting the implementation of TWF throughout the CMR, fostering the creation of more than 200 TWFs in the PUI-Tuy alone.[57]

Local community participation through the TWF takes place throughout the whole planning process, starting from the community water needs assessment and the elaboration of a joint diagnosis with Hidrocapital professionals, through the design of specific projects for the rehabilitation and/or expansion of the network, to the monitoring of the service provided, the state of the network, and the use of water in a sensible way. The projects engendered differ greatly in technical

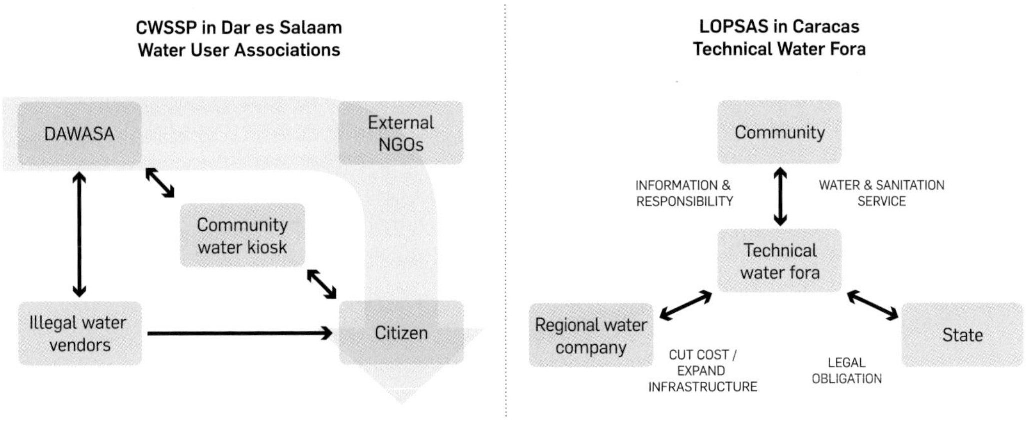

Figure 13. Institutional mechanisms for state-citizen water coproduction.

difficulty, cost, and complexity, ranging from small-scale water distribution systems to large-scale systems complete with pumping stations, rural water supply systems, wastewater collectors, and others. Within this process, the project represents a common vision of a concrete future and allows for the necessary organization of its implementation. The TWF is in charge of the financial comanagement of the projects in collaboration with various state agencies and are also responsible for negotiating and regularizing water tariffs agreed to within each community.

In the case of Dar es Salaam, the provisions for community self-provision in the context of privatization present a very different picture. Here the interaction between the state and lower-income communities was structured in a more instrumental fashion. Mediated by the support of external NGOs, a number of selected communities were given the possibility to access a marginal percentage of the financial resources allocated to the improvement of the metropolitan water system.[58] Not only was the interface between the state and local communities set up in a hierarchical way, but no link was established between the community-managed distribution networks and the main operating company.

A recent random sampling study by Mwakalila Shadrack in low- and middle-income settlements reveals that only about 10 percent of interviewed residents in Greater Dar es Salaam perceive DAWASCO as a satisfactory water provider.[59] The majority of respondents (47 percent) identify water user associations as the most adequate and legitimate channel to improve water services because of their capacity to reach unplanned settlement dwellers through flexible arrangements. However, for a long time during the operation of CWSSP, these were marginally considered and supported by the state, though more recently, DAWASCO has introduced a pro-poor unit based on the success of the program.

Table 2 summarizes the differences between the two case studies under examination in terms of roles, rights, and responsibilities. The comparison shows that when citizen coproduction mechanisms are framed within a predominantly instrumental rationale and subordinated to the single logic of cost recovery, significant asymmetries between the poor as self-providers and

Table 2. Roles, rights, and responsibilities

	DAR ES SALAAM (CWSSP)	CARACAS (LOPSA)
Policymaking	• Private contract terminated • Public company driven by cost recovery • Water as a right in theory but an economic good in practice	• Public regional agency directly linked to the technical water fora (TWF) • Guiding principles: social equity and democratic control • Water as a social right, not a subsidized gift
Financing	• General pricing mechanisms (tariffs) aimed at covering new investments and water production costs (full cost recovery) • Ad hoc public funding (CWSSP) matched by 5 percent community contributions	• New investments funding by the state • Water tariff reflecting the true cost of water production (transparent operating costs) linked to a new water culture • Cross-subsidies and public investment prioritize social needs
Capacity-building	• NGO-driven and community-targeted	• Driven by interaction between Hidrocapital and TWF
Planning	• Public company, limited forward planning	• Water local plans formulated by TWF in association with Hidrocapital
Regulation	• DAWASA /DAWASCO	• Hidrocapital and TWF
Implementation	• Communities from selected subward (Mtaas)	• Open to various agents but mainly by public agency

formal public-private providers are likely to persist, leading to inequality in the control over water resources and service provision.

What Is the Impact of Coproduction on the Poor?

The impact of citizen coproduction on the poor does not simply refer to whether or not they gain better access to certain services, but also to their status as citizens vis-à-vis the state and other citizens. For the urban and peri-urban poor, access to water is often not an individual concern but a collective problem. In this sense, the promotion and reward of collective action around water provision is potentially a powerful way to meet not just their practical needs but also their strategic needs.[60]

In the two case studies examined, the implementation of coproduction mechanisms in water provision is fairly recent, and, therefore, there is not enough information to assess their impact over a lengthy period. However, a number of achievements and shortcomings—summarized in table 3—seem to be emerging.

Despite the problems highlighted before, the CWSSP in Greater Dar es Salaam has been reported to have achieved some successful results. According to the government, the program has mobilized so far a total of sixty-six communities, supporting the construction of thirteen subprojects. More than US$43,000 has been collected from the communities as part of their 5 percent contribution to the total project cost. In 2007 the World Bank reported on its website some of the

Table 3. Impact of coproduction

	DAR ES SALAAM	CARACAS
Achievements	• Improved water access through public kiosks in some communities (66 communities mobilized) • Reduction in the price of water in selected projects reduced from US$0.40 to US$0.02 for 20 liters of water • Financial contribution from the communities amounting to US$43,000 (5 percent of the project's cost)	• MDG already achieved: water supply coverage in urban and peri-urban areas increased from 88 percent (1998) to 92 percent (2003) • Technical expertise combined with social responsibility • Needs-driven public investment and transparent system of water costing • Political clientelism challenged and emergency of new community organizations and new leadership, particularly among women. • Responsible citizenship and a new water culture
Shortcomings	• About 120,000 out of a projected 200,000 households remain completely unserved • About 2 percent of the total budget for 80 percent of people • Hierarchical interaction between public agencies and citizens • Mixed reactions from unserved communities • Residents prefer the flexibility of other means of provision, such as water vendors • Informal vendors wary of losing trade	• Fluctuations in the emergence and consolidation of TWFs, still affected by participation fatigue and emergency-driven organization • Lower rate of achievements in better-off areas in terms of water provision • Need to rework the framework in terms of transfer of responsibilities

results achieved in the case of JUWABERI, a water users association participating under CWSSP in the Kitunda Settlement, in the Ilala District. According to the JUWABERI's chairman: "Before the project came into being, we used to buy water from mostly shallow, privately-owned boreholes and from private vendors. . . . Apart from being unreliable, some of this water was not clean and was very expensive."[61] In this case, the community has benefited from a substantial reduction in the price of water, from an average price of US$0.40 to US$0.02 for twenty liters of water, reducing their reliance on informal vendors.

In its latest evaluation report, the World Bank also highlighted the operation of the CWSSP as one of the most effective and efficient components. This was in sharp contrast with the unsatisfactory performance of the Dar Es Salaam Water Supply and Sanitation Project as a whole. By 2010, the original target of completing fifty small water-supply schemes had been exceeded, with about 275,000 persons accessing the CWSSP's facilities. In addition, the scheme proved to be financially sustainable with revenues collected from the WUAs covering the operations, maintenance and expansion. As previously mentioned, the potential of the scheme materialized in further institutionalization through a pro-poor unit within DAWASCO. The unit emphasizes strengthening the management capacity of WUA to ensure the sustainability of the scheme, as well as providing oversight of off-network water schemes to ensure the proper operations of kiosks and to promote social connections.[62] Beside accounts like the one above, there are no other independent assessments so far of the CWSSP performance in reaching unserved low-income communities in Great Dar Salaam, though its success has also been acknowledged by other organisations, such as the IRC International Water and Sanitation Centre. However, DAWASCO has implemented some of the draconian provisions stipulated under the original contract signed with the World Bank.[63] In January 2008 the Tanzanian water minister publicly criticized the corporation for uprooting water pipes to make its customers pay their bills.[64] The total estimated water demand in Dar es Salaam is 400 million liters per day, but the system pumps about 281 million liters per day, of which only 16 percent is delivered to paying customers; the rest goes to illegal connections and is lost through leakages.[65] In this context, and given that cost recovery is the leading concern, it is not difficult to predict that the current focus on cutting off nonpayers and illegal connections is likely to have a negative impact on a large percentage of the population for whom the only alternatives are to rely on water vendors and other forms of self-provision.

Despite the success of the CWSSP, sanitation remains marginalized. Interventions in the pro-poor sanitation sector are becoming increasingly urgent in order to upgrade living conditions among the low income population. Dar es Salaam is below the national Tanzanian rate for sanitation coverage, which is already less than 50 percent. International organizations agree that the millennium development goals for sanitation will not be achieved.[66]

In the case of Caracas, TWF have helped improve coverage of water services. Although not easily attributable to the TWF alone, in Venezuela, the government claims that the millennium development goal of halving the population without access to water and sanitation by 2015 were already met in 2005. By 2010 the World Health Organization (WHO) / United Nations Children's Fund (UNICEF) Joint Monitoring Programme (JMP) for Water Supply and Sanitation showed a national figure of 92 percent improved drinking water and 89 percent improved sanitation.[67]

Miguel Lacabana and Cecilia Cariola argue that the introduction of TWF in the CMR has brought about significant transformations in four areas: (1) accountability—the management and monitoring of the service by Hidrocapital reflects the mechanisms laid down and adopted by the communities themselves; (2) transparency—the decision-making process relies on improved communication channels between communities and professionals; (3) synergy between citizens as professionals—through the articulation of the company's technical know-how with the communities' knowledge of their own networks and sources of water supply; and (4) higher professional responsiveness within the water bureaucracy, committed not only to high levels of performance and efficiency but also to a socially inclusive orientation to ensure high-quality service for all.[68] In addition, TWFs have arguably helped reduce the impact of patronage politics, historically facilitated by the high revenues of the oil-rich Venezuelan state to which local and national politicians have had access as means of providing infrastructure in exchange for votes.

Lacabana and Cariola also highlight that cultural change undertaken by Hidrocapital in the CMR was a key step toward the resolution of conflicts over water, especially in the lower-income communities. Before the institutionalization of TWFs, frequent breakdowns of service were settled by activating growing protest mechanisms that ranged from blocking roads and highways to violent occupation of water company facilities. In this sense, a reactive management approach—which sought only to keep problems under control—was replaced by a new mechanism of public action. Through TWFs, Hidrocapital and the communities gained a new channel to articulate responses, to solve service problems and to anticipate new demands and solutions.[69] As a result, TWFs have become effective platforms for negotiation and resolution of disputes, not only in the provision of water service but also regarding other problems involving community life, as expressed by a neighborhood leader in the PUI Tuy:

> The experiences I've had with the technical water forum are not just about water. That has opened many other doors for us, because as soon as they see the communities are well organized, the institutions take more of an interest in reaching those communities.[70]

In the public sector, both the water supply company and the local and state governments claim benefits from the introduction of the TWF. These are linked to the reduction of open conflict, which had characterized their relationship with the population, and the reduction of the costs of providing water by tank truck.

At the community level, TWFs have strengthened solidarity ties while providing examples of participatory democracy where not only rights but also duties of community members are stressed. In addition, within the communities, TWFs have encompassed the emergence of women's mobilization. Women represent approximately 75 percent of the TWF members and also the majority of the leaders within these organizations.[71] However, the emergence and consolidation of TWFs is still challenged by long-term practices of political clientelism and patronage relationships, as well as by participation fatigue and an emergency-driven culture among the communities. This implies that while some TWFs have become a strong basis to expand community mobilization from water to other areas, others have disappeared after meeting their most immediate objectives.

Concluding Remarks

The extent to which the institutional arrangements analyzed in this chapter have the capacity to empower the poor as citizens—breaking down the status quo and reasserting their right to the city—can be assessed by examining the way in which such arrangements transform the political space that frames their access to and control over service production.

Partnerships or Coproduction?

The notions of public-private community partnerships and government-citizens coproduction present two very different sets of assumptions. Although both concepts have been discussed within the coproduction literature, the former is closely linked with the New Public Management (NPM) school and is primarily concerned with the principle of efficiency, while the latter has been advanced from innovations within the Public Policy school of analysis and is centrally concerned with questions of social equality and political accountability.

A differentiation of these two discourses in service provision is important because each of them places people in different positions vis-à-vis the state and the private sector. From the former perspective, individuals, groups, and even communities are defined as clients, with the potential to chip in with various resources and assets in the process of service delivery. Moreover, they are often seen as the civic branch of the private sector. Citizen coproduction, by contrast, refers to people's involvement in the process of governing the production and delivery of services, paying particular attention to the need to reformulate citizens' rights and responsibilities vis-à-vis the state's. A second difference between these two discourses is that in the first case, water provision is conceptualized as a good or commodity, while in the second case it is viewed as a universal entitlement guaranteed by the state.

The search for alternative forms of service provision in developing countries is often associated with contexts "where state authority is weak, and public agencies struggled hard to fulfill the roles we take for granted in OECD countries."[72] Although this is often a precise characterization, citizen coproduction should be seen not just as an institutional arrangement that emerges out of the limited (e.g., political, financial, and regulatory) capacity of the state to provide universal services—as in the case of Greater Dar es Salaam—but, as demonstrated in the case of Caracas, out of a political project, in which coproduction is intentionally (and not by default) conceived as a way of transforming governance within the realm of participatory democracy.

Do Institutional Mechanisms Matter?

So, what does the above mean in terms of the political space opened or constrained by specific institutional mechanisms like the ones analyzed throughout this chapter? According to Joshi and Moore, in comparison to conventional state or private service production, citizen coproduction as an institutional mechanism offers several advantages.[73] First, it allows users and communities to supplement government provision in those cases where a particular service is not reaching certain groups or individuals. Second, it can help in the development of an effective interface between public/professional service providers and users/communities creating a mechanism for interaction and feedback that allows the reformulation of policy design and implementation to meet the particular needs and expectations of the end beneficiaries. Third, it can empower citizens to fully exercise their rights and to become agents of change, fostering a type of governance that is not producer-centered but people-centered. The previous analysis tells us that the extent to which these three functions are met depends of the institutional design of the mechanism in question (e.g., the way in which it establishes roles and responsibilities) and, above all, the political process and discourse within which coproduction is embedded.

In Dar es Salaam, service coproduction has been defined as a targeted strategy aimed at reaching the poor or, in other words, those unlikely to access water provision through the market mechanisms institutionalized with the failed attempt to privatize the service. This implies the coexistence of two systems: (1) a mainstream system in which water is treated as an economic good, delivered by a private and later public company through a water tariff system; and (2) an ad-hoc channel aimed at guaranteeing access by the poor, to be administered by NGOs, with cash and in-kind contributions by the targeted communities. Therefore, service delivery is structured through market mechanisms aimed to reach those who can pay, with a residual coproduction component for those who cannot be reached by the formal system. In this case, service coproduction has only delivered results in terms of supplementing government provision among some of the peri-urban communities in Greater Dar es Salaam, though the gradual institutionalization of a pro-poor approach within DAWASCO might in turn lead to a more substantial reorganization of the operation of this agency as a whole.

By contrast, in the case of Caracas, service coproduction was framed within a political and institutional attempt to retreat from service privatization as a prevailing paradigm. This does not imply the exclusion of cost-recovery mechanisms; rather, it involves the introduction of new forms of regulation in activities like water provision, defined by the state as a strategic right and entitlement to be guaranteed to all citizens. In this case, the three advantages outlined above have been performed by the establishment and consolidation of the TWF, ranging from material improvements in service delivery to the emergence of an institutionalized space for negotiation between the poor and the state.

Instrumentalization or Transformation?

What is then the scope of coproduction to activate the transformative capacity of the social and political practices of the poor beyond the improvement of service delivery?

The notion of citizens' participation in service coproduction has been contested by many authors, who fear that this might after all become just another means of invited participation by which users and communities are dumped with the responsibility of filling in gaps where governments are unwilling or unable to deliver. Geoff Mulgan contends that "it is hardly progressive to distribute responsibilities to the powerless."[74] The central concern here refers to the potential misuse of service coproduction, demanding the active engagement of the less well-off in society to produce services to which they should already have a right as citizens.

In Caracas, TWFs establish a relationship between citizens and Hidrocapital that is based on the notion of coresponsibility. For the peri-urban poor, the new institutional structure represents an opportunity to improve service, not only in terms of frequency of delivery but also through their official recognition as legally entitled citizens. In addition, as these citizen organizations consolidate, they generate practices giving way to a new water culture—a new understanding of water in environmental, social, and economic terms—involving rights and obligations that result in new forms of social inclusion and citizenship building. In this sense, the TWF's most important accomplishment, is "obtaining the service while building citizenship."[75]

In Dar es Salaam, by contrast, there is a more conventional and instrumental approach to the participation of the poor, in which access to water is still framed within a market system, with a particular outlet to alleviate the needs of those outside the market but with the capacity to contribute financially to the establishment of public kiosks. Nevertheless, it is important to acknowledge that the CWSSP has moved from being seen as a marginal initiative to being recognized as an efficient and effective alternative to respond to the demands of the poor and unserviced.

The two experiences reviewed are based on the introduction of potentially positive mechanisms to reach the poor, where they deeply differ is on the way in which they frame citizen coproduction. Their comparison suggests that, when genuinely applied, coproduction is a highly political process with the ability to promote participative democracy, challenge professional expertise, and empower users and communities. In the case of the TWF, communities were empowered through an institutionalized channel that allows them to be active players and have a voice in the decision making process. Of course, one could argue that the TWF in Caracas could become over time yet another instrument of bureaucratic control and political clientelism and that the water users associations in Dar es Salaam could evolve into a legitimate vehicle to encompass a deeper process of negotiation with the state as far as water provision and other issues, such as land management and regularization, are concerned.

While the outcomes of relatively or entirely self-organized forms of cooperation and negotiation among citizens and the state are difficult to predict, in the two case analyzed institutionalized coproduction platforms appeared to have extended the 'opportunity space' for those typically disenfranchised from the decision making process to establish regular channels of communication and negotiation with the state. Building on the notions of practical and strategic needs, it could be argued that citizen coproduction might have a positive impact on the practical needs of the poor—for instance, by improving service provision and widening the practical choices among users (e.g., drawing on different technical options, reducing provision costs, improving the quality/quantity and regularity of the service provided, and opening their access to alternative providers)—or on their strategic needs, promoting inclusive forms of state-citizen interaction, enabling their entitlements as citizens, and valuing and nurturing their knowledge vis-à-vis that of professionals. Their longlasting transformative power depends on the depth and scale of the political process they generate and sustain.

NOTES

The author would like to thank her colleagues at the UCL Development Planning Unit and in Dar es Salaam and Caracas, with whom she worked during a three-year research project, whose findings provided the basis for the reflections presented throughout this chapter. Among them, special thanks to Pascale Hofmann, Julio Dávila, Miguel Lacabana, and Wilbard Kombe and also to Diana Daste Marmolejo, for her assistance in updating some of the details provided in the analysis of the two case studies. Sincere thanks are also due to my colleagues Caren Levy and Michael Mattingly, and to the editor of this book, Igor Vojnovic, who read earlier versions of this chapter and provided useful comments and suggestions. The usual disclaimers nevertheless apply.

1. Caren Levy, Defining Strategic Action Planning Led by Civil Society Organisations: The Case of CLIFF, India," a paper presented at the 8th N-AERUS Conference, September 6–8, 2007, London.
2. These were two of the five case studies examined under a three-year research project concerned with the governance of water and sanitation in the peri-urban interface (PUI) of metropolitan regions in the developing world. The project was funded by the Department for International Development (DFID) of the British Government and led by the Development Planning Unit (DPU), University College London. The project partners in Caracas and Dar es Salaam were respectively the Centre for Development Studies (CENDES) and the University College of Lands and Architectural Studies (UCLAS). For more information, visit http://www.ucl.ac.uk/dpu/pui.
3. Adriana Allen, Julio D. Dávila, and Pascale Hofmann, *Governance of Water and Sanitation for the Peri-Urban Poor: A Framework for Understanding and Action in Metropolitan* Regions (London: Development Planning Unit, 2006).
4. Anuradha Joshi and Mick Moore, Institutionalized Co-Production: Unorthodox Public Service Delivery in Challenging Environments, *Journal of Development Studies* 40:4 (2004): 31–49.
5. NPM emerged as a response to the context of the economic and fiscal crises that afflicted a number of Western states in the late 1970s, which were largely attributed to the bureaucratic failures of the Keynesian welfare state. Over time, the principles of this school of thought were spread throughout the developing world, through the promotion of civil-service reform, privatization, management decentralization, and a host of other measures

focusing on the rolling back of the state.

6. Joshi and Moore, Institutionalized Co-Production, 31–49.
7. Jessica Budds and Gordon McGranahan, Are the Debates on Water Privatization Missing the Point? Experiences from Africa, Asia and Latin America, *Environment and Urbanization* 15:2 (2003): 87–113.
8. K. Bakker, *Good Governance in Restructuring Water Supply: A Handbook* (Ottawa: Federation of Canadian Municipalities, 2002).
9. E. Gutierrez, B. Calaguas, J. Green, and V. Roaf, *New Rules, New Roles: Does Private Sector Participation Benefit the Poor?* Synthesis Report (London: WaterAid and Tearfund, 2003).
10. Matthias Finger, The New Water Paradigm: The Privatisation of Governance and the Instrumentalisation of the State, in *The Business of Global Environmental Governance*, ed. David Levy and Peter Newell (Cambridge, MA: MIT Press, 2005), 275–328.
11. Bakker, *Good Governance in Restructuring Water Supply*.
12. Adriana Allen, Julio D. Dávila, and Pascale Hofmann, The Peri-Urban Poor: Citizens or Consumers? *Environment and Urbanization* 18:2 (2006): 333–51.
13. Elinor Ostrom, *Community Organisation and the Provision of Police Services* (Beverly Hills: Sage, 1973).
14. G. Whitaker, Co-Production: Citizen Participation in Service Delivery, *Public Administration Review* 40 (1980): 240–246; S. L. Percy, Citizen Participation in the Co-Production of Urban Services, *Urban Affairs Review* 19:4 (1984): 431–46.
15. Elinor Ostrom, Crossing the Great Divide: Co-Production, Synergy and Development, *World Development* 24:6 (1996): 1073–87.
16. Anuradha Joshi and Mick Moore, Institutionalized Co-Production: Unorthodox Public Service Delivery in Challenging Environments, *Journal of Development Studies* 40:4 (2004): 31–49.
17. Ibid., 40.
18. Isabelle Lemaire, Deliberative Democracies through Co-Production: The Case of Caracas Water Provision in the Peri-Urban Interface, unpublished work at Development Planning Unit, University College London, 2008.
19. N. Webster and L. Engberg-Pedersen, ed., In the Name of the Poor: Contesting Political Space for Poverty Reduction (London: Zed Books, 2002).
20. In terms of population growth, the highest rates in the PUI Tuy were recorded for the intercensus periods 1971–1981 and 1981–1990 at 7.0 and 7.1 percent respectively, decreasing to 3.5 percent during the 1990–2001 interval.
21. Miguel Lacabana and Cecilia Cariola, *Entre la ciudad global y la periferia en transicion: Caracas—Valles del Tuy Medio* (Caracas: Ministerio del Poder Popular para Ciencia y Tecnologia, 2006).
22. Miguel Lacabana and Cecilia Cariola, Globalisation and Metropolitan Expansion: Residential Strategies and Livelihoods in Caracas and Its Periphery, *Environment and Urbanization* 15 (2003): 65–74.
23. Ibid.
24. Cecilia Cariola and Miguel Lacabana, An Overview of the Water Supply and Sanitation System at Metropolitan and Peri-Urban Level: The Case of Caracas, report prepared for the Research Project Service Provision Governance in the Peri-Urban Interface of Metropolitan Areas (London: Development Planning Unit, University College London, 2004).
25. WaterAid and Tearfund, *New Rules, New Roles: Does PSP Benefit the Poor? Water Reforms and PSP in Dar es Salaam*, WaterAid-Tanzania, 2003, at http://www.wateraid.org/documents/plugin_documents/waterreformsandpsptanz.pdf.
26. Francos Halla, A Century of Urban Development Planning for Dar es Salaam City in Tanzania, *Journal of Building and Land Development* 9:1 (2002): 28–46.
27. V. Kreibich, Informal Land Management: An Introduction, *Habitat International* 24 (2000): 121–25.
28. Wilbard Kombe and John Lupala, An Overview of the Water Supply and Sanitation System at Metropolitan and Peri-Urban Level: The Case of Dar es Salaam, report prepared for the Research Project Service Provision Governance in the Peri-Urban Interface of Metropolitan Areas (London: Development Planning Unit, University College London, 2004).
29. Wilbard Kombe and John Lupala, WSS Practices and Living Conditions in the Peri-Urban Interface of Metropolitan Dar es Salaam: The Cases Tungi and Stakishari, report prepared for the Research Project Service Provision Governance in the Peri-Urban Interface of Metropolitan Areas (London: Development Planning Unit, University College London, 2004).
30. Wilbard Kombe, Land Use Dynamics in Peri-Urban Areas and Their Implications on the Urban Growth and Form: The Case of Dar es Salaam, Tanzania, *Habitat International* 29 (2005): 113.
31. Focus group session in the Paso Real 2000 Community; Cariola and Lacabana, WSS Practices and Living Conditions.
32. Ibid.
33. Kombe and Lupala, WSS Practices and Living Conditions.

34. Discussion with Zainabu Saidi, Tungi subward chairperson, on February 5, 2004, at Tungi Subward Office; Kombe and Lupala, WSS Practices and Living Conditions.
35. Discussion with Mr. Rugenzi, on February 6, 2004, at Tungi; Kombe and Lupala, WSS Practices and Living Conditions.
36. Discussion with Mzee Abraham Juma, a resident in Tungi since 2001, on February 5, 2004; Kombe and Lupala, WSS Practices and Living Conditions.
37. Davis Mwamfupe and J. Briggs, Peri Urban Development in an Era of Structural Adjustment in Africa: The City of Dar es Salaam, *Urban Studies* 37:4 (2000): 797–809.
38. Focus group discussion involving Suleiman Lolila, Rajabu Shemweta, Julieth Kianesh, Petronilla Milanzi, Fatuma Chande, Hatibu Mavura, Hamis Chande, and Glorious Luoga, all residents of Stakishari settlements, in September 2003; Kombe and Lupala, WSS Practices and Living Conditions.
39. Cristóbal Francisco, Hidroven dará paso a las nuevas instituciones de regulación y planificación del sector, *Vertientes* 11 (December 2002): 15–19.
40. A long tradition of public water supply without charge means that at the time of the fieldwork in 2003–2004, 50 percent of water bills were not collected in the Caracas Metropolitan Region, and only 10 percent of the water distributed in the Valles del Tuy region was paid for. Cariola and Lacabana, WSS Practices and Living Conditions.
41. The largest operating cost is electric power due to the pumping needs posed by the altitude differences between extraction areas and the distributional network. About 40 percent (US$53 million in 2002) of this cost is subsidized by the national government. Jacqueline Farías, Navegando Hacia Otras Aguas, *Vertientes* 11 (December 2002): 20–24.
42. Angela González , Informe nacional sobre la gestión del agua en Venezuela, *Caracas* 83 (January 2000).
43. Francisco, Hidroven Dará Paso, 19.
44. Pers. comm. with Professor Miguel Lacabana, April 1, 2008.
45. ActionAid, Turning Off the Taps: Donor Conditionality and Water Privatisation in Dar es Salaam, ActionAid Report, 2004, http://www.actionaid.org.uk/_content/documents/TurningofftheTAps.pdf.
46. John Davies, Report of the Short-term Adviser on the Privatisation of DAWASA, London, November 1997.
47. This utility rehabilitation project was cofinanced by the World Bank, the African Development Bank, and the European Investment Bank.
48. World Bank, Project appraisal document on a proposed credit in the amount of SDR 45.0 million (US$61.5 million equivalent) to the United Republic of Tanzania for the Dar es Salaam Water and sanitation project, WB Africa Regional Office Report No 25249-TA (April 2003): 16, http://www.worldbank.org/afr/padi/TZ_PAD.pdf].
49. Ibid., 17.
50. Ibid., 6.
51. Ibid.
52. Anuradha Joshi and Mick Moore, Organisations That Reach the Poor: Why Co-Production Matters, paper prepared and presented at the *Making Services Work for Poor People, World Development Report (WDR) 2003/04 Workshop*, Oxford, November 4–5, 2002.
53. Tony Bovaird, Beyond Engagement and Participation, User and Community Co-Production of Services, report produced for UK Carnegie Trust, 2007, http://rural.carnegieuktrust.org.uk/files/rural/Beyond%20Engagement%20and%20Participation-%20T%20Bovaird.pdf.
54. ActionAid, Turning Off the Taps, 15. http://www.actionaid.org.uk/_content/documents/TurningofftheTAps.pdf.
55. WaterAid and Tearfund. 2003. Op. cit. p. 7.
56. Ibid., 8.
57. Cariola and Lacabana, WSS Practices and Living Conditions.
58. The criteria for selection considered water and sanitation supply and water supply vulnerability based on five categories: low income households with inadequate access to services; cholera prone locations; dangerous free land; areas with deficient water supply; and areas distant from water sources.
59. Mwakalila Shadrack, Residents' Perceptions of Institutional Performance in Water Supply in Dar es Salaam, *Physics and Chemistry of the Earth, Parts A/B/C* 32:15–18 (2007): 1285–90.
60. Borrowing from the gender literature, the notion of practical needs is used here to signify those needs which are related to satisfying both men's women's, girls and boys basic material needs (e.g., food, water, clothing and shelter) while strategic needs refer to the changes required to challenge the roots of social exclusion and inequality.
61. http://go.worldbank.org/3ECC6990J0.
62. The World Bank (2011) Implementation completion and results report (ida-37710 and ida-3771a) on a credit in the amount of sdr 45 million (US$61.5 million equivalent) to the United Republic of Tanzania for a Dar es Salaam water supply and sanitation project. Water and urban unit Country department , Africa Regional Office.
63. DAWASCO took over CWS in 2005, and a new lease

contract and subloan agreement for US$6 million was approved by the World Bank in the same year to support the implementation of a so-called 100 Day Rescue Plan.

64. Peter Felister, Dawasco Too Harsh on Water Bills—Minister, *Guardian*, January 16, 2008, http://www.ippmedia.com/ipp/guardian/2008/01/16/106404.html.
65. Brian Mathew, Dar es Salaam Water: What to Do? *Tanzanian Affairs* 81 (September 1, 2005), http://www.tzaffairs.org/?p=172.
66. ICR (2009) Local government and communities at work: questioning the Community Water Supply and Sanitation Project Dar es Salaam, Tanzania
67. World Health Organization (WHO) / United Nations Children's Fund (UNICEF) Joint Monitoring Programme (JMP) for Water Supply and Sanitation in http://www.wssinfo.org/ (Last accessed: March 2012)
68. Lacabana and Cariola, Construyendo la participacion popular, 111–33.
69. Cariola and Lacabana, WSS Practices and Living Conditions.
70. Interview with a female neighborhood leader, El Carmen, CMR, 2003; Cariola and Lacabana, WSS Practices and Living Conditions.
71. Interview with the Community Coordinator of the Hidrocapital Losada-Ocumarito System, CRM, 2003; Cariola and Lacabana, WSS Practices and Living Conditions.
72. Joshi and Moore, Institutionalized Co-Production, 32–33.
73. Joshi and Moore, Organisations That Reach the Poor.
74. G. Mulgan, Citizens and Responsibilities, in *Citizenship*, ed. G. Andrews (London: Lawrence & Wishart, 1991), 45.
75. Cecilia Cariola, Las mesas técnicas de agua, primer consejo comunitario del agua de la región capital, working paper for CENDES-UCV, May 2003, 3.

REFERENCES

ActionAid. Turning Off the Taps. Donor conditionality and Water Privatisation in Dar es Salaam. ActionAid Report, 2004. http://www.actionaid.org.uk/_content/documents/TurningofftheTAps.pdf.

Allen, Adriana, Julio D. Dávila, and Pascale Hofmann. *Governance of Water and Sanitation for the Peri-urban Poor: A Framework for Understanding and Action in Metropolitan Regions.* London: Development Planning Unit, 2006.

Allen, Adriana, Julio D. Dávila, and Pascale Hofmann. The Peri-urban Poor: Citizens or Consumers? *Environment and Urbanization* 18:2 (2006): 333–51.

Bakker, K. *Good Governance in Restructuring Water Supply: A Handbook.* Ottawa: Federation of Canadian Municipalities, 2002.

Bovaird, Tony. Beyond Engagement and Participation. User and Community Co-production of Services. Report produced for UK Carnegie Trust, 2007. http://rural.carnegieuktrust.org.uk/files/rural/Beyond%20Engagement%20and%20Participation-%20T%20Bovaird.pdf.

Budds, Jessica, and Gordon McGranahan. Are the Debates on Water Privatization Missing the Point? Experiences from Africa, Asia and Latin America. *Environment and Urbanization* 15:2 (2003): 87–113.

Cariola, Cecilia, and Miguel Lacabana. *An Overview of the Water Supply and Sanitation System at Metropolitan and Peri-urban Level: The Case of Caracas.* Report prepared for the Research Project Service Provision Governance in the Peri-urban Interface of Metropolitan Areas. London: Development Planning Unit, University College London, 2004.

Cariola, Cecilia, and Miguel Lacabana. *WSS Practices and Living Conditions in the Peri-urban Interface of Metropolitan Caracas: The Cases of Bachaquero and Paso Real 2000.* Report prepared for the Research Project Service Provision Governance in the Peri-urban Interface of Metropolitan Areas. London: Development Planning Unit, University College London, 2004.

Cariola, Cecilia. Notas sobre las Mesas Técnicas de agua. Primer consejo comunitario del agua de la Región Capital. Working paper for CENDES-UCV, May 2003 (mimeo).

Davies, John. November. Report of the Short-Term Adviser on the Privatisation of DAWASA. London, 1997.

Felister, Peter. Dawasco Too Harsh on Water Bills—Minister. *Guardian*, 2008–01–16. http://www.ippmedia.com/ipp/guardian/2008/01/16/106404.html.

Finger, Matthias. The New Water Paradigm: The Privatisation of governance and the Instrumentalisation of the State. In *The Business of Global Environmental Governance*, ed. David Levy and Peter Newell, 275–328. Cambridge, MA: MIT Press, 2005.

Francisco, Cristóbal. Hidroven dará paso a las nuevas instituciones de regulación y planificación del sector. *Vertientes* 11 (2002): 15–19.

González, Angela L. Informe nacional sobre la gestión del agua en Venezuela. *Caracas* 83 (January 2000).

Gutierrez, E., B. Calaguas, J. Green and V. Roaf. *New Rules, New Roles: Does Private Sector Participation Benefit the Poor? Synthesis Report.* London: WaterAid and Tearfund, 2003.

Halla, Francos. A Century of Urban Development Planning for Dar es Salaam City in Tanzania. *Journal of Building and Land Development* 9:1 (2002): 28–46.

Joshi, Anuradha, and Mick Moore. Organisations that Reach the Poor: Why Co-production Matters. Paper prepared and presented at the Making Services Work for Poor People, World Development Report (WDR) 2003/04 Workshop, Oxford, November 4–5, 2002.

Joshi, Anuradha, and Mick Moore. Institutionalized Co-production: Unorthodox Public Service Delivery in Challenging Environments. *Journal of Development Studies* 40:4 (2004): 31–49.

Kombe, Wilbard, and John Lupala. *An Overview of the Water Supply and Sanitation System at Metropolitan and Peri-urban Level: The Case of Dar es Salaam.* Report prepared for the Research Project Service Provision Governance in the Peri-urban interface of Metropolitan Areas. London: Development Planning Unit, University College London, 2004.

Kombe, Wilbard, and John Lupala. *WSS Practices and Living Conditions in the Peri-urban Interface of Metropolitan Dar es Salaam: The Cases Tungi and Stakishari.* Report prepared for the Research Project Service Provision Governance in the Peri-urban Interface of Metropolitan Areas. London: Development Planning Unit, University College London, 2004.

Kombe, Wilbard. Land Use Dynamics in Peri-urban Areas and Their Implications on the Urban Growth and Form: The Case of Dar es Salaam, Tanzania. *Habitat International* 29 (2005): 113–35.

Kreibich, V. Informal Land Management: An Introduction. *Habitat International* 24 (2000): 121–25.

Lacabana, Miguel, and Cecilia Cariola. Construyendo la participacion popular y una nueva cultura del agua en Venezuela. *Cuadernos del CENDES* 22:59 (2005): 111–33.

———. *Entre la ciudad global y la periferia en transicion. Caracas—Valles del Tuy Medio.* Caracas: Ministerio del Poder Popular para Ciencia y Tecnologia, 2006.

———. Globalisation and Metropolitan Expansion: Residential Strategies and Livelihoods in Caracas and Its Periphery. *Environment and Urbanization* 15 (2003): 65–74.

Lemaire, Isabelle. Deliberative Democracies through Co-Production: The Case of Caracas Water Provision in the Peri-Urban Interface. Unpublished work at Development Planning Unit, University College London, 2008.

Levy, Caren. Defining Strategic Action Planning Led by Civil Society Organisations: The case of CLIFF, India. A paper presented at the 8th N-AERUS Conference, September 6–8, 2007, London.

Mathew, Brian. Dar es Salaam Water: What to Do? *Tanzanian Affairs* 81 (2005). http://www.tzaffairs.org/?p=172.

Mulgan, G. Citizens and Responsibilities. In *Citizenship*, ed. G. Andrews, 37–49. London: Lawrence and Wishart, 1991.

Mwamfupe, Davis, and J. Briggs. Peri Urban Development in an Era of Structural Adjustment in Africa: The City of Dar es Salaam. *Urban Studies* 37:4 (2000): 797–809.

Ostrom, Elinor. *Community Organisation and the Provision of Police Services.* Beverly Hills, CA: Sage, 1973.

———. Crossing the Great Divide: Co-production, Synergy and Development. *World Development* 24:6 (1996): 1073–87.

Percy, S. L. Citizen Participation in the Co-production of Urban Services. *Urban Affairs Review* 19:4 (1984): 431–46.

Shadrack, Mwakalila. Residents' Perceptions of Institutional Performance in Water Supply in Dar es Salaam. *Physics and Chemistry of the Earth, Parts A/B/C* 32:15–18 (2007): 1285–90.

WaterAid and Tearfund. New Rules, New Roles: Does PSP Benefit the Poor? Water Reforms and PSP in Dar es Salaam, WaterAid-Tanzania. 2003. http://www.wateraid.org/documents/plugin_documents/waterreformsandpsptanz.pdf.

Webster, N., and L. Engberg-Pedersen, eds. *In the Name of the Poor: Contesting Political Space for Poverty Reduction.* London: Zed Books, 2002.

Whitaker, G. Co-production: Citizen Participation in Service Delivery. *Public Administration Review* 40 (1980): 240–46.

■ RICARDO GOMEZ-INSAUSTI / ANALIA S. CONTE

Economic Reorganization, Social Transformation, and Urban Sustainability in Argentina

THE CASE OF METROPOLITAN BUENOS AIRES

The market-driven policies of macroeconomic adjustment that the Argentinean governments carried out in the 1990s deepened the country's socioeconomic disparities, reaching the most dramatic turning point during the political-economic crisis of 2001–2002, which resulted in violent protests and the fall of Fernando de la Rua's government. The execution of this type of economic reform was not new in Argentina. The World Bank (WB) and the International Monetary Fund (IMF) have encouraged the implementation of neoliberal policies since the 1970s. However, the magnitude of the socioeconomic and spatial transformation was unusually high in the 1990s. Argentina's largest urban centers became the foci of deep social conflicts as poverty, sociospatial fragmentation and segregation, crime, and insecurity reached levels previously unknown.

The structure of metropolitan Buenos Aires, a second-tier world city within a peripheral capitalist economy, changed dramatically at the end of the twentieth century. The forces of globalization and the disjointed local planning system combined to deeply transform the sociospatial organization of the metropolis. Buenos Aires city, the country's capital, lost population while the outer suburbs—the third ring in particular—more than doubled in growth (table 1, fig. 1).

The transition of Buenos Aires toward its new role in the global economy was not straightforward. The restructuring of its metropolitan space was affected by factors external to the city and even to the country, over which not much control can be exerted.[1] On the one hand, the macroeconomic policies of stabilization, flexibilization, and deregulation within the context of the market ideology improved the environment for private investment, foreign and domestic alike. The new strategy favored the modernization of urban services and the revitalization of real estate developments wherever profitability was granted or already available. On the other hand, the contraction of public spending and the privatization of state-run firms such as the utility companies had a negative impact on social and public infrastructure, affecting mainly the poorer sectors of

Table 1. Population distribution of Metropolitan Buenos Aires

	1991	2001	GROWTH (%)
Buenos Aires city	2,965,403	2,768,772	–6.6
Suburban ring 1	4,614,113	4,726,311	2.4
Suburban ring 2	3,310,311	3,839,726	16.0
Suburban ring 3	452,848	804,095	77.6

Source: Marcela Cerrutti and Alejandro Grimson, Buenos Aires, neoliberalismo y después: Cambios socioeconómicos y respuestas populares, Working Paper 04-04d.2 The Center for Migration and Development. Princeton, NJ: Princeton University, 2004.

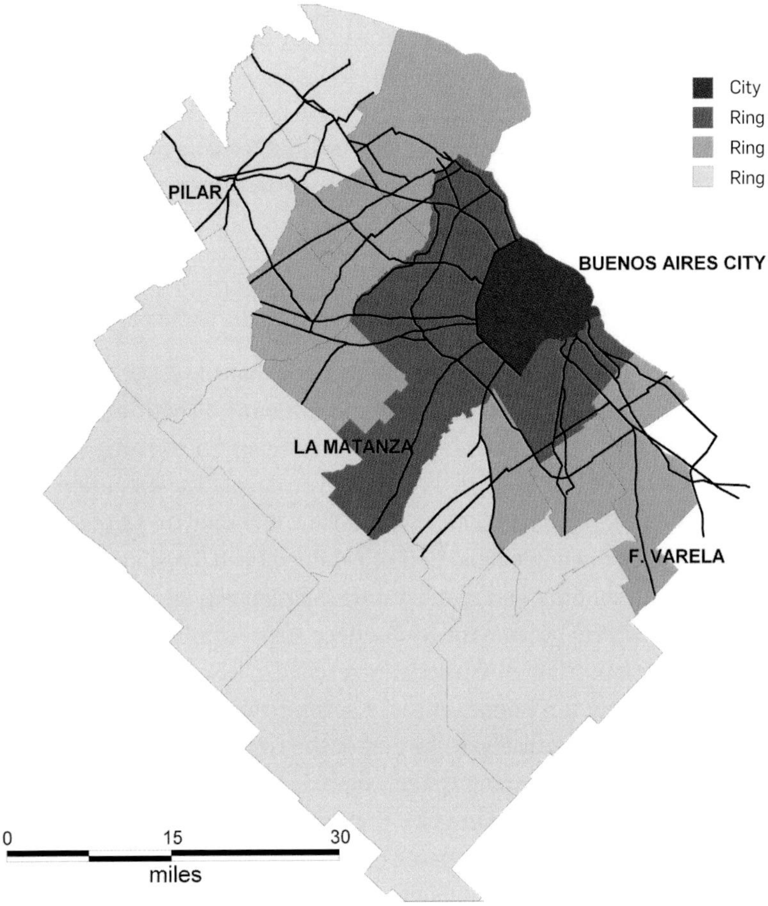

Figure 1. Metropolitan Buenos Aires, spatial configuration.

the population.[2] Privatization virtually meant transferring infrastructure and service planning to private companies operating for profit.

The new market-driven policies did not affect everybody similarly. The large urban middle-income groups formed during the post–World War II industrialization process of import substitution shrank dramatically. They moved down in the social scale, contributing to the enlargement of the lower income groups. Social polarization skyrocketed, making sociospatial fragmentation and segregation in Buenos Aires as noticeable as it is in other Latin American metropolises. Islands of wealth developed in a restless sea of poverty.[3]

The new layers of foreign and allied-domestic private investment concentrated at the core and along the northern sector of the metropolis, where the privileged tend to work and live. Old railway, waterfront, and port areas near the financial district suddenly became valuable commercial or residential land, and the northern sector the preferred space for urban revalorization. Upscale residences, shopping spaces, luxurious international-chain hotels, and corporate headquarters developed in recently revalorized pieces of land. It is estimated that 75 percent or 80 percent of the US$28.4 billion invested in metropolitan Buenos Aires between 1990 and 1998 went to these areas.[4]

The urban landscape that emerged in the 1990s was shaped by a set of distinctive and conflictive social processes: (1) the impoverishment of the middle- and low-income groups that was accompanied by new forms of social conflict, protests, crime, and violence; (2) the escalation

Figure 2. Revalorization of Buenos Aires' landscape.

Figure 3. New corporate and residential buildings in the redeveloped area of Puerto Madero.

of urban insecurity as disparities in social capital formation produced frictions between the privileged and underprivileged; (3) the revalorization of exclusive spaces at the core and the suburban expansion of gated communities in the northern suburbs that contrasted with the generalized deterioration of the urban space in the rest of the metropolis; and, (4) the frantic use of the environment as the market took any space available, either suitable or unsuitable, for human living.

Material, social, and environmental deterioration characterized the living conditions of a large portion of the population in metropolitan Buenos Aires during the 1990s.[5] These sociospatial changes are the symptoms of a process of growth that goes against some of the basic principles of urban sustainability: inclusiveness, equitability, stability, and citizenry empowerment. The market-driven policies of economic adjustment implemented in the 1990s pushed the metropolitan region of Buenos Aires further away from any fruitful path toward sustainable urban growth.

Urban Growth and Sustainability

According to the United Nations' Habitat program for sustainable cities, urban sustainability pursues an integrated approach to the production and management of the urban space. All parts of the urban landscape and the relationship between them are to be considered in the building of a livable city for today and tomorrow. Persons and institutions produce and manage the urban space where natural and human processes are intimately intertwined. The urban environment should be a cohesive integrated space where environmental and social conditions interrelate organically.

For many years, Argentinean scholars and practitioners have discussed the constrains and contradictions that the economic system brings to sustainable development and urban sustainability in particular. Many documents were produced on these topics in Argentina, and metropolitan Buenos Aires, in particular. From as early as the mid-1970s, several institutions and many individuals have been concerned not only with the preservation of the environment but also with the achievement of social equitability, stability, and citizenry empowerment in the country.[6]

Many official documents on sustainability were produced—often reviewed and updated or discarded with each change of political authorities. The politics behind sustainability are immense. Universities and research centers have undergone in one way or another alternate cycles of silence and assertion in relation to political swings. State monies are the most common sources of funding for research projects. The discussion of ideas or projects considered destabilizing by authoritarian and nondemocratic governments was not a straightforward option within the country's political-institutional system. Only from the 1980s onward, urban sustainability has been consistently discussed in many Argentinean political and institutional forums.

The formation of the United Nations Environment Programme (UNEP) in 1979, the World Commission on Environment and Development (WCED) in 1983 and Commission on Sustainable Development in 1992 brought the discourse on sustainability to mainstream political discussions in Argentina as much as it did in other peripheral economies. The specificities of urban sustainability in peripheral countries demanded not only international but full domestic attention as well.

Urban growth problems in peripheral economies have added stresses when compared to growth problems faced by urban regions in central economies. Consumerism, resource overexploitation, and pollution are only part of the problems that peripheral economies face. Underdeveloped countries also deal with acute levels of poverty, lack of basic infrastructure and services, and a chaotic use of the urban land. These challenges are immediate imperatives for the state to guarantee respectable conditions of human well-being. The achievement of collective goals can hardly be transferred to the market, where the economic and political powers are so unevenly balanced.

The state plays a critical role in creating favorable conditions for urban sustainability. The achievement of individual goals through the working of the market and the realization of collective goals through state mechanisms lie on a markedly uneven relationship of power in peripheral economies. This relationship has become even rougher since the restructuring of global capitalism in the 1970s. International financial organizations—the WB and IMF—have permanently conditioned any assistance to the adoption of neoliberal policies of economic adjustment. In one way or another, these policies favored the concentration of socioeconomic power in a few private hands while debilitating the role of state as an agent of collective action and transformation.

Argentina moved from a highly protected semi-industrialized country into a virtually open economy in less than a decade. From the mid-1970s to the early 1980s, under the military administration, strong interventionist but market-inspired policies adjusted the production system drastically, with manufacturing being the sector most negatively affected.[7] Buenos Aires, the country's major industrial agglomeration with almost 30 percent of the total population, suffered the immediate impact of deindustrialization.

However, the deepening of the market-driven initiatives only took a definitive turn in the 1990s. The democratic government in power-controlled inflation through a fixed exchange rate linked to the American dollar (Convertibility Law), debilitated unions, privatized state-run businesses, and tightened public spending severely through the decentralization of functions. These changes were quickly implemented but not necessarily thoroughly planned. Provinces and municipalities suddenly faced new responsibilities without sufficient political and economic support.

The social costs of the adjustment policies of the 1990s reached levels totally unknown in metropolitan Buenos Aires. Poverty, crime, violence, and insecurity increased, steeply deteriorating the urban environment. The liberalization of basic services and infrastructure development and the internationalization of their assets introduced new economic and environmental standards. Profitability and quality started being determined by the market while the underprivileged began to be excluded from most of the benefits of the market.

Poverty and Social Polarization

The levels of poverty, income disparity, and social fragmentation in the metropolis grew in parallel to the deterioration of the labor market. Unemployment grew from 6.7 percent in 1992 to 19.0 percent in 2001, while full-time employment decreased from 30.5 percent to 24.9 percent respectively (table 2).[8] The dismantling of the highly protected import-substitution system of industrial production and the privatization of state-run businesses affected negatively the employment income of many low- and middle-income families.

The new economic environment favored, on the one hand, investments in production technology of intermediate goods, particularly by large capital-intensive firms, pushing down the demand of low-skilled workers while maintaining only a small number of highly skilled jobs. The adoption of new production technologies contributed to split the labor force along socioeconomic lines. The most competitive industries paid their managers and highly qualified laborers far better than their low-skilled workers. Oil, mining, wholesale, transportation, finance, and civil services were the economic sectors that contributed the most to increase income disparities.[9]

On the other hand, in the new market-oriented environment for production, the number of small and medium size manufacturing firms continued to decline following the negative trend that started in the early 1980s with the opening up of the economy. Many small businesses could not survive the competition from imports that the peso-dollar parity facilitated. Within the already contracted labor market of metropolitan Buenos Aires, salaried jobs in firms under five employees went down from 20.8 percent in 1991 to 17.5 percent in 2001, and in larger firms from 41.0 percent to 39.2 percent, respectively.[10]

The reduction of employment income generation that resulted from the decline of jobs in manufacturing and public services had a negative impact on many low- and middle-income families. Disparities in income distribution jumped considerably. The ratio between the fifth and the first quintile moved up from 9.2 in 1991 to 13.4 in 2001 and the Gini coefficient climbed from 0.432 to 0.508, surpassing the critical 0.50 threshold. The Gini coefficient of income distribution grew almost constantly during the 1990s, indicating that the market-driven economic growth did not generate viable options for the individuals to develop their capacities (table 3).[11]

The increasing gap in income generation between those favored by the new policies of

Table 2. Metropolitan Buenos Aires labor conditions (%)

YEAR	UNEMPLOYMENT	FULL-TIME EMPLOYMENT	YEAR	UNEMPLOYMENT	FULL-TIME EMPLOYMENT
1992	6.7	30.5	1997	14.3	28.9
1993	9.6	30.3	1998	13.3	28.5
1994	13.1	29.0	1999	14.4	28.2
1995	17.4	27.1	2000	14.7	27.8
1996	18.8	26.9	2001	19.0	24.9

Source: INDEC, October waves, several years, Encuesta Permamente de Hogares.

Table 3. Metropolitan Buenos Aires income disparity

YEAR	GINI COEFFICIENT	YEAR	GINI COEFFICIENT
1991	0.432	1997	0.458
1992	0.419	1998	0.478
1993	0.432	1999	0.463
1994	0.436	2000	0.479
1995	0.465	2001	0.508
1996	0.463		

Source: Guillermo Paraje, Crisis, reforma estructural y . . . nuevamente crisis: desigualdad y bienestar en el gran Buenos Aires, *Desarrollo Económico* 45:179 (2005): 379.

Table 4. Metropolitan Buenos Aires population under the poverty line (%)

	BUENOS AIRES CITY	OUTSIDE THE CITY		BUENOS AIRES CITY	OUTSIDE THE CITY
1992	9.4	27.4	1997	8.0	39.9
1993	6.9	26.3	1998	7.8	36.9
1994	7.5	23.6	1999	10.1	42.6
1995	9.2	33.9	2000	13.0	44.7
1996	10.6	41.5	2001	12.6	52.4

Source: INDEC, October waves, several years, Encuesta Permamente de Hogares.

economic growth and those that did not is at the root of many social conflicts. The process of acute polarization, or bipolarization, that took place in Buenos Aires in the 1990s supports the hypothesis of a centrifuging society.[12] The contraction of the middle-income group contributes to the formation of two poles at each end of the income distribution scale, with the low end being the one that grows faster.

Outside Buenos Aires city, in the suburbs, the proportion of households under the poverty line as defined by the Argentinean statistics bureau (INDEC) increased to 52.4 percent in 2001 from 27.4 percent in 1992 (table 4).[13] However, the poverty level in some of the southern municipalities such as La Matanza, Florencio Varela, easily overpassed 60 percent of the population, bearing the formation of the new urban poor.[14] The poor and the newly impoverished middle-income groups grew to be more visible in the urban arena as conflicts and protests erupted almost everywhere. Unemployment, poverty, crime, and insecurity became common headlines on the front page of daily newspapers.

The privatization of basic services such as water and energy supply, waste collection, and transportation infrastructure also added pressure on the living conditions of the poor. The underprivileged remained virtually excluded from the improvement or even from the formal provision of basic infrastructure and services as previous subsidies and levels of tolerance to clandestine connections virtually disappeared under private ownership. Even shantytowns—*villas miseria*—within Buenos Aires city, just a few blocks away from luxurious hotels and corporate buildings, remained excluded from basic services (e.g., figs. 4 and 5).

The newly privatized systems remained uncoordinated and poorly regulated, as no organic planning procedures were clearly enunciated by the state. Metropolitan Buenos Aires is formed by a conglomerate of separated political administrative jurisdictions reporting to three different organizational levels: municipal, provincial (also applicable to the Autonomous City of Buenos Aires), and federal. Some infrastructure and service provisions are controlled by the municipalities (e.g., solid waste collection), while others by the province or the federal government (e.g., power distribution, water supply). Despite the complexity of the territorial structure, no regional planning body was effectively put in place to rationally coordinate the provision and development of services and infrastructure. The Metropolitan Area of Buenos Aires (AMBA) and later the National Commission for the Metropolitan Area of Buenos Aires (CONAMBA) were mere consulting bodies without any regulatory power. The incumbencies and duties of each government level of operation were blurrily defined. Only short-term strategies dominated the planning environment in municipalities where uncompensated decentralization and unconsulted privatization processes had their hardest impact.

The privatization of basic infrastructure and services reinforced sociospatial disparities within the urban space. Users in residential areas with higher purchasing power and a greater level of consumption benefited more than the others.[15] The adoption of the market ideology in the organization and management of infrastructure and services meant that the poorest inhabitants had no longer legal or illegal access to basic services. The living standards of the underprivileged got worse once again.

Municipal, provincial, and federal social programs to alleviate the declining living conditions of the poor came late. By the end of the 1990s many low- and middle-income groups found almost spontaneously ways to organize alternative forms of income redistribution. Palliatives embraced a full spectrum of options, from the provision of daily meals by community associations to the recovery of abandoned factories by laid-off workers. Disappointment in political representation and social conflicts and violence reached a climax in the early 2000s. New popular uprising leaders (e.g., *piqueteros*) confronted social conflicts with new forms of struggle for political power. Unexpected road blockages, a unique form of protest particularly exercised in Buenos Aires, increased from 51 in 1998 to 2,336 in 2002.[16] The access to the city and circulation in the metropolis were no longer easily guaranteed. Disruptions in the production system started being more frequently related to road blockages than to strikes organized by the weakened labor unions.

PHOTOGRAPH BY RICARDO GOMEZ-INSAUSTI

Figure 4. Villa Miseria Retiro near the upscale Barrio Norte in the background, city of Buenos Aires.

PHOTOGRAPH BY RICARDO GOMEZ-INSAUSTI

Figure 5. The extensive scale of Villa Miseria Retiro contrasting with the higher densities of the affluent Barrio Norte, city of Buenos Aires.

Insecurity and Social Conflicts

Significant levels of inequality and deprivation rather than absolute poverty are assumed to be prime determinants of crime when the gap between culturally desirable goals and legal means to attain them diverges constantly.[17] Although the lack of employment income may not necessarily explain the growth of crime, disparities in income distribution may.[18] Criminality frequently arises

PHOTOGRAPH BY FERNANDO VASQUEZ

Figure 6. Street blocked by piqueteros.

when underprivileged groups in society take matters into their own hands to overcome absolute or relative deprivation. The urban space of world cities in peripheral economies is the place where the international consumption style of the wealthy and the deprivation of the poor brutally converge. It is the place where the marketing of new consumption styles concentrates, offering illusions to everybody but selling attainable opportunities to a few.

The contradictory relationship between both poles of the social spectrum and the rise of criminality appear to be interrelated in metropolitan Buenos Aires. Crime rates had been historically low until the drastic neoliberal economic adjustments of the 1990s. Reported felonies jumped between 1991 and 2001 from 1,500 per 100,000 inhabitants to 6,600 per 100,000 inhabitants, and property crimes (mostly robbery and thefts) from 1,000 per 100,000 inhabitants to 4,800 per 100,000 inhabitants.[19] In 2001, 39.6 percent of the inhabitants of Buenos Aires city reported they had suffered from some sort of crime; 29.1 percent reported property crimes.[20] In 2002 only, more than 140,000 property crimes were committed in Buenos Aires city, with 52 percent robbery, 43 percent thefts, and the remaining 5 percent other related property crimes.[21] Notably, crimes to property were more common against the middle- and lower-middle income groups than against the upper-income groups, as the latter were able to better protect their homes.[22]

Although the perception of crime levels in the city is similar by all income groups, it has been the wealthy who have acted accordingly by creating fortified housing, buildings, or communities.[23]

The rise in criminality produced defensive mechanisms that were translated into spatial segregation and the formation of exclusionary urban spaces. Gated communities, protected neighborhoods, and secured buildings grew as the sense of insecurity in the urban space spread out. Physical barriers and limited accessibility were raised to intimidate the intruders—that is, "the others." Rather than building an inclusive and integrated urban space, the economic environment of the 1990s generated the opposite.

Social Exclusion and Gated Communities

In Buenos Aires, sociospatial segregation has always existed to some extent and under different forms over the years. Several exclusive but open neighborhoods developed during the twentieth century along the northern sector of the city, where accessibility has always been better.[24] However, the trends of the housing market for the wealthy took a completely different path in the 1990s. Gated communities bloomed in the northern outer suburbs of Buenos Aires, producing a major transformation of the metropolitan landscape.

Walled housing areas, planned as a whole and designed with high levels of security, have been of great success as social polarization, conflicts, crime, and violence intensified in the metropolis. The total number of built gated communities grew from about 100 in 1995 to 351 in 2000.[25] In the 1990s the privileged started moving away from Buenos Aires city, breaking the European tradition of living close to the core, as they had done until then. By the end of the 1990s, it is estimated that about 130,000 people had already left the city for the suburbs.[26] In 2004, it was estimated that 500,000 people lived in some sort of gated community (e.g., enclosed neighborhood, new cities, country-clubs, or *chacras*—exurban farms).[27]

Marketing campaigns for gated communities or closed neighborhoods targeted the well-off young families that wanted to avoid the highly dense and increasingly unsafe urban core. Real-estate developers encouraged the rush for suburbia by emphasizing the importance of a new lifestyle in a safer and greener environment while still having access to the city through recently improved privatized highways. The northern access to the city—the Pan-Americana road—was one of the first highways to be upgraded in 1993.[28]

The development of gated communities basically reflects one end of the opposed lifestyles that started blooming in Buenos Aires. The fear of rising city crime was explicitly or implicitly behind the sense of security that the wealthy began seeking in walled housing areas. For the privileged, the housing space is an important factor to maintaining a high standard of living. However, this type of reclusive housing environment and lifestyle bring up extensive social consequences.

The fragmented organization of the different social groups over space influences the way the most powerful sectors interact and relate to other sectors of society. Within the walls, everything is known, safe, and controlled; outside, everything is unknown, dangerous, and uncontrolled. The privileged do not need to go outside the community; their everyday life occurs within the walls. These well-organized gated housing areas fairly often have hypermarkets, bank branches, health centers, rugby, hockey, and soccer fields, sometimes even riding facilities, private schools, and universities.

The inhabitants of these walled spaces perceive their communities not only as private and protected, but also as socially homogenous. Protection and social homogeneity are likely the most important factors behind the development of gated communities. They give the impression of a stable and secure environment to those that can bypass shared public spaces and services. Closed neighborhoods with private educational and health services, secured shopping, and entertainment spaces protect the privileged from their eventual exposure to the others. However, walled spaces do not contribute to social coherence and solidarity in the urban arena.

The northern zone of Buenos Aires has always been the preferred residential area of the privileged. Exclusive communities of different scales have been progressively concentrated along the northern suburbs from the 1970s onward. Sufficient availability of land, an attractive landscape, and improved accessibility through highways have been decisive factors in the suburban development of the housing areas for the wealthy in the 1990s.[29]

The municipality of Pilar, about thirty miles away from the downtown, offers the best example of gated community growth in the 1990s. Since the late 1980s, Pilar has been the top choice among the easy-commute municipalities surrounding Buenos Aires city. Between 1991 and 2001, Pilar increased the number of private dwellings by 187 percent (i.e., over 27,000 dwellings), population by 79 percent (i.e., over 100,000 inhabitants), and gated communities by 383 percent (i.e., eighty-five

Figure 7. Pilar's gated communities.

new communities). Real estate developers took low-priced, underserviced land in poor municipalities such as Pilar to build fenced communities in vacant lands surrounded by low-income neighborhoods. Pilar received the largest portion of direct investment in the province of Buenos Aires; yet, 80 percent of the population—the others—still lacks piped water and sewage.[30]

The 8912 Provincial Law of Territorial Reorganization enacted in 1977 by the province of Buenos Aires was sanctioned to limit the consumption of land without infrastructure, which characterized the post–World War II process of suburbanization of Buenos Aires city over the neighboring territory of Buenos Aires province. As a result, it favored the development of well-planned gated communities.[31] The 1977 law explained in detail the formation of gated communities, while neither industrial and commercial land use nor affordable housing were given a careful consideration. This legal body that was created during a nondemocratic government has influenced the way suburban municipalities surrounding Buenos Aires city have managed urban growth since then. The 1977 provincial law virtually left to the discretion of municipal authorities the implementation of urban policies without responding organically to any higher level of planning. No planning authority organically coordinated the growth of Buenos Aires City and its surrounding municipalities. The decentralized planning structure framed by the 1977 law did not encourage local participation but rather gave unrestricted powers to local authorities. In one way or another, through different practices of clientelism, the sociospatial dynamics of the localities shaped the planning framework that reinforced social disparities within the urban space.

Authorities in poor municipalities such as Pilar have seen the development of gated communities as a source of increasing revenues and the low-income neighbors as a source of employment. Municipal discretionary practices made possible numerous exceptions to planning requirements, as no opposition usually rose against developments without on-time-approval.[32]

The Frantic Use of the Environment

The environmental degradation of the urban space in Buenos Aires was intrinsically reinforced by the emerging bipolarity in society. The socioeconomic profile of the inhabitants, wealth and power conditions, configured the use of the space. Most social actors have been more concerned with their daily survival strategies than with the perdurability of the environment where they live. The rational production and use of the urban environment does not easily flourish when social disparities bloom.

With the lack of green space, air pollution, and noise pollution, incompatible land uses became the main characteristics of many densely populated middle-income neighborhoods in Buenos Aires.[33] In contrast, the living space of the poor expanded in whatever space was available, legally or illegally. They occupied spaces from contaminated areas and flood-risk zones, to underserviced spaces, vacant dwellings, and low-end hotels (e.g., in old parts of town like San Telmo). The poor and the newly impoverished low-middle income groups formed the new urban poor, whose living conditions deteriorated sharply. Educational and health infrastructure and service quality declined in the poorest neighborhoods. The lack access to basic services such as primary health in Buenos Aires went up to 26.2 percent of the population in 2001, from 19.7 percent in 1991.[34]

The use of the urban space by the upper-income groups was not environmentally less problematic. They moved to the third suburban ring, contributing to the deterioration of the agricultural and natural ecosystems in the richest agricultural region of the country and one of the most fertile in the world. The new gated communities, retail megacenters, and large educational complexes reshaped the use of formerly agricultural spaces. Formal and informal settlements on stream banks have contributed to decreased water infiltration and increased floods downstream within the metropolitan region.[35]

The absence of a planning system organically structured, involving all political-administrative levels and geographies, did not help to rationally control the use of the space within the metropolis. Resource allocation often mismatches needs in the disjointly planned urban space of metropolitan Buenos Aires. Land use functionality and environmental problems are trans-territorial; they overpass administrative jurisdictions and geographies.

State (Re)Actions

Argentina's severe economic crisis in the early 2000s, corroborated by the neoliberal policies of the 1990s, did not deliver sustainable and equitable growth. The whole political-institutional system as it was known until then collapsed. As a consequence, the search for stable governance pushed the state to have a more active role in all jurisdictional levels: national, provincial, and municipal.

The transfer of responsibilities to achieve collective goals to the market in the 1990s did not contribute to a sustainable management of the urban space. Authorities had no choice but to try and regain political representativeness and pursue economic equitability and social stability. The state in Argentina began once again to intervene more actively in the economy. At the metropolitan level, contracts with foreign basic-service suppliers were renegotiated and some agreements called off.[36] However, the new state actions have to now deal with forms of foreign and domestic private capital that did not exist before.

Original ad-hoc and experimental state and nongovernmental initiatives appeared on many fronts within metropolitan Buenos Aires. In order to deal with the new challenges, many new programs were developed within the context of urban sustainability. Experimental plans to reduce poverty were developed in the suburbs, integrated management of water resources were attempted at the municipal level, and sustainable urban designs for housing tested within Buenos Aires city.[37]

Improving governance became a major challenge in order to develop a sustainable metropolis. Disbelief in the formal political system pushed authorities toward a more participative approach to urban decision-making. However, the institutional and political complexity of metropolitan Buenos Aires, where national, provincial, and municipal jurisdictions converged, makes improvements in governance a tough job.

Conclusions

The market-driven policies of economic adjustment that the governments implemented in the 1990s did not improve the welfare of the population. The economic adjustment produced a form of urban development that can be characterized by its fragmented structure. The territory of the wealthy has been organized in isolated living spaces interconnected through highways that act as functional social bridges to be transited for work or leisure purposes in the city. Their dominant time-space construct is virtually disconnected from the rest of the metropolitan space. By contrast, the territory of the poor with no access to the exclusionary spaces of the wealthy prompts a subdominant time-space construct that is basically configured by barriers of secured environments that marginalize them from the most desirable forms of metropolitan life.

The restructuring of metropolitan Buenos Aires in the 1990s has been basically the result of three major contradictory global-local relationships within the urban space: the tension generated by the fulfillment of global and local needs that produced a fragmented urban landscape disconnected from any organic planning system; the allocation of international and allied local resources through market-driven policies that does not match the local needs of the underprivileged, but that has been shaped by the desires of the privileged; the fragmentation of the citizenry by global and local forces that compartmentalizes and deteriorates their formal channels of political representation and participation, encouraging new forms of popular reaction and reorganization from below, in the metropolis.

Summing up, the process of metropolitan growth in Buenos Aires has been defined by strong sociospatial disparities, a fragmented organization of social power and political representation over space, a disregard for the environment supported by market-driven actions, and a disarticulated planning system framed by the market ideology.

However, the lack of state planning policies that favored social equity does not mean the state was absent. All levels of government were active players in the transformation of metropolitan Buenos Aires by supporting the market ideology that framed the policies of the 1990s. The forces of globalization certainly affected the urban landscape of Buenos Aires, but the local mechanisms used to produce and reproduce the urban space are an essential part of the transformation. Certainly, the forces behind the urban transformation of the 1990s were not those in pursuit of urban sustainability.

NOTES

1. Pablo Cicolella and Iliana Mignaqui, Economía global y reestructuración metropolitana. Buenos Aires: ¿Ciudad global o ciudad dual del siglo XXI? *Cuadernos del Cendes* 17:43 (2000): 29–50.
2. James Haselip, Isaac Dyner, and Judith Cherni, Electricity Market Reform in Argentina: Assessing the Impact for the Poor in Buenos Aires, *Utilities Policy* 13 (2005): 1–14.
3. Martin Coy and Martin Pöhler, Gated Communities in Latin American Megacities: Case Studies in Brazil and Argentina, *Environment and Planning B: Planning and Design* 29 (2002): 355–70.
4. Pablo Cicolella, Globalización y dualización en la región metropolitana de Buenos Airs: Grandes inversiones y restructuración socioterritorial en los años noventa, *EURE* 25:76 (1999).
5. Elías Rosenfeld, Medio ambiente y calidad de vida: ¿Desarrollo sustentable o trampa discursiva? in *Fragmentos sociales: Problemas urbanos de la Argentina*, ed. B. Cuenya, C. Fidel, and H. Herzer Buenos Aires, SXXI Argentina, 2004.
6. A comprehensive recount of milestones in sustainability in Argentina is provided by Alejandro Rofman in *Actualización crítica del enfoque del desarrollo sustentable: Su aplicación al ámbito de la ciudad de Buenos Aires,* CEUR, Centro de Estudios Avanzados, Universidad de Buenos Aires 2001 , and by Luis Ainstein in *Urban Sustainability within the*

Framework of Institutional Vacuums? International Workshop, Cities of the South: Sustainable for Whom?, European Science Foundation/N-AERUS, UNRISD, IREC-DA/EPFL, Geneva, May 3-6, 2000.
7. Ricardo Gomez Insausti, The Impact of State Actions on Urban/Regional Growth in Argentina, 1970–1990, *Acta Wasaensia 45, Geography 6* (1995): 193–206.
8. INDEC, October Waves, *Encuesta permanente de hogares,* Buenos Aires 1992-2001.
9. James K. Galbraith and Laura T. Spagnolo, Economic Inequality and Political Power: A Comparative Analysis of Argentina and Brazil, *Business and Politics* 9:1 (2007): Art. 3.
10. INDEC, October Waves.
11. Ibid.; Guillermo Paraje, Crisis, reforma estructural y . . . nuevamente crisis: desigualdad y bienestar en el gran Buenos Aires, *Desarrollo Económico* 45:179 (2005): 373–402; Laura Tedesco, La Ñata Contra el Vidrio: Urban Violence and Democratic Governability in Argentina, *Bulletin of Latin American Research* 19 (2000): 527–45.
12. Guillermo Paraje, Inequality, Welfare and Polarisation in the Greater Buenos Aires, 1986–1999, University of Cambridge, Faculty of Economics and Politics (2002).
13. Marcela Cerrutti and Alejandro Grimson, Buenos Aires, neoliberalismo y después: Cambios socioeconómicos y respuestas populares, Working Paper 04–04d.2, Center for Migration and Development, Princeton University 2004.
14. Marie-France Prévôt Schapira, Buenos Aires en los años '90: Metropolización y desigualdades, *EURE* 28:85 (2002).
15. Pedro Pírez, Gestión de servicios y calidad urbana en la ciudad de Buenos Aires, *EURE* 25:76 (1999).
16. Cerrutti and Grimson, Buenos Aires.
17. Alejandro Portes and Bryan R. Roberts, The Free-Market City: Latin American Urbanization in the Years of the Neoliberal Experiment, *Studies in Comparative International Development* 40:1 (2005): 43–82.
18. David E. Hojman, Explaining Crime in Buenos Aires: The Roles of Inequality, Unemployment, and Structural Change, *Bulletin of Latin American Research* 21:1 (2002): 121–28.
19. Portes and Roberts, The Free-Market City, 43–82.
20. Cerrutti and Grimson, Buenos Aires.
21. Hugo Spinelli, Marcio Alazraqui, Gabriela Zunino, H. Olaeta, H. Poggese, C. Concaro, and S. Porterie, Firearm-Related Deaths and Crime in the Autonomous City of Buenos Aires, 2002 *Ciência and Saúde Coletiva* 11: 2 (2006): 327–38
22. Rafael di Tella, Sebastian Galiani, and Ernesto Schrgradosky, Crime Victimization and Income Distribution, Universidad de San Andres, Bs. As, 2002.
23. Lucía Dammert, Construyendo ciudades inseguras: Temor y violencia en Argentina, *EURE* 27:82 (2001).
24. J. Ricardo Gomez Insausti, Caracterización del sector norte del Gran Buenos Aires, Buenos Aires, Oikos (1982).
25. Guy Thuillier, Gated Communities in the Metropolitan Area of Buenos Aires, Argentina: A Challenge for Town Planning, *Housing Studies* 20:2 (2005): 255–71.
26. Sonia Vidal-Koppman, La articulación global-local o cuando los actores privados construyen una nueva ciudad, *Scripta Nova X* 218:39 (2006).
27. María C. Arizaga, Espacialización, estilos de vida y clases medias: Procesos de suburbanización en la region metropolitana de Buenos Aires, *Perfiles Latinomericanos* 25 (2004): 46.
28. Nora Libertun de Duren, Planning à la Carte: The Location Patterns of Gated Communities around Buenos Aires in a Decentralized Planning Context, *International Journal of Urban and Regional Research* 30:2 (2006): 308–27.
29. Gomez-Insausti, Caracterización del sector norte del Gran Buenos Aires.
30. INDEC, *Censo nacional de población y vivienda* , Buenos Aires (2001); Libertun de Duren, Planning à la Carte, 308–27.
31. Nora Clichevsky, Tierra vacante en Buenos Aires: Entre los "loteos populares" y las "áreas exclusivas," in *Tierra Vacante en ciudades Latinoamericanas,* ed. N. Clichesvky (Cambridge, MA: Lincoln Institute of Land Policy, 2002).
32. Laurence Crot, "Scenographic" and "Cosmetic" Planning: Globalization and Territorial Restructuring in Buenos Aires, *Journal of Urban Affairs* 28:3 (2006): 227–51.
33. Rofman, *Actualización Crítica del Enfoque.*
34. INDEC, *Censo Nacional de Población y Vivienda.*
35. Jorge Morello, Silvia D. Matteucci, and Andrea Rodríguez, Development and Urban Growth in the Argentine Pampas Region, *Annals of the American Academy of Political and Social Science* 590 (2003): 116–30.
36. David Westendorff, Sustainable Development for Urban Poor: Applying a Human Rights Approach to the Problem, in *From Unsustainable to Inclusive Cities,* ed. D. Westendorff (Geneva: UNRISD, 2004).
37. Ricardo Schusterman, F. Almansi, A. Hardoy, C. Monti, and G. Urquiza, Poverty Reduction in Action: Participatory Planning in San Fernando, Buenos Aires, Argentina, Human Settlement

Working Paper 6 on Poverty Reduction in Urban Areas, IIED, London (2002); Ana Hardoy, J. Hardoy, G. Pandiella, and G. Urquiza, Governance for Water and Sanitation Services in Low-Income Settlements: Experiences with Partnership-Based Management in Moreno, Buenos Aires, *Environment and Urbanization* 17 (2005): 183–200; Silvia de Schiller, Supporting Sustainability Issues in Urban Transformation, *Urban Design International* 9 (2004): 53–60.

REFERENCES

Ainstein, Luis. Urban Sustainability within the Framework of Institutional Vacuums? International Workshop, Cities of the South: Sustainable for Whom?, European Science Foundation/N-AERUS, UNRISD, IREC-DA/EPFL, Geneva, May 3-6, 2000.

Arizaga, María C. Espacialización, estilos de vida y clases medias: Procesos de suburbanización en la region metropolitana de Buenos Aires. *Perfiles Latinomericanos* 25 (2004): 43–58.

Cerrutti, Marcela, and Alejandro Grimson. Buenos Aires, neoliberalismo y después. Cambios socioeconómicos y respuestas populares. Working Paper 04–04d.2. Princeton University, Center for Migration and Development, 2004.

Cicolella Pablo. Globalización y dualización en la Región Metropolitana de Buenos Airs. Grandes inversiones y restructuración socioterritorial en los años noventa. *EURE* 25 (1999): 76.

Cicolella, Pablo, and Iliana Mignaqui. Economía global y reestructuración metropolitana. Buenos Aires: Ciudad global o ciudad dual del siglo XXI. *Cuadernos del Cendes* 17:43 (2000): 29–50.

Clichevsky, Nora. Tierra Vacante en Buenos Aires. Entre los "loteos populares" y las "áreas exclusivas." In *Tierra Vacante en ciudades Latinoamericanas*, ed. N. Clichesvky. Cambridge, MA: Lincoln Institute of Land Policy, 2002.

Coy, Martin, and Martin Pöhler. Gated Communities in Latin American Megacities: Case Studies in Brazil and Argentina. *Environment and Planning B: Planning and Design* 29 (2002): 355–70.

Crot, Laurence. "Scenographic" and "Cosmetic" Planning: Globalization and Territorial Restructuring in Buenos Aires. *Journal of Urban Affairs* 28:3 (2006): 227–51.

Dammert, Lucía. Construyendo ciudades inseguras: Temor y violencia en Argentina. *EURE* 27:82 (2001): 5–20.

Galbraith, James K., and Laura T. Spagnolo. Economic Inequality and Political Power: A Comparative Analysis of Argentina and Brazil. *Business and Politics* 9:1 (2007): Art. 3.

Gomez-Insausti, J. Ricardo. *Caracterización del Sector Norte del Gran Buenos Aires.* Buenos Aires: Oikos, 1982.

———. The Impact of State Actions on Urban/Regional Growth in Argentina, 1970–1990. *Acta Wasaensia* 45, *Geography* 6 (1995): 193–206.

Hardoy, Ana, J. Hardoy, G. Pandiella, and G. Urquiza. Governance for Water and Sanitation Services in Low-Income Settlements: Experiences with Partnership-Based Management in Moreno, Buenos Aires. *Environment and Urbanization* 17 (2005): 183–200.

Haselip, James, Isaac Dyner and Judith Cherni. Electricity Market Reform in Argentina: Assessing the impact for the poor in Buenos Aires. *Utilities Policy* 13 (2005): 1–14.

Hojman, David E. Explaining Crime in Buenos Aires: The Roles of Inequality, Unemployment, and Structural Change. *Bulletin of Latin American Research* 21:1 (2002): 121–28.

INDEC. Censo Nacional de población y vivienda. Buenos Aires: 2001.

———. Encuesta permanente de hogares. October Waves 1992-2001.

Libertun de Duren, Nora. Planning à la Carte: The Location Patterns of Gated Communities around Buenos Aires in a Decentralized Planning Context. *International Journal of Urban and Regional Research* 30:2 (2006): 308–27.

Morello, Jorge, Silvia D. Matteucci, and Andrea Rodríguez. Development and Urban Growth in the Argentine Pampas Region. *Annals of the American Academy of Political and Social Science* 590 (2003): 116–30.

Paraje, Guillermo. Crisis, reforma estructural y . . . nuevamente crisis: Desigualdad y bienestar en el Gran Buenos Aires. *Desarrollo Económico* 45:179 (2005): 373–402.

———. *Inequality, Welfare and Polarisation in the Greater Buenos Aires, 1986–1999.* University of Cambridge, Faculty of Economics and Politics (2002).

Pírez, Pedro. Gestión de servicios y calidad urbana en la ciudad de Buenos Aires. *EURE* 25:76 (1999).

Prévôt Schapira, Marie-France. Buenos Aires en los años '90: Metropolización y desigualdades. *EURE* 28:85 (2002): 31–50.

Portes, Alejandro, and Bryan R. Roberts. The Free-Market

City: Latin American Urbanization in the Years of the Neoliberal Experiment. *Studies in Comparative International Development* 40:1 (2005): 43–82.

Rofman, Alejandro. Actualización crítica del enfoque del desarrollo sustentable: Su aplicación al ámbito de la ciudad de Buenos Aires. CEUR, Centro de Estudios Avanzados, Universidad de Buenos Aires 2001.

Rosenfeld, Elías. Medio ambiente y calidad de vida. Desarrollo sustentable o trampa discursive. In *Fragmentos sociales. Problemas urbanos de la Argentina*, ed. B. Cuenya, C. Fidel and H. Herzer. Buenos Aires: SXXI Argentina (2004).

de Schiller, Silvia. Supporting Sustainability Issues in Urban Transformation. *Urban Design International* 9 (2004): 53–60.

Schusterman, Ricardo, F. Almansi, A. Hardoy, C. Monti, and G. Urquiza.. Poverty Reduction in Action: Participatory Planning in San Fernando, Buenos Aires, Argentina. *Human Settlement Working Paper 6 on Poverty Reduction in Urban Areas.* London: IIED, 2002.

Spinelli, Hugo, Marcio Alazraqui, Gabriela Zunino, H. Olaeta, H. Poggese, C. Concaro and S. Porterie. Firearm-Related Deaths and Crime in the Autonomous City of Buenos Aires, 2002. *Ciência and Saúde Coletiva* 11:2 (2006): 327–38.

Tedesco, Laura. La ñata contra el vidrio: Urban Violence and Democratic Governability in Argentina. *Bulletin of Latin American Research* 19 (2000): 527–545.

di Tella, Rafael, Sebastian Galiani, and Ernesto Schrgradosky. Crime Victimization and Income Distribution Universidad de San Andres, Buenos Aires, 2002.

Thuillier, Guy. Gated Communities in the Metropolitan Area of Buenos Aires, Argentina: A Challenge for Town Planning. *Housing Studies* 20:2 (2005): 255–71.

Vidal-Koppman, Sonia. La articulación global-local o cuando los actores privados construyen una nueva ciudad. *Scripta Nova* 10:218 (2006): 239.

Westendorff, David. Sustainable Development for Urban Poor: Applying a Human Rights Approach to the Problem. In *From Unsustainable to Inclusive Cities*, ed. D. Westendorff. Geneva: UNRISD (2004): 191–256.

■ BRIAN J. GODFREY

Urban Renewal, *Favelas*, and Guanabara Bay

ENVIRONMENTAL JUSTICE AND SUSTAINABILITY IN RIO DE JANEIRO

Famous for its dramatic landscapes and cultural contrasts, Rio de Janeiro evokes images of towering mountains, luxuriant tropical vegetation, white beaches and scenic lagoons, and exuberant carnival celebrations with a pulsating samba beat. The city's panorama exhilarates visitors landing by plane, although the time-honored arrival by sea remains even more aweinspiring, as vessels sail past Sugarloaf Mountain to behold the breathtaking tableau of Guanabara Bay. The need to preserve the city's beautiful natural setting led the United Nations to inscribe "Rio de Janeiro, Carioca Landscapes between the Mountain and the Sea" as a world heritage site in 2012. Amid these spectacular surroundings, travelers may note unsightly trash and wastewater in the bay or on nearby beaches. Sightseers also notice the ramshackle shantytowns, known as *favelas,* set on the city's hills or wetlands. While picturesque from a distance, at close range these informal settlements bring to mind poverty, crime, and violence, as popularized by such films as *City of God* and reinforced by the news media. Rio's stunning views, so enthralling at first sight, ultimately display a metropolis divided by wealth and poverty (fig.1).

For all its exceptional scenery, Rio de Janeiro highlights ecological problems of rapid urbanization common in developing countries. For centuries visitors have rhapsodized about the city's great bay, but it has long served as a dumping ground. Literally meaning "breast of the sea" in the native Tupí-Guaraní language, Guanabara Bay shrank from 180 square miles (466 square kilometers) in 1500 to 154 square miles (399 square kilometers) in 2000—a decrease of 15 percent—due to shoreline expansion. Shaped like an oval, the bay narrows to 1.1 miles (1.8 kilometers) at its entrance, then broadens to about 15 miles (24 kilometers) at its widest east-west spot; its north-south distance is approximately 18.6 miles (30 kilometers).[1] This enclosure shelters the port from Atlantic storms, but also inhibits the ocean's natural flushing action in the bay, particularly in the context of mounting landfill, pollution, and sedimentation. As the city's original raison d'être and

Figure 1. Rio's classic postcard of Sugarloaf Mountain at the entrance to Guanabara Bay, taken from Corcovado Mountain above the city, obscures the marked socioeconomic disparities evident from below.

continuing economic hub, Guanabara Bay's margins are highly urbanized and contain most of the metropolitan population, industries, oil refineries, two major airports, the seaport and naval base, and the main campus of the Federal University of Rio de Janeiro (fig. 2).

When a Portuguese expedition visited the bay in January 1502, the explorers named it Rio de Janeiro. According to tradition, the mariners mistook Guanabara Bay's entrance for the mouth of a great river, although a rival interpretation suggests that they recognized a drowned river valley, or "ria." Certainly the bay once had been a river in prehistoric times. During the Holocene period, when the sea level was some 425 feet (130 meters) lower than at present, a river system developed in Guanabara Valley, only to be flooded by rising oceans about 12,000 years ago as the last ice age ended. This submerged Guanabara paleoriver forms the central trough where the bay reaches its greatest depths of some 164 feet (50 meters). Otherwise, depths on the irregular bottom of this drowned river valley vary from about 56 feet (17 meters) at the entrance, to less than 10 feet (3 meters) away from the navigation channels. The bay's average depth has been variously estimated between 19 feet (5.7 meters) and 25 feet (7.6 meters), but it is much less in the shallow northwestern parts. Officials have warned that half of the bay is "only about a foot and a half deep and runs the risk of drying up" (fig. 3).[2]

Such dire projections contrast with an unspoiled state upon European arrival five centuries ago, when the bay and nearby lagoons and mangrove forests teemed with fish and wildlife, including dolphins, whales, birds, and shellfish. Tupí-Guaraní groups, locally called Tupinambás or Tamoios, clustered in agricultural villages around Guanabara Bay. The Portuguese founded São

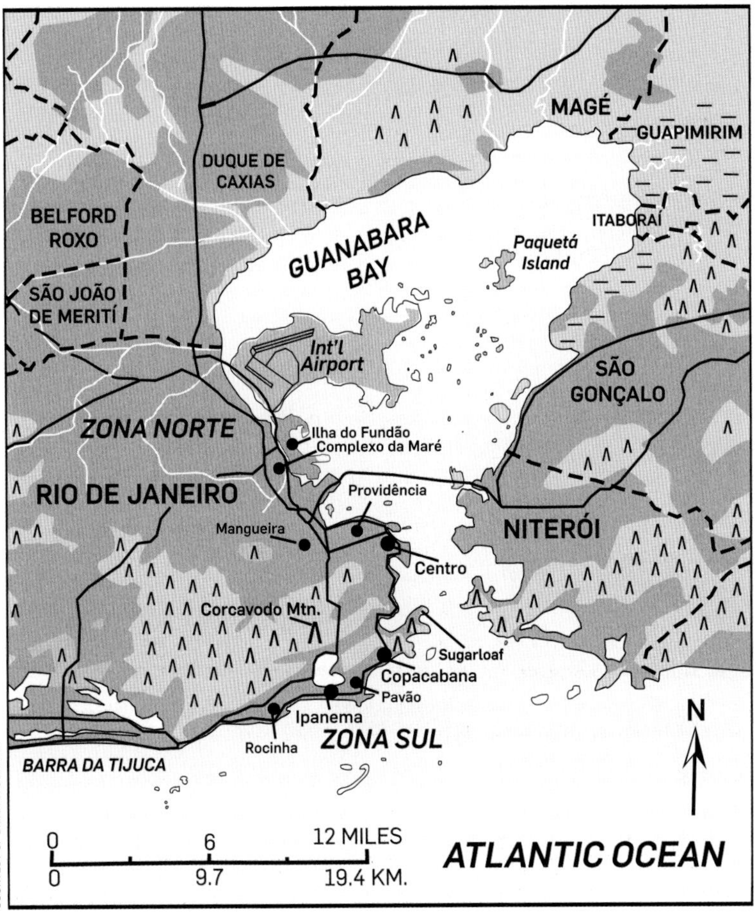

COURTESY OF BRIAN J. GODFREY

Figure 2. Metropolitan Rio de Janeiro.

Sebastião do Rio de Janeiro in 1565, which began a long process of urbanization—along with deforestation, wildlife extinction, wastewater contamination, and tropical disease. By 1850, when Herman Melville visited and praised "the Bay of all Rivers—the Bay of all Delights—the Bay of all Beauties," overexploitation of the whale population, which once found an ideal breeding ground here, had already ended a local industry in whale meat and oil that had flourished for two centuries.[3] Environmental degradation mounted as Rio grew into a megacity: hillside erosion, sedimentation, and landfill steadily encroached on the bay's shorelines, while pollution by industry, shipping, oil spills, and untreated sewage rendered its once-pristine beaches unsafe for swimming. Rio's mountains, historic hills, and national forests were declared national landmarks in 1973, but Guanabara Bay remained without such protection.[4] State agencies now monitor the bay, and nongovernmental organizations (NGOs) advocate its restoration, but political obstacles, economic realities, and the task's daunting scale stifle progress. During the 1992 United Nations Conference on Environment and Development, Rio's "Earth Summit," signatories of an Alternative Treaty famously proposed "that Guanabara Bay and its surrounding environments be declared a World Heritage Site."[5]

COURTESY OF BRIAN J. GODFREY

Figure 3. Downtown Rio de Janeiro with the Rio-Niterói Bridge (8.25 miles or 13.2 kilometers long) in the background; despite modern shoreline consolidation, sixty-five islands still dot Guanabara Bay.

In that spirit, this chapter examines Rio de Janeiro's urban sustainability with regard to the interactions of urban renewal programs, *favela* communities, and Guanabara Bay. As popularized by the Earth Summit's "Agenda 21" program, sustainability has been widely regarded as equitably meeting "the developmental and environmental needs of present and future generations."[6] Despite the concept's ambiguities and contradictions, sustainability has the virtue of linking environmental quality to human welfare. While mainstream environmentalism has at times been criticized for downplaying issues of social justice, sustainable development attempts to reconcile, at least in principle, the "three Es" of environment, economy, and equity. Thus arise concerns for environmental justice, as defined by the U.S. Environmental Protection Agency (EPA): "The fair treatment and meaningful involvement of all people regardless of race, color, national origin, or income with respect to the development, implementation, and enforcement of environmental laws, regulations and policies."[7]

As in other cities, the problems of Rio's *favelas* underscore how unsustainable urban growth results from environmental injustice—spatial (dis)placement, inadequate housing, landslides and other environmental hazards, and lack of such urban services as potable water, electricity, and sewage treatment.[8] Indeed, since *favela* residents are overwhelmingly poor and people of color, their communities reflect deprivations of both race and class. Robert Bullard's appraisal of the U.S.

applies equally well to Brazil: "institutional racism and discriminatory land-use policies and practices of government—at all levels—influence the creation and perpetuation of racially separate and unequal residential areas for people of color and whites." Environmental justice, he goes on, would ensure "equal protection of environmental, health, employment, housing, transportation, and civil rights laws."[9] By juxtaposing the degradation of Guanabara Bay and the infrastructural problems of the port, industry, and *favelas* nearby, this chapter analyzes the coevolution of Rio's most pressing sustainability issues in both ecological and socioeconomic terms.

Urban Metabolism, Environmental Justice, and Rio's *Favelas*

As ecological communities, cities can be viewed as organisms that require a variety of inputs to survive and thrive, resulting in outputs of unwanted waste products. Urban centers need materials and resources to sustain inhabitants, to maintain the built environment, and to operate machines, transportation, and other moving parts. As Herbert Girardet reminds us, a city's sustainability can be gauged by the efficiency and renewability of its metabolism—"the flow of resources and products through the urban system for the benefit of urban populations." On one hand, natural ecosystems feature *circular metabolisms* in which local outputs become inputs (and viceversa) in largely self-contained chains of mutual benefit. Unfortunately, modern cities favor *linear metabolisms,* as resources are directed "through the urban system without much concern about their origin or about the destination of wastes, resulting in the discharge of vast amounts of waste products incompatible with natural systems." Hence urban ecologists like Girardet emphasize the importance of closing the open-ended resource loops of modern cities through recycling and reusing materials, rather than dumping unwanted "externalities" in landfills, incinerators, and waterways.[10]

Water is of particular importance. Since citydwellers require potable water for drinking, cooking, and sanitation, metropolises cannot grow without systems to provide fresh water and then to discharge domestic and industrial wastewater. Metabolic infrastructures must collect, treat, and dispose of wastes before they expose residents to pathogens resulting in such diseases as cholera, typhoid, and dysentery, which historically plagued London, New York, and other early industrial metropolises. At present, such waterborne diseases still threaten poor communities in Mexico City, São Paulo, Lagos, and other rapidly growing cities of the developing world, where much of the urban population lacks sewerage. Of course, sewage treatment and safe disposal of sludge is essential for economic growth as well as public health.[11]

In Brazil, sewage systems reached only 50 percent of the urban population in 2004—and even then most of the discharged sewage remained untreated—although 85 percent benefited from public water provision. The half of the urban population with sewerage generally coincides with what has been called the "organized city" of relatively affluent populations, paved streets, high-rise buildings, and urban services. The other half without access to sewage systems tends to be low-income and to reside in either peripheral areas of legal subdivisions with many unpaved streets and few services, or in self-constructed *favelas* of uncertain legal title as well as a lack of basic infrastructures. Foreigners tend to view *favelas* as synonymous with "slums," but in Brazilian parlance they differ from deteriorated inner cities and peri-urban residential subdivisions by appearance and location. Typically, *favelas* arise on steep hillsides, low-lying wetlands, along railroad lines or highways, or on other undesirable sites.[12]

Officially 18.7 percent of Rio's population lived in 513 *favelas* in 2000, but these figures were conservative. In 2002 Rio's planning agency found 39.4 percent of the city's dwelling units (839,855 houses or apartments) "irregular" and without legal title, although clearly not all were *favelas*.[13] Legislation of 1937 recognized *favelas* as "groups of two or more irregular shacks, constructed of improvised materials." Since 1950, the Brazilian census has considered *favelas* to be groups of 50 or more dwellings of a "rustic appearance" without land title, full or partial absence of public services, and lack of street paving, numbers, and signage.[14] The initial rudimentary shacks often give way in time to improved dwellings, if the *favela* is secure from landslides, flooding, and eviction. Indeed, Brazilian elites and policymakers have tried alternatively to ignore, eradicate, or upgrade and integrate *favelas*, while their residents or *favelados* have continued to provide cheap labor and services for the urban economy.

Despite policy changes, *favelados* continue to be viewed in largely negative ways by society at large. Janice Perlman once famously argued that such views reflected dominant ideologies, which steadfastly ignored evidence that *favelados* were not passive and marginal but rather were "in fact integrated into society, albeit in a manner detrimental to their own interests."[15] Follow-up interviews based on the original 1968–1969 study, more than three decades later (1999–2003), found a transformation from "the myth of marginality" among aspiring recent migrants to "the reality of marginality" among continuing residents faced with few prospects of social mobility. Although objective living standards, urban services, and education had improved among those interviewed in three selected *favelas*, previously upbeat attitudes had soured: the inability to move into affluent neighborhoods and to achieve better jobs frustrated *favelados*, while pervasive fear of gang violence heightened their pessimism. Other scholars also have noted ominous trends in urban segregation, income inequality, rates of violent crime, and social and racial polarization under neoliberalism since Brazil's return to democracy in 1985.[16]

This attitudinal downturn among *favelados* also reflects environmental injustice, including a dearth of vital urban services among low-income communities. Such ecological lapses highlight the city's social geography of north-south polarization, which contrasts the industrial working-class districts (both peripheral subdivisions and *favelas*) concentrated around Guanabara Bay with the affluent districts near the scenic Atlantic beaches. Densely inhabited and highly segregated by socioeconomic status and race, the city of Rio reached a population of 6.1 million in 2006—over half the 11.5 million residents in the metropolitan region, comprised of twenty municipalities covering 1,809 square miles (4,686 square kilometers). The city's Southern Zone (Zona Sul), centered on such beachfront communities as Copacabana and Ipanema, includes 27 *favelas*, according to 2000 data. The rapidly growing Western Zone (Zona Oeste) encompasses Barra da Tijuca and other wealthy beachfront districts, along with such struggling communities as the City of God and 262 other *favelas*. Central Rio includes the downtown business district, diverse residential districts, and 61 hillside *favelas*. The city's Northern Zone (Zona Norte) and suburbs of the Fluminense Lowlands (Baixada Fluminense) encompass a vast urban region with the port, shipyards, oil refineries, chemical plants and other industries, and 354 *favelas*.[17]

At a metropolitan scale, human development indices (HDI)—including education, health, income, and housing—are highest in populous Rio and Niterói, which now have relatively low rates of demographic growth. These cities rank second and first in HDI, respectively, among the state's ninety-two municipalities. Table 1 compares the seven *municípios* encircling Guanabara Bay: while not encompassing the bay's entire watershed, they comprise three-quarters of the metropolitan population. Beyond the core cities of Rio and Niterói, the others are poorer, offer fewer urban services, and generally have lower quality of life. Much of the peripheral urban populations remain unconnected to the public water supply and sewerage systems. City residents without sewage connections in 2000 officially ranged from 43 percent in Duque de Caxias, 60 percent in São Gonçalo, to even higher proportions elsewhere. Even in relatively well-served Rio de Janeiro, 22 percent of the urban population lacked sewerage, while in Niterói the figure rose to 27 percent.[18] Community groups argue that official figures understate such problems:

> Currently about 12 percent of households in Rio de Janeiro do not have running water, over 30 percent do not have sewage connections, and official electricity connections reach only 70 percent of the population. In *favelas*—which make up the bulk of the households without these urban services—residents use illegal connections (*gatos*) to water and electricity, and sewage is often dumped straight into rivers, drainage ditches, and lagoons.[19]

After this metropolitan overview, we shift to the environmental history of Rio de Janeiro's urbanization with a focus on evolving perceptions and policies. Basically, I argue that elite ideologies have shifted successively from the *favelas'* assumed disease, filth, and moral depravity in the

Table 1. Population and human development in Greater Rio de Janeiro, 1996–2006

MUNICIPALITIES ON GUANABARA BAY	AREA (MI² / KM²)	POPULATION % URBAN 2000	POPULATION TOTAL 2006	POPULATION % ANNUAL CHANGE 1996–2006	PUBLIC WATER 2000*	PUBLIC SEWERAGE 2000*	STATE HDI RANK**
Duque de Caxias	180 / 465	99.6	854,509	1.9	69.5	56.6	52/92
Guapimirim	139 / 361	67.4	45,251	3.9	49.0	25.6	63/92
Itaboraí	164 / 424	94.5	222,722	3.9	23.8	28.9	67/92
Magé	149 / 386	94.2	236,748	2.9	47.5	31.1	57/92
Niterói	50 / 129	100	476,561	0.6	78.3	73.0	1/92
Rio de Janeiro	456 / 1,182	100	6,134,892	1.0	97.8	78.0	2/92
São Gonçalo	96 / 249	100	972,854	1.7	80.4	40.3	23/92
7 municipalities on bay (total)	1,234 / 3,196	99.6	8,943,537	1.3	—	—	—
20 municipalities, Rio de Janiero metro region (total)	1,809 / 4,686	99.3	11,460,463	1.4	—	—	15/33

Sources: Instituto Brasileiro de Geografia e Estatística, http://www.ibge.gov.br/; Fundação CIDE—Centro de Informações e Dados do Rio de Janeiro, *Rio de Janeiro em Dados*, http://200.156.34.70/cide/index.php; Instituto da Baía de Guanabara, http://www.portalbaiadeguanabara.com.br/; United Nations Development Program, Brazil, *Atlas do Desenvolvimento Humano do Brasil—2003*, http://www.pnud.org.br/home/.

* Percent of urban population.

**The United National Human Development Index combines various quality-of-life indicators, including education, health, income, and housing. Municipalities are ranked according to the ninety-two jurisdictions in Rio de Janeiro state (x/92); the metropolitan region is ranked according to the thirty-three such areas studied in Brazil (x/33).

nineteenth- and early twentieth-century sanitary city, to their supposed social marginalization, behavioral deviance, economic dependence, and general pathology in the mid-twentieth-century "modernist city," and more recently to the environmental problems, geohazards, and violent threats they purportedly pose to the contemporary sustainable city. Biases against *favelas* have been reconfigured according to the pressing problems of each historic era: policies have evolved, but *favelas* have consistently been diagnosed in negative terms that reinforced stereotypes and stigmatized residents. The following brief historical geography examines the emergence of Rio's contemporary ecological problems with regard to long-term issues of social equity, spatial segregation, and environmental justice.

The Sanitary City: Urban Reforms to "Civilize" Rio (1808–1920)

Concern with pollution, sanitation, and tropical disease first arose in colonial Rio de Janeiro. Despite a splendid natural harbor, the irregular site and uneven topography—composed of coastal inlets, low-lying marshes and lagoons, and steep hills—constrained urban expansion, while the humid tropical climate and uneven terrain created problems of stagnant water, ideal for the proliferation of mosquitoes and other insect vectors of disease. As early as 1613 a yellow fever epidemic caused high mortality rates, especially among slaves. Soon thereafter, the filling of central lagoons and construction of drainage ditches began to modify the city's natural landscape. Despite such early efforts, ecological problems steadily mounted along with urban growth.[20] The 1763 transfer of the viceregal capital from Salvador da Bahia to Rio de Janeiro, which featured a convenient port of entry to the inland gold and diamond mines of Minas Gerais, reflected the city's increasing size and status. As Preston James once noted: "Gold made Rio de Janeiro, as surely as sugar made São Salvador and Recife and, as later, coffee made São Paulo."[21]

The royal family's sudden arrival in 1808, after fleeing Lisbon to escape the Napoleonic invasions, overnight made Rio the capital of Portugal's vast overseas empire. Under this centralized power, one historian notes, "Rio's landscape began a process of monumental change that would extend well into the twentieth century."[22] Finding a city of narrow and irregular streets, unhealthy swamps, crowded housing, and few urban amenities, Dom João VI ordered the building of roads, botanical gardens, parade grounds at Campo Santana, and other parks, monuments, and buildings. Powered by slave labor, royal projects also included filling swamps, leveling low hills, and shoreline landfills. The influx of some 10,000 Portuguese with the court, coupled with liberalization of foreign trade, dramatically accelerated urbanization. The Bragança royal family and leading aristocrats began an exodus of the wealthy from the city center: the monarch set up court at Quinta da Boa Vista on the city's outskirts, returning to the Imperial Palace downtown only for ceremonial functions, while nobles built luxurious hillside estates (fig. 4).[23]

Rio's population more than doubled from about 50,000 in 1808 to 112,000 by 1821, when a Portuguese constitutionalist revolt forced King João VI's return to Lisbon. He left his heir, Dom Pedro I, to govern Brazil. As imperial capital, main port, and cultural center of an independent Brazil after 1822, Rio de Janeiro overshadowed the country's other nineteenth-century cities. Rio boasted a population of 274,972 in 1872, compared with 31,385 in São Paulo. Spurred by the rural-urban migration resulting from railroad expansion and abolition of slavery in 1888, the city's

Figure 4. Rio de Janeiro, 1812–1817.

growth continued unabated after the Republic's proclamation in 1889. As Rio's population grew by nearly 7 percent annually from 1872 to 1900 (table 2), infrastructural deficiencies mounted in the provision of fresh water, sewerage, and transportation. One-quarter of the city's population crowded into central tenements called *cortiços* (literally, "beehives"), which raised concerns for public health. For example, a smallpox epidemic killed 4,160 people in 1849, and recurring epidemics of yellow fever, malaria, typhoid, and cholera led to periodic international quarantines that damaged commerce. Sanitation was abysmal. Dirty water was disposed by throwing it from windows into the street, often with little more than a shouted warning to passersby: "Agua Vai!" Fecal material was stored in barrels and dumped by slaves known as "tigers" for the brown streaks

Table 2. City and metropolitan populations of Rio de Janeiro, 1808–2010

YEAR	CITY OF RIO DE JANEIRO		RIO DE JANEIRO METROPOLITAN REGION	
	POPULATION	% ANNUAL CHANGE	POPULATION	% ANNUAL CHANGE
1808	50,000	—	—	—
1821	113,000	9.7	—	—
1836	139,000	1.5	—	—
1850	180,000	2.1	—	—
1872	274,972	2.4	—	—
1900	811,443	6.9	—	—
1920	1,157,873	2.1	—	—
1940	1,764,141	2.6	—	—
1960	3,281,908	4.3	4,874,619	—
1980	5,090,700	2.7	9,014,274	4.2
2000	5,857,904	0.7	10,894,156	1.0
2010	6,320,446	0.8	11,835,708	0.9

Note: Populations of metropolitan regions are available starting in 1960.

Sources: *Anuário Estatístico do Brasil 1984*, Rio de Janeiro: Instituto Brasileiro de Geografia e Estatística (IBGE), 1985, 81–82; *Contagem da População 1996*, Rio de Janeiro: IBGE, 1997, vol. 1, 25–26; *Anuário Estatístico do Brasil 1996*, Rio de Janeiro: IBGE, 1997, 42; Cities@ IBGE, http://www.ibge.gov.br/cidadesat/topwindow.htm?1; and *Sinopse do Censo Demográfico 2010*, http://www.ibge.gov.br/home/estatistica/populacao/censo2010/ [accessed April 23, 2010].

that often stained their clothes. As historian Lise Sedrez notes: "Sanitation predates beautification as the Holy Grail of *Carioca* engineers in the 19th century."[24]

In 1862 the government contracted a British firm, the City Improvements Company, to provide sewers and waste treatment. Initially three districts were established, each with sewers and treatment plants—known as Casas das Máquinas—based on the latest European designs. Despite the chemical treatment and filtering of wastes, critics complained of nauseating odors, rains overwhelming the system, and generally dubious sanitary effects. Growing concerns with sanitation, disease, and social problems in the urban core continued the suburban exodus of elites. Transportation improvements allowed affluent classes to gravitate to the Zona Sul, where speculative real-estate development steadily increased the residential densities.[25] By 1902 nine sewerage districts struggled to process mounting wastes: eight districts released 6.4 million liters (1.7 million gallons) of waste per hour in Guanabara Bay, while the Leblon station dumped refuse into the Atlantic Ocean. Still, sewers served only about 60 percent of buildings.[26]

Hillside shantytowns also arose during this period of rapid urbanization. Although informal settlements began as early as the 1870s, the first one actually called a *favela* appeared in 1897–1898, when squatters occupied the Morro da Providência, then known as the Morro da Favella. One account explains the settlement as resulting from the demolition of a central tenement called Cabeça do Porco ("Pig's Head"), whose dislocated residents then occupied the hillside. Another popular explanation points to returning veterans of a war against the separatist movement of Antônio Conselheiro in Bahia: the name of the Rio shantytown recalled a plant common in the northeastern backlands, identified with the Alto da Favela battlefield at Canudos. In fact, other informal settlements emerged during this period, but Favela Hill came to symbolize the phenomena.[27] Valladares argues that this persistent myth of origin arose as public intellectuals and journalists read *Os Sertões,* Euclides da Cunha's classic account of the Canudos rebellion, first published in 1902 and later translated into English as *Rebellion in the Backlands.* Historian Bradford Burns argues that da Cunha emphasized "the struggle of man against nature, of civilization against barbarism. . . . The villain of the plot was the cities; the victims were Antônio Conselheiro and his rustic followers."[28] By extension, then, the *favela* arose just as rural-urban migration projected barbarism into Rio de Janeiro.

Whatever the precise historical and etymological origins, the term *favela* soon became generalized as informal communities grew from a shortage of affordable housing, exacerbated by displacement from central tenements. As the city's population approached a million in 1900, downtown was increasingly congested, the outmoded port delayed shipping, and pressure mounted for new housing and transportation arteries. In response, new President Rodriguez Alves announced ambitious urban reforms in 1902. Francisco Pereira Passos, appointed mayor of the Federal District, acquired sweeping powers of eminent domain to allow expropriation and demolition without judicial review. As mayor from 1902 to 1906, Passos and backers in the influential Engineering Club aspired to make Rio into a "tropical Paris." The city administration worked with federal public health authorities, under Oswaldo Cruz, in a campaign to end yellow fever. Health experts and civil engineers stressed the need to vanquish disease through sanitation and science, which conveniently complemented general elite concerns with "civilizing" Rio.[29]

Turn-of-the-century reformers regarded Rio's narrow streets, dating from colonial days, as dangerous, unsanitary, and backward. Despite popular discontent, authorities demolished over 500 buildings to carve Avenida Central (now Avenida Rio Branco) through downtown, allowing construction of the School of Fine Arts, the National Library, the Supreme Court, the Municipal Theater, and other neoclassical buildings along what quickly became a fashionable thoroughfare. Jeffrey Needell notes: "Much of the *Cidade Velha's* narrow, dank, and muddled working-class world was destroyed: it's streets were widened, given light and air, and better connected by demolishing old buildings, changing old streets, and building new ones."[30] Not coincidentally, the short-lived but violent "Revolt of the Vaccine," a destructive spree by rampaging downtown mobs in 1904, prompted by popular indignation over mandatory yellow-fever inoculation, also reflected widespread displacement from the renovated central district. Protestors targeted the municipal streetcars for destruction, along with streetlights and new buildings downtown.[31]

Fin-de-siècle reforms also modified the city's shoreline (fig. 5). Previously the marshes and swamps, common in low-lying areas, were the primary focus of filling and leveling. With the Pereira Passos reforms, authorities began using landfills *(aterros)* to reclaim broad swaths of Guanabara Bay for urban development. The port was transferred from the cramped urban core, around Praça XV de Novembro, to enlarged facilities with railroad connections on the north side. Completed by 1920, the expanded port complex straightened the northern shoreline and eliminated the historic inlets. South of the central district, the Passos administration completed the Avenida Beira-Mar, the "Seaside Avenue," built on a landfill behind a seawall from downtown to Botafogo. Coupled with subsequent twentieth-century landfills, traditional beaches here disappeared under

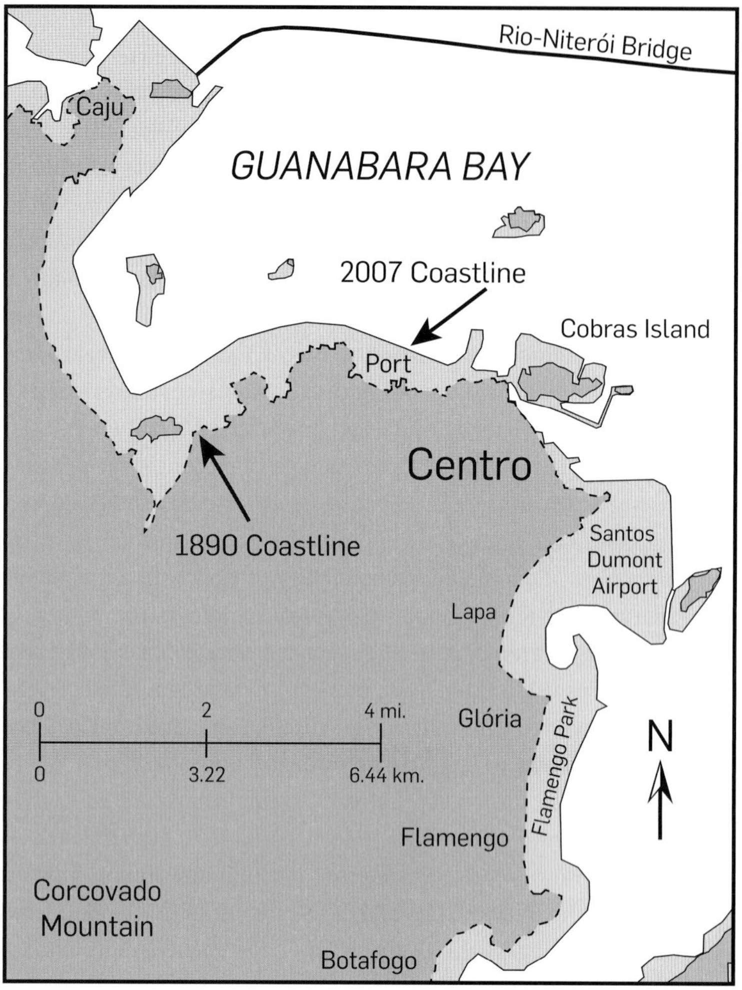

COURTESY OF BRIAN J. GODFREY

Figure 5. Coastlines of Central Rio de Janeiro, 1890 and 2007.

new roads, parks, and buildings. Venerable churches and other landmarks, once located on the shoreline, were located a halfmile or more from the water's edge after 1910.[32]

The Modernist City: Twentieth Century Urban Renewal (1920–1985)

While turn-of-the-century urban reforms removed the poor from the central business district in the interests of sanitation and beautification, subsequent twentieth-century urban renewal emphasized the needs for "modernization and development." Urban planners at midcentury continued to reshape the urban built environment and to promote sociospatial polarization by race and class, but the dominant rationale shifted somewhat. While concerns about public health and "social hygiene" continued, reference to "civilizing" the masses fell out of favor with the rise of populism. This ideological shift became noticeable during the 1922 Modern Art Week of São Paulo, which depicted such Brazilian realities as social conflict, racial diversity, urbanization, and popular culture. The modernist influence was particularly strong among painters and poets, but other intellectuals collaborated in rethinking national life. Urban planners and architects, inspired by the Radiant City of modernist master Le Corbusier, proposed leveling large parts of the city to make way for new traffic arteries and high-rise buildings. The Agache Plan of French architect Donat-Alfred Agache proposed in 1926–1930 to transform Rio into a "monumental city" through redevelopment, land-use rationalization, and *favela* removal:

> Built contrary to all rules of hygiene, without piped water, without sewerage, without garbage collection, without order, with irregular materials, the *favelas* constitute a permanent risk of fire and epidemic infections for neighborhoods they infiltrate. Their leprosy fouls the beaches and neighborhoods gracefully endowed by nature, strips the hills of their adorning greenery, and corrodes even the edges of the forest on the lower slopes of the coastal hill range . . . [Their destruction is important] for social order and security, as well as the general hygiene of the city, to say nothing of aesthetics.[33]

With the Revolution of 1930 and the rise of Getúlio Vargas, the Agache Plan was never fully implemented. Given his populist leanings, Vargas generally left the *favelas* intact as he centralized political control from 1930 to 1945, although Rio became his urban showcase for modernization. With the expansion of state power under the Estado Novo, modernist urban renewal took on a new transformative scale (table 3). The leveling of historic Castelo Hill during the 1920s "in the

Table 3. Historical periods of physical transformation in Rio de Janeiro

PERIOD	INTERVENTIONS	OBJECTIVES	CONSEQUENCES
17th–19th centuries	Demolition of low hills, filling of wetlands, waterfront development	Occupation of irregular site, defense, commerce, political centralization	Urban expansion, port development, environmental degradation, tropical disease
1902–1906	Urban renewal, Pereira Passos administration	Sanitation, public health, beautification, functional efficiency	Transport and port efficiencies, tenement (*cortiço*) removal, favela growth, demolition of historic patrimony
1920s–1940s	Castelo Hill leveled, expansion of central business district (CBD), opening of Avenida Presidente Vargas	Urban expansion, high-rise commercial and real estate development, new transportation arterials	Destruction of Rio's colonial historic patrimony, social displacement, verticalization of CBD
1950s–1960s	Santo Antônio Hill razed, diverse traffic arterials, Flamengo Park landscaped	CBD modernization, vehicular circulation, public recreation, real estate development	New high-rises and parks, bay pollution, shoreline expansion, CBD-waterfront separation, affluent move to Zona Sul, removal of selected *favelas*
1970s	Construction of Rio-Niterói Bridge, opening of metro/subway system	Mass transport, metropolitan integration, suburbanization, multiple urban nuclei	Destruction of historic structures, formation of open spaces, bay pollution, further urban decentralization
1980s	CBD Cultural Corredor, renovation of historic squares and buildings, tenements (*cortiços*)	Historic preservation, urban revitalization	Preservation of built heritage, commercial displacement of central housing by the Decree 322/76
1990s	Guanabara Bay conservation programs, waterfront renewal, cultural projects	Upgrading, commercial revitalization, renewed urban centrality	Cultural renewal of CBD, restoration waterfront linkages, occupation of open spaces

COURTESY OF BRIAN J. GODFREY

Figure 6. Flamengo Park, built on a landfill that expanded the shoreline dramatically, opened in the early 1960s.

interests of ventilation and hygiene" destroyed the city's site of colonial foundation but provided debris for construction of the Santos Dumont Airport on Guanabara Bay and opened space for new modernist buildings, such as the Ministry of Education and Health between 1936 and 1945.[34] A monumental boulevard, Avenida Presidente Vargas, torn through the city's historic core between 1941 and 1944, improved downtown's access to growing northern districts. Several new railroad lines of the Central do Brasil, along with opening of Avenida Brasil in 1946, attracted more migrants to the burgeoning informal settlements of the Zona Norte and northern *subúrbios*.[35]

Subsequent urban programs continued to increase the social distance among the city's diverse socioeconomic groups. During the 1950s, demolition of Santo Antonio Hill provided landfill to widen the shoreline along Flamengo Beach: beside the seaside boulevard of Passos, Governor Carlos Lacerda opened massive Flamengo Park, landscaped by Roberto Burle Marx, in the early 1960s (fig. 6). Such urban amenities encouraged further realestate development in the southern zone, as beachfront towers for affluent classes sprouted along the water. Meanwhile, construction of elevated roadways along the central waterfronts, expansion of Avenida Brazil and other highways in the northern zones, and expansion of the two airports, ruptured urban linkages with Guanabara Bay. These projects further segregated the city, as racial disparities increasingly coincided with patterns of residence.

Table 4. Number of *favelas* in Rio de Janeiro, 1950–2000

URBAN ZONE	1950		1980		2000	
	NUMBER	%	NUMBER	%	NUMBER	%
Central (Centro)	20	19.0	45	12.1	61	8.7
Southern (Zona Sul)	26	24.8	25	6.7	27	3.8
Western (Zona Oeste)	11	10.5	86	23.1	262	37.2
Northern Rio and Suburbs (Zona Norte/Subúrbios)	48	45.7	216	58.1	354	50.3
Total	**105**	**100.0**	**372**	**100.0**	**704**	**100.0**

Sources: Favela Tem Memória, http://www.favelatemmemoria.com.br/; Instituto Brasileiro de Geografia e Estatística, 1991 and 2000 censuses.

Favelas, first legally defined in 1937, were systematically counted by the Federal District in 1949. The city initially found 119 such informal settlements with a population of 280,000 inhabitants. Using somewhat different criteria, the demographic census of 1950 found 105 *favelas* with 169,305 residents, or 7 percent of Rio's population. The postwar decades, characterized by industrialization and urban renewal, saw the number of *favelas* rise dramatically. By 1980 the number of *favelas* officially rose to 372, representing 628,170 residents, or 12 percent of the city's total. While growth stabilized downtown and in the Zona Sul, the number of favelas in the Zona Norte and its northern suburbs reached 58 percent of the total (table 4).[36] This growing North-South socioeconomic divide had dire consequences for Guanabara Bay, as one observer has noted:

> Squatter settlements throughout much of the Guanabara Bay basin, an almost complete lack of basic sanitation systems able to service urbanized areas, industrial pollution, landfills covering large areas of the bay, clear-cut hillsides, silting up and reductions in depth—all this took place during the 20th century, mainly from the 1950s onwards.[37]

Government policy has called for the eradication of *favelas* since 1937, and the 1947 Commission for the Eradication of the *Favelas* even proposed "returning *favela* residents to their states of origin, committing *favela* residents over the age of 60 to State Institutions, and expelling from the *favela* all families whose income exceeded a minimum." Although a shortage of resources previously prevented such draconian measures, the military *coup d'état* of 1964 provided the central authority required for a massive program of *favela* removal. Along with the National Housing Bank (NHB), the military regime created the Coordination of Social Interest Housing of the Greater Rio Metropolitan Area (CHISAM) to assure that there would be "no more people living in the slums of Rio de Janeiro by 1976."[38] With funding from the NHB, CHISAM began to demolish *favela* communities in the Zona Sul, where real estate interests most benefited from urban redevelopment. The agency's goal was to remove 100 families each day, and between 1962 and 1974 almost 140,000 residents from eighty different communities were displaced from their homes.[39] Despite the massive displacement of *favelados* from affluent districts, overall the *favela* populations tripled between 1950 and 1970, reaching 13.3 percent of the population. Consistently, *favelas* have grown much faster than the city's general rate of demographic increase: *favelados*

Table 5. Population growth in *favelas* of Rio de Janeiro, 1950–2000

YEAR	*FAVELA* POPULATION	*FAVELAS* AS PART OF RIO POPULATION (%)	ANNUAL CHANGE IN *FAVELA* POPULATION (%)	ANNUAL CHANGE IN RIO POPULATION (%)
1950	169,305	7.2	—	—
1960	337,412	10.2	9.9	4.1
1970	563,970	13.3	6.7	2.9
1980	628,170	12.3	1.1	2.0
1990	882,483	16.1	4.0	0.8
2000	1,092,958	18.7	2.4	0.7

Sources: Favela Tem Memória, http://www.favelatemmemoria.com.br/; Instituto Brasileiro de Geografia e Estatística, 1991 and 2000 censuses.

officially represented over a million residents, or nearly 20 percent of Rio's total population, by 2000 (table 5).

To the military regime (1964–1985), urban renewal would integrate *favelados* into society: "The first objective is the economic, social, moral, and hygienic reclaiming of the slum families . . . These

COURTESY OF BRIAN J. GODFREY

Figure 7. View of a small section of Rocinha, one of Brazil's largest *favelas*, with an official population of 56,313 in 2000, although unofficial estimates go as high as 150,000.

COURTESY OF BRIAN J. GODFREY

Figure 8. The view of a narrow and winding passageway in the hilly terrain of Rocinha, illustrating the improvised character of this informal settlement.

families then become completely integrated in the community, especially in the way that they live and think."[40] Such stereotypes were inaccurate, since in fact *favelados* were thoroughly integrated into the workforce and social institutions, if excluded from participation on equal terms. Behind the rhetoric, *favela* eradication concentrated on valuable real estate in the Zona Sul. Such urban renewal further marginalized the poor: a 1966 study found that relocated residents had to travel two hours each way on public transportation, costing one-third of their wages. Policies of *favela* removal waned as the military gradually allowed a return to democratic government with local and state elections after 1983, when political parties began to court the *favela* vote by promising infrastructure improvements and land security.[41] Large *favelas* such as Rocinha increasingly have been viewed as established urban neighborhoods, although disparities in service provision and drug-related violence still set them apart (figs. 7 and 8).[42]

Modernist programs of urban renewal struggled to provide sewage treatment for the growing city. In 1947, as the ninety-year contract with the City Improvements Company ended, the Federal District's new Water and Sewers Service (Serviço de Aguas e Esgotos) inherited 440 miles

(708 kilometers) of sewers and seven treatment stations. Service had deteriorated due to lack of investments, leaving the public sector to modernize and expand the dilapidated system. By 1960, as the Federal District moved to Brasília, Rio's network of sewers had grown to 710 miles (1,142 kilometers). The most significant subsequent accomplishment was the 1969–1975 construction of the Ipanema offshore discharge, which carried sewage 2.7 miles (4.3 kilometers) into the Atlantic Ocean. Serving one million city customers, peak capacity of the Ipanema system reached 424 cubic feet per second (12 cubic meters per second).[43]

The Sustainable City: Contemporary Programs of Environmental Justice (1985–present)

In contrast to the modernist city's emphasis on economic development, urban renewal, and *favela* removal, contemporary proposals for sustainability stress goals of economic development with social equity and environmental protection. Concern with the growth of inequality, pollution, and deforestation during the Brazilian "economic miracle" (1967–1973) gave rise to new institutions. In 1975 the state of Rio de Janeiro created the Environmental Engineering Foundation (FEEMA), one of the country's first environmental agencies. In 1985 a civilian was elected president, and subsequent democratic politics allowed nongovernmental groups to also become active in promoting environmental protection. For example, the Guanabara Bay Institute, founded in 1993, became one of the most active NGOs working "to study and resolve the environmental, social, and urban problems of the bay and its watershed."[44]

With democratization came new state programs aimed at sustainable development. In the wake of the 1992 "Earth Summit" in Rio, authorities launched in 1994 a massive, ten-year Guanabara Bay Cleanup Program (Programa de Despoluição da Baia de Guanabara) with a budget of US$793 million, funded largely by US$350 million from the Inter-American Development Bank and US$237 million from Japan's Overseas Economic Cooperation Fund. Plans called for a 90 percent reduction in industrial pollution by 1999, as well as drastic reductions in untreated domestic sewage discharges. About half of the funds were destined for residential sewage systems, including plans to connect twenty-nine *favelas,* along with other underserved areas around the bay. The most encouraging results came in better monitoring and reducing pollution from some 400 polluting industries—including textiles and food-processing plants, the naval and port facilities, shipyards, and several oil refineries. Yet results in the residential sector remained disappointing. Even in the informal communities served by sewerage, residents often could not pay sanitation fees and resisted domestic hookups; without sewers, wastewater drained into the surface runoff—often ending up as dark streaks on public beaches.[45]

Although the 1994–2004 cleanup program promised the bay's salvation, it soon lagged behind schedule and ultimately fell far short of expectations. Pollution continued from various sources. In 1975 and 2000, oil spills befouled the bay's beaches, marine life, and mangroves. Tankers often wash out their hulls at night in the bay. In addition to such port activities, continuing contamination comes from the discharge of domestic and industrial wastewater. Guanabara Bay received about 706 cubic feet per second (20 cubic meters per second) of wastewater in 2005: about 30 percent received primary treatment and only 15 percent benefited from further secondary

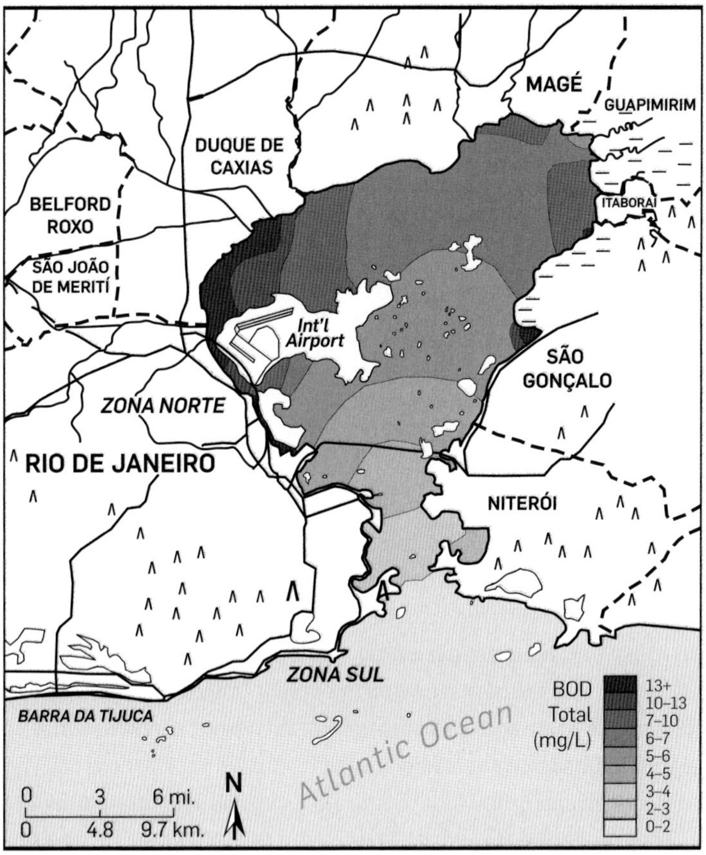

Figure 9. Water Quality in Guanabara Bay.

treatment. Industry now accounts for about 20 percent of the solid waste deposited in the bay, while the remainder stems largely from untreated residential wastewater. In 2005, at the end of the cleanup program, the bay still received some 881,849 pounds (400 tons) of untreated sewage, 141,095 pounds (64 tons) of industrial waste, 22,046 pounds (10 tons) of oil, and 661 pounds (300 kilograms) of heavy metals. Since 2005, Guanabara Bay's water quality continues to worsen and its beaches remain polluted. Given the bay's narrow entrance and shallow depths, it takes 200 days for the water to be fully renewed outside of deep shipping channels.[46] If such trends continue, the bay will suffer a dramatic reduction in size during coming decades, particularly in the heavily polluted northwestern parts (fig. 9).[47]

Besides the scenic, recreational, and economic impacts of pollution, the widespread lack of basic sanitation—especially sewerage and trash removal—endangers the health of *favelados* and other low-income residents. For example, infant mortality rates vary according to socioeconomic status. Rio's affluent Zona Sul had an infant mortality rate of 17 per 1,000 live births in 1986, while the rate was 45 per 1,000 in the Fluminense suburbs; among the 7,000 infants who died under one year of age in metropolitan Rio that year, only 230 (3.2 percent) occurred in the Zona Sul, while 2,764 (39 percent) were in the Baixada Fluminense. Clearly, the human toll of pollution remains enormous among the poor populations of urban Brazil.[48]

Despite such problems, there has been an encouraging shift in public discourse. At least rhetorically, sustainable development has emerged as the preferred policy framework. For example, concern for social and environmental justice has been evident in the Favela-Bairro (shantytown-neighborhood) program, administered by Rio de Janeiro with funding from the Inter-American Development Bank and the European Union. Begun in 1994, Favela-Bairro initially sought to upgrade infrastructures in thirty-eight *favelas.* The first phase sought to work with existing physical structures and social networks to improve water pipelines, sewage lines, and pathways. The program's second phase began in 2000, when Favela-Bairro II introduced job training, health clinics, and other forms of community development. One anthropologist emphasized: "There is a change in the attitude of officials . . . *Favelas* are there to stay; they cannot be eradicated or ignored."[49] Residents of the affected communities often have mixed reviews, as in Santa Marta after eleven years of the Favela-Bairro program: "To many of the community's residents the unfinished stairs and tram symbolized another era of the government's broken promises. Hundreds of power lines ran through the streets, the result of illegally tapping power. The urbanization program includes providing light and power, but like the other objectives, they have yet to be completed."[50]

Critics assert that Favela-Bairro's limited infrastructural improvements, while largely ignoring social services, limit social mobility and segregate the city. Indeed, calls for *favela* removal have reemerged in recent years. Based in part on concern over drug-related violence and impacts on nearby property values, discussions have also relied on "environmentalist" arguments of developers, the Globo chain and other news media, state agencies, and community groups. With the rise of environmentalist discourse, conservation has become a new tool to displace or at least control the *favelas.* As Mario Fuks noted: "the declared aim is now not to 'socially integrate' the 'contaminated' sectors, but to protect or recover environmental resources. That is, the *favela* dweller is not seen simply as contaminated by the surrounding filth, but as a causative agent of pollution of the urban environment."[51]

This argument for *favela* removal stresses environmental degradation, including increased pollution and deforestation: removal of vegetation along with the dumping of trash and inadequate sewage allegedly make the *favelas* detrimental to the city's general sustainability, reduce the urban quality of life, and devalue potentially valuable property. Indeed, realestate interests have long argued that the prime locations made available through the *favela* eradication would allow construction of luxury condominiums, thus making the areas safer and more "sustainable." Interestingly, such arguments are not made with regard to *favelas* in the Zona Norte and the Fluminense Lowlands but to the affluent Zona Sul, pointing to social class and racial difference as implicit concerns. For example, after torrential rains led to widespread landslides and the collapse of scores of hillside shacks in February 1998, Rio's leading newspaper, *O Jornal do Brasil,* called *favelas* the city's "biggest urban problem":

> The city has 223 areas of risk, which every summer create floods and landslides. There are *favelas* like Rocinha in which urbanization is the only solution, such is the area occupied. But a *favela* like Santa Marta should be eradicated, as it poses an eternal threat to its residents. . . . Before being swallowed by *favelas,* Rio needs to revive old plans to urbanize *favelas* that are urbanizable, and to remove *favelas* that are removable.[52]

After the disastrous summer rains of 1988, the Reconstruct Rio Program (Programa Reconstrução Rio) funded infrastructure improvements with US$150 million loans from the World Bank and federal governments.[53] The underlying ecological problems, however, resisted easy resolution: deforestation and compaction of soil on Rio's hillsides have increased flooding during the summer storms. Fifty years ago, the city's forested hills would have absorbed roughly 70 percent of the rainfall, but today perhaps only 30 percent—leaving 70 percent of precipitation to run off into swollen streams and storm drains during heavy rains.[54] To call for *favela* removal, as did the *Jornal do Brasil,* effectively blamed the victims for causing environmental hazards. Such ideologically charged rhetoric reflects how the environment can be constituted as a social problem in an era of sustainable development. The new calls for *favela* removal reflect the increasing social polarization of contemporary Brazilian cities, given trends toward social exclusion, segregation, and inequality since the country's return to democracy.[55]

Certainly the expansion of informal communities, badly served by sewage treatment, complicates environmental protection. The most serious problems lie in the Zona Norte and northern suburbs. For example, the vast informal settlement at Complexo da Maré ("Slum of the Tide"), which arose on tidal flats after World War II, now releases a steady stream of raw sewage into the Cunha Canal. Emitting an acrid stench, this toxic stream empties into the shallow waters around Fundão Island (site of the Federal University) and Governador Island (site of the international

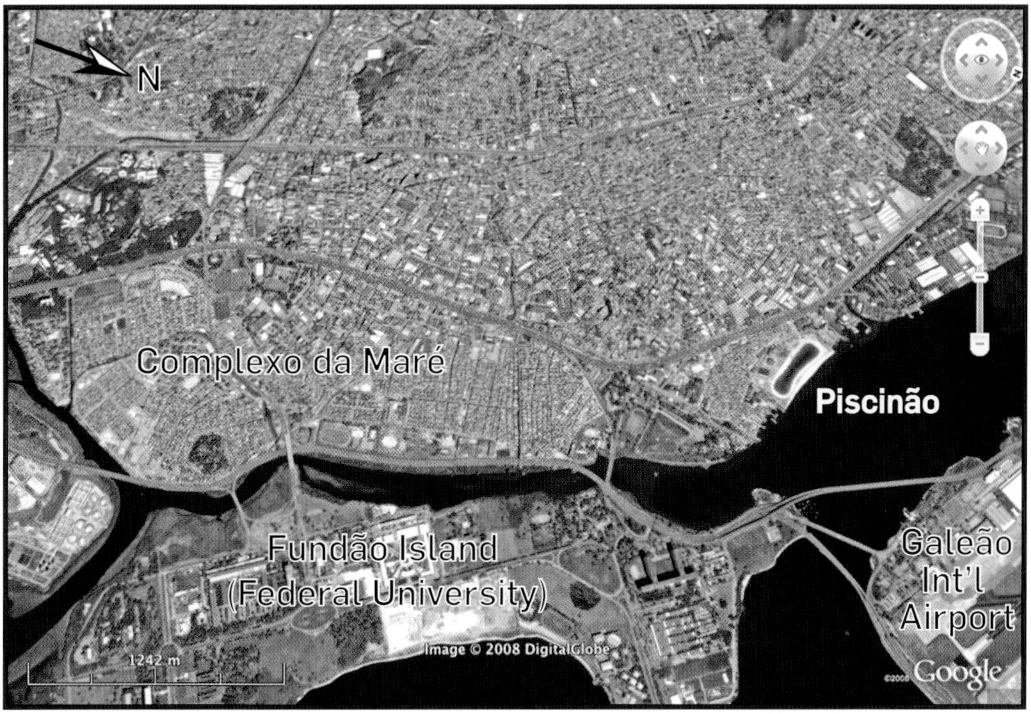

COURTESY OF BRIAN J. GODFREY

Figure 10. Complexo do Maré, showing the Piscinão, parts of the international airport, and the Federal University of Rio de Janeiro on Fundão Island.

airport). Fifty years ago the waters here were safe to swim in, but today they pose a threat to public health. During this period, the Maré Complex has become one of the city's largest *favelas,* with a population variously estimated at between 70,000 and 130,000.[56] Given the heavy local pollution, in 2002 the city opened a large artificial swimming pool, the Piscinão de Ramos, on the bayshore nearby. Despite reported problems with the maintenance of clean water, the pool has become popular among local residents, who are spared the long trip to southern beaches. Critics claim that this project keeps the poor away from the Zona Sul and thus maintains segregation by class and race (fig. 10).

Although mainstream media—newspapers, magazines, travel guides, and television newscasts—routinely depict horrific violence in Rio's *favelas* and stigmatize *favelados,* a significant contemporary counternarrative has emerged. Vibrant Afro-Brazilian samba, hip-hop, and funk subcultures emanate from *favelas* and strive to affirm the everyday struggles of residents. While television news, feature films, and documentaries often sensationalize *favelas,* some do depict life sympathetically. For example, the televised miniseries and subsequent feature film *City of Men (Cidade dos Homens),* tell fictionalized stories of young *favelados* who struggle to fulfill their aspirations amidst poverty, gangsters, and police corruption. *Favela Rising* documents the formation of the Grupo Cultural AfroReggae (AfroReggae Cultural Group), which used musical genres and dance—including hip-hop, rap, soul, percussion, and *capoeira*—to offer young *favelados* educational alternatives to drug traffic and gang violence in the violent district of Vigário Geral.[57] The term "Favela chic" suggests cultural currents that glorify and even commodify this image of urban poverty in music, fashion, and entertainment.

At the local level, community groups also have been active in representing *favelas* in positive terms. NGOs have developed innovative programs with websites offering oral histories, photography, statistics, and other materials to challenge the public's prejudices while enhancing pride of place among residents. For example, the Viva Favela program and the related website, *Favelas Have Heritage (Favela Tem Memória),* feature social histories and ongoing community issues. Another group, Favela Faces, focuses on "the problems facing *favela* residents, the ways in which they are working to overcome them, and how they have and continue to improve their communities with the limited resources available to them." While mentioning violence and drugs, depictions emphasize the circumstances forcing residents into the *favelas,* including the government's forced removals from affluent southern districts, as well as current community struggles. The Favela Painting program began in 2006 to improve the image of the *favelas* by enhancing and beautifying them: "In order for the lives of people living in the *favelas* to improve, the popular perception of their neighborhoods must improve. The core of our idea is to help this happen by painting an entire hillside *favela.*" Since its inception in 2000, Catalytic Communities, or CatComm, has facilitated more than 130 community-based projects in nine countries. The program's founder, Theresa Williamson, traces her inspiration "to direct observation of positive things that were going on in our communities here in Rio de Janeiro." The work of such NGOs for positive social change at the community level, despite largely negative media representations of the urban poor, suggests the importance of community groups currently struggling to improve life in the *favelas.*[58]

Retrospect and Prospect for Guanabara Bay

Rio de Janeiro's mounting ecological problems have motivated the razing of hills, construction of drainage ditches, filling of wetlands, and landfills to extend the shoreline—starting in the seventeenth century and continuing with increasing environmental impacts. The massive urban renewal projects of the twentieth century intensified these long-term ecological processes with such ominous negative consequences as industrial and domestic pollution, socioeconomic inequity, and governmental negligence. The uneven distribution of environmental amenities and services, such as sewage treatment and potable water, coupled with continued erosion and runoff from the Guanabara watershed, threatens to reduce further the size and quality of the city's great bay. Environmental agencies and NGOs, while working to save Guanabara Bay, have been frustrated by a lack of funding and political influence. Despite marginal improvements, the bay's continued degradation reflects an unhealthy urban metabolism in need of corrective action.

The major contributing role of informal communities in the bay's degradation cannot be denied, but it raises politically charged debates about environmental causation, culpability, and social responsibility. Created by forces of regional migration, urbanization, and urban renewal, *favelas* arose as a way to house low-income populations whom the realestate market and government had not accommodated. In some ways, *favela* ecology has favored a healthy circular metabolism, since poverty has meant high levels of recycling, reliance on scavenged and used building materials, collective transport, sharing among households, and community collaboration. Undoubtedly, affluent districts are comparatively wasteful in their use of resources. What *favelas* have lacked are the vital services and infrastructures necessary to reduce levels of pollution. In this context, it seems cruelly ironic that elites have blamed *favelados* for a host of ills since the late nineteenth century. Arguments for *favela* removal have taken various forms over the decades, but consistently have attempted to relocate informal communities away from affluent sectors. This chapter has identified three major periods of public policy and political ecology:

The Sanitary City (1808–1920): Since the late colonial period's surge in urbanization, abysmal sanitation and tropical disease have given rise to public interventions, engineering projects, and urban reforms. As pollution became problematic, the British City Improvements Company began a long-term contract to provide sewerage in 1862. With the abolition of slavery in 1888 and the resulting rural-urban migration, elites emphasized the importance of "civilizing" the burgeoning poor and migrant classes. A prime strategy was to remove impoverished people of color from expanding downtowns and affluent districts. During and after the urban reforms of Pereira Passos from 1902 to 1906, images of rampant disease, hygienic problems, and social pathology among the city's poor and rural migrants justified their displacement from downtown tenement *cortiços* to peripheral shantytowns. The expanding northern districts, near Guanabara Bay, became the main recipients of the working classes.

The Modernist City (1920–1985): During the mid twentieth century, hygienic concerns gave way to greater stress on large-scale urban renewal projects and efforts to "integrate" the "marginal" *favela* populations into the socioeconomic mainstream. Given social biases of this period, the military regime aggressively sought to extricate *favelas* from the Zona Sul and to concentrate them in Rio's mushrooming northern and western zones. The poor were represented as criminal and marginal elements of society, whom government policies sought to educate and if necessary remove. It was during this phase that spatial segregation became most pronounced and Rio's contemporary north-south divide emerged in stark relief, leaving large informal communities with inadequate urban services, concentrated largely around Guanabara Bay.

The Sustainable City (1985–Present): Since the end of the military regime, democratic politics and economic neoliberalism have given rise to concerns about sustainable development. On the one hand, the "sustainable city" has provided new forms of citizen participation, social organizing, and environmental advocacy. NGOs and community groups now work for social and environmental justice in ways that would have been unimaginable a generation ago. Unfortunately, the increasing levels of urban violence and growing awareness of environmental degradation also have given rise to a new set of rationales for *favela* exclusion. This ideological stance incorporates aspects of previous arguments, based on the unsightly buildings, lack of sanitation, danger of disease, fear of crime, and accusations of environmental ruin. Reflecting class prejudice and racial prejudice, these particular "environmentalist" contentions continue long-term efforts to promote urban segregation and distance the poor from wealthy communities. Although the Favela-Bairro program has marginally improved infrastructures and social services, the results have not remedied general problems of social immobility, lack of services, and violence that continue to trouble *favelas*.

Amid the long-term policy shifts, Guanabara Bay's degradation has continued largely unabated. Ambitious restoration plans have not succeeded, as witnessed by shortcomings of the 1994–2004 cleanup program. This unhealthy urban metabolism results largely from environmental injustice: the provision of vital urban services among the masses of the Zona Norte and its northern suburbs would do much to enhance Rio's general sustainability. The continuing devastation of Guanabara Bay threatens a vital scenic, recreational, and natural resource well worth saving. While governmental agencies and community groups have made significant efforts to address these problems, greater efforts are required to improve the prospects for social equity and ecological sustainability in this global megacity.

NOTES

Portuguese-English translations are my responsibility, unless otherwise noted. I thank John Browder, Colin Crawford, Maria Clara Dias, Carlos Alejandro Echeverria, Jurandyr Florentino Miguez, Maureen Hays-Mitchell, Rômulo S.R. Sampaio, Lise Sedrez, Igor Vojnovic, and Antoinette Winkler-Prins for their help at various stages of the research, presentation, writing, and editing of this chapter.

1. Coelho, *Baía de Guanabara*, 36–44; Eliane Canedo de Freitas Pinheiro, *Baía de Guanabara: Biografia de uma Paisagem* (Rio de Janeiro: Andrea Jakobsson Estúdio, 2005), 262; Instituto da Baía de Guanabara, Espelho d'Agua, http://www.portalbaiadeguanabara.org.br/portal/espelho1.asp.
2. Marlise Simons, Rio Journal: The Bay's a Thing of Beauty; Pity It's a Cesspool, *New York Times*, September 16, 1987; Pinheiro, *Baía de Guanabara*, 262.
3. Herman Melville, *White-Jacket; or, The World in a Man-of-War* (New York: Harper & Bros, 1850), http://www.melville.org/hmwjack.htm; Coelho, *Baía de Guanabara*, 19.
4. In 1973 the Brazilian National Institute of Historic and Artistic Patrimony (IPHAN) granted landmark status to Corcovado Mountain, five historic hills (Babilônia, Cara de Cão, Dois Irmãos, Pão de Açúcar [Sugarloaf], and Urca), and Tijuca National Park and Forest. Guanabara Bay, however, still does not figure in the list of 127 natural and cultural landmarks for

Rio de Janeiro (http://www.iphan.gov.br/).

5. Information Habitat, *The NGO Alternative Treaties from the Global Forum at Rio de Janeiro*, 1992.
6. Stephen M. Wheeler and Timothy Beatley, eds., *The Sustainable Urban Development Reader* (New York: Routledge, 2004), 59.
7. Robert Bullard, "People-of-Color Environmentalism," in Wheeler and Beatley, *Urban Sustainability Reader, Sustainable Urban Development Reader*, 144.
8. On informal communities elsewhere in the developing world, see J. Hardoy, D. Mitlin, and D. Satterthwaite, *Environmental Problems in an Urbanizing World*, 2001; and K. Pezzoli, *Human Settlements and Planning for Ecological Sustainability*, 1998.
9. Bullard, People-of-Color Environmentalism, 144.
10. Herbert Giarardet, The Metabolism of Cities, quoted in Wheeler and Beatley, *Urban Sustainability Reader*, 125–26.
11. See Gerard T. Koeppel, *Water for Gotham: A History* (Princeton, NJ: Princeton University Press, 2001); E. Ezcurra, M. Mazari-Hiriart, I. Pisanty, and A.G. Aguilar, *The Basin of Mexico: Critical Environmental Issues and Sustainability* (New York: United Nations Press, 1999); Margaret Keck, Water, Water, Everywhere, and Not a Drop to Drink: Land Use and Water Policy in São Paulo, Brazil, in *Livable Cities? Urban Struggles for Livelihood and Sustainability*, ed. Peter Evans (Berkeley: University of California Press, 2002), 162–94.
12. Coelho, *Baía de Guanabara*, 58–72. According to this source, in southeastern Brazil the "organized city" accounts for 55 percent of the urban population, "peripheral areas" for 30 percent, and *favelas* for the remaining 15 percent. In my view, such figures are at best approximations.
13. Selma Schmidt, Mais de 800 mil casas irregulares: Estudo mostra que cidade informal vem crescendo e domicílios sem licença Já São 40%, *O Globo*, Rio de Janeiro, January 13, 2002, 15.
14. Licia Valladares, A gênese da favela carioca, *Revista Brasileira de ciências socialis* 15:44 (2000); Maria Lais Pereira Silva, *Favelas* do Rio de Janeiro: Localização e expansão através do espaço urbano (1928–1964), in *Rio de Janeiro: Formas, movimentos, representações—Estudos de geografia histórica carioca*, ed. Maurício de Almeida Abreu (Rio de Janeiro: Da Fonseca Comunicação, 2005), 176–78.
15. Janice Perlman, *The Myth of Marginality: Urban Poverty and Politics in Rio de Janeiro* (Berkeley: University of California Press, 1976), 195.
16. Janice Perlman, The Metamorphosis of Marginality: Four Generations in the *Favelas* of Rio de Janeiro, *Annals of the American Academy of Political and Social Science* 606 (2006): 154–77. See also T. Caldeira, *City of Walls: Crime, Segregation, and Citizenship in São Paulo* (University of California Press, 2000); and Robert Gay, *Popular Organization and Democracy in Rio de Janeiro: A Tale of Two Favelas* (Philadelphia: Temple University Press, 1994).
17. Instituto Brasileiro de Geografia e Estatística, 2007, http://www.ibge.gov.br/home/; Favela tem Memoria, http://www.favelatemmemoria.com/br/.
18. Ibid.; Fundação CIDE—Centro de Informações e Dados do Rio de Janeiro, *Rio de Janeiro em Dados*, 2007, http://200.156.34.70/cide/index.php.
19. Favela Faces, A Tale of Two Cities: The Asphalt and the Favela, http://www.favelafaces.org/.
20. Coelho, *Baía de Guanabara*, 19–22.
21. P. James, Rio de Janeiro and São Paulo, *Geographical Review* 23:2 (1933): 274–75.
22. Patrick Wilcken, *Empire Adrift: The Portuguese Court in Rio de Janeiro, 1808–1821* (London: Bloomsbury, 2004), 175.
23. B. Godfrey, Spanish and Portuguese Colonial Cities in the Americas: A Historical-Geographical Approach to Urban Morphology, in *Cities and Urban Geography in Latin America*, ed. Vicent Ortells Chabrara, Robert B. Kent, and Javier Soriano Marti, 8–29 (Barcelona: Publicacions de la Universitat Jaime I, 2005); Brian J. Godfrey, Revisiting Rio de Janeiro and São Paulo, *Geographical Review* 89:1 (January 1999): 94–121; Brian J. Godfrey, Modernizing the Brazilian City, *Geographical Review* 81:1 (January 1991): 18–34.
24. Lise Sedrez, The Bay of All Beauties: State and Nature in Guanabara Bay, Rio de Janeiro, Brazil, 1875–1975, PhD diss., Stanford University, 2004, 84; for demographic figures, see E. Bradford Burns, *A History of Brazil* (New York: Columbia University Press, 1980), 144–51; Coelho, *Baía de Guanabara*, 46; Pinheiro, *Baía de Guanabara*, 252; Júlio César Pino, *Family and Favela: The Reproduction of Poverty in Rio de Janeiro* (Westport, CT: Greenwood Press, 1987), 40.
25. Christopher G. Boone, Streetcars and Politics in Rio de Janeiro: Private Enterprise versus Municipal Government in Mass Transit Delivery, 1903–1920, *Journal of Latin American Studies* 27 (May 1995): 343–65; Christopher G. Boone, Streetcars and Popular Protest in Rio de Janeiro: The Case of the Rio de Janeiro Tramway, Light and Power Company, 1903–1920, *Conference of Latin Americanist Geographers Yearbook* (October 1994): 49–57.

26. Isabelle Macedo Gomes, Dois séculos em busca de Uma Solução: Esgotos sanitários e meio ambiente na cidade do Rio de Janeiro, in Abreu, *Rio de Janeiro,* 56–71.
27. Valladares, A gênese da favela carioca; Silva, *Favelas* do Rio de Janeiro, 176–78; Fabio Soares and Yuri Soares, The Socio-Economic Impact of Favela-Bairro: What Do the Data Say? Office of Evaluation and Oversight (OVE), Inter-American Development Bank, 2005; Pino, *Family and Favela,* 37; Favela Faces, A Tale of Two Cities: The Asphalt and the Favela, http://www.favelafaces.org/.
28. Burns, *A History of Brazil,* 317.
29. Teresa A. Meade, *"Civilizing" Rio: Reform and Resistance in a Brazilian City, 1889–1930* (University Park: Penn State University Press, 1997), 28; Sedrez, The Bay of All Beauties, 85.
30. Jeffrey D. Needell, *A Tropical Belle Epoque: Elite Culture and Society in Turn-of-the-Century Rio de Janeiro* (New York: Cambridge University Press, 1987), 34.
31. Meade, *"Civilizing" Rio,* 110; Boone, Streetcars and Popular Protest, 49–57.
32. John Deal, Brazil Brazil, http://www.brazilbrazil.com/rio440y.html.
33. Quoted in Mauricio de Almeida Abreu, *Evolução Urbana do Rio de Janeiro* (Rio de Janeiro, IPLANRIO/ZAHAR, 1987), 89.
34. Ibid., 76; David Underwood, *Oscar Niemeyer and Brazilian Free-Form Modernism* (New York: George Braziller, 1994).
35. Pino, *Family and Favela,* 42.
36. Valladares, A gênese da favela carioca, 23–24; Pino, *Family and Favela,* 44; Favela tem Memoria, http://www.favelatemmemoria.com/br/.
37. Pinheiro, *Baía de Guanabara,* 242.
38. Perlman, *The Myth of Marginality,* 200–2.
39. Gay, *Popular Organization,* 19.
40. Quoted in Soares and Soares, The Socio-Economic Impact of Favela-Bairro, 5.
41. Gay, *Popular Organization;* Perlman, *The Myth of Marginality.*
42. The Favela Tem Memória website indicates that Rocinha and other selected *favelas* have glaring disparities in socioeconomic status (income, employment, and literacy) and service provision (trash collection, sewage, and water provision) compared to citywide averages. See http://www.favelatemmemoria.com.br/.
43. Coelho, *Baía de Guanabara,* 57.
44. Instituto da Baía de Guanabara, http://www.portalbaiadeguanabara.com.br/sitenovo/.
45. Banco Interamericano de Desenvolvimento. *Relatório Final de Projeto: Programa de Saneamento Básico da Bacia da Baía da Guanabara (PDBG),* 1–39;Coelho, *Baía de Guanabara,* 68–70.
46. Coelho, Baía de Guanabara, 62–68; Sedrez, The Bay of All Beauties, 249–51; Tom Phillips, Sewage, Algae, and Rubbish Stain the Once-Pristine White Beaches of Rio, *Guardian International,* April 28, 2007, 28; Pinheiro, *Baía de Guanabara,* 263; Simons, Rio Journal: The Bay's a Thing of Beauty.
47. Map adapted from the Instituto Baía de Guanabara, based on tests of biochemical oxygen demand (BOD) in February 2000; concentrations of over eight milligrams per liter, considered highly polluted, encompass much of the bay's northern and western quadrants.
48. Coelho, *Baía de Guanabara,* 72.
49. Susie Seefelt Lesieutre, From Favela to Bairro: Rio's Neighborhoods in Transition, *ReVista-Harvard Review of Latin America* (winter 2001), http://drclas.fas.harvard.edu/revista/articles/view/530.
50. Kelly E. Graham, The Asphalt and the Favela: A Critical Examination of Contemporary Urban Segregation, senior thesis, Vassar College, 2007, 38–39.
51. Mario Fuks, Environmental Litigation in Rio de Janeiro: Shaping Frames for a New Social Problem, *International Journal of Urban and Regional Research* 22:3 (September 1998): 394–408.
52. Cabeça de Avestruz, *Jornal do Brasil* (February 13, 1998): 8.
53. Coelho, *Baía de Guanabara,* 60.
54. Uma Cidade Despreparada, *O Globo,* February 21, 1998, 12.
55. Perlman, The Metamorphosis of Marginality, 154–77; Caldeira, *City of Walls.*
56. Tom Phillips, Sewage, Algae, and Rubbish Stain the Once-Pristine White Beaches of Rio, *Guardian International,* April 28, 2007, 28; Viva Rio/Viva Favela, Retrato Matemático, 2008, http://www.favelatemmemoria.com.br/. The official Brazilian census indicates that Maré's population in 2000 was 69,851, but unofficial estimates put the figure much higher.
57. See the official film websites at http://www.palmpictures.com/film/city-of-men.php,http://cidadedoshomens.globo.com/, and http://www.favelarising.com/index.html.
58. See the diverse organization websites: http://www.vivafavela.com.br/; http://www.favelatemmemoria.com.br/; http://www.favelafaces.org/; http://www.favelapainting.com/; and http://www.comcat.org/novo/sobreacomcat.asp.

REFERENCES

Abreu, Mauricio de Almeida. *Evolução Urbana do Rio de Janeiro.* Rio de Janeiro: IPLANRIO/ZAHAR, 1987.

Banco Interamericano de Desenvolvimento. *Relatório Final de Projeto: Programa de Saneamento Básico da Bacia da Baía da Guanabara (PDBG).* Brazil, 2006.

Boone, Christopher G. Streetcars and Politics in Rio de Janeiro: Private Enterprise versus Municipal Government in Mass Transit Delivery, 1903–1920. *Journal of Latin American Studies* 27 (May 1995): 343–65.

———. Streetcars and Popular Protest in Rio de Janeiro: The Case of the Rio de Janeiro Tramway, Light and Power Company, 1903–1920. *Conference of Latin Americanist Geographers Yearbook* (October 1994): 49–57.

Bullard, Robert. People-of-Color Environmentalism. Reprinted in *The Sustainable Urban Development Reader,* ed. Stephen M. Wheeler and Timothy Beatley, 143–49. New York: Routledge, 2004.

Burns, E. Bradford. *A History of Brazil.* New York: Columbia University Press, 1980.

Caldeira, T. *City of Walls: Crime, Segregation, and Citizenship in São Paulo.* University of California Press, 2000.

Coelho, Victor. *Baía de Guanabara: Uma História de Agressão Ambiental.* Rio de Janeiro: Casa da Palavra, 2007.

Deal, John. *Brazil Brazil.* 2008. http://www.brazilbrazil.com/rio440y.html.

Ezcurra, E., M. Mazari-Hiriart, I. Pisanty, and A.G. Aguilar. *The Basin of Mexico: Critical Environmental Issues and Sustainability.* New York: United Nations Press, 1999.

Favela Faces. A Tale of Two Cities: The Asphalt and the *Favela.* http://www.favelafaces.org/intro_eng.html.

Figueiredo, L.H.M. *Problemas Ambientais Globais: Conceitos Fundamentais e Instrumentos de Análise Ambiental.* Programa de Despoluição da Baía de Guanabara. Capacitação em Educação para a Gestão Ambiental. Rio de Janeiro: CEPUERJ/UERJ, 1997.

Fuks, Mario. Environmental Litigation in Rio de Janeiro: Shaping Frames for a New Social Problem. *International Journal of Urban and Regional Research* 22:3 (1998): 394–408.

Fundação CIDE (Centro de Informações e Dados do Rio de Janeiro). *Rio de Janeiro em Dados.*2007. http://200.156.34.70/cide/index.php.

Gay, Robert. *Popular Organization and Democracy in Rio de Janeiro: A Tale of Two Favelas.* Philadelphia: Temple University Press, 1994.

Giarardet, Herbert. The Metabolism of Cities. Quoted in *Urban Sustainability Reader,* ed. Stephen M. Wheeler and Timothy Beatley, 125–32. New York: Routledge, 2004.

Godfrey, Brian J. Modernizing the Brazilian City. *Geographical Review* 81:1 (January 1991): 18–34.

———. Revisiting Rio de Janeiro and São Paulo. *Geographical Review* 89:1 (January 1999): 94–121.

———. Spanish and Portuguese Colonial Cities in the Americas: A Historical-Geographical Approach to Urban Morphology. In *Cities and Urban Geography in Latin America,* ed. Vicent Ortells Chabrara, Robert B. Kent, and Javier Soriano Marti, 8–29. Barcelona: Publicacions de la Universitat Jaime I, 2005.

Graham, Kelly E. The Asphalt and the Favela: A Critical Examination of Contemporary Urban Segregation. Senior thesis, Vassar College, 2007.

Gomes, Isabelle Macedo. Dois Séculos em Busca de Uma Solução: Esgotos Sanitários e Meio Ambiente na Cidade do Rio de Janeiro. In *Rio de Janeiro: Formas, Movimentos, Representações—Estudos de Geografia Histórica Carioca,* ed. Maurício de Almeida Abreu, 56–71. Rio de Janeiro, RJ: Da Fonseca Comunicação, 2005.

Gouvêa, Ronaldo Guimarães. *A Questão Metropolitana no Brasil.* Rio de Janeiro: Editoria Fundação Getúlio Vargas, 2005.

Hardoy, Jorge E. Two Thousand Years of Latin American Urbanization. In *Urbanization in Latin America: Approaches and Issues,* ed. J. E. Hardoy, 3–56. Garden City, NY: Anchor Books, 1975.

Hardoy, Jorge, Diana Mitlin, and David Satterthwaite. *Environmental Problems in an Urbanizing World: Finding Solutions in Africa, Asia, and Latin America.* Sterling, VA: Earthscan, 2001.

Information Habitat. Concerning Guanabara Bay: Humankind's Heritage. *The NGO Alternative Treaties from the Global Forum at Rio de Janeiro.* 1992. http://habitat.igc.org/treaties/at-34.htm.

Instituto Brasileiro de Geografia e Estatística (IBGE). 2007. http://www.ibge.gov.br/.

Instituto da Baía de Guanabara. 2007. http://www.portalbaiadeguanabara.com.br/.

IPHAN (National Institute of Historic and Artistic Patrimony). 2008. http://www.iphan.gov.br/.

James, Preston E. Rio de Janeiro and São Paulo. *Geographical Review* 23:2 (1933): 271–98.

Keck, Margaret. Water, Water, Everywhere, and Not a Drop to Drink: Land Use and Water Policy in São Paulo, Brazil. In *Livable Cities? Urban Struggles for Livelihood and Sustainability,* ed. Peter Evans, 162–94. Berkeley: University of California Press,

2002.
Koeppel, Gerard T. *Water for Gotham: A History.* Princeton, NJ: Princeton University Press, 2001.
Lesieutre, Susie Seefelt. From Favela to Bairro: Rio's Neighborhoods in Transition. *ReVista: Harvard Review of Latin America* (winter 2001). http://drclas.fas.harvard.edu/revista/articles/view/530.
Meade, Teresa A. *"Civilizing" Rio: Reform and Resistance in a Brazilian City, 1889–1930.* University Park: Pennsylvania State University Press, 1997.
Melville, Herman. *White-Jacket; or, The World in a Man-of-War.* New York: Harper & Brothers, 1850. http://www.melville.org/hmwjack.htm.
Needell, Jeffrey D. *A Tropical Belle Epoque: Elite Culture and Society in Turn-of-the-Century Rio de Janeiro.* New York: Cambridge University Press, 1987.
Perlman, Janice. The Metamorphosis of Marginality: Four Generations in the *Favelas* of Rio de Janeiro. *Annals of the American Academy of Political and Social Science* 606 (2006): 154–77.
———. *The Myth of Marginality: Urban Poverty and Politics in Rio de Janeiro.* Berkeley: University of California Press, 1976.
Pezzoli, Keith. *Human Settlements and Planning for Ecological Sustainability: The Case of Mexico City.* Cambridge: MIT Press, 1998.
Phillips, Tom. Sewage, Algae, and Rubbish Stain the Once-Pristine White Beaches of Rio. *Guardian International,* April 28, 2007, 28.
Pinheiro, Eliane Canedo de Freitas. *Baía de Guanabara: Biografia de uma Paisagem.* Rio de Janeiro: Andrea Jakobsson Estúdio, 2005.
Pino, Júlio César. *Family and Favela: The Reproduction of Poverty in Rio de Janeiro.* Westport, CT: Greenwood Press, 1987.
Schmidt, Selma. Mais de 800 Mil Casas Irregulares: Estudo Mostra Que Cidade Informal Vem Crescendo e Domicílios Sem Licença Já São 40%. *O Globo,* Rio de Janeiro, January 13, 2002, 15.
Sedrez, Lise. The Bay of All Beauties: State and Nature in Guanabara Bay, Rio de Janeiro, Brazil, 1875–1975. PhD diss., Stanford University, 2004.
Silva, Maria Lais Pereira. *Favelas* do Rio de Janeiro: Localização e Expansão Através do Espaço Urbano (1928–1964). In *Rio de Janeiro: Formas, Movimentos, Representações—Estudos de Geografia Histórica Carioca,* ed. Maurício de Almeida Abreu, 176–201. Rio de Janeiro: Da Fonseca Comunicação, 2005.
Simons, Marlise. Rio Journal: The Bay's a Thing of Beauty; Pity It's a Cesspool. *New York Times,* September 16, 1987.
Soares, Fabio, and Yuri Soares. The Socio-Economic Impact of Favela-Bairro: What Do the Data Say? Office of Evaluation and Oversight (OVE), Inter-American Development Bank, 2005.
Underwood, David. *Oscar Niemeyer and Brazilian Free-Form Modernism.* New York: George Braziller, 1994.
United Nations Development Program (UNDP). *Atlas do Desenvolvimento Humano do Brasil—2003.* 2003. http://www.pnud.org.br/home/.
Valladares, Licia. A gênese da Favela carioca. *Revista Brasileira de ciências socialis* 15:44 (2000): 5–34.
Viva Rio/Viva Favela. Retrato Matemático. 2008. http://www.favelatemmemoria.com.br/.
Wheeler, Stephen M., and Timothy Beatley, eds. *The Sustainable Urban Development Reader.* New York: Routledge, 2004.
Wilcken, Patrick. *Empire Adrift: The Portuguese Court in Rio de Janeiro, 1808–1821.* London: Bloomsbury, 2004.

■ BEVERLEY MULLINGS

Neoliberal Restructuring, Poverty, and Urban Sustainability in Kingston, Jamaica

Like many other Caribbean and Latin American countries, Jamaica is highly urbanized. In 2007 53 percent of its population of 2.5 million lived in an urban area.[1] Not only is Jamaica highly urbanized, its urban population has continued to grow each year. Thus, in the 1960s an average of 37 percent of the population was urban, rising to 44 percent in the 1970s, and to 48 percent and to 50 percent, respectively, throughout the 1980s and 1990s.[2] Jamaica's large and growing urban population represents a significant challenge to the sustainability of its cities, because urbanization is occurring in the context of declining real wages and high unemployment. Unlike rapidly industrializing countries where urbanization has followed the expansion of the manufacturing sector and rising levels of agricultural productivity, Jamaica's high level of urbanization is the spatial expression of the strategies that many employ to counter declining economic opportunities on the island.

As Jamaica's largest cities grow, their sustainability is increasingly under threat. Low rates of economic growth since the 1980s have made it difficult for the state to provide the social and physical infrastructure needed to meet the needs of its growing urban population. Cities like Kingston, Portmore, Spanish Town, and Montego Bay, for example, are faced with increasing demands for basic collective services, such as the provision of clean water, affordable housing, and sewage disposal, but with few resources to meet them. Combined with the high levels of long-term structural unemployment that have characterized its inner-city neighborhoods for the past twenty years, the prospects of urban sustainability in Jamaica are particularly low.

In order to fully understand the factors that have constrained Jamaica's ability to secure the economic, environmental, and social health of its cities—the conditions for long-term improvements in the quality of life of its urban population—we need to examine how the development strategy pursued by the Jamaican government for the past thirty years has affected the urban sustainability of its cities. Focusing on the Kingston Metropolitan Area (KMA), the largest of the urban regions on the island, I shall examine the ways that Jamaica's liberalization strategy, with its emphasis on a reduced role for government in the provision of welfare-oriented investments, and greater service provision by the private sector has eroded the social networks and relations that foster social stability. In doing so, I will pay particular attention to the ways that policymakers have relied on women's unpaid labor to maintain the human and social investments needed for social cohesion and the long-term impact that the continued devaluation of social reproduction is having on the goal of urban sustainability as a whole.

Economic and Social Sustainability—Contradictory Objectives?

Goodland notes that the criteria for social and economic sustainability, though overlapping, are sufficiently different as to require separate consideration.[3] Defining economic sustainability as the ability to generate the capital required to maintain levels of consumption, while preserving "natural capital," he argues that economic policy should err on the side of uncertainty and caution if the regenerative capacity of people is ever at stake.[4] Robert Goodland defines social sustainability, on the other hand, as the maintenance and the replenishment of the investments and services needed to facilitate cooperation among community members of a society. Influenced by the work of Pierre Bourdieu, Goodland views such investments as a form of social capital that protects societies from violent social breakdown and mistrust.[5] Goodland's work focuses on the relationship between socioeconomic sustainability and environmental sustainability. As a result, it does not examine the relationship between economic sustainability and social sustainability. Yet, as many scholars of political economy have argued, the relationship between the production of capital and the reproduction of labor is crucial to not only environmental sustainability, but also to sustainable development as a whole.[6] Cindi Katz for example, argues that social reproduction is crucial to the reproduction of the labor force at a certain level of differentiation and expertise.[7] Social reproduction is also crucial to economic development to the extent that it maintains the cultural forms and practices that reinforce and naturalize social relations within a community and, in so doing, generates the levels of stability required for economic growth.

Cities in Jamaica

Like many other countries in the region, Jamaica has a primate city urban structure, where the capital city is the focal point of national influence and activity. Established in 1892 as the national capital, Kingston is located in the southeast quadrant of the island, bounded by the Blue Mountain range to the east and the Caribbean Sea to the south (fig. 1). Since its inception in 1692, the population of this port city has continuously expanded. By the 1930s Kingston had grown to incorporate the northeastern parish of St. Andrew, and by the 1970s it had spilled southwest, across a number of rural fishing and agricultural villages in the adjoining parish of St. Catherine. This area, the city of Portmore, has since become a major area of urban growth.

Today the Kingston Metropolitan Area is an amalgamation of the parish of Kingston and parts of the parish of St. Andrew. Much of the early city is now considered part of downtown Kingston, while much of the parish of St. Andrew now constitutes the residential and commercial heartland

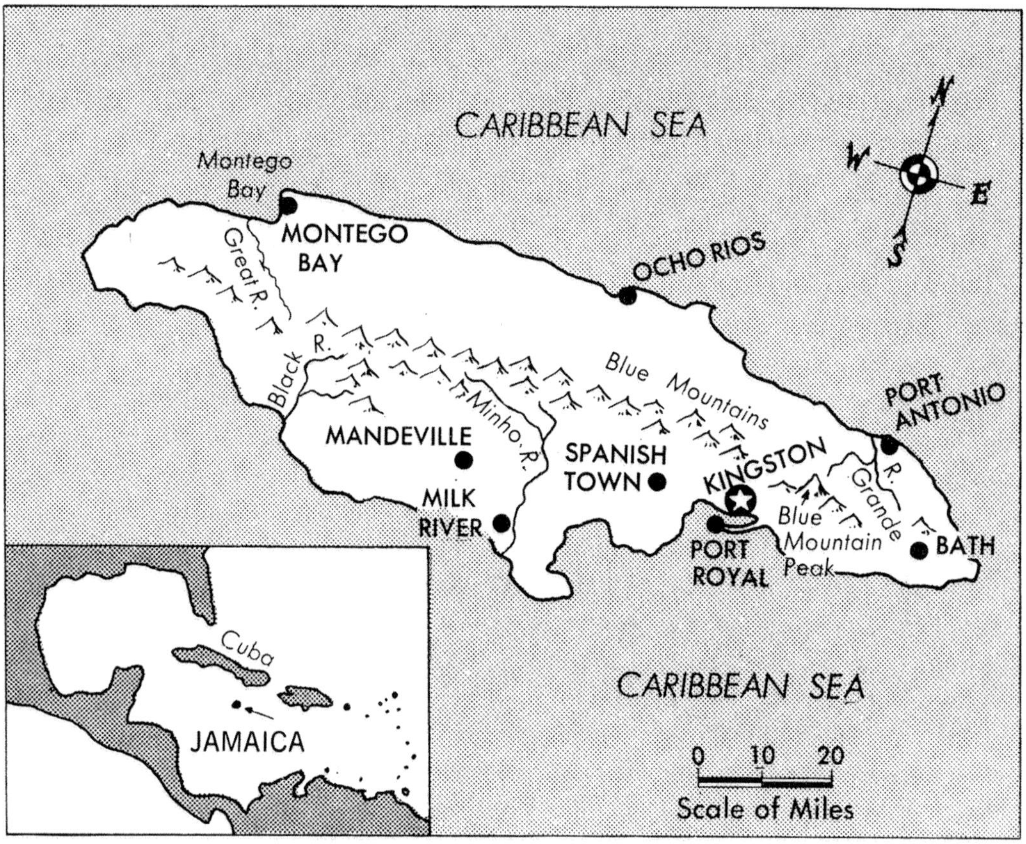

Figure 1. Map of Jamaica with major cities.

of the city. The 2001 census calculated the population of the Kingston Metropolitan Area to be 579,137, of which 483,085 lived in the parish of St. Andrew.[8]

The westward spread of Kingston's urban population into the parish of St. Catherine and the creation of the city of Portmore reflects one of the early efforts of the state to alleviate the shortage of land and affordable housing facing the Kingston Metropolitan Area. Faced with a shortage of housing to meet the need of its burgeoning population, in 1967 the government endorsed the private construction of a causeway and a bridge across Kingston Harbor that would link the downtown commercial and industrial areas of western Kingston to southern St. Catherine. Completed in 1969, the causeway facilitated the development of at least ten privately built housing schemes between 1969 and 1978, which today form part of the municipality of Portmore. Further state investment in housing and community development throughout the 1980s and 1990s have contributed to the spectacular growth of Portmore since its early inception. In 1970 the population of Portmore was estimated to be 2,200, but by 1982 this number had risen to 73,000, to 100,000 in 1991 and in 2001 to 160,000.[9] The growth of Portmore has also transformed the traditional class patterns residential settlement. As Anderson and colleagues note, whereas in traditional urban residential patterns of settlement in Jamaica, the very poor tend to live on peripheral lands abutting middle class and wealthy areas, the development of Portmore created new areas of middle- and working-class housing that excluded the very poor in slum settlements altogether. In 2003 Portmore became a municipality, a designation that recognizes its status as a functioning city and grants a degree of autonomy.

The urban pressures of Kingston have also led to the growth of Spanish Town, the former capital of the island. Spurred on by the construction of the Twickenham Park housing estate and the Nelson Mandela Highway linking West Kingston to Spanish Town, the population of this city has also expanded significantly. From a population of 14,700 in 1960, Colin Clarke states that Spanish Town grew to 39,200 in 1970, 89,100 in 1982 to 131,515 in 2001, a figure that is larger than that of Jamaica's second official city Montego Bay.[10]

As Kingston has urbanized it has increasingly encompassed or stimulated urban growth in other adjacent parishes. Clarke argues that this pattern of urban sprawl is reminiscent of that of other North American cities and has contributed to the formation of the Kingston Metropolitan Region, a contiguous urban zone that includes not only the Kingston Metropolitan Area, but also Portmore and Spanish Town and its suburbs.

The city of Montego Bay, located in the northwestern quadrant of the island, is the second largest urban area outside the Kingston metropolitan region, and Jamaica's second official city. Proclaimed a city in 1980, Montego Bay functions as both a major hub for the island's tourism industry and the location of the island's main offshore freezone area. The population of Montego Bay has also increased steadily over time, rising from 70,265 in 1982, to 83,400 in 1991, to 96,488 in 2001 and in 2008 to 121,000. Currently Montego Bay is the fourth largest city in Jamaica.

An Urban Profile of the Kingston Metropolitan Area

Kingston functioned from the 1800s onward as the center of government, commerce, and cultural exchange and a magnet for new immigrants from the surrounding countryside. As early as the 1840s, Kingston could be characterized as a highly unequal and stratified city where wealthy white elites lived in relatively luxurious mansions but a stone's throw away from runaway slaves and freed black persons living in squalor-filled slum settlements. Other early nonwhite immigrants to the city—namely, Jews and free coloreds, and later on in the early 1900s, Chinese and Syrians—settled in areas of the city close to the retail districts, where most such newcomers were economically engaged.

The highly unequal and racialized pattern of settlement that emerged in the early years of the city changed substantially in the years that followed the emancipation of slavery in 1838, the First World War and the 1930s Great Depression. By the 1950s wealth, rather than race, increasingly determined the quality and range of resources that different ethnoracial groups in the city could access. But the stark inequalities between the resources enjoyed by the handful of white or "closer to white" ethnoracial groups and their absence for large groups of predominantly black households persist to this day.

Kingston has suffered from high levels of unemployment as far back as the mid-1930s. Clarke, for example, states that in 1936, of the 45,000 estimated to comprise the city's labor force, approximately 11 percent were unemployed.[11] While international migration has historically acted as a

PHOTOGRAPH BY EMMA THOMPSON

Figure 2. Affluent housing in the Beverly Hills suburban community to the northeast of Kingston.

safety valve, relieving the social tensions associated with poverty and inequality during the 1920s, 1960s, 1980s, and 1990s, unemployment remains a significant source of social instability across the Kingston Metropolitan Region. Persistently high levels of unemployment and poverty continue to characterize the large zone of deprivation that stretches across East and West Kingston and a number of squatter settlements adjacent to the wealthy suburbs of Beverly Hills and Norbrook, to the north of the city (fig. 2).

Although rates of poverty are higher in rural areas (poverty rates in 2007 were estimated to be 15.3 percent in rural areas, compared to 6.2 percent in Kingston and 9.9 percent in other urban areas), urban poverty in Jamaica tends to be more entrenched, politically linked, and socially corrosive.[12] The chronic nature of urban poverty in Jamaica can be seen in the increasing proportion of the urban population that is concentrated in Kingston's inner-city slums—heavily populated areas of settlement where the inhabitants' needs for adequate housing and basic services are poorly addressed by the state (figs. 3, 4, and 5). In 1990 the proportion of Jamaica's urban population living in slum conditions was approximately 30 percent but has since doubled to 61 percent in 2005.[13]

Between the 1960s and 1970s, Jamaica's newly independent government invested significantly in much-needed social welfare. Investments during this period included not only roads and bridges, but also housing to alleviate the urban stresses associated with the continuous influx of

PHOTOGRAPH BY JACOB VOORTHUIS

Figure 3. Trench Town, a poor inner-city community where Bob Marley was born.

PHOTOGRAPH BY JACOB VOORTHUIS

Figure 4. Riverton City, a poor inner-city community adjacent to the city garbage dump, on the edge of Kingston.

PHOTOGRAPH BY ST. RACHEL E. USTANNY

Figure 5. Public showers in Majestic Gardens, a politically aligned garrison community.

unskilled and semiskilled labor from surrounding rural areas. During the 1960s and 1970s the state funded the construction of a number of residential projects to provide mass housing opportunities for both its growing middle-class population and the urban poor. Middle-class housing developments were largely located in suburban locations, away from the inner-city confines of Kingston mass housing for poor households that remained primarily within West Kingston, on sites that were previously tenement yards and squatter settlements. Government funded mass housing estates such as Tivoli Gardens built in the mid-1960s on the former Back o' Wall slum (fig. 6), or Arnett Gardens, built in the 1970s, provided poor households with solid concrete dwelling structures and amenities such as running water and indoor toilet facilities.

Other welfare investments were aimed at enhancing levels of education and health and reducing the historically high levels of inequality across class and ethnoracial groups, patterns that were the legacy of the colonial plantation system. For example, in 1972 the state established a national literacy program that reduced functional illiteracy levels by 40 percent within two years; free secondary and tertiary education in 1973; increases in social security for the poor in 1974; a fund in 1977 for housing construction through compulsory contributions; and in 1979 a policy of paid maternity leave that facilitated the entry of women into the labor force.[14] These specific social programs in health and education, combined with a general system of subsidies for basic food items like cooking oil, flour, and condensed milk, made it possible for even the poorest to access the basic levels of social welfare needed to sustain their daily and intergenerational reproductive needs.

PHOTOGRAPH BY JACOB VOORTHUIS

Figure 6. Tivoli Gardens, a government housing estate built in the mid-1960s that is today a politically aligned garrison community.

The Impact of Neoliberalization on Urban Sustainability

The gains brought about by housing construction, adult literacy programs, universal health care, and social security came abruptly to a halt after the 1974 oil price crisis, and the subsequent upward spiral of debt in the region. Under World Bank and International Monetary Fund (IMF) guided programs of structural adjustment, public spending was drastically reduced throughout the 1980s. For example, between 1982/1983 and 1987/1988, government spending in real terms on public health services declined by 71 percent and by approximately 57 percent on education between 1982/1983 and 1986/1987. Similarly, between 1979/1980 and 1987/1988 drastic declines in government spending on housing diminished what was an already inadequate level of provision by 200 percent.

As the state retreated from the provision of universal forms of social security, targeted social safety nets in the form of food stamps and school feeding programs were instituted, but these programs were largely unsuccessful in reaching these more narrowly defined target populations. The 2001 survey of living conditions by the Planning Institute of Jamaica and Statistical Institute of Jamaica (PIOJ/STATIN), for example, indicates that only 5 percent of individuals in Jamaica received welfare assistance through the food stamp program, and, with the exception of children under six, less than half of those eligible for welfare assistance under the food stamp program actually took up these benefits.[15] It was believed that the low level of take-up was attributable to the low economic value of these benefits and the stigma attached to those who appeared to fail to secure their welfare through the market rather than the state.

Neoliberalization and the Feminization of Poverty

The effect of the early neoliberal reforms in Jamaica can be seen in the rising levels of poverty during the late 1980s. Households, particularly in the rural areas, experienced increasing levels of income deprivation that restricted the access of many to the resources that were necessary to maintain a socially acceptable standard of living. These early forms of neoliberal restructuring also had a profoundly negative effect on poor urban communities and, in particular, on women. As Helen Safa and Peggy Antrobus document, women were affected not only by the loss of employment that they experienced as unemployment and underemployment levels rose, they also suffered from the unequal burden that the rising cost of living exacted as subsidies on basic food items were removed.[16] Women also bore the brunt of the loss of access to public services like health and education, as public expenditure on these forms of social reproduction declined. Women in particular compensated for the loss of publicly provided social welfare by increasing the amount of their time and unpaid labor devoted to social reproduction. They compensated for the loss of public health care with their time when regional hospitals closed, traveling further afield to reach health care facilities.

By the end of the 1980s the social effects of the decline in state spending in areas directly linked to social sustainability became clear as the gap between the rich and the poor widened and as the incomes of increasing numbers of Jamaicans fell below the poverty line.[17] Although quantitative studies in the 1980s indicated no significant gender differences in the proportion of males and females living in poverty, feminist scholars throughout the 1990s continued to qualitatively document how the burdens associated with structural adjustment, and, in particular, declining state involvement in social welfare disproportionately and negatively affected Jamaican women.[18] Women experienced not only higher levels of unemployment and wage discrimination, but also higher levels of poverty, because they tended to assume greater levels of responsibility for the social well-being of households than men.[19] The disproportionate level of responsibility for family and community welfare assumed by Jamaican women was argued to be a reflection of the matrifocality of Jamaican society—the traditional way that social and community life revolved around women. But matrifocality in the context of crisis increased the burden shouldered by women, because they were also more likely than men to be single heads of households with dependants and more likely to be poor (households headed by women account for 66 percent of single-headed households in poverty).[20] For example, figures based on the 1999 Survey of Living Conditions show that households headed by women (73 percent) were more likely than those headed by men (65 percent) to have experienced financial difficulties that forced them to forgo food and the payment of utility bills and health expenses.[21] The survey also indicated that these financial difficulties were persistent, with 41 percent of households reporting having faced such a situation for the past five years. Faced with little state support, many households reported that they had no choice but to turn to alternative sources of social and economic support. While male household heads were more likely than female-headed ones to draw on savings, sell assets, or take on additional employment to survive, women household heads were more likely to delay bill payments, seek assistance from relatives and friends at home and abroad, or pray for support.

How households, particularly those headed by women, coped with these hardships over the long term offers important insights into the factors that continue to affect the sustainability of Jamaica's urban communities. While women devised short-term responses, such as work in the informal and grey sectors, or by pooling incomes and care responsibilities among extended household and family members, they also developed longer-term survival strategies that involved migration and the transnationalization of social reproduction. It is the social sustainability of these longer-term strategies that I would like to examine in further detail.

Migration and Social Sustainability

Jamaican women have been active participants in migration streams since as early as the 1950s, when many were recruited to Britain to alleviate the postwar shortages of workers in care sectors such as nursing.[22] These early migrants often left the country without their children, leaving them behind with close relatives such as grandmothers and siblings until they could be reunited. This transnational pattern of parenthood not only provided women with better chances of gaining access to British labor markets, it also improved the livelihoods of families who benefited from the remittances that women sent back home. The size, intensity, and frequency of these social and financial exchanges increased significantly in the 1980s as the economic crisis forced larger numbers of men and women to migrate, and as families became more and more dependent on remittances to meet everyday expenses, such as rent, food, utility bills, and medical and school expenses. Emigration rates among women increased during the 1990s as women responded to the growing demand for low-cost caring labor in the global north, rising, in the case of migrants to the United States, from 52 percent to 54 percent between 1991 and 1996 (table 1). The proliferation of money transfer agencies in neighborhoods with high concentrations of Jamaican migrants in cities like London, Toronto, and New York attests to the transnationalization of the Jamaican family, and the extent to which families abroad actively participated in sustaining the economic needs of family members in Jamaica.

The emigration of increasing numbers of women and men during the 1990s, however, has had contradictory effects on the social sustainability of households and communities in Jamaica. Many households left behind have benefited from the remittances of family members abroad and in so doing have survived the impoverishing effects of the soaring cost of food, clothing, and housing. The World Bank estimates that of countries in Latin America and the Caribbean, remittances per capita were highest in Jamaica, accounting for approximately $550 per person in 2004, relative to $128 per capita in the rest of the region (table 2).[23] More than simply a cash flow, Jenny Burman argues that remittances should be considered affective investments that are as important to maintaining the psychological welfare of family members disconnected across borders as their physical well-being.[24] Regular financial remittances are an important mechanism for ensuring that children left behind are provided with the highest levels of care and opportunities for social development possible. For, as Karen Fog Olwig documents, the social well-being of children left behind is often contingent on the frequency and volume of remittances.[25] Drawing on the childhood memories of people left behind by migrating parents, she notes:

Table 1. Migration of Jamaicans to the United States

	TOTAL	WOMEN	MEN	% OF WOMEN
1973	9,963	4,992	4,971	50
1979	19,714	10,345	9,369	52
1985	18,923	9,881	9,042	52
1991	18,914	9,807	9,107	52
1996	19,089	10,280	8,809	54
2004	14,430	7,809	6,605	54

Source: U.S. Department of Homeland Security, various years.

life stories show that while the children may miss their parents, due to the latter's physical absence in distant migration destinations, they can develop close relations to their parents and a secure sense of belonging in the family home if the parents maintain a strong social and economic presence in this home. Those children whose parents have a very limited presence in the family home, on the other hand, will more than likely experience both the economic hardship that results from their parents' neglect, and become targets of the moral condemnation which is directed at their absent parents. The children left behind therefore remain strongly dependent upon having a continued relationship with their parents.[26]

The economic sustainability that remittances have produced in the twenty years or more since Jamaica's economic restructuring began, however, has not been sufficient to avert the corrosive effects of the retreat of the state from the provision of social welfare in Kingston. While remittances played an important role in the 9 percent reduction in the number of Jamaicans living below the national poverty line between 1995 and 2000 (table 3), these financial transfers were not as successful in preserving the social norms and rules governing social interaction that have traditionally regulated the city's dominant social order. In the following section I shall demonstrate how changes to the functioning of three social institutions that have been affected by the retreat of the state are threatening levels of urban sustainability of Kingston.

Table 2. Remittances to selected Caribbean countries ($US millions)

YEAR	2001	2002	2003
Dominican Republic	1,807	2,206	2,217
Jamaica	967	1,288	1,425
Cuba	930	1,265	1,194
Haiti	810	931	977
Guyana	n/a	119	137
Trinidad and Tobago	n/a	59	88
Caribbean	4,514	5,868	6,038

Source: Inter-American Development Bank, *Sending Money Home: Remittance to Latin America and the Caribbean* (Washington, DC: IDB, 2004).

Table 3. Poverty statistics

	1995	2000	% CHANGE
Poverty headcount at national poverty line (% population)	28	19	–9
Poverty headcount at rural poverty line (% rural population)	37	25	–12
Poverty headcount at urban poverty line (% urban population)	19	13	–6

Source: World Bank Online Database, 2008.

Education and Employment

The years of underinvestment in education during the period of structural adjustment have significantly eroded the quality of Jamaica's stock of human capital. Recent studies, for example, suggest that despite the fact that 78 percent of young people between the ages of fifteen and sixteen are enrolled in primary school, as many as 40 percent are functionally illiterate when they leave.[27] Low levels of achievement in school disproportionately affect boys, who are more likely to drop out of school during their high school years or irregularly attend.[28] Barry Chevannes states that the poor record of achievement among boys can be explained by the different ways in which boys and girls are socialized in Jamaica.[29] He argues that while girls are socialized to follow rules and to cooperate in ways that are conducive to traditional school routines, boys are often expected to be able to fend for themselves in ways that are not conducive to classroom discipline. A number of studies also suggest that there is a relationship between educational underachievement among boys and violence in Jamaica.[30] These studies suggest that underachievement in school often masks learning impediments that are rarely recognized as such. Boys in such situations often drop out of school or resort to violence in response to the frustration and anger they experience in the school system. As one recent study by the Ministry of Education and Youth notes, as many as 35 percent of students involved in violent incidents at school were not functionally literate.[31] The consequences of educational underachievement go far beyond the school system. As figures from the World Bank indicate, underachievement and leaving school early contributed to the situation, where in 2004 despite the fact that total unemployment rates had fallen from 15.4 percent to 11.4 percent, 26 percent of Jamaicans between the ages of fifteen and twenty-four years of age remained unemployed.[32]

Faced with limited prospects of employment as they become adults, young men are increasingly forced into the underground sector, where opportunities of earning living wages are significantly greater, though infinitely more risky and violent. The low levels of educational achievement and employment among young Jamaicans can be partially attributed to the weak levels of investment in education during the 1980s and 1990s. But the relationship between low levels of education, violence, and social disorder is also the product of the slow erosion of the family and community networks that historically maintained social cohesion in Jamaican society. Like education, this erosion is the indirect outcome of the priority that the state has given to private sector strategies to boost economic sustainability to the detriment of social sustainability.

Family Networks and Social Capital

The long-term effects of state social disinvestment can be seen in the changing structure of Jamaican households and the vulnerabilities this has created for young people, particularly those in inner-city communities. While the internationalization of the Jamaican household through migration allowed households and communities to meet the everyday consumption needs of their members, this practice is declining in its ability to maintain the long-term social well-being of all household members. It is estimated that three out of every ten households in Jamaica have children whose parents no longer live on the island.[33] While large numbers of these so-called barrel kids live in stable households with relatives and friends who rely on parental remittances to finance their care, reports suggest that a small but increasing number are at risk because they are in precarious housing arrangements where they frequently are shifted among guardians.[34] Children, and especially girls, who live in such inadequate surrogate parental living environments are more vulnerable to both physical and sexual abuse and to heightened feelings of loneliness and abandonment.

It is important to note that the increasing number of children in inadequate parenting arrangements is neither indicative of the inadequacy or dysfunctionality of the Jamaican family, nor a predictor of future aggression as some popularly argue. The transnational household is, on the contrary, a symbol of the value of the social capital that has been accumulated throughout the region's history in response to crisis. Much depends, as Joy Moncrieffe states, on the quality of the relationships maintained between migrating parents and the children they leave behind.[35] But what appears to be challenging the sustainability of the practice of transnational parenting is the increasing demands that the ongoing economic crisis has placed on the ability of families and communities to maintain the levels of reciprocity and care entailed in these relationships. For as increasing members of family units migrate, children are more likely to be placed in precarious living arrangements where investments in health, care, and the intergenerational transfer of social norms may be scarce or altogether absent.

Studies by the Violence Prevention Alliance, a network of government, nongovernmental, and community-based organizations that work together to prevent violence, found that children were not only victims of violence but increasingly also perpetrators. For example, in 2004, of the 1,471 homicides recorded, 119 were children, of whom 86 percent were boys, but in that same year, 2,003 children were also arrested for committing major crimes such as murder (44) and rape (57).[36] These studies also indicated that while boys were more likely to experience intentional injuries and murder, girls were more likely to have experienced sexual violence.

Social Exclusion in Kingston's Inner Cities

Alongside the erosion of the networks that once maintained the social sustainability of urban households and communities have been widening levels of social polarization in Kingston. Levels of income inequality, for example, grew significantly between the 1980s and 1990s as Jamaicans responded to the withdrawal of the state from the provision of social welfare. Neoliberalization

Table 4. Inequality, GINI index

YEAR	1988	1989	1990	1991	1993	1996	1999	2000	2002	2003	2004
GINI	43	42	42	41	36	40	44	43	48	48	46

Source: World Bank Online Database, 2008.

has intensified the social tensions that historically existed between the upper, and middle classes in Uptown Kingston and the poor, many of whom are concentrated in Kingston's old downtown core. These policies have had the effect of deepening the divide between the highly skilled and entrepreneurial who could successfully maneuver their way around an increasingly export-oriented, private sector–based service economy and the unskilled and less-educated, who were faced with few opportunities outside the informal and grey economy. Among Jamaica's middle classes the outcome has been mixed. While some successfully joined the upper classes in private sector jobs, others fled the country, leaving those who were less successful in a rapidly shrinking public sector starved of personnel and resources. Thus as table 4 indicates, between 1988 and 1993 levels of inequality fell from forty-three to thirty-six, but between 1996 and 2003—as the Jamaican government intensified the pace and scale of liberalization—levels of inequality rose dramatically from forty to forty-eight. With the middle classes fleeing the country, either the very rich or the very poor were left behind. The number of poor people living in Jamaica's urban slums increased significantly from 29.2 percent in 1990 to 35.7 percent by 2001.[37]

Already a society with significant ethnoracial and class divisions originating in slavery and colonial rule, levels of social polarization in Kingston have become the primary threat to the city's sustainability since the 1990s as the heightened levels of deprivation and violence previously contained in Kingston's inner-city slums have spilled out to every part of the city itself. Combined with rising emigration rates, especially among women, and the increasing vulnerability to violence of young people in households where transnational parenting networks have broken down, many of Kingston's poorest residents have turned to the social networks of support and welfare found in garrison communities. A product of the pork barrel politics of the 1950s–1970s, when competing politicians sought geopolitical control by awarding public contracts exclusively to party supporters within their electoral constituencies, particular slums evolved in the 1980s into garrison communities.[38] These are ghettoized urban spaces of poverty and violent political sectarian control. Ruled by self-appointed local gang leaders popularly know as Dons and closed to state regulation or governance, garrison communities became the geographic expression of the long-term retreat of the state from social welfare. Garrison communities suffer from extreme levels of deprivation with limited access to basic urban infrastructure such as sewage systems, electricity, health facilities, and supermarkets. While communities living inside garrison communities might be afforded protection and limited amounts of welfare assistance from Dons, these forms of social and physical security exist within a state of warfare that restricts movement, relationships, and opportunities to participate in everyday life outside these conflict zones. For many young people in garrison communities, home has increasingly become a space of insecurity and loss, because many have lost close family members to the ongoing conflict situation.[39]

For young men already excluded from participation in the formal economy because of their low levels of educational achievement, their social exclusion is compounded by the fact that they are often shunned by prospective employers once it becomes known that they are from garrison communities. With so few opportunities for making a living, it is therefore not surprising that increasing numbers of young men have become workers in the international transshipment of crack cocaine, or as foot soldiers in the ongoing low-intensity war between rival gangs for control of local income-generating activities such as extortion.

The social sustainability of these urban areas is impossible in the current neoliberal environment where social investments in inner-city housing, water, or education have become the preserve of nongovernmental organizations, philanthropic charities, or local dons.

Conclusion

Accounts of the deteriorating urban environment in Jamaica tend to overwhelmingly locate the source of the problem in the highly deprived garrison communities or in homes where parents are physically absent. The state in these accounts is portrayed as a victim, powerless and unable to provide the investments to sustain the levels of social capital in communities. There is some truth to this narrative. Under the burden of debt, the Jamaican government in the 1980s and early 1990s had few options other than to accept the neoliberal policies embedded in the conditional loans they received from the IMF, World Bank, and other development institutions. But the daily abuses of the rights of the urban poor and, in particular, those concentrated in Kingston's urban slums, is also reflection of the ongoing importance of the post-plantation social divisions between Jamaica's upper- and middle-class "brown" elites and its poor- and working-class "black" urban population and the state's scant regard for them. Few in Jamaica are prepared to acknowledge the extent to which the post-plantation social order has remained an important referent in an emerging social structure that is increasingly driven, as Carl Stone notes, by the singular drive to generate income and wealth regardless of the means.[40] Many prefer instead to draw upon the visible presence of black middle-class elites as evidence of the demise of the plantation social order. Yet, what appears to be clear is that Kingston's black elite that emerged as a result of the liberalization of the Jamaican economy have not challenged the racialized class system of the post-plantation period; rather, they have reinforced its boundaries, particularly with regard to the black inner-city poor. The resentment felt by people in Kingston's poorest communities is increasingly finding expression in forms of violence that are extending themselves to the middle classes; but these acts are not significantly different from the structural violence of the neoliberal policies that have made the market, and success within it, the only medium through which social relations are valued.

Since the 1990s increasing levels of attention have turned to the rising levels of violence, particularly among young people in the urban areas. Homicide levels, for example, more than doubled between 1982 and 1997, and in 2006, at a rate of 49 per 100,000 persons, Jamaica ranked as one of the most violent places in the world.[41] The heightened levels of violence have been attributed to the dependence of many, directly and indirectly, on the profits generated from organized crime, and in particular the international transshipment of illicit drugs. Rising violence, however, should also be seen as the long-term outcome of the divestment of the state's responsibility for social welfare and the consequent erosion of the social institutions and conventions that have historically regulated Jamaica's post-plantation social order. Without social cohesion, urban sustainability cannot be achieved, and without a state committed to significant welfare-oriented social investments that narrow the gap between the rich and poor in Jamaica, social cohesion will not be possible.

NOTES

1. World Bank Online Database, http://www.worldbank.org/data/onlinedatabases/onlinedatabases.html.
2. Ibid.
3. Robert Goodland and Herman Daly, Poverty Alleviation Is Essential for Environmental Sustainability, *International Journal of Sustainable Development* 2 (1995): 31–48; Robert Goodland, Sustainability: Human, Social, Economic and Environmental, in *Encyclopedia of Global Environmental Change, Social and Economic dimensions of Global Environmental Change*, ed. Peter Timmerman (New York: John Wiley & Sons, 2002).
4. The regenerative capacities of material and energy resources from the environment.
5. Pierre Bourdieu, *Distinction: A Critique of the Judgement of Taste* (London: Routledge & Kegan Paul, 1984).
6. David Harvey, *Justice, Nature and the Geography of Difference* (Oxford: Blackwell Publishers, 1996); Cindi Katz, Vagabond Capitalism and the Necessity of Social Reproduction, *Antipode* 33:4 (2001): 709–28; Isabella Bakker and Stephen Gill, *Power, Production, and Social Reproduction: Human In/Security in the Global Political Economy* (New York: Palgrave Macmillan, 2003).
7. Katz, Vagabond Capitalism, 709–28.
8. STATIN, *Population Census 2001—Jamaica, Volume 1, Country Report* (Kingston: Statistical Institute of Jamaica, 2002).
9. Patricia Anderson and Michael Witter, Crisis, Adjustment and Social Change: A Case Study of Jamaica, in *The Consequences of Structural Adjustment: A Review of the Jamaican Experience*, ed. Elsie LeFranc (Kingston: Canoe Press, 1994); Colin Clarke, *Decolonizing the Colonial City: Urbanization and Stratification in Kingston, Jamaica* (Oxford: Oxford University Press, 2006).
10. Clarke, *Decolonizing the Colonial City.*
11. Ibid.
12. Survey Says Living Standards Improved in '07, *Jamaica Observer*, January 15, 2009.
13. United Nations, UN Data Statistical Database, 2008, http://data.un.org/Data.aspx?d=MDG&f=seriesRowID%3A711.
14. Carl Stone, *Electoral Behaviour and Public Opinion in Jamaica* (Kingston: Institute of Social and Economic Research, 1973); Evelyn Huber Stephens and John Stephens, *Democratic Socialism in Jamaica: The Political Movement and Social Transformation in Dependent Capitalism* (London: Macmillan, 1986).
15. PIOJ/STATIN, *Jamaica Survey of Living Conditions, 2001* (Kingston: Planning Institute of Jamaica and Statistical Institute of Jamaica, 2002).
16. Helen Safa and Peggy Antrobus, Women and Economic Crisis in the Caribbean, in *Unequal Burden: Economic Crises, Persistent Poverty and Women's Work*, ed. Lourdes Benería and Shelley Feldman (Oxford: Westview Press, 1992), 49–82.
17. World Bank, Jamaica: A Strategy for Growth and Poverty Reduction, Country Economic Memorandum (Washington, DC: World Bank, 1994); Caribbean Group for Cooperation in Economic Development (CGCED), Macroeconomic Volatility, Household Vulnerability, and Institutional and Policy Responses—Report No. 24165-LAC (Washington, DC: World Bank, 2002).
18. Frederic Louat, Margaret Grosh, and Jacques Van Der Gaag, *Welfare Implications of Female Headship in Jamaican Households* (Washington, DC: World Bank, 1993); Lyn Bolles, Kitchens Hit by Priorities: Employed Working-Class Women Confront the IMF, in *Women, Men and the International Division of Labor*, ed. June C. Nash and Maria P. Fernandez-Kelly (Albany: State University of New York Press, 1983); Lyn Bolles, *Sister Jamaica: A Study of Women, Work, and Households in Kingston* (Lanham, MD: University Press of America, 1996); Faye Harrison, Women in Jamaica's Urban Informal Economy: Insights from a Kingston Slum, in *Third World Women and the Politics of Feminism*, ed.

Chandra Mohanty, Ann Russo, and Lourdes Torres (Bloomington: Indiana University Press, 1991); Faye Harrison, The Gendered Politics and Violence of Structural Adjustment, in *Situated Lives: Gender and Culture in Everyday Lives*, ed. Louise Lamphere, Helena Ragoné, and Patricia Zavella (New York: Routledge, 1997).

19. Helen Safa, *The Myth of the Male Breadwinner: Women and Industrialization in the Caribbean, Conflict and Social Change Series* (Boulder: Westview Press, 1995); Safa and Antrobus, Women and Economic Crisis; Bolles, *Sister Jamaica.*
20. PIOJ/STATIN, *Jamaica Survey of Living Conditions.*
21. Ibid.
22. Wendy Webster, *Imagining Home: Gender, "Race" and National Identity, 1945–1964* (London: UCL Press, 1998).
23. World Bank, International Migration, Remittances and the Brain Drain: A Study of 24 Labor-Exporting Countries, Policy Research Working Paper 3069 (Washington, DC: World Bank, 2003).
24. Jenny Burman, Remittance: Or Diasporic Economies of Yearning, *Small Axe* 2 (2002): 49–71.
25. Isa Maria Soto, West Indian Child Fostering and Its Role in Migrant Exchanges, in *Caribbean Life in New York City*, ed. Elsa M. Chaney and Constance R. Sutton (New York: Center for Migration Studies, 1987), 131–49; Karen Fog Olwig, Narratives of the Children Left Behind: Home and Identity in Globalised Caribbean Families, *Journal of Ethnic and Migration Studies* 25 (1999): 267–84.
26. Fog Olwig, Narratives, 297.
27. World Bank, The Road to Sustained Growth in Jamaica, edited by A. W. B. C. S. Report, 2004.
28. Government of Jamaica, Youth in Jamaica: Meeting their Development Needs: National Centre for Youth Development, Ministry of Education, Youth and Culture, Jamaica, 2002.
29. Barry Chevannes, *What We Sow and What We Reap—Problems in the Cultivation of Male Identity in Jamaica* (Kingston: Grace, Kennedy Foundation, 1999).
30. Maureen Samms-Vaughan, M. A. Jackson, and D. E. Ashley, Urban Jamaican Children's Exposure to Community Violence, *West Indian Medical Journal* 54:1 (2005): 14–21; Jyotsna Jha and Fatimah Kelleher, *Boys' Underachievement in Education: An Exploration in Selected Commonwealth Countries* (London: Commonwealth Secretariat and Commonwealth of Learning, 2006).
31. Gareth Manning, Special Educators to Target Illiteracy in Schools, *Gleaner*, April 7, 2007, 1.
32. World Bank, Crime, Violence and Development: Trends, Costs and Policy Options in the Caribbean, in A Joint Report by the United Nations Office on Drugs and Crime and the Latin America and the Caribbean Region of the World Bank (Washington, DC: World Bank, 2007).
33. Audrey M. Pottinger, Children's Experience of Loss by Parental Migration in Inner-City Jamaica, *American Journal of Orthopsychiatry* 75:4 (2005): 485–96.
34. Named after the receptacles used by their parents to send everyday household items to Jamaica, "barrel kids" are defined as children who have one or both parents living abroad who regularly send goods from abroad to meet the material needs of their children and caregivers in Jamaica. Claudette Crawford-Brown, The Impact of Migration on the Rights of Children and Families in the Caribbean, in *Children's Rights Caribbean Realities*, ed. Christine Barrow (Kingston: Ian Randle, 2002); Claudette Crawford-Brown, Beyond the Barrel Children Phenomenon, paper read at Bridgetown, Barbados, August 2003.
35. Joy Moncrieffe, Making and Unmaking the Young "Shotta" [Shooter]: Boundaries and (Counter)-Actions in the "Garrisons," IDS working paper, 2008, 297.
36. Ministry of Health, *Jamaica Injury Surveillance System: Report on Violence Related Injuries 2003* (Kingston: Ministry of Health, 2004).
37. United Nations, UN Data Statistical Database, 2008, http://data.un.org/Data.aspx?d=MDG&f=seriesRowID%3A711.
38. Throughout the 1980s a growing number of young persons within Garrison communities began to earn their livelihoods through Dons, who provided them with access public contracts as well as to incomes through extortion and the export of marijuana. By the 1990s, as dons became more reliant on the lucrative opportunities offered by the transshipment of crack cocaine, and as competition between rival gangs increased, the levels of violence generated by these young recruits not only grew in frequency but also in intensity.
39. Moncrieffe, Making and Unmaking the Young "Shotta," 297.
40. Carl Stone, Values, Norms and Personality Development in Jamaica, *Political Scientist*, March 23, 1992.
41. World Bank, Crime, Violence and Development.

REFERENCES

Anderson, Patricia, and Michael Witter. Crisis, Adjustment and Social Change: A Case Study of Jamaica. In *The Consequences of Structural Adjustment: A Review of the Jamaican Experience*, ed. Elsie LeFranc. Kingston: Canoe Press, 1994.

Antrobus, Peggy. Crisis, Challenge and the Experiences of Caribbean Women. *Caribbean Quarterly* 35:1/2 (1989): 17–28.

Bakker, Isabella, and Stephen Gill. *Power, Production, and Social Reproduction: Human In/Security in the Global Political Economy.* New York: Palgrave Macmillan, 2003.

Bolles, Lyn. Kitchens Hit by Priorities: Employed Working-Class Women Confront the IMF. In *Women, Men and the International Division of Labor*, ed. June C. Nash and Maria P. Fernandez-Kelly. Albany: State University of New York Press, 1983.

———. *Sister Jamaica: A Study of Women, Work, and Households in Kingston.* Lanham, MD: University Press of America, 1996.

Bourdieu, Pierre. *Distinction: A Critique of the Judgement of Taste.* London: Routledge & Kegan Paul, 1984.

Burman, Jenny. Remittance: Or Diasporic Economies of Yearning. *Small Axe* 2 (2002): 49–71.

Caribbean Group for Cooperation in Economic Development (CGCED). Macroeconomic Volatility. Household Vulnerability, and Institutional and Policy Responses—Report No. 24165-LAC (Washington, DC: World Bank, 2002).

Chevannes, Barry. *What We Sow and What We Reap—Problems in the Cultivation of Male Identity in Jamaica.* Kingston, Jamaica: Grace, Kennedy Foundation, 1999.

Clarke, Colin. *Decolonizing the Colonial City: Urbanization and Stratification in Kingston, Jamaica.* Oxford: Oxford University Press, 2006.

———. *Kingston, Jamaica: Urban Development and Social Change 1692–1962.* Berkeley: University of California, 1975.

Crawford-Brown, Claudette. Beyond the Barrel Children Phenomenon. Paper read at Bridgetown, Barbados. August 2003.

———. The Impact of Migration on the Rights of Children and Families in the Caribbean. In *Children's Rights Caribbean Realities*, ed. Christine Barrow. Kingston, Jamaica: Ian Randle, 2002.

Fog Olwig, Karen. Narratives of the Children Left Behind: Home and Identity in Globalised Caribbean Families. *Journal of Ethnic and Migration Studies* 25 (1999): 267–84.

Goodland, Robert. Sustainability: Human, Social, Economic and Environmental. In *Encyclopedia of Global Environmental Change, Social and Economic Dimensions of Global Environmental Change*, ed. Peter Timmerman. New York: John Wiley & Sons, 2002.

Goodland, Robert, and Herman Daly. Poverty Alleviation Is Essential for Environmental Sustainability. *International Journal of Sustainable Development* 2 (1995): 31–48.

Gordon, Derek, Patricia Anderson, and Don Robotham. Jamaica: Urbanization during the Years of Crisis. In *The Urban Caribbean: Transition to the New Global Economy*, ed. Alejandro Portes, Carlos Dore, and Patricia L. Cabral. London: Johns Hopkins University Press, 1997.

Government of Jamaica. Youth in Jamaica: Meeting their Development Needs: National Centre for Youth Development, Ministry of Education, Youth and Culture, Jamaica, 2002.

Harrison, Faye. The Gendered Politics and Violence of Structural Adjustment. In *Situated Lives: Gender and Culture in Everyday Lives*, ed. Louise Lamphere, Helena Ragoné, and Patricia Zavella. New York: Routledge, 1997.

———. Women in Jamaica's Urban Informal Economy: Insights from a Kingston Slum. In *Third World Women and the Politics of Feminism*, ed. Chandra Mohanty, Ann Russo, and Lourdes Torres. Bloomington: Indiana University Press, 1991.

Harvey, David. *Justice, Nature and the Geography of Difference.* Oxford: Blackwell Publishers, 1996.

Huber Stephens, Evelyn, and John Stephens. *Democratic Socialism in Jamaica: The Political Movement and Social Transformation in Dependent Capitalism.* London: Macmillan, 1986.

Inter-American Development Bank. *Sending Money Home: Remittance to Latin America and the Caribbean.* Washington, DC: IDB, 2004.

Jamaica Observer. Survey Says Living Standards Improved in '07. January 15, 2009.

Jha, Jyotsna, and Fatimah Kelleher. *Boys' Underachievement in Education an Exploration in Selected Commonwealth Countries.* London: Commonwealth Secretariat and Commonwealth of Learning, 2006.

Katz, Cindi. Vagabond Capitalism and the Necessity of Social Reproduction. *Antipode* 33:4 (2001): 709–28.

Louat, Frederic, Margaret Grosh, and Jacques Van Der Gaag. *Welfare Implications of Female Headship in Jamaican Households.* Washington, DC: World Bank, 1993.

Manning, Gareth. Special Educators to Target Illiteracy in

Schools. *Gleaner,* April 7, 2007: 1.

Ministry of Health. *Jamaica Injury Surveillance System: Report on Violence Related Injuries 2003.* Kingston, Jamaica: Ministry of Health, 2004.

Mitchell, Kathryn, Sallie Marston, and Cindi Katz. Introduction: Life's Work: An Introduction, Review and Critique. *Antipode* 35:3 (2003): 415–42.

Moncrieffe, Joy. Making and Unmaking the Young "Shotta" [Shooter]: Boundaries and (Counter)- Actions in the "Garrisons." IDS working paper, 2008.

Peterson, V. Spike. *A Critical Rewriting of Global Political Economy: Integrating Productive, Reproductive and Virtual Economies.* New York: Routledge, 2003.

PIOJ/STATIN. *Jamaica Survey of Living Conditions 1999* Kingston: Planning Institute of Jamaica and Statistical Institute of Jamaica, 2000.

———. *Jamaica Survey of Living Conditions 2001.* Kingston: Planning Institute of Jamaica and Statistical Institute of Jamaica, 2002.

Pottinger, Audrey M. Children's Experience of Loss by Parental Migration in Inner-City Jamaica. *American Journal of Orthopsychiatry* 75:4 (2005): 485–96.

Safa, Helen. *The Myth of the Male Breadwinner: Women and Industrialization in the Caribbean, Conflict and Social Change Series.* Boulder: Westview Press, 1995.

Safa, Helen, and Peggy Antrobus. Women and Economic Crisis in the Caribbean. In *Unequal Burden: Economic Crises, Persistent Poverty and Women's Work,* ed. Lourdes Benería and Shelley Feldman, 49–82. Oxford: Westview Press, 1992.

Samms-Vaughan, Maureen, Maria A. Jackson, and Deanna E. Ashley. Urban Jamaican Children's Exposure to Community Violence. *West Indian Medical Journal* 54:1 (2005): 14–21.

Soto, Isa Maria. West Indian Child Fostering and Its Role in Migrant Exchanges. In *Caribbean Life in New York City,* ed. Elsa M. Chaney and Constance R. Sutton, 131–49. New York: Center for Migration Studies of New York, 1987.

STATIN. *Population Census 2001—Jamaica, Volume 1 Country Report.* Kingston: Statistical Institute of Jamaica, 2002.

Stone, Carl. *Electoral Behaviour and Public Opinion in Jamaica.* Kingston: Institute of Social and Economic Research, 1973.

———. Values, Norms and Personality Development in Jamaica. *Political Scientist,* March 23, 1992.

U.S. Department of Homeland Security. *Yearbook of Immigration Statistics: 2004.* Washington, DC: U.S. Department of Homeland Security, Office of Immigration Statistics, 2006.

United Nations. UN Data Statistical Database. 2008. http://data.un.org/Data.aspx?d=MDG&f=seriesRowID%3A711.

United Nations/Habitat. 2003. The Challenge of Slums—Global Report on Human Settlements 2003. London: Earthscan.

Webster, Wendy. *Imagining Home: Gender, "Race" and National Identity, 1945–1964.* London: UCL Press, 1998.

World Bank. Crime, Violence and Development: Trends, Costs and Policy Options in the Caribbean. In A Joint Report by the United Nations Office on Drugs and Crime and the Latin America and the Caribbean Region of the World Bank Washington, DC: World Bank, 2007.

———. International Migration, Remittances and the Brain Drain. A Study of 24 Labor-Exporting Countries. Policy Research Working Paper 3069. Washington, DC: World Bank, 2003.

———. Jamaica: A Strategy for Growth and Poverty Reduction, Country Economic Memorandum. Washington, DC: World Bank, 1994.

———. The Road to Sustained Growth in Jamaica. Washington, DC: World Bank, 2004.

———. World Bank Online Database. 2008. http://www.worldbank.org/data/onlinedatabases/onlinedatabases.

■ VICTORIA BASOLO

Housing and Urban Sustainability

A LOS ANGELES CASE STUDY

Housing plays a central role in urbanization and urban sustainability in the United States. Population growth in and migration to urbanized areas is accompanied by demand for housing. The response to this demand, housing development, in turn consumes increasingly more land, spurring urbanization and fostering sprawling development patterns. With over fifty years of growth, mass housing production, and a cultural propensity for consumptive behavior, the United States serves as an exemplary case through which to examine urbanization and the featured role of housing within this larger process. This case also reveals the effects of decisions by housing producers, consumers, and regulators on urban form, the environment, and social structure and thus provides knowledge for the formulation of strategies to achieve urban sustainability.

Producers and consumers of housing in the United States have contributed to a changing urban form. The traditional form, with urban (central city) and suburban living environments, has given way to exurbs and edgeless cities. Urban sprawl—the seemingly unrestricted outward movement of new development and people from traditional urban cores to the hinterlands—spawned these new types of cities and has been defended as the market expression of individual choice; conversely, it has been condemned as a wasteful and inefficient pattern of development.[1]

Demand for housing results from population increase, whether this increase is due to natural change (births in existing population), immigration, or a combination of both. Urbanization, therefore, reflects to some extent consumers' demand for housing. This demand, as discussed later in the chapter, is shaped in the United States by both a culture of consumption and a preference for homeownership and single-family detached housing.

Housing production was not simply a response to demand. The urbanization of the United States, with its attendant changing urban form, was affected by private sector production of housing and public policies supporting it. In their practices and policies, the real estate development industry and government significantly influenced the locations and types of housing available to consumers. Thus, understanding the relationship between housing and urbanization (examining in particular the cultural norms, private practices, and public policies influencing housing) is critical to thinking about urban sustainability.

In this chapter, I discuss the importance of housing to urban sustainability. In doing so, I argue that cultural norms, associated with the emergence of mass consumption in the United States, coincided with, and was fostered by, private practices and public policies related to housing; and that these forces and mechanisms contributed to a process of urbanization that has numerous implications for urban sustainability. The chapter concludes with some thoughts about promoting urban sustainability by rethinking governmental policies toward housing.

The Centrality of Housing to Urban Sustainability

Census 2000 reported that 79 percent of the total U.S. population was living in urbanized areas or urban clusters. Housing in urban areas is linked to spatial structure, transportation, environmental issues, social inequalities, and regional economies; therefore, housing is vital to the functioning and outcomes of urban regions. The linkages within urban areas, however, are not simple relationships; rather, they are so interconnected that market-oriented actions and public policies in one domain can trigger effects in one or more other domains. I argue that, within this complex environment, housing is central to urban sustainability; such a claim, of course, requires further explanation.[2]

The importance of housing in the United States can be observed at multiple levels of analysis. First, it is part (as well as a determinant) of the physical, social, and economic structure of regions; it also has direct and indirect implications for regional environments. It is at this scale that housing is embedded in a web of regional relationships. Furthermore, housing reflects and influences individuals' social statuses, preferences, and feelings of security, life satisfaction, and belonging.[3] Finally, through industries such as construction and lending, housing plays a role in macroeconomic conditions.[4] Thus, housing directly impacts regional economies through employment; it can also have indirect and reciprocative effects on urbanized regions through impacts on the national economy and the financial sector.

The potential impacts of housing on regions and their populations support the argument that housing is central to urban regions and their sustainability. To make such a claim, however, one must provide a definition of urban sustainability. "Sustainability" has numerous definitions; in defining the concept, much of the emphasis has been on the natural environment. Increasingly, however, the concept is used to examine the built environment, including cities and regions, transportation, and housing.[5] In general, the various definitions of sustainability reflect a philosophy concerned with preservation and protection of natural environments for future generations, and this perspective is associated with goals that include renewable resources, appropriate technologies, and overall balance.[6] These larger concepts have been employed in the area of housing as well. For example, the use of construction technologies that favor renewable resources or increase energy efficiency are an increasingly important area of research and practice.[7] While "green" housing exemplifies sustainability concepts, it applies to sustainability in general rather than specifically in an urban context. To understand *urban* sustainability as a concept, one must recognize the interdependence of the processes and outcomes occurring within urbanized regions (the urban). Moreover, achieving urban sustainability requires fostering structural arrangements that promote the well-being of urbanized regions and their inhabitants both now and in the future (sustainability).

The connections among urban activities, as well as the manner in which housing has always been inextricably tangled in a web of regional relationships, are evident in the effects of the private practices and public policies related to housing in the United States. These effects, of course, have been cumulative and coupled with changing cultural norms. Therefore, to understand the centrality of housing to urban sustainability requires a historical perspective.

In the next section, I consider both the evolution of private practices and public policies related to housing and the ways these activities interacted with changing cultural norms over time. While this historical perspective is critical to understanding the position of housing in a discussion of urban sustainability, it also provides insights about the processes that have shaped housing and urbanized environments more generally. These processes, which still operate today, are useful in thinking about urban sustainability and strategies to support this goal.

Private Practices, Public Policies, and Changing Cultural Norms

The private and public sectors influenced the development of cities in the United States. Housing, employment, and services in U.S. cities were within relatively short distances of each other in the nineteenth century and into the first part of the twentieth century. Outward growth from the city center tended to follow streetcars lines. The first streetcars were powered by horses and thus had limited range; however, the advent of the electric streetcar expanded service to more distant locations. "Streetcar suburbs" appeared in many regions (including areas around Boston, Los Angeles, Chicago, and New York) and foreshadowed the development patterns of future decades. Despite the influence of streetcars, however, urban development remained relatively compact.[8]

The private sector dominated the provision of housing in the late nineteenth and early twentieth century, although charitable organizations and the public sector responded in limited ways to the housing needs and conditions of the poor. Renting was the most common form of tenure during this period. In many cities, very low-income renters, often immigrants, occupied privately-owned, tenement housing. Overcrowding and the poor physical conditions of this type of housing raised concerns among social reformers and legislators. As a result, laws were passed to ensure a minimum room size and some level of ventilation and sanitation in tenements, and the separation of land uses (particularly residential from noxious uses such as slaughterhouses) became an increasingly common practice.[9] The governmental regulation of land use gained official legitimacy in 1926, and local zoning incrementally expanded thereafter.[10]

The role of government in housing provision changed dramatically during the 1930s when the U.S. economy sank into depression. Public solutions to economic problems gained prominence during this era. Due to pressure from urban leadership and a desire to sustain employment levels, President Franklin Roosevelt created a slew of development initiatives, including housing programs serving renters and owners.[11]

This period also witnessed the establishment of a financial infrastructure to support homeownership. The federal government created a number of permanent institutions, including the Federal Housing Administration (FHA) in 1934. FHA's purpose was to insure mortgages and reduce risk for investors.[12] It was followed by the creation of the Federal National Mortgage Association (FNMA) in 1938. FNMA purchased insured mortgages from lenders, reducing the risk for banks and freeing funds for more loans.[13]

These new institutions supporting homeownership were accompanied by additional policies. Homes had previously been owned outright or had short repayment periods, often five years, but with support of government policy, the thirty-year amortized mortgage loan was born and quickly established as the standard in mortgage lending. The federal income tax code also helped by allowing for deduction of all types of interest, including interest on mortgage loans. This tax policy effectively reduces the cost of ownership housing for households with mortgages.[14]

Government policies during the 1930s institutionalized public support for both rental and ownership housing. In the decades that followed, the federal government initiated many new housing programs and supported and modified existing ones. At the same time, the United States experienced tremendous social changes that significantly affected urban housing and patterns of urban development. The development of the interstate highway system provided infrastructure for the growth outward from central cities; the landmark ruling in *Brown v. Board of Education* fostered racial desegregation and "white flight" from cities; and urban renewal replaced older sections of cities and displaced many poor urban residents.[15]

The private provision of housing was fueled in the postwar era by economic growth and prosperity. Within this context, the demand for homeownership exploded as households sought more living space and an outward expression of their fortunes. Robert Fogelson, an urban historian, recalls the reason his parents sought a home in the suburbs during the 1950s: "they were unhappy with the apartment house in the West Bronx into which they had moved during the Great Depression. . . . I later learned that they found their two-bedroom apartment too small to raise three boys—though it was much bigger than the Manhattan tenements in which their parents had raised larger families."[16]Another historian, Lizabeth Cohen, writing about the same period, offers a harsher recollection of her parents' "serial acquisition of more expensive homes" and the growth of suburbia, or, as she characterizes it, "the landscape of mass consumption."[17]

The emerging culture of consumption and the growth of the middle class clearly supported the production of suburban housing in the postwar period. Subdivisions sprang up in new suburbs throughout the United States, with over 12 million units added to the housing stock between 1950 and 1960. Another 57 million housing units, a near 100 percent increase, were added by the end of the millennium.[18]

The latter half of the twentieth century was marked by growth and change in development patterns. Central cities deteriorated as middle-class households moved in large numbers to the suburbs, leaving a concentration of poor minorities behind. Even minorities within reach of suburban housing opportunities faced racial discrimination, which reduced their access to the suburbs. When minorities did move out of the central cities, many found themselves in mature, "inner-ring" suburbs: areas of older housing and lower quality that were experiencing decline similar to that of central cities.[19]

PHOTOGRAPH BY SUSAN WELSH

Figure 1. Mature Los Angeles suburban neighborhood.

The federal role in housing continued as suburbanization progressed, but its focus shifted over the decades. In the 1980s and after, rental subsidies were favored over the production of publicly-owned units. Meanwhile, federal tax policies were altered, making multifamily housing less attractive as an investment; this resulted in a harrowing drop in the market production of this type of housing. Federal policies during this period promoted homeownership, even for low-income households.[20] A major initiative to support the production of multifamily rental housing, the Low-Income Housing Tax Credit (LIHTC), was created as a temporary program in 1986. The purpose of the program was to encourage private capital investment in low-income housing.[21] The LIHTC was subsequently made permanent, with over 1.5 million units produced between 1987 and 2005.[22]

As a result of these changes to federal policy, current housing assistance generally benefits two subpopulations: very low-income households (with subsidized rental housing) and households with sufficient incomes and credit histories to qualify for mortgages (with tax and other homeownership subsidies). Moreover, the federal government increasingly has withdrawn from its leadership role in housing policy, looking to private and nonprofit developers as well as states and localities to address lower-income housing needs.[23] Devolution in housing policy, however, has not resulted in major policy change. Similar to federal policymakers, state and local government leaders tend to show a preference for homeownership in their public statements and in their financial support. This preference is based on beliefs about the societal and individual benefits of homeownership, which range from improved community participation to wealth accumulation.[24]

Homeownership also received a boost from the finance industry over the last thirty years. The proliferation of loan products, such as interest-only loans and adjustable rate mortgages, made it easier for more households to qualify for mortgage loans and thus created demand for ownership housing. While looser credit provided access for more lower-income households to enter the ownership market, it also allowed some middle-class borrowers to eschew smaller homes closer to regional centers for larger homes in outlying areas. This demand for larger homes contributed to the growth of exurban communities, which often exhibit the extremes of consumptive culture. In writing about Temecula, California, an exurban community about ninety minutes from Los Angeles, journalist Scott Gold observes: "Atop onion fields and grazing pastures, they've built a parade of 4,000- and 5,000-square-foot houses—palaces many of them, with turrets and faux backyard grottoes, with six-car garages and children's playrooms larger than the average Manhattan apartment."[25] Clearly, in the early part of the twenty-first century, homeownership, including "conspicuous consumption" of housing, was deeply embedded in American culture and contributed to sprawling urbanization across the nation.

The brief history provided here is intended to place housing in context; that is, part of a process of urbanization that was spurred by private and public actions interacting with changing cultural norms. In the following section, I examine the effects of past and present practices, policies, and cultural norms as they relate to housing, urbanization, and urban sustainability.

The Effects of Private and Public Actions and Changing Cultural Norms

After World War II, private development responded to urban growth with mass construction of detached, single-family housing on wide tracts of cheaper land beyond central cities. Public policies encouraged this form of urbanization through highway development and the support of homeownership. Private and public actions not only created new development patterns; they also helped to stoke and feed an emerging culture of consumption and shaped norms, especially in terms of tenure. Figure 2 shows the homeownership rate in the United States for 1900 through 2000. In 1940, following the Depression, the national homeownership rate was at a low of 43.6 percent. By 1950 the homeownership rate had increased by almost 12 percentage points, making the country a majority homeowner nation for the first time. This majority continued to grow, and by 2000 the homeownership rate reached 66.2 percent.

The cultural propensity for homeownership was cultivated by a history of linking certain rights with land ownership, individuals' desires for privacy, control, community, and, more generally, the good life.[26] However, assistance from government subsidies (including tax deductions) and the establishment of a financing infrastructure (specifically the secondary market) catalyzed homeownership and ensured it would be the dominant form of tenure. In the process, housing became more of a commodity and more associated with economic advantages.[27]

Homeownership's economic advantages through tax deductions are significant. In 2007, according to the Office of Management and Budget, over $79.9 billion in tax expenditures resulted from the mortgage interest deduction for owner-occupied housing.[28] The notion of homeownership as a commodity is best captured by the belief that it is a good investment for building wealth. In other words, homeowners invest in a home and expect a substantial return through increasing housing prices.

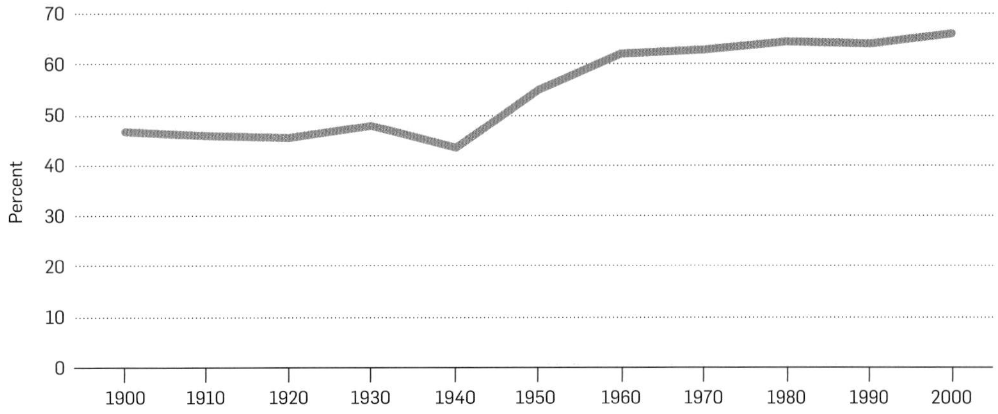

Figure 2. Homeownership rate, United States, 1900–2000.

Source: U.S. Census Bureau, Census of Housing (Washington, DC: U.S. Census Bureau, Housing and Household Economic Statistics Division, 2011).

This tendency to think of ownership as an investment vehicle is revealed in data from a 2007 survey of residents in both Miami-Dade County, Florida, and Los Angeles County, California. As shown in table 1, over 50 percent of the respondents in both areas identified financial investment as the main reason to own a home. These findings are consistent with a 2003 representative national sample of U.S. adults that found 61 percent of the respondents thought housing was a safe investment. Ironically, economist Robert Shiller, using housing sales price data for the United States from 1890 to 2004 (with the exception of two boom periods immediately after World War II and the late 1990s) shows, "real home prices overall have been mostly flat or declining." Nevertheless, homeowners and potential homeowners view housing as an important investment.[29]

Whether real or imagined, the benefits attributed to homeownership have shaped tenure choices. Homeownership undeniably has long been the preference of most households. In 2003, with the homeownership rate topping 68 percent, a representative sample survey of U.S. adults revealed that 57 percent of renters reported that they were likely to buy a home within three years.[30] Although these responses proved overly optimistic, they are illustrative of the lure of homeownership in the United States. By default, renting (especially in multifamily developments) is the less attractive form of tenure.

Table 1. Main reason for choosing to own a home

	LOS ANGELES COUNTY		MIAMI-DADE COUNTY	
	NUMBER	PERCENTAGE	NUMBER	PERCENTAGE
Good financial investment	171	56.3	177	52.4
Control of own living space	67	22.0	84	24.8
Sense of community	12	3.9	18	5.3
Other	54	17.8	59	17.5
Total	**304**	**100.0**	**338**	**100.0**

Federal tax policies have not only supported ownership housing; they have also affected the production of multifamily rental units. The Tax Reform Act of 1986 contained a number of provisions that made multifamily rental housing less attractive to investors. As Kent Colton and Kate Collignon note, earlier tax policies "resulted in the rental housing market becoming overbuilt, largely among higher end units."[31] Changing the tax code was one response to this problem, but the effects were profound and arguably too severe. Figure 3 shows the number of units by type authorized by building permits from 1980 to 2000. Clearly, in absolute numbers and relative to single-family units, far fewer multifamily units have been produced since the tax policy change. In 1983, under the old tax law, the ratio of authorized multifamily to single-family units was 0.831 to 1.0. By 1993, this ratio had fallen to 0.215 to 1.0 and remained relatively low in 2000 at 0.329 to 1.0.

The federal government significantly influenced tenure choice and development patterns, but policies at the local level also supported ownership and sprawling single-family development. The application of zoning evolved from earlier regulations that separated uses such as slaughterhouses from residential uses to dividing types of housing by density. It became standard to have both a single-family zoning designation and a multifamily designation in local zoning codes. This separation of living spaces was consistent with the vaunted status of detached, single-family ownership housing as a cultural icon—a symbol of success and status to be distinguished from other housing types and renting.

The extension in scope and proliferation of zoning interacted with the market propensity for outward development to promote sprawl. Zoning also became a force unto itself, creating rigidity in local government approaches to development planning. In his book *Zoned Out,* Jonathan Levine argues that single-family zones are hallowed ground in U.S. municipalities; his empirical evidence indicates that local land-use regulations are a barrier to developers producing more compact development.[32]

The intersection and interactions of private practices, public policies, and a cultural propensity for homeownership ensured the emergence and growth of the suburbs. The preference for detached, single-family homes and suburban homeownership, of course, implicitly assumes acceptance of a tradeoff: continued outward growth or sprawl for increased homeownership opportunities.[33] This tradeoff has been acceptable thanks to the mass consumption culture of the United States. However, this tradeoff may not be considered advantageous if the analysis accounts for the social, economic, and environmental consequences associated with it.

The private and public activities affecting housing and urbanization in the United States, and the post–World War II shift in cultural norms, have contributed to significant social consequences. Many central cities have experienced population and job losses, as well as segregation of minorities in poor, inner-city neighborhoods.[34] These conditions have resulted in limited (programmatically and geographically) public programs to increase the opportunities for the poor and minorities by assisting their mobility from "bad" inner-city neighborhoods to "good" (sometimes suburban) neighborhoods.[35] However, the consequences of long-term private practices and public policies are not easily rectified with limited programs. Thus, the attendant social problems persist without sufficient attention to the well-being of an entire subset of urban residents.

Economic impacts from the interaction of private practices, public policies, and changing cultural norms related to housing and urbanization are numerous. First, some central cities

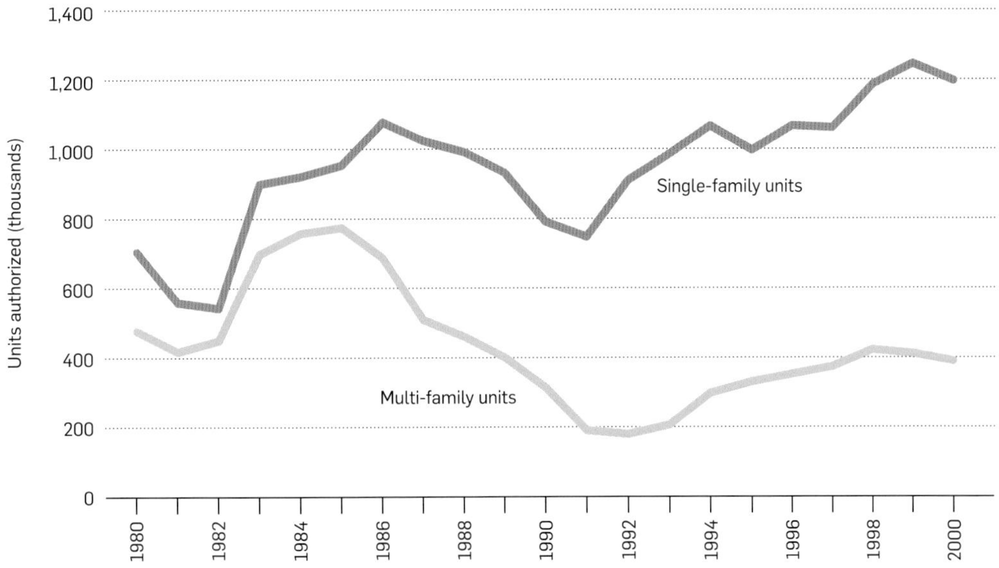

Figure 3. Residential units authorized by type, United States, 1980–2000.

Source: U.S. Census Bureau, Building Permits Survey (Washington, DC: U.S. Census Bureau, 2008).

experiencing population and job losses were deprived of their revenue base, sending them into fiscal crisis.[36] Second, the horizontal development pattern resulted in longer commute times and loss of productive hours. Between 1980 and 2000, the average travel time to work in the United States increased; almost 53 million hours were devoted to commuting in 2000.[37] Third, the lack of desirable and affordable housing (ownership and rental) within reasonable distances of job centers is creating what is labeled a workforce housing crisis in many urbanized regions.[38]

The lack of workforce housing is increasingly problematic for employers and employees. The high cost of housing in many regions leaves employees with limited alternatives. They can ask for higher wages, leave the area for employment elsewhere, commute long distances between home and work, or share housing with others. The first two alternatives affect the employers and could prompt them to relocate their businesses to areas with affordable housing for their employees. The third alternative affects employees and employers: employees lose productive hours, often with their families, and employers may experience a stressed and fatigued workforce. The fourth alternative can lead to overcrowding and thus is unattractive for workers with families.

The threat of losing the labor pool (and hence losing employers) due to the unavailability of affordable housing is a serious problem for some regional economies and the cities within these regions. Currently, the dialogue about workforce housing tends to focus on the lack of affordable housing for professions such as teachers, fire and police personnel, and nurses, and it increasingly includes discussion about strategies to house these workers.[39] However, equally important, workforce housing is needed for the low-wage workers employed in the hospitality, retail, and other service industries. Clearly, these workforce housing needs, as well as city fiscal concerns and loss of productive hours to commuting, threaten the welfare of regional economies and their residents.

The loss of employees and employers are not the only local government fiscal concern associated with sprawling development. As Robert Burchell, Anthony Downs, Sahan Mukherji, and Barbara McCann observe: "A fundamental characteristic of sprawl is that two sets of infrastructure are being created that are underused: the ones that Americans have been running away from (cities and older developed suburbs) and the one they never catch up with (the new sprawling development)."[40] These authors emphasize the costs associated with improving aging infrastructure and the high costs of extending infrastructure. They note infrastructure costs are increasing and consuming a larger proportion of city budgets. They also find that these costs are presenting significant challenges to city managers.

In addition to fiscal costs, sprawling housing development spurred by the interaction of cultural norms and private and public actions has direct and indirect effects on the natural environment.[41] A direct effect is the loss of hinterlands, in many cases land suited to agriculture, which have been consumed by the outward movement of development. In fact, the average acreage per housing unit has increased, and land consumption through settlement of exurban areas at lower densities has been tremendous. As Theobald comments: "In 2000 roughly 38 million acres were settled at urban densities, and nearly ten times that much land was settled at rates from low, exurban density (as low as one house per forty acres) to higher rates (up to one per acre)."[42] The loss of land to housing development has consequences for agricultural output. In a study of the reduction of net primary productivity (a measure of photosynthetic production), researchers found that the annual conversion of agricultural land to urban uses in the United States resulted in a loss of "food products capable of satisfying the caloric needs of 16.5 million people or about 6 percent of the U.S. population."[43]

A major indirect effect of suburban sprawl is pollution stemming from vehicle emissions. Increased commuting contributes to higher levels of emissions, which affect air quality, aquatic sediment, and climate change.[44] The health risk of pollutants from vehicles and other sources of air emissions associated with population growth raise significant concerns. For example, using the Health Index (HI), where a value exceeding 1 indicates the potential for adverse health effects, researchers estimate an increase in "the number of Americans with a respiratory HI for mobile source air toxics above one, from 250 million in 1999 to 273 million in 2030."[45] Sprawling development patterns reliant on gasoline-powered vehicles for commuting clearly contribute to poorer air quality. Furthermore, this degradation of air quality, and the environment more generally, creates externalities for all people living in the affected area. In other words, air pollution generated by commuters from distant suburbs is an uncompensated cost to everyone in the affected region.

In some areas of the country, urban sprawl slowed in 2006–2008 as housing construction waned or ceased completely. A combination of mortgage products with escalating interest rates, conspicuous consumption of homes, and overheated housing markets contributed to a mortgage foreclosure crisis that saw foreclosures jump 53 percent between 2006 and 2007, and a high volume of foreclosures continued through 2011.[46] This crisis has been significant enough to seriously affect the national economy (and global economy), but the physical evidence is visible in many communities. In one exurban community outside Los Angles, an observer noted vacant homes with faux lawns (unwatered yards, painted green, to maintain an illusion) and untended swimming pools becoming mosquito breeding ponds.[47]

The foreclosure crisis will not end urban sprawl. Comments from economists, builders, policymakers, and the general public characterize current conditions as a market correction, cyclical trough, or similar temporary condition with the presumption that conditions will return to normal in time. Thus, as the housing industry and the economy overall recovers from the current downturn, it can be expected that sprawling development will continue.

The social, economic, and environmental consequences of over five decades of suburban development and promotion of homeownership are alarming. Combined, these two forces and a cultural norm favoring single-family homeownership in the United States have produced deteriorating urban environments. Sprawling regions work against the interdependence of urban activities, such as housing, transportation, and the economy. Sprawl taxes the regional system with negative externalities that fail to promote the well-being of regions and their populations. In the next section, I use the Los Angeles region as an illustrative example of an unsustainable development pattern and discuss the externalities arising from private and public practices and changing cultural norms.

Los Angeles: The Unsustainable Region?

The Los Angeles region provides a fascinating example of the processes described in previous sections, and its development has captivated many urban scholars from across disciplines. In writing about Los Angeles, historian Scott Bottles comments, "Los Angeles' close association with the automobile and its sprawling urban form make it a natural case study of twentieth-century urban development."[48] One variable shaping the city's decentralized urban form, and enforcing its close association with the car, was its relatively late development within the U.S. urban context. In 1900, for instance, the city of Los Angeles had a population of only 102,479, which over the next three decades, by the 1930 census, increased to some 1.24 million.[49] Los Angeles, as a result, was largely developed after the introduction of the automobile. The local reliance on the car (see table 2) enabled a new level of mobility and facilitated the low-density outward expansion of the city, which became characterized largely by single-family homes. In 1930, Los Angeles' single-family housing stock made up 93.9 percent of the city's housing. In comparison, 49.5 percent of Boston's housing stock consisted of single-family homes, and in Chicago and New York the figures were 52 and 52.8 percent.[50]

Table 2. Residents per automobile

	UNITED STATES	LOS ANGELES	CHICAGO
1915	43.1	8.2	61.0
1920	13.1	3.6	30.0
1925	6.6	1.8	11.0
1930	5.3	1.5	8.0
1935	5.6	1.6	—
1940	4.8	1.4	—

Source: Scott Bottles, *Los Angeles and the Automobile: The Making of the Modern City* (Berkeley: University of California Press, 1987).

It was not only that the city was being built outward at low densities, but increasingly both residents and businesses began leaving the city of Los Angeles for its suburbs. This impacted the city's urban form; local travel patterns; the material, land, and energy consumption of the area; as well as regional pollution emissions. As maintained by Peter Hall: "Progressively, Los Angeles emptied itself out: not merely residences, but also jobs, left the central business district and the industrial zone immediately around it. By the late 1930s there was a traffic pattern never before seen in any city: one of multiple origins and multiple destinations and multiple travel corridors, the product but also the generator of an automobile-dependent economy and society."[51]

Urban scholars describe the Los Angeles' urban form as low density and polycentric (consisting of multiple subcenters of employment activity); however, some researchers challenge these characterizations.[52] Part of the disagreement in the urban literature about the Los Angeles area is the result of the differences in measures of density and the geographic scope of different studies.

Local Economic Profile: Foundations of Development

It has been argued that variables such as natural features and climate (sunshine, mountains, coast, and ocean), soil quality, a seaport, effective boosterism, and proximity to Mexico (which allowed for a quick escape for those engaged in clandestine activity) were some of the early variables that facilitated the economic growth of Los Angeles. By the 1920s the city had been developing around petroleum and movie production. Early aircraft manufacturing was also evident in the area, driven by local entrepreneurs such as Douglas, Loughhead (later renamed Lockheed), and Northrup.[53] By the 1940s Los Angeles also became a concentration point of Fordist assembly-line industries, including consumer durables, steel, glass, tires, and automobile assembly. During the post–World War II economic boom, these industries were developing rapidly and facilitating the growth of the region.

During the 1970s, the region's fortunes in industrial production changed, and Los Angeles experienced a process of deindustrialization that was occurring across the United States. Traditional Fordist industries that the region had relied upon during the 1950s and 1960s almost completely disappeared, decimating the area's working-class neighborhoods. During this period of deindustrialization, however, this loss in the region's traditional industries was being countered with a growth in services, finance, insurance, and real estate. In fact, the Los Angeles region would proceed to develop into its current status as a major metropolitan financial and business center, a service industry–hub for not only the western United States but also the Pacific Rim.

In addition, during the early- to mid-1980s, the Los Angeles area began to experience a reindustrialization, which was particularly evident in two industries. The first was in high-tech production, led by aerospace and defense electronics, and the second was in labor-intensive craft-based industries, which included clothing, jewelry, leather working, motion pictures, and music production. Into the twenty-first century, the city had firmly established a "legendary quality" in the fashion and entertainment industries that few global cities paralleled.[54]

The economic robustness of the region was key in accommodating both the rapid population growth and existing urban development patterns. In addition, the character of local development was also heavily influenced by globalization and increasing global migration into the region, shaping the Los Angeles area into a cosmopolitan metropolis.

CARTOGRAPHY BY ELLEN WHITE

Figure 4. Five-county Los Angeles region.

Local Development, Housing, and Urban Form

In this section, I present a number of indicators of growth and change in the region with attention to housing development and differences among the counties within the region. For convenience, I define the region as consisting of the counties of Los Angeles, Ventura, Orange, San Bernardino, and Riverside. (see fig.4).

The entire five-county region encompasses an area of over 33,950 square miles and is home to over 16 million people, making it one of the largest urban areas in the United States. Growth in terms of population and housing, as well as horizontal growth outward from the historical center of the region, the city of Los Angeles, is a dominant characteristic of the region.

The area is generally considered diverse in terms of race and ethnicity. Of the five counties in the region, Los Angeles County clearly is the most racially and ethnically diverse (see the appendix for percentages by race and Hispanic/Latino ethnicity for 1990 and 2000).[55] As the older county containing the central city and early suburbs, it represents a demographic pattern consistent with the "white flight" phenomenon. However, the region's demographic picture is much more complex for a number of reasons, including substantial immigration of people from Latin America and Asia. From 1990 to 2000, the proportion of the white population decreased in all five counties, the percentage of African Americans decreased in the counties of Los Angeles, Orange, and Ventura, but increased in the rapidly growing Riverside and San Bernardino counties. From 1990 to 2000, the proportion of Latinos grew in all five counties, with Riverside and San Bernardino posting the largest increases during the period.

The rate of growth has changed over the years, with the outlying counties, particularly Riverside and San Bernardino, exhibiting much higher growth rates than Los Angeles County, as measured by the percentage change in population and housing units (see table 3).

Figure 5. Los Angeles, the sprawling metropolis.

Growth is evident in the number of residential units authorized by building permits. Between 1990 and 2007, for the region as a whole, approximately 933,000 residential units were authorized.[56] These permit data provide insights to the location and type of growth occurring in the region. Overall, about 70.5 percent of the permitted units were single-family, but the proportion of single-family units to total units authorized by permit varied among the region's counties. As shown in table 4, it is clear that Los Angeles County was tending toward multifamily development or a balance between single-family and multifamily, while the outlying counties, especially Riverside and San Bernardino, consistently favored single-family residential development. In other words, Los Angeles County was increasing housing density, while the Counties of Riverside and San Bernardino embraced the more sprawling, single-family development.

Table 3. Population and housing units, Los Angeles region, 1990 and 2000

	POPULATION			HOUSING UNITS		
COUNTY	1990	2000	CHANGE (%)	1990	2000	CHANGE (%)
Los Angeles	8,863,164	9,519,338	7.40	3,163,343	3,270,909	3.40
Orange	2,410,556	2,846,289	18.08	875,072	969,484	10.79
Riverside	1,170,413	1,545,387	32.04	483,847	584,674	20.84
San Bernardino	1,418,380	1,709,434	20.52	542,332	601,369	10.89
Ventura	669,016	753,197	12.58	228,478	251,712	10.17

Source: U.S. Census Bureau, 1990 and 2000 Dencennial Censuses.

Table 4. Single-family residential units authorized by permit, Los Angeles region, 1990–2005

	1990		1995		2000		2005	
COUNTY	**NUMBER**	**%**	**NUMBER**	**%**	**NUMBER**	**%**	**NUMBER**	**%**
Los Angeles	8,887	35.99	4,543	63.49	8,173	49.09	11,819	54.01
Orange	4,378	36.54	5,935	72.72	6,761	55.04	4,051	57.36
Riverside	12,085	78.94	6,666	99.15	13,104	88.67	28,982	88.56
San Bernardino	10,990	82.94	3,765	96.74	5,720	89.21	14,929	93.05
Ventura	1,360	52.07	1,935	90.34	2,984	75.35	2,297	57.10

Source: U.S. Census Bureau. Accessed at: http://censtats.census.gov/cgi-bin/bldgprmt/bldgdisp.pl.

Single-family development provided opportunities for homeownership throughout the region. In all but Los Angeles County, the homeownership rates exceeded the State of California's rate as a whole (56.9 percent in 2000). Furthermore, from 1990 to 2000, the rates in these counties increased, while they fell in Los Angeles County (see table 5). The pattern of building permits and homeownership rates suggest the suburban counties continue a trend of single-family development and homeownership, while the older urbanized area of Los Angeles County appears to be taking another track.

The sprawling development pattern is reflected in county-to-county commuting between home and work. The two fastest-growing counties in the region, Riverside and San Bernardino, also had the highest intercounty commuter rates in 2000 (see table 6). In fact, they are the only counties in Southern California to have 25 percent or more of their working residents making intercounty commutes. For the Los Angeles region as a whole, slightly more than 11 percent of the commuters reported journey-to-work times exceeding sixty minutes, ranking the region sixth in the nation among major metropolitan areas for these long commutes.[57]

The sprawling development pattern contributes to high levels of commuting and therefore to vehicle emissions and air quality concerns. Citing growth, sprawl, and annual vehicle miles traveled as contributing factors to air pollution, Ed Avol, writes, "Southern California has been a perennial competitor for the dubious distinction of 'poorest air quality in the nation.' Ambient

Table 5. Homeownership rates, Los Angeles region, 1990 and 2000

	HOMEOWNERSHIP RATE (%)		
COUNTY	**1990**	**2000**	**CHANGE**
Los Angeles	48.2	47.9	–0.3
Orange	60.1	61.4	1.3
Riverside	67.4	68.9	1.5
San Bernardino	63.3	64.5	1.2
Ventura	65.5	67.6	2.1

Source: U.S. Census Bureau, 1990 and 2000 Decennial Censuses.

Table 6. County-to-county worker flow (residence to workplace), Los Angeles region, 2000

COUNTY OF RESIDENCE	COUNTY OF WORKPLACE				
	LOS ANGELES (%)	ORANGE (%)	RIVERSIDE (%)	SAN BERNARDINO (%)	VENTURA (%)
Los Angeles	92.7	4.2	0.2	1.1	0.8
Orange	14.1	83.0	0.9	0.7	0.1
Riverside	6.2	8.7	70.6	10.2	< 0.1
San Bernardino	16.9	4.4	7.9	69.3	< 0.1
Ventura	19.8	0.2	0.1	< 0.1	76.2

Source: U.S. Census Bureau, County-to-County Worker Flow Files, 2000.

(outdoor) ozone and particulate levels have historically been among the highest in the country."[58] He also draws attention to recent research that raises real concerns about health problems from longer-term exposure to air pollution.

For instance, in the South Coast Air Basin in California (covering Los Angeles, Orange, Riverside, and San Bernardino counties) research on health impacts of air pollution by Rachel

PHOTOGRAPH BY SUSAN WELSH

Figure 6. Los Angeles commuter traffic.

Morello-Frosch and colleagues has shown that estimated lifetime cancer risks associated with outdoor air toxins to residents of the region are ubiquitously high. Overall cancer risks in the South Coast Air Basin exceed the Clean Air Act goal between one and three orders of magnitude. As noted by Morello-Frosch, Manuel Pastor, and James Sadd, "nearly 8,000 excess cancer cases were estimated for the South Coast region based on cancer risk and population per tract."[59] Their research also shows that there is a racial and ethnic dimension to the cancer risk. In the tracts with the highest quartile of estimated cancer risk, 68 percent are people of color, while only 32 percent are Anglo. They go on to note that "the probability of a person of color in Southern California living in a high cancer risk neighborhood is nearly one in three, but the probability for an Anglo resident is about one in seven."[60]

The Los Angeles area exhibits the characteristics of an unsustainable region. The population and housing growth, physical size, and commuting patterns of the Los Angeles region confirm a sprawling urbanized area. Moreover, the pattern of building permits and homeownership rates reflect the region's propensity to foster sprawl by favoring single-family housing and ownership. As historian Kenneth Jackson writes, "Los Angeles, in particular, provides the nation's most dramatic example of urban sprawl. . . . Its vast, amorphous conglomeration of housing tracts, shopping centers, industrial parks, freeways, and independent towns blend into each other in a seamless fabric of concrete and asphalt."[61] He cites "cheap land . . . and the desire for single-family houses" as factors in the relatively early development of sprawl in Los Angeles. As land values have increased in more urbanized areas over the past several decades, it is clear that public and private actors have sought development in outlying areas to provide single-family houses to consumers, and, in turn, fostered continued sprawl and higher levels of commuting.

The consequences of sprawl in the Los Angeles region are clearly visible, and continued outward growth without intervening measures makes for an unsustainable region. Strategies to address commuting, such as high occupancy vehicle lanes and the regionwide Metrolink train system, are efforts to reduce vehicles on the roads. Also, some improvements have been made in air quality, but air pollution remains a significant concern in the region.

In addition to air pollution, another area of concern in the Los Angeles region resulting from the rapid decentralization is growing infrastructure requirements. Robert Burchell and colleagues show that considerable savings in infrastructure outlay—such as water, sewage, and road—would be evident if new developments would concentrate in the already developed urban and suburban areas, as opposed to expanding outward on to new and undeveloped lands.[62] In fact, the Los Angeles area is considered the urban region in the United States that would realize some of the greatest cost savings if it curtailed its low-density decentralization. If the Los Angeles region promoted a more compact growth model, as opposed to the existing rate of outward expansion, between the years 2000 to 2025 the region would require 18,375 fewer lanemiles and would save a total of $15.9 billion in road construction costs alone.[63]

Similar resource and cost savings are also evident in water and sewage provision. If the existing rate of decentralization persists over the next two decades, the region will require more water and sewer capacity than any other metropolitan region in the nation. By adopting the more compact growth model, the Los Angeles region by 2025 could save 15.4 million gallons in water capacity each day and could require 477,000 fewer water and sewer laterals, a total savings of $1.26

PHOTOGRAPH BY SUSAN WELSH

Figure 7. Metrolink.

billion in water and sewer infrastructure outlay.[64] While considerable environmental and fiscal benefits would result from the more compact urban form, it must be recognized that the likely impact of promoting greater compactness would translate into upward pressures on land values, and hence housing, within the region.

While efforts to address specific problems are important, the larger issue of the region's development pattern, particularly the proliferation of single-family housing development in outlying counties, is the central problem in terms of sustainability. Redirecting focus to this problem may be more likely as a result of the subprime mortgage and foreclosure crisis that began in 2005. The Los Angeles region has been particularly hard hit in this crisis with Los Angeles, Riverside, and San Bernardino counties[65] topping the list of California counties in terms of numbers of subprime loans outstanding in 2005–2006, and these counties in 2011 had the highest number of foreclosures among the counties in the region (with 25,020 in Los Angeles County, 17,496 in Riverside County, and 14,171 in San Bernardino County).[66]

The foreclosure and concomitant financial crises are serious for individuals, developers, and the finance industry, and recovery will be a long process. Without diminishing the severity of the crisis, the recovery period is an opportunity, as it provides time to rethink planning and development in the region and develop strategies for urban sustainability.

In the Los Angeles region and the nation as a whole, our past and recent private practices, public polices, and consumptive culture hold little promise for urban sustainability. However, they do suggest a direction for change. In the final section of this chapter, I discuss practices

PHOTOGRAPH BY VICTORIA BEARD

Figure 8. Foreclosure sign.

and policies related to housing that have potential to move U.S. urban regions toward the goal of sustainability.

Conclusion: Housing and Urban Sustainability

Housing is not only essential to the proper functioning of urban regions; it is also central to their sustainability. As discussed in this chapter, private development practices, public policies, and cultural norms promoted horizontal growth patterns, which have resulted in a range of negative consequences. One response to this problem would be to slow sprawl by controlling development through governmental regulation, but this approach has a number of shortcomings. First, local governments control land use regulation in most of the United States. Many of the outlying localities desire growth for identity and economic reasons. Thus, at worst, voluntary growth controls would have little effect; at best, with only a portion of outlying localities likely to adopt growth controls, the result would be uneven, but still outward, development.

Second, if growth regulations did prevail widely without countermeasures, they would increase the price of existing housing, at least in the short- to middle-term.[67] Therefore, the limit on outward growth would need to be counterbalanced with intensive housing development in areas closer to the center of a region. This solution has been proffered by some planners under the rubric of compact development. While compact development is intuitively appealing as a sustainability goal, it would require local governments to adopt regulatory frameworks to support more intensive development; it would also require public incentives such as tax breaks to producers and consumers of housing, to counteract existing preferences for the traditional, single-family, suburban form.

Another response to some of the negative impacts of sprawl would be to link employees to job centers via fast and efficient mass transit, such as high-speed trains. Alone, this response has a number of drawbacks. First, in the many sprawling areas without existing rail, the cost of building a rail system is enormous. Second, building a public rail system does not ensure people will use the system, although incentives could be offered to increase use. Third, the development of a rail system would provide additional access and encourage further housing development outward; this, in turn, would bring about a need to extend rail lines.

Changes in federal policies could have a significant effect on housing development patterns. A return to pre-1986 tax law to encourage multifamily development, for example, would increase availability of rental housing and provide more affordability to low- and moderate-income workers. Furthermore, this could be coupled with tax breaks to developers who build near job centers and renters who reside close to their place of employment. Of course, this strategy assumes that local governments would plan and zone their communities to accommodate workforce housing near job centers. Additionally, the current policy of a $1 million cap on the mortgage interest deduction could be modified to lower the cap significantly. This reduction in the cap would need to be amortized over a period of years to reduce the impacts on the high-end housing market. The tax laws also could be modified to scale the mortgage interest deduction by the distance between work and home; that is, provide a higher mortgage interest deduction for households living within proximity of their places of employment. To set such a scale, research that used simulations and took transportation networks and other context-specific attributes into account would be necessary to determine the effective threshold distances for different urbanized regions across the country.

There are many more strategies related to housing that could promote sustainable development patterns. These approaches, however, require a change in the way we think about housing in the United States. Through years of private practices and public policies, housing has been promoted as a commodity, an investment vehicle, and developed to separate people, by distance, tenure, and class. In the present and future, governmental policies could reorient private practices and, in general, reshape thinking, possibly changing cultural norms, about housing and development patterns in urbanized areas. The federal government needs to expand its effort beyond the relatively limited "Sustainable Communities" initiative and adopt an ambitious agenda for urban sustainability that recognizes housing as central to sustaining urban regions as well as promote effective, integrated policies that will help reverse or stem the negative social, economic, and environmental consequences of sprawling development. In the face of the foreclosure and financial crises, such an agenda could be placed on the back burner, but these problems actually could be the starting point for a more sound housing policy that would foster sustainable development patterns.

Appendix

Changes to the census form from 1990 to 2000 affect analyses of race and ethnicity. "Mixed race" was included as a choice in the 2000 census, and some of the change in racial proportions between

Table 7. Race, Los Angeles region, 1990 and 2000

	RACE (BY PERCENT)								
	AFRICAN AMERICAN			ASIAN			WHITE		
COUNTY	1990	2000	CHANGE	1990	2000	CHANGE	1990	2000	CHANGE
Los Angeles	11.2	9.8	−1.4	10.8	11.9	1.2	56.8	48.7	−8.1
Orange	1.8	1.7	−0.1	10.3	13.6	3.3	78.6	64.8	−13.8
Riverside	5.4	6.2	0.8	3.6	3.7	0.1	76.4	65.6	−10.9
San Bernardino	8.1	9.1	1.0	4.2	4.7	0.5	73.0	58.9	−14.1
Ventura	2.3	1.9	−0.4	5.2	5.3	0.2	79.1	69.9	−9.2

Source: U.S. Census Bureau, 1990 and 2000 Decennial Censuses.

Table 8. Hispanic origin/Latino, Los Angeles region, 1990 and 2000

	HISPANIC/LATINO (BY PERCENT)		
COUNTY	1990	2000	CHANGE
Los Angeles	37.8	44.6	6.8
Orange	23.4	30.8	7.3
Riverside	26.3	36.2	9.9
San Bernardino	26.7	39.2	12.5
Ventura	26.4	33.4	7.0

Source: U.S. Census Bureau, 1990 and 2000 Decennial Censuses.

the two censuses is likely due to providing this category. "Hispanic origin" was used in the 1990 census, and "Hispanic or Latino" was used in the 2000 census. As a result, comparison between the two census years is imperfect and should be analyzed only in general terms.

NOTES

The author thanks James Basolo, Victoria Beard, Susan Welsh, and two anonymous reviewers for their contributions to this chapter.

1. Judy S. Davis, Arthur C. Nelson, and Kenneth J. Dueker, The New "Burbs": The Exurbs and Their Implications for Planning Policy, *Journal of the American Planning Association* 60:1 (1994): 45–59; Robert E. Lang, *Edgeless Cities: Exploring the Elusive Metropolis* (Washington, DC: Brookings Institution Press, 2003); see George Galster, Royce Hanson, Michael R. Ratcliffe, Harold Wolman, Stephen Coleman, and Jason Freihage, Wrestling Sprawl to the Ground: Defining and Measuring an Elusive Concept, *Housing Policy Debate* 12:4 (2007): 681–717; Peter Gordon and Harry W. Richardson, Where's the Sprawl? Letter to the Editor, *Journal of the American Planning Association* 63:2 (1997): 275–78; Jonathan C. Levine, *Zoned Out: Regulation, Markets, and Choices in Transportation and Metropolitan Land-Use* (Washington, DC: Resources for the Future, 2006).
2. U.S. Census Bureau, Census 2000, SF1 and SF3, 2000; Susan B. Hansen, Carolyn Ban, and Leonard Huggins, Explaining the "Brain Drain" from Older Industrial Cities: The Pittsburg Experience, *Economic Development Quarterly* 17:2 (2003): 132–47;

Mark W. Horner, Spatial Dimensions of Urban Commuting: A Review of Major Issues and Their Implications for Future Geographic Research, *The Professional Geographer* 56:2 (2004): 160–73; Yosef Rafeq Jabareen, Sustainable Urban Forms—Their Typologies, Models, and Concepts, *Journal of Planning Education and Research* 26:1 (2006): 38–52; Ooi Giok Ling, *Sustainability and Cities: Concept and Assessment* (Singapore: Institute of Policy Studies and World Scientific Publishing, 2005); André Sorensen, Peter J. Marcotullio, and Jill Grant, Towards Sustainable Cities, in *Towards Sustainable Cities: East Asian, North American and European Perspectives on Managing Urban Regions*, ed. André Sorensen, Peter J. Marcotullio, and Jill Grant (Aldershot, UK: Ashgate, 2004), 3–23.

3. See Clare Cooper Marcus, *Housing as a Mirror of Self: Exploring the Deeper Meaning of Home* (Berkeley, CA: Conari Press, 1995); Roberta M. Feldman, Settlement-Identity: Psychological Bonds with Home Places in a Mobile Society, *Environment and Behavior* 22:2 (1990): 183–229.
4. Darryl Getter (2006) illustrates this point when he writes about comments by Dr. Frank Nothaft, chief economist at Freddie Mac (a secondary market conduit of funds that ensures availability of capital for mortgage lenders by purchasing home loans from lenders and selling them to investors). Getter notes, "Dr. Nothaft pointed out that about one-fifth of GDP growth was tied to the housing sector and that the recent decline in housing market activity has shaved 1% off recent growth" (Darryl E. Getter, November 2006 SGE Monthly Luncheon, Society of Government Economists (n.p.), http://www.sge-econ.org/meet/archives/0611Nothaft.html).
5. See Peter Evans, ed., *Livable Cities? Urban Struggles for Livelihood and Sustainability* (Berkeley: University of California Press, 2002); Sang-Dae Lee, Urban Growth Management and Housing Supply in the Capital Region of South Korea, in Sorensen et al., *Towards Sustainable Cities*, 285–98; John Mason, *Sustainable Agriculture* (Collingwood, AU: Landlinks Press, 2003); Anna Nagurney, *Sustainable Transportation Networks* (Cheltenham, UK: Edwin Elgar Publishing, 2000).
6. Charles L. Choguill, The Search for Policies to Support Sustainable Housing, *Habitat International* 31 (2007): 143–49; Ling, *Sustainability and Cities*.
7. The development of sustainable buildings, including housing, is one of the key objectives of the U.S. Green Building Council. This nonprofit organization is probably best known for its Leadership in Energy and Environmental Design (LEED) Green Building Rating System. See, for example, R. M. Pulselli, E. Simoncini, F. M. Pulselli, and S. Bastianoni, Emergy Analysis of Building Manufacturing, Maintenance and Use: Em-Building Indices to Evaluate Housing Sustainability, *Energy and Buildings* 39:5 (2007): 620–28.
8. Igor Vojnovic, Shaping Metropolitan Toronto: A Study of Linear Infrastructure Subsidies, 1954–66, *Environment and Planning B: Planning and Design* 27:2 (2000): 197–230; Sam Bass Warner, *Streetcar Suburbs: The Process of Growth in Boston, 1870–1900* (Cambridge, MA: Harvard University Press, 1978).
9. Settlement houses operated by charitable organizations addressed housing problems by providing a decent home to some of the urban poor. See Allen Davis, *Spearheads for Reform: The Social Settlements and the Progressive Movement, 1890–1914* (Oxford: Oxford University Press, 1967); Frank S. So and Judith Getzels, Introduction to the Context and History of Comprehensive Planning, in *The Practice of Local Government Planning*, ed. Frank S. So and Judith Getzels (Washington, DC: International City Management Association, 1988); Margaret E. Woods, Housing and Cities: 1790 to 1890, in *The Story of Housing*, ed. Gertrude S. Fish (New York: Macmillan, 1979); Mel Scott, *American City Planning* (Berkeley: University of California Press, 1969); Frank S. So and Judith Getzels, Introduction to the Context and History of Comprehensive Planning, in *The Practice of Local Government Planning*, ed. Frank S. So and Judith Getzels (Washington, DC: International City Management Association, 1988).
10. By ruling of the U.S. Supreme Court in *Village of Euclid, Ohio v. Ambler Realty Company*.
11. Mark I. Gelfand, *A Nation of Cities: The Federal Government and Urban America, 1933–1965* (New York: Oxford University Press, 1975); Paul Kantor, *The Dependent City* (Glenview, IL: Scott, Foresman & Co., 1988); J. Paul Mitchell, The Historical Context for Housing Policy, in *Federal Housing Policy and Programs*, ed. J. Paul Mitchell (New Brunswick, NJ: Center for Urban Policy Research, 1985); Eric H. Monkkonen, *America Becomes Urban* (Berkeley: University of California Press, 1988).
12. Scott, *American City Planning*; Milton P. Semer, Julian H. Zimmerman, Ashley Foard, and John M. Frantz, Evolution of Federal Legislative Policy in Housing: Housing Credits, in *Federal Housing Policy and Programs*, ed. J. Paul Mitchell (New Brunswick, NJ: Center for Urban Policy Research, 1985), 69–106.
13. Today, Fannie Mae, formerly known as FNMA, is one of the government-sponsored enterprises (Freddie Mac and Ginnie Mae are the others) operating in

the secondary market. These entities package loans made by banks into pools (MBS, or mortgage-backed securities) to sell to investors, thus ensuring a flow of capital for mortgage finance; Annand K. Bhattacharya, Frank J. Fabozzi, and S. Esther Chang, Overview of the Mortgage Market, in *The Handbook of Mortgage-Backed Securities*, ed. Frank J. Fabozzi (New York: McGraw Hill, 2001). Despite its long time status as an innovative approach to ensuring mortgage capital, the future of Fannie Mae is uncertain as a result of the foreclosure crisis and its attendant effects.

14. This policy continues today with up to $1 million allowed as a deduction for mortgage interest. Edward G. Goetz, *Shelter Burden: Local Politics and Progressive Housing Policy* (Philadelphia: Temple University Press, 1993); Gerald Prante, The History of the Mortgage Interest Deduction (March 6, 2006), *Tax Foundation*, http://www.taxfoundation.org/blog/show/1382.html.
15. Kenneth T. Jackson, *Crabgrass Frontier: The Suburbanization of the United States* (New York: Oxford University Press, 1985); William H. Frey, Central City White Flight: Racial and Nonracial Causes, *American Sociological Review* 44 (June1979): 425–48; Oliver Gillham, *The Limitless City: A Primer on the Urban Sprawl Debate* (Washington, DC: Island Press, 2002); Michael J. Klarman, *Brown v. Board of Education and the Civil Rights Movement* (New York: Oxford University Press, 2007); Mitchell, The Historical Context; Dan McNichol, *The Roads That Built America: The Incredible Story of the U.S. Interstate System* (New York: Sterling, 2005).
16. Robert M. Fogelson, *Bourgeois Nightmares* (New Haven, CT: Yale University Press, 2005), 1.
17. Lizabeth Cohen, *A Consumer's Republic: The Politics of Mass Consumption in Postwar America* (New York: Vintage Books, 2003), 6.
18. U.S. Census Bureau, Census of Population and Housing, Population and Housing Unit Counts: United States (CPH 2–1–1), 1990; U.S. Census Bureau, Census 2000, SF1 and SF3, 2000.
19. John Yinger, *Closed Doors, Opportunities Lost: The Continuing Costs of Housing Discrimination* (New York: Russell Sage Foundation, 1997); Anthony Downs, The Challenges of Our Declining Big Cities, *Housing Policy Debate* 8:2 (1997): 359–408.
20. William M. Rohe and Victoria Basolo, Long Term Effects of Homeownership on the Self-Perceptions and Social Interaction of Low-Income Persons, *Environment and Behavior* 29:6 (1997): 793–819.
21. Victoria Basolo and Corianne Scally, State Innovations in Affordable Housing Policy: Lessons from California and New Jersey, *Housing Policy Debate* 19:4 (2008); Kirk McClure, The Low-Income Housing Tax Credit as an Aid to Housing Finance: How Well Has It Worked? *Housing Policy Debate* 11:1 (2000): 91–114.
22. Department of Housing and Urban Development, http://www.huduser.org/datasets/lihtc.html.
23. Basolo and Scally, State Innovations in Affordable Housing.
24. Victoria Basolo, Explaining the Support for Homeownership in U.S. Cities: A Political Economy Perspective, *Housing Studies* 22:1 (2007): 99–119.
25. Scott Gold, A Jolt to Comfy Temecula, *Los Angeles Times* (June 6, 2008): B-1.
26. Jackson, *Crabgrass Frontier*; Nicolas P. Retsinas and Eric S. Belsky, Examining the Unexamined Goal, in *Low-Income Homeownership: Examining the Unexamined Goal*, ed. Nicolas P. Retsinas and Eric S. Belsky (Washington, DC: Brookings Institution, 2002).
27. Political rhetoric, however, praises homeownership for additional benefits, including bringing stability to communities and making neighborhoods safer for children. See Basolo, Explaining the Support for Homeownership, 99–119.
28. There also was an additional $15.54 billion in tax expenditures from deductions of state and local property taxes on owner-occupied housing. Executive Office of the President, Office of Management and Budget, Analytical Perspectives of the FY 2008 Budget (table 19-1), Washington, DC: U.S. Government Printing Office, 2007, http://www.whitehouse.gov/omb/.
29. I report results from homeowners only. The survey is part of a larger research project of disaster preparedness. The research is supported by the National Science Foundation under Grant No. 0429454. The author is thankful for this support and acknowledges that the opinions, interpretations, findings, and conclusions contained in this publication are those of the author and do not necessarily reflect the views of the National Science Foundation. The data were collected via a random digit dialing telephone survey of over 1,000 households from the two areas. While the study used randomly generated telephone numbers, it was designed as a quota survey (to achieve 500 responses from each area). Therefore, it cannot be considered representative of the population of households in the two counties. If fact, analyses of the responses indicate that respondents in the samples tended to be nonminority with higher incomes than the populations as a whole. Fannie

Mae, Understanding America's Homeownership Gaps: 2003 Fannie Mae National Housing Survey, 2003, http://www.fanniemae.com/global/pdf/media/survey/survey2003.pdf; Robert J. Shiller, *Irrational Exuberance*, 2d ed. (Princeton, NJ: Princeton University Press, 2005), 20. His estimate of the 1890–2004 (without the two boom periods) real housing price increase on an annual basis is 0.4 percent.

30. This percentage includes respondents answering "very" or "somewhat likely" to the question. Fannie Mae, Understanding America's Homeownership Gaps: 2003 Fannie Mae National Housing Survey, http://www.fanniemae.com/global/pdf/media/survey/survey2003.pdf.
31. Kent W. Colton and Kate Collignon, Multifamily Rental Housing in the 21st Century, Working Paper (W01–1), Joint Center for Housing Studies, Harvard University, 2001, http://www.jchs.harvard.edu/publications/finance/colton_w01–1.pdf.
32. Levine, *Zoned Out*.
33. Outward growth sometimes meant "leapfrogging" more expensive suburban land for more distant, cheaper land.
34. See Robert Burchell, Anthony Downs, Sahan Mukherji, and Barbara McCann, *Sprawl Costs: Economic Impacts of Unchecked Development* (Washington, DC: Island Press, 2005); Frey, Central City White Flight, 425–48; John F. Kain, A Pioneer's Perspective on the Spatial Mismatch Literature, *Urban Studies* 3:2 (2004): 7–32; John D. Kasarda and Kwok-fai Ting, Joblessness and Poverty in America's Central Cities: Causes and Policy Prescriptions, *Housing Policy Debate* 7:2 (1996): 387–419; David Rusk, *Cities without Suburbs* (Baltimore: Johns Hopkins University Press, 1995).
35. See Leonard S. Rubinowitz and James E. Rosenbaum, *Crossing the Class and Color Lines: From Public Housing to White Suburbia* (Chicago: University of Chicago Press, 2002); John Goering and Judith D. Feins, *Choosing a Better Life? Evaluating the Moving to Opportunity Social Experiment* (Washington, DC: Urban Institute Press, 2003).
36. See Helen Ladd and John Yinger, *America's Ailing Cities: Fiscal Health and the Design of Urban Policy* (Baltimore: Johns Hopkins University Press, 1989).
37. U.S. Census Bureau, Census of Population, General Social and Economic Characteristics, United States Summary, 1980; U.S. Census Bureau, Census of Population, STF3C, 1990; U.S. Census Bureau, Census 2000, SF1 and SF3, 2000.
38. See Orange County Business Council, Workforce Housing Scorecard, Irvine, CA, 2007.
39. See, for example, Richard Haughey, *Developing Housing for the Workforce: A Tool Kit* (Washington, DC: Urban Land Institute, 2007).
40. Burchell et al., *Sprawl Costs*, 4.
41. See Adam Rome, *The Bulldozer in the Countryside: Suburban Sprawl and the Rise of American Environmentalism* (New York: Cambridge University Press, 2001).
42. David M. Theobald, Land-Use Dynamics beyond the American Urban Fringe, *Geographical Review* 91:3 (2001): 544.
43. Mark L. Imhoff, Lahouari Bounoua, Ruth DeFries, William T. Lawrence, David Stutzer, Compton J. Tucker, and Taylor Ricketts, The Consequences of Urban Land Transformation on Net Primary Productivity in the United States, *Remote Sensing of Environment* 89:4 (2004): 442.
44. Sudhir C. Rajan, Climate Change Dilemma: Technology, Social Change or Both? An Examination of Long-Term Transport Policy Choices in the United States, *Energy Policy* 34:6 (2006): 664–79; Peter S. Van Metre, Barbara J. Mahler, and Edward T. Furlong, Urban Sprawl Leaves Its PAH Signature, *Environmental Science and Technology* 34 (2000): 4064–70.
45. Richard Cook, Madeleine Strum, Jawad S. Touma, Ted Palma, James Thurman, Darrell Ensley, and Roy Smith, Inhalation Exposure and Risk from Mobile Source Air Toxics in Future Years, *Journal of Exposure Science and Environmental Epidemiology* 17 (2007): 104.
46. It is premature at this time to argue a complete, causal understanding of the foreclosure crisis; therefore, I suggest some, but not all, of the contributing factors. From a speech by Ben Bernanke, chairman of the Federal Reserve Bank, in New York City on May 5, 2008, http://www.federalreserve.gov/newsevents/speech/Bernanke20080505a.htm. The rate of foreclosures was lower in 2011 than during earlier periods of the crisis, however, foreclosures continue in 2012 with no clear point of return to normal, historical levels.
47. See Gold, A Jolt to Comfy Temecula.
48. Scott L. Bottles, *Los Angeles and the Automobile* (Berkeley: University of California Press, 1987), 4.
49. U.S. Bureau of the Census, *Population of the 100 Largest Cities and Other Urban Places in the United States: 1790 to 1990* (Washington, DC: U.S. Census Bureau Population Division, 1998).
50. Peter Hall, *Cities in Civilization* (New York: Fromm International, 2001), 815.
51. Ibid., 816.
52. See, for example, Roger W. Lotchin, Population

Concentration in Los Angeles, 1940–2000, *Pacific Historical Review* 77:1 (2008): 87–101; Peter Gordon and Harry W. Richardson, Beyond Polycentricity—The Dispersed Metropolis, Los Angeles, 1970–1990, *Journal of the American Planning Association* 62:3 (1996): 289–95.

53. Edward Soja, *Postmetropolis: Critical Studies of Cities and Regions* (Malden, MA: Blackwell Publishing, 2000), 128.
54. Hall, *Cities in Civilization*, 605.
55. Diversity does not imply the absence of residential segregation. In 2000, the Los Angeles-Long Beach Metropolitan Area ranked nineteenth worst of forty-three metropolitan areas (MAs) for African Americans and fifth worst of thirty-six MAs for Latinos on the dissimilarity index, a measure of evenness in the spatial distribution of groups (i.e., racial and ethnic groups). See John Iceland, Daniel H. Weinberg, and Erika Steinmetz, Racial and Ethnic Residential Segregation in the United States: 1980–2000, 2002, http://www.census.gov/hhes/www/housing/housing_patterns/working_papers.html.
56. This figure is based on reported authorized permits, which are lower than estimated authorized building permits. Data come from the Census Bureau, http://censtats.census.gov/cgi-bin/bldgprmt/bldgdisp.pl.
57. Alan E. Pisarski, Commuting in America III (Washington, DC: Transportation Research Board, 2006), 107.
58. Ed Avol, Air Quality and Health in the Greater Los Angeles Area: A Region in Crisis, in *The State of the Region 2007* (report) (Los Angeles: Southern California Association of Governments, 2007), 120.
59. Rachel Morello-Frosch, Manuel Pastor, and James Sadd, Environmental Justice and Southern California's "Riskcape": The Distribution of Air Toxics Exposures and Health Risks among Diverse Communities, *Urban Affairs Review* 36 (2001): 560.
60. Ibid., 565.
61. Jackson, *Crabgrass Frontier*.
62. Burchell et al., *Sprawl Costs*.
63. Ibid. According to this population density and urban form model, the historical relationship between population density and the density of the road network is used to determine future development and road requirements. Under the compact growth model, 9.2 percent of the expected new housing construction nationally is concentrated in the already developed urban and suburban areas.
64. Burchell et al., *Sprawl Costs*, 57–58.
65. The subprime loan and foreclosure crisis is likely to impact lower-income and minority homeowners most severely, especially in the outlying counties. Detailed data to fully assess disproportional impacts are currently unavailable.
66. Rani Isaac, *Foreclosures in California: The Current Crisis Is More Severe than Previous Corrections* (Sacramento: California Research Bureau, 2008), 5.
67. Eventually such a solution would result in high housing prices, driving out workers and employers. The long-term effect, therefore, is the loss of an economic base, deterioration of the region, and a decrease in housing prices.

REFERENCES

Avol, Ed. Air Quality and Health in the Greater Los Angeles Area: A Region in Crisis. In *The State of the Region 2007* (report). Los Angeles: Southern California Association of Governments, 2007.

Basolo, Victoria. Explaining the Support for Homeownership in U.S. Cities: A Political Economy Perspective. *Housing Studies* 22:1 (2007): 99–119.

Basolo, Victoria, and Corianne Scally. State Innovations in Affordable Housing Policy: Lessons from California and New Jersey. *Housing Policy Debate* 19:4 (2008): 741–74.

Bhattacharya, Annand K., Frank J. Fabozzi, and S. Esther Chang. Overview of the Mortgage Market. In *The Handbook of Mortgage-Backed Securities*, ed. Frank J. Fabozzi, 3–24. New York: McGraw Hill, 2001.

Bottles, Scott L. *Los Angeles and the Automobile*. Berkeley: University of California Press, 1987.

Burchell, Robert, Anthony Downs, Sahan Mukherji, and Barbara McCann. *Sprawl Costs: Economic Impacts of Unchecked Development*. Washington, DC: Island Press, 2005.

Choguill, Charles L. The Search for Policies to Support Sustainable Housing. *Habitat International* 31 (2007): 143–49.

Cohen, Lizabeth. *A Consumer's Republic: The Politics of Mass Consumption in Postwar America*. New York: Vintage Books, 2003.

Colton, Kent W., and Kate Collignon. Multifamily Rental Housing in the 21st Century. Working Paper (W01–1). Joint Center for Housing Studies, Harvard University, 2001. http://www.jchs.harvard.edu/publications/finance/colton_w01–1.pdf.

Cook, Richard, Madeleine Strum, Jawad S. Touma, Ted Palma, James Thurman, Darrell Ensley, and Roy Smith. Inhalation Exposure and Risk from Mobile Source Air Toxics in Future Years. *Journal of Exposure Science and Environmental Epidemiology* 17 (2007): 95–105.

Davis, Allen. *Spearheads for Reform: The Social Settlements and the Progressive Movement, 1890–1914*. Oxford: Oxford University Press, 1967.

Davis, Judy S., Arthur C. Nelson, and Kenneth J. Dueker. The New "Burbs": The Exurbs and Their Implications for Planning Policy. *Journal of the American Planning Association* 60:1 (1994): 45–59.

Downs, Anthony. The Challenges of Our Declining Big Cities. *Housing Policy Debate* 8:2 (1997): 359–408.

Evans, Peter, ed. *Livable Cities? Urban Struggles for Livelihood and Sustainability*. Berkeley: University of California Press, 2002.

Executive Office of the President, Office of Management and Budget. Analytical Perspectives of the FY 2008 Budget (table 19-1). Washington, DC: U.S. Government Printing Office, 2007. http://www.whitehouse.gov/omb/.

Fannie Mae. Understanding America's Homeownership Gaps: 2003 Fannie Mae National Housing Survey, 2003. http://www.fanniemae.com/global/pdf/media/survey/survey2003.pdf.

Feldman, Roberta M. Settlement-Identity: Psychological Bonds with Home Places in a Mobile Society. *Environment and Behavior* 22:2 (1990): 183–229.

Fogelson, Robert M. *Bourgeois Nightmares*. New Haven, CT: Yale University Press, 2005.

Frey, William H. Central City White Flight: Racial and Nonracial Causes. *American Sociological Review* 44 (June 1979): 425–48.

Galster, George, Royce Hanson, Michael R. Ratcliffe, Harold Wolman, Stephen Coleman, and Jason Freihage. Wrestling Sprawl to the Ground: Defining and Measuring an Elusive Concept. *Housing Policy Debate* 12:4 (2007): 681–717.

Gelfand, Mark I. *A Nation of Cities: The Federal Government and Urban America, 1933–1965*. New York: Oxford University Press, 1975.

Getter, Darrly E. November 2006 SGE Monthly Luncheon. Society of Government Economists, 2006. http://www.sge-econ.org/meet/archives/0611Nothaft.html.

Gillham, Oliver. *The Limitless City: A Primer on the Urban Sprawl Debate*. Washington, DC: Island Press, 2002.

Goering, John, and Judith D. Feins. *Choosing a Better Life? Evaluating the Moving to Opportunity Social Experiment*. Washington, DC: Urban Institute Press, 2003.

Goetz, Edward G. *Shelter Burden: Local Politics and Progressive Housing Policy*. Philadelphia: Temple University Press, 1993.

Gold, Scott. A Jolt to Comfy Temecula. *Los Angeles Times*, June 6, 2008, B-1.

Gordon, Peter, and Harry W. Richardson. Where's the Sprawl? Letter to the Editor. *Journal of the American Planning Association* 63:2 (1997): 275–78.

Hansen, Susan B., Carolyn Ban, and Leonard Huggins. Explaining the "Brain Drain" from Older Industrial Cities: The Pittsburg Experience. *Economic Development Quarterly* 17:2 (2003): 132–47.

Haughey, Richard. *Developing Housing for the Workforce: A Tool Kit*. Washington, DC: Urban Land Institute, 2007.

Horner, Mark W. Spatial Dimensions of Urban Commuting: A Review of Major Issues and Their Implications for Future Geographic Research. *Professional Geographer* 56:2 (2004): 160–73.

Iceland, John, Daniel H. Weinberg, and Erika Steinmetz. Racial and Ethnic Residential Segregation in the United States: 1980–2000. Paper presented at the annual meeting of the Population Association of America, 2002.

Imhoff, Mark L., Lahouari Bounoua, Ruth DeFries, William T. Lawrence, David Stutzer, Compton J. Tucker, and Taylor Ricketts. The Consequences of Urban Land Transformation on Net Primary Productivity in the United States. *Remote Sensing of Environment* 89:4 (2004): 434–43.

Isaac, Rani. Foreclosures in California: The Current Crisis Is More Severe than Previous Corrections. Sacramento: California Research Bureau, 2008.

Jabareen, Yosef Rafeq. Sustainable Urban Forms—Their Typologies, Models, and Concepts. *Journal of Planning Education and Research* 26:1 (2006): 38–52.

Jackson, Kenneth T. *Crabgrass Frontier: The Suburbanization of the United States*. New York: Oxford University Press, 1985.

Kain, John F. A Pioneer's Perspective on the Spatial Mismatch Literature. *Urban Studies* 3:2 (2004): 7–32.

Kantor, Paul. *The Dependent City*. Glenview, IL: Scott, Foresman and Co., 1988.

Kasarda, John D., and Kwok-fai Ting. Joblessness and Poverty in America's Central Cities: Causes and Policy Prescriptions. *Housing Policy Debate* 7:2 (1996): 387–419.

Klarman, Michael J. *Brown v. Board of Education and the Civil Rights Movement*. New York: Oxford University Press, 2007.

Ladd, Helen, and John Yinger. *America's Ailing Cities: Fiscal Health and the Design of Urban Policy*. Baltimore: Johns Hopkins University Press, 1989.

Lang, Robert E. *Edgeless Cities: Exploring the Elusive*

Metropolis. Washington, DC: Brookings Institution Press, 2003.

Lee, Sang-Dae. Urban Growth Management and Housing Supply in the Capital Region of South Korea. In *Towards Sustainable Cities: East Asian, North American and European Perspectives on Managing Urban Regions*, ed. Andre Sorensen, Peter J. Marcotullio, and Jill Grant, 285–98. Aldershot, UK: Ashgate, 2004.

Levine, Jonathan C. *Zoned Out: Regulation, Markets, and Choices in Transportation and Metropolitan Land-Use*. Washington, DC: Resources for the Future, 2006.

Ling, Ooi Giok. *Sustainability and Cities: Concept and Assessment*. Singapore: Institute of Policy Studies and World Scientific Publishing, 2005.

Marcus, Clare Cooper. *Housing as a Mirror of Self: Exploring the Deeper Meaning of Home*. Berkeley, CA: Conari Press, 1995.

Mason, John. *Sustainable Agriculture*. Collingwood, Australia: Landlinks Press, 2003.

McClure, Kirk. The Low-Income Housing Tax Credit as an Aid to Housing Finance: How Well Has It Worked? *Housing Policy Debate* 11:1 (2000): 91–114.

McNichol, Dan. *The Roads That Built America: The Incredible Story of the U.S. Interstate System*. New York: Sterling Publishing, 2005.

Mitchell, J. Paul. The Historical Context for Housing Policy. In *Federal Housing Policy and Programs*, ed. J. Paul Mitchell, 3–17. New Brunswick, NJ: Center for Urban Policy Research, 1985.

Monkkonen, Eric H. *America Becomes Urban*. Berkeley: University of California Press, 1988.

Nagurney, Anna. *Sustainable Transportation Networks*. Cheltenham, UK: Edwin Elgar Publishing, 2000.

Orange County Business Council. Workforce Housing Scorecard. Irvine, CA: Orange County Business Council, 2007.

Pisarski, Alan E. Commuting in America III. Washington, DC: Transportation Research Board, 2006.

Prante, Gerald. The History of the Mortgage Interest Deduction (March 6, 2006). *The Tax Foundation*. http://www.taxfoundation.org/blog/show/1382.html.

Pulselli, R.M., E. Simoncini, F.M. Pulselli, and S. Bastianoni. Emergy Analysis of Building Manufacturing, Maintenance and Use: Em-building Indices to Evaluate Housing Sustainability. *Energy and Buildings* 39:5 (2007): 620–28.

Rajan, Sudhir C. Climate Change Dilemma: Technology, Social Change or Both? An Examination of Long-term Transport Policy Choices in the United States. *Energy Policy* 34:6 (2006): 664–79.

Retsinas, Nicolas P., and Eric S. Belsky. Examining the Unexamined Goal. In *Low-Income Homeownership: Examining the Unexamined Goal*, ed. Nicolas P. Retsinas and Eric S. Belsky. Washington, DC: Brookings Institution, 2002.

Rohe, William M., and Victoria Basolo. Long Term Effects of Homeownership on the Self-Perceptions and Social Interaction of Low-Income Persons. *Environment and Behavior* 29:6 (1997): 793–819.

Rome, Adam. *The Bulldozer in the Countryside: Suburban Sprawl and the Rise of American Environmentalism*. New York: Cambridge University Press, 2001.

Rubinowitz, Leonard S., and James E. Rosenbaum. *Crossing the Class and Color Lines: From Public Housing to White Suburbia*. Chicago: University of Chicago Press, 2002.

Rusk, David. *Cities without Suburbs*. Baltimore: Johns Hopkins University Press, 1995.

Scott, Mel. *American City Planning*. Berkeley: University of California Press, 1969.

Shiller, Robert J. *Irrational Exuberance*. 2d ed. Princeton, NJ: Princeton University Press, 2005.

Semer, Milton P., Julian H. Zimmerman, Ashley Foard, and John M. Frantz. Evolution of Federal Legislative Policy in Housing: Housing Credits. In *Federal Housing Policy and Programs: Past and Present*, ed. J. Paul Mitchell, 69–106. New Brunswick, NJ: Center for Urban Policy Research, 1985.

So, Frank S., and Judith Getzels. Introduction to the Context and History of Comprehensive Planning. In *The Practice of Local Government Planning*, ed. Frank S. So and Judith Getzels. Washington, DC: International City Management Association, 1988.

Sorensen, André, Peter J. Marcotullio, and Jill Grant. Towards Sustainable Cities. In *Towards Sustainable Cities: East Asian, North American and European Perspectives on Managing Urban Regions*, ed. André Sorensen, Peter J. Marcotullio, and Jill Grant, 3–23. Aldershot, UK: Ashgate, 2004.

Theobald, David M. Land-Use Dynamics beyond the American Urban Fringe. *Geographical Review* 91:3 (2001): 544–64.

U.S. Census Bureau. 1980 Census of Population, General Social and Economic Characteristics, United States Summary. Washington, DC: Population Division, U.S. Census Bureau, 1983.

———. 1990 Census of Population and Housing. Population and Housing Unit Counts: United States (CPH 2-1-1). Washington, DC: Population Division, U.S. Census Bureau, 1993.

———. 1990 Census of Population, STF3C.Washington, DC: Population Division, U.S. Census Bureau, 1993.

———. 2000 Census, SF1 and SF3.Washington, DC: Population Division, U.S. Census Bureau, 2002.

———. 2000 Census, County-to-County Worker Flow Files. Washington, DC: Population Division, U.S. Census Bureau, 2003.

———. Building Permits Survey. Washington, DC: U.S. Census Bureau, 2008.

Van Metre, Peter S., Barbara J. Mahler, and Edward T. Furlong. Urban Sprawl Leaves Its PAH Signature. *Environmental Science and Technology* 34 (2000): 4064–70.

Vojnovic, Igor. Shaping Metropolitan Toronto: A Study of Linear Infrastructure Subsidies, 1954–66. *Environment and Planning B: Planning and Design* 27:2 (2000): 197–230.

Warner, Sam Bass. *Streetcar Suburbs: The Process of Growth in Boston, 1870–1900*. Cambridge, MA: Harvard University Press, 1978.

Woods, Margaret E. Housing and Cities: 1790 to 1890. In *The Story of Housing*, ed. Gertrude S. Fish, 43–122. New York: Macmillan, 1979.

Yinger, John. *Closed Doors, Opportunities Lost: The Continuing Costs of Housing Discrimination*. New York: Russell Sage Foundation, 1997.

■ IGOR VOJNOVIC / JOE T. DARDEN

The Colors That Shaped a City

THE ROLE OF RACIAL AND CLASS TENSIONS IN INHIBITING URBAN SUSTAINABILITY, THE DETROIT CONTEXT

A topic of particular interest in the U.S. discourse on sustainable cities focuses on urban form, the physical fabric of the city. On the one hand, it is difficult to argue that there is a generic American city, since developments in high-density, pedestrian-oriented cities (such as New York and Boston) are very different from development patterns in low-density cities that were shaped by the automobile (cities such as Houston and Phoenix). On the other hand, over half of the U.S. population lives in suburbs, with the rest split between urban and rural areas, creating a concrete demographic and physical settlement pattern that reveals the scale of suburbanization in America.[1]

This decentralization reflects a spatial arrangement that began to shape the U.S. urban landscape particularly after World War II. This spatial arrangement also has very clear racial overtones. Since the early 1970s, the majority of the U.S. population living in metropolitan areas lived in suburbs, and this majority was overwhelmingly white. Although the suburbs are still predominantly white, there has been growing racial and ethnic diversity in suburbs changing the demographic composition. The 2010 census revealed that more blacks and other racial/ethnic minority groups have been leaving the central cities for the suburbs. Detroit, however, remains the American city with the highest portion of blacks (82.7 percent) in 2010.[2] Blacks represented only 12 percent of Detroit's suburban population compared to a white representation of 80 percent[3] (see figs. 1, 2, 3, 4, 5, and 6).[4]

Following the wealth, businesses also began to suburbanize. For instance, 25 percent of the office stock in U.S. metropolitan areas was located in the suburbs in 1970. This figure passed a major threshold in 1993 as the office stock in the suburbs increased to 53 percent.[5] Thus, minority and lower-income groups became spatially isolated in inner cities, while middle- and upper-income whites, businesses, and jobs increasingly suburbanized.

The Detroit region reflects perhaps the most dramatic U.S. example of excessive urban

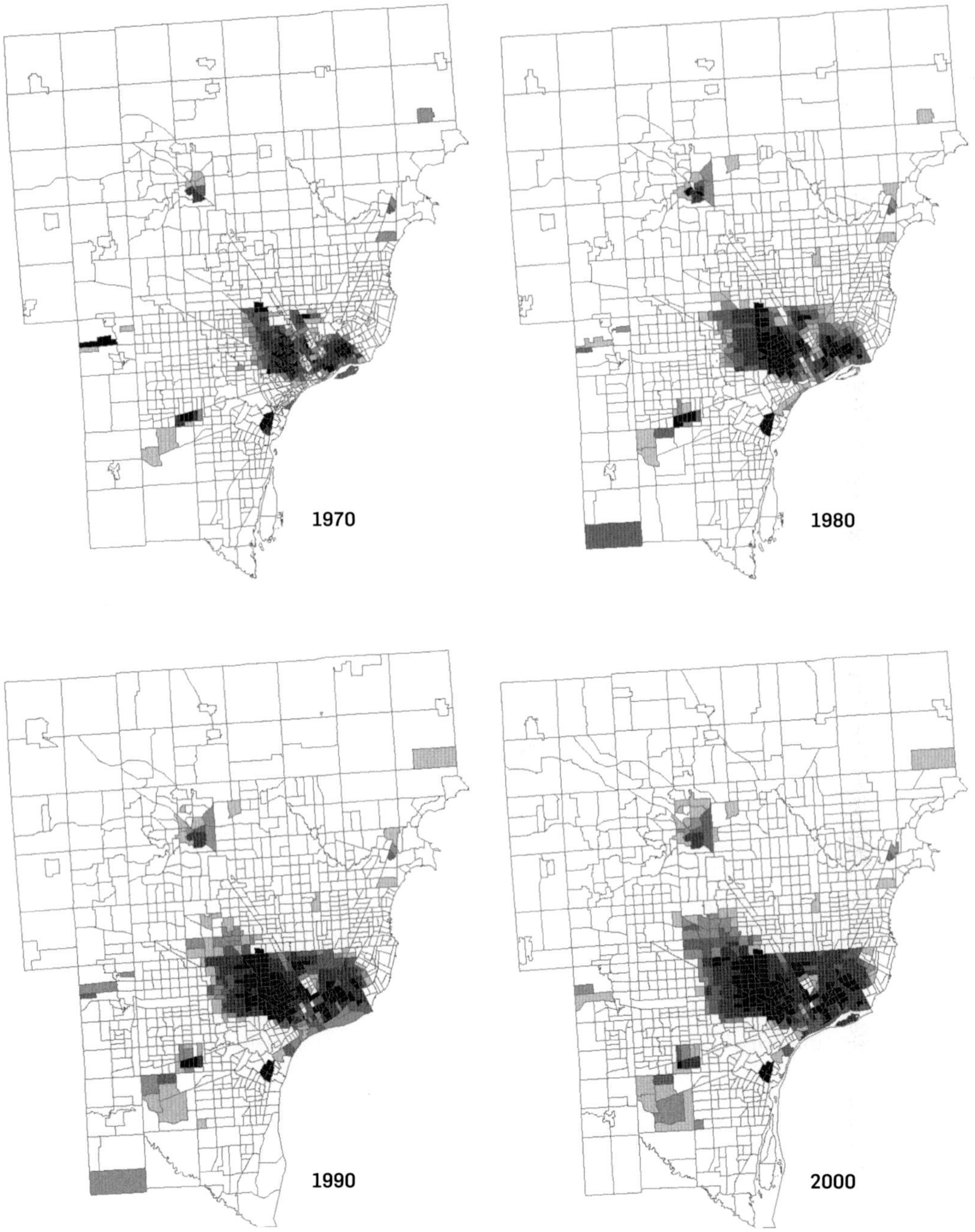

Figure 1. Metro Detroit percentage black.

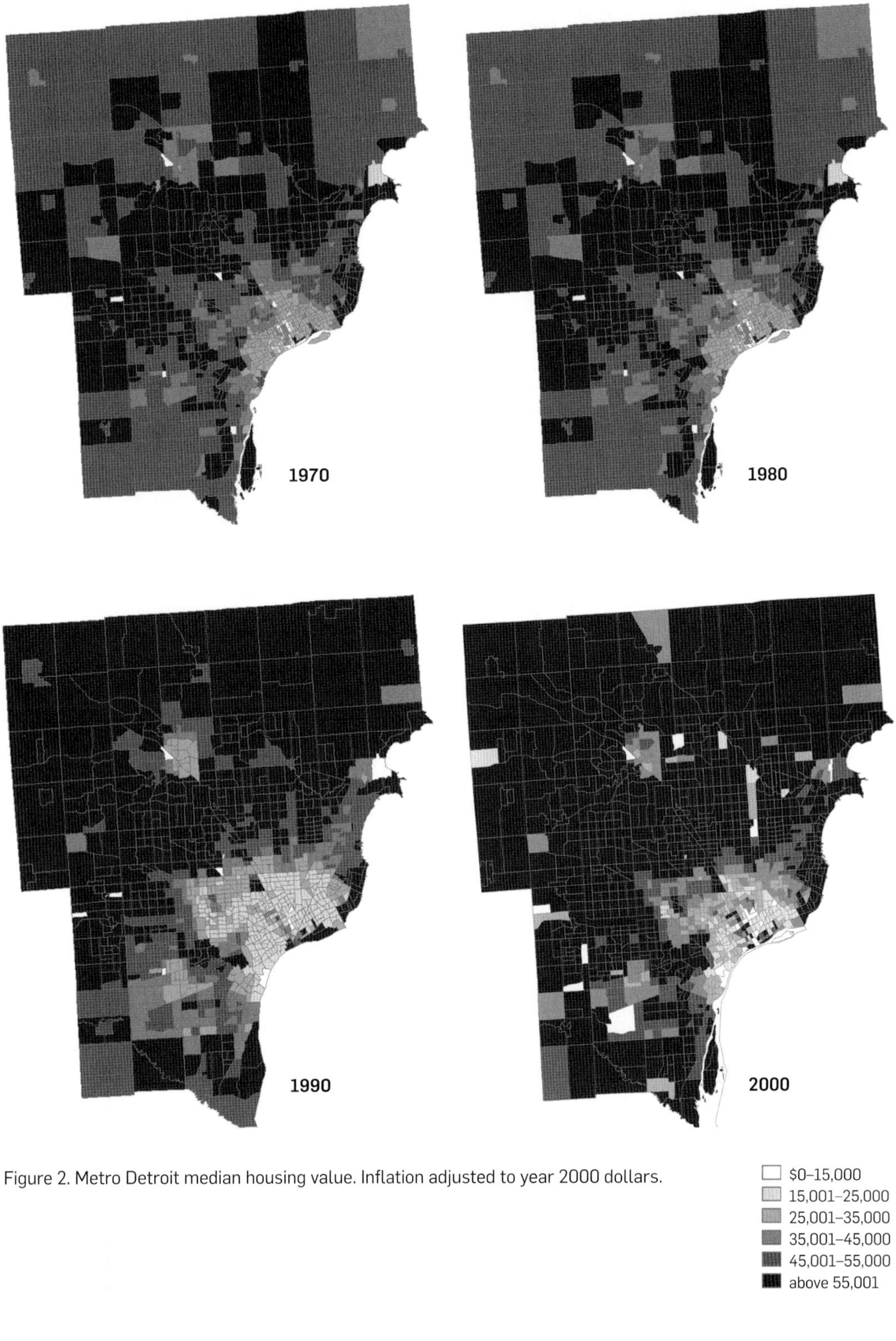

Figure 2. Metro Detroit median housing value. Inflation adjusted to year 2000 dollars.

PHOTOGRAPH BY IGOR VOJNOVIC

Figure 3. Detroit, a rapidly deteriorating urban landscape.

PHOTOGRAPH BY IGOR VOJNOVIC

Figure 4. Abandoned high-rises in Detroit.

PHOTOGRAPH BY IGOR VOJNOVIC

Figure 5. Closed stores and vacant buildings in proximity to the city center.

PHOTOGRAPH BY IGOR VOJNOVIC

Figure 6. Derelict and deserted former public buildings, from fire departments to schools, are found throughout Detroit.

decentralization and urban decline, creating an urban core characterized by extreme poverty and blight. Just between the years 2000 and 2010, the city of Detroit lost approximately a quarter of its population, decreasing in size from 951,270 residents in 2000 to 713,777 in 2010. This is a population loss in the city of close to 3 people every hour throughout the decade, and among those who left the city during this period, some 80 percent were black.

Since the city hit its population high of some 1.85 million during the 1950s, its population has been cut by more than 60 percent. The city of Detroit has lost over 1.1 million people in a little over five decades, and its average residential density has declined from 13,249 people per square mile (ppsm) in 1950 to some 5,170 ppsm in 2010.[6] But, as noted earlier, it has been a particular population type that has been lost from this city over the past five decades: the whites.

Severe local pressures are evident with the city given that it has been built to accommodate 1.85 million people, and now there are only some 700,000 that live within its administrative jurisdiction. While the Detroit region continues to decentralize and suburbanize, there are ongoing discussions within the city itself on how to reduce Detroit's boundaries. The layers of local government simply do not have the fiscal capacity to maintain basic public services—from police protection to snow removal to street lighting—in a city whose population is rapidly declining and where large areas of the city are abandoned.

The review in chapter 1 of inter- and intragenerational equity illustrates the inherent coupling between environmental and social equity in the pursuit of urban sustainability. This chapter explores one particular aspect of this relationship: the role of racial and class discrimination that is manifested in distortions in the urban built environment, which generates resource-inefficient and environmentally destructive human behavior. Racial and class conflicts shape urban form as one population group, largely white and upper-income, attempts to distance itself from another population group that it considers incompatible or a threat to its neighborhoods and way of life. This process of driving excessive suburbanization, as whites seek homogenous urban environments and use space to increase the distance between themselves and the black population, is a decentralization process known as white flight. The nature of resulting developments (inefficient low-density suburbanization) not only facilitates excessive degradation of natural ecological systems, but also reduces the economic performance and overall welfare of cities.

After exploring suburbanization in metropolitan Detroit (see fig. 7), the chapter examines the complex dimensions—natural environmental, built, social, and economic—of racially driven urban processes and outcomes that hinder the pursuit of urban sustainability.[7] The review will reinforce the inherent coupling between inter- and intragenerational equity by illustrating that by not pursuing intragenerational equity, communities will encourage resource-inefficient and environmentally destructive human behavior. The chapter concludes by assessing necessary changes in the urban built form, culture, and regional cooperation in setting a more sustainable pathway for development in the Detroit region.

Race, Class, and the Environment

Within the context of urban sustainability, environmental, social, and racial equity are inherently coupled. This is best evident in the work on environmental injustice and racism. The notion that

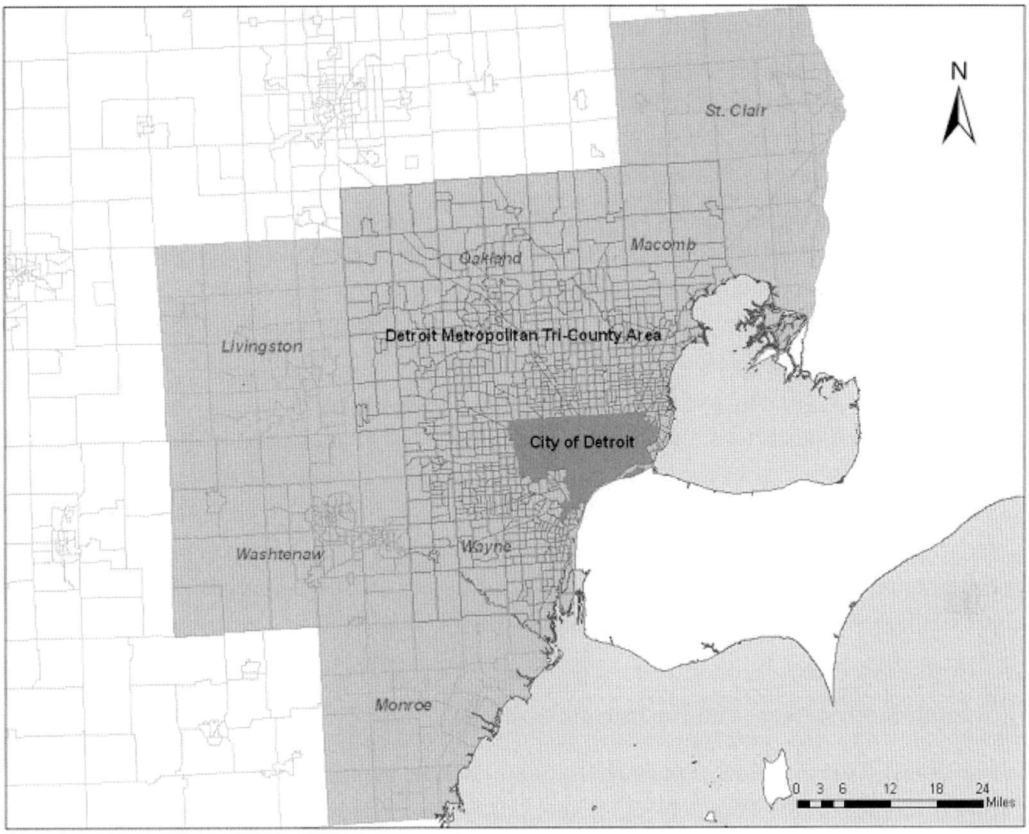

Figure 7. Metropolitan Detroit refers to the tricounty area of Macomb, Oakland, and Wayne counties. The broader Detroit regional government also includes St. Clair, Livingston, Washtenaw, and Monroe counties and is also known as the Southeast Michigan Region.

subgroup populations, and especially those of lower socioeconomic status and nonwhites, are disproportionately exposed to environmental burdens began to receive national attention during the 1980s. A lawsuit and two studies are credited for giving this topic its prominence.

In 1979 the residents of Northwood Manor, a black Houston neighborhood, filed what is considered the first environmental racism lawsuit on grounds of civil rights violation, *Bean versus Southwestern Waste Management*.[8] The legal action was brought against racially biased waste facility citing practices in the city of Houston. Between 1920 and 1978, seventeen solid-waste facilities were located in Houston's black neighborhoods. The city also operated eight garbage incinerators—six located in black neighborhoods, one in a Hispanic neighborhood, and one in a white neighborhood. While the plaintiffs lost the lawsuit, the case did attract national attention to the disproportionate exposure to environmental burdens among nonwhites.

Over the next decade, two studies further raised the prominence of environmental racism. In 1983, a report by the U.S. General Accounting Office revealed the inequities in the location of hazardous waste sites by showing that three of the four largest commercial landfills among eight southern U.S. states—which received hazardous waste from across the U.S. and internationally—were located in communities of color.[9] In 1987 the United Church of Christ's report *Toxic Wastes and Race in the United States* reached a similar conclusion, but added that among the numerous indicators evaluated, it was race that was the best predictor of hazardous facility location.[10] While studies on environmental exposure date back to the 1960s, these two reports were critical in establishing nationwide consciousness to the class and racial dimensions of environmental hazards.[11]

A distinction is made between environmental racism, which places an emphasis on nonwhites being disproportionately burdened with hazardous exposure, and environmental injustice, which is dependent on socioeconomic status as the variable determining inequitable and harmful environmental exposure. Beginning with the United Church of Christ's report, there has been general agreement that it is race and not class that more effectively predicts risk.[12] In understanding this bias, it is argued that environmental racism should be seen as part of wider racial oppression, shaped by the racist nature of socioeconomic structure and institutional organization in America.[13]

While research linking the environment and racism spans some four decades, it has been largely limited to the study of inequitable exposure of nonwhites to environmental hazards. This chapter explores the role of racial conflicts and oppression within the broader context of urban sustainability.

Sustainability, Race, and the Detroit Region

In the United States, an early engagement in a national discourse on sustainability occurred during the 1990s, when President Bill Clinton and Vice President Al Gore created the President's Council on Sustainable Development.[14] It consisted of members from private enterprise, nonprofits, and government, ranging from Kenneth Derr (chair and CEO of Chevron) to Michele Perrault (international vice president of Sierra Club). The council advanced ten goals in the pursuit of sustainability, including the pursuit of social and economic equity, equal access to education, improvements in public and environmental health, resource conservation, and habitat protection.[15] An initiative promoting similar sustainability goals is evident with the 2009 Partnership for Sustainable Communities, which over a three year period has provided some $3.5 billion in federal funding to over 700 communities in support of projects promoting sustainability.[16] With ongoing urban decentralization, increasing resource consumption, and growing wealth disparities, U.S. cities could do much more to advance toward these goals. However, Detroit remains a unique case in the scale to which it has and continues to distance itself from the sustainability condition.

The Detroit region illustrates the extent to which racial tensions, conflicts, and oppression facilitate and accelerate excessive and inefficient suburbanization, inhibiting any potential advancement toward sustainability. This review will also show that urban policy promoting inter- and intragenerational equity is strongly dependent on the encouragement of greater racial and class integration, which could facilitate urban compactness. This one initiative can advance equity while concurrently reducing resource consumption and environmental degradation (along with its broader global environmental impacts), illustrating the classic integrative environmental, social, and economic dimension of sustainability. However, an important element in the Detroit region preventing it from pursuing this policy direction is cultural: the absence of ethnic/racial tolerance and pluralistic ideals.

Decentralizing Urban America

The affordable automobile, public investment in roads and highways, increases in real incomes, and reduced real energy prices all encouraged decentralization. In addition, while the car facilitated residential suburbanization, the transport truck encouraged the decentralization of industry and retail. Given the concentration of automobile manufacturers in the region—including Ford, Dodge Brothers, and General Motors (which by 1920 included Chevrolet, Buick, Oldsmobile, and Cadillac)—the car industry was particularly influential in Detroit. The success of many of Detroit's automobile makers was also founded on the production of affordable cars, which enabled mass private transport, a corporate objective in direct conflict with mass transit.

In 1923, when Detroit's Rapid Transit Commission (RTC) introduced a comprehensive transportation plan (an integrated network of highways, subways, and streetcars) the City Council rejected the proposal due to costs. Given the opposition, Sidney Waldon, a retired automobile company executive who chaired the RTC, began to emphasize the "highway phase of the plan because of pressure from his former colleagues in the automobile industry."[17] Despite these efforts, a scaled-down version of the plan was rejected in 1926. In 1929 Detroit voters also rejected a bond proposition to build a subway. The opposition to mass transit in Detroit had successfully argued that while roads were a public good and required government aid, mass transit was a private good and should not be supported by government. As Kenneth Jackson noted, "Americans taxed and harassed public transportation, even while subsidizing the automobile like a pampered child."[18]

While many cities of Detroit's size and vintage built subways, Detroit never made such an investment. As a result, Detroit never developed the increasing capacity to move its population, and by freeing its roads, an increasing capacity to transport goods. Without a subway, Detroit was not able to achieve the residential and business concentrations in its core that other cities realized as a result of robust rapid rail networks.[19] However, the region's emphasis on roads and mass transportation by car, which became a status symbol and a defining commodity of the local culture, fueled suburbanization.

Suburbanization in Detroit, and in the United States as a whole, was also encouraged by the Federal Housing Administration and Veterans Administration mortgage guarantees, and by federal income tax deduction programs, which deduct interest of the mortgage and the property tax from income taxes. Other factors facilitating decentralization include increases in incomes, the subsidization of suburban public services, zoning bylaws that encouraged single-family detached housing, high crime rates within cities, reductions in the quality of urban schools, and residential preferences for large homes on large lots.[20] Particularly from the mid-1940s onward, homes and lots became larger, streets became wider, and new developments began to increasingly scatter and leapfrog.

By 1960 urban areas in the United States were using twice as much land as in 1950, yet the population had increased by only 38 percent. Average urban density, which was 5,410 people per square mile (ppsm) in 1950, was reduced to 3,759 ppsm by 1960. The proliferation of the suburbs would continue throughout the rest of the century. For instance, while the population in the United States increased by only 11 percent between 1982 and 1992, urban land increased by more than 25 percent during the same period.[21] Urban land consumption was also developing at an increasing rate. Between 1982 and 1997, while the population grew by 17 percent, urbanized land grew by 47 percent.[22] By 2000 lots were averaging 14,000 square feet and house sizes were averaging 2,400 square feet, twice the average lot and house size in comparison to just 1970.[23]

Municipal Fragmentation, Suburbanization, and the Tax Base

With a highly fragmented municipal structure, as in Metro Detroit, when the urban population and their tax base move into the suburbs, the reduced tax base in the city facilitates urban decline. In certain contexts, suburban residents are especially interested in a municipally fragmented

Table 1. Municipalities with the highest and lowest per capita assessed taxable values in the Detroit region, 2000

MUNICIPALITIES WITH THE *HIGHEST* PER CAPITA TAXABLE VALUES	TAXABLE VALUE PER CAPITA 2000	CHANGE IN TAXABLE VALUE 1990–2000 (INFLATION ADJUSTED)
Bloomfield Hills	$165,794	$88,066,682
Bingham Farms	$160,905	–$5,370,033
Lake Angelus	$132,393	$13,613,645
China Township	$128,835	–$211,070,756
Barton Hills	$119,187	$6,051,530
Orchard Lake Village	$119,049	$76,505,575
East China Township	$114,057	$2,637,179
Grosse Point Shores	$112,935	$640,509
Ann Arbor Township	$70,420	$64,531,029
Birmingham	$66,535	$170,392,931
MUNICIPALITIES WITH THE *LOWEST* PER CAPITA TAXABLE VALUES	**TAXABLE VALUE PER CAPITA 2000**	**CHANGE IN TAXABLE VALUE 1990–2000 (INFLATION ADJUSTED)**
Highland Park	$7,012	–$160,893,645
Hamtramck	$7,346	$20,497,092
Detroit	$7,573	–$147,128,602
Inkster	$8,401	–$2,258,755
New Haven	$10,875	$13,786,984
Hazel Park	$12,175	$18,616,127
Capac	$12,988	$5,299,744
Ypsilanti	$13,130	$8,689,726
Petersburg	$13,588	$4,278,398
Yale	$13,743	$8,798,688

Source: Southeast Michigan Council of Governments, Fiscal Capacity of Southeast Michigan Communities: Taxable Value and Its Implications (Detroit: SEMCOG, 2003).

Table 2. Instructional expenditure differences among Metro Detroit municipalities, 2003

MUNICIPALITIES WITH *HIGHEST* EXPENDITURES PER PUPIL	INSTRUCTIONAL SPENDING PER PUPIL	MUNICIPALITIES WITH *LOWEST* EXPENDITURES PER PUPIL	INSTRUCTIONAL SPENDING PER PUPIL
Bloomfield Hills	$6,148	Clintondale	$2,030
Southfield	$5,518	Redford Union	$2,444
Birmingham	$5,271	New Haven	$2,699
Grosse Pointe	$4,973	Holly	$2,907
Troy	$4,963	Highland Park	$3,054
Farmington	$4,856	Detroit	$3,100
Mt. Clemens	$4,851	Southgate	$3,120
Trenton	$4,737	Pontiac	$3,158
Dearborn	$4,731	Hamtramck	$3,171
West Bloomfield	$4,704	Richmond	$3,197

Note: These educational instruction expenditure distinctions are still evident a decade after Michigan voters approved Proposal A, an initiative that reduced what were then even greater funding capacity differences that existed between wealthier and poorer school districts.

Source: B. Heath, Michigan Still Shortchanges Poor Schools, *Detroit News*, May 25, 2003, 1A.

region because of their disinterest in supporting public services in the urban core. This fragmentation enables the development of exclusive suburbs with a rich property tax base and decaying urban cores that maintain high concentrations of poverty, crime, minorities, and deficient public services. Thus, despite the fact that many suburban residents earn their living in the urban core and make extensive use of its public services, they contribute minimally to the support of services in the city.[24]

Fiscal disparities in the region are evident in the comparison of taxable assessment (table 1). Not only is the per capita taxable assessment in Detroit only $7,573, but the city continues to confront a tax base exodus. These fiscal disparities have a direct impact on the capacity of municipalities to fund services and infrastructure investment.[25]

One public service that is of particular relevance is education, not only because of the implications of withholding adequate educational services from populations, but also because of the importance of educational funding in shaping urban form. Because of fiscal discrepancies, the quality of education that one receives is highly dependent on where one lives (see table 2). Since K–12 education is one of the most important variables in affecting housing demand by homebuyers with school age children, the lower spending and poorer quality of education in fiscally distressed cities encourages families to move into suburbs with better schools, further driving decentralization.

Exploring Race and Class in Shaping the Urban Environment

Racial and class inequality has been an important variable that has been intensified by the process of urban decentralization within the United States. The Detroit region emerges as an important case study, since it is not only one of the most extreme cases of urban decentralization and resulting inner-city decline, but also one of the best cases where metropolitan fragmentation so clearly reveals institutional oppression by race and place, separate and unequal economic and political power, and sharp differences along racial lines by neighborhood socioeconomic characteristics.

The factors of race, class, and place inequality and the process of urban decentralization, urban decay, and uneven development in metropolitan Detroit are best understood within the theoretical framework of the ideology of white supremacy.[26]

This ideology maintains that in any relationship involving the white population and the black population, the white population must have the superior position and the competitive advantage. In other words, the ideology of white supremacy provides inherited privilege to those with white skin despite their acquired status. Thus, when blacks have tried to demonstrate their acquired status of racial equality by competing for high level jobs, quality housing, and quality education, which have been traditionally a privilege of whites, resistance often occurs, leading to racial conflict and racial discrimination. This has been the history of metropolitan Detroit, which has created a deep racial divide as most whites have used the suburbs (a geographic boundary) to separate themselves from blacks in the city and to maintain their unequal status, especially after antidiscrimination in housing legislation passed during the sixties.[27]

Policy makers in metropolitan Detroit and in the state of Michigan have failed to address the problems. Their primary interests have not been providing racial equity to the disadvantaged black minority, but rather stability in the city and preservation of their own privileged position. In the meantime, the trend of out-migration of whites from the city to the suburbs continues along with uneven economic growth and decline and unequal opportunities for advancement and social mobility for blacks in metropolitan Detroit.

Metropolitan Detroit: Race, Class, and the Shaping of the Urban Built Environment

Detroit was thriving as a city in 1950. The population growth and economic investment were closely associated with the location of the auto industry in the city. As the auto industry grew in Detroit, so did the population and its economic well-being. In 1950, for example, because of work

Table 3. Population growth, city of Detroit, 1900–1950

YEAR	TOTAL POPULATION	TOTAL % CHANGE	BLACK POPULATION*	BLACK % OF TOTAL POPULATION
1900	285,704	38.8	4,111	1.4
1910	465,766	63.0	5,741	1.2
1920	993,678	113.3	40,838	4.1
1930	1,568,662	57.9	120,066	7.7
1940	1,623,452	3.5	149,119	9.2
1950	1,849,568	13.9	300,506	16.2

Source: U.S. Department of Commerce, Bureau of the Census, Michigan, 1900–1950 (Washington, DC: U.S. Government Printing Office, 1906, 1913, 1922, 1932, 1943, 1952.

* Black or African American alone.

Table 4. Population decline, city of Detroit, 1960–2010

YEAR	TOTAL POPULATION	TOTAL % CHANGE	BLACK POPULATION*	BLACK % OF TOTAL POPULATION
1960	1,670,144	−9.7	482,229	28.9
1970	1,511,482	−9.5	660,428	43.7
1980	1,203,339	−20.5	758,939	63.0
1990	1,026,670	−15.0	774,529	76.0
2000	951,270	−0.07	775,772	81.5
2010	713,777	−25.0	590,226	82.7

Source: U.S. Bureau of the Census, *Population and Housing 1960–2000: Michigan* (Washington, DC: U.S. Government Printing Office, 1963, 1972, 1982, 1992, 2002); U.S. Census Bureau, 2010 Census Redistricting Data (Washington, DC: U.S. Government Printing Office, 2011).

* Black or African American alone.

in the auto industry, the poverty rate in the city of Detroit was actually lower than the poverty rate in the suburbs, and the median household income was about the same.[28]

Living in the city of Detroit near the auto plants had certain advantages. As long as these advantages existed, the population of Detroit continued to grow (table 3). Population growth was clearly linked to investment in the auto industry. As new auto plants were built further outward spatially, residential development also spread and became increasingly differential by race, class, and place.

Between 1947 and 1955, for example, Ford, Chrysler, and General Motors constructed twenty new plants in suburban Detroit.[29] Ford Motor Company contributed to the decentralization of the auto industry and to the suburbanization of housing in response to military orders for the Korean War.[30] The suburban pattern of auto investment at the expense of the city had a severe impact on the population, driving its continual decline.

Associated with population decline is a continual drain of resources out of the city and into the suburbs. Although largely unmeasured, the drain includes human resources and capital. As a result, the declining area is left without the most important resources needed for development and growth, and the economic infrastructure is seriously deficient.[31]

The drain of human resources happens because professionals often leave the declining areas first, followed by many of the most capable and most educated. The drain of capital is equally striking. A substantial portion of the savings of the declining central city goes into financial institutions such as banks and savings associations, whose investment policies often drain funds out of the central city area and into business loans, mortgages, and other investments in the suburbs. Perhaps one of the most important aspects of the flow of capital out of the central city takes place in housing.[32] One deteriorated building draws down the value of surrounding property. Deterioration often leads to even less investment in the neighborhood, where the neighborhood soon follows in a self-perpetuating cycle of decay. Home-improvement loans are often denied in the declining area.[33] This leads to poor maintenance, as growth breeds growth and decline breeds decline. Just as population growth was related to investment in the city's auto industry, population decline was related to disinvestment in the city and disproportionate investment in the suburbs (table 4).

Race Matters in Influencing City/Suburban Residential Patterns

In 2010 the Detroit metropolitan area (Wayne, Oakland, and Macomb) consisted of 3,863,924 people. Of this total, 2,598,821, or 67.3 percent, were white, while 974,744, or 25.2 percent, were black.[34] Of these, 97.1 percent of all whites lived in the suburbs and only 2.9 percent resided in the city. This made an already predominantly black city even blacker. By 2000 the city of Detroit had declined in population from 1 million people in 1990 to a total of 951,270 and dropped to 713,777 by 2010.[35] It had also become 81.3 percent black in 2000 and 82.7 percent black in 2010.[36] This was up from 75 percent in 1990. Thus, blacks and whites in metropolitan Detroit continued to live in separate neighborhoods. To determine just how segregated blacks and whites in Metro Detroit were in 2010, we computed an index of dissimilarity.

The index of dissimilarity is a method to determine the extent of unevenness in the spatial distribution of two groups over subunits (census tracts). If the two groups are evenly distributed (i.e., their proportions of the population are equal in the tracts), the index would be "0," reflecting no residential segregation. If, on the other hand, the two groups do not share residential space (i.e., they live in completely different census tracts), the index would be "100," reflecting complete residential segregation. As the index increases, so does the degree of racial residential segregation.[37] Although other indexes have also been used to measure residential segregation, such as the isolation index, the index of dissimilarity is the most widely used index. In 2010 the index of dissimilarity between blacks and whites in the Detroit metropolitan area was 79.6. This index for blacks and whites was higher than the index for any other racial minority group in Metropolitan Detroit.[38]

Central City and Suburban Blacks and Whites

Patterns of race and class segregation evolved over time and did not occur by chance. The patterns were created primarily by white real estate brokers, apartment managers, and builders who controlled the housing market and who had the capital to invest in economic development projects. They made the decision to exclude most blacks from purchasing or renting housing in the suburbs while allowing and even encouraging most whites to leave the city for the suburbs. At the same time, most white investors disinvested in the city and invested overwhelmingly in economic development and housing projects in the suburbs.[39]

The exclusion of blacks from the suburbs also involved the federal government, through the use of Federal Housing Administration (FHA) insured mortgages. Xavier Briggs edited volume has presented a comprehensive discussion of the important role of the federal government's involvement in furthering the facilitation of white suburbanization in metropolitan areas. Most of the federal housing programs subsidized by the government had regulations that encouraged or specified homogeneous neighborhoods based on race and class. These programs primarily benefited white middle- and working-class residents, since the FHA adopted a racially segregationist policy and refused to insure properties that did not comply. White appraisers were told to look for physical barriers between the races or find and honor racially restrictive covenants. The race of the applicant and the racial composition of the neighborhoods were officially listed as valid reasons for rejecting a mortgage. Thus, most blacks were denied equal access to Detroit's growing suburbs. Research on metropolitan Detroit shows that neither socioeconomic inequality between blacks and whites nor racial preferences of blacks explain the bulk of the residential segregation of blacks in the city of Detroit.

With the demographic and geographic structure of the Detroit metropolitan area fixed primarily by years of racial discrimination in housing, from 1950 to 1980, at least fifty incorporated places were added to Detroit's metropolitan area. The population of those suburban places consisted of 737,007 whites and only 4,852 blacks.[40] With the movement to the suburbs of the white population after 1950, the city of Detroit started to decline in total population.

In 2010 metropolitan Detroit and Milwaukee were two of the most racially segregated large metropolitan areas in the United States. With such extreme racial residential segregation has come extreme class segregation. The city of Detroit ranked at the top of the scale in the percent of the population below the poverty level (about 35 percent) in 2010. Nationally, the poverty rate was 15.1 percent.

The stark inequality between poor blacks in the central city and the more affluent whites in the suburbs makes metropolitan Detroit unusual. All but three of the forty-eight concentrated poverty neighborhoods (defined as census tracts where 40 percent or more of the population is poor) were located in the city of Detroit in 1999. On the other hand, all of the eleven concentrated affluent neighborhoods (defined as census tracts where more than 50 percent of the residents had median family incomes above 150 percent of the median family income for the Detroit metropolitan area as a whole) were located in suburban Oakland County.[41]

The city of Detroit has been experiencing an economic decline related to globalization, auto industry disinvestment, and economic restructuring, while the suburbs located in Oakland County remain comparatively prosperous. Indeed, Oakland County is one of the wealthiest counties in the United States. Thus, population growth, social and spatial mobility, and economic development in metropolitan Detroit have been uneven, and this unevenness is most visible by race, place, and quality of life.[42]

Urban Decentralization: Exploring the Impacts of Unsustainable Development Processes

It is at multiple dimensions (environmental, economic, and social) that excessive decentralization hinders sustainability.

Environmental Implications of Suburbanization

The concentration of residents and employment within a city will determine the amount of land necessary to accommodate a population. A city characterized by low densities will require more land to accommodate the same number of people when compared to a city characterized by a more compact urban form. While some, such as Peter Gordon and Harry W. Richardson, argue that the geographic size of the United States makes the issue of land consumption trivial, this land conversion cannot be viewed as insignificant. For instance, between 1997 and 2001 more than 1 million acres of U.S. forestland was developed. In Michigan, between 1982 and 1992 the state lost

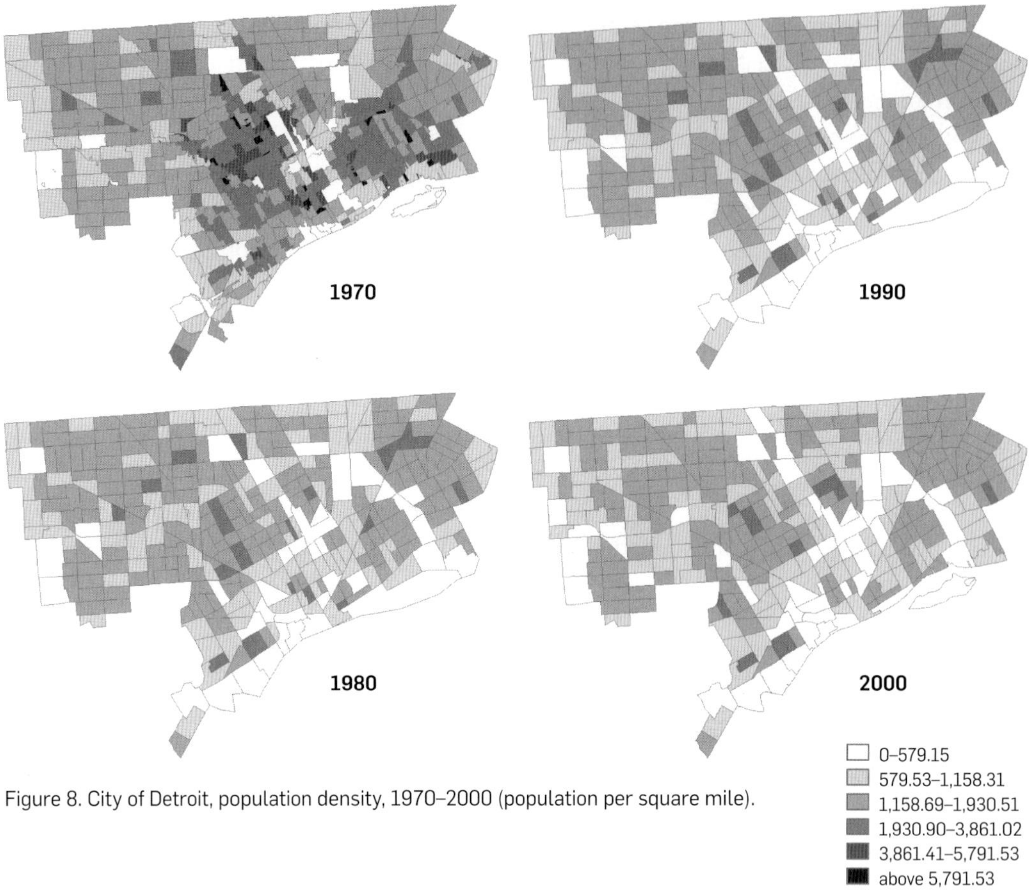

Figure 8. City of Detroit, population density, 1970–2000 (population per square mile).

854,000 acres of farmland to urban development, an average of 10 acres every hour. In addition to land consumption, the separation of activities in decentralizing cities generates resource-intensive transportation patterns, greater automobile-dependence, increased energy use for heating and cooling buildings, and greater infrastructure requirements.[43]

In the Detroit region, the conversion of natural and agricultural lands to urban uses occurred at a rate thirteen times greater than population growth between 1960 and 1990. While developments in the Detroit region maintained an average residential density of 2.84 housing units per acre in 1990, the density of new housing construction during the 1990s was cut to less than half, to 1.26 housing units per acre.[44] The average residential density in the city of Detroit proper, which was 13,249 people per square mile (ppsm) in 1950, was reduced to 10,953 ppsm in 1970, and 5,170 ppsm in 2010 (see fig. 8 for changes in population density to year 2000).

At the regional scale, local spatial structure effectively illustrates options for regional development (fig. 9). Two structures that are efficient in terms of land and resource use are monocentric and polycentric regions. These built forms accommodate concentrated activity nodes, employment and housing clusters that enable high-density concentrations while facilitating lower density peripheral housing options. The monocentric spatial structure is appropriate for smaller centers,

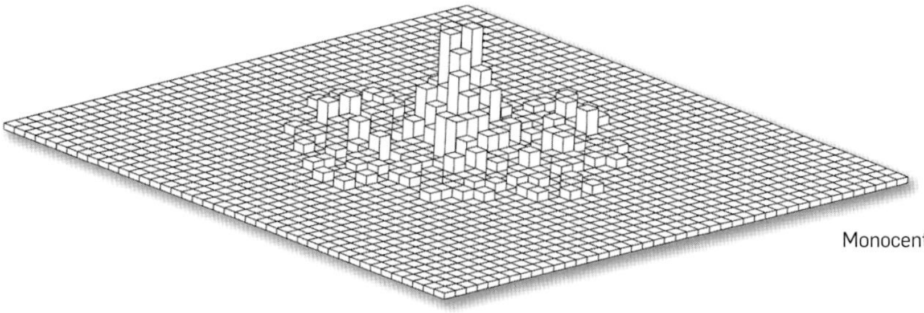

Monocentric urban region.

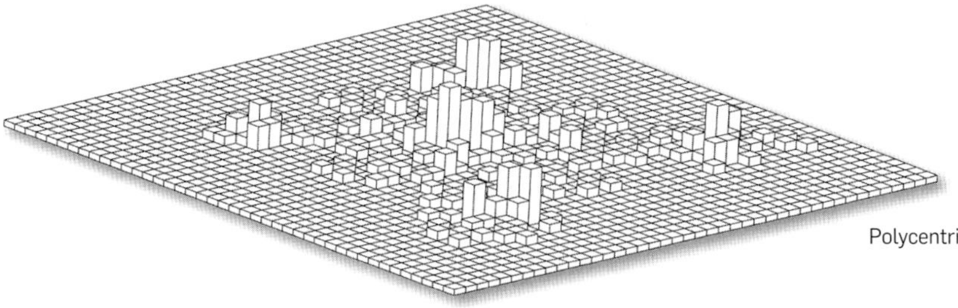

Polycentric urban region.

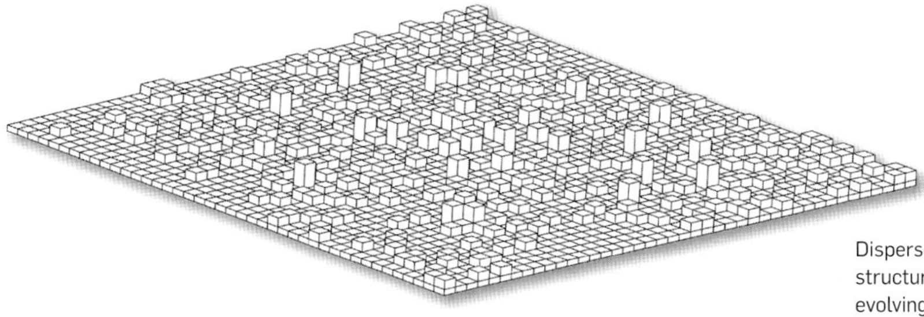

Dispersed urban region, the regional structure that the Detroit region is evolving toward.

Figure 9. Residential and employment concentrations in monocentric, polycentric, and dispersed urban regions.

but as a region grows, congestion makes the polycentric structure a more suitable alternative. In comparison, a dispersed, low-density built environment uses land relatively inefficiently. Los Angeles was the first large U.S. metropolitan center recognized as evolving toward a uniformly dispersed region. Table 5 shows patterns of employment and population concentrations in the Detroit region, illustrating that the Detroit area is also evolving toward a dispersed regional structure, but at half the density of Metropolitan Los Angeles.[45]

The increasingly dispersed nature of developments in the region—in addition to the degradation of farmlands, forests, and wetlands—increases distances between destinations and encourages automobile dependence. In 1960, for instance, vehicle ownership in the Detroit region averaged 365.5 cars per 1,000 people. By 1990 this figure had almost doubled to 693.4 cars per 1,000 people. During the same period, the percentage of the population in the region that walked or cycled to work was cut by more than two-thirds, from 6.4 percent to 2.0 percent. In addition, the proportion of the regional population that used public transit to get to work was reduced from 13.8 percent in 1960 to 2.6 percent in 1990.[46]

Table 5. Major employment and population nodes in the Detroit region, 1970 and 2000

1970

CITIES	EMPLOYMENT	% OF REGION	POPULATION	% OF REGION
Detroit	735,104	37.9	1,514,063	32.0
Dearborn	105,532	5.4	104,199	2.2
Warren	93,821	4.8	179,260	3.8
Pontiac	68,127	3.5	85,279	1.8
Southfield	55,912	2.9	69,285	1.5
Ann Arbor	52,499	2.7	100,035	2.1
Livonia	50,858	2.6	110,109	2.3
Highland Park	33,997	1.8	35,444	0.8
Ecorse	31,464	1.6	17,515	0.4
Sterling Heights	26,037	1.3	61,365	1.3
Top ten total	**1,253,351**	**64.7**	**2,276,554**	**48.1**
Region	**1,938,512**	**100.0**	**4,736,008**	**100.0**

2000

CITIES	EMPLOYMENT	% OF REGION	POPULATION	% OF REGION
Detroit	345,424	12.9	951,270	19.7
Troy	135,977	5.1	80,959	1.7
Southfield	128,407	4.8	78,296	1.6
Ann Arbor	124,378	4.7	114,024	2.4
Dearborn	108,418	4.1	97,775	2.0
Livonia	105,019	3.9	100,545	2.1
Warren	101,187	3.8	138,247	2.9
Farmington Hills	78,835	2.9	82,111	1.7
Sterling Heights	68,008	2.5	124,471	2.6
Pontiac	63,070	2.4	66,337	1.4
Top ten total	**1,258,723**	**47.1**	**1,834,035**	**37.9**
Region	**2,673,052**	**100.0**	**4,833,493**	**100.0**

Source: Southeast Michigan Council of Governments, *Historical Population and Employment by Minor Civil Division, Southeast Michigan* (Detroit: SEMCOG, 2002).

Tables 6 and 7 illustrate environmental impacts associated with Detroit's excessive decentralization. The resource demands of this built environment are evident in longer travel distances (with a Detroit resident annually traveling about twice the distance of a typical European urban resident and three times the distance of an Asian resident), greater petroleum use, higher emissions, and greater infrastructure requirements. While a typical Detroit resident will travel an average of over 9,953 miles annually, a typical Toronto resident will travel 5,717 miles, a London resident will travel 5,001 miles, and a Hong Kong resident only 2,856 miles. In turn, the greater travel distances result in greater automobile dependence and higher levels of energy consumption and pollutant emissions. The Detroit travel patterns also result in a greater ecological footprint and increasing global environmental burdens.

Economic Implications of Suburbanization

Greater urban compactness not only reduces resource use and minimizes the degradation of natural ecosystems, but such an urban form can also improve the economic performance of urban regions. The increased material and energy requirements in the construction and the maintenance of decentralized urban forms—associated with material use for the built structures, physical infrastructure provision, and operating costs of servicing decentralization—results in higher municipal costs and also higher housing costs. The Southeast Michigan Council of Governments (SEMCOG) explored the economics of decentralization in eighteen Michigan communities, including the Detroit area.[47]

There are considerable benefits associated with compact developments in the Detroit region, Southeast Michigan.[48] These include cost savings in local and state road provision, in water and sewage provision, and in private development costs (table 8). Environmental benefits are also evident with the preservation of farmlands, natural lands, and sensitive ecosystems. With greater development compactness, by 2020 local governments in the Detroit region would save approximately $1.7 million dollars in servicing costs and a total of 2,386 acres of farmland and 832 acres of natural land. In addition, residential housing costs would be reduced by an average of $11,400 per unit, associated with the use of less land and on-site infrastructure. This shows, again, that beneficial social, economic, and environmental outcomes can be achieved simultaneously. Simply, less resource use in the development process reduces costs. This relationship is consistent with the global comparison in tables 6 and 7, with high-density centers requiring less infrastructure (such as roads), lower levels of energy, and less pollution generation.

There are also extensive private costs associated with the automobile. In 1997 (when petroleum prices were considerably below current levels) the average American spent some 25 percent of annual income, about $6,500, on automobile ownership.[49] For a family that does not own property, an increase of $6,500 in disposable income would make the purchase of a house more accessible. This would be a much wiser investment than a car, as long as the family lives in a transit- or walking-friendly city.

Finally, economic costs of excessive suburbanization are also evident in regional competitiveness. By the 1980s, after decades of unyielding decentralization, it was argued that the information economy (with telecommuting, teleconferencing, and e-shopping) would facilitate the continued dispersal of urban America, making cities increasingly irrelevant. While Detroit has fulfilled this prognosis, the most economically competitive urban centers (cities with the highest levels of investment and employment) have pursued the exact opposite development direction, urban intensification. Both in the United States (evident with New York and San Francisco) and globally (apparent with London and Tokyo) infrastructure investment, businesses, and residents began concentrating in cities that emerged as dominant economic centers. In contrast to the prediction of urban decentralization and urban irrelevancy, since the 1980s residential and employment densities increased within these urban regions and their cores.

Table 6. Global comparison of urban densities, travel behavior, gasoline use, CO_2 emissions, and infrastructure provision

CITY	POPULATION DENSITY[1]		EMPLOYMENT DENSITY[1]		ANNUAL TRAVEL[2]			GASOLINE USE[3]	TOTAL TRANSPORTATION ENERGY[4]	CO_2 EMISSIONS[5]	ROAD SUPPLY[6]	CBD PARKING SPACES[7]
	METRO	INNER-AREA[8]	METRO	INNER-AREA	TOTAL	IN PRIVATE CARS	IN PUBLIC TRANSIT					
Sacramento	5.1	7.9	2.8	5.1	12,027	11,955	73	65,351	76,673	12,178	28.9	777
Houston	3.9	7.5	2.3	8.7	11,942	11,809	134	63,800	71,624	11,449	38.4	612
San Diego	5.3	13.0	2.8	7.9	11,816	11,655	161	61,004	67,248	10,684	18.0	688
Phoenix	4.3	6.6	2.1	12.6	9,958	9,882	77	59,832	64,641	10,260	31.5	906
San Francisco	6.5	24.2	3.4	19.6	10,643	10,084	559	58,493	65,890	11,292	15.1	137
Portland	4.7	9.6	3.4	9.5	9,290	9,112	178	57,699	70,698	11,230	34.8	403
Denver	5.2	6.6	3.5	5.9	8,522	8,398	124	56,132	68,286	10,937	24.9	606
Los Angeles	9.7	11.6	5.0	6.3	10,586	10,368	219	55,246	62,167	9,868	12.5	520
Detroit	5.2	11.6	2.5	4.4	9,953	9,846	106	54,817	62,744	9,960	19.7	706
Boston	4.9	17.5	2.9	13.8	11,185	10,795	390	50,617	58,391	9,343	22.0	285
Washington	5.5	15.4	3.8	18.3	10,556	10,075	481	49,593	60,454	9,707	17.1	253
Chicago	6.7	19.2	3.5	9.6	9,260	8,759	500	46,498	56,121	8,971	17.1	128
New York	7.8	37.0	4.5	21.2	7,703	6,874	829	46,409	51,626	8,331	15.1	60
American average	**5.7**	**14.4**	**3.3**	**11.0**	**10,264**	**9,970**	**295**	**55,807**	**64,351**	**10,324**	**22.6**	**468**
Calgary	8.4	9.2	4.9	9.6	7,365	6,884	482	35,684	47,133	7,480	16.1	522
Winnipeg	8.6	16.7	3.6	11.8	6,372	5,978	395	32,018	39,366	6,248	13.8	546
Edmonton	12.1	10.9	6.4	—	6,684	6,231	452	31,848	44,060	6,993	15.7	593
Vancouver	8.4	16.8	4.3	12.1	8,334	7,793	541	31,544	37,211	5,893	16.7	443
Toronto	16.8	24.3	9.4	17.9	5,717	4,366	1,350	30,746	33,613	5,366	8.5	176
Montreal	13.7	25.6	6.0	17.3	4,632	4,040	592	27,706	—	5,331	14.8	347
Ottawa	12.7	19.9	6.4	39.6	5,646	5,118	528	26,705	33,562	5,342	23.3	230
Canadian average	**11.5**	**17.7**	**5.8**	**18.1**	**6,393**	**5,773**	**620**	**30,893**	**39,173**	**6,094**	**15.4**	**408**
Canberra	3.8	3.5	2.0	5.5	7,366	6,956	410	40,699	44,995	7,143	28.9	842
Perth	4.3	6.6	1.8	6.4	7,813	7,474	338	34,579	41,395	6,570	35.1	631
Brisbane	4.0	8.2	1.6	8.4	7,511	6,952	559	31,290	39,277	6,391	26.9	322
Melbourne	6.0	11.0	2.4	17.4	6,603	6,078	524	33,527	38,890	6,429	25.3	337
Adelaide	4.8	7.6	2.1	10.5	7,298	6,946	355	31,784	37,103	5,891	26.2	580
Sydney	6.8	15.9	2.9	15.4	6,951	5,851	1,099	29,491	35,074	5,706	20.3	222
Australian average	**4.9**	**8.8**	**2.2**	**10.6**	**7,257**	**6,709**	**548**	**33,562**	**39,456**	**6,356**	**27.2**	**489**

CITY	POPULATION DENSITY[1]		EMPLOYMENT DENSITY[1]		ANNUAL TRAVEL[2]			GASOLINE USE[3]	TOTAL TRANSPORTATION ENERGY[4]	CO_2 EMISSIONS[5]	ROAD SUPPLY[6]	CBD PARKING SPACES[7]
	METRO	INNER-AREA[8]	METRO	INNER-AREA	TOTAL	IN PRIVATE CARS	IN PUBLIC TRANSIT					
Frankfurt	18.9	24.7	17.5	37.9	5,877	5,163	714	24,779	38,293	6,202	6.6	246
Brussels	30.3	36.8	18.9	33.4	5,118	4,231	887	21,080	28,895	4,661	6.9	314
Hamburg	16.1	34.7	9.6	38.5	5,572	4,717	854	20,344	36,716	5,908	8.5	177
Zurich	19.1	29.8	14.3	29.5	6,308	4,780	1,528	19,947	25,244	3,889	13.1	137
Stockholm	21.5	37.1	15.9	51.2	5,351	3,890	1,461	18,362	26,817	4,396	7.2	193
Vienna	27.7	52.1	15.1	44.7	4,786	3,276	1,510	14,990	20,603	3,318	5.9	186
Copenhagen	11.6	21.8	6.5	14.3	5,814	4,815	999	14,609	20,385	3,404	15.1	223
Paris	18.7	39.2	8.9	22.7	4,327	3,009	1,318	14,269	24,241	3,799	3.0	199
Munich	21.7	43.3	15.1	60.8	5,212	3,682	1,530	14,224	18,197	3,177	5.9	266
Amsterdam	19.8	36.2	9.0	17.5	4,712	4,053	659	13,915	19,843	3,252	8.5	354
London	17.1	31.6	9.6	25.8	5,001	3,507	1,494	12,884	23,374	3,757	6.6	—
European average	**20.2**	**35.2**	**12.8**	**34.2**	**5,279**	**4,102**	**1,178**	**17,218**	**25,692**	**4,160**	**7.9**	**230**
Kuala Lumpur	23.8	27.9	9.1	14.5	4,893	3,914	980	11,643	20,017	3,139	4.9	297
Singapore	35.1	50.3	20.0	53.8	3,693	1,969	1,724	11,383	18,079	2,903	3.6	164
Tokyo	28.7	53.5	29.6	43.8	5,391	1,973	3,418	8,015	18,243	3,080	12.8	43
Bangkok	60.5	116.8	25.3	48.4	4,317	2,879	1,437	7,742	18,176	2,875	2.0	397
Seoul	99.1	121.0	41.1	84.9	3,327	1,531	1,796	5,293	9,615	1,554	2.6	49
Jakarta	69.2	108.0	23.8	54.7	1,783	961	822	4,787	9,072	1,440	1.6	—
Manila	80.2	150.8	27.4	45.1	2,392	796	1,596	2,896	7,335	1,166	2.0	27
Surabaya	71.6	107.3	31.5	—	1,319	974	345	2,633	5,611	891	1.0	—
Hong Kong	121.7	325.5	56.7	313.8	2,856	505	2,351	2,406	9,612	1,676	1.0	33
Asian average	**65.5**	**117.9**	**29.4**	**82.4**	**3,330**	**1,722**	**1,608**	**6,311**	**12,862**	**2,081**	**3.6**	**144**

1. Population per acre.
2. Passenger miles per capita.
3. Per capita; private transportation (MJ).
4. Per capita; public and private (MJ).
5. Per capita; total transportation (lbs.)
6. Feet per person.
7. Per 1,000 jobs.
8. The inner-area density refers to the pre–World War II city area developed mostly before the emergence of automobile-dependent lifestyles.

Sources: Jeffrey Kenworthy and Felix Laube, *An International Sourcebook of Automobile Dependence in Cities, 1960–1990* (Boulder: University Press of Colorado, 1999); Peter Newman and Jeffrey Kenworthy, *Sustainability and Cities: Overcoming Automobile Dependence* (Washington DC: Island Press, 1999).

Table 7. Global urban comparison of annual air pollutant emissions

CITY	CO PER CAPITA (LB.)	NO_x PER CAPITA (LB.)	SO_2 PER CAPITA (LB.)	VHC* PER CAPITA (LB.)
Phoenix	365.9	47.4	3.7	52.0
Denver	520.1	42.5	3.2	46.5
Boston	490.9	56.2	4.0	48.7
Houston	531.8	58.6	4.4	60.9
Washington	405.7	48.5	3.5	45.2
San Francisco	432.3	46.9	3.8	47.8
Detroit	543.9	54.2	3.8	54.2
Chicago	406.9	45.6	3.1	44.3
Los Angeles	399.0	43.9	3.5	47.6
New York	412.3	46.7	3.3	45.0
American Average	**450.8**	**49.2**	**3.5**	**49.2**
Perth	412.7	44.8	0.9	52.0
Adelaide	370.6	40.1	0.9	46.7
Brisbane	412.9	64.8	2.4	54.5
Melbourne	395.1	39.7	1.1	50.0
Sydney	456.4	52.0	1.3	49.8
Australian Average	**409.6**	**48.3**	**1.3**	**50.7**
Frankfurt	150.4	44.3	2.0	26.7
Amsterdam	75.4	28.2	—	12.6
Zurich	71.4	26.7	0.9	19.0
Brussels	145.3	36.8	2.7	22.7
Munich	138.9	28.2	1.8	21.6
Stockholm	457.7	39.2	2.2	58.9
Vienna	110.2	9.3	7.1	11.5
Hamburg	118.0	28.2	17.6	18.3
Copenhagen	129.2	15.7	—	7.5
London	213.9	36.2	2.0	37.5
Paris	150.6	23.4	3.5	44.3
European Average	**160.1**	**28.7**	**4.4**	**25.6**
Singapore	—	—	—	—
Tokyo	31.5	9.7	1.7	4.4
Hong Kong	55.6	17.6	3.7	5.3
Wealthy Asian Average	**43.7**	**13.7**	**2.9**	**4.9**
Kuala Lumpur	198.4	24.7	2.2	50.3
Surabaya	92.6	6.8	2.0	25.8
Jakarta	127.1	35.7	2.0	20.5
Bangkok	186.5	7.9	4.0	51.2
Seoul	63.5	19.6	3.3	7.9
Beijing	—	—	—	—
Manila	148.8	20.3	3.3	24.7
Poor Asian Average	**136.3**	**19.2**	**2.9**	**30.0**

* Volatile hydrocarbons

Source: Jeffrey Kenworthy and Felix Laube, *An International Sourcebook of Automobile Dependence in Cities 1960–1990* (Boulder: University Press of Colorado, 1999).

Table 8. Annual cost savings of compact versus current growth in Michigan by the year 2020

	CURRENT			COMPACT			BENEFITS OF COMPACT GROWTH		
COMMUNITY	ADDED COSTS ($)	ADDED REVENUES ($)	COST REVENUE IMPACT ($)	ADDED COSTS ($)	ADDED REVENUES ($)	COST REVENUE IMPACT ($)	ANNUAL MUNICIPAL COST SAVINGS ($)	RESIDENTIAL CONSTRUCTION SAVINGS ($ PER UNIT)	ACRES OF LAND SAVED
Southeast Michigan municipalities									
Harrison	1,542,388	861,076	−681,312	1,490,966	820,540	−670,426	10,886	11,952	152
Macomb	5,091,515	4,379,449	−712,067	4,053,520	3,969,190	−84,330	627,737	18,646	−66
Bedford	996,846	1,134,165	137,319	965,328	1,121,665	156,337	19,018	1,402	101
Novi	14,769,424	11,766,829	−3,002,594	14,653,446	11,807,116	−2,846,331	156,264	−1,989	711
Pittsfield	3,719,980	7,490,948	3,770,967	3,734,848	7,514,031	3,779,183	8,216	−2,029	516
Canton	9,275,327	5,419,323	−3,856,004	7,924,363	4,942,195	−2,982,168	873,836	30,456	1,820
Grand Rapids/Muskegon region									
Kentwood	3,572,526	1,998,102	−1,574,424	3,390,741	1,962,729	−1,428,012	146,413	798	571
Allendale	912,787	1,113,150	200,363	845,180	1,058,339	213,159	12,796	9,585	981
Montague	339,440	330,129	−9,311	327,076	309,401	−17,675	−8,364	5,384	37
Muskegon	1,632,708	2,505,778	873,070	1,585,668	2,409,922	824,254	−48,816	3,767	50
Traverse City region									
Bear Creek	221,193	274,641	53,448	215,853	271,439	55,586	2,139	−118	87
Petoskey	452,279	161,444	−290,835	430,191	153,176	277,015	13,819	6,221	11
Resort	271,442	119,814	−151,628	265,515	121,504	144,011	7,617	−5,258	266
Garfield	1,925,993	1,998,648	72,655	1,776,888	1,925,961	149,073	76,418	5,964	1,700
Communities in other regions									
Portage	6,006,245	6,086,134	79,889	5,611,165	5,603,079	−8,086	−87,975	14,770	485
Hartford	82,057	79,616	−2,441	81,236	77,675	−3,561	−1,120	2,604	5
Meridian	1,920,088	1,582,411	−337,677	1,843,368	1,509,790	−333,578	4,099	7,764	625
Mt. Pleasant	2,697,763	3,740,532	1,042,769	2,548,033	3,575,147	1,027,113	−15,656	19,870	111
Total	**55,430,002**	**51,042,190**	**−4,387,812**	**51,743,387**	**49,152,900**	**−2,590,487**	**1,797,326**	**10,466**	**8,164**

Source: SEMCOG. 1997. Fiscal Impacts of Alternative Land Development Patterns in Michigan. Detroit: Southeast Michigan Council of Governments.

A number of reasons explain the economic competitiveness of metropolitan regions with strong urban cores over centers with declining inner cities, like Detroit. Regions with weak urban cores generally maintain low investment in public infrastructure—such as transportation (mass transit, airports, ports, and rail), communications, and education—reducing the operating regional capacities of retail, commerce, and manufacturing. In a high-tech and specialized services economy, investment in education is particularly relevant, which both trains local labor and provides research and development support for local firms. The variability in in-class spending in Detroit Metro is common in U.S. cities with declining cores; in turn, the poorer quality of educational infrastructure will affect the competitiveness of local labor. Ultimately, infrastructure is critical for effective corporate performance. In 2007, for instance, Volkswagen announced the move of its headquarters from the Detroit area to Herndon, Virginia. The move was the result of "Virginia's high-quality schools, skilled workforce and proximity to the airport," all infrastructure related factors.[50]

Urban regions with weak and decaying inner cities also lose the advantage of agglomeration economies. Two types of agglomeration effects are recognized. *Localization economies* are realized with the concentration of firms in a single industry, which increases total output of the industry at that location due to variables such as increased innovation, specialization in input and output markets, and lower supply costs. *Urbanization economies* are evident with the concentration of firms in different industries at one location, producing increases in total economic size (output, income, and/or wealth) as a result of agglomeration.[51]

Finally, an important loss in economic competitiveness of regions shaped by decaying inner cities is their image. Regions characterized by declining cores develop a poor image, and this reduces capital investment in plant expansions and start-ups.

During the 1970s and 1980s, other traditional industrial centers in the United States, including New York and Boston, also experienced declining urban cores as local plants closed due to market deregulation and globalization. With focused public and private investment, these cities rebuilt their cores and successfully transitioned from a manufacturing to a high-tech and services economy. Residential and business concentrations again increased in these city centers, since services and high-tech, like manufacturing, benefit from agglomeration.[52]

In addition, the Nagoya example, discussed earlier in this volume, reveals that the fate of cities in traditionally industrial economies does not need to result in the loss of manufacturing. Traditional industrial economies (with appropriate cultural, corporate, and government interest) can ensure the preservation of manufacturing as an essential element of the regional economy despite globalizing pressures. Japan is among the most competitive global economies, with a strong national interest in preserving manufacturing and employment in manufacturing, which ensures the survival and competitiveness of this sector.

Social Implications of Suburbanization

As recognized in the earlier discussion on educational spending, where a person lives is important in determining his or her opportunities. It is, in part, the reduced access to amenities and adequate infrastructure in decaying inner cities that perpetuates poverty. For instance, the relatively low in-class educational spending in Detroit is likely a significant factor in the city's less than 25 percent high school graduation rate (table 9).[53] Within the region, access to employment, public services, safe urban environments, and even competitively priced and quality produce are all dependent on where one lives, with the least opportunities offered to the low-income, black population living in the declining urban core (figs. 10, 11, and 12).

There are numerous social benefits that are recognized in cities with strong urban cores and compact regions. For one, as shown in table 8, higher densities—and less land and infrastructure used in development—reduces the unit cost of housing construction. While units would still be maintained at the same size and standard, the cost savings from using less land and infrastructure would amount to about 7 percent, an average saving of $11,407 on every house built in the Detroit region. Thus, by being resource-efficient both economic and social benefits can be realized, at least if builders pass some cost savings to consumers. This example illustrates once again the inherent environmental, economic, and social integration in advancing sustainability. Simply, less resource use results in lower economic costs and allows greater affordability.

It should be recognized, however, that the racial and class conflicts ensure that upper-income earners in the suburbs have little interest in encouraging lower priced housing within their

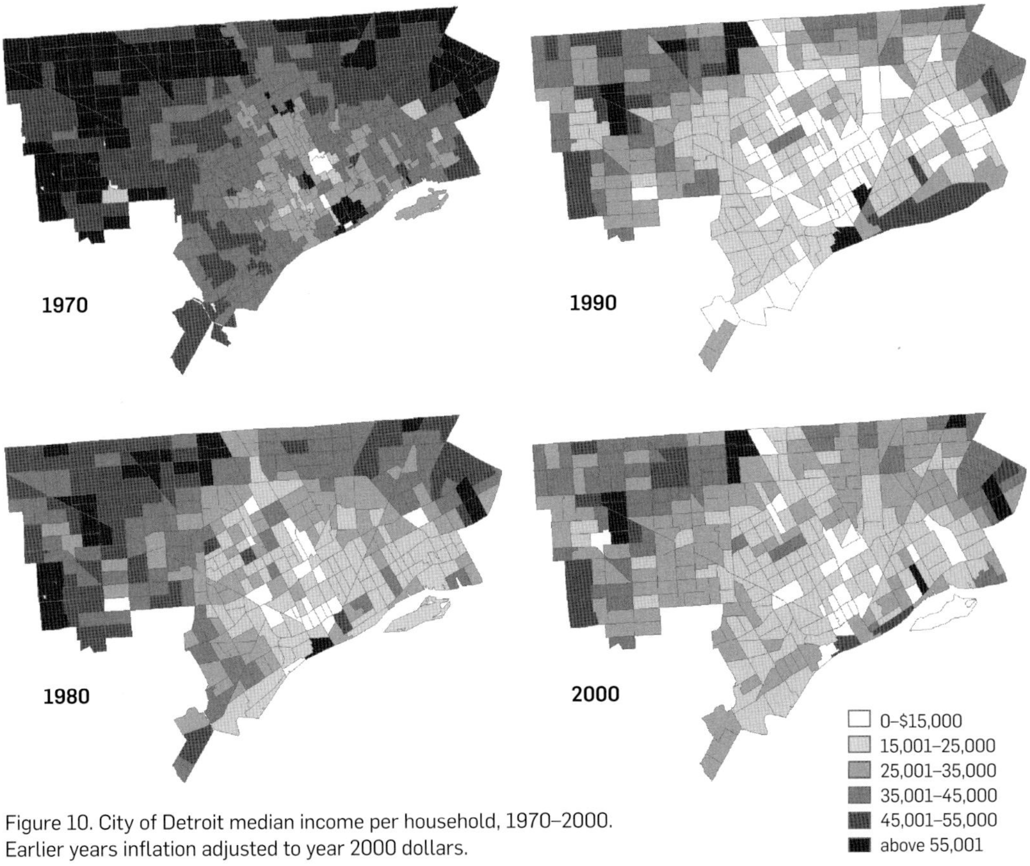

Figure 10. City of Detroit median income per household, 1970–2000. Earlier years inflation adjusted to year 2000 dollars.

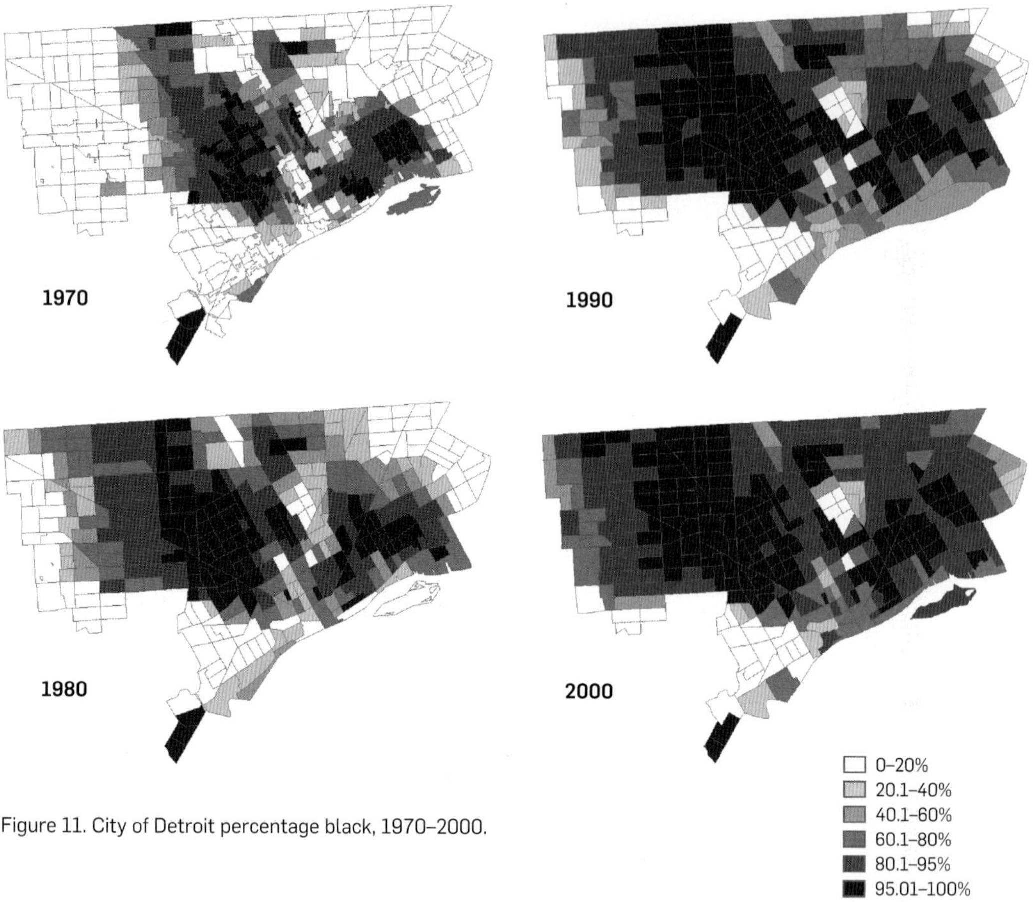

Figure 11. City of Detroit percentage black, 1970–2000.

jurisdiction. In fact, municipalities have historically used zoning ordinances to restrict developments to single family homes on large lots in order to limit affordable housing.[54] In many cases where municipalities have adopted more compact designs, such as row houses, the housing is made acceptable to local residents through goldplating.[55] This involves upgrading the dwellings with customized materials and high-end appliances, ensuring that the dwellings are marketed to the wealthy.

Inequities in public funding allocation, disproportionately favoring upper-income earners living in suburbs, are an added social implication of suburbanization. Research has shown that excessive suburbanization is supported by public infrastructure subsidies that reduce the costs of suburban homeownership, making costly low-density developments more attractive. In the process, however, the inequitable subsidies distort local markets and urban form.[56]

In Michigan specifically, research has shown that the state's Unrestricted Revenue Sharing Program, which has transferred billions of dollars from the state to municipalities ($1.4 billion in the 1999–2000 fiscal year alone), strongly favors infrastructure investment in the suburbs over fiscally distressed central cities and their poorer population.[57] This not only raises fundamental issues of inequities in financing practices, since disproportionate benefits from this program go

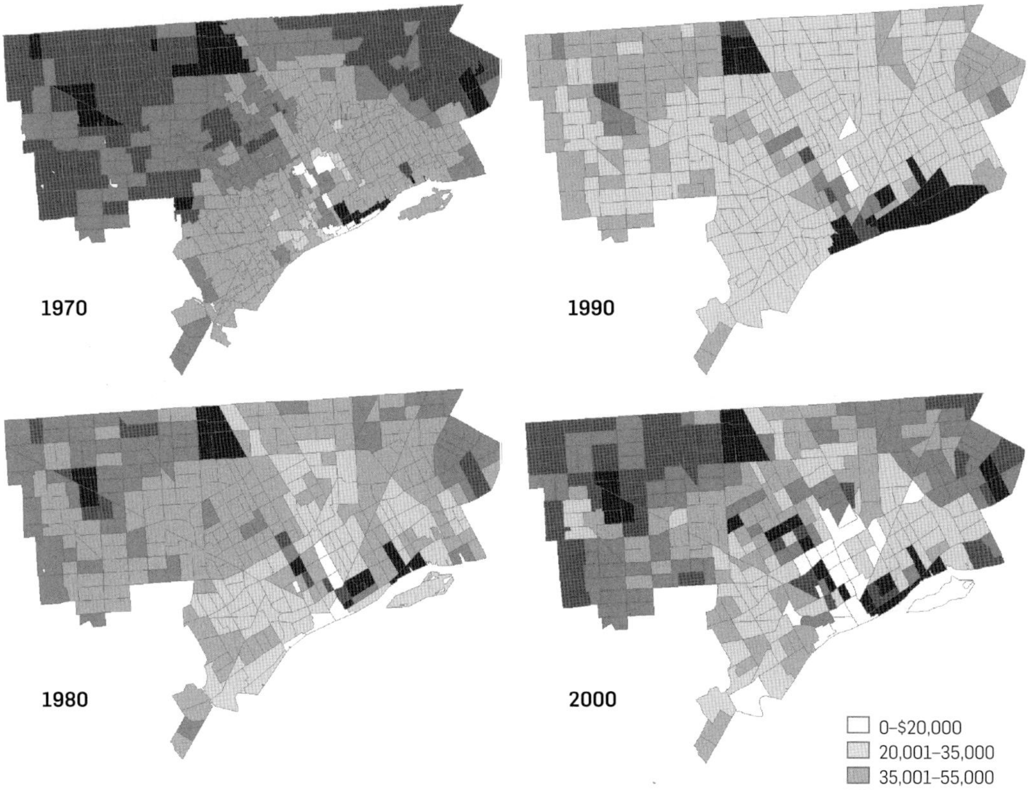

Figure 12. City of Detroit median housing value, 1970–2000. Earlier years inflation adjusted to year 2000 dollars.

to white upper-income earners, but it also illustrates how inequitable funding drives inefficient suburbanization.[58]

U.S. federal income tax deduction programs also subsidize suburban lifestyles. In 1995, according to the U.S. Congress, the federal subsidy for homeowners was $83.2 billion, whereas the federal subsidy for public housing and rental assistance was only $24.9 billion.[59] Some 38.9 percent of homeowners' subsidies were allocated to households with annual incomes of over $100,000. Therefore, this small upper-income group, about 5 percent of the U.S. population, received more federal housing aid than all renters in America. In addition, most of the homeowner subsidy goes to the suburbs, "where homeownership rates far exceed those in the central city, and houses are generally more expensive."[60]

Social costs of excessive decentralization are also associated with mobility among populations that do not have access to a car or that cannot drive. The elderly, children, and poor are disproportionately affected by suburbanization. For instance, many retirees move to suburbs, but in the process they become automobile dependent. Since individuals can walk later in life than they can drive, they lose their independence sooner and are usually forced to move into assisted living. Social isolation of the elderly, in fact, is considered a critical national public health concern.[61]

Table 9. Graduation rates for fifty largest U.S. cities, 2003–2004

CITY	PRINCIPAL SCHOOL DISTRICT	GRADUATION RATE (%)
Mesa	Mesa Unified District	77.1
San Jose	San Jose Unified	77.0
Nashville-Davidson County	Nashville-Davidson County School District	77.0
Colorado Springs	Colorado Springs School District	76.0
San Francisco	San Francisco Unified	73.1
Tucson	Tucson Unified District	71.7
Seattle	Seattle School District	67.6
Virginia Beach	Virginia Beach City Public Schools	67.4
Sacramento	Sacramento City Unified	66.7
Honolulu	Hawaii Department of Education	64.1
Louisville/Jefferson County	Jefferson County School District	63.7
Long Beach	Long Beach Unified	63.5
Arlington	Arlington Independent School District	62.7
Memphis	Memphis City School District	61.7
San Diego	San Diego Unified	61.6
Albuquerque	Albuquerque Public Schools	60.8
El Paso	El Paso Independent School District	60.5
Charlotte	Charlotte-Mecklenburg Schools	59.8
Wichita	Wichita Public Schools	59.6
Phoenix	Phoenix Union High School District	58.3
Austin	Austin Independent School District	58.2
Washington	District of Columbia Public Schools	58.2
Fresno	Fresno Unified	57.4
Boston	Boston Public Schools	57.0
Fort Worth	Fort Worth Independent School District	55.5
Omaha	Omaha Public Schools	55.1
Houston	Houston Independent School District	54.6
Portland	Portland School District	53.6
Las Vegas	Clark County School District	53.1
San Antonio	San Antonio Independent School District	51.9
Chicago	City of Chicago School District	51.5
Tulsa	Tulsa Public Schools	50.6
Jacksonville	Duval County School District	50.2
Philadelphia	Philadelphia City School District	49.6
Miami	Dade County School District	49.0
Oklahoma City	Oklahoma City Public Schools	47.5
Denver	Denver County School District	46.3
Milwaukee	Milwaukee Public Schools	46.1
Atlanta	Atlanta City School District	46.0
Kansas City	Kansas City School District	45.7
Oakland	Oakland Unified	45.6
Los Angeles	Los Angeles Unified	45.3
New York	New York City Public Schools	45.2
Dallas	Dallas Independent School District	44.4
Minneapolis	Minneapolis Public Schools	43.7
Columbus	Columbus Public Schools	40.9
Baltimore	Baltimore City Public School System	34.6
Cleveland	Cleveland Municipal School District	34.1
Indianapolis	Indianapolis Public Schools	30.5
Detroit	Detroit City School District	24.9
50-City Average		**51.8**

Source: Christopher B. Swanson, *Cities in Crisis: A Special Analytical Report on High School Graduation* (Bethesda, MD: Education Research Center, 2008).

Table 10. Residential segregation, black suburbanization, black spatial mismatch, and black-white income inequality in Metropolitan Detroit, 2000

	DISSIMILARITY INDEX	% BLACKS IN SUBURBS	SPATIAL MISMATCH INDEX	BLACK/WHITE INCOME DISPARITY[a]
Detroit	85.0	6.6	71.4	0.599
Mean[b]	72.1	8.7	63.0	0.576

a. A ratio of 1.00 = equality of income; a ratio < 1.00 = inequality in favor of whites
b. Based on eighteen metropolitan areas

Sources: S. Raphael and M. Stoll, *Moderate Progress in Narrowing Spatial Mismatch between Blacks and Jobs in the 1990s* (Washington, DC: Brookings Institution, 2002); J. Logan, Separate and Unequal: The Neighborhood Gap for Blacks and Hispanics in Metropolitan America (Washington, DC: Brookings Institution, 2000).

Alternatively, if retirees move into pedestrian-oriented neighborhoods, with close access to amenities such as shopping, they would have greater independence and would engage in healthier lifestyles by regularly walking.

A mobility issue that marginalized populations confront is access to employment. An important element of suburbanization is the decentralization of commercial activity and associated jobs. This spatial separation between minority, lower-income populations, and their potential jobs is known as spatial mismatch. Such development patterns place the already marginalized at a further disadvantage, since they confront greater costs in terms of time or money of reaching employment.

According to John Kain, the lack of equal access to jobs, particularly in manufacturing, reduced the employment opportunities of blacks. The impact of the spatial mismatch was magnified in cities such as Detroit, where blacks faced both employer and housing discrimination.[62] Table 10 shows the relationship between residential segregation, black suburbanization, black spatial mismatch, and black/white income disparity. Compared to similar metropolitan areas, blacks in metropolitan Detroit are more residentially segregated, are least represented in the suburbs (where most of the jobs are located), and have a higher spatial mismatch index.

The suburbanization of retail in Detroit has produced another accessibility issue among lower-income groups: access to competitively priced and healthy foods. Research in Detroit Metro has shown that lower income urban neighborhoods have fewer supermarkets than the white outer suburbs. The limited access to supermarkets in the inner city leads to reduced fresh fruit and vegetable intake among the poor, leading to direct impacts on public health.[63] Kami Pothukuchi and colleagues have also shown that in addition to the limited shopping options, stores in the poorer black Detroit neighborhoods had a higher rate of food safety violations.[64] Moreover, the greater reliance on smaller grocery stores in the city results in lower income groups paying more than the wealthy suburbanites for the same produce. A market-basket price survey across U.S. cities has shown that grocery prices in lower-income neighborhoods are 41 percent higher than prices of the same produce in upper-income neighborhoods.[65]

Advancing toward Sustainability: Urban Form, Social Justice, Equal Opportunity, and Regional Cooperation

If the Detroit region is to advance toward sustainability, new development standards need to be introduced in order to rebuild the urban core and promote greater compactness. However, to achieve this built environment, the local culture also needs to reexamine its position on racial and regional cooperation.

Urban Form, Growth Controls, and Regional Cooperation

If the Detroit region is to develop away from the current path of dispersal and toward a polycentric spatial structure, suburban municipalities that maintain an interest—and that could develop into commercial activity nodes—need to make changes to zoning in order to promote higher densities, a fine-grained land use mix, and increased connectivity. Such built environments are not only rare in the Detroit region, they are also illegal in many Detroit area municipalities.

The Detroit region needs to accommodate streetscapes that are more successful in striking a balance between different modes of travel, motorized and nonmotorized. Over the past six decades, Metro Detroit has been built emphasizing travel by automobile. Given the low densities and single-use zoning, these design choices have ensured that the car is the only reasonable choice of travel. New design standards that emphasize a grid street system, a fine-grained land use and building mix (allowing greater integration among commercial and residential uses), minimal streetscape barriers (such as expansive parking lots), and minimal building setbacks (to bring buildings closer to the street and closer to one another) are needed. Adopting such design standards will ensure shorter distances between destinations, encouraging walking, cycling, and the use of mass transit.[66]

Governments can facilitate the shaping of the new urban environment by strategically guiding infrastructure investment. Investment in public transit, schools, higher education (such as university hospitals), telecommunication networks, and cultural infrastructure in the urban core will facilitate inner-city revitalization by increasing urban amenities and employment opportunities. Concentrating urban amenities in the core is considered critical to bringing private investment back into the city, as evident in San Francisco, Boston, and New York.

A key advocacy of twentieth-century American city planning has been urban decentralization, as reflected in housing policies, infrastructure investment, and zoning. In part, initiatives promoting decentralization were a response to the hyperintensification and overcrowding in early industrial cities. In part, these initiatives were also intended to create homogenous urban environments, particularly for whites. Hyperintensification is not an issue in Metro Detroit, yet investment policies encouraging suburbanization persist, in part, since lack of tolerance continues to permeate the regional culture. In fact, current urban stresses in Detroit are a result of excessive suburbanization and inner-city decline, implying the need of the exact opposite policy direction, reinvestment in the urban core.

Evidence shows that land use controls, particularly regional initiatives, can curtail decentralization and encourage the redevelopment of activity nodes.[67] For instance, during the 1960s

Portland was rapidly suburbanizing, leading to a declining urban core. In response to the increased suburbanization throughout the state, Oregon introduced Senate Bills 10 and 100, which required all municipalities to develop comprehensive plans and land use regulations. Responding to the state, in 1979 Portland area voters introduced Metro, a regional governing body currently consisting of twenty-five cities with a population of some 1.4 million. To curtail suburbanization, Metro adopted an urban growth boundary, forcing new development within the growth area and limiting peripheral expansion.[68] The average residential lot in Metro, which in 1979 was approximately 13,000 square feet, by the late-1990s was reduced to 7,400 square feet. At the state level, agricultural land loss, which used to be 30,000 acres annually, was reduced to 2,000 acres per year by the mid-1990s.[69]

Urban regions in other U.S. states (including Maryland, Washington, Colorado, and California) have also introduced urban growth boundaries. Cities have also initiated other measures to curtail suburbanization—such as infrastructure charges and incentives promoting higher densities—and research has shown that many have been effective. Ensuring regional cooperation has been considered vital in the success of such initiatives. However, while some cities and states maintain considerable interest in limiting suburbanization there are many parts of the U.S. that have little interest in curbing decentralization. In the Michigan context, it is clear that the state and its cities could do more to curtail inefficient suburbanization.[70]

Despite decentralization trends throughout Michigan, a unique example emerges in the state that illustrates the role of regional cooperation in limiting suburbanization. Like most other regions in Michigan, the Grand Rapids Metropolitan area was rapidly decentralizing. In recognition of the difficulties that the region would face unless this trend was reversed, in 1989 three counties and twenty-six cities and towns formed the Grand Valley Metro Council. It currently consists of thirty-two member governments, with a mandate to strengthen urban centers and restrain suburbanization. Facilitated through interjurisdictional cooperation, the council has been successful in promoting inner-city revival and increasing the economic performance of the area. Throughout the 1990s the Grand Rapids region faced a 16 percent increase in population, the second largest regional population growth in Michigan, and a 32 percent increase in jobs, the most rapid employment increase in the state. Despite its uniqueness in Michigan, suburbanization in Grand Rapids still persists, as do racial and class disparities.[71] The Grand Rapids cooperative regional structure, however, has been considered important in facilitating the revival of its core and the region's economic success.

Ultimately, greater regional cooperation in Metro Detroit will also be essential to address the decline of its urban core and ensure the well-being of the region. It should be acknowledged that in 2002, fourteen Detroit area municipalities formed the Michigan Suburbs Alliance (MSA) in recognition that municipal fragmentation and excessive municipal competition has been a driver of economic inefficiencies and excessive suburbanization. The MSA, under the leadership of Conan Smith, currently consists of twenty-three municipalities and has been an effective regional voice for the inner suburbs. Even broader regional cooperation, which would encompass Detroit and the outer suburbs, remains critical in the revitalization of the region, but regional cooperation continues to be difficult.[72] Racial and class tensions are considered key variables in limiting broader regional collaboration.

Racial and Social Justice and Equal Opportunity

If the Detroit region is to encourage urban compactness and advance toward sustainability, the physical characteristics in the urban built environment are only secondary considerations to local socioeconomic and racial intolerance. Detroit area residents need to embrace increased social, ethnic, and racial diversity, and pluralistic ideals as a principal strategy in the pursuit of urban sustainability. The acceptance of such ideals are necessary in a region that is so socially, ethnically, and racially diverse. The pursuit of intragenerational equity (particularly social justice, racial equality, and equal opportunity) is the only option that the region has if it is to end its excessive decentralization and its environmentally destructive and economically inefficient development patterns.

In addition, there is considerable evidence that ethnic acceptance, new immigrants, and the ability to learn from other cultures is a means of fostering socially productive societies. Evident nationally (New York and San Francisco) and globally (Toronto and London), by utilizing the cultural, artistic, and intellectual richness of ethnic diversity, cities can improve their economic well-being while becoming more culturally and socially robust. This has also been evident historically, as with ancient Rome and medieval Cordoba, where ethnic diversity fostered prosperity and cultural richness.[73] In fact, the Detroit region has little choice but to embrace pluralistic ideals if it is to ensure its own stability and economic survival.

Commentary and Conclusion

As in other American cities, suburbanization in Detroit has been driven by technological innovations, increases in real incomes, reductions in real energy prices, changing consumer preferences, and public policy. The region has also been uniquely and extensively shaped by the automobile industry, and a local culture that has been extremely embracing of the car while dismissive of mass transit. The scale of racial, ethnic, and social intolerance in the region is also unique and has accelerated suburbanization, as whites attempt to increase the distance between themselves and Detroit's black population, who they view as incompatible and a threat.

The suburbanization has been also accommodated by a highly fragmented regional municipal structure, with little interest in interjurisdictional cooperation to promote a regional vision of development and well-being. This fragmentation has enabled wealthier Detroit suburbanites to maintain a disinterest in the welfare and economic performance of the city. The decaying core, however, has facilitated a decline in the well-being and competitiveness of the whole Detroit region.

Like a perfect storm, the combination of variables facilitating suburbanization in the Detroit area has produced a unique urban form in the scale of decentralization and inner-city decline. In turn, a highly resource inefficient, pollution intensive, and environmentally destructive built form has been produced, with broad detrimental global environmental impacts.

The Detroit region illustrates that any discourse in curtailing suburbanization is irrelevant unless the local population can address class and racial intolerance. By facilitating distortions in the urban form, evident with inefficient urban decentralization, racial and class conflicts have encouraged excessive ecological degradation and losses in regional economic well-being. Excessive suburbanization limits the advantages of urban lifestyles, while exacerbating the socioeconomic and environmental pressures of urban growth. This inherent coupling between social and environmental equity reinforces the pursuit of equity—in this case, addressing class and racial discrimination and oppression—among existing generations as a precondition for achieving equity between generations and in advancing toward urban sustainability.[74]

The U.S. experience also shows that depending on political interest, local and state governments have taken different positions on suburbanization. Some parts of the country have been active in curtailing inefficient decentralization, while other local and state governments have little interest in such policies. In Michigan, it is perhaps the lack of class and racial tolerance in the region that has limited policies curtailing suburbanization at both the local and state level.

If the Detroit region becomes serious in revitalizing its core and promoting greater compactness, a number of issues need to be considered. Due to the supradurable nature of urban form, any change in the built environment should be considered a long-term process. It took over six decades to produce a dispersed regional structure, and it will take as long, and likely longer, to produce a more compact regional urban form.

An issue within the context of redevelopment in Detroit will be the integration of any new population with the existing African American community in a process that will ensure the rights of the traditional urban residents. Recently, cities across the United States have celebrated a new urban renaissance. Detroit has also been doing its best to engage in these revival efforts, with several downtown development projects already completed. A consistent theme with these revival initiatives has been the physical and cultural aesthetic necessary to attract the new middle class.[75] Celebrated developments in Detroit, such as the Merchant Row Lofts and the Cadillac Center (currently on hold) are similarly marketed to upper-income groups and reflect the new middle-class aesthetic.

In this celebration of urban, however, there has been little interest focused on displaced traditional populations. The homeless, the poor, and Africa American residents are not part of the new middle-class aesthetic or the celebration of cities. Within this context, Detroit offers a unique opportunity. The degree of vacant land—which is so extensive that there are discussions of reducing the municipal boundary—would enable new populations to move into the city without requiring struggles over space occupied by traditional residents. However, if the rebuilding of Detroit is achieved with the displacement of the traditional African American population (as many other U.S. cities are trying to do) it would be difficult to conclude that the city has advanced toward sustainability.[76]

Addressing social and racial inequities and pursuing regional compactness will not in itself enable Detroit to achieve sustainability. This can be seen as a necessary first step to alleviate critical social and environmental stresses. It will enable advancement toward sustainability and generate nontrivial improvements in community welfare and environmental quality. Social, economic, and natural environmental advantages would be realized if the city could advance toward a profile (in terms of land, energy, and material use) similar to its Midwest counterpart, Chicago, or its Canadian neighbor, Toronto. Future generations could then reconsider how to further advance toward sustainability. However, without the pursuit of basic intragenerational equity—with the realization of racially and socially just societies being critical—intergenerational inequities will persist and the Detroit region will continue to move away from the sustainability condition.

NOTES

We would like to thank our chapter reviewers—Professors June Thomas, Pierre Filion, and Andrew James Jacobs—for their wisdom and constructive input on the draft. We would also like to thank the National Science Foundation for the Human Social Dynamics (SES 0624263) grant that is funding our research in Detroit.

1. U.S. Census Bureau, Population Estimates of Metropolitan Areas, Metropolitan Areas Inside Central Cities, Metropolitan Areas Outside Central Cities, and Nonmetropolitan Areas by State (MA-99–6) (Washington, DC: Population Division, U.S. Census Bureau, 2000).
2. U.S. Census Bureau, *2010 Census Redistricting Data* (Washington, DC: U.S. Government Printing Office, 2011).
3. U.S. Bureau of the Census. American Community–Survey 2006-2010 5–Year Estimates. Washington, DC: U.S. Government Printing Office, 2011.
4. U.S. Bureau of the Census, 2010 Census Shows Black Population Has Highest Concentration in the South. CB11-CN.185 (Washington, DC: U.S. Government Printing Office, 2011), http://2010.census.gov/news/releases/operations/cb11-cn185.html.
5. Congress of the United States, Office of Technology Assessment, The Technological Reshaping of Metropolitan America (Washington, D.C.: U.S. Government Printing Offices, 1995).
6. U.S. Bureau of the Census, 1950 Census Population Census Report (Washington, DC: U.S. Government Printing Office, 1952); U.S. Bureau of the Census, Census Redistricting Data (Public Law 94-171) Summary File (Washington, DC: U.S. Government Printing Office, 2010).
7. Throughout the chapter, when we refer to Metropolitan Detroit (or Metro Detroit) we are referring to the tricounty area of Macomb, Oakland, and Wayne counties. There is, however, the wider SEMCOG (Michigan Council of Governments) region, which throughout the chapter we will make reference to as the Detroit region. SEMCOG consists of Macomb, Oakland, Wayne, St. Clair, Livingston, Washtenaw, and Monroe counties, and is also known as the southeast Michigan region. When we refer to the Detroit region, we are specifically referencing the SEMCOG regional boundary.
8. R. Bullard, Dumping on Houston's Black Neighborhoods, in *Energy Metropolis: An Environmental History of Houston and the Gulf Coast*, ed. M. Melosi and J. Pratt, 207–23 (Pittsburgh: University of Pittsburgh Press, 2007).
9. U.S. General Accounting Office, Siting of Hazardous Waste Landfills and Their Correlation with Racial and Economic Status of Surrounding Communities (Washington, DC: U.S. General Accounting Office, 1983). The states reviewed consisted of Alabama, Florida, Georgia, Kentucky, Mississippi, North Carolina, South Carolina, and Tennessee.
10. Commission for Racial Justice, *Toxic Wastes and Race in the United States: A National Report on Racial and Socio-Economic Characteristics of Communities with Hazardous Waste Sites* (New York: United Church of Christ Commissions for Racial Justice, 1987).
11. W. Hoffman, H. Adler, W. Fishbein, and F. Bauer, Relation of Pesticide Concentration in Fat to Pathological Changes in Tissues, archives of *Environmental Health* 15 (1967): 758–62; B. A. Goldman, *Not Just Prosperity: Achieving Sustainability with Environmental Justice* (Washington, DC: National Wildlife Foundation, 1993); P. Asch and J. J. Seneca, Some Evidence on the Distribution of Air Quality, *Land Economics* 54 (1978): 278–97.
12. L. Westra and B. E. Lawson, ed., *Faces of Environmental Racism: Confronting Issues of Global Justice* (Lanham: Rowman & Littlefield, 2001); P. Mohai and B. Bryant, Environmental Racism: Reviewing the Evidence, in *Race and the Incidence of Environmental Hazards: A Time for Discourse*, ed. B. Bryant and P. Mohai (Boulder: Westview Press, 1992), 163–76; R. Bullard, *Confronting Environmental Racism: Voices from the Grassroots* (Boston: South End Press, 1993).
13. L. Pulido, Rethinking Environmental Racism: White Privilege and Urban Development in Southern California, *Annals of the Association of American Geographers* 90:1 (2000): 12–40; R. Bullard, Environmental Justice: It's More Than Waste Facility Siting, *Social Science Quarterly* 77 (1996): 493–99.
14. The council was formed in 1993 and existed until 1999.
15. The President's Council on Sustainable Development, Sustainable America: A New Consensus (Washington, DC: President's Council on Sustainable Development, 1996).
16. Partnership for Sustainable Communities, Three Years of Helping Communities Achieve Their Visions for Growth and Prosperity (Washington, DC: U.S. Environmental Protection Agency, 2012).
17. M. S. Foster, *From Streetcar to Superhighway: American City Planners and Urban Transportation, 1900–1940* (Philadelphia: Temple University Press, 1982), 82.

18. Political pressure was one strategy that the automobile industry used in displacing rail. In addition, General Motors had developed a subsidiary that purchased streetcar companies in fiscal difficulties and converted their lines to GM-manufactured bus lines. By 1950 GM had been involved in the conversion of more than 100 streetcar operations to buses in the United States. K. Jackson, *Grabgrass Frontier: The Suburbanization of the United States* (New York: Oxford University Press, 1985); M. S. Foster, *From Streetcar to Superhighway: American City Planners and Urban Transportation, 1900–1940* (Philadelphia: Temple University Press, 1981), 82.
19. I. Vojnovic, Urban Infrastructures, in *Canadian Cities in Transition: Local through Global Perspectives*, ed. T. Bunting and P. Filion (New York: Oxford University Press, 2006), 123–37.
20. I. Vojnovic, The Environmental Costs of Modernism, *Cities* 16 (1999): 301–13; I. Vojnovic, Shaping Metropolitan Toronto: A Study of Linear Infrastructure Subsidies, *Environment and Planning B* 27 (2000): 197–230; I. Vojnovic, The Transitional Impacts of Municipal Consolidations, *Journal of Urban Affairs* 22 (2000): 385–417; J. Levine, *Zoned Out: Regulation, Markets, and Choices in Transportation and Metropolitan Land-Use* (Washington, DC: Resources for the Future, 2006).
21. R. R. Boyce, Myth Versus Reality in Urban Planning, *Land Economics* 39 (1963): 241–51; R. Pendall, Do Land Use Controls Cause Sprawl? *Environment and Planning B: Planning and Design* 26 (1999): 555–71.
22. R. Burchell, A. Downs, B. McCann, and S. Mukherji, *Sprawl Costs: Economic Impacts of Unchecked Development* (Washington, DC: Island Press, 2005), 38.
23. R. Burchell, G. Lowenstein, W. Dolphin, C. Galley, A. Downs, S. Seskin, K. Still, and T. Moore, *Costs of Sprawl 2000* (Washington, DC: National Academy Press, 2002), 36.
24. In Detroit, an infrastructure exists that was built to support about 2 million people and yet some 1 million people are missing. The remaining population thus faces higher per capita costs just to maintain the city's extensive and rapidly deteriorating infrastructure (I. Vojnovic, Urban Settlements in Michigan: Suburbanization and the Future, in *Michigan: A Geography and Geology*, ed. R. Schaetzl, J. Darden, and D. Brandt (Cambridge: Pearson Publishing Group, 2009), 487–507.
25. Municipalities across the United States vary widely in terms of per capita taxation and per capita public expenditures. Cities like Houston and Phoenix maintain low per capita local taxes and low per capita public expenditures, while cities like San Francisco and Minneapolis maintain much higher per capita local taxes and provide a much richer bundle of public services. These are political decisions made within the municipality that in part reflect local cultural preferences. For instance, locally in Houston, per capita expenditures on public welfare were maintained at $6.70 per capita in 1996, while in the same year per capita expenditures on public welfare were $489 in San Francisco and $1,026 in New York City (Vojnovic, The Transitional Impacts, 385–417). See also I. Vojnovic, Government and Urban Management in the 20th Century: Policies, Contradictions, and Weaknesses of the New Right, *GeoJournal* 69 (2007): 271–300; I. Vojnovic, Laissez-Faire Governance and the Archetype Laissez-Faire City in the USA: Exploring Houston, *Geografiska Annaler B* 85 (2003): 19–38.
26. J. T. Darden, *The Significance of White Supremacy in the Canadian Metropolis of Toronto* (Lewiston, NY: Edwin Mellen Press, 2004).
27. E. J. Rose, and Associates, *Colour and Citizenship* (London: Oxford University Press, 1969); Darden, *The Significance of White Supremacy*; J. T. Darden, R. Hill, J. Thomas, and R. Thomas, *Detroit: Race and Uneven Development* (Philadelphia: Temple University Press, 1987).
28. R. Farley, S. Danzinger, and H. Holzer, *Detroit Divided* (New York: Russell Sage Foundation, 2000).
29. Darden et al., *Detroit: Race and Uneven Development.*
30. A. J. Jacobs, Intergovernmental Relations and Uneven Development in the Detroit and Nagoya Auto Regions (Ph.D. diss., Michigan State University, East Lansing, 1999).
31. D. Fusfeld, The Economy of the Urban Ghetto, in *The Ghetto: Readings with Interpretations*, ed. J. T. Darden (Port Washington: Kennikat Press, 1981), 131–55.
32. Ibid.
33. J. T. Darden, Changes in Black Residential Segregation in Metropolitan Areas of Michigan, 1990—2000, in *The State of Black Michigan, 1967–2007*, ed. J. T. Darden, C. Stokes, and R. Thomas (East Lansing: Michigan State University Press, 2007), 147–60.
34. U.S. Bureau of the Census. American Community—Survey 2006–2010 5-Year Estimates. Washington, DC: U.S. Government Printing Office, 2011.
35. U.S. Bureau of the Census, 2000 Census Summary File 3 (SF3), State of Michigan (Washington, DC: U.S. Government Printing Office, 2002); U.S. Census Bureau, *2010 Census Redistricting Data* (Washington,

DC: U.S. Government Printing Office, 2011).

36. Ibid.
37. For computation of the index, see J. T. Darden and A. Tabachneck, Algorithm 8: Graphic and Mathematical Descriptions of Inequality, Dissimilarity, Segregation, or Concentration, *Environment and Planning A* 12 (1980): 227–34.
38. J. T. Darden and S. Kamel, Black Residential Segregation in the City and Suburbs of Detroit: Does Socioeconomic Status Matter? *Journal of Urban Affairs* 22 (2000): 1–13; J. T. Darden, C. Stokes, and R. Thomas, eds., *The State of Black Michigan, 1967—2007* (East Lansing: Michigan State University Press, 2007).
39. Farley, Danzinger, and Holzer, *Detroit Divided*; Darden et al., *Detroit: Race and Uneven Development.*
40. Darden et al., *Detroit: Race and Uneven Development.*
41. Darden, Stokes, and Thomas, eds., *The State of Black Michigan*; U. S. Bureau of the Census, American Community Survey 2006, Washington, DC: U.S. Government Printing Office, 2007; Farley, Danzinger, and Holzer, *Detroit Divided.*
42. Darden et al., *Detroit: Race and Uneven Development.*
43. A comparison of land uses in the cities of Chicago and Houston, the third and fourth largest U.S. cities, provides an effective example of how variations in urban densities affect land consumption. Chicago houses 2.89 million people on 229 square miles of land. In contrast, Houston uses almost three times the land, over 620 square miles, to house 1.95 million people, almost 1 million fewer residents. P. Gordon and H. Richardson, Are Compact Cities a Desirable Planning Goal? *Journal of the American Planning Association* 63 (1997): 95–106; R. Burchell, A. Downs, B. McCann, and S. Mukherji, *Sprawl Costs: Economic Impacts of Unchecked Development* (Washington DC: Island Press, 2005), 42.
44. SEMCOG, *Land Use Change in Michigan: Causes and Consequences* (Detroit: Michigan Council of Governments, 2003).
45. While in 2000 the population density of the Los Angeles primary metropolitan statistical area (PMSA) was 2,344 people per square mile, the Detroit PMSA maintained a population density of only 1,140 people per square mile.
46. J. Kenworthy and F. Laube, *An International Sourcebook of Automobile Dependence in Cities 1960–1990* (Boulder: University Press of Colorado, 1999).
47. SEMCOG, *Fiscal Impacts of Alternative Land Development Patterns in Michigan* (Detroit: Michigan Council of Governments, 1997).
48. The compact development scenario assumes that only 10 percent of new development will be built in the periphery. Designs characterized by higher density developments and clustering facilitate the expected population growth while reducing agricultural and natural land use.
49. J. Holts Kay, *Asphalt Nation: How the Automobile Took Over America and How We Can Take It Back* (Berkeley: University of California Press, 1998).
50. Z. Goldfarb, Volkswagen Moving to Herndon, *Washington Post,* September 6, 2007, D01.
51. E. Glaeser, H. D. Kallal, J. A. Scheinkman, and A. Shleifer, Growth in Cities, *Journal of Political Economy* 100 (1992): 1125–52.
52. A. J. Scott, *Regions and the World Economy: The Coming Shape of Global Production, Competition, and Political Order* (Oxford: Oxford University Press, 2000).
53. C. B. Swanson, *Cities in Crisis: A Special Analytical Report on High School Graduation* (Bethesda, MD: Education Research Center, 2008).
54. I. Vojnovic, Shaping Metropolitan Toronto: A Study of Linear Infrastructure Subsidies, *Environment and Planning B* 27 (2000): 197–230; I. Vojnovic, Building Communities to Promote Physical Activity: A Multi-Scale Geographic Analysis, *Geografiska Annaler Series B* 88:1 (2006): 67–90; I. Vojnovic, C. Jackson-Elmoore, J. Holtrop, and S. Bruch, The Renewed Interest in Urban Form and Public Health: Promoting Increased Physical Activity in Michigan, *Cities* 23 (2006): 1–17.
55. I. Vojnovic, Energy Conservation in New Subdivision Designs (Toronto: University of Toronto, Program in Planning, 1992).
56. Vojnovic, Shaping Metropolitan Toronto, 197–230.
57. CRC (Citizens Research Council of Michigan), Michigan's Unrestricted Revenue Sharing Program (Livonia: Citizens Research Council of Michigan, Livonia, 2000); G. Taylor and C. Weissert, Are We Supporting Sprawl through Aid to High-Growth Communities? Revisiting the 1998 State Revenue Sharing Formula Changes, in *Urban Policy Choices for Michigan Leaders*, ed. D. Thornton and C. Weissert (East Lansing: Institute for Public Policy and Social Research and Urban Affairs Program, Michigan State University, 2002).
58. I. Vojnovic, Urban Settlements in Michigan: Suburbanization and the Future, in *Michigan: A Geography and Geology*, ed. R. Schaetzl, J. Darden, and D. Brandt (Cambridge: Pearson, 2009), 487–507.
59. In Michigan, renters can claim a small portion of rent paid as credit (about 20 percent), which is considered property tax and is part of the rental assistance data. U.S. Congress, The Technological

Reshaping of Metropolitan America (Washington DC: Office of Technology Assessment, U.S. Congress, 1995).

60. Ibid.
61. L. C. Mullins, C. H. Elston, and S. M. Gutkowski, Social Determinants of Loneliness among Older Americans, *Genetic, Social, and General Psychology Monograms* 122 (1996): 453–73.
62. J. F. Kain, Housing Segregation, Negro Employment and Metropolitan Decentralization, *Quarterly Journal of Economics* 82 (1968): 175–97; S. C. Turner, Race, Space and Skills in Metropolitan Detroit: Explanations for Growing Wage and Employment Gaps between Black and White Workers, Ph.D. diss., Ann Arbor: University of Michigan, 1995; Farley, Danzinger, and Holzer, *Detroit Divided.*
63. S. Zenk, A. J. Schulz, T. Hollis-Neely, R. T. Campbell, N. Holmes, G. Watkins, R. Nwankwo, and A. Odoms-Young, Fruit and Vegetable Intake in African Americans: Income and Store Characteristics, *American Journal of Preventative Medicine* 29 (2005): 1–9.
64. K. Pothukuchi, R. Mohamed, and D. A. Gebben, Explaining Disparities in Food Safety Compliance by Food Stores: Does Community Matter? *Agriculture and Human Values* (2008): 319–32.
65. J. Bell and B. M. Burlin, In Urban Areas: Many of the Poor Still Pay More for Food, *Journal of Public Policy and Marketing* 12 (1993): 260–70.
66. I. Vojnovic, Building Communities to Promote Physical Activity: A Multi-Scale Geographic Analysis, *Geografiska Annaler Series B* 88 (2006): 67–90.
67. R. Pendall, Do Land Use Controls Cause Sprawl? *Environment and Planning B: Planning and Design* 26 (1999): 555–71; Q. Shen and F. Zhang, Land-Use Changes in a Pro-Smart-Growth State: Maryland, USA, *Environment and Planning A* 36 (2007): 1457–77.
68. B. Stephenson, A Vision of Green: Lewis Mumford's Legacy in Portland, Oregon, *Journal of American Planning Association* 65:3 (1999): 259–69.
69. P. Nivola, *Laws of the Landscape: How Policies Shape Cities in Europe and America* (Washington, DC: Brookings Institution, 1999).
70. Q. Shen and F. Zhang, Land-Use Changes in a Pro-Smart-Growth State: Maryland, USA, *Environment and Planning A* 36 (2007): 1457–77; J. Carruthers and G. Ulfarsson, Fragmentation and Sprawl: Evidence from Interregional Analysis, *Growth and Change* 33 (2002): 312–40. Perhaps the most extreme example in the U.S. is Houston, which despite having a Department of Planning and Development has no formal zoning or comprehensive plan, an important variable driving Houston's extreme low-density suburbanization.
71. M. Orfield and T. Luce, *Michigan Metropatterns* (Minneapolis, MN: Ameregis, 2003).
72. For the efficient and equitable design of regional tax structures, see I. Vojnovic, Municipal Restructuring, Regional Planning, and Fiscal Accountability: Designing Municipal Tax Zones in Two Maritime Regions, *Canadian Journal of Regional Science* 23 (2000): 49–72.
73. X. Briggs, Civilization in Color: The Multicultural City in Three Millennia, *City and Community* 3 (2004): 311–42.
74. I. Vojnovic, Inter-Generational and Intra-Generational Equity Requirements for Sustainable Development, *Environmental Conservation* 22 (1995): 223–28.
75. This is evident, for instance, in Richard Florida's discourse on environments necessary to retain the finicky creatives.
76. A. Podagrosi and I. Vojnovic, Tearing Down Freedmen's Town and African-American Displacement in Houston: The Good, the Bad, and the Ugly of Urban Revival, *Urban Geography* 29 (2008): 371–401.

REFERENCES

Asch, P., and J. J. Seneca. Some Evidence on the Distribution of Air Quality. *Land Economics* 54 (1978): 278–97.

Bell, J., and B. M. Burlin. In Urban Areas: Many of the Poor Still Pay More for Food. *Journal of Public Policy and Marketing* 12 (1993): 260–70.

Boyce, R. R. Myth versus Reality in Urban Planning. *Land Economics* 39 (1963): 241–51.

Briggs, X. Civilization in Color: The Multicultural City in Three Millennia. *City and Community* 3 (2004): 311–42.

———, ed. *The Geography of Opportunity.* Washington, DC: Brookings Institute, 2005.

Bullard, R. *Confronting Environmental Racism: Voices from the Grassroots.* Boston: South End Press, 1993.

———. Dumping on Houston's Black Neighborhoods. In *Energy Metropolis: An Environmental History of Houston and the Gulf Coast*, ed. M. Melosi and J. Pratt, 207–23. Pittsburgh: University of Pittsburgh Press, 2007.

———. Environmental Justice: It's More Than Waste

Facility Siting. *Social Science Quarterly* 77 (1996): 493–99.

Burchell, R., A. Downs, B. McCann, and S. Mukherji. *Sprawl Costs: Economic Impacts of Unchecked Development.* Washington, DC: Island Press, 2005.

Burchell, R., G. Lowenstein, W. Dolphin, C. Galley, A. Downs, S. Seskin, K. Still, and T. Moore. *Costs of Sprawl 2000.* Washington, DC: National Academy Press, 2002.

Carruthers, J., and G. Ulfarsson. Fragmentation and Sprawl: Evidence from Interregional Analysis. *Growth and Change* 33 (2002): 312–40.

Charles, C. Z. Can We Live Together? Racial Preferences and Neighborhood Outcomes. In *The Geography of Opportunity*, ed. X. Briggs, 45–80. Washington, DC: Brookings Institute, 2005.

Commission for Racial Justice. *Toxic Wastes and Race in the United States: A National Report on Racial and Socio-Economic Characteristics of Communities with Hazardous Waste Sites.* New York: United Church of Christ Commissions for Racial Justice, 1987.

Congress of the United States, Office of Technology Assessment. *The Technological Reshaping of Metropolitan America.* Washington DC: U.S. Government Printing Office, 1995.

Citizens Research Council of Michigan. *Michigan's Unrestricted Revenue Sharing Program.* Livonia, MI: CRC, 2000.

Darden, J. T. Changes in Black Residential Segregation in Metropolitan Areas of Michigan, 1990–2000. In *The State of Black Michigan, 1967–2007*, ed. J. T. Darden, C. Stokes, and R. Thomas, 147–60. East Lansing: Michigan State University Press, 2007.

———. *The Significance of White Supremacy in the Canadian Metropolis of Toronto* Lewiston, NY: Edwin Mellen Press, 2004.

Darden, J. T., R. Hill, J. Thomas, and R. Thomas. *Detroit: Race and Uneven Development.* Philadelphia: Temple University Press, 1987.

Darden, J. T., and S. Kamel. Black Residential Segregation in the City and Suburbs of Detroit: Does Socioeconomic Status Matter? *Journal of Urban Affairs* 22 (2000): 1–13.

Darden, J. T., C. Stokes, and R. Thomas, eds. *The State of Black Michigan, 1967—2007.* East Lansing: Michigan State University Press, 2007.

Darden, J. T., and A. Tabachneck. Algorithm 8: Graphic and Mathematical Descriptions of Inequality, Dissimilarity, Segregation, or Concentration. *Environment and Planning A* 12 (1980): 227–34.

Farley, R., S. Danzinger, and H. Holzer. *Detroit Divided.* New York: Russell Sage Foundation 2000.

Foster, M. S. *From Streetcar to Superhighway: American City Planners and Urban Transportation, 1900–1940.* Philadelphia: Temple University Press, 1981.

Fusfeld, D. The Economy of the Urban Ghetto. In *The Ghetto: Readings with Interpretations*, ed. J. T. Darden, 131–55. Port Washington: Kennikat Press, 1981.

Glaeser, E., H. D. Kallal, J. A. Scheinkman, and A. Shleifer. Growth in Cities. *Journal of Political Economy* 100 (1992): 1125–52.

Goldfarb, Z. Volkswagen Moving to Herndon. *Washington Post*, September 6, 2007, D01.

Goldman, B. A. *Not Just Prosperity: Achieving Sustainability with Environmental Justice.* Washington, DC: National Wildlife Foundation, 1993.

Gordon, P., and H. Richardson. Are Compact Cities a Desirable Planning Goal? *Journal of the American Planning Association* 63 (1997): 95–106.

Hoffman, W., H. Adler, W. Fishbein, and F. Bauer. Relation of Pesticide Concentration in Fat to Pathological Changes in Tissues. *Archives of Environmental Health* 15 (1967): 758–62.

Holts Kay, J. *Asphalt Nation: How the Automobile Took Over America and How We Can Take It Back.* Berkeley: University of California Press, 1998.

Jackson, K. *Grabgrass Frontier: The Suburbanization of the United States.* New York: Oxford University Press, 1985.

Jacobs, A. J. Intergovernmental Relations and Uneven Development in the Detroit and Nagoya Auto Regions. Ph.D. diss., Michigan State University, East Lansing, 1999.

Kain, J. F. Housing Segregation, Negro Employment and Metropolitan Decentralization. *Quarterly Journal of Economics* 82 (1968): 175–97.

Kenworthy, J., and F. Laube. *An International Sourcebook of Automobile Dependence in Cities 1960–1990.* Boulder: University Press of Colorado, 1999.

Levine, J. *Zoned Out: Regulation, Markets, and Choices in Transportation and Metropolitan Land-Use.* Washington, DC: Resources for the Future, 2006.

Logan, J. *Separate and Unequal: The Neighborhood Gap for Blacks and Hispanics in Metropolitan America.* Washington, DC: Brookings Institution, 2000.

Mohai, P., and B. Bryant. Environmental Racism: Reviewing the Evidence. In *Race and the Incidence of Environmental Hazards: A Time for Discourse*, ed. B. Bryant and P. Mohai, 163–76. Boulder: Westview Press, 1992.

Mullins, L. C., C. H. Elston, and S. M. Gutkowski. Social Determinants of Loneliness among Older Americans. *Genetic, Social, and General Psychology Monograms* 122 (1996): 453–73.

Nivola, P. *Laws of the Landscape: How Policies Shape Cities in Europe and America.* Washington, DC: Brookings Institution, 1999.

Orfield, M., and T. Luce. *Michigan Metropatterns.* Minneapolis, MN: Ameregis, 2003.

Partnership for Sustainable Communities, Three Years of Helping Communities Achieve Their Visions for Growth and Prosperity. Washington, D.C.: U.S. Environmental Protection Agency, 2012.

Pendall, R. Do Land Use Controls Cause Sprawl? *Environment and Planning B: Planning and Design* 26 (1999): 555–71.

Podagrosi, A., and I. Vojnovic. Tearing Down Freedmen's Town and African-American Displacement in Houston: The Good, the Bad, and the Ugly of Urban Revival. *Urban Geography* 29 (2008): 371–401.

Pothukuchi, K., R. Mohamed, and D. A. Gebben. Explaining Disparities in Food Safety Compliance by Food Stores: Does Community Matter? *Agriculture and Human Values* 25 (2008): 319–32.

President's Council on Sustainable Development. Sustainable America: A New Consensus. Washington, DC: President's Council on Sustainable Development, 1996.

Pulido, L. Rethinking Environmental Racism: White Privilege and Urban Development in Southern California. *Annals of the Association of American Geographers* 90:1 (2000): 12–40.

Rose, E. J., and Associates. *Colour and Citizenship.* London: Oxford University Press, 1969.

Scott, A. J. *Regions and the World Economy: The Coming Shape of Global Production, Competition, and Political Order.* Oxford: Oxford University Press, 2000.

SEMCOG. *Fiscal Impacts of Alternative Land Development Patterns in Michigan.* Detroit: Southeast Michigan Council of Governments, 1997.

———. *Land Use Change in Southeast Michigan: Causes and Consequences.* Detroit: Southeast Michigan Council of Governments, 2003.

Shen, Q., and F. Zhang. Land-Use Changes in a Pro-Smart-Growth State: Maryland, USA. *Environment and Planning A* 36 (2007): 1457–77.

Stephenson, B. A Vision of Green: Lewis Mumford's Legacy in Portland, Oregon. *Journal of American Planning Association* 65:3 (1999): 259–69.

Swanson, C. B. Cities in Crisis: A Special Analytical Report on High School Graduation. Bethesda, MD: Education Research Center, 2008.

Taylor, G., and C. Weissert. Are We Supporting Sprawl through Aid to High-Growth Communities? Revisiting the 1998 State Revenue Sharing Formula Changes. In *Urban Policy Choices for Michigan Leaders,* ed. D. Thornton and C. Weissert, 159–182. East Lansing: Institute for Public Policy and Social Research and Urban Affairs Program, Michigan State University, 2002.

Thomas, J. *Redevelopment and Race: Planning a Finer City in Postwar Detroit.* Baltimore: Johns Hopkins University Press, 1997.

Turner, S. C. Race, Space and Skills in Metropolitan Detroit: Explanations for Growing Wage and Employment Gaps between Black and White Workers. Ph.D. diss., University of Michigan, Ann Arbor, 1995.

U.S. Bureau of the Census. American Community—Survey 2006–2010 5-Year Estimates. Washington, DC: U.S. Government Printing Office, 2011.

———. American Community Survey 2006. Washington, DC: U.S. Government Printing Office, 2007.

———. 2010 Census Redistricting Data. (Public Law 94-171) Summary File. Washington, DC: U.S. Government Printing Office, 2011.

———. 2010 Census Shows Black Population Has Highest Concentration in the South. CB11-CN.185. Washington, DC: U.S. Government Printing Office, 2011. http://2010.census.gov/news/releases/operations/cb11-cn185.html.

———. 2000 Census Summary File 3 (SF3). State of Michigan. Washington, DC: U.S. Government Printing Office, 2002.

———. 1950 Census Population Census Report. Washington, DC: U.S. Government Printing Office, 1952.

———. Population Estimates of Metropolitan Areas, Metropolitan Areas Inside Central Cities, Metropolitan Areas Outside Central Cities, and Nonmetropolitan Areas by State (MA-99–6). Washington, DC: Population Division, U.S. Census Bureau, 2000.

U.S. Congress. The Technological Reshaping of Metropolitan America. Washington, DC: Office of Technology Assessment, U.S. Congress, 1995.

U.S. General Accounting Office. Siting of Hazardous Waste Landfills and Their Correlation with Racial and Economic Status of Surrounding Communities. Washington, DC: U.S. General Accounting Office, 1983.

Vojnovic, I. Building Communities to Promote Physical Activity: A Multi-Scale Geographic Analysis. *Geografiska Annaler Series B* 88:1 (2006): 67–90.

———. Energy Conservation in New Subdivision Designs. Toronto: University of Toronto, Program in Planning, 1992.

———. The Environmental Costs of Modernism. *Cities* 16 (1999): 301–13.

———. Government and Urban Management in the 20th Century: Policies, Contradictions, and Weaknesses

of the New Right. *GeoJournal* 69 (2007): 271–300.
———. Inter-Generational and Intra-Generational Equity Requirements for Sustainable Development. *Environmental Conservation* 22 (1995): 223–28.
———. Laissez-Faire Governance and the Archetype Laissez-Faire City in the USA: Exploring Houston. *Geografiska Annaler B* 85 (2003): 19–38.
———. Municipal Restructuring, Regional Planning, and Fiscal Accountability: Designing Municipal Tax Zones in Two Maritime Regions. *Canadian Journal of Regional Science* 23 (2000): 49–72.
———. Shaping Metropolitan Toronto: A Study of Linear Infrastructure Subsidies. *Environment and Planning B* 27 (2000): 197–230.
———. The Transitional Impacts of Municipal Consolidations. *Journal of Urban Affairs* 22 (2000): 385–417.
———. Urban Infrastructures. In *Canadian Cities in Transition: Local through Global Perspectives*, ed. T. Bunting and P. Filion, 123–37. New York: Oxford University Press, 2006.
———. Urban Settlements in Michigan: Suburbanization and the Future. In *Michigan: A Geography and Geology*, ed. R. Schaetzl, J. Darden, and D. Brandt, 487–507. Cambridge: Pearson, 2009.
Vojnovic, I., C. Jackson-Elmoore, J. Holtrop, and S. Bruch. The Renewed Interest in Urban Form and Public Health: Promoting Increased Physical Activity in Michigan. *Cities* 23 (2006): 1–17.
Westra, L., and B. E. Lawson, ed. *Faces of Environmental Racism: Confronting Issues of Global Justice*. Lanham: Rowman & Littlefield, 2001.
Zenk, S., A. J. Schulz, T. Hollis-Neely, R. T. Campbell, N. Holmes, G. Watkins, R. Nwankwo, and A. Odoms-Young. Fruit and Vegetable Intake in African Americans: Income and Store Characteristics. *American Journal of Preventative Medicine* 29 (2005): 1–9.

■ JUNE MANNING THOMAS

The Role of Ethnicity and Race in Supporting Sustainable Urban Environments

The title of this chapter, suggested by the editor, offers the opportunity to think about race, ethnicity, and urban sustainability in an uncommon way. What exactly are the contributions of ethnicity and race to sustainable urban settings? Social equity is a component of environmental sustainability, and it is important to consider issues of race and ethnicity when discussing social equity, but these topics are not usually offered as necessary to "support" sustainable urban environments. Indeed, they have emerged largely in discussions concerning the deleterious effects of environmental degradation and its uneven distribution, with large burdens falling upon minority races and ethnicities. An extensive environmental justice literature has emerged that has documented inequity by race, ethnicity, or class, in varying locales throughout the world, thus providing a crucial link between environmental and social justice concerns.[1]

This chapter reviews some ways in which the concepts of race and ethnicity connect with the idea of sustainability in urban environments. It suggests that considerations of social equity are important components of urban sustainability, but not solely because of unjust treatment of certain categories of people—the active and even clustered presence of different racial and ethnic minority groups may indeed be an important characteristic of healthy, vibrant, and sustainable cities. This different way of thinking about ethnicity, race, and urban sustainability should become more apparent once we review first the concepts of social equity and environmental justice, the traditional realm for considering matters of race and ethnicity in relation to sustainability, and then explore in more detail recent observations about immigrants and ethnic enclaves and the effects these are having on metropolitan and central-city economies and neighborhoods. As will be shown, immigrants and residents of various ethnic origins have great potential to enhance urban sustainability because of their potential contributions to the economy in general, neighborhoods, and specific industries such as tourism. We will use largely North American examples and end with a short discussion of Chicago to illustrate these points.

By way of definition concerning race and ethnicity, it should be noted that "race" has little biological justification as a way to classify human beings, but it has very strong social grounding. One problem with the concept of race is that, especially in multiracial societies, genetic intermixing has often occurred to the extent that it is not always clear how to classify a person by "race."[2] The U.S. census bureau has changed its definition several times over the last few decades, now settling on self-definition by respondents; it counts whites, African Americans, American Indians, and Asians as separate "races," but each of these contains populations of wide variability, in terms of national origin, skin color, physical features, and other characteristics often associated with "race." Asians can have very different backgrounds depending on whether they originated in China, Vietnam, Japan, or Indonesia, and China itself recognizes over eighty ethnic groups within its national population. In North America, the language grouping "Hispanics" can include several races; many Native American or First Nations people of varied ethnic (or national or tribal) backgrounds reside in urban and rural areas.

For reasons of flexibility some scholars have suggested replacing the word "race" with "ethnicity," which allows for subtler gradations, but here too problems of definition abound, especially for such matters as the census.[3] The term "ethnicity" implies a shared history, culture, and sense of identity that may form in a group enclosed within a nation, as with the many Chinese ethnic groups; or cross national boundaries, as with the Kurds in the Middle East; or match nationality pretty closely if not completely, as with the Japanese. In this chapter we will refer to both race and ethnicity. Oren Yiftachel suggests that ethnic differences often provide more conflict and uneven development in Southern and Eastern parts of the world than do racial differences, which may be more of a problem in many Northern and Western countries, but our largely North American discussion sometimes necessitates identifying ethnic differences as well, and we treat larger nationality groupings (e.g., immigrant Chinese and their progeny) as one ethnic group.[4]

Urban Sustainability and Social Equity

Many other chapters of this book define sustainability in general and urban sustainability in particular. Here we will not repeat these discussions, but rather select some aspects that relate to justice and equity as a necessary background for discussion of race and ethnicity.

Although many definitions of sustainability exist, one source includes both environmental and equity considerations: sustainability is the need to "ensure a better quality of life for all, now, and into the future, in a just and equitable manner, while living within the limits of supporting ecosystems."[5] Tim Brindley notes that urban sustainability requires greater residential density, a reduced need for mobility, and a greater mixing of social functions and activities, all in a relatively compact urban form. Timothy Beatley further argues that sustainability implies equity in the distribution of goods and services, a resurgent spirit of communitarian connection, and levying of appropriate costs (e.g., taxes) to account for the social and environmental effects of public and private decisions. Under these views, a sustainable urban community would minimize its ecological impact on the landscape, exhibit compactness and efficient use of existing land, and promote

PHOTOGRAPH BY JUNE THOMAS

Figure 1. Compact urban form includes housing with multifamily units or little space between lots and single-family houses, as shown in this photograph of an alley in Chicago's Pilsen neighborhood.

efficient urban transport, all in the context of justice. This definition also implies that a spatial prerequisite for a sustainable urban area would be at least one central core *able* to attract or keep populations living in compact contexts as opposed to endlessly decentralized locales.[6]

Some authors refer to three main components of sustainability: environmental protection, social equity, and economic growth. Some, such as Julian Agyeman and Tom Evans, define the intersection of these three spheres of influence as sustainable development, but others point out that this trilogy generates considerable conflicts of values, goals, and practice that do not intersect easily.[7] Brindley suggests viewing urban sustainability in a way that relies on a similar trilogy of concerns and yet considers "the social dimension of the urban village."[8] In this view, urban sustainability does indeed have three major components: he calls these environmental sustainability, economic sustainability, and social sustainability. Although the labels are very similar to Scott Campbell's, however, the content is less so. Environmental sustainability involves components such as a compact urban form, little use of energy, low reliance on long distance travel, and low pollution. For economic sustainability, rather than term this economic growth and efficiency, he suggests mixed uses and activities, work for home-based endeavors, and local jobs in the "compact economy." Social sustainability would involve not just social equity in terms of distribution, but also higher residential densities, viable community life in healthy social systems, and a social mix that includes some degree of social integration. Brindley then notes that this vision of sustainability relies on a concept of community that is quite different from trends in residential lifestyles, which tend to be decentralized, dispersive, and segregated.

Although some authors use the terms "social equity" and "social justice" interchangeably, others look at "social justice" as a process-oriented concept. Graham Haughton makes conditions of social equity between contemporary human beings in the same metropolitan area only one of five ways to view social equity, while Harvey Jacobs suggests that we can see equity as an allocative process, focused on distribution, or as a procedural process, focused on participation. Michael Gunder has charged that some people have used the concept of sustainability as an excuse to abandon traditional concerns about social justice, which he defined based on the concept of need, such as concerns about homelessness, housing for the working class, or racial injustice, and to focus instead on balancing economic growth, environmental protection, and future social equity.[9]

This brief overview suggests why it is not a simple matter to discuss the intersections of race, ethnicity, and sustainability. With so many possible ways to define and pursue equity and justice, it is little wonder that action to connect these concepts with sustainability is difficult. (In fact, the "sustainable development" movement has other challenges as well.)[10] It is for such reasons that the environmental justice movement is important. Environmental justice advocates have forced the issue of definition to some operational conclusion, defining social equity and justice as important largely to the extent that they concern human beings in need, particularly those disadvantaged by race, ethnicity, or income. Although the environmental justice movement is not the only way to view the potential role of race and ethnicity in sustainability, and although the environmental justice movement has not necessarily focused on urban sustainability, we now turn to it briefly as an important part of this discussion.

Role of the Environmental Justice Movement

A major concern about sustainable development is that the criteria described here—economic growth, environmental protection, and social equity, which Agyeman, Robert Bullard, and Evans, as well as Scott Campbell, reference, or environmental, economic, and social sustainability, which Brindley describes—do not receive equal attention from the sustainability movement, which tends to focus on the environment without consideration of allocation of risk affecting minority racial and ethnic communities. This was a major reason for the creation of the environmental justice movement.[11]

In part, the split in focus was possible because the modern environmental movement has often been made up of middle- or upper-class white citizens, with little membership from or expressed concern about other classes or racial groups, and with little focus on either allocation or participation by powerless groups. Furthermore, "environmental justice" and "environmental sustainability" are not always compatible, and in many ways these two goals are diametrically opposed to each other. An overriding goal for environmental justice would be to rectify the uneven distribution of pollutants (and other nuisances such as trash dumps), but a primary goal of environmental sustainability would call for reducing overall levels of pollutants rather than rectifying their uneven impact.[12]

Early U.S.-based components of the environmental justice movement joined together the modern environmental movement and the U.S. civil rights movement. A landmark 1987 study sponsored by the Commission on Racial Justice of the United Church of Christ, which demonstrated that hazardous waste sites were disproportionately located in U.S. black communities, is one of the earliest manifestations of this movement. Researchers such as Robert Bullard, Paul Mohai, and Bunyan Bryant began to study additional instances of disproportionate proximity to environmental problems.[13] Such concerns led to several key reports and conferences, including a conference organized in 1991, the First National People of Color Environmental Leadership Summit, where participants of several minority races reported on varied experiences of environmental degradation in or near their communities. A series of books, studies, and local activities flowed from this initiative and ensured that the environmental justice movement became a force of moral suasion in the United States and in many countries abroad.

The basic concern of the environmental justice movement is the uneven distribution of noxious environmental land uses or other activities, with the burden of hosting such noxious activities placed most heavily upon racial-minority and low-income communities, which then suffer associated health problems. Although community activists and a few researchers were the first to call attention to this situation, subsequent empirical studies demonstrated disparities in exposure to hazardous waste, air pollution, toxic and radioactive releases, solid waste, and other issues. One example is a study of twenty years of data concerning the location of toxic waste sites, summarized in a 2007 report prepared for the United Church of Christ that showed that people of color make up the majority of the population living in "host neighborhoods" (within 1.8 miles) of toxic waste facilities in the United States.[14]

Observers have suggested that room exists for improved research in this area. Although some, such as Benjamin Goldman, have suggested that empirical studies overwhelmingly demonstrate that toxic exposure is associated with income and, to a much greater extent, race, and that such exposure has led to higher levels of lead and other toxins in minority people, other researchers have pointed out conceptual problems with "environmental justice" research that need further investigation. William Bowen and Michael Wells note that some early studies in particular failed to prove adequately a causative link between observations and supposed effects—as have more recent studies, such as that of Morello-Frosch, Manuel Pastor, and James Sadd—or could not be replicated. Bowen and Wells furthermore argue that studies of this genre have only demonstrated how little is known about "the health risks posed by environmentally hazardous sites, and even less is known about differences in these risks in terms of race or class." Lisa Schweitzer and Max Stephenson offer a more nuanced set of questions, seeking to improve research related to environment and social justice. They accept, as do most researchers, the preponderance of evidence that suggests that racial minorities suffer disproportionately from diseases associated with pollution, and that the main difficulties of race and poverty are intertwined. They point out, however, that much environmental justice research has failed to acknowledge "the larger context of urbanization and prejudice," given insufficient attention to the contribution of industrial clustering patterns in environmental inequality, and offered insufficient analysis of the role of race and residential segregation in urban distribution patterns.[15]

Even so, the environmental justice movement itself has elevated consciousness about the equity dimension of sustainability in important ways. Books, articles, and reports have offered convincing evidence of higher-than-normal proximity to hazardous land use by racial and ethnic minorities, and at least anecdotal (if not always stronger) evidence of health repercussions due to such proximity, both in this country and abroad.[16] Community protests over these conditions have made it likelier that discussions about environmentalism and sustainability include considerations of social equity, defined as fair treatment of those in need, with environmental risks shared fairly by all. Although U.S. government actions taken in response have not been completely effective, and in fact the federal government's role in environmental justice faded significantly in the 2000s, the movement has at least placed items related to environmental justice on the agenda in the United States and elsewhere.[17]

The environmental justice movement has also raised consciousness about environmental justice within racial and ethnic populations themselves. At first some sentiments within environmental organizations were that racial minorities and low-income people were not interested in environmental issues.[18] As sustainability was often erroneously defined as environmentalism, the implication would have been that minorities were not interested in sustainability. As we have seen, however, the concept of sustainability is considerably broader than environmentalism, and lack of action in environmental movements does not necessarily mean lack of interest or action in sustainability.

One study of white and African American respondents in metropolitan Detroit determined that African Americans were very concerned about environmental quality issues.[19] The researchers expected that blacks would be less concerned than whites about certain issues, such as nature preservation or water pollution, but even there concern was high. Where the two races did express some difference, it related to local environmental problems that were actually broader community development issues, about which African Americans expressed more concern than whites. In addition to such concern about traditional environmental concerns, such as water and waste pollution, nature preservation, or the need for recycling, African American respondents were significantly likelier to highlight specific local or neighborhood environmental conditions, such as air pollution, trash/litter, noise, abandoned houses, or household pests. The problems they identified related in great part, then, to the environmental deterioration of Detroit, in which African Americans predominate.

Another useful article concerning this issue comes from Great Britain. There, Agyeman investigated the environmental perspectives of a range of ethnic minorities.[20] He found that the respondents, many of whom came from various parts of the world, were involved in multiple activities designed to improve the urban environment, covering such issues as drugs, crime, and housing. As with the Detroit respondents, their vision of sustainability was a broad one, focusing on urban communities in which it was safe to live, free from a range of everyday hazards.

In sum, two conclusions evolve from this portion of the discussion: first, the environmental justice movement helps us to look at urban sustainability at least partially in terms of whether or not specific racial and ethnic minorities suffer disproportionately from the worst effects of environmental toxicity. This is an important antidote to the tendency to view urban sustainability solely in terms of improving overall environmental performance, or creating sustainable or efficient economic growth, or designing better, more compact cities. This movement has likewise helped to make the vague concept of "social equity" more specific in the real world. Secondly, minorities who are not necessarily associated with either environmental or environmental justice organizations may support urban sustainability, an important consideration in a democratic society. This support would be not only for the efficient reuse of existing central cities, where much infrastructure already exists, but also for enhancing basic livability in those cities, through provision of such basic needs as safe neighborhoods and housing.

Racial and Ethnic Contributions to Cities

One could argue that racial and ethnic minorities contribute to urban sustainability in several ways, in part because they have lived in many undesirable sections of urban areas, maintaining a certain level of residence, when majority-race populations were fleeing central cities in a steady pattern of suburbanization. This settlement pattern for some minority people, such as African Americans in the United States, has not usually been a voluntary process, but its effects are important nonetheless. In addition, and the focus for this discussion, immigration by foreign-born ethnic groups has been a key factor in allowing certain central cities to replace decentralizing populations, as well as to support social and economic sustainability.

At first glance the claim that what has often been an involuntary process of segregation or conglomeration can be a benefit to urban sustainability may seem bold. The extent of historically enforced residential segregation of minority-race groups makes it hard to justify minority-race conglomeration as a positive development. A number of studies have demonstrated the deleterious effects of racial segregation in U.S. urban areas—for example, in metropolitan areas and in their cities. Metropolitan areas with a relatively high percentage of African Americans have lower incomes, lower educational levels, and higher poverty than do other metropolitan areas.[21] Both William Wilson and coauthors Douglas Massey and Nancy Denton have extensively documented the lingering negative effects of racial segregation and of concentrated poverty.[22] This situation leads to the obvious conclusion that urban areas characterized by high racial segregation and concentrated poverty are not sustainable on many levels; they tend to collapse in the core as populations leave central cities for greener suburbs. Central-city municipal, economic, and social systems may suffer declining tax revenues as middle-class families flee either because of the attractions of newer suburban areas, or because they are escaping what they perceive to be declining public safety and public education, deteriorating neighborhoods and public services, or increasing taxes. Urban infrastructure, once constructed, however, is difficult to contract and so declining numbers of tax-paying people can cause serious declines in public services and lead to further exodus. The demographic pattern of urban decentralization, now fairly established in many places of the world, feeds the suburban sprawl that makes urban sustainability difficult.[23]

Such situations have been well described elsewhere in copious detail. Less discussed is the fact that, when certain racial and ethnic groups populate sections of otherwise depopulating

PHOTOGRAPH BY JUNE THOMAS

Figure 2. Hispanic culture has contributed to U.S. central cities through murals in public spaces.

central cities, they have sometimes been able to provide tangible benefits that enhanced many aspects of urban sustainability. In considering this possibility, it might be helpful to review the idea of the urban village, as explained by Brindley, who argued that the concept of an urban village existing within a larger central city or metropolitan area is an old one.[24] He suggested that true urban sustainability would require the replication of the essential elements of such an urban village. This would involve such outward manifestations as high residential density, but also what he called social sustainability, acquired through a healthy social system and a high degree of social integration. He suggests that the common perception has been that such social integration could best occur with a diversity of people, leading to calls for mixed-income and other heterogeneous central-city development projects. As he points out, however, the sociological literature suggests that such heterogeneous communities will be very difficult to form at a time when populations are decentralizing and community is become less place-based. He illustrates his points by examining three mixed-income housing proposals in the United Kingdom.

Here it is necessary to point out, however, that the traditional definition of an urban village has involved the clustered living of fairly homogeneous, not necessarily heterogeneous, populations. An example might be the ethnic Italian American community researched by Herbert Gans in his classical work, *The Urban Villagers*.[25] The ties of community and family may have provided many benefits, including ongoing residence in an area abandoned by more prosperous middle-class Anglo-Saxon families. This community was not sustainable over time, in part because of misguided application of urban renewal, but also because the children of such families were already beginning to move to the suburbs—a process supported by U.S. federal tax incentives and other policies—when Herbert Gans did his work. However, the community he described, of people living and working together, bound by strong family and ethnic networks, is close to the modern concept of social sustainability.[26]

A valuable key that links the conversation about race and ethnicity to the concept of urban sustainability is the literature on immigration. This discusses a specific form of diversity in the postmodern era that has the potential to bring many benefits, particularly to central cities. William Clark and Sarah Blue examined the population dynamics of five large (over 1 million in the central city) U.S. metropolitan areas that they called "immigrant gateway cities," using data that included these cities' metropolitan areas to demonstrate how vital immigrant populations were to population growth.[27] In 2000 as table 1 shows, the proportion foreign-born in these five metropolitan areas ranged from a high of 40.2 percent of Miami's population to 30.9 percent of Los Angeles, 29.3 percent of San Francisco, 28.0 percent of New York/New Jersey, and 17.2 percent of Chicago, and these figures underestimate the foreign-born percentages located in the central city.[28] As table 1 illustrates, for a metropolitan area such as Los Angeles, only 10 percent of non-Hispanic whites were foreign-born, and 5.4 percent of blacks, but fully 69.2 percent of Asians and 46.6 percent of Hispanics came from other countries. These numbers were not always as high by the 2010 census but remained similarly impressive. By that time 37 percent of metropolitan Miami residents were foreign-born, and 18 percent of metropolitan Chicago, but the percentage of foreign-born had increased to 34 percent in metropolitan Los Angeles.[29] Different nationality profiles characterized each of the metropolitan areas. For example, the Asians in Los Angeles came from Korea, Japan, China, and the Philippines, but China and India were the primary Asian countries of origin in New York/New Jersey.

Immigration and Economic Innovation

One way that different races and ethnic groups support urban sustainability is by bringing economic benefits to the cities and regions in which immigrants settle. One strong proponent of the

Table 1. Immigrant population composition of U.S. metropolitan areas with more than 1 million people (percentages), 2000

	ALL	NON-HISPANIC WHITE		BLACK		ASIAN		HISPANIC	
	FOREIGN-BORN	TOTAL	FOREIGN-BORN	TOTAL	FOREIGN-BORN	TOTAL	FOREIGN-BORN	TOTAL	FOREIGN-BORN
Los Angeles	30.9	40.1	10.0	7.7	5.4	10.7	69.2	41.6	46.6
San Francisco	29.3	49.7	10.0	7.8	5.1	22.0	68.1	20.5	44.6
Miami	40.2	36.8	11.1	20.4	30.9	1.8	76.9	40.9	68.3
Chicago	17.2	58.9	10.7	19.0	2.2	4.7	72.3	17.4	47.2
New York/New Jersey	28.0	51.2	14.1	19.9	25.3	7.6	76.6	21.3	44.1

Source: William Clark and Sarah Blue, Race, Class, and Segregation Patterns in Immigrant Gateway Cities, *Urban Affairs Review* 39 (2004): 6, 673.

view that residents born in other countries can be an important factor in the economic viability of metropolitan areas is Richard Florida. He calls the "melting pot" index, or relative proportion of foreign-born people in a metropolitan area, an important predictor of economic viability as measured by extraordinary high-technology economic activity, his primary determination of a successful "creative-class city." He suggests a connection between the presence of contemporary advanced technology and foreign-born populations in many of the foremost global cities, such as New York, Toronto, Dubai, Los Angeles, London, and Amsterdam, although it is not clear in his analysis which came first, the technological jobs or the immigrants. Several critics have suggested that parts of Florida's conclusions about the "creative class" are not valid, but his highlighting of the economic importance of immigrants, in particular, has support in the literature.[30]

Joel Kotkin argues that the linkage between immigration and economic performance is key, and that this is not a new phenomenon: immigrants have been important for city economic viability in times dating back to the early periods of human civilization, as in Sumer and Alexandria, and during the medieval period, as with Venice, Amsterdam, and London.[31] In societies as diverse as ancient Greece and the medieval Islamic Middle East, foreign people supported the marketplace when local people, especially those of high birth, would not. Kotkin further suggests that the cutting off of foreign markets and immigration pools was a critical factor in the economic decline of post-fifteenth-century cities in China and Japan.

Khalid Koser and John Salt reviewed data sets from around the world concerning "the geography of highly skilled international migration," including such people as visiting technicians, academics, corporate transferees, and clergy/missionaries.[32] They concluded that migrants gravitated toward a few "global cities" in large part because of the presence of high-level and specialist jobs, but that in turn these cities became more attractive to firms seeking a diverse pool of skilled labor. Such skilled foreign workers, then, were both attracted to global cities and part of the production of global cities.

For more specifics about racial and ethnic characteristics of such migrants, it helps to turn to national studies or case studies of specific regions. AnnaLee Saxenian documented the role of highly skilled immigrants for California's Silicon Valley. She found that, in 1990, 11 percent of total Silicon Valley workers were foreign-born Asians, as were 21 percent of the scientists and engineers in high-technology work.[33] Immigration was fairly recent; 71 percent of the Chinese and 87 percent of those from India working in high-technology arrived after 1970. As further evidence of foreign-born contributions to innovation, Chinese- and Indian-run companies made up an increasing share of Silicon Valley high-technology start-ups from 1980 to 1998; for example, Chinese-run companies made up 9 percent of the start-ups from 1980 to 1984, but 20 percent from 1995 to 1998. Canada was so convinced of economic value of immigrants that it set up a program designed to attract immigrant entrepreneurs from Pacific Rim countries. Although the positive results of this program are not clear, policymakers claim that the venture has brought benefits.[34]

In the United States, immigration flows have changed in racial and ethnic composition markedly over the years. It has been established practice in the United States to limit legal immigration, and historically policies have favored certain (usually "developed") source countries. Many U.S. restrictions relaxed after the 1965 Hart-Cellar Immigration Act, which pegged immigration to skill levels and to family ties with existing U.S. residents rather than previous national-origin quotas.

Again immigration arose during the 1990s, and during that decade the U.S. foreign-born population grew by 57 percent, so that by 2010, 12.9 percent of the U.S. population was foreign-born. Although some were highly skilled, as in the Silicon Valley, California, many were not.[35]

Foreign-born immigration has become a major factor in many parts of the contemporary world, but the process has brought both benefits and controversy. In the United States, specific concerns have been real or imagined competition with domestic workers, the importation of an underground economy that does not always operate within the tax system, and competition for public services, especially for low-income immigrants from developing countries.[36]

George Borjas examined whether immigrants depressed native-born Americans' wages, as some claimed, or had other measurable effects.[37] Using several decades of data comparing wages for immigrants and for natives, for men twenty-five to sixty-four years old in the labor force, he found that the percentage of white (European-origin) immigrants fell drastically, from 62 percent in 1970 to 21 percent in 1990. The new overall composition of immigrants in 1990 included 26 percent Mexicans, 16 percent other Hispanics, and 21.7 percent Asian. Publishing much of his work in the midst of the 1990s immigration wave, which included many workers with lower wages and skill levels than previous immigrants, he explored both potentially negative distributional effects, such as the strong possibility that immigrant workers were lowering native workers' wages, and positive immigration surpluses, such as efficiency and potentially lower production costs gained from new workers. His models suggested that immigration had many benefits: it promoted efficiency, expanded the size of the market, introduced new interactions between workers and firms, and provided complementarities between immigrant workers and other aspects of production. He concluded that the effects of immigration varied greatly by time and place, but that it was, on balance, beneficial to the U.S. national economy.

Cities crucial to the global economy do appear to serve as magnets for certain skilled immigrants, who then contribute to the local economies. We know this in large part from global cities analysts such as Saskia Sassen, but also from a number of anecdotal accounts and case studies. Kotkin notes that the five U.S. cities listed in table 1 received over half of the total estimated immigrants to the United States (20 million legal and 3–5 million illegal) during the twenty-five years preceding the writing of his book, illustrating that U.S. immigration is largely a targeted metropolitan phenomenon. He tells of experiences in these and other cities, such as Houston and St. Louis, that demonstrate the economic boost immigrants provided to cities suffering population loss and economic decline.[38]

For example, in Los Angeles, an area just east of downtown comprising fifteen square blocks suffered near dereliction and abandonment, but now it is a "toy town," a bustling center of economic activity involving the storage and distribution of imported toys. Languages spoken there for daily business dealings include Chinese, Vietnamese, Korean, Farsi, and Spanish, evidence of diverse ethnic origin. A physics doctoral student of Chinese origin started the first toy distribution firm in the area, because of the district's incredibly cheap space, and soon leveraged overseas and domestic connections to build a business that had annual sales of over $30 million.[39] Other firms gravitated toward this area because of his business, and soon Los Angeles developed other nearby districts focusing on such products as flowers, food, and fashion. Middle Easterners, with a very high rate of self-employment, have also become extremely influential in Los Angeles retail, wholesale, and distribution centers, particularly for the apparel industry, and they own many of the high-end stores in that industry. These ethnic entrepreneurs have provided a major boost to the local economy and have helped recycle previously underused geographic areas of the city. Kotkin describes comparable results in other cities such as Miami and New York.

Although the example from Los Angeles is instructive, it illustrates the creation of economic sectors not necessarily associated with ethnic neighborhoods. It would also be helpful to look at further evidence concerning ethnic enclaves as well.

Ethnic Enclaves and Economic Growth

John Logan, Richard Alba, and Brian Stults provided a useful classification scheme for ethnic economies that helps us understand their economic functions. Their four categories: employment niches, enclave economies, entrepreneurial niches, and nonethnic sectors. Of these four types, employment niches refer to the fact that different ethnic groups may be overrepresented in certain employment sectors, such as African Americans and Puerto Ricans in the public sector in Los Angeles and New York. Entrepreneurial niches arise when ethnic entrepreneurs cluster in certain businesses for which they have developed expertise, as with the Chaldeans in Detroit, who specialize in small grocery stores, and Chinese in the toy industry or Middle Easterners in the garment industry in Los Angeles. In the enclave economy, ethnic group members may serve as both owners and workers in a spatially concentrated area, such as a neighborhood, that may include a number of different economic sectors, a situation leading to visibility and variety for the enclave. Enclave economies vary greatly because of specialization: for New York City, the African American enclave specializes in social services; the Chinese enclave has a high rate of apparel and restaurant businesses; and the Dominican enclave relies heavily on food, bakery, and dairy stores, as well as repair services. Such enclaves add vibrancy and purpose to urban areas in which they are located.[40]

"Portal neighborhoods" often turn into ethnic enclaves and are often the first places of arrival for new immigrants, providing a culturally familiar locale that allows them to establish themselves. Among the characteristics of these neighborhoods are relatively low per capita income, high density, limited English proficiency rates, the presence of informal and formal services, and commerce tailored for the immigrant population, but they shelter a population with substantial buying power, in spite of low incomes, and a high rate of entrepreneurship. Paul Brophy and Joy Borkholder found a 10–20 percent higher self-employment rate compared to native-born counterparts in such neighborhoods, although they also found that many of these neighborhoods and businesses were fragile, suggesting the need for focused support.[41]

Ethnic enclaves may provide economic benefits even if they do not lead to new economic ventures, as happened in Los Angeles, and even if they are economically stressed portal neighborhoods. This is true not just in immigrant gateway cities, but also in other places. In Detroit, the U.S. city discussed in some detail in another chapter of this book, the development of segregated, spatially isolated, low-income African American neighborhoods has been the death-knell of several areas of the city, leading to failure to attract incoming homeowners, abandonment, vacancy, poor access to economic or employment opportunities for remaining residents, and resulting social distress. Detroit's historic southwest Mexicantown neighborhood, divided in half by expressway construction, has also experienced a great deal of abandonment and vacancy, and its bifurcated restaurant row district has suffered as well. However, in other sections of southwest Detroit, diverse businesses and neighborhoods have survived in islands of urbanity that exist in large part because of the concentrated presence of the local Hispanic community, a community populated in large part by Mexican immigrants and their families. Furthermore, in seven counties of southeast Michigan, which is the larger Detroit metropolitan area as defined by the regional planning agency, net domestic migration from 2000 to 2003 was minus 27,000, but the net international migration was plus 18,000. This demonstrates that population loss in the Detroit metropolitan area would have been far worse without the foreign-born residents who moved there. The largest number of international in-migrants for the region, 1995–2000, came from Mexico (10,584 people aged five and over), followed in numbers by residents of India, Canada, Germany, and Japan. Although the migrants from Mexico were not as likely to have college degrees as some other nationalities, they brought other benefits, such as willingness to live in southwest Detroit and set up or work in businesses there.[42]

Ceri Peach and Frederick Boal explain part of the contradictory phenomenon of detriments and benefits stemming from ethnic conglomeration by noting that different forms of assimilation and pluralism characterize different cities and countries, as well as different racial and ethnic groups. Peach, who critiqued the Chicago School of social ecology dating back to the 1920s, noted that one problem with that school of thought was its argument that social elevation of various socioeconomic and ethnic groups led necessarily to suburbanization, and that blacks in the American ghetto would follow these patterns as well. Even in the 1920s, he notes, the American black ghetto was a fairly unique form of settlement historically, with its residents segregated in two ways: first, nearly all metropolitan blacks lived in confined central-city areas, and, second, these areas were fairly homogeneous and racially isolated from other groups. The classic American ghetto was (is) not voluntary, had very few benefits for those residents left behind or for their cities, and persisted over a long period of time. With ethnic enclaves, in contrast, concentration and isolation from other groups were both much less pronounced. Such enclaves were often voluntary and provided support systems for their residents. Many minority ethnic groups, he noted, live in enclaves rather than ghettos.[43]

Ethnic enclaves often host businesses specifically associated with immigrants of that ethnicity, providing familiar goods and services, as well as employment for immigrants with poor language skills in the greater society. Although some scholars, such as Clark and Blue, continue to view the clustered presence of Hispanics, Asians, and blacks as evidence of residential isolation and segregation that is by implication negative, all the results of such clustering may not be negative, particularly concerning entrepreneurism.[44]

The literature on immigration offers many examples. Mohammed Qadeer used Toronto as a reference point in order to argue that cities with a diversity of immigrant groups could experience heightened economic development because of largely voluntary enclaves. Especially in those areas where immigrants move to sections abandoned by more prosperous groups, new residents can serve to put trickle-down housing and infrastructure to good use, and generate new economic activities supported by lower-cost labor and family support systems. This suggests that ethnic enclaves can bring new energy to a city and help create the kind of social sustainability and economic

PHOTOGRAPH BY JUNE THOMAS

Figure 3. Reuse of older buildings in new ways, as with this bookstore in Chicago's Pilsen neighborhood, is another feature of immigrant enclaves in central cities.

sustainability that Brindley describes. In addition, in some cases, as with Asian immigrants to California and Chicago, ethnic business networks and associations, whether based in ethnic enclaves or not, may generate increased business with home countries, becoming a boon to the whole regional economy.[45]

Ethnic Enclaves and Tourism

Ethnic enclaves have provided not only increased population and support for incoming immigrants, but also, in many cases, visibility for the tourist industry. For example, Chinatowns have long been an attraction for non-Chinese residents and nonresidents alike, as a locus for unique restaurants and shops, as well as an opportunity for majority-race people to visit a "foreign" culture in a controlled and easily accessible environment. The natural economic benefits that stem from agglomeration may increase as the very presence of the enclave becomes something close to a basic industry, generating tourist dollars from afar. Such tourism may provide additional opportunities for ethnic entrepreneurs to create new businesses.

Jan Rath suggests that the intersections of ethnicity and tourism have been understudied and need further attention. He argues that tourism is an essential part of the postindustrial economy in many parts of the world, but notes that ethnic communities play an important role in urban tourism, as becomes evident in his compelling if somewhat contradictory case studies from New Orleans, Boston, Birmingham (UK), Sydney, Lisbon, Istanbul, and Miami. New Orleans claimed ethnic heritage tourism even though the population was not particularly multicultural, and Istanbul tapped considerable ethnic diversity to support tourism even though it did not have genuine tourist-oriented ethnic enclaves. In New York City, quarrels arose when certain commercial areas, Harlem (African American), Little Italy, and Chinatown, received municipal publicity in official materials and others did not, demonstrating exclusion of some ethnic enclaves but inclusion of one historic racial ghetto, treated as an ethnic enclave for tourist purposes. In Boston, Sydney, and countless communities, however, civic boosters highlighted whatever ethnic diversity they had to buttress tourism aimed rather successfully at majority-race tourists as well as tourists from other ethnic groups.[46]

Min-Jung Kwak and Daniel Hiebert offer a fascinating case study of tourism in Vancouver that demonstrates that the possibilities are much broader than promotion of tourism based on native populations who may be interested in seeing the enclaves of others seen as foreign. As they note, tourism is becoming global in the sense that resident populations in one country, such as Koreans in Canada, can generate tourism with populations transplanted from their homeland to new venues, such as the city of Vancouver, linking in creative ways tourism, ethnic enclaves, and ethnic entrepreneurism. Canadian Koreans created very successful businesses tailored to Korean students studying in Canada, their families, and Koreans who wanted to send their children to North America to study, generating local economic growth.[47]

These discussions support the argument that ethnic communities have or could have a substantial role to play in helping to maintain the social and economic viability of central cities. As we have seen, immigrant populations can be an important presence for cities, in great part because of their continued influx into central cities, establishment of ethnic enclaves, and attendant economic activities, such as entrepreneurship, self-employment, and tourism. However, the interactions of race, ethnicity, and economic growth can be complex, and ethnic diversity may not resolve many of the problems that face cities. For example, many immigrants to the United States no longer use portal central-city neighborhoods, heading straight to the suburbs. Furthermore, ethnic enclaves face many threats to their existence and may in fact resist attempts to enhance growth through such means as ethnic tourism. It will be easier to describe some of these trends and concerns by briefly discussing one such U.S. city.

Chicago

Discussing Chicago in detail shows how race and ethnicity have supported urban sustainability even in the face of significant challenges. Chicago manifests some important characteristics of a sustainable city; while the Chicago metropolitan area is not compact, the use of residential space

Table 2. Immigrant populations in Metropolitan Chicago, 1940–2010

YEAR	METRO CHICAGO NUMBER	METRO CHICAGO PERCENTAGE OF POPULATION	CHICAGO NUMBER	CHICAGO PERCENTAGE OF POPULATION	SUBURBS NUMBER	SUBURBS PERCENTAGE OF POPULATION
1950	669,158	12.9	526,058	14.5	143,100	9.2
1960	601,015	9.7	438,392	12.3	162,623	6.1
1970	563,176	8.1	373,919	11.1	189,257	5.2
1980	744,930	10.5	435,232	14.5	309,698	7.6
1990	879,863	12.1	469,187	16.9	410,676	9.2
2000	1,416,890	17.5	628,903	21.7	787,987	15.2
2010	1,669,752	17.6	557,674	20.7	1,112,078	16.4

Source: Rob Paral and Michael Norkewicz, *Metro Chicago Immigration Fact Book* (Chicago: Institute for Metropolitan Affairs, Roosevelt University, 2003), 79. U. S. Census 2010, one-year estimates.

within its central city is relatively compact compared to that of many U.S. cities.[48] The city's light rail system allows for transportation within the central city besides automobiles and buses, and it connects with regional rail service for some suburbs; Chicago's core central business district (the Loop) and its satellites or extensions (e.g., the Magnificent Mile) have survived economic decentralization to remain important centers for commercial and office use, as are many of its neighborhood commercial areas; and the city in other aspects represents both a diverse, sustainable economy and social diversity. Chicago is one of the few large rust belt central cities in the Midwest to grow in population from 1990 to 2000, suggesting that it was able to hold on to its population or to attract new people at least for that decade; and even though population fell 7 percent during the following decade, this is relatively low by Midwest standards.[49] Edward Glaeser has called the city of Chicago an important success story. The relative absence of land-use controls and a pro-growth mayor have supported increased housing opportunities for middle-income people and allowed developers to bring high-rise, densely constructed condos to market in key areas.[50]

Migration, Segregation, and Enclaves in Chicago

Chicago has a reputation as a city of immigrants and has received successive waves of foreign-born residents throughout its history. Immigrants were only 11.1 percent of the city in 1970 but 21.7 percent in 2000 and 20.7 percent in 2010. As table 2 shows, however, not only the city of Chicago relies on immigrants; the metropolitan area does as well, including many suburbs, which as of recently are receiving large numbers of immigrants compared to previous decades.

Many of these immigrants have settled in geographic clusters, with neighborhoods largely populated by people who speak a language other than English, or who are associated with one particular ethnic group. The city's population increase in the 1990s was due to the increase of Hispanic/Latino and Asian minorities. The city expanded by 112,000 people, growing for the first time since the 1940s, but the white population fell by 149,000 between 1990 and 2000, and by 392,000

PHOTOGRAPH BY JUNE THOMAS

Figure 4. A mural with a portrait of a Hispanic family cooking together decorates the wall of a parking lot in Chicago's Pilsen neighborhood.

between 1980 and 2000, and the African American population fell very slightly as well. As noted in table 3, the number of Hispanics/Latinos rose by over 207,000 persons in 1990–2000, becoming 27 percent of the city's population, compared to non-Hispanic whites, who made up only 31.3 percent of the city's total. Proportions in 2010 were very similar: 28.3 percent for Hispanics/Latinos, and 31.6 percent non-Hispanic whites, but the rate of increase had slowed drastically. As late as the 1960s, whites made up 73.4 percent of the city's population.[51]

The city has become more diverse, but this diversity has not translated into diverse neighborhoods where segregation between several large racial and ethnic groupings is high. James Lewis,

Table 3. Latino or Hispanic population increase by decades: City of Chicago

1960–1970	161,181	1990–2000	207,792
1970–1980	174,720	2000–2010	25,218
1980–1990	128,789		

Source: James Lewis, Michael Maly, Paul Kleppner, and Ruth Tobias, *Race and Residence in the Chicago Metropolitan Area, 1980 to 2000* (Chicago: Institute for Metropolitan Affairs, Roosevelt University, and Office for Social Policy Research, Northern Illinois University, 2002), 72. Updated by author with U.S. Census 2010 one-year estimates and 2000 100 percent data.

PHOTOGRAPH BY JUNE THOMAS

Figure 5. A compact house in Chicago's Pilsen neighborhood displays creative use of upgrade materials, as well as the below-grade access characteristic of older Chicago buildings.

Michael Maly, Paul Kleppner, and Ruth Anne Tobias calculate that the dissimilarity indices for 2000 were in the high 80s on a 100-point scale for several racial and ethnic groups. Clark and Blue found similar results for the dissimilarity index, which was high for blacks and whites across all educational levels in the core city and in the suburbs, but with somewhat lower segregation scores for Asians compared to whites and for Hispanics compared to whites. They also found low levels of relative exposure, another indication of segregation, particularly for African Americans in Chicago. Preliminary figures from 2010 are not much better. But are these findings due to racial ghettos or to voluntary ethnic enclaves? Although different Chicago community areas have different stories, observers have found evidence that for at least one group, African Americans, segregation occurs in great part because of white flight from neighborhoods into which blacks move. Although white flight abated in the 1970s, it occurred again in later decades in those places where black population increased, and the resulting segregation was not due to voluntary agglomeration by African Americans. As for gentrification, either by income or by transition from African American to white, a small but controversial trend documented for several Chicago community areas, this process has resembled reclamation by white professionals of areas close to the central business district and has not necessarily led to neighborhoods variegated by race and class.[52]

For other ethnic populations, it is not so clear that residential segregation is either involuntary or due to a history of racial or ethnic prejudice. In Chicago many true ethnic enclaves exist, with ethnic-oriented businesses as well as residents, and these emerged not so much to attract tourists or to protect against exclusion as to shelter immigrants and provide economic opportunities. These enclaves include Chinese settlements in two distinctive ethnic enclaves or Chinatowns, anchored by businesses and also by substantial Chinese-ancestry residence. A significant presence of Arabs of various Middle Eastern national origins, who as just 1 percent of the population owned perhaps 20 percent of small liquor and grocery stores in Chicago by the early 1970s, have since gone on to venture into several commercial venues such as taxis, limousines, and restaurants. Asian Indians, of Indian, Pakistan, and other nationalities, transformed the city's north side Devon Avenue into an international marketplace and in the process developed a dynamic microcosm of Chicago itself. African Americans have also retained a dominant presence in Bronzeville, a richly historic and socioeconomically diverse community just to the south of the center of Chicago, as a viable locale taking important steps toward self-protection and cultural tourism. Time and space will not permit a description of these fascinating communities, each of which has distinctly unique characteristics, but they demonstrate the value of population influx associated with both ethnic enclave and ethnic entrepreneurial economies, all of which have contributed to Chicago's economic sustainability, as well as the value of supporting established African American communities. Instead, this chapter will describe in more detail the Latino population, which in itself reflects a diversity of various Latin American nationalities as well as advantages and limitations of ethnicity as a strategy for urban sustainability. In both sheer numbers and in social and cultural contributions, the Latino presence has been significant for both city and suburbs, but with a particularly telling effect on the city of Chicago.[53]

Chicago's Latino Community

The U.S. census now relies on the language- and ancestry-grouping term "Hispanic," with a separate tally by race. Latinos are Hispanics with family origins in Latin America. Research in other locales and the United States as a whole has shown that Latinos have a high rate of upward mobility. Poor English-speaking skills of those who have recently arrived diminish greatly after several decades of residence in the United States, and over thirty years their poverty rates have declined from 28.7 percent to 11.8 percent. Latinos also progress quickly into home ownership. This makes them a particularly valuable asset in city and other locales where the aging of the U.S.-born baby boomer population leaves gaping holes in the housing market and many employment venues.[54]

Although suburbanization is increasing among Chicago-area Latinos, and their immigration to the city has slowed, they remain in large numbers in the city of Chicago. Several Latino subgroupings are associated with different countries of origin, but the largest group in 2010 was of Mexican ancestry, with 1,546,171 persons in the Chicago metropolitan area and 37 percent of those living in the city (578,100 people). The city also hosted people of Guatemalan (17,973), Ecuadorian (15,466), and Cuban (8,331) ancestry, along with people with origins in the U. S. territory of Puerto Rico (102,703). These different groups have exhibited very different experiences and settlement patterns.[55]

PHOTOGRAPH BY JUNE THOMAS

Figure 6. The Dominican Shrine of St. Jude Thaddeus, located on the south side of Chicago, symbolizes the importance of the Catholic Church in Hispanic neighborhoods and street-culture activities, such as clothing retail.

Puerto Ricans, for example, have a distinctive social culture tied to their island heritage. They have the rights of U.S. citizens and are not technically immigrants, even though they may speak Spanish. While their legal situation therefore has been privileged compared to other Latino groups, their economic status has not been, and many who came to Chicago seeking economic opportunity ended up working in menial and light manufacturing jobs. Puerto Ricans settled in several northwest Chicago neighborhoods, including West Town, Humboldt Park, and Logan Square areas, which had been virtually abandoned by white residents in both commercial and residential sections. Some parts of these areas became Hispanic barrios, or ghettos, with low-income working families, concentrated poverty, and disenchanted youth, leading to a number of gang-related flare-ups in the late 1970s and 1980s. A noticeable exodus to the suburbs by well-to-do Puerto Ricans followed the familiar pattern of upward mobility outward and away from impoverished neighborhoods.[56]

In recent years, however, Puerto Rican heritage has served as a rallying point for several community-building efforts in historic Puerto Rican neighborhoods, including the creation of the Division Street Business Development Association and the Puerto Rican Cultural Center. According to the executive director of the business association, the segment of Division Street now renamed Paseo Boricua has experienced a marked increase in the number of restaurants and other businesses and has supported the retention and revitalization of several municipal assets, including the multipurpose Humboldt Park. Although the community has struggled in the face of middle-class flight and, in very recent years, gentrification via condo development, an almost inevitable situation in Chicago because of the area's proximity to the downtown and to rapid transit lines, Puerto Rican affiliation has apparently served as a focal point for community revitalization.[57]

As evidence of the diversity in the Latino community, consider the Cubans, a relatively small group, who represent an entirely different cultural experience but have also made major contributions to Chicago's economic and social diversity. Cubans came in large numbers to the United States as political refugees from Fidel Castro's socialist Cuba, beginning in the 1960s. They arrived with a number of advantages over other Latino groups, including the sympathy and support of the U.S. government and their own backgrounds. Many early arrivals were entrepreneurs and

PHOTOGRAPH BY JUNE THOMAS

Figure 7. This beautiful mural, "Bless the Children of Pilsen," is actually a door leading to a sidewalk or alleyway between two buildings. It symbolizes the power of paint to beautify humble surroundings, another contribution of Chicago's Hispanic community.

professionals with flexible skills, and they soon tapped into the Hispanic market and demand for bilingual professionals, although particularly recent arrivals have been more disadvantaged. In overall socioeconomic status Cubans have been the most successful Latino immigrants. Less likely to congregate in ethnic neighborhoods, with a few exceptions, they have settled in scattered neighborhoods in northern Chicago and nearby suburbs. However Cuban-owned businesses have clustered in areas such as Logan Square on the near northwest side of the city and other business strips throughout the city, making this Latino population another visible part of the retail fabric of the city.[58]

By far the largest Latino cultural group is Mexican. Rates of immigration to metropolitan Chicago from Mexico have been high and rising, but the first immigrants arrived early in the twentieth century. Because of their large population size, Mexicans live in several community areas of Chicago, although historically key locales have been located on the near southwest and west side, just south of the Puerto Rican areas described earlier. In 1990 most Mexicans still lived in the city, particularly in the South Lawndale community area known as Little Village, and in the lower west side area known as Pilsen, although they lived in some other areas as well, such as Logan Square on the north side. By the 2000s heavy concentrations remain in South Lawndale and the lower West Side, as well as Logan Square, but they had extended south of South Lawndale into Brighton Park, further consolidating their presence in the west and southwest areas of Chicago.[59]

In general, Mexican immigrants have had lower educational levels and higher poverty levels than other immigrants to the Chicago area, but they are highly visible in both the city and its suburbs, in great part because their rate of business ownership is high. Their presence in southwest Chicago is a story of ethnic succession: the lower west side, bound by several railroad tracks and part of the Chicago River, housed several large manufacturing plants but remained a relatively isolated working-class neighborhood from the 1870s until construction of the Adlai Stevenson expressway in 1964. Early settlers were Bohemian immigrants, dating from the Chicago Fire of 1871, but parts of the area were populated by German immigrants as well. As Bohemians moved westward out of the neighborhood in the 1920s, immigrants from Poland, Yugoslavia, and other Eastern European locales took their place. From the 1930s neighborhoods in the lower west side declined markedly in population size, but because of urban renewal in other parts of the city Mexican families began to move into the area in the 1950s and the 1960s, soon establishing a strongly Mexican enclave characterized by thriving businesses and community institutions.[60]

A visit to an established Mexican-ancestry neighborhood, such as Pilsen or Little Village, offers immersion into a colorful, dynamic community environment that gives hope to promoters of urban sustainability. As one would find in Chinatown, where Chinese-language characters herald the shopping district storefronts, one indication of the ethnic character of the neighborhood is the high number of storefront signs that are bilingual or non-English. Unlike Chicago's main Chinatown, however, which is organized in a way that would be attractive to tourists, with relatively dispersed Chinese residential patterns, the environmental flavor in Pilsen is one of a one-time working-class European enclave, now Mexican, with a high proportion of children and youth (from Catholic families), nestled near or within an industrial district. Industrial buildings, schools, Catholic churches, social halls, school buildings, and commercial businesses offer visible signs of the dominant Latino culture, and commercial ventures are a glorious juxtaposition

PHOTOGRAPH BY JUNE THOMAS

Figure 8. The front of a restaurant in Chicago's Pilsen neighborhood exudes cultural influence.

of indigenous restaurants, laundromats, furniture stores, and shops selling clothes and religious relics. Shelter to both legal and undocumented immigrants, Pilsen and other Mexican enclaves also provide an array of working-class and low-income housing, affordable for workers in the hidden economy. A number of studies have documented the resulting creative networks in Chicago, with strong self-identification related to cultural and artistic production, bilingual skills even among youth born in the United States, ongoing linkages among people who came from the same village or city in Mexico, and other strong social networks. One survey found that local art and culture had a great role to play in enhancing community identity as well as individuals' social life.[61]

As Latinos and other Hispanics increased their socioeconomic status, as did European immigrants before them, many of them purchased middle-class homes in nearby city neighborhoods or in nearby suburbs. Nevertheless, many still live in the central city, creating a rich urban fabric that is densely populated, economically diverse, visually interesting, and socially useful. However, this settlement pattern has both advantages and disadvantages, and the price for maintenance of central-city enclaves has sometimes been the perceived necessity to keep "others" out. In the case of Pilsen, the others have sometimes been tourists or developers who wanted to spur more gentrification.

This juxtaposition between the creation of a viable ethnic enclave and the protection of that enclave from outsiders is part of the dilemma associated with racial and ethnic diversity. Homogeneous ethnic communities can indeed create the sustainable urban village that helps promote social sustainability, and they can do this in ways that bring many benefits to old and new residents alike, but they also by definition create a form of social isolation, which can have benefits as well as detriments.

Among the ways to explore this dilemma is to consider the battle over spatiality, development, and tourism that has taken place in the Mexican-American community of Pilsen, located in the Lower West Side of Chicago. Mexican Americans have done much to create population stability in this neighborhood; population numbers remained fairly steady after 1970, over at least thirty years. But unemployment rates grew, as did the percentage of households below poverty and the percentage of substandard dwelling units. Particularly problematic for this area was the loss of industrial jobs. Chicago lost 100,000 manufacturing jobs between 1970 and 1980, and many were located in or near Pilsen. The shutdown of worksites such as U.S. Steels' plant led to a severe "spiral of poverty" for this working-class neighborhood.[62]

As described by David Wilson, Jared Wouters, and Dennis Grammenos, in the 1980s Pilsen became particularly attractive to developers because of its nearness to downtown and the University of Illinois–Chicago, relatively good housing stock, and low-cost land. Pressures to gentrify neighborhoods within striking distance of the downtown Loop were a driving force, and that force gained impetus from a new postindustrial global economy that brought in new professionals actively seeking housing. But organized opposition within Pilsen halted many development initiatives during that time period, when Pilsen gained a reputation for neighborhood opposition to development schemes. More recently, attempts have been made to enhance the area's commercial areas in order to attract tourism, but again community opposition has arisen, and merchants who seemed open to the ideas presented by tourism promoters have had their minds changed by community activists who actively objected to the commodification of a commercial sector set up largely to serve indigenous people, not outside tourists. As one organizer noted: "What I tell residents and neighbors is straightforward. The Chamber would make Pilsen a community of fake Mexican icons and people. They want sombrero-clad, smiling people who happily munch on tortillas."[63]

In a campaign that called up old images of ethnic stereotyping, promoters of development and commodified tourism have fought their battles in part by claiming that Pilsen was a broken-down slum in need of upgrading, but community activists have rallied support among Mexican Americans by highlighting the considerable assets and high level of social bonding evident in this enclave. This group has portrayed Pilsen as populated by a proud people who have built a community that they want to keep, and who benefit from a rich and ancient culture, reflected in part by their current urban fabric. They actively draw on the concepts of social capital and sense of community in order to protect the enclave from people they see as potential invaders: developers

PHOTOGRAPH BY JUNE THOMAS

Figure 9. This antigentrification mural in Pilsen features the clawed hand of oppression. Visible in the background is the Chicago skyline, including Willis Tower.

and the Chicago Office of Tourism. In turn, developers have backed off their pursuit of projects in this area in order to avoid confrontation and active hostility. Therefore some gentrified housing is available, but not much, some of it sponsored by the University of Illinois and located on the periphery of the historic community. A few upscale or garishly decorated shopping venues catering to tourists exist, but only in isolated venues, while homegrown retail operations with more modest façades predominate. On the whole, the community has succeeded in protecting itself, at least in the short term.

The example of Pilsen captures one facet of the dilemmas of the modern ethnic enclave. Pilsen as urban village has brought many benefits to Chicago as a city. It has served as a gateway for the influx of an important immigrant group, one that tends to remain within the central city even as it sends many of its members outward toward the suburbs. Its artistic, cultural, and social life is rich and variegated, and it houses a group that has a history of upward mobility and strong motivation to succeed economically, all good things in a formerly industrial city. And yet in order to protect itself the community opposes things often seen as necessary for the modern urban community: the workers associated with the postindustrial economy, painted as gentrifiers, and the promoters of urban tourism, seen as destructive of core community values.

Conclusion

In summary, racial and ethnic groups may help provide concrete benefits for cities, helping them to become sustainable in special ways. From the environmental sustainability perspective, healthy enclaves can reuse housing and other public infrastructure and public investments to help create new, healthy communities. From the economic sustainability perspective, such communities can generate economic activity and provide the kind of economic functions that take place close to home and neighborhood. In terms of social sustainability, in conditions of homogeneity the bonds of community and social life can still exist, and in conditions of heterogeneity such groups can help provide the diversity needed to create and sustain a healthily mixed population. This leads to a new, dynamic view of social sustainability, one that varies by nation and continent but has, as its essence, a lasting appreciation of diversity.[64]

In such ways different ethnic and racial groups may indeed support sustainable urban environments. Sustainability has several potential meanings, and a common definition given for urban sustainability references such factors as residential density, efficient transportation systems, and mixed-use development. A broader definition of sustainability, however, suggests that environmental protection, economic growth, and social equity are necessary in order to create a sustainable environment. A variant of this definition suggests that we look more closely at such issues as economic sustainability involving compact economies, environmental sustainability involving low reliance on long distance travel and minimal pollution, and social sustainability characterized by viable community life and healthy social interaction.[65] The concern that sustainability is not easily attained in the context of decentralized residential lifestyles opens an opportunity to think about alternative definitions of community, in which racial or ethnic enclaves may in fact exemplify many of the characteristics of sustainable urban villages.

This is not to deny that other important issues relating to race and ethnicity affect sustainability, however. Environmental justice advocates point out that justice and environmental matters relate not only to future generations or to natural resources but also to vulnerable populations needing protection from environmental degradation. They bring to life the otherwise dangerously nebulous concept of social equity. None of this discussion offers an excuse for the creation and maintenance of communities characterized by concentrated poverty and enforced segregation. Suburban populations do more to jeopardize sustainability by running away from central cities than meager efforts such as cities' sustainability initiatives or immigrant communities' building up of ethnic businesses can overcome. Patterns of suburban decentralization jeopardizing urbanity are well funded and strongly entrenched and show no signs of turning around.[66] Immigrant communities themselves are, as we have shown, decentralizing, suggesting that the incentives to move to the suburbs are strong even in the face of less ethnic solidarity.

While not ignoring these sobering facts, we suggest thinking about the role of race and ethnicity in a different way. One main challenge that will face society in future years is the fact that such positive benefits as have come forth from racial and ethnic populations have been almost accidental if not necessitated by very difficult circumstances. The fact that some racial or ethnic enclaves have managed to survive, thrive, and even prosper under adverse situations does not mean that they will do so in the future, or that other minority communities will be able to do so. Furthermore, although researchers are uncovering the positive effects of immigration, mobility between countries is still difficult and heavily discouraged in some circumstances. The anti-immigrant sentiment in Western Europe is quite high, and nativism still affects U.S. politics and popular opinion. Many people view racial and ethnic enclaves as necessary evils rather than the foundations for advancing urban sustainability.

As times change, however, and as it becomes necessary to define more precisely the social implications of urban sustainability, such misconceptions could change. As a society grows to see the benefits of compactness, and to recognize the positive contributions that different racial and ethnic groups, allowed to thrive in healthy contexts, and supported in their efforts to protect community and heritage, can make to a city as well as to metropolitan areas, views may change yet again. More and more people may come to appreciate the power of racial and ethnic diversity to support healthy, sustainable urban environments.

NOTES

1. Julian Agyeman, Robert Bullard, and Tom Evans, Joined-up Thinking: Bringing Together Sustainability, Environmental Justice and Equity, in *Just Sustainabilities: Development in an Unequal World*, ed. Julian Agyeman, Robert Bullard, and Tom Evans (Cambridge: MIT Press, 2003), 1–16.
2. For many years in parts of the United States, if a person had any traceable sub-Saharan black African ancestry ("one drop"), this led to the social classification of "black," now often termed "African American." Different states had varying guidelines for the definition of what were then called colored or Negro people (e.g., one-sixteenth African heritage in one state, one-eighth or "one drop"—any drop of black blood qualifies one as black—in another) during the nineteenth and much of the twentieth century. In the twenty-first century the "one-drop" rule still applies socially in some contexts, even though the resulting label may bear no necessary relationship to a person's physical characteristics.
3. Charles Hirshmann, The Origins and Demise of the Concept of Race, *Population and Development Review* 30:3 (2004): 385–415.
4. Oren Yiftachel, Re-engaging Planning Theory? Towards "South-Eastern" Perspectives, *Planning Theory* 5:3 (2006): 211–22.
5. Agyeman, Bullard, and Evans, Joined-up Thinking, 2.
6. Tim Brindley, The Social Dimension of the Urban Village: A Comparison of Models for Sustainable Urban Development, *Urban Design International* 8 (2003): 53–65; Timothy Beatley, Planning and Sustainability: The Elements of a New (Improved?) Paradigm, *Journal of Planning Literature* 9:4 (1995): 383–94.
7. Julian Agyeman and Tom Evans, Toward Just Sustainability in Urban Communities: Building Equity Rights with Sustainable Solutions, *The Annals of the American Academy of Political and Social Science* 590 (2003): 35–53; see also Scott Campbell, Green Cities, Growing Cities, Just Cities? Urban Planning and the Contradictions of Sustainable Development, *Journal of the American Planning Association* 62:3 (1996): 296–312.
8. Brindley, The Social Dimension, 53.
9. Graham Haughton, Environmental Justice and the Sustainable City, *Journal of Planning Education and Research* 18 (1999): 233–43; Harvey Jacobs, Social Equity in Agricultural Land Protection, *Landscape and Urban Planning* 17 (1989): 21–33; Michael Gunder, Sustainability: Planning's Saving Grace or Road to Perdition? *Journal of Planning Education and Research* 26 (2006): 208–21.
10. Victor suggests that the concept has become subject to unclear thinking and co-opted by special interest groups. Citing specific actions associated with international efforts sponsored by the United Nation, he also decries the environmental bias of the movement, noting that the failure to address social equity dimensions is only one part of the problem (David G. Victor, Recovering Sustainable Development, *Foreign Affairs* 85:1 [2006]: 91–103).
11. Agyeman, Bullard, and Evans, *Joined-up Thinking*, 2; Campbell, *Green Cities, Growing Cities*, 296–312; Brindley, *The Social Dimension*, 53.
12. Robert D. Bullard, Anatomy of Environmental Racism and the Environmental Justice Movement, in

Confronting Environmental Racism: Voices from the Grassroots, ed. Robert Bullard (Boston: South End Press, 1993), 15–39; David Newton, *Environmental Justice: A Reference Handbook,* Contemporary World Issues series (Santa Barbara, CA: ABC-CLIO, 1996); Andrew Dobson, Social Justice and Environmental Sustainability: Ne'er the Twain Shall Meet? in *Just Sustainabilities: Development in an Unequal World,* ed. Julian Agyeman, Robert Bullard, and Tom Evans (Cambridge: MIT Press, 2003), 83–98.

13. Newton, *Environmental Justice.*
14. Robert D. Bullard, Paul Mohai, Robin Saha, and Beverly Wright, Toxic Wastes and Race at Twenty, 1987–2007: Grassroots Struggles to Dismantle Environmental Racism in the United States, Executive Summary: Special Preview Release, February, 2007.
15. Benjamin A. Goldman, *Not Just Prosperity: Achieving Sustainability with Environmental Justice* (Washington, DC: National Wildlife Federation, 1993); Newton, *Environmental Justice*, 29; William Bowen and Michael Wells, The Politics and Reality of Environmental Justice: A History and Considerations for Public Administrators and Policy Makers, *Public Administration Review* 62:6 (2002): 688–98; Lisa Schweitzer and Max Stephenson Jr., Right Answers, Wrong Questions: Environmental Justice as Urban Research, *Urban Studies* 44:2 (2007): 319–37; Rachel Morello-Frosch, Manuel Pastor, and James Sadd, Environmental Justice and Southern California's "Riskscape": The Distribution of Air Toxics Exposures and Health Risks among Diverse Communities, *Urban Affairs Review* 36:4 (2001): 551–78; Lisa Schweitzer and Max Stephenson Jr., Right Answers, Wrong Questions: Environmental Justice as Urban Research, *Urban Studies* 44:2 (2007): 319–37; Susan A. Perlin, Ken Sexton, and David W. S. Wong, An Examination of Race and Poverty for Populations Living Near Industrial Sources of Air Pollution, *Journal of Exposure Analysis and Environmental Epidemiology* 9 (1999): 29–48.
16. Agyeman, Bullard, and Evans, Joined-up Thinking, 1–16; Bullard, Anatomy of Environmental Racism, 15–39.
17. Newton, *Environmental Justice*; U.S. Environmental Protection Agency, *Toward an Environmental Justice Collaborative Model: An Evaluation of the Use of Partnerships to Address Environmental Justice Issues in Communities*, 2003, http://www.epa.gov/evaluate/ejevalcs.pdf; U.S. Environmental Protection Agency, Fiscal Year 2006 Performance and Accountability Report, 2007, 101, http://www.epa.gov/ocfo/finstatement/2006par/index.htm; Julian Agyeman and Tom Evans, "Just Sustainability": The Emerging Discourse of Environmental Justice in Britain? *Geographical Journal* 170:2 (2004): 155–64.
18. Paul Mohai and Bunyan Bryant, Is There a "Race" Effect on Concern for Environmental Quality? *Public Opinion Quarterly* 62 (1998): 475–505.
19. Ibid.
20. Julian Agyeman, Ethnic Minorities in Britain: Short Change, Systematic Indifference and Sustainable Development, *Journal of Environmental Policy and Planning* 3 (2001): 15–20.
21. Sheldon Danziger, Determinants of the Level and Distribution of Family Income in Metropolitan Areas, 1969, *Land Economics* 52:4 (1976): 467–78; Janice Madden, Do Racial Composition and Segregation Affect Economic Outcomes in Metropolitan Areas? in *Problem of the Century: Racial Stratification in the United States*, ed. E. Anderson and Denton Massey (New York: Russell Sage Foundation, 2001), 290–316.
22. William J. Wilson, *The Declining Significance of Race: Blacks and Changing American Institutions* (Chicago: University of Chicago Press, 1980); William J. Wilson, *The Truly Disadvantaged: The Inner City, the Underclass and Public Policy* (Chicago: University of Chicago Press, 1987); Douglas S. Massey and Nancy Denton, *American Apartheid: Segregation and the Making of the Underclass* (Cambridge, MA: Harvard University Press, 1993).
23. Brindley, The Social Dimension, 53–65.
24. Ibid.
25. Herbert Gans, *The Urban Villagers: Group and Class in the Life of Italian-Americans* (New York: Free Press, 1962).
26. Brindley, The Social Dimension, 53–65.
27. William Clark and Sarah Blue, Race, Class, and Segregation Patterns in U.S. Immigrant Gateway Cities, *Urban Affairs Review* 39:6 (2004): 667–88.
28. According to Richard Florida (*The Flight of the Creative Class: The New Global Competition for Talent* [New York: Harper Business, 2005]), over half of the central city of Miami, and over 35 percent of the Los Angeles city population, was foreign-born. Florida also presents findings for what he calls the "mosaic index" for many world cities; this index looks not just at foreign-born percentage, but also at a weighted measure that accounts for other factors such as the percentage foreign-born not from a neighboring country. He credits development of the mosaic index results to another source: the team of Lisa Benton-Short, Marie Price, and Samantha Friedman, A Global Perspective on the Connections between Immigrants and World Cities, George

Washington Center for the Study of Globalization, 2004.

29. As of the writing of this chapter updated census data from U. S. Census is available for Los Angeles and Chicago, but information for the Miami metropolitan area posted at American FactFinder2 is based on 2006 estimates.
30. Richard Florida, *The Rise of the Creative Class: And How It's Transforming Work, Leisure, Community and Everyday Life* (New York: Basic Books, 2004); Florida, *The Flight of the Creative Class*, 172; Stephen Rausch and Cynthia Negrey, Does the Creative Engine Run? A Consideration of the Effect of Creative Class on Economic Strength and Growth, *Journal of Urban Affairs* 28:5 (2006): 473–89; June Thomas and Julia Darnton, Social Diversity and Economic Development in the Metropolis, *Journal of Planning Literature* 21:2 (2006): 153–68.
31. Joel Kotkin, Movers and Shakers: How Immigrants Are Reviving Neighborhoods Given Up for Dead, *Reason* 32:7 (2000): 40–46.
32. Khalid Koser and John Salt, The Geography of Highly Skilled International Immigration, *International Journal of Population Geography* 3 (1997): 285–303.
33. AnnaLee Saxenian, Silicon Valley's New Immigrant High-Growth Entrepreneurs, *Economic Development Quarterly* 16:1 (2002): 20–31.
34. David Ley, Seeking Homo Economicus: The Canadian State and the Strange Story of the Business Immigration Program, *Annals of the Association of American Geographers* 93:2 (2003): 426–41.
35. U. S. Census. See also Ayse Pamuk, Geography of Immigrant Clusters in Global Cities: A Case Study of San Francisco, 2000, *International Journal of Urban and Regional Research* 28:2 (2004): 287–307; Paul C. Brophy and Joy Borkholder, Strengthening Portal Neighborhoods, Published by CEOs for Cities, 2007, http://www.ceosforcities.org/files/CEOsForCitiesPortalNeighborhoodsFinal2006.pdf.
36. Albert Saiz, The Impact of Immigration on American Cities: An Introduction to the Issues, *Business Review* [Federal Reserve] Fourth Quarter (2003): 14–22; Kotkin, Movers and Shakers, 40–46.
37. George Borjas, The Economics of Immigration, *Journal of Economic Literature* 32 (1994): 1667–717; George Borjas, The Economic Benefits of Immigration, *Journal of Economic Perspectives* 9:2 (1995): 3–22.
38. Saskia Sassen, Cities in a World Economy, in *Readings in Urban Theory*, 2nd ed., ed. Susan Fainstein and Scott Campbell (Malden, MA: Blackwell, 2002), 32–56; Joel Kotkin, Movers and Shakers, 40–46.
39. Kotkin, Movers and Shakers, 40–46.
40. John R. Logan, Richard Alba, and Brian Stults, Enclaves and Entrepreneurs: Assessing the Payoff for Immigrants and Minorities, *International Migration Review* 37:2 (2003): 344–88.
41. Brophy and Borkholder, Strengthening Portal Neighborhoods.
42. Southeast Michigan Council of Governments, *Migration and Its Impact on Southeast Michigan, 1990–2003* (Detroit: SEMCOG, November, 2004); Nichole Christian, Detroit Journal: Mexican Immigrants Lead a Revival, *New York Times*, May 21, 2000, http://query.nytimes.com/gst/fullpage.html?res=9F00EEDB133AF932A15756C0A9669C8B63&sec=&spon=&pagewanted=1.
43. Ceri Peach, The Ghetto and the Ethnic Enclave, in *Desegregating the City: Ghettos, Enclaves and Inequality*, ed. David Varady (Albany: State University of New York, 2005), 31–48; Frederick Boal, Urban Ethnic Segregation and the Scenarios Spectrum, in *Desegregating the City: Ghettos, Enclaves and Inequality*, ed. Dave Varady (Albany: State University of Albany Press, 2005), 62–78.
44. Clark and Blue, Race, Class, and Segregation Patterns, 667–88.
45. Mohammed Qadeer, Ethnic Segregation in a Multicultural City, in *Desegregating the City: Ghettos, Enclaves and Inequality*, ed. David Varady (Albany: State University of New York, 2005), 49–61; Brindley, The Social Dimension, 53–65; Kotkin, Movers and Shakers, 40–46; Ivan Light, Immigrant Place Entrepreneurs in Los Angeles, 1970–99, *International Journal of Urban and Regional Research* 26:2 (2002): 215–28; Saxenian, Silicon Valley's New Immigrant, 20–31; Isham Ashutosh, (Re-)creating the Community: South Asian Transnationalism on Chicago's Devon Avenue, *Urban Geography* 29:3 (2008): 224–45.
46. Jan Rath, ed., *Tourism, Ethnic Diversity and the City* (New York: Routledge, 2007); Michael C. Hall and Jan Rath, Tourism, Migration and Place Advantage in the Global Cultural Economy, in Rath, *Tourism, Ethnic Diversity and the City*, 1–24; Kevin F. Gotham, Ethnic Heritage Tourism and Global-local Connections in New Orleans, in Rath, *Tourism, Ethnic Diversity and the City*, 125–42; Volkan Aytar, Caterers of the Consumed Metropolis: Ethnicized Tourism and Entertainment Landscapes in Istanbul, in Rath, *Tourism, Ethnic Diversity and the City*, 89–100; Susan Fainstein and John C. Powers, Tourism and New York's Ethnic Diversity: An Underutilized Resource? in Rath, *Tourism, Ethnic Diversity and the City*, 143–63; Marilyn Halter, Tourists 'R' Us:

Immigrants, Ethnic Tourism and the Marketing of Metropolitan Boston, in Rath, *Tourism, Ethnic Diversity and the City*, 199–215; Jock Collins, Ethnic Precincts as Contradictory Tourist Spaces, in Rath, *Tourism, Ethnic Diversity and the City*, 67–86; Larry Ford, Florinda Klevisser, and Francesca Carli, Ethnic Neighborhoods and Urban Revitalization: Can Europe Use the American Model? *Geographical Review* 98:1 (2008): 82–102.

47. Min-Jung Kwak and Daniel Hiebert, Making the New Economy: Immigrant Entrepreneurs and Merging Transnational Networks of International Education and Tourism in Seoul and Vancouver, in Rath, *Tourism, Ethnic Diversity and the City*, 27–49.
48. Edward Glaeser, interviewed in Kelly Evans, State of the City, *Wall Street Journal*, July 28, 2008, http://online.wsj.com/article/SB121676446070675115.html.
49. U. S. Census 2010 1-Year Estimates.
50. Ibid.; City of Chicago, Downtown Density Bonus Generates Millions for Affordable Housing in Neighborhoods, press release, January 31, 2006, http://www.cityofchicago.org/city/webportal/portalContentItemAction.do?contenTypeName=COC_EDITORIAL&contentOID=536935544&topChannelName=HomePage.
51. Hiromi Ishizawa and Gillian Stevens, Non-English Language Neighborhoods in Chicago, Illinois: 2000, *Social Science Research* 36 (2007): 1042–64; Dominic Pacyga and Ellen Skerrett, *Chicago, City of Neighborhoods: Histories and Tours* (Chicago: Loyola University Press, 1986); Melvin G. Holli and Peter d'A. Jones, *Ethnic Chicago: A Multicultural Portrait* (Grand Rapids: William B. Eerdmans, 1995); John Koval, Larry Bennett, Michael Bennett, Fassil Demissie, Roberta Garner, and Kiljoong Kim, ed., *The New Chicago: A Social and Cultural Analysis* (Philadelphia: Temple University Press, 2006); James Lewis, Michael Maly, Paul Kleppner, and Ruth Anne Tobias, *Race and Residence in the Chicago Metropolitan Area* (Chicago: Institute for Metropolitan Affairs, Roosevelt University, and Office for Social Policy Research, Northern Illinois University, 2002), 72.
52. Lewis et al., Race and Residence, 72; Clark and Blue, Race, Class, and Segregation Patterns, 667–88.
53. Yvonne Lau, Chicago's Chinese Americans: From Chinatown and Beyond, in Koval et al., *The New Chicago*, 168–81; Susan Moy, The Chinese in Chicago: The First One Hundred Years, in Holli and Jones, *Ethnic Chicago: A Multicultural Portrait*, 378–408; Louise Cainkar, Immigrants from the Arab World, in Koval et al., *The New Chicago*, 224–45; Padma Rangaswamy, Asian Indians in Chicago: Growth and Change in a Model Minority, in Holli and Jones, *Ethnic Chicago: A Multicultural Portrait*, 438–62; Padma Rangaswamy, Asian Indians in Chicago, in Koval et al., *The New Chicago*, 128–40.
54. Dowell Myers, Immigrants' Contributions in an Aging America, *Communities and Banking*, Summer 2008, www.bos.frb.org/commdev/c&b/2008/summer/myers_immigrants_and_boomers.pdf.
55. U. S. Census 2010, 1-Year Estimates. The numbers of Cubans dropped by half from 2000. For data on 2000 and commentary, see Rob Paral, Latinos of New Chicago, in Koval et al., *The New Chicago*, 105–144.
56. Jorge Casuso and Eduardo Camacho, Latino Chicago, in Holli and Jones, *Ethnic Chicago*, 346–77.
57. Enrique Salgado, Remarks offered to a tour group of the Association of Collegiate Schools of Planning, accompanied by organizational brochures for the Division Street Business Development Association, July 9, 2008.
58. Jorge Casuso and Eduardo Camacho, Latino Chicago, in Holli and Jones, *Ethnic Chicago*, 346–77.
59. Rob Paral, Latinos of New Chicago, in Koval et al., *The New Chicago*, 105–44; Jorge Casuso and Eduardo Camacho, Latino Chicago, in Holli and Jones, *Ethnic Chicago*, 346–77.
60. Paral, Latinos of New Chicago, 105–44; Pacyga and Skerrett, *Chicago, City of Neighborhoods*.
61. Ishizawa and Stevens, Non-English Language Neighborhoods in Chicago, 1042–64; Center for Cultural Understanding and Change, The Field Museum Team Engineering Collaboratory, et al., Creative Networks: Mexican Immigrant Assets in Chicago, research report for the Rockefeller Foundation, 2006, http://www.fieldmuseum.org/creativenetworks/pdfs/MIA_fullreport.pdf.
62. David Wilson, Jared Wouters, and Dennis Grammenos, Successful Protect-Community Discourse: Spatiality and Politics in Chicago's Pilsen Neighborhood, *Environment and Planning A* 36 (2004): 1176.
63. Ibid., 1173–90.
64. Mario Polese and Richard Stren, *The Social Sustainability of Cities: Diversity and the Management of Change* (Toronto: University of Toronto Press, 2000).
65. Brindley, The Social Dimension, 53–65.
66. Anthony Downs, Smart Growth: Why We Discuss It More Than We Do It, *Journal of the American Planning Association* 71:4 (2005): 367–80.

REFERENCES

Agyeman, Julian. Ethnic Minorities in Britain: Short Change, Systematic Indifference and Sustainable Development. *Journal of Environmental Policy and Planning* 3 (2001): 15–20.

Agyeman, Julian, Robert Bullard, and Tom Evans. Joined-up Thinking: Bringing Together Sustainability, Environmental Justice and Equity. In *Just Sustainabilities: Development in an Unequal World*, ed. Julian Agyeman, Robert Bullard, and Tom Evans, 1–16. Cambridge: MIT Press, 2003.

Agyeman, Julian, and Tom Evans. "Just Sustainability": The Emerging Discourse of Environmental Justice in Britain? *Geographical Journal* 170:2 (2004): 155–64.

———. Toward Just Sustainability in Urban Communities: Building Equity Rights with Sustainable Solutions. *The Annals of the American Academy of Political and Social Science* 590 (2003): 35–53.

Ashutosh, Isham. (Re-)creating the Community: South Asian Trans-nationalism on Chicago's Devon Avenue. *Urban Geography* 29:3 (2008): 224–45.

Aytar, Volkan. Caterers of the Consumed Metropolis: Ethnicized Tourism and Entertainment Landscapes in Istanbul. In *Tourism, Ethnic Diversity and the City*, ed. Jan Rath, 89–106. New York: Routledge, 2007.

Beatley, Timothy. Planning and Sustainability: The Elements of a New (Improved?) Paradigm. *Journal of Planning Literature* 9:4 (1995): 383–94.

Boal, Frederick. Urban Ethnic Segregation and the Scenarios Spectrum. In *Desegregating the City: Ghettos, Enclaves and Inequality*, ed. Dave Varady, 62–78. Albany: State University of Albany Press, 2005.

Borjas, George. The Economic Benefits of Immigration. *Journal of Economic Perspectives* 9:2 (1995): 3–22.

———. The Economics of Immigration. *Journal of Economic Literature* 32 (1994): 1667–717.

Bowen, William, and Michael Wells. The Politics and Reality of Environmental Justice: A History and Considerations for Public Administrators and Policy Makers. *Public Administration Review* 62:6 (2002): 688–98.

Brindley, Tim. The Social Dimension of the Urban Village: A Comparison of Models for Sustainable Urban Development. *Urban Design International* 8 (2003): 53–65.

Brophy, Paul C., and Joy Borkholder. Strengthening Portal Neighborhoods. Published by CEOs for Cities. February 19, 2007. http://www.ceosforcities.org/files/CEOsForCitiesPortalNeighborhoodsFinal2006.pdf.

Bullard, Robert D. Anatomy of Environmental Racism and the Environmental Justice Movement. In *Confronting Environmental Racism: Voices from the Grassroots*, ed. Robert Bullard, 15–39. Boston: South End Press, 1993.

Bullard, Robert D., Paul Mohai, Robin Saha, and Beverly Wright. Toxic Wastes and Race at Twenty, 1987–2007: Grassroots Struggles to Dismantle Environmental Racism in the United States. Executive Summary: Special Preview Release, February 2007.

Cainkar, Louise. Immigrants from the Arab World. In *The New Chicago: A Social and Cultural Analysis*, ed. John Koval, Larry Bennett, Michael Bennett, Fassil Demissie, Roberta Garner, and Kiljoong Kim, 182–96. Philadelphia: Temple University Press, 2006.

Campbell, Scott. Green Cities, Growing Cities, Just Cities? Urban Planning and the Contradictions of Sustainable Development. *Journal of the American Planning Association* 62:3 (1996): 296–312.

Casuso, Jorge, and Eduardo Camacho. Latino Chicago. In *Ethnic Chicago: A Multicultural Portrait*, ed. Melvin G. Holli and Peter d'A. Jones, 346–377. Grand Rapids: William B. Eerdmans, 1995.

Center for Cultural Understanding and Change, The Field Museum Team Engineering Collaboratory, Science of Networks in Communities Research Group, Creative Networks: Mexican Immigrant Assets in Chicago. Grant # 2004 CC 034 Research Report for the Rockefeller Foundation. University of Illinois, Urbana-Champaign. December 2006. http://archive.fieldmuseum.org/creativenetworks/pdfs/MIA_fullreport.pdf.

Christian, Nichole. Detroit Journal: Mexican Immigrants Lead a Revival. *New York Times*, May 21, 2000. http://query.nytimes.com/gst/fullpage.html?res=9F00EEDB133AF932A15756C0A9669C8B63&sec=&spon=&pagewanted=1.

City of Chicago. Downtown Density Bonus Generates Millions for Affordable Housing in Neighborhoods. Press Release, January 31, 2006. http://www.cityofchicago.org/city/webportal/portalContentItemAction.do?contenTypeName=COC_EDITORIAL&contentOID=536935544&topChannelName=HomePage.

Clark, William, and Sarah Blue. Race, Class, and Segregation Patterns in U.S. Immigrant Gateway Cities. *Urban Affairs Review* 39:6 (2004): 667–88.

Collins, Jock. Ethnic Precincts as Contradictory Tourist Spaces. In *Tourism, Ethnic Diversity and the City*, ed. Jan Rath, 67–86. New York: Routledge, 2007.

Danziger, Sheldon. Determinants of the Level and Distribution of Family Income in Metropolitan Areas, 1969. *Land Economics* 52:4 (1976): 467–78.

Dobson, Andrew. Social Justice and Environmental Sustainability: Ne'er the Twain Shall Meet? In *Just Sustainabilities: Development in an Unequal World*, ed. Julian Agyeman, Robert Bullard, and Tom Evans, 83–98. Cambridge: MIT Press, 2003.

Downs, Anthony. Smart Growth: Why We Discuss It More Than We Do It. *Journal of the American Planning Association* 71:4 (2005): 367–80.

Fainstein, Susan, and John C. Powers. Tourism and New York's Ethnic Diversity: An Underutilized Resource? In *Tourism, Ethnic Diversity and the City*, ed. Jan Rath, 143–63. New York: Routledge, 2007.

Ford, Larry, Florinda Klevisser, and Francesca Carli. Ethnic Neighborhoods and Urban Revitalization: Can Europe Use the American Model? *Geographical Review* 98:1 (2008): 82–102.

Florida, Richard. *The Flight of the Creative Class: The New Global Competition for Talent*. New York: Harper Business, 2005.

———. *The Rise of the Creative Class: And How It's Transforming Work, Leisure, Community and Everyday Life*. New York: Basic Books, 2004.

Gans, Herbert. *The Urban Villagers: Group and Class in the Life of Italian-Americans*. New York: Free Press, 1962.

Glaeser, Edward. Interviewed in Kelly Evans, State of the City, *The Wall Street Journal*, July 28, 2008. http://online.wsj.com/article/SB121676446070675115.html.

Goldman, Benjamin A. *Not Just Prosperity: Achieving Sustainability with Environmental Justice*. Washington, DC: National Wildlife Federation, 1993.

Gotham, Kevin F. Ethnic Heritage Tourism and Global-local Connections in New Orleans. In *Tourism, Ethnic Diversity and the City*, ed. Jan Rath, 125–42. New York: Routledge, 2007.

Gunder, Michael. Sustainability: Planning's Saving Grace or Road to Perdition? *Journal of Planning Education and Research* 26 (2006): 208–21.

Hall, Michael C., and Jan Rath. Tourism, Migration and Place Advantage in the Global Cultural Economy. In *Tourism, Ethnic Diversity and the City*, ed. Jan Rath, 1–24. New York: Routledge, 2007.

Halter, Marilyn. Tourists 'R' Us: Immigrants, Ethnic Tourism and the Marketing of Metropolitan Boston. In *Tourism, Ethnic Diversity and the City*, ed. Jan Rath, 199–215. New York: Routledge, 2007.

Haughton, Graham. Environmental Justice and the Sustainable City. *Journal of Planning Education and Research* 18 (1999): 233–43.

Hirshmann, Charles. The Origins and Demise of the Concept of Race. *Population and Development Review* 30:3 (2004): 385–415.

Holli, Melvin G., and Peter d'A. Jones. *Ethnic Chicago: A Multicultural Portrait*. Grand Rapids: William B. Eerdmans, 1995.

Ishizawa, Hiromi, and Gillian Stevens. Non-English Language Neighborhoods in Chicago, Illinois: 2000. *Social Science Research* 36 (2007): 1042–64.

Jacobs, Harvey. Social Equity in Agricultural Land Protection. *Landscape and Urban Planning* 17 (1989): 21–33.

Koser, Khalid, and John Salt. The Geography of Highly Skilled International Immigration. *International Journal of Population Geography* 3 (1997): 285–303.

Kotkin, Joel. Movers and Shakers: How Immigrants Are Reviving Neighborhoods Given Up for Dead. *Reason* 32:7 (2000): 40–46.

Koval, John, Larry Bennett, Michael Bennett, Fassil Demissie, Roberta Garner, and Kiljoong Kim, eds. *The New Chicago: A Social and Cultural Analysis*. Philadelphia: Temple University Press, 2006.

Kwak, Min-Jung, and Daniel Hiebert. Making the New Economy: Immigrant Entrepreneurs and Merging Transnational Networks of International Education and Tourism in Seoul and Vancouver. In *Tourism, Ethnic Diversity and the City*, ed. Jan Rath, 27–49. New York: Routledge, 2007.

Lau, Yvonne. Chicago's Chinese Americans: From Chinatown and Beyond. In *The New Chicago: A Social and Cultural Analysis*, ed. John Koval, Larry Bennett, Michael Bennett, Fassil Demissie, Roberta Garner, and Kiljoong Kim , 168–81. Philadelphia: Temple University Press, 2006.

Lewis, James, Michael Maly, Paul Kleppner, and Ruth Anne Tobias. *Race and Residence in the Chicago Metropolitan Area*. Chicago: Institute for Metropolitan Affairs, Roosevelt University, and Office for Social Policy Research, Northern Illinois University, 2002.

Ley, David. Seeking Homo Economicus: The Canadian State and the Strange Story of the Business Immigration Program. *Annals of the Association of American Geographers* 93:2 (2003): 426–41.

Light, Ivan. Immigrant Place Entrepreneurs in Los Angeles, 1970–99. *International Journal of Urban and Regional Research* 26:2 (2002): 215–28.

Logan, John R., Richard Alba, and Brian Stults. Enclaves and Entrepreneurs: Assessing the Payoff for Immigrants and Minorities. *International Migration Review* 37:2 (2003): 344–88.

Madden, Janice. Do Racial Composition and Segregation Affect Economic Outcomes in Metropolitan Areas? In *Problem of the Century: Racial Stratification in the United States*, ed. E. Anderson and Denton Massey, 290–316. New York: Russell Sage Foundation, 2001.

Massey, Douglas S., and Nancy Denton. *American Apartheid: Segregation and the Making of the*

Underclass. Cambridge, MA: Harvard University Press, 1993.

Mohai, Paul, and Bunyan Bryant. Is There a "Race" Effect on Concern for Environmental Quality? *Public Opinion Quarterly* 62 (1998): 475–505.

Morello-Frosch, Rachel, Manuel Pastor, and James Sadd. Environmental Justice and Southern California's "Riskscape": The Distribution of Air Toxics Exposures and Health Risks among Diverse Communities. *Urban Affairs Review* 36:4 (2001): 551–78.

Moy, Susan. The Chinese in Chicago: The First One Hundred Years. In *Ethnic Chicago: A Multicultural Portrait*, ed. Melvin G. Holli and Peter d'A. Jones, 378–408. Grand Rapids: William B. Eerdmans, 1995.

Myers, Dowell. Immigrants' Contributions in an Aging America. *Communities and Banking*. Summer 2008. http://www.bos.frb.org/commdev/c&b/2008/summer/myers_immigrants_and_boomers.pdf.

Newton, David. *Environmental Justice: A Reference Handbook*. Contemporary World Issues series. Santa Barbara, CA: ABC-CLIO, 1996.

Pacyga, Dominic, and Ellen Skerrett. *Chicago, City of Neighborhoods: Histories and Tours*. Chicago: Loyola University Press, 1986.

Pamuk, Ayse. Geography of Immigrant Clusters in Global Cities: A Case Study of San Francisco, 2000. *International Journal of Urban and Regional Research* 28:2 (2004): 287–307.

Paral, Rob. Latinos of New Chicago. In *The New Chicago: A Social and Cultural Analysis*, ed. John Koval, Larry Bennett, Michael Bennett, Fassil Demissie, Roberta Garner, and Kiljoong Kim, 105–44. Philadelphia: Temple University Press, 2006.

Paral, Rob, and Michael Norkewicz. *The Metro Chicago Immigration Fact Book*. Chicago: Institute for Metropolitan Affairs, Roosevelt University, 2003.

Peach, Ceri. The Ghetto and the Ethnic Enclave. In *Desegregating the City: Ghettos, Enclaves and Inequality*, ed. David Varady, 31–48. Albany: State University of New York, 2005.

Perlin, Susan A., Ken Sexton, and David W. S. Wong. An Examination of Race and Poverty for Populations Living Near Industrial Sources of Air Pollution. *Journal of Exposure Analysis and Environmental Epidemiology* 9 (1999): 29–48.

Polese, Mario, and Richard Stren. *The Social Sustainability of Cities: Diversity and the Management of Change*. Toronto: University of Toronto Press, 2000.

Qadeer, Mohammed. Ethnic Segregation in a Multicultural City. In *Desegregating the City: Ghettos, Enclaves and Inequality*, ed. David Varady, 49–61. Albany: State University of New York, 2005.

Rangaswamy, Padma. Asian Indians in Chicago. In *The New Chicago: A Social and Cultural Analysis*, ed. John Koval, Larry Bennett, Michael Bennett, Fassil Demissie, Roberta Garner, and Kiljoong Kim, 128–140. Philadelphia: Temple University Press, 2006.

———. Asian Indians in Chicago: Growth and Change in a Model Minority. In *Ethnic Chicago: A Multicultural Portrait*, ed. Melvin G. Holli and Peter d'A. Jones, 438–62. Grand Rapids: William B. Eerdmans, 1995.

Rath, Jan, ed. *Tourism, Ethnic Diversity and the City*. New York: Routledge, 2007.

Rausch, Stephen, and Cynthia Negrey. Does the Creative Engine Run? A Consideration of the Effect of Creative Class on Economic Strength and Growth. *Journal of Urban Affairs* 28:5 (2006): 473–89.

Saiz, Albert. The Impact of Immigration on American Cities: An Introduction to the Issues. *Business Review* [Federal Reserve] Fourth Quarter (2003): 14–22.

Salgado, Enrique. Remarks offered to a tour group of the Association of Collegiate Schools of Planning, accompanied by organizational brochures for the Division Street Business Development Association. July 9, 2008.

Sassen, Saskia. Cities in a World Economy. In *Readings in Urban Theory*, 2d ed., ed. Susan Fainstein and Scott Campbell, 32–56. Malden, MA: Blackwell, 2002.

Saxenian, AnnaLee. Silicon Valley's New Immigrant High-Growth Entrepreneurs. *Economic Development Quarterly* 16:1 (2002): 20–31.

Schweitzer, Lisa, and Max Stephenson Jr. Right Answers, Wrong Questions: Environmental Justice as Urban Research. *Urban Studies* 44:2 (2007): 319–37.

Southeast Michigan Council of Governments (SEMCOG). *Migration and Its Impact on Southeast Michigan, 1990–2003*. Detroit: SEMCOG, 2004.

Thomas, June, and Julia Darnton. Social Diversity and Economic Development in the Metropolis. *Journal of Planning Literature* 21:2 (2006): 153–68.

U. S. Census. 2010 American Community Survey 1-Year Estimates. Washington, DC.

U.S. Environmental Protection Agency. Fiscal Year 2006 Performance and Accountability Report. 2007. http://www.epa.gov/ocfo/finstatement/2006par/index.htm.

———. Toward an Environmental Justice Collaborative Model: An Evaluation of the Use of Partnerships to Address Environmental Justice Issues in Communities. 2003. http://www.epa.gov/evaluate/ejevalcs.pdf.

Victor, David G. Recovering Sustainable Development. *Foreign Affairs* 85:1 (2006): 91–103.

Wilson, David, Jared Wouters, and Dennis Grammenos.

Successful Protect-Community Discourse: Spatiality and Politics in Chicago's Pilsen Neighborhood. *Environment and Planning A* 36 (2004): 1173–90.

Wilson, William J. *The Declining Significance of Race: Blacks and Changing American Institutions*. Chicago: University of Chicago Press, 1980.

———. *The Truly Disadvantaged: The Inner City, the Underclass and Public Policy*. Chicago: University of Chicago Press, 1987.

Yiftachel, Oren. Re-engaging Planning Theory? Towards "South-Eastern" Perspectives. *Planning Theory* 5:3 (2006): 211–22.

■ PIERRE FILION

Recent Planning and Development in Toronto

MOVING TOWARD SMART GROWTH?

There is a growing gap between, on the one hand, the political and planning discourse, that calls for alternatives to urban sprawl and automobile dependence, and, on the other hand, the reality of urban development. Despite efforts to raise density, public transit use, and reliance on walking, relatively low-density, single-use, and automobile-dependent forms still prevail. The chapter addresses this gap within the context of the Toronto metropolitan region.

I identify major attempts over the 2001–2007 period at achieving alternative models of urban development, which feature rising densities, multifunctionality, high levels of transit use and walking, along with the preservation of natural areas. Findings indicate residential density increments in the core, thanks to a high-rise condominium boom, and in outer suburbs, where the density of subdivisions is higher than in older suburban developments. There have also been notable public transit improvements, but they fall well short of needs arising from accelerated population growth. Finally, among all efforts at modifying urban development trends, the preservation of natural and rural land is most successful. Major obstacles to the realization of alternative forms of development include prevailing urban dynamics, habits and expectations, and the suitability of conventional urban forms to requirements of the economy and prevailing lifestyles. But the two most frequently recurring obstacles are NIMBY (Not In My Back Yard) reactions and limited public sector finances. Overall, density increments, public transit investments, and natural area conservation are much more successful at achieving their respective immediate objectives than at modifying metropolitan-wide relations between transportation and land use, and behavioral patterns, in a fashion that is consistent with smart growth.

Pressures for Urban Change

There is growing awareness of the adverse consequences of conventional patterns of urban development—specifically, their relatively low-density, single-use development and near universal reliance on the automobile. Concern about this form of growth is of course driven by its environmental sequels, but increasing attention goes to infrastructure and service delivery costs, and quality of life and health implications.[1] In development scenarios the spread option comes out as costlier in terms of infrastructures and services than more concentrated alternatives, and time spent on roads and highways eats into possibilities of engaging in leisure and cultural activities, and in family life.[2] From a health perspective, a growing body of research links obesity and associated ailments to insufficient exercise due to urban forms that force generalized dependence on the car.[3] Other consequences of sprawl include an inequitable distribution of fiscal revenues between peripheral and central jurisdictions, and accessibility difficulties experienced by many social groups in a car-oriented environment.[4]

Especially in large metropolitan regions, where negative sides of conventional urban development are exacerbated, there is a growing feeling that business as usual cannot continue. Mounting opposition to further growth—seen as responsible for worsening congestion and pollution—and perceptions of declining quality of life have fed pressures for alternative forms of development.[5]

Since 1970 we have witnessed a succession of alternative models in reaction to prevailing patterns of development. These alternatives have been inspired successively by attempts to reduce energy needs in the wake of the oil crises of the 1970s and early 1980s, sustainable development, and, most recently, the smart growth movement.[6] Smart growth is differentiated from earlier attempts at modifying urban development by its simultaneous focus on environmental, financial, and quality-of-life aspects of urban development. But despite valiant attempts at formulating and promoting this succession of alternatives (such as different forms of intensification and nonautomobile travel options), their impact on development has been limited. Not only does urbanization persistently adhere for the most part to post–World War II models, but tendencies initiated over these years keep on gaining ground. This is notably the case of ever increasing automobile dependency.

Forces of Inertia

Why is it proving so difficult to reorient development when there is apparently so much support for a transition in urban form? I identify five categories of factors responsible for the limited implementation and success of alternative urban patterns.

Changes in Economic Circumstances and Political Priorities

The 1950s and 1960s were favorable to massive investments in infrastructures. Rapid productivity gains assured rising prosperity, which in turn filled public sector coffers, thus fostering expanded government intervention capacity.[7] Moreover, infrastructure development was high on governments' priority lists.[8] Along with their key role in supporting rising productivity (for example, the impact of the Interstate Highway System on the manufacturing sector), infrastructure expenditures played a central part within Keynesian strategies, the macroeconomic orthodoxy of the time.[9] Not only did investments in infrastructure create employment and thereby bolster consumer demand, but they equally contributed to adapt the urban environment to the mass consumption of durable goods—above all, the automobile.

From the 1970s, changing circumstances challenged these arrangements. At first, oil crises and stagflation triggered recessions with dire consequences for the public purse. Later, with economic globalization and waning faith in interventionism, Keynesianism fell out of favor.[10] Infrastructure investments were further affected by growing resistance to tax increases and the reduced priority given to infrastructure as other sectors of expenditure, notably healthcare, assumed more importance. Such a situation casts doubt on the possibility of creating alternative infrastructure systems of a scale sufficient to counteract the dynamics generated by existing networks, conceived during post–World War II decades.

Transportation and Land Use Relationship

The key issue from the perspective of present attempts at modifying urban form and journey patterns is the deep entrenchment of the auto-oriented land use–transportation relationship.[11] Small-scale attempts at modifying this relationship will either fail or be of limited consequence. To be effective they must be sufficiently extensive to have an effect at points of origin and destination, and have a simultaneous impact on transportation and land use. The need for interventions that are large scale and comprehensive harks back to the first factor of inertia: difficulties in finding resources to carry out such interventions.

Habits and Expectations

Reliance on habits reduces the complexity of life while instilling ontological security.[12] Habits are integral to how people organize their lives and they prevent having to engage in repeated learning processes. Likewise, expectations within the urban environment are shaped by previous experiences and familiarity with available options. Of most relevance to the present discussion is the fact that a large proportion of residents of metropolitan regions have been raised in a suburban environment and are most familiar with this type of setting.[13] Accordingly, living environment preferences are largely molded by this familiarity. In a circular fashion, developers typically respond to expectation (and preference) patterns, and these patterns are themselves fashioned by products from the development industry.[14] Both habits and expectations thus have a conservative influence on urban environments.

Vested Interests

A focus on economic benefits distinguishes the present from the previous category of factors of inertia. Land speculators, the segment of the development and building industry that specializes in low-density structures, as well as road and highway contractors, all have economic interests vested in conventional forms of urban growth.[15] As expected, they use their political and economic leverage to influence policymaking.[16] This is also the case of certain consumer lobbies, with most relevance here, automobile associations.

Vested interests advocate not only for a perpetuation of present forms of development, but also against modifications to existing urban environments, especially intensification. Such conservationist vested interests are generally made of homeowners preoccupied with possible adverse impacts on property values. Resulting NIMBY activism constitutes a foremost obstacle to alternative forms of development.[17]

Economic Requirements and Lifestyles

For all their environmental sequels and infrastructure expenses, present development patterns are generally successful in producing affordable locales for different types of activities.[18] Accessibility to the periphery warranted by automobile-oriented development indeed contributes to an abundance of available land for different types of activities, and thereby to relatively low land costs.[19] But congestion and resulting impaired peripheral accessibility challenge land affordability.

Conventional development yields a wide range of forms of housing and commercial facilities, appealing to households and businesses with various needs and means. The homely commercial strip perhaps best illustrates the flexibility of the automobile-oriented model.[20] This haphazard assemblage of structures set in a sea of parking offers an unequaled range of opportunities for businesses and consumers: for example, fast-food outlets, used-car dealerships, inexpensive motels, cheek and jowl with a wide range of services, including medical offices, dance or karate schools, not-for-profit establishments, and shopping malls occupied by department stores and national and international chains.

The discussion on forces of inertia underscores difficulties in changing urban development tendencies. Overcoming these barriers requires considerable and persistent efforts, most likely to take place and be effective in periods of perceived crisis. It is when the status quo no longer appears to be viable that shifts in urban development are most likely to happen.

The Toronto Case Study

Confrontations between forces of innovation and of inertia play themselves out differently according to the metropolitan regions under consideration, due to their respective history, economic base, urban structure, values, and political system and dynamics. At the same time, however, one can expect similarities across the Canada–U.S. metropolitan system. The spread of best practices within the planning community, the car-orientation of most post–World War II development, and the tendency for all metropolitan regions to compete in the same economic arena, assure shared features across all metros.

Toronto stands out in North America by the early formation of a two-tier government structure. From its inception in 1954 until the creation in the early 1970s of regional governments at its borders, Metro Toronto enjoyed planning power over the totality of the metropolitan region.[21]

Toronto was also distinguished by the adoption of planning strategies aiming at promoting a balanced form of development, at once centralized and decentralized, and involving both low- and high-density areas, as well as pockets of public housing in all developing suburban municipalities. Perhaps the aspect of the Toronto balanced approach that most influenced urban structure was a dual focus on expressway and subway development at a time when transportation funding across North America went nearly exclusively to highway projects.[22]

If the inner suburbs (built between 1946 and 1971) reflect these Toronto planning particularities, the outer suburbs conform much more closely to the North American norm.[23] They developed at a time when metropolitan-wide planning was impeded by the absence of agency operating at this level.[24] Provincial attempts to play this role were episodic and generally unsuccessful. In addition, outlying municipalities failed to subscribe to the Metro Toronto balanced planning vision, producing instead a relatively low-density car-reliant urban environment. With substantial cutbacks to subsidized housing and public transportation funding, senior governments also contributed to the demise of the balanced planning approach.[25]

Especially since the 1980s, the gap between ongoing urban growth and investment in infrastructures has widened. The problem is exacerbated by a rise in automobile ownership and use far in excess of population growth.[26] Consequences for the economic performance of Toronto and its quality of life are dire. It is estimated that the metropolitan region loses $2 billion annually in reduced productivity due to traffic congestion.[27] And once a North American beacon of public transit performance, Toronto Transit Commission services (responsible for over 80 percent of the transit journeys within the metropolitan region) have slipped seriously over the 1990s. Service cuts have caused a severe loss of patronage during this period, only partially recaptured by a rebound over the 2000s.[28]

There have been numerous attempts since 1970 to formulate and implement alternative forms of urban development. Foremost examples include the Toronto Centered Region plan, which proposed a linear urban form for the metropolitan region, contained by a green belt and surrounded by a limited number of satellite towns;[29] the Metro Toronto plan for the urban structure, which advanced a network of mixed-use nodes adjacent to subway lines;[30] and the Office for the Greater Toronto Area proposal for a system of twenty-three nodes and of rail transit expanded at the scale of the entire metropolitan region.[31] In the end, rail transit was expanded but did not keep pace with the rise in population and unabated outward urban expansion, and of all the proposed nodes, only three large and a few smaller ones materialized.

Since the turn of the century, two planning exercises converged to produce a new vision of metropolitan growth. The first culminated in the 2002 City of Toronto Official Plan, which proposed to direct over the following thirty years 20 percent of the growth of the metropolitan region to the City of Toronto (a fully built-out urban area with a population of 2.4 million, about half of the region).[32] The additional 537,000 residents are to be accommodated in redeveloped sectors consisting of brownfields, the waterfront, downtown Toronto, nodes, and arterial roads where low-rise commercial structures with abundant surface parking would be redeveloped into six- to eight-story residential structures with ground-level retailing.

The second vision emanated from the provincial government. Confronted with pressures to address high rates of rural and natural land absorption, traffic congestion, and the prospect for further deterioration to the environment and quality of life with the anticipated arrival of 3.7 million new residents within the Greater Golden Horseshoe (an extended Toronto-centered region), in 2006 the province adopted the Places to Grow plan. The plan prescribes the creation of about a 1.8 million acre (728,430 hectare) greenbelt, a nodal pattern of development destined to absorb the 40 percent of the population growth to be channeled to existing built-up areas and major expansions of public transit systems.[33]

Smart Growth Compatible Planning in Toronto: 2001–2007

It is clearly too early to assess the smart growth impacts of these recent visions. Still, lessons can be learned by verifying how development in Toronto responded to mounting pressures for the adoption of alternative forms of development, at a time of rising concern over the adverse effects of prevailing growth patterns. Recall that by 2001 there had already been a long search for alternative development patterns and numerous implementation attempts. Research is based on a survey of Toronto newspaper articles from January 2001 to June 2007. The newspaper search has allowed the identification and documentation of issues. Consultation of plans and reports contributed further information on the issues.[34] Identified alternative patterns of development fall into three categories: intensification, transportation, and protection of the natural environment (see figs. 1 and 2 for the location of these alternative patterns).

Intensification

The 2001–2007 period witnessed an important surge in high-rise condominium development, concentrated largely in downtown Toronto, the waterfront, other parts of the inner city, and inner-city and suburban nodes. Proximity to rail public transit attracts such development as illustrated by massive clusters of high-rise condominium buildings in North York Centre (served by three subway stations) and along the new Sheppard subway line (see fig. 3).[35] Different forms of condominium structures—high-, medium-, and low-rise, as well as townhouses—are also found in redeveloped brownfield sites, as well as in new suburban developments. Within an enabling legal context set by official plans and zoning, it is the private sector that carries out these developments. In one instance, however, the impetus came from the public sector. Regent Park, a 1950s inner-city public housing complex, separated from the street grid and provided with abundant green space (albeit poorly used and maintained), is presently being redeveloped at a higher density with a combination of street-aligned public and market housing.[36]

Developer interest for high-density housing is supported by a robust demand from downsizing baby boomers, members of the echo generation trying to gain a foothold in the property market, and large inflows of immigrants accustomed to high-density living.[37] In the many sites where high-rise condominium developments are isolated from low-density neighborhoods, NIMBY reactions tend to be muted. In other instances, however, such projects can be delayed or scuttled by vociferous opposition from nearby residents.[38]

The present wave of high-density residential development has caused an increase in multiples

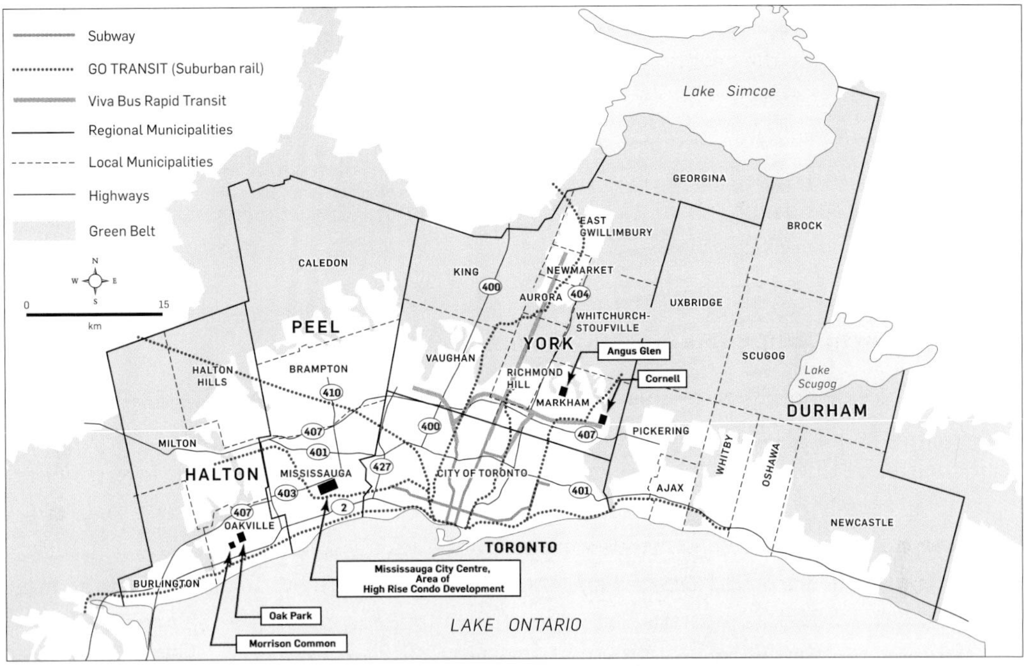

Figure 1. Smart growth inspired planning initiatives in the Greater Toronto Area, 2001–2007.

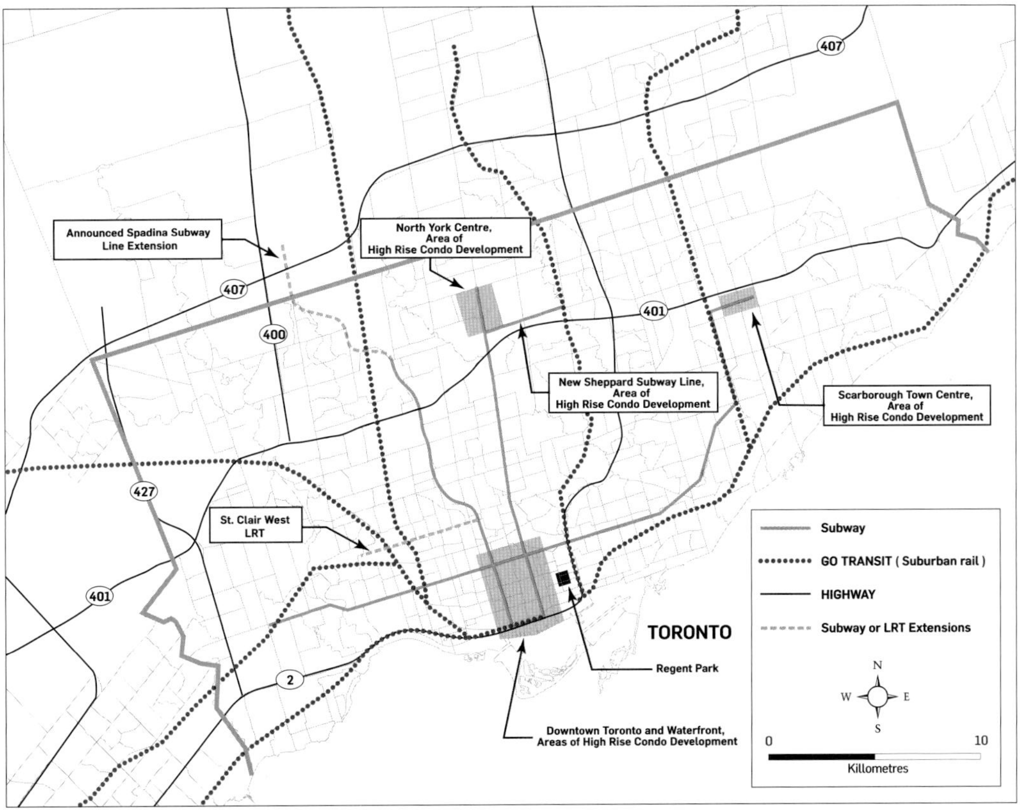

Figure 2. Smart growth inspired planning initiatives in the Greater Toronto Area, 2001–2007.

PHOTOGRAPH BY PIERRE FILION

Figure 3. High-rise condominium clusters along new Sheppard subway line. North York Centre has experienced considerable high-rise condominium development over the past years.

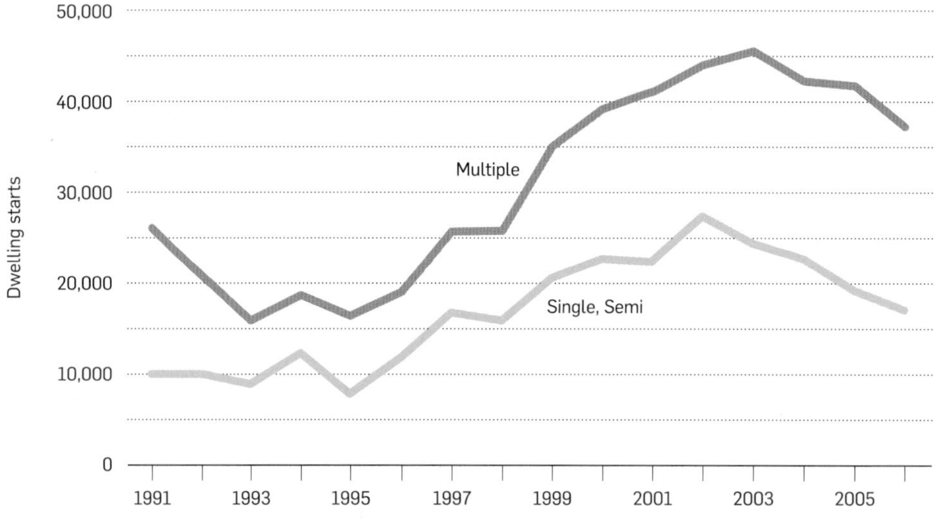

Figure 4. Dwelling starts, Toronto Metropolitan Region, 1991–2006.

Source: Canada Mortgage and Housing Corporation, *Monthly Housing Statistics* (Ottawa: CMHC, various dates).

as a proportion of all new units (see fig. 4). Given the erection of many such units within the built perimeter, current figures appear to be consistent with Places to Grow intensification objectives.

New subdivisions also register higher densities. Such a trend is in part attributable to new urbanism master planned communities. One, the Beach Neighborhood, is an inner-city redevelopment of a former racetrack, and Cornell, Angus Glen, Morrison Common, and Oak Park are outer-suburban greenfield developments (see fig. 5). The town of Markham was most ambitious among suburban municipalities in its promotion of residential intensification. As a result, Markham features narrow lot subdivisions (fully or partly inspired by new urbanism), shallow lot subdivisions, and high-density condominium units in its city center, presently under development.[39] But given the small proportion of all new homes that is built in new urbanism communities, suburban subdivision intensification is far more a function of a generalized shrinkage of single-family home lot sizes, along with an additional presence of multiples.

Such intensification is a function of planning regulations (as those adopted in Markham), but, above all, of escalating land prices. Because the development is taking place on green fields, NIMBY is rarely an obstacle to the building of subdivisions with densities that exceed the previous suburban norm.

PHOTOGRAPH BY PIERRE FILION

Figure 5. Higher-density new subdivisions following development patterns of new urbanism master planned communities. New urbanism neighborhood, Cornell in Markham.

Public Transportation

The foremost public transit expansion over 2001–2007 was the new Sheppard subway line, opened in 2002. The 3.4 mile (5.5 kilometer) line was built at the cost of nearly $1 billion. The Sheppard line runs eastward from North York Centre, where it connects with the north-south Yonge line. Low in the Toronto Transit Commission list of priorities, the Sheppard line was built largely for political reasons. The mayor of Toronto, formerly the preamalgamation mayor of North York, had a personal interest in a line improving access to North York Centre.[40] The Sheppard line has attracted limited ridership (40,000 passengers a day).[41] However, considerable high-rise condominium development is taking place along its route (13,000 units either recently completed, being built, or in the preconstruction stage), which bodes well for future patronage.[42]

Another Toronto transit investment included the creation of a 4.2 mile (6.7 kilometer) streetcar right-of-way on St. Clair Street West (already served by streetcars, but without their own right-of-way), at the cost of $65 million. The project is an early stage of a Toronto Transit Commission City of Toronto-wide seventy-five mile (120 kilometer) light rail transit (LRT) network plan labeled Transit City.[43] The proposed network is meant to stem worsening road congestion likely to result from the anticipated intensification of the city. The LRT option was presented as a cheaper substitute to subway expansion—about one-tenth the cost of a tunneled subway. However, merchants along St. Clair West objected fiercely to the loss of traffic lanes and reduced parking spaces, and thus to less automobile accessibility. The battle against the right-of-way was fought in the political and legal arenas from 2002 until 2006. In the end, with the approval of the Toronto City Council and of the courts, the project went ahead. The smart growth impact of the new right-of-way will be limited—a few minutes off the journey time and a more efficient and predictable operation of streetcars on the line. But its effect will be far more important if, as planned, it constitutes a link in a comprehensive future LRT network.

A third major transit investment took place in York Region, a suburban regional municipality north of Toronto. In 2002 York Region launched the Viva bus rapid transit network, consisting of five lines crisscrossing York Region along a north-south and an east-west axis, and connecting with subway and GO (commuter train) stations. The buses run at maximum headways of fifteen minutes. The original investment was $180 million, with contributions from all three levels of government. One year after the inception of Viva, public transit patronage in York Region had increased by 38 percent (albeit from a low 5 percent modal share base value).[44] Bus rights-of-way along the network and an eventual upgrading to light rail transit are projected.[45] Thanks to the possibility of widening arterial roads in a less densely developed environment, bus and LRT rights-of-way in York Region are unlikely to trigger the adverse reactions observed in the St. Clair West case.

For all their merits, the three projects fall well short from expectations regarding public transit expansion within the Toronto metropolitan region. Plans from the 1980s recommended considerable subway extensions: the Yonge-Spadina loop line, the Eglinton line, and the downtown line.[46] Due to fiscal constraints, public transit expansion has not kept pace with population growth. But even with profuse funding, it would have been difficult to extend viable transit services into low-density auto-oriented suburbs, where much of Toronto's development takes place.

Financial constraints do not only affect capital expenditures, they also have an impact on the operation of public transit systems. Since the 1990s' interlevel redistribution of responsibilities and revenues, local (or regional) administrations are fully accountable for transit operation subsidies. The more passengers public transit systems attract, an eminent smart growth objective, the heavier the burden on the municipal purse. Over the summer of 2007, while the province was extolling the virtues of smart growth, the City of Toronto Council considered tackling its $413 million structural deficit by, among other things, closing down the Sheppard line and eliminating over twenty bus lines.[47] Council instead opted for a fare increase while acknowledging that this measure failed to provide a long-term solution to its budget woes.[48]

It is important to realize that road investments are much more attuned than public transit expansion to urban growth. Local road and arterial networks must indeed be in place for a new development to happen and expressway networks are extended and widened as urban development reaches farther outward.

The 2001–2007 period has witnessed the announcement of two major public transit projects. One is a bus rapid transit network running along expressways (on its own right-of-way or on high-occupancy-vehicle lanes) and the other is an extension of the Spadina subway line to the Vaughan Corporate Centre (the first subway to reach beyond Toronto boundaries).[49]

Protection of the Natural Environment

It is by far the creation of a greenbelt, assuring the future preservation of the Oak Ridges Moraine, an environmentally sensitive area to the north of the Toronto built perimeter, that has garnered most attention within this category of initiatives.[50] The greenbelt is indeed a mainstay of the Places to Grow plan. At a smaller scale, similar concerns for natural environments have also influenced the morphology of suburban areas. Since the 1980s, the tendency has been for an increased protection of natural features within subdivisions. Woods are preserved, and creeks and their riparian zones kept in their natural state, in stark contrast with past practices. In consequence, the contemporary subdivision features much more natural space than its earlier emanations. Meanwhile, yards and conventional parks tend to occupy less space.

The activism of environmental groups and the popularity of their views have been instrumental in the protection of natural areas. The conservation of large expanses of green space, such as the Oak Ridges Moraine, has been the object of epic battles (the Ontario Greenbelt Alliance groups more than eighty member organizations).[51] Likewise, the adoption of an environmental approach is often a condition for the acceptance of subdivision plans by city councils feeling pressure from environmental groups.

Of the three categories of smart growth–related measures, this is arguably the one that has been most successfully implemented in Toronto. Strong reservations about the greenbelt on the part of the home building industry and the farming community were offset by a highly supportive public attitude, and the protection of natural features within subdivisions generated little opposition. These measures thus avoid the frequent disapproval of local effects of intensification and resulting NIMBY reactions, as well as benefit from low implementation costs compared with transit development. Instead of buying out the greenbelt land owned by developers, the Province of Ontario has engaged in a land swap, and the protection of natural features has become part of the normal subdivision approval process.

Implementation and Outcomes of Alternative Development Models

Figure 6 presents a six-stage model that runs from the original perception of problems leading to the formulation of policies, to the eventual smart growth impacts of resulting policies. The model is meant to demonstrate the need for consistency at these different stages, which involve different processes and actors, in order to achieve desired smart growth effects. It is within this succession of stages that forces of urban change and of inertia play themselves out. If attempts at achieving alternative development and dynamics fail, because of direct obstruction from forces of inertia or perhaps due to incompetence, shifting political priorities or unanticipated outcomes, growth reverts back to conventional patterns due to the overwhelming influence of these forces.

The different smart growth-oriented initiatives are broken down in figure 7 into the stages described in the previous table. Naturally, there is no evidence of blockages at the early stages of the initiatives, for such blockages would have caused the initiatives to abort and thus fall below the chapter's methodological radar. Figure 7 shows that the initiatives tend to attain their immediate smart growth objectives. Areas targeted for intensified residential development do attract developers and residents while reducing the per capita urban footprint. The Viva bus service is successful in raising York Region public transit modal shares, and the greenbelt and the preservation of natural features in subdivisions are reaching their conservation objectives. It is too early, however, to pass judgment on the Sheppard subway line ridership level because its corridor is undergoing accelerated redevelopment, and the performance and impact of the St. Clair West LRT is still unknown, the line being under construction.

The situation regarding broad smart growth consequences, beyond immediate objectives, of land-use interventions is less favorable. If high-rise condominium developments can raise

1 **Original impetus**: Demand for intervention on the part of pressure groups, influence of the media, potential impact on the electoral process.

2 **Planning formulation and discourse**: Planning process (public participation, preparation of report or plan) leads to the formulation of proposals.

3 **Political decision making**: Proposals enter the political sphere. Debates around the proposals. Political pressures. Uneven distribution of political influence affects outcome.

4 **Implementation of political decisions**: Full or partial implementation, subjected to financial constraints and changes of priorities.

5 **Capacity to achieve development objectives**: Often need a favorable market response or to modify behaviors to meet objectives.

6 **Impact of developments on behavior and on urban dynamics**: Are fully implemented interventions inducing desired smart growth effects, or are unexpected outcomes impeding these effects?

Figure 6. Stages in the formulation, implementation, and smart growth impacts of planning interventions.

Residential intensification

	HIGH-RISE CONDOMINIUM DEVELOPMENTS	SUBDIVISION INTENSIFICATION
Original impetus	Part of intensification strategy: save rural land and favor alternatives to car use.	Part of intensification strategy: save rural land and favor alternatives to car use.
Planning formulation and discourse	Identification of sectors adapted to high-density redevelopment: downtown or close to public transit.	Higher subdivision density thresholds in official plans. Some municipalities are more engaged than others.
Political decision making	Many NIMBY objections due to effects on nearby low-density neighborhoods. Some projects are canceled but most go ahead.	Few NIMBY objections because located on greenfields.
Implementation of political decision	Public sector aspect of intensification based on regulations and infrastructure support. In some cases, public transit upgrading lags, hence congestion and NIMBY reactions.	Based on planning regulations. No problem from a public expenditure perspective.
Capacity to achieve development objectives	High-rise condos most common formula because most profitable for developers.	Achievement of higher density objectives facilitated by increased land values. Limited market for new urbanist developments.
Impact of developments on behavior and urban dynamics	In downtown Toronto residential intensification contributes to reliance on walking. Where there is quality public transit, it contributes to transit use. Elsewhere, little effect on modal shares.	Density is not sufficiently high to raise public transit use or to foster activity distributions favorable to walking.

Public transit

	SHEPPARD SUBWAY LINE	ST. CLAIR WEST LRT	VIVA BUS RAPID TRANSIT
Original impetus	Low priority in the TTC subway expansion strategy. Provincial funding becomes available in the 1990s. Political influence assures the choice of this line.	Part of ambitious citywide LRT system, seen as essential to intensification strategy.	Objective is to raise very low outer-suburban public transit use.
Planning formulation and discourse	TTC prepares subway plans when funding becomes available.	St. Clair West seen as ideally suited as early stage of the LRT network: wide street and presence of streetcars.	Part of land use strategy involving high-density mixed-use nodes. Bus rapid transit possibly to be upgraded to LRT over time.
Political decision making	Influence of mayor of Toronto, former mayor of North York, who was favorable to Sheppard Line because it served North York Centre.	Opposition of local merchants who try to scuttle the LRT due to perceived impediments to car access and parking.	Promoted by the regional government and funded in large part by the province.
Implementation of political decision	The line has been constructed.	The project receives support from the courts and from council, presently under construction.	Early phases in place.
Capacity to achieve development objectives	The subway line is short and does not connect with major activity centers. The line is a catalyst for high-density residential developments.	Will improve reliability of services but have minor effect on journey time. Possible major impact if full LRT network is achieved.	Factor in increasing public transit ridership and may provide support for nodal development.
Impact of developments on behavior and urban dynamics	Relatively little use of the line, but things may change as considerable redevelopment takes place along the line.	Too early to judge.	Ridership is still too low to have a major impact on land use, but things may change in the future.

Protection of the natural environment

	GREENBELT	PRESERVATION OF NATURAL FEATURES IN SUBDIVISIONS
Original impetus	Well-organized environmental activism calls for a protection of the Oak Ridges Moraine. Major trigger of the planning exercise that led to Places to Grow.	Local pressures to preserve natural features. Such a protection makes development acceptable.
Planning formulation and discourse	Province engages in regional planning. Much emphasis given to the protection of the moraine in Places to Grow.	New discourse about development: Associated with a respect of the environment interpreted as a protection of natural features.
Political decision making	Development freeze and land swap with developers.	Most regional and local governments adhere to this approach, but with different levels of commitment.
Implementation of political decision	Legislation is adopted to protect the Greenbelt. Most regional and local governments support the concept.	Part of official plans and of subdivision planning process.
Capacity to achieve development objectives	Maintain current uses so limited direct expenditure.	Local objectives are attained: Environmental features, especially those that are related to water, are protected.
Impact of developments on behavior and urban dynamics	Greenbelt will likely achieve water quality objectives, but doubts about capacity to contain urban development. Development will likely jump the green belt as suggested by present development trends.	This approach contributes to lower density and separate land uses, running counter to land use and walking objectives.

Figure 7. Smart growth–oriented interventions and developments in Toronto, 2001–2007: From formulation to implementation and impacts.

public transit patronage and walking when appropriate conditions are present—mixed use, as best exemplified by downtown Toronto, and proximity to quality public transit services—the effect of other initiatives on urban dynamics are less positive from a smart growth perspective.[52] Without quality public transit and multifunctional environments, even high-rise condominium developments have little effect on modal shares. Meanwhile, intensified subdivisions remain short of density thresholds needed to alter modal shares. The prominence of cars in new subdivisions illustrates the negligible effect higher single-family home densities have on automobile use. Notwithstanding new urbanism neighborhoods, where design devices deemphasize the presence of the car, the tendency is for "snout houses" on narrow lots, devoting most of their façades to garage space. In intensified subdivisions, density remains insufficient to support retail and service distributions that encourage walking.

Overall, possible smart growth benefits from residential intensification are compromised by enduring land use specialization, an obstacle to the reliance on alternatives to the car, and by the fact that most urban space is occupied by nonresidential land uses. Evidence suggests that, rather than intensifying, workplaces and retailing are increasingly opting for low-density automobile-oriented formats (business parks and big-box stores, for example).[53]

In the absence of a profound redistribution of density and functional patterns, a prodigal conservation of natural areas reduces the density of metropolitan regions and further separates land uses, thereby contributing to longer journeys and dependence on the automobile. Finally, likely land use–transportation outcomes of public transit investments offer reason for optimism, provided that new services remain attractive to high-density redevelopments.

Within the City of Toronto, however, decision-making regarding public transit planning has stalled since the 2010 election of Mayor Robert Ford. To prevent any infringement on automobile circulation, Mayor Ford opposes LRT development. For him tunnelled subways are the only acceptable form of rail public transit. Fourteen months into Mayor Ford's term council overturned his transit vision and has returned to the largely LRT-based Transit City proposal.

Conclusion: Smart Growth Lessons from Toronto

Attempts to substitute smart growth–inspired urban development in place of conventional styles require mobilization of agents of change, whether in the public, private, or community sectors, in order to counteract resistance from forces of inertia. Conventional patterns, characterized by automobile orientation, low density, and functional specialization, are the default in terms of urban development. Whenever commitment to change falters, development reverts back to conventional models. The promotion of alternative forms of growth is aided by the perception of a state of crisis. Escalating energy costs have played a role in the past and will likely have a greater impact in the future, as will the environmental consequences of urbanization, especially the emission of greenhouse gases. Clearly, these factors are important in the adoption of smart growth–inspired policies in Toronto, but so is concern about the quality of life and economic consequences of anticipated growth rates if present forms of development persist.

Recent Toronto cases have exposed two types of outcomes associated with interventions consistent with smart growth principles. These interventions have generally been successful in reaching their immediate objectives—density levels, the conservation of natural areas, and, in one case, ridership goals. However, the achievement of behavioral changes mirrored in shorter journeys and higher reliance on nonautomobile modes, and a mutual adaptation between land use and public transit in expending suburbs, all of which are of most significance to smart growth, have proven to be more elusive.

Yet, we may be at a juncture. If the ambitious proposals contained in recent plans are implemented, and if coordination is improved to assure that all scales of planning contribute to smart growth outcomes, the Toronto region could substantially improve its smart growth performance. It could lower per-capita land use, assure the preservation of natural areas, and raise public transit and walking modal shares, thus abating traffic congestion and air pollution.

NOTES

1. R. Ewing, R. Pendall, and D. Chen, *Measuring Sprawl and Its Impact*, 2002, http://www.smartgrowthamerica.org/sprawlindex/sprawlreport.html; O. Gillham, *The Limitless City: A Primer on the Urban Sprawl Debate* (Washington, DC: Island Press, 2002); D. E. Morris, *It's a Sprawl World After All: The Human Cost of Unplanned Growth—And Visions of a Better Future* (Gabriola Island, BC: New Society Publishers, 2005); H. N. Richardson and C-H. Bae, *Urban Sprawl in Western Europe and the United States* (Burlington, VT: Ashgate, 2004); Sierra Club, *Sprawl Costs Us All*, 2000, http://www.sierraclub.org/sprawl/report00/; G. D. Squires, ed., *Urban Sprawl: Causes, Consequences, and Policy Responses* (Washington, DC: Urban Institute Press, 2002).
2. D. Bannister, Energy, Quality of Life and the Environment: The Role of Transport, *Transport Reviews* 16 (1996): 23–35; P. Blais, The Economics of Urban Form (background report for the GTA Task Force), in GTA Task Force Report (Toronto: Queen's Printer, 1996); D. Levinson and Y. Wu, The Rational Locator Re-Examined: Are Travel Times Still Stable? *Transportation* 32 (2005): 187–202.
3. A. Abelsohn, R. Bray, C. Vakil, and D. Elliott, *Report on Public Health and Urban Sprawl in Ontario: A Review of the Pertinent Literature* (Toronto: Environment Health Committee, Ontario College of Family Physicians, 2005), http://www.ocfp.on.ca/local/files/Communications/Current%20Issues/UrbanSprawl.pdf; H. Frumkin, L. Frank, and R. J. Jackson, *Urban Sprawl and Public Health: Designing, Planning, and Building for Healthy Communities* (Washington, DC: Island Press, 2004).
4. C. Leo, M. A. Beavis, H. Carver, and R. Turner, Local Growth Control, Regional Growth Management, and Politics, *Urban Affairs Review* 34 (1998): 179–212; C. Leo and K. Anderson, Being Realistic about Urban Growth, in *Canadian Cities in Transition: Local through Global Perspectives*, ed. T. Bunting and P. Filion (Toronto: Oxford University Press, 2006), 393–407; B. K. Ray and D. Rose, Cities of the Everyday: Socio-Spatial Perspectives on Gender, Difference and Diversity, in *Canadian Cities in Transition: The Twenty-First Century*, ed. T. Bunting and P. Filion (Toronto: Oxford University Press, 2000), 502–24.
5. M. Baldassare, The Suburban Movement to Limit Growth: Reasons for Support in Orange County, *Policy Studies Review* 4 (1985): 613–25; M. Baldassare and G. Wilson, More Trouble in Paradise: Urbanization and the Decline in Suburban Quality-of-Life Ratings, *Urban Affairs Review* 30 (1995): 690–708; M. Baldassare and G. Wilson, Changing Sources of Suburban Support for Local Growth Controls, *Urban Studies* 33 (1996): 459–71; E. Fodor, *Better Not Bigger: How to Take Control of Urban Growth and Improve Your Community* (Gabriola Island, BC: New Society Publishers, 1999); L. Gilbert, G. R. Wekerle, and L. A. Sandberg, Local Responses to Development Pressures: Conflictual Politics of Sprawl and Environmental Conservation, *Cahiers de Géographie du Québec* 49:138 (2005): 377–92; B. M. Green and Y. Schreuder, Growth, Zoning, and Neighborhood Organizations: Land Use Conflict in Wilmington, Delaware, *Journal of Urban Affairs* 13 (1991): 97–110; A. Power, Social Exclusion and Urban Sprawl: Is the Rescue of Cities Possible? *Regional Studies* 35 (2001): 731–42.
6. S. E. Owens, *Energy, Planning and Urban Form* (London: Pion, 1986); M. Roseland, *Toward Sustainable Communities: A Resource Book for*

Municipal and Local Governments (Ottawa: National Round Table on the Environment and the Economy, 1992); World Commission on Environment and Development, *Our Common Future* (Oxford: Oxford University Press, 1987).

7. W. Bonefield and J. Holloway, ed., *Post-Fordism and Social Form: A Marxist Debate on the Post-Fordist State* (Basingstoke: Macmillan, 1991).
8. I. Vojnovic, Shaping Metropolitan Toronto: A Study of Linear Infrastructure Subsidies, 1954–1966, *Environment and Planning B* 27 (2000): 197–230.
9. C. Holleyman, Industry Studies of the Relationship between Highway Infrastructure Investment and Productivity, *Logistics and Transportation Review* 32 (1996): 93–117.
10. M. Goodwin and J. Painter, Local Governance, the Crisis of Fordism and the Changing Geographies of Regulation, *Transactions of the Institute of British Geographers NS* 21 (1996): 635–48; J. Hirsch, From the Fordist to the Post-Fordist State, in *The Politics of Flexibility: Restructuring State and Industry in Britain, Germany and Scandinavia*, ed. B. Jessop, H. Katendiek, K. Nielsen, and O. K. Pedersen (Aldershot: Edward Elgar, 1991), 67–81; A. Lipietz, *Mirages and Miracles: The Crises of Global Fordism* (London: Verso, 1987); A. Tickell and J. Peck, Social Regulation after Fordism: Regulation Theory, Neo-Liberalism and the Global-Local Nexus, *Economy and Society* 24 (1995): 357–86.
11. D. A. Badoe and E. J. Miller, Transportation-Land Use Interaction: Empirical Findings in North America, and Their Implications for Modeling, *Transportation Research Part D* 5 (2000): 235–63; M. G. Boarnet and R. Crane, *The Influence of Urban Form on Travel* (Oxford: Oxford University Press, 2001); R. Cervero, Built Environment and Mode Choice: Toward a Normative Framework, *Transportation Research Part D* 7 (2002): 265–84; R. Crane, The Influence of Urban Form on Travel: An Interpretive View, *Journal of Planning Literature* 15 (2000): 3–23; E. Ewing and R. Cervero, Travel and the Built Environment: A Synthesis, *Transportation Research Record* 1780 (2001): 87–114.
12. See, for example, P. Bourdieu, *Outline of a Theory of Practice* (Cambridge: Cambridge University Press, 1977).
13. K. R. Cox, J. J. McCarthy, and F. Nartowicz, The Cognitive Organization of the North American City: Empirical Evidence, *Environment and Planning A* 11 (1979): 327–34.
14. P. Filion, T. Bunting, and K. Warriner, The Entrenchment of Urban Dispersion: Residential Location Patterns and Preferences in the Dispersed City, *Urban Studies* 36 (1999): 1317–47.
15. For statements from the Greater Toronto Home Builders' Association, see D. Auciello, *Land Supply: Cost Concerns Builders* (Toronto: Greater Toronto Home Builders' Association, 2006), http://www.newhomes.org/articles_sun.asp?id=416&SearchType=ExactPhrase&terms=places%20to20grow; M. Parson, *Affordable Housing Depends on Land Supply* (Toronto: Greater Toronto Home Builders' Association, 2004), http://www.newhomes.org/NewHomes/uploadedFiles/Articles/2004/July_31_04.pdf.
16. J. R. Logan and H. L. Molotch, *Urban Fortunes: The Political Economy of Place* (Berkeley: University of California Press, 1987).
17. T. T. Curic and T. E. Bunting, Does Compatibility Mean Same As? Lessons Learned from the Residential Intensification of Surplus Hydro Lands in Four Older Neighbourhoods in the City of Toronto, *Canadian Journal of Urban Research* 15 (2006): 202–24; A. Garde, Designing and Developing New Urbanist Projects in the United States: Insights and Implication, *Journal of Urban Design* 11 (2006): 33–54; R. Pendall, Opposition to Housing: NIMBY and Beyond, *Urban Affairs Review* 35 (1999): 112–36.
18. P. Gordon and H. W. Richardson, Beyond Polycentricity: The Dispersed Metropolis, Los Angeles, 1970–1990, *Journal of the American Planning Association* 62 (1996): 289–95.
19. Herein lies a major rationale for libertarian perspectives objecting to growth control; see R. O'Toole, *The Vanishing Automobile and Other Myths: How Smart Growth Will Harm American Cities* (Bandon, OR: Thoreau Institute, 2001).
20. K. E. McHugh, Oh, the Places They'll Go! Mobility, Place and Landscape in the Film *This Is Nowhere*, *Journal of Cultural Geography* 23 (2005): 71–90.
21. B. Donald, Spinning Toronto's Golden Age: The Making of the City That Worked, *Environment and Planning A* 34 (2002): 2127–54; A. Rose, *Governing Metropolitan Toronto: A Social and Political Analysis, 1953–1971* (Berkeley: University of California Press, 1972).
22. Filion, Balancing Concentration and Dispersion?, 163–89; J. Pill, Toronto: Thirty Years of Transit Development, in *Transit Land Use and Urban Form*, ed. W. Attoe (Austin: Center for the Study of American Architecture, 1998), 57–62.
23. P. Filion, T. Bunting, K. McSpurren, and A. Tse, Canada-U.S. Metropolitan Density Patterns: Zonal Convergence and Divergence, *Urban Geography* 25 (2004): 42–65.
24. R. Keil, Toronto in the 1990s: Dissociated

Governance, *Studies in Political Economy* 56 (1998): 151–68.
25. R. Keil, "Common-Sense Neoliberalism": Progressive Conservative Urbanism in Toronto, Canada, *Antipode* 34 (2002): 578–601; G. Williams, Institutional Capacity and Metropolitan Governance, *Cities* 16 (1999): 171–80.
26. Joint Program in Transportation (Data Management Group), *1986–1996 Travel Trends in the GTA and Hamilton-Wentworth* (Toronto: Joint Program in Transportation, 1998), http://www.jpint.utoronto.ca/PDF/trend.pdf; E. J. Miller and A. Shalaby, *Travel in the GTA: Past and Current Behavioural Relation to Urban Form* (Toronto: Neptis Foundation and University of Toronto Joint Program in Transportation, 2000).
27. The Toronto Board of Trade, *A Strategy for Rail-Based Transit* (Toronto: Toronto Board of Trade, 2001), http://www.bot.com/assets/staticassets/documents/pdf/policy/botrailwayreport.pdf.
28. A. Perl and J. Pucher, Transit in Trouble? The Policy Challenge Posed by Canada's Changing Urban Mobility, *Canadian Public Policy* 21 (1995): 261–83.
29. Government of Ontario, *Design for Development: The Toronto-Centred Region* (Toronto: Queen's Printer and Publisher, 1970).
30. Metro Toronto, *Official Plan for the Urban Structure* (Toronto: Metro Toronto, 1981).
31. Office for the Greater Toronto Area, *Growing Together: Towards an Urban Consensus in the Greater Toronto Area* (Toronto: OGTA, 1991); Office for the Greater Toronto Area, *The Challenge of Our Future—A Working Document* (Toronto: OGTA, 1992).
32. City of Toronto, *Toronto Official Plan* (Toronto: City of Toronto, 2002) (approved, in part, with modifications by the Ontario Municipal Board, June 2006), http://www.toronto.ca/planning/official_plan/pdf.
33. Government of Ontario, Ministry of Public Infrastructure Renewal, *Growth Plan for the Greater Golden Horseshoe* (Toronto: Queen's Printer for Ontario, 2006), http://www.pir.gov.on.ca/English/growth/gghdols/FPLAN-ENG-WEB-ALL.pdf.
34. The content of three Toronto dailies (the *Toronto Star*, the *Globe and Mail*, and the *Toronto Sun*) was scanned using the following key words: "smart growth," "intensification," and "new urbanism." Overall, 871 articles were identified. Only issues that were the object of clusters of articles are considered in this chapter. Still, nearly all the identified articles related to issues presented in this section.
35. P. Filion, *The Urban Growth Centres Strategy in the Greater Golden Horseshoe: Lessons from Downtowns, Nodes, and Corridors* (Toronto: Neptis Foundation / Neptis Studies on the Toronto Metropolitan Region, 2007).
36. Regent Park Collaborative Team, *Regent Park Revitalization Study* (Toronto: Toronto Community Housing Corporation, 2002); Regent Park Collaborative Team, *Regent Park Revitalization Study: Summary Report on Action Plan and Implementation Strategy* (Toronto: Toronto Community Housing Corp., 2003).
37. Canada Mortgage and Housing Corporation, *Housing the Boom, Bust and Echo Generations*, Socioeconomic series 77 (Ottawa: CMHC, 2002); D. K. Foot and D. Stoffman, *Boom, Bust and Echo 2000: Profiting from the Demographic Shift in the New Millennium* (Toronto: Macfarlane Walter and Ross, 1998).
38. See, for example, K. Gillespie, Uproar Over Twin Tower OK—Condo Project to Go Ahead Despite Opposition, *Toronto Star*, September 20, 2002, A01; M. Parson, A Place Where Hume and GTA Builders Agree, *Toronto Star*, May 8, 2004, K04.
39. D. Gordon and S. Vipond, Gross Density and New Urbanism: Comparing Conventional and New Urbanist Suburbs in Markham, Ontario, *Journal of the American Planning Association* 71 (2005): 41–55.
40. A. Dobrota, The Mayor's Knife: The Sheppard Line, Subway Project Nearly Derailed Before, *Globe and Mail*, July 21, 2007, A12.
41. J. Lewington and J. Gray, The Mayor's Knife: TTC Asked to Slash $30 Million to Help Make Up for Defeated Tax Proposals, *Globe and Mail*, July 20, 2007, A1.
42. D. Raymaker, New Digs: Condo Corridor, *Globe and Mail*, July 27, 2007, G7.
43. Toronto Transit Commission, *Toronto Transit City—Light Rail Plan*, 2007, http://www.toronto.ca/ttc/pdf/toronto_transit_city_light_rail_plan.pdf; Toronto Transit Commission, *Transit City Light Rail Plan—Implementation Work Plan Update*, 2007, http://www.ttc.ca/postings/gso-comprt/.
44. J. Wilkes, Planners Try for Live-Work Balance, *Toronto Star*, September 11, 2006, B01.
45. York Region, *Viva Rapid Transit*, 2005, http://www.york.ca/publications/news/2005/september+6%2c+2005+viva+fact+sheet.htm.
46. Metro Toronto, *Future Transportation Needs in the GTA: A Joint Report* (Toronto: Metro Toronto, 1987); Toronto Transit Commission, *Network 2011: A Rapid Transit Plan for Metropolitan Toronto* (Toronto: TTC, 1985).
47. T. Kalinowski and J. Byers, Closing Sheppard Subway

Line, Cutting Bus Routes and Trimming Police Budget Are All on the Table; Miller's Axe Looms over TTC, *Toronto Star,* July 20, 2007, A01.

48. T. Kalinowski, TTC Hikes Metropass Fare $9.25; Transit Commissioners Okay "Bitter" Increase in Attempt to Stave Off Deep Cuts to Service, *Toronto Star,* September 13, 2007, A01.
49. J. Hall, Fast Buses Seen as Key to GTA's Transit Future—Report Suggests Network of Reserved Lanes, *Toronto Star,* April 6, 2001, F05; J. Hall, Bus-Only Roadways Called Transit Solution—System Linking All of GTA Could Be Ready within a Decade, *Toronto Star,* June 15, 2002, B03.
50. Government of Ontario, Greenbelt Act (Bill 135) Royal Assent, February 24, 2005.
51. Gilbert, Wekerle, and Sandberg, Local Responses to Development Pressures, 377–92.
52. Filion, *The Urban Growth Centres*; D. M. Nowlan and G. Steuart, Downtown Population Growth and Commuting Trips: Recent Experience in Toronto, *Journal of the American Planning Association* 57 (1991): 165–82.
53. T. Hernandez, T. Erguden, and P. Bermingham, *Power Retail Growth in Canada and the GTA* (Toronto: Ryerson University, Centre for the Study of Commercial Activity, 2006); R. E. Lang, *Edgeless Cities: Exploring the Elusive Metropolis* (Washington, DC: Brookings Institution Press, 2003).

REFERENCES

Abelsohn, A., R. Bray, C. Vakil. and D. Elliott. Report on Public Health and Urban Sprawl in Ontario: A Review of the Pertinent Literature. Toronto: Environment Health Committee, Ontario College of Family Physicians, 2005. http://www.ocfp.on.ca/local/files/Communications/Current%20Issues/UrbanSprawl.pdf.

Auciello, D. *Land Supply: Cost Concerns Builders.* Toronto: Greater Toronto Home Builders' Association, 2006. http://www.newhomes.org/articles_sun.asp?id=416&SearchType=ExactPhrase&terms=places%20to20grow.

Badoe, D. A., and E. J. Miller. Transportation-Land Use Interaction: Empirical Findings in North America, and Their Implications for Modeling. *Transportation Research Part D* 5 (2000): 35–263.

Baldassare, M. The Suburban Movement to Limit Growth: Reasons for Support in Orange County. *Policy Studies Review* 4 (1985): 613–25.

Baldassare, M., and G. Wilson. Changing Sources of Suburban Support for Local Growth Controls. *Urban Studies* 33 (1996): 459–71.

———. More Trouble in Paradise: Urbanization and the Decline in Suburban Quality-of-Life Ratings. *Urban Affairs Review* 30 (1995): 690–708.

Bannister, D., Energy, Quality of Life and the Environment: The Role of Transport. *Transport Reviews* 16 (1996): 23–35.

Blais, P., The Economics of Urban Form (Background Report for the GTA Task Force), in GTA Task Force Report. Toronto: Queen's Printer, 1996.

Boarnet, M. G., and R. Crane. *The Influence of Urban Form on Travel.* Oxford: Oxford University Press, 2001.

Bonefield, W., and J. Holloway, eds. *Post-Fordism and Social Form: A Marxist Debate on the Post-Fordist State.* Basingstoke: Macmillan, 1991.

Bourdieu, P. *Outline of a Theory of Practice.* Cambridge: Cambridge University Press, 1977.

Canada Mortgage and Housing Corporation. *Housing the Boom, Bust and Echo Generations.* Socioeconomic series, 77. Ottawa: CMHC, 2002.

Cervero, R. Built Environment and Mode Choice: Toward a Normative Framework. *Transportation Research Part D* 7 (2002): 265–84.

Cox, K. R., J. J. McCarthy, and F. Nartowicz. The Cognitive Organization of the North American City: Empirical Evidence. *Environment and Planning A* 11 (1979): 327–34.

Crane, R. The Influence of Urban Form on Travel: An Interpretive View. *Journal of Planning Literature* 15 (2000): 3–23.

Curic, T. T., and T. E. Bunting. Does Compatibility Mean Same As? Lessons Learned from the Residential Intensification of Surplus Hydro Lands in Four Older Neighbourhoods in the City of Toronto. *Canadian Journal of Urban Research* 15 (2006): 202–24.

Dobrota, A. The Mayor's Knife: The Sheppard Line, Subway Project Nearly Derailed Before. *Globe and Mail,* July 21, 2007. A12.

Donald, B. Spinning Toronto's Golden Age: The Making of the City That Worked. *Environment and Planning A* 34 (2002): 2127–54.

Ewing, E., and R. Cervero. Travel and the Built Environment: A Synthesis. *Transportation Research Record* 1780 (2001): 87–114.

Ewing, R., R. Pendall, and D. Chen. Measuring Sprawl and Its Impact. 2002. http://www.smartgrowthamerica.org/sprawlindex/sprawlreport.html.

Filion, P. Balancing Concentration and Dispersion? Public Policy and Urban Structure in Toronto. *Environment and Planning C* 18 (2000): 163–89.

———. *The Urban Growth Centres Strategy in the Greater Golden Horseshoe: Lessons from Downtowns, Nodes, and Corridors.* Toronto: Neptis Foundation (Neptis Studies on the Toronto Metropolitan Region, 2007.

Filion, P., T. Bunting, K. McSpurren, and A. Tse. Canada-U.S. Metropolitan Density Patterns: Zonal Convergence and Divergence. *Urban Geography* 25 (2004): 42–65.

Filion, P., T. Bunting, and K. Warriner. The Entrenchment of Urban Dispersion: Residential Location Patterns and Preferences in the Dispersed City. *Urban Studies* 36 (1999): 1317–47.

Fodor, E. *Better Not bigger: How to Take Control of Urban Growth and Improve Your Community.* Gabriola Island, BC: New Society Publishers, 1999.

Foot, D. K., and D. Stoffman. *Boom, Bust and Echo 2000: Profiting from the Demographic Shift in the New Millennium.* Toronto: Macfarlane Walter & Ross, 1998.

Frumkin, H., L. Frank, and R. J. Jackson. *Urban Sprawl and Public Health: Designing, Planning, and Building for Healthy Communities.* Washington, DC: Island Press, 2004.

Garde, A. Designing and Developing New Urbanist Projects in the United States: Insights and Implication. *Journal of Urban Design* 11 (2006): 33–54.

Gilbert, L., G. R. Wekerle, and L. A. Sandberg. Local Responses to Development Pressures: Conflictual Politics of Sprawl and Environmental Conservation. *Cahiers de Géographie du Québec* 49:138 (2005): 377–92.

Gillespie, K. Uproar Over Twin Tower OK—Condo Project to Go Ahead Despite Opposition. *Toronto Star,* September 20, 2002, A01.

Gillham, O. *The Limitless City: A Primer on the Urban Sprawl Debate.* Washington, DC: Island Press, 2002.

Goodwin, M., and J. Painter. Local Governance, the Crisis of Fordism and the Changing Geographies of Regulation. *Transactions of the Institute of British Geographers* 21 (1996): 635–48.

Gordon, D., and S. Vipond. Gross Density and New Urbanism: Comparing Conventional and New Urbanist Suburbs in Markham, Ontario. *Journal of the American Planning Association* 71 (2005): 41–55.

Gordon, P., and H. W. Richardson. Beyond Polycentricity: The Dispersed Metropolis, Los Angeles, 1970–1990. *Journal of the American Planning Association* 62 (1996): 289–95.

Green, B. M., and Y. Schreuder. Growth, Zoning, and Neighborhood Organizations: Land Use Conflict in Wilmington, Delaware. *Journal of Urban Affairs* 13 (1991): 97–110.

Hall, J. Bus-Only Roadways Called Transit Solution—System Linking All of GTA Could Be Ready within a Decade. *Toronto Star,* June 15, 2002, B03.

———. Fast Buses Seen as Key to GTA's Transit Future—Report Suggests Network of Reserved Lanes. *Toronto Star,* April 6, 2001, F05.

Hernandez, T., T. Erguden, and P. Bermingham. *Power Retail Growth in Canada and the GTA.* Toronto: Ryerson University, Centre for the Study of Commercial Activity, 2006.

Hirsch, J. From the Fordist to the Post-Fordist State. In *The Politics of Flexibility: Restructuring State and Industry in Britain, Germany and Scandinavia,* ed. B. Jessop, H. Katendiek, K. Nielsen, and O. K. Pedersen, 67–81. Aldershot: Edward Elgar, 1991.

Holleyman, C. Industry Studies of the Relationship between Highway Infrastructure Investment and Productivity. *Logistics and Transportation Review* 32 (1996): 93–117.

Joint Program in Transportation (Data Management Group). 1986–1996 Travel Trends in the GTA and Hamilton-Wentworth. Toronto: Joint Program in Transportation. 1998. http://www.jpint.utoronto.ca/PDF/trend.pdf.

Kalinowski, T. TTC Hikes Metropass Fare $9.25; Transit Commissioners Okay "Bitter" Increase in Attempt to Stave Off Deep Cuts to Service. *Toronto Star,* September 13, 2007, A01.

Kalinowski, T., and J. Byers. Closing Sheppard Subway Line, Cutting Bus Routes and Trimming Police Budget Are All on the Table; Miller's Axe Looms over TTC, *Toronto Star,* July 20, 2007, A01.

Keil, R. "Common-Sense Neoliberalism": Progressive Conservative Urbanism in Toronto, Canada. *Antipode* 34 (2002): 578–601.

———. Toronto in the 1990s: Dissociated Governance. *Studies in Political Economy* 56 (1998): 151–68.

Lang, R. E. *Edgeless Cities: Exploring the Elusive Metropolis.* Washington, DC: Brookings Institution Press, 2003.

Leo, C., and K. Anderson. Being Realistic about Urban Growth. In *Canadian Cities in Transition: Local through Global Perspectives,* ed. T. Bunting and P. Filion, 393–407. Toronto: Oxford University Press, 2006.

Leo, C., M. A. Beavis, H. Carver, and R. Turner. Local Growth Control, Regional Growth Management, and Politics. *Urban Affairs Review* 34 (1998): 179–212.

Levinson, D., and Y. Wu. The Rational Locator Re-Examined: Are Travel Times Still Stable? *Transportation* 32 (2005): 187–202.

Lewington, J., and J. Gray. The Mayor's Knife: TTC Asked to Slash $30 Million to Help Make Up for Defeated Tax

Proposals. *Globe and Mail*, July 20, 2007, A1.

Lipietz, A. *Mirages and Miracles: The Crises of Global Fordism*. London: Verso, 1987.

Logan, J. R., and H. L. Molotch. *Urban Fortunes: The Political Economy of Place*. Berkeley: University of California Press, 1987.

McHugh, K. E. Oh, the Places They'll Go! Mobility, Place and Landscape in the Film *This Is Nowhere*. *Journal of Cultural Geography* 23 (2005): 71–90.

Metro Toronto. *Future Transportation Needs in the GTA: A Joint Report*. Toronto: Metro Toronto, 1987.

———. *Official Plan for the Urban Structure*. Toronto: Metro Toronto, 1981.

Miller, E. J., and A. Shalaby. *Travel in the GTA: Past and Current Behavioural Relation to Urban Form*. Toronto: Neptis Foundation and University of Toronto Joint Program in Transportation, 2000.

Morris, D. E. *It's a Sprawl World After All: The Human Cost of Unplanned Growth—And Visions of a Better Future*. Gabriola Island, BC: New Society Publishers, 2005.

Nowlan, D. M., and G. Steuart. Downtown Population Growth and Commuting Trips: Recent Experience in Toronto. *Journal of the American Planning Association* 57 (1991): 165–82.

Office for the Greater Toronto Area. *The Challenge of Our Future—A Working Document*. Toronto: OGTA, 1992.

———. *Growing Together: Towards an Urban Consensus in the Greater Toronto Area*. Toronto: OGTA, 1991.

Ontario (Government of). *Design for Development: The Toronto-Centred Region*. Toronto: Queen's Printer and Publisher, 1970.

———. Greenbelt Act (Bill 135) Royal Assent, February 24, 2005.

Ontario (Government of), Ministry of Public Infrastructure Renewal. *Growth Plan for the Greater Golden Horseshoe*. Toronto: Queen's Printer for Ontario, 2006. http://www.pir.gov.on.ca/English/growth/gghdols/FPLAN-ENG-WEB-ALL.pdf.

O'Toole, R. *The Vanishing Automobile and Other Myths: How Smart Growth Will Harm American Cities*. Bandon, OR: Thoreau Institute, 2001.

Owens, S. E. *Energy, Planning and Urban Form*. London: Pion, 1986.

Parson, M. *Affordable Housing Depends on Land Supply*. Toronto: Greater Toronto Home Builders' Association, 2004. http://www.newhomes.org/NewHomes/uploadedFiles/Articles/2004/July_31_04.pdf.

———. A Place Where Hume and GTA Builders Agree. *Toronto Star*, May 8, 2004, K04.

Pendall, R. Opposition to Housing: NIMBY and Beyond. *Urban Affairs Review* 35 (1999): 112–36.

Perl, A., and J. Pucher. Transit in Trouble? The Policy Challenge Posed by Canada's Changing Urban Mobility. *Canadian Public Policy* 21 (1995): 261–83.

Pill, J. Toronto: Thirty Years of Transit Development. In *Transit Land Use and Urban Form*, ed. W. Attoe, 57–62. Austin: Center for the Study of American Architecture, 1998.

Power, A. Social Exclusion and Urban Sprawl: Is the Rescue of Cities Possible? *Regional Studies* 35 (2001): 731–42.

Ray, B. K., and D. Rose. Cities of the Everyday: Socio-Spatial Perspectives on Gender, Difference and Diversity. In *Canadian Cities in Transition: The Twenty-First Century*, ed. T. Bunting and P. Filion, 502–24. Toronto: Oxford University Press, 2000.

Raymaker, D. New Digs: Condo Corridor. *Globe and Mail*, July 27, 2007, G7.

Regent Park Collaborative Team. *Regent Park Revitalization Study*. Toronto: Toronto Community Housing Corporation, 2002.

———. *Regent Park Revitalization Study: Summary Report on Action Plan and Implementation Strategy*. Toronto: Toronto Community Housing Corporation, 2003.

Richardson, H. N., and C-H. Bae. *Urban Sprawl in Western Europe and the United States*. Burlington, VT: Ashgate, 2004.

Rose, A. *Governing Metropolitan Toronto: A Social and Political Analysis, 1953–1971*. Berkeley: University of California Press, 1972.

Roseland, M. *Toward Sustainable Communities: A Resource Book for Municipal and Local Governments*. Ottawa: National Round Table on the Environment and the Economy, 1992.

Sierra Club. *Sprawl Costs Us All*. 2000. http://www.sierraclub.org/sprawl/report00/.

Squires, G. D. ed. *Urban Sprawl: Causes, Consequences, and Policy Responses*. Washington, DC: Urban Institute Press, 2002.

Tickell, A., and J. Peck. Social Regulation after Fordism: Regulation Theory, Neo-Liberalism and the Global-Local Nexus. *Economy and Society* 24 (1995): 357–86.

Toronto Board of Trade. *A Strategy for Rail-Based Transit*. Toronto: Toronto Board of Trade, 2001. http://www.bot.com/assets/staticassets/documents/pdf/policy/botrailwayreport.pdf.

Toronto (City of). Toronto Official Plan. Toronto: City of Toronto (approved, in part, with modifications by the Ontario Municipal Board, June 2006). 2002. http://www.toronto.ca/planning/official_plan/pdf.

Toronto Transit Commission. Network 2011: A Rapid Transit Plan for Metropolitan Toronto. Toronto: TTC, 1985.

———. Toronto Transit City—Light Rail Plan. 2007. http://www.toronto.ca/ttc/pdf/

toronto_transit_city_light_rail_plan.pdf.
———. Transit City Light Rail Plan—Implementation Work Plan Update. 2007. Online at http://www.ttc.ca/postings/gso-comprt/.
Vojnovic, I. Shaping Metropolitan Toronto: A Study of Linear Infrastructure Subsidies, 1954–1966. *Environment and Planning B* 27 (2000): 197–230.
Wilkes, J. Planners Try for Live-Work Balance. *Toronto Star*, September 11, 2006, B01.
Williams, G. Institutional Capacity and Metropolitan Governance. *Cities* 16 (1999): 171–80.
World Commission on Environment and Development. *Our Common Future*. Oxford: Oxford University Press, 1987.
York Region. Viva Rapid Transit. 2005. http://www.york.ca/publications/news/2005/september+6%2c+2005+viva+fact+sheet.htm

■ RAPHAËL FISCHLER / JEANNE M. WOLFE

Planning for Sustainable Development in Montreal

A QUALIFIED SUCCESS

Sustainable development has become the leading paradigm for urban planning and management in Canada at least since the publication and adoption by the United Nations of the Brundtland report in 1987.[1] This chapter looks at the ways in which the city-region of Montreal has integrated the concept of sustainability in its policies and practices. As with most metropolitan areas, Montreal is subdivided into a large number of local and regional jurisdictions, each with its own fields of interest and agenda, but rarely united on precise political, economic, or social objectives, much less on the way to achieve them. All actors, however, find it the politically correct thing, if not the politically necessary thing, to affirm their allegiance to the doctrine of sustainable development.

Montreal is the primate city of the province of Quebec and the second largest city-region of Canada, a country with a federal system of government. Both senior levels of government, the federal and the provincial, have articulated policies on sustainability. Quebec even has a Ministry of Sustainable Development, Environment and Parks. Like other Canadians, Quebecers see climate change as the most pressing public-policy issue in the coming decade, and environmental matters are the objects of much expert attention in Montreal.[2]

The city is host to several organizations that have leading roles in international environmental policymaking. For instance, the Montreal Protocol on Substances that deplete the Ozone Layer was adopted on September 16, 1987, at the headquarters of the International Civil Aviation Organization. The first binding international agreement on environmental responsibility, the protocol laid the groundwork for the Kyoto Protocol, which was adopted ten years later. Montreal is also the home of the Commission for Environmental Cooperation, an outcome of the North American Free Trade Agreement (NAFTA) between the United States, Mexico, and Canada, and established under the North American Agreement on Environmental Cooperation (NAAEC). Since 1996 the city has also housed the secretariat of the UN Convention on Biodiversity, an initiative started at the Earth Summit on Sustainable Development in Rio de Janeiro in 1992. The city also hosted the UN Convention on Climatic Change Council of the Parties (COP 11) in 2005. This event included a large meeting of big city mayors, chaired by the mayor of Montreal, devoted to ways and means of combating climate change at the municipal level. Most recently, the Montreal Stock Exchange has started carbon credit trading at the Montreal Climate Exchange (MCex) in conjunction with the Chicago Exchange. At the same time, Montreal's four major universities have between them several internationally known research centers in earth and atmospheric sciences, urban studies, and environment, including Ouranos. Also present is the Montreal Centre of Excellence in Brownfields Rehabilitation, a nonprofit corporation that brings together scientists from governments, institutions, and industry involved in the rehabilitation of contaminated sites.

With so many international or national organizations in town, not to mention the numerous local nongovernmental organizations (NGOs) promoting environmental prudence and sustainable development, one would expect that sustainability issues should be well known, just from local media reporting, both by decision makers and the local population. However, despite all ongoing activities and intermittent surges of enthusiasm by the business community, progress in applying sustainable development principles in the region has been slow.

This chapter begins with a brief outline of the role of the senior levels of government in matters of sustainable development and their relationship to local government. It then moves on to examine the planning structures, strategies, and activities in metropolitan Montreal and at the City of Montreal proper, the focus of this chapter. The city has both an urban development plan and a plan for sustainable development. It has adopted many innovative approaches toward the goal of sustainability, including decentralization; widespread and ongoing consultation with many stakeholders from the business community, the social sector, and civil society; and the forging of partnerships and "*ententes*" (understandings) with many diverse actors on the urban scene. Although it is premature to evaluate the results of all this action in any detail, the chapter ends by taking stock of what has been done so far and speculating on the future. The conclusion is that Montreal's success lies in its ability to put sustainable development on the agenda and to translate this interest into an impressive set of policy and planning documents. This success is qualified, however, by the lack of effective change in decision making and implementation due to political-economic limitations. With its high average densities, well-functioning neighborhoods, enviable public-transit services, and community facilities, Montreal can, for a large part of its territory, serve as a model of sustainable development for North America. But unsustainable fiscal constraints limit the ability of the city (like other Quebec and Canadian municipalities in general) to live up to its promises.

The Governmental Context

It is not the purpose of this chapter to explore the complexities of intergovernmental relationships in a federal state, but when examining such a multifaceted subject as sustainability, some discussion is inevitable. The federal government, based in Ottawa, is responsible for foreign affairs, defense, fiscal and monetary policy, national transportation and communications, the northern territories, native populations, immigration, and other matters of national importance. Ottawa

PHOTOGRAPH BY MICHAEL AFAR

Figure 1. View from the summit of Mount Royal: the western part of downtown, with the St. Lawrence River and the Victoria Bridge in the background.

represents Canadians at global forums and signs international agreements in their name. It is in this context, for instance, that Canada signed the Kyoto Protocol. But having done so, the federal government had to persuade each of the ten provincial governments to agree to support it too—not an easy task in the case of Alberta, home of the oil-rich tar sands.

Provincial governments are in charge of natural-resource management, all aspects of local government, education, health care, social services, land-use planning, and transportation.[3] On the environmental front, joint measures with the federal government are necessary: migratory birds, weather systems, and watercourses know no provincial boundaries. For example, Ottawa and Quebec have been working together on the St. Lawrence Plan since 1988, in a joint effort (together with partners in the business and social sectors) to clean up the St. Lawrence River and restore its ecological habitats.[4] There are intergovernmental councils of environmental and natural-resource ministries that coordinate work in these areas in a spirit of cooperative federalism.

Local governments are completely under the control of the provinces, which can create and abolish municipalities and establish the exact extent of their powers and responsibilities. The provinces also set policy for local and regional governments to follow in matters of development. Municipalities are largely financed by own-source means, by far the most important being local property taxes, although some grants are made available for special projects or new programs, often on a cost-shared basis. Their major responsibilities are urban management, land-use

PHOTOGRAPH BY MICHAEL AFAR

Figure 2. Rue St. Paul in Old Montreal: nineteenth-century commercial buildings serving the postindustrial creative and leisure economy.

planning, infrastructure, parks and playgrounds, economic development, public security, social housing, and cultural facilities.

It is worth noting, in the context of sustainable development, that the federal government has little direct contact with local governments: federal programs related to municipalities must usually be channeled through the provincial ministry responsible, usually a Department of Municipal Affairs, or by other means. The Federation of Canadian Municipalities, a powerful national support, research, and advocacy group with almost 2,000 members, runs two programs, the Green Municipal Fund and Partners for Climate Protection, which are funded by Ottawa, thus forming an indirect bridge between the federal and local levels of government.[5]

The Province of Quebec

Though a province rather than a state, Quebec has been party to the Earth Summits since the Rio de Janeiro meeting in 1992. It has been signatory to many of the agreements relating to environmental action, and this has influenced policy, as is shown in table 1. The first action of note was a plan of the Ministry for Sustainable Development for protected areas, probably the easiest measure to adopt, since most of those areas designated so far are in remote, scarcely populated parts of the province. More demanding is the comprehensive sustainable development policy of the ministry, which contains principles that must be taken up by local governments. Additional policies were brought forward in the Strategy and Action Plan for Biodiversity and in the Climate Change Action Plan. These plans are not merely policy statements; they detail strategies and contain timetables of precise actions to be undertaken by the various agencies and organizations of government. They must also be followed up by progress reports. Their implementation is often dependent on making formal agreements—"government by contract"—with other players. The striking of such *ententes* is becoming more and more common in the activities of the Quebec Ministry for Sustainable Development and is reflected in those of the city of Montreal.[6]

The relationship between land use planning and sustainable development has been well documented, even though there is much ongoing debate on cause and effect. The provincial legislation guiding municipal planning, the Act Respecting Land Use Planning and Development, was amended in the early 1990s to include economic and social development planning alongside the usual land-use planning. The law has also been amended to include Agenda 21 principles, and

Table 1. Milestones in Quebec's pathway toward sustainable development

YEAR	ACTIONS/COMMISSIONS	ROLES/OUTCOMES/DOCUMENTS
1988	Table ronde québécoise sur l'environnement et l'économie	Forum for debate: government, business, social sector
1991	Interministerial committee on sustainable development	Coordination of sustainable development activities within government
1992	Participation in the Earth Summit, Rio	Adoption of *Agenda 21* principles
1992	State of the environment reporting	*État de l'environnement au Québec 1992* (pub. 1993)
1996	Participation in Agenda 21 reporting, Earth Summit	*Mise en oeuvre d'Action 21: exemple . . . du Québec*
1996	EcoSummit	*Le Québec et le développement durable*
1997	Agence de l'efficacité énergétique	Revised energy policy
1997	Nikan convention	Recognition of the roles played by native peoples
2000	Fonds d'action québécois pour le développement durable (FAQDD)	Supports for initiatives by NGOs, municipalities, etc. on 50-50 basis
2000	Policy on protected areas	*Stratégie québécoise sur les aires protégées: Plan d'action stratégique*
2002	Participation in Earth Summit, Johannesburg	Pledge to draw up sustainable development strategies by 2005
2004	Action plan on biodiversity	*Plan d'action québécois sur la diversité biologique 2004–2007*
2005	Public consultation on Quebec's Sustainable Development Plan	*Quebec Sustainable Development Plan, Consultation Document*
2006	Sustainable Development Act	*Sustainable Development Act*
2006	Climate Change Action Plan, 2006-2012	*Le Québec et les changements climatiques: Un défi pour l'avenir*
2007	Climate change progress report	*Bilan de la première année*

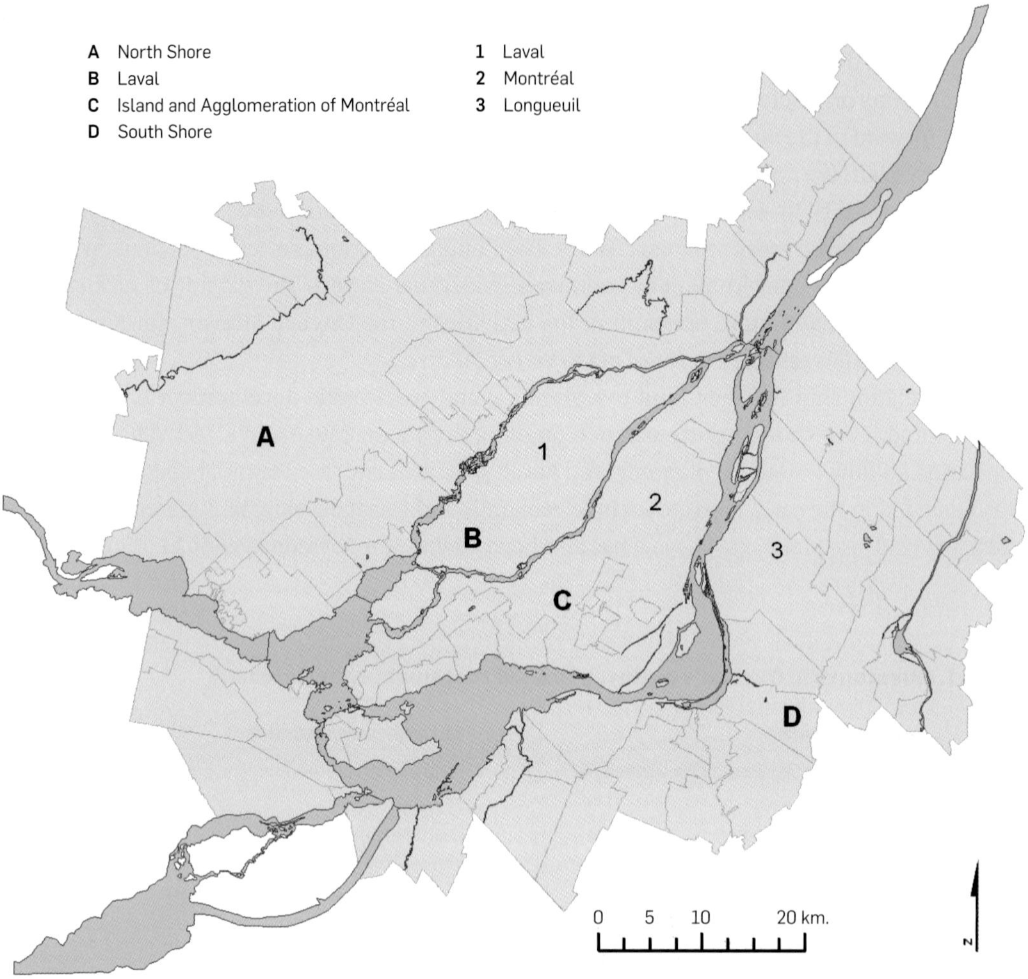

Figure 3. Map of the CMM, a metropolitan area that comprises four geographic subregions and contains eighty-two municipalities, of which three cities have over 300,000 people in population.

Source: Walter Hitschfeld Geographic Information Centre, McGill University Library.

a thorough guidebook on land use planning and adaptation to climate change has been produced along with directives on Agenda 21 for use by municipalities.[7] The usual prescriptions, stopping sprawl, favoring higher densities and mixed uses, protecting natural milieus, promoting nonmotorized travel, and the like are all clearly laid out.

The Montreal Metropolitan Community

The region of Montreal occupies an archipelago in the St. Lawrence River and extends across the fertile lands of its north and south shores. The city of Montreal itself is located on an island that until recently it shared with twenty-seven other municipalities. Between 1979 and 2001, the central city and its near suburbs were members of the Montreal Urban Community, a regional body

Table 2. The CMM at a glance

1	METROPOLITAN COMMUNITY Since January 1, 2001	120	CULTURAL COMMUNITIES
14	REGIONAL COUNTY MUNICIPALITIES four of which are cities with RCM jurisdiction	19.4%	OF INHABITANTS OVER THE AGE OF 20 have a university degree
82	LOCAL MUNICIPALITIES	C$139 billion	METROPOLITAN GDP (at market prices) or C$38,000 per capita in 2006
1 (out of 82)	CITY (Montreal) with more than 1.6 million inhabitants in 2007	1.86 million	JOBS IN 2006 or 49% of Quebec's jobs
2 (out of 82)	CITIES (Laval and Longueuil) with 200,000 to 400,000 inhabitants in 2007	136,400	JOBS IN THE NEW ECONOMY IN 2005 including 88,500 in the information technology industry, 29,000 in aerospace and 18,900 in biopharmaceuticals
34 (out of 82)	MUNICIPALITIES with 15,000 to 100,000 inhabitants in 2007		
45 (out of 82)	MUNICIPALITIES with fewer than 15,000 inhabitants in 2007	14 million	VISITORS IN 2005 in Montréal RMR
5	ADMINISTRATIVE REGIONS three of which are partial (Laurentians, Lanaudière, Montérégie)	80 million	CONSUMERS within a 1,000 km radius
7	REGIONAL CONFERENCES OF ELECTED OFFICIALS (CRÉ) four of which are partial (Laurentians, Lanaudière, and two in Montérégie)		
4,360 km^2	TOTAL AREA including 525 km^2 of water resources and 2,218 km^2 of protected farmland, or 58% of the entire region	1.84 million	AUTOMOBILES or 1.23 cars per dwelling in 2003
3.6 million	POPULATION IN 2007 or nearly 50% of the Quebec population	7.3 million	TRIPS in 24 hours in 2003, including 67.6% by car, 16.4% by public transit, 12.2% nonmotorized and 5.1% by other modes
926	PEOPLE PER km^2 IN 2007	1	INTERNATIONAL AIRPORT with traffic of 11.4 million travelers in 2006
1.39 million	PRIVATE DWELLINGS 49.9% are rented	1	PORT with traffic of 25.1 million metric tons of cargo in 2006, 45% of it containerized
2.4	PERSONS PER HOUSEHOLD	5	UNIVERSITIES three French-speaking and two English-speaking, seven affiliated schools and research institutes, for a total of 170,000 students in 2005
18.7%	OF THE POPULATION ARE IMMIGRANTS one-third of whom arrived less than 10 years ago	66	CEGEPs AND COLLEGES public and private
75	LANGUAGES SPOKEN mostly French, then English	201	RESEARCH CENTERS
20.6%	OF INHABITANTS SPEAK AT LEAST TWO LANGUAGES AT HOME IN 2001 one of which is neither French nor English	60	CONSULATES AND FOREIGN DELEGATIONS

Source: Communauté Métropolitaine de Montréal, http://www.cmm.qc.ca/index.php?id=334.

in charge of planning for the island as a whole and of administering shared infrastructure and services, such as main roads and cultural facilities, policing, and property valuation (see table 2).

In 2000 the Quebec government, then run by the Parti Québécois, introduced sweeping and radical local government reform to the major cities of the province.[8] The arguments presented for the reform were both greater efficiency and greater equity—that is, more effective planning for regionwide infrastructure, cost-sharing between rich and poor municipalities, cooperative economic development, sound environmental management, and the need to make Quebec's large cities, especially Montreal, more competitive on the world scene.

In the region of Montreal, the reform first meant dissolving the Montreal Urban Community and replacing it with a more extensive metropolitan body. The Montreal Metropolitan Community (MMC or CMM, as it is known in its French acronym), which has been in operation since January 1, 2001, is made up of eighty-two municipalities and has jurisdiction over an area of about 18.6 miles (30 kilometers) in radius, roughly contiguous with the Census Metropolitan Area. Its mandate covers regional land-use planning, economic development, cultural development, social housing, management of metropolitan facilities, and regional planning for infrastructure, waste management, and the remediation of air and water quality. So far, it has produced an economic development plan, a regional land-use plan that is still awaiting formal adoption, a policy on social housing, a solid waste disposal plan, and a policy on waste water yet to be ratified.[9] Regional public transport is in the hands of the Agence métropolitaine de transport (AMT), an organization that answers to the Québec Ministry of Transport. The CMM is supposed to endorse the AMT's plans and actions and perhaps one day take over its control. One of the interesting things the CMM has done is to sign an agreement with the Québec government on the management of "blue and green" assets (water bodies and shorelines, and natural habitats), air and water quality, and recycling. Among its objectives is the remediation of the extensive shorelines of the region of Montreal, in the interests of both ecology and recreation. Whether this agreement will prove to be binding remains to be seen.

The City of Montreal

The second important aspect of Quebec's municipal reform of 2001 was the merger of all twenty-eight municipalities on the island of Montreal to become the new "megacity" of Montreal, and the merger of six municipalities on the South Shore to form an enlarged city of Longueuil. (The city of Laval was created by a similar merger in 1966.) Although the merger of Montreal and its suburbs in 2001 was a victory for mayor Pierre Bourque, the champion of "One island, one city" lost the first election in the megacity. His successor, Gérald Tremblay, a former Liberal provincial minister of industry, was elected by a loose coalition of urbanites and suburbanites, social progressives and conservatives, all opposed to the centralized governance model that Bourque had hoped to impose. The third element of the reform, therefore, was the decentralization of administration and service delivery in the city of Montreal into twenty-seven boroughs (*arrondissements*), nine of them carved out of the old central city and eighteen representing annexed municipalities.

The forced amalgamation of municipalities, which took effect on January 1, 2001, elicited much anger. Capitalizing on that resentment, the Liberal Party won the 2003 provincial election, in part by promising to allow merged municipalities to secede. On the island of Montreal, fifteen municipalities elected to reconstitute themselves, despite the fact that they would not get back all their original powers. Merged services would remain regional in scale and would be run by an island-wide body, the Agglomeration Council (Conseil d'Agglomération). The reconstituted municipalities, which regained independence on January 1, 2006, make up 13 percent of the population of the Island of Montreal, occupy 28 percent of its area, and of course are completely overwhelmed by the central city in Agglomeration Council deliberations. The residents of the boroughs of Montreal now effectively live under four layers of local government: the Montreal Metropolitan Community, the Agglomeration Council, the City of Montreal, and their own Borough Council.

Facing the trauma of two episodes of structural reorganization (merger and demerger), Tremblay has clearly had his hands full with complicated administrative, staffing, and financial rearrangements. Despite this, the mayor and his administration have set an ambitious policy agenda and have implemented part of it—in particular, with respect to sustainable development.

The first dramatic action of Gérald Tremblay was to inaugurate the "Sommet de Montréal," a series of workshops and consultative meetings to which people from all walks of life were invited in a major effort to promote consensus, solidarity, and buy-in to the new city. Participants included representatives of the business, social, community and government sectors, including people from youth groups, unions (including those involving city workers historically in conflict with the administration), advocacy groups for the disabled, women's organizations, and the gay community, in addition to the predictable specialists and activists in environment, conservation, housing, planning, public finance, and the like.

The first round of meetings in April 2002 were arranged around fourteen themes, such as housing, local democracy, sustainable development, urban planning, economic development, public security, community life, public finance, and parks and recreation—in fact, each one of the major operations of the city. Background papers outlining the facts and issues were debated, recommendations made and prioritized. Written reports were prepared on the spot and made available widely. A similar procedure was undertaken in each of the (then) twenty-seven boroughs, where residents were able to put forward their ideas about the future of their community.[10]

The second round of consultations (the summit of summits, so to speak), in June 2002, brought together representatives from all the thematic deliberations for an intensive three-day workshop, focusing on five goals for the city that had emerged as top priorities from the first round. These were to foster economic growth, promote sustainable development, improve quality of life and inclusiveness, strengthen democracy and transparency, and aim for sound administration. These became the foundations for the vision statement for the new city.[11] Under these headings, projects were identified, and nineteen ongoing working groups (*chantiers*) were set up to pursue various issues. Some of these have proved livelier than others. One of the most successful is that on democracy: it has succeeded in having Montreal adopt a Charter of Rights and Responsibilities toward its citizens in 2005 (which the administration would like to see included in the city charter), appoint an ombudsman, and reopen the Office de Consultation Publique de Montréal, which is responsible for holding public hearings to evaluate major development projects—all significant steps on the road to sustainability.[12]

One of the major outcomes of the Montreal Summit was the adoption of a policy on sustainable development and the preparation of a Sustainable Development Plan.[13] Here, as in other policy realms, the approach of the Tremblay administration is strategic. It involves consulting the public on key goals, identifying priority projects, establishing partnerships and signing agreements, setting targets and timetables for implementation, reporting on progress, and revising the plan every two years.[14]

Policies, Planning Frameworks, and Plans

According to Quebec's Land Use Planning and Development Act, the provincial government is obliged to issue guidelines to any planning authority preparatory to the preparation of a local or regional plan in order to identify both the provincial policy orientations for that jurisdiction and the major projects that the government intends to implement in the near future. Such guidelines were published by the Ministry of Municipal Affairs for the region of Montreal in its "Planning Framework and Government Orientations" for 2001–2012, and the CMM draft plan follows these guidelines closely.[15] CMM regulations relating to solid waste management and wastewater discharge into watercourses also adhere closely to provincial norms and guidelines.

The official planning policy of the government of Quebec for the Montreal region is that of sustainable development. It entails consolidation of the center of the metropolitan area, limitation of urban sprawl within growth boundaries (first set by the protective agricultural zoning of 1978), and concentration of infrastructure investment in already serviced urban areas, a policy that has been restated several times.[16] But the province has not used its power to oversee local planning as well as it could in order to implement its sustainable-development policies. It has been quite lax at times in protecting agricultural land, most notably under Liberal administrations during 1985–1994, and in ensuring conformity of local plans with regional ones and of regional plans with provincial frameworks.[17] At the same time, it has continued to build road infrastructure, such as the extension of highways 25 and 30, and health and educational facilities in distant suburbs, which encourage further sprawl.

Likewise, at the level of discourse, both the CMM and the City of Montreal are totally committed to the ideal of sustainable development, although their actions also reflect political expediency and fiscal realism. In its "Strategic Vision Statement," Vision 2025, the CMM presents the Montreal metropolitan region as "a community focused on sustainable development . . . where quality of life, solidarity and tolerance are valued; . . . a responsible community endowed with transparent institutions and participatory democracy."[18] With respect to physical planning, realizing the vision of "a Competitive, Attractive, Interdependent and Responsible Community" will require that Montreal's downtown core be strengthened, that the existing urban fabric be consolidated, that the use of mass transit be promoted, that built and natural heritage areas be protected, and that housing areas offer all residents a high quality of life and adequate public services.[19]

The CMM is trying to give some teeth to this policy by means of a *Plan métropolitain d'aménagement et de développement* (PMAD), adopted on December 8, 2011 over the objections of a number of suburban mayors. The plan contains regulatory provisions that all local governments, regional county municipalities, municipalities, and boroughs are expected to comply. The major directives of the plan are essentially smart-growth principles:

Table 3. Policies, plans and strategies of the City of Montreal, 2003–2008

TITLE AND YEAR	DESCRIPTION
Public Consultation and Participation Policy, 2003	Outlines ways by which the city "aims to foster . . . the exercise of participatory democracy" and thereby enable citizens "to influence the decisions that affect them and to participate in the development of their community."
Master Plan, 2004	"Presents a planning and development vision for the city, as well as measures for implementing the goals and objectives resulting from that vision."
Strategic plan for Sustainable Development, 2005	"Sets forth an orientation and an action plan for Montreal regarding sustainable development."
Cultural Development Policy, 2005	Shows how "culture is a driving force behind [Montreal's] development, its economic dynamics and its future prosperity."
Economic Development Strategy, 2005	Proposes ways "to make Montreal a leader among North American metropolises by 2025 in standard of living and in quality of life."
Heritage Policy, 2005	Outlines ways to foster "the development of a collective vision and a shared responsibility for Montreal's heritage and to make heritage a lever of cultural, social and economic development."
Tree Policy, 2005	"Provides everyone [—] municipal authorities, citizens and land owners [—] with the tools necessary to protect and develop the island's arboreal heritage."
Action Plan for Universal Accessibility, 2006	Lists "a series of measures and programs [by which] the city intends to reduce problems of access to public buildings and spaces," as well as to jobs, information, programs, and services for citizens and employees.
Montreal Charter of Rights and Responsibilities, 2006	Specifies the respective rights and responsibilities of citizens and municipal authorities with respect to "democracy, economic and social life, cultural life, recreation, physical activities and sports, environment and sustainable development, security and municipal services."
Policy on the Protection and Enhancement of Natural Habitats, 2006	Presents strategies to reach the goal of permanently protecting six per cent of the city's territory, especially in ten "ecoterritories," which are not in public ownership but have been identified as having "large concentration of natural environments and . . . high ecological value."
Transport Plan, 2007	Outlines "the means of transportation [required] to meet the needs of all Montréalers and [make] their city a pleasant city to live [*sic*] while promoting economic prosperity and respecting the environment."
Corporate Plan for Climate Protection, 2007	Synthesizes the ways in which the City of Montreal will help to limit the local emission of greenhouse gases in its own operations.
Affordable Housing Inclusion Strategy, 2007	Lists tools currently available to the city to ensure that new residential projects include affordable units and that, overall, "30 per cent of all new housing built be affordable."
Purchasing Policy, 2007	Presents how the city will improve its business transactions according to "four guiding principles: ethics, quality, performance and sustainable development."
Policy for a peaceful and safe environment, 2008	Spells out the city's approach to public safety, based on outreach, prevention, and collaboration.
Policy for the equal participation of women and men in Montreal, 2008	Expresses the commitment of the City of Montreal to ensure gender equality in governance, municipal employment, public services, economic development, and international representation.
Draft master plan for waste management of the Agglomeration of Montreal, 2008	Shows how the City of Montreal and neighboring municipalities on the island of Montreal intend to implement the metropolitan waste management plan of the Montreal Metropolitan Community in terms of reduction, reuse, recycling, composting, etc.

Note: All citations are from the Ville de Montréal website, section les "Les grands dossiers" ("Key Issues"), at http://ville.montreal.qc.ca/portal/page?_pageid=132,231220&_dad=portal&_schema=PORTAL. Some citations were taken from the English-language version where available; others were taken from the French-language version, which has a more definitive list, and were translated by the authors.

- Priority must be given to the consolidation of existing urban areas and densification of existing centers;
- new development must be concentrated in transit-oriented developments (TODs);
- minimum average dwelling densities must be set in local regulations for various types of TODs and for residential areas outside of TODs;
- major transit infrastructure investment must help to increase the modal share of transit; and
- forests, wetlands and other environmental areas, as well as the existing agricultural zone, must be protected.[20]

The PMAD echoes the Places to Grow Act that the Province of Ontario adopted for the Toronto region. It translates broad policy goals into planning requirements for local governments and in so doing introduces a metropolitan level of control over land use that local officials find extremely hard to accept. It is no wonder that it took the latter ten years to fulfill their provincial mandate to adopt a metropolitan plan.

It remains to be seen how much change the PMAD will bring to the metropolitan coordination and regulation of development. Municipalities enjoy their power to adopt their own plans and to approve local projects on their own. Such is certainly the case for Montreal, which has issued a flurry of plans between 2003 and 2007, from a new Master Plan to plan for economic development, cultural development, and environmental preservation. These plans are discussed below. All of them are expected to show, of course, that the policies of Mayor Tremblay's administration are "based on two fundamental values: sustainable development and solidarity."[21] Individual boroughs have shown different levels of interest in sustainable development. Rates of recycling vary greatly, and levels of funding or political support for environmental initiatives are variable.

In 2007–2008, the website of the City of Montreal highlighted a set of "key issues" receiving the attention of the Tremblay administration. To address these problems, the city adopted a whole set of policies, plans, and strategies (see table 3). The plethora of documents, the myriad goals and objectives, and the multitude of projects that the city has put forward since the Montreal Summit of 2002 are impressive. There is, of course, much overlap between the different plans. Many of the goals of the updated Strategic Plan for Sustainable Development for 2007–2009 are common in other documents.[22] For example, enhancing the quality of residential areas, preserving green space, and reducing greenhouse gas emissions are identified as policy objectives in many documents.

Montreal's Master Plan of 2004, in particular, offers much of what a believer in sustainable development would expect from such a document. (This was not the case with the city's first Master Plan, adopted in 1991.) "The Master Plan," the mayor contends in a glossy presentation brochure, is nothing but "a sustainable master plan" whose measures are "in keeping with the *Kyoto Protocol.*" It includes measures to increase urban densities along transit corridors and integrate various land uses, thereby increasing transit use and reducing reliance on the private automobile.[23]

The Master Plan of 2004 earned an award of excellence from the Canadian Institute of Planners. But it does show a major weakness: it is too comprehensive, really, to convey a sense of strategic priorities. This is ironic, as Mayor Tremblay, who heads both the city and the metropolitan community of Montreal, holds a particularly strong belief in the value of large-scale, "structuring" projects, both public and private, for economic development. To a large extent, his strategy is and must be one of real estate development—in particular, the reuse of brownfield sites for high-technology campuses—to attract companies in leading-edge industrial clusters ("*grappes de compétitivité de calibre international*").[24] Thus the actual contents of Montreal 2025, a game plan to raise Montreal in the hierarchy of world cities, is a list of over a hundred "major projects that will transform the city."[25] Their implementation will be promoted by the newly created Strategic and Tactical Intervention Group (Groupe d'Intervention Stratégique et Tactique)—a team of guerillas in the bureaucracy?—whose mission is to facilitate the work of public and private developers, ensure the urban-design integration of their projects, and maximize the leverage obtained for the community at large.

A similar case may be made about the city's new transport plan.[26] Hailed as "another important moment of [Montreal's] history,"[27] the plan is in fact an elaboration of the transportation chapter of the Master Plan. Despite the lofty rhetoric on historic significance and on visions and goals, the essence of the plan, like that of Montreal 2025, is a list of projects. Realizing these would confirm the importance of Montreal as an economic center; but it would also confirm Montreal's fiscal dependency on the provincial and federal governments. The call for action to "reinvent" the city (the plan is called Réinventer Montréal), for example by reintroducing tramways, is accompanied by a call for access to new sources of funding—for instance, by reinstating bridge tolls for suburban motorists coming into the city. Clearly, the fiscal means of the administration are no match for its ambitions.

Implementation Programs and Processes

The key question, apart from those of municipal regulation and city expenditures to further the *grands projets*, is how to get all these policies implemented. Sustainable development is often defined as a reconciliation of the demands of society, the economy, and the environment, or as Jennifer Wolch has said, recasting urban citizenship to promote social and ecological justice, redesigning systems of production and consumption, and restoring the city's ecological integrity.[28] Montreal has interesting programs under all these categories, some devised by the city, some by provincial-level agencies, some by NGOs, some by the private sector, and some produced as joint ventures.

In terms of social sustainability, it should be noted that in Canada, health, welfare, and education are controlled by provincial governments, although some responsibilities may be devolved to local boards. Generally speaking, Quebec has remained a fairly progressive province. Although it, too, took a conservative turn in the 1990s, its policies continue to display a concern with redistribution (e.g., in affordable day care and housing) and with prevention (e.g., in youth violence and in public health). The province also has a long tradition of citizen participation in public inquiries, environmental assessments, and other forums.

Montreal, which has worked as a junior partner with the province on social issues in its neighborhoods, has pursued a three-pronged effort to nurture urban citizenship. It began in 2000 with decentralization, the creation of boroughs in the new, merged city of Montreal, providing a more accessible local government at an understandable scale (although some boroughs have populations of well over 100,000).[29] This is the first step toward Agenda 21, which advocates local control and civic engagement as essential ingredients in urban improvement. Some boroughs, going beyond their mandated responsibilities in local planning and service delivery, have introduced their own promising innovations. The Plateau Mont-Royal, for instance, is experimenting both with participatory budgeting and with local mobilization for sustainability.[30]

Greater transparency in government, the organization of public hearings on some (though not all) large development projects, the chance to complain through the ombudsman, and the adoption of a Charter of Rights and Responsibilities have already been mentioned. Along with these are many special programs to better meet the particular needs of immigrants, the disabled, women, youth, and the elderly; a family policy, too, has been the object of much attention recently.[31] Such actions, which promote participatory democracy, cultural integration, and the egalitarian sharing of social space in the city, are devised to contribute to the empowerment of residents, another ingredient of Agenda 21.

On a small scale, the city has long fostered local groups who want to improve the wholesomeness and beauty of their neighborhood, either through Healthy Cities initiatives (Quartiers en Santé) or through the Eco-Quartier program. The latter provides funding to help community groups educate residents to recycle, reduce, and reuse. Some groups also sensitize school children to the potential of appropriate consumption habits and waste reduction, teach greening and composting, and generally promote environmental citizenship. With the new sustainable development policy, this program is being extended by another initiative, Quartiers 21, in conjunction with the Public Health Department. Neighborhood groups that subscribe to Agenda 21 principles will be subsidized by $50,000 per year to promote local sustainability; three Quartiers 21 are to be selected each year by competition.[32]

Because of a low birth rate, both Montreal and Quebec as a whole are facing the prospect of a decreasing and aging population. This has a direct impact on economic sustainability as well. In Montreal itself, the problem is being compounded by the departure of younger households to the suburbs, while in the outer regions of the province it is worsened by migration to the Montreal metropolitan area. To stem the exodus to the suburbs, Montreal has recently adopted a "family policy" that individual boroughs are implementing in their own action plans. These aim to make Montreal more attractive to families in terms of housing, community services, safety and security, sports and recreation, and other elements of the living environment. The city has also put in place an affordable-housing policy, one based essentially on voluntary agreements with developers rather than on set requirements. After the first year of implementation, the target of 15 percent affordable units in market-rate projects was reached, but this was owed in large part to the construction of small units. How family-sized housing units, preferably with private outdoor space, can be provided at affordable cost remains one of the main puzzles the city has to solve.[33]

Officials and planners tend to place greater hope for salvation from the looming demographic peril in the attraction of international immigrants. This influx is fairly limited outside Montreal, where population decline has become a fact—as it has in other parts of Canada—but it is quite substantial in the Montreal area, where about 85 percent of all immigrants to Québec choose to plant roots.[34] Of those, nearly the same proportion settles on the island of Montreal and thereby helps to achieve positive demographic change. Montreal is ranked fifth in North America (after

Toronto, Vancouver, Miami, and Calgary) for its international immigration rate and ninth for its proportion of the population born outside the country. But the city and metropolitan area do not perform well in giving new residents steady employment. Recent immigrants (those who have been in Canada for less than five years) suffer an unemployment rate three times as high as that of Canadian-born workers. Although the discrepancy between recent immigrants and native residents is as large in Toronto and in Vancouver, the unemployment rate among recent immigrants is much higher in Montreal. In general, poverty rates well above the Canadian or North American average remain one of Montreal's main hurdles in its search for sustained, generalized well-being.[35]

In the face of such handicaps, both the Metropolitan Community and the City of Montreal have prepared ambitious economic development plans.[36] These are largely designed to entice global capital investment to the region by attracting high-tech enterprises, of which there are already well-known clusters in biotechnology, pharmaceuticals, and aeronautics. At the other end of the economic scale, activists in community groups and urban social movements have been promoting local economic development since the 1980s to bring back employment and improve social conditions in neighborhoods hard hit by deindustrialization. Much advocacy work has been done on the potential of local economic development, both by local organizations and by government agencies.[37]

Grassroots participation in economic development takes place through nine community development corporations or CDECs (*corporations de développement économique communautaire*) on the Island of Montreal, through many community organizations that are recognized by the provincial Ministry of Health and Social Services as reliable service providers, and through the province's *Secretariat à l'action communautaire autonome,* which promotes and supports community action initiatives and volunteerism, with a special focus on collective rights advocacy organizations. How much of all this actually compensates for the downloading of service delivery from senior levels of government to local jurisdictions in the 1990s is a moot point. The social economy, once understood as the activity of not-for-profit and cooperative enterprises only, is now broadly seen to include all development projects that help to pursue both economic and social goals and that produce goods and services of social utility that contribute to a net increase in collective wealth. The recent funding by the federal and provincial governments of the Fonds d'Économie Sociale du Sud-Ouest (FESSO), for example, is an acknowledgment of the power of the social economy and an important contribution to sustainability. Whether such an initiative represents only a palliative solution to socioeconomic exclusion or the start of a regime shift in the style advocated by Wolch remains to be seen.[38]

On the administrative front, the city has been revising its own practices. It encourages environmentally sustainable procurement, has a civic plan for the reduction of energy consumption in all city departments and buildings, and, perhaps because of its fragile financial situation, has engaged in long-term budgeting (over seven years), presumably with an eye to lifetime costing of facilities.[39]

The third facet of sustainable development, enhancement of the environment, has largely found expression in the provisions of the Sustainable Development Plan, in addition to many handy guidelines on subjects such as green building, excessive automobile use, water use, and nonresidential garbage management.[40] A key implementation strategy of the city, aside from the adoption of much stronger environmental regulations, is to be proactive in forging partnerships and exchanging information with businesses, institutions, government agencies at all levels, and nongovernmental and community-based organizations, with the aim of getting them to change their own ways of operation and become more sustainable. An example is McGill University: in revising the development plan of its downtown campus, it has undertaken to reduce the number of parking spots, keep the lower campus yard open for public use, and continue to improve its programs relating to recycling, composting, ecological maintenance, greening, and the like.[41] Over eighty organizations signed up in the first round of partnerships, and the city is hoping for a "domino effect" among other potential participants. The partners' actions will be monitored and assessed against their promises.

Climate change has received special attention from the Public Health Department of Montreal, which actually comes under the aegis of the provincial Agence (formerly Régie Régionale) de la Santé et des Services Sociaux de Montréal. Heat-island effects leading to hyperthermia, the possible migration of disease vectors northward into the region, respiratory diseases related to air quality, and disasters caused by extreme weather events are all being examined. The Conseil Régional de l'Environnement de Montréal, an NGO, has started a neighborhood tree-planting program to combat heat islands. Meanwhile, the city has adopted a tree-preservation and tree-planting policy of its own, and, in an attempt to preserve biodiversity in compliance with Quebec policies, has designated ten "ecoterritories," areas of significant ecological significance (and mostly privately owned), for protection from development. Citizen-led initiatives to clean up the banks of the St. Lawrence River and its tributaries are encouraged through grants by the St. Lawrence Plan.[42]

Efforts to reduce the use of private automobiles include private initiatives such as Commun-Auto, a community car-sharing operation for people who need cars irregularly. It is very popular, especially because parking is scarce in most of the older parts of the city, making car ownership trying even for higher-income households. The city has recently opened a dedicated bicycle path right through the downtown core, making three universities and four colleges in particular more accessible by bike. It has also adopted a charter protecting the rights of pedestrians.[43] The impact of all these endeavors remains to be seen.

Conclusion

Achieving economic, social, and environmental sustainability requires that the right collective choices be made with respect to public investment, income redistribution, and resource conservation. As former Maryland governor Parris Glendening, a champion of Smart Growth, recognized recently, the extent to which a city-region grows in a sustainable manner is a function, first and foremost, of its political culture.[44] Limiting sprawl and focusing development in already urbanized areas requires popular support for unpopular measures that constrain local autonomy in planning and zoning and in infrastructure development. Higher-level oversight on municipal land-use decision making is an essential element of the CMM's draft master plan for the greater Montreal region; it is also the main reason why the plan has not been officially adopted, three years after it was first issued.

The exhaustive research of Tomalty and Alexander on Smart Growth in Canada bears out the fact that sustainable development is very present as a concept in public discourse but rather discrete as a reality in practice on the ground.[45] Actions and results remain far more modest than statements and goals, especially when it comes to achieving more mixed land uses and higher densities of employment. Housing affordability has in fact gone down and dependency on the automobile gone up in many metropolitan areas.[46] For Montreal, Tomalty and Alexander found that the record is less dismal than in other city-regions and actually reasonable in some respects. It may be too early to judge how well the city has done, given that most of its sustainable-development initiatives are very recent. Still, what the mayor of Montreal said of his city's Policy on the Protection and Enhancement of Natural Habitats may be said of the set of policies, plans, and programs adopted in the region of Montreal as a whole: their "implementation [has been] a qualified success."[47]

On the positive side, the loss of population from the central city to peripheral municipalities has been slowed, as has the loss of agricultural land; the vitality of Montreal's downtown and other employment poles has been maintained; the number of transit riders has been increased (after many years of decline); and the dramatic deficit in wastewater treatment capacity has been remedied. Air quality in Montreal is improving; and the amount of particulate matter in the central areas is decreasing, as are the number of days with unacceptable pollution levels.[48] Despite a setback in 2006, due to extraordinarily heavy rainfall that washed in detritus, the quality of water for recreation is improving.[49] Even Montreal's long-standing problem of high unemployment, a major issue in social and economic sustainability, seems to be lessening; although the unemployment rate remains higher than in Toronto and Vancouver, it has diminished significantly in the past years. Here, of course, Canada-wide trends and policies may account for more of the change than do local ones, though the robustness of the diversified regional economy is certainly a factor as well.

On the negative side, much development still occurs outside zones officially targeted for densification, often on environmentally valuable land (forests, wetlands, and agricultural land).[50] Also, suburban densities and urban forms are not more conducive to the provision of public transit than before, and dependency on the car has therefore remained high. All in all, provincial planning frameworks and oversight have not significantly influenced the decisions of municipalities in search of fiscally beneficial development or the actions of private developers in search of profit from greenfield construction. Despite the institution of new mechanisms of coordination over the years, decision-making in the Montreal metropolitan area is still fragmented, both horizontally (among provincial ministries and among regional and municipal authorities) and vertically (between different levels of government), and is still heavily influenced by intermunicipal competition.

Despite the promotion of more sustainable development practices and greener lifestyles, many private decisions remain informed by the dream of an affordable home in the suburbs or by the search for cheap land for commercial and industrial facilities. The rate of growth of the population on the island of Montreal is much smaller than the rate experienced on the North Shore and on the South Shore. Hence the share of the population of greater Montreal that resides on the island of Montreal has continued to decline; it went from 59.4 percent in 1986 to just above

50 percent in 2010. This means that, although the number of trips made on public transit has grown, the number of cars on the road and the dependency on the private car have continued to increase, as has the number of acres of peripheral land taken over by low-density urbanization. Waste removal and recycling also show a relative meager record of achievement. Although the population of the Island of Montreal increased by a mere 2.3 percent between 2002 and 2006, the amount of trash it sent to landfills rose by 7 percent; and while the Quebec government would like to see all municipalities recycle at least 60 percent of recyclable waste, no municipality on the island reaches this goal (a couple of boroughs within Montreal do come close to that target); some recycle only a mere 20 percent.[51]

When we compare Montreal to other large Canadian cities, the picture is mixed as well. Historically, Montrealers and their elected officials have displayed a weaker commitment to environmental preservation than, say, their counterparts in Vancouver. Judging from the documents reviewed here, this difference has been greatly lessened in the past few years. Local leadership certainly accounts for this positive evolution, at least in part. Elected officials and professional planners have been promoting an agenda of sustainable development and have been in turn pushed forward by environmental activists. Alongside the stronger environmental ethos that seems to be spreading in Quebecois society, the growing realization of local and regional players that Montreal must be better positioned in the new global economy, and that it has the potential to compete as a high-tech, high-culture center, has prompted officials to adopt a "greener" mind-set and message.[52]

At the same time, rates of growth that are below those of other Canadian cities (and that express the shift of the country's economic center of gravity to Toronto and toward the West) have left the city and its region relatively poorer; but they may also have limited the damage done by growth over the past decades because of lower rates of home and automobile ownership. Although housing starts picked up significantly in 2002, the lower rate of growth relative to other cities over many years may have made it easier in some ways to manage growth in a sustainable manner. But it has made it all the more necessary for Montreal to be attractive to investors and immigrants in order to secure economic development. At the same time, the economic integration of immigrant workers remains uncertain, even when they master the French language.[53]

Despite the urgency of collective action, intrametropolitan competition in Montreal is acting at cross-purposes with interregional competition. The heavy dependence of Quebecois and other Canadian municipalities on the property tax for their revenues fuels competition for development irrespective of spatial location and splinters action into locally meaningful yet regionally inconsistent measures.[54] The lack of political will in Quebec and the absence of directly elected metropolitan leadership both diminish the likelihood that political and economic players will reach constructive compromises, let alone make hard choices, at the metropolitan level. At the local level, however, the division of Montreal in boroughs has allowed for interesting experimentation while also making the implementation of central-city initiatives more difficult.

Patterns of spatial development, habits of resource utilization, and practices of decision making as they are currently found in Montreal and its region are probably not sustainable on a global scale. Locally, however, they still seem to be acceptable: the price to pay for them does not strike government officials, citizens, and businesspeople as too onerous. For instance, the commuting times of most suburbanites, except for those stuck at rush hour on a bridge to the island of Montreal, are not longer, on average, than the commuting times of residents of Montreal proper, especially of those who take public transit to work. The loss of natural and agricultural areas, though ongoing, does not arouse major outcries. And although the decentralization of employment continues to lower the density of commercial and industrial development and to increase people's dependence on the automobile, average housing densities are actually increasing in residential subdivisions, a fact observed elsewhere in Canada as well. In 2009 and 2010, about 62 percent of all housing units built in the metropolitan region of Montreal have been in multifamily structures. The stagnation of middle-class incomes and the rising price of gasoline are likely to have a stronger impact on behaviors than will policies and programs.[55]

The least sustainable elements of the current situation, from the public point of view, are regional migration patterns and the fiscal predicament of cities. Between 1991 and 2007, the most outlying regions of the province lost between 10 and 18 percent of their population, mostly to the Montreal metropolitan area; the island of Montreal, meanwhile, lost over 8 percent of its population to the South Shore, Laval, and the North Shore.[56] In Montreal, international migration has more than compensated for this loss. However, the integration of residents from foreign lands and cultures is a task that cities are ill-equipped and ill-financed to handle. The discrepancy between mandates and means is characteristic of municipal finances in general, in Canada as a whole. The City of Montreal spends about 20 percent of every dollar to service its debt, is facing billions of dollars worth of work to upgrade its infrastructure, and struggles every year to close its budget. Like other big-city mayors, Gérald Tremblay has been demanding a grant of new taxation powers from the province, which would give his city a more diverse tax base and provide revenues more commensurate with its responsibilities. It is not surprising, therefore, that Tremblay's recent statement on "Sustainable Solutions for Montreal" speaks to a basic requirement: "straighten the finances of the City." The fiscal imbalance between the city and the province, not sprawl or greenhouse gas emission, is "the most urgent crisis."[57]

Sustainable development is both rhetoric and reality. How much it will be the latter rather than the former depends not just on local leadership but also on the intensity of political pressure that local and regional officials will experience from the grassroots up and from the government ministries down, and on the amount of political support that they will receive for their initiatives. In theory, sustainable development is good for the economy, for society at large, and for the environment. In practice, fiscal constraints and lifestyle preferences can stand in the way of the best intentions. In the greater Montreal region, spotty ideological commitment, fragmented governance structures, and a favorable urban and regional ecology make sustainable development less of a political urgency than it is in other places. Despite these limitations, officials, planners, researchers, and activists have started to put Montreal on the map as a center of thought and action on sustainable development. That qualifies as success.

Appendix 1. The Nineteen Objectives of the Montreal Master Plan

1. Improve the quality of existing living environments.
2. Foster the construction of 60,000 to 75,000 housing units between 2004 and 2014.
3. Consolidate and exploit the potential of the urban territory in relation with existing and projected transportation networks.
4. Enlarge the metropolitan, national, and international vocation of the city center.
5. Reinforce the coherence of the city center.
6. Consolidate employment areas by fostering the arrival of new, dynamic businesses and by improving transportation links.
7. Diversify and reinforce activities in the center's immediate periphery to support a more intensive use of existing infrastructure.
8. Foster the implementation of institutional employment areas that are well integrated in the city.
9. Highlight Mount Royal, the island topography, and other elements of the urban landscape.
10. Favor architectural quality and consolidate the built environment in harmony with the character of each area.
11. Improve the public realm by coherent design of the street and other public spaces.
12. Ensure that large-scale transport infrastructure contributes positively to the improvement of the urban landscape.
13. Ensure the conservation and full use of built and archeological heritage.
14. Preserve and put to full use the natural heritage of the city.
15. Ensure the optimal use of resources in an urban context.
16. Reduce nuisances generated by urban activities on the environment.
17. Ensure proper development in areas with natural constraints.

Source: Montreal, *Plan d'urbanisme* (Montréal: Ville de Montréal, 2004). Goals taken from the English version of the plan.

Appendix 2. Actions to Improve Air Quality and Reduce Greenhouse Gas Emissions, 2007–2009

- Eliminate unnecessary idling of motor vehicles: apply new regulation to that effect.
- Reduce the supply of parking by eliminating illegal spots in parking lots and garages downtown.
- Minimize automobile traffic on roads crossing Mount Royal.
- Enlarge bicycle infrastructure by expanding the Montreal-wide bicycle network and by developing bicycle facilities in businesses.
- Foster the growth of car-sharing.
- Implement measures favoring sustainable transport in businesses (public transit, ride-sharing, bicycling, walking).
- Implement measures to reduce greenhouse gas emissions: adopt municipal action plan to achieve a reduction of 20 percent in 2012 compared to 2002; create joint strategy with large industrial actors.
- Continue the greening of the municipal vehicle fleet: adopt greening policy; replace 500 subcompact cars with environmentally friendly vehicles and replace 106 six-cylinder gas-engine vans with four-cylinder vehicles by 2011; use alternative fuels whose environmental benefit is recognized.
- Put in place compensation mechanisms for business trips that are carbon-neutral: adhere to the compensation program for business trips by airplane.

Source: Montréal, *Premier plan stratégique de développement durable de la collectivité Montréalaise—phase 2007–2009* (Montréal: Ville de Montréal, 2007), 6; translated and adapted by the authors.

NOTES

In memory of Jeanne M. Wolfe, 1934–2009

1. World Commission on Environment and Development, *Our Common Future* (Brundtland report) (Oxford: Oxford University Press, 1987).
2. CBC, In Depth: Canada 2020, National Public Opinion Survey, June 2006, http://www.cbc.ca/news/background/canada2020/poll-pt1.html.
3. See also Donald Lidstone, *Assessment of the Municipal Acts of the Provinces and Territories* (Ottawa: Federation of Canadian Municipalities, 2004).
4. Environment Canada and MDDEP, *St. Lawrence Plan for a Sustainable Development* (Ottawa: Environment Canada / Ministère du Développement Durable, de l'Environnement et des Parcs, 2008).
5. FCM, *Partners for Climate Protection* (Ottawa: Federation of Canadian Municipalities, 2006); FCM, *Municipal Governments and Sustainable Communities: A Best Practices Guide* (Ottawa: Federation of Canadian Municipalities, 2006).
6. MDDEP, *Stratégie Québécoise sur les Aires Protégées: Plan d'Action Stratégique* (Quebec: Ministère du Développement Durable, de l'Environnement et des Parcs, 2000); MDDEP, *Plan de Développement Durable (Document de Consultation)* (Quebec: Ministère du Développement Durable, de l'Environnement et des Parcs, 2004); MDDEP, *Stratégie et Plan d'Action Québécois sur la Diversité Biologique, 2004–2007* (Quebec: Ministère du Développement Durable, de l'Environnement et des Parcs, 2004); MDDEP, *Québec and Climate Change: A Challenge for the Future—Action Plan 2006–2012* (Quebec: Ministère du Développement durable, de l'Environnement et des Parcs, 2002); MDDEP, *Stratégie québécoise sur les aires protégées: Plan d'action stratégique, premiers résultats* (Quebec: Ministère du Développement Durable, de l'Environnement et des Parcs, 2006); MDDEP, *Rapport Annuel 2004–2005 sur la Mise en Oeuvre de la Stratégie et Plan d'Action Québécois sur la Diversité Biologique 2004–2007* (Quebec: Ministère du Développement Durable, de l'Environnement et des Parcs, 2006); MDDEP, *Bilan de la Première Année du Plan d'Action Québécois 2006–2012* (Quebec: Ministère du Développement Durable, de l'Environnement et des Parcs, 2007). Much activity on climate change and its impact on urban and regional development has taken place at the federal level as well. See, for example, NRTEE, *Environmental Quality in Canadian Cities: The Federal Role* (Ottawa: National Round Table on the Environment and the Economy, 2003); NRCAN, *Climate Change Impacts and Adaptation: A Canadian Perspective* (Ottawa: Natural Resources Canada—Climate Change Impacts and Adaptation Directorate, 2004); C–CIARN, *Adapting to Climate Change: An Introduction for Canadian Municipalities* (Ottawa: Canadian Climate Impacts and Adaptation Network, 2006); Environment Canada, *Turning the Corner: An Action Plan to Reduce Greenhouse Gases and Air Pollution* (Ottawa: Environment Canada, 2007).
7. MAMR, *Reduction of Greenhouse Gas Emissions and Land Use Planning: Best Practices Guide* (Quebec: Ministère des Affaires Municipales et des Régions, 2004); MAMR, *La réduction des émissions de gaz à effet de serre et l'aménagement du territoire: Faits saillants—fiche d'information* (Quebec: Ministère des Affaires Municipales et des Régions, 2005); MAMR, *Agenda 21 Local, schéma d'aménagement et de développement et plan d'urbanisme: Trois outils d'une même démarche?* (Quebec: Ministère des Affaires Municipales et des Régions, 2007).
8. MAMM, *Municipal Reorganization: Changing the Ways to Better Serve the Public* (Quebec: Ministère des Affaires Municipales et de la Métropole, 2000).
9. CMM, *Charting Our International Future: A Competitive Montréal Metropolitan Region—Economic Development Plan* (Montreal: Montréal Metropolitan Community, 2005); CMM, *Cap sur le monde: Pour une region métropolitaine de Montréal attractive—Projet de schéma métropolitain d'aménagement et de développement* (Montreal: Communauté Métropolitaine de Montréal, 2005); CMM, *Orientations de la CMM en matière de logement social et abordable* (Montreal: Communauté Métropolitaine de Montréal, 2005); CMM, *Plan métropolitain de gestion des matières résiduelles* (Montreal: Communauté Métropolitaine de Montréal, 2006); CMM, *Projet de règlement sur le contrôle des déversements d'eaux usées dans les ouvrages d'assainissement et cours d'eau* (Montreal: Communauté Métropolitaine de Montréal, 2007).
10. Montreal, *Le sommet de Montréal* (Montreal: Ville de Montréal, 2002).
11. Montreal, *Imaginer—Réaliser Montréal 2025* (Montreal: Ville de Montréal, 2005).
12. Montreal, *Sommet de Montréal 2002: Bilan des réalisations 2002–2005* (Montreal: Ville de Montréal, 2005); *Montreal, La charte Montréalaise des droits et responsabilités* (Montreal: Ville de Montréal, 2006).

13. Montreal, Premier plan stratégique de développement durable de la collectivité Montréalaise (Montreal: Ville de Montréal, 2005).
14. Montreal, *Premier plan stratégique de développement durable de la collectivité Montréalaise—Phase 2007–2009* (Montreal: Ville de Montréal, 2007).
15. MAMM, *Planning Framework and Government Orientations, Montréal Metropolitan Region 2001–2021* (Quebec: Ministère des Affaires Municipales et de la Métropole, 2001).
16. François Charbonneau, Pierre Hamel, and Michel Barcelo, *Urban Sprawl in the Montréal Area—Policies and Trends, in The Changing Canadian Metropolis: A Public Policy Perspective,* vol. 2, ed. Frances Frisken, 459–95 (Berkeley: Institute of Governmental Studies Press, University of California/Canadian Urban Institute, 1994).
17. CPTA, *Les enjeux de la protection du territoire agricole dans la région de Montréal après 25 ans de zonage agricole (rapport annuel de gestion 2003–2004, document complémentaire)* (Quebec: La Commission de Protection du Territoire Agricole du Québec, 2004). See also Ray Tomalty and Don Alexander, *Smart Growth in Canada: Implementation of a Planning Concept* (Ottawa: Canada Mortgage and Housing Corp., 2005).
18. CMM, *Vision 2025—Charting Our International Future: Building a Competitive, Attractive, Interdependent and Responsible Community—Strategic Vision Statement* (Montreal: Montréal Metropolitan Community, 2003).
19. CMM, *Cap sur le monde: Pour une région métropolitaine de Montréal attractive—Projet de schéma métropolitain d'aménagement et de développement* (Montreal: Communauté Métropolitaine de Montréal, 2005).
20. CMM, *Plan métropolitain d'aménagement et de développement* (Montreal: Communauté Métropolitaine de Montréal, 2011).
21. Gérald Tremblay, *Allocution de Monsieur Gérald Tremblay, Maire de Montréal, Président de la Communauté métropolitaine de Montréal, lors du colloque Réinventer Montréal organisé dans le cadre du 30e anniversaire du Départment des études urbaines et touristiques de l'UQÀM, le jeudi 27 avril 2006* (Montreal: Ville de Montréal, 2006); translation by the authors.
22. Montreal, *Premier plan stratégique de développement durable de la collectivité Montréalaise—Phase 2007–2009* (Montreal: Ville de Montréal, 2007).
23. Montreal, *Plan d'urbanisme* (Montreal: Ville de Montréal, 2004); Gérald Domon, Michel Gariépy, and Peter Jacobs, Développement viable en milieu urbain: Vers une stratégie de gestion des interventions, *Plan Canada* (January 1992): 4–17; Montreal, *Montréal Adopts Its Vision of the Future with the Master Plan* (English Summary) (Montreal: Ville de Montréal, 2004).
24. Gérald Tremblay, *Notes pour une allocation du Maire de Montréal, Monsieur Gérald Tremblay, Sommet Immobilier de Montréal, le mercredi 29 mars 2006* (Montreal: Ville de Montréal, 2006), 6.
25. Montreal, *Imaginer—Réaliser Montréal 2025* (Montreal: Ville de Montréal, 2005), 9; translation by the authors.
26. Montreal, *Réinventer Montreal: Plan de transport 2007—Document de consultation* (Montreal: Ville de Montréal, 2007).
27. Montreal, *Priorité au transport collectif et actif: Montréal se dote d'un premier plan de transport ambitieux, press release, May 17, 2007* (Montreal: Ville de Montréal, 2007), 1.
28. Jennifer Wolch, Green Urban Worlds, *Annals of the American Association of Geographers* 97:2 (2007): 373–84.
29. Jean-Pierre Collin and Mélanie Robertson, The Borough System of Consolidated Montreal: Revisiting Urban Governance in a Composite Metropolis, *Journal of Urban Affairs* 27:3 (2005): 307–34.
30. Alain Perron, *Un premier budget participatif positif, le Plateau* (Montreal: Arrondissement du Plateau Mont-Royal, 2006). See also Alex Josza and David Brown, *Neighbourhood Sustainability Indicators: Report on a Best Practice Workshop* (Montreal: McGill University, School of Urban Planning and Urban Ecology Centre/SodecM, 2005).
31. Montreal, *La ville de Montréal et les personnes handicapées et les personnes à mobilité réduite* (Montreal: Ville de Montréal, 2000); Montreal, *The Challenge of Participation: Montréal's Public Consultation and Participation Policy* (Montreal: Ville de Montréal, 2003); Montreal, *Déclaration de Montréal pour la diversité culturelle et l'inclusion* (Montreal: Ville de Montréal, 2004); Montreal, *Poursuivons le virage de l'accessibilité universelle* (Montreal: Ville de Montréal, 2006); Montreal, *Montréal, Ville de familles: Cadre de référence de la politique familiale de la ville de Montréal* (Montreal: Ville de Montréal, 2007); Montreal, *Pour grandir à Montreal: Politique familiale de Montréal 2008* (Montreal: Ville de Montréal, 2008).
32. G. Sénécal, Montréal's Eco-quartier Environmental Program: Local Action and Municipal Management,

Environmental Management 30:1 (2002): 46–58; Montreal, Montréal passe à l'ère des Quartiers 21, press release, October 20, 2005 (Montreal: Ville de Montréal, 2005); *Montreal, Premier plan stratégique de développement durable de la collectivité Montréalaise—phase 2007–2009* (Montreal: Ville de Montréal, 2007).

33. Claude Picher, L'hémorragie, *Montreal La Presse Affaires*, June 12, 2008; Montreal, *Montréal, Ville de familles: Cadre de référence de la politique familiale de la ville de Montréal* (Montreal: Ville de Montréal, 2007); Montreal, *Stratégie d'inclusion de logements abordables* (Montreal: Ville de Montréal, 2005); Montreal, *Stratégie d'inclusion de logements abordables dans les nouveaux projets résidentiels: Avancement de sa mise en œuvre* (Montreal: Ville de Montréal, 2007).
34. John Simmons and Larry S. Bourne, Living with Population Growth and Decline, *Plan Canada* 47:2 (2007): 13–21.
35. CMM, *Portrait du Grand Montréal, Édition 2010, Cahiers Métropolitains* (December 2010); Statistics Canada, Study: Canada's Immigrant Labour Market, *Daily*, September 10, 2007; Montreal, *Bilan économique 2006 de l'agglomération de Montréal* (Montreal: Ville de Montréal, 2007).
36. CMM, *Charting Our International Future: A Competitive Montréal Metropolitan Region—Economic Development Plan* (Montreal: Montréal Metropolitan Community, 2005); Montreal, *Stratégie de développement économique 2005–2010 de la Ville de Montréal* (Montreal: Ville de Montréal, 2005).
37. Nancy Neamtan, Le chantier de l'économie sociale: Un bilan, in *Objectif plein-emploi: Le marché, la social-démocratie ou l'économie sociale?*, ed. Diane-Gabriel Tremblay, 157–66 (Ste-Foy: Presses de l'Université du Québec, 1998).
38. Jean-Marc Fontan, Pierre Hamel, Richard Morin, and Eric Shragge, The Institutionalization of Montréal's CEDECs: From Grassroots Organizations to State Apparatus, *Canadian Journal of Urban Research* 12:1 (2003): 58–76; ASSSM, various documents on climate change, sustainable development, transport, urban planning and health, 2007, consulted at http://www.santepubmtl.qc.ca/Environnement/index.html and http://www.santepubmtl.qc.ca/Publication/environpub.html; MESSF, *Le plan d'action gouvernemental en matière d'action communautaire* (Quebec: Ministère de l'Emploi, de la Solidarité Sociale et de la Famille, 2004). See also Comité Aviseur de l'Action Communautaire Autonome, *Dix ans de luttes pour la reconnaissance* (Montreal: Comité Aviseur de l'Action Communautaire Autonome, 2006); D. Lidstone, *Assessment of the Municipal Acts of the Provinces and Territories* (Ottawa: Federation of Canadian Municipalities, 2004); RESO, *Fonds d'économie sociale du sud-ouest* (Montreal: Regroupement Economique et Social du Sud-Ouest, 2007); J. Wolch, Green Urban Worlds, *Annals of the American Association of Geographers* 97:2 (2007): 373–84.
39. Montreal, *Intégrer des critères de développement durable dans les processus décisionnels et l'achat de biens et de services* (Montreal: Ville de Montréal, 2007); Montreal, *Quelques tendances dans l'amélioration de l'efficacité énergétique des véhicules* (Montreal: Ville de Montréal, 2005); Montreal, *Plan d'action corporatif: Pour préserver le climat* (Montreal: Ville de Montréal, 2007); Montreal, *Projection des grands postes de revenus et dépenses et grands enjeux sur un horizon de 7 ans* (Montreal: Ville de Montréal, 2007).
40. Montreal, *Premier plan stratégique de développement durable de la collectivité Montréalaise* (Montreal: Ville de Montréal, 2005); Montreal, *Les bâtiments verts ont la cote* (Montreal: Ville de Montréal, 2006); Montreal, *Quelques tendances dans l'amélioration de l'efficacité énergétique des véhicules* (Montreal: Ville de Montréal, 2005); Montreal, *Des mesures pour réduire les émissions de GES dans les déplacements d'affaires* (Montreal: Ville de Montréal, 2006); Montreal, *Les économies d'eau potable: Une responsabilité individuelle et collective* (Montreal: Ville de Montréal, 2006); Montreal, *Mieux gérer les déchets dans les industries, commerces et institutions (ICI)* (Montreal: Ville de Montréal, 2006).
41. The university has declared its commitment to making its two campuses "welcoming places, fully accessible and safe for pedestrians, persons with disabilities, and cyclists," and to ensuring that "future development will be carried out in accordance with principles of sustainability, respectful of the environment and the need to preserve natural resources" (McGill University, *University Master Plan: Guiding Principles* [Montreal: McGill University, 2005]).
42. RRSSS—*Montréal, Urban Health: A Vital Factor in Montreal's Development (2002 Annual Report on the Health of the Population)* (Montreal: Régie Régional de Santé et des Services Sociaux de Montréal Centre, Direction de la Santé Publique, 2002); CRE—Montréal, *Projet de lutte aux îlots de chaleur urbains: Les outils développés pour sensibiliser et faciliter l'action de verdissement* (Montreal: Conseil Régional de l'Environnement de Montréal, 2007); Montreal, *La politique de l'arbre de Montréal* (Montreal:

Ville de Montréal, 2005); Montreal, *Policy on the Protection and Enhancement of Natural Habitats of Montreal: Results to Date and Current Priorities* (Montreal: Ville de Montréal, 2006); St. Lawrence Plan, *The St. Lawrence Plan for a Sustainable Development 2005–2010* (Ottawa: Environment Canada, Fisheries and Oceans Canada / Ministère du Développement Durable, de l'Environnement et des Parcs, 2005).

43. Montreal, *Charte du piéton: Document de consultation* (Montreal: Ville de Montréal, 2006). The document issued for public consultation was subsequently adopted as part of the overall transportation plan of the city.
44. Tim B. Wheeler, Smart Growth Policy Defended, *Baltimore Sun*, October 4, 2007.
45. Ray Tomalty and Don Alexander, *Smart Growth in Canada: Implementation of a Planning Concept* (Ottawa: Canada Mortgage and Housing Corp., 2005).
46. For a summary of the findings of the Tomalty and Alexander study, see also Fanis Grammenos, The Smart Growth Gap, *Plan Canada* 47:2 (2007): 41–44.
47. Montreal, *Policy on the Protection and Enhancement of Natural Habitats of Montreal: Results to Date and Current Priorities* (Montreal: Ville de Montréal, 2006), 2.
48. Montreal, *Qualité de l'air à Montréal—Rapport annuel 2006* (Montreal: Ville de Montréal, 2007).
49. Montreal, *Qualité des cours d'eau de Montréal—Rapport annuel 2007* (Montreal: Ville de Montréal, 2008).
50. Jean Boivin, Gilles Sénécal, Pierre J. Hamel, and Ludovic Guerpillon, *Évolution des surfaces boisées et des espaces verts dans la région métropolitaine de Montréal* (Montreal: INRS—Urbanisation, Culture et Société & Intélec Géomatique, 2002).
51. CMM, *Portrait du Grand Montréal, Édition 2010, Cahiers Métropolitains* (December 2010); CPTA, *Les enjeux de la protection du territoire agricole dans la région de Montréal après 25 ans de zonage agricole—Rapport annuel de gestion 2003–2004, document complementaire* (Quebec: Commission de Protection du Territoire Agricole du Québec, 2004); Linda Gyulai, City Recycling Takes a Turn for the Better, The Montreal *Gazette*, March 29, 2008. See also Montreal, *Le plan métropolitain de gestion des matières résiduelles du grand Montréal* (Montreal: Ville de Montréal, 2007).
52. Ray Tomalty, *The Compact Metropolis: Growth Management and Intensification in Vancouver, Toronto, and Montreal* (Toronto: ICURR Press, 1997); Louise Leduc, Les québécois sont sensibilisés, *La Presse*, March 31, 2008; Kevin Stolarick, Richard Florida, and Louis Musante, *Montreal's Capacity for Creative Connectivity: Outlook and Opportunities* (Montreal: Culture Montréal, 2005).
53. CMM, *Vision 2025—Cap sur le monde: Bâtir une communauté compétitive, attractive, solidaire et responsable* (Montreal: Communauté Métropolitaine de Montréal, 2002); CMHC, *CHS—Residential Building Activity: Dwelling Starts, Completions, Under Construction and Newly Completed and Unabsorbed Dwellings, 2006* (Ottawa: Canada Mortgage and Housing Corp., 2007), table 3; Elizabeth Thompson, French No Boon for Allophones: Study, The Montreal *Gazette*, April 14, 2008.
54. Enid Slack, *Fiscal Imbalance: The Case for Cities* (Toronto: Institute on Municipal Finance and Governance, Munk Centre for International Studies, University of Toronto, 2006).
55. *La Presse*, Le nouveau visage de la banlieue (dossier), October 12, 2007, A2–A5; Larry S. Bourne, The Urban Sprawl Debate: Myths, Realities and Hidden Agendas, *Plan Canada* 41:4 (2001): 26–28; CMHC, *CHS—Residential Building Activity: Dwelling Starts, Completions, Under Construction and Newly Completed and Unabsorbed Dwellings, 2010* (Ottawa: Canada Mortgage and Housing Corp., 2011), table 10.
56. Claude Picher, L'hémorragie, *La Presse (Affaires)*, June 12, 2008.
57. Enid Slack, *Fiscal Imbalance: The Case for Cities* (Toronto: Institute on Municipal Finance and Governance, Munk Centre for International Studies, University of Toronto, 2006); Montreal, *Vos taxes 2007: Immeubles toutes catégories* (pamphlet included with tax bills) (Montreal: Ville de Montréal, 2007); Montreal, *Sustainable Solutions for Montréal* (Montreal: Ville de Montréal, 2007), 1.

REFERENCES

Agence de Santé et des Services Sociaux de Montréal. Various Documents: Climate Change, Sustainable Development, Forum Transport, *Aménagement urbain et santé*, May 2006. Montreal: ASSSM, 2007. http://www.santepubmtl.qc.ca/Environnement/index.html.

Aubin, H. Editorial. The Montreal *Gazette*, July 21, 2007.

Boivin, J., G. Sénécal, P. J. Hamel and L. Guerpillon. *Évolution des surfaces boisées et des espaces verts dans la région métropolitaine de Montréal.* Montreal: Institut National de la Recherche Scientifique-Urbanisation, 2002. http://www.vrm.ca.

World Commission on Environment and Development. *Our Common Future* (Brundtland Report). Oxford: Oxford University Press, 1987.

Bourne, L. S. The Urban Sprawl Debate: Myths, Realities and Hidden Agendas. *Plan Canada* 41:4 (2001): 26–28.

Buttle, J., T. Muir, and J. Frain. Economic Impacts of Climate Change on the Canadian Great Lakes Hydro-Electric Power Producers: A Supply Analysis. *Canadian Water Resources Journal* 29:2 (2004): 89–110.

Canada. *Climate Change Plan for Canada.* 2002. http://www.climatechangegc.ca/plan_for_canada/index.html.

Canada. *Turning the Corner: An Action Plan to Reduce Greenhouse Gases and Air Pollution.* Ottawa: Environment Canada, 2007. http://www.ecoaction.gc.ca/news-nouvels/20070426-eng.cfm.

Canadian Climate Impacts and Adaptation Network. *Adapting to Climate Change: An Introduction for Canadian Municipalities.* Ottawa: C-CIARN, February 2006. http://www.c-ciarn.ca/adapting_e.html.

Charbonneau, F., P. Hamel, and M. Barcelo. Urban Sprawl in the Montréal Area—Policies and Trends, in *The Changing Canadian Metropolis: A Public Policy Perspective,* vol. 2, ed. Frances Frisken, 459–95. Berkeley: Institute of Governmental Studies Press, University of California and Toronto: Canadian Urban Institute, 1994.

Canada Mortgage and Housing Corporation. *CHS—Residential Building Activity: Dwelling Starts, Completions, Under Construction and Newly Completed and Unabsorbed Dwellings—2006.* Ottawa: CMHC, 2007.

Communauté métropolitaine de Montréal. *Cap sur le monde: Bâtir une communauté compétitive, attractive, solidaire et responsable.* Tome 1: *Diagnostic et défis.* Montreal: Communauté métropolitaine de Montréal / CMM and Ministère des Affaires municipales et des Régions et Ministère de l'Environnement, 2002.

———. *Cap sur le monde: pour une region métropolitaine de Montréal attractive. Projet de schéma métropolitain d'aménagement et de développement.* CMM and Ministère des Affaires municipales et des Régions et Ministère de l'Environnement, 2005. http://www.cmm.qc.ca/index.php?id=8.

———. *Charting Our International Future: A Competitive Montréal Metropolitan Region. Economic Development Plan.* CMM and Ministère des Affaires municipales et des Régions et Ministère de l'Environnement, 2005. http://www.cmm.qc.ca/index.php?id=316.

———. *Entente de Communauté sur le développement durable: Un nouveau partenariat Québec/Communauté métropolitaine de Montréal.* Montreal: CMM and Ministère des Affaires municipales et des Régions et Ministère de l'Environnement, 2002. http://www.cmm.qc.ca/index.php?id=216.

———. *Orientations de la CMM en matière de logement social et abordable.* CMM and Ministère des Affaires municipales et des Régions et Ministère de l'Environnement, 2002. http://www.cmm.qc.ca/index.php?id=143.

———. *Plan métropolitain de gestion des matières résiduelles.* Montreal: CMM and Ministère des Affaires municipales et des Régions et Ministère de l'Environnement, 2006. http://www.cmm.qc.ca/index.php?id=143.

———. *Perspective Grand Montréal* 2:1 (January 2008).

———. *Plan métropolitain d'aménagement et de développement.* Montreal: Communauté Métropolitaine de Montréal, 2011.

———. *Portrait du Grand Montreal, Édition 2010, Cahiers Métropolitains* (December 2010).

———. *Projet de règlement sur le contrôle des déversements d'eaux usées dans les ouvrages d'assainissement et cours d'eau.* Montreal: CMM and Ministère des Affaires municipales et des Régions et Ministère de l'Environnement, 2007. http://www.cmm.qc.ca/index.php?id=143.

———. *Vision 2025. Charting Our International Future: Building a Competitive, Attractive, Interdependent and Responsible Community. Strategic Vision Statement.* Montreal: CMM and Ministère des Affaires municipales et des Régions et Ministère de l'Environnement, 2003. http://cmm.qc.ca/index.php?id=323&type=98&cond=&cond2=&sujet=&typedoc=&tx_ttnews[tt_news]=&tx_ttnews[pS]=&tx_ttnews[pL]=&tx_ttnews[arc]=&tx_ttnews[pointer]=}&pageNum.

CPTA. *Les enjeux de la protection du territoire agricole dans la région de Montréal après 25 ans de zonage agricole. Rapport annuel de gestion 2003–2004, Document complementaire.* Quebec: La Commission de protection du territoire agricole du Québec, 2004. http://www.cptaq.gouv.qc.ca/fileadmin/doc/pdf/publications/rannuel/rap_annuel2003–2004/enjeux7.html.

Collin, J.-P., and Robertson, M. The Borough System of Consolidated Montreal: Revisiting Urban Governance in a Composite Metropolis. *Journal of Urban Affairs* 27:3 (2005): 307–34.

Conseil Régional de l'Environnement de Montréal. *Projet de lutte aux ilots de chaleur urbains. Les outils développés pour sensibiliser et faciliter l'action de verdissement.* Montreal: CRE-Montréal, 2007.

D'Arcy, P., J. F. Bibeault, and R. Raffa. *Changements climatiques et transport maritime sur le St. Laurent: Étude exploratoire d'options d'adaptation* (Réalisée pour le Comité de concertation navigation du Plan d'action St. Laurent). Ottawa: Plan St. Laurent, 2005.

Deschamps, G., J. P. Lafleur, C. Juteau, R. Mallet, and C. Tremblay. *Qualité des cours d'eau de Montreal: Rapport annuel 2006.* Montreal: Ville de Montréal, Service des Infrastructures, Transport et Environnement, Direction de l'Environnement et du Développement Durable, 2006. http://ville.Montréal.qc.ca/pls/portal/docs/page/rsma_fr/media/documents/Bilan_q_r_2006.pdf.

Domon, Gérald, Michel Gariépy, and Peter Jacobs. Développement viable en milieu urbain: Vers une stratégie de gestion des interventions. *Plan Canada* (January 1992): 4–17.

Duchemin, M., A. N. Rousseau, R. Majdoub, and R. Quilbé. Impacts des changements climatiques sur l'érosion hydrique des sols. *Vecteur Environ* 34:4 (2004): 26–32.

Faure, A. Montréal, l'île laboratoire: Les politiques publiques à l'épreuve du bien commun urbain. *Canadian Journal of Urban Research* 12:1 (2003): 35–57.

Federation of Canadian Municipalities. *Municipal Governments and Sustainable Communities: A Best Practices Guide.* Ottawa: FCM, 2006. http://www.sustainablecommunities.fcm.ca.

———. *Partners for Climate Protection.* Ottawa: FCM, 2006. http://sustainablecommunities.fcm.ca/Partners-for-Climate-Protection/.

Fontan, J.-M., P. Hamel, R. Morin, and E. Shragge. The Institutionalization of Montréal's CEDECS: From Grassroots Organizations to State Apparatus. *Canadian Journal of Urban Research* 12:1 (2003): 58–76.

Gagnon, C., C. Bessette, Y. Garneau, R. Mallet, and P. Paquette. *Qualité de l'air à Montreal: Rapport annuel 2006.* Montreal: Ville de Montréal, Service des Infrastructures, Transport et Environnement, Direction de l'Environnement et du Développement Durable, 2006. http://www.rsqa.qc.ca/framville.asp?url=framrsqf.asp.

Grammenos, F. The Smart Growth Gap. *Plan Canada* 47:2 (2007): 41–44.

Gyulai, Linda. City Recycling Takes a Turn for the Better. The Montreal *Gazette,* March 29, 2008, A7.

Intergovernmental Panel on Climate Change Secretariat. *Climate Change 2007: The Physical Science Basis. Summary for Policy Makers.* Geneva: IPCC, 2007.

Josza, A., and D. Brown. *Neighbourhood Sustainability Indicators: Report on a Best Practice Workshop.* Montreal: McGill University, School of Urban Planning and Urban Ecology Centre/SodecM, 2005.

La Presse. Le nouveau visage de la banlieue. October 12, 2007, A2–A5.

Lavoie, I., I. Laurion, A. Warren, and W. Vincent. *Les fleurs d'eau de cyanobactéries, revue de littérature.* Quebec: INRS Eau, Terre et Environnement Rapport de Recherché 916, 2007.

Leduc, Louise. Les Québécois sont sensibilisés. *La Presse,* March 31, 2008, A3.

Lidstone, D. *Assessment of the Municipal Acts of the Provinces and Territories.* Ottawa: Federation of Canadian Municipalities, 2004. http://www.fcm.ca/english/documents/assess.html.

Mailhot, A., G. Rivard, S. Duchesne, and J.-P. Villeneuve. *Impacts et adaptation liés aux changements climatiques en matière de drainage urbain au Québec.* Quebec: INRS-Eau, Terre et Environnement, 2007. http://www.ouranos.ca/doc/produit_e.html.

Ministère des Affaires Municipales et de la Métropole. *Municipal Reorganization: Changing the Ways to Better Serve the Public.* Quebec: MAMM, 2000.

———. *Planning Framework and Government Orientations, Montréal Metropolitan Region 2001–2021.* Quebec: MAMM, 2001. http://www.mamr.gouv.qc.ca/publications/recherche_publications/themes.asp?noTheme=39.

Ministère des Affaires Municipales et des Régions. *Agenda 21 local, schéma d'aménagement et de développement et plan d'urbanisme:trois outils d'une même démarche?* Quebec: MAMR, 2007. http://www.mamr.gouv.qc.ca/publications/recherche_publications/themes.asp?noTheme=39.

———. *La réduction des émissions de gaz à effet de serre et l'aménagement du territoire—Faits saillants–Fiche d'information.* Quebec: MAMR, 2005. http://www.mamr.gouv.qc.ca/publications/recherche_publications/themes.asp?noTheme=39.

———. *Reduction of Greenhouse Gas Emissions and Land Use Planning—Best Practices Guide.* Quebec: MAMR, 2004. http://www.mamr.gouv.qc.ca/publications/recherche_publications/themes.asp?noTheme=39.

McGill University. University Master Plan: Guiding Principles. Montreal: McGill University, 2005. http://www.mcgill.ca/masterplan/principles.

Ministère du Développement Durable, de l'Environnement et des Parcs. *Bilan de la première année du plan d'action québécois 2006–2012.* Quebec: MDDEP, 2007. http://www.mddep.gouv.qc.ca/changements/plan_action/index.htm, 28.

———. *Plan de développement durable (document de consultation)*. Quebec: MDDEP, 2004. http://www.menv.gouv.qc.ca/developpement/inter.htm.

———. *Québec and Climate Change—A Challenge for the Future. Action Plan 2006–2012*. Quebec: MDDEP, 2006. http://www.menv.gouv.qc.ca/changements/plan_action/2006-2012_en.pdf.

———. *Rapport annuel 2004–2005 sur la mise en œuvre de la stratégie et plan d'action québécois sur la diversité biologique 2004–2007*. Quebec: MDDEP, 2006. http://www.menv.gouv.qc.ca/biodiversite/voir.htm.

———. *Stratégie québécoise sur les aires protégées: Plan d'action stratégique*. Quebec: MDDEP, 2000. http://www.menv.gouv.qc.ca/biodiversite/aires_protegees/index.htm.

———. *Stratégie québécoise sur les aires protégées: Plan d'action stratégique. Premiers résultats* Quebec: MDDEP, 2002. http://www.menv.gouv.qc.ca/biodiversite/aires_protegees/index.htm.

———. *Stratégie et Plan d'action québécois sur la diversité biologique 2004–2007*. Quebec: MDDEP, 2004. http://www.menv.gouv.qc.ca/biodiversite/inter.htm.

Ministère du Développement économique, de l'Innovation et de l'Exportation. *Ministère du Développement économique, de l'innovation et de l'exportation: Plan stratégique 2005–2008*. Quebec: MDEIE, 2005. http://www.mdeie.gouv.qc.ca/page/web/portail/exportation/nav/publications.html?&page=details_publication.jsp&iddoc=64171.

Mehdi, Bano, ed. *Adapting to Climate Change: An Introduction for Canadian Municipalities*. Ottawa: Canadian Climate Impacts and Adaptation Network, 2006. http://www.c-ciarn.ca/adapting_e.html.

Ministère de l'Emploi, de la Solidarité Sociale et de la Famille. *Le Plan d'action gouvernemental en matière d'action communautaire*. Quebec: MESSF, 2004. http://www.mess.gouv.qc.ca/saca/action-communautaire/plan-action.asp.

Ministère des Ressources Naturelles et de la Faune. *L'énergie pour construire le Québec de demain: La stratégie énergétique du Québec 2006–2015*. Quebec: MRNF, 2006. http://www.aee.gouv.qc.ca/innovations/promotion/projets/projets.jsp.

Montreal. Montreal: Ville de Montréal, Développement Durable, Dossiers Thématiques, 2006. http://ville.Montréal.qc.ca/portal/page?_pageid=736,10105648&_dad=portal&_schema=PORTAL.

———. *Bilan économique 2006 de l'agglomération de Montréal*. Montreal: Ville de Montréal, 2007. http://ville.Montréal.qc.ca/portal/page?_pageid=65,3929842&_dad=portal&_schema=PORTAL.

———. *The Challenge of Participation: Montréal's Public Consultation and Participation Policy*. Montreal: Ville de Montréal, 2003. http://ville.Montréal.qc.ca/pls/portal/docs/page/Bureau_Du_Maire_En/media/documents/consultation_participation_en.pdf.

———. *Charte du piéton: Document de consultation*. Montreal: Ville de Montréal, 2006. http://ville.montreal.qc.ca/pls/portal/docs/page/transport_v2_fr/media/documents/Charte_pieton.pdf.

———. *La Charte montréalaise des droits et responsabilités*. Montreal: Ville de Montréal, 2006. http://ville.Montréal.qc.ca/portal/page?_pageid=65,48130&_dad=portal&_schema=PORTAL.

———. *Déclaration de Montréal pour la diversité culturelle et l'inclusion*. Montreal: Ville de Montréal, 2004. http://ville.Montréal.qc.ca/portal/page?_pageid=65,401435&_dad=portal&_schema=PORTAL.

———. *Les économies d'eau potable: Une responsabilité individuelle et collective*. Montreal: Ville de Montréal, Développement Durable, Dossiers Thématiques, 2006. http://ville.Montréal.qc.ca/portal/page?_pageid=736,10105584&_dad=portal&_schema=PORTAL.

———. *Imaginer—Réaliser Montréal 2025*. Montreal: Ville de Montréal, 2002.

———. *Des mesures pour réduire les émissions de GES dans les déplacements d'affaires*. Montreal: Ville de Montréal, Développement Durable, Dossiers Thématiques, 2006. http://ville.Montréal.qc.ca/portal/page?_pageid=736,10105579&_dad=portal&_schema=PORTAL.

———. *Mieux gérer les déchets dans les industries, commerces et institutions (ICI)*. Montreal: Ville de Montréal, Développement Durable, Dossiers Thématiques, 2006. http://ville.Montréal.qc.ca/portal/page?_pageid=736,10105574&_dad=portal&_schema=PORTAL.

———. *Montréal Adopts Its Vision of the Future with the Master Plan*. Montreal: Ville de Montréal, 2004. English summary. http://ville.Montréal.qc.ca/pls/portal/docs/page/plan_urbanisme_en/media/documents/041200_summary_plan_en.pdf.

———. *Montréal passe à l'ère des Quartiers 21*. Montreal: Ville de Montréal, 2005. Communiqué 2005:10:20.

———. *Plan d'action corporatif: Pour préserver le climat*. Montreal: Ville de Montréal, 2007. http://ville.Montréal.qc.ca/portal/page?_pageid=916,1615443&_dad=portal&_schema=PORTAL.

———. *Le Plan d'urbanisme*. Montreal: Ville de Montréal, Service d'Urbanisme, 2004. http://ville.Montréal.qc.ca/portal/page?_pageid=2761,3098694&_dad=portal&_schema=PORTAL.

———. *Policy on the Protection and Enhancement of Natural Habitats of Montreal: Results to Date and Current Priorities.* Montreal: Ville de Montréal, 2006. http://ville.Montréal.qc.ca/portal/page?_dad=portal&_pageid=174,1181440&_schema=PORTAL.

———. *Politique de développement culturel de la Ville de Montréal 2005–2015.* Montreal: Ville de Montréal, 2005. http://ville.Montréal.qc.ca/portal/page?_pageid=1576,1746206&_dad=portal&_schema=PORTAL.

———. *La Politique de l'arbre de Montréal.* Montreal: Ville de Montréal, 2005. http://ville.Montréal.qc.ca/pls/portal/docs/page/conseil_patrimoine_mtl_fr/media/documents/politique_arbre.pdf.

———. *Politique du Patrimoine.* Montreal: Ville de Montréal, 2005. http://ville.Montréal.qc.ca/pls/portal/docs/page/patrimoine_urbain_fr/media/documents/politique.pdf.

———. *Pour relancer la Métropole: Des solutions nouvelles et durables.* Montreal: Ville de Montréal, 2007. http://ville.Montréal.qc.ca/portal/page?_pageid=162,301525&_dad=portal&_schema=PORTAL.

———. *Poursuivons le virage de l'accessibilité universelle.* Montreal: Ville de Montréal, 2006. http://servicesenligne2.ville.Montréal.qc.ca/sel/publications/htdocs/porteaccespublication_Fr/porteaccespublication.jsp?systemName=3902047.

———. *Premier plan stratégique de développement durable de la collectivité montréalaise.* Montreal: Ville de Montréal, 2005. http://ville.Montréal.qc.ca/portal/page?_pageid=736,4732369&_dad=portal&_schema=PORTAL.

———. *Premier plan stratégique de développement durable de la collectivité montréalaise—Phase 2007–2009.* Montreal: Ville de Montréal, 2007. http://ville.Montréal.qc.ca/portal/page?_pageid=736,4732369&_dad=portal&_schema=PORTAL.

———. "Priorité au transport collectif et actif, Montréal se dote d'un premier plan de transport ambitieux." Press release from the Mayor's office and the Executive Committee, May 17, 2007. Montreal: Ville de Montréal, 2007.

———. *Quelques tendances dans l'amélioration de l'efficacité énergétique des véhicules.* Montreal: Ville de Montréal, Développement Durable, Dossiers Thématiques, 2005. http://ville.Montréal.qc.ca/portal/page?_pageid=736,10105651&_dad=portal&_schema=PORTAL.

———. *Réinventer Montréal. Plan de transport 2007—Document de consultation.* Montreal: Ville de Montréal, 2007. http://ville.Montréal.qc.ca/portal/page?_pageid=4577,7761568&_dad=portal&_schema=PORTAL.

———. *Le Sommet de Montréal.* Montreal: Ville de Montréal, 2002. http://ville.Montréal.qc.ca/portal/page?_pageid=2137,2657439&_dad=portal&_schema=PORTAL.

———. *Sommet de Montréal 2002:Bilan des réalisations 2002–2005.* Montreal: Ville de Montréal, 2005. http://ville.Montréal.qc.ca/portal/page?_pageid=2137,2656577&_dad=portal&_schema=PORTAL.

———. *Stratégie de développement économique 2005–2010 de la Ville de Montréal.* Montreal: Ville de Montréal, 2005. http://ville.Montréal.qc.ca/portal/page?_pageid=65,3929842&_dad=portal&_schema=PORTAL.

———. *Stratégie d'inclusion de logements abordables—Habiter Montréal* Montreal: Ville de Montréal, 2005. http://servicesenligne2.ville.Montréal.qc.ca/sel/publications/htdocs/porteaccespublication_Fr/porteaccespublication.jsp?systemName=4795969.

———. *Stratégie d'inclusion de logements abordables dans les nouveaux projets résidentiels: Avancement de sa mise en œuvre.* Montreal: Ville de Montréal, 2007. http://servicesenligne2.ville.Montréal.qc.ca/sel/publications/htdocs/porteaccespublication_Fr/porteaccespublication.jsp?systemName=9771578.

———. *Sustainable Solutions for Montréal.* Montreal: Ville de Montréal, 2007.

———. "Vos taxes 2007: Immeubles toutes catégories" (pamphlet included with tax bills). Montreal: Ville de Montréal, 2007.

———. *La Ville de Montréal et les personnes handicapées et les personnes à mobilité réduite.* Montreal: Ville de Montréal, 2000. http://servicesenligne2.ville.Montréal.qc.ca/sel/publications/PorteAccesTelechargement?lng=Fr&systemName=2729584&client=Serv_corp.

Montréal. *Intégrer des critères de développement durable dans les processus décisionnels et l'achat de biens et de services.* Montreal: Ville de Montréal, Développement Durable, Dossiers Thématiques, 2007. http://ville.Montréal.qc.ca/portal/page?_pageid=736,4733137&_dad=portal&_schema=PORTAL.

———. *Montréal, ville de familles. Cadre de référence de la Politique familiale de la Ville de Montréal.* Montreal: Ville de Montréal, 2007. http://ville.montreal.qc.ca/pls/portal/docs/page/librairie_fr/documents/cadre_de_reference.pdf.

———. *Plan d'action de la Ville de Montréal en matière d'accessibilité universelle et Bilan 2006.* Montreal: Ville de Montréal, Service du Développement

Culture, de la Qualité du Milieu de Vie et de la Diversité Ethnoculturelle, 2007. https://servicesenligne2.ville.montreal.qc.ca/sel/publications/PorteAccesTelechargement?lng=Fr&systemName=9819561&client=Serv_corp.

———. *Le Plan métropolitain de gestion des matières résiduelles du Grand Montréal.* Montreal: Ville de Montréal, Développement Durable, Dossiers Thématiques, 2007. http://ville.Montréal.qc.ca/portal/page?_pageid=736,11173613&_dad=portal&_schema=PORTAL.

———. *Politique pour un environnement paisible et sécuritaire à Montréal. Montreal:* Ville de Montréal, Service des Communication et des Relations Avec les Citoyens, 2008. https://servicesenligne2.ville.montreal.qc.ca/sel/publications/PorteAccesTelechargement?lng=Fr&systemName=15339811&client=Serv_corp.

———. *Politique pour une participation égalitaire des femmes et des hommes à la vie de Montréal.* Montreal: Ville de Montréal, Service des Communications et des Relations Avec les Citoyens, 2008. https://servicesenligne2.ville.montreal.qc.ca/sel/publications/PorteAccesTelechargement?lng=Fr&systemName=15935576&client=Serv_corp.

———. *Projection des grands postes de revenus et dépenses et grands enjeux sur un horizon de 7 ans.* Montreal: Ville de Montréal, 2007. http://ville.Montréal.qc.ca/portal/page?_pageid=162,301525&_dad=portal&_schema=PORTAL.

———. *Projet de plan directeur de gestion des matières résiduelles de l'agglomération de Montréal, 2008–2012.* Montreal: Ville de Montréal, Service des Infrastructures, Transport et Environnement, 2008. http://ville.montreal.qc.ca/pls/portal/docs/page/Environnement_Fr/media/documents/PDGMR_final.pdf.

Montréal Stock Exchange. Montreal Exchange Files for Regulatory Approval of Market Rules for Trading of MCeX Environmental Products (press release). Montreal: Montréal Stock Exchange, 2007. http://m-x.ca/f_comm_press_en/29–07_en.pdf.

Neamtan, Nancy. Le Chantier de l'économie sociale: Un bilan, in *Objectif Plein-Emploi: Le marché, la social-démocratie ou l'économie sociale?* ed. Diane-Gabriel Tremblay, 157–66. Ste-Foy: Presses de l'Université du Québec, 1998.

Natural Resources Canada. *Climate Change Impacts and Adaptation: A Canadian Perspective.* Ottawa: NRCAN, Climate Change Impacts and Adaptation Directorate, 2004. http://adaptation.nrcan.gc.ca/perspective_e.asp.

National Round Table on the Environment and the Economy. *Advice on a Long-term Strategy on Energy and Climate Change.* Ottawa: NRTEE, 2006. http://www.nrtee-trnee.ca/.

———. *Environmental Quality in Canadian Cities: The Federal Role.* Ottawa: NRTEE, 2003. http://www.nrtee-trnee.ca/.

Ouranos. *S'adapter aux changements climatiques.* Montreal: Ouranos, 2004. http://www.ouranos.ca/intro/changclim9.pdf.

Perron, Alain. *Un premier budget participatif positif, Le Plateau.* Montreal: Arrondissement du Plateau Mont-Royal, 2006.

Picher, Claude. L'hémorragie. *La Presse (Affaires),* April 12, 2008, 5.

Plan Canada. Planning for Uneven Urban Growth (thematic issue) 47:2 (summer 2007).

Premil, S., F. Bertrand, A. Smargiassi, and M. Daniel. Socio-economic Correlates of Municipal-Level Pollution Emissions on Montréal Island. *Canadian Journal of Public Health* 98:2 (2007): 138–42.

Robert, B., S. Forget, and J. Rousselle. The Effectiveness of Flood Damage Reduction Measures in the Montréal Region, *Natural Hazards* 28:2–3 (2003): 367–85.

Regroupement Economique et Social du Sud-Ouest. *Fonds d'économie sociale du Sud-Ouest.* Montreal: RESO, 2007. http://www.resomtl.com/fr/default.aspx?sortcode=1.4.10.

———. *Plan d'action local pour l'économie et l'emploi 2007–2010 (PALÉE).* Montreal: Regroupement économique et social du Sud-Ouest, 2007. http://www.resomtl.com/fr/accueil.aspx.

RRSSS-Montréal. *Urban Health: A Vital Factor in Montréal's Development* (2002 Annual Report on the Health of the Population). Montreal: Régie Régional de Santé et des Services Sociaux de Montréal Centre, Direction de la Santé publique, 2002.

Rousseau, A. N. Gestion de l'eau dans la région sud du Québec—Impacts appréhendés et stratégies d'adaptation, in Ouranos, *S'adapter aux changements climatique,* 43–45. Montréal: Bibliothèque nationales du Québec, 2004.

Rousseau, A. N., A. Mailhot, M. Slivitzky, J. P. Villeneuve, M. J. Rodriguez, and A. Bourque. Usages et approvisionnement en eau dans le sud du Quebec: Niveau des connaissances et axes de recherche à privilégier dans une perspective de changements climatiques. *Canadian Water Resources Journal* 29:2 (2004): 121–34.

Sénécal, G. Montréal's Éco-quartier Environmental Program: Local Action and Municipal Management. *Environmental Management* 30:1 (2002): 46–58.

Sénécal, G., R. Haf, P. J. Hamel, C. Poitras, M. Ponton, D. Saint-Laurent, and N. Vachon, with J. Archambault.

Le Portrait environnemental de l'ile de Montréal au regard de la durabilité urbaine. Montreal: INRS-Urbanisation, pour le Comité environnement du Conseil Régional de Développement de l'île de Montréal, 1999. http://www.vrm.ca.

Sénécal, G., R. Haf, P. J. Hamel, C. Poitras, and N. Vachon. La forme de l'agglomération montréalaise et la réduction des gaz à effet de serre: La polycentricité est-elle durable? *Revue Canadienne de Sciences Régionales* 2:2 (2002): 135–52.

———. La forme de l'agglomération montréalaise et la réduction des gaz à effet de serre: La polycentricité est-elle durable? *Revue Canadienne de Sciences Régionales* 25:2 (2002): 135–52.

Sénécal, G., P. J. Hamel, R. Haf, C. Poitras, N. Vachon, with J. Archambault and J. Mongeau. *L'étude sur la problématique québécoise concernant l'aménagement du territoire et les changements climatiques.* Montreal: INRS-Urbanisation, 2000. http://www.vrm.ca.

Sénécal, G., D. Latouche, G. Côté, and S. Reyburn 2002. La compétitivité durable des métropoles: Le facteur de la mobilité. Montreal: INRS-Urbanisation. http://www.vrm.ca.

Sénécal, G., and D. Saint-Laurent. *Les espaces dégradés, Contraintes et conquêtes.* Sainte-Foy: Presses de l'Université du Québec, 2000.

Simmons, J., and L. Bourne. Living with Population Growth and Decline. *Plan Canada* 47:2 (2007): 13–21.

Slack, Enid. Fiscal Imbalance: The Case for Cities. Unpublished paper. Toronto: Institute on Municipal Finance and Governance, Munk Centre for International Studies, University of Toronto, 2006. http://www.utoronto.ca/mcis/imfg/pdf/municipal percent20fisal percent20imbalance percent20paper percent20Jun percent2006.pdf.

SLP. *The St. Lawrence Plan for a Sustainable Development 2005–2010.* Ottawa: Environment Canada and Fisheries and Oceans Canada / Ministère du Développement Durable, de l'Environnement et des Parcs, 2005. http://www.planstlaurent.qc.ca.

Sotomayor, E., and M. Lacombe. *Dix ans de luttes pour la reconnaissance.* Montreal: Comité Aviseur de l'Action Communautaire, 2006.

Statistics Canada. Study: Canada's Immigrant Labour Market, *Daily,* September 10, 2007. http://www.statcan.ca/Daily/English/070910/d070910a.htm.

Stolarick, Kevin, Richard Florida, and Louis Musante. Montreal's Capacity for Creative Connectivity: Outlook and Opportunities. Toronto: Martin Prosperity Institute, 2005. http://www.culturemontreal.ca/pdf/050127_catalytix_eng.pdf.

Thompson, Elizabeth. French No Boon for Allophones: Study. The Montreal *Gazette,* April 14, 2008. http://www.canada.com/montrealgazette/news/story.html?id=9699d0af-af72–48fb-9ae5-b9277a0f5f3e&k=36078.

Tomalty, R., and D. Alexander. *Smart Growth in Canada: Implementation of a Planning Concept.* Ottawa: Canada Mortgage and Housing Corp., 2005.

Tomalty, Ray. *The Compact Metropolis: Growth Management and Intensification in Vancouver, Toronto, and Montreal.* Toronto: ICURR Press, 1997.

Tremblay, Gérald. Allocution de Monsieur Gérald Tremblay, Maire de Montréal, Président de la Communauté métropolitaine de Montréal, lors du colloque *Réinventer Montréal* organisé dans le cadre du 30e anniversaire du Départment des études urbaines et touristiques de l'UQÀM, le jeudi 27 avril 2006. http://www.ville.montreal.qc.ca.

———. Notes pour une allocation du Maire de Montréal, Monsieur Gérald Tremblay, Sommet Immobilier de Montréal, le mercredi 29 mars 2006. http://www.ville.montreal.qc.ca.

Wolch, J. Green Urban Worlds. *Annals of the American Association of Geographers* 97:2 (2007): 373–84.

Wheeler, T. B. Smart Growth Policy Defended. *Baltimore Sun,* October 4, 2007. http://www.baltimoresun.com.

NAIRNE CAMERON / KAREN E. SMOYER-TOMIC / VLADIMIR YASENOVSKIY / CARL AMRHEIN

Oil for Food—Energy, Equity, and Evolution of Urban Supermarket Locations

AN EDMONTON, ALBERTA, CASE STUDY

This chapter explores the connections between urban sustainability and public health in the context of the physical manifestations of economic, sociocultural, and demographic processes shaping developed world cities, with a focus on a case study of supermarket access in the Canadian city of Edmonton, Alberta. Sustainability refers to the ability for both human and ecological systems to coexist and function effectively over time. Health is viewed here following the World Health Organization in terms of overall well-being, and not merely the absence of illness or infirmity. Public health is defined broadly as "the art and science of preventing disease, and protecting and promoting the health of the community."[1]

Since World War II, populations in urban areas have decentralized and services have dispersed. This chapter focuses on supermarkets—a key source of healthy food—and explores the environmental and health issues; in particular, the rise in obesity rates that have coincided with decentralization. We examine the theoretical links between sustainability, equity, efficiency, and public health and illustrate these connections in our case study. We then discuss the consequences and future implications of changes in supermarket distribution.

Over time, new health challenges arise, and in turn the means of addressing the challenges change, but the goal of public health remains "to reduce the amount of disease, premature death, and disease-produced discomfort and disability in the population."[2] For example, while early public health efforts focused on drinking water quality (which is still a concern today), new health issues continue to evolve, such as a global obesity epidemic, affected in part by behavioral factors like diet and physical activity. The World Health Organization (WHO) estimated that as of 2005 there were 1.6 billion overweight adults, 400 million of whom were obese, with the numbers continuing to increase, including among children.[3] Researchers are examining ecological factors of individual behaviors in the causal pathway for obesity, including physical activity and accessibility of food retail resources.[4] Our focus here is on human health and urban sustainability as they relate to urban sprawl and the modes of transportation used to access supermarkets, a major source of nutritious food for the majority of Canadian households.

Urbanization and Public Health

As of 2007 over half of the world's population now lives in cities, and the trend is expected to continue, with 60 percent of the global population being urban by 2030.[5] Urban life offers benefits such as social and employment opportunities and a range of services. However, dating back to the ancient city of Jericho, urban areas have exhibited a particular set of health risks, including crowding, infectious disease, wastes, social problems, and poor housing quality.[6] Cities in developed economies (the focus here) share some of these problems, but the health risks are often negative externalities arising from economic standards.

The modern public health movement began to combat infectious disease that had arisen as a result of overcrowding and poor sanitation in cities during the industrial revolution. Along with water and sewer systems, a lower density of residential living and the separation of industry and businesses from homes were advocated. This separation of land uses continues to be legally enforced in many North American jurisdictions, despite the transition to a service economy with less noxious industries. For example, the city of Edmonton's Zoning Bylaw does not permit commercial and residential uses to coincide (e.g., housing above street-level shops) in standard zoning classes. Only in certain cases can a site-specific zoning class be applied to allow for mixed uses.[7]

Following World War II, increasing car ownership, combined with automobile-centered federal and state policies and subsidies, promoted a lower density in many cities, especially in Canada and the United States. With the mushrooming demand for larger homes and properties, residential development spread out from central cities into suburbs and exurbs.

Employment centers have also dispersed. These decentralizing forces have led to complex suburb-to-suburb travel patterns and have been compounded by a higher overall number of workers and a greater number of work trips. Such trends have lengthened commuting times and contributed to greater traffic congestion, and increased overall travel time, mainly in cars.

As the decentralization of urban development has progressed and car use has increased, there has been a parallel enlargement in both the physical size and trade area of supermarkets in Edmonton and similarly across Canada and the United States, as traced by Edward Egyedy, Zy Weinberg, and Mark Epstein. Replacing small specialty stores, the modern-day supermarket debuted in the 1930s, ranging between 4,000 and 10,000 square feet. Then, in the 1950s, small neighborhood supermarkets (15,000–20,000 square feet) serving 5,000–10,000 customers were the norm. In the 1960s and 1970s larger supermarkets of 30,000–40,000 square feet with a wider product range and catering to 20,000 customers were introduced. Even bigger supermarkets, up to 50,000 square feet, emerged in the late 1970s.[8]

Then, the 1980s saw the entrance of suburban megafood stores (75,000–100,000 square feet) designed to serve a greater customer base and selling more and more nonfood products, in addition to standard groceries. Profit margins in the grocery business are extremely low, and thus a high volume of sales is required to turn a profit. These large stores with a wide product range sought to increase customer volume in the store so that the food shoppers would also purchase the higher-margin nonfood items. They also enhanced the companies' competitive edge through greater purchasing power and standardization of their store layouts, and introduction of information technologies that link directly to manufacturers across their national and international networks. With a larger scale of operation, profits could be increased through marketing the retailers' own private label products. The Edmonton megafood stores were sited in the suburbs due to the availability of large developable tracts of land with lower taxation rates and less zoning restrictions than inner-city locations. And, they were located along major travel arterials, offering easy accessibility and attracting shoppers from across the city and also from outlying regions, thus requiring large parking areas. As a result, these stores caused changes in citywide travel behavior and increases in overall traffic volumes. On an individual level, Egyedy notes that the megafood stores led Edmonton consumers to "the acceptance of travelling greater distances for food items."[9]

Thus getting out of the city, one of the advocated cures for solving health problems associated with industrialization and urban congestion, has led to unanticipated health consequences. With increasing dependency on personal automobiles for accessing jobs, schools, services, and recreation from suburban and exurban residential communities comes a suite of public health and sustainability concerns. Car use has led to traffic accident injuries and deaths, respiratory illnesses and mortality from increased air pollution, and less time spent walking to destinations.[10]

In a community workshop on healthy neighborhoods, representatives from a variety of Edmonton agencies and organizations noted that "residents are simply doing less and less in their own neighborhood, opting to drive elsewhere for most of their daily activities." The participants also expressed concern about "the decline in interaction between neighbors, as community meeting places such as schools and shops are either disappearing or falling into disuse in older areas and never materializing in new neighborhoods." These observations point to the link between fewer local services and increased driving. Conversely, the presence of local services, such as stores within walking distance, provides residents with the option not to drive and can result in some substitution of walking and cycling for car travel.[11]

A drive-through culture with direct automobile access to services, including coffee outlets, fast-food restaurants, banks, and pharmacies, has developed in Edmonton and in other cities across Canada. These convenience-driven facilities remove the need for occupants to ever leave their cars. The cities of Toronto and Vancouver have regulated drive-throughs near residential areas and retail areas geared toward pedestrians. Several Canadian municipalities, including Ajax, Hamilton, London, North Vancouver, and Sarnia have debated restricting new facilities due to the local traffic congestion, noise, idling-related greenhouse gas emissions, and human health effects of car exhaust, as well as the antipedestrian environment associated with drive-throughs. Some Edmonton city councilors have also discussed the possibility of regulating the practice. In June 2008, the city of Calgary voted to prohibit any new drive-through services around a light rail transit station in a South Calgary redevelopment area. City Alderman Brian Pincott commented that an eventual phase-out of drive-throughs would be beneficial for "building community again and getting people out of their cars, forcing people to interact with each other."[12]

The health effects of urban sprawl are being documented. An in-depth literature review found that there were few Canadian studies linking sprawl and health, but studies from the United States point to potential health effects of the continued sprawl of Canadian cities. Youth as well as adults living in sprawling counties in the United States have higher body mass indices (BMI) and are more likely to be obese than those in compact counties. Recent Canadian research found higher BMI scores for men (but not for women) living in sprawling metropolitan areas. A potential mechanism for these relationships is time spent traveling by car, which has been linked to obesity. For example, Lawrence Frank et al. found that the likelihood of obesity rose 6 percent for each hour of daily car travel, but decreased 4.8 percent for each .62 mile (one kilometer) of walking.[13]

Increased consumerism has coincided with dual incomes and a marked rise in female participation in the workforce over the last few decades. In Canada, the proportion of employed females aged fifteen or over rose from 42 percent to 58 percent between 1976 and 2006. Thus in many households, two or more family members commute to work with increasing travel times. These dual-income households shop less frequently than single-earner households. Also, many households stockpile food in their homes, enabled by personal vehicles to transport bulk purchases and household technologies such as freezers to store food. These hypermodern convenience devices may also decrease shopping trip frequency. So, less frequent shopping of certain segments of the population and consumers' bulk purchases may also be contributing to the trend toward new, larger automobile-accessible warehouse stores that can hold bulk product volumes. More time at work, less time at home, and rising incomes have increased the demand for household services such as prepared food. For example, the number of fast-food outlets in the United States doubled between 1972 and 1997, and the number of meals consumed outside the home continued to climb through the 1980s and 1990s, although there is some Canadian evidence from 2003 of a reversal in this trend. Consumption of processed foods, which are inexpensive, readily available, and automobile accessible, leads to poor nutrition. Overconsumption of fast-food has been linked to overweight, obesity, and other health conditions.[14]

Land use, transportation, employment patterns, and food retail trends have helped to set the conditions for a host of negative implications for urban sustainability and public health. These are manifested in part by a growing dependence on internal combustion engines, especially automobiles, which replace walking to destinations, and thus a noted decrease in physical activity.

Sustainability, Equity, and Their Links to Public Health

Equity over time is a key element of sustainable development, coined by the Brundtland Commission as "development that meets the needs of the present without compromising the ability of future generations to meet their own needs." Intergenerational equity refers to fairness *between* generations and is often related to ongoing availability of physical or natural resources. Intragenerational equity is fairness *within* a generation and is often referred to as social equity. "The social dimension is critical since the unjust society is unlikely to be sustainable in environmental or economic terms: the social tensions that are created undermine the recognition of reciprocal rights and obligations leading to environmental degradation and ultimately to political breakdown." Equity is an important consideration in both sustainability and public health.[15]

The health of a population depends on the economic, social, and biophysical environment, and thus any inequalities in accessing or participating in these environments will affect health. Health inequalities can in turn threaten the cohesion of communities. By contrast, a more egalitarian society has greater social stability and resources to work toward sustainable development, which can result in more equitable health status.[16]

While addressing social inequities was highlighted as a priority over twenty years ago in the Ottawa Charter for Health Promotion, there has been little progress in operationalizing the concept. Income inequities continue to exist between and within countries, and within cities. For example, in some American cities, there has been a "doughnut effect" whereby wealthier residents depart the inner city for the suburbs, leaving poverty, abandoned buildings, social problems, vandalism, and crime in the city centers. In general, there is less social and economic segregation within Canadian cities than American ones, but economic polarization is increasing in Canadian urban areas. Baum calls for a New Public Health to address health threats posed by social inequities and globalization.[17]

In addition to social equity, spatial equity to health promoting amenities (ranging from parks to supermarkets to health clinics) is a critical element of public health. As Baum notes: "Our problem is not insufficient food but uneven distribution; there is enough wealth to go around, but it is concentrated in the hands of a few . . . health could be more evenly distributed if only the resources that create it were." Spatial equity entails the ease with which amenities can be reached, in terms of physical distances and time, as well as social, cultural, and gender-based constraints. It also reflects the quality, quantity, and type of activities offered by the amenities. In this chapter, we are focusing on the spatial equity in accessing supermarkets by walking—a sustainable and health-promoting form of transport.[18]

Igor Vojnovic outlines five equity requirements of sustainability that are applied here to illustrate the environmental sustainability (and health benefits) of pedestrian trips compared to car use for supermarket shopping.[19] Access to supermarkets by walking would reduce fossil fuel use and thus would encourage lower resource consumption rates, and would allow the substitution of renewable human energy for nonrenewable fossil fuels (and provide the health advantage of physical activity). Walking to the supermarket would also reduce greenhouse gas emissions and pollutants from motorized vehicles. Fossil fuels are a nonrenewable resource, and as such are in limited supply. Some forecasters indicate that we have already reached "peak oil," and oil prices will increasingly rise and become unstable as they are priced relative to their scarcity.[20] When this occurs, it may encourage a higher residential density, and thus it may be profitable for the supermarkets to have a finer network of stores. Finally, having a supermarket within walking distance provides transportation and health equity, since the vast majority of the population can travel by this mode and can benefit from the physical activity that a walking trip to the supermarket entails.

Integrating walking and biking into everyday living (such as traveling to the store), termed "active transport," provides moderate physical activity without the dedication of free time that recreational sports require. In particular, active transport can yield important health benefits for the elderly, sedentary, and obese. The World Health Organization estimates that in North America, changes to the environment, such as promoting walking and biking, could reduce physical inactivity levels by 31 percent.[21]

Equity and Efficiency

Our current Western economic system allows for social and environmental costs to be externalized from business operations.[22] Globalization of business means that many stores on the local landscape are actually part of larger networks such as national and international chains. These expansive networks, plus larger stores at a city level, enable the retailers on the supply side to gain economies of scale. Efficiency is the mantra of the private sector, along with the goal to maximize profits and a focus on increasing short-term returns to shareholders. This efficiency arises not just from cost minimization but by shifting certain costs on to society. For example, the construction of large retail outlets on the perimeters of cities requires local governments to build access roads and assume road maintenance costs, as well as create and run new transit routes to reach the stores. And customers often require cars to reach the retail outlets. This shifting economic balance means that consumers and governments on the demand side are now assuming costs previously covered by the retailers.

The public sector is also concerned with efficiency, but in addition they have the added consideration of equity. Marie Truelove differentiates the two terms as follows: "efficiency refers to the distribution of services among the population and equity refers to the distribution of the effects of these services."[23] How much efficiency should be exchanged for equity? And, how can the public sector influence private sector location practices especially with national and multinational chains?

The links between urban sustainability, equity, efficiency, and public health will be elaborated through a case study of supermarket access in Edmonton, Alberta. To provide context for the case study, the next section discusses the current status of urban sustainability in Alberta and more specifically in Edmonton.

Sustainability: The Alberta and Edmonton Experience

The case study is based in Edmonton, the capital of the western prairie province of Alberta (fig. 1), and the sixth largest Census Metropolitan Area in Canada. Edmonton is a servicing, and increasingly a processing, center for oil sands operations in northern Alberta, as well as a hub for other resource industries in Canada's north. Close to three-quarters of Alberta's population is concentrated in a 249 mile (400 kilometer) corridor that runs between Edmonton and Calgary to the south. The population of Alberta grew 10.6 percent to over 3 million residents between 2001 and 2006, with the fast pace of growth stimulated by the rapidly expanding oil industry. This increased economic activity luring new workers has spurred the demand for housing and all related infrastructure and services dramatically. With few geographical barriers, and flat, easily developed land encircling many urban areas, sprawl has continued unimpeded. The province of Alberta has lagged behind other Canadian jurisdictions on the sustainability front, as noted by Alan Bolstad: "On the road toward Smart Growth, Alberta can barely make out the tail lights of provinces like B.C. and Ontario." Until recently, the province was not involved in any provincial land use planning and support for regional planning was discontinued by the Province in the mid-1990s.[24]

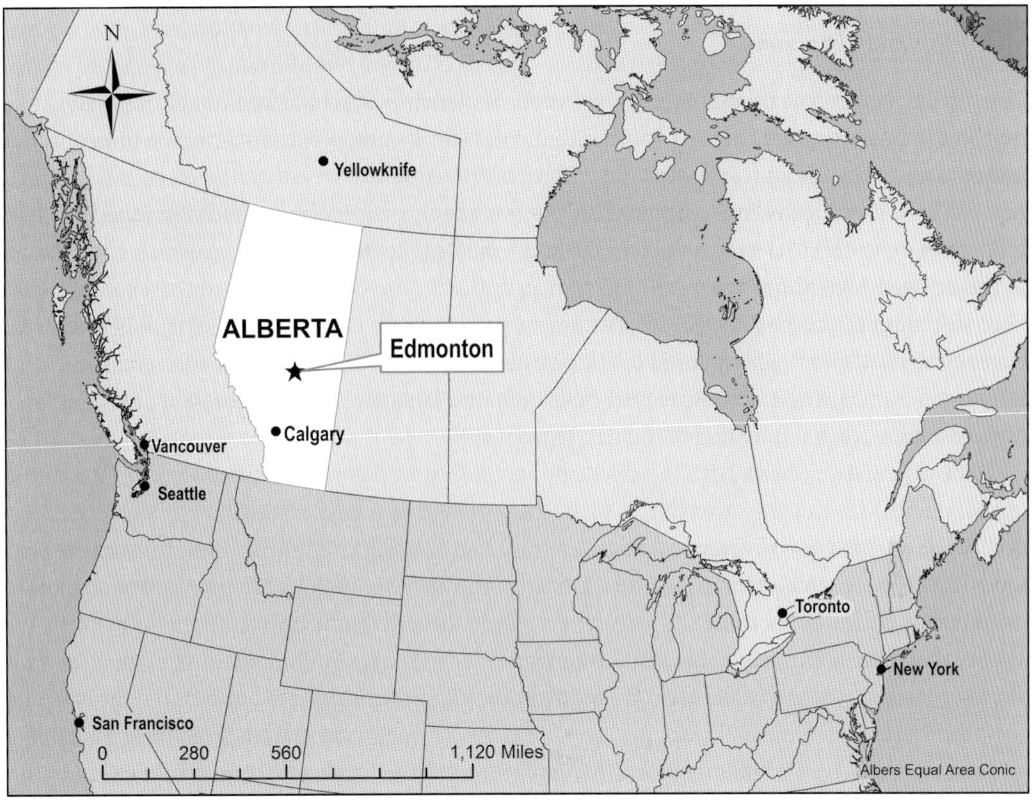

Figure 1. Location of Edmonton, Alberta.

Source: Government of Canada; Instituto Nacional de Estadística, Geografía e Informática (INEGI); U.S. Geological Survey. *North American Atlas—Political Boundaries and Populated Places*. Ottawa, Ontario, Canada; Aguascalientes, Aguascalientes, Mexico; Reston, Virginia, USA, 2006.

Since the installation of Ed Stelmach as the provincial premier in December 2006, the province has become more engaged in land use planning in an attempt to manage the rapid population growth. Two initiatives are of note. The first is the development of a provincial land-use framework. The draft framework was released in May 2008 delineating six provincial land-use zones, and recommending a cabinet committee, a land-use secretariat, regional advisory councils, and a monitoring and reporting system. The second initiative is the creation of a board made up of representatives from the city of Edmonton and surrounding municipalities to coordinate land use, road, and public transit planning in the Edmonton area.[25]

Groups active in the dialogue on urban sustainability in Alberta are the Canada-West Foundation, Alberta Urban Municipalities Association, Capital Health, social groups and environmental organizations such as Sierra Club, and innovative developers.[26]

Urban sustainability initiatives by the city of Edmonton include Smart Choices, launched in 2004. This program is similar to Smart Growth in that it promotes compact development through infill and redevelopment of commercial and industrial lands and encourages transit-oriented development and walkability. Smart Growth developments are considered to be health promoting since they have been associated with more walking and biking and less driving compared to car-oriented communities. However, Edmonton's program deviates from Smart Growth principles in that it does not specifically promote "energy efficiency of buildings; sustainable wastewater management; the development of complete and environmentally sustainable new suburban neighborhoods; the preservation of agricultural lands for local food production; the protection of natural areas; heritage conservation; and, affordable housing."[27]

While Smart Choices promotes walkability, it makes little mention of encouraging local retail and community services such as neighborhood schools or stores to which residents could walk, beyond mixed-use development around transit stations. The city has initiated a separate Walkability Strategy supported by the Smart Choices program and Capital Health that will develop a walkability plan specifically tailored to the northern climate of Edmonton. In addition, the city of Edmonton is preparing a new Municipal Development Plan slated to be released in 2008 that may include a more substantial Smart Growth component.[28]

The city of Edmonton is in the midst of expanding its light rail transit system. A 2.9 mile (4.7 kilometer) southward extension is being constructed at a cost of US$439 million (CAD$675 million, based on a 2001 currency conversion rate that is being used throughout this chapter). In June 2008, the city voted to end (by 2010) electric trolley service which had routes through mature neighborhoods and to acquire forty-seven new hybrid diesel-electric buses.[29]

Another recent initiative between the University of Alberta, Grant MacEwan College and their student unions, the city of Edmonton, and the adjoining counties of St. Albert and Strathcona, was the "U-Pass," a universal student transit pass. In September 2007, students were assigned a mandatory fee as part of their tuition that provided unlimited travel by transit in the Edmonton area during the school year.[30]

High growth, easily developed land, and the regional political environment have created prime conditions for urban sprawl in Edmonton and across Alberta, and consequently substantial urban sustainability issues. Gradually, there has been greater recognition of these challenges and some initiatives to address the issues are being launched.

Next, the connections between urban sustainability, decentralized development patterns, equity, and health are explored in a case study tracking neighborhood-level changes in Edmonton supermarket accessibility between 1970 and 2000.

Case Study: Changes in Supermarket Accessibility in Edmonton

Canadian obesity rates have increased sharply from 9.7 to 14.9 percent between 1970–1972 and 1998. Obesity is now a serious public health concern, having been linked to health conditions such as heart disease and type 2 diabetes. A nutritious diet can help prevent obesity, and access to healthy and affordable food is one of the factors that have been associated with a healthy diet. For example, Barbara Laraia et al. found that pregnant women living closer to a supermarket had a higher quality diet. Conversely, poor accessibility to healthy and low-cost food contributes to food insecurity, poor nutrition, and high-calorie consumption among vulnerable groups. Though the link between obesity and food availability and accessibility has not been fully substantiated, perhaps due to a lack of research, the existing evidence suggests an association.[31]

Almost all food access research has been cross-sectional, except for a before-after United

Kingdom neighborhood comparison by Neil Wrigley et al. and a recent study in London, Ontario, by Kristian Larsen and Jason Gilliland. This research examines how supermarket locations have changed over time. In addition, we report on qualitative research portraying a neighborhood perspective on the changing supermarket landscape.[32]

Edmonton, Alberta, has grown in population from 436,264 in 1971 to 666,104 in 2001. The city has a low-density sprawling form with a central core built around the North Saskatchewan River. Edmonton's downtown experienced a decline between the 1970s and 1990s, having few residents and high commercial vacancies, but in recent years there has been an upswing with a revitalization plan and more residents and business activity. There are 109 mature neighborhoods surrounding the downtown. These mainly residential neighborhoods were built before 1970 and the advent of traffic engineering and thus are reasonably walkable. Newer, suburban areas developed for car use lie outside the mature zone.[33]

The majority of weekday trips in Edmonton in 2005 (similar to 1994) were by car (78 percent), with only 11 percent by walking and 9 percent by transit.[34] Edmontonians are more likely to make all of their daily trips by car (as a driver or passenger) than residents of any other large Canadian census metropolitan area (Toronto, Montreal, Vancouver, Ottawa-Gatineau, Calgary, Quebec City, and Winnipeg).[35]

Market Conditions

Supermarkets are the focus of this study since they can provide healthy, low-calorie food (although they of course offer many processed, calorie-dense, and low-nutrient foods) and are currently the main retail food source for Canadians. Included in the study are chain supermarkets and banner stores, which together accounted for the majority (≥80 percent) of retail food sales over the study time period.[36]

Data

Supermarket addresses were captured from a search of historical telephone books for four time periods (1970, 1982, 1991, and 1999/2000), which roughly correspond with the years for which historical census data are available (1971, 1981, 1991, and 2001). Further refinement of the dates of store openings and closings was accomplished by consulting archival newspaper articles. The store addresses were geocoded to point locations using GeoPinpoint software. The store locations (categorized by time period) were then imported into ArcGIS 9.1.[37]

Census tracts were chosen as the unit of analysis, as they are designed to allow comparison across censuses. As population in an area increases, census tracts are divided into smaller areas with the new census tracts, including a reference to the original census tract code. Edmonton census tract cartographic boundary files by Statistics Canada (1971, 1981, 1991, and 2001) were obtained, and census tract attribute data for the same years was sourced from CHASS and E-STAT. To track changes in the number of people within walking distance of a supermarket, the number of residents of each census tract whose centroid fell within half a mile (800 meters) in Euclidean distance from a supermarket was calculated for each time period.[38]

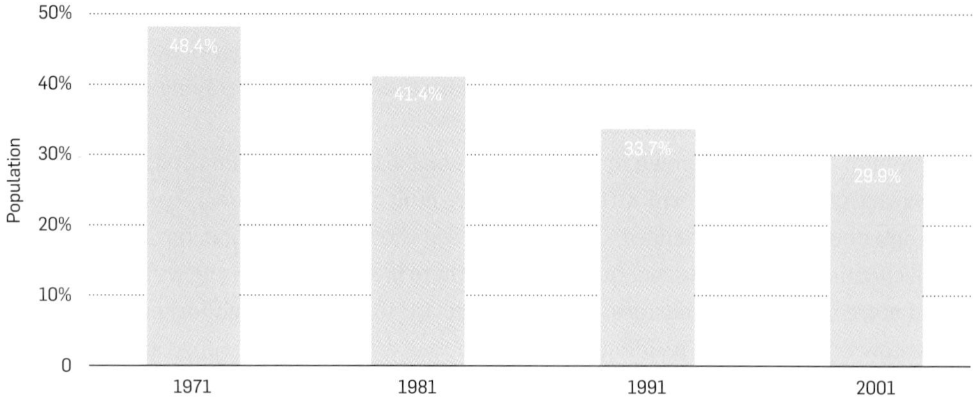

Figure 2. Percent population within walking distance of a supermarket.

RESULTS AND DISCUSSION. The percentage of the city's population within walking distance of a supermarket has steadily decreased over the study period, from 48.4 percent in 1971 to 41.4 percent in 1981, then to 33.7 percent in 1991, and finally to 29.9 percent in 2001 (fig.2). A progressive dispersion outward from the central city with increasing spacing between supermarkets is evident between 1971 and 2001, as illustrated in figures 3–6. This trend is consistent with Canadian statistics that reveal an increase of 40 percent in supermarket size between 1991 and 1996, and a 15 percent decrease in the number of grocery outlets (excluding specialty stores) between 1989 and 1997 due to the closure of smaller independent stores. A Vancouver study documents this trend of supermarkets becoming larger and trade areas for supermarkets increasing to draw shoppers from greater distances. The car has enabled trade area expansion, and consumers have been attracted to the larger stores by the choices offered and lower prices.[39]

Between 1998 and 2004, Canadian food stores expanded their offerings, catering to one-stop shoppers. Over this time period, they maintained their market share of consumer food spending mainly through sales of health and personal care products, including medications, but also through wider offerings of prepared and frozen foods and nonfood items. However, there is recent increased competition in the food retail sector from general merchandisers. Canadian retail chains are preparing themselves to compete against Walmart's new supercenters that will sell groceries.[40]

Between 1971 and 1996, Edmonton's population decentralized, with population losses in the central business district (and census tracts within walking distance of approximately .93 mile) and inner city (the core plus surrounding census tracts developed before 1946), and a population increase in the suburbs (only those tracts with a population density of at least 2,072 people per square mile [800 people per square kilometer]).[41] There was a decrease in population density in all three zones. This sprawl and loss in population density likely contributed to the expansion of supermarket trade areas. See table 1.

Power centers have now emerged as a retail force in Edmonton targeting the growing suburban population and high consumer spending power. These centers comprise several big-box (large stand-alone) anchor stores such as warehouse and discount department stores. Since the big-box

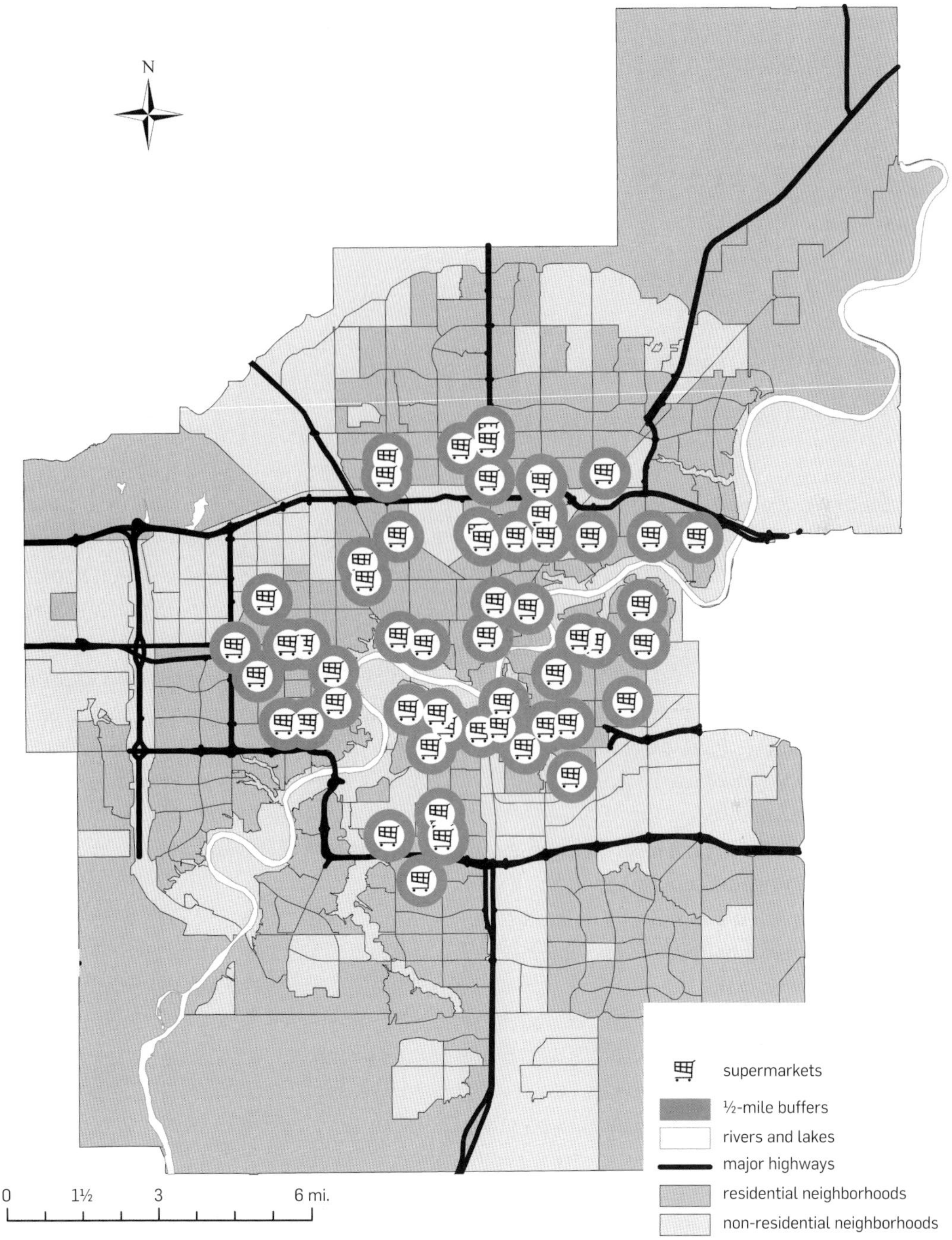

Figure 3. Areas within walking distance of supermarkets in Edmonton, 1971.

Note: Neighborhoods shown as of 2004.

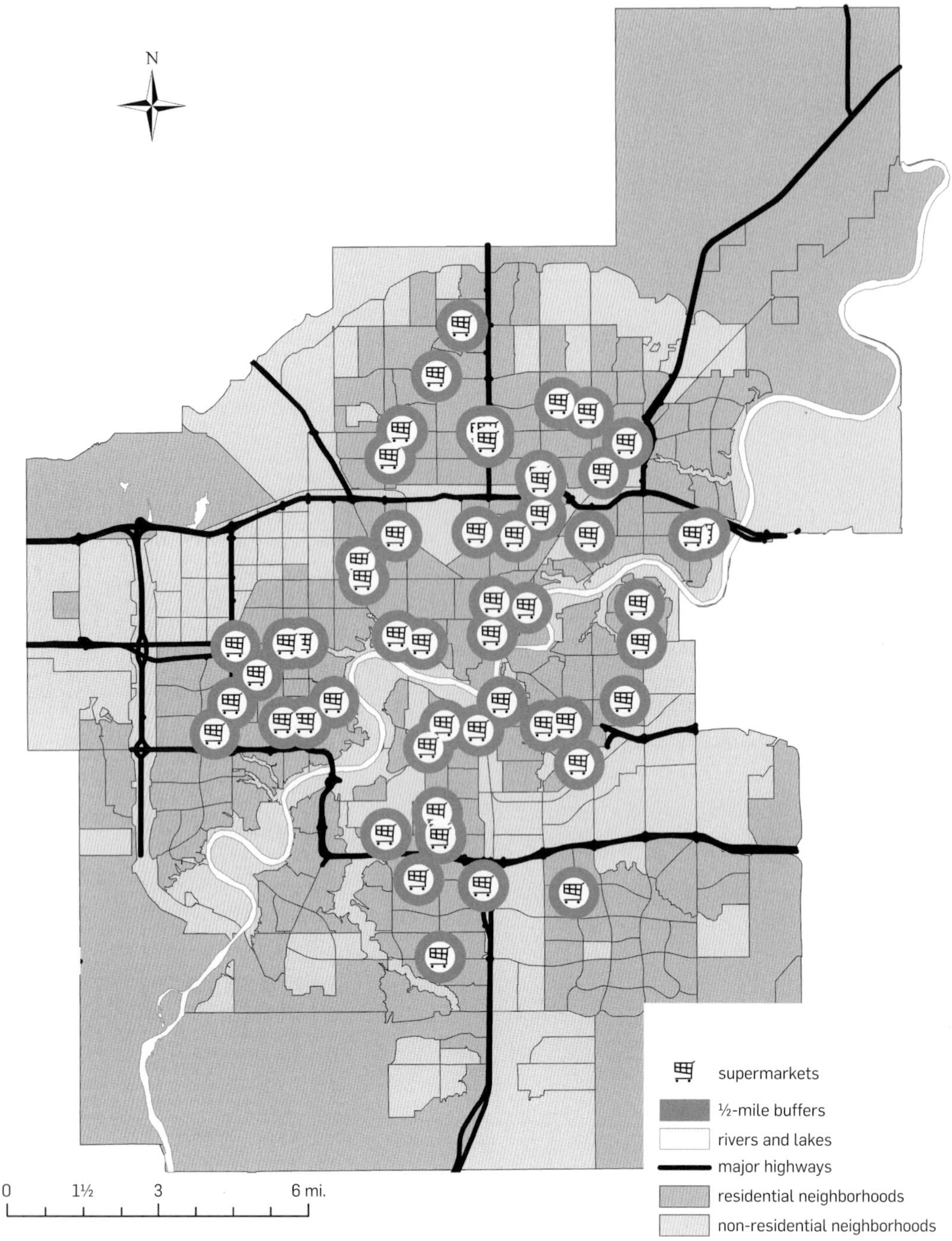

Figure 4. Areas within walking distance of supermarkets in Edmonton, 1981.

Note: Neighborhoods shown as of 2004.

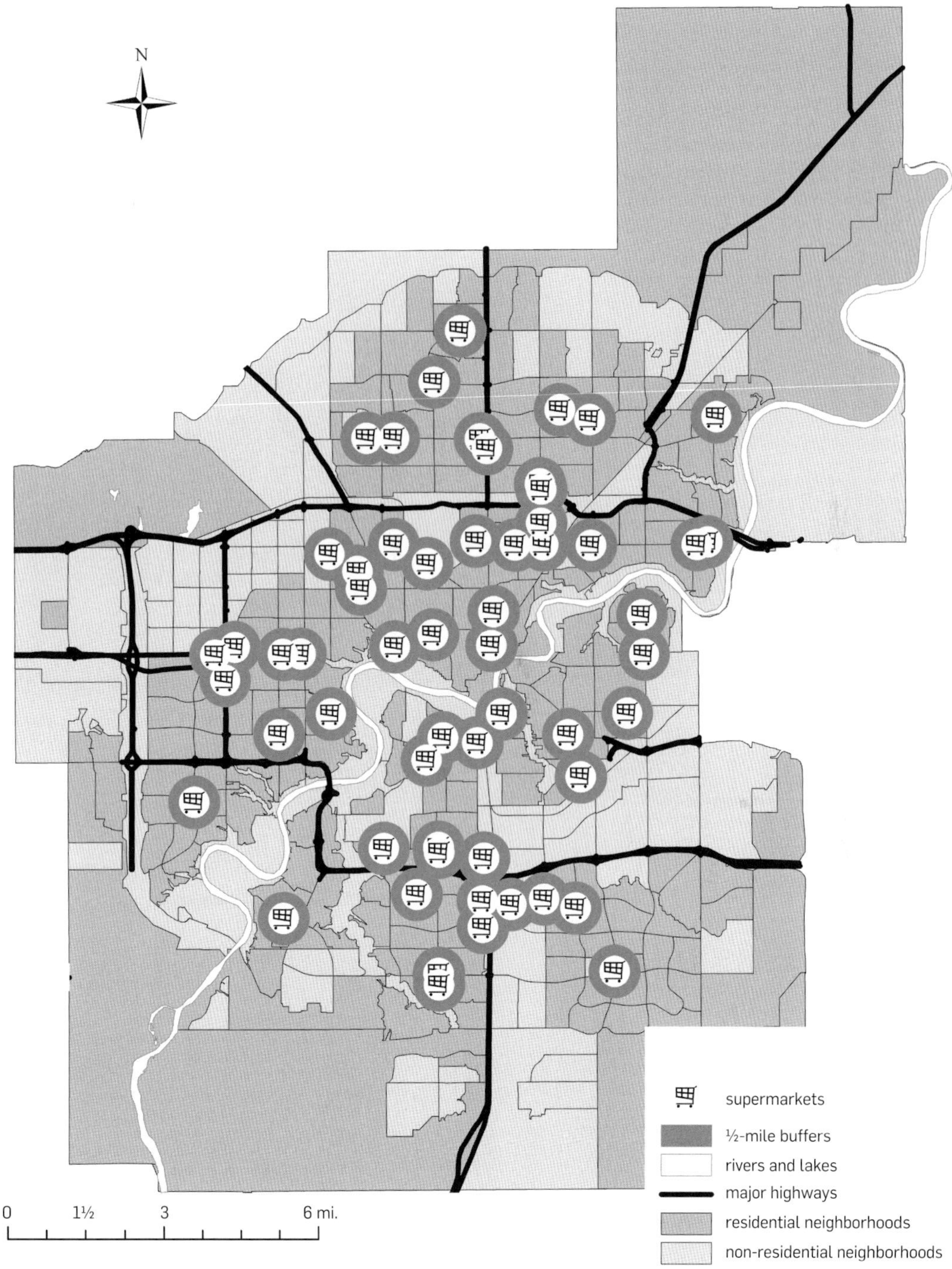

Figure 5. Areas within walking distance of supermarkets in Edmonton, 1991.

Note: Neighborhoods shown as of 2004.

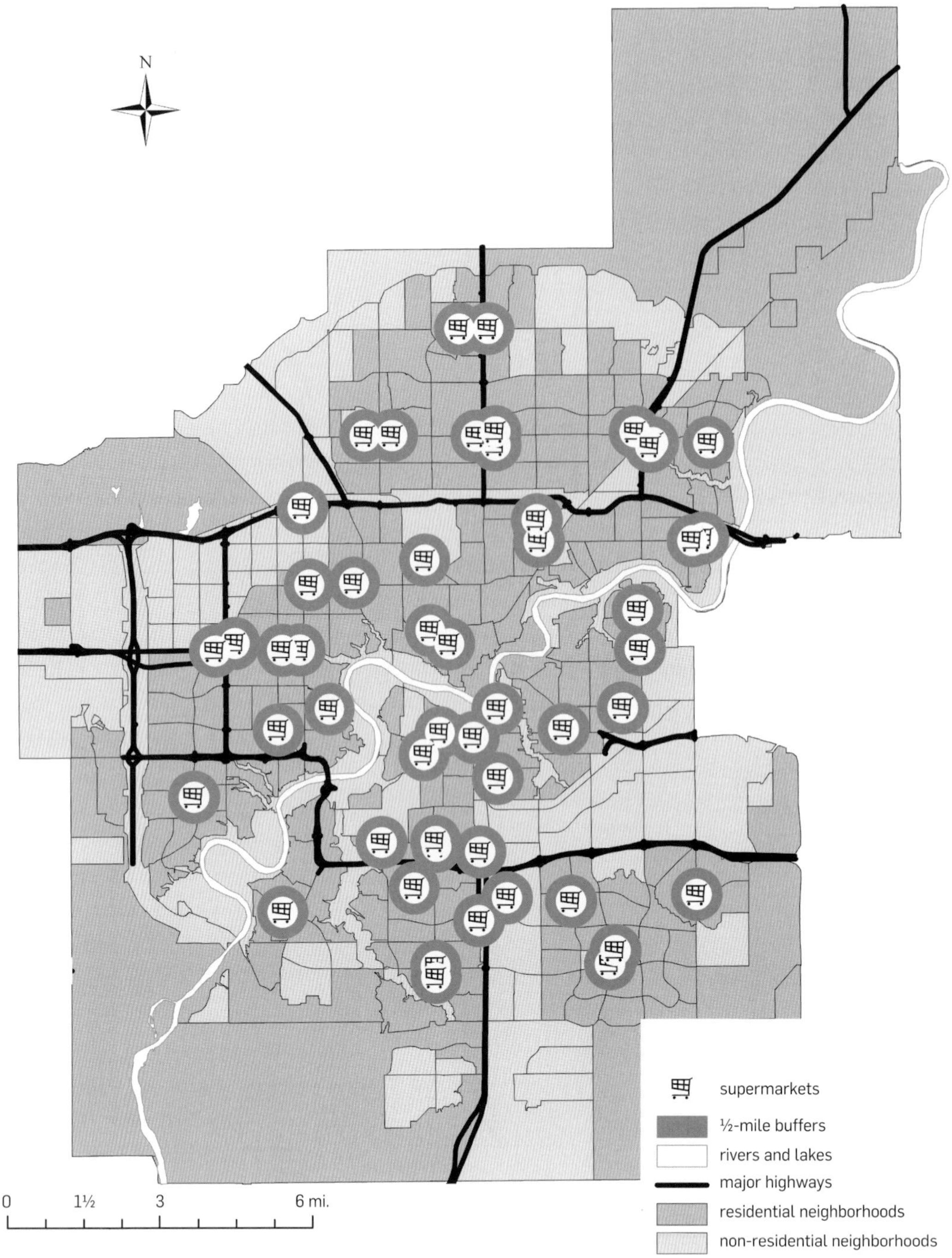

Figure 6. Areas within walking distance of supermarkets in Edmonton, 2001.

Note: Neighborhoods shown as of 2004.

Table 1. Changes in Edmonton's population and population density, 1971–1996

	CORE AREA	INNER CITY	SUBURBS
1971 population	27,790	50,675	366,255
1971 density: persons per mi.^{2} / (km^2)	9,461 / (3,653)	9,946 / (3,840)	6,180 / (2,386)
1996 population	24,057	42,587	530,287
1996 density: persons per mi.^{2} / (km^2)	8,192 / (3,163)	8,358 / (3,227)	5,602 / (2,163)
Change in population density	−13.4%	−16.0%	−9.4%

Source: T. Bunting, P. Filion, and H. Priston, Density Gradients in Canadian Metropolitan Regions, 1971–96: Differential Patterns of Central Area and Suburban Growth and Change, *Urban Studies* 39:13 (2002): 2531–52.

outlets are unconnected, these developments cater to the automobile with large parking areas outside each store. South Edmonton Common, one of Canada's largest power centers, opened its first anchor store in 1998. The center is located in the southeast corner of Edmonton on a major intersection of a route linking the downtown to the airport and a recently completed interstate-quality ring road. Since the rising volumes of traffic accessing the center have resulted in congestion and a high accident rate, the city has now started construction on a costly US$169 million (CAD$260 million) interchange to remedy the problem. The city, with provincial funds, is covering the costs of the interchange, with no contribution from the developers of South Edmonton Common. Retail food is available in two hypermarkets (a large store of 150,000 square feet or more combining food and nonfood items), one of which is a Walmart Supercenter.[42]

There is also a new power center (Skyview) in the city's northwest, with another (Windermere) being constructed in southwest Edmonton, and one more (The Meadows) planned for southeast Edmonton, and there is an opportunity to build yet another in the western neighborhood of Granville. As a gateway to northern communities, the power centers also appear to cater to populations as far north as Yellowknife in the Northwest Territories, a distance of 932 miles. So the picture is complex.[43]

Comparing Edmonton's mature and suburban neighborhoods in 2001 (fig. 7) reveals a younger population in the suburbs (22.5 percent of the suburban population is zero to fourteen years of age, compared to 15.4 percent in mature neighborhoods).[44] Suburban neighborhoods also have a higher average number of persons per household (2.91), in contrast to mature neighborhoods (2.33). Furthermore, the suburbs have wealthier residents on average, with a 2001 median family income of US$39,086.13 (CAD$60,132.50) in the suburbs, versus US$34,017.75 (CAD$52,335.00) in mature neighborhoods. Thus purchasing power per household is higher in the suburbs, although the higher population densities in the core area and inner city offset this to some extent. However, supermarket operators are less sensitive to the demographics of potential supermarket sites than the actual site location characteristics, due to the fact that the entire population requires food, independent of their age, wealth, or ethnicity. The important site factors, most frequently found together in suburban locations, include a large, relatively inexpensive lot on a major traffic route, easy accessibility, and minimal competition.[45]

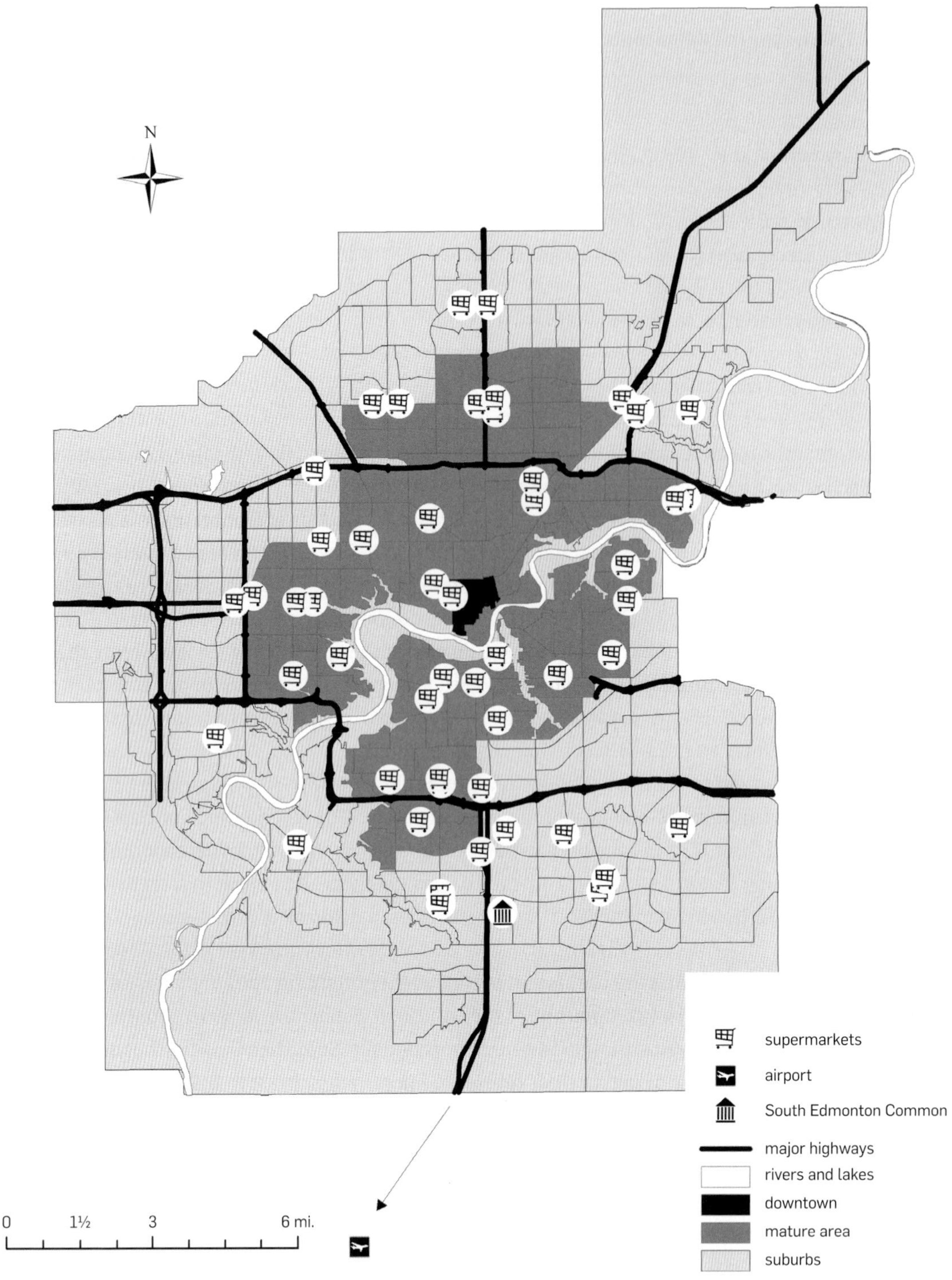

Figure 7. Edmonton city zones.

Supermarkets are shown as of 2001. Neighborhoods are shown as of 2004.

What fills the gap between supermarkets? There has been an increase in food sales from nontraditional food retailers, including pharmacies, discount stores, and gas stations. Their offerings are largely nonperishable, processed food with limited produce or meat. Also, fast-food outlets are proliferating in Edmonton (and elsewhere), with 761 fast-food outlets compared to only 61 supermarkets in 2001, with low income neighborhoods having notably higher exposure to fast-food outlets.[46]

On a citywide scale, supermarket access in Edmonton appears equitable in that low income and car ownership neighborhoods generally had a supermarket closer to them than other areas of the city.[47] However, the study found that a handful of low income areas had limited supermarket accessibility, and our work here shows that less than one-third of Edmonton's population (30 percent in 2001) is within walking distance of a supermarket. This creates a dichotomous city population of "walking-enabled" and "energy-dependent" food shoppers. At a street-corridor scale, store closures have left some neighborhoods without a supermarket. For example, the mature neighborhood of Highlands had been the site of a supermarket since the 1930s. However, the store was closed in 1993, causing considerable community distress, as expressed in focus-group interviews with residents. The departure of the supermarket left the community with walkable options only to convenience stores, a pharmacy, and, for a time, a fruit and vegetable store. Now, to obtain healthy food the residents have no other option but to drive or take a bus to a full-line supermarket.

A period of cheap oil in the last half of the twentieth century has facilitated a car-centered culture and has influenced the urban form and infrastructure placement in North American cities. Many urban neighborhoods now lack shops and services to walk to, creating fewer possibilities of physical activity and more dependence on driving. Our findings show that Edmonton's current population has an increased dependence on and consumption of external energy to reach supermarkets, compared to 1970. Since the trend toward fewer, larger supermarkets is reported at a national level, this same energy dependence likely exists in other Canadian cities. "Oil for food" is a modern reality.

The current trend in supermarket structure with larger and fewer supermarkets has been an efficiency and profit gain for the chains, as they have been able to close smaller, lower-volume stores. With larger facilities, the chains can benefit from economies of scale and transfer transportation costs to consumers and governments. While these store closures have been private sector decisions, they have implications for urban health and quality of life of urban residents shifting costs to others such as the health care system. Can there be a better balance between equity and efficiency?

Truelove notes that there is no single measure able to generate a single solution combining efficiency and equity, but rather there are a range of solutions with varying levels of efficiency and equity. Truelove suggests that one option to increase equity is to add a greater number of smaller facilities in closer proximity.[48]

A denser network of supermarkets would allow a greater percentage of the city's population to be within walking distance and would bring more supermarket anchors into neighborhoods. Neighborhood supermarkets increase community social interaction and also encourage the viability of other community business ventures.[49]

But since supermarkets are operated by the private sector, how can the trend toward larger and fewer outlets be reversed? Supermarket companies might be motivated by profits to open more stores if there were an increase in residential population density. The city of Edmonton is working to do this. Its Municipal Development Plan states that it is "promoting infill development in existing neighborhoods and business areas and accommodating higher density land uses along transportation corridors."[50]

Supermarkets might also open additional stores if profitable market segments exist. For instance, while there has been some urban infill with a few new supermarkets, these have tended to be in more affluent rather than in the lowest income areas. In May 2008, a small 18,000 square foot store opened in a formerly depressed area of downtown Edmonton to serve its expanding residential population.[51] However, the store caters to well-heeled grocery shoppers with wares including "duck breasts, frog legs, lobster tails and sheep's milk cheese infused with truffles."[52] Infill development is often costly, and it is difficult to assemble enough commercially zoned land in fully built-up mature neighborhoods. Even if land is available, old buildings may have to be demolished and the site remediated. Zoning approval also takes longer in inner-city locations than in suburban locations.[53] Thus, it will take time to intensify overall development and add more infill supermarkets, which still may not adequately serve low-income neighborhoods.

Also, the city could possibly intervene by providing zoning for new supermarkets. However, there is pressure in exactly the opposite direction through applications to remove commercial zoning. In Rutherford, a developing neighborhood in the south of Edmonton, there was a recent proposal by a developer to eliminate commercial zoning located in the center of the neighborhood, and thus rule out the future possibility of walking to a nearby convenience or grocery store. The proposal sought to replace the neighborhood commercial zoning with residential, and transfer the commercial zoning over half a mile (about one kilometer) away (Euclidean distance) to a larger mall located at the far south end of the neighborhood. The developer argued that the neighborhood site was not commercially viable. Following an intervention by the Sierra Club, the city and developer agreed to mixed-use zoning on the site for residential apartments with shops on the ground floor.[54]

For incorporation of supermarkets into new neighborhoods, design standards entitled LEED-ND (Leadership in Energy and Environmental Design—Neighborhood Development) which are currently being developed may exert an influence in the future. A research report on the association between neighborhood planning and public health by Reid Ewing et al. was prepared for and considered by the LEED-ND committee as it developed the rating system. Supermarkets are among the services recognized to be an important element of a neighborhood. Developments are rated according to the number of amenities such as supermarkets that are within a half mile walking distance of half the housing units. Two Edmonton projects (Strathearn Masterplan and the Village at Griesbach, Stage 8) are part of the pilot study for the rating system.[55]

Public-private partnerships could be formed or financial incentives could also be offered to attract supermarkets, as well as smaller grocery and produce stores. Another possibility is to encourage local convenience stores to sell healthier food options.[56]

However, change may occur spontaneously as a result of oil price increases. Willingness to drive longer distances to save money on groceries has been made possible by the wide availability of cars, relatively inexpensive gasoline prices, and low density residential patterns. But if there are fewer cars, higher gas prices, or higher residential densities, there may be less motivation to travel longer distances, and the market would be forced to respond.

Simon Szreter notes that previous public health advances have been made when social relations within communities are solidified to a point where political responses can address public health problems on a community level. This tendency underlines the need for the political inclusion of all residents in tackling the underlying causes (especially environmental ones) of rising obesity rates.[57]

In Edmonton, large shopping developments, such as power centers with big-box supermarkets and hypermarkets, are being designed to serve multiple new neighborhoods on the city's periphery, rendering many suburban food shoppers energy dependent. A few older areas of Edmonton that are being revitalized have attracted new upmarket grocery stores, increasing the food walkability in the local area. By contrast, some mature neighborhoods have lost supermarkets, forcing food shoppers to travel longer distances by motorized transport, or to rely on nearby convenience stores, pharmacies, and discount stores, which may not provide nutritious food options.

With more of the world's population concentrating in cities, and with the increasing resource demands and wastes created by cities, global ecological integrity depends on citizens' behavior within cities. One way to develop more sustainable, equitable, and healthy cities is to promote walkable access to nutritious food sources such as supermarkets, as well as other services and employment. Sustainability, equity, and health could be enhanced together with less oil and more walking for food and fitness.

NOTES

This work has been supported by the Centre for Urban Health Initiatives (Toronto, Canada). We would also like to thank Sirina Hamilton and Lee Yen Chong, both undergraduate research assistants at the University of Alberta. An earlier version of this chapter was presented at the 2007 Association of American Geographers Meeting in San Francisco, California.

1. Valerie A. Brown, John Grootjans, Jan Ritchie, Mardie Townsend, and Glenda Verrinder, *Sustainability and Health: Supporting Global Ecological Integrity in Public Health* (London: Earthscan, 2005), xvi.
2. John M. Last, *Public Health and Human Ecology*, 2d ed. (Stamford, CT: Appleton & Lange, 1998), 6.
3. World Health Organization (WHO), Obesity and Overweight Factsheet, Factsheet no. 311. 2006, http://www.who.int/mediacentre/factsheets/fs311/en/index.html.
4. Boyd Swinburn, Garry Egger, and Fezeela Raza, Dissecting Obesogenic Environments: The Development and Application of a Framework for Identifying and Prioritizing Environmental Interventions for Obesity, *Preventive Medicine* 29 (1999): 563–70.
5. UN-Habitat, The State of the World's Cities 2006/2007 (London, UK: Earthscan, 2007); UN-Habitat, The State of the World's Cities 2004/2005 (London, UK: Earthscan, 2004).
6. Anthony J. McMichael, *Planetary Overload: Global Environmental Change and the Health of the Human Species* (Cambridge, UK: Cambridge University Press, 1993).
7. Jill Grant, Mixed Use in Theory and Practice, *Journal of the American Planning Association* 68:1 (2002): 71–84; Tom Young, Alex Regiec, and Erik Backstrom, Anatomy of A TOD: Greyfield Redevelopment in Edmonton, *Taking the Pulse of . . . Planning Practice: Case-In-Point* (Manitoba Professional Planners Institute, 2005), http://www.mppi.mb.ca/assets/pdfs/Young2005.pdf.
8. William J. Coffey and Richard G. Shearmur, Employment in Canadian Cities, in *Canadian Cities*

in Transition: Local through Global Perspective, 3d ed., ed. Trudi Bunting and Pierre Filion (Don Mills, ON: Oxford University Press, 2006), 249–71; Statistics Canada, Work and Commuting in Census Metropolitan Areas, 1996–2001, Catalogue No. 89–613-MIE, No. 007 (Ottawa, ON: Statistics Canada, 2005); David Levinson and Ajay Kumar, Activity, Travel and the Allocation of Time, *Journal of the American Planning Association* 61:4 (1995): 458–70; Statistics Canada, Work and Commuting in Census Metropolitan Areas, 1996–2001, Catalogue No. 89–613-MIE, No. 007 (Ottawa, ON: Statistics Canada, 2005); Lawrence D. Frank, Economic Determinants of Urban Form: Resulting Trade-offs between Active and Sedentary Forms of Travel, *American Journal of Preventive Medicine* 27:3S (2004): 146–53; Edward Egyedy, Land Use and Market Area Analyses of Mega-Food Stores in Edmonton, Research Paper 22, Corporate Forecasting Group, Long Range Planning Branch, Planning and Building Department (City of Edmonton, 1988); Zy Weinberg and Mark S. Epstein, *No Place to Shop: Challenges and Opportunities Facing the Development of Supermarkets in Urban America* (Washington, DC: Public Voice for Food & Health Policy, 1996).

9. City of Vancouver, Trends and Futures in the Retail Grocery Business in Vancouver: A Dialogue (proceedings of a conference held May 10, 2000, draft); William H. Borghesani, Peter L. de la Cruz, and David B, Berry, Controlling the Chain: Buyer Power, Distributive Control, and New Dynamics in Retailing, *Business Horizons* 40:4 (1997): 17–24; Egyedy, Land Use and Market Area Analyses, 3.
10. Howard Frumkin, Lawrence Frank, and Richard Jackson, *Urban Sprawl and Public Health: Designing, Planning, and Building for Healthy Communities* (Washington, DC: Island Press, 2004).
11. Alan Bolstad, *The Alberta Smart Growth Report* (Sierra Club of Canada Prairie Chapter, 2005) 16, 47; Susan L. Handy and Kelly J. Clifton, Local Shopping as a Strategy for Reducing Automobile Travel, *Transportation* 28:4 (2001): 317–46; Lawrence Frank, Sarah Kavage, and Todd Litman, *Promoting Public Health through Smart Growth: Building Healthier Communities through Transportation and Land Use Policies and Practices* (Vancouver, BC: SmartGrowth BC, 2006), http://www.smartgrowth.bc.ca/Portals/0/Downloads/SGBC_Health_Report_FINAL.pdf; James F. Sallis, Lawrence D. Frank, Brian E. Saelens, and M. Katherine Kraft, Active Transportation and Physical Activity: Opportunities for Collaboration on Transportation and Public Health Research, *Transportation Research Part A* 38 (2004): 249–68.
12. City of Toronto, Council Highlights—City Council Meeting of October 1, 2002, http://www.toronto.ca/council_highlights/2002/100102.htm; City of Vancouver, Drive-In Restaurant and Drive-Through Service Guidelines, November 4, 1986, http://vancouver.ca/commsvcs/Guidelines/D009.pdf; Town of Ajax, Inside Ajax, June, 2008, http://www.townofajax.com/AssetFactory.aspx?did=4863; City of Hamilton, Economic Development and Planning Committee Minutes 07–021, December 4, 2007, http://www.myhamilton.ca/NR/rdonlyres/B33FD4B2–6E71–4936-A8DD-C8F856C2E7B3/0/Dec04Minutes.pdf; City of London, Official Plan/Zoning Refinement Review. Regulation of Drive-Through Facilities. Revised Official Plan Amendment. July 10, 2008, http://www.london.ca/By-laws/PDFs/drivethru_july14.pdf; City of North Vancouver, Minutes of the Regular Meeting of Council, January 21, 2008, http://www.cnv.org/c/DATA/1/88/2008%2001%2021.PDF; City of Sarnia, Council Minutes, June 23, 2008, http://www.city.sarnia.on.ca/pdf/Minutes%2020080623.pdf; Frank Landry, Drive-Thru Ban No Idle Threat, *Edmonton Sun*, January 25, 2008; CBC News, Drive-Thrus Not "Viable" for Strong Communities, Says Alderman, June 25, 2008, http://www.cbc.ca/canada/calgary/story/2008/06/25/drive-thrus.html#socialcomments.
13. Riina Bray, Catherine Vakil, and David Elliott, *Report on Public Health and Urban Sprawl in Ontario: A Review of the Pertinent Literature* (Environmental Health Committee, Ontario College of Family Physicians, 2005); Reid Ewing, Ross C. Brownson, and David Berrigan, Relationship between Urban Sprawl and Weight of United States Youth, *American Journal of Preventive Medicine* 31:6 (2006): 464–74. Reid Ewing, Tom Schmid, Richard Killingsworth, Amy Zlot, and Stephen Raudenbush, Relationship between Urban Sprawl and Physical Activity, Obesity, and Morbidity, *American Journal of Health Promotion* 18 (2003): 47–57; Alexia C. Kelly-Schwartz, Jean Stockard, Scott Doyle, and Marc Schlossberg, Is Sprawl Unhealthy? A Multilevel Analysis of the Relationship of Metropolitan Sprawl to the Health of Individuals, *Journal of Planning Education Research* 24:2 (2004): 184–96; Russ Lopez, Urban Sprawl and Risk for Being Overweight or Obese, *American Journal of Public Health* 94:9 (2004): 1574–79; Lawrence D. Frank, Martin A. Andresen, and Thomas L. Schmid, Obesity Relationships with Community Design, Physical Activity, and Time Spent in Cars, *American Journal of Preventive Medicine* 27 (2004): 87–96; Nancy A. Ross, Stephane Tremblay, Saeeda

Khan, Daniel Crouse, Mark Tremblay, and Jean-Marie Berthelot, Body Mass Index in Urban Canada: Neighborhood and Metropolitan Area Effects, *American Journal of Public Health* 97:3 (2007): 500–8.

14. Statistics Canada, Women in Canada: Work Chapter Updates. Catalogue no. 89F0133XIE (Ottawa, ON: Statistics Canada, 2006) http://www.statcan.ca/english/freepub/89F0133XIE/89F0133XIE2006000.htm; Statistics Canada, Work and Commuting in Census Metropolitan Areas, 1996–2001, Catalogue No. 89–613-MIE, No. 007 (Ottawa, ON: Statistics Canada, 2005); Kapil Bawa and Avijit Ghosh, A Model of Household Grocery Shopping Behaviour, *Marketing Letters* 10:2 (1999): 149–60; Margaret E. Beck, Dinner Preparation in the Modern United States, *British Food Journal* 109:7 (2007): 531–47; Alan Warde, Convenience Food: Space and Timing, *British Food Journal* 101:7 (1999): 518–27; Levinson and Kumar, Activity, Travel and the Allocation of Time, 458–70; Shin-Yi Chou, Michael Grossman, and Henry Saffer, An Economic Analysis of Adult Obesity: Results from the Behavioral Risk Factor Surveillance System, *Journal of Health Economics* 23 (2004): 565–87; Samara J. Nielsen and Barry M. Popkin, Changes in Beverage Intake between 1977 and 2001, *American Journal of Preventive Medicine* 27:3 (2004): 205–10; Guillaume Dubé, Canadian Retailers Competing for the Consumer's Food Dollar, Catalogue no. 11–621-MIE2006038 (Ottawa, ON: Statistics Canada, 2006), http://www.statcan.ca/english/research/11–621-MIE/11–621-MIE2006038.htm; Robert W. Jeffery and Simone A. French, Epidemic Obesity in the United States: Are Fast Foods and Television Viewing Contributing? *American Journal of Public Health* 88:2 (1998): 277–80; Mark A. Pereira, Alex I. Kartashov, Cara B. Ebbeling, Linda Van Horn, Martha L. Slattery, David R. Jacobs Jr., and David S. Ludwig, Fast-food Habits, Weight Gain, and Insulin Resistance (The CARDIA Study): 15-Year Prospective Analysis, *Lancet* 365 (2005): 36–42.

15. World Commission on Environment and Development, *Our Common Future* (Oxford: Oxford University Press, 1987), 43; Igor Vojnovic, Intergenerational and Intragenerational Equity Requirements for Sustainability, *Environmental Conservation* 22:3 (1995): 223–28; Owiti A. K'Akumu, Sustain No City: An Ecological Conceptualization of Urban Development, *City* 11:2 (2007): 221–28; Graham Haughton, Environmental Justice and the Sustainable City, *Journal of Planning Education and Research* 18 (1999): 233–43.

16. John Duncan Middleton, Health, Environmental and Social Justice, *Local Environment* 8:2 (2003): 155–65; Yasmin Von Schirnding, Health and Sustainable Development: Can We Rise to the Challenge? *Lancet* 360 (2002): 632–37; Richard G. Wilkinson, *Unhealthy Societies: The Afflictions of Inequality* (London: Routledge, 1996).

17. World Health Organization, Health and Welfare Canada, and the Canadian Public Health Association, Ottawa Charter for Health Promotion, *Canadian Journal of Public Health* 77:12 (1986): 425–30; Valéry Ridde, Anne Guichard, and David Houéto, Social Inequalities in Health from Ottawa to Vancouver: Action for Fair Equality of Opportunity, IUHPE—Promotion and Education Supplement 2, 2007; Ann Robertson and Meredith Minkler, New Health Promotion Movement: A Critical Examination, *Health Education Quarterly* 21:3 (1994): 295–312; UN-Habitat, *The State of the World's Cities 2006/2007* (London: Earthscan, 2007); Hugo Priemus, Changing Urban Housing Markets in Advanced Economies, *Housing, Theory and Society* 21:1 (2004): 2–16; Kim England and John Mercer, Canadian Cities in Continental Context: Global and Continental Perspectives on Canadian Urban Development, in *Canadian Cities in Transition*, ed. Bunting and Filion, 24–39; Larry S. Bourne, Alternative Future for Urban Canada: Challenges and Opportunities, in ed. Bunting and Filion, *Canadian Cities in Transition*, 450–463; Fran Baum, *The New Public Health* (South Melbourne: Oxford University Press, 2002).

18. Baum, *The New Public Health*, xiv; Don Mitchell, Introduction: Public Space and the City, *Urban Geography* 17:2 (1996): 127–31; Greg Lindsey, Maltie Maraj, and Son Cheong Kuan, Access, Equity, and Urban Greenways: An Exploratory Investigation, *Professional Geographer* 53:5 (2001): 332–46; Susan L. Handy and Debbie A. Niemeier, Measuring Accessibility: An Exploration of Issues and Alternatives, *Environment and Planning A* 29:7 (1997): 1175–94.

19. Vojnovic, Intergenerational, 223–28.

20. Kenneth S. Deffeyes, *Beyond Oil: The View from Hubbert's Peak* (New York: Hill & Wang, 2005); Richard Gilbert and Anthony Perl, *Transport Revolutions: Moving People and Freight Without Oil* (London: Earthscan, 2007).

21. Lawrence D. Frank and Peter Engelke, Multiple Impacts of the Built Environment on Public Health: Walkable Places and the Exposure to Air Pollution, *International Regional Science Review* 28:2 (2005): 193–216; Roy J. Shephard, What Is the Optimal Type

of Physical Activity to Enhance Health? *British Journal of Sports Medicine* 31 (1997): 277–84; Annette Prüss-Üstün and Carlos F. Corvalán, *Preventing Disease through Healthy Environments: Towards an Estimate of the Environmental Burden of Disease* (Geneva: World Health Organization, 2006), http://www.who.int/quantifying_ehimpacts/publications/preventingdisease.pdf.

22. Haughton, Environmental Justice, 233–43.
23. Marie Truelove, Measurement of Spatial Equity, *Environment and Planning C: Government and Policy* 11 (1993): 19–34.
24. Statistics Canada, Portrait of the Canadian Population in 2006: Subprovincial Population Dynamics (Ottawa, ON: Statistics Canada, 2006), http://www12.statcan.ca/english/census06/analysis/popdwell/tables/table3.htm; Edmonton Economic Development Corporation, Transportation and Logistics, http://www.edmonton.com/business/page.asp?page=751; Statistics Canada, A Profile of the Canadian Population: Where We Live, Catalogue No.: 96F0030XIE2001001 (Ottawa, ON: Statistics Canada, 2002), http://geodepot.statcan.ca/Diss/Highlights/Page9/Page9d_e.cfm; Statistics Canada, Portrait of the Canadian Population in 2006 Census, Catalogue no. 97–550-XWE2006001 (Ottawa, ON: Statistics Canada, 2007), http://www12.statcan.ca/english/census06/analysis/popdwell/ProvTerr5.cfm; City of Edmonton, Working in Edmonton: Edmonton Economic Facts, 2008, http://www.movetoedmonton.com/working/economicfacts/; Bolstad, *The Alberta Smart Growth Report*, 5; Edward C. LeSage Jr. and Lorna Stefanick, New Regionalist Metropolitan Action: The Case of the Alberta Capital Region Alliance (Canadian Political Science Association Meetings, Winnipeg, 2004), http://www.cpsa-acsp.ca/papers-2004/Stefanick-LeSage.pdf; Regional Planning Commissions, established by the Province of Alberta, were overseen by Alberta Municipal Affairs. In the early 1990s, small urban and rural municipalities had expressed discontent with the Commissions, even though their jurisdictions were overrepresented. In 1995 Ralph Klein's Conservative government eliminated the Commissions and mandatory regional planning in the second installment of the province's *Municipal Government Act*.
25. Government of Alberta, Draft Land-Use Framework, 2008, http://www.landuse.gov.ab.ca/docs/LUF%20Draft%20Document%20may%2016%20FINAL.pdf; Ed Stelmach, New Board First Step in Capital Region Planning, December 19, 2007, http://premier.alberta.ca/news/news-2007-dec-19-Capital_Region_plan.cfm.
26. As of May 15, 2008, the boards of Capital Health, and the other eight regional health authorities in Alberta have been eliminated, and will be transitioning to a single provincial board, the Alberta Health Service Board (Government of Alberta 2008b). Government of Alberta, One Provincial Board to Govern Alberta's Health System, News Release, May 15, 2008, http://alberta.ca/home/NewsFrame.cfm?ReleaseID=/acn/200805/23523ED9498C0–0827–451C-E98A0B8430DC1879.html. Capital Health Edmonton Area, Designing Healthy Places: Land Use Planning and Public Health (Population Health, 2007).
27. City of Edmonton, Smart Choices for Developing Our Community—Recommendations, Planning and Development Report 2004PDP006, February 18, 2004, http://www.edmonton.ca/InfraPlan/SmartChoices/Documents/Recommendations%202004.pdf; City of Edmonton, 2008, Smart Choices Program, http://www.edmonton.ca/portal/server.pt/gateway/PTARGS_0_0_284_220_0_43/http%3B/CMSServer/COEWeb/infrastructure+planning+and+building/planning/smart+choices/; Frank, Kavage, and Litman, *Promoting Public Health*; City of Edmonton, Sustainable Development Practices: Planning and Development Report 2007PDP003, January 24, 2007, http://www.edmonton.ca/InfraPlan/SmartChoices/2007PDP003%20Sustainable%20Development%20Practices.pdf, 3.
28. City of Edmonton, Smart Choices for Developing Our Community—Recommendations, Planning and Development Report 2004PDP006, February 18, 2004, http://www.edmonton.ca/InfraPlan/SmartChoices/Documents/Recommendations%202004.pdf; City of Edmonton, Walkability Strategy Project, 2008, http://www.smartcity.edmonton.ab.ca/portal/server.pt/gateway/PTARGS_0_0_266_211_0_43/http%3B/CMSServer/COEWeb/city+government/departments+and+branches/community+services/plans+and+initiatives/walkabilitystrategyproject.htm; City of Edmonton, Focus Edmonton City Plan, 2008, http://www.focusedmonton.ca/home.html.
29. The currency exchange throughout the chapter was based on the U.S. Federal Reserve Bank of New York's average 2001 exchange rate of .65 Canadian to the US Dollar. In 2012, the exchange rate is around one-to-one. City of Edmonton, Fact Sheet: South LRT Extension, 2008, http://www.edmonton.ca/RoadsTraffic/LRT%20Projects/SLRT-Documents/Fact%20Sheet-SLRTExtension-Jun'08.pdf.; City of Edmonton, City Council Minutes, (Draft), June 18, 2008, http://www.edmonton.ca/meetings/

minutes_council/cc20080618mn.doc.

30. University of Alberta, U-Pass History, http://www.uofaweb.ualberta.ca/u-pass/u-passhistory.cfm. Grant MacEwan College, U-Pass, http://www.macewan.ca/web/services/sa/home/DetailsPage.cfm?ID=6839&utm_source=upass&utm_medium=redirect.
31. Peter Katzmarzyk, The Canadian Obesity Epidemic: An Historical Perspective, *Obesity Research* 10:7 (2002): 666–74; Kimberly Morland, Steve Wing, and Ana Diez Roux, The Contextual Effect of the Local Food Environment on Residents' Diets: The Atherosclerosis Risk in Communities Study, *American Journal of Public Health* 92:11 (2002): 1761–67; Barbara A. Laraia, Anna Maria Siega-Riz, Jay S. Kaufman, and Sonya J. Jones, Proximity of Supermarkets Is Positively Associated with Diet Quality Index for Pregnancy, *Preventive Medicine* 39:5 (2004): 869–75; Kim. D. Travers, Using Qualitative Research to Understand the Socio-Cultural Origins of Diabetes among Cape Breton Mi'kmaq, *Chronic Diseases in Canada* 16:4 (1995): 140–43; K. Gebel, L. King, A. Bauman, P. Vita, T. Gill, A. Rigby, and A. Capon, *Creating Healthy Environments: A Review of Links between the Physical Environment, Physical Activity and Obesity* (Sydney: Health Department and NSW Centre for Overweight and Obesity, 2005), http://www.coo.health.usyd.edu.au/pdf/2005_creating_healthy_environments.pdf; Kim Raine, John C. Spence, John Church, Normand Boulé, Linda Slater, Josh Marko, Karyn Gibbons, and Eric Hemphill, *State of the Evidence Review on Urban Health and Healthy Weights* (Ottawa: Canadian Institute for Health Information [CIHI], 2008), http://secure.cihi.ca/cihiweb/products/Urban%20Health%20and%20Healthy%20Weights.pdf; Capital Health Edmonton Area, *Designing Healthy Places: Land Use Planning and Public Health* (Population Health, 2007).
32. Neil Wrigley, Daniel Warm, Barrie Margetts, and Amanda Whelan, Assessing the Impact of Improved Retail Access on Diet in a "Food Desert": A Preliminary Report, *Urban Studies* 39:11 (2002): 2061–82; Kristian Larsen and Jason Gilliland, Mapping the Evolution of "Food Deserts" in a Canadian City: Supermarket Accessibility in London, Ontario, 1961–2005, *International Journal of Health Geographics* 7 (2008): 16.
33. City of Edmonton, City of Edmonton Population, Historical, 2007, http://www.edmonton.ca/infraplan/demographic/Edmonton%20Population%20Historical.pdf; T. Bunting, P. Filion, and H. Priston, Density Gradients in Canadian Metropolitan Regions, 1971–96: Differential Patterns of Central Area and Suburban Growth and Change, *Urban Studies* 39:13 (2002): 2531–52; Adam Farr, Strategically Implementing the Capital City Downtown Plan, *Alberta Association Canadian Institute of Planners, Planning Digest* 6:3 (2002): 8–10, http://www.aacip.com/members/AACIP%20Digest%20V6–3-B&W-Part%201.pdf; City of Edmonton, Edmonton City Trends, 2008, Growth Analysis Unit, Corporate Planning and Policy Section, Planning and Policy Services Branch, Planning and Development Department, http://www.edmonton.ca/infraplan/Monthly%20Economic%20Review/2008/February%202008.pdf.
34. City of Edmonton, 2005 Edmonton Household Travel Survey: Summary Report on Weekday Travel by Edmonton Residents.
35. Martin Turcotte, Life in Metropolitan Areas: Dependence on Cars in Urban Neighborhoods, Canadian Social Trends, Catalogue no. 11–008-XIE (Ottawa, ON: Statistics Canada, 2008), http://www.statcan.ca/english/freepub/11–008-XIE/2008001/article/10503-en.pdf.
36. Agriculture and Agri-Food Canada, Market and Industry Services Branch, Food Bureau, 1999, The Food Marketing and Distribution Sector in Canada; Ralph Ferguson, *Compare the Share Phase II: The Comparisons Continue* (Ottawa, ON: n.p., 2002). Banner stores are independently owned yet, tied closely to a sponsoring company by legal contracts, making them similar to chain supermarkets. With the introduction of banner stores in the early 1970s, the percentage of retail food sales by "true" independents decreased markedly from approximately 50 percent in 1969 to approximately 15 percent in 1974 (Ferguson, *Compare the Share*).
37. EDTEL, 1995–1996 (EDTEL Phone Book 1995, 1996; EDTEL Yellow Pages 1996); Edmonton Telephones, 1970–1994 (Edmonton Classified Telephone Directory 1970; Edmonton and Vicinity Telephone Directory 1970; Edmonton Phone Book 1973, 1976, 1979; Edmonton and Vicinity Yellow Pages 1982–1984; Edmonton and Vicinity White Pages 1982, 1985, 1988, 1991, 1994); Henderson Directories, 1982–1999 (Edmonton Alberta City Directories 1982, 1984/1985, 1998/1999); Telus, 1997–2004 (Edmonton Phone Book 1997; Edmonton Yellow Pages 1997/1998, 1999/2000; Edmonton and Area TELUS Telephone Directory 1998/1999, 2003/2004); *Edmonton Journal*, 1981–2006; DMTI Spatial Inc., 2004, GeoPinpoint Suite software, Version 5.4.00; ESRI 2005; ArcGIS software, Version 9.1.
38. Statistics Canada, Cartographic Boundary Files for

Edmonton, 1971, 1981, 1991, 2001; Computing in the Humanities and Social Sciences (CHASS), Canadian Census Profiles (Census Tract Level), originally released by Statistics Canada, Canadian Census Analyzer, University of Toronto, http://dc1.chass.utoronto.ca/census/ct.html; E-STAT 2006, Statistics Canada Census Data, http://www.statcan.ca/english/Estat/licence.htm.

39. Agriculture and Agri-Food Canada, Market and Industry Services Branch, Food Bureau, 1999, The Food Marketing and Distribution Sector in Canada; Eileen Krakar and Kim Longtin, *An Overview of the Canadian Agriculture and Agri-Food System* (Ottawa, ON: Agriculture and Agri-Food Canada, 2005); City of Vancouver, Policy Report: Urban Structure, Supermarkets in Vancouver, November 3, 1998, http://www.city.vancouver.bc.ca/ctyclerk/cclerk/981117/p1.htm.

40. Dubé, Canadian Retailers; Mario Toneguzzi, Wal-Mart Super-sizes Five Alberta Stores; Airdrie Outlet Also Expanding as "Supercentre," *Calgary Herald*, September 20, 2007; Canadian Grocer, Price Battle Spreads to Alberta, *Canadian Grocery E-Newsletter*, September 21, 2007; Loblaw Results Plummet on Costs, *Star*, November 15, 2007.

41. Bunting, Filion, and Priston, Density Gradients, 2531–52.

42. International Council of Shopping Centers, ICSC Shopping Center Definitions, http://www.icsc.org/srch/lib/SCDefinitions99.pdf; Young, Regiec, and Backstrom, Anatomy of A TOD; Mairi MacLean, South-Side Mega Cineplex Set to Open: 16-Screen Complex Newest Attraction in Big-Box Retail Centre, *Edmonton Journal*, August 2, 2000, Final Edition, F7; Keith Gerein, Price Soars for Traffic Interchange at 23rd Ave, *Edmonton Journal*, May 13, 2006, Final Edition, A1; Interchange Breaks Ground: Construction Begins on $260M Road Project, *Edmonton Journal*, April 3, 2008, B2; U.S. Department of Agriculture, Food Marketing System in the U.S.: Retail Food Glossary, http://www.ers.usda.gov/Briefing/FoodMarketingSystem/foodretailingglossary.htm.

43. City of Edmonton, Windermere Neighborhood Structure Plan, Planning and Development Department, October 2006, http://www.edmonton.ca/InfraPlan/Consolidations/PDF%20Consolidations/Windermere%20NSP%20Consolidation.pdf; Bill Mah, More Edmonton Malls in Store; 1.7M Square Feet of New Space Coming to Busy Southern Suburbs Alone, *Edmonton Journal*, April 30, 2008, E1; City of Edmonton, Adoption of the Granville Neighborhood Structure Plan, Planning and Development Department Report 2007PDP507, Bylaw 14699, July 16, 2007, http://www.edmonton.ca/OcctopusDocs/Public/Complete/Reports/CC/CSAM/2007–08–21/2007PDP507.doc.

44. Statistics Canada, 2001 Basic Profile of Edmonton Neighborhoods, Components 1–7, 2001 Census (20% Sample) (Ottawa, ON: Statistics Canada, 2001). Analysis conducted with 215 residential neighborhoods in the city of Edmonton, having nonsuppressed data comprising of 109 mature neighborhoods, and 106 suburban neighborhoods.

45. City of Vancouver, Trends and Futures in the Retail Grocery Business in Vancouver.

46. Agriculture and Agri-Food Canada, An Overview of the Canadian Agriculture and Agri-Food System 2007, http://www4.agr.gc.ca/AAFC-AAC/display-afficher.do?id=1205781159471&lang=e; Phil R. Kaufman, Nontraditional Retailers Are Challenging Traditional Grocery Stores, *FoodReview* 21:3 (1999): 31–33, http://www.ers.usda.gov/publications/foodreview/sep1998/frsept98g.pdf; Karen E. Smoyer-Tomic, John C. Spence, Kim D. Raine, Carl Amrhein, Nairne Cameron, Vladimir Yasenovskiy, Nicoleta Cutumisu, Eric Hemphill, and Julia Healy, The Association between Neighborhood Socioeconomic Status and Exposure to Supermarkets and Fast Food Outlets, *Health and Place* 14:4 (2008): 740–54.

47. Karen E. Smoyer-Tomic, John C. Spence, and Carl A. Amrhein, Food Deserts in the Prairies? Supermarket Accessibility and Neighborhood Need in Edmonton, Canada, *Professional Geographer* 58 (2006): 307–26.

48. Truelove, Measurement of Spatial Equity, 19–34.

49. Elizabeth Eisenhauer, In Poor Health: Supermarket Redlining and Urban Nutrition, *GeoJournal* 53 (2001): 125–33.

50. City of Edmonton, Plan Edmonton: Edmonton's Municipal Development Plan. Bylaw No. 11777, Approved August 31, 1998, with Amendments to January 22, 2007 (Edmonton, AB: City of Edmonton, 2007), 11, http://www.edmonton.ca/InfraPlan/Plan%20Edmonton/Amended%20MDP%20FINAL%20PLAN%20Jan%202007.pdf.

51. Paula Simons, Downtown Food Store Will Cater to Gourmet Tastes; Customers Will Also Be Able to Dine On-Site, *Edmonton Journal*, May 6, 2008.

52. Simons, Downtown Food Store Will Cater to Gourmet Tastes.

53. Weinberg and Epstein, *No Place to Shop*.

54. City of Edmonton, Amendment to the Rutherford Neighborhood Area Structure Plan, City Council Agenda Public Hearing, F16, Bylaw 14856, February 25, 2008; Sierra Club, Speaking Notes from Sierra Club Canada Prairie Chapter, Intervention at City

Council, February 25, 2008; Susan Ruttan, No Takers for Rutherford Retail Space: City Agrees to Allow Apartments with Stores on Main Floor as Compromise, *Edmonton Journal*, February 26, 2008.

55. U.S. Green Building Council, LEED for Neighborhood Development, 2008, http://www.usgbc.org/DisplayPage.aspx?CMSPageID=148; Reid Ewing, Lawrence Frank, and Richard Kreutzer, Understanding the Relationship between Public Health and the Built Environment: A Report Prepared for the LEED-ND Core Committee, May, 2006, http://www.usgbc.org/ShowFile.aspx?DocumentID=1736; U.S. Green Building Council, LEED for Neighborhood Development Registered Pilot Project List, 2008, http://www.usgbc.org/ShowFile.aspx?DocumentID=3546.
56. Pennsylvania Fresh Food Financing Initiative (FFFI), Brief (Philadelphia, PA), http://www.thefoodtrust.org/pdf/FFFI%20Brief.pdf; Food Trust, Corner Store Campaign (Philadelphia, PA), http://www.thefoodtrust.org/php/programs/corner.store.campaign.php.
57. Simon Szreter, Economic Growth, Disruption, Deprivation, Disease, and Death: On the Importance of the Politics of Public Health for Development, *Population and Development Review* 23:4 (1997): 693–728.

REFERENCES

Agriculture and Agri-Food Canada. An Overview of the Canadian Agriculture and Agri-Food System 2007. http://www4.agr.gc.ca/AAFC-AAC/display-afficher.do?id=1205781159471&lang=e.

Ajax (Town of). Inside Ajax. June 2008. http://www.townofajax.com/AssetFactory.aspx?did=4863.

Baum, Fran. *The New Public Health*. South Melbourne: Oxford University Press, 2002.

Bawa, Kapil, and Avijit Ghosh. A Model of Household Grocery Shopping Behaviour. *Marketing Letters* 10:2 (1999): 149–60.

Beck, Margaret E. Dinner Preparation in the Modern United States. *British Food Journal* 109:7 (2007): 531–47.

Bolstad, Alan. *The Alberta Smart Growth Report*. Sierra Club of Canada Prairie Chapter, 2005.

Borghesani, William H., Peter L. de la Cruz, and David B. Berry. Controlling the Chain: Buyer Power, Distributive Control, and New Dynamics in Retailing. *Business Horizons* 40:4 (1997): 17–24.

Bourne, Larry S. Alternative Future for Urban Canada: Challenges and Opportunities. In *Canadian Cities in Transition: Local through Global Perspective*, 3d ed., ed. Trudi Bunting and Pierre Filion, 450–63. Don Mills, ON: Oxford University Press, 2006.

Bray, Riina, Catherine Vakil, and David Elliott. Report on Public Health and Urban Sprawl in Ontario: A Review of the Pertinent Literature. Environmental Health Committee, Ontario College of Family Physicians, 2005.

Brown, Valerie A., John Grootjans, Jan Ritchie, Mardie Townsend, and Glenda Verrinder. *Sustainability and Health: Supporting Global Ecological Integrity in Public Health*. Sterling, VA: Earthscan, 2005.

Bunting, T., P. Filion, and H. Priston. Density Gradients in Canadian Metropolitan Regions, 1971–96: Differential Patterns of Central Area and Suburban Growth and Change. *Urban Studies* 39:13 (2002): 2531–52.

Canadian Grocer. Price Battle Spreads to Alberta. *Canadian Grocery E-Newsletter*, September 21, 2007.

Capital Health Edmonton Area. Designing Healthy Places: Land Use Planning and Public Health. *Population Health* (2007).

CBC News. Drive-Thrus Not "Viable" for Strong Communities, Says Alderman. June 25, 2008. http://www.cbc.ca/canada/calgary/story/2008/06/25/drive-thrus.html#socialcomments.

Chou, Shin-Yi, Michael Grossman, and Henry Saffer. An Economic Analysis of Adult Obesity: Results from the Behavioral Risk Factor Surveillance System. *Journal of Health Economics* 23 (2004): 565–87.

Coffey, William J., and Richard G. Shearmur. Employment in Canadian Cities. In *Canadian Cities in Transition: Local through Global Perspective*, 3d ed., ed. Trudi Bunting and Pierre Filion, 249–71. Don Mills, ON: Oxford University Press, 2006.

Computing in the Humanities and Social Sciences (CHASS). Canadian Census Profiles (Census Tract Level). Originally released by Statistics Canada. Canadian Census Analyzer. University of Toronto. http://dc1.chass.utoronto.ca/census/ct.html.

Deffeyes, Kenneth S. *Beyond Oil: The View from Hubbert's Peak*. New York: Hill & Wang, 2005.

Dubé, Guillaume. Canadian Retailers Competing for the Consumer's Food Dollar. Catalogue no. 11-621-MIE2006038. Ottawa, ON: Statistics Canada, 2006. http://www.statcan.ca/english/research/11-621-MIE/11-621-MIE2006038.htm.

Edmonton (City of). Adoption of the Granville Neighborhood Structure Plan. Planning and Development Department Report 2007PDP507. Bylaw 14699, July 16, 2007. http://www.edmonton.ca/OcctopusDocs/Public/Complete/Reports/CC/CSAM/2007-08-21/2007PDP507.doc.

———. City Council Minutes, (Draft). June 18, 2008. http://www.edmonton.ca/meetings/minutes_council/cc20080618mn.doc.

———. City of Edmonton Population, Historical. 2007. http://www.edmonton.ca/infraplan/demographic/Edmonton%20Population%20Historical.pdf.

———. Edmonton City Trends. Growth Analysis Unit, Corporate Planning and Policy Section, Planning and Policy Services Branch, Planning and Development Department. 2008. http://www.edmonton.ca/infraplan/Monthly%20Economic%20Review/2008/February%202008.pdf.

———. Fact Sheet: South LRT Extension. 2008. http://www.edmonton.ca/RoadsTraffic/LRT%20Projects/SLRT-Documents/Fact%20Sheet-SLRTExtension-Jun'08.pdf.

———. Focus Edmonton City Plan. 2008. http://www.focusedmonton.ca/home.html.

———. Plan Edmonton: Edmonton's Municipal Development Plan. Bylaw No. 11777, Approved August 31, 1998, with Amendments to January 22, 2007. Edmonton, AB: City of Edmonton. 2007. Online at http://www.edmonton.ca/InfraPlan/Plan%20Edmonton/Amended%20MDP%20FINAL%20PLAN%20Jan%202007.pdf.

———. Smart Choices for Developing Our Community—Recommendations. Planning and Development Report 2004PDP006. February 18, 2004. http://www.edmonton.ca/InfraPlan/SmartChoices/Documents/Recommendations%202004.pdf.

———. Smart Choices Program. 2008. http://www.edmonton.ca/portal/server.pt/gateway/PTARGS_0_0_284_220_0_43/http%3B/CMSServer/COEWeb/infrastructure+planning+and+building/planning/smart+choices/.

———. Sustainable Development Practices: Planning and Development Report 2007PDP003. January 24, 2007. http://www.edmonton.ca/InfraPlan/SmartChoices/2007PDP003%20Sustainable%20Development%20Practices.pdf.

———. 2005 Edmonton Household Travel Survey: Summary Report on Weekday Travel by Edmonton Residents. 2006.

———. Walkability Strategy Project. 2008. http://www.smartcity.edmonton.ab.ca/portal/server.pt/gateway/PTARGS_0_0_266_211_0_43/http%3B/CMSServer/COEWeb/city+government/departments+and+branches/community+services/plans+and+initiatives/walkabilitystrategyproject.htm.

———. Windermere Neighborhood Structure Plan. Planning and Development Department. October 2006. http://www.edmonton.ca/InfraPlan/Consolidations/PDF%20Consolidations/Windermere%20NSP%20Consolidation.pdf.

———. Working In Edmonton: Edmonton Economic Facts. 2008. http://www.movetoedmonton.com/working/economicfacts/.

Edmonton Journal. Interchange Breaks Ground; Construction Begins on $260M Road Project. April 3, 2008, B2.

Egyedy, Edward. Land Use and Market Area Analyses of Mega-Food Stores in Edmonton. Research Paper 22. Corporate Forecasting Group, Long Range Planning Branch, Planning and Building Department, City of Edmonton, 1988.

Eisenhauer, Elizabeth. In Poor Health: Supermarket Redlining and Urban Nutrition. *GeoJournal* 53 (2001): 125–33.

England, Kim, and John Mercer. 2006. Canadian Cities in Continental Context: Global and Continental Perspectives on Canadian Urban Development. In *Canadian Cities in Transition: Local through Global Perspective,* 3d ed., ed. Trudi Bunting and Pierre Filion, 24–39. Don Mills, ON: Oxford University Press.

Ewing, Reid, Ross C. Brownson, and David Berrigan. Relationship between Urban Sprawl and Weight of United States Youth. *American Journal of Preventive Medicine* 31:6 (2006): 464–74.

Ewing, Reid, Lawrence Frank, and Richard Kreutzer. Understanding the Relationship between Public Health and the Built Environment. A Report Prepared for the LEED-ND Core Committee. 2006. http://www.usgbc.org/ShowFile.aspx?DocumentID=1736.

Ewing, Reid, Tom Schmid, Richard Killingsworth, Amy Zlot, and Stephen Raudenbush. Relationship between Urban Sprawl and Physical Activity, Obesity, and Morbidity. *American Journal of Health Promotion* 18 (2003): 47–57.

Farr, Adam. Strategically Implementing the Capital City Downtown Plan. Alberta Association, Canadian Institute of Planners, *Planning Digest* 6:3 (2002): 8–10. http://www.aacip.com/members/AACIP%20Digest%20V6–3-B&W-Part%201.pdf.

Ferguson, Ralph. *Compare the Share Phase II: The Comparisons Continue*. Ottawa, ON: n.p., 1992.

Frank, Lawrence D. Economic Determinants of Urban Form: Resulting Trade-offs between Active and Sedentary

Forms of Travel. *American Journal of Preventive Medicine* 27:3S (2004): 146–53.

Frank, Lawrence D., Martin A. Andresen, and Thomas L. Schmid. Obesity Relationships with Community Design, Physical Activity, and Time Spent in Cars. *American Journal of Preventive Medicine* 27 (2004): 87–96.

Frank, Lawrence D., and Peter Engelke. Multiple Impacts of the Built Environment on Public Health: Walkable Places and the Exposure to Air Pollution. *International Regional Science Review* 28:2 (2005): 193–216.

Frank, Lawrence, Sarah Kavage, and Todd Litman. Promoting Public Health through Smart Growth: Building Healthier Communities through Transportation and Land Use Policies and Practices. Vancouver: SmartGrowth B.C., 2006. http://www.smartgrowth.bc.ca/Portals/0/Downloads/SGBC_Health_Report_FINAL.pdf.

Frumkin, Howard, Lawrence Frank, and Richard Jackson. *Urban Sprawl and Public Health: Designing, Planning, and Building for Healthy Communities.* Washington, DC: Island Press, 2004.

Gebel, K., L. King, A. Bauman, P. Vita, T. Gill, A. Rigby, and A. Capon. *Creating Healthy Environments: A Review of Links between the Physical Environment, Physical Activity and Obesity.* Sydney: NSW: Health Department and NSW Centre for Overweight and Obesity, 2005. http://www.coo.health.usyd.edu.au/pdf/2005_creating_healthy_environments.pdf.

Gerein, Keith. Price Soars for Traffic Interchange at 23rd Ave. May 13, 2006. *Edmonton Journal*, Final Edition, A1.

Gilbert, Richard, and Anthony Perl. *Transport Revolutions: Moving People and Freight without Oil.* London: Earthscan, 2007.

Government of Alberta. Draft Land-Use Framework. 2008. http://www.landuse.gov.ab.ca/docs/LUF%20Draft%20Document%20may%2016%20FINAL.pdf.

———. One Provincial Board to Govern Alberta's Health System. News Release. May 15, 2008. http://alberta.ca/home/NewsFrame.cfm?ReleaseID=/acn/200805/23523ED9498C0–0827–451C-E98A0B8430DC1879.html.

Grant, Jill. Mixed Use in Theory and Practice. *Journal of the American Planning Association* 68:1 (2002): 71–84.

Grant MacEwan College. U-Pass. http://www.macewan.ca/web/services/sa/home/DetailsPage.cfm?ID=6839&utm_source=upass&utm_medium=redirect.

Hamilton (City of). Economic Development and Planning Committee Minutes 07–021, December 4, 2007. http://www.myhamilton.ca/NR/rdonlyres/B33FD4B2–6E71–4936-A8DD-C8F856C2E7B3/0/Dec04Minutes.pdf.

Handy, Susan L., and Kelly J. Clifton. Local Shopping as a Strategy for Reducing Automobile Travel. *Transportation* 28:4 (2001): 317–46.

Handy, Susan L., and Debbie A. Niemeier. Measuring Accessibility: An Exploration of Issues and Alternatives. *Environment and Planning A* 29:7 (1997): 1175–94.

Haughton, Graham. Environmental Justice and the Sustainable City. *Journal of Planning Education and Research* 18 (1999): 233–43.

International Council of Shopping Centers. ICSC Shopping Center Definitions. http://www.icsc.org/srch/lib/SCDefinitions99.pdf.

Jeffery, Robert W., and Simone A. French. Epidemic Obesity in the United States: Are Fast Foods and Television Viewing Contributing? *American Journal of Public Health* 88:2 (1998): 277–80.

K'Akumu, Owiti A. Sustain No City: An Ecological Conceptualization of Urban Development. *City* 11:2 (2007): 221–28.

Katzmarzyk, Peter. The Canadian Obesity Epidemic: An Historical Perspective. *Obesity Research* 10:7 (2002): 666–74.

Kaufman, Phil R. Nontraditional Retailers Are Challenging Traditional Grocery Stores. *FoodReview* 21:3 (1999): 31–33. http://www.ers.usda.gov/publications/foodreview/sep1998/frsept98g.pdf.

Kelly-Schwartz, Alexia C., Jean Stockard, Scott Doyle, and Marc Schlossberg. Is Sprawl Unhealthy? A Multilevel Analysis of the Relationship of Metropolitan Sprawl to the Health of Individuals. *Journal of Planning Education Research* 24:2 (2004): 184–96.

Krakar, Eileen, and Kim Longtin. An Overview of the Canadian Agriculture and Agri-Food System. Ottawa, ON: Agriculture and Agri-Food Canada, 2005.

Landry, Frank. Drive-Thru Ban No Idle Threat. *Edmonton Sun*, January 25, 2008.

Laraia, Barbara A., Anna Maria Siega-Riz, Jay S. Kaufman, and Sonya J. Jones. Proximity of Supermarkets Is Positively Associated with Diet Quality Index for Pregnancy. *Preventive Medicine* 39:5 (2004): 869–75.

Larsen, Kristian, and Jason Gilliland. Mapping the Evolution of "Food Deserts" in a Canadian City: Supermarket Accessibility in London, Ontario, 1961–2005. *International Journal of Health Geographics* 7 (2008): 16.

Last, John M. *Public Health and Human Ecology.* 2nd ed. Stamford, CT: Appleton & Lange, 1998.

LeSage, Edward C., Jr., and Lorna Stefanick. New Regionalist Metropolitan Action: The Case of the Alberta

Capital Region Alliance. Canadian Political Science Association Meetings, Winnipeg. 2004. http://www.cpsa-acsp.ca/papers-2004/Stefanick-LeSage.pdf.

Levinson, David, and Ajay Kumar. Activity, Travel and the Allocation of Time. *Journal of the American Planning Association* 61:4 (1995): 458–70.

Lindsey, Greg, Maltie Maraj, and SonCheong Kuan. Access, Equity, and Urban Greenways: An Exploratory Investigation. *Professional Geographer* 53:5 (2001): 332–46.

London (City of). Official Plan/Zoning Refinement Review. Regulation of Drive-Through Facilities. Revised Official Plan Amendment. July 10, 2008. http://www.london.ca/By-laws/PDFs/drivethru_july14.pdf.

Lopez, Russ. Urban Sprawl and Risk for Being Overweight or Obese. *American Journal of Public Health* 94:9 (2004): 1574–79.

MacLean, Mairi. South-Side Mega Cineplex Set to Open: 16-Screen Complex Newest Attraction in Big-Box Retail Centre. *Edmonton Journal*, Final Edition, August 2, 2000.

Mah, Bill. More Edmonton Malls in Store; 1.7M Square Feet of New Space Coming to Busy Southern Suburbs Alone. *Edmonton Journal*, April 30, 2008, E1.

McMichael, Anthony J. *Planetary Overload: Global Environmental Change and the Health of the Human Species*. Cambridge, UK: Cambridge University Press, 1993.

Middleton, John Duncan. Health, Environmental and Social Justice. *Local Environment* 8:2 (2003): 155–65.

Mitchell, Don. Introduction: Public Space and The City. *Urban Geography* 17:2 (1996): 127–31.

Morland, Kimberly, Steve Wing, and Ana Diez Roux. The Contextual Effect of the Local Food Environment on Residents' Diets: The Atherosclerosis Risk in Communities Study. *American Journal of Public Health* 92:11 (2002): 1761–67.

Nielsen, Samara J., and Barry M. Popkin. Changes in Beverage Intake between 1977 and 2001. *American Journal of Preventive Medicine* 27:3 (2004): 205–10.

North Vancouver (City of). Minutes Of The Regular Meeting Of Council. January 21, 2008. Online at http://www.cnv.org/c/DATA/1/88/2008%2001%2021.PDF.

Pereira, Mark A., Alex I. Kartashov, Cara B. Ebbeling, Linda Van Horn, Martha L. Slattery, David R. Jacobs Jr., and David S. Ludwig. Fast-food Habits, Weight Gain, and Insulin Resistance (The CARDIA Study): 15-Year Prospective Analysis. *Lancet* 365 (2005): 36–42.

Priemus, Hugo. Changing Urban Housing Markets in Advanced Economies. *Housing, Theory and Society* 21:1 (2004): 2–16.

Prüss-Üstün, Annette, and Carlos F. Corvalán. *Preventing Disease through Healthy Environments: Towards an Estimate of the Environmental Burden of Disease*. Geneva: World Health Organization, 2006. http://www.who.int/quantifying_ehimpacts/publications/preventingdisease.pdf.

Raine, Kim, John C. Spence, John Church, Normand Boulé, Linda Slater, Josh Marko, Karyn Gibbons, and Eric Hemphill. *State of the Evidence Review on Urban Health and Healthy Weights*. Ottawa: Canadian Institute for Health Information (CIHI), 2008. http://secure.cihi.ca/cihiweb/products/Urban%20Health%20and%20Healthy%20Weights.pdf.

Ridde, Valéry, Anne Guichard, and David Houéto. Social Inequalities in Health From Ottawa to Vancouver: Action for Fair Equality of Opportunity. IUHPE—Promotion and Education Supplement 2, 2007.

Robertson, Ann, and Meredith Minkler. New Health Promotion Movement: A Critical Examination. *Health Education Quarterly* 21:3 (1994): 295–312.

Ross, Nancy A., Stephane Tremblay, Saeeda Khan, Daniel Crouse, Mark Tremblay, and Jean-Marie Berthelot. Body Mass Index in Urban Canada: Neighborhood and Metropolitan Area Effects. *American Journal of Public Health* 97:3 (2007): 500–8.

Ruttan, Susan. No Takers for Rutherford Retail Space: City Agrees to Allow Apartments with Stores on Main Floor as Compromise. *Edmonton Journal*, February 26, 2008.

Sallis, James F., Lawrence D. Frank, Brian E. Saelens, and M. Katherine Kraft. 2004. Active Transportation and Physical Activity: Opportunities for Collaboration on Transportation and Public Health Research. *Transportation Research Part A. Policy and Practice* 38 (2004): 249–68.

Sarnia (City of). Council Minutes. June 23, 2008. http://www.city.sarnia.on.ca/pdf/Minutes%2020080623.pdf.

Shephard, Roy J. What Is the Optimal Type of Physical Activity to Enhance Health? *British Journal of Sports Medicine* 31 (1997): 277–84.

Simons, Paula. Downtown Food Store Will Cater to Gourmet Tastes; Customers Will Also Be Able to Dine On-Site. *Edmonton Journal*, May 6, 2008.

Smoyer-Tomic, Karen E., John C. Spence, and Carl A. Amrhein. Food Deserts in the Prairies? Supermarket Accessibility and Neighborhood Need in Edmonton, Canada. *Professional Geographer* 58 (2006): 307–26.

Smoyer-Tomic, Karen E., John C. Spence, Kim D. Raine, Carl Amrhein, Nairne Cameron, Vladimir Yasenovskiy, Nicoleta Cutumisu, Eric Hemphill, and Julia Healy. The Association between Neighborhood Socioeconomic Status and Exposure to Supermarkets and Fast Food Outlets. *Health and Place* 14:4 (2008): 740–54.

The Star. Loblaw Results Plummet on Costs. November 15,

2007.

Statistics Canada. Portrait of the Canadian Population in 2006 Census. Catalogue no. 97–550-XWE2006001. Ottawa, ON: Statistics Canada, 2007. http://www12.statcan.ca/english/census06/analysis/popdwell/ProvTerr5.cfm.

———. Portrait of the Canadian Population in 2006: Subprovincial Population Dynamics. Ottawa, ON: Statistics Canada, 2006. http://www12.statcan.ca/english/census06/analysis/popdwell/tables/table3.htm.

———. A Profile of the Canadian Population: Where We Live. Catalogue No.: 96F0030XIE2001001. Ottawa, ON: Statistics Canada, 2002. http://geodepot.statcan.ca/Diss/Highlights/Page9/Page9d_e.cfm.

———. 2001 Basic Profile of Edmonton Neighborhoods, Components 1–7, 2001 Census (20% Sample). Ottawa, ON. Statistics Canada, 2001.

———. Women in Canada: Work Chapter Updates. Catalogue no. 89F0133XIE. Ottawa, ON: Statistics Canada, 2006. http://www.statcan.ca/english/freepub/89F0133XIE/89F0133XIE2006000.htm.

———. Work and Commuting in Census Metropolitan Areas, 1996–2001. Catalogue No. 89–613-MIE, No. 007. Ottawa, ON: Statistics Canada, 2005.

Stelmach, Ed. New Board First Step in Capital Region Planning. December 19, 2007. http://premier.alberta.ca/news/news-2007-dec-19-Capital_Region_plan.cfm.

Swinburn, Boyd, Garry Egger, and Fezeela Raza. Dissecting Obesogenic Environments: The Development and Application of a Framework for Identifying and Prioritizing Environmental Interventions for Obesity. *Preventive Medicine* 29 (1999): 563–70.

Szreter, Simon. Economic Growth, Disruption, Deprivation, Disease, and Death: On the Importance of the Politics of Public Health for Development. *Population and Development Review* 23:4 (1997): 693–728.

Toneguzzi, Mario. Wal-Mart Super-sizes Five Alberta Stores; Airdrie Outlet Also Expanding as "Supercentre." *Calgary Herald*, September 20, 2007.

Toronto (City of). Council Highlights—City Council Meeting of October 1, 2002. http://www.toronto.ca/council_highlights/2002/100102.htm.

Travers, Kim D. Using Qualitative Research to Understand the Socio-Cultural Origins of Diabetes among Cape Breton Mi'kmaq. *Chronic Diseases in Canada* 16:4 (1995): 140–43.

Truelove, Marie. Measurement of Spatial Equity. *Environment and Planning C: Government and Policy* 11 (1993): 19–34.

Turcotte, Martin. Life in Metropolitan Areas: Dependence on Cars in Urban Neighborhoods. Canadian Social Trends. Catalogue no. 11–008-XIE. Ottawa, ON: Statistics Canada, 2008. http://www.statcan.ca/english/freepub/11–008-XIE/2008001/article/10503-en.pdf.

UN-Habitat. The State of the World's Cities 2004/2005. London, UK: Earthscan, 2004.

———. The State of the World's Cities 2006/2007. London, UK: Earthscan, 2007.

University of Alberta. U-Pass History. http://www.uofaweb.ualberta.ca/u-pass/u-passhistory.cfm.

U.S. Department of Agriculture. Food Marketing System in the U.S.: Retail Food Glossary. http://www.ers.usda.gov/Briefing/FoodMarketingSystem/foodretailingglossary.htm.

U.S. Green Building Council. LEED for Neighborhood Development. 2008. http://www.usgbc.org/DisplayPage.aspx?CMSPageID=148.

———. LEED for Neighborhood Development Registered Pilot Project List. 2008. http://www.usgbc.org/ShowFile.aspx?DocumentID=3546.

Vancouver (City of). Drive-In Restaurant and Drive-Through Service Guidelines. November 4, 1986. http://vancouver.ca/commsvcs/Guidelines/D009.pdf.

———. Policy Report: Urban Structure. Supermarkets in Vancouver. November 3, 1998. http://www.city.vancouver.bc.ca/ctyclerk/cclerk/981117/p1.htm.

———. Trends and Futures in the Retail Grocery Business in Vancouver: A Dialogue. Proceedings of a Conference Held May 10, 2000. Draft.

Vojnovic, Igor. Intergenerational and Intragenerational Equity Requirements for Sustainability. *Environmental Conservation* 22:3 (1995): 223–28.

Von Schirnding, Yasmin. Health and Sustainable Development: Can We Rise to the Challenge? *Lancet* 360 (2002): 632–37.

Warde, Alan. Convenience Food: Space and Timing. *British Food Journal* 101:7 (1999): 518–27.

Weinberg, Zy, and Mark S. Epstein. *No Place to Shop: Challenges and Opportunities Facing the Development of Supermarkets in Urban America.* Washington, DC: Public Voice for Food and Health Policy, 1996.

Wilkinson, Richard G. *Unhealthy Societies: The Afflictions of Inequality*. London: Routledge, 1996.

World Commission on Environment and Development. *Our Common Future.* Oxford: Oxford University Press, 1987.

World Health Organization (WHO). Obesity and Overweight Factsheet. Factsheet no. 311. 2006. http://www.who.int/mediacentre/factsheets/fs311/en/index.html.

World Health Organization, Health and Welfare Canada, and the Canadian Public Health Association. Ottawa

Charter for Health Promotion. *Canadian Journal of Public Health* 77:12 (1986): 425–30.

Wrigley, Neil, Daniel Warm, Barrie Margetts, and Amanda Whelan. Assessing the Impact of Improved Retail Access on Diet in a "Food Desert": A Preliminary Report. *Urban Studies* 39:11 (2002): 2061–82.

Young, Tom, Alex Regiec, and Erik Backstrom. Anatomy of A TOD: Greyfield Redevelopment in Edmonton. Taking the Pulse of . . . Planning Practice: Case-In-Point. Manitoba Professional Planners Institute, 2005. http://www.mppi.mb.ca/assets/pdfs/Young2005.pdf.

■ STEFAN ANDERBERG / ERIC CLARK

Green Sustainable Øresund Region

OR ECO-BRANDING COPENHAGEN AND MALMÖ?

A positive image of a city or region attracts people, investors, and enterprises. High-quality environment and local sustainability initiatives can be used for creating a positive image. A growing number of regions and cities around the world have in recent years attempted to exploit this opportunity through sustainable development strategies and innovative environmental initiatives combined with green image marketing. The Øresund region in southern Scandinavia is an example of an area that has gone to great effort to brand itself as green and sustainable. One of the central visions for the region when the Øresund cooperation was launched in 1994—after the decision to build a bridge across the sound (Øresund) connecting Denmark and Sweden—was to become "one of the cleanest big city regions in Europe."[1] This goal was representative of the new environmental policy agenda that had emerged in the early 1990s. Environmental efforts came to be considered important not only for the sake of health, quality of life, and sustainability, but also for stimulating growth and enhancing attractiveness of the region. Stimulating environmentally sustainable development signals that this is an advanced region and encourages environmental innovations and export of related products and services. Particularly the major cities Copenhagen and Malmö have developed sustainability profiles and eco-branding strategies. They are often mentioned, particularly in European contexts, as eco-city forerunners and achieve high rankings in international comparisons.

In this chapter we discuss the recent development of the region and analyze the relation between environmental quality in the region and policy programs to undergird the image of Øresund, Copenhagen, and Malmö as green environmental forerunners of urban sustainability. Have the latter had marked impact on the environment? Or has eco-branding primarily capitalized on previous environmental improvement—much of which was exogenously driven? Is this a place where sustainable living is in the becoming? Our aim is not to provide exhaustive answers to these

Figure 1. Map of the Øresund region.

questions, but more modestly to present an analysis supporting the relevance of these questions while indicating conclusions that more thorough analyses may reach.

The Øresund Region

Copenhagen is the capital of Denmark (540,000 inhabitants, with 1.7 million inhabitants in the capital region), while Malmö is the third largest city in Sweden (303,000 inhabitants, with 663,000 in the greater metropolitan area). Together with their surrounding regions (Zealand in Denmark and Scania in Sweden), they form the transboundary Øresund region with 3.7 million inhabitants in an area of 20,689 square kilometers (7,988 square miles)—the largest and most densely populated urban region in Scandinavia. Other cities in the region include Helsingborg (124,000, center of Northwestern Scania), Lund (103,000), and Kristianstad (77,000, center of Northeastern Scania) in Sweden, and Roskilde (81,000) and Elsinore (Helsingør, 61,000) in Denmark.

The Øresund region accounts for 26 percent of Denmark's and Sweden's combined GNP, with an employed labor force of about 1.7 million (1.2 million on the Danish side, 500,000 on the Swedish side).[2] The region is home of twelve universities, organizationally connected through Øresund

PHOTOGRAPH BY JAN KOFOD WINTHER

Figure 2. Øresund Bridge, view from Denmark toward Sweden. Artificial Pepper Island in foreground, where bridge and tunnel meet. The southern tip of Salt Island is on the left, with Malmö in the background.

University, with some 150,000 students, 6,500 PhD candidates and 12,000 researchers.[3] Both sides of the Øresund region are rich in agricultural land. About half of Denmark's and Sweden's combined employment in pharmaceutical industries and in medical technological industries is located in the region, which also includes strong clusters of firms within life science, IT, design, logistics, food industries, and environmental technology.

Copenhagen is in many ways the primary city in Scandinavia. Compared to Malmö and Scania, Greater Copenhagen has a much larger and more diversified labor market, especially in state and business administration, banking and finance, consultancy, culture and tourism, and has in recent years become an important labor market for the population of Scania. Crossing the Øresund was greatly facilitated by the opening of the bridge in 2000. In 2007 some 25 million trips were made across the sound via the bridge (nearly 10 million of which were by train), about twice as many trips as in 2001.[4]

The Breakthrough of Sustainability Goals

It was not surprising that sustainability became a central part of the Øresund cooperation from the start. Both Denmark and Sweden endeavor to be perceived internationally as leaders of environmental policy and management. During the 1980s, environmental politics had reached its second and definite breakthrough in Western Europe. While the first wave, the "environmental awakening" in the 1960s, was characterized by discovery and debate on local environmental problems, the emphasis during the 1980s was on large-scale international issues. Dying forests in Central Europe, the discovery of the ozone hole and mass death among fish and seals in the Baltic Sea made large-scale threats concrete, and these threats were perceived as urgent.[5] International cooperation intensified in the early 1990s with the Earth Summit in Rio de Janeiro, and environmental issues became in many countries a much more important policy area.

In both Sweden and Denmark, environmental policies were radicalized during the 1990s.[6] Ambitious water plans and programs for radical reduction of greenhouse gas emissions were introduced in Denmark, and the Ecocycle and Green People's Home programs were launched in Sweden.[7] The Ecocycle vision was a national vision for sustainable Swedish society based on closing cycles and minimizing road transport while improving public transport coverage and regional economic growth potentials. The Green People's Home policy incorporated the goal of sustainable development into the traditional social democratic People's Home program. The most concrete result was the Local Investment Program, which supported innovative sustainability efforts in Swedish municipalities.[8] Local Agenda 21 was actively supported by governments in both countries.

Ecological Modernization, Ecocities and Place Branding

The *Environmental Program for the Øresund Region* states the following:

> A good environment is a goal in itself. In the Øresund region it is, however, more than that—it is also one of the most important preconditions for a positive and dynamic development. With this environmental program it is our intention not only to take a first step toward breaking the relation between wealth and negative environmental impact, but to establish that a good environment is a prerequisite for desirable development in the Øresund region.[9]

This program evidently assumes that it is possible to combine sustainability with economic growth, and that active environmental initiatives can contribute to growth. In this it adheres to a perspective that has gained considerable influence in environmental politics: ecological modernization.[10] Ecological modernization optimistically emphasizes potentials for combining environmental and economic goals by identifying and exploiting win-win situations. Links are thereby forged between environmental policy and regional development programs. Programs of environmental innovation, local sustainability investment, development of alternative energy sources, and green industry initiatives are seen not only to improve environmental performance, but also to stimulate regional economic competitiveness and growth by making regions more attractive to tourists (which account for increasing shares of urban economies), investors, and the creative class (commonly perceived as a key factor in urban development).[11]

These visions provide market actors a central role in developing society in an ecologically sustainable direction. Environmental consciousness is important not only for influencing legislation, but also for stimulating change in behavior such as choosing environmentally friendly products and sorting waste. Sustainable technology and enhanced efficiency of resource utilization are

PHOTOGRAPH BY PER WESSEL

Figure 3. Banner for Copenhagen's Eco-Metropole vision.

seen to increase competitiveness and provide market advantages. Private enterprise and political bodies at various scales are called to seize upon sustainable development as an opportunity, and the image is propagated that there is much to gain for those who start early and keep ahead.[12] Environmental programs have to a lesser degree been characterized by traditional command and control measures via legislation and regulation. Other types of measures have become more important, aiming at increasing consciousness, mobilizing industry and the public, and creating incentives for cooperation and proactive engagement in solutions based on improved control and efficiency of resource flows rather than conventional end-of-pipe pollution control. Local Agenda 21, information campaigns, recycling programs, local investment programs for stimulating environmental innovation, green networks linking public authorities and industry, and branch treaties are examples of policy initiatives introduced in Denmark and Sweden in the 1990s.

This new type of environmental policy also implies new roles and challenges for local authorities. Decentralization has given municipalities in both Denmark and Sweden increasing responsibility for environmental protection and natural resource management. Municipalities are responsible for information and for initiating local collaboration in various ways. Such collaboration is often encouraged and supported by central government but is largely dependent on voluntary local initiatives.

This breakthrough in environmental policy based on ecological modernization was paralleled in the 1990s by advances in urban ecology, eco-city movements and sustainable city visions.[13] The European Sustainable Cities and Towns Conference was held in Aalborg in Denmark in 1994. The Aalborg Charter states that cities play a central role in ensuring sustainable development and encourages cities to develop a more integrated approach to local policymaking, harmonizing environmental, social, cultural, and economic objectives. The task for cities is to integrate principles of sustainability into all policy areas and to formulate locally appropriate strategies based on their respective strengths. Supported by national programs, cities began to develop sustainability activities with inspiration from Local Agenda 21, the Aalborg Charter, and urban ecology. Such initiatives have also been supported by the European Union (EU), which, despite limited power over local and regional planning, selected sustainable urban development as a central area for environmental and sustainability policy activities. The sustainability programs of the EU are based on Open Method of Coordination (OMC), a "soft form of governance" by which the EU makes efforts to encourage innovative initiatives through economic support and benchmarking.[14]

Environmental quality and awareness have also become an increasingly important element in competition between metropolitan regions.[15] Scandinavian cities are no exception to the global move toward investment in place marketing, "imagineering," and branding.[16] This involves defining a sharp city profile and making efforts to ensure consistent communication of that profile. Some features of a city are emphasized in a city brand, while others remain unacknowledged—not least, the geographical locations of the city's ecological footprint. The brand may be based on an emerging or desirable characteristic, a vision or goal, rather than current reality, but in order to be credible and successful it needs to be backed up by consistent actions.

The underlying thesis of ecological modernization theory—"that the only possible way out of the ecological crisis is by going further into industrialization"—has aroused considerable debate.[17] The debate on ecological modernization has been helpful in highlighting nuances in the subtle complexities involved in institutional responses of industrial capitalist societies to ecological crises. Richard York and Eugene Rosa detail some logical, methodological, and empirical inadequacies in the theory and caution against uncritical commitment to ecological modernization, "because it may blind us to other options that have greater potential for bringing about ecological sustainability."[18] Our aim here is not to contribute to one side or the other in this debate. The relevance of ecological modernization theory for analyses of eco-branding is simply that eco-branding constitutes a common form in which "ecological modernisation appears in its guise of a pragmatic programme for business and government...a cover for business-as-usual with a slight green tinge."[19] Eco-branding presents images that are meant to strike us as very positive for the environment, but we stand to be reminded that we "should not assume that an appearance of environmental commitment necessarily corresponds with ecologically sustainable outcomes."[20]

Sustainability Activities in the Region

In order to gain an overview and evaluate the status of environmental and sustainability activities and programs in the Øresund region, Stefan Anderberg conducted an Internet-based inventory of programs and activities in municipalities in the region.[21] The inventory involved searches using environmental keywords and selected organizations, corporations, and municipalities, mostly in English, Danish, and Swedish, but also in German and French. The Internet provides remarkable opportunities for quick overviews, but one must be careful not to draw far-reaching conclusions. The uneven development of Internet use limits the value of this source for reliable comparisons. Material accessible on the Web is very heterogeneous, often arbitrary, and not comprehensive. Documents presenting general aims and priorities are common, while detailed documentation of activities is rare. The results of such inventories may say more about branding and imagineering than about real activities. Firms and municipalities engaged in similar activities may prioritize differently given variation in resource capacity for producing information and materials for public relations. Furthermore, terminology is not standardized but rather often improvised. The same phenomenon may be referred to by different names in various contexts—for example, green merchandise, ecological products, or environmentally friendly goods—and missing just one can skew the results of such an inventory.

This inventory shows that especially the major cities of Copenhagen, Malmö, and Lund, but also other major cities in the region, such as Helsingborg, Kristianstad, Landskrona, Frederiksberg, Roskilde, Køge, and Helsingør, have ambitious environmental profiling activities.[22] There are also examples of suburban municipalities in Greater Copenhagen, such as Albertslund, Ballerup, and Glostrup, that have invested in environmental profiling in order to replace their traditional images as sites of large polluting industries. These municipalities strive, however, to maintain their industry and present themselves as attractive industrial locations. Landskrona is a similar Swedish example. There are also a few dispersed rural municipalities that declare high environmental ambitions, but their activities are difficult to assess in comparison with the more documented cities.

Danish municipalities have generally developed more environmental interests and are engaged in a broader array of sustainability activities than their Swedish counterparts. It is more common that Danish municipalities have programs for green procurement, green industry, environmental regulation, ecological information, and ecological housing and planning. About one-third of the Swedish municipalities appear somewhat uncommitted and passive, compared to one-fifth of the Danish municipalities. These passive municipalities are predominantly located in the periphery. Already associated with clean environments and nature, they do not see any pressing need to improve their green image.

In Denmark, Local Agenda 21 is compulsory by law and has therefore become an integrated part of municipal development plans. Since the discontinuation of central government support for Local Agenda 21 in Sweden, it remains in operation almost exclusively in larger cities, where it has a similar status as in Denmark. In Scania there are nine eco-communes that are part of a national network to stimulate local sustainability efforts (Scania consists of thirty-three municipalities). The Local Investment Program was an important Swedish venture, whereby nearly US$1 billion (six billion kronor) was distributed to Swedish municipalities for implementing Agenda 21 plans.[23] About half of all Swedish municipalities—seventeen in Scania—received support from this program, most of which are part of or close to major cities.

The Region on the International Sustainability Scene

The international visibility of the Øresund region as environmentally progressive—a place where sustainable development and ecological planning are deep-seated—is striking. Hosting international conferences and participating in international projects and networks have contributed to this visibility. In addition, there are organizations with highly visible programs, most notably the Øresund Environment Academy and Sustainable Business Hub, which seek to combine environmental initiatives with business development.[24] Furthermore, there are several international companies with home bases in the region that in various ways have developed or improved their environmental/sustainability image—for example, Hartmanns, Mærsk, Arla, and Tetra Pak.

Copenhagen, Malmö, and Lund dominate visibility (see table 1). These cities are also more likely to be found on German and French language websites and literature on Ökostadt/ecovilles. Helsingborg, Landskrona, Roskilde, and Kristianstad, with its Water Kingdom, are also fairly visible on English-language Internet sites.

Copenhagen is well known as a bicycle city, but it has many other sustainability strengths in housing, energy, and transportation. EMAS-certification of the municipality in 1998 clearly signaled its environmental profiling ambitions and aspirations to become the (unofficial) environmental capital of Europe.[25] In Sweden, Lund was one of the first cities to develop a green

Table 1. Internet hits of municipal environmental and sustainability programs and activities in the Øresund region.

Sustainable city		+ Lund	819,000	+ Øresund	18,700
+ Malmö	20,300	+ Malmö	249,000	**Water**	
+ Copenhagen	17,300	+ Roskilde	166,000	+ Kristianstad	206,000
+ Lund	14,300	+ Kristianstad	80,800	**Environment**	
Sustainable		+ Helsingborg	54,900	+ Øresund	46,700
+ Copenhagen	1,760,000	+ Landskrona	20,100		

Source: Google, September 9, 2007.

profile. But today it has been surpassed by Malmö, which in European contexts is often recognized as a sustainable city front-runner—a fact that is probably surprising to many citizens in the region. Malmö's visibility is primarily a result of consistently being very active in EU-sponsored international network projects, hosting and participating in conferences, and investing in eco-imagineering. Malmö has received much attention for a few flagship urban renewal projects emphasizing sustainable energy—namely, Augustenborg and Västra Hamnen (waterfront redevelopment in the harbor), but also for green roofs (Green Roof Center) and, most recently, the City Tunnel rail project.

PHOTOGRAPH BY TINE HARDEN

Figure 4. From brochure: "Eco-Metropole: Our Vision for Copenhagen 2015."

While sustainability branding of the region has had some success, it is clearly the major cities that have most successfully penetrated international attention. Recently, the American environmental magazine *Grist* published a list of fifteen green cities in the world.[26] Malmö ranked fourth place and Copenhagen sixth place. Such rankings are commonly based less on careful measurements of environmental quality than on subjectivity and coincidence. Nevertheless, the results are not merely coincidental, since they are not an isolated event but rather an outcome of deliberate imagineering and eco-branding.

The Ecocity Forerunners: Copenhagen and Malmö

Copenhagen is a much larger city than Malmö, although there are significant similarities in the development of the two cities—and of other cities in Northwestern Europe. Manufacturing industries were severely hit by restructuring in the 1970s. Both cities stagnated but have since the mid-1980s experienced renewed growth. In recent years, growth in Malmö has been stimulated particularly by the construction of the Øresund Bridge, expansion of education, and strong growth in the Danish economy.

The Traditional Image: Crowded, Industrial, and Polluted Cities

Neither city has a long-standing reputation as clean and healthy. Both had large centrally located industries right into the 1980s, as well as large harbor areas which during the postwar period expanded rapidly on landfill in Øresund. For over a century, until the crisis of the 1970s, Malmö consistently remained among the fastest growing cities in Sweden. As late as 1949, 37 percent of manufacturing employment in Denmark was located in the inner city of Copenhagen.[27] Copenhagen long had been among the most densely populated cities in Europe. In the crowded inner city, housing was mixed with industry, and most of the problems of the early industrial European city still existed into the 1950s: crowdedness, unhealthy apartments, lack of light and fresh air, and related health problems.

During the postwar economic boom, pollution problems became more evident and received increasing attention. Coal and coke remained the dominant source of energy, and air pollution was a severe problem. The first air pollution measurements in the 1940s showed that areas in the center of Copenhagen were more polluted than London.[28] When regular air quality measurements started in the early 1960s, the average SO_2 (sulfur dioxide) level in central Copenhagen was about 80 $\mu g/m^3$ (micrograms per cubic meter) in the summer and 120 $\mu g/m^3$ in the winter, which can be compared with WHO's recommended ceiling of 50 $\mu g/m^3$ SO_2. Malmö had similar levels until the early 1970s. Industry made noise and created high-risk situations in connection with transportation and the use of chemicals in the vicinity of housing areas. Coke was also widely used in Malmö for heating, gas production, and some industries, but the energy sector diversified earlier in Sweden with electrification based on hydropower resources in the northern part of the country.

Movement out from the crowded inner city commenced in the 1950s, both industry and people finding space for expansion in the periphery. In Copenhagen, the inner-city population decreased by approximately 40 percent between the 1950s and the 1980s, and today less than half

Figure 5. Øresund Bridge, view from Sweden toward Denmark. Salt Island on the right, with artificial Pepper Island on the left. Copenhagen is in the distant background.

the population of Greater Copenhagen live in the inner city. In Malmö, a dramatic expansion of the city took place with construction of large peripheral housing estates during the so-called million program (the construction of over 1 million dwellings between 1965 and 1974 in a country of about 8 million inhabitants). Parallel to the peripheral expansion of both cities, the inner cities became the object of large-scale renewal. In Malmö, a radical reshaping of large areas of the inner city took place through demolition and new construction, while in Copenhagen inner-city transformation more commonly took the form of renovations. In both cases, inner-city revitalization included new infrastructure and green areas.

Improved Urban Environmental Quality

As in most North European cities, air quality has improved considerably since the 1960s (see fig. 6.) In both Copenhagen and Malmö, levels of sulfur dioxide (SO_2) have generally been below 5 μg/

m^3 since the 1990s, and concentrations of most other pollutants have also decreased in recent decades. This improvement in air quality started in the 1960s with the substitution of coal and coke with oil and large-scale investment in district heating. Today, 96 percent of Copenhagen's apartment buildings and 90 percent of Malmö's are connected to extensive district heating networks. Improvement continued in the 1970s with pollution control, closing of heavily polluting factories, and new types of fuel for heating. Today, the main source of air pollution is road traffic. Atmospheric concentrations of the typically car-related pollutants nitrogen dioxide and ozone have been relatively stable since the 1980s. In central Copenhagen it remains, however, a challenge to reach NO_2 levels below 40 µg/m^3.

The development of water quality is more remarkable. Both cities have centrally located beaches that are very popular and crowded during summer. In Malmö, investment in new sewage treatment plants in the 1970s and continuous refinement of water management has resulted in cleaner water in Malmö's beaches than most beaches along Swedish coasts. In Denmark, water pollution control developed more slowly, but emissions to Øresund have been reduced by 80–90 percent since the 1980s, and beaches have recently been opened in the South Harbor.

The major trend in the regional pollution landscape is a dramatic change from a traditional emission landscape with a distinct difference between the polluted city and the clean countryside, to a more complex emission landscape in which pollution sources are more diffuse and primarily generated by traffic, consumption, and agriculture.[29]

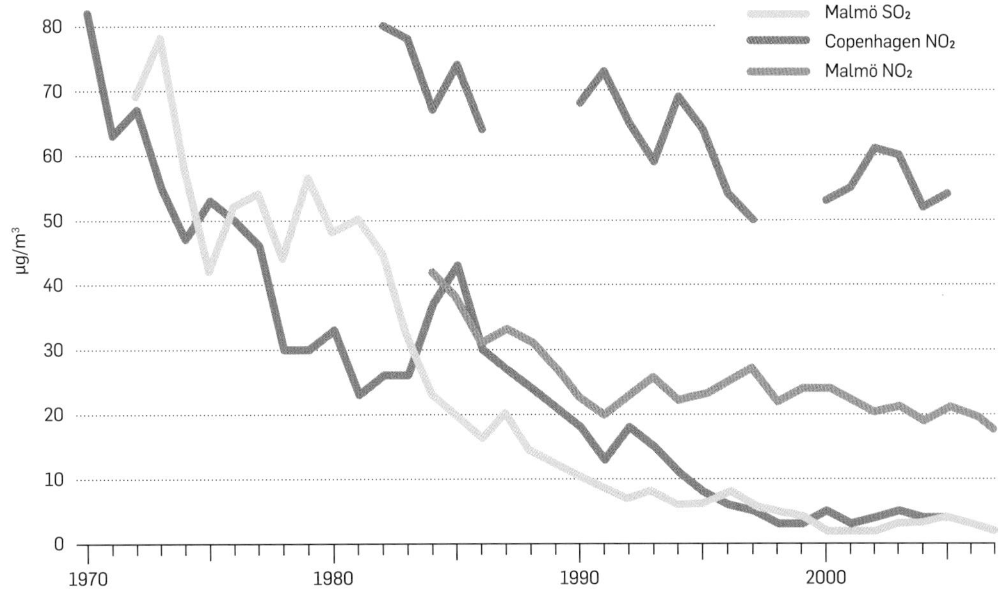

Figure 6. Atmospheric concentrations of sulphur dioxide (SO_2) and nitrogen dioxide (NO_2) in the city centers of Copenhagen and Malmö.

Source: Luftkvaliteten i Malmö 2007, Malmö stad, Miljöförvaltningen, Historiske data om luftforurening (H.C. Andersens Boulevard), Københavns Kommune, Miljøkontrollen.

Transformation—Search for New Identities

With the economic crisis of the 1970s, population in both cities stagnated and the tax revenue base deteriorated as high-income groups moved out to residential suburbs and peripheral municipalities. Important industries such as textile and shipyards closed, regional policies disadvantaged the big cities, and new industrial development took place elsewhere. For Scania, this was a period of regional decline: from being one of the wealthiest regions in the country in the 1960s, it had become one of the poorest in the 1990s. However, since the mid-1980s Copenhagen and Malmö have experienced renewed growth in which immigration, education and research, trade, finance, and cultural activities have played key roles. Presently the Øresund region has a concentration of biotech education, research, and development, making it among the leading biotech regions worldwide.[30] For Malmö, the establishment of a new university college, the construction of the Øresund Bridge, and improved connections to Copenhagen and the booming Danish economy have been especially important.

This transformation has also involved a shift in city governance and a search for new identities, visions, and brands for the cities. Local governments became much more active in branding their cities in order to attract new investments and residents. "Wonderful" Copenhagen has a long history of presenting itself for tourists and international visitors. For Malmö, however, this was more of a challenge. In their search for a new identity and brand for place-marketing, both cities discovered that their previous environmental achievements were an asset, and they set about to utilize and refine that asset.

The Sustainability Branding of Two Cities

As home to many research milieus, environmental and development consultancy firms, and modern investments in environmental infrastructure, Copenhagen has reflected Denmark's self-image as an environmental pioneer. The capital city has been a center for showcasing Danish innovations and exporting Danish technology and environmental management tools. But it was not until the 1990s that the municipality and region began to actively draw on this potential for creating a green image of the city. Well initiated, its ambitions became grandiose. The location of the European Environmental Agency, opened in 1994, rendered legitimacy to Copenhagen being the environmental capital of Europe. Biking has been the most consistent and successful element in the green marketing of Copenhagen, but the city has cultivated other good practices of sustainable urban development, including ecological housing, green consumerism, development of green and recreational areas, and waste and water management. Copenhagen became the first EMAS-certified municipality in 1998. According to the present official vision, "Miljømetropolen" Copenhagen will be the world's most environmentally sound metropolis by 2015 and stand as proof that environmental care can fuel developmental dynamics.

Malmö has long been at the frontier of Swedish environmental initiatives. The sewage treatment plant and the remote heating system were among the most advanced in the world in the 1970s. However, the city was then more a site for implementing central state policies than

PHOTOGRAPH BY TINE HARDEN

Figure 7. A Copenhagen brochure.

it was initiator of environmental projects. It was not until the mid-1990s that the city started to independently develop its green profile. This was facilitated by the central state and EU in the form of funding for Bo01 in Västra Hamnen (a national housing exhibition in the West Harbor) and Augustenborg (known for the Green Roof Center), and by emerging forms of cooperation with Copenhagen. These projects and cooperation with Copenhagen opened the door to many important networks. Malmö developed its sustainable development agenda and administration, and became an active partner in many networks. The city regularly hosts international workshops, meetings, and conferences, often with a high political profile—for example, Global Ministerial Environment Forum in 2000 and International Sustainable City Development Conferences in 2005 and 2007, boosting international exposure. Together with Malmö University College and other local and regional partners, the city founded a Center for Sustainable Urban Development, spanning research and business-related sustainability activities. In 2006 Malmö became Sweden's first Fairtrade city. Not surprisingly, Malmö was among the nominees for the Nordic Council's Nature and Environment Prize, which for the first time targeted cities in 2007. Malmö's explicit ambitions as a green and sustainable city are, however, more modest than Copenhagen's. City plans focus more on implementing national goals than developing Malmö's image as a sustainability city forerunner.

Figure 8. A Copenhagen brochure: "The World's Best City for Biking."

The Great Unsolved Problem

The great unsolved environmental problem in the Øresund region, a problem it shares with many other regions, concerns road traffic. Road traffic has continued to grow in both Greater Copenhagen and Malmö, and problems of road congestion have increased dramatically in recent years, especially in Copenhagen—disturbing its ambitions to be an environmental metropolis. While major infrastructural investments have increased rail capacity on both sides of Øresund, there are few signs of any structural shift away from car traffic. It is only in the inner cities where public transport, biking, and walking play significant roles for daily transport. New peripheral shopping and business zones accessible only by motorway are developed and allowed to expand.

Copenhagen has long-held ambitions to reduce car traffic by developing public transport. Car traffic continues to grow, however, in spite of increasing use of public transport. The number of vehicles passing the municipal boundary increased 30 percent between 1985 and 2005, while the average speed on major roads decreased by more than 20 percent, from 34 to 27 km/h (21 to 17 mph) (see fig. 9).

With continued economic growth in Greater Copenhagen, car ownership and commuting has increased dramatically. The number of cars in the metropolitan area (Hovedstadsområdet) increased 28 percent between 1992 and 2004. Regional commuting patterns have become more dispersed, complex, and difficult to cover with public transport. Figure 10 shows daily commuting in Greater Copenhagen in 1970 and 2005. The two inner-city municipalities are Copenhagen and Frederiksberg (shown in yellow). The inner suburbs are shown in green, and the periphery of the city region is shown in blue.

In figure 10 the width of the arrows corresponds to the number of daily commuters. Traditional

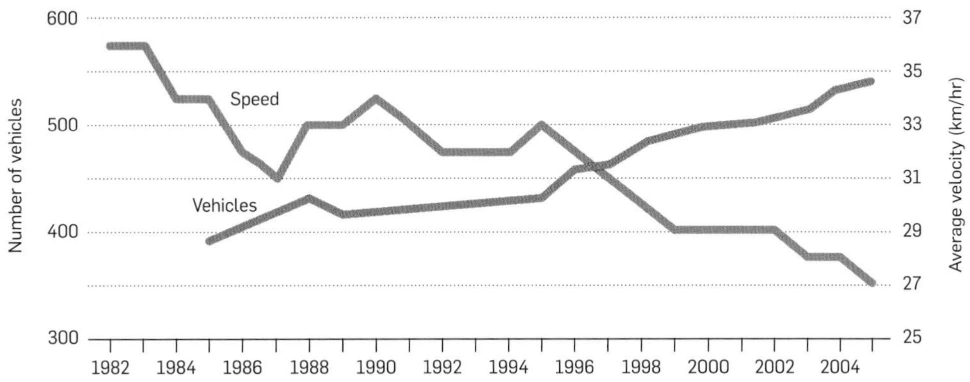

Figure 9. Number of vehicles passing the Copenhagen municipal boundary 6 A.M.–6 P.M. daily.

Source: Københavns Kommune, Teknik-og Miljøforvaltningen, Center for Trafik, 2008.

commuting from the inner suburbs to the city center peaked in the 1970s. In 1970 these commuter flows varied from 7,300 to 120,000, and in 2005 from 20,000 to 85,000. Today about 60 percent of the working population in the region works outside their municipality of residence. During the last decade the flows that grew the most were commuting into the region from areas outside the metropolitan area (including Sweden) and the commuting of residents in the inner city.

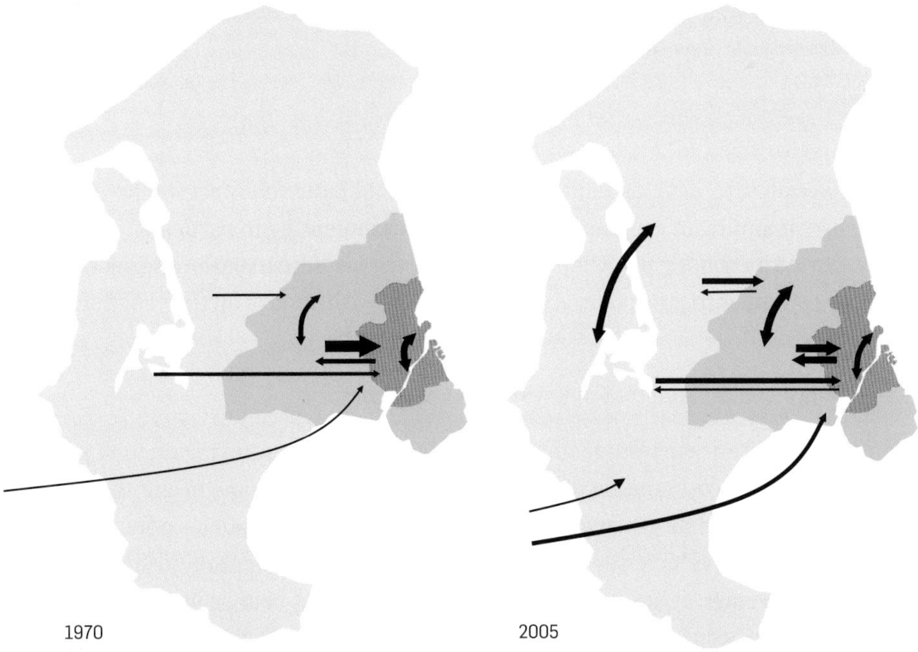

Figure 10. Commuting between the inner city, the suburbs, and the periphery of the city region, and between municipalities within these areas in 1970 and 2005.

Source: Data from Danmarks Statistik, http://www.statistikbanken.dk.

Figure 11. Lilla Fiskaregatan, the main shopping street in Lund.
PHOTOGRAPH BY HUEI-MIN TSAI

On the Swedish side, development around Malmö and Lund follows a similar pattern, with a marked rise in commuting in general and long-distance commuting in particular. Public transport in Scania increased by about 7 percent per year during the last fifteen years, and yet car traffic and car ownership continues to grow. Cars account for about two-thirds of all travel in the region.

Material Flows and Geographies of Environmental Impacts

Most of the major postwar environmental improvements in the Øresund region took place well before sustainability and eco-branding of places came into vogue. To some extent the eco-branding of the region can be seen as greenwashing, not unlike that of private corporations marketing products such as motor vehicles as especially green and environmentally friendly even if they pollute more than average. It has been suggested that "the risk of being conned by slick corporate greenwash has never been greater."[31] As cities vie for flows of capital and the so-called creative class, this risk appears to extend to political bodies of cities and regions.

Furthermore, a sizable share of these improvements were exogenously generated, through economic restructuring or national policy. While most pollutants continue to decrease, albeit at a slower pace, it is difficult to connect these improvements to the local initiatives highlighted in the region's and cities' recent efforts at eco-branding.

The shift from an industrial to a postindustrial economic base had major impacts on the environment. Consumption of industrial products in the region has, however, not diminished, but rather increased. This raises issues of environmental load displacement and ecologically unequal exchange, which in turn problematizes sustainability from a perspective of scale.[32] In a global system in which all places are economically connected, can any place claim to be sustainable based on local measures alone, without consideration of material linkages with other less sustainable places? Is local sustainability an oxymoron?

Unequal exchange entails "moving accumulated capital from politically weak regions to politically strong regions."[33] The concept of ecologically unequal exchange leaves the issue of value aside, focusing instead on material flows of trade and their ecological consequences. To paraphrase Immanuel Wallerstein, it entails moving the ecological footprint of politically and economically strong regions to politically and economically weak regions.[34] Ecologically unequal exchange takes place when societal relations of power allow for the physical transfer of environmental degradation—upon which much of our daily consumption rests—to places far away from our environmentally clean (and therefore often presumed sustainable) homes, cities, and regions. Helga Weisz's empirical analysis of Denmark's ecological trade balances corroborates the view that Copenhagen's greenness is achieved partly through ecologically unequal trade and the time-space appropriation of distant places.[35]

Conclusion

The goals of the Øresund region to become "one of the cleanest big city regions in Europe" and to "break the relation between wealth and negative environmental impact" were neither bold nor creative. The Øresund region was already one of the cleanest densely populated regions in the world and had for decades combined remarkable environmental improvements with economic growth. The difference between today and when the goals were formulated a decade ago is that now the Øresund region has a much stronger international position as a forerunner of urban sustainability. The region, and in particular Copenhagen and Malmö, have successfully eco-branded themselves and become visible on the global sustainability scene. It is difficult however to distinguish this from previous efforts to attract capital investment in competition with other cities.

This is certainly not to deny that there is a long list of municipal, regional, national, and EU initiatives, investments, programs, and activities with positive environmental impacts. But in a broader view it appears that the geopolitical economy of global economic restructuring and environmental load displacement through ecologically unequal exchange also play important roles in the region's recent environmental history. We have not been able here to even begin to determine with any precision the relative importance of these forces, and must leave that an open question for further research. But the analysis does suggest that the comet careers of Copenhagen and Malmö on the eco-branding scene are based as much on capitalizing preexisting conditions as on remarkable successes of environmental policies and measures taken after the high-pitched goals were formulated.

NOTES

We gratefully acknowledge funding by a Linnaeus Research Grant (http://www.lucid.lu.se) from The Swedish Research Council, Formas.

1. *Øresund—En region bliver til* (Copenhagen: Erhvervsministeriet, 1999), 69.
2. http://www.oresundskomiteen.dk/regionen-i-ciffror-statistik/se/html/00_00.html.
3. http://www.uni.oresund.org/sw2006.asp.
4. Värt att veta om Øresundsbron, Øresundsbro Konsortiet 2008, http://www.oresundsbron.com/library/?obj=6216
5. Stefan Anderberg, Sylvia Prieler, Krzysztof Olendrzynski, and Sander de Bruyn, *Old Sins—Industrial Metabolism, Heavy Metal Pollution and Environmental Transition in Central Europe* (Tokyo: United Nations University Press, 2000).
6. Andrew Jamison and Erik Baark, National Shades of Green: Comparing the Swedish and Danish Styles in Ecological Modernization, *Environmental Values* 8 (1999): 199–218.
7. Colin Fudge and Janet Rowe, Ecological Modernisation as a Framework for Sustainable Development: A Case Study in Sweden, *Environment and Planning A* 33 (2001): 1527–46.
8. Jonas R. Bylund, *Planning, Projects, Practice: A Human Geography of the Stockholm Local Investment Programme in Hammarby Sjöstad* (Stockholm: Stockholm University, 2006).
9. Miljöprogram för Öresundsregionen, Rapport från Miljöprogrammets styrgrupp, Öresundskomitteen, 2000, 5.
10. Joseph Huber, *Die verlorene unschuld der Ökologie: Neue teknologien und superindustrielle entwicklung* (Frankfurt am Main: Fischer Verlag, 1982); Maarten A. Hajer, *The Politics of Environmental Discourse: Ecological Modernization and the Policy Process* (Oxford: Oxford University Press, 1995).
11. Richard Florida, *The Rise of the Creative Class: And How It's Transforming Work, Leisure and Everyday Life* (New York: Basic Books, 2002).
12. Michael E. Porter and Claas van der Linde, Green and Competitive: Ending the Stalemate, *Harvard Business Review* 73 (1995): 120–34.
13. Graham Haughton and Colin Hunter, *Sustainable Cities* (London: Jessica Kingsley Publishers / Regional Studies Association, 1994).
14. Introduced by the European Council of Lisbon in March 2000, this term recognized and formalized previously established practices more than it contributed to forging new practices.
15. Christian Wichmann Matthiessen, Henrik Søgaard, and Stefan Anderberg, Environmental Performance and European Cities—A New Key Parameter in Competition between Metropolitan Centers, in *Monitoring Cities—International Perspectives*, ed. Wayne K. D. Davies and Ivan J. Townshend (Calgary: International Geographical Union, 2002), 119–41.
16. Søren Smidt-Jensen, Branding Medium-Sized Cities in Transition, in *Restructuring of Medium Sized Cities—Lessons from the Baltic Sea Region*, ed. Niels Boje Groth, Thilo Lang, Mats Johansson, Vesa Kanninen, Stefan Anderberg, and Andreas Cornett (Copenhagen: Danish Centre for Forest, Landscape and Planning, 2005), 159–70.
17. Gert Spargaren and Arthur P. J. Mol, Sociology, Environment and Modernity: Ecological Modernization as a Theory of Social Change, *Society and Natural Resources* 5 (1992): 323–44.
18. Richard York and Eugene A. Rosa, Key Challenges to Ecological Modernization Theory: Institutional Efficacy, Case Study Evidence, Units of Analysis and the Pace of Eco-efficiency, *Organization and Environment* 16 (2003): 273–88.
19. David Gibbs, Ecological Modernisation, Regional Economic Development and Regional Development Agencies, *Geoforum* 31 (2000): 9–19.
20. York and Rosa, Key Challenges to Ecological Modernization Theory, 273–88.
21. Stefan Anderberg, Ekologisk modernisering i Øresundsregionen? Miljø—Centralt i Øresundssamarbetet, in *Geografers forskningsbidrag til det Øresundsregionale udviklingsprojekt*, ed. Christian Wichmann Matthiessen, 67-80 (Copenhagen: Reitzels Forlag, 2005).
22. The municipalities of Frederiksberg and Copenhagen together form the inner city of Greater Copenhagen.
23. Daniel Nilsson, The LIP Programme—A Prerequisite for the Environmental Initiatives, in *Sustainable City of Tomorrow—Bo01—Experiences from a Swedish Housing Exhibition*, ed. Bengt Persson (Stockholm: Formas, 2005).
24. http://www.oresundscienceregion.org/sw13743.asp and http://www.sbhub.se/SbHub_eng/index.html.
25. Eco-Management and Audit Scheme is an EU voluntary instrument for recognizing organizations that continuously improve their environmental performance.
26. *Grist*, 15 Green Cities, July 19, 2007, http://www.grist.org/news/maindish/2007/07/19/cities/.
27. Stefan Anderberg and Erik Slentø, Stof og

energistrømme i landskabet—Storkøbenhavns miljøhistorie, in *Byen i landskabet—Landskabet i byen*, ed. Sten Engelstoft (Odense: Geografforlaget, 2009).

28. Jes Fenger, *Luftforureningens historie: Fra et indendørs til et globalt problem*, 2d ed. (Denmark: Hovedland, 2004).
29. Ulrik Lohm, Stefan Anderberg, and Bo Bergbäck, Industrial Metabolism at the National Level: A Case-Study on Chromium and Lead Pollution in Sweden, 1880–1980, in *Industrial Metabolism: Restructuring for Sustainable Development*, ed. Robert U. Ayres and Udo E. Simonis (Tokyo: United Nations University Press, 1994), 103–18.
30. Steve Garlick, Peter Kresl, and Peter Vaessen, The Øresund Science Region: A Cross-Border Partnership between Denmark and Sweden, Peer Review Report, Programme on Institutional Management of Higher Education (IMHE), Organisation for Economic Co-operation and Development, Directorate for Education, 2006.
31. Fred Pearce, The Great Green Swindle, *Guardian*, October 23, 2008.
32. Alf Hornborg, Footprints in the Cotton Fields: The Industrial Revolution as Time-Space Appropriation and Environmental Load Displacement, *Ecological Economics* 59 (2006): 74–81; Alf Hornborg, Environmental Load Displacement in World History, in *Sustainable Development in a Globalized World*, ed. Björn Hettne (New York: Palgrave Macmillan, 2007); Helmut Haberl, Marina Fischer-Kowalski, Fridolin Krausmann, Helga Weisz, and Verena Winiwarter, Progress towards Sustainability? What the Conceptual Framework of Material and Energy Flow Accounting (MEFA) Can Offer, *Land Use Policy* 21 (2004): 199–213; Helga Weisz, Combining Social Metabolism and Input-Output Analysis to Account for Ecologically Unequal Trade, in *Rethinking Environmental History: World-System History and Global Environmental Change*, ed. Alf Hornborg, J. R. McNeill, and Joan Martinez-Alier, 289–306 (Lanham, MD: AltaMira, 2007).
33. Immanuel Wallerstein, *World-Systems Analysis: An Introduction* (Durham, NC: Duke University Press, 2004), 28.
34. Alf Hornborg, Towards an Ecological Theory of Unequal Exchange: Articulating World System Theory and Ecological Economics, *Ecological Economics* 25 (1998): 127–36.
35. Weisz, Combining Social Metabolism, 289–306 (Lanham, MD: AltaMira, 2007).

REFERENCES

Anderberg, Stefan. Ekologisk modernisering i Øresundsregionen? Miljø—Centralt i Øresunds-samarbetet. In *Geografers forskningsbidrag til det Øresundsregionale udviklingsprojekt. Kulturgeografiske skrifter, bd. 14*, ed. Christian Wichmann Matthiessen, 67–80. Copenhagen: Reitzels Forlag, 2005.

Anderberg, Stefan, Sylvia Prieler, Krzysztof Olendrzynski, and Sander de Bruyn. *Old Sins—Industrial Metabolism, Heavy Metal Pollution and Environmental Transition in Central Europe*. Tokyo: United Nations University Press, 2000.

Anderberg, Stefan, and Erik Slentø. Stof og energistrømme i landskabet—Storkøbenhavns miljøhistorie. In *Byen i landskabet—Landskabet i byen*, ed. Sten Engelstoft. Odense: Geografforlaget, 2009.

Bylund, Jonas R. *Planning, Projects, Practice: A Human Geography of the Stockholm Local Investment Programme in Hammarby Sjöstad*. Stockholm: Stockholm University, 2006.

Fenger, Jes. *Luftforureningens historie: Fra et indendørs til et globalt problem*. 2d ed. Denmark: Hovedland, 2004.

Florida, Richard. *The Rise of the Creative Class: And How It's Transforming Work, Leisure and Everyday Life*. New York: Basic Books, 2002.

Fudge, Colin, and Janet Rowe. Ecological Modernisation as a Framework for Sustainable Development: A Case Study in Sweden. *Environment and Planning A* 33 (2001): 1527–46.

Garlick, Steve, Peter Kresl and Peter Vaessen. 2006. The Øresund Science Region: A Cross-Border Partnership between Denmark and Sweden. Peer review report. Programme on Institutional Management of Higher Education (IMHE), Organisation for Economic Co-operation and Development, Directorate for Education.

Gibbs, David. Ecological Modernisation, Regional Economic Development and Regional Development Agencies. *Geoforum* 31 (2000): 9–19.

Haberl, Helmut, Marina Fischer-Kowalski, Fridolin Krausmann, Helga Weisz, and Verena Winiwarter. Progress towards Sustainability? What the Conceptual Framework of Material and Energy Flow Accounting (MEFA) Can Offer. *Land Use Policy* 21 (2004): 199–213.

Hajer, Maarten A. *The Politics of Environmental Discourse:*

Ecological Modernization and the Policy Process. Oxford: Oxford University Press, 1995.

Haughton, Graham, and Colin Hunter. *Sustainable Cities.* London: Jessica Kingsley Publishers / Regional Studies Association, 1994.

Hornborg, Alf. Environmental Load Displacement in World History. In *Sustainable Development in a Globalized World,* ed. Björn Hettne. New York: Palgrave Macmillan, 2007.

———. Footprints in the Cotton Fields: The Industrial Revolution as Time-Space Appropriation and Environmental Load Displacement. *Ecological Economics* 59 (2006): 74–81.

———. Towards an Ecological Theory of Unequal Exchange: Articulating World System Theory and Ecological Economics. *Ecological Economics* 25 (1998): 127–36.

Huber, Joseph. *Die Verlorene Unschuld der Ökologie: Neue Teknologien und Superindustrielle Entwicklung.* Frankfurt am Main: Fischer Verlag, 1982.

Jamison, Andrew, and Erik Baark. National Shades of Green: Comparing the Swedish and Danish Styles in Ecological Modernization. *Environmental Values* 8 (1999): 199–218.

Lohm, Ulrik, Stefan Anderberg, and Bo Bergbäck. 1994. Industrial Metabolism at the National Level: A Case-Study on Chromium and Lead Pollution in Sweden, 1880–1980. In *Industrial Metabolism: Restructuring for Sustainable Development,* ed. Robert U. Ayres and Udo E. Simonis, 103–18. Tokyo: United Nations University Press, 1994.

Miljöprogram för Öresundsregionen. 2000. Rapport från Miljöprogrammets styrgrupp. Öresundskomitteen.

Nilsson, Daniel. The LIP Programme—A Prerequisite for the Environmental Initiatives. In *Sustainable City of Tomorrow—Bo01—Experiences from a Swedish Housing Exhibition,* ed. Bengt Persson, 11–15. Stockholm: Formas, 2005.

Pearce, Fred. The Great Green Swindle. *Guardian,* October 23, 2008.

Porter, Michael E., and Claas van der Linde. Green and Competitive: Ending the Stalemate. *Harvard Business Review* 73 (1995): 120–34.

Smidt-Jensen, Søren. Branding Medium-Sized Cities in Transition. In *Restructuring of Medium Sized Cities—Lessons from the Baltic Sea region,* ed. Niels Boje Groth, Thilo Lang, Mats Johansson, Vesa Kanninen, Stefan Anderberg and Andreas Cornett, 159–70. Copenhagen: Danish Centre for Forest, Landscape and Planning, 2005.

Spargaren, Gert, and Arthur P. J. Mol. Sociology, Environment, and Modernity: Ecological Modernization as a Theory of Social Change. *Society and Natural Resources* 5 (1992): 323–44.

Wallerstein, Immanuel. *World-Systems Analysis: An Introduction.* Durham: Duke University Press, 2004.

Weisz, Helga. Combining Social Metabolism and Input-Output Analysis to Account for Ecologically Unequal Trade. In *Rethinking Environmental History: World-System History and Global Environmental Change,* ed. Alf Hornborg, J. R. McNeill, and Joan Martinez-Alier, 289–306. Lanham: AltaMira, 2007.

Wichmann Matthiessen, Christian, Henrik Søgaard, and Stefan Anderberg. Environmental Performance and European Cities—A New Key Parameter in Competition between Metropolitan Centers. In *Monitoring Cities—International Perspectives,* ed. Wayne K. D. Davies and Ivan J. Townshend, 119–41. Calgary: International Geographical Union, 2002.

York, Richard, and Eugene A. Rosa. Key Challenges to Ecological Modernization Theory: Institutional Efficacy, Case Study Evidence, Units of Analysis and the Pace of Eco-efficiency. *Organization and Environment* 16 (2003): 273–88.

■ MICHAEL PACIONE

Urban Sustainability in the United Kingdom

The majority of the Earth's population lives in urban areas. Consequently, the pursuit of sustainable urban development (SUD) has emerged as a major challenge for governments throughout the contemporary world. The concept of sustainable development, in general terms, aims to meet "the needs of the present without compromising the ability of future generations to meet their own needs."[1] In seeking to achieve the goal of sustainable urban change, society must aim to achieve a balance between economic priorities on the one hand and social and environmental priorities on the other.

The ideal world envisaged at the Rio Earth Summit in 1992 was one in which the objectives of sustainable development would be fulfilled at all levels of spatial organization. Agenda 21 of the Earth Summit focused particular attention on the challenge of sustainable development at the urban scale. In 1994 the Global Forum on Cities and Sustainable Development considered reports from fifty cities on progress being made toward sustainable development,[2] and in 1996 the UN City Summit (Habitat II) monitored progress on achieving sustainability in cities across the globe.[3] Following the Rio+10Earth Summit of 2002 SUD was embraced as a goal by numerous international agencies and governments. The Organisation for Economic Cooperation and Development (OECD), the European Community, and the World Bank now all have sustainable cities programs. In contrast to the level of attention directed to the principles of sustainable development, however, implementation of policies to achieve SUD on the ground is less widespread. As the European Community's Expert Group on the Urban Environment–Sustainable Cities Project concluded, "the gap between public declarations and concepts on the one hand, and concrete measures taken on the other hand, remains large in most cities." In this chapter we examine the rhetoric and reality of sustainable urban development in the United Kingdom.[4]

Sidebar 1. The Major Dimensions of Sustainable Urban Development

Economic sustainability. The ability of the local economy to sustain itself without causing irreversible damage to the natural resource base on which it depends. This implies maximizing the productivity of a local (urban or regional) economy not in absolute terms (e.g., profit maximization), but in relation to the sustainability of the other four dimensions. The difficulty of achieving economic sustainability in capitalist societies is compounded by economic globalization that is promoting competition among cities, as well as between cities and their surrounding regions.

Social sustainability. A set of actions and policies aimed at the improvement of quality of life and at fair access to and distribution of rights over the use and appropriation of the natural and built environment. This implies the improvement of local living conditions by reducing poverty and increasing satisfaction of basic needs.

Natural sustainability. The rational management of natural resources and of the pressures exerted by the waste produced by every society. Overexploitation of natural capital and growing inequality in access to, and rights over, the natural resources of a city or region compromises the sustainability of natural capital.

Physical sustainability. The capacity of the urban built environment to support human life and productive activities. Crises of physical sustainability are evident, particularly in metropolitan areas of the Third World, as a result of the imbalance between in-migration of population and the carrying capacity of the cities.

Political sustainability. The democratization and participation of the local civil society in urban governance. Attainment of this goal may be undermined by the increasing influence of nonlocal and market forces in urban change.

Conceptualizing Urban Sustainability

Interrogation of the concept of sustainability is considered elsewhere in this volume and need not be rehearsed here. In general, the concept of urban sustainability may be viewed as comprising five dimensions (see sidebar 1). Figure 1 illustrates the relationship among the five main dimensions of urban sustainability.

In this concept, political sustainability plays a central role as the governance framework regulating the performance of the other four dimensions. The fundamental political character of sustainability is also evident in how different societies and governments define the concept of sustainability both as a problem and as a desired objective; identify and characterize the origins and causes of problems that undermine sustainability; and delineate solutions conducive to sustainability. In brief, "the definition of the problem, its causes and possible outcomes are all inherently and inescapably political projects."[5]

In practice, creating a sustainable and livable city requires both an integrated planning and decision-making framework, and a fundamental shift in traditional values and perspectives. There needs to be a change in focus from curative measures such as pollution reduction to measures based on prevention, from consumption to conservation, and from managing the environment to managing the demands on the environment. This will require change at the individual, community, business, and urban levels. In the following discussion, we examine how UK government policy has approached this goal.

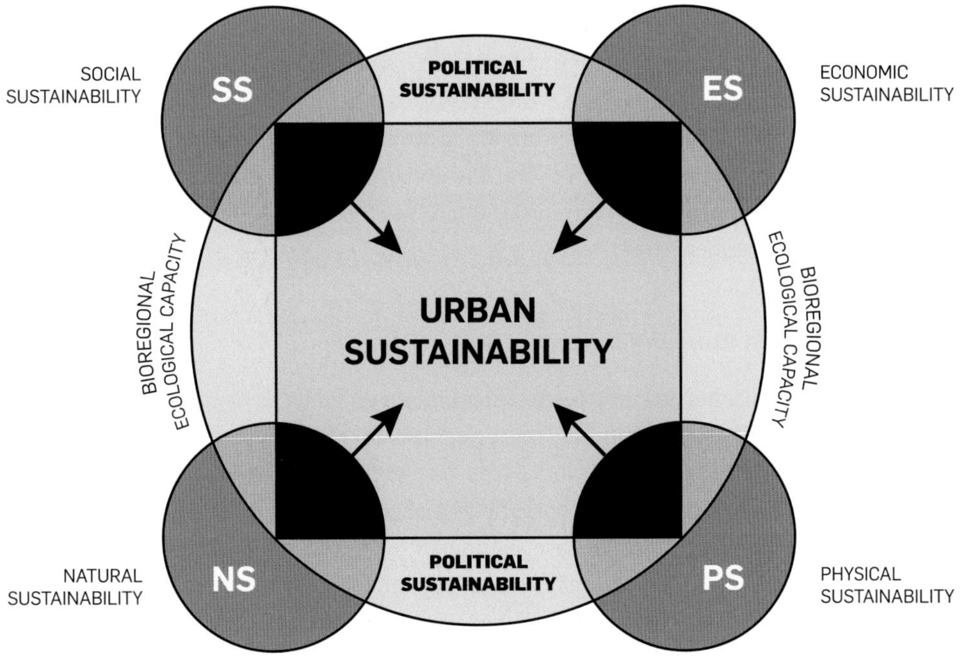

Figure 1. Major dimensions of urban sustainability.

The Policy Framework for SUD in the United Kingdom

The Brundtland report gave credibility to the concept of sustainable development and emphasized the interdependence of economic prosperity, equity, and environmental quality.[6] These principles were embraced by the UK government in its policy document *This Common Inheritance*.[7] The second major global level document that impacted on sustainable development policy in the United Kingdom was Agenda 21. This challenged national and local governments to respond to its recommendations by preparing National Sustainable Development Strategies and Local Agenda 21s.

The detailed response of the United Kingdom to the Earth Summit was set out in *Sustainable Development: The UK Strategy,* a strategy document (deliberately) unclear about whether it advocates a weak or strong form of sustainable development (SD).[8] While both require intergenerational transfer of capital stock not less than that currently in existence, in weak SD all forms of capital are interchangeable so that environmental capital may be traded for economic or social capital. Strong SD, on the other hand, maintains that there are limits to the extent to which environmental capital may be substituted by man-made capital. On one hand, the document states that "sometimes environmental costs have to be accepted as the price of economic development"—the epitome of weak SD. On the other hand, it acknowledges that "on other occasions a site, or an ecosystem, or some other aspect of the environment, has to be regarded as so valuable that it should be protected from exploitation."[9] This ambivalence may be interpreted as the political equivalent of attempting to be all things to all people. The document resonates with the concerns of the broad constituency (business and electorate) at whom the message is directed—by keeping their future social and economic well-being as central to the argument for SUD; and by promoting social gain rather than echoing the environmental threats of the 1960s and 1970s, the message is made more attractive to citizens who are most likely to differentiate between the tangible local benefits of SUD and less apparent global problems affecting distant others. The document is much clearer about the means of delivering on the strategy—the UK planning system is seen as a key instrument in implementing the government's commitment to SUD.

The Role of the UK Planning System in SUD

In the UK, SUD is approached via a plan-led system based on a hierarchy of national policies and guidance notes, regional spatial planning strategies (including the spatial development plan for London), and local development frameworks. The UK government provides framework guidance for SD/SUD through establishing national principles and goals, and by operating through the planning system in which local authorities have significant delegated powers to effect change within their areas. As Planning Policy Statement 1 states, "sustainable development is the core principle underpinning planning. At the heart of sustainable development is the simple idea of ensuring a better quality of life for everyone, now and for future generations."[10]

Two key features of the UK approach is that a spatial planning approach should be at the heart of planning for SD and community involvement is an essential element in delivering SD and in creating sustainable and safe communities. This approach resonates with the goals of Agenda 21 that (founded on the principle of subsidiarity) sought to promote SUD through the twin ideals of increased democratization and decentralization, with action at the local level through establishment of Local Agenda 21 plans. Significantly, the Agenda 21 document highlighted the existing system of local authorities as a suitable delivery framework, with the potential for partnerships among all sectors of the community in seeking to achieve SUD. It did not envisage citizen control but rather a process of devolution taking place within the framework set by each local authority.[11]

In 1999 the UK government published its updated strategy on SD entitled *A Better Quality of Life—Strategy for Sustainable Development for the UK—1999*. In preparing this strategy, the government built on the foundations of the 1994 strategy but took the view that "a new approach is needed, which emphasizes the social dimension of sustainable development alongside economic issues, the environment and resource use." The 1999 strategy document also set a target for all local authorities to prepare local sustainable development Local Agenda 21 (LA21) strategies by the end of 2000. By 2002 over 400 LA21 programs had been developed, although most have struggled to involve marginal groups such as deprived communities, ethnic minorities, youth, and elderly sections of the population. In a similar vein, in 2005 the UK government introduced a new program entitled *Community Action 2020—Together We Can* in an effort to revitalize local community action in support of SUD.[12]

The 1999 strategy document unequivocally sought to focus attention on social dimensions of sustainable development to balance a perceived overemphasis on environmental-ecological issues:

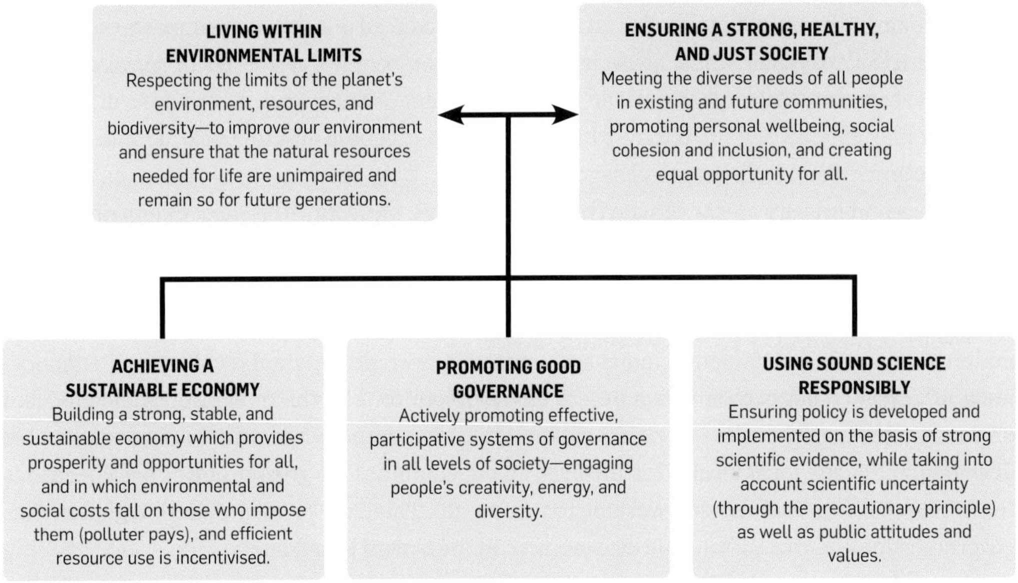

LIVING WITHIN ENVIRONMENTAL LIMITS
Respecting the limits of the planet's environment, resources, and biodiversity—to improve our environment and ensure that the natural resources needed for life are unimpaired and remain so for future generations.
ENSURING A STRONG, HEALTHY, AND JUST SOCIETY
Meeting the diverse needs of all people in existing and future communities, promoting personal wellbeing, social cohesion and inclusion, and creating equal opportunity for all.
ACHIEVING A SUSTAINABLE ECONOMY
Building a strong, stable, and sustainable economy which provides prosperity and opportunities for all, and in which environmental and social costs fall on those who impose them (polluter pays), and efficient resource use is incentivised.
PROMOTING GOOD GOVERNANCE
Actively promoting effective, participative systems of governance in all levels of society—engaging people's creativity, energy, and diversity.
USING SOUND SCIENCE RESPONSIBLY
Ensuring policy is developed and implemented on the basis of strong scientific evidence, while taking into account scientific uncertainty (through the precautionary principle) as well as public attitudes and values.

Figure 2. Guiding principles of UK government's sustainable development strategy.

> Sometimes discussion of sustainable development, particularly in richer countries, has focused mainly on environmental limits. But economic and social boundaries must also be recognised. An economy in long term recession is not sustainable. Nor is a situation where many people are denied opportunity and face poverty and exclusion. Development which ignores the essential needs of the poorest people, whether in this country or abroad, is not sustainable development at all.[13]

This policy statement signaled a focus on the creation of sustainable communities that has permeated subsequent UK government urban development policy. Significantly, for the translation of SUD rhetoric into praxis, it also provided a clear indication of the relative importance afforded to SUD in the wider context of urban development policy in the United Kingdom.

The 1999 strategy document was superseded in 2005 by *The UK Government Sustainable Development Strategy.*[14] In updating the previous document this retained the four central aims of the 1999 strategy. They include social progress that recognizes the needs of all, effective protection of the environment, prudent use of natural resources, and maintenance of high and stable levels of economic growth and employment. The new set of guiding principles (fig. 2) sets out to integrate socioeconomic and environmental concerns within the ethos of a developed world nation—"living within environmental limits while ensuring a strong economy and healthy society." More explicitly, it states that "for a policy to be sustainable it must respect all five of these principles, though we recognise that some policies, while underpinned by all five, will place more emphasis on certain principles than others."

The 2005 strategy document identified four priority areas for immediate action. The first focuses on sustainable consumption and production: achieving more with less. This approach means looking not only at how goods and services are produced but also at the impacts of products and materials across their whole lifecycle and building on people's awareness of social and environmental concerns. This includes reducing the inefficient use of resources that are a drag on the economy and thereby helping to boost business competitiveness and to break the link between economic growth and environmental degradation.

The second priority area is climate change and energy, mitigating the effect of greenhouse gas emissions on the atmosphere by changing the way energy is generated and used, while at the same time preparing for the unavoidable impacts of climate change. The third area of action centers on natural resource protection and environmental enhancement. The key is developing a better understanding of environmental limits and undertaking environmental recovery and enhancement of degraded lands to ensure a decent environment for all. The final priority area focuses on sustainable communities—creating communities that embody the principles of sustainable development at the local level. This involves giving communities greater power over decisions that affect them and partnership working to achieve SD. This final priority objective underwrites government policies for sustainable development in the United Kingdom.[15]

Creating Sustainable Communities

The HMGSD strategy identifies sustainable communities as "places where people want to live and work, now and in the future. They meet the diverse needs of existing and future residents, are sensitive to their environment, and contribute to a high quality of life. They are safe and inclusive, well planned, built and run, and offer equality of opportunity and good services for all."[16]

In detail, sustainable communities should be the following:

- *Active, inclusive, and safe:* fair, tolerant, and cohesive, with a strong local culture and other shared community activities
- *Well run:* with effective and inclusive participation, representation, and leadership
- *Environmentally sensitive:* providing places for people to live that are considerate of the environment
- *Well designed and built:* featuring a quality built and natural environment
- *Well connected:* with good transport services and communications linking people to jobs, schools, health, and other services
- *Thriving:* with a flourishing and diverse local economy
- *Well served:* with public, private, community, and voluntary services that are appropriate to people's needs and accessible to all
- *Fair for everyone:* including those in other communities, now and in the future

The complete list of sustainable community characteristics runs to forty-three items. While there is some unavoidable overlap in that—for example, a well-designed built environment can also promote a sense of place and reduce the need for car travel—it is instructive to note the balance of concerns within the listing of sustainable community characteristics. There are seven

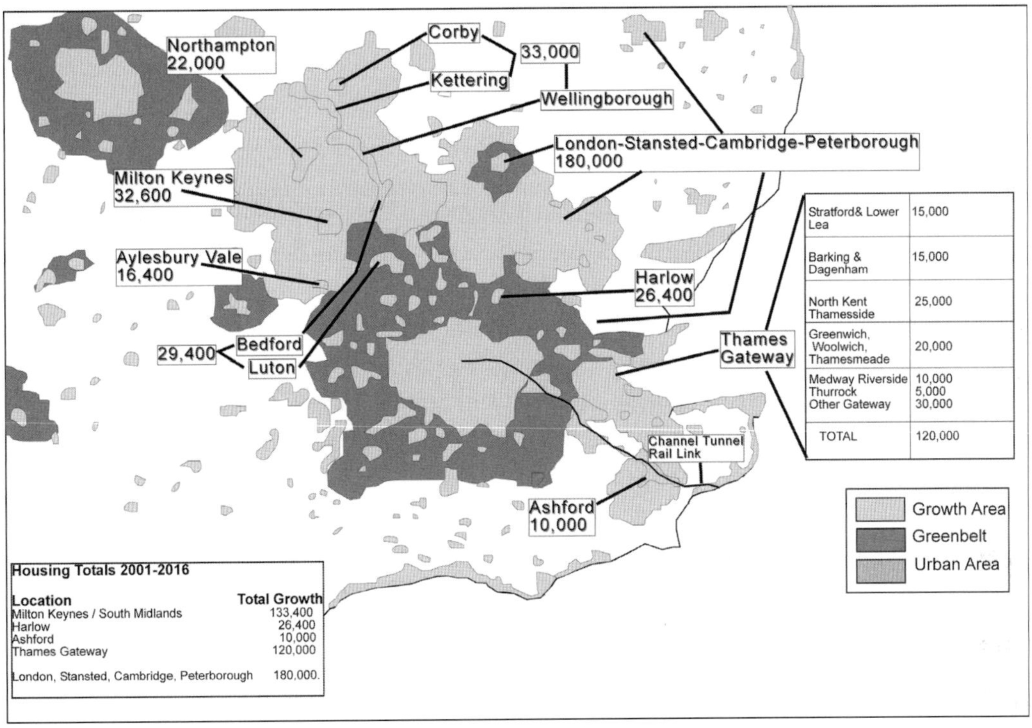

Figure 3. Major growth areas in South East England.

that are related explicitly to the condition of the environment, twenty to community cohesion and safety, six to design, five to traffic, and five to the local economy.

This reflects the consistent ethos of UK SD policy—to move toward SUD within the context and standards of living commensurate with a developed world urban economy. This policy perspective is embedded in a belief that environmental costs may have to be accepted as the price of economic development; that social and economic dimensions of SUD are as important as environmental and resource use issues; and in a commitment to high and stable levels of economic growth and employment. This governmental ethos is indicative of a more general national population view of the place of SD in urban development. The rhetoric of SD should not cloud the fact that most people will not relinquish voluntarily a cherished lifestyle. Further, the goal of sustainability is not an integral element of market capitalism and will inevitably encounter opposition from other interests. The primary objective of UK urban policy is to promote sound and sustainable growth. In pursuit of this goal, a consistent feature of urban policy in the United Kingdom over recent decades is the prominent role played by public-private partnerships (such as London Docklands Development Corporation, the Isle of Dogs Enterprise Zone, and the more recent London Thames Gateway Development Corporation) and the focus on area-based initiatives. How these principles are translated into practice on the ground may be illustrated with reference to the example of the Lower Lea Valley area of the Thames Gateway region in London.[17]

Case Study—SUD in the Thames Gateway

The UK government in partnership with other agencies, including the Greater London Authority (GLA) and its functioning agencies (including the London Development Authority; and Transport for London); the Thames Gateway Development Corporation; the London boroughs; and national bodies such as the Housing Corporation and English Partnerships is seeking to implement a sustainable development agenda in the Thames Gateway. This is one of several major designated growth areas in the South East of England (fig. 3).

Thames Gateway is the largest brownfield urban development opportunity in Europe (fig. 4). Within this area six strategic development locations have been identified "where the private sector is ready to invest" (fig. 5).[18] One of these areas, the East London Gateway around Stratford and the Lower Lea Valley (LLV), has received an additional boost with its selection as the site for the 2012 Olympic Games.

The London Sustainable Development Commission established by the GLA in 2002 to advise on sustainability issues promotes a vision of London as "an exemplary sustainable world city." This is based on three interlocking elements of strong and diverse economic growth, social inclusion, and fundamental improvements in environmental management and use of resources.

PHOTOGRAPH BY MICHAEL PACIONE

Figure 4. Derelict former industrial land in East London.

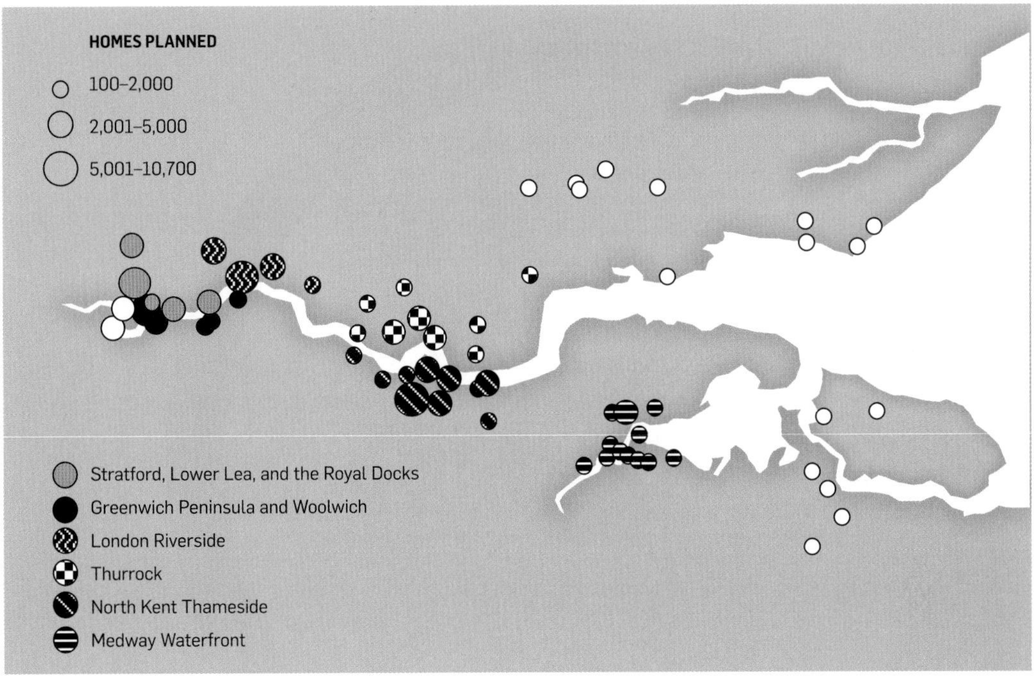

Figure 5. Strategic development locations in the Thames Gateway.

It is worthy of note that the national government sees the main strategic challenges facing London to be "to accommodate growth and to alleviate poverty and deprivation, and reduce the long-standing imbalance in prosperity between East and West London, with a focus on homes, transport, education and crime reduction" (sidebar 2).[19] In contrast, the GLA, under the charismatic leadership of former mayor Ken Livingstone, presents an agenda that incorporates more explicit attention to ecological concerns. The London Sustainable Development Commission (LSDC) has identified a set of quality-of-life indicators against which to monitor progress toward a more sustainable form of urban development (fig. 6).

Sidebar 2. National Government Objectives for SUD in the Thames Gateway

- To make more effective use of the skills and resources of a sector of London that is performing at a much lower level than more prosperous areas in the metropolis
- To redevelop brownfield land left by the contraction of traditional docks and manufacturing industry
- To link the regeneration of underused land with improvements in transport systems, including the Channel Tunnel Rail Link (CTRL) that was routed through the area in order to serve as a catalyst for redevelopment
- To promote sustainable mixed-use communities, generating new jobs and better housing
- To achieve a sustainable legacy of new housing, employment, transport, leisure facilities, and open space following the Olympic Games of 2012

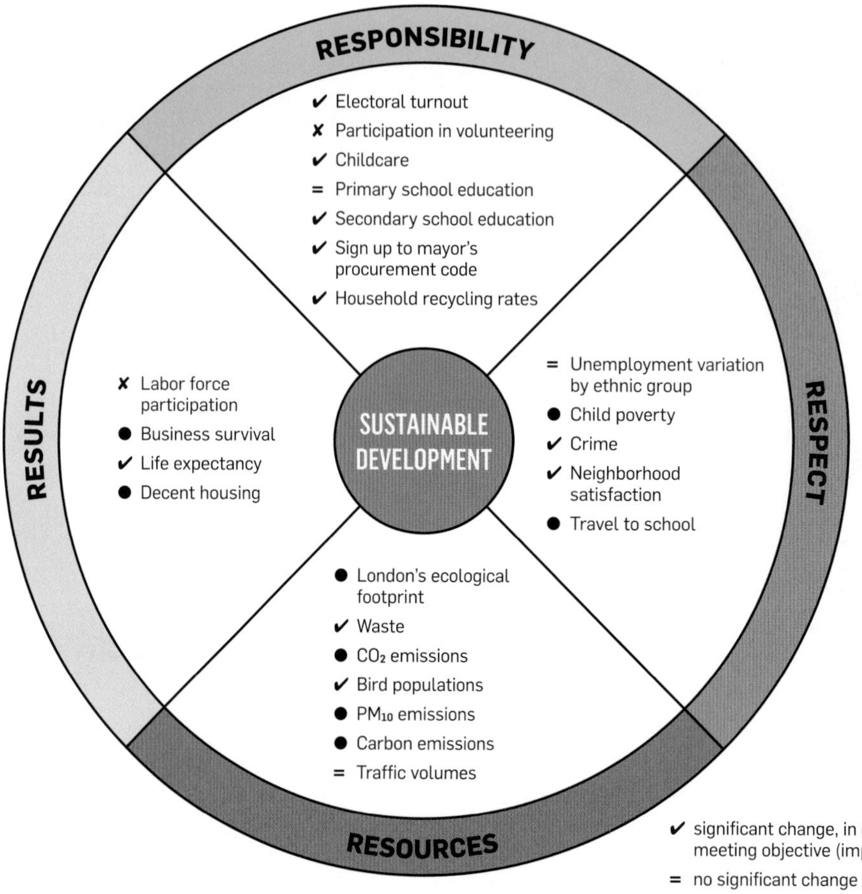

✔ significant change, in direction of meeting objective (improvement)
= no significant change (little or no change)
✘ significant change, in direction away from meeting objective (detrioration)
● insufficient or no comparable data

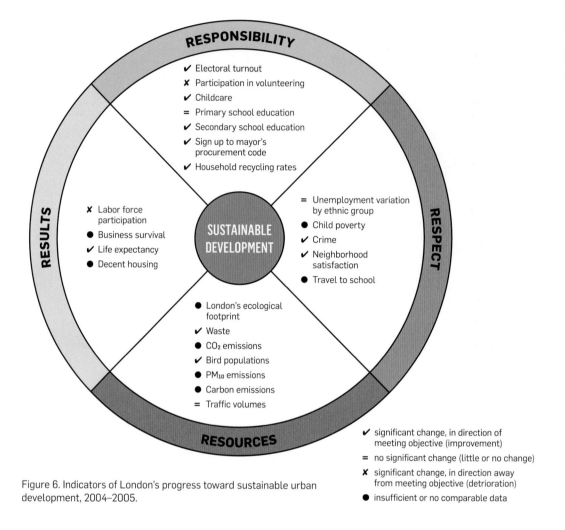

Figure 6. Indicators of London's progress toward sustainable urban development, 2004–2005.

We may illustrate the ways in which these principles are to be put into practice with reference to the Lower Lea Valley (see fig. 7), which is the largest (3,583 acres) remaining regeneration opportunity in inner London. Located three miles from central London, it runs north-south from Stratford to Canary Wharf, taking in parts of the boroughs of Hackney, Tower Hamlets, Newham, and Waltham Forest. The area is one of the most deprived in the United Kingdom, with unemployment on some estates running at 35 percent. Skill levels are low, and the area has one of the highest levels of black and minority ethnic populations in London. Over the next twenty years the Lower Lea Valley will be one of the main growth areas in London, with the potential to provide 30,000–40,000 new homes. As discussed below, the vision is to transform the LLV into a "vibrant, high quality and sustainable mixed use city district that is fully integrated into the urban fabric of London and is set within an unrivalled landscape that contains high quality parkland and water features."[20]

PHOTOGRAPH BY MICHAEL PACIONE

Figure 7. Aerial view of the Lower Lea Valley looking south from the Olympic Park toward Canary Wharf.

SUD is an integral element of the Lower Lea Valley's regeneration strategy centered on the Olympic Games. Specific sustainability goals for the games are to have the following:

- *Low carbon games* to reduce energy demand and meet it from low carbon and renewable sources
- *Zero-waste games* to avoid landfill by reducing waste at source, then recycling and recovering all remaining waste
- *Conservation of biodiversity* to conserve natural habitats and wildlife and to improve the quality of urban green space
- *Sustainable transport* to reduce the need for travel and provide sustainable alternatives to the private car
- *Sustainable legacy* to promote health and well-being through a package of sporting, environmental, and cultural initiatives

Hosting the Olympic Games will accelerate plans to regenerate the area. There are a number of projects that had to be completed before 2012. They include the extension of the Docklands Light Railway (DLR), enhancement of DLR capacity, and refurbishment of all London Underground stations to create car-free games; environmental benefits through reclamation of contaminated and disused industrial land; construction of 9,000 new houses in the Olympic Park, along with schools and other community facilities; the provision of leisure and sports facilities, including the Olympic stadium, indoor sports centers, and an aquatic center; and the creation of the largest new park in London since Victorian times.

As indicated, the longer-term vision for the Lower Lea Valley is to develop a new water city. There are a number of main components to this initiative, ranging from the revitalization of waterways to housing provision.

Water resources—Water is key to the character of the LLV. There are almost four miles of tidal and nontidal rivers and canals in the Lea Valley creating islands and peninsulas from Stratford in the north to Leamouth on the Thames. While many of these waterways are currently of low environmental and ecological value, culverted over, or boxed in by concrete walls, they represent a potential asset. Revitalization of the waterways is central to regeneration of the LLV. Under redevelopment, where the river flows through the built-up area, buildings will face onto the water, with wharfs and moorings for boats installed. As in waterfront developments elsewhere, canals and canal basins provide a focus for new mixed-use areas accommodating light industries, high-density residential developments, and social and entertainment facilities that will help to promote the waterfront as active social space. The Lea Valley Park that currently extends from Hertfordshire twenty miles south along the river to Hackney will be extended down to the Thames so that the revitalized Lea Valley will have at its core a series of open spaces linked by waterways (fig. 8). The new linear park will provide additional neighborhood green spaces, some designed for active sport and recreation, including Olympic legacy sports facilities, and others created as wetlands and wildlife refuges. All will be accessible via a network of green paths, footpaths, and cycleways. This will require significant investment in flood risk management using sustainable land drainage systems.

Urban centers—The aim is to strengthen existing town and neighborhood centers and create new ones to become the foci for regeneration, maximizing good public transport links to Canary Wharf and central London. A major development node is at Stratford, twenty minutes from the city and ten minutes from Canary Wharf. Stratford is already a transport hub with national rail, underground, DLR, and bus termini, and opening of the Channel Tunnel Rail Link (CTRL) and new international station will further enhance this function. The Stratford city master plan aims to extend the existing town center to create a high density mixed-use center with construction of over 1.5 million square feet of shopping and over 5 million square feet of commercial space generating 34,000 new jobs and 5,000 new homes and a network of open spaces. The 1.88 million square foot Westfield Stratford shopping center that opened in 2011 has 300 shops, 70 restaurants, a cinema and a hotel and provides 10,000 jobs; 2,000 of which were filled by local people. It is also one of the first developments to use Pavegen floor tiles to harness the kinetic energy of pedestrian foot traffic to generate usable electricity. Other major urban centers in the area include Canning Town, another key transport node adjacent to a main trunk road (A13), and with direct access via underground and DLR to Canary Wharf, the Greenwich Peninsula, Stratford, and London city airport. Canning Town is likely to grow into the second largest center and, complementing Stratford to the north, will form the primary focus for the southern part of the LLV. The Local Plan provides for the construction of 7,000 new houses in Canning Town. The smaller neighborhood centers of Bromley by Bow, Hackney Wick and West Ham will also be expanded through provision of new civic spaces, shopping, business, leisure, and community facilities to create district centers.

PHOTOGRAPH BY MICHAEL PACIONE

Figure 8. The East India Dock Basin at the southern end of the planned Lea Valley park, with the financial center of Canary Wharf in the background and new residential development at Virginia Quay in the foreground.

Housing—London faces a shortage of good quality homes of all sizes suitable for different types of households, from families to singles with a range of incomes. As noted above, over the next twenty years the Lower Lea Valley will be one of the major growth areas in the city, with the potential to provide up to 40,000 new homes. The SUD plan is to make new and existing neighborhoods part of a network of sustainable balanced communities within walking distance of open space, local shopping, and community facilities integrated with employment areas and with good access to public transport. Accordingly, a key objective is to offer a wide choice of housing types from urban apartments to homes with gardens in order to provide flexibility in the housing stock to accommodate changing demands over time. The new housing will be provided at a range of densities, with higher density developments in town center locations at Stratford and Canning Town to take advantage of the concentrations of shops, service facilities, and access to good public transport. Further out from the town centers development densities will be lower, with a greater proportion of family housing related to schools, health facilities, and leisure space. While most of the new housing will be in newly developed areas, a significant amount will come from redevelopment of existing housing areas in need of modernization, including renewal of entire estates of decaying social housing (fig. 9).

PHOTOGRAPH BY MICHAEL PACIONE

Figure 9. A rundown council housing estate in the Lower Lea Valley, East London.

The regeneration strategy will promote new mixed-use development in appropriate locations, (e.g., Stratford and Canning Town), in which housing will be integrated with shops, offices, and other business uses. Furthermore, in an attempt to foster stable and balanced communities, 40 percent of all new housing will be of a form suitable for families. In addition, in recognition of the high cost of housing in the private market and extreme levels of deprivation in the area, 50 percent of new housing will be affordable housing for rent or shared ownership.

Employment—The Lower Lea Valley, long part of the industrial East End of London remains one of the key inner industrial locations in London and plays a significant role in accommodating industry that serves London-wide needs, such as food processing, printing, and recycling. Clearly, the changing structure of labor demand will pose a major challenge for many residents without the skills required to compete successfully in a postindustrial economy. Because of their local and regional importance, a number of the existing industrial areas of the LLV have been identified as strategic employment locations (SELs). This central valley industrial corridor, focused on five key concentrations—Lea Bridge Gateway, Fish Island, Cody Road, Hackney Wick, and Thameside West—will be retained and developed for industrial use.

While such activities remain important, the declining traditional industrial base also needs to diversify into tertiary sector activities, such as creative industries (fig. 10), and companies providing a range of support services to the city and Canary Wharf. In addition to the existing 30,000 jobs, the Lea Valley has the potential to accommodate 50,000 new jobs. The bulk of these (30,000) primarily in business and financial services and the retail sector will be linked to the Stratford city development that will see Stratford evolve into an important metropolitan subcenter in proximity to Canary Wharf and the City of London, and linked to Europe by the CTRL and nearby London city airport. In addition to the planned developments at Stratford, diversification of the area's economic base can be facilitated through release of almost 432 acres (40 percent) of existing industrial land. Outside of the SELs mixed-use higher-density industrial redevelopment will be encouraged. This will also involve relocation of businesses displaced by the Olympic Games developments.

Transport—Transport and the concept of transit-oriented development is of central importance to SUD. While the Lower Lea Valley has good public transport provision, and planned extensions to the DLR and East London line, the absence of a comprehensive street network aggravated by the barrier effects of waterways, railways, and flyovers has served to disconnect the area from surrounding neighborhoods. Improvements to local circulation both within and beyond the LLV are essential to create a more cohesive sense of community and to integrate the valley with surrounding areas. New infrastructure required to reconnect various parts of the LLV will include a new north-south spine road to connect Stratford with Canary Wharf, and new road, rail, and river crossings to ease pedestrian and vehicular circulation throughout the valley. In the context of SUD

PHOTOGRAPH BY MICHAEL PACIONE

Figure 10. Film and television production studios in the Three Mills creative industries quarter on the River Lea.

the particular needs of the elderly, disabled, and parents with children will be incorporated into the design of these new routeways to facilitate mobility for all.

Environment—Improving the quality of the physical environment is a central goal of SUD. To ensure that the planned new developments in the Lower Lea Valley have minimum impacts on the environment will require innovative approaches to provision of energy, water, and waste disposal systems that will reduce carbon emissions, water demand, and waste production. In an effort to make the Lower Lea Valley an exemplar for SUD in other parts of London, these initiatives will include reduction of energy consumption and carbon emissions by incorporating sustainable principles in building design; combining heat and power schemes as a low carbon energy strategy; reducing demand for water by cutting losses through leakage, drawing water from boreholes and rainwater, and recycling grey water; and cutting the amount of waste sent to landfills for final disposal by maximizing opportunities for reuse, recycling, and recovery. These include energy recovery from waste treatment, recycling of domestic and industrial waste, and reuse of waste materials at the construction stage. The LLV currently accommodates many waste processing businesses, and there is potential for the valley to develop new modern waste management facilities for waste recycling and processing that could also generate long-term local employment opportunities and help meet landfill reduction targets.

The Olympic Legacy and SUD

As Michael Pacione explains, the concept of legacy is at the core of the Olympic Games-led sustainable regeneration of the LLV area.[21] The emphasis placed on the sustainable legacy of the 2012 Games is in marked contrast with the commercially driven model of regeneration typified by the nearby Canary Wharf development. As stated in the 2011 London Plan, "the Mayor will work with partners to develop and implement a visible and sustainable legacy for the Olympic and Paralympic games to deliver fundamental economic, social and environmental change within east London, and to close the deprivation gap between the Olympic host boroughs and the rest of London. This will be London's single most important regeneration project for the next 25 years. It will sustain existing stable communities and promote local economic investment to create job opportunities, especially for young people, driven by community engagement."[22]

In general, the Lower Lea Valley, boosted by the impulse of the 2012 Olympic Games, has the potential to be an exemplar for SUD initiatives in London over the next twenty years. As Pacione points out, however, a key question is the extent to which the policy rhetoric will be realized in practice.[23] The most obvious legacy of event-led regeneration is the new facilities and environmental improvements of former brownfield land. However in creating a sustainable legacy it is also necessary to focus on economic and social regeneration as in skills training for local people to enable them to compete in the modern economy. In the particular context of the sustainable regeneration of the Lower Lea Valley several challenges emerged early in the process. In cost terms by 2007 the initial operational budget of about 4.8 billion U.S. dollars (£2.4 billion) had to be revised to 6.6 billion U.S. dollars (£3.3 billion) with the additional costs to be covered by sale of part of the Olympic Park land to private developers on completion of the event rather than remaining part of the open green space as envisaged in the original scheme.

In relation to housing the Olympic legacy will provide 9,000 new units, 50 percent of which will be affordable housing. While the 'Olympic effect' will improve the quality of the local housing stock it may also accentuate socio-spatial segregation if increasing costs of the event delivers responsibility for parts of the legacy into the hands of private developers for whom gentrification is a desirable outcome. In terms of employment impact the three boroughs closest to the Olympic development site—Hackney, Newham, and Tower Hamlets—have an above city average of the workforce with no qualifications and a lower proportion of knowledge workers. This creates the potential for employment polarization with local people filling low-skill jobs and higher paid specialist labor being recruited from elsewhere. These challenges illustrate the difficulties of delivering a sustainable legacy that positively impact existing patterns of social division in the area.

Conclusion

Despite or perhaps because of its vagueness, SD has become a central component of national and local planning philosophy in many states, including the United Kingdom. There is, however, ongoing debate on whether the lack of conceptual precision benefits or handicaps progress toward the goals of SD/SUD. Lack of a conceptual consensus may be viewed both as an advantage (embracing multiple perspectives and goals under the rubric of sustainable development), and as a disadvantage (hindering social and political efforts to advance toward the goals of urban sustainability). Politics is central to the issue. As Mathis Wackernagel and William Rees state, "the deliberate vagueness of the concept, even as defined by Brundtland, is a reflection of power politics and political bargaining, not a manifestation of insurmountable intellectual difficulty."[24]

SD/SUD is an attractive political philosophy because it enables governments to display their green credentials and at the same time to bring a plethora of existing and new policies under the umbrella of SD/SUD. Most political representations of SD/SUD portray a win-win philosophy in which economic prosperity and environmental enlightenment go hand in hand.[25] Indeed, it can be argued that SD is something of a political Trojan horse—that the very vagueness of the concept leads to general acceptance of, or at least acquiescence with, the SD principles embedded within national policy and land use planning, to the extent that the political commitments to SD/SUD "may prove difficult to abandon when their more uncomfortable implications become clear."[26]

Sustainable development draws its political sustenance from its unifying, consensual, and essentially conservative connotations. The breadth of the construct enables it to serve a variety of purposes. It provides status and support in the scientific community, endows environmentalists with much-desired credibility, creates a platform for politicians, and transforms the image of business.[27] Efforts aimed at maintaining consensus, however, could mean that "effective action in the pursuit of sustainable development is likely to be strictly limited."[28] On the other hand, introduction of stronger measures to implement SUD raises the question of whether general enthusiasm for the concept of SD is likely to decline as the full implications for our urban lifestyle become evident—for example, in the London congestion charge, carbon taxes, water metering, and smart garbage bins that monitor the amount and type of waste generated by households.

Within the framework of UK national policy guidance, local authorities are key actors in action toward SUD. Central to this role has been a shift toward multiagency working that brings together actors and agencies at local, national, and international scales across public, private, and voluntary sectors. In this context successful implementation of policies for SUD will require a combination of top-down and bottom-up approaches that embraces the principle of subsidiarity, whereby action is taken at the lowest feasible level. In practice, however, mobilizing popular support for SUD in a context of uncertainty over other dimensions of quality of life, including job security and a contracting welfare state, is difficult. The task is further complicated by declining levels of trust in those wielding political and economic power.[29] Local communities must feel that they are being supported and empowered in their activity and not merely exploited as sources of volunteer labor to assist governments to achieve token results.[30] Another potential barrier to citizen participation in SUD is the perennial question of the representativeness of those community members who sit on local committees, and the reality that participation in local affairs is often a minority sport.[31] A further obstacle to successful implementation of SUD strategies is that many members of the general public remain confused about the idea of SD, not least because of conflicting expert opinion on the causes and consequences of environmental problems, and this can militate against grassroots participation. Finally, since citizens identify more readily with local issues, on-the-ground neighborhood examples of SUD, by demonstrating potential benefits for local residents, can be of paramount importance in translating the rhetoric of SUD into reality.

Sustainable urban development is an inextricable part of the political process that decides the fundamental human, and quintessentially geographical, question of who gets what where and how. To extend current levels of implementation of the principles of SUD will require sensitivity to the locally embedded meanings of the concept, and construction of initiatives that address the broad concerns of SUD within local contexts, and that provide recognizable improvements in the quality of life of local stakeholders. Sustainable urban development in the United Kingdom is very much a work in progress. Green shoots are evident in national policy statements, in many urban areas including the widespread adoption of Local Agenda 21 programs, and in policy initiatives such as those of the GLA and its partner agencies, but widespread implementation of the precepts of SUD remains a long-term objective rather than a current reality.

NOTES

1. World Commission on Sustainable Development, *Our Common Future* (Oxford: Oxford University Press, 1987).
2. Diane Mitlin and David Satterthwaite, *Cities and Sustainable Development Discussion Paper for UN Global Forum* (Manchester, UK: IIED, 1994).
3. United Nations Centre for Human Settlements, *An Urbanising World: Global Review of Human Settlements 1996* (Nairobi: Habitat, 1996).
4. Organisation for Economic Cooperation and Development, *Cities for the 21st Century* (Paris: OECD, 2001). OECD, *Strategies for Sustainable Development* (Paris: OECD, 1996); European Community, *A Sustainable Europe for a Better World—A European Strategy for Sustainable Development* (Brussels: EC, 2001); World Bank, *The Human Face of the Urban Environment* (Washington, DC: World Bank, 1995); European Community Expert Group on the Urban Environment-Sustainable Cities Project, *European Sustainable Cities* (Brussels: EC, 1994).
5. National Science Foundation, *Towards A*

Comprehensive Geographical Perspective on Urban Sustainability Final Report of the 1998 NSF Workshop on Urban Sustainability (New York: Center for Urban Policy Research, 2000).
6. World Commission on Sustainable Development, *Our Common Future.*
7. Her Majesty's Government, *This Common Inheritance*, Cm 2068 (London: HMSO, 1992).
8. HMG, *Sustainable Development: The UK Strategy*, Cm 2426 (London: HMSO, 1994).
9. Ibid., para. 15.
10. HMG, *The UK Government Sustainable Development Strategy*, Cm 6467 (London: HMSO, 2005); Office of the Deputy Prime Minister, PPS 11, *Regional Spatial Strategies* (London: HMSO, 2004); ODPM, PPS 12, *Local Development Frameworks* (London: HMSO, 2004); ODPM, *Planning Policy Statement 1: Delivering Sustainable Development* (London: HMSO, 2005).
11. Ibid.; ODPM, *The Egan Review: Skills for Sustainable Communities* (London: ODPM, 2004); UCED, *Agenda 21—Action Plan for the Next Century* (New York: UN, 1992); Local Government Management Board, Earth Summit: Rio 92 Supplement No. 2 Agenda 21—A Guide for Local Authorities in the UK (London: LGMB, 1992).
12. HMG, *A Better Quality of Life—Strategy for Sustainable Development for the UK—1999*, Cm 4345 (London: HMSO, 1999); Joseph Rowntree Foundation, *Thinking Locally, Acting Globally* (York: JRF, 2002); JRF, *What's in a Name? Local Agenda 21, Community Planning and Neighbourhood Renewal* (York: JRF, 2003); Department for Environment, Food and Rural Affairs, *Community Action 2020—Together We Can* (London: DEFRA, 2005).
13. See, for example, OECD, *Environmental Policies for Cities in the 1990s* (Paris: OECD, 1990); HMG, *A Better Quality of Life.*
14. HMG, *The UK Government Sustainable Development Strategy.*
15. See, for example, Department of the Environment, Transport and the Regions ETR, *Sustainable Communities for the 21st Century* (London: DETR, 1998); Department for Communities and Local Government, *Millennium Villages and Sustainable Communities* (London: HMSO, 2000); ODPM, *Sustainable Communities: People, Places and Prosperity* (London: ODPM, 2005).
16. HMG, *The UK Government Sustainable Development Strategy.*
17. HMG, *Sustainable Development: The UK Strategy*; HMG, *This Common Inheritance*; HMG, *The UK Government Sustainable Development Strategy*; Andrew Church and Martin Frost, The Thames Gateway, *Geographical Journal* 161 (1995):199–209; Peter Daniels and J. Boke, Extending the Boundary of the City of London, *Environment and Planning A* 25 (1993): 539–52; Philip Ogden, *London Docklands* (Cambridge: Cambridge University Press, 1995).
18. ODPM, *Creating Sustainable Communities: Making It Happen: Thames Gateway and the Growth Areas* (London: ODPM, 2003).
19. ODPM, *Creating Sustainable Communities in London: Making It Happen* (London: ODPM, 2004).
20. London Thames Gateway Development Corporation, *Vision for the Lower Lea Valley* (London: LTGDC, 2006).
21. Michael Pacione, The role of events in urban regeneration, in *Handbook Events London*, ed. S. Page and J. Connell (London: Routledge, 2012), 385–400.
22. Mayor of London, *The London Plan: Spatial Development Strategy for Greater London* (London: Greater London Authority, 2012).
23. Michael Pacione, Sustainable urban development in the United Kingdom: Rhetoric or reality, *Geography* 92 (2007): 246–63.
24. Mathis Wackernagel and William Rees, *One Ecological Footprint: Reducing Human Impact on the Earth* (Gabricola, Canada: New Society Publishers, 1995).
25. DETR, *Towards a Better Quality of Life: A Strategy for Sustainable Development for the UK* (London: HMSO, 1999); HMG, *Sustainable Development: The UK Strategy.*
26. Susan Owens, Land, Limits and Sustainability: A Conceptual Framework and Some Dilemmas for the Planning System, *Transactions of the Institute of British Geographers* 19 (1994): 439–56.
27. Frederick Buttel, A. Hawkins and A. Power, From Limits to Growth to Global Change: Constraints and Contradictions in the Evolution of Environmental Science and Ideology, *Global Environmental Change, Human and Policy Dimensions* 1 (1990): 57–66.
28. Andrew Blowers, Sustainable Urban Development: The Political Prospects, in *Sustainable Development and Urban Form*, ed. Michael Breheny, 24–38 (London: Pion, 1992).
29. Richard Munton, Engaging Sustainable Development Progress, *Human Geography* 21 (1997): 147–63.
30. Paul Selman, *Local Sustainability* (London: PCP, 1996).
31. R. MacFarlane, *Community Involvement in City Challenge: A Good Practice Report* (London: NCVO Publications, 1993).

REFERENCES

Blowers, Andrew. Sustainable Urban Development: The Political Prospects, in *Sustainable Development and Urban Form*, ed. Michael Breheny, 24–32. London: Pion, 1992.

Buttel, Frederick, Ann Hawkins, and Alison Power. From Limits to Growth to Global Change: Constraints and Contradictions in the Evolution of Environmental Science and Ideology. *Global Environmental Change, Human and Policy Dimensions* 1 (1990): 57–66.

Church, Andrew, and Martin Frost. The Thames Gateway. *Geographical Journal* 161 (1995): 199–209.

Daniels, Peter, and J. Bobe. Extending the Boundary of the City of London. *Environment and Planning A* 25 (1993): 539–52.

Department for Communities and Local Government. *Millennium Villages and Sustainable Communities.* London: HMSO, 2000.

Department for Environment, Food and Rural Affairs. *Community Action 2020—Together We Can.* London: DEFRA, 2005.

Department of the Environment, Transport and the Regions. *Sustainable Communities for the 21st Century.* London: DETR, 1998.

———. *Towards a Better Quality of Life: A Strategy for Sustainable Development for the UK.* London: HMSO, 1999.

DOE. *Sustainable Development: The UK Strategy,* Cm 2426. London: HMSO, 1994.

European Community. *A Sustainable Europe for a Better World—A European Strategy for Sustainable Development.* Brussels: EC, 2001.

European Community Expert Group on the Urban Environment–Sustainable Cities Project. *European Sustainable Cities.* Brussels: EC, 1994.

Her Majesty's Government. *A Better Quality of Life—Strategy for Sustainable Development for the UK—1999 Cm 4345.* London: HMSO, 1999.

———. *This Common Inheritance Cm 2068.* London: HMSO, 1992.

———. *Sustainable Development: The UK Strategy Cm 2426.* London: HMSO, 1994.

———. *The UK Government Sustainable Development Strategy Cm 6467.* London: HMSO, 2005.

Joseph Rowntree Foundation. *Thinking Locally, Acting Globally.* York: Joseph Rowntree Foundation, 2002.

———. *What's in a Name? Local Agenda 21, Community Planning and Neighbourhood Renewal.* York: Joseph Rowntree Foundation, 2003.

Local Government Management Board. *Earth Summit: Rio 92 Supplement No. 2 Agenda 21—A Guide for Local Authorities in the UK.* London: LGMB, 1992.

London Thames Gateway Development Corporation. *Vision for the Lower Lea Valley.* London: LTGDC, 2006.

MacFarlane, R. *Community Involvement in City Challenge: A Good Practice Report.* London: National Council for Voluntary Organization Publications, 1993.

Mayor of London. *The London Plan: Spatial Development Strategy for Greater London* London: Greater London Authority, 2012.

Mitlin, Diane, and David Satterthwaite. Cities and Sustainable Development. Discussion Paper for UN Global Forum. Manchester, London: International Institute for Environment and Development, 1994.

Munton, Richard. Engaging Sustainable Development. *Progress in Human Geography* 21 (1997): 147–63.

National Science Foundation. *Towards a Comprehensive Geographical Perspective on Urban Sustainability Final Report of the 1998 NSF Workshop on Urban Sustainability.* New York: Center for Urban Policy Research, 2000.

Office of the Deputy Prime Minister. *Creating Sustainable Communities: Making It Happen: Thames Gateway and the Growth Areas.* London: ODPM, 2003.

———. *Creating Sustainable Communities in London: Making It Happen.* London: ODPM, 2004.

———. *The Egan Review: Skills for Sustainable Communities.* London: ODPM, 2004.

———. *Planning Policy Statement 1: Delivering Sustainable Development.* London: HMSO, 2005.

———. *PPS 11 Regional Spatial Strategies.* London: HMSO, 2004.

———. *PPS 12 Local Development Frameworks.* London: HMSO, 2004.

———. *Sustainable Communities: People, Places and Prosperity.* London: ODPM, 2005.

Ogden, Philip. *London Docklands.* Cambridge: Cambridge University Press, 1995.

Organisation for Economic Cooperation and Development. *Cities for the 21st Century.* Paris: OECD, 1996.

———. *Environmental Policies for Cities in the 1990s.* Paris: OECD, 1990.

———. *Strategies for Sustainable Development.* Paris: OECD, 2001.

Owens, Susan. Land, Limits and Sustainability: A Conceptual Framework and Some Dilemmas for the Planning System. *Transactions of the Institute of British Geographers* 19 (1994): 439–56.

Pacione, Michael. Sustainable Urban Development in the United Kingdom: Rhetoric or Reality. *Geography* 92 (2007): 246–63.

———. The Role of Events in Urban Regeneration. In *Handbook Events London*, ed. S. Page and J. Connell,

385–400. London: Routledge, 2012.
Selman, Paul. *Local Sustainability*. London: PCP, 1996.
UCED. *Agenda 21—Action Plan for the Next Century*. New York: United Nations, 1992.
United Nations Centre for Human Settlements. *An Urbanising World: Global Review of Human Settlements 1996*. Nairobi: Habitat, 1996.
Wackernagel, Mathis, and William Rees. *One Ecological Footprint: Reducing Human Impact on the Earth*. Gabricola, Canada: New Society Publishers, 1995.
World Bank. *The Human Face of the Urban Environment*. Washington, DC: World Bank, 1995.
World Commission on Sustainable Development. *Our Common Future*. Oxford: Oxford University Press, 1987.

CARLOS BALSAS

Sustainable Development in Portugal

AN ANALYSIS OF LISBON AND PORTO

Portugal is in the process of developing and implementing a more integrated national planning strategy so that the country can become both more sustainable and more competitive. However, becoming more sustainable and more competitive can impose some constraints on the pace of development and make the country disrespect previously agreed-upon green gas emission targets. It is estimated that Portugal will surpass the national target for green gas emissions from 8 percent to 14 percent. The Kyoto Protocol requires Portugal to comply with only a 27 percent increase in relation to the 1990 target for CO_2 emissions for 2008–2012. However, the new estimates point to a possible 41 percent increase.[1] Unless the country quickly adopts a more energy efficient and balanced urban growth stand, the current dilemma seems to be the possible curbing of development opportunities and a decrease in the quality of urban life. This is an important time for politicians and decision makers to understand how sustainability goals can help to improve the effectiveness of current development strategies without burdening natural and built systems.

The purpose of this chapter is to review some of the most important sustainability dilemmas in Portugal and to analyze how cities in the two main metropolitan areas are addressing them. This research is guided by the following three questions: What are the most important sustainable development challenges in Portugal? How are the two main metropolitan areas using sustainable development to address urban development problems? And how can Portugal use the sustainable development framework to advance the implementation of a sustainability agenda?

Sustainable development has become such a broad concept that it almost resembles an ultimate goal instead of a constant process of devising and evaluating a combination of public policies and societal responses and behaviors.[2] In this chapter, I argue that Portugal needs to move from the development of a national sustainability strategy to the implementation of that strategy through locally based and inclusive public participation processes. The planning of the coastal zone, anchored by the metropolitan areas of Lisbon and Porto, will be critical to a more balanced and harmonious national development. The development of sustainable metropolitan planning programs and their institutional governance practices will likely define the country's success in meeting the green gas emission targets imposed by the Kyoto Protocol.[3]

Sustainable Development in Portugal

The beginning of the sustainability movement is usually associated with the publication of the report *Our Common Future* by the World Commission on Environment and Development (WCED), an independent body charged by the United Nations to devise a global agenda for environmental, economic, and social change.[4] Sustainable development was readily embraced in Portugal from its inception. As it has been recognized, "in the first half of 1992, Portugal assumed the presidency of the European Union (EU), and as leader of the EU delegation at the Rio Summit wanted to be seen as a country with a forward-looking environmental agenda."[5] The participation in the Rio Summit led to the development of environmental agendas for all sectors of government. To mark this milestone, the chairwoman of the WCED, Gro Brundtland, was given an honorary doctorate by the Portuguese University of Aveiro. After the publication of the European Green Book on Urban Environment, local governments started adopting the Aalborg Charter of Sustainable Cities and Towns in 1994.[6] The city of Lisbon organized the second European conference on sustainable cities and towns in 1996, where more than 1,000 participants representing 250 municipalities endorsed an action plan for the Aalborg Charter of Sustainable Cities and Towns.[7]

By the fourth European conference, called Aalborg+10, in 2004, the number of signatory municipalities had risen to 2,300. In ten years of Local Agenda 21 (LA21) there were about 6,500 LA21s, of which 5,200 were European.[8] However, Portugal did not show very successful numbers when it came to devising and implementing LA21 processes. Many LA21s started as mere environmental plans and then evolved to slightly more comprehensive action plans. It has been argued that "there are not more than twenty LA21 processes running in Portugal and most of them do not fulfill all the parameters required."[9] In fact, it has been recognized that Portugal is the country with fewer LA21s in Europe. The number of LA21s in Portugal evolved from ten in 1997 to seventy-nine in 2007.[10] But many of these might not have had continuity after the making of the action plan. The reasons for such a slow progress have been attributed to structural political conditions in local governance and public participation, despite efforts by the national association of Portuguese municipalities (ANMP) to encourage cities and towns to develop their own LA21 plans.

At the national level, the concept of sustainable development was introduced in the revision of the constitution of the country, and the government created a National Council of the Environment and Sustainable Development (CNADS) in 1997.[11] This council is an independent body created to advise the government, public entities, and NGOs on all matters associated with the environment and sustainable development policies. Mainly due to political reasons, this council had a somewhat passive role in the promotion of a sustainable development framework in Portugal. Its activity was confined mainly to providing comments on different laws and studies related to environmental planning. The LA21 in Portugal is characterized by the following: "1) a lack of support and promotional framework by the government at the central level (there is no state entity in charge of leading the promotion and implementation of LA21); 2) a lack of stimulus, technical support, and campaigns for spreading out LA21 initiatives over the territory; and 3) a lack of financial or other kinds of resource incentives."[12]

A national sustainability strategy had been requested as early as 2002, but it took five years to have it fully adopted.[13] After successful lobbying by some environmental groups and the opposition parties, the Portuguese government approved a National Strategy for Sustainable Development (ENDS) and its Implementation Plan (PIENDS). The main goal is to place Portugal amongst the twenty most competitive and attractive European Union countries by 2015 (currently Portugal ranks twenty-ninth) and to have an ecological deficit lower than its present one. The main goal of the strategy is a better coordination between sustainable development issues and technological innovation, employment, competitiveness, and the emergence of a new model of economic growth.

This strategy was developed in articulation with the revamped Strategy of Lisbon, which included a national action plan for growth and employment, a technological plan, a national plan for employment, a national strategy for the sea, a strategic plan for rural development, and more important, a national program for territorial planning (PNPOT). The National Strategy for Sustainable Development (ENDS) is a very comprehensive plan, with a SWOT analysis, a series of socioeconomic and environmental indicators, and objectives detailed in strategic priorities, subobjectives, and quantified targets with very specific time frames.

In terms of urban planning, the ENDS advocates urban dynamics less destructive of the environment and socially more solidary, and the making of regional and LA21 plans for the entire country, as well as an urban revitalization approach with visible benefits in terms of air quality. It is too early to assess how this strategy will be implemented, but it is not too late to note that the document and all its objectives and subobjectives do not clearly indicate which ministry or secretary of state will be responsible for achieving the stated objectives and targeting how much funds they will have for implementation.

The sustainable development theme, together with the revamping of the Lisbon Strategy, was among the main flagships of the Portuguese presidency of the European Union in the second half of 2007. There are hopes that the Leipzig Charter of Sustainable European Cities approved during the German presidency of the European Union in the first half of 2007 will give an additional boost to the creation of more sustainable and just cities in Europe.[14]

Planning Frameworks and Programs in Portugal

Portugal saw many advances in its urban, regional, and national planning frameworks during the last two decades.[15] The Portuguese entry into the European Union brought many administrative reforms and societal changes. Several authors have argued that "it was a historical opportunity due to the types of intervention that it rendered possible in the environmental domains, and for enabling the start and continuous existence of an increasingly integrated, active and systematic inclusion of the environment in the national public policy agenda."[16] This translated into "a rapid evolution of environmental consciousness within Portuguese society and a deep transformation of the institutional framework."[17] Two of the most important planning and sustainable development frameworks are the Legal Framework for the Environment (*Lei de Bases do Ambiente*), approved in

1987, and the Legal Framework for Territorial Planning (*Lei de Bases da Política do Ordenamento do Território*), approved in 1999. Despite these two national frameworks, it has been argued that "strategic spatial planning is still at an infant stage and environmental concerns, recently introduced largely under the influence of the European Union, adopted essentially a restrictive and reactive stance."[18]

The Portuguese planning system is based on a hierarchical approach of plans, from neighborhood plans (*Planos de Pormenor—PPs*), to master plans (Planos *Directores Municipal—PDMs*) and regional plans (*Planos Regional de Ordenamento do Território—PROTs*), to a national plan (*Plano Nacional de Política de Ordenamento do Território—PNPOT*).[19] Although many municipalities had developed their master plans by the late 1990s, the country only approved its national plan in 2007. According to Jorge Gaspar, the plan identifies seven challenges currently faced by the Portuguese society: (1) the demographic challenge, where because of a decrease in fertility rates the country might experience a considerable reduction in its total population; (2) the need to value human resources appropriately, otherwise brain drain and emigration processes might lead to decreases in total population; (3) the challenge created by the current economic model, which requires the country not only to produce more but also to increase its productivity by being more innovative; (4) the urbanization challenge that includes the migrations from the countryside to the major urban centers; (5) the social and cultural cohesion challenge that includes the need to revamp the Portuguese identity and to foster socioeconomic cohesion; (6) the environmental challenge that addresses the need to decrease pollution emissions and to alleviate mounting pressures on natural resources; and, (7) the challenge of being responsible for the implementation of appropriate solutions to solve the identified problems.[20]

The PNPOT presents specific territorial strategies for the different Portuguese regions. The PNPOT is perceived as a privileged instrument for the implementation of the National Sustainable Development Strategy (ENDS), so that Portugal can fulfill the following main objectives: a sustainable and orderly country, a competitive and integrated economy, an equitable territory in terms of development and societal well-being, and a creative society with an active citizenship. Finally, the PNPOT also identifies a territorial model for the country in the year 2025. This model is based on prevention and reduction of natural and man-made risks; the preservation of natural resources; the strengthening of the urban system based on four main urban agglomerations (Porto, Central Coast, Lisbon, and Algarve), and the improvement of accessibilities and international connectivity through the building of a new international airport and a new high speed train network connection to Europe.

One of the most important national programs to integrate urban and environmental regeneration objectives at the local scale was the POLIS Program. The POLIS program was initiated in 2000 with the major goal of improving the quality of life in twenty-eight selected cities through urban and environmental interventions. Such interventions were aimed at increasing the attractiveness and competitiveness of those cities in the national urban system. The POLIS program had four main objectives: (1) to develop a major urban regeneration program with an integrated approach toward significant environmental improvements; (2) to develop actions to rehabilitate and improve the quality of urban centers and promote their multifunctionality; (3) to support activities that improve the urban environment and increase the value of environmental landmarks, such as riverbanks or the coastline; and (4) to promote initiatives that contribute to an increase in green and pedestrian areas and a reduction in traffic in urban centers.[21]

The POLIS Program led to urban space improvements, urban signage, improved accessibility favoring public transportation and the construction of parking spaces, the implementation of better traffic management schemes through telematics, the renovation of historic centers, the creation of parks and greenways, the renovation of river and ocean fronts, and the building of bicycle lanes and pedestrian-only precincts. An innovative feature of this program was the creation of partnership arrangements between the central government and local municipalities as a creative way of channeling EU funds. A new follow-up program called POLIS XXI was launched in the first half of 2007.

POLIS XXI is to be financed with EU funds between the years 2007–2013. Special emphasis will be given to sustainable urban regeneration schemes in line with the orientations of the Leipzig Charter approved during the German presidency of the European Union. This new program will only finance projects that integrate physical, environmental, social, economic, and cultural dimensions. The partnership led by a municipality should also include other national, regional, and local stakeholders, such as chambers of commerce, nonprofit organizations, and universities.[22]

The current urban policy framework is based on four dimensions: urban regeneration, competitiveness and differentiation, integration of city-regions, and innovative solutions to urban problems.[23] Portugal seems to be giving increasing attention to urban regeneration activities.[24] In fact, the political priorities of the XVII government clearly stated the support of interventions and programs that favor the urban regeneration of dilapidated areas. The creation of urban rehabilitation corporations (SRUs) to expedite and simplify the revitalization of urban neighborhoods in downtown areas and the broadening of the mission of the National Institute of Housing to address urban revitalization issues are two additional examples of a growing interest in urban revitalization.

Urban Development in Portugal

Portugal has a population of 10 million people, with the majority living on the coast (see fig. 1). Most urban development in Portugal occurs along the coast and is anchored by the metropolitan areas of Lisbon and Porto (see figs. 2 and 3). The coastal area of Portugal represents about 28 percent of the country, with a population in the order of 60 percent in 2001. The rest of the population lives mainly in medium-size cities throughout the country. The two metropolitan areas suffered a late suburbanization process, which occurred mainly after the political revolution of 1974. Their main cities lost population to the suburbs between 1981 and 2001; Lisbon lost 30 percent and Porto lost 20 percent. These numbers contrast sharply with regular regional gains in demographics from 1951 to 2001. In the Lisbon Metropolitan Area the population increased by 104 percent, and in the Porto Metropolitan Area it increased by 72 percent. The growth of the urban population in Portugal from 1990 to 1999 was 2.7 percent, a much higher increase than those found in many other European countries. In fact, it has been argued that this growth rate resembles those of some developing countries where urban growth creates added pressure on urban services and infrastructure.[25]

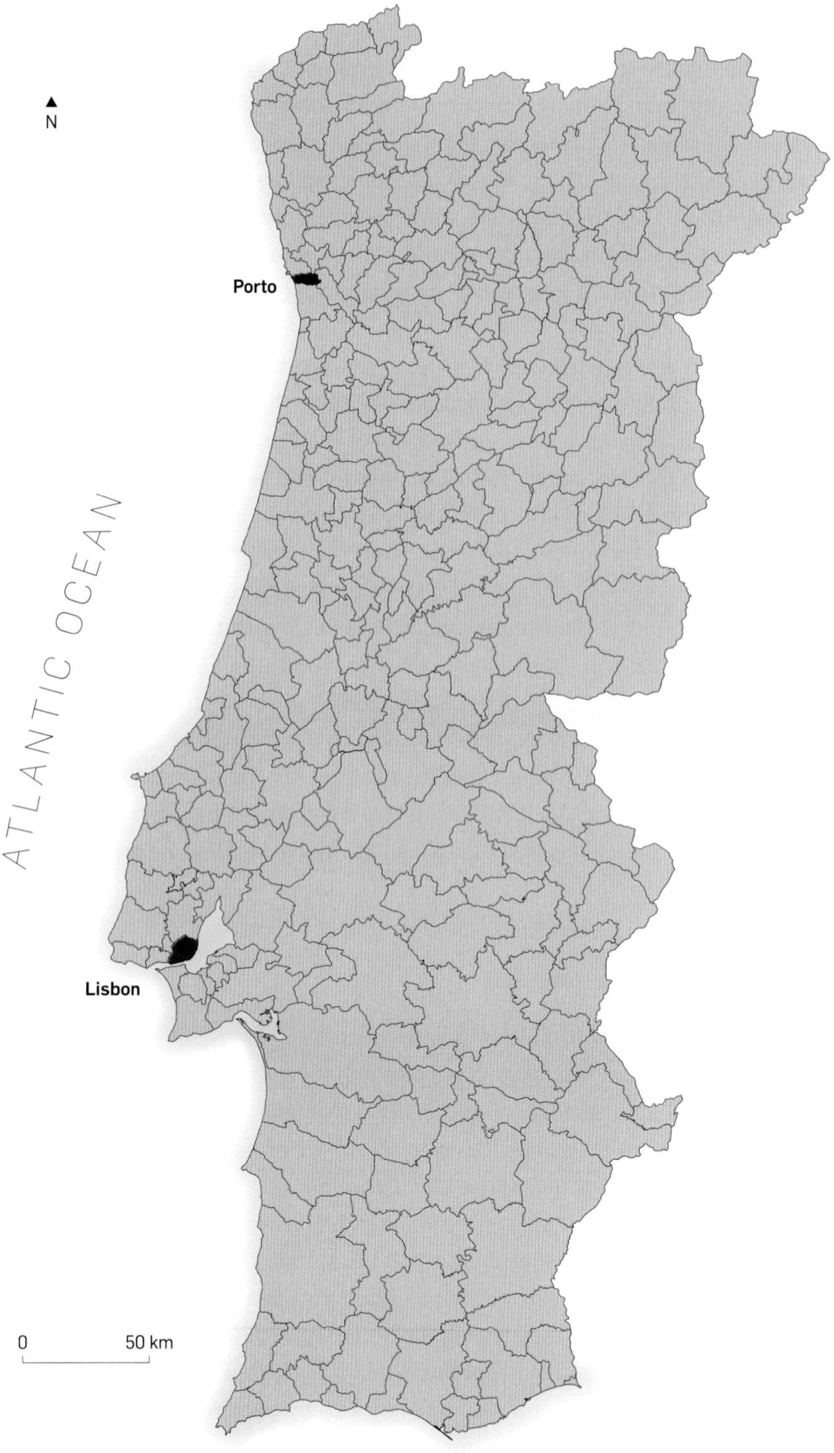

CARTOGRAPHY BY HERCULANO CACHINHO

Figure 1. Map of continental Portugal.

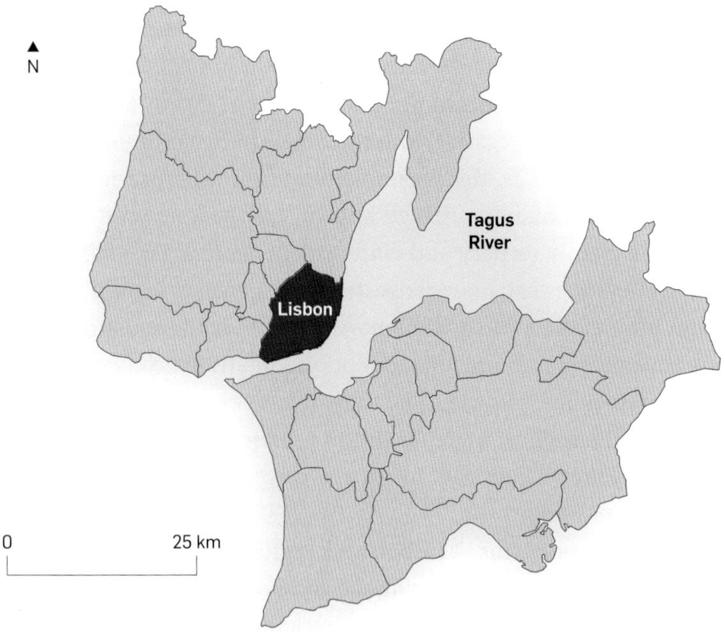

CARTOGRAPHY BY HERCULANO CACHINHO

Figure 2. Map of the Lisbon Metropolitan Area.

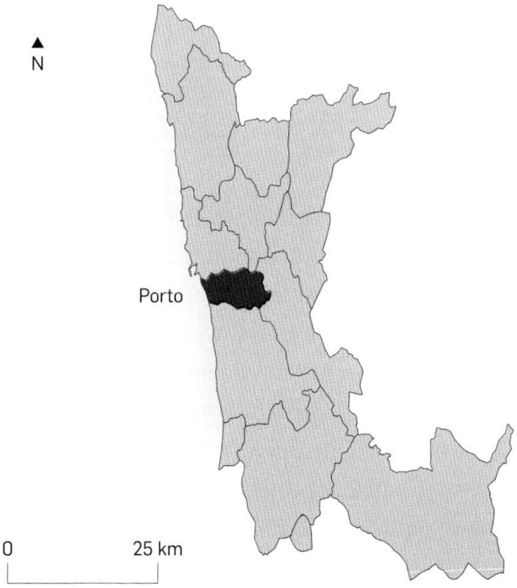

CARTOGRAPHY BY HERCULANO CACHINHO

Figure 3. Map of the Porto Metropolitan Area.

Nonetheless, the suburbanization processes in Portugal were partly similar to those of major Western European cities.[26] The growth of the suburbs allowed people to own newer and bigger homes and apartments, but it also led to the decline of the city centers. Two other factors in this decentralization movement were the increase in motorization rates and the boom in service-oriented and shopping malls in peripheral areas of cities. This boom in real estate led to unbalanced land uses with negative consequences on urban living. With the exception of incipient returns to central areas, the phenomenon of suburbanization is still under way. The consequences of this phenomenon are well known. City centers tend to lose their residential activities and become mainly tertiary and employment centers. People start commuting to and from the suburbs, generating rush hour congestion and increases in air pollution. In fact, surveys of environmental problems in Portugal demonstrated that the most often cited examples of environmental problems were air and noise pollution from traffic congestion, due to an excessive use of individual automobiles.[27] At the same time, it has been recognized that Portugal was one of the countries with the highest increase in the production of green house gases associated with transportation in Europe from 1991 to 2001, 97 percent compared to an increase of only 26 percent for the European Union.[28]

The two largest cities in Portugal, Lisbon and Porto, experienced some attempts at revitalizing their riverfronts and city centers during the second half of the 1990s. These revitalizations complemented the renovation of the historic districts, which had already started during the 1980s. In Lisbon, the World Exposition EXPO '98 was instrumental in regenerating a riverfront area in the eastern part of the capital. The revitalization of the central business district, known as *baixa* (or downtown), included urban design interventions in several squares. In Porto the 2001 European Capital of Culture revitalized the public space of four main squares and many streets in the *baixa*. In both cities, the revitalization of city centers included improvements to public spaces, streetscaping, pedestrianization schemes, urban furniture, limited housing rehabilitation, some retail modernizations, and embryonic attempts at implementing city center management partnerships.[29]

Lisbon

Lisbon is the capital of Portugal and the main metropolitan area in the country. Its 2.6 million people represent about 25 percent of the population in the country. The metropolitan area comprises eighteen municipalities and is centered around the Tagus estuary, with the city of Lisbon located on the north bank of the river (see fig. 4). In the words of a former minister of environment and planning, the metropolitan area suffered from the following problems: an increase in the prices of real estate, leading to the decline of city centers; congested roads and highways; an overall decline of the environment; a decrease of public open spaces; the growth of social exclusion processes; and a decline in the quality of urban landscapes.[30] In the metropolitan area, the automobile mode share increased from 26 to 46 percent, and the public transport mode share decreased from 51 to 36 percent from 1991 to 2001.[31]

Lisbon's central location in the metropolitan area disproportionately impacts its growth and decline problems.[32] The city has been actively engaged in the development of different types of

PHOTOGRAPHY BY CARLOS BALSAS

Figure 4. Overview of Lisbon's western riverfront area.

plans to properly guide its development. In fact, Lisbon was the first city in Portugal to approve a strategic plan in 1992. One of the unique features of this plan was the creation of a stakeholders' council to give input and help prioritize strategic options. The work of this council was also critical to the approval of the city's master plan in 1994.[33] These two plans targeted an abandoned riverfront area on the eastern part of Lisbon as the site for the future World Exposition EXPO '98. The redevelopment of this site is probably the most successful example of sustainable urban regeneration in Portugal. More recently, the renovation of several main squares and streets in downtown Lisbon can also be seen as examples of urban regeneration projects (see fig. 5). Nonetheless, there are still plenty of problems with the urban fabric of the downtown area, its adjacent historic districts, and their functional activities.

It has been claimed that the environmental plan produced between 1997 and 2000 resembled a true Local Agenda 21 process, with vision statements, the participation of interested stakeholders, and the production of local action plans for key thematic areas.[34] According to a former city councilmember, this environmental plan established actions in the following key areas: the improvement and renovation of public spaces, the development of a green structure for the city, the planning of urban landscape thematic trails, the improvement of consolidated residential neighborhoods, the rehabilitation of historic districts, the development of a noise charter for the

Figure 5. D. Pedro IV Square in Lisbon.

city of Lisbon, the redefinition of a selective recycling scheme, and the development of a strategy to minimize air pollution.[35]

Changes in political leadership can very often interrupt the continuity of planning programs and policies. Despite some leadership changes in Lisbon during the last decade, two Portuguese urbanists have synthesized the following list of revitalization activities in Lisbon:[36]

- Several pilot housing projects on Rua da Madalena and Rua de São Bento;
- The launching of major renovation works, called "Mega Empreitadas;"
- An exhaustive building inventory on selected thoroughfares in the city;
- A system of coercive summons for building repairs and indictments;
- The launching of three urban rehabilitation companies—SRUs (Baixa Pombalina, Alcântara/Ajuda, and Zona Oriental);
- The creation of a number of cofunded rehabilitation programs, such as RECRIA, REHABITA, and RECRIPH;
- The candidacy of Baixa Pombalina as a UNESCO World Heritage Site;
- And the restriction of vehicle accessibility and parking alternatives in three of the most popular historic neighborhoods: Alfama, Bairro Alto, and Santa Catarina.

At the regional level, the Lisbon Metropolitan Area Authority has limited regional planning powers. The governance capabilities of this authority are intermingled with the competencies of a different regional planning organization, the Comissão de Coordenação e Desenvolvimento da Região de Lisboa e Vale do Tejo (CCDR-LVT). The regional plan for the Lisbon Metropolitan Area (PROTAML) was approved in 2002. A new regional strategy for metropolitan Lisbon called "Lisboa 2020" was finalized recently. This plan is less technical and more action oriented than PROTAML.[37] It is based on a 4Cs strategy for the Lisbon Metropolitan Area: cohesion, connections, cosmopolitanism, and competitiveness. This plan also emphasizes the following broad goals: innovation and knowledge, environmental intelligence, connected metropolis, metropolis for people, qualified metropolis, a metropolis of tourism, and heritage and culture. Nonetheless, the suburbanization process and unbalanced urban growth seem to be uncontrollable. Apparently, the cities in the metropolitan area do not recognize much value in the making of municipal and regional plans. In fact, a former president of CCDR-LVT has even questioned the need for so many plans when they have not been implemented by the different cities in the metropolitan area.[38]

Despite the lack of effective metropolitan governance processes hampering the development of a single and unified sustainable metropolitan development strategy, different municipalities have made important progress in the development and implementation of their own sustainable development strategies. The cities of Almada and Oeiras have been identified as the two municipalities that have been promoting local sustainable development agendas with "considerable positive impact for their inhabitants."[39] Their LA21 plans were led by independent teams (with intensive cooperation and input from the municipalities) from universities and with very comprehensive public participation processes.

Finally, an important sustainability document in Lisbon is the Energy and Environmental Strategy, which targets a reduction in primary energy consumption of 7 percent and a reduction in water consumption of 25 percent by 2020. This strategy also includes a 6 percent reduction in building energy, a 9 percent reduction in transport related energy, and a 25 percent reduction in public lighting. If these targets are achieved, the total citywide reduction in carbon dioxide emissions can be as high as 10 percent.[40]

Porto

Porto is the main city in the northern part of the country. The metropolitan area comprises 1.3 million people within sixteen municipalities. Like the Lisbon metropolitan area, the Porto metropolitan area is centered on a river estuary. The city of Porto is located on the northern bank of the River Douro, while the famous Port wine cellars are on the south bank in the city of Vila Nova de Gaia (see fig. 6). The historic district of Porto was awarded the UNESCO's designation of World Heritage Site of the Humanity in 1996 for its unique built and cultural heritage.

The centuries-old urban fabric in the historic district is both a blessing and a curse for the city; a blessing because it represents the layers of history that have shaped this important city and a curse because it is difficult for planners and public officials to renovate and adapt it to contemporary living conditions. Many of the buildings in the historic district have very small rooms. The majority do not have elevators or appropriate bathrooms and parking garages. These structural

PHOTOGRAPH BY CARLOS BALSAS

Figure 6. Porto riverfront area.

problems have influenced the new generations to leave the city center for new suburban developments with new apartments, more space to build single-family homes, new shopping malls, and more highway accessibility. In fact, the city center has a large percentage of elderly people without a lot of resources to renovate their homes. In addition, one can also observe the worsening of social vulnerability situations with obvious problems in terms of urban crime and homelessness, mainly due to unemployment.[41]

Similar to the development of the EXPO '98 in Lisbon, the city of Porto also used a mega-event to renovate its urban core and promote the city to outside visitors. Porto organized the event European Capital of Culture in 2001. This event not only served to celebrate cultural and artistic achievements in the city, but it also helped to regenerate the downtown area, located just north of the historic district. New utility systems were installed, public squares were renovated, sidewalks were widened, and new parking garages were built (see fig. 7). One of the shortcomings of this event was that the urban fabric was not greatly improved. Despite successful small-scale improvements and building renovations, previous city administrations had a difficult time marketing the city center to private investors. Apparently, too many regulations and problems of property ownership made it difficult to attract private investors to renovate the building stock in the historic district. This situation seems to have been improved with the creation of the urban rehabilitation corporation called SRU Porto Vivo.

The SRU Porto Vivo rehabilitation corporation's main goal is to convert the city center of Porto into a space of sociability and residency with diverse and competitive economic activities and high standards of urban living. The strategy currently under way focuses on urban rehabilitation, the promotion of business entrepreneurship, the promotion of retail activities, the fostering of tourism and leisure experiences, and the renovation of public spaces. After a very detailed master plan for the intervention area, Porto Vivo is now implementing the revitalization of several urban blocks and street corridors in the downtown area. Due to recent changes in fiscal laws, the corporation Porto Vivo estimates that new construction in greenfield sites costs 30 percent more than urban rehabilitation in the city center, and that new construction has on average 28 percent more fiscal burdens than rehabilitation in the city center.[42] A particularly interesting example of the work conducted by Porto Vivo is the current renovation of a public market called Mercado do Bolhão into a modern and convenient retail space.

Another trend in Porto is the increase in car ownership and its negative consequences in terms of congestion and air pollution emissions. In the Porto Metropolitan Area, the automobile mode share increased from 31 percent to 52 percent between 1991 and 2001, while the public transport mode share decreased from 42 percent to 28 percent during the same period.[43] To improve accessibility and mobility in the metropolitan area, a new modern light rail system was recently

PHOTOGRAPH BY CARLOS BALSAS

Figure 7. Aliados Avenue in downtown Porto.

built. This light rail system was a very successful accomplishment not only for the city, but also for the entire metropolitan area. The light rail system is about thirty-seven miles (sixty kilometers) long, and it has served almost 40 million passengers since the launching of its first line in 2003.

In terms of environmental planning and contrary to what is happening in the Lisbon metropolitan area, the residents in Porto have been quite active in the development of an environmental strategic plan for the greater Porto area. For the purpose of their study, the authors identified Greater Porto as comprising nine municipalities. This plan was initiated in 2003, and it was promoted by the solid waste corporation of Greater Porto (LIPOR) and coordinated by the Biotech School of the Portuguese Catholic University. This plan has had broad public participation, which until now has included more than 4,000 citizens. The diagnosis and main analyses have focused on four main components: water, education for sustainability, mobility and air quality, and urban planning, open spaces, and forestry. In 2005, this collective effort was recognized with a best practice award from the International Council for Local Environmental Initiatives (ICLEI). This plan is innovative in not only scale but also public participation practices. The main priorities identified in the public participation processes were the need to have more environmental education, to recycle waste, to prevent wildfires, and to achieve more orderly urban development.[44]

Discussion

The following discussion addresses three commonly known dimensions of sustainable development: economic, environmental, and social.[45] The economic impact of the two metropolitan areas can be observed by their strong pull over the countryside, and by their growing total population and increases in living standards.[46] The cities of Lisbon and Porto seem to be very keen on balancing their public finances in order to provide adequate services and enable the proper functioning of urban and metropolitan economies. The role of national and European Union programs in the improvement of living conditions and the fostering of more competitive economic sectors in both metropolitan areas is also quite noticeable.[47] It is worth emphasizing the role of several European Union funded urban revitalization programs—such as URBCOM, POLIS, and SRUs—in the creation of more vital neighborhoods in the metropolitan areas of Lisbon and Porto.

The negative environmental impacts in Lisbon and Porto seem to be a direct consequence of metropolitan expansion and inadequate implementation of existing plans and policies. The negative environmental impacts result mainly from increasing pollution levels associated not only with urban living but also with growing energy usage. Transportation, in particular the rise of private automobiles, seems to be a major problem in these two metropolitan areas. The transportation impacts can be measured by their growing congestion levels, vehicle emissions, energy consumption, and lost productivity. Both cities have made considerable progress in addressing mobility issues through the implementation of clean-fuel vehicles fleets, smart real-time systems, the building of a light rail in Porto, and the expansion of the subway system in Lisbon. The stringent implementation of the Lisbon Energy and Environmental Strategy should also lead to major reductions in energy usage both in transportation and in buildings.

The social impact of sustainable development practices in both metropolitan areas can be observed by the growing number of social programs currently under way. The city of Lisbon developed a very coherent and comprehensive strategic plan for social sustainable development in 2007.[48] This plan not only articulated the city's responsibilities in the social sphere, but also advanced recommendations for partnerships with other charitable groups in the city (e.g., sisters of mercy, church groups, and private foundations). Many of the programs are being implemented with European Union funds and resources collected through the hard work of civic-minded and solidary individuals and organizations. In Porto, the social conditions for homeless people seem to be deteriorating with the termination of a drug rehab partnership between the central government and the nonprofit organization Porto Feliz. About five hundred *arrumadores* have been displaced on the streets of Porto because of the termination of this collaboration. *Arrumadores* is the name given to many homeless people who make a living by helping people park cars in exchange for small monetary donations. Unfortunately, many of these people have health issues and use that money to buy drugs and alcohol.[49]

Although it is difficult to make direct comparisons between the two metropolitan areas, one can observe that they are both attempting to develop a better understanding of what more sustainable development practices might entail. These practices can be better achieved with clearer and more committed political objectives, better integrated governance practices, and more inclusive public participation processes.[50] A more detailed assessment of past programs and a better understanding of innovative ways to move forward will allow citizens and the Portuguese society to recognize the real relevance of sustainable development behaviors to their daily lives. Only more sustainable behaviors will facilitate a collective move toward the successful implementation of the national sustainable development strategy.

Conclusion

The main objective of this chapter was to highlight how Portugal—and its two main metropolitan areas in particular—is addressing the challenges of moving toward more sustainable development practices. It was argued that Portugal is attempting to implement a more integrated national planning strategy to create a more sustainable and competitive country. This process presents some unique challenges that will require more leadership, commitment, inclusive practices, and measured progress.

The most important sustainable development issues the country faces at this time seem to be the translation of broad based national planning goals and programs into executable regional and local level strategies capable of changing deep-rooted routines and behaviors.[51] Overall, "Portuguese municipalities have been slow in developing integrated environmental policies that go beyond sectoral and specific actions to solve particular problems or to provide amenities."[52]

The two main Portuguese metropolitan areas show different levels of progress in the development of Local Agenda 21 plans and strategies. Greater Porto, with its strategic environmental plan, seems to be making some positive progress toward the identification of environmental vulnerabilities and the development of appropriate action plans. The Lisbon Energy and Environmental Strategy is an innovative attempt at reducing energy consumption and complying with the targets imposed by the Kyoto Protocol. Different municipalities in the two metropolitan areas show different degrees of commitment toward sustainable development plans and practices. It has been recognized that "there is a strong relation between the more urbanized and wealthy areas and the importance given to environmental issues."[53] This claim is still true today.

The Portuguese economy is very heterogeneous, and its industry is still very resource and energy driven. The more the economy transitions to more value-added goods, the more effective the relationship between the environment and the economy will be. The apparently slow progress for the country as a whole might be reflective of a relatively young democratic regime characterized as being able to meet "the lowest levels of implementation in what concerns...participatory processes for local sustainability."[54]

After a period of relative inactivity at the central level, the 2007 Portuguese sustainable development strategy has identified very ambitious goals and targets. The seventy-page document seems to have been well received by environmental and economic groups, and since it has a broad scope, it does promise to become a sustainability milestone by European standards. In conclusion, sustainable development is on the agenda in Portugal. Now it needs to be brought down to the regional and local levels, with the understanding that changes in individual and collective behaviors will lead to a more prosperous, environmentally sound, and responsible society.

NOTES

1. Diário de noticias, Deputados contribuem para diminuir dióxido de carbono, August 21, 2007.
2. P. Newman and J. Kenworthy, *Sustainability and Cities: Overcoming Automobile Dependence* (Washington, DC: Island Press, 1999); R. Kemp and P. Martens, Sustainable Development: How to Manage Something That Is Subjective and Never Can Be Achieved? *Sustainability: Science, Practice and Policy* 3:2 (2007): 1–10; Reed, Shifting from Sustainability to Regeneration, 674–80.
3. Published literature on sustainable development in Portugal is very slim. With the exception of several papers and surveys, I found mainly technical reports on environmental planning and specific papers on sustainability related aspects of urban development in Lisbon and Porto. I did not, however, find any published research comparatively analyzing the evolution and implementation of sustainability plans and programs in both metropolitan areas. The methodology used in this chapter included extensive literature and newspaper reviews, meetings in Portugal, and the review of official documents, regulations, and plans. N. Carter, F. Silva, F. Magalhães, Local Agenda 21: Progress in Portugal, *European Urban and Regional Studies* 7:2 (2000): 181–86; J. Almeida et al., II Inquérito nacional os Portugueses e o ambiente, OBSERVA—Ambiente, sociedade e opinião pública, 2001, http://observa.iscte.pt/index.php; S. Valente and L. Schmidt, 2004, Áreas metropolitanas, vivências, mobilidades e qualidade de vida, http://observa.iscte.pt/index.php; L. Schmidt, J. Nave, and J. Guerra, Who's Afraid of Local Agenda 21, *Journal of Environment and Sustainable Development* 5:2 (2006): 181–98.
4. WCED, *Our Common Future* (New York: Oxford University Press, 1987).
5. N. Carter, F. Silva, F. Magalhães, Local Agenda 21: Progress in Portugal, *European Urban and Regional Studies* 7:2 (2000): 181.
6. T. Beatley, *Green Urbanism, Learning from European Cities* (Washington, DC: Island Press, 1999).
7. R. Godinho, Desenvolvimento Sustentável: As cidades como solução (paper presented at the NUTAU Conference, São Paulo, Brazil, October 7–11, 2002).
8. G. Begin, European Cities Move towards Sustainability Achievements and Prospects 1992–2012 (paper presented at the 2006 ICLEI Seminar, Kyoto), http://lorc.ryukoku.ac.jp/iclei_seminars2006.html.
9. Schmidt, Nave, and Guerra, Who's Afraid of Local Agenda 21?, 181.
10. M. Pinto, 2006, Agenda 21 Local—Plataforma na Internet sobre Agenda21 Local ou uma Utopia do Trabalho em Colaboração, http://www.agenda21local.info/http://www.eu2007.de/en/.
11. V. Soromenho-Marques, M. Queirós, and M. Vale, National Report: Regional Sustainable Development,

REGIONET—Thematic Network: Strategies for Regional Sustainable Development, 2004, 11.
12. Schmidt, Nave, and Guerra, Who's Afraid of Local Agenda 21?, 185.
13. Portuguese Government, Estratégia Nacional de Desenvolvimento Sustentável—ENDS 2015 and Plano de Implementação. Resolução do Conselho de Ministros. Diário da República, 1ª Série, No.159, August 20, 2007.
14. German Presidency of the European Union, Leipzig Charter on Sustainable European Cities, Leipzig, May 24–25, 2007, http://www.eu2007.de/en/.
15. R. Cardoso and I. Breda-Vázquez, Social Justice as a Guide to Planning Theory and Practice: Analyzing the Portuguese Planning System, *International Journal of Urban and Regional Research* 31:2 (2007): 384–400.
16. Soromenho-Marques, Queirós, and Vale, National Report, 10.
17. Ibid.
18. A. Pires, The Fragile Foundations of European Spatial Planning in Portugal, *European Planning Studies* 13:2 (2005): 237.
19. See Decree Law 380/99, September 22, and Decree Law 310/03, December 10.
20. J. Gaspar, Notas em torno do processo de elaboração do PNPOT, *Sociedade e território* 40 (2007): 74–86.
21. M. Partidário and F. Correia, POLIS—The Portuguese Programme on Urban Environment. A Contribution to the Discussion on European Urban Policy, *European Planning Studies* 12:3 (2004): 413.
22. MAOTDR, Política de cidades POLIS XXI, 2007, http://www.dgotdu.pt/http://www.eu2007.de/en/.
23. MAOTDR, Balanço de dois anos (2005–2007): XVII Governo constitucional (Lisbon: Ministério do Ambiente, Ordenamento do Território e do Desenvolvimento Regional, 2007), 84.
24. B. Reed, Shifting from Sustainability to Regeneration, *Building Research and Information* 35:6 (2007): 674–80.
25. L. Souza et al., Cidades sustentáveis: Um desafio comum para Brasil e Portugal. III ENECS—Encontro nacional sobre edificações e comunidades sustentáveis, São Carlos, Brazil, September 21–24, 2003, http://repositorium.sdum.uminho.pt/.
26. N. Portas, A. Domingues, and J. Cabral, *Políticas urbanas, tendências, estratégias e oportunidades* (Lisbon: Fundação Calouste Gulbenkian, 2003).
27. Valente and Schmidt, Áreas metropolitanas, vivências.
28. A. Vitorino, Transportes para um Desenvolvimento Sustentável (paper presented at the Conference TDeS'07, LNEC, Lisbon, June 22, 2007), http://tdes07.lnec.pt/.
29. C. Balsas, City Center Revitalization in Portugal: A Study of Lisbon and Porto, *Journal of Urban Design* 12:2 (2007): 231–59.
30. F. Correia, Lisboa 2020—Uma estratégia de Lisboa para a região de Lisboa (keynote speech at the Centro de Congressos da FIL, Lisbon, June, 4, 2007), http://www.portugal.gov.pt/.
31. Vitorino, Transportes para um Desenvolvimento Sustentável.
32. T. Salgueiro, *Lisboa, Periferia e centralidades* (Oeiras: Celta Editora, 2001).
33. V. Oliveira and P. Pinho, Urban Form and Planning in Lisbon and Oporto, *Planning Perspectives* 23 (2008): 81–105.
34. R. Godinho, Desenvolvimento sustentável: As cidades como solução (paper presented at the NUTAU Conference, São Paulo, Brazil, October 7–11, 2002).
35. Ibid., 9–10.
36. T. Craveiro and M. Lobo, Integrating the City—A 3rd Solution for the Periphery of Lisbon (paper presented at the 42nd ISOCARP Congress, 2006), http://www.isocarp.org/.
37. A. Ferreira, *Gestão estratégica de cidades e regiões* (Lisbon: Fundação Calouste Gulbenkian, 2005); A. Ferreira, Área metropolitana de Lisboa: Dilemas e oportunidades, *Sociedade e território* 40 (2007): 63–71.
38. Ferreira, Área metropolitana, 63–71.
39. Soromenho-Marques, Queirós, and Vale, National Report, 23.
40. L. Tirone, Estratégia energético-ambiental para a cidade de Lisboa (paper presented at the Conference Metas de Desempenho Energético-Ambientais, November, 22, 2007), http://lisboaenova.org/ http://www.eu2007.de/en/; N. Rodrigues, Cidades sustentáveis: Lisboa define metas energéticas, *Jornal Arquitecturas Suplemento*, February 21, 2007, 4.
41. J. Fernandes, (Des)Ordenamento metropolitano: Dos problemas ás soluções (paper presented at the PEAGP, Maia, June 17, 2005), http://www.futurosustentavel.org/; Porto, Governo suspendeu apoio ao tratamento de "arrumadores," 16–17.
42. SRU—Porto Vivo, reabilitação da baixa portuense—Uma oportunidade, Uma obrigação (presentation made at IMOBITUR, May 11, 2007), http://repositorium.sdum.uminho.pt/http://www.eu2007.de/en/.
43. Vitorino, Transportes para um Desenvolvimento Sustentável.
44. Futurosustentavel.org, Futuro sustentável, diagnóstico de ambiente do grande

Porto—ordenamento do território, espaços verdes e áreas naturais, 2006, http://www.futurosustentavel.org/http://www.eu2007.de/en/.

45. P. Newman and J. Kenworthy, *Sustainability and Cities: Overcoming Automobile Dependence* (Washington, DC: Island Press, 1999); T. Fidélis, *Planeamento territorial e ambiental* (Cascais: Principia, 2001).
46. J. Ferrão, Uma metrópole em transição: Novo perfil produtivo, novos espaços económicos, in *Atlas da área metropolitana de Lisboa*, ed. A. Tenedório, 2004, http://www.forumdourbanismo.info/.
47. A. Domingues, *Cidade e democracia—30 anos de transformação em Portugal* (Porto: Argumentum, 2006).
48. Câmara Municipal de Lisboa, *Plano Estratégico de desenvolvimento social sustentado* (Lisbon: CML, 2007).
49. Porto, Governo suspendeu apoio ao tratamento de "arrumadores," 16–17.
50. J. Seixas, A cidade não governada: Motivações públicas e governação urbana, *Cidades, comunidades e territórios* 1 (2000): 57–72; N. Quental, M. Silva, and J. Lourenço, Integração de critérios objectivos de sustentabilidade ambiental na elaboração de planos regionais de ordenamento do território (paper presented at the 11th AUP Conference, Santa Maria da Feira, October, 13–15, 2004), http://repositorium.sdum.uminho.pt/.
51. Soromenho-Marques, Queirós, and Vale, National Report.
52. N. Carter, F. Silva, F. Magalhães, Local Agenda 21: Progress in Portugal, *European Urban and Regional Studies* 7:2 (2000): 182.
53. Ibid.
54. Schmidt, Nave, and Guerra, Who's Afraid of Local Agenda 21?, 183.

REFERENCES

Balsas, Carlos. City Center Revitalization in Portugal: A Study of Lisbon and Porto. *Journal of Urban Design* 12:2 (2007): 231–59.

Beatley, Timothy. *Green Urbanism, Learning from European Cities.* Washington, DC: Island Press, 1999.

Begin, G. European Cities Move towards Sustainability Achievements and Prospects 1992–2012. Paper presented at the 2006 ICLEI Seminar, Kyoto. http://lorc.ryukoku.ac.jp/iclei_seminars2006.html.

Câmara Municipal de Lisboa. *Plano estratégico de desenvolvimento social sustentado.* Lisbon: CML, 2007.

Cardoso, Ricardo, and Isabel Breda-Vázquez. Social Justice as a Guide to Planning Theory and Practice: Analyzing the Portuguese Planning System. *International Journal of Urban and Regional Research* 31:2 (2007): 384–400.

Carter, Norma, Fernando Nunes da Silva, and Fernanda Magalhães. Local Agenda 21: Progress in Portugal. *European Urban and Regional Studies* 7:2 (2000): 181–86.

Correia, F. Lisboa 2020—Uma estratégia de Lisboa para a região de Lisboa. Keynote Speech at the Centro de Congressos da FIL. Lisbon, June, 4, 2007. http://www.portugal.gov.pt/.

Craveiro, T., and M. Lobo. Integrating the City—A 3rd Solution for the Periphery of Lisbon. Paper presented at the 42nd ISOCARP Congress, 2006. http://www.isocarp.org/.

Diário de noticias. Deputados contribuem para diminuir dióxido de carbono. August 21, 2007.

Domingues, A. *Cidade e democracia—30 anos de transformação em Portugal.* Porto: Argumentum, 2006.

Farreira de Almeida, J., et al. 2001. II Inquérito nacional os Portugueses e o ambiente. OBSERVA—Ambiente, sociedade e opinião pública. http://observa.iscte.pt/index.php.

Fernandes, Jose A. Rio. (Des)Ordenamento metropolitano: Dos problemas ás soluções. Paper presented at the PEAGP, Maia, June 17, 2005. http://www.futurosustentavel.org/.

Ferrão, J. Uma Metrópole em transição: Novo perfil produtivo, novos espaços económicos. In *Atlas da área metropolitana de Lisboa*, ed. A. Tenedório. http://www.forumdourbanismo.info/1.

Ferreira, A. Área metropolitana de Lisboa: Dilemas e oportunidades. *Sociedade e território* 40 (2007): 63–71.

———. *Gestão estratégica de cidades e regiões.* Lisbon: Fundação Calouste Gulbenkian, 2005.

Fidélis, T. *Planeamento territorial e ambiental.* Cascais: Principia, 2001.

Futurosustentavel.org. 2006. Futuro sustentável, diagnóstico de ambiente do grande Porto—Ordenamento do território, espaços verdes e áreas naturais. http://www.futurosustentavel.org/.

Gaspar, Jorge. Notas em torno do processo de elaboração do

PNPOT. *Sociedade e território* 40 (2007): 74–86.
German Presidency of the European Union. Leipzig Charter on Sustainable European Cities. Leipzig, May 24–25, 2007. http://www.eu2007.de/en/.
Godinho, Ricardo. Desenvolvimento sustentável: As cidades como solução. Paper presented at the NUTAU Conference. São Paulo, Brazil, October 7–11, 2002.
Kemp, Rene, and Pim Martens. Sustainable Development: How to Manage Something That Is Subjective and Never Can Be Achieved? *Sustainability: Science, Practice and Policy* 3:2 (2007): 1–10.
Ministério do Ambiente, Ordenamento do Território e do Desenvolvimento Regional (MAOTDR). Balanço de Dois Anos (2005–2007). XVII Governo Constitucional. Lisbon: MAOTDR, 2007.
———. Política de Cidades POLIS XXI. 2007. http://www.dgotdu.pt/.
Newman, Peter, and Jeffrey Kenworthy. *Sustainability and Cities: Overcoming Automobile Dependence.* Washington, DC: Island Press, 1999.
Oliveira, Vitor, and Paulo Pinho. Urban Form and Planning in Lisbon and Oporto. *Planning Perspectives* 23 (2008): 81–105.
Partidário, Maria Do Rosario, and Francisco Nunes Correia. POLIS—The Portuguese Programme on Urban Environment. A Contribution to the Discussion on European Urban Policy. *European Planning Studies* 12:3 (2004): 409–24.
Pinto, M. Agenda 21 Local—Plataforma na Internet sobre Agenda21 Local ou uma Utopia do Trabalho em Colaboração. 2006. http://www.agenda21local.info/.
Pires, Artur. The Fragile Foundations of European Spatial Planning in Portugal. *European Planning Studies* 13:2 (2005): 237–52.
Portas, N., A. Domingues, and J. Cabral. *Políticas Urbanas, Tendências, Estratégias e Oportunidades.* Lisbon: Fundação Calouste Gulbenkian, 2003.
Porto. Governo suspendeu apoio ao tratamento de "arrumadores." Porto Sempre, October 16–17, 2007.
Portuguese Government. Estratégia Nacional de Desenvolvimento Sustentável—ENDS 2015 and Plano de Implementação. Resolução do Conselho de Ministros. Diário da República, 1ª Série, No.159, August 20, 2007.
Quental, Nuno, Margarida Silva, and Julia Lourenço. Integração de critérios objectivos de sustentabilidade ambiental na elaboração de planos regionais de ordenamento do território. Paper presented at the 11th AUP Conference. Santa Maria da Feira, October, 13–15, 2004. http://repositorium.sdum.uminho.pt/.
Reed, Bill. Shifting from Sustainability to Regeneration. *Building Research and Information* 35:6 (2007): 674–80.
Rodrigues, N. Cidades sustentáveis: Lisboa define metas energéticas. *Jornal arquitecturas suplemento,* February 21, 2007, 4.
Salgueiro, Teresa Barata. *Lisboa, Periferia e centralidades.* Oeiras: Celta Editora, 2001.
Schmidt, Luisa, Joaquim Nave, and Joao Guerra. Who's Afraid of Local Agenda 21? *Journal of Environment and Sustainable Development* 5:2 (2006): 181–98.
Seixas, J. A cidade não governada: Motivações públicas e governação urbana. *Cidades, comunidades e territórios* 1 (2000): 57–72.
Soromenho-Marques, Viriato, Margarida Queirós, Mario Vale. 2004. National Report: Regional Sustainable Development. REGIONET—Thematic Network: Strategies for Regional Sustainable Development.
Souza, Lea Cristina Lucas, Rui A. R. Ramos, Antonio Nelson Rodriguez da Silva, Jose F. G. Mendes. 2003. Cidades sustentáveis: Um desafio comum para Brasil e Portugal. III ENECS—Encontro nacional sobre edificações e comunidades sustentáveis. São Carlos, Brasil, September 21–24. http://repositorium.sdum.uminho.pt/.
SRU—Porto Vivo. Reabilitação da baixa portuense—Uma oportunidade, uma obrigação. Presentation made at IMOBITUR. May 11, 2007. http://repositorium.sdum.uminho.pt/.
Tirone, L. Estratégia energético-ambiental para a cidade de Lisboa. Paper presented at the Conference Metas de Desempenho Energético-Ambientais, November, 22, 2007. http://lisboaenova.org/.
Valente, S., and J. Schmidt. 2004. Áreas metropolitanas, vivências, mobilidades e qualidade de vida. http://observa.iscte.pt/index.php.
Vitorino, A. Transportes para um desenvolvimento sustentável. Paper presented at the Conference TDeS'07. LNEC, Lisbon, June 22, 2007. http://tdes07.lnec.pt/.
WCED. *Our Common Future.* New York: Oxford University Press, 1987.

■ GIOVANNA CODATO / ZENIA KOTVAL / ELENA FRANCO

Sustainable Development in Traditional Harbor Communities

THE CASE OF GENOA AND NAPLES

Sustainable development at both the national and global levels has been the focus of European Union (EU) discussion and policymaking. In 1997 sustainability was included as a main objective in the Treaty of Amsterdam. Then the first comprehensive sustainable development strategy was proposed by the European Commission in June 2001 at the European Council at Gothenburg. In June 2006 the European Council adopted a renewed sustainable development strategy for an enlarged EU, which is based on the preceding Gothenburg strategy and is adapted for the present inclusion of twenty-five nations in the union.

This renewed strategy aims to direct EU actions in a sustainable direction, defined as that which achieves "meeting the needs of present generations without jeopardizing the needs of future generations—a better quality of life for everyone, now and for generations to come."[1] It takes into account the interconnectedness of local and global, social, economic, and environmental needs. The renewed strategy focuses on seven priority challenges: climate change and clean energy; sustainable transport; sustainable consumption and production; public health threats; better management of natural resources; social inclusion, demography, and migration; and fighting global poverty.

In order to realize this goal of sustainable development, the cooperation at all levels of government, with citizens, businesses, and nongovernmental organizations (NGOs), is emphasized. The EU's sustainable development strategy calls for a more integrated policymaking approach that emphasizes improved regulations, such as the implementation of impact assessments. Impact assessments are a political decision-making process that informs decision makers by identifying relevant problems and objectives to be pursued. Then "it identifies the main options for achieving the objective and analyzes their likely impacts in the economic, environmental and social fields. It outlines advantages and disadvantages of each option and examines possible synergies and trade-offs."[2]

Regarding changes in how policy is made, the 2001 sustainable development strategy and the renewed strategy emphasize the importance of improving policy coherence (as with the impact and environmental impact assessments), establishment of energy taxes to encourage alternative energy sources, investment in science and technology, and, finally, improving communication and mobilization of citizens and businesses. The EU has also taken a proactive stance on environmental issues in a variety of ways, such as through the European Climate Change Program and in signing the Kyoto Treaty.

Sustainable European Port City Development

The EU's emphasis on sustainable development translates into the development of the region's many port cities. While Europe is the smallest continent in the world, it also has the longest coastline, and hence the development of its port cities has significant effect on the continent as a whole. Economic, environmental, and social development of port cities have been the emphasis of the recent NEW EPOC response to the EU's green paper "Towards a Future Maritime Policy for the Union: A European Vision for the Ocean and Seas,"[3] and of the International Association Cities and Ports' Charter for the Sustainable Development of Port Cities, presented at the Sydney conference in 2006 and approved at the general assembly in Le Havre in 2007.

The Renewing Economic Prosperity for Port Cities (NEW EPOC) project addresses the issues of economic and environmental urban challenges, maritime cultural heritage, social inclusion, and a working toolset/data exchange. The project recognizes the diminishing role of port cities in today's global economy but argues that this does not warrant the neglect from the EU's maritime policies. Instead, the project asserts that changing technology and the shifting structure of port cities present new opportunities for port city development, but this reinvention will require the support of strong EU policies.

From the environmental angle, stricter regulatory standards are requiring ports and shipping companies to invest in technological improvements that will reduce the environmental impacts of operations. These improvements are expected to lead to cost savings with time. The project also recognizes the importance of environmentally conscious actions for establishing positive relationships with communities. The project has established guides that enable port cities to garner economic as well as social benefits from environmentally conscious activities, enabling port activities to flourish under the increasingly stringent environmental regulations of the EU. The suggested environmental measures state that "all ports should ensure that adequate facilities are available to accept and deal with all forms of recovered and recyclable waste," and that "a full study should be carried out to ascertain whether vessels switching to shore power whilst in port could help reduce emissions and noise levels and whether this is an environmentally sound option."[4]

The EU has taken action to mitigate climate change caused by human activities. Existing and new policies likely to emerge could affect port cities by shifting toward low-carbon energy, reducing investment in carbon-intensive industries and investing in coastal protection to protect against the predicted rise in sea level. These kinds of measures (such as the Climate Change Levy) could negatively impact the amount of carbon-intensive industry in ports. Alternatively, if water becomes a preferred method of low-carbon transport, port cities could benefit. The report notes that fragmentation of EU environmental policies makes waterfront planning and development efforts confusing and can actually hinder investment in port cities.

From the social angle, systematic unemployment is a problem for European port cities. The establishment of high-tech and knowledge-based jobs in port cities will be essential to improving the perception of port cities as places where modern and competitive jobs can be found. Measures such as workforce pooling and reskilling of older workers, plus the creation of new jobs through "effective measures for labor market integration," are facilitated by EU funding but could be enhanced with cooperation of public and private entities.

At an international scope, port cities could benefit from international cooperation in technology and environmental disciplines. The report points to increasing the number of training courses in integrated coastal zone management, and bringing in students from poorer countries to generate jobs and incomes.

The project also calls for the EU to take the well-being of port cities into consideration when implementing policies that affect ports. Port cities are in a time of transition, from being port cities to maritime cities, with the broad maritime economy now at their centers. The paper concludes with three attitudinal changes that could help port cities thrive in the midst of physical and political changes. These changes include bringing people to the water through appealing infrastructure and the use of water for public transportation; modernizing cultural heritage through maritime museums and other tourism or leisure opportunities; and using brownfield sites as a sustainable development alternative to traditional (and often costly) bluefield and greenfield development.[5]

Charter for Sustainable Development of Port Cities

The Charter for Sustainable Development of Port Cities addresses sustainable port city development in the context of globalization. In this context, port cities are primary players in the path of global economic transit. Shareholders with a stake in the successful sustainable development of port cities identified in the charter are the cities, the ports, and all related economic and institutional partners. The charter is based on the intentions of these various stakeholders to engage in sustainable development practices. The charter provides a description of sustainability tailored to port-city development, which includes the following components: "Work together to find solutions for sustainable development of each and of all; cooperate with the national and international organizations seeking to devise rules to protect the earth's natural resources and at the same time improve its populations' quality of life; become initiators of proposals to promote a new political, economic, social and environmental approach to global economic trade and to the management of port cities, growing at an ever faster pace; establish a privileged relationship with global maritime operators competing in the race for ever huger ships."

The six chapters of the charter call for port cities to take action through various means, expressed broadly per chapter followed by detailed courses of action in the following articles. The first chapter calls for port cities "to ensure coherence of projects on the scale of port cities and regions"[6] through, for example, drawing institutional ties and maintaining a dialogue with the public. The second chapter calls port cities "to deal with port interfaces from the viewpoint of mixity [diversity]," including the respect of site identity and management of differing dimensions of port and urban life. The third chapter calls cities "to respect the equilibriums between port cities and their natural environment," by protecting the natural environment, guaranteeing clean maritime and river transport and developing renewable energy. The fourth chapter calls "to strengthen social cohesion and stimulate employment," by opening ports and port city spaces to everyone, creating a diversity of housing options, placing emphasis on knowledge and training and employing fair trade. The fifth chapter calls "to promote innovative port and urban economic development," by, for example, securing safety in port facilities, boosting economic activities, and implementing a new tourism strategy. The final chapter calls port cities "to foster cooperation among port cities," by working together to attain sustainable development, by setting a positive example, and by supporting the International Association of Cities and Ports (IACP) actions.

Italy's Port Cities

Italy's 148 ports, along its more than 4,598 miles (7,400 kilometers) of coastline, handle 85 million passengers and 463 tons of freight every year. Seen as a huge platform stretching out into the Mediterranean, Italy has the potential to attract and handle large numbers of the new-generation vessels that are increasingly a feature of today's maritime traffic.

Port cities have recently been at the center stage of planning practices, from the ports themselves that open up considerably to new cruising routes, to the infrastructures connected to them, to their relationship with the urban fabric of the city centers around which they developed. In Italy, the coexistence of urban activities and port functions is quite common. Nonetheless, often a physical separation between city and port still exists. Port planning is starting to take into account economic and social issues as well as mandatory environmental matters, sometimes contemplating conversions of old industrial activities due to global economic changes, or of their main activities due to lifestyle changes. Ports are beginning to tackle mobility and transit issues, not only in terms of cargos and container transit, but also concerning pedestrian transit, mainly due to the growing sector of the cruising activities. Cruise terminals usually can have up to 2,500 people arriving at the same time, thus they need adequate parking and connections to major destinations, such as the city center and airports. The conversion of some of their brownfields in commercial and recreational sites with hotels and retail is also aimed at offering pre- and post-cruise activities, especially in those cities that have chosen to invest on the fairs and convention industry. The two, cruises and fairs, contribute to relevant synergies. Port infrastructures need to be renewed given the increased size of large cargo ships. Issues such as security, due to the recent terrorist events, are starting to be taken more seriously as well.

It is clear that the Italian government believes that the key to successful port development is comprehensive and integrated planning. This chapter looks at some of the key principles of good port development and then offers two case studies of harbor cities in Italy: Genoa and Naples.

Key Principles of Sustainable Port Development

Traditional harbor cities are facing new challenges and opportunities due to changes in coastal shipping practices, fishing treaties, international shipping laws, and security issues, not to mention the increase in size of vessels and increased dredging requirements. Under the control of port authorities, ports in these harbor cities were traditionally separate from the city itself, and their development was not coordinated with the development and planning of the city. Today, however, demands for space and the need to improve old areas that do not meet modern requirements are making integration and cooperation a necessity.

Waterfronts differ in many ways, but they share certain common challenges as they undertake revitalization in accordance with the principles of sustainable development. These challenges include financing, conflicts over land use and acquisition, underutilization, unclear government jurisdictions, aging infrastructure, pollution and environmental issues, public access issues, ownership, and the overall complexities relating to master plan development, construction, and community/business acceptance.[7]

Sustainable port planning discerns from the more ample concept of "sustainable development," a process by which changes in economic structure, organization, and activity of an economic ecological system are directed toward maximum welfare and can be sustained by available resources.[8] Within this context, a number of planning practices can be pursued.

National and International Trends

Port planning can no longer take place in isolation, nor is redevelopment feasible without assessing its impact on the hinterlands. Ports are still the economic lifeblood of many of these communities. Urban planners must understand ports' changing needs—for example, new and larger types of containers require different handling facilities.

An Intelligent Master Plan and Appropriate Zoning Regulations

A successful harbor requires a long-range harbor plan and comprehensive zoning regulations to enforce it. Harbors must be planned with the water as a unifying element. Once water-dependent and water-related uses are satisfied, then other uses can be considered. Furthermore, harbors must plan for twenty-four-hour operations. Ports that are dependent on tidal flows or are accustomed to a shortened operational day will be at a disadvantage. Amongst the critical elements that must be addressed are history and culture, inland integration, and design principles.

Many harbor communities are rich in history and culture; many have historic forts and castles right on the waterfront. Lighthouses and maritime museums add to the charm and attraction of a harbor. Such historic and cultural structures draw tourists and can make visiting the harbor an educational experience. Maintenance and management of these elements, therefore, are important to harbor planning.

Harbors should be integrated inland as extensively as possible. The daylighting (the opening up of these water bodies for public viewing) of channels, canals, rivers, and streams can add value

PHOTOGRAPH BY ZENIA KOTVAL

Figure 1. History, culture and inland integration.

to communities and, perhaps more important, can integrate the harbor more fully into the fabric of the community.

Zoning regulations, architecture and design controls, and site planning regulations can all help preserve and enhance a harbor's historical, cultural, and aesthetic attributes and will encourage the optimal mix of uses.

The master plan should call for a stepping down in the height of buildings. Too frequently, the views of harbors are blocked by high-rise buildings. Cities should maintain a low-rise profile along the waterfront and, if necessary, increase the height as one moves inland. Waterfronts belong to the public, yet too often access is de facto denied by private interests or the practical everyday work that takes place along the waterfront. It is important, as a planning principle, that public access be emphasized. Walking and bike paths should be developed as close as possible to the water. Reconciling this imperative with recognition of and respect for private property rights is, unfortunately, no easy task.

Mixed Uses Can Be Complementary If Well Positioned

Planners should aim for multiple uses of harbors, including fishing, fish processing, recreational boating, shipbuilding and repair, and tourist activities. These uses need not be mutually exclusive.

A harbor can be both a working harbor and a recreational harbor if it is well planned and managed. In fact, mixed uses can actually complement each other. Unfortunately, a lack of careful planning often has led to conflict between fishermen and recreationalists. Where this conflict exists, it is the fishermen who typically suffer.

People benefit from a working harbor. Not only does it provide jobs and a tax base for the community, it attracts water-related industries and supporting businesses. Furthermore, a safe and well-maintained and managed section of a working harbor can actually be a draw for tourists curious to learn about and observe the working of various industries. A shipping fleet preparing to go out to sea or returning with a fresh catch can be a fascinating spectacle that provides a valuable learning experience.

Museums, aquariums, and teaching programs would also certainly be a draw for tourists and residents alike, and teaching and research programs would be highly beneficial to harbor-related industries. A research laboratory for a specialized trade such as aquaculture could make the harbor a special destination for professional groups as well as students.

When considering mixed-use development, there are three things planners should bear in mind. First, working harbors must be protected. Tensions over international fishing and the market sensitivity of the shipbuilding industry put working harbors at risk in many countries.

PHOTOGRAPH BY ZENIA KOTVAL

Figure 2. Mixed uses including retail, boating, office, and residential.

PHOTOGRAPH BY ZENIA KOTVAL

Figure 3. Boat repair facility.

Second, harbors have terrific potential to serve as teaching centers for marine activities, aquaculture, and other water-related topics, and these teaching activities can coexist nicely with both work and recreational functions, but these functions do have very different needs and serve very different populations. Regulations need to address areas of potential conflict clearly.

Third, tourist activities typically provide extensive local benefit along harbor fronts. Visitors tend to support ancillary activities. Furthermore, local residents can enjoy other related amenities that are associated with harbor tourism.

Connecting the Harbor to the Community Center

To maximize the potential of the harbor, it should be connected to the downtown area. As tourist harbors tend to be catalysts for growth in tourism-related activities, the whole community can thereby benefit. Downtown stores, hotels, and restaurants become an integral part of the tourist experience. Wide roads or large paved parking areas that separate the rest of the community from the waterfront are obstacles to tourists traveling inward from the harbor and therefore should be avoided. When direct connections are not possible due to the historic layout of the harbor and the community, good signage and design elements (such as period streetlights or walkways and bridges) can help draw people from one area to another.

PHOTOGRAPH BY ZENIA KOTVAL

Figure 4. Food and entertainment at the waterfront.

PHOTOGRAPH BY ZENIA KOTVAL

Figure 5. Fishing activities at the waterfront.

PHOTOGRAPH BY ZENIA KOTVAL

Figure 6. Transportation networks integrating pedestrians and vehicles.

Key Transportation Systems and Traffic Management Policies

If the harbor lacks good access to rail systems or major roads, it will be less able to reach its full potential. We have noted harbors, for example, that require that goods be off-loaded onto trucks for a short journey and then reloaded onto rail facilities. This inevitably adds costs to the products. Similarly, if trucks must pass through crowded streets or if there are outdated cranes or no rail or roll-off/roll-on capabilities, then the harbor will be at a disadvantage.

Unplanned traffic circulation can be chaotic for both vehicles and pedestrians. Some traffic management will always be necessary, regardless of the harbor's use. This becomes more imperative if there are mixed uses. Adequate parking, well-defined walkways, and (optionally) bike paths and jogging trails need to be established. Managed circulation is a requirement not only for the aesthetics and functionality of the harbor but also for safety reasons. If it is not possible to entirely separate vehicle traffic from pedestrians, strategies such as traffic calming or specific time limits for service vehicles would be beneficial.

Waterfront developers face a much greater array of environmental regulations than their predecessors did. Great care must be taken to ensure that sewer and/or combined sewer/storm water outflows are treated. Too frequently lack of treatment creates less than optimal conditions.

Public-Private Partnerships

Given a harbor's varied functions and clientele, public and private partnerships are in order. In most cases, a port or harbor authority oversees day-to-day running and management. However, that authority needs to work closely with other agencies. The chamber of commerce and/or local tourism boards play a role in the recreational and tourist aspects of harbor management. The police, coast guard, fire departments, and parking authorities also play important roles. Established merchants, associations, and recreational clubs are also generally involved, as are special-interest groups. Good communication between all these entities is crucial to the management and success of the harbor and the community as a whole.

Case Studies

We now present two major Italian port cities and discuss how they are implementing some of the sustainable factors discussed above and how these cities and their ports are planning for the future.

Genoa: The City Wins Its Sea Back from the Port

Genoa, located in the Gulf of Genoa, has been one of the most important Italian ports since the eleventh century. Today, the port extends along 12.4 miles (20 kilometers) of coastline.

The Old Port area includes the ferry and cruise terminal, a small tourist port, and a former industrial site that was converted into a public recreational space in the early 1990s. The Multedo Oil Terminal, one of the biggest oil terminals in the Mediterranean, is well sheltered from the sea by a long breakwater, a quiet water channel, and a large airport's esplanade. The Voltri Container Terminal, with a surface area of 519 acres (2.1 square kilometers), is one of the most important container terminals in the Mediterranean.[9]

The Port of Genoa is a strategic resource for the city and region's economy. Planners would like to see the port, which is host to many and varied related activities, grow alongside the city in an integrated manner; they would also like to see a balance between the port's needs and the needs of the city (enhancement of quality of life, development of its tourism potential, and improvement of the city-sea relationship).

In the late 1980s, a movement began to "return the sea to the city" in the Old Port. This was taken up by Renzo Piano in his "Fresco," a vision of the port and the city presented in May 2004 to commemorate Genoa's celebration as the "European Capital of Culture." After a number of adjustments to align Piano's plan with local needs, it was adopted by the Genoa Port Authority and other local institutions.[10] Its goals were to enhance the port's potential and resources, improve tourist and recreational spaces, improve livability and mobility in the city center, and eliminate environmental risk factors. Piano's plan took into account several of the principles mentioned above.

PUBLIC-PRIVATE PARTNERSHIPS. The port authority, the local administration, and major stakeholders worked in partnership to lay the basis for Piano's waterfront project, which is expected to transform the city and port with its harmonious, coherent development.

To carry out the project, the Genoa Port Authority, acting with the Region of Liguria and the Genoa provincial and municipal administrations, set up the Waterfront and Territorial Agency in 2004. This agency provides technical support and coordinates operations. It also works to ensure that Piano's plans are compatible with the various territorial planning instruments at the regional, provincial, and municipal levels, as well as with the Port Zoning Scheme. In addition, the agency also assesses the plans' consistency with current initiatives.[11] In 2005 the agency began detailed feasibility studies on the Fresco waterfront project, looking into the competitive positioning of the port, the technical and urban planning framework, the engineering feasibility of the maritime works, and the land/airport infrastructure, in addition to the financial feasibility of the project as a whole.

CAREFUL MASTER PLANNING. The project is attempting to reconfigure the complex and delicate relationships between Genoa, the sea, and the port, striving to reconcile the various urban, environmental, and economic needs involved. This entails cross-category work that affects the entire local area.

The port's master plan guidelines were undersigned in March 2007 by representatives of regional, county, and local governments, the Labor Unions, and local stakeholders. The guidelines aim to solve possible conflicts between port versus city planning. To understand the new role of the port in relation to shipping across the globe, the plan looks at various critical issues, including resizing the docking areas to handle a projected 6 million TEUs (twenty-foot equivalent units), accommodating the growth of cruising industry traffic, and planning new infrastructure.[12] Prioritizing interventions, guaranteeing a positive environmental impact, and agreeing on a commonly shared vision of the port's development are part of the critical issues discussed in the plan as well.

The planned urban redevelopment initiatives involve first and foremost the creation of a series of parks and green areas along the 13.7 miles (22 kilometers) of waterfront, closing the gap that separates the city from the sea.

Today the system of public green areas in Genoa is both limited in size and separated from the city's seafront. The project aims to create three large parks closer to the coastline. The first park, planned in Voltri, will stretch for about 1.9 miles (3 kilometers) in the area between the old railway station and the sea, representing a continuation of the public green area already created in the free zone and extending up to the planned fish market and small fishing boat dock. The second park, between Multedo and Sestri Ponente, will occupy the area between the existing petrochemical plant, the naval construction sites area, and the airport, reestablishing a link between Multedo and the sea with boulevards and tree-lined pathways. The third park will run from the Old Port to the trade fair complex, creating an unbroken pathway. The planned redevelopment of the existing airport runway as a site for port activities offers the possibility of creating a new berthing area for oil tankers on its western side. The areas now used for this purpose could be partially filled in to create the areas needed for shipyard expansion and partially developed into urban areas. The area currently occupied by the petrochemical products handling facilities will be redeveloped into a

PHOTOGRAPH BY ZENIA KOTVAL

Figure 7. Public promenade along the eastern side of the trade fair complex, Genoa.

marina, a green, sports facilities, and a promenade and will include an extension of the existing beach. With the elimination of the industrial sheds, an area of urban parkland can be created and be restored to the city.

The waterfront project embraces some other major works along the city's waterfront, the most significant being the transfer of the airport runway to a utilitarian island, making it possible to create a linear port without the constraints imposed by the airport landing cone. This project will also drastically increase the space devoted to port activities. Another key initiative is the creation of the Ship Repair island, a bigger, better organized area than the current one, creating the conditions for industrial development in the segment.

Finally, to the east, Città del Mare (literally, City of the Sea) will be created exclusively for pleasure craft, with new tourist marinas and a significant increase in the number of moorings available, in addition to facilities for maxi yachts. Plans for the Città del Mare also include the new Yacht Club, which will transform the original site into a permanent exhibition, a seafront promenade, a public precinct along the eastern side of the trade fair complex, an underground car park, and a new public beach.

CONNECTING THE HARBOR TO THE COMMUNITY CENTER. The Old Port area, located in the heart of the historic center, was converted in the early nineties into an exhibition area (aquarium, congress

PHOTOGRAPH BY ZENIA KOTVAL

Figure 8. Bigo structure over the sea in old Genoa harbor. Panoramic lift by the architect Renzo Piano.

center, cinema). At its center, the architectural monument Piano's Bigo, an homage to Columbus' discovery of the Americas, stands out. The facilities in the area are responsible for the movement of over 3 million people every year, thanks to its proximity to the passenger terminal.

Another element, the elevated highway that runs east to west along the coast, though quite efficient, has a physically devastating effect on the relationship between the sea and the urban fabric, dividing the city from the port. In Piano's new vision of the city, an indisputable condition for returning the waterfront to the city and its inhabitants is its complete removal and replacement with an underwater tunnel that will cross the port.

TRANSPORTATION SYSTEMS AND TRAFFIC MANAGEMENT POLICIES. Given the urban layout of the city, squeezed between the mountains and the sea, it was crucial to reorganize transit according to the different types of traffic and to guarantee a high level of accessibility. The plan foresees both rail and road transits reorganized according to the classic principles of functional hierarchy and the new urban design, in the belief that traffic related to the old town should be routed via the mountains rather than along the sea, as is currently the case. Moreover, mobility systems are identified and integrated in the broader geographical context by strategically located park-and-ride facilities to absorb some of the vehicle traffic entering the city, offering users high frequency public transport to complete their journeys. The park and ride facilities are planned on four main access routes from the east and west of the city.

IN SUMMARY: GENOA AND THE CHARTER FOR SUSTAINABLE DEVELOPMENT OF PORT CITIES. The adopted plan for Genoa's port city development embodies many principles that align with the International Association Cities and Ports' Charter for Sustainable Development of Port Cities. Chapter 1 of the charter calls for cities "to ensure coherence of projects on the scale of port cities and regions," through the cooperation of different institutions and the consideration of the needs of the population, as well as the metropolitan scale of port city projects. In the plan for Genoa, this will be accomplished through the creation of the collaborative Waterfront Territorial Agency and through the integration of the port plan with other city projects.

Through these integrated projects, the development also undertakes the task of dealing "with port interfaces from the viewpoint of mixity [diversity]" (chap. 2). The plan addresses this goal by respecting site identity (art. 2.1) through extending existing successful projects and by maintaining and integrating older components such as the railway station. Throughout, the project creates connections between the old and new. Also, different dimensions of port and urban life (art. 2.3) are celebrated with a variety of available activities, from the serenity of open urban park space to marinas for tourists, and the expansion of facilities for industrial and passenger port functions.

PHOTOGRAPH BY ZENIA KOTVAL

Figure 9. Elevated highway and view of the city.

PHOTOGRAPH BY ZENIA KOTVAL

Figure 10. Integrating old and new artifacts of port and urban life.

As outlined in the goals of Piano's project and included in the master plan guidelines, the plan would not only serve social and economic functions, but would also eliminate environmental risks and create a positive environmental impact, consistent with the third chapter of the charter, which calls for respect for the "equilibriums between port cities and their natural environment." Finally, by creating more green open parkland and creating the more discrete, tunneled transit line, the city/port spaces are made more accessible to everyone (art. 4.1), including those using the port for economic purposes.

Through its consideration of conflicts between the planning of the port and city, its call for increased understanding of the importance of port activities in relation to the global economy, and its prioritization of new and environmentally conscious infrastructure development, the plan for Genoa undertakes many of the guidelines provided in the charter for sustainable development of port cities.

Naples and the Port's Strengthening Economy

The third most populated city in Italy and the biggest city in southern Italy, Naples, owes its popularity to its port, which represents the entryway to countries on the southern Mediterranean shores. While Genoa centers its future development on the reconnection between the urban fabric and its old port, keeping the more maritime and port activities away from the center and rediscovering its relationship with the sea through the old port, Naples has not been focusing on its physical connection to the city until recently. Nevertheless, this is a successful example of port planning as reflected in a number of initiatives.

NATIONAL AND INTERNATIONAL TRENDS. Still investing on the role that the port has in the regional economy, the Naples Port Authority has recently presented a new regulatory plan of the port area. The plan aims to consolidate the role of Naples' port as a port of international importance through a clearly targeted policy of investments that expands the infrastructure and improves the services. The plan confirms the multifunctional nature of the port as a resource: cruise liners, shipyards for nautical repairs, and commercial traffic are the main sectors of the port's activity.[13] Taking from the regulatory plan, and proceeding along the lines of the previous operational plan, a new three-year operation program was set up with the aim to strengthen the multipurpose nature of the port by enhancing and expanding the three most dynamic sectors. The plan intends to restore and rationalize all three sectors of the port economy (passenger, shipyard, and commercial sectors). More specifically, it focuses on the sector of coastal navigation-sea highways, which is enjoying significant expansion, the new security and safety plan and environmental initiatives, and the establishment of new companies.

COMPLEMENTARY MIXED USES. To redesign the urban layout of an area where all port functions coexist, from passenger traffic, commercial traffic, and industrial repair and shipyard activities is complex. The plan was devised to be a flexible instrument in regards to the use of port spaces, and it foresees a rationalization and transformation of the operational areas and maritime traffic. In the passenger area (western area), the focus is on rationalization and the specialization of quays and wharves through the creation of new terminals especially designed for different types of traffic. A terminal for the cruise ships of the Harbour Station (including the establishment of a new public/private company for its management, Terminal Napoli Inc., which comprises the main holiday cruise companies in the world and of which Naples Port Authority maintains a minority controlling share), and a terminal for coastal navigation have been constructed.

The central area of the port, designed for shipyard activities, will also be rationalized by assigning new especially equipped and specialized wharves to ship repairs, with the modernization and modification of the dry docks. For this area, the objective of the plan is to restore the port as a point of reference for ship repairs for the whole Mediterranean area. To achieve this, not only infrastructural initiatives but also organizational schemes are necessary. The sector is one of the main sources of employment for the port (it provides work for 2,500 people, either directly or indirectly).

The commercial area, situated in the eastern zone of the port, will be subject to works aimed at enhancing all sectors of traffic—in particular, those related to container traffic. Container traffic is enjoying a period of substantial expansion due to the central position of the Naples port in the Mediterranean, the contacts with the hinterland, and the quality of the services provided. Some of the work has already been completed, such as the new railway track. Other works will be starting briefly to modernize and expand facilities and infrastructure. The executive project

PHOTOGRAPH BY ZENIA KOTVAL

Figure 11. Container traffic in the port of Naples.

for the establishment of the new terminal of the eastern zone will provide ample space for the development of commercial activities. In the medium to long term, there are also plans for further development in the western area of the port, with the possible delocalization of the oil terminal. Another objective of the plan is to create a system of landing places for pleasure boats and yachts, which meets the pressing need for mooring places for boats and equipment along the whole coastline of the city of Naples.

KEY TRANSPORTATION SYSTEMS. Much attention is also being focused on all the works necessary for improving links with the hinterland, with the eventual aim of the most efficient possible integration with the Italian transport system in order to improve the effectiveness and efficiency of intermodal services. Nevertheless, although recent history has not witnessed Naples at center stage, the port of Naples has been gradually rediscovering its wide-ranging role not merely concerned with the sea but also with adjacent cities. A strong connection has now returned between Naples and its port: the elimination of the barriers around the port and the pedestrianization of the tourist area will help to link the city with its port and, as a consequence, with the seashore.

REESTABLISHING A CONNECTION BETWEEN THE HARBOR AND THE CITY. Now no longer an "obstacle," the port of Naples has a wide range of activities (commercial, productive, tourist, and cultural) that all use the sea as a point of exchange, transformation, and growth. The idea to reconnect the city center with the port, by interrupting the physical barrier represented by the railroad, especially where new train stations will be built, is a step in such a direction.

Another positive sign in this sense is the one reflected in French architect Michel Euvé's 2005 prize-winning waterfront restoration project along the historic coastal development. This project introduces the concept of the "filtering line" of pathways that connect the port to the city center. A demarcation line between these two different places that must converge allows the continuation of their own specific activities. New facilities and parking areas will be located along this line in order to reorganize the mobility separating the port from the city. Pedestrian routes and connections between the city and the port will be arranged to rationalize access to the port. Along this line, services, multiuse spaces, and underground parking will be created. Over the filtering line, the project foresees the creation of a new urban layout, which develops at different levels, with gardens, shopping areas, restaurants, and other recreational activities alongside office spaces, stretching along the waterfront for approximately one mile (one and a half kilometers).

NEW ENVIRONMENTAL MEASURES AND CLEANLINESS OPERATIONS. The Port Authority has drawn up a plan for waste collection and discharge residues produced by ships. The plan regulates collection, transport, recycling and/or disposal activities and improves the availability and the function of the Port collection systems, implementing and making the differentiation of waste by the ships a priority.

PHOTOGRAPH BY ZENIA KOTVAL

Figure 12. Mixed-use functions dominated by tourist activities.

IN SUMMARY: NAPLES AND THE CHARTER FOR SUSTAINABLE PORT CITY DEVELOPMENT. The plan for port city development in Naples has a strong economic emphasis. Through the development of expanded infrastructure and improved services, the port will be better suited for multiple industrial uses, actions highly consistent with the charter's call for "innovative port and urban economic development" (chap. 6). The city's development also attempts to realize the maximum potential of its location, carefully positioning complementary uses. Safety and security is specifically mentioned in chapter 5 of the charter (art. 5.3) and is a priority in the development plan for Naples.

The plan also supports intermodal transportation (art. 5.2), which led to renewed consideration for the synergy among port and city activities, an important component of the charter's criteria for sustainable port city development (chaps. 2 and 4). This synergy will be achieved by creating connections between the maritime and land uses, through creation of parks, improved pedestrian accessibility, and increasing the availability of social activities. The new urban layout of Naples' development will incorporate a variety of urban activities, accessible and appealing to a variety of people, many of which integrate the port with the city (chap. 2 and art. 4.1).

Finally, the Port Authority's specific plan for ship wastes addresses the charter's call for "clean maritime and river transport" in the sought-after equilibrium between the port city and the environment.

Conclusion

European and global attention is shifting toward concerns for environment as well as economic development and social issues. The EU has implemented a variety of policies addressing these various components of sustainability, some individually and some as part of a comprehensive sustainable development strategy. While these strategies may prove to benefit the nation, the effect on port cities may be variable. European port cities face challenges as globalization changes their place and relevance within their nations and the world. The unique characteristics of port cities necessitate that these cities recognize the areas in which EU policies could be detrimental and the areas in which they might be beneficial.

The integration of sustainable development strategies for port cities can complement the EU objectives of sustainable development. Some common themes across general EU policy and the mentioned port-city specific initiatives are the emphasis on communication among various stakeholders, nations and governments at all levels; the need for education in knowledge and new technology; and utilization of alternative energy sources. The case studies illustrated here show that harbor redevelopment projects should be market driven and address the critical issues of sustainability.

The plans for development of both Genoa and Naples address issues important to sustainable port city development. In Genoa, the plan prioritizes both the connection between port and city uses and the area's accessibility for economic as well as social activities. The plan encourages ample green space, and a variety of social activities and uses, and it incorporates the considerations of various parties that have a vested interest in the development of the port city.

In Naples, economic concerns have long been the driving force for development, though in the interest of bolstering economically beneficial intermodal transportation, the importance of the synergy among port and city activities has been realized.

Both cities have taken the environmental impact of current activities and future development into consideration, with the goal of reducing impact or, in some instances, creating a positive impact on the environment. Both cities also present a heightened consciousness for how the port and city uses play off of one another, on the notion that sustainable development occurs when the two realms are integrated and accessible.

Neither plan, however, addresses the charter's call for developing renewable energy (chap. 3), which ties in with chapter 5's call to take advantage of new technologies. This is an area that will increase in importance as energy prices rise. According to CIBC World Markets, the shipping industry is closely tied with energy costs, and for "every one dollar rise in world oil prices," over the past three years there has been a 1 percent rise in transportation costs. The report notes that, for example, the same standard container that cost $3,000 (inland transport costs included) to ship from China to the United States in 2000 now costs $8,000 to ship, attributed largely to rising energy costs. At $200 per barrel, the shipping/transport cost for that container would be almost $15,000, or five times the 2000 cost.[14]

Many Port Authorities in the United States and Europe are actively pursuing ways to reduce the sensitivity of port activities to energy prices. From installing renewable energy generators at port sites to implementing innovations in energy efficiency, these efforts are aimed at reducing the costly blow that $200 per barrel of oil would otherwise deliver.[15] For example, increasingly popular devices for capturing energy are attached to rubber-tired gantry (RTG) cranes that store (then provide) energy through the motion of lifting and setting containers at ports.[16] This illustrates that while the rise of energy costs may not limit the potential of port activities, it does call for new technological innovations and planning considerations for any port city.

While rising energy prices do push the operating costs for the shipping industry up as well, shipping by water can still have a cost advantage over shipping on land, where transport costs might be even more sensitive to the energy price hike. As a result, some major European companies that generally transport goods by road are looking to expand their operations to water, seeking the enhancement of canals and other waterways, since shipping by water can be less costly.[17] Many of those interested in increasing their water activity have faced problems attributed to insufficient plans or active government support for the issue. As such, incorporating plans for creating or expanding shipping potential could be considered in the plans of both Genoa and Naples.

It is clear that harbor cities are undergoing dramatic changes as a result of trade agreements, greater environmental awareness, marketing trends, and consumer preferences, among other factors. At the same time, these ports are fragile. They are old, full of history and culture, have dated infrastructure systems, and must struggle to accommodate new transportation and production technologies. For these reasons, they must be carefully protected and planned. They are special places.

NOTES

1. European Commission, Sustainable Development: Europa, 2007, http://ec.europa.eu/environment/eussd/.
2. European Commission, Secretariat General, Impact Assessment: Political Context, 2007, http://ec.europa.eu/governance/impact/index_en.htm.
3. Commission of the European Communities, Green Paper: Towards a Future Maritime Policy for the Union: A European Vision for the Oceans and Seas—How Inappropriate to Call This Planet Earth When It Is Quite Clearly Ocean, vol. 2, attributed to Arthur C. Clarke (Brussles: Commission of the European Communities, 2006).
4. NEW EPOC, Renewing Economic Prosperity for Port Cities, Final Response to EU Green Paper, Towards a Future Maritime Policy for the Union: A European Vision for the Oceans and Seas (Rennes, France: Channel Arc Manche, June 29, 2007).
5. Association Internationale Villes Et Ports, Plan the City with the Port, concluding seminar of the project Hanse Passage (Le Havre: AIVP, May 25, 2007).
6. International Association of Cities and Ports, Charter for Sustainable Development of Port Cities (Sydney: IACP, 2007).
7. Zenia Kotval and John Mullin, The Once and Future of Medium Sized Harbours, in *Environmental Challenges in an Expanding Urban World and the Role of Emerging Information Technologies*, ed. Jack Ahern and Joao Reis Machado, 231–35 (Lisbon: CNIG-National Centre for Geographical Information, 1997); Zenia Kotval and John Mullin, Waterfront Planning as a Strategic Incentive to Downtown Enhancement and Livability, in *Downtowns: Revitalizing the Centers of Small Urban Communities*, Michael Burayidi, 179–96 (New York: Routledge, 2001).
8. Leon C. Braat and Ineke Steetskamp, Ecological-Economic Analysis for Regional Sustainable Development, in *Ecological Economics*, ed. Robert Costanza, 269–88 (New York: Columbia University Press, 1991).
9. I Porti d'Italia, ed., L'Autorità Portuale di Genova approva il nuovo Piano Operativo Triennale, *I Porti d'Italia*. Newsletter, March (2002): 11–15.
10. Autorità Portuale di Genova, *Costruiamo insieme il porto di domani* (Genoa: Autorità Portuale di Genova, 2006).
11. Suzanna Scarabicchi, Renzo Piano, Stefano D'Atri, Criatiano Zaccaria, and Silvia Picariello, *Genova e il suo porto: La città che cambia* (Genoa: Renzo Piano Building Workshop, 2006).
12. TEU is a standard way of measuring cargo loads. One TEU is the equivalent of the cargo capacity of a standard shipping container that is twenty feet long by eight feet wide.
13. Comune di Napoli, Piano regolatore generale: Relazione illustrativa, capitolo 3. Le scelte a scala cittadini (Naples: Comune di Napoli, 1996).
14. Jeff Rubin and Benjamin Tal, Will Soaring Transport Costs Reverse Globalization? *StrategEcon* . CIBC World Markets Inc. May 27, 2008: 4.
15. Patrik Wheater, Port Powerhouses, *Port Strategy Online Edition*, 2008, http://www.portstrategy.com.
16. Benedict Young, Bigger, Smarter, Greener. *Port Strategy Online Edition*, 2006, http://www.portstrategy.com.
17. Hannah Godfrey, Soaring Fuel Prices and Green Pressures Herald Comeback for Britain's Waterways, *Independent*, 2008, http://www.independent.co.uk/news/uk/.

REFERENCES

Association Internationale Villes Et Ports. Plan the City with the Port. Concluding seminar of the project Hanse Passage. Le Havre: AIVP, May 27, 2007.

Autorità Portuale di Genova. Costruiamo insieme il porto di domani. Genoa: Autorità Portuale di Genova, 2006.

Braat, Leon C., and Ineke Steetskamp. Ecological-Economic Analysis for Regional Sustainable Development. In *Ecological Economics*, ed. Robert Costanza, 269–88. New York: Columbia University Press, 1991.

Commission of the European Communities. Green Paper: Towards a Future Maritime Policy for the Union: A European Vision for the Oceans and Seas—How Inappropriate to Call This Planet Earth When It Is Quite Clearly Ocean. Vol. 2. Attributed to Arthur C. Clarke. Brussles: Commission of the European Communities, 2006.

Comune di Napoli. Piano regolatore generale. Relazione illustrativa, capitolo 3. Le scelte a scala cittadini. Naples: Comune di Napoli, 1996.

European Commission. Sustainable Development: Europa. 2007. http://ec.europa.eu/environment/eussd/.

———. Secretariat General. Impact Assessment: Political

Context. 2007. http://ec.europa.eu/governance/impact/index_en.htm.

Godfrey, Hannah. Soaring Fuel Prices and Green Pressures Herald Comeback for Britain's Waterways. *Independent,* August 10, 2008. http://www.independent.co.uk/news/uk/.

I Porti d'Italia, ed. L'Autorità Portuale di Genova approva il nuovo Piano Operativo Triennale. *I Porti d'Italia,* Newsletter, March 2002.

International Association of Cities and Ports. Charter for Sustainable Development of Port Cities. Sydney: IACP, 2007.

Kotval, Zenia, and John Mullin. The Once and Future of Medium Sized Harbours. In *Environmental Challenges in an Expanding Urban World and the Role of Emerging Information Technologies*, ed. Jack Ahern and Joao Reis Machado, 231–35. Lisbon: CNIG-National Centre for Geographical Information, 1997.

Kotval, Zenia, and John Mullin. Waterfront Planning as a Strategic Incentive to Downtown Enhancement and Livability. In *Downtowns: Revitalizing the Centers of Small Urban Communities*, ed. Michael Burayidi, 179–96. New York: Routledge, 2001.

NEW EPOC. Renewing Economic Prosperity for Port Cities. Final Response to EU Green Paper, Towards a Future Maritime Policy for the Union: A European Vision for the Oceans and Seas. Rennes, France: Channel Arc Manche. June 29, 2007.

Rubin, Jeff, and Benjamin Tal. Will Soaring Transport Costs Reverse Globalization? *StrategEcon.* CIBC World Markets Inc., May 27, 2008: 4.

Scarabicchi, Suzanna, Renzo Piano, Stefano D'Atri, Criatiano Zaccaria, and Silvia Picariello. *Genova e il suo porto: La città che cambia.* Genoa: Renzo Piano Building Workshop, 2006.

Wheater, Patrik. Port Powerhouses. *Port Strategy Online Edition,* 2008. http://www.portstrategy.com.

Young, Benedict. Bigger, Smarter, Greener. *Port Strategy Online Edition,* 2006 http://www.portstrategy.com.

CONTRIBUTORS

Adriana Allen is currently a senior lecturer at the Development Planning Unit, University College London. She has over twenty years of work experience in issues related to sustainable urbanization and environmental justice in the context of development. Her work covers Latin America, Asia, Africa, and the Middle East. One of her main current areas of research is on the governance of service provision for the urban poor, with a focus on citizen coproduction in water and sanitation.

Carl Amrhein is in his second term as provost and vice president (academic) at the University of Alberta. He came to the University of Alberta in 2003 following seventeen years at the University of Toronto. He holds a bachelor of science degree in geography from Pennsylvania State University (1978) and a PhD in geography from State University of New York at Buffalo (1984), with research interest in economic geography, labor markets, decision theory, migration, and quantitative methods. He recently received the Ami de la Francophonie Award and the German-Canadian Friendship Award.

Stefan Anderberg is codirector of the Lund University Centre for Sustainability Studies. His prior appointment was as associate professor at the Department of Geography, University of Copenhagen (1996–2008). Before that, he was affiliated with the International Institute for Applied Systems Analysis, Laxenburg, Austria, where he was involved in studies on resource use and the environment in varying spatial and temporal scales. His current research focuses on industrial ecology, regional and urban transformation, and water management. Other research interests include global sustainability issues, environmental history, and rural development.

Carlos Balsas is an assistant professor at Arizona State University. He has graduate degrees in regional planning from the University of Massachusetts at Amherst, as well as an undergraduate degree in urban and regional planning from the University of Aveiro, Portugal. His main research interests include urban revitalization and nonmotorized transportation planning. He has published two books on commercial urbanism and city center revitalization and currently teaches introduction to urban planning, planning theory, advanced urban studio, and sustainable transportation planning.

Victoria Basolo is an associate professor of urban planning at the University of California, Irvine. Her research investigates decision making around housing and neighborhoods, urban development, governance, and disaster preparedness. Professor Basolo is particularly interested in the formulation and implementation of housing and community development policies and the effects of policymaking processes and adopted policies on individual and societal outcomes. Her work has been published in numerous journals, including *Housing Policy Debate, Housing Studies, Journal of Urban Affairs, Urban Affairs Review, and Urban Studies.*

Jeb Brugmann is an urban and business strategist who has worked for twenty-six years with cities worldwide. In 1990 he founded ICLEI—Local Governments for Sustainability and served as its chief executive until 2000. He also cofounded the worldwide Local Agenda 21 initiative and the Cities for Climate Protection Campaign, which now supports more than 1,000 cities in a coordinated effort to reduce urban greenhouse gas emissions. His new book, *Welcome to the Urban Revolution: How Cities Are Changing the World,* was published in 2009.

Nairne Cameron is an assistant professor of geography at Algoma University and an adjunct assistant professor in the Centre for Health Promotion Studies at the University of Alberta. Her research interests include food and health geography, spatial analysis, and urban and regional development. She holds a bachelor of science degree from Queen's University, and a master's and PhD from the University of Ottawa.

Xi Chen received his PhD from Wuhan University in China in 2003. He has worked at Xinjiang Institute of Ecology and Geography of the Chinese Academy of Science since 1988. In 2002 he was appointed as the academy's associate director and as its director in 2006. He is recognized as an expert on the assessment of ecological processes and urbanization impacts in arid and semiarid regions, with a focus on ecological and societal sustainability.

Eric Clark is professor and head of the Department of Human Geography at Lund University and Fellow of the Royal Society of Letters at Lund. His research interests include gentrification, the political economy of space, and, more recently, island studies and historical political ecology. Clark edited *Geografiska Annaler B* 1999–2008. He is board member of the Danish Centre for Strategic Urban Research and steering committee member of the International Critical Geography Group, the International Small Island Studies Association, and the International Geographical Union Commission on Islands.

Giovanna Codato is the commissioner for Land and Urban Planning, Mobility in Ivrea, Italy. She graduated in architecture at the Polytechnic of Turin, where she worked as a research associate in the field of strategic urban and land use planning until 2007. She is the cofounder and president of the scientific committee of AGeCC, the Italian association of town center management, and is an ex-officio international board member of the International Downtown Association. She also serves on the scientific committee of the *Centri commerciali &* and on the Editorial Advisory Board of the *Journal of Place Management and Development.*

Analia S. Conte is a research fellow of the Consejo Nacional de Investigaciones Científicas y Técnicas-CONICET and associate professor at the Universidad Nacional de la Plata, Argentina. She is the vice president of the Sociedad Argentina de Estudios Geográficos-GÆA and member of the Academia Nacional de Geografía, Argentina. She has been the director of projects on technology transfer and GIS development and consultant to Argentinean government agencies. She is author of numerous publications on economic geography and research methodology.

Joe T. Darden is professor of geography at Michigan State University and former dean of Urban Affairs Programs, 1984–1997. He is a former Fulbright Scholar, Department of Geography, University of Toronto, 1997–1998. His research interests are urban social geography, residential segregation, and socioeconomic neighborhood inequality in multiracial societies. He is the author or coauthor of seven books. His most recent book, coauthored with John Frazier and Noah Henry, is *The African Diaspora in the United States and Canada at the Dawn of the 21st Century.*

Harm de Blij is a Visiting John A. Hannah Distinguished University Professor in the Department of Geography at Michigan State University. Author, professor, and television personality, Harm de Blij was the Geography Editor for *Good Morning America* and Geography Analyst for NBC News. He was writer and commentator for the original PBS Series *The Power of Place.* He has published more than 30 books including scientific, educational, and trade titles, and over 100 articles.

Peilei Fan is an assistant professor of Urban and Regional Planning at the School of Planning, Design, and Construction, Michigan State University. She holds a PhD in economic development and an MS in Electrical Engineering Computer Science, both from MIT. Her research interests are international planning and development, high-tech industrialization, and urbanization in Asia.

Pierre Filion is professor of urban planning at the School of Planning of the University of Waterloo. His research interests include metropolitan scale planning, the transportation/land-use relationship, downtown areas, and connections between urban planning and major societal trends. His present work involves an assessment of the obstacles to the achievement of smart growth objectives in southern Ontario as well as a survey of the land-use models present in regional plans across North America.

Raphaël Fischler was trained in architecture and in urban planning, in the Netherlands and in the United States. He is the director of the School of Urban Planning at McGill University, where he teaches community planning and land development, as well as planning history and theory. He is a consultant to local, regional, and provincial agencies and an adviser to community groups. He serves on Montreal's design review committee, on the board of the Ordre des Urbanistes du Québec, and on the Policy Committee of the Canadian Institute of Planners.

Elena Franco is founder and CEO of TCM Italia. Educated as an architect, she has extensive experience in mounting private-public partnerships, especially related to urban regeneration and city renewals. She has also developed several methodologies and tools for urban design and retail cores. She has been committed to town center management, urban retail clusters, and development since 1998. As an expert in these areas, she is asked to intervene on national and international levels.

Tegegne Gebre-Egziabher is a professor of regional and urban development and planning at Addis Ababa University. He earned his PhD from Ohio State University. He teaches urbanization and urban planning, regional development and policy, and local economic development at the Department of Geography and Environmental Studies and at the Centre for Regional and Local Development Studies. His research interests lie in regional and urban development, industrial and value chain development, decentralization and governance, and urban poverty. His recent book is entitled *Livelihood and Urban Poverty Reduction in Ethiopia.*

Brian J. Godfrey studies urban and regional change, heritage and historic preservation, and sustainable development in the Americas. Given his training in history (BA, Pomona College) and geography (MA and PhD, University of California, Berkeley), he takes a historical-geographical approach to scholarship on Latin America and the United States. Currently he is writing a book on contested urban heritages of Brazil. He is professor of geography at Vassar College, where he also teaches courses in environmental studies, Latin American studies, and urban studies.

Ricardo Gomez-Insausti is the vice president of research at BBM Canada. Before joining BBM, he held academic positions at Ryerson University, York University, and Syracuse University. He was Research Fellow of the Consejo Nacional de Investigaciones Científicas y Técnicas-CONICET and associate professor at the Universidad Nacional de La Plata, Argentina. He received his PhD from the University of Toronto and has authored numerous papers on urban/regional economics, retail/service geography, and market research. He is a member of the Advisory Council of the Department of Geography, Ryerson University, and of the Board of Directors of Access Alliance, Multicultural Health and Community Services, Toronto, Canada.

Sultan Khan is associate professor of sociology in the School of Sociology and Social Studies at the University of KwaZulu-Natal, South Africa. He teaches social issues and urban sociology. Currently he is undertaking research on public transport and investigating sustainable and livable human settlements in the province of KwaZulu-Natal. In 2007 he coedited the book *Undressing Durban,* which discusses social life and issues in the postapartheid city.

Ronald Kalafsky is an associate professor in the Department of Geography at the University of Tennessee. Research interests include the geographies of manufacturing and the export strategies of manufacturers. Of particular interest are the challenges and performance of manufacturers located in mature industrial regions, including Japan and the southern United States. Research on these topics has appeared in journals such as the *Asia Pacific Business Review* and *Tijdschrift voor Economische en Sociale Geografie*. He is the coeditor of the *Industrial Geographer* and also serves on the editorial board of the *American Review of Canadian Studies*.

Jeffrey Kenworthy is professor of sustainable cities at the Curtin University Sustainability Policy Institute (CUSP) at Curtin University in Perth. He teaches courses and supervises postgraduate research students in the area of urban sustainability. He has thirty years experience in urban transport and land-use policy and over 200 publications in the field. He is particularly noted for his international comparisons of cities around the theme of reducing automobile dependence.

Zenia Kotval is professor of Urban and Regional Planning, School of Planning Design and Construction at Michigan State University. She is the author of several articles and reports on economic impact assessments, economic development, and planning. Her expertise is in redevelopment of older regions, including brownfields, old ports, and downtowns. She is an adjunct professor at the University of Massachusetts and a teaching fellow with the Lincoln Institute of Land Policy in Cambridge, Massachusetts. She is a member of the American Institute of Certified Planners and the Economic Development Track Chair for the Associated Collegiate Schools of Planning.

Weichun Ma is an associate professor in the Department of Environmental Science and Engineering, Fudan University. His research interests include the applications of GIS and RS in environmental assessment, strategic environmental assessment, and environmental planning and management. He also conducts research on atmospheric environmental modeling and land use/cover change, with a particular focus on urban areas. He teaches environmental assessment and environmental information system courses at Fudan University.

Darshini Mahadevia teaches at the Faculty of Planning and Public Policy, CEPT University, Ahmedabad. She holds a PhD from Jawaharlal Nehru University, New Delhi, and has been a visiting scholar at the Graduate School of Architecture and Urban Planning, University of California, Los Angeles; School of Urban Planning, McGill University; and Tsinghua University, Beijing. She has been the recipient of a number of international fellowships. She also has extensive experience working with nongovernmental organizations in India. She has numerous publications in books and academic journals on urban and environmental issues, and human and gender development.

Brij Maharaj is professor and discipline chair (geography) at the University of KwaZulu-Natal (PMB) in the School of Environmental Studies. In addition to coediting four books, he has published over 100 scholarly papers in *Urban Studies, International Journal of Urban and Regional Studies, Political Geography, Urban Geography, Antipode, Polity and Space,* and *GeoJournal,* as well as numerous book chapters. He presently serves on the editorial board of *Geoforum, Antipode, Indian Ocean Survey,* and *Open Areas Studies Journal.* He is also consulting editor of the *Journal of Immigration and Refugee Studies.* He is chair of South African Netherlands Research Programme on Alternatives in Development.

Assefa Mehretu is professor of geography and African studies at Michigan State University. He is an economic geographer with a PhD from the Johns Hopkins University. Most recently, he served as associate dean of the College of Social Science and director of the Center for Integrative Studies in Social Science at Michigan State University. He teaches economic geography, geography of Africa, and global relations. His research interests lie in African development, regional development, and theories and patterns of socioeconomic marginality in both developed and less developed societies.

Joseph Messina has a PhD from the University of North Carolina, Chapel Hill, and is an associate professor of geography at Michigan State University. He also holds appointments with the Michigan Agricultural Experiment Station and the Center for Global Change and Earth Observations. Recent research activities have included infectious disease modeling and climate change in East Africa, simulation of urban environments, health care planning, and land-use and cover change research in China.

Beverley Mullings is an associate professor of geography at Queen's University in Canada. Her research generally examines how contemporary capitalism systems are transforming labor, bodies, and the nature of work. Framed within feminist political economy, past research has examined the impact of neoliberalism on the gender division of labor in the Caribbean; export oriented services and women's work; social reproduction, crisis, and violence; and neoliberalism, governmentality, and the role of diaspora. Her research has appeared in a number of geographical journals, including the *Annals of the Association of American Geographers, the Journal of Economic Geography, Geoforum,* and *Global Networks.*

Peter Newman is the professor of sustainability at Curtin University and is on the board of Infrastructure Australia, which is funding infrastructure for the long-term sustainability of Australian cities. In 2001–2003 he directed the production of WA's Sustainability Strategy in the Department of the Premier and Cabinet, the first state sustainability strategy in the world. In 2004–2005 he was a sustainability commissioner in Sydney advising the government on planning issues. In 2006–2007 he was a Fulbright Senior Scholar at the University of Virginia, Charlottesville. Peter's book with Jeffrey Kenworthy, *Sustainability and Cities: Overcoming Automobile Dependence,* was launched in the White House in 1999.

Michael Pacione is the chair of geography at the University of Strathclyde in Glasgow. His principal research interest is in the field of urban geography. He has published twenty-five books and more than 125 research papers in an international range of academic and professional journals. His most recent books include *Glasgow: The Socio-Spatial Development of the City; Britain's Cities:*

Geographies of Division in Urban Britain; *Applied Geography: Principles and Practice*; and *Urban Geography: A Global Perspective.*

Jiaguo Qi is director of the Center for Global Change and Earth Observations and professor in the Department of Geography at Michigan State University. He also serves as a project scientist in the NASA-MAIRS program. He received a BS degree from Harbin Teacher's Normal University (physics) in 1981, and MS and PhD degrees from the University of Arizona's Department of Soil and Water Science in 1989 and 1993, respectively. His research focuses on two areas: integrating biophysical and social processes and methods in understanding land use and land cover change, and transforming data into information and knowledge.

Eran Razin teaches in the Department of Geography and the Institute of Urban and Regional Studies of the Hebrew University of Jerusalem. He is the head of Floersheimer Studies, specializing in policy studies on society, space, and governance. He focuses primarily on the study of local government and urban development, and of metropolitan dynamics, particularly debates over suburbanization and sprawl, emphasizing a cross-national comparative perspective. He has coauthored and edited several books and numerous articles in journals such *Environment and Planning A & C, Urban Studies, Political Geography, Urban Affairs Review,* and *Journal of Urban Affairs.*

Imad Salamey is assistant professor of political science and international affairs at the Lebanese American University. He is the current director of Middle East Partnership Initiative's sponsored Young Women Leaders Program at the Lebanese American University and the president of the Center for Arab Research and Development. He received his PhD in political science from Wayne State University in 2003. His research interests focus on topics of ethnic relations, democracy, and governance. He has various publications related to the advancement of ethnosectarian relations, democracy, and electoral reforms in Lebanon and the Middle East.

Daniel Sui is a professor of geography and Distinguished Professor of Social and Behavioral Sciences at Ohio State University. He is also the director of the Center for Urban and Regional Analysis and the chair of the Department of Geography at Ohio State University. His research interests include the integration of spatial analysis and modeling with GIS for socioeconomic and environmental applications, theoretical issues in GIScience, urban geography, and emerging geographies of the information society. He teaches courses in GIScience, urban and economic geography, environment and resources, and geography of East Asia.

June Manning Thomas is Centennial Professor of Urban and Regional Planning at the University of Michigan, Ann Arbor; she is also professor emeritus at Michigan State University, East Lansing. Her books include *Redevelopment and Race: Planning a Finer City in Postwar Detroit; Planning Progress: Lessons from Shoghi Effendi;* and the coedited *Urban Planning and the African American Community: In the Shadows.* She writes about diversification of the planning profession, planning history, social equity, and urban revitalization.

Karen E. Smoyer-Tomic is a senior research analyst for HealthCore, a wholly owned subsidiary of WellPoint, Inc. She is also an adjunct associate professor in the Department of Geography at the University of Delaware. Her research interests include disparities in spatial accessibility to health resources; the pathways by which the physical, built, and social environment affect diverse health outcomes, including heat-related mortality and overweight/obesity; and the role of urban sprawl on population and environmental health.

Wei Tu is an associate professor in geography at Georgia Southern University. His research interests include input-output analysis, urban environmental management and policy, and GIS and spatial analysis for economic, environmental, and public health issues. He is currently working on low birth weight prevalence in Georgia using a combined spatial and multilevel modeling approach. He has teaching duties in GIS/cartography, economic geography, and geography of Asia.

Pariwate Varnakovida holds an appointment as assistant professor at Lake Superior State University in the Division of Chemistry, Environmental Sciences, Geology, and Physics. He has a BSc in mathematics with minors in computer science, and an MS degree with a focus on Information System Management for Environmental and Natural Resource Management. Varnakovida entered the PhD program at Michigan State University in fall 2003. His research program focuses on characterizing urban morphology, development associated with the unexplored rural region urbanization processes, and Southeast Asian sustainable development.

Igor Vojnovic is an associate professor in the Department of Geography at Michigan State University. He holds cross-appointments and affiliations with the Global Urban Studies Program, Environmental Science and Policy, the Center for Global Change and Earth Observation, and Urban and Regional Planning. His areas of research include metropolitan environments, urban form, urban design, and local governance. His work has been published in journals such as *Environmental Conservation, Environment and Planning A, Environment and Planning B, Urban Geography, Cities, Journal of Urban Design, Health & Place, Journal of Urban Affairs, GeoJournal,* and *Geografiska Annaler Series B.* He is also an associate editor for the *Journal of Urban Affairs.*

Jeanne M. Wolfe was director of the School of Urban Planning at McGill University from 1988 to 1999 and became professor emerita in 2000. She passed away in December 2009. She had been a leader in the field in Montreal, Quebec, and Canada, and she had published widely in the areas of land-use planning, housing policy, urban and metropolitan governance, and planning history and theory. In the last two decades of her life, she did most of her research on urban planning and sustainable development in the Caribbean and Central America and in India and China. Her contributions to planning research, teaching, and practice earned her the Prix Jean-Claude La Haye of the Ordre des Urbanistes du Québec (2004), the President's Award of the Canadian Institute of Planners (2007), and a designation as a member of the Order of Canada (2009).

Vladimir Yasenovskiy is a PhD candidate at the University of Alberta as well as an analyst at Alberta Gaming and Liquor Commission. He received his undergraduate and graduate degrees from Moscow State University and has been working in the field of GIS research and applications for more than twelve years. His research interests include methods of spatial accessibility, spatial interaction theory and models, advanced GIS methodology and applications, and business geography. In his PhD dissertation, he is developing new spatial accessibility indicators accounting for some specific features of the gambling industry and designed for explaining and predicting patronage at gambling facilities.